George Whitefield Clark

Romans and I. and II. Corinthians

A Popular Commentary upon a Critical Basis, Especially Designed for Pastors and Sunday Schools

George Whitefield Clark

Romans and I. and II. Corinthians
A Popular Commentary upon a Critical Basis, Especially Designed for Pastors and Sunday Schools

ISBN/EAN: 9783337020811

Printed in Europe, USA, Canada, Australia, Japan

Cover: Foto ©Lupo / pixelio.de

More available books at **www.hansebooks.com**

SECTION OF ROME SHOWING FORUM AND RUINED COLOSSEUM

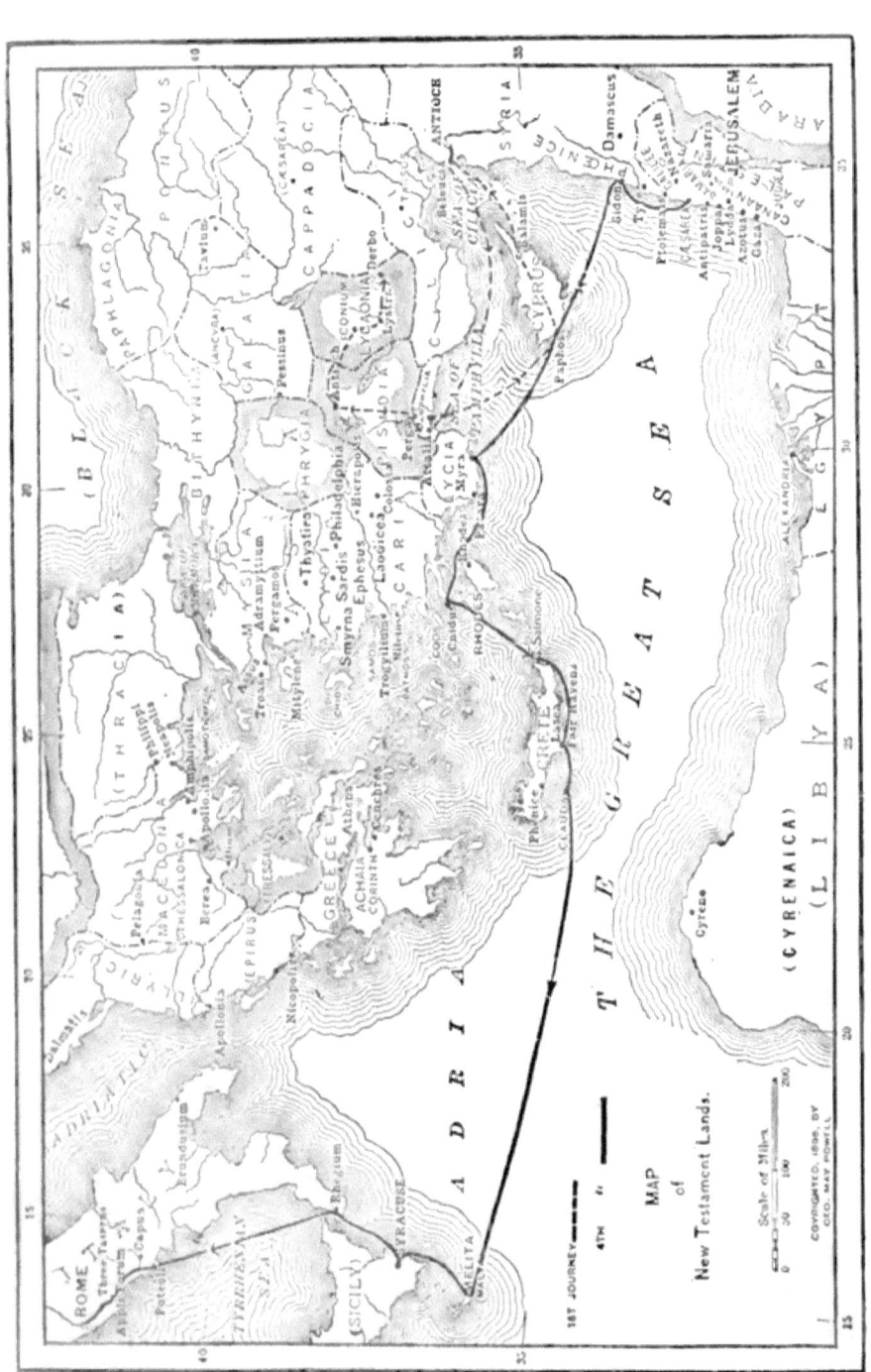

A People's Commentary

ROMANS

AND

I. AND II. CORINTHIANS

A POPULAR COMMENTARY UPON A CRITICAL
BASIS, ESPECIALLY DESIGNED FOR PASTORS
AND SUNDAY SCHOOLS ◊◊◊◊◊◊◊◊◊◊◊◊◊◊

BY

GEO. W. CLARK, D. D.

Author of "A New Harmony of the Gospels," and a "Harmony of the Acts," etc.

PHILADELPHIA
AMERICAN BAPTIST PUBLICATION SOCIETY
1420 Chestnut Street
1897

PREFACE

It is proposed to complete the work entitled "A People's Commentary" on the New Testament, by issuing four volumes on the Epistles and Revelation. Like the preceding volumes on the Gospels and the Acts of the Apostles, they will be popular commentaries on a critical basis, designed for that large class of Sunday-school workers and pastors who are unable, or have not the time, to consult original sources, and yet wish the best results of latest scholarship. To do this is a difficult task; in selecting material from many sources, in deciding what to admit and what to reject, and what explanations are needed. A certain simplicity and fullness are required; for what is plain to one may be obscure to another. But to keep the work within the limits proposed, a certain brevity is necessary. To meet these requirements the paraphrase is sometimes adopted, brief explanations are thrown in between words and clauses, and often a literal, a free, or a full rendering of a passage is given. Often brief sentences, quite independent of each other, are arranged together.

In this volume four questions have been kept in view: What did the writer intend to express? What was the idea that he conveyed to the Christian readers whom he addressed? What did the Spirit intend to say through him? How can the thought thus attained be best expressed now? The grammatical form and logical connection of the original have been carefully studied throughout; and it has been the endeavor to give the course of thought and the true meaning of every passage. This has been done, it is believed, in that devout and prayerful spirit which brings the mind into sympathy with the object and source of Divine truth. There is deep meaning and much truth in that old saying: "To have prayed well is to have studied well." Prayer fits for reverent study, and the sincere desire that accompanies prayer and the Spirit granted in answer to prayer, are adapted to clear the spiritual vision and prepare it to apprehend spiritual truth. The best helps, both earlier and later, have been sought and used. The author, however, is conscious of having come short of this high standard; but he feels assured of having come nearer to it than he would if his aim had been lower.

Four years ago the Publication Society authorized me to obtain any assistance I needed for the completion of this Commentary on the New Testament. I have been fortunate in securing the services of Rev. O. P. Eaches, D. D., whose scholarly instincts and habits, teaching ability and pastoral experience, spiritual insight and devotion to the truth, clearness and simplicity of style, fit him for the work. He has prepared the notes for the Epistles to the Hebrews, James, and Peter, which volume will follow this. If the Lord will, two additional volumes, one by Dr. Eaches, and one by myself, will complete the series.

Hightstown, N. J., 1897.

INTRODUCTION

THE EPISTLES IN GENERAL

The Epistles and the Apocalypse supplement the four Gospels and the Acts, and complete the revelations regarding the divine scheme of salvation. In them we may discover the progressive manifestation of truth, and the last and fullest revelations of the Divine will. Addressed publicly to churches, or privately to individuals, or generally to Christians, they rescue from uncertain tradition the certain inspired teachings of the apostles. They deal with doctrinal and practical questions pertaining to the nature of our Lord's kingdom, to his sufferings, death, and resurrection, to his calling of the Gentiles, and to his second coming and final glory. Twenty-two in number, they naturally fall into the three groups of Peter, Paul, and John. With the Gospels of Matthew and Mark as a basis, Peter, with James and Jude, presents the simplest and earliest form of Gospel apostolic teaching. Paul, building upon the foundation laid by Peter in the Jewish and Gentile world, writes more largely and develops more fully than the others the great doctrines of grace and redemption. With him must be associated the writings of Luke, the address of Stephen, and the Epistle to the Hebrews, as kindred in thought and doctrine. John, the profoundest yet most childlike of all, is remarkable for his spiritual contemplation of the heights and depths of the mysteries of godliness, and for the power with which he presents the manifestation of the incarnate Word and the revelation of the glorified Son of Man. Peter has been aptly styled the apostle of hope; Paul, the apostle of faith; and John, the apostle of love.

The addresses in the Acts are to those who are not Christians, except the debate in the council at Jerusalem and the charge to the elders at Miletus; but the Epistles are addressed to Christians for their instruction in doctrine and their upbuilding in their inner and outer life. As an apostle of the circumcision and a witness of the resurrection, Peter appeals constantly to the Old Testament Scriptures, and makes prominent the earthly and heavenly life of our Lord. Paul, while using largely the law and prophets in illustrating and confirming the doctrines of salvation by grace, refers but little to the earthly life of our Lord, but makes prominent the risen and glorified Christ. John, starting with the eternal Logos as a fundamental and central fact, dwells upon him as the light and life of men, resulting in their spiritual fellowship with the Father and with his Son, Jesus Christ, and with one another. In practice Peter emphasizes repentance toward God; Paul, faith in our Lord Jesus Christ; and John, love to God and for our fellow-men. These three great leaders of spiritual thought in the New Testament, while exhibiting diversity of gifts, manifest unity of spirit.

"They are unlike in regard to their point of departure and the method and depth of their teaching, but agree in their convictions in regard to faith in their principles and expectations; their color is varied, but not so the original light; their tones change, but thereby the higher harmony is rather increased than disturbed. The Jewish Christian cast of thought of the one writer is by no means irreconcilably opposed to the more Grecian coloring of thought in the other; and a continued investigation always leads to the discovery of a harmony even in those cases where it was before doubted, perhaps entirely overlooked" (VAN OOSTERZEE). Each wrote independently of the other, at different times and in different places, but without contradiction and with such unity of purpose and spirit and harmony of thought as to indicate the truth coming from Christ as a common source and that the writers themselves were under the guidance of the Holy Spirit.

In the study of the Epistles we discover in the writers growth in grace and in the knowledge of the truth. It is best therefore to study them in the order in which they were written. After the Gospels and the Acts, first Peter, then Paul, then John. Chronological order should especially be observed in studying the writings of the Apostle Paul. During the thirteen years between his first and last Epistle, Paul evidently had deep experiences, rich revelations, and increasing insight into divine truth. His thirteen or perhaps fourteen Epistles should probably be arranged as follows: First and Second Thessalonians, Galatians, First and Second Corinthians, Romans, Ephesians, Colossians, Philippians, Philemon, First Timothy, Titus, and Second Timothy. Dr. Lightfoot places Philippians before Ephesians, and some would place Galatians after Second Corinthians. The Epistle to the Hebrews, whether written under the direction of Paul or not, may be profitably studied after the Epistle to the Romans.

PAUL THE WRITER OF EPISTLES.

If we would fully understand Paul we must know Paul. Born a Jew, and yet a Roman citizen (Acts 22:28), he was thus connected with the better and more influential of Jewish families. Spending his childhood at Tarsus, a city classed with Athens and Alexandria, the three forming the great centers of the world's learning, he must have known something of Grecian culture and felt its influence, while he was carefully trained by his devout parents according to the precepts and doctrines of the strictest Pharisees (2 Tim. 1:3; Phil. 3:5; Acts 23:6). Passing his youth and early manhood at Jerusalem under the great Gamaliel (Acts 22:3), and instructed in the law of the fathers, and again at Tarsus, both doubtless before and certainly after his conversion (Acts 9:30; 11:25), he enjoyed the best advantages of his times. Of quick intellect and with great powers of acquisition (Gal. 1:14), taught in Jewish Scriptures and Jewish tradition and having the Greek perfectly at command, he was eminently fitted by nature, position, and education to meet and influence both Jews and Gentiles. Possessing a keen, logical mind with a strong, emotional nature, he was a man of clear and deep convictions, naturally following premise to conclusion; before his conversion a zealot for God and the traditions of the fathers (Acts 22:3; Gal. 1:14), and after, consecrated absolutely to Christ and intensely devoted to his apostolic and missionary work; before, his whole soul bent in the line of Jewish narrowness; after, toward all the objects of Christ's love, without distinction of race or nation.

Paul's Epistles are in a sense parts of himself. We cannot read them to-day, after eighteen centuries, without still feeling the impulse he imparted to them. For (1) he wrote and spoke *out of his own experience*. At his conversion Christ was revealed in him (Gal. 1:16) as the Saviour of the sinner, whether Jew or Gentile. The thought grew as a living reality until we find it in its highest development in the Epistles of the imprisonment, which have been aptly styled the "Christological Epistles." He had found the gospel to be the power of God unto salvation, and he knew the truth of its doctrines and the value of its precepts from a rich experience. Two of his addresses in the Acts were accounts of his own conversion, and but a cursory reading of his Epistles will reveal how largely they were the transcripts and results of soul-struggles and soul-victories.

(2) Connected with his experience were *Divine revelations*. These he had enjoyed in great abundance (2 Cor. 12:2-7) as well as the supernatural gifts of the Spirit (1 Cor. 14:18,19). Many things he had received directly from the Lord, such as the manner of celebrating the Lord's Supper (1 Cor. 11:23) and the gospel which he preached (Gal. 1:12). The hidden things connected with the redemption of the race had been made known to him. He had been so entrusted with these treasures, and so commissioned to proclaim them that he could speak of them as "my gospel" (Rom. 2:16; 16:25; 2 Tim. 2:8; 1 Cor. 15:1; Gal. 1:11; 2:2; 2 Thess. 2:14).

(3) Connected with his experience also was *an intense love for souls*. Abbott speaks of Paul as more a philanthropist than a philosopher. He was indeed a lover of men, but more a lover of the souls of men. And all this because of Christ, the Saviour and elder brother. For the Jews, his persecuting kinsmen, he poured forth his earnest prayers that they might be saved, and would even willingly have died in their behalf. To the Gentiles he devoted his life in labors incessant, not counting his life dear to himself; admonishing in tears, weeping over sinners, becoming all things to all men that he might gain some.

(4) He was also however a philosopher, in that he was *a lover of truth*. Whatever was opposed to the truth he treated with the utmost abhorrence (Gal. 1:8,9; 2:14). While not giving a systematic theology he gave the most systematic presentation of truth found in the New Testament. A Christian philosophy pervades and gives color to all his writings.

(5) And added to this was *vehemence*. Truth he often enforced with powerful logic; but whether in argument or persuasion he drove in his points with vehemence. Thoughts often came forth in torrents, which would not always yield easily to the rules of grammar. With an object before him he pushed toward it with the fervor and energy of his whole being. And the more since (6) his Epistles are largely *of the nature of oral discourse*. Employing an amanuensis his Epistles were dictated for the most part and addressed as if speaking to his readers face to face. Often rising to the fervor of the most impassioned oratory, with richness of thought and feeling he plunged into irregular and complex sentences, or into a sudden and unexpected burst of eloquence, or some digression suggested by a word or a reminiscence. The Epistles of Paul need to be studied as combining the elements of written letters and oral addresses.

THE EPISTLE TO THE ROMANS

Paul has been universally regarded as the author of the Epistle to the Romans. The Jewish Christian sects of old who opposed its distinctive doctrines admitted this, and the skeptical school of modern Germany has not assailed its Pauline authorship. The Epistle is found in the oldest manuscripts, which proves its existence before the fourth century. It is quoted by the early Christian writers as Paul's, among them by Eusebius of Cæsarea in Palestine, about the end of the third century; by Tertullian, who lived both before and after A. D. 200 at Carthage in North Africa; by Clement of Alexandria, who died there about A. D. 220; and by Origen, who lived in Egypt and Palestine (A. D. 186-254) and wrote a commentary on this Epistle, a translation of which in Latin has come down to us. Irenæus of Lyons, the latter part of the second century, frequently speaks of Paul as writing to the Romans. The Muratorian fragment, written before A. D. 170, gives a list of Paul's Epistles, among which is that to the Romans. Marcion of Sinope, the Gnostic, about the middle of the second century, includes this Epistle in his list of Paul's Epistles. Justin, early in the second century, appears to quote freely from Rom. 4 : 11, 12 (*Dial.* 23); and Clement of Rome, near the close of the first century, in his Epistle to the Corinthians (chap. 35) plainly summarizes Rom. 1 : 27-32. He appears also to make some reference to 2 Peter 2 : 5; and Peter (2 Peter 3 : 15, 16) speaks of the letters of Paul.

Some, however, during the past hundred years, while regarding the whole Epistle as Paul's, have thought the closing chapters (some the last five, others the last two) either mutilated, or misplaced. Their reasons are insufficient and their views have met with but little favor. It has been suggested that the sixteenth chapter belonged to some epistle sent to Ephesus, or to some Asiatic church. The suggestion has been made because of the number of persons greeted, and especially because of the mention of Aquila and Priscilla, who had been recently at Ephesus, and of the church at their house. But Strabo (XVI., 5) says that many Tarsians were at Rome and that Rome swarmed with Asiatics. Communication was easy and frequent between Ephesus, Corinth, and Rome. Aquila doubtless went to Rome either soon after the tumult at Ephesus (Acts 20 : 1), or possibly before, when Paul definitely purposed to visit Rome (Acts 19 : 21). There was abundance of time therefore for Aquila to have gone to Rome, arranged matters, and sent back word to Paul. He may have taken some of his helpers in his business with him, who were Christians, and, having room in his establishment, may have commenced meetings at once and interested and gathered in other believers also. That Aquila and his wife were adapted to this kind of work, and successful, is evident from their instruction of Apollos (Acts 18 : 26. See introductory remarks to chap. 15, and note on 16 : 3, 14).

TO WHOM ADDRESSED.

The Epistle is addressed " to all the beloved of God, called to be saints, that are in Rome." They are nowhere in the New Testament spoken of as a church, though there appear to have been several church assemblies in the city (16 : 5, 14, 15). It is very probable that there was no place sufficiently large at their com-

INTRODUCTION

mand, where the entire discipleship could conveniently meet. Rome is variously estimated to have contained from one to two million inhabitants. The streets were generally narrow and crooked, and the tenement houses were built to a great height, and densely crowded. Nero decreed that dwelling-houses should not be more than seventy feet high. Under such surroundings but few believers, like Aquila, would have rooms for religious gatherings except very small ones. Such circumstances and the changing character of the population may have prevented them from having one central organization, and a great central meeting place. They seemed however to have moved in concert, and, if not in fact, they were really one body of Christian believers, with their several bishops or pastors (1:8; 16:17. See note on 16:5, 16).

The *composition* of the Christian congregation at Rome has been much discussed. It is evident from the Epistle that it comprised both Jewish and Gentile elements. The former is implied in the appeal of 2:17, but the general tone of the Epistle (1:13; 11:13; 15:15, 16) implies a majority of the latter. The number of Jews at Rome in the apostolic age, has been variously estimated at from twenty to sixty thousand. They lived in their own quarter beyond the Tiber, and had at least seven synagogues. That but few Jews were Christians, who kept themselves mostly separate from the others, seems evident from Acts 28:17-22. It was doubtless the best policy for them to ignore Christianity as much as possible (Acts 28:22). But there was also a large number of proselytes, and especially of devout Gentiles like Cornelius at Rome and elsewhere. This is the testimony of Josephus and the historians of that day. These pious Gentiles accepted and studied the law of Moses and practised many of its precepts. From this class most of the early Gentile converts were drawn. They were prepared to appreciate Paul's quotations and arguments from the Old Testament Scriptures and to receive the doctrines he taught. It would seem that the Christians at Rome had not been subjected to such Judaizing influences as had those in Galatia, nor had serious error grown up among them. What they had taught met with his general approval (1:8; 6:17; 15:14), and their views were so far accordant with his own, that they were well prepared to receive and profit by the great doctrines of this Epistle. Their type of Christianity appears to have been not widely different from that proclaimed by Paul himself.

The *origin* of Christianity at Rome is unknown. It must have existed there some time before this Epistle was written. Its adherents there had already become famous everywhere. This however is accounted for in part by the fact that from every place there was a road to Rome. Some of these believers also had been long in the faith (16:7). That Paul should have addressed his most systematic and longest letter to them indicates growth, standing, intellectual and spiritual attainments in his readers—not only of the leaders but also of the better part of the brethren at large. An unreliable tradition makes Peter the founder of the church in A. D. 42 and continuing as its bishop for twenty-five years till his martyrdom. But every known evidence is against such a supposition. It finds no support in this Epistle, indeed it is excluded by Paul's principle of not building on another man's foundation (15:20). The Acts proves that Peter was at Jerusalem in A. D. 44 (Acts 12) and in about A. D. 50 (Acts 15), and at Antioch about

A. D. 54 (Gal. 2:11). There is no mention of Peter's labors at Rome in the Acts or in any of the Epistles. He was probably in Babylon in Chaldea, in A. D. 66 (1 Peter 5:13). Paul makes no mention of Peter, nor implies his presence at Rome either in this or in any of his Epistles. He would not have written as he did, nor passed over his name in silence, if Peter had founded the church at Rome or if he had been the pastor or bishop of the church. Of all places Rome was the most likely to have the gospel take root without apostolic help. Its close connection with all parts of the empire would bring its inhabitants, both Jews and Gentiles, into contact with the gospel. Converts would come to sojourn there. Some of the sojourners from Rome, both Jews and proselytes (Acts 2:10), who witnessed the outpouring of the Spirit at Pentecost, doubtless returned, bringing the gospel with them. Thus doubtless the seed was first carried to Rome; and so it would continue to be by pilgrims returning from the feasts, and by converts in the leading cities where the gospel was successfully preached.

The *language* of the saints at Rome appears to have been principally Greek. The Jews were Hellenists, or foreign Jews who spoke that language. The names mentioned in the sixteenth chapter of the Epistle are mostly of Greek origin. A very large proportion of the population of Rome was from the Greek-speaking provinces. The most enterprising, intelligent, and energetic of the middle classes and common people were Greek. From these the Christian converts would most likely be gathered. The early Christian literature of the Roman church was Greek. The first Latin version of the Bible was not made for Rome, but for North Africa and the provinces. The Epistle to the Romans would naturally be written in Greek, both because it was more familiar to Paul, and because it would be more generally understood by believers at Rome and to a large extent in Italy.

WHEN AND WHERE WRITTEN.

This Epistle was written in anticipation of Paul's going to Rome (15:26) by way of Jerusalem. He purposed this visit at Ephesus in the spring of A. D. 57 (Acts 19:21); but he spent a year in Ephesus, Macedonia, and Greece, before leaving the last-named for Jerusalem (Acts 20:5) in the spring of A. D. 58. The Epistle therefore must have been written between these two dates. So long and systematic an Epistle may have been prepared from time to time. But when it was completed he had done his work in Macedonia and the East (15:19, 23), and he was about to leave Greece, where he had spent three months, for Jerusalem (15:25). Phœbe, the bearer of the Epistle, was of Cenchræa, the eastern port of Corinth (16:1); Gaius, who was Paul's host, appears to have been of Corinth (16:23; 1 Cor. 1:14). The phrase "the city" (16:23), where Paul was, points also to Corinth as the capital. It seems evident therefore that Paul completed this Epistle and sent it from Corinth in the spring of A. D. 58.

OCCASION AND DESIGN OF THE EPISTLE.

Paul had long desired to visit Rome, but had been hindered from so doing. As his third missionary tour was nearing its close, he formed the design of visiting Spain, taking Rome on his way. With a view to this he probably sent Aquila and Priscilla to Rome to open a business and prepare an abode for him.

Still later Phœbe, a deaconess of Cenchræa, was going to Rome. He also knew a goodly number there; and his expected visit would be short. All these circumstances gave him an occasion for writing this Epistle and an opportunity of sending it ahead as a forerunner of himself.

Rome was the metropolis of the world, where were found, as residents and visitors, the representatives of all nations. Through the Christians at Rome Paul could reach a greater variety and larger number of peoples than in any other city. He therefore presents the gospel which he preached in a more extended and systematic way than he had done in any other writing. His gospel was cosmopolitan, and Rome the most cosmopolitan of cities was the place in which to unfold it. He presents salvation through Christ alone adapted to the whole human race, to both Jews and Gentiles, a salvation solely through grace and by faith, in harmony with God's declaration and conduct as recorded in the Old Testament, and applicable to the inner and outer life of the Christian, as a member of a church and of the kingdom and a citizen of the world. Very likely the apostle desired to anticipate any possible error by presenting the truth, and to guard them against the assaults of Judaizing teachers. Very likely also he would fortify them in some instructions which he had but recently found very needful at Corinth (1 Cor. 6:1 ff.; 12:1 ff.). Doubtless he wished to comfort and confirm the disciples at Rome (1:11, 12), but he evidently had a wider and more general design.

CONTENTS AND ANALYSIS.

This Epistle is Paul's masterpiece, and the fullest presentation of his theology. It is an advance upon the Epistle to the Galatians, deeper and broader. In that the contrast is between Moses and Christ; in this between Adam and Christ. That has special reference to Judaism; this deals more with the race. The errors and the evils he combats in this are such as he had found everywhere, and which would naturally be expected to exist to some extent in Rome. Very probably the discussions in this Epistle were largely anticipatory and preventive. Thus he meets the points of controversy with Judaizers logically and systematically and in a conciliatory manner, fitted to disarm prejudice and obtain the favor of the Jewish element among Christians. As Rome was the seat of justice for the whole world Paul naturally presented the gospel in relation to law and righteousness. He also deals with the bearing of the gospel on the Jewish people and upon the Gentile world, presenting an interesting lesson on the philosophy of history (11:32).

Briefly and generally the Epistle may be divided into six parts: I. The *introduction*, in which is presented God's righteousness and salvation by faith alone, the leading thought of the Epistle (1:1-17). II. The *ruin* and *guilt* of the whole human race (1:18–3:20). III. The *remedy* provided by God in the gospel for the justification, sanctification, and complete salvation of believers in Jesus (3:21–8:39). IV. A *vindication* of God's dealing with the Jews and the Gentiles (9:1–11:36). V. *Practical* and *ethical lessons* regarding the inner and outer life, among Christians and in the world (12:1–15:13). VI. *Personal* and *concluding* matters (15:14–16:27).

A FULLER ANALYSIS.

I. INTRODUCTION.
1. Salutation to saints at Rome, 1 : 1-7.
2. Paul's long-cherished desire to preach to them, 1 : 8-15.
3. The Theme: *The gospel God's power to save all who believe*, 1 : 16, 17.

II. THE RUIN AND GUILT OF THE WHOLE RACE, 1 : 18-3 : 20.
   Hence the necessity of a salvation and righteousness such as the gospel reveals.
1. God's wrath against the sins of men, 1 : 18.
2. The downfall and degradation of mankind, 1 : 19-23.
3. Judicially given over to a reprobate mind, 1 : 24-32.
4. The self-righteous and censorious self-condemned, 2 : 1-16.
5. The Jew fails to keep God's law, 2 : 17-24.
6. Circumcision cannot save him, 2 : 25-29.
7. Yet the Jews have a certain advantage, 3 : 1-8.
8. But they and Gentiles are both condemned by the law, 3 : 9-18.
9. Hence all men are sinners and condemned, 3 : 19, 20.

III. THE REMEDY: RIGHTEOUSNESS AND SALVATION ALONE THROUGH FAITH IN CHRIST, 3 : 21-8 : 39.

JUSTIFICATION.
1. Its nature: gratuitous, 3 : 21-24.
2. Its ground: the redemption and sacrifice of Christ, 3 : 25.
3. Its object: to enable a righteous God to save sinners, 3 : 26.
4. Its results: exclude boasting, etc., 3 : 27-31.
5. Illustrated and confirmed from the Old Testament, 4 : 1-25.
6. Results of justification upon the individual, 5 : 1-11.
7. Results upon the race, 5 : 12-21.

SANCTIFICATION.
1. In Christ's death the believer died to sin, 6 : 1, 2.
2. Illustrated by his baptism, 6 : 3-11.
3. Let him not serve sin any more, 6 : 12-14.
4. A servant of righteousness constrained to loving obedience, 6 : 15-23.
5. The new life illustrated from Jewish law, 7 : 1-6.
6. Sinful passions excited by the holy restraints of the law, 7 : 5.
7. Yet the law is not evil but holy, 7 : 7, 12.
8. Illustrated by his experience before conversion, 7 : 7-12.
9. The evil not in the law but in man, 7 : 13.
10. Illustrated in experience both before and after conversion, 7 : 13-25.
11. Justified, and having a new life in Christ, no condemnation, 8 : 1, 2.
12. Grace has accomplished what the law could not, 8 : 3, 4.
13. A changed nature insures a changed life, 8 : 5-8.
14. The Spirit dwelling in and actuating believers, 8 : 9-13.
15. The sons of God with the spirit of sonship, 8 : 14-17.
16. Grounds of encouragement in the midst of suffering, 8 : 18-30.
17. Final issue assured, complete salvation, 8 : 31-39.

IV. VINDICATION OF GOD'S DEALINGS WITH JEWS AND GENTILES, 9:1–11:36.
The problem in respect to the passing over of Israel and the calling of the Gentiles.
1. Paul's interest and deep sorrow for Israel, 9 : 1–5.
2. Yet God's promise had not failed, 9 : 6–13.
3. No unrighteousness with God, 9 : 14–18.
4. God's justice and mercy displayed, 9 : 19–24.
5. According to prophecy, 9 : 20–29.
6. How Israel failed and Gentiles succeeded, 9 : 30–33.
7. Israel savable, yet unsaved. Why? 10 : 1–4.
8. The gospel adapted and designed for all, 10 : 5–13.
9. The gospel should be preached to all, 10 : 14–21.
10. God has not wholly passed over his people, 11 : 1–10.
11. Israel's fall not final; an occasion of salvation to the Gentiles, 11 : 11–16.
12. Gentiles should be humble, reverent, and grateful, 11 : 17–24.
13. Gentiles gathered in, and Israel restored, 11 : 25–32.
14. Praise to God at this sublime mystery, 11 : 33–35.
End of the doctrinal portion of the Epistle.

V. PRACTICAL AND ETHICAL LESSONS, 12 : 1–15 : 13.
1. A consecrated body and a renewed mind, 12 : 1, 2.
2. The right use of spiritual gifts, 12 : 3–8.
3. Duties to one another, 12 : 9–13.
4. Duties to the world, 12 : 14–21.
5. Subjection to rightful civil authority, 13 : 1–5.
6. Faithful attention to civil duties, 13 : 6–10.
7. Motives: brevity of life; approaching salvation, 13 : 11–14.
8. Conduct toward weak and overscrupulous brethren, 14 : 1–12.
9. A stumbling-block should not be put in the way of the weak, 14 : 13–18.
10. Should exercise self-sacrifice for the weak, 14 : 19–23.
11. Enforced by the example of Christ, 15 : 1–13.

VI. PERSONAL AND CONCLUDING MATTERS, 15 : 14–16 : 27.
1. Paul's apostolic labors among the Gentiles, 15 : 14–21.
2. Plans for the future, 15 : 22–24.
3. Present plans and work, 15 : 25–29.
4. Entreats their prayers. A benediction, 15 : 30–33.
5. Concluding words. Phœbe commended, 16 : 1, 2.
6. Salutations of Paul, 16 : 3–16.
7. Warnings against false teachers and divisions, 16 : 17–20.
8. Salutations from Paul's companions, and others, 16 : 21–24.
9. Doxology, 16 : 25–27.

THE EPISTLES TO THE CORINTHIANS

No Epistles of the New Testament have come down to us better attested than the two to the Corinthians. They bear the evident marks of the times in which they were written, of the state of the Corinthian church, and of the character of Paul as the writer. Clement of Rome, quite generally regarded as a friend and companion of Paul (Phil. 4:3), wrote his first Epistle to the Corinthians about A. D. 97, in which (chap. 47) he refers to Paul's first Epistle to them. And Polycarp, a disciple of John, and perhaps pastor of the church at Smyrna when John wrote the Revelation (Rev. 2:8), in his Epistle to the Philippians (chap. 11) about A. D. 116, quotes 1 Cor. 6:2 as the words of Paul. So also, about the same time, in the shorter Greek Epistles of Ignatius, who was pastor of the church at Antioch, there are several quotations from the same Epistle. Irenæus, a disciple of Polycarp, Athenagoras of Athens, Clement of Alexandria, and Tertullian of Carthage, all belonging to the second century, give their testimony to both the First and the Second Epistle to the Corinthians, as those of Paul. From that time onward they have been unhesitatingly accepted as the genuine writings of the apostle.

The genuineness of these Epistles is confirmed by the *undesigned coincidences* between them and the Acts of the Apostles. These have been exhaustively treated by Paley in his "*Horæ Paulinæ*," and they are brought to view in the author's "Harmonic Arrangement of the Acts." (See §§ 26, 27, 30, 31, 34, 36, 37, 38, 39, 40, 42, 49, and notes.) They form decisive arguments for the genuineness and truthfulness of these books of Scripture. A reference may here be made to some of them:

Paul at Corinth before Apollos, 1 Cor. 1:12; 3:6; Acts 18:27, 28.
Paul's baptism of Crispus, 1 Cor. 1:14; Acts 18:8.
Paul's laboring with his own hands, 1 Cor. 4:12; Acts 18:3.
Paul's sending Timothy to Corinth, 1 Cor. 4:17; Acts 19:22.
To the Jews becoming as a Jew, 1 Cor. 9:20; Acts 16:3; 21:23-26.
The churches of Galatia, 1 Cor. 16:1; Acts 18:23; 19:1.
Paul's going to Macedonia, 2 Cor. 1:15, 16; 9:2, 4; Acts 20:1.
Brethren coming from Macedonia, 2 Cor. 11:9; Acts 18:5.
Silas, or Silvanus and Timothy, 2 Cor. 1:19; Acts 18:5.
Paul stoned once, 2 Cor. 11:25; Acts 14:19.
Letters of commendation, 2 Cor. 3:1; Acts 18:27.
Paul's escape from Damascus, 2 Cor. 11:32, 33; Acts 9:23-25.

In these and many other passages the variations and agreements are so marked, without contradiction, as to stamp them as genuine writings of the times and the truthful exhibitions of matters as they then existed.

TO WHOM ADDRESSED.

Both Epistles are addressed to "The Church of God which is at Corinth." It was in A. D. 52 that Paul, on his second missionary journey, first visited Corinth. There he continued for eighteen months, then three months (Acts 18:11, 18) with perhaps a short visit to Athens between (2 Cor. 12 : 14; 13 : 1). He gathered many disciples, some of them being Jews (Acts 18 : 5), but the majority being Gentiles of Greek and Roman descent (1 Cor. 12 : 2). They were mostly from the poorer classes (1 Cor. 1 : 26) and of slender intellectual attainments, but Crispus, the ruler of the synagogue (Acts 18 : 8), Erastus, the chamberlain of the city (Rom. 16 : 23), and Gaius, Paul's host, formed exceptions. After Paul left them they were ministered to by Apollos and others. Factions arose in the church and questions upon Christian morality and doctrine, which are discussed in these Epistles.

The *subsequent history* of the church is brought to view by the letter of Clement, pastor at Rome (about A. D. 97. See above). It was addressed to this church, and indicates that after a period of harmony the church had been again divided into factions by ambitious leaders. A copy of the Epistle is found in the Alexandrine manuscript of the New Testament. Hegesippus, an ecclesiastical writer about the middle of the second century, speaks of the church of Corinth as having kept the true faith; and Dionysius, a most noted pastor at Corinth (about A. D. 170), in one of his letters, speaks of their Lord's Day's observances. It would seem that for a long time the church maintained apostolic doctrines, and usually enjoyed a good degree of prosperity.

CORINTH.

Some knowledge of the city of Corinth will help us to understand better the church there and these Epistles. It was not the ancient Greek Corinth which Paul visited. That had been taken and destroyed by L. Mummius, a Roman consul, B. C. 146. For one hundred years it lay in total ruin, till Julius Cæsar, B. C. 46, rebuilt it and colonized it largely with veterans and Roman freedmen. Standing on the isthmus with two harbors, Cenchreæ, the eastern, about nine miles distant, and Lechæum, the western, only a mile and a-half distant, it invited the commerce both from the East and the West. It soon regained more than its ancient opulence and was the metropolis of Achaia, embracing Southern and Central Greece. The Roman proconsul of Achaia fixed his seat there (Acts 18 : 12), the city having a population of from four to five hundred thousand. Jews were drawn thither by its merchandise, and Greeks by its ancient reputation and the glory of its Isthmian games. Its marts were filled with objects of luxury, and visited by every nation of the civilized world. The worship of Venus, which had given Corinth an infamous pre-eminence, was restored, and a thousand priestesses were dedicated to its licentious and shameful worship. The very name of Corinthian was synonymous with profligacy. A declining Greek philosophy prevailed among the Greeks and wealthier classes, and more or less affected the mass of the people. It was with such difficulties that Paul, his associates, and the disciples gathered there, had to contend. In these Epistles we find indications of a general looseness of manners and morals (1 Cor. 5 : 11; 6 : 9-11), a denial of a future life and the making of this life one of unlimited enjoyment (1 Cor. 15 : 32), rivalries and personal vanity (1 Cor. 4 : 6. 7; 5 : 6; 2 Cor. 11 : 12), and a worldly philosophy and strife of words (1 Cor. 1 : 17; 2 : 13; 2 Cor. 12 : 20).

THE FIRST EPISTLE

Apollos had returned from Corinth to Ephesus (1 Cor. 16:12). The church had degenerated, and some had fallen into immoral practices. Paul had written them a letter, charging them not to keep company with fornicators (1 Cor. 5:8). Judaizing teachers came to Corinth (2 Cor. 11:22), who brought letters of recommendation from other churches (2 Cor. 3:1) and who opposed the authority and teaching of Paul. This led to unduly extolling and following different religious leaders (1 Cor. 1:12). Some were carrying their views of Christian liberty so far as to tolerate notorious immorality (1 Cor. 5:1), and to attend idolatrous feasts (1 Cor. 8:10). Others were going to law against their brethren in heathen courts (1 Cor. 6:6). Christian women, transgressing the customary rules of modesty, were casting aside their veils in the public congregation (1 Cor. 11:5). The Lord's Supper was degenerating into a common and disorderly meal (1 Cor. 11:18, 19). Besides all this, spiritual gifts had been shamefully misused, and had become occasions of envy and strife. Doubtless under the influence of heathen philosophy and perhaps Sadducean influence, the doctrine of the resurrection had been denied or questioned by some (1 Cor. 15:12). There were, however, many members of the church of sincere piety and exemplary lives, whom the apostle could conscientiously commend (1 Cor. 1:4-9). Certain brethren had come to him, who had been a source of great comfort to him (1 Cor. 16:17, 18).

Deeply solicitous for the church Paul sent Timothy with instructions to proceed to Corinth after transacting some necessary business in Macedonia. Soon after this he received a letter from Corinth asking questions on certain subjects discussed there, without referring to the disorders among them (1 Cor. 7:1). From others however he heard of the factions in the church and of immoral excesses (1 Cor. 1:11; 5:1). As he could not leave Ephesus at that time (1 Cor. 16:9), he at once sends Titus and a brother not named, very probably in charge of this Epistle which these circumstances of the church had called forth (2 Cor. 2:13; 8:6, 16-18, 22, 23; 12:18).

His *design* in writing was to restore harmony in the church, to correct errors of doctrine and practice, to vindicate his authority as an apostle, and the character and style of his preaching from the attacks of his enemies, and to confirm the Christians of Corinth and Greece in their allegiance to Christ. He would have them realize the true ideas as a church and as Christians.

TIME AND PLACE OF WRITING.

Paul wrote the First Epistle to the Corinthians from Ephesus (16:8, 19) a little time before Pentecost, shortly after sending Timothy to Corinth by way of Macedonia (16:10, 11). A considerable interval must have elapsed since his ministry at Corinth; for Apollos had labored there (3:6; Acts 19:1) and had returned to Ephesus (16:12); divisions and disorders had grown up in the church; and Paul had written a previous letter which now is lost (5:9). All this would lead us to put this letter near the close of Paul's ministry at Ephesus. Now from Acts 19:21, 22, we learn that near the end of his stay at Ephesus he was proposing to visit Macedonia and Greece, and he sent on before Timothy and Erastus into Macedonia. He was in Ephesus from A. D. 54 to 57. From all this it appears that he wrote this Epistle at Ephesus, probably in the spring of A. D. 57.

FEATURES OF THE EPISTLE.

In the Epistle to the Romans doctrine predominates; in those to the Corinthians the practical prevails. Peculiar circumstances of a church in a pagan city called them forth. Did we not have these Epistles we should know far less than we do of apostolic churches in general, and of Gentile churches in particular; of their struggles and temptations, of the trials of apostolic missionaries and the difficulties of their work. The *first* Epistle brings more especially to view the church and its relations; the *second* brings into prominence Paul as an individual. But both present different sides of the church at Corinth, and also most remarkable characteristics of the apostle. The wisdom and shrewd common sense of Paul are marked in the first Epistle. It is applied Christianity in practical matters and to ordinary life. At the same time no Epistle presents better specimens of sublime thought or eloquent language. How he speaks of the wisdom of God and the foolishness of men (1:20 f.); of the ministers of Christ (4:1 f.); and of the shortness of time (7:29 f.). How magnificent his panegyric on love (chap. 13), and how unsurpassed in force of argument and happy illustration his defense and development of the doctrine of the resurrection. Paul appears as the settler of great principles and the preacher of great doctrines, the guide, the instructor, and the counselor of churches.

CONTENTS.

In the first six chapters Paul speaks of the divisions and disorders of the church at Corinth; and from the beginning of the seventh chapter on he answers the series of questions which the church had sent him. The following analysis is given.

FIRST PART.—Divisions and disorders in the church at Corinth, 1 : 1–6 : 20.
I. Salutation and thanksgiving, 1 : 1-9.
II. Divisions from party spirit, 1 : 10-4 : 21.
  1. Exhortation to unity, and a statement of their divisions, 1 : 10-12.
  2. Paul disclaims his own headship of the Christian system, 1 : 13-17.
  3. The preaching of the Cross abasing to pride, 1 : 18-23.
  4. But it is the power and wisdom of God, 1 : 24, 25.
  5. Illustrated in the Corinthian converts, 1 : 26-31.
  6. Paul preached not himself but Christ crucified, 2 : 1-5.
  7. Held up as the wisdom of God, 2 : 6-9.
  8. Revealed by God's Spirit, 2 : 10-13.
  9. Must be spiritually received, 2 : 14-16.
  10. But their party spirit proved their carnal-mindedness, 3 : 1-4.
  11. Christian ministers only workmen; God the master, 3 : 5-9.
  12. They must build on Christ, the only foundation, 3 : 10-15.
  13. Their danger and responsibility, 3 : 16, 17.
  14. Must renounce human wisdom, that they may be wise, 3 : 18-20.
  15. Therefore they must not glory in men, 3 : 21-23.

16. Paul and Apollos servants and stewards, 4 : 1–4.
17. Accountable to God and judged by him, 4 : 5.
18. Let there be no strife about teachers, 4 : 6–8.
19. The Corinthian arrogance and their self-denying labors contrasted, 4 : 9–13.
20. Paul speaks with apostolic authority, 4 : 14–21.

III. Moral disorders in the Corinthian church, 5 : 1–6 : 20.
    1. Case of incest. Failure of discipline, 5 : 1–8.
    2. Directions of a previous letter, 5 : 9–11.
    3. The offender to be expelled, 5 : 12, 13.
    4. Lawsuits at heathen tribunals, 6 : 1–7.
    5. The inconsistency of such conduct, 6 : 8–11.
    6. Fornication not a matter of indifference, 6 : 12–14.
    7. A sin against their own body, which belongs to Christ, and the temple of the Spirit, 6 : 15–18.
    8. A redeemed body should be used to God's glory, 6 : 19, 20.

SECOND PART.—Answers to certain questions asked in a letter from Corinth.

I. In regard to marriage, divorce, and celibacy, 7 : 1–40.
    1. Advice as to marriage and celibacy, 7 : 1–7.
    2. General advice to the unmarried, 7 : 8, 9.
    3. General advice as to divorce, 7 : 10, 11.
    4. As to the separation of married persons, 7 : 12–16.
    5. Generally, let each one abide in his calling, 7 : 17–24.
    6. Regarding marriage under present circumstances, especially of maiden daughters, 7 : 25–34.
    7. Duty of parents to unmarried daughters, 7 : 35–38.
    8. The duty of widows, 7 : 39, 40.

II. Concerning things offered in sacrifice to idols, 8 : 1–11 : 1.
    1. To be settled by love rather than by knowledge, 8 : 1–3.
    2. Really a matter of indifference, 8 : 4–6.
    3. But all not enlightened in regard to this, 8 : 7.
    4. Sin against a brother's conscience a sin against Christ, 8 : 8–12.
    5. Paul's principle of abstinence for the sake of others, 8 : 13.
    6. Illustrated by his own conduct.
        (a) Foregoing his rights as an apostle for others' good, 9 : 1–12.
        (b) His freedom and self-denial, 9 : 13–23.
    7. Self-restraint needful for their own safety, 9 : 24–27.
    8. Want of self-restraint was fatal to their highly favored fathers, 10 : 1–10.
    9. An example and warning to Christians, 10 : 11–13.
    10. Fellowship cannot exist with both Christ and demons, 10 : 14–22.
    11. Consideration for others our rule of action, 10 : 23–30.
    12. Seek God's glory and our neighbor's good, 10 : 31–11 : 1.

III. Concerning public worship, 11 : 2–34.
    1. The conduct and dress of women in public services, 11 : 2–16.
        (a) Praising the Corinthians for observing his instructions, 11 : 2.
        (b) Women veiled in public worship, 11 : 3–6.
        (c) Because of her relation to man, 11 : 7–12.

(d) From a sense of natural fitness, 11 : 13-15.
   (e) From the custom of the churches, 11 : 16.
  2. Disorders at the Lord's Supper, and its proper observance, 11 : 17-34.
   (a) Their abuse of the Lord's Supper, 11 : 17-22.
   (b) History, nature, and purpose of the Lord's Supper, 11 : 23-26.
   (c) Manner in which it should be observed, 11 : 27-34.
IV. Concerning exercises of spiritual gifts, 12 : 1-14 : 40.
  1. How to discern their nature, 12 : 1-3.
  2. Unity and diversity of spiritual gifts, 12 : 4-11.
  3. Illustrated by the human body, 12 : 12-26.
   (a) Many members in one body, 12 : 12-14.
   (b) None to be overrated or despised, 12 : 15-26.
  4. Application of these principles, 12 : 27-31.
  5. The superiority of love, 13 : 1-13.
   (a) Love pre-eminently essential to religion, 13 : 1-3.
   (b) Characteristics of love, 13 : 4-7.
   (c) Permanence of love, 13 : 8-12.
   (d) Pre-eminence of love, 13 : 13.
  6. Prophecy superior to gift of tongues, 14 : 1-25.
   (a) Prophecy a means of edification, 14 : 1-5.
   (b) Unknown tongues not understood, 14 : 6-9.
   (c) If not understood they tend to confusion, 14 : 10-19.
   (d) They are a sign to unbelievers, 14 : 20-22.
   (e) Prophecy especially for believers, 14 : 22-25.
  7. Directions to insure decency and order, 14 : 26-40.
   (a) Rules for the use of tongues and prophecy, 14 : 26-33.
   (b) As to the public ministrations of women, 14 : 34-36.
   (c) Exhortation to obedience and order, 14 : 36-40.
V. Concerning the resurrection of the dead, 15 : 11-58.
  1. Christ's resurrection a primal theme of Paul's preaching, 15 : 1-4.
  2. The fact of Christ's resurrection established, 15 : 5-11.
  3. Christ's resurrection implies a general resurrection, 15 : 12-19.
  4. The resurrection essential to the scheme of redemption, 15 : 20-28.
  5. Argument from the lives of believers, 15 : 29-34.
  6. Manner of the resurrection, 15 : 35-49.
  7. Result of the resurrection, 15 : 50-58.
VI. Concerning collections. Sundry matters, 16 : 1-24.
  1. Directions about the collection, 16 : 1-4.
  2. Paul's proposed visit to them, 16 : 5-9.
  3. Regarding Timothy, Apollos, and others, 16 : 10-18.
  4. Salutations, warning, and benediction, 16 : 19-24.

THE SECOND EPISTLE

TIME, PLACE, OCCASION, AND OBJECT

This Epistle is addressed to the church of God at Corinth, and to "all the saints which are in all Achaia." It was therefore a matter of interest to the churches throughout Greece, including that of Athens, and it impliedly met a want in them. With Paul was associated Timothy (2 Cor. 2:1), whom he had sent from Ephesus into Macedonia and Achaia to prepare for his coming (Acts 19:21, 22; 1 Cor. 16:10). After this Paul left Ephesus and went to Troas and into Macedonia, where he wrote this Epistle (Acts 20:1; 2 Cor. 2:12, 13; 8:1; 9:2, 4). Titus, who also had been sent to Corinth, returned bringing favorable tidings regarding the state of the church (2 Cor. 7:6; 8:16, 23). After sending this Epistle Paul visited Corinth and spent the winter of A. D. 58 there (2 Cor. 13:1; Acts 20:3, 4; Rom. 15:19, 23, 26). From all this it appears that Paul wrote this letter in the autumn of A. D. 57.

The *place* where he wrote it cannot be so definitely determined. It has been common to fix it at Philippi; but Paul speaks of the liberality of the churches of Macedonia (2 Cor. 8:1; 9:2) as though he had visited more than one of them, whereas Philippi would be the first in his way from Troas (Acts 16:11,12). An examination of the Epistle indicates a change of feeling and tone with the beginning of the seventh chapter. The first six chapters imply that Paul had learned some things favorable from Corinth, but that he was left in a state of some uncertainty and anxiety regarding their condition. The remaining chapters indicate a fuller and more favorable report of the church, and a clearer view of the opposition of his opponents. He is filled with greater joy and greater boldness in defending his apostolic authority, and answering taunts and accusations against himself. May we not then suppose that upon coming to Philippi he met with Timothy, who had returned from a brief visit to Corinth (1 Cor. 4:17; 16:10, 11), and who informed him of the exclusion and repentance of the incestuous person, as well as of some other matters in the church. Paul at once begins his letter, and after writing the first six chapters passes on to Thessalonica, where he meets Titus returning from a longer mission to Corinth, who gives him a full account of the church there. He is filled with joy, and he sees just what is needed to complete the work already going on at Corinth. From the fullness of his heart he completes the Epistle and sends it at once, perhaps by Titus (2 Cor. 8:23, 24), preparatory to his speedily following himself. If this theory is correct then the Epistle was begun at Philippi and finished at Thessalonica. It should be noted also that the situation as to parties in the church had changed since his writing the first Epistle. Then there were four parties, though his own followers and those of Apollos appear to receive his principal attention. Now in the second Epistle his bitter opposers seem to center in the Christ-party, who made light of his apostolic authority, some of whom claimed a special relationship to Jesus, and very probably were Jews who had seen Christ in the flesh (2 Cor. 10:7; 11:23). These largely made this Epistle necessary.

Paul's *object* in writing this Epistle seems to have been to develop in believers at Corinth a proper state of mind; to promote in them the reformation

INTRODUCTION

already begun; to guard them against the influences of false teachers, and thus render severity unnecessary on his part, when he should come to them. His own language is, "This also we pray for, even your perfection. For this cause I write these things while absent, that when present I may not deal sharply according to the authority which the Lord gave me for building up, and not casting down" (2 Cor. 13 : 9, 10). It was intended to prepare the way for the visit which he was soon to make them.

ITS CHARACTERISTICS.

This Epistle was evidently written in haste. Hence it is the least methodical of all of Paul's Epistles. It is the outpouring of a soul filled with affection, burdened with anxiety, schooled in affliction, and terribly in earnest. It is distinguished by its variety of gentleness and severity, calmness and vehemence, earnestness and irony. Nowhere do we see so much of Paul as an individual and as an apostolic missionary. He lays open his heart, discovers to us his soul-struggles, and the inner and outer conflicts in his planting and training of the churches. At the same time we get an inner view of the Corinthian church, with its praiseworthy characteristics and its glaring defects, and having a membership with different attitudes toward himself. How wisely he addresses different classes and how skillfully he anticipates argument and meets objections. How is the whole interspersed with the most delicate touches of thought and the sublimest eloquence. "Now he boils up," says Erasmus, "like a limpid spring, suddenly he rolls away with a great noise like a mighty torrent bearing all before it, and then he flows gently along, or expands like a placid lake over all the land."

SPECIAL PRACTICAL USES.

The two Epistles to the Corinthians were pre-eminently tracts for the times; yet they are suited, in a greater or less degree, to churches and believers of every age.

1. As to *churches*. The word church occurs more frequently in these Epistles than elsewhere in the New Testament. It is generally applied to the local church (1 Cor. 4 : 17; 2 Cor. 11 : 8, etc.), though it is also applied to the collective membership everywhere (1 Cor. 12 : 28; 1 Cor. 15 : 9). It is styled "the church of God," bringing into view its high position (1 Cor. 1 : 1 ; 2 Cor. 1 : 1). It is the dwelling-place of the Spirit (1 Cor. 3 : 16) ; a cultivated field (1 Cor. 3 : 9) ; a building, a temple (1 Cor. 3 : 11-17). Baptism, as related to Christ, is implied in 1 Cor. 10 : 1 ff. The institution and administration of the Lord's Supper in the church is given more fully than elsewhere in 1 Cor. 11 : 23-29. Ordinary and extraordinary gifts have their fullest presentation in chapters 12, 13, and 14 of 1 Corinthians. Church discipline is noted (1 Cor. 5 : 7-13), and the duty to the returning penitent (2 Cor. 2 : 5-8). Liberty is enjoyed, but must not be exercised to the injury of others, but guided by the highest law of love (1 Cor., chap. 8 and 9). Christian benevolence is treated in 1 Cor. 16 : 1-4 and 2 Cor., chap. 8 and 9. Social life in the church is brought to view in 1 Cor. 7 : 16-24 ; 2 Cor. 6 : 14-16, etc.

2. As to the *ministry*. The nature, character, motives, responsibilities, and work of the Christian ministry are treated in 2 Cor., chap. 4, 5, and 6 ; by whom

to be exercised (1 Cor. 11 : 4, 5, 16; 14 : 24). They are to be supported by the churches (1 Cor. 9 : 13, 14; 2 Cor. 11 : 7-9).

3. As to our *own age and country*. As Corinth was a place of great mental activity, celebrated for its wealth and commercial and manufacturing enterprises, the obstacles to the gospel were in many respects similar to those in our own age. As Corinth lay between two seas, so our own great country lies between two oceans, drawing toward it the commerce and enterprises of the world. A spirit of pride and worldly wisdom, a lowering of moral standards, and losing sight of the headship of Christ, are affecting our Christianity. There is a tendency on the part of many to undervalue the simplicity of the gospel, to neglect spiritual gifts, to cover up immoral practices, to fail in the grace of Christian giving, to engender party strifes and insubordination in churches and to pastors, to prefer a brilliant to a godly and experienced ministry, and to make both church and ministry subserve a worldly interest. The zeal, humility, consecration, self-denial, love, and earnest labor, such as Paul exercised, and the gospel he preached at Corinth, are needed to counteract and overcome these evils of our day.

CONTENTS.

This Epistle naturally divides itself into three parts. In the first seven chapters Paul explains his conduct in not coming immediately to them, but going to Troas, and how he exercised his ministry toward them. In the eighth and ninth chapters he treats the grace of giving and the collection for the poor. Beginning with the tenth chapter, and on to the end of the Epistle, he vindicates his apostolic authority and character. The Epistle has also a historical setting, the past, present, and future, corresponding to its three divisions. (See 1 : 8, 15; 2 : 12, 13; 7 : 5; 8 : 1; 10 : 1; 13 : 1.)

FIRST PART.—Explains why Paul first went to Troas instead of coming to Corinth, and the principles upon which he exercised his ministry, 1 : 1-7 : 16.
  I. Salutation, 1 : 1, 2.
  II. Reasons for first going to Troas, 1 : 3-2 : 17.
    1. Divine consolation in suffering, 1 : 3, 4.
    2. Enabled thereby to console others, 1 : 5-7.
    3. Paul's affliction in Asia and their sympathy, 1 : 8-14.
    4. Reasons for delaying his visit, 1 : 15-2 : 17.
      (a) Not fickleness on his part, 1 : 15-22.
      (b) But to spare them and help them, 1 : 23, 24.
      (c) And that he might not come in sorrow, 2 : 1-4.
      (d) So now advises the forgiveness and restoration of the penitent offender, 2 : 5-11.
    5. Why he left Troas and came into Macedonia, 2 : 12, 13.
    6. Exults in the triumphs of his ministry, 2 : 14-16.
    7. His insufficiency, yet sincerity, 2 : 16, 17.
  III Explains his ministry; its principles, character, and results, 3 : 1-7 : 16.
    1. His ministry accredited by his converts, 3 : 1-3.
    2. Its sufficiency not in himself, but from God, 3 : 4-6.
    3. Superiority to the ministry of the law, 3 : 7-11.

4. He and his fellow-laborers superior to Moses, 3 : 12-18.
5. His ministry true and genuine, 4 : 1, 2.
6. They that perish shut their eyes to the glory of Christ, 4 : 3-6.
7. The weakness of the minister but sets off the power of his ministry, 4 : 7-15.
8. But sustained by the hope of glorious immortality, 4 : 16-5 : 10.
   (a) Cheered by the prospects of eternal life, 4 : 16-18.
   (b) Looking for the future glorified body, 5 : 1-4.
   (c) Having an earnest of this, though as yet absent from the Lord, 5 : 5-8.
   (d) And stimulated by the thought of the judgment, 5 : 9, 10.
9. The motives : fear of the Lord, love of Christ, 5 : 11-15.
10. Their ministry one of reconciliation, 5 : 16-19.
11. Therefore preaches earnestly the Divine reconciliation, 5 : 20, 21.
12. How he aims to give effect to this ministry, 6 : 1-10.
13. Appeals for an affectionate response, 6 : 11-13.
14. Warning against evil associations, 6 : 14-18.
15. Exhorting the pursuit of inward holiness, 7 : 1.
16. Exhorts them to trust him, 7 : 2-4.
17. His affection proved by his experience in Macedonia, 7 : 5-16.
   (a) Anxiety gave way to joy through the report of Titus, 7 : 5-7.
   (b) His former letter designed for their reformation, 7 : 8-12.
   (c) The end attained awakened his joy and hope, 7 : 13-16.

SECOND PART.—Paul urges upon them to exercise the grace of giving for the poor of the saints of Jerusalem, 8 : 1-9 : 15.
1. By the example of the Macedonian Christians, 8 : 1-6.
2. By the example of Christ, 8 : 7-11.
3. Let there be a fair proportionment, 8 : 12-15.
4. The brethren in charge of this are trustworthy, 8 : 16-24.
5. Wishes them to sustain his boasts of them, 9 : 1-5.
6. Rich blessings will be returned to them, 9 : 6-11.
7. Will redound to God's glory, 9 : 12-15.

THIRD PART.—Paul vindicates his apostolic authority and character, 10 : 1-13 : 14.
I. His authority as an apostle, 10 : 1-18.
   1. Declares his spiritual power, 10 : 1-6.
   2. His authority a reality, 10 : 7-11.
   3. Does not imitate the false pretenses of his opposers, 10 : 12-18.
II. Paul's defense against his accusers, 11 : 1-12 : 13.
   1. Apologizes for his boasting, 11 : 1-20.
      (a) He does it out of interest and anxiety for them, 11 : 1-6.
      (b) His disinterested love, 11 : 7-11.
      (c) Guarding against dishonest men, 11 : 12-20.
   2. Equal and superior to his opponents, 11 : 21-33.
      (a) Equal to them in race, 11 : 21, 22.
      (b) Superior to them in labors, sufferings, and deliverances, 11 : 23-33.

3. Abundant revelations, 12 : 1-6.
   4. Continued suffering and promised grace, 12 : 7-10.
   5. The signs of his apostleship wrought among them, 12 : 11-13.
III. His proposed apostolic conduct, exhortations, and warnings, 12 : 14-13 : 14.
   1. Will still act disinterestedly and honestly, 12 : 14-18.
   2. His object their reformation, 12 : 19-21.
   3. When he comes will enforce discipline, 13 : 1-4.
   4. Exhorts to self-examination, 13 : 5, 6.
   5. Prays for their perfection, 13 : 7-9.
   6. Writes in order to avoid using severity, 13 : 10.
   7. Closing words, salutations, and benediction, 13 : 11-14.

The comments in the commentary are on the Common version and the original Greek. But the Improved version is placed in parallel columns. This will be found valuable for comparison and reference.

PAUL'S EPISTLE TO THE ROMANS

Introduction, salutation, and theme of the Epistle.

1 PAUL, ᵃa servant of Jesus Christ,

1 PAUL, a servant of Jesus Christ,

a 15:16.

TITLE. The oldest known title is simply *To the Romans*. Later it was enlarged to designate the writer of the Epistle. The fuller form is included and implied in the first and seventh verses of the salutation.

CHAPTER I.

The apostle begins with a marvelously full and rich salutation; and then after a few introductory words of personal interest passes, in ver. 16 and 17, to the ground thought of the Epistle. Through the remainder of the chapter he shows the need of the gospel, with the salvation it brings and the righteousness it reveals, from the base moral condition of the Gentiles.

1–17. SALUTATION TO THE SAINTS AT ROME, AND THE PARTICULAR INTRODUCTION TO THE EPISTLE. The salutation presents very strikingly Paul's manner. Ver. 1 and 7 form a complete sentence by themselves, the rest being parenthetic or relative sentences. Thoughts crowd upon him and press for utterance. Christ is the center, and around him thought suggesting thought revolves. In the introduction Paul expresses his thanksgiving for the well-known faith of the saints at Rome, and his prayerful desire for the mutual benefit which would arise from seeing and knowing them. This desire had been a well-formed purpose which he had been hindered from carrying out; but it was kept alive by a sense of duty to preach the gospel to all classes and everywhere. This he could readily and even joyfully do, since the gospel makes known to men the divine salvation, revealing God's righteousness by faith.

1. Paul—meaning *little*; his Roman name, which he uses in all his Epistles to the churches and fellow-laborers among the Gentiles, and is applied to him in the account of his Gentile work in the Acts. Saul was his Hebrew name, meaning *the asked for*, and was applied to him in his connection with the Jews, and in his earlier and less distinctive work. See "Notes on the Acts," 13:9, where the change of his name first appears, for further discussion. According to the custom of his time Paul inscribes his name at the beginning instead of at the end of his letter. With his name he writes the statement of his official position as a *servant* and an *apostle* of Jesus Christ. This he did because most of the church at Rome were not personally acquainted with him, and because he was about to discuss the great doctrines under Divine direction and by apostolic authority. Compare the opening salutations of his other Epistles, especially those to the Galatians, the Philippians, and to Titus. **Servant**—literally, *a slave*, one who serves, answering in the Scriptures to a *bond-servant*. The word has the twofold idea of belonging to a master and of service as a bondsman. Paul regarded himself as belonging to Christ, to whom he owed the service of obedience (1 Cor. 6:20; 7:23). But such service was true freedom (Gal. 5:1). The service of sin was slavery (6:16-19; John 8:34). The word servant is frequently applied in the New Testament to believers in general (1 Cor. 7:22; Eph. 6:6; 1 Peter 2:16); but Paul appears here to apply it to his general official position in the kingdom of God, just as in the

b called *to be* an apostle, separated unto
2 the gospel of God, (*c* which he had
promised afore *d* by his prophets in the
3 Holy Scriptures,) concerning *e* his Son
Jesus Christ our Lord, *f* which was
made of the seed of David according
4 to the flesh; and declared *to be* the Son

called to be an apostle, set apart to the
2 gospel of God, which he promised before through his prophets in the Holy
3 Scriptures, concerning his Son, who
was born of the seed of David according to the flesh, who was instated as

b See refs. Acts 22 : 21. *c* See refs. Acts 26 : 6. *d* 16 : 26; Gal. 3 : 8.
e Ps. 2 : 7; John 5 : 17-30; Heb. 1 : 2, 3. *f* Matt. 1 : 1; Luke 1 : 32.

Old Testament it was applied to prophets (Deut. 34 : 5; Jer. 25 : 4), and in the New frequently to ministers of the gospel and to apostles (Col. 4 : 12; 2 Tim. 2 : 24; James 1 : 1; 2 Peter 1 : 1). It was a high honor to be a servant of **Jesus Christ.** Paul gloried in being spiritually and officially thus connected with such a Master. **Called to be an apostle**—divinely selected and appointed to the office. From the general designation of servant, Paul goes on to specify what kind of a servant, namely, an *apostle*. He had been called by Christ himself to the office, like the other apostles (Acts 9 : 15; 26 16-18; Gal. 1 : 1, 15, 16). The apostles were eye-witnesses of Christ's ministry, death, and resurrection. (See Acts 1 : 21, and note). Paul speaks of having seen the Lord after his resurrection, and of the signs of his apostleship (1 Cor. 9 : 1; 2 Cor. 12 : 12). The apostles had their three years' preparation with the Lord; Paul, his three years in Arabia and Damascus (Gal. 1 : 17, 18), and also an abundance of revelations (Gal. 1 : 12; 2 Cor. 12 : 1, 7). **Separated**—*set apart* from the mass of men unto the work of preaching the gospel by God's choice and call (Acts 9 : 15; Gal. 1 : 15.) There seems also to be a special reference to the act of the church at Antioch under the Spirit's direction (Acts 13 : 1, 2). This Paul specifies still more: not only called to the apostolic office, but set apart to the particular calling of preaching *the glad tidings*. **Of God**—as the author and giver of the gospel, showing its dignity and authority (15 : 16; 1 Thess. 2 : 2, 8, 9). This verse may be paraphrased thus: *Paul, who has the honor to be a servant*, or bondman, *of Jesus who is the Christ*, to whom he and his service absolutely belong, yet in whom he finds his highest freedom and glory, *chosen* and appointed by him *to be an apostle, set apart* from among men, from his birth (Gal. 1 : 14), at his conversion, and by the Spirit through the church at Antioch, *to the* particular work of *announcing*

the glad tidings of which *God* himself is the author.
2. This verse should not be put in a parenthesis, as in the Common version. In this and the two following verses Paul gives a brief description of the gospel, **which had been promised** or *announced beforehand*, amounting to a promise, *through* **his prophets in the Holy Scriptures.** These prophets included all who had uttered Messianic predictions in the Old Testament. Paul holds up the gospel as no human invention, no afterthought, but as coming from God, and long before promised through inspired men (Acts 3 : 22-24). The phrase, *Holy Scriptures*, in the original is without the article, but the adjective *holy* makes the noun definite. But Meyer renders literally, *in holy writings*, that is, in the prophetic portions of the Old Testament. In either rendering the thought is essentially the same.
3. Concerning his Son—the great theme of the gospel and of Messianic promises, without whom there could have been no gospel. The *Son* is presented in two aspects, the Son of Man in this verse, and the Son of God in the next verse. According to the highest critical authorities, **Jesus Christ our Lord** does not belong here, but at the end of ver. 4. **Which was made**, rather, *who became* or *was born*, **of the seed of David**, intimating his high kingly character. It is also implied that in his birth there was a change of relation, that he had a previous existence in another relation (John 1 : 14). **According to the** flesh—in respect to his human nature, body, soul, and spirit, distinguished from his divine nature brought to view in the next verse (1 Tim. 3 : 16; Phil. 2 : 7). Thus he was David's noblest son, pre-eminently *the Son*, among the sons of men. (See Ps. 89 : 26-37; 2 Tim. 2 : 8.)
4. And declared—*determined*, it was manifestly settled, that he was **the**

of God with power, according ᵉ to the spirit of holiness, ᵇ by the resurrec-
5 tion from the dead: by whom ⁱ we have received grace and apostleship, for obedience to the faith ᵏ among all nations,

the Son of God with power according to the Spirit of holiness, by resurrection of the dead, Jesus Christ our Lord;
5 through whom we received grace and apostleship, for obedience of faith among all the nations, for his name's

g Heb. 9 : 14. h Acts 13 : 33-37. i Gal. 2 : 9; Eph. 3 : 2-9; 1 Tim. 1 : 11, 12. k Mark 16 : 15; Acts 9 : 15.

Son of God. Although he was the Son of God before his resurrection, yet he was openly defined and manifested as such by that great and crowning event. **With power**—literally, *in power*. Some would join this as an adverbial phrase with the preceding verb: *Declared*, or *determined powerfully to be*, etc., as in Rev. 1 : 16, "The sun shines *in his strength*." But it is better to join it with *Son*. It was manifestly settled and shown by the resurrection that he was the Son of God *in power*, exalted and having all authority in heaven and on earth (Matt. 28 : 18; Phil. 2 : 9-11). It appears to refer to Christ's condition after his resurrection, with *power*, such as he did not have in his earthly condition and as born of the seed of David. Compare "in glory" (Phil. 4 : 19). **Spirit of holiness**—presenting holiness as an essential quality, a spirit to which belongs holiness. Holiness in the abstract is ascribed only to God (Exod. 15 : 11; Isa. 6 : 3; Rev. 15 : 4). The reference here is not to the Holy Spirit, but to Christ's divine nature which is contrasted with *the flesh*, his human nature, in the preceding verse. In his divine nature he is spirit (John 4 : 24), and the phrase *spirit of holiness* is evidently applied to him as the Word who in the beginning was with God and was God (John 1 : 1. Compare 9 : 5). **By the resurrection from the dead.** The resurrection is here spoken of generally, which had its most glorious illustration in the resurrection of Christ. He is its author (John 11 : 25, 26) and its first-fruits (1 Cor. 15 : 20). Christ's resurrection is constantly appealed to as a proof of his Messiahship (Acts 2 : 31-36; 17 : 31, etc.). And so at this point, according to the best text, comes in, **Jesus Christ our Lord,** in apposition with "*his son*" of verse 3. The son, in his two-fold nature, Son of David and Son of God, is here emphatically presented in his familiar three-fold title: **Jesus,** *Saviour*; **Christ,** the promised *Anointed* or *Messiah*; **our Lord,** our *Lord and Master*, the Lord of the gospel dispensation, the Head of the church, to whom all believers owe allegiance and obedience. Paraphrase ver. 3 and 4 as follows: *Concerning his Son*, the great theme of the gospel, *who*, being pre-existent, *became by birth of the royal seed*, the noblest Son *of David according to his human nature, the flesh, who was* manifestly *determined* and shown *to be the Son of God with power* and authority in heaven and on earth, peculiar to himself, *according to* his divine nature, *the spirit of holiness, by virtue of the resurrection of the dead* of which his own resurrection was a proof and firstfruit (1 Cor. 15), even *Jesus Christ* our great anointed Saviour and *our* Supreme Master and *Lord*. On "Son of God," see note on John 1 : 34.

5. By (*through*) **whom.** Christ is viewed mediatorially, through whom he had received grace and the high calling of God (15 : 15). **We**—Paul uses the plural in speaking of himself, as was frequently done by Greek authors, though perhaps of himself as one of a class. Compare 3 : 9; Gal. 1 : 8, 9, etc., where Paul refers to himself by the plural "we." **We have received**—rather, *we received*, at a definite time in his past history. **Grace and apostleship.** Some take this as a figure of speech to mean, *the grace* or *gift* of *apostleship* (Eph. 3 : 2, 7). It is better and more natural however to take *grace*, generally, the *favor* of God which he received at conversion and as a Christian, and *apostleship* as something in addition which he received particularly and officially from the Lord (Acts 9 : 15; 26 : 16-18; Gal. 1 : 1). **For obedience to the faith**—rather, *unto obedience of faith*, expressing the design for which grace and apostleship had been conferred on Paul. It is better to take *faith* here, not as a system of Christian doctrine, but as that exercise of belief and trust in Christ by which the gospel is accepted and with which obedience is invariably

6 ¹for his name; among whom are ye also ᵐ the called of Jesus Christ:
7 To all that be in Rome, ⁿ beloved of God, ᵒ called *to be* saints;

6 sake; among whom are ye also, called
7 to be Jesus Christ's—to all the beloved of God that are in Rome, called to be saints: Grace to you and peace from

l Mal. 1 : 11.　　*m* 5 : 28-30 ; 1 Peter 5 : 10.　　*n* Deut. 33 : 12 ; Col. 3 : 12.　　*o* 1 Cor. 1 : 2 ; 2 Peter 1 : 3.

connected. Faith is the controlling principle. To receive and act on faith is to obey. And as it is the design that Christ and the whole gospel should be received by faith, so the obedience required of all by Christ is embraced in the gospel. **Among all nations.** Many regard this as including all nations, according to the last Commission (Matt. 28 : 19) and Paul's general treatment of the gospel as for both Jews and Gentiles. This accords also with the fact that the salutation was to all the saints at Rome, Jews and Gentiles (ver. 7), and that his work among Gentiles is not definitely introduced until ver. 13. Others, however, with strong reasons take it to mean: *Among all the Gentiles.* For so the word translated *nations* is commonly used in Paul's Epistles, occurring, according to Prof. J. R. Boise, fifty-five times, of which forty-four times it is translated *Gentiles*, four times *heathen*, and in other places *nations*. The corresponding Hebrew word also always means Gentiles or pagan nations. Moreover, the apostleship of Paul had special reference to the Gentiles and is so presented in this Epistle (11 : 13 ; 15 : 16). A strict interpretation would seem to demand this view. Yet may not the apostle have designed a certain indefiniteness of expression in the salutation of the Epistle, in deference to the two classes of his readers? Elsewhere he shows great conciliatory tact, especially in his address recorded in the Acts. **For his name**—*for his name's sake*, for all that name implies, the human and divine Christ (Acts 3 : 16 ; 5 : 41). These words are most closely connected in thought with "obedience of faith" (2 Cor. 5 : 20, 21). Paul had for years exercised his apostleship most earnestly among all nations, especially the Gentile nations, to bring them into faith and obedience for the sake of honoring and knowing Christ—for what he was in himself, what he had done and could do, to whom also he himself as a Christian and an apostle owed so much (2 Thess. 1 : 11, 12).

6. Paul intimates the reason for addressing them: **Among whom** (the nations, ver. 5) **are ye also the called** *ones* **of Jesus Christ,** or, called to be Jesus Christ's. They are represented not as called *by* Jesus Christ, but as *belonging* to him. Paul generally regards the calling as coming from God the Father (9 : 24 ; Gal. 1 : 15 ; 2 Thess. 2 : 14 ; 2 Tim. 1 : 9). The calling also is not that which is general and external, but that which is internal and effectual; the called ones being made partakers of the blessings which Christ bestows. (Compare 8 : 28-35 ; Heb. 3 : 1.)

7. This verse contains the salutation and is connected with the first. All the clauses that intervene came forth from his richly stored mind, and prevented him from sooner finishing the sentence he had begun. **To all that be in Rome,** etc. A clearer and preferable rendering is: *To all the beloved of God that are in Rome.* (See note ending ver. 13.) Paul addressed the Epistle to Christians, not to the church as a collective body, at Rome. It was doubtless made up of two or more congregations (16 : 5). So in his later Epistles "to the saints" (Eph. 1 : 1 ; Phil. 1 : 1 ; Col. 1 : 2). His earlier Epistles were addressed to churches (1 Thess. 1 : 1 ; Gal. 1 : 2, etc.). **Beloved of God.** As reconciled with God through Christ they are *beloved* (5 : 31-39). God's people are thus often honorably named (Deut. 33 : 12 ; Col. 3 : 12). **Called to be saints,** or *called, chosen saints.* The word saint includes the ideas of separation from the world and consecration to God. Christians are so called, as those who are called out from the world (John 17 : 16-19) to be a chosen, holy people (1 Peter 2 : 9). Their consecration is not only by an external profession, but also by the regenerating power of the Holy Spirit, and the cultivation of spiritual worship and holiness.

Grace to you, etc. This is the beginning of the salutation proper, and should commence a new sentence. All that precedes is the inscription. Salutations in letters among the ancients were brief. The Greeks simply sent *greetings*, as in Acts 15 : 23 ; James 1 : 1 ;

ᵖ Grace to you and peace from God our Father, and the Lord Jesus Christ.
8 First, ᑫ I thank my God through Jesus Christ for you all, that ʳ your faith is spoken of throughout the whole world.
9 For God is my witness, whom I serve with my spirit in ˢ the gospel of his Son, that ᵗ without ceasing I make mention
10 of you always in my prayers; ᵘ making request, if by any means now at length

God our Father and the Lord Jesus Christ.
8 First, I thank my God through Jesus Christ for you all, that your faith is
9 proclaimed in all the world. For God is my witness, whom I serve in my spirit in the gospel of his Son, how unceasingly I make mention of you, al-
10 ways in my prayers making request, if in any way now at length I may be

ᵖ 1 Cor. 1 : 3; 2 Peter 1 : 2; Rev. 1 : 4, 5.
ᵗ 1 Sam. 12 : 23.
ᑫ 1 Cor. 1 : 4.   ʳ 16 : 19.   ˢ 1 John 5 : 9–11.
ᵘ 1 Thess. 3 : 10.

the Hebrews, *Peace be with thee.* (Compare Dan. 4 : 1; 6 : 25; 3 John 14.) The Christian salutation combines the two, and enriches them from the infinite fountain of God's love. (Compare 2 John 3 : Jude 2.) **Grace**—the favor of God with all its attendant spiritual blessings. **Peace**—the fruit of grace, the sense of inward security and the blessedness which flows from the Divine favor. **God our Father** and the **Lord Jesus Christ** are equally the source of grace and peace. "God the Father is the Author, Christ the mediator and procurer, the Holy Spirit the applier or imparter, of grace and peace. The Spirit takes them from Christ and shows them to the believer (John 16 : 14). The latter may be the reason why the Holy Spirit is not especially mentioned in the epistolary salutations, except 2 Cor. 13 : 13, 14; 1 Peter 1 : 2" (DR. SCHAFF in *Lange*). This concludes the salutation. How full of Christ! How rich in doctrine! Where in profane writers can we find so much compressed within so small a compass?

8. The special introduction begins with this verse. **First** *of all*—absolutely—without intending to state subsequent points in numerical order. As was usual with Paul's Epistles, with the exception of that to the Galatians, he begins with conciliatory and commendatory words. **I thank my God.** How he appropriates God to himself personally, conscious of reconciliation and communion with him! No pagan religion thus brings God endearingly to the soul, and no heathen writer thus appropriates him. (Compare Acts 27 : 23; 1 Cor. 1 : 4, etc.) **Through Jesus Christ,** as mediator, we approach God in prayer, praise, and thanksgiving (Eph. 5 : 20). **That your faith** in the gospel, including trust in Christ and its legitimate fruits, **is spoken of,** or *proclaimed,* **throughout the whole world.** A popular expression and at the same time the language of ardent feeling, meaning *everywhere,* wherever Christians were found. (Compare Col. 1 : 6; 1 Thess. 1 : 8.) The Roman empire was generally regarded as the whole world (Luke 2 : 1), and the gospel had already been preached in its chief cities (10 : 18; 15 : 19). Rome was the center of the empire and there was a going and coming from all the provinces. News could be easily transmitted.

9. For introduces the proof of his statement in ver. 8. **God is my witness.** Such solemn affirmations, made in the warmth of feeling, are common in Paul's writings (2 Cor. 1 : 23; Gal. 1 : 20; Phil. 1 : 8; 1 Thess. 2 : 5, 10). God was his only witness and his only appeal in regard to his secret prayers. **Whom I serve with my spirit**—rather, *in my spirit,* implying a spiritual heart service. (Compare John 4 : 24.) The word translated *serve* denotes *religious* service, or *worship.* Compare "Whose I am and whom I serve" (Acts 27 : 23, and note). **In the gospel of his Son**—in the field assigned me in proclaiming and defending the glad tidings of his Son. Thus both inwardly and outwardly he was engaged in serving God and spreading the gospel. All this thus far is closely connected with "God is my witness" and strengthens that solemn assertion. So also what follows: *My witness . . . how unceasingly* **I make mention of you always in my prayers**—never forgetful of you whenever I pray. (Compare Phil. 1 : 3; 2 Tim. 1 : 3.)

10. Paul notes a special subject of prayer connected with his incessant praying for them: **Making request,** etc. **If by any means,** or *in any*

I might have a prosperous journey by
11 the will of God to come unto you. For
I long to see you, that *I may impart
unto you some spiritual gift, to the end
12 ye may be established; that is, that
I may be comforted together with you
by *y* the mutual faith both of you and
me.
13 Now I would not have you ignorant,
brethren, that *z* oftentimes I purposed

prospered by the will of God to come
11 to you. For I long to see you, that I
may impart to you some spiritual gift,
to the end that ye may be established;
12 that is, to be comforted together in
you, through each other's faith, both
13 yours and mine. And I do not wish you
to be ignorant, brethren, that oftentimes I purposed to come to you, (and

---

x 15 : 29.   *y* 2 Peter 1 : 1.   *z* See refs. Acts 19 : 21.

way, implying a strong desire. If **now at length,** after so long a delay, **I may have a prosperous journey,** *the way made clear,* and *prospered* **by the will of God to come unto you.** It is implied that he had long desired to visit them, but had thus far been unable to carry out his purpose. Literally, *in the will of God*—the determining however being within the Divine will, and upon that his coming to them depended (15 : 32; Acts 18 : 21).

11. Giving an explanatory reason for what he had just said about coming to them, he adds, **For I long** earnestly **to see you** (compare 2 Cor. 9 : 14; Phil. 1 : 8; 2 : 26; 2 Tim. 1 : 3) not from curiosity, nor for personal advantage, nor for mere social friendship, but **that I may impart** *to you something, a* **spiritual gift,** to each one according to his faith and the will of God, **to the end that ye may be established** in Christian doctrine and life, and fortified against every temptation to swerve from them (1 Thess. 3 : 2, 3; 2 Thess. 3 : 3). *Spiritual gifts,* bestowed by the Holy Spirit, included both the miraculous (1 Cor. 12 : 10) and the ordinary gifts of teaching, exhortation, faith, and the like (12 : 6-8; 1 Cor. 12 : 8, 9). Miraculous gifts were endowments communicated by laying on of hands of the apostles (Acts 8 : 17; 19 : 6), and were common in apostolic churches (1 Cor. 1 : 7; Gal. 3 : 5); the ordinary were the edifying and comforting influences of the Holy Spirit and those endowments which were needed for service in the churches (1 Peter 4 : 10, 11). In this passage the word may refer to all kinds of gifts, but more especially to every religious benefit, of faith, knowledge, holiness, consolation, virtue, of which the apostle might be the means of bestowing. Paul's desire was that they might be "comforted together" (ver. 12), that he might "preach the gospel" to them at Rome. In his ministry he valued most highly the ordinary gifts of the Spirit (1 Cor. 13). *To the end ye may be established.* This word *established* occurs at the end of this Epistle (16 : 25), and is suggestive both of Paul's desire and hope that this Epistle, as well as his visit to them, would result in building them up in the Christian life.

12. That is, in other words, to speak modestly and without seeming to assume too much, to **be comforted** and helped *together among you* privately and in your assemblies *through each other's faith* in Christ and the gospel—the **faith both of you and me.** Paul expresses himself with delicate courtesy to brethren who were mostly strangers to him, lest he should seem to put too high an estimate on himself and too low upon them. The advantageous result of his visit would by no means be one-sided. In being a blessing to them they would be a blessing to him. There would be a mutual strengthening of the faith of each and his heart would be consoled as well as theirs. The full meaning of the verb translated *to be comforted together* cannot easily be expressed in English. It includes the ideas of enlivening, encouraging, and consoling. It has two corresponding nouns. One is used to express *exhortation, encouragement, consolation, comfort.* The other is the one that Jesus applies to the Holy Spirit *the Comforter, Advocate,* or *Helper* (John 14 : 16). While Paul hoped to impart spiritual gifts to the strengthening of his Roman brethren, he was not unmindful of his own dependence on Christian communion and fellowship for encouragement and comfort.

13. Now not only have I longed to come to you, but *I do not wish you to be* **ignorant, brethren.** This is the first time that the word *brethren* is found in

to come unto you, (but *a* was let hitherto,) that I might have some *b* fruit among you also, even as among other 14 Gentiles. *c* I am debtor both to the Greeks, and to the Barbarians; both to 15 the wise, and to the unwise. So, as much as in me is, I am ready to preach the gospel to you that are at Rome also.

was hindered hitherto,) that I might have some fruit in you also, even as 14 in the rest of the Gentiles. Both to Greeks and Barbarians, both to wise 15 and foolish, I am debtor; so, as far as lies in me, I am ready to preach the gospel to you also who are in Rome.

a See refs, Acts 16 : 6, 7.   *b* John 15 . 16 , Phil. 4 : 17.   *c* 1 Cor. 9 : 16–23.

the Epistles. It is much more frequent than any other designation of Christians, suggestive of their relation in the churches, and of their union in Christ (Eph. 2 : 19; 5 : 23, 30). They are generallly called disciples in the Gospels, frequently in the Acts, but never in the Epistles. They are never styled *saints* in the Gospels, only four times in the Acts, and fifty-five times in the Epistles. But they are termed brethren about fifteen times in the Gospels, thirty times in the Acts, and about one hundred and ninety times in the Epistles. The term *sister* is sometimes used (Rom. 16 : 1; 1 Cor. 7 : 15; James 2 : 15; Matt. 12 : 50. See on Acts 9 : 13; 11 : 29). *That oftentimes* during many years (15 : 23) *I purposed to come to you* (Acts 19 : 21) *and* **was** *hindered* **hitherto,** especially by the urgent calls from nearer fields, where the gospel had not been preached, being ambitious to preach Christ in such places (15 : 20). Doubtless the Spirit at times was directing otherwise (Acts 16 : 6), and Satan at other times was hindering (1 Thess. 2 : 18). But had it not been for these many hindrances we might not have had this Epistle to the Romans. **Let** is the old English word for *hindered.* Paul adds the object he had in view. **That I might have some fruit**—as a harvest, *in you also* and among you, in building you up in Christian graces and activities, and in the consequent conversion of souls (6 : 22; John 4 : 35–38; 15 : 16; Ps. 51 : 12, 13), **even as among** or *in the rest of the* **Gentiles** (15 : 14, 19. See note on ver. 5). Paul speaks as the apostle to the Gentiles. It would seem that the brethren at Rome were mostly Gentiles.

Rome was the leading Gentile city of the world, and the brethren there were largely Gentiles (15 : 15, 16). It contained about two million inhabitants, one-half of whom were slaves. Representatives of all nations were found there, among whom were about sixty thousand Jews. The Greeks were its most enterprising inhabitants. The names in the last chapter of this Epistle would indicate that the Christians there were mostly Greek. Indeed this seems to have been its character during the first two centuries.

14. Having introduced himself as the apostle to the Gentiles, Paul in this verse and the next expresses his sense of obligation to preach the gospel to Gentiles everywhere, including those at Rome. **I am a debtor,** under obligation from gratitude to Christ for graciously calling me into his kingdom (Gal. 1 : 15, 16; 1 Tim. 1 : 12–16), and from my commission (ver. 5; Acts 9 : 15; 26 : 16–18; 2 Tim. 1 : 11) to preach the gospel *both to the* **Greeks and Barbarians,** to cultivated and uncultivated nations without distinctions of race, *both to* **wise and unwise** or *foolish*, without regard to conditions of life, to natural intelligence and culture among the people. Paul is speaking of Gentiles. The Jews would naturally be reached to some extent as they were scattered among the Gentiles. "The question whether the Romans belonged to the Greeks or the Barbarians is scarcely in place, probably did not occur to the mind of Paul" (J. R. BOISE). *Barbarian* meant originally a foreigner, a man speaking a strange tongue, and is so used in 1 Cor. 14 : 11; Acts 28 : 2, 4. But the Greeks in their pride of race and culture and the Romans in their pride of power, came to look upon all outside of themselves as rude and uncultured foreigners. *Debtor* —held under obligation to do something for some one (8 : 12; 15 : 27). This obligation was imposed by Christ and by the lost condition of men. In preaching the gospel he was paying a debt to God and his fellow-men. He had received, and must give forth.

15. So, under this sense of obligation, **as far** *as it respects me*, on my part as far as I have the ability and the opportunity, **I am ready** and desirous

16 For ᵈ I am not ashamed of the gospel of Christ: for ᵉ it is the power of God unto salvation ᶠ to every one that believeth; ᵍ to the Jew first, and also to the 17 Greek. For ʰ therein is the righteousness of God revealed from faith to faith:

d Ps. 40 : 9, 10 ; 1 Cor. 2 : 2 ; 1 Tim. 1 : 8, 12.
f John 3 : 15, 16.   *g* 2 : 9 ; Luke 2 : 30–32 ; Acts 3 : 26.

e 1 Cor. 1 : 18 ; 2 Cor. 10 : 4, 5 ; 1 Thess. 2 : 13.
h 3 : 21–30 ; 4 : 5 ; Gal. 2 : 16 ; 5 : 5 ; Phil. 3 : 8, 9.

to preach the gospel to you *also that are at Rome*—where are found the representatives of all nations and classes of the world. Paul's *readiness* corresponded with his sense of obligation. To YOU—refers primarily to the Christians at Rome (ver. 7) who would profit by his evangelistic labors, but *you*, used generally and popularly, includes all who should be disposed to hear the gospel from him. *To preach the gospel* here is one word, *to evangelize* (Acts 8 : 25), announcing the glad tidings concerning Jesus as the Messiah and of salvation through him.

16. Paul passes naturally and informally to the leading thought or theme which he intended to develop in his letter: The gospel is the power of God for saving men, both Jews and Gentiles, on condition of faith, since it reveals a righteousness from God through faith alone. For introduces the reason for his readiness to preach the gospel at Rome, where there was so much grandeur and politeness, human learning and superstition. I am not ashamed of the gospel, though it is galling to human pride to meet the contempt cast upon the doctrine of the world's Messiah crucified as a malefactor (1 Cor. 2 : 1-5). Paul had met it wherever he went; at Philippi, which was a colony, a miniature of Rome (Acts 16 : 12, 21 ; Phil. 1 : 30) ; at Athens, where he was called "a babbler" (Acts 17 : 18) ; at Corinth and throughout Greece, where Christ crucified was a stumbling-block to Jews and foolishness to Gentiles (1 Cor. 1 : 23). Of Christ—should be omitted according to the best Greek text. The *gospel* which Paul preached included all about Christ, his life, death, resurrection, and ascension ; that he was the Messiah, the Saviour of the world, the Son of the living God; that salvation was through him alone by faith in him, by which man could be justified from all things that he was not able to be justified by the law of Moses (Acts 13 : 39). For, rather than be ashamed of the gospel, it becomes me to glory in its divine excellency, it being the power of God, superior to anything that man has ever devised; efficaciously working and leading into complete and eternal salvation of the soul from sin and death, to every one that believeth, without regard to national distinctions, to the Jew first in priority of time and in precedence of national privilege, and also to the Greek, the rest of mankind, the Gentiles (Luke 24 : 47 ; Acts 13 : 46). Notice that the gospel itself is *the power of God*, great, glorious, and efficacious (2 Cor. 10 : 3-6) ; the whole provision made in the gospel is meant, including the influences of the Holy Spirit accompanying the word (1 Cor. 1. 18; Heb. 4: 12; James 1 : 18; Jer. 23 : 29). To the Romans, the most powerful of men, it was fitting to style the gospel "the *power* of God," but to the Greek the most eminent for human wisdom, Paul adds, "the *wisdom* of God" (1 Cor. 1 : 24). *To every one that believeth*—that *has* faith in the gospel, which of course includes faith in Christ. Faith is not the ground of merit, but the medium of receiving Christ and salvation as proclaimed in the gospel (Rom. 5 : 1 ; Phil. 3 : 9).

17. The gospel is the power of God unto salvation, For therein is *a* righteousness of God revealed—or *God's righteousness*, that which proceeds from him as its author, is imparted by him to the believer, and is only acceptable to him. This righteousness was foreshadowed in Abraham (4 : 9), predicted in prophecy (Isa. 56 : 1), but was not fully made known to men till it was revealed in the gospel (Eph. 2 : 8, 9). It is from faith to faith, literally, *out of faith into faith*, beginning with faith and leading on to faith. It is from beginning to end of faith (9 : 30; 10 : 6 ; Phil. 3 : 9). It is appropriated so as to be personally available at first and ever after by faith. To the believer

as it is written, 'The just shall live by faith.

from faith to faith; as it is written, But the righteous shall live by faith.

¹ See refs. Hab. 2 : 4.

this righteousness becomes more and more a reality, a personal realization, but only by faith. Compare the phrase "from glory to glory" (2 Cor. 3 : 18) and "from strength to strength" (Ps. 84 : 7). Also "of death unto death" (2 Cor. 2 : 16). Faith is an exercise of the soul including *belief* and *trust*. **As it is written,** in Hab. 2 : 4, *The righteous shall have life from faith*. Quoted also in Gal. 3 : 11; Heb. 10 : 38. In the Hebrew, Habakkuk says, "The righteous by his faith," or "*his faithfulness*," shall live." Faith is implied and really included in *faithfulness*. "This *faithfulness* in the prophet's sense, and *faith* in the Christian sense, have the same fundamental idea, *trustful self-surrender to God*" (MEYER). The faith of a heart accepted with God is always the same in its nature under whatever circumstances exercised. Paul uses this expression as a brief summary of the Old Testament on this point, without reference to its particular use and application in Habakkuk. Some place a comma after faith. "The righteous by faith, shall live." It seems better, if a comma is used, to put it after "righteous"; but it is best to have no comma at all.

Righteousness and four kindred words, translated *just* or *righteous, justify* and *justification*, are of first importance in Paul's writings. A clear understanding of these terms is needful in the exposition especially of Romans and Galatians. They must therefore be briefly noticed here. They are derived from a Greek word (δίκη, *dikē*), meaning *right*, as follows:

(1) *Righteous* or *just* (*dikaios*, δίκαιος). This is used absolutely of God, as perfectly righteous and holy, and is thus applied to Christ (3 : 26; 2 Tim. 4 : 8; 1 John 2 : 29; Acts 3 : 14). In this sense it can be rightly said of mankind, that there is not one righteous (3 : 10). In a relative sense, however, *righteous* can be applied to men, as upright, virtuous, and serving God (Acts 10 : 22; Titus 1 : 8). It is applied to them as approved of God (5 : 7), as acceptable to him by faith (this verse; Gal. 3 : 11; Heb. 10 : 38). Thus they are spoken of as "righteous before God"

(2 : 13). This word occurs eighty-one times in the New Testament. In the Revised version it is translated sixty-three times *righteous*, eleven times *just* (nine of which are translated righteous in the Improved Bible Union version), and seven times *right*.

(2) *Righteousness* (*dikaiosune*, δικαιοσύνη), denoting the abstract idea or quality or state of one who is righteous. It never means justification, but simply *righteousness*, and is always so translated in both the Common and the Revised versions. This sense varies in its application. Sometimes it means the righteousness or holiness in the Divine character (3 : 5); sometimes godliness or true piety in man (6 : 13). Sometimes it is that righteousness which is reckoned to us on Christ's account (4 : 6), and sometimes that which, through and in connection with this imputation of Christ's righteousness, has become an effect in us (6 : 16, 19). Both of these ideas are at times united in this word, the righteousness which is reckoned to the believer and that resultant moral condition inseparably connected with it (2 Cor. 5 : 21). *Righteousness* in this passage (ver. 17) appears to include this double meaning. As *salvation* in the preceding verse is a full and complete salvation of the soul, so righteousness here includes what Christ does for us and in us. Both of these ideas Paul discusses and develops in this Epistle. So Dr. A. H. Strong, "Systematic Theology," p. 486 (f.): "This righteousness includes sanctification as well as justification, and the subject of the Epistle to the Romans is not simply justification by faith, but rather righteousness by faith, or salvation by faith. Justification by faith is the subject of chap. 1-7; sanctification by faith is the subject of chap. 8-16. We are not sanctified by efforts of our own any more than we are justified by efforts of our own." The particular application of this word in different passages, and Paul's use of it, will appear more exactly as we proceed in these notes. It occurs thirty-six times in this Epistle.

(3) *To justify* (*dikaioō*, δικαιόω) in New Testament usage means to *show*,

The ruin and guilt of the Gentiles.

18 ᵃ FOR the wrath of God is revealed | 18 For God's wrath is revealed from

a 2 : 5, 6, 8, 9 ; Ezek. 18 : 4 ; Col. 3 : 6.

or *declare righteous*. The former meaning is occasional and occurs in 3 : 4 ; 1 Cor. 4 : 4 ; 1 Tim. 3 : 16 ; Matt. 11 : 19 ; Luke 7 : 35 ; 10 : 29. The latter meaning, in a judicial sense, *to declare one righteous* and treat him accordingly, is found elsewhere in Paul's Epistles, and is the predominant idea of the word elsewhere in the New Testament. This act of God declaring and treating one as righteous for Christ's sake, carries along with it the forgiveness of sins. The sinner is not only released from punishment, but accepted as though he had committed no offense (3 : 25 ; 4 : 6-8 ; 8 : 33). It also implies regeneration and the impartation of righteousness (8 : 30 ; Phil. 3 : 9 ; 2 Cor. 5 : 17-19 ; Gal. 6 : 15 ; John 5 : 21).

(4) *Justification* (*dikaiōsis*, δικαίωσις) expressing the abstract idea of the verb *justify*. The act of God *declaring men free from guilt and acceptable to him*. This word occurs only twice in the New Testament (4 : 25 ; 5 : 18).

(5) *Justification* (*dikaiōma*, δικαίωμα) that which is divinely accounted right, namely, a divine *requirement* or *ordinance* (1 : 32 ; 2 : 26 ; 8 : 4 ; Luke 1 : 6 ; Heb. 9 : 1, 10). Also that which the law regards or accounts right, *a righteous act* (5 : 18 ; Rev. 15 : 4 ; 19 : 8). Once it means *justification* (5 : 16), a favorable sentence, by which God acquits men and declares them acceptable to him, and restored to his favor. By this and the two preceding words God is represented in the New Testament as acquitting the believer from all guilt and restoring him to the Divine favor on the ground of Christ's obedience, death, and intercession, irrespective of the believer's personal merit. Yet when justification is explained and treated as an actual experience in man it at once appears as inseparable from a moral change of the justified (6 : 7-11, 18, 22 ; 8 : 1-4). The fact seems to be that when Paul addressed those who trusted in themselves that they were righteous, he preached the judicial doctrine of justification by faith alone, salvation attainable only through trust in Jesus Christ; but when he explained and enforced this doctrine it was a salvation attained alone by a personal trust and union of the justified with his Saviour, which necessarily implied and involved a renewal of his nature. Acquitting the sinner and accounting him righteous, forgiveness, regeneration, and faith, though we may distinguish and treat them separately, in order to understand them clearly, yet in our conception of them should not be divorced from one another, and in actual experience, they are inseparable.

The five words, above considered, relating to righteousness and justification, should be clearly understood in order to an intelligent reading or study of Paul's writings.

The subject of the Epistle as here presented may be thus stated : THE GOSPEL REVEALS SALVATION THROUGH A RIGHTEOUSNESS BY FAITH IN CHRIST ALONE, IRRESPECTIVE OF WORKS OF LAW. From this point the doctrinal portion of the Epistle begins and extends to the end of the eleventh chapter. The necessity of this righteousness in order to salvation is shown in 1 : 18 to 3 : 20. This righteousness through Christ is presented and illustrated, for the justification, sanctification, and complete salvation of believers in Jesus in 3 : 21 to the end of the eighth chapter. The rejection of Israel as a peculiar covenant people, and the extension of the offer of salvation to all men are considered in chap. 9 to 11 inclusive. The remainder of the Epistle contains the practical part ; various precepts, directions in regard to the treatment of weak brethren, personal explanations and exhortation, messages and salutations.

18–32. THE NECESSITY OF SALVATION AND OF A RIGHTEOUSNESS such as the gospel reveals SHOWN FROM THE SINFULNESS OF the human race with special reference to THE GENTILE WORLD. Divine wrath against the ungodliness and unrighteousness of men (ver. 18) ; historical view of the downfall and degradation of mankind (ver. 19-23) ; judicially given over to vileness and to a reprobate mind (ver. 24-32). Paul views the race as having sunk down from a

ROMANS

from heaven against all ungodliness and unrighteousness of men, *who hold
19 the truth in unrighteousness. Because *that which may be known of God is manifest in them; for *God hath
20 showed *it* unto them. For *the invisible things of him from the creation of the world are clearly seen, being understood by the things *p* that are made, *even* his eternal power and Godhead: so that

heaven against all ungodliness and unrighteousness of men, who hold back
19 the truth in unrighteousness; because that which may be known of God is manifest in them; for God manifested
20 it to them. For, since the creation of the world, his invisible things are clearly seen, being perceived by the things that are made, even his eternal power and divinity; that they may be

l Luke 12:46, 47; John 3:19–21.   *m* Acts 14:17.   *n* 1 John 1:9.   *o* Ps. 19:1-6, Acts 14:17.   *p* 2:15.

primeval state in which a true knowledge of God was enjoyed.

18. Having presented s a l v a t i o n through a righteousness by faith alone, Paul proceeds to prove the necessity of just such a provision. This is evident from man's condition as a sinner, and as such condemned before God, **For the wrath of God,** etc. *The wrath* of God is his antagonism against sin, and is infinitely removed from the malignity of human anger. God's holiness and justice, and indeed his love and his entire nature, are diametrically opposed to all that is evil. **Is revealed** through man's conscience, through Divine interpositions and revelations **from heaven,** where God dwells. Paul assumes the existence of God and his primitive justice as truths which exist in human consciousness, and force themselves on the knowledge and convictions of men. See ver. 24–32 for an illustration of how God has revealed his wrath. Such wrath from heaven should certainly suggest the necessity of a righteousness from heaven. **Against all** kinds of **ungodliness,** impiety toward God, **and unrighteousness,** *immorality* and *injustice* among men. These two classes are a comprehensive summary of the objects of the Divine displeasure. **Who hold the truth in unrighteousness**—who possess the truth yet remain in sin, who know it yet refuse to obey it. So the verb *hold* is used in 1 Cor. 7:30; 2 Cor. 6:10. (Compare James 2:1.) This view is favored by ver. 21, 28. This wrath is revealed against those who know something of God's will and disregard it. Others, however, would translate more literally, *hold back the truth, repress* it, in their reason and conscience, not allowing what they do know concerning God and his attributes, to have its proper influence, (ver. 21, 28). "Truth repressed is soon forgotten or perverted.

(Compare John 7:17.)" There need be no conflict between these views as stated above; for they who possess the truth and remain in sin must in a certain measure repress it, and *vice versa.*

19. Because introduces the reason of the statement of ver. 18. They were not ignorant of the truth which they disregarded and repressed, therefore "the wrath of God is revealed," etc. **That which may be known of God**—from nature and providence; or as many translate, *That which is known of God* from creation and providence. **Is manifest in them**—within their minds, in their hearts. **For God hath shewed,** rather, *manifested* or *made it known,* **unto them** by his works and providence from the time man became an inhabitant of the earth (ver. 20). The historic or indefinite past tense is used. The knowledge of God among men preceded heathenism. This is the teaching of Scripture (Gen. 1, 2; Eccl. 7:29) and is confirmed by tradition. God's revelation is threefold: (1) To the reason and conscience (2:15; John 1:9); (2) through creation and providence (ver. 20; Acts 14:17; 17:25-28); and (3) through the Holy Scriptures including the gospel of the manifestation of Christ. The first two are here meant in distinction from the last.

20. For confirms the statement just made. **The invisible things of him**—the attributes and perfections of his being which are not seen by the senses, **from,** rather, *since*, **the creation of the world** (compare Acts 15:17) **are clearly seen** by the mind, **being understood,** or better, *being perceived,* **by the things that are made**—by means of his works. There has been no time or circumstance since the world was created at or in which men could have excuse, since the knowledge of God from his works was within their reach. Heathen writers have expressed simi-

21 they are without excuse: because that, q when they knew God, they glorified *him* not as God, neither were thankful; but r became vain in their imaginations, and their foolish heart was 22 darkened. *Professing themselves to 23 be wise, they became fools, and changed the glory of the uncorruptible t God into an image made like to corruptible man, and to birds, and fourfooted beasts, and creeping things.

21 without excuse. Because, knowing God, they glorified him not as God, nor gave thanks; but became vain in their reasonings, and their stupid 22 heart was darkened. Affirming themselves to be wise, they became fools; 23 and changed the glory of the incorruptible God for the likeness of an image of corruptible man, and of birds and fourfooted beasts and creeping things.

q Ver. 28. r 2 Kings 17:15; Jer. 2:5; Eph. 4:17, 18. s Jer. 10:14; 1 Cor. 1:19-21.
t See refs, Exod. 20:4; Ps. 106:20; Ezek. 8:10.

lar sentiments. **Even his eternal power**—the first and prominent attribute which the works of creation would impress on the mind; **and Godhead,** *Divinity,* the divine nature and character. These are the invisible things just spoken of. **So that they are,** or *So that they may be,* **without excuse.** Professor Boise suggests that both ideas, result and purpose, may be included here. Some may shut their eyes to the light; others may not go through the process of reasoning. But even then where knowledge is attainable ignorance is no excuse. Or even if a whole nation is found utterly ignorant of God it only shows how man through sin has degenerated, and sunk into spiritual darkness. See Fish's "Masterpieces," Vol. II., p. 463, sermon by President Maxey; also "Christian Review," Vol. XXV., p. 105 ff. on Rom. 1:18-23.

21. Because introduces more emphatically and more fully why they are without excuse. *Because that having known* or *knowing* the true *God,* in contrast to false gods, in the early history of the race and from time to time in all ages. Knowing of his existence and his chief perfections. Paul treats now of a matter of fact and shows what men did, although they had this knowledge. Heathen mythologies indicate the doctrine of the Divine unity to have been universally held among all nations in their early history. So also the Scriptures indicate this. Before the flood. (See Gen. 4:26; 5:24; 6:8.) After the flood for indications of the knowledge of the true God among the early nations. (See Gen. 14:18-20; 20:5, 10; Num. 22: 8, 24; Jonah 3:5.) **They glorified him not as God,** by worshiping and obeying him as such, **neither were they thankful,** they did not give thanks to him as the source of all good. (Compare Dan. 5:23.) Thus they totally rejected God. **But became vain in their imaginations**—*in their reasonings* and speculations; *became vain* referring to their foolish and base conceptions of God, especially in their idol worship. Heathen gods and their worship are spoken of in Scriptures as *vanities.* (Acts 14:15; 1 Kings 16:13; 2 Kings 17:15; Jer. 8:19.) **And their foolish heart,** stupid and senseless, as to their whole inward being, **was darkened;** losing all right views of God, their moral conceptions became more and more degraded (1 Cor. 3:20).

22. This sentence enlarges and proves the statement just made. **Professing,** or *affirming,* **themselves to be wise,** making high pretensions to wisdom, **they became fools,** or *foolish,* in their conceit of wisdom. Such were the idle speculations of the early Greek philosophers who were justly condemned by Socrates. But special reference is had to the origin of idolatry, and to that worldly wisdom which engenders pride, separates from God, brings on spiritual blindness, and results in the worship of the creature rather than the Creator (1 Cor. 1:21; Jer. 10:14).

23. The sentence continuing from the preceding verse illustrates their folly: **And changed the glory of the uncorruptible God,** the imperishable, eternal God with his glorious perfections, whom they ought to have worshiped, **into an image,** etc. In their conceptions they degraded God into the likeness of human beings, and even of the meanest creatures, and carried out these conceptions in making objects of worship. Or translate, *And exchanged . . . for the likeness of an image,* something similar to the form *of corruptible man,* etc. Of **birds**—as the ibis or stork. **Four-footed beasts**—

24 "Wherefore God also gave them up to uncleanness through the lusts of their own hearts, to dishonour their own 25 bodies between themselves: who changed the truth of God into a lie, and worshipped and served the creature more than the Creator, who is 26 blessed for ever. Amen. For this cause God gave them up unto vile af-

24 Wherefore God delivered them up in the desires of their hearts to uncleanness, to dishonor their bodies among 25 themselves; who changed the truth of God into falsehood; and worshiped and served the creature rather than the Creator, who is blessed forever. 26 Amen. For this cause God delivered them up to shameful passions; for

u See refs. Ps. 81 : 12 ; Hosea 4 : 17 ; Eph. 4 : 18, 19. *v* 1 Cor. 6 : 18, 1 Peter 4 : 3. *w* Lev. 18 : 22.
x 1 John 5 : 20. *y* Isa. 44 : 20 ; Jer. 10 : 14 ; Amos 2 : 4 ; Hab. 2 : 18. *z* Ps. 72 : 19.
a Ver. 24 ; Eph. 5 : 12 ; Jude 10.

as the cat and the dog and the sacred ox. **Creeping things**—as the crocodile and the serpent. In Greece, idols of the human form prevailed; in Egypt, those of birds, beasts and reptiles; in Rome, the former largely, though at that time both were united. (See on ver. 25.) Though the intelligent "defender of such worship may plead that it is offered only to the Divine Being, as manifested or brought to mind by objects (a plea which the Bible nowhere admits), yet the mass of the people everywhere unquestionably worship the idol itself as a god." (Compare Acts 19 : 26, 35.)

24. Thus far Paul had made prominent the *ungodliness* of men (ver. 18); from this point to the end of the chapter he brings into prominence *the unrighteousness*, the immorality, and injustice of men (ver. 18). **Wherefore,** in righteous retribution upon the heathen for their idolatry, **God gave them up,** abandoned them, unrestrained, to their own wicked passions. **To uncleanness,** the impurity of lustful, profligate living, **through,** rather, *in*, **the lusts** or *the desires of their hearts*, in this terrible state or condition they were in, degraded but voluntary on their part. Here Paul presents the judicial act of God; in Eph. 4 : 19 he presents the manward side of the heathen, by their own act delivering "themselves up to wantonness, to work all uncleanness in greediness." (See Acts 28 : 27, and note.) **To dishonour their bodies between,** rather, *among*, **themselves.** In their foolish speculations they had dishonored God (ver. 21-23); and now following their desires they dishonor their own bodies. Paul refers here and farther on to those crimes against nature which were common to pagan nations, and was the reproach of pagan civilization.

25. Who—*As they who*, indicating the class to which they belonged, and implying the reason why God gave them over: because they **changed the truth of God,** which he had revealed respecting himself (see ver. 19-21), **into a lie,** the very essence and atmosphere of idolatry (2 Thess. 2 : 11; Rev. 22 : 15). The verse may be rendered: *As those who exchanged the truth of God for a lie*, that is, the true God for false gods. The term *falsehood* is applied to false gods in the Old Testament (Jer. 13 : 25; Ps. 31 : 6; compare Rev. 21 : 8). Paul views idolatry in the heart (Ezek. 14 : 3) and in practice as the root of all heathen degradation (ver. 18-23.) From it come the sins of impurity (ver. 24-27), and all other sins (ver. 28-32). **And,** enlarging the idea of the preceding clause, **worshipped,** internally from the heart, and **served,** externally by words and sacrificial rites, **the creature,** or *the created, rather than the Creator*. **More than** should be translated *rather than*, implying the entire exclusion of **the Creator** from their worship. In holy horror at the thought of thus dethroning God and in reverence to his name, Paul exclaims, **who is blessed for ever**—surrounded with the perpetual praise and homage of the heavenly world and worthy thus to be. To which also he adds in deep devotion his solemn affirmation and prayer, **Amen,** *so it is* and *so let it be*. Compare Paul's doxologies elsewhere (9 : 5; 11 : 36; 1 Tim. 1 : 17; 2 Tim. 4 : 18).

26. For this cause, because of their idolatrous apostasy just spoken of in ver. 25, **God gave them up.** Paul repeats what he had said in ver. 24 (on which see) with greater force and delineation. It was necessary thus to do in order to prove the utterly lost condition of the heathen, and that their salvation could only be attained through

fections: for even their women did change the natural use into that which ²⁷ is against nature: and likewise also the men, leaving the natural use of the woman, burned in their lust one toward another; men with men working that which is unseemly, and receiving in themselves that recompense of their ²⁸ error which was meet. And even ᵇas they did not like to retain God in *their* knowledge, ᶜGod gave them over to ᵈa reprobate mind, to do those things ²⁹ ᵉwhich are not convenient; being filled

their women changed the natural use ²⁷ into that which is against nature; and in like manner the men also, leaving the natural use of the woman, burned in their desire one toward another; men with men working that which is unseemly, and receiving in themselves the recompense of their error which ²⁸ was due. And as they did not choose to retain God in their knowledge, God delivered them up to a reprobate mind, ²⁹ to do those things which are not becoming; being filled with all unright-

b Ver. 21.   *c* Ver. 24.   *d* Jer. 6 : 30.   *e* Eph. 5 : 4.

the power of God and his righteousness by faith (ver. 16, 17). Yet with great delicacy he alludes to those vile practices of which he says elsewhere it is a shame to speak (Eph. 5 : 12). **To vile affections**—to vile passions and unnatural sins. This was true of both sexes. **For even their women**—*their females*. Omit *even*. He may speak of these first, because such unnatural sensual abominations were the more horrible in that sex whose chief adornment was modesty and sobriety (1 Tim. 2:9); yet at the same time not more flagrant than that among men (ver. 27). **Did change**, etc. This unnatural vice among females was common in pagan Greece and Rome, even in the time of their highest civilization and refinement.

27. And likewise also the men, or, *their males*—the prominent idea is the shameful abuse of their sex. **Burned**—*were inflamed*. **Unseemly** —shameful and indecent. The vice here mentioned was that which has been called *sodomy* from the shameful sin of Sodom (Gen. 19 : 5; Lev. 18 : 22 · 1 Cor. 6 : 9). **And receiving in themselves that recompense of their error which was meet,** *justly their due*. Their *error* was their departure from the true God into idolatry; and this *recompense* was a necessary consequence and a just penalty, received in their own persons—physical diseases and degeneracy, mental weaknesses and disorders and moral degradation. The unnatural crime here spoken of was common in the highest periods of pagan civilization. The picture here given in these and the following verses represent truly the morals of the heathen world at that time. This may be proved by contemporary Greek and Latin writers as gathered and quoted by Tholuck and Döllinger. It is confirmed by the excavations and disclosures of the buried cities of Herculaneum and Pompeii. That it is a true portraiture of the fearful moral results of idolatry is shown by the condition of the heathen to-day. Missionaries affirm the present truthfulness of the likeness, and the heathen recognize it as descriptive of themselves.

28. Paul now proceeds to enumerate other general vices to which God had given them over. **And even as**—*accordingly*. *Corresponding* to their rejection of the knowledge of God was their punishment. **As they did not like,** or *choose*, **to retain God in their knowledge,** as they *reprobated*, rejected the knowledge of God (ver. 22-25), **God gave them over to a reprobate mind.** The force of the sentence is increased in the original by different forms of the same Greek word, translated *like* and *reprobate*. It may be rendered, "As they did not think God *worthy* to be kept in knowledge, God gave them up to an *unworthy* mind," the moral unfitness extending to the deepest springs of life. They are represented as bringing this abandonment by God upon themselves. **To do,** *to the doing* habitually, **those things which are not convenient,** *not becoming* moral and intelligent creatures, hence *immoralities*, such as are named in ver. 29-32. Notice this is the third time he says *God gave them up* (ver. 24, 26).

29. This summary of the more common passions, feelings, and acts, furnishes examples of what departure from God has produced. As a whole they are characteristic of **our** race, since none can plead exemption from all of them, and they indicate our fallen

with all unrighteousness, fornication, wickedness, covetousness, maliciousness; full of envy, murder, ᶠdebate, de- 30 ceit, malignity; ᵍ whisperers, backbiters, haters of God, despiteful, proud, boasters; inventors of evil things, dis- 31 obedient to parents; without understanding, covenant breakers, ʰ without natural affection, implacable, unmer- 32 ciful: who ⁱ knowing the judgment of God, that they which commit such things ᵏ are worthy of death, not only do the same, but ˡ have pleasure in them that do them.

eousness, wickedness, covetousness, maliciousness; full of envy, murder, strife, deceit, malignity; whisperers, 30 slanderers, hateful to God, insolent, proud, boasters, devisers of evil 31 things, disobedient to parents, without understanding, covenant-breakers, without natural affection, unmerciful; 32 who, knowing the judgment of God, that they who practice such things are worthy of death, not only do them, but also have pleasure in those who practice them.

f See 13 : 13 ; 1 Tim. 6 : 4.   *g* See refs. Ps. 41 : 7.   *h* Ps. 106 : 37, 38.   *i* 2 : 2, 14, 15.   *k* 6 : 21.
l Ps. 50 : 18 ; Hosea 7 : 3.

and depraved condition by nature. These sins are not named according to any particular order, but rather for rhetorical effect; accumulated according as Paul's emotions bore him on toward the climax of his thought. Words denoting general sins and particular sins are mingled together. See a similar catalogue of sins in 2 Cor. 12 : 20; Gal. 5 : 19-21 ; 2 Tim. 3 : 2-4. **Being filled**—a strong expression, extending to the whole being. **With all unrighteousness** of heart and life. **Fornication**—not found in the best manuscripts. **Wickedness**—the *badness* of a vicious disposition. **Covetousness**—*avarice*, a greedy desire of gain; a sin especially condemned by Paul (Eph. 5 : 3; Col. 3 : 5). **Maliciousness**—a spirit of malice, a disposition to inflict evil. The apostle proceeds to specify more particularly: **Full of envy, murder** (in the heart, a spirit of murder), **debate**, rather, *strife*, **deceit, malignity**—a malicious fault-finding, putting the worst construction on everything. Paul continues his catalogue by designating persons by their most characteristic sins. **Whisperers**—who hint and slander in low tones and secretly.

30. Backbiters—who publicly speak ill and slander those who are absent. **Haters of God**, or *hateful to God*—exceptionally impious and wicked. **Despiteful**—*insolent* in words and acts. **Proud**—*haughty*, despising others and even treating them with contempt. **Boasters**—empty pretenders. **Inventors of evil things**—of new devices to practise evil; authors of mischief (2 Macc. 7 : 31). **Disobedient to parents**—breakers of the fourth com-

mandment, and especially displeasing to God.

31. Paul concludes his catalogue by designating persons by some prevailing principle or sentiment that actuates their lives. **Without understanding** —stupid morally. **Covenant breakers**—faithless, false to their contracts. **Without natural affection** of love—heartless. (See Ps. 106 : 37, 38.) As "mothers who exposed their children, emperors or satraps who put their brothers to death."—*Jowett*. **Implacable**. This word is not found in the best manuscripts, and should be omitted. **Unmerciful**—"The dark places of the earth are full of the habitations of cruelty" (Ps. 74 : 20). *Merciless* in the treatment of children and slaves, of the sick and the aged, and in their gladiatorial combats.

32. Who, knowing the judgment, or *ordinance*, **of God**—an appointment of God having the force of law. See note on the word justification (5) on ver. 17. **That they** *who practise* **such things are worthy of death**—they know this from their own consciences and from the lessons of their wisest teachers. It had been taught our first parents at the fall (Gen. 2 : 17), and it had been recognized in the laws and mythologies of the heathen. Compare Acts 28 : 4, where we may discover this moral sense of retribution in the natives of Melita. **Not only do the same, but have pleasure in**, or *applaud those who practise them*. Here, then, is the climax of depravity. They know the Divine ordinance of death for such sins, yet they practise them! And deeper and more shameful still, they even applaud others who practise them. Many will condemn in others what they do themselves; but these rejoice in iniquity.

Thus Paul has shown that the heathen are willful sinners, exposed to Divine wrath and suffering from the results of their own depravity.

PRACTICAL REMARKS.

1. To be a servant of Christ is a greater honor than to be a lord or king among men (ver. 1; Luke 7 : 28; 1 John 4 : 4).

2. The gospel was the soul of the old dispensation (ver. 2; Rev. 19 : 10; Acts 26 : 22, 23).

3. Christ is the center and circumference of the gospel (ver. 3; Rev. 1 : 8; Heb. 1 : 2; 1 Cor. 2 : 1).

4. Christ is human and divine, the God-man, attested both by his birth and his resurrection (ver. 4; 2 Tim. 2 : 8; Phil. 2 : 5-10).

5. The ministry and the means of grace are designed to lead men everywhere to believe and obey God (ver. 5; 15 : 18; James 2 : 22, 26).

6. Christians are saints, called to be Jesus Christ's, and beloved of God on his account (ver. 6, 7; 1 Cor. 3 : 21; Rom. 8 : 16, 39; Eph. 5 : 1).

7. The Father and the Son are equally the source of grace and peace, and equally the objects of prayer (ver. 7; 1 Tim. 1 : 2; Rev. 1 : 4; 5 : 13).

8. Christ is our Mediator, through whom our prayers and thanksgiving must ascend to God (ver. 8; John 14 : 4; Eph. 5 : 20; Heb. 13 : 15).

9. We should be unceasing in our prayers for God's people everywhere (ver. 9; Gal. 6 : 16; 1 Thess. 1 : 3, 4).

10. We should make journeying and the ordinary affairs of life subjects of prayer, and dependent on the will of God (ver. 10; James 4 : 14, 15).

11. One of the designs of the Christian ministry is to build up and strengthen believers (ver. 11; 15 : 29; Eph. 4 : 11-13).

12. In spiritual friendship we both give and receive (ver 12; 3 John 4-8; 1 Cor. 9 : 23).

13. As Christian workers we should ever be solicitous for fruit, the salvation of souls (ver. 13; John 15 : 16).

14. What Christ has done for us makes us debtors to preach the gospel to the world he came to save (ver. 14, 15; 1 Cor. 9 : 16-23).

15. There is something in the gospel of which the natural man is ashamed. Only the renewed soul can glory in the gospel (ver. 16; 1 Cor. 2 : 14; Gal. 6 : 14).

16. The power of the gospel is in the truth which embodies Christ, and reveals Christ to the soul (ver. 16; John 17 : 3; 2 Cor. 3 : 18; James 1 : 18).

17. The gospel produces not mere temporary effects, but extends unto salvation, a complete deliverance from sin and its consequences (ver. 16, 17; 1 Peter 1 : 5).

18. Unless we become united with Christ by faith, and receive heartily the righteousness which is of God, as the ground of our acceptance, we have no part in the salvation of the gospel (ver. 17; Acts 4 : 12; 8 : 20-23).

19. Sin is two-sided—being against God and against man. In the very nature of things, human and divine, it merits wrath and punishment (ver. 18; Eph. 5 : 6; Col. 3 : 6; Job 36 : 18).

20. There is nothing that prevents the spread and triumph of truth but sin (ver. 18, 19; John 3 : 20, 21; 2 Tim. 3 : 8).

21. God has never left himself without a witness to the reason and consciences of men (ver. 19; John 1 : 5, 9; Acts 14 : 17).

22. The visible creation is a proof of the existence of God though he is invisible (ver. 20; Ps. 19 : 1-6).

23. Sins committed against the light, and in spite of the light, are doubly without excuse (ver. 21; Ps. 14 : 1; John 9 : 41).

24. The tendency of the race, even in the highest civilization and wisdom, has been away from God. Reformations have ever been followed by declensions (ver. 22; 1 Cor. 1 : 20, 21; Jer. 8 : 8, 9).

25. Idolatry is senseless, and betrays both mental and moral degradation (ver. 23, 25; Isa. 44 : 9-20).

26. God needs but to give up the sinner to his own desires to ensure his degradation and punishment (ver. 24; Ps. 81 : 11, 12; Hosea 4 : 17).

27. God abandons those who willfully abandon him. Irreligion and immorality are likely to go together (ver. 26, 28; Isa. 66 : 3, 4; 1 Sam. 2 : 30).

The greater guilt of the Jews; and the impossibility of justification by the Law.

2 THEREFORE thou art ᵐ inexcusable, O man, whosoever thou art that judgest: ⁿ for wherein thou judgest another, thou condemnest thyself; for thou that judgest doest the same things. But we are sure that the judgment of God is according to truth against them which commit such things. And thinkest

2 WHEREFORE thou art without excuse, O man, whoever thou art that judgest; for wherein thou judgest another, thou condemnest thyself; for thou that judgest dost practice the same things. Now we know that the judgment of God is according to truth, upon those who practice such things.

m 1 : 20. n 2 Sam. 12 : 5–7; Matt. 7 : 1, 2; John 8 : 9.

28. The sins of uncleanness are scriptural evidences of human depravity and God's disfavor (ver. 27; Eccl. 7 : 26; Prov. 22 : 14).

29. Sin is often its own punishment, engendering other sins, and leading to physical, mental, and moral degeneracy (ver. 29–31; Prov. 14 : 14; Gal. 6 : 7, 8).

30. The moral degradation of the heathen proves their need of a religion of divine power and a righteousness from God (ver. 30; 16, 17; 1 John 5 : 19; 2 Tim. 3 : 13).

31. If the apostasy of the heathen was so terrible, how much more aggravating must apostasy be under the light of Christianity (ver. 29–31; Matt. 11 : 22; 2 Thess. 2 : 8–12).

32. Sinners evince the climax of depravity when they not only sin knowingly themselves, but also help others to do the same (ver. 32; Isa. 5 : 18–24).

33. The wrath of God is a revealer not against ignorance but against sin, disregard and disobedience of the truth (ver. 18–32).

CHAPTER II.

Having shown that the heathen are inexcusably guilty, Paul proceeds in this chapter to show first, that those who exhibit their superior knowledge in judging others, whether Jews or enlightened Gentiles, must be inexcusable too. Then with this transition of thought he passes (ver. 17) to a pointed application to the Jew, showing that he is thereby the more guilty and the more inexcusable, and that circumcision cannot save him.

1–16. APPLICATION TO THE SELF-RIGHTEOUS, WHETHER JEW OR GENTILE, who condemn in others what they themselves practise, showing that they are guilty and inexcusable. Paul lays down general principles regarding Divine forbearance and justice to which they, especially the Jew, must assent. So that this section forms a transition in his discussion between the sinful and lost condition of the Gentile and the sinful and lost condition of the Jew.

1. Therefore, in view of what I have just said (1 : 18–32) **thou art inexcusable, O man.** This sudden and unexpected application is a peculiarity of Paul's style (ver. 17). **Whosoever thou art that judgest**—implying that they had that knowledge of God and of the ill-desert of sin spoken of in 1 : 20, 21, 32. The class addressed would be found both among Jews and Gentiles. **For wherein thou judgest another**—*passeth unfavorable judgment on the other,* thy fellow-man, thy neighbor. **Condemnest**—a little stronger word than *judgest.* **For thou that judgest doest,** *dost practise,* **the same things**—the same in nature, not necessarily the same act, but equally sinful. The direct appeal to the conscience makes it the more forcible. The fact that he judges another shows that he has all the light necessary to render his own sinful practice without excuse. Knowing the right and doing the wrong, was indeed holding the truth in unrighteousness (1 : 18).

2. But we are sure—*we know;* Christians, Jews, and intelligent Gentiles must at once assent to the statement he is about to make. **That the judgment of God is according to truth,** to right. There can be no error nor injustice possible in God's judgment. This truth, confirmed alike by reason, conscience, and the Old Testament Scriptures, he makes the foundation of the application that follows. **Against,** or *upon,* **them which commit,** or *practise,* **such things,**

thou this, O man, that judgest them which do °such things, and doest the same, that thou shalt escape the judg-
4 ment of God? Or, ᵖdespisest thou ᵠthe riches of his goodness and ʳforbearance and ˢlongsuffering; ᵗnot knowing that the goodness of God leadeth thee to re-
5 pentance? But after thy hardness and impenitent heart ᵘtreasurest up unto thyself wrath against the day of wrath and revelation of the righteous judg-
6 ment of God; ˣwho will render to every
7 man according to his deeds: to them

3 And reckonest thou this, O man, that judgest those who practice such things, and doest them, that thou shalt
4 escape the judgment of God? Or despisest thou the riches of his kindness, and forbearance, and long-suffering, not knowing that the goodness of God
5 is leading thee to repentance; and after thy hardness and impenitent heart, art laying up for thyself wrath in the day of wrath and of the revelation of the righteous judgment of
6 God; who will render to every man
7 according to his works; to those

o 1 : 32.　　p 6 : 1, 15; Eccl. 8 : 11.　　q 9 : 23; Eph. 1 : 7, 2, 4, 7.　　r 3 : 25.　　s See refs. Exod. 34 : 6.
t Job 33 : 27-30; Jer. 3 : 12, 13; Hosea 5 : 15; 2 Peter 3 : 9, 15.　　u Deut. 32 : 34; James 5 : 3.
x 14 : 12; see refs. Job 34 : 11; Jer. 17 : 10; 1 Cor. 3 : 8; Rev. 20 : 12.

every enlightened man, whether Jew or Gentile, admits this statement.

3. And can there be any escape according to the principle laid down? If so it must be either on man's side (this verse) or on God's side (next verse). **And thinkest thou this**—*but reckonest thou*, in face of the proposition, that the judgment of God is according to truth, **that thou shalt escape**, etc. Since God is just and righteous will he not condemn those sins which ye yourselves condemn, and condemn them in you as well as in others? The mere question was sufficient answer. Reason, conscience, and the word of God, would promptly respond. There is no escape so far as what man can do is concerned. As to the Jew hiding himself within the Abrahamic covenant, Paul notices that farther on, in ver. 25-29, in which he shows that circumcision cannot protect the sinner.

4. Or, if thou art not counting on thus escaping, art thou thinking that the goodness of God is so great that he will forbear to punish thee? Thus to do was to *despise* his goodness: **Despisest thou the riches**, the wealth, the abundance (9 ²³) **of his goodness,** etc. *Goodness* is the kindness which God exercises toward men. **Forbearance** is tolerating and enduring, holding back, as it were, his vengeance. **Longsuffering** is his patient waiting, his slowness in avenging wrongs (2 Peter 3 : 5-9; Ps. 103 : 8). How vast Paul's conception of Divine indulgence! One word could not express it, nor three. It was the abundance of them all. **Not knowing**—*not recognizing* and ignoring the design of God's goodness to them. Instead of encouraging them to hope that God would not punish them, its design was to *lead* them gently **to repentance,** that they might humble themselves, and turning to him might forsake their sins. Notice that *riches* is a favorite word with Paul (11 : 33; Eph. 1 : 7; 3 : 16, etc.). This pointed question was well fitted to any Jewish reader.

5. But God's mercy has its limits, **and after,** *according to,* **thy hardness,** the *obstinacy* which resists the influences of Divine kindness, and **impenitent heart,** thy firm persistence in evil, thou **treasurest up,** thou *art treasuring up for thyself*, **wrath**, etc. (See Luke 12 : 21.) The sinner is willfully heaping up this fearful treasure just in proportion to his obstinacy toward good influence and his persistence in evil. He is accumulating for himself personally *wrath* which will come upon him **against,** rather *in,* **the day of wrath,** the day of judgment (Rev. 6 : 17; Amos 3 : 10; Zeph. 1 : 15). God's displeasure against sin is now revealed (1 : 18), but there is to be a day of final reckoning, which will also be a day of *revealing* the **righteous judgment of God,** showing that his dealings with all men are in strict accordance with truth and justice. This is further exhibited in the next six verses. This great principle of God's moral government accords with the teachings of the Old Testament. The Jews must assent to it; the intelligent Gentile could not deny it.

6. Who will *fully* **render,** be he Jew or Gentile, **according to his deeds,** in opposition to any other ground of judgment. Paul is not speaking here of the provisions of the gospel, but is expounding the law, and

who by patient continuance in well-doing seek for glory and honour and 8 immortality, eternal life: but unto them that are contentious, and ʲdo not obey the truth, but obey unrighteous- 9 ness, indignation and wrath, tribulation and anguish, upon every soul of man that doeth evil, of the Jew ᵃfirst,

who by patient continuance in well doing seek for glory and honor and 8 immortality, eternal life; but to those who are contentious, and do not obey the truth, but obey unrighteous- 9 ness, wrath and indignation, tribulation and distress, on every soul of man that works evil, of the Jew first, and

y Job 24 : 11 ; 2 Thess. 1 : 8.   *z* Mat. 11 . 20-24 ; Luke 12 : 47, 48 ; 1 Peter 4 : 17.

righteousness by the law. In this and the following five verses he teaches that the Divine awards will be not according to race or rank, relations or professions, but according to their works, which will indicate their real character. The honest Gentile would naturally assent, for why, he might say, should God deal partially with the Jew. The Jew could not but admit that this was taught in their own Scriptures. Indeed this verse is a quotation from Prov. 24 : 12. (Comp. Job 34 : 11 ; Ps. 62 : 12 ; Jer. 17 : 10, etc.) The Christian reader must also assent (1 Cor. 3 : 13 ; 2 Cor. 5 : 10 ; Gal. 6 : 7, 8). But Paul does not here speak of works as a ground of merit. (See on ver. 13.) Faith also is a work of God (John 6 : 29 ; Rom. 4 : 3 ; James 2 : 21-26), but Paul had no occasion to speak of it in this part of the discussion (3 : 31).

7. Paul proceeds to explain in detail. **To them,** on the one hand, **who by patient continuance,** or *constancy,* **in well doing,** in conduct, in every good work which piety begets and demands. They who are unswerved, even by the greatest trials and sufferings, from their deliberate purpose and loyalty to God and the truth (Luke 8 : 15 ; 2 Thess. 1 : 4 ; James 5 : 11 ; Rev. 13 : 10). **Seek,** by this persevering life of piety in God's service, **glory, honor, and immortality.** These three words form a full and complete description of future salvation. The *glory* is the splendor of that perfected life (Matt. 13 : 43), the *honor* that comes to it like a prize to a victor (1 Cor. 9 : 25 ; James 1 : 12 ; 1 Peter 5 : 4), and *immortality* is its imperishableness (1 Peter 1 : 4). Man at first was crowned with glory and honor (Ps. 8 : 5) which he lost, but these seek to regain them with that immortality which will free them from all that is perishable. To those thus seeking he will render (ver. 6) **eternal life,** life in the highest and truest sense, spiritual, in holy and loving harmony with God, and everlasting. The gospel reveals also that it consists in knowing Jesus Christ (John 17 : 2). Paul, from his higher Christian viewpoint, describes future blessedness.

8. **But unto them,** on the other hand, **who are contentious,** or *factions,* having a *self-seeking* and *partisan* spirit, corresponding very closely to that described in ver. 5. With their stubbornness they **do not obey the truth** (1 : 18), and in their persistence they **obey unrighteousness**—and hence are the servants of sin and Satan (6 : 17 ; John 8 : 44). Thus directly and indirectly they factiously contend against God's revealed will, a sin committed indeed by Gentiles, but often by the Jews as well (Isa. 1 : 2-4 ; Jer. 5 : 23 ; Acts 7 : 51). To such shall be rendered (according to the best Greek text) **indignation and wrath.** The former word expresses the internal heat and the more permanent feeling; the latter the sudden bursting forth of feeling and the stronger passion. But both words as expressing the just retribution of sin, and as connected with God, must be regarded as the outbursting of his holiness and justice against sin.

9. In this and the next verse Paul recapitulates what he had said in the two preceding, inverting the order and emphasizing the universality of the retribution. The change gives vividness and force to his language. **Tribulation and anguish.** The first word expresses that *affliction* that comes from without; the second, that *distress* and *hopelessness* which is felt within. **Upon every soul of man,** whoever, **doeth,** *is working,* practising **evil.** *Soul,* while it may suggest that part of man which feels pain, seems to be used as in chap. 13 : 1 for the whole man, and calls to mind the formulas of the law, and gives solemnity to the warning (Lev. 5 : 1). This should come, according to the principles of truth and righteousness, upon every soul of this class, **of the Jew first,** who, so far from enjoying special favor, should on account of

10 and also of the Gentile; *but glory, honour, and peace, to every man that worketh good, to the Jew first, and
11 also to the Gentile. For *there is no respect of persons with God.
12 For as many as have sinned *without law shall also perish without law; and as many as have *sinned in the law
13 shall be judged by the law; For *not the hearers of the law *are* just before God, *but the doers of the law shall be justified. For when the Gentiles, *which

10 also of the Greek; but glory and honor and peace to every man that works good, to the Jew first, also to the Greek.
11 For there is no respect of persons with God. For as many as sinned without law will also perish without law; and as many as sinned with
13 law will be judged by law; for not the hearers of the law are righteous before God, but the doers of law will
14 be justified: (for when Gentiles, who

a 1 Peter 1 : 7. *b* See refs. Deut. 10 : 17. *c* 1 : 19, 20. *d* Gal. 2 : 16-19 ; 3 : 10 ; James 2 : 10, 11.
e Matt. 7 : 21-27 ; James 1 : 22-25. *f* 10 : 5 ; Lev. 18 : 5 ; Gal. 3 : 11, 12. *g* Eph. 2 : 12.

greater light and higher privileges be first in condemnation and punishment (1 : 16 ; Luke 12 : 47, 48). **And also of the Gentile,** rather, *of the Greek*. None of this class shall escape this impartial tribunal.

10. But glory, honour. (See on ver. 7.) **Peace** is used here instead of immortality in ver. 7, and refers to the *tranquil, blessed state* of the righteous after death. **To every man that worketh good.** In the original *worketh* is not so full and strong as its compound word "worketh" in ver. 9. There the idea is of *accomplishing, perpetuating*, evil ; here the idea is the giving of one's strength to doing the good, working for it. **To the Jew first**—having received the oracles of God (3 : 2) and the first offers of salvation. **And also to the Gentile**—*the Greek*, who on this account shall not be excluded.

11. This verse forms a connecting link between the preceding verses of this chapter and the next five verses. This equitable distribution without partiality must be made, **For there is no respect of persons,** *partiality* on account of outward conditions such as rank or race, **with God.** (James 2 : 1-4 ; Eph. 6 : 9 ; Col. 3 : 25.) This was taught in the Old Testament (Deut. 10 : 17), but the Jew limited this to God's dealings with his chosen people. Paul uses it with a broader application, as also did Peter to Cornelius at Cæsarea. See Acts 10 : 34 and note, where a kindred word of the same formation is used.

12. This principle of impartiality in the divine government is explained and illustrated in respect to both Jew and Gentile (ver. 12-16). **For** introduces the reason and confirmation of the statement of the preceding verse, with special reference to future condemnation. All shall be treated according to the light they have, and their opportunity of knowing their duty. For **as many as have sinned,** rather, *as sinned*, being viewed in the past with reference to the future judgment. **Without law**—the written law, referring to the law of Moses. **Shall perish**—be condemned and punished **without** written **law**, with due allowance for the circumstances under which they sinned. *Perish* means here *shall incur the loss of true* or *eternal life* (ver. 7 ; John 3 : 16). **And as many** *as sinned* **in the law,** in possession and with the knowledge of it, **shall be judged by the law,** their condemnation being implied. Paul here states a general fact in regard to the impartiality of the rule by which men are to be judged. It would commend itself to the reason and conscience of both Gentile and Jew, and it also accorded with the Scriptures of the latter (Dan. 12 : 2).

13. Paul enforces the declaration in the last clause of ver. 12, showing that it was useless to possess and know the law unless it was obeyed. **For not the hearers of the law,** like the Jew who heard it read constantly in their synagogues, **are just,** or *righteous*, **before God,** but the doers of **the law shall be justified,** *shall be counted righteous*, that is, actually so (James 1 : 22 ; 4 : 11). Paul is not here speaking of gospel justification, but of a legal principle in God's government. The law required perfect obedience; and this included sinlessness in heart and life. "This do and thou shalt live" (Luke 10 : 28, on which see note). The Jew is taken upon his own ground. The possession of the law could not make him righteous unless he obeyed it. He

have not the law, *b* do by nature the things contained in the law, these, having not the law, are a law unto
15 themselves: which shew the work of the law *i* written in their hearts, their conscience also bearing witness, and *their* thoughts the meanwhile *k* accus-
16 ing or else excusing one another; *l* in the day when God shall judge the se-

have no law, do by nature the things required by law, these, having no law,
15 are a law to themselves; who shew the work of law written in their hearts, their conscience testifying with it, and between one another their thoughts
16 accusing or also excusing;) in the day when God will judge the secrets of

h Ver. 27. *i* 1 : 18–20. *k* Gen. 3 : 8–11; Eccl. 7 : 22; 1 John 3 : 19–21.
l Eccl. 12 : 14; 1 Cor. 4 : 5; Rev. 20 : 12.

could not count upon certain privileges as a Jew; he must rigidly keep the requirements of the law. "The thoughtful Jew must have felt how impossible it was for him to be justified on this principle; and to create this conviction was the object of the apostle in this entire connection" (BOISE).

14. In this and the next verse the apostle illustrates and defends the statement in the first clause of ver. 12 in respect to the Gentiles who without the written law have the light of nature for their guide. **For when Gentiles,** *pagans,* (omit **the**)—some of them—*who have no* revealed *law,* **do by nature,** from their natural impulses without any higher instruction, *the things required by law,* moral duties toward God and man. Pagans perform many virtuous deeds. He does not say that they fully obey the law, but he only means so far as they do this. They have the law of nature or conscience—their own innate perceptions of what is right and wrong, guided by conscience; and by this law they are to be judged. Whether any one ever actually attained to eternal life without the gospel revelation is not the question, and is not here referred to. *Having no law,* in the sense that the Jew has it, **are a law unto themselves**—the voice of their own moral nature is their rule, which the constitution of their minds teaches them to revere as the law of Him who formed it. God is author of both the written and unwritten law, and so far as they run parallel, they must agree. (See next verse.)

15. *Inasmuch as they* **shew the work** *of law,* its *operation,* not so much by what it requires as by what it performs, **written in their hearts**—in their inner intelligent being. They show the work and office of law, in their inner perceptions of right and wrong, corresponding to the more important precepts of that law written on tables of stone. Note that it is not *on* but *in* their hearts. **Their conscience,** their moral sense or judgment, **also bearing witness,** rather, *witnessing therewith,* with the outer manifestation of this inner law, and confirming it by its testimony. **And their thoughts the meanwhile,** better, *And between one another,* that is, between these pagans, *their thoughts,* in reviewing one another's conduct, *accusing or also excusing,* according to the decisions of their moral judgment. Thus this inner law is shown by its outer operations, by conscience, and by the mutual judgment of their thoughts regarding one another.

16. There is a difference of opinion among expositors in respect to the connection of this verse with what goes before. Some would connect it directly with ver. 15, which is manifestly impossible unless we suppose that Paul omitted some connecting thought he had in mind. There evidently precedes this a parenthetic passage or thought. But where to begin it is the question. Alford would begin with ver. 11. But this seems too remote; Meyer begins with ver. 15; Beza with ver. 14. It would seem that with the end of ver. 12, Paul proceeds in ver. 13 to explain the last clause of ver. 12, beginning with *For;* and having done this, it occurred to him that the first clause of ver. 12 equally needed explanation, which he does in verses 14, 15, beginning again with *For.* Having thus explained the two clauses of ver. 12, he proceeds in ver. 16 with his regular course of thought. Thus the parenthetic passage seems to be ver. 13, 14, and 15. It was a peculiarity of Paul to throw in parenthetic thoughts. It indicates the high state of spiritual emotion in which he wrote. **In the day**—connect with ver. 12; *will be judged by law in the*

crets of men — by Jesus Christ, according-
ing to my gospel.
17 Behold, thou art called a Jew, and
restest in the law, and makest thy
18 boast of God, and knowest his will,
and approvest the things that are
more excellent, being instructed out
19 of the law; and art confident that

men, according to my gospel, through
Jesus Christ.
17 But if thou art called a Jew, and
restest on law, and gloriest in God,
18 and knowest his will, and approvest
the things that are excellent, being in-
19 structed out of the law; and believest

m See refs. John 5 : 22–29.　　*n* 16 : 25; 2 Tim. 2 : 8.　　　　　　　　　　*o* See refs. Luke 3 : 8.　　*p* 9 : 1; John 9 : 28, 29.
　　　　　　q Isa. 45 : 25; Micah 3 : 11; John 8 : 41.　　　　　　　　　　　*r* 3 : 2; Deut. 4 : 8.　　*s* Phil. 1 : 10.

day; that is, at the final judgment, according to the universal usage of the
New Testament (Matt. 7 : 22, etc.). **Shall
judge the secrets of men**—what
human judges cannot detect, what the
sinner hides from others, and even what
he himself may blindly fail to see.
According to my gospel—which he
was commissioned to preach (Gal. 1 : 1, 9,
11, 12). A day of judgment by **Jesus
Christ** was one of its doctrines (Acts
17 : 31; 2 Cor. 5 : 10; 2 Thess. 4 : 1; John 5 : 22; Acts
10 : 42). *In that day*, also would be verified the great principle which he has
explained in ver. 13–15. So doubtless
it vividly appeared to Paul as he passed
from his parenthetic thoughts to this
verse.

17-29. THE JEW, DIRECTLY AD-
DRESSED KNOWS GOD'S LAW BETTER,
BUT KEEPS IT STILL LESS. NOR CAN
CIRCUMCISION SAVE HIM. His need
of God's righteousness is therefore
apparent. In the preceding section
Paul had passed gradually and skil-
fully to the Jew, naming him first in
ver. 9, having secured his co-operating
conscience. The Jewish reader must
have felt that he was being addressed,
when now Paul turns suddenly upon
him in ver. 17. Such carefulness and
such surprises were characteristic of
Paul (Compare Acts 13 : 46; 17 : 31; 22 : 21.)

17. Behold—*If*, according to the
oldest and best manuscripts. **Thou**—
emphatic. Notice how it is repeated in
ver. 21. *If thou* **art called**, *sur-
named*, or *denominated*, **a Jew**—*if thou
art entitled* in addition to your personal
name *a Jew*. The name Jew, meaning *praised*, was a matter of national
and religious pride (Rev. 2 : 9). Paul's
object in thus addressing the Jew pointedly and by name, was to arrest his
attention to the fact that by his sinning
against his superior knowledge and his
larger means of grace he was more
guilty than the Gentile who sinned only

against the light of nature. **And restest confidently in the law,** *upon law*,
and makest thy boast exultantly,
gloriest in **God**, in the true God, Jehovah, as the exclusive guardian and protector of Israel. The gods of the Gentiles were but idols and vanity (1 : 21).
There is a true and right glorying in
God (Isa. 45 : 25; Gal. 6 : 14); and there is a
false and self-righteous boasting (Gal. 6 :
13; John 8 : 41, 42). Notice how Paul rises
in each clause toward a climax. He
enumerates the superior advantages of
the Jew in the Jew's own boastful language, in order to try him on the highest ground he chooses to claim.

18. And knowest his will—having a distinct knowledge of the things
willed by God. **And approvest the
things that are more excellent**—
and as one who has power to decide in
regard to points of duty and to *recognize*
what is *genuine* after examination,—
*thou approvest the things that are excel-
lent, even as one who is instructed
out of the law*, which is the form, or
the true expression of knowledge and
truth (ver. 20). Another rendering equally grammatical is: *And distinguishest
the things that differ,* that is, *And art
able to discriminate* rightly between
what is lawful and unlawful, *being instructed*, etc. Meyer prefers the first of
these renderings; Alford the second.
The first however seems to suit the
connection better, and forms a better
climax in the thought. (Comp. Phil. 1 : 10.)
Being instructed, orally, **out of
the law**—by hearing it read publicly in the synagogues (Acts 18 : 25; 21
21; 1 Cor. 14 : 19).

19, 20. Notice how the clauses in
these two verses are thrown in one after
another without any conjunctions, thus
giving vividness and strength to the
description. **And art confident**—
exhibiting the high opinion the Jew
had of himself, especially as a teacher

thou thyself art *a guide of the blind,
a light of them which are in darkness,
20 an instructor of the foolish, a teacher
of babes, *which hast the form of
knowledge and of the truth in the
21 law. *Thou therefore which teachest
another, teachest thou not thyself?
Thou that preachest a man should not
22 steal, dost thou steal? Thou that sayest a man should not commit adultery,
dost thou commit adultery? Thou that
abhorrest idols, dost thou commit sac-

thyself to be a guide of the blind, a
20 light of those who are in darkness, an
instructor of the foolish, a teacher of
babes, having in the law the form of
21 knowledge and of the truth; thou then
that teachest another, dost thou not
teach thyself? thou that preachest a
man should not steal, dost thou steal?
22 thou that sayest a man should not
commit adultery, dost thou commit
adultery? thou that abhorrest idols,

t Matt. 15 : 14 ; John 9 : 31, 40, 41.   *u* 6 : 17.   *x* Ps. 50 : 16, etc. ; Matt. 23 : 3, etc.

of the Gentile world. **That thou thyself art a guide** *of blind persons.* This and the other titles may have been those which Jewish teachers assumed, gathered from such passages as Isa. 42 : 6, 7 (Matt. 15 : 14). He regarded himself as blessed with spiritual vision while others were blind, especially Gentiles. **A light to them which are in darkness** of heathenism (Isa. 9 : 1, 2; 60 : 2). **An instructor of the foolish** —*stupid* in regard to divine things. **A teacher of babes**—untaught, having a low degree of spiritual knowledge and development in general. Jews styled Gentiles *blind*, *foolish*, *baby*, the last applied to proselytes. Thus the proud Jew spoke of himself in comparison with Gentiles. **Which hast**, rather, *having*, **the form,** *the embodiment* as it were, **of knowledge and of the truth in the law.** *Knowledge*— what is known of divine things and human things. *Truth*—moral truth, of the highest kind, which the Jew sought in the Mosaic law. Knowledge and truth were embodied and typically represented in the law; but they are essentially revealed in the gospel (John 1 : 17; 17 : 3). The word translated *form* is only found elsewhere in the New Testament in 2 Tim. 3 : 5. May not the word here, as there, be used reproachfully? As the proud self-righteous Jew held the law, it was but an embodiment of a dead system, an organic structure without life.

21. Thou therefore — introduces the conclusion, in an unusual form, of the preceding four verses. The interrogative form gives point and vividness to the argument. *Thou then that art teaching another, art thou not teaching thyself?* The present tense expresses what they were habitually doing. The inference was: If you are what you claim to be, your guilt in sinning must be proportionately greater. **Thou that art preaching** or *heralding*, **a man should not steal, dost thou steal?** —*art thou stealing?* Paul uses striking and extreme examples to illustrate his position, and yet such as would force itself upon the Jewish conscience. "Grotius on the text proves from Josephus that some of the Jewish priests lived by rapine, depriving others of their due share of the tithes, and even suffering them to perish in want" (DODDRIDGE). (Compare 1 Sam. 2 : 13-16.) See what James (5 : 1-6) says of the rich fraudulently keeping back the hire of the reaper; and the words of our Lord regarding the rapacity and excess of the Pharisees (Matt. 23 : 23-25).

22. Thou that *art saying* and enjoining, **a man should not commit adultery,** *art thou committing* **adultery?** That this crime was common among the Jews seems evident from our Lord's discourses (Matt. 19 : 8, 9; 23 : 15); and the Talmudists even charge adultery on some of the most celebrated rabbins (James 4 : 4). **Thou that abhorrest idols** and their contamination, turning away from them as polluted and detestable, **dost thou commit sacrilege,** or *rob temples*, not hesitating to plunder their shrines and sacred places. The question has arisen whether Paul refers to the specific crime of temple robbery or more generally to the profane abuse of sacred places and things. He probably refers primarily to the former without entirely excluding the latter. The Sermon on the Mount shows that even definite crimes extend wider and deeper than the mere outward act (Matt. 5 : 21, 22). That Jews might have become temple-robbers appears from Acts 19 : 37 and Josephus (Ant., Bk. IV., 8, 10). They were forbid-

23 rilege? Thou that makest thy boast of the law, through breaking the law
24 dishonourest thou God? For the name of God is blasphemed among the Gentiles through you, as it is ʸ written.
25 ᵃ For circumcision verily profiteth, if thou keep the law: but if thou be a breaker of the law, thy circumcision is

23 dost thou rob temples? thou that gloriest in law, through the transgression
24 of the law dishonourest thou God? For, the name of God is blasphemed among the Gentiles because of you, as it is written.
25 For circumcision indeed profits, if thou doest the law; but if thou art a transgressor of law, thy circumcision

y Ver. 17.   z 2 Sam. 12:14.   a 3:1, 2; Deut. 30:6; Gal. 5:3-6.

den to take the gold and silver ornaments of idols (Deut. 7:25). As they did not regard heathen temples sacred, and these contained many things of great value, it is altogether probable that they often took valuables from them. They shrank in abhorrence from the pollution of idols, but neither their pollution nor that of the idol temples would deter them if they could only get the gold and silver. The same spirit led them to make the house of God a den of robbers (Matt. 21:13), and to commit the sin of robbing God by withholding from him what was his due (Mal. 3:8, 9).

23. Thou that makest thy boast, or, *that gloriest in the law, through the transgression of* **the law dishonourest thou God?** Thus showing inconsistency and hypocrisy in their contemptuous treatment of the true God, the author and giver of the law. Meyer regards this verse as the answer of the four preceding questions, and punctuates it as such. It might be so taken. But the climax of thought appears better, by regarding this also as a question. It includes all the preceding questions and m u c h m o r e. Notice the gradation: *Steal, commit adultery, robbing temples and sacrilege, and contemptuous treatment of God.* Against thy neighbor, thyself, things sacred, God. Similarly Bengel.

24. For connects the s t a t e m e n t made in the preceding verse with the quotation here given. **The name of God is blasphemed,** brought into contempt and reviled, **among the Gentiles through you,** better, *on account of you,* because of your wicked lives and immoralities. They would say that Jehovah was corrupt and impure like their own heathen gods. **As it is written**—as true now as when first written. This comes after the quotation, indicating both that it is a general quotation, and used descriptively of the then present condition of things.

It is better to take it, not as a quotation of any particular passage, but the substance of several passages (Is. 52:5; Ezek. 36:20-23; Neh. 5:9; Mal. 1:12).

25. The Jew could not but assent to the force of the apostle's reasoning, and acknowledge consequent guilt, but was he not on account of his connection with Abraham and circumcision entitled to favor and certain immunities from the strict construction of the law? This was the ceremonial distinction to which the Jew attached the most importance. It was a common opinion among the Jews that no circumcised man would go to hell. Paul therefore proceeds to show that even this could not save the Jewish sinner. **For I** grant that **circumcision** *indeed* **profiteth, if thou keep,** or *doest,* **the law,** if thou habitually do the requirements of the law. (See on ver. 13.) Circumcision was indeed an advantage to the Jew if he were a good man; it was profitable to him spiritually to be thus connected with God's c h o s e n people, to be the first to whom Christ and the gospel should be presented (1 16); it gave him special advantages for becoming a Christian, and if his obedience were perfect he would be entitled to all the blessings promised by the law. **But if thou be a breaker,** or *transgressor,* **of the law, thy circumcision is made,** or *has become,* **uncircumcision.** As a sign of a covenant it was of value only as the covenant was kept; but through a violation of the covenant circumcision becomes in effect uncircumcision; the Jew comes into the same condition morally as the Gentile. As a mere rite it had no merit. It might indicate a righteousness by faith in the heart, on the promise of God to the heirs by faith (4:11-15). But Paul had not reached these points in his discussion.

26. Paul draws a logical inference from the statement just made. *If,*

26 made uncircumcision. Therefore ^b if the uncircumcision keep the righteousness of the law, shall not his uncircumcision be counted for circumcision?
27 And shall not uncircumcision which is by nature, if it fulfil the law, ^c judge thee, who ^d by the letter and circumcision dost transgress the law? For ^e he is
28 not a Jew, ^f which is one outwardly; neither is that circumcision, which is
29 outward in the flesh; but he is a Jew, which is one inwardly; and ^g circumcision is that of the heart, ^h in the spirit, and not in the letter; ⁱ whose praise is not of men, but of God.

26 has become uncircumcision. If then the uncircumcision keep the requirements of the law, shall not his uncircumcision be reckoned for circumci-
27 sion? And shall not the uncircumcision that is by nature, if it fulfils the law, judge thee, who with the letter and circumcision art a transgressor of law?
28 For he is not a Jew, who is one outwardly; nor is that circumcision,
29 which is outward in the flesh. But he is a Jew, who is one inwardly; and circumcision is that of the heart, in spirit not in letter; whose praise is not from men, but from God.

b Isa. 56 : 6, 7; Matt. 8 : 11, 17; Acts 10 : 34, 35; 1 Cor. 7 : 18, 19.   *c* Matt. 12 : 41, 42.   *d* 7 : 6.   *e* 9 : 6–8; Matt. 3 : 9; Gal. 6 : 15.   *f* Matt. 23 : 25–28.   *g* Deut. 10 : 16; 30 : 6; Phil. 3 : 3; Col. 2 : 11.   *h* 7 : 6; John 3 : 5–8; 2 Cor. 3 : 6.   *i* 1 Sam. 16 : 7; 1 Cor. 4 : 5; 2 Cor. 10 : 18.

therefore, by parity of reason, **the uncircumcision keep the righteousness,** *the things accounted right*, that is, *the requirements* **of the law** (see on 1 : 17 (5)), **shall not his uncircumcision** *be accounted*, or *be reckoned*, **for circumcision?** A fine illustration of the phraseology of 4 : 3; Gal. 3 : 6. The moral requirements of the law are here meant. In such a case would not the Gentile be treated as favorably by God as the Jew? (Compare Acts 10 : 35.) The Jew could hardly deny the conclusion.

27. This verse can be punctuated as a question or as a period. Each is supported by eminent authorities. The latter regards this as an answer to the preceding question, the affirmative being self-evident: *And the uncircumcision by nature*, etc. The interrogative form naturally follows the preceding question and gives a certain vivacity and force, and is preferred in these notes. **And shall not** *the* **uncircumcision, which is by nature**—occasioned by the circumstances of birth, a Gentile. **Judge**, *condemn*, **thee** (Matt. 12 : 41). **Who by the letter**, rather, *who with a written law*, **and circumcision**, descriptive of his state or condition in contrast to the Gentile; who possessing these, and impliedly in spite of them, **dost transgress the law** (1 Sam. 15 : 22; Matt. 12 : 42. See ver. 14, 15).

28. This verse and the next are explanatory and confirmatory of the preceding two verses. They also give us a beautiful specimen of Paul's condensed and vigorous style. **For he is not a Jew**, a genuine Jew, a true child of God, **which is one outwardly**—one in mere form and outward show. *Nor is that circumcision* truly, **which is outward in the flesh**—this is not the true circumcision which indicates one to be beloved of God. Mere outward religion and forms are denounced in the Old Testament (Isa. 29 : 13).

29. Having made the statement negatively (ver. 28), he now makes it affirmatively. The former being accepted as true, the latter must be also accepted. **But he is a** true and genuine **Jew, which is one inwardly**, in the hidden parts, in the soul (Ps. 51 : 6); **and circumcision is that of the heart**, or *and there is a circumcision of the heart*. "Circumcise therefore the foreskin of your heart" (Deut. 10 : 16). "And the Lord thy God will circumcise thy heart" (Deut. 30 : 6). **In the spirit**—in the spiritual nature effecting a purification of it, instead of in the flesh (ver. 28). Compare what is said elsewhere in Scripture of the uncircumcised in heart (Lev. 26 : 41; Jer. 9 : 26; Ezek. 44 : 9; Acts 7 : 51). Some refer this to the Holy Spirit. This circumcision is, of course, effected by the Holy Spirit, but it is performed upon the spiritual nature of man. **Not in the letter**—not in the literal observance of mere rites (2 Cor. 3 : 6). **Whose praise is not of men**—that is, of the true Jew (John 1 : 47). The truly pious does not thus seek honor from men, but rather **of God.** A rebuke to Jewish pride and vain-glory (John 5 : 44; Gal. 6 : 12).

The above views would be well understood by the more pious and spiritually enlightened Jews, who looked beyond the letter of the law to its deeper and spiritual meaning (Micah 6 : 6-8). See the scribe's answer to Jesus in Mark 12 : 32-34. "The Jew consists in the innermost parts of the heart," is quoted from the Talmud. Paul therefore appeals to the conscience on the ground of well-known and admitted truths; and shows that the Jew as well as the Gentile was inexcusably guilty, that he could hope nothing from external observances either in obtaining salvation or in exemption from condemnation, and hence needed the righteousness of God (ver. 1 : 17).

PRACTICAL REMARKS.

1. The self-righteous, who are generally censorious and hypocrites, are inexcusable and self-condemned (ver. 1 ; Matt. 23 : 23 ; 29-31 ; Luke 18 : 9-14).

2. God is just ; without partiality on the one hand, or prejudice on the other (ver. 2 ; Ps. 89 : 14 ; Isa. 45 : 21).

3. The refuges of a deceived and deceitful heart will fail men at last (ver. 3 ; Isa. 28 : 17 ; 44 : 20).

4. God's goodness is despised and perverted by any who hope thereby to escape just punishment (ver. 4 ; 10 : 21 ; Ps. 78 : 36-41, 61).

5. The goodness of God is designed to lead sinners to repentance, but if it fails the fault is their own (ver. 4 ; Matt. 23 : 37 ; John 5 : 40).

6. If God's goodness does not soften, it will harden the heart and aggravate the guilt (ver. 5 ; Eccl. 8 : 11 ; 2 Peter 3 : 3-7).

7. The day of judgment will be to the finally impenitent a day of wrath and woe (ver. 5 ; Rev. 6 : 17 ; Matt. 25 : 41-43).

8. The retributions and rewards of the judgment will be according to those works which are an index of the character and life (ver. 6-8 ; Prov. 24 : 12 ; Jer. 32 : 19 ; Matt. 25 : 14-29).

9. The truly righteous are indicated by their perseverance in well-doing and in seeking heavenly things (ver. 7 ; Rev. 2 : 10 ; Heb. 10 : 38, 39).

10. The wicked are rebellious toward God, disobedient to the truth, and workers of evil (ver. 8, 9 ; Isa. 1 : 2 ; 2 Thess. 1 : 8).

11. Whether Jew or Gentile, Christian or heathen, none will be saved but the truly good ; none lost but the truly wicked (ver. 6-10 ; 2 Thess. 1 : 6-9 ; 1 Peter 4 : 17, 18).

12. The heathen are in a perishing condition and need the salvation offered in the gospel (ver. 12 ; Jer. 10 : 25).

13. Nothing short of perfect obedience can satisfy the claims of the law (ver. 13 ; James 2 : 10).

14. The heathen are not to be judged by a law they never had, but by that standard revealed in the works of creation and to their own reason and conscience (ver. 14, 15 ; 1 : 20 ; Isa. 40 : 21-26).

15. There is in every man that which accuses and excuses, call it what we may, which is not the result of education, since it can itself be educated (ver. 15 ; 9 : 1 ; 13 : 5 ; 2 Cor. 4 : 2).

16. The fact that the secrets of the heart are to be manifested and that Jesus Christ is to be the Judge, invests the judgment with an awful character (ver. 16 ; 1 Cor. 4 : 5 ; Matt. 10 : 26, 28).

17. Character and conduct, and not outward professions, are the tests before God now, and will be at the judgment (ver. 17 ; Matt. 7 : 21, 22 ; 1 Sam. 16 : 7).

18. Boasting instead of gratitude, despising others instead of wishing to save them, are evidences of formalism and self-righteousness (ver. 17-20 ; Luke 18 : 9).

19. Neither the knowledge of the truth, nor teaching the truth, but doing and keeping the truth, is what God requires (ver. 18-20 ; Micah 6 : 8 ; John 13 : 17).

20. Back of a form of knowledge and truth there is a spiritual discernment and life (ver. 20 ; 2 Tim. 3 : 5 ; 1 Cor. 2 : 14).

21. We should illustrate godly teaching by godly living (ver. 21 ; Matt. 23 : 3).

22. A man's life and practice do more than his words to honor or disgrace religion (ver. 22, 23 ; Matt. 5 : 16 ; 15 : 8, 9, 14).

23. The inconsistent lives of many professed Christians afford the strongest arguments to infidelity and the greatest cause of reproach of religion among unbelievers (ver. 23, 24 ; Neh. 5 : 9).

24. No religious rite is of profit unless it tends to produce holiness of heart and life (ver. 25 ; Titus 1 : 16 ; Isa. 1 : 11-16).

25. Outward ordinances have their place and value, but dependence on them for salvation will result in certain ruin (ver. 26, 27 ; Gal. 5 : 6 ; 6 : 15).

3 ᵏWHAT advantage then hath the Jew; or what profit *is there* of circum-
2 cision? Much every way: chiefly, because that ˡ unto them were committed
3 the oracles of God. For what if some did not believe; ᵐ shall their unbelief make the faith of God without effect?

3 WHAT then is the advantage of the Jew? Or what is the profit of circum-
2 cision? Much every way: first, indeed, that they were intrusted with the
3 oracles of God. For what if some disbelieved? Shall their disbelief make
4 void the faithfulness of God? Far be

k 2 : 25–29.   l 2 : 18, 9 : 4 ; Deut. 4 : 7, 8 ; Acts 7 : 38.   m 9 : 6, 2 Tim. 2 : 13.

26. The essence of religion is not in any ritual, but in the loving service of an obedient heart (ver. 26–28; 11 : 17 ; 1 Tim. 1 : 5).

27. Spiritual religion is of the first importance, and will manifest itself necessarily in outward religion (ver. 27 ; 10 : 9, 10).

28. The greatest boon of a man of God is a right heart, and the highest honor the praise that cometh from God (ver. 28 ; John 5 : 44 ; 8 : 54).

CHAPTER III.

In this chapter Paul completes his argument begun with 1 : 18, showing that Jews and Gentiles are alike under sin. He then (ver. 21) proceeds to exhibit and discuss the doctrine of salvation by Christ, in whom there is revealed a righteousness from God to be received through faith, not earned by works.

1-20. CONCLUSION OF THE DISCUSSION PROVING THAT JEWS AND GENTILES ARE ALIKE SINNERS AND CONDEMNED, and hence in need of God's righteousness. The apostle answers certain objections which might be brought against the preceding view: *First,* That it takes away from God's chosen people all their advantages over Gentiles. *Second,* That it makes God unfaithful to his holy covenant. *Third,* That God cannot justly inflict punishment upon his chosen people, since their sinfulness redounds to his glory (ver. 1-8). He then resumes his argument and proves from Scripture the universal sinfulness of men, both Jews and Gentiles.

1. What then, in view of what he had said regarding Jews and Gentiles, circumcision and uncircumcision, *is the* advantage, or *superiority, of* **the** Jew? Or, changing the question and putting it in a different and more specific form, *What is the profit,* or *benefit of* circumcision? These questions would naturally arise in the mind of a Jew, and doubtless had been met and answered in Paul's own experience. He had admitted that circumcision did profit (2 : 25). But how? To put Jew and Gentile both under condemnation and on a level before God was offensive to Jewish pride. The objection that would at once arise he therefore asks and answers.

2. Much every way—however you may look at it. This he admits is strictly true and needs no abatement. But it makes no difference in regard to the essential point of his argument. **Chiefly**—literally, *First indeed,* used absolutely as in 1 : 8, meaning, *First of all,* as much as to say, I need mention this only. There is no probability that Paul thought of enumerating other points. He, however, specifies some other advantages in 9 : 4, 5. He also implied certain advantages in 2 : 17–20 ; and discusses circumcision somewhat in 4 : 1 ff. *For first of all,* they had this advantage, in which the Jew especially gloried, *that they were entrusted with the* **oracles of God**—the divine *utterances* of his word ; the commands of the Mosaic law and especially the Messianic *promises,* as is evident from the next verse (Heb. 5 : 12 ; 1 Peter 4 : 11 ; Acts 7 : 38, on which compare note).

3. This verse is differently punctuated by different critical editors, without substantially altering the sense. That used in the Common, Revised, and Bible Union versions is preferred here. **For what,** introduces a vigorous question, implying that nothing could be said to the contrary. *For what* **if some did not believe?** rather, *if some disbelieved;* positively and actively exercised their unbelief in, and hence their rejection of, the promises contained in the oracles of God (ver. 2). **Shall their unbelief,** better, *their disbelief,* **make the faith,** rather, *the faithfulness* or *fidelity* (Titus 2 : 10) of **God of none effect?**—*make it inoperative* and useless in fulfilling his promises to his chosen people? The form of the question in the original de-

l God forbid; yea, let *m* God be true, but *n* every man a liar; as it is written,
That thou mightest be justified in thy sayings, and mightest overcome when
5 thou art judged. But *o* if our unrighteousness commend the righteousness of God, what shall we say? *q* Is God unrighteous who taketh vengeance?
6 (*r* I speak as a man) God forbid: for

it. But let God be true, and every man a liar, as it is written,
That thou mayest be justified in thy words,
And mayest overcome when thou art judged.
5 But if our unrighteousness commends God's righteousness, what shall we say? Is God unrighteous who visits
6 wrath? (I speak as a man.) Far be

n See refs. Num. 23 : 19; Deut. 32 : 4; John 3 : 33.   *o* Ps. 62 : 9; 116 : 11.   *p* Ver. 25, 26, 5 : 8, 20, 21
q Gen. 18 : 25.   *r* 6 : 19; Gal. 3 : 15.

---

mands a negative answer. Their disbelieving rejection of the Messiah does not show that God is unfaithful to his promises or to his covenant (9 : 6 ff.). They surely, on their part, had broken their covenant obligations. Some such objections as these would naturally arise in the Jewish mind. What were the Scriptures with all their promises of the Messiah to the Jews, if when he came they for the most part rejected him? Does not this imply in some way unfaithfulness on the part of God to his holy covenant? Or that he has been thwarted in fulfilling his covenant? The answer is given in the next verse.

4. But even the thought of questioning the faithfulness of God is repulsive. **God forbid!** *Far be it! Away the thought!* The translation of this exclamation is unfortunate, since the name of God does not occur in the original, and its literal translation is, *Let it not be*—named or thought of. It occurs thirteen times in Paul's Epistles and in Luke 20 : 16. It generally follows a question, as here, implying a negative answer. It prepares the way for a strong assertion of God's prerogative as the God of truth: **Yea,** better, *But,* rather than harbor such a thought **let God be true,** *be found true,* in his words and faithful to his promises, and acknowledged as such, **and every man** be found **a liar.** Let God be true though all else be false. Compare the similar thought in 2 Tim. 2 : 13. **As it is written,** in Ps. 51 : 4. The quotation is from the Septuagint version, and is sufficiently true to the Hebrew to answer Paul's purpose. **That thou mightest be justified**—*that thou mayest be shown to be righteous in thy words*—actually so of course in God's case. (1 : 17 (3).) **And mightest**

(*mayest*) **overcome when thou art judged,** *or when thou comest into judgment.* The idea is, that God is righteous in all his doings, and will most certainly come off victorious over any who may enter into judgment with him. How great then the folly of arraigning the conduct of God!

5. At this point an objection faces the apostle, one which he had doubtless felt in his own experience, and which was perfectly suited to the arrogant and self-righteous Jew, and could be made a pretext for every wicked indulgence: If according to the Scripture just quoted, the sinfulness of God's people renders conspicuous God's righteousness and redounds to his glory, how can he therefore justly inflict punishment? Paul therefore asks, **But if our unrighteousness commends,** or *shows forth,* renders conspicuous, **the righteousness of God,** the righteousness or holiness of his divine character (note, 1 : 17 (2)), **what shall we say?** Are we to *say* or infer that God is unrighteous in inflicting punishment? The question, *What shall we say?* was after the manner of Jewish teachers, and occurs seven times in this Epistle, and nowhere else in Paul's writings (4 : 1; 6 : 1; 7 : 7; 8 : 31; 9 : 14, 30). Shall we say **Is God unrighteous who taketh vengeance?** *who visits wrath?* The word for *vengeance* is that rendered *wrath* in 1 : 18; 2 : 5. The form of the question demands a negative answer. But Paul would not utter such an impious sentiment without a form of an apology. And so he adds, **I speak as a man,** *after the manner of men,* as men speak; here, as such impiety leads men to feel and speak.

6. God forbid. *By no means.* Away the thought! This negative assertion is proved in this and the next

then *how shall God judge the world?
7 For if the truth of God hath more abounded through my lie unto his glory; ᵗwhy yet am I also judged as a
8 sinner? And not *rather*, (as we be slanderously reported, and as some affirm that we say,) ᵘ Let us do evil, that good ma_` come? Whose damnation is just.
9 What then? ˣ Are we better *than they?* No, in no wise: for ʸ we have before

it! For then how shall God judge the
7 world? For if the truth of God, through my lie, abounded unto his glory, why am I also still judged as a
8 sinner? And why should we not (as we are slanderously reported, and as some affirm that we say,) do evil, that good may come? Whose condemnation is just.
9 What then? Are we better? No, in

ₛ Ps. 9 : 8.   ₜ 9 : 19, 20.   ᵤ 6 : 1, 15.   ₓ Ver. 22, 23; 1 Cor. 4 : 7.   ᵧ 1 : 18-32; chap. 2.

two verses. **For then**—in that case, **how shall God judge the world?** He could not judge at all, since every man might escape punishment on the same ground. *The world* is all mankind; not limited to Gentiles as some have maintained. Some suppose that Paul here assumes the righteousness of God as a judge to be a self-evident truth, which must be admitted by all (Gen. 18 : 25); and that to admit God to be unrighteous would incapacitate him for the office of judge of the world. The former view I regard as better suited to the connection. The argument appears to be this: If God cannot punish sinful Jews, then (ver. 6) he cannot judge the world, for (ver. 7) every one might say, God has been glorified and his truth made conspicuous by my sinful conduct. Why then am I condemned as a sinner and not exempted from punishment? And why (ver. 8) should we not adopt the sentiment slanderously ascribed to us, etc.?

7. This verse applies still further the principle stated in ver. 5, and naturally carries on the argument begun in ver. 6. **For if the truth of God,** his *moral truth,* righteousness, holiness. **Through my lie,** that *falsity* by which man by sinning breaks faith with God. Here it is equivalent to immorality, wickedness. **Hath more abounded**—more exactly, *abounded unto his glory,* making his truthfulness more conspicuous. **Why yet am I**—why am *I also still judged* and condemned **as a sinner?** In this verse the thought naturally passes to the Gentile, whom the Jew usually designated *a sinner.* Thus by the false principle of ver. 5 not only Jews but all sinners might escape punishment. Some of the oldest manuscripts begin this verse with *But* instead of *For.* In that case the word rendered *But* can be regarded as continuative, and rendered *And.* It thus indicates the continuance of the argument and the amplification of ver. 5. But there are strong reasons for retaining the reading *For.*

8. And not rather—better, *And why should we not* (**as we be slanderously,** *blasphemously,* **reported, and as some affirm we say,**) **Let us do evil, that good may come?** This sentiment and impious slander, Paul does not stop to refute. Its bare statement was its own refutation. The form of the question shows that Paul regarded it as untrue and the statement basely false. He only adds, **Whose damnation,** rather, *condemnation,* **is just;** that is, those who follow this principle. He strongly denounces it as subversive of all morality and its perpetrators as deservedly condemned. Thus he repels the slander on the one hand and condemns the slanderers on the other.

In reviewing ver. 1-8, it appears evident that Paul does not introduce an objector into his discourse, but carries on the argument in his own person, meeting objection which he sees would arise. An objector would have put his questions in a form looking for an affirmative answer, and not a negative one, as in ver. 3, 5, 7.

9. What then?—what conclusion shall we come to in regard to our condition as Jews? **Are we better**—than they, the Gentiles. Meyer and a few others translate, *Have we any excuse* or *defense?* that is, to make before a just judge. But this is not well sustained, and is not followed by most leading commentators. "The translation of the English revisers, *Are we in worse condition than they,* is far removed from the ordinary meaning of the word" (BOISE). *Are we better?* is the most natural rendering, and one which the context demands. **No, in no wise**—*not at all,* an emphatic de-

proved both Jews and Gentiles, that
10 *they are all under sin; as it is written,
*There is none righteous, no, not one;
11 there is none that understandeth, there
12 is none that seeketh after God. They
are all gone out of the way, they are
together become unprofitable; there is
none that doeth good, no, not one.
13 Their throat *is* an open sepulchre; with
their tongues they have used deceit;
the poison of asps *is* under their lips;
14 whose mouth *is* full of cursing and
15 bitterness; ᵇtheir feet *are* swift to
16 shed blood; destruction and misery
17 *are* in their ways; and ᶜthe way of
18 peace have they not known; there is
no fear of God before their eyes.

no wise; for we before charged, that
both Jews and Greeks are all under
10 sin. As it is written,
There is none righteous, no, not one;
11 There is none that understands,
There is none that seeks after God;
12 They are all gone out of the way,
they are together become unprofitable;
There is none that does good, there is
not so much as one;
13 Their throat is an open sepulchre;
With their tongues they have used
deceit;
The poison of asps is under their
lips;
14 Whose mouth is full of cursing and
bitterness;
15 Their feet are swift to shed blood;
16 Destruction and misery are in their
ways;
17 And the way of peace they have not
known;
18 There is no fear of God before their
eyes.

z Ver. 23; Gal. 3 : 22.   *a* Ps. 53 : 1; Eph. 2 : 1-3; 1 John 1 : 8-10.   *b* Prov. 1 : 16.   *c* Isa. 57 : 21.

nial. The Jews had the advantage of the Gentiles in respect to privilege (ver. 2), but not in regard to acceptance with God. **For we have before proved,** rather, *for we have before made the charge,* in presenting the proof of it, *that* **both Jews** (2 : 1-24) **and Gentiles** (1 : 18-32) *are all* **under sin—**under the power and slavery of sin (6 : 16; 7 : 24; Gal. 3 : 22). They were as a consequence exposed to condemnation. In this great, essential respect both Jews and Gentiles were alike.

10-18. The discussion brings the apostle back to his position that all are sinners. He had argued this from the general degeneracy of the race and the universal downward sinful tendency of both Jew and Gentile. He now turns to the Scripture proof that Jews as well as Gentiles are under sin, and that in this respect the former have no advantage over the latter. The quotations apply especially to the Jews (ver. 19) although not exclusively. They are quoted freely, for the most part, from the Septuagint version. **As it is written.** Ver. 10, 11, and 12 are from Ps. 14 : 1-3. There is here a general reference to all men, showing *the universal sinfulness* and corruption of mankind. **None that understandeth.** It is the part of true wisdom to *seek after God.* In departing from God they have all become **unprofitable,** useless.

(Compare 1 : 28-31). The universal prevalence of *the sins of the tongue* is presented in ver. 13, 14. The first two clauses of ver. 13 are from Ps. 5 : 9, the last clause from Ps. 140 : 3. Ver. 14 is from Ps. 10 : 7. **Their throat is an open sepulchre**—standing ready to swallow up or to send forth its corruptive influence. **They have used,** *they were* and are *using,* **deceit—**with habitual hypocrisy. **The poison of asps—**a small and venomous serpent whose bite is very fatal, representing slandering, and backbiting, while perhaps professing friendship. **Full of cursing—**imprecations and malignant utterances. **Bitterness**—hateful speech. In ver. 15-17 are recounted their wicked deeds, *sins of violence.* The quotation is from Isa. 59 : 7, 8. **Swift,** quick, **to shed blood—**committing murder on the slightest provocation. They carry **destruction,** *ruin,* and consequent **misery** wherever they go. And in opposition to this way which leads to wretchedness, they have not known **the way of peace,** which leads to peace, a course of life promoting harmony. In ver. 18 is presented *the source* of this universal wickedness. Quoted from Ps. 36 : 1. **There is no fear,** *no reverence,* of **God—**no respect for his authority, none which leads them to love and obey him, and would have preserved them

19 Now we know that what things soever ᵈthe law saith, it saith to them who are under the law: that ᵉevery mouth may be stopped, and ᶠall the world may become guilty before God. 20 Therefore ᵍby the deeds of the law there shall no flesh be justified in his

19 Now we know that whatever the law says, it speaks to those under the law; that every mouth may be stopped, and all the world may be subject to condemnation before God. Because by works of law no flesh will be justified in

ᵈ 2 : 12.   ᵉ 1 : 20, 2 : 1; Job 9 : 2–4; Ezek. 16 : 63, 1 Cor. 1 : 29.   ᶠ Gal. 3 : 10, 22.
ᵍ 9 : 31, 32; Acts 13 : 39; Gal. 3 : 10–13; Eph. 2 : 8, 9.

from their wicked conduct. (Compare Ps. 111 : 10.) These quotations prove from Scripture: (1) The universal sinfulness of the race. (2) That one may be outwardly a Jew and yet a great sinner. (3) That great numbers and at times the nation as such have been in that condition. (See ver. 15-17, and compare Isa. chap. 58 and 59.) (4) The inevitable inference follows, That the Jew as such is not exempt from the penalty of God's broken law.

19. In this and the next verse Paul concludes his argument from the history of the race, from observation, from human consciousness, and from Scripture, that all men are sinners without excuse, justly exposed to the Divine condemnation and therefore in need of a righteousness from God. The conclusion would readily be admitted in respect to the Gentile; but lest the Jew might say that such passages, as above quoted, are not applicable to him, Paul in a single sentence shows that they are intended to apply to the Jews. **Now we know that whatever the law saith, it saith to them under the law,** or *within the sphere of the law*. The *law* here includes the whole Old Testament, which is evident from the passages quoted. Such passages found in their own law and addressed to them must have reference to them. **That**—*in order that*—one of the purposes of the law, and the one applicable at this point. **Every mouth may be stopped**—having nothing to answer before God. It was the Divine intention to take away every excuse from Jew as well as Gentile. **And all the world may become guilty**—*may be under indictment*, or *subject to condemnation before God*, to whom satisfaction for sin is due. *All the world* includes both Jews and Gentiles.

20. Therefore—rather, *Because*, giving the reason for what he had just said in ver. 19, drawn from the whole discussion thus far: Because none will

be justified on the ground of works' **By the deeds of the law**—better, *by works of law*—by any works, whatever they may be, prescribed by any law, though the Mosaic law would be chiefly in mind. *Law* here includes both the written law as quoted in ver. 10–18, and the law written on the conscience (2 : 14, 15). Every man is under the law in one or both of these respects. There is no distinction implied here between the ceremonial and moral law. It is law as a whole. The Scriptures make no such distinction. Neither are *works* here to be limited to those done before regeneration, since "works of law" include good works of every kind, even of the greatest excellence. Those that are the fruit of a regenerate state are consequent upon justification, because they are the evidences of a living, saving, and justifying faith (James 2 : 18–22). **There shall no flesh**—with reference to our weakness, frailty, and mortality—*no mortal man shall* **be justified**—*declared* or *accounted righteous* **in his sight**, being such as God shall look upon as righteous. This is a partial quotation from Ps. 143 : 2, "For in thy sight no one living shall be justified." (*Justified*, see note on 1 : 17.) There is no contradiction here between Paul and James (2 : 22–25). Paul treats of justification as the act of God (8 : 22) and as God looks upon it: James treats of it as it is manifested and evidenced to men by consequent works. Paul looks at the ground of justification which is not of works but through faith; James, at the result in the experience of the individual. James does not combat a justification by a living faith which shows itself by works, but a nominal faith, which being without works is dead. To be justified *by the works of the law* means more than obedience to the law, for God looks upon the heart (1 Sam. 16 : 7). Both heart and life must from the beginning be perfectly conformed to the holy law of

sight: for ʰ by the law *is* the knowledge of sin.

The remedy. God's righteousness freely given to the believer in Christ, as to believers in former times.

21 BUT now ⁱ the righteousness of God without the law is manifested, ᵏ being witnessed by the Law ˡ and the Proph-
22 ets; even the righteousness of God his sight; for through law is knowl-
21 edge of sin. But now, apart from law, a righteousness of God has been manifested, being witnessed by the law and
22 the prophets; even a righteousness of

ʰ 7 : 7-9.   ⁱ 1 : 17; 10 : 3, 4.   ᵏ Gen. 15 : 6; John 5 : 46.   ˡ 1 : 2; Jer. 23 : 5, 6; Dan. 9 : 24.

God. (See note on 2 : 13.) But Paul is not speaking concerning the justification of innocent beings like our first parents before the fall, but of men as they actually are, of sinners, as is evident from what follows: **For by**, or *through*, **the law** *cometh a full* **knowledge of sin**—one comes to know his true character and condition as a sinner by the law. Its office and effect is to convince of sin; pardon, the spirit of obedience, and consequent peace, it cannot give. Paul could speak regarding this from experience, for he says (7 : 7), "I had not known sin except through law"; and "the law has become our schoolmaster," or *tutor*, "unto Christ, that we may be justified by faith" (Gal. 3 : 24). And in 1 Tim. 1 : 8-10 he describes the functions of the law: That its lawful use is good, but that it exists not for righteous men, but for sinners. Such being the office of the law, and its effect upon fallen men, it is evident that it cannot be a ground of their justification. It rather condemns, and cuts off all hope; for it is written, "Cursed is every one that continues not in all the things written in the book of the law, to do them" (Gal. 3 : 10).

21-31. Having shown that all men are sinners and in need of God's righteousness, Paul proceeds to present the WAY OF SALVATION THROUGH FAITH IN CHRIST in the following respects: Its *nature*, not of works but through faith; offered and adapted to all men alike; gratuitous. Its *ground*, the propitiatory sacrifice and redemption which is in Jesus Christ. Its *object*, to enable a righteous God to pardon and save sinners. Its *results*, excludes boasting; presents God exercising justifying mercy to both Jews and Gentiles; establishing, not subverting, the law.

21. But now, since man has no righteousness of his own under law, **without the law**, *apart from law,* without any connection or dependence on law, whether Mosaic or natural, there is now under the gospel **manifested,** fully and plainly made known, *a* **righteousness of God.** Of which God is the Author, as in 1 : 17, which is from him and which he imparts. See note on 1 : 17, especially that (2) on "righteousness." This righteousness was manifested in and through Jesus Christ, who is "the Lord our righteousness" (Jer. 23 : 6). Being not only perfectly innocent (John 8 : 46), but positively holy (John 7 : 18; 7 : 26), he was able by his voluntary and holy obedience, both in living and in suffering even unto death, to meet all the demands of God's holy law (Rom. 5 : 19; Phil. 2 : 8; Heb. 5 : 8). Actively and passively, in character and life, he exhibited all that moral excellence which God and his law requires. His righteousness was spotless, perfect, and complete (Heb. 9 : 14; 1 Peter 1 : 19; Rev. 5 : 6-14). **Being witnessed**, or *testified to*, **by the law and the prophets**—the Old Testament Scriptures (Gen. 3 : 15; Exod. 34 : 6, 7; Ps. 32 : 1, 2; 103 : 8, 9, 10; Isa. 53 : 5, 11; Jer. 31 : 34). See also the illustrations from Abraham and David (4 : 6, 13). There was also the continual testimony of the expiatory sacrifices in the Old Testament. It was therefore not a new doctrine, but one which had been gleaming through the types and shadows of the law, and the brief and indistinct utterances of the prophets. Hence the phrase, literally, *has been manifested*, is eminently suitable. That which was previously but dimly and partially seen has now been made plain fully and completely in the gospel.

22. Even a righteousness of God. In the preceding verse Paul teaches that this righteousness is not attained by works of law; in this verse, that it is attained through faith in Christ. Its emphatic repetition joins it

which is ᵐby faith of Jesus Christ unto all and upon all them that believe: 23 (for ⁿthere is no difference: for °all have sinned, and come short of the 24 glory of God;) being justified freely ᵖby his grace ᑫthrough the redemption 25 that is in Christ Jesus: whom God hath God through faith in Jesus Christ, to all that believe; for there is no dis- 23 tinction; for all have sinned, and fall 24 short of the glory of God; being justi- fied freely by his grace, through the re- 25 demption that is in Christ Jesus; whom

ᵐ Chap. 4; 5:1.　ⁿ Gal. 3:25.　° See refs. 1 Kings 8:46.　ᵖ 5. 16-19; Eph. 2:7-9; Titus 3:5-7. ᑫ Matt. 20:28; Col. 1:14; Heb. 9:12.

with and emphasizes faith. **By,** rather, *through faith in Jesus Christ.* It is through faith as the medium; or faith may be regarded as the appropriating organ through which the righteousness is received. Through faith also we re- ceive Christ and become united with him; Christ becomes ours with his atonement and righteousness. "Salva- tion comes not because our faith saves us, but because it links us to the Christ who saves; and believing is the link. There is no more merit in it than in the beggar's stretching forth his hand to re- ceive the offered purse, or the drown- ing man's grasping the rope that is thrown to him" (STRONG'S "Theol- ogy," p. 481). **Unto all and upon all**—extending to all and coming upon all **that believe.** But some of the old- est and best manuscripts read simply, *unto all that believe.* A reason is given for what he had just said: **For there is no difference** or distinction in this respect between Jews and Gentiles (10:12), for they are all alike con- demned, and the one has no moral su- periority over the other.
23. Further reason for the above: **For all have sinned**—more exactly, *For all sinned.* A historic fact of the past, including the first sin in the gar- den and the sinful disposition and acts flowing out of it. *All are sinners.* The preceding arguments had shown this. **And come short,** *do come short* con- tinually, **of the glory of God.** This is differently interpreted. Some regard it as the glory which belongs to God and which he imparts to the believer. Similar in construction to "righteousness of God" (1:17; 3:21). Others suppose it to mean that all are failing to receive the *approbation* of God—the praise and honor which he bestows (John 5:44; 12:43). But it seems better to take it to mean *in re- spect to the glory of God*—that glory which is due to him: They all do fail of glorifying God. (Compare 1:21.) "Be-

cause, knowing God they glorified him not as God." Also the rebuke of Bel- shazzar, "And the God in whose hand thy breath is ... hast thou not glori- fied" (Dan. 5:23).
24. Being justified — *declared* or *accounted righteous*—grammatically connected with *all* (ver. 23), but by a well- known usage referring back in thought to ver. 22, to those who through faith receive God's righteousness (ver. 22). The statement of ver. 23, that all are sin- ners and are failing continually of ren- dering to God the glory that is his due, makes the gratuitous justification of this verse stand out the more promi- nently. **Freely**—gratuitously. **By** or *through* **his grace** adds greater in- tensity to the expression. They are justified, as a free gift, without any equivalent on their part in the exercise of his grace toward the undeserving, being merely an act of mercy. This is a hard thing for men in their sins and self-righteousness to accept. **Through the redemption that is in Christ Jesus.** *Redemption* is deliverance by the payment of a ransom (Job 33:24; Isa. 35:10; 1 Tim. 2:6), and in the New Testa- ment is applied to deliverance from the guilt of sin (Eph. 1:7; Col. 1:14), from the curse of the law (Gal. 3:13; 4:5), and from the wrath of God (5:9; 1 Thess. 1:10; 5:9). It also includes deliverance from the power, dominion, and consequences of sin (Titus 2:14; 1 Peter 1:18), including the redemption of the body (8:23). This redemption is said to be *in Jesus Christ,* or according to a better reading, *in Christ Jesus,* in his person as the Mes- siah—the redeeming act being per- formed by him personally in what he did and suffered. It is entirely in Christ and in no other. All human agency is excluded. Justification is *through* or *by means of* this redemption in Christ Jesus. (See ANDREW FUL- LER'S "Works," Vol. I., p. 276 ff. Three Sermons on Justification.)
25. *Whom God set forth for himself*

set forth *to be* a propitiation *through faith in his blood, to declare his right-*

r Lev. 16 : 15, 16; 1 John 2 : 2; 4 : 10.

as it were into public view. The expression includes the idea that it was *his own*, his own Son, he set forth, especially in his death, his crucifixion. **To be**, or *as*, **a propitiation,** involving the idea of *appeasing, expiating*. In the Septuagint (Exod. 25 : 18, etc.) and in Heb. 9 : 5, it is applied to the cover of the ark of the covenant in the Holy of Holies, which was sprinkled with the blood of the expiatory victim on the day of the atonement, signifying that the life of the people, the loss of which they had merited on account of their sins, was offered to God in the blood as the life of the victim, and that thus God was appeased and their sins expiated. Hence it was called the *expiatory—the lid of expiation*, or as translated in our version, *the mercy seat*, the place of mercy. Some transfer this meaning to this passage: That Christ, besprinkled with his own blood, was truly that which this lid of expiation typified, namely, the Atoner and Mediator. Hodge objects to this meaning of the word, because "Christ is nowhere else called the mercy seat," and because "it is common to speak of the blood of a sacrifice, but not of the blood of the mercy seat." It may also be added that the mercy-seat is *hidden* rather than *set forth*. Others therefore with good reason take the word to mean *propitiatory sacrifice*. It is strictly an adjective, meaning *propitiatory*, and implies some noun as *sacrifice* or *offering* understood, the connection suggesting the sense. Meyer refers to the analogous terms used, where *offering* is understood, as the word *pertaining* to *thanks* used for *thank-offering*, etc. Or if used as a noun it would very naturally mean *a victim of expiation*. The context suggests the idea of an atoning sacrifice by the words "in his blood" (Lev. 17 : 11). This view accords with the fact that the Mosaic sacrifices were typical of Christ (1 Cor. 5 : 7; Heb. 10 : 1-10), and that he was styled by John "the Lamb of God that taketh away the sin of the world" (John 1 : 29), and that the Old Testament prophecies foretold a suffering Messiah who should make an atonement for the sins of the world (Isa. 53 : 4-12; Dan. 9 : 24-26).

God set forth as a propitiation, through faith, in his blood, for the exhibition of

s John 6 : 53-58; Col. 1 : 20.

Zech. 13 : 1 ff.; Ps. 16 : 22, 40; Luke 24 : 26, 27, 46, etc.). Christ also is expressly declared to be a sacrifice and offering unto God for a sweet-smelling savor (Eph. 5 : 2), and he is also said to have offered himself without spot or blemish unto God (Heb. 9 : 14). This view is also confirmed by the use of its kindred words elsewhere in the New Testament. Thus the verb from which it is derived means to *appease*, to *propitiate*. In Heb. 2 : 17 it is correctly translated in the Revised and the Bible Union versions, to *make propitiation*; and in Luke 18 : 13, *Be merciful* or *be propitiated*; and in the Septuagint it is used six times with the same essential meaning. So also its kindred noun derived from the above verb, means *an appeasing, a propitiating*, and is used of an expiatory sacrifice in 2 Macc. 3 : 33; and of Christ as a *propitiation* of our sins in 1 John 2 : 2; 4 : 10. Notice that while it is said that Christ offered himself, that it was God who gave and sent his Son (John 3 : 16, 17), and the Son voluntarily obeyed (Heb. 10 : 5-8). And also that here Paul says not *offered*, but *whom God set forth, as a propitiatory* sacrifice. **Through faith**—connected most naturally with *propitiation*. Christ the propitiatory sacrifice becomes such to the believer through faith. **In**, or *by*, **his blood**—by means of his blood, meaning his life which he offered to God for the sins of men (Deut. 12 : 23; Heb. 9 : 22).

Observe here that there was something in God to be propitiated, and that Christ by his sacrifice made the propitiation. The holy wrath of God was aroused against sin and the sinner (1 : 18; 5 : 9; Ps. 7 : 11; Gal. 3 : 13), which was removed by the death of Christ. The Bible everywhere represents sin as abominable in God's sight. There is a holy displeasure of God superadded to the penalties of the law (2 : 4, 5, 8, 9; 3 : 5; Eph. 5 : 6; Col. 3 : 6; 1 Thess. 2 : 16). It is but the natural outworkings of God's holiness and justice against sin. Christ so satisfies these as to deliver us from wrath (Rom. 5 : 9; 1 Thess. 1 : 10; 5 : 9). It should also be noted that it was not God offering up a propitiatory sacrifice to himself, but that it was the second Adam

eousness ʰfor the remission of ᵘsins that are past, through the forbearance of God; to declare, *I say*, at this time his righteousness: ˣthat he might be just, and the justifier of him which believeth in Jesus.

his righteousness, because of the passing over of the sins formerly committed in the forbearance of God; for the exhibition of his righteousness in this present time, that he may be righteous, and the justifier of him who believes in Jesus.

t Acts 13 : 38, 39.   *u* Acts 17 : 30; Heb. 9 : 15.   *x* Isa. 42 : 21.

representing the race (1 Tim. 2 : 5, 6; Phil. 2 : 7, 8; 1 Cor. 15 : 22, 45).

To declare—*for the exhibition;* that is, *in order to exhibit* **his righteousness.** His holiness, justice, hatred of sin, and his infinite love are all exhibited, as nowhere else, in the sacrificial offering of his son; especially his "judicial righteousness in both its aspects, of sin-condemning and sin-forgiving righteousness" (SCHAFF). In order to show that his righteousness was maintained while he remitted the penalty of violated law. **For the remission,** etc. The rest of this verse constitutes one clause, and is better rendered: *Because of the passing over* (compare *overlooked* (Acts 17 : 30); observe also that the word does not mean *remission*) *of the sins previously committed* (before the expiatory death of Christ) *in the long-suffering of God*—while God in his long-suffering forbore to inflict punishment. For four thousand years God had tolerated sin and sinners, (Comp. Acts 14 : 16.) His holiness and justice were in danger of being lost sight of, and the conception of them obscured (2 : 2; 2 Peter 3 : 3, 4). The same conscience also that condemned the sin would condemn the judge who should remit the penalty. There was a necessity therefore for a solemn manifestation of God's righteousness as exhibited in the expiatory death of Christ. Of the benefits which godly men of old derived from looking forward to a coming Saviour Paul is not now speaking. He is showing the need of displaying God's righteousness.

26. Paul repeats for another purpose a thought of the preceding verse. **To declare, I say,** etc. Better, *For the exhibition of* **his righteousness** *at this present time,* in this critical period of the world's history under the gospel. *At this present time* is emphatic, and contrasted with the passing over of sins previously committed (ver. 25). Then there was a passing over and a forbearance in punishment; now, a full forgiveness through the atoning sacrifice, which if rejected would bring swift destruction (Acts 13 : 40, 41). *Exhibition of his righteousness* in the Divine character—see on preceding verse. We must not separate the justice and mercy of God; nor suppose that any of his attributes are antagonistic. His holiness, justice, mercy, and love, are all in perfect harmony, and all made conspicuous in the suffering and death of Christ. In this sacrifice Christ was exhibited as well pleasing and acceptable to God (John 10 : 17, 18), as voluntarily making it on his part (Heb. 10 : 5-7), as sustaining a twofold relation to God and man (1 Tim. 2 : 5, 6; Phil. 2 : 6 ff.), and both these relations were conspicuous in his life (John 1 : 14), in his sufferings and death (Matt. 27 : 50-54), and in his resurrection (1 : 4; 4 : 25; Acts 13 : 33), and still conspicuous in his exaltation (Acts 5 : 31; Phil. 2 : 9-11; Rev. 5 : 9-14). Thus was God honored as much as if his holy displeasure and the penalty of his law had been visited on the sinner himself.

The object or end in view of all this ("whom God set forth as a propitiation," etc.), is now stated: **That he might be just and the justifier of him which believeth in Jesus.** Or more exactly, *in order that he may himself be righteous* (really and manifestly so) *and making him righteous who is of faith in Jesus.* A difficulty here is that there is no single word in English to render the word translated *justify* corresponding with the word *righteous*. "We have here the greatest paradox of the gospel; for in the law God is seen *just* and *condemning*; in the gospel as being himself *just* and *justifying* the sinner" (BENGEL). In the act of justification the righteousness of Christ (ver. 21) is accounted to the believer, so that he is pardoned and treated as if he had never sinned. Through faith this righteousness is accepted and the soul becomes united with Christ (ver. 22), in-

27 ʸ Where *is* boasting then? It is excluded. By what law? Of works?
28 ᶻ Nay: but by the law of faith. Therefore we conclude that a man is justified by faith without the deeds of the law.
29 *Is* he the God of the Jews only? *Is* he not also of the Gentiles? ᵃ Yes, of
30 the Gentiles also: seeing ᵇ *it is* one God which shall justify the circumcision by faith, and uncircumcision through faith.

27 Where then is the glorying? It is excluded. By what kind of law? Of works? Nay; but by a law of faith.
28 For we reckon that a man is justified
29 by faith apart from works of law. Or is God the God of Jews only? Is he not also of Gentiles? Yes, of Gentiles
30 also; since God is one, who will justify the circumcision by faith, and the uncircumcision through faith. Do we
31

ʸ 1 Cor. 1 : 29-31.　ᶻ 9 : 32; Gal. 2 : 16.　ᵃ 9 : 24-26; Mal. 1 : 11; Eph. 3 : 6.　ᵇ Gal. 3 : 28; 5 : 6.

volving regeneration and adoption (8 : 15-18; 2 Cor. 5 : 17) and a partaking of the Divine nature (2 Peter 1 : 4; Heb. 12 : 10). Justification includes both the forgiveness of sins and restoration to the Divine favor. But through faith, by virtue of union with Christ, this righteousness is received in growth in grace and sanctification. "Being made free from sin," that is, *justified*, "ye have your fruit unto holiness," that is, unto *sanctification* (6 : 23; see on 1 : 17 and 3 : 24). This passage (ver. 25, 26) is one of the richest in doctrinal instruction in all Paul's writings. Nowhere else is he, or any other writer in the New Testament, so full or so explicit on the atoning efficacy of Christ's death. Nowhere else is the great question of the ages, which human wisdom never solved, so clearly answered, "How can man be just with God?" (Job 9 : 2.) What consolation has this brought to troubled and believing hearts. "On reading it," says Cowper, "I immediately received power to believe. . . I saw the complete sufficiency of the expiation which Christ had wrought for my pardon and justification. . . My eyes filled with tears, transports choked my utterance. I could only look up to heaven in silent fear, overflowing with love and wonder."

27. Paul now draws his conclusions in a number of spirited questions and answers. **Where is** *the* **boasting then?** that is, of the Jew (2 : 17; 3 : 19. See below on ver. 29). *Where?* It is not to be found or seen, so confident is Paul in the strength of his position. **It is excluded.** The gospel plan of redemption leaves no ground of boasting. How then is it excluded? How can its spirit be suppressed? **By what** *kind of* **law?** By a law of works? one which demands works as a ground of merit? **Nay;** emphatically; for that

would lead to self-righteousness. **But by** *a* **law of faith**—a principle or rule which requires faith. Only thus will a person learn to glory in the Lord and not in self (Eph. 2 : 8, 9). But Paul only discarded legal works; he held as strongly as James to the works which are evidences of a living faith, the fruit in a Christian life (Eph. 2 : 10; Titus 3 : 8).

28. Therefore, in view of what has just been said, and confirmatory of it, **we conclude,** rather, *we reckon* or *hold,* **that a man is justified,** or *accounted righteous,* **by faith,** *apart from works of law,* as a ground of acceptance with God. (See on ver. 20, 21.)

29. Is he the God, etc. Rather, *Or,* if this statement (ver. 2ᵇ) is doubted or not admitted, *is God the God of Jews only?* "If righteousness comes through works of law, as the Jews only had the law, the absurd conclusion follows that he was the God of the Jews only" (BOISE). Thus this verse and the next strikingly confirm the statement in ver. 28. **Is he not also** *of* **Gentiles?** The form of the question in the original anticipates an affirmative answer. **Yes,** *of Gentiles* **also.** This authoritative assertion is founded on numerous passages in the Old Testament (Gen. 12 : 3; Ps. 2 : 8; 82 : 8; Isa. 49 : 5-7, etc.).

30. The statement of this verse, grounded on the unity of God, is closely connected with the preceding verse. **Seeing**—*since God is one,* a doctrine firmly held by the Jews. Hence he must be God of both Jews and Gentiles, or the absurd conclusion would follow that Gentiles had no God! As there is one God of all, so there is but one way of justification for all. *Who will* **justify the circumcision by,** or *out of,* **faith, and** *the* **uncircumcision through** *the* **faith,** the very same faith as that by which the Jew is

31 Do we then *make void the law through faith? God forbid: yea, ᵈwe establish the law.

then make void law through faith? Far be it! Yea, we establish law.

c Gal. 3 : 17-19.   d 7. 7-14 ; 8. 4.

justified, or *accounted as righteous.* Most take *by* and *through* as equivalent in meaning. *By* or *out of* may point rather to faith as the *source* by which Jews were justified and thus made truly the sons of Abraham (Gal. 3 : 6, 7), their circumcision being but an outward sign or seal of that faith (4 : 11). *Through* may point to faith as the *means* or *medium* by which others received the benefits of justification, independent of any outward sign or any ancient covenant.

31. This verse forms the conclusion of what precedes, and a transition to the discussion in the next chapter. An objection would arise in the minds of many, as doubtless it had in Paul's own experience, that such a gratuitous justification by faith alone, would do away with the obligations of the law. **Do we then make void the law,** make it inoperative and useless, **through faith? God forbid.** *Away the thought!* Impossible! It is not to be once named. **Yea, we establish the law.** But how? (1) God's displeasure against sin and his justice receive their highest manifestation on Calvary and in the gospel. (2) Through the gospel a spirit of obedience to the Divine will is produced in man, and thus the law which represents the will of God is established. (3) Christ also honored it and gave it a perfect obedience. He came not to destroy it, but to fulfill it. (4) The law as illustrated in Abraham (4 : 3), involved the same principle of faith, and is therefore confirmed thereby.

PRACTICAL REMARKS.

1. The advantages of belonging to the church, or of living in a Christian community, are many, and the responsibility is great (ver. 1 ; Deut. 4 : 7-9 ; Ps. 147 : 19, 20).

2. Since the Bible is such a boon to any people, how important to give it to all nations (ver. 2 ; Ps. 119 : 97-104 ; Rev. 22 : 6, 7, 10).

3. God is faithful to his promises; and it is man's fault if he fails of its blessings (ver. 3, 4 ; 2 Tim. 2 : 11-13 ; 1 John 1 : 9).

4. It is a mark of true piety to justify God rather than ourselves (ver. 4 ; Job 42 : 5, 6).

5. That God makes the wrath of man to praise him does not lessen the guilt of the sinner (ver. 5 ; Ps. 76 : 7-10 ; Prov. 9 : 12).

6. The final judgment will be impartial and founded in truth and righteousness (ver. 6 ; Ps. 72 : 2 ; Rev. 19 : 2).

7. Sinners may comfort themselves by false reasonings about God, but they cannot thereby escape condemnation and punishment (ver. 7 ; Exod. 34 : 7).

8. That practice cannot be good, nor that doctrine true, whose tendency is immoral (ver. 8 ; Matt. 7 : 16-20 ; 1 Cor. 15 : 33).

9. Whatever advantages the people of Christian countries may have over the heathen, all are alike sinners (ver. 9, 23 ; 1 Kings 8 : 46).

10. Paul regarded the Old Testament as the word of God and an ultimate standard of appeal (ver. 10-18 ; 2 Tim. 3 : 16).

11. The Bible's description of the human heart and life before Christ is equally true at the present day (ver. 10-18 ; 2 Tim. 3 : 1, 2 ; 2 Peter 3 : 3).

12. The Bible teaches explicitly human depravity, involving the *tongue, mouth, lips, feet,* the entire body (ver. 10-18 ; Jer. 17 : 9 ; James 3 : 6).

13. The law was intended neither to justify nor sanctify. It gives no hope of salvation ; but only speaks condemnation to the sinner (ver. 19, 20 ; Gal. 3 : 22).

14. Conviction of sin and a feeling that if we are saved it must be by other merit and power than our own, are a needed preparation for the reception of the gospel (ver. 20 ; Gal. 3 : 23, 24).

15. The doctrine of salvation by grace through faith is a doctrine of the Old Testament as well as the New (ver. 21 ; Hab. 2 : 4 ; Isa. 28 : 16 ; Zech. 4 : 7).

16. Christ has wrought out a perfect righteousness by his obedience unto death,

4 WHAT shall we then say that *Abraham our father, [f]as pertaining to the flesh, hath found?

[e] Isa. 51:2; Matt. 3:9.

4 WHAT then shall we say that Abraham, our forefather according to the

[f] Phil. 3:3, 4.

which is accounted to the believer in justification, and of which by a personal union with Christ, the believer becomes partaker in sanctification (ver. 21, 22; Gal. 2:16, 20; Phil. 1:11; Rev. 19:8).

17. The Bible teaches that all men are sinners. Sin robs God of his glory, and takes for self that which belongs to God (ver. 23; 5:12; Mal. 1:6; Gal. 3:22).

18. Justification is an act of grace on God's part, gratuitously exercised toward men, and made available by means of the ransom which Christ personally paid for us (ver. 24; Gal. 4:4, 5).

19. All human agency is excluded in justification. It is an act of God solely because of what Christ has done for us (ver. 24-26; 8:33; Phil. 1:8, 9; Eph 2:8).

20. In the atonement Christ is set forth as expiating sin and satisfying the justice and holiness of God (ver. 25, 26; Heb. 9:14).

21. The death of Christ displays and vindicates the righteous character and perfections of God, in his treatment of sinners, both in the former dispensation and in the present (ver. 25, 26).

22. Christ obeyed and suffered in our stead in order that we might through him be pardoned and saved (ver. 22-26; 4:25).

23. It was only as Christ was set forth as a propitiation that God could be righteous in exercising justifying mercy (ver. 26; Matt. 26:39, 42).

24. Both justification and sanctification are of God. The former is God's gracious act toward us; the latter is what he graciously does within us (ver. 22-26; John 17:17).

25. All the attributes of God were in glorious harmony in providing and accomplishing the great work of redemption (ver 22-26, 31; Ps. 10, 11).

26. Gospel justification tends to humble men and exalt God (ver. 27, 28; 1 Cor. 1:31).

27. God is the universal Father and all men are brethren in the flesh (ver. 29; Acts 17:28, 29).

28. Justification by faith is without partiality, and open to all (ver. 30; Mal. 1:11).

29. The law, in its spiritual character and righteous requirements, abides, and is in perfect harmony with the gospel (ver. 31; Mark 12:28-34).

CHAPTER IV.

In this chapter we have the expanding of the truth brought to view in the last verse of the preceding chapter. The law and the gospel are in perfect accord. The former is confirmed by the latter. The doctrine of salvation by grace through faith is the same in both; but it finds its highest development in the gospel through Jesus Christ.

1-25. THE DOCTRINE OF SALVATION BY GRACE THROUGH JUSTIFICATION BY FAITH ILLUSTRATED AND CONFIRMED FROM THE OLD TESTAMENT. Abraham justified by faith (ver. 1-5). David recognized a righteousness apart from works (ver. 6-8). This faith and this reckoned righteousness of justification in Abraham preceded circumcision (ver. 9-13). Circumcision a sign and a seal of the righteousness of Abraham's faith. Through the righteousness of faith also Abraham was the heir of the world (ver. 13-22), which now may also be ours.

1. Paul anticipates an objection which would naturally arise in the mind of a Jew, and which he had felt in his own experience: If such a view be correct, **What shall we then say that Abraham** *our forefather* **hath found?** obtained *as to the flesh?*—as to external observances affecting the body only, within the sphere of works, such as circumcision, ablutions, fastings, etc., on which the Jew laid so much stress (Gal. 6:12; Phil. 3:4, 5). Some with the Revised version read, *our forefather according to the flesh hath found*—what benefit hath he gained? Others without sufficient reason omit *hath found*, and translate, *What then shall we say of Abraham our forefather?* The general sense of these various read-

2 For if Abraham were justified by works, he hath *whereof* to glory.
3 not before God; for what saith the Scripture? *Abraham believed God, and it was counted unto him for right-
4 eousness*. Now ᵇ to him that worketh is the reward not reckoned of grace,
5 but of debt; but ⁱ to him that worketh not, but believeth on him that justifieth the ungodly, ᵏ his faith is counted for righteousness.

g Gal. 3 : 6; James 2 : 23.   *h* 11 : 6.

2 flesh, has found? For if Abraham was justified by works, he has ground of glo-
3 rying; but not towards God. For what says the Scripture? And Abraham believed God, and it was reckoned to
4 him for righteousness. Now to him that works, the reward is not reckoned
5 as of grace, but as of debt. But to him that works not, but believes on him who justifies the ungodly, his faith is
6 reckoned for righteousness. As also

i Ver. 24 ; 3 : 22.   *k* Ver. 3.

ings is nearly the same. The answer implied to the question is, Nothing as regards righteousness and justification. To the Jew Abraham was the highest authority; and this question of the first importance.

2. A negative answer to the preceding question being implied, *For* introduces the reason for this answer. This verse and the next afford a good illustration of Paul's brief elliptical style, which makes the interpretation difficult. **For if Abraham** *was* **justified,** or *accounted righteous,* **by works** *he hath ground of glorying* and of *boasting*—with an evident allusion to 3 : 27. **But not before,** or *toward,* **God.** Some interpret: In that case he has occasion of glorying, not toward God, but only toward himself. Even then whatever merit he may have in the sight of men, he has no ground of boasting before an infinitely holy God. But the most natural and satisfactory explanation seems to be: For if Abraham was justified by works, as the Jews commonly supposed, he would have ground of boasting; but he has no such ground before or toward God; and therefore he was not justified by works; for what saith the Scripture, etc. This is the view of Calvin and Hodge.

3. For introduces the proof of the negative assertion implied above. *For what saith the Scripture* in regard to the ground of Abraham's justification? **Abraham believed God, and it was counted,** or *reckoned,* **to him for righteousness** (Gal. 3 : 6; James 2 : 23). Quoted from Gen 15 : 6, from the Septuagint. *Believed* is emphatic, and thus Abraham's faith is distinguished from works, and merit on his part is excluded. Abraham's faith being *reckoned to him for righteousness* implies that he was justified, or accounted righteous and treated as such.

(Compare 2 : 26 ; 9 : 8 ; 8 : 36.) Abraham's faith included both his filial trust in God, and his belief in God's promise (Gen. 15 : 5, 6). How strong it was may be learned from ver. 18 and from Gen. 12 : 1–4 and Heb. 11 : 8–10. At this point it was only necessary to Paul's argument to contrast faith and works; and to show that as the gospel makes known a righteousness by faith apart from works, so Abraham in like manner obtained righteousness by faith apart from works. From other parts of Scripture we learn that Abraham's faith in God rested on the Promised Seed (Gal. 3 : 8), and the promises which were seen from afar (John 8 : 56; Heb. 11 : 13). See closing note on ver. 10.

4, 5. These two verses illustrate the essential difference between a reward of works, and a favor bestowed without any equivalent in return. They illustrate and confirm ver. 3. **Now to him that worketh**—for wages or hire. This is the natural meaning, as shown by the use of the word **reward,** *the pay of a hireling.* To such the pay is *not reckoned as* a matter *of grace* or *favor, but as* **of debt. But to him,** who like Abraham, **worketh not,** as a hireling for pay, but renouncing all claim to reward and merit, **believeth on him** *who* **justifieth,** or *accounts the ungodly as righteous,* to such a one, **his faith** *is reckoned* **for righteousness,** and necessarily gratuitous. (See on ver. 3.) Then he is no longer regarded as *ungodly* but *reconciled* (5 : 10), regenerated and adopted into God's family (8 : 15. See on 3 : 26). Faith is here presented as entirely separate from works, and as opposed to all trust in works, not as supplementing defective works (11 : 6). The final statement of ver. 5 prepares the way for the argument in the next verse.

6. David is quoted an authority

6 Even as David also describeth the blessedness of the man unto whom God imputeth righteousness *without works, saying,* Blessed *are* they whose iniquities are forgiven, and whose sins
8 are covered. Blessed *is* the man to whom the Lord will not impute sin.
9 ᵐ *Cometh* this blessedness then upon the circumcision *only,* or upon the uncircumcision also? ⁿ For we say that faith was reckoned to Abraham for righteousness.
10 How was it then reckoned: when he was in circumcision, or in uncircum-

David speaks of the happiness of the man, to whom God reckons righteousness, apart from works.
7 Happy they, whose iniquities have been forgiven,
   And whose sins have been covered;
8 Happy the man to whom the Lord will not reckon sin!
9 Comes this happiness then on the circumcision, or also on the uncircumcision? For we say, Faith was reckoned
10 to Abraham for righteousness. How then was it reckoned? When he was in circumcision, or in uncircumcision?

l 3 : 20, 21, 27.   *m* 3 : 29, 30.   *n* Ver. 3.

among the Jews hardly second to Abraham, and especially revered for his Messianic relations and predictions (Ps. 2 : 2; Matt. 1 : 1), **Even as David describeth**—*speaks* or *asserts.* His testimony is appealed to as a proof and in elucidation of a righteousness apart from works. *Just as David speaks of* **the blessedness of,** or *upon,* **the man unto whom God imputeth,** or *reckoneth,* **righteousness without works,** *apart from works.* The word rendered *blessedness* occurs in the New Testament only three times (here, ver. 9, and Gal. 4 : 15), and means *a declaration of blessedness* or *happiness.* Thus David utters a *declaration of happiness upon the man.* " Nearly equivalent to saying, *congratulates the man,*" etc. (BOISE).

7, 8. The quotation is from the Septuagint (Ps. 32 : 1, 2). **Blessed,** or *Happy,* **they whose iniquities were** (and are) **forgiven, and whose sins were** (and are) **covered** *completely.* This implies man's absolute need of forgiveness, and that he could in nowise demand justice at God's hands (Job 9 : 2, 3). **Blessed,** or *Happy,* **the man to whom the Lord will** *in no wise* **impute,** rather, *reckon,* **sin.** This implies that his only hope is in God's forbearing to bring him into judgment—to account sin against him. The two passages regarding Abraham and David in a measure supplement each other. Justification is the central point (ver. 5). Gratuitously performed through faith and a reckoned righteousness are the points brought to view in the case of Abraham. The full and gracious forgiveness of sins is made prominent in the words of David. It is implied, and so Paul affirms, that to such a one

righteousness is reckoned apart from works (ver. 6). It has been noted that in the Hebrew of the quotation from David there are three different words used to express sin. Thus " sin is viewed as a wrong against God (transgression) which needs to be *forgiven,* as a loathsome thing (sin) which needs to be *covered,* and as a crime (iniquity) which needs to be avenged unless some satisfaction is rendered to justice; or to express substantially the same distinctions more briefly, sin is represented as an offense against God's majesty, his purity, and his justice" (A. N. ARNOLD, "Am. Com."). (See Ps. 32 : 1, 2.)

9. Paul proceeds to prove from Abraham's case that circumcision is not a necessary condition of that happy state in which righteousness is reckoned to a believer, implying his justification. Having shown how Abraham was accounted righteous (ver. 3–5), and given the testimony of David to the same effect, the question naturally arises: **Cometh this blessedness then upon the circumcision only, or upon the uncircumcision also?** This is not the language of a supposed objector, but rather Paul's statement of the point in question. No direct answer is given, but it is implied : Upon the circumcision also; **for we say,** etc. On *this blessedness.* (See on ver. 6.) *For* begins the discussion, repeating the Scripture statement of ver. 3 as a fundamental starting point. In the words, *we say,* Paul assumes the assent of the reader to this position. (See on ver. 3.)

10. How, under what circumstances, **was it then reckoned? when he was in circumcision,**

cision? Not in circumcision, but in
11 uncircumcision. And ᵒhe received the sign of circumcision, ᵖa seal of ᑫthe righteousness of the faith which *he had yet* being uncircumcised: that ʳhe might be the father of all them that believe, though they be not circumcised; that righteousness might be im-
12 puted unto them also: and the father of circumcision ˢto them who are not of the circumcision only, but who also walk in the steps of that faith of our father Abraham, which *he had* being *yet* uncircumcised.

Not in circumcision, but in uncircumcision. And he received the sign of
11 cision. And he received the sign of circumcision, a seal of the righteousness of the faith which he had while in uncircumcision; that he might be father of all that believe while in uncircumcision, that the righteousness
12 might be reckoned to them also; and father of circumcision to those who not only are of the circumcision, but who also walk in the steps of the faith of our father Abraham, which he had while in uncircumcision.

o Gen. 17 : 10, 11.　p 2 Cor. 1 : 22; Eph. 1 : 13, 14.　q Phil. 3 : 9.　r Luke 19 : 9; Gal. 3 : 7.　s 9 : 6, 7.

or in uncircumcision? This was a question of so great importance to the Jew, that a direct question and a positive answer are given. **Not in circumcision, but in uncircumcision.** From a comparison of Gen. 15 : 6; 16 : 16; 17 : 13, it appears that it was some months before the birth of Ishmael that the faith of Abraham was counted to him for righteousness, that Abraham was eighty-six years old when Ishmael was born, and ninety-nine years old when he was circumcised. Thus this great spiritual era in his life occurred at least fourteen years before his circumcision, clearly showing that circumcision had nothing to do with it. It should be noted that Gen. 15 : 6 does not necessarily fix the time of his justification. It was then that it became an assured and a revealed fact to him. About ten years before this, when he left his own country and came into the land of Canaan (Gen. 12 : 4; 14 : 18-20; 16 : 3), he believed God, and he should then be regarded as justified. But it was not till later that he came to know experimentally and as a revealed fact a righteousness obtained through faith.

11. So far from this circumcision was given in consequence of it, and as a seal in attestation of the righteousness of faith which he had while in uncircumcision. **And,** consequently, **he received the sign,** or token, **of circumcision**—a token of the covenant formed with him as "the father of a multitude of nations" (Gen. 17 : 4-10). **A seal**—a stamp by which anything is attested (1 Cor. 9 : 2). Circumcision was a *seal*, an outward token, attesting the fact **of the righteousness of faith** (faith having been reckoned to him for righteousness) **which he had**

being uncircumcised. Circumcision to him and to his descendants was a sign of God's covenant made with Abraham, but only to Abraham was it a seal of the righteousness of his faith exercised before his circumcision. It was therefore to him what it could not be to any of his descendants who were circumcised when eight days old.

The argument is now complete in Abraham's case that he was accounted righteous before he received circumcision. Now comes the application of his case to this discussion. **That he might be the father**—spiritually, a conspicuous example to those exercising faith and a leader of the faithful. The great doctrine of righteousness through faith was the more fully revealed to him, handed down from him, and traced back to him. As father and sons are animated by the same spirit to a common faith, so a like spirit and a righteousness apart from works characterized Abraham and the faithful after him (Gal. 3 : 7; Ps. 51 : 10, 16, 17). His faith was accounted for righteousness when he was uncircumcised, of which fact circumcision became to him an attesting seal in order that he might be the father **of all them that believe, though they be not circumcised, that** *the* **righteousness might be imputed,** or *reckoned*, **unto them also.**

12. The construction in this verse is very difficult in the original. Its meaning is brought out in the following translation: *And father in relation to circumcision*, to *those who not only are of circumcision* (having been circumcised), *but who also walk in the steps* (after the example) *of the faith of our father, Abraham, which he had when yet in*

E

13 For the promise that he should be the *heir of the world, was not to Abraham, or to his seed, through the law, but through the righteousness of
14 faith. For if they which are of the law be heirs, faith is made void, and
15 the promise made of none effect: because the law worketh wrath: for where no law is, there is no transgression.
16 Therefore it is of faith, that it might be by grace; to the end the promise might be sure to all the seed;

13 For not through law was the promise to Abraham, or to his seed, that he should be heir of the world, but
14 through righteousness of faith. For if they that are of law are heirs, faith is made void, and the promise is made of
15 no effect. For the law works wrath; but where there is no law, neither is
16 there transgression. For this cause it is of faith, that it may be according to grace; in order that the promise may be sure to all the seed; not to that only

t Gen. 12 : 1-3 ; 17 : 4, etc.; Gal. 3 : 29.   *u* Gal. 3 : 16-18.   *x* Ver. 11.   *y* Gal. 2 : 21 ; 5 : 4.
z See 3 : 31.   *a* 3 : 19, 20 ; 5 : 13, 20 ; 1 Cor. 15 : 56 ; 2 Cor. 3 : 7, 9.   *b* 5 : 13.   *c* 3 : 24-26 ; 5 : 1.
d Gal. 3 : 22 ; Heb. 6 : 13-20.

uncircumcision. In the preceding verse Abraham is declared to be father of believing Gentiles; in this verse, father of believing Jews; and unbelieving Jews are excluded from this relation. So John the Baptist emphasized this spiritual relationship: "Begin not to say within yourselves, We have Abraham for our father," etc. (Luke 3 : 8). Our Saviour also: "If ye were Abraham's children, ye would do the works of Abraham" (John 8 : 39). The true children of Abraham are not his natural descendants, but those who have faith.

13. The great fact that Abraham was father of believing Jews and Gentiles is confirmed by another reason: The promise to Abraham and his seed was grounded on faith, not on works of law. **For the promise** *to Abraham and his seed* **that he should be the heir of the world** *was not through law,* demanding works and obedience, *but through righteousness* **of faith,** that obtained by means of faith. The phrase "heir of the world" is not used in the promises to Abraham, but is a summary of their import (Gen. 12 : 2, 3 ; 13 : 14-17 ; 15 : 18 ; 17 : 8 ; 22 : 18 ; compare Ps. 89). They centered in the promise, "In thee shall all families of the earth be blessed." It was only in Christ, the seed of the promise (Gal. 3 : 16, 17), that Abraham truly became "the heir of the world" (8 : 17 ; 1 Cor. 15 : 24). Compare also: "For all things are yours . . . and ye are Christ's and Christ is God's" (1 Cor. 3 : 21-23).

14. For if they *that are of law,* especially those who depend on the works of the Mosaic law, *are* **heirs, faith is made void,** rendered useless, **and the promise made of none effect** (Gal. 3 : 18). If the inheritance comes through obedience to law then the faith ascribed to Abraham is useless and the promise too is inoperative and of no value, since the inheritance might be claimed as due for service, just as if no promise had been made. What God promised as a gratuity would be claimed as a reward.

15. Another reason given why the inheritance does not come by works of law. **Because the law worketh wrath,** is the occasion of God's wrath, and exposes us to punishment as transgressors, inasmuch as no one fully meets its claims. If it therefore only aggravates man's case, how then could it secure to him the blessings of the inheritance? *For,* rather, *But where there is no law neither is there transgression* of any specific law, hence no wrath and no punishment. It is the law that gives the knowledge of sin (3 : 20) and to sin its condemning power. It must be outside and independent of law that the promised inheritance can be secured. Paul here is careful and guarded in the use of the word *transgression,* which means a violation of a specific law. There is another word for sin in its broader and deeper meaning (5 : 13), which has reference to wrong moral emotions and character, and to the underlying corrupt moral nature.

16. Recurring to ver. 13, Paul applies what he had just said. **Therefore—** *on account of this*—such being the case that the law works wrath and cannot confer heirship, **it,** the inheritance, **is of faith, that** *it may be according to* **grace**—free, unmerited favor, not as a debt, but as a gift. **To the end,** or *In order that* **the promise** *may be* **sure to all the seed.** Only in this way could it be sure. Never could it be if dependent on imperfect, chang-

not to that only which is of the law, but to that also which is of the faith of Abraham; *who is the father of us all, 17 (as it is written, I have made thee a father of many nations,) before him whom he believeth, *even* God, ʰwho quickeneth the dead, and calleth those ᵍthings which be not as though they 18 were. Who against hope believed in hope, that he might become the father of many nations, according to that which was spoken, So shall thy seed

which is of the law, but to that also which is of the faith of Abraham; who 17 is the father of us all, (as it is written, A father of many nations have I made thee,) before God whom he believed, who makes alive the dead, and calls the things that are not as though they 18 were; who against hope believed in hope, to the end that he might become father of many nations, according to that which was spoken, So shall thy

e 9 : 8; Isa. 51 : 2.   *f* 5 : 14; Eph. 2 : 1–5.   *g* 9 : 26; 1 Cor. 1 : 28; 1 Peter 2 : 10.

ing, sinful man; but ever would it be, if it rested on the faithful word of the eternal and unchanging God. The *seed* are the spiritual ones through faith (ver. 13). **All** is emphatic, and expanded in the next clause. The meaning is: That the promise may be sure to *all* the spiritual seed, **not to that seed only which is of the law,** (that is, believing Jews), **but to that seed also which is of the faith of Abraham** (believing Gentiles (ver. 12)). "Both the grace and the certainty of the promise required that it should be connected with faith alone. But this implies that it is *universal* to *all* who believe." **Who is the father of us all**—who believe (Gal. 3 : 29).

17. **As it is written**—corroborating what he had just said. *This* and the quotation that follows are generally put in a parenthesis. **I have made thee a father of many nations** (Gen. 17 : 5 quoted from the Septuagint version). The primary reference of this promise appears to have been to his natural descendants; but all the promises to Abraham had also their spiritual significance. They had their letter and their spirit (2 : 28, 29). Abraham was the natural ancestor of the Edomites, Ishmaelites, and many Arabian tribes, as well as of the Israelites (Gen. 25 : 1–4); but spiritually of a numerous posterity of believers from all nations (ver. 11). The connection of thought makes the reference here to the latter. The word translated *nations* means also *Gentiles*, which makes the quotation the more striking. **Before him whom he believed, even God.** This is a very difficult phrase. The word translated *before* means strictly *over against*, but according to a Hebrew idiom, *before, in the sight of*, and so it is commonly regarded. It can therefore be rendered, *Before God in whom he believed*, meaning, He was father of many nations, before or in the sight of God in whom he believed. But another explanation is worthy of notice, though not without its difficulties. According to an Aramean idiom, an example occurring in Ezra 6 : 13, where the form corresponds exactly with this phrase in the Greek, it may be rendered, *Because*, or *according as he believed God*. With this translation there need be no parenthesis. A colon may be placed at the end of ver. 16 and after "nations." **Who quickeneth the dead**—with reference to Abraham and Sarah (ver. 19; Heb. 11 : 11, 12, 19). God's almighty power and his omniscience were the ground of Abraham's faith. **And calleth** *the* **things** *that are not* **as though they were**—referring to unborn generations, the descendants of Abraham and Sarah. To God the future is as present; the unborn as if existing. Many render, *And calleth into being the things that are not*, with reference to his omnipotent, creative power. But the former is the simpler and more natural explanation (Acts 7 : 5). "The nations which should spring, physically or spiritually, from him God spoke of as having an existence, which word Abraham believed" (ALFORD).

18. Abraham is exhibited as a remarkable example of faith. **Who against hope,** and *contrary* to hope, **believed in hope,** *resting upon hope.* Contrary to all human grounds of reasoning he notwithstanding believed, resting his hope on the ground of the Divine promise. A good illustration of what faith is. (Compare Heb. 11 : 1, 8–10.) **That he might,** etc. His faith extending thus far, *that he might* or *should become father of many nations* (see on ver. 17), **according to that which was**

19 be. And being not weak in faith, ʰ he considered not his own body now dead, when he was about an hundred years old, neither yet the deadness of Sarah's
20 womb: he staggered not at the promise of God through unbelief; but was strong in faith, giving glory to God;
21 and being fully persuaded that, what he had promised, ⁱ he was able also to
22 perform. And therefore ᵏ it was imputed to him for righteousness.
23 Now ˡ it was not written for his sake
24 alone, that it was imputed to him; but for us also, to whom it shall be imputed, if we believe on him that raised

19 seed be. And being not weakened in faith, he considered his own body already dead, being about a hundred years old, and the deadness of Sarah's
20 womb; but in view of the promise of God he wavered not through unbelief, but was made strong in faith, giving
21 glory to God, and being fully assured, that what he had promised he was able
22 also to perform. Wherefore also it was reckoned to him for righteousness.
23 And it was not written for his sake alone, that it was reckoned to him;
24 but for ours also, to whom it will be reckoned, if we believe on him who raised Jesus our Lord from the dead:

ʰ Gen. 17 : 17 ; 18 : 11-14 ; Heb. 11 : 11, 12.   ⁱ Luke 1 : 37, 45.   ᵏ Ver. 3, 6.
ˡ 15 : 4 ; 1 Cor. 10 : 6, 11 ; 2 Tim. 3 : 16, 17.

spoken, **So,** as the stars for multitude, **shall thy seed be** (Gen. 15 : 5, quoted from the Septuagint; Heb. 11 : 12).

19. And being not weak, but on the contrary strong, **in faith, he considered not,** *he did not regard*—he made no account of **his own body now dead** (figuratively), etc., but against all human probabilities and all human analogies, rested on God's promise. But the highest critical authorities omit *not* after *considered*, and translate, *he considered his own body now as good as dead . . . but staggered not*, etc. Not being weak in faith he was well aware of and considered well the impossibilities as to nature, but as to the promise of God he wavered not through unbelief. His faith was not shaken. This reading and the interpretation growing out of it accords well with ver. 18, where Abraham is said to rest upon hope in God, when no hope appeared on the human side, and also with Gen. 17 : 17, one of the surprises in Abraham's faith, but only a surprise, for he showed his steadfast faith in his immediate obedience in being circumcised himself, and circumcising Ishmael and all the males in his house.

20. He staggered not, etc. If *not* is omitted after *considered*, in the preceding verse, then translate, *but as to the promise of God, he wavered not through unbelief*, he did not look upon it distrustfully, neither did he doubt through lack of faith, *but waxed* **strong in faith.** So far from wavering he increased in faith, **giving glory to God,** doubtless in oral praise and adoration, and in honoring his faithfulness and power by his conduct and life.

21. And being fully persuaded, or *assured*, **that what he had promised, he was able also to perform** —a general truth, applicable in our day as well as in Abraham's or Paul's.

22. And therefore, etc., *wherefore also,* on account of this faith, this simple, unconditional confidence in God and his promise, **it was imputed,** *reckoned,* **to him for righteousness.** Notice how emphasis is put upon Abraham's strong faith, as illustrated in ver. 13-21; and that an important element in his faith was "giving glory to God" (ver. 20). Whatever merit there might be in it was not on his part but belonged wholly to God, to whom he gave glory, since it was his work in him (Eph. 2 : 8; see further on ver. 3).

23. Application of what has been said regarding Abraham to Christians —**Now it was not written,** when it was first recorded, **for his sake alone** —its design was not merely to record a historical fact and do honor to that illustrious patriarch, **that it was imputed,** *accounted,* **to him,** but rather that he should be a type and pattern to believers in every age. (Comp. 1 Cor. 9 : 10; 10 : 6, 11; Gal. 3 : 8.)

24. But for us also—for our benefit and profit, *to whom it will be reckoned,* **if we believe on him who raised up Jesus our Lord from the dead.** Faith in God is required in us as well as in Abraham. This is the parallel which Paul wished here to draw. Under the gospel to believe in God is to believe in Christ, for Christ is the way to God; and to believe in Christ is to believe in God, for Christ is

25 up Jesus our Lord from the dead; ᵐ who was delivered for our offences, and ⁿ was raised again for our justification. | 25 who was delivered up for our trespasses, and was raised for our justification.

m 5 : 6-8 ; 8 : 32 ; Isa. 53 : 5, 6, 10-12 ; 2 Cor. 5 : 21.   n 8 : 33, 34 ; 1 Cor. 15 : 17.

God manifested in the flesh (John 1 : 1, 14 ; 12 : 44, 45 ; 14 : 1, 6, 9). Abraham too looked forward to Christ (John 8 : 56). Notice also the emphasis put upon Christ's resurrection. It was the great decisive evidence of his divine mission as the Christ, the Saviour of the world (10 : 9 ; Acts 1 : 22 ; 4 : 33, etc.). It was the greatest of miracles, and an exhibition of Divine power here paralleled with that inferior one in the birth of Isaac. And the birth of Isaac was not stranger to the Jew than the spiritual birth of Gentiles through faith alone.

25. This verse contains the very heart of the gospel. **Who was delivered** *up* unto death. Delivered up by Judas (Matt. 26 : 48-50) and by the Jewish authorities (Matt. 27 : 2), by God's fixed purpose and foreknowledge (Acts 2 : 23) and voluntarily by himself, acting in accordance with the will of the Father (John 10 : 17, 18 ; 18 : 11), **For,** *on account of,* **our offenses,** because we had sinned and to make expiation for sin (Isa. 53 : 5, 6 ; Heb. 9 : 28 ; 1 Peter 2 : 24). The word *offenses,* translated *trespasses* in the Revised version, includes any deviation from truth and uprightness. **And was raised for our justification,** *for the sake of*—to secure *our justification*—the forgiveness of sins and restoration to the Divine favor, our being accounted as righteous and our acceptance with God. The word here translated justification occurs only here and in 5 : 18. (See on 1 : 17 (4) ; also on 3 : 26.) But how was Christ's resurrection necessary to our justification? (1) A *dead* Christ would have shown that sin and death had been triumphant ; the *living* Christ implies a victor who is able to save to the uttermost (1 : 4 ; 7 : 24, 25 ; 8 : 34 ; 1 Cor. 15 : 55-57). (2) Christ's atoning death would have been in vain if he had not risen to be a human and divine mediator and intercessor ; to be also exalted as a Prince and a Saviour to give repentance and the remission of sins, and to bestow the promised Holy Spirit (1 Cor. 15 : 17 ; Acts 2 : 33 ; 5 : 31 ; Heb. 7 : 25). (3) We need Christ as our life as well as our death. We die to sin and self in him, and we rise with him to newness of life (6 : 3, 4, 7-11). (4) His great work as a Redeemer was not complete without his resurrection. He must rise to continue his work personally before God in heaven, and through the Holy Spirit among men on earth (Heb. 9 : 9-15, 23-26 ; 10 : 12-18).

PRACTICAL REMARKS.

1. The righteousness by faith was exemplified in Abraham and David (ver. 1-8 ; Heb. 11 : 17, 32, 33).

2. God's method of saving sinners takes away all boasting, even from the best of men (ver. 2, 3 ; Eph. 2 : 8-10).

3. Justification by works and justification by faith are diametrically opposed to each other, and cannot be even partially united (ver. 5, 6 ; 11 : 6).

4. Persons are justified as undeserving and ungodly without any merit of their own, but for what Christ has done for them and is to them (ver. 5 ; 5 : 6 ; Phil. 3 : 9).

5. Saving faith is the same in all ages and dispensations (ver. 5-8 ; Heb. 11 : 1, 5, 6, etc.).

6. True happiness comes only to those to whom God reckons not sin but righteousness (ver. 6-8 ; 5 : 1, 2 ; 8 : 1, 5).

7. True happiness does not depend on outward conditions or mere externals (ver. 9-11 ; Matt. 5 : 3-11).

8. Justification, by which a righteousness is accounted to us by faith, is a doctrine both of the Old and New Testament, and is suited to all men (ver. 8, 9 ; Hab. 2 : 4 ; Isa. 53 : 11).

9. The perversion of rites, ceremonies, and means of grace, by regarding them as meritorious, has been common under the gospel as well as under the law (ver. 9-12 ; Gal. 1 : 6 : 3 : 2-4).

10. In God's covenants with his ancient people, we should distinguish the letter from the Spirit, the shadow from the substance (ver. 11, 12 ; Heb. 10 : 16 ; Gal. 4 : 21-27).

11. There appears to have been two covenants made with Abraham, the one

by which, as progenitor of the Messiah and father of the faithful, he was constituted heir of the world (ver. 13), the other "the covenant of circumcision" (Acts 7:8), which was to mark his natural descendants and be a bond of a national organization (ver. 11–13; Gen. 12:3; 15:5, 6; 17:10–14; 22:18).

12. Circumcision of the descendants of Abraham in all ages attests his faith which he exercised before he was circumcised (ver. 11; Gen. 15:5–18; ver. 17; 17:2–11).

13. Baptism did not take the place of circumcision. The latter was a national rite for all the male descendants of Abraham; the former is a gospel rite for believers, both male and female. Circumcision was a seal of Abraham's faith alone (ver. 11); baptism is not a seal but a symbol of the inward change of those who are to receive it (6:3, 4). If Paul and the other New Testament writers had known of this relation existing between circumcision and baptism, how strange it is that they never refer to it. It would have been most natural at the apostolic conference (Acts 15), and at other times, for them to say: Baptism takes the place of circumcision. But they neither said nor hinted anything of the kind, showing that the thought never occurred to them (ver. 11, 12).

14. Spiritual service of the heart has been required in all dispensations, and has ever been essential to godliness (ver. 11–13; 1 Sam. 15:22; Micah 6:8; Heb. 11:5).

15. All true believers are of the seed of Abraham, and are brethren, and with Christ their Head are heirs of the wolrd (ver. 11–13; Gal. 3:29).

16. God's people are not restricted by national limits. The spiritual nature of Christ's kingdom and of church-membership are against all national, sacramental, and hereditary theories of the church (ver. 11–13; John 4:21; 18:36).

17. God has made no promises of salvation on account of morality or mere forms of religion. They afford no ground of faith or of justification (ver. 14; 10:2–4; 2 Tim. 3:5).

18. There can be no justification by the law which works wrath. That which condemns cannot justify (ver. 15; 7:7–11).

19. It is the *gratuitousness* of salvation through *faith* that renders it suited to all men in all ages (ver. 16; 10:11–13).

20. Our faith should be strong, since we have the promises of God backed by his omnipotence, omnipresence, and all the infinite resources of his being (ver. 17–21; 1:16; Eph. 3:20).

21. Giving glory to God is an important element in all true worship. Distrust of God's power, wisdom, and goodness is the highest dishonor we can cast on his name (ver. 20; John 16:9; 1 John 5:10).

22. We should rest implicitly on the promises of God. No obstacle in their way should cause us to doubt their fulfillment (ver. 21, 22; Isa. 40:8; 46:9, 10; 2 Cor. 1:20).

23. The Scriptures are for our instruction, that we might know the way to God through Jesus Christ (ver. 23, 24; 2 Cor. 5:19; Isa. 61:10).

24. The resurrection of Christ was the crowning miracle of the gospel, and the mainspring of our hopes of salvation (ver. 24; 2 Tim. 1:10; 1 Peter 1:3, 21; 1 Thess. 4:14; John 14:19).

25. The death and resurrection of Christ are inseparably connected with man's salvation. Without his death there could have been no expiation of sin, and without his resurrection no object of faith and no justification (ver. 25; Acts 17:3; 20:21).

CHAPTER V.

Thus far the argument is complete. The gospel is the power of God unto salvation, for in it is revealed a righteousness of God which can be obtained through faith. All men are sinners and under condemnation, and need this righteousness (1:18–3:20). It can be obtained through grace, entirely independent of works of law, by faith in Christ Jesus, who has redeemed us and offered up himself as a propitiatory sacrifice. Thus all the demands on the part of God are satisfied, and his holy and righteous character in his relations and dealings with sinful men is so exhibited before all intelligent creatures, that he can be righteous and accept as righteous believers in Jesus. The doctrine of justification by faith is thus brought into view, on the one hand excluding all boasting, yet on the other

The results of justification to the believer, and as to the race.

5 THEREFORE °being justified by faith, we have ᵖ peace with God through
2 our Lord Jesus Christ; ᑫ by whom also we have access by faith into this grace wherein we stand, and ʳ rejoice in hope of the glory of God.
3 And not only so, but ˢ we glory in

5 BEING justified therefore by faith, let us have peace with God through
2 our Lord Jesus Christ; through whom we have had our access also by faith into this grace in which we stand, and let us exult in hope of the glory of God.
3 God. And not only so, but let us exult

o See refs. 1 : 17.   p Isa. 32 : 17; John 16 : 33; 2 Cor. 5 : 18–20.   q John 10 : 9; Eph. 3 : 12.
r 1 Peter 1 : 3–8.   s 8 : 35–37; Matt. 5 : 11, 12; 2 Cor. 12 : 10.

establishing the law (3 : 21-31). This doctrine of salvation by grace, through justification by faith, is further confirmed and illustrated from the Old Testament Scriptures, showing that the law and gospel in this respect are in perfect accord, and that the former is preparatory to the latter (4 : 1-25). In this chapter Paul notices the results of justification by faith first upon the individual (ver. 1-11), and second upon the race parallel with the ruin through Adam (ver. 12-21).

1-11. JUSTIFICATION BY FAITH RESULTS IN PEACE WITH GOD, HOPE, JOY IN AFFLICTIONS, AND ASSURANCE OF SALVATION.

1. Therefore—in accordance with what has been said in 3 : 21–4 : 25. **Being justified,** or *accounted righteous*, **by faith.** The position of these words is emphatic, and closely connected with "justification" in 4 : 25. Paul regards this doctrine as an established fact, and the foundation of the results of which he is about to speak. The tense of the word translated *being justified* is such in the original as to indicate that it is not a progressive, but a single and completed act in connection with the exercise of faith. **We have peace.** Most manuscripts read, *Let us have peace*—retain, hold fast peace (1 : 28; 1 Tim. 3 : 9; 2 Tim. 1 : 13). This is an immediate and abiding result of justification; this they should have, and hold fast to as a possession. So the American revisers and the Improved Bible Union version translate. Internal evidence and the context, however, rather favor the common reading, *We have peace*. A statement of fact is more suitable to the connection. Some ancient transcriber could easily and inadvertently have made the change, there being a difference only of a single similar letter with probably no difference in pronunciation. Whichever form is used in the text, the other reading should be put in the margin. **Peace with God**—conscious of being reconciled to God, and no longer conscious of enmity between ourselves and God (2 Cor. 5 : 17–19). **Through our Lord Jesus Christ**—the one through whom this peace with God is effected. Christ has died for our sins, satisfied all of God's claims upon us, removed his righteous displeasure, and wrought out a righteousness for us, and God for his sake has accepted us as righteous. Conscious of the fact that we are forgiven and restored to the Divine favor, we are delivered from all fear of Divine wrath, and through Christ brought into loving union with God (Matt. 11 : 28).

2. By whom also we have had *our access*, or, *admission*, **by means of faith into this grace,** this state of gratuitous justification, **wherein we stand**—have been and are standing (Eph. 2 : 18; 3 : 12). This takes us back to our first *admission*, or as Meyer translates *our introduction*, into this gracious state within which we have since been standing, enjoying friendly relations and intercourse with God. **And rejoice,** or *glory*. If we translate in the preceding verse, *Let us have peace*, then in this verse we must translate, *And let us rejoice*. Either rendering is allowable. A triumphant, exultant joy is meant. **In hope,** or *upon hope*, of sharing **the glory of God** —that glory which God will impart to the believer in the future world (8 : 18). Three benefits are thus far specified in connection with justification; admission into this gracious state, peace with God (ver. 1), and the exultant hope of glory hereafter.

3. And not only so, do we exult in hope of glory, **but we glory**—*rejoice* exultingly—**in tribulations,** or

72   ROMANS   [CH. V.

tribulations also: knowing that tribula-
1 tion worketh patience; ¹and patience,
experience; ᵘand experience, hope:
5 ˣand hope maketh not ashamed; ᶻ because the love of God is shed abroad in
our hearts by the Holy Ghost which is
given unto us.
6 For ʸ when we were yet without
strength, ᶻ in due time Christ died for

in afflictions also; knowing that afflic-
4 tion worketh patience; and patience ap-
5 proval; and approval hope; and hope
makes not ashamed; because the love
of God has been poured forth in our
hearts, through the Holy Spirit which
was given to us.
6 For when we were yet weak, in due
season Christ died for the ungodly.

t 1 Peter 1 : 6, 7.   *u* Lam. 3 : 22-25.   *v* Isa. 49 : 23; Phil. 1 : 20.   *x* Tim. 1 : 12.
x 8 : 14-17; 2 Cor. 1 : 22; Gal. 4 : 6.   *y* Isa. 1 : 4, 5; Hosea 13 : 9; Eph. 2 : 1-5.   *z* Gal. 4 : 4.

afflictions, **also**. If we adopt in ver. 1 the reading, "Let us have peace," then we must translate here, *Let us glory*, or *rejoice*. In our justified state our relations are so changed to God that our afflictions become proofs of his love and **matters** of joy and thankfulness (s : 18; Heb. 12 : 6). They develop Christian graces, as the apostle goes on to show. **Knowing**—because we know—**that tribulation**, or *affliction*, **worketh patience**—*endurance*, as a trait of character and habit of mind. This is exhibited in the Christian, developed even in the greatest **trials** and sufferings (2 Cor. 8 : 2). Compare **the** words of our Lord (Matt. 5 : 4, 10-12), and the **experience of the apostles** (Acts 5 : 41; 2 Cor. 12 : 10, 11; 1 Peter 4 : 13, 14).

4. And patience, experience; *an approved* or *tried character* (2 Cor. 2 : 9; Phil. 2 : 22). The Bible Union version translates *approval*, a condition of **approval**, with a consciousness of it (Eph. 1 : 13). Patience works what? That which is *tested, tried, approved*, in **the mind** and character of the individual; hence *a tried character*, one **which has** stood the test, and through *endurance* has become hardened to **trials, and** strong to meet and overcome them. **And experience,** *tried character*, **hope.** To the Christian himself his own state of mind and character produces fresh hope, and sustains and develops hope, by the proof he has of the truth and value of religion and of God's approbation (James 1 : 3, 4. See on hope in ver. 2).

5. And hope maketh not ashamed—it does not put us to shame by ending in disappointment (Ps. 22 : 5). **Because**, introducing a reason for the foregoing statement. The ground of this assurance of these developed benefits of afflictions, and especially of our hope, is found not in our strength of purpose or of character, but in God's

love to us; and this is brought out in what follows as far as ver. 11. **Because the love of God**—not our love to God, but God's love to us, which **is shed abroad, rather,** which *has been poured forth*, as it were, **in our hearts by** means of **the Holy Spirit** (John 16 : 14; 1 Cor. 2 : 9, 10), filling our hearts with the blissful consciousness of his favor and the enjoyment of his unparalleled love. **Which is given unto us**—rather, *which was given to us*, referring to the pentecostal outpouring of the Spirit. The Christian has in himself the pledge that his hope shall be realized in the manifestation of God's love in his own heart, through the Holy Spirit the Comforter given him as promised in John 15 : 26. (Comp. Eph. 1 : 14.) It should be noted, however, that God's love does **not** exclude, but rather **produces, our love to** him. The two must exist together in the heart (John 4 : 10, 19).

6. In this and the two following verses, **Paul** shows the greatness **and** the disinterestedness of God's love to us from the circumstances under which it was exercised. **For,** introduces the proof of God's love to us in Christ. *For while we were still* **without strength,** spiritually *helpless*, entirely unable to free ourselves from sin and its consequences, **in due time,** in the proper and right season of the world's history (Gal. 4 : 2, 4), **Christ died for the ungodly,** *in behalf of the impious*, those *without reverence* toward God. How strikingly Paul presents the Divine love toward us. God gave his Son to die for us, when we were without help in ourselves, and without any claim on either his justice or goodness. It was at the time appointed by God, when everything called for it, and everything in human history was ripe for it (Heb. 9 : 26; 1 Peter 1 : 20). While the preposition in Greek translated *For*,

7 the ungodly. For scarcely for a righteous man will one die: yet peradventure for a good man some would even
8 dare to die. But *b* God commendeth his love toward us, in that, while we were yet sinners, Christ died for us.
9 Much more then, being now justified *c* by his blood, we shall be saved from
10 wrath through him. For if, when we were enemies, *d* we were reconciled to God by the death of his Son: much more, being reconciled, we shall be saved *e* by his life.

7 For scarcely for a righteous man will one die; though, for the good man, perhaps some one does even dare
8 to die. But God commends his own love toward us, in that, while we were
9 yet sinners, Christ died for us. Much more, therefore, being now justified by his blood, shall we be saved from
10 the wrath through him. For if, being enemies, we were reconciled to God through the death of his Son; much more, being reconciled, shall we be

a See 16 : 4 ; 2 Sam. 23 : 14-17.　　*b* 1 John 3 : 16 ; 4 : 9, 10.　　*c* 3 : 25 ; Eph. 2 : 13.
d 2 Cor. 5 : 18, 19 ; Eph. 2 : 16 ; Col. 1 : 20, 21.　　*e* John 14 : 19 ; Col. 3 : 4.

or, *in behalf of*, does not fully express the idea of substitution, yet it points toward it. That Christ died in our stead is taught by Paul (3 : 25; Eph. 5 : 2; 1 Tim. 2 : 6) and by John (1 John 2 : 2 ; 4 : 10). Jesus also taught that he gave himself a substitute for us (Matt. 20 : 28; Mark 10 : 45). The idea of substitution appears also to be involved in the next two verses.

7. **For**, introducing a noble human example from which to illustrate the infinite condescension and love of God. *For* **scarcely**, *in behalf of*, **a righteous man**, in the usual sense of a strictly just or righteous person, **will one die;** implying that much less would he die for an ungodly man. **Yet peradventure;** translate: *Though I grant in behalf of the good man perhaps some one even dares to die.* The *good man* is here regarded as doing more than the righteous man. The latter does what the law or justice requires; the former in addition does deeds of kindness. The one calls forth our respect; the other our love. For the one hardly would one die; but perhaps for the other earthly affection would make the sacrifice.

8. **But**, introduces something unheard of, something divinely noble! *But* **God commendeth,** *proves* and *makes conspicuous,* now and for all time, **his** *own* **love**, in contrast to human love, **in that while we were yet sinners,** in contrast to "a righteous man" and "the good man" (ver. 7), **Christ died for us,** *in our behalf. Sinners* in this verse is equivalent to the *ungodly* and those *without strength* (ver. 6). Yet "ungodly" is there used more generally with reference to the race, while the word "sinners" here has a more personal and individual reference. Notice in this unequaled exhibition of love how *God* and *Christ* are united and yet distinct in doing each his part. God's love was exhibited in Christ's love, and Christ's death was an exhibition of God's infinite sacrifice on our behalf.

9. In this verse and the one following Paul argues the certainty of the final salvation of believers. **Much more then**—much more probable is it, and reasonable to expect, **being now**—in contrast to the past when we were ungodly, **justified,** or *accounted righteous*, **by his blood,** through the merits of his atoning death (3 : 25; 4 : 25), **we shall be saved** from the well-known and deserved **wrath** to come **through him.** If God's love was exhibited toward us so wonderfully when we were sinners, much more can we depend on it when we are reconciled and accepted through Christ as righteous. The word *justified*, as in ver. 1, denotes an accomplished, not a progressive, work.

10. The argument is repeated more pointedly. **For if,** *being* **enemies,** being actually such in ourselves and necessarily regarded as such by God, **we were reconciled to God,** our enmity being overcome and his wrath removed **by,** or *through,* **the death of his Son** (Eph. 2 : 1-6)**; much more** being **reconciled,** in this changed condition and changed relation, **we shall be saved by,** or *in,* **his life,** while he lives and exerts his power and love for our safety. (Comp. Heb. 7 : 25.) The word *enemies* may be taken to mean either haters of God or the objects of his displeasure. The former is the more common meaning and the one that would first suggest itself to the

11 And not only so, but we also ¹joy in God through our Lord Jesus Christ, by whom we have now received the atonement [*or*, reconciliation ᵍ].

11 saved by his life; and not only so, but also exulting in God through our Lord Jesus Christ, through whom we have now received the reconciliation.

f Isa. 61 : 10; Hab. 3 : 18.   *g* 2 Cor. 5 : 18, 19.

mind. The death of Christ and the amazing love exhibited thereby are the great instruments in the hands of the Spirit in overcoming and destroying this enmity (John 12 : 32). Yet the Divine displeasure must also be included since this was propitiated and removed in the death of his Son (3 : 25). Both ideas seem to unite; we were actual enemies, having enmity against God (8 : 7) and objects of the Divine displeasure (1 : 18. Comp. Eph. 2 : 14-16; Col. 1 : 20, 21). So also the words *reconciled to God*, include, as it seems to me, both God's changed relation to us and our changed condition toward him. The latter is included in our justification (3 : 26). Both sides are beautifully exhibited (2 Cor. 5 : 18-20. Comp. 1 Cor. 7 : 11). The argument of the apostle is complete and irresistible. If being enemies Divine love has secured justification, much more now being friends it would secure our final salvation. Christ died to make an atonement and effect our reconciliation to God; and now he lives forever to shield us from all evil and to consummate that for which he died. Thus our final salvation is assured.

11. And more than this: we have triumphant confidence in God. **And not only so**—being reconciled to God, *but also rejoicing* or *glorying* **in God,** in the assurance that our salvation is certain. And this too becomes a present fact to the Christian, *exulting in God* now, since we are reconciled to him and his love is abiding in us (ver. 5). And this joy can only come **through our Lord Jesus Christ** *through whom we have now*, at the present time, **received the atonement**—rather, *the reconciliation*, as a foretaste and pledge of our final salvation and future glorification. The word *atonement* is found only here in the New Testament, and its theological meaning does not give the sense of the original here. The Greek word means *adjustment of a difference*, *reconciliation*, and is also found in 11 : 15; 2 Cor. 5 : 18, 19. (Cf. 1 Cor. 7 : 11.) It was through Christ that the *adjustment of difference* or the reconciliation was effected on God's part, so that the sinner could be restored to the Divine favor. It is by faith that he accepts this adjustment on his part, and through the Holy Spirit and the truth he himself comes into a reconciled condition. By a living union with Christ the believer comes into a consciousness of a reconciled God and of an assured and glorious hope of eternal salvation (8 : 11; Gal. 2 : 20; John 14 : 19). "Reconciliation may be viewed from two sides: it removes God's indignation against us (2 Cor. 5 : 19), and our alienation from God (2 Cor. 5 : 20)" (BENGEL on **3 : 24**).

12-21. RESULTS OF SALVATION THROUGH JUSTIFICATION BY FAITH UPON THE RACE COMPARED WITH THE RUIN THROUGH ADAM. The former is shown to be the exact counterpart of the latter, and as all who believed in the Old Testament admitted the latter, so they could not object to the principle involved in the former. The course of thought is broken off abruptly at the end of ver. 12 and is not resumed till ver. 18. Ver. 13–17 are suggested by the statement of ver. 12, and are somewhat parenthetic both in thought and form. The leading thought of ver. 12 is explained in ver. 13, 14; and the gospel doctrine of salvation is incidentally illustrated in ver. 15-17, by some points of difference in the resemblance between Adam and Christ. In ver. 18 the thought of ver. 12 is resumed in a form somewhat affected by the thought of the intervening verses, and for the sake of presenting a complete analogy Paul employs a universal form of expression, which he limits in ver. 19 in order to adapt it to the real facts in the case. To complete the view he notices in ver. 20, 21 the design and effect of the law in relation to sin and grace. Throughout this whole section the one essential point of the analogy holds perfectly that the condition of the many depends on the act of the one. To put it briefly, so also, as through Adam came death, so through Christ comes life.

12 Wherefore, as [h] by one man sin entered into the world, and [i] death by sin; and so death passed upon all men, 13 for that [k] all have sinned. For until

12 Therefore, as through one man sin entered into the world, and death through sin; and so death passed unto 13 all men, for that all sinned: for until

h Gen. 3 : 6.   i Gen. 2 : 17; James 1 : 15.   k See refs. 3 : 23.

12. Wherefore—*on account of this* reconciliation (ver. 11) ensuring triumphant joy in the trials of life and final salvation to the justified (ver. 1-11). As if Paul had said, *accordingly*, then there is an analogy between the loss of God's favor through the sin of one and its recovery through the obedience of one. **As**—naturally introduces a comparison; but where do we find a *so* introducing the second member of the comparison? Some would find it virtually in ver. 14, which speaks of Christ as the antitype of Adam. But this construction seems harsh and unnatural. The corresponsive *so* does not seem to appear till ver. 18, where Paul resumes the main subject of his discourse. *As* **by,** or *through,* **one man sin entered into the world.** Paul does not mean to exclude Eve as a partaker in the transgression, for Adam was the head and representative of his family (1 Cor. 11 : 3; Eph. 5 : 23). Besides the word Adam, or *man* (Gen. 5 : 2), is applied to both Adam and Eve, including the two sexes, "And called their name Adam," or *man,* "in the day when they were created." The word *sin* is personified, and action is attributed to it. It *entered into the world,* implying a permanent change and a new element introduced into the world. This is confirmed in the next verse by the expression, "sin was in the world," which implies a permanent state. It cannot therefore mean a single act of transgression, that one man committed a single act of sin; but rather that sin entered into our world as a ruling power or principle. It is distinguished from "transgression" (ver. 14) and "offense" or *trespass* (ver. 15, 16, 17, 18, 20). **And death** entered into the world, a ruling power **by,** or *through,* sin. Comp. ver. 14, "Death *reigned* from Adam to Moses." The selection of this term was occasioned by Gen. 2 : 17, "In the day that thou eatest thereof thou shalt surely die." In this passage and throughout the Scriptures *sin* and *death* are regarded as *cause* and *effect* (Jer. 31 : 30; Rom. 6 : 16, 21, 24; 8 : 13; James 1 : 15; Rev. 2 : 11).

Thus *death* includes all the penal consequences of sin, physical and spiritual death (1 Cor. 15 : 21, 56). As the one is the separation of soul and body, so the other is separation of the soul from God, and this continued and fixed forever is *eternal death,* which is also called the *second* death. The loss of God's favor was the greatest and the immediate result of sin (Gen. 3 : 7-13), although the decree of physical death was at once passed (Gen. 3 : 19). Paul evidently takes the temporal penalty of physical death as the representative of all and the ground of his reasoning (ver. 14). "Adam, if he had not sinned, might have passed to higher forms of life, but without a violent separation of soul and body, without being 'unclothed,' but by being 'clothed upon' (2 Cor. 5 : 2-4), or in the beautiful figure of the rabbins, 'by a kiss of the Almighty'" (SCHAFF in *Lange*). **And so**—*And thus,* in the way as stated, **death passed** *through unto* **all men,** none escaping his power. This accords with what he had just stated, "sin entered the world" and "death entered by sin." The universality of sin and death is here described. **For that**—an old rendering, *in whom,* that is, in Adam, is now generally given up. It is now almost unanimously agreed that it means, *On the ground that, because that.* The rendering in the Common version, *For that,* expresses the true idea. Death extended unto all men, *on the ground that,* or *for that* **all have sinned,** rather, *all sinned*—a statement of a historical fact, naturally referring to the one act by which sin entered into the world. Paul states a fact but does not stop to explain it. "The question *how* the entire race became involved in the consequences of the one act of the one man, is not discussed by the apostle. The fact alone is affirmed. Godet well remarks: 'In the revelation given to the apostle of the system of salvation, this mysterious connection was supposed but not explained'" (J. R. BOISE). Almost numberless volumes have been

the law sin was in the world: but sin is not imputed when there is no law. | the law sin was in the world; but sin is not reckoned when there is no law.

---

written in defense of various theories explaining this question; but whatever defects there may be in theories, the fact remains. Dr. A. H. STRONG in his "Theology" (p. 331) thus puts it: "In connection with this problem a central fact is announced in Scripture, which we feel compelled to believe upon divine testimony, even though every attempted explanation should prove unsatisfactory. That central fact, which constitutes the substance of the Scripture doctrine of original sin is simply this: That the sin of Adam is the immediate cause and ground of inborn depravity, guilt, and condemnation to the whole human race." In this passage Paul presents Adam as the head of the race, and appears plainly to teach that the race sinned in him, and that he acted for the race. The most natural explanation seems to me to be, that the race was germinally included in Adam as its natural head. (See also ver. 18; 1 Cor. 15 : 22; Heb. 7 : 5, 10; Ps. 51 : 5.) Paul certainly does not teach that all have consciously and personally sinned in Adam; for this is opposed to the whole passage, which repeatedly says that *one* sin, not numberless sins, is the cause of death passing upon all men; and also to ver. 13, 14 which treat of certain persons suffering death, who did not commit sin after the likeness of Adam's transgression. Paul teaches the great fact that through Adam both sin and death became universal, the lot of all, adding the last clause, *For that all sinned,* implying a certain union of the race in him, and showing that sin as well as death is universal; for the penalty which is the effect could not extend farther than the cause extended. With this statement that the universal depravity of the race is the consequence of the sinful act of one, the way is prepared for the parallel in ver. 18 and throughout the passage.

13. The phrase "For that all sinned," might suggest, as in 2 : 14, a seeming paradox of sin in absence of law. The apostle therefore breaks off the regular course of thought to illustrate and confirm what he had just said. **For until the law**—the Mo-

saic law would be naturally understood, and this agrees well with the period mentioned in the next verse, "from Adam to Moses." **Sin was in the world**—that introduced by Adam continued as a resident of the world (ver. 12). **But sin is not imputed.** The verb in Greek occurs nowhere else except in an inscription. A verb almost identical, with the same derivation, is found in Philem. 18, " put that to my account." It means *to reckon* or *set to one's account*. But by whom is sin taken into account? Augustine, Luther, Calvin, and others, answer, by the sinner himself. Men did *not reckon it against* themselves, they did not come to the consciousness of it, for through the law is the knowledge of sin (3 : 20; 7 : 9). But this is foreign to the context and to the argument of the whole section. Paul is not treating of the inward sense of sin, but rather of sin and its penalty. Inconsistent also with 2 : 15. Hence Meyer, Alford, Hodge, Olshausen, and others regard God as the one who here *does not take sin into account*, with reference to its punishment, *when there is no law*. This seems to be the meaning required by the passage. But Alford and a few others think they see a modified sense of the verb, *is not formally, fully,* or *strictly reckoned* by God, that is, in the relative absence of law sin is not held to its full accountability. In support of this Acts 17 : 30, "God's overlooking the time of ignorance," and Rom. 2 : 12; 3 : 25, are appealed to. This meaning of the verb is possible, but it is not best to found an interpretation of so important a passage on the somewhat doubtful meaning of a word. To return then to the beginning of the verse Paul explains and confirms what he had just said by a fact. *For until the law sin was in the world.* This every believer in the Old Testament would acknowledge. The wickedness of men before the flood (Gen. 6 : 5), of Sodom (Gen. 18 : 20), and of the Canaanites (Lev. 18 : 25), was a proof of this. The apostle then states a common principle of justice : *Sin cannot be imputed or reckoned against one* and its penalty inflicted, *when there is no law*. But it

CH. V.]   ROMANS   77

14 Nevertheless ᵐdeath reigned from Adam to Moses, even over them that had not sinned after the similitude of Adam's transgression; ⁿwho is the figure of him that was to come. But

14 But yet death reigned from Adam until Moses, even over those who sinned not after the likeness of Adam's transgression, who is a type of the Coming

---
m Ver. 17, 21.   *n* 1 Cor. 15 : 21, 22, 45.

would easily occur to every one familiar with the period between Adam and Moses, that sin was during that time reckoned or imputed. Such examples as the deluge, Sodom and Gomorrah, Pharaoh, and the Canaanites, prove that God did bring the sins of men to a terrible reckoning. But then against what law? Was it the law written in men's hearts and consciences, referred to in 2 : 14, 15? But the line of Paul's parallelism and argument did not require him to notice this. (See next ver.)
14. Having stated a principle, without applying it, Paul asserts another fact, **Nevertheless**—*But* though this principle is true and the Mosaic law had not been given, *yet* **death,** the very penalty inflicted on Adam, **reigned,** held sway like a monarch, **from Adam to Moses,** showing that sin was reckoned and some law was transgressed. Was it not the law Adam transgressed? We must restrict the thought just as Paul restricts it and not broaden its application. For while it is evident that men between Adam and Moses transgressed the law written in their hearts and consciences (see last ver.), yet it does not appear that Paul is speaking of the penalty of that law here. *Death,* the penalty of *Adam's sin,* had come upon his descendants, showing that in some way they had broken that law, and the sin had been reckoned against them. This appears still more clearly in the next clause, **Even over them that had not sinned,** or, *sinned not,* **after the similitude,** or, *likeness* **of Adam's transgression,** that is, who sinned not personally and consciously as Adam did. The reference to the unwritten law in the heart and conscience seems to be entirely excluded here, not only by Paul's logical reasoning, but also from his assertion that *All sinned* (ver. 12), which must include multitudes of infants and idiots who did not sin in their own persons, consciously breaking some known law. The language used, *who sinned not after the likeness of Adam's transgression,* describes exactly such persons who were not in a state of moral consciousness or who had not arrived at that state. Paul does not specify infants, because he wished to include others in much the same moral condition; and therefore he uses general language. But if their sin was not against the unwritten law, it must have been against the Eden command; if it was not after the likeness of Adam's transgression, then it was the same as his. What other law or statute was there besides these for which sin could be reckoned? The conclusion seems irresistible. *All sinned* in Adam. And if true of the race till Moses, it would be true for all time. Paul however states facts, and in his brief arguments leaves conclusions to be drawn by his readers. He propounds no philosophical explanations. We may well believe that the race lay in the loins of their great progenitor and shared in his transgression (see on ver. 12, end); that his trespass when he fell was the trespass of the race. There was a personal union in him, just as we may believe there is a vital connection with him, by which the characteristics of Adam, physically, mentally, and morally, have descended to his posterity. Adam being himself sinful and mortal could beget only those who were such.
Who is the figure—rather, *a type, of him who was to come*; that is, of Christ (Matt. 11 : 3). Adam was the type or likeness of Christ by contrast. (See 1 Cor. 15 : 21, 22.) But Abbott takes the phrase to mean *who was the type of the future,* that is, of the oncoming race of man, in his fall, sin, and punishment. But the context and the thought of the whole section rather require a reference to *the Coming One,* the Christ. The comparison which began with ver. 12 is broken off abruptly at the end of the verse. In ver. 15 it is referred to as if well understood. It was prominent in the apostle's mind, and most naturally he indicates it here in saying that Adam was the type of

78 ROMANS [CH. V.

not as the offence, so also *is* the free gift. For if through the offence of one ᵒmany be dead, much more the grace of God, and ᵖthe gift by grace, *which is* by one man, Jesus Christ, hath 16 abounded ᑫ unto many. And not as *it was* by one that sinned, *so is* the gift: for ʳthe judgment *was* by one to condemnation, but the free gift *is* ˢof 17 many offences unto justification. For

15 On But not as the trespass, so also is the gift; for if by the trespass of the one the many died, much more did the grace of God, and the gift by the grace of the one man, Jesus Christ, abound 16 to the many. And not as through one that sinned, is the gift; for the judgment came of one unto condemnation, but the gift came of many trespasses 17 unto justification. For if by the tres-

o Ver. 12, 18.   p 6 : 23 ; 2 Cor. 9 : 15.   q Matt. 20 : 28 ; 26 : 28..   r Gen. 3 : 6-19.
s Luke 7 : 47 ; 1 Cor. 6 : 10, 11.

the coming One. The same thought is brought out in 1 Cor. 15 : 45-47, where the apostle contrasts the first and the second Adam. As Adam was the head of the human race, so Christ is the head especially of his redeemed people. The next verse seems to imply and demand such a reference here. See Practical Remark 15, at the end of the chapter.

15. Having referred to Adam and Christ, each standing at the head of a long line, as type and antitype, Paul stops to state in this and the two following verses some contrasts in these two relations, in which that of the believer to Christ is the more fully unfolded. The language is remarkably concise, its structure peculiar, and its meaning somewhat obscure. **But not as the offence,** or *the trespass* of Adam, including also the idea of the consequences of his sin. **So also the free gift** of eternal life (John 10 : 28), including the idea of its consequences likewise. The meaning seems to be this: There is a difference, however, between the case of Adam, through whose trespass all fell, and that of Christ, through whom the gift of eternal life is offered to all. On *offense* see on 4 : 25. **For if through,** rather, *by*, **the offence of one many be dead,** rather, *the many died*. The conclusion is from the less to the greater. **Much more.** This may be, much more in degree did grace abound, or much more logically, that is, with stronger reason or probability. Either is appropriate, and each is defended by eminent expositors. The latter, however, accords with similar language in ver. 9, 10, and 17, and also commends itself by its fitness and propriety of thought: If the many suffer from the fall of one, much more reasonable and probable is it that the many should be benefited by the grace of God and the gift of one. " For God far rather allows his goodness to prevail than his severity. On this presupposition the conclusion rests" (MEYER). **The grace of God,** the source of the gift, **and the gift by** *the grace of the one man* **Jesus Christ.** (See 2 Cor. 8 : 9.) "*Grace* is opposed to the *offence*; the *gift* to *they that are dead*, and it is the *gift of life*" (BENGEL). **Abounded,** or *did abound*—richly extending *unto the* **many.** This too was the echo of his own experience (1 Tim. 1 : 13, 14). *The many* regain more in Christ than *the many* lost in Adam. The believer is more than restored to the state in which Adam originally was. How gloriously does the *grace* and the *gift by grace* contrast in richness and greatness with the *offense.*

16. Paul presents another contrast. **And not as** *through one* **that sinned is the gift.** The consequences in Adam's case were occasioned by *one sin;* that in Christ's case by *many offenses* of individuals and the race. Only a hint of the meaning is given in this first clause, to be supplied from what follows. **For the judgment,** the judicial sentence, **came from one offense unto condemnation.** The one trespass came to be the occasion of a sentence of condemnation. **But,** on the contrary, **the free,** or *gracious,* **gift** *came* **of many offences unto justification.** In a certain sense it may be said that the many trespasses were the occasion of the justification—a gracious sentence of acquittal. Without them there would have been no need of it. They made it necessary. Thus the contrast is briefly brought to view. On the one hand one transgression occasions the condemnation, on the other hand numerous transgressions occasion and give the opportunity of their gracious forgiveness. (Comp. ver. 20.) On *justification,* see 1 : 17 (5).

if by one man's offence death reigned by one; much more they which receive abundance of grace and of the gift of righteousness *shall reign in 18 life by one, Jesus Christ. Therefore as by the offence of one *judgment came* upon all men to condemnation; even so by the righteousness of one *the free gift came* ᵘupon all men unto justifica- 19 tion of life. For as by one man's disobedience many were made sinners,

pass of the one, death reigned through the one; much more they who receive the abundance of the grace, and of the gift of righteousness, will reign in life through the one, Jesus Christ.
18 So then, as through one trespass it came to all men unto condemnation; so also through one righteous act it came to all men unto justification of 19 life. For as through the disobedience of the one man the many were constituted

t Matt. 25 : 31; Rev. 5 : 9, 10.　　　ᵘ John 12 : 32; 1 Tim. 2 : 4–6; Heb. 2 : 9.

---

17. For, to enlarge upon and confirm the contrasts just made in the two preceding verses. *For* **if by one man's offence,** rather, *For if by the trespass of the one death reigned through the one.* (See ver. 15.) **Reigned** —held sway as a monarch (ver. 14). **Much more** reasonable and probable is it, that **they who receive** *the* **abundance of grace and of the gift of righteousness,** etc. The righteousness is that wrought out through the obedience of Jesus Christ in his life and death. (See 1 : 17 (2).) Both the grace of God and the righteousness of Christ are a free gift, and both bestowed abundantly, resulting in eternal life. **Shall reign**—*will reign in life through the one, Jesus Christ.* Notice how the apostle brings out the full name of Jesus Christ as in holy exultation. "An air of rapturous triumph pervades the closing part of this verse" (BOISE). The degradation of sin and death is surpassed by the superabundance of righteousness and life.

18. The parallelism commenced in ver. 12 is here resumed under a form suggested by the preceding context. Compare Gal. 2 : 6 for a similar style. This verse and the next contain a concise comparison of the results between Adam and Christ. **Therefore**—*Accordingly then,* in view of what just precedes and resuming the sentence begun in ver. 12. **As by the offence,** etc. A mere summary is given; the verbs are omitted; the construction is the most concise possible. Only the words which are pointers and to be kept in mind are given. To complete the sense some words must be supplied. The Revised version, like our Common version, supplies *judgment came*, and *the free gift came.* The Improved Bible Union simply supplies *it came* in each case. *It was* may

be supplied, as perhaps nearest the apostle's thought. The verse may be rendered: *Accordingly then as through one trespass it was unto all men unto condemnation, so also through one righteous act it was unto all men unto justification of life.* Notice that in the first half of this verse the sin of all in ver. 12 is carried over into the *condemnation* of all, as in ver. 16. *The one righteous act* is a better rendering than **the righteousness of one.** (See on 1 : 17 (5).) Christ's meritorious obedience, culminating in giving himself up to death, is presented as a whole (Gal. 1 : 4; Phil. 2 : 8), and set over against Adam's disobedience. **Justification.** (See on 1 : 17 (4); also 4 : 25.) *Justification of life* is that acquittal and restoration to the Divine favor which is connected with eternal life in its present beginning and future results, just as eternal death begins with and results from condemnation. *Unto all men.* The apostle gives universality to both cases in order to make the analogy perfect. It is also true that the death of Christ had reference to all men. It atoned for the sins of all men so far as they sinned in Adam, and hence a full satisfaction is made for all who die in infancy; and the atonement in reference to all mankind is such that the provisions and offers of justification are for all. In the next verse the actual results of Christ's work is stated and there Paul makes the necessary limitation to *many* instead of *all*. This change itself stands opposed to the doctrine of universal salvation. The change in form appears intentional, and the limitation accords with Paul's doctrine elsewhere.

19. For introduces the ground and proof of the statement of the preceding verse. This verse contains also the summary of ver. 12-18. It includes

x so by the obedience of one shall many be made righteous.
20 Moreover y the law entered, that the offence might abound. But z where sin abounded, grace did much more
21 abound: that as sin hath reigned unto

sinners, so also through the obedience of the one will the many be constituted righteous. But the law came in beside, that the trespass might abound. But where sin abounded, grace superabounded; that as sin reigned in

x Isa. 53 : 10-12 ; Dan. 9 : 24 ; 2 Cor. 5 : 21.
y 3 : 19, 20 ; John 15 : 22 ; Gal. 3 : 19-25.
z See 2 Chron. 33 : 9-13 ; Luke 7 : 47 ; 23 : 39-43.

in the parallelism the real facts in their exactness, *the* **many**, the natural descendants of Adam, *the* **many**, the spiritual descendants of Christ. *The many* may mean the whole, the greater part, or a large number, and which of these it means in any given case must be learned from the evident intention of the writer and from the known facts in the case. When we take into account the half of the race that die before the age of spiritual accountability, and the vast multitude that will be saved in the days of the millennial glory, *the many* of the redeemed will doubtless include the larger part of the human race. *The disobedience of the one man*, as in ver. 12, points to Adam's sin. **The obedience of** *the one*, like "the one righteous act" of ver. 18, points to **Christ's meritorious obedience.** Were **made, or** *constituted*, **sinners . . . shall be made,** or *constituted*, **righteous.** By virtue of their union with Adam the race became sinners actually and personally *through* his disobedience. So also by virtue of a spiritual union with Christ the redeemed will become virtually such in their justification and actually and personally such in their sanctification. It is common for expositors to limit the meaning of *will be constituted* to *being accounted righteous* and dealt with as such. But Paul is speaking, in this chapter, of the happy results of justification, and it was perfectly natural that he should go beyond the mere act of justification itself. And as he is about to treat of things pertaining to sanctification in the next chapter, it was natural that he should anticipate in thought what was already filling his mind. See also how his mind passes on to the superabounding grace of eternal life in ver. 21. BOISE, who prefers to translate *established* instead of *constitute*, says: "In the one case, the certainty became determined in the very beginning of the race; in the other, it will be determined at the very end, when all the redeemed shall be gathered in."

20. It was necessary to a full view of the results of justification, in this comparison of Adam and Christ, to notice the design and effect of the Mosaic law and the position it held in the religious history of the race. This is the point unfolded in this and the next verse. **Moreover,** or rather, *But law came in alongside* of sin which was already in the world (ver. 13). *Law* in the original is emphatic but without the article. It is evident from ver. 13, 14, that the Mosaic law is meant, in which law was revealed and enforced anew. It corresponds also with Gal. 3 : 19, where the law of Moses is plainly meant. Sin was holding sway in the world (ver. 13), but the law came in beside it incidentally and tributary to it. That the offence, or *trespass*, might abound. *Trespass* here is a violation of a specific law, and may be referred to Adam's first transgression, which was the root of all the sins of the race, or to the specific sins of the individuals of the race. *Trespass* is the outward expression of *sin* (ver. 12), the inward depraved principle (next clause). A design of the law is here given. The law is primarily designed to be obeyed. But in the plan of redemption of a fallen race it had an additional necessary design, that the evils of our nature might be manifested, be brought out and exposed by their opposition to and violation of a specific law, which is holy, righteous, and true (7 : 7-12 ; Gal. 3 : 19 ; Matt. 10 : 34, 35). **But where sin abounded, grace did much more abound**, *abounded over and above it*. An ultimate design or result of the law is here brought into view. How grace superabounded in Paul's own experience (1 Tim. 1 : 13, 14). Thus the law in the purpose of God prepared the way for Christ and for the reception of the gospel (7 : 24, 25 ; Gal. 3 : 10, 24).

death, even so might *grace reign through righteousness unto eternal life by Jesus Christ our Lord.

death, so also might grace reign through righteousness unto eternal life, through Jesus Christ our Lord.

a John 1 : 16, 17 : Titus 2 : 11.

21. The thought of the preceding verse is continued, and sin and grace are contrasted. **That as sin,** *reigned in death*. Sin (ver. 12) is the real destroyer of man, the real antagonist of God's grace. Death is its result, its wages (6:23). *So also* **grace might reign**—hold sway, a conqueror, greater and stronger than sin and death (ver. 13, 14). **Through,** by means of **righteousness,** the righteousness revealed in the gospel (1 : 17). Grace reigns not only by accepting the believer as righteous, and restoring him to the Divine favor, but also by maintaining in him holiness of heart and conduct, and leading him safely *unto life eternal;* and all this is effected *through* **Jesus Christ our Lord.** Notice how Paul closes this wonderful parallel and his wonderful experience (7:25) alike, *through Jesus Christ our Lord*, with whom the believer has a real, living, and spiritual union. Notice also that the last two verses of this chapter prepare the way for the two following chapters (6:1, 15; 7:7).

PRACTICAL REMARKS.

1. True peace with God can only come to the sinner through justification by faith in Jesus Christ (ver. 1; Eph. 2 : 14–16).

2. Future glory is the hope and joy of God's believing people (ver. 2; 8 : 18).

3. Joy in afflictions is a privilege and a precious boon of the child of God (ver. 3 ; 2 Cor. 4 : 17, 18).

4. The blessed results of a justified state are inseparably linked together and are developed from one another (ver. 1–5; Gal. 5 : 22, 23 ; 2 Peter 1 : 5).

5. In the present condition of our race no character can become great without suffering (ver. 3–5; 1 Peter 1 : 6; Heb. 2 : 9, 10).

6. The hope of the believer is like an anchor; that of the sinner like a spider's web (ver. 5; Heb. 6 : 19 ; Job 8 : 14).

7. The love of God pervading the heart is an evidence of the presence of the Holy Spirit and of acceptance with God (ver. 5; 1 John 4 : 7–10).

8. It is the privilege of the believer to be assured of his own salvation (ver. 6–8; 1 John 3 : 14; Eph. 3 : 18, 19).

9. The love of God lies at the foundation of the plan of redemption, and of all our hopes (ver. 7, 8; 8 : 34–39; 1 John 4 : 19).

10. Redemption is not through the moral influence of Christ's example, teachings, and life, but through his blood (ver. 9; Heb. 9 : 22; Rev. 5 : 9).

11. The final perseverance of the saints, resting on God's infinite grace and love, is a doctrine of the Scriptures (ver. 9–11 ; John 10 : 25, 29; Isa. 49 : 15).

12. How terrible is sin, that in and through its one commission the whole race became estranged from God (ver. 12 ; 3 : 10–18).

13. Death like a tyrant holds sway over the bodies and souls of men, giving evidence of the presence, power, and unspeakable evil of sin (ver. 13, 15; 8 : 6, 13 ; James 1 : 15).

14. "While God will judge men impartially, and 'render to every man according to his works,' yet in respect to certain general principles and conditions of our being, he deals with his creature *man* as a *race*, he regards *humanity* as a *unit*" (A. N. ARNOLD). (Ver. 12–17; 1 Cor. 15 : 22.)

15. Christ was head of the race in that he created man in his own image and after his likeness (Gen. 1 : 26; John 1 : 1–3; Col. 1 : 16); and thus the race bears to him the relation of kinship (Acts 17 : 29 ; Heb. 2 : 11), he the head and they of like nature with him. Most fittingly therefore is Christ also the head of the redeemed, who, in their salvation, more than overcomes their ruin in the fall (ver. 14–16; 8 : 18, 23 ; 1 Cor. 15 : 55–57).

16. The parallelism of what Adam and Christ have done for the race seems necessarily to imply the salvation of infants and of all who die before coming into a state of moral accountability. No one, we may well believe, will be held accountable for the sin of Adam, until he has made it his own by personal and actual sinning (ver. 14–21 ; comp. Mark 10 : 14;

F

Sanctification; the believer made holy by his union with Christ, who frees him from the power of sin.

6 WHAT shall we say then? ᵇShall we continue in sin, that grace may abound? God forbid. How shall we, that are ᶜdead to sin, ᵈlive any

6 WHAT then shall we say? Are we to continue in sin, that grace may abound? Far be it! How shall we, who died to sin, live any longer

b 3 : 8; Gal. 5 : 13; 1 Peter 2 : 16.   c Col. 3 : 3; 1 Peter 2 : 24.   d 1 Peter 4 : 1–3.

Matt. 18 : 2; Deut. 1 : 39; Isa. 7 : 15, 16; Jonah 4 : 11; Heb. 5 : 13, 14).

17. Both sin and salvation are two great facts in our world. All as they grow up exhibit early sinful traits. The gospel saves and its offers are to all; and whoever perishes, perishes through his own sin (ver. 15–19; Ps. 58 : 3; Rev. 22 : 17; Ezek. 18 : 4, 20).

18. The fact that all are sinners and under condemnation, renders the work of Christ and a complete salvation a necessity (ver. 18, 19; Acts 4 : 12).

19. Every one should humbly accept the fact that he is a sinner, and gratefully embrace the means provided for his salvation (ver. 18–20; 2 Cor. 6 : 2; Acts 2 : 40).

20. As the law had an important work in the religious history of our sinful race, so it has in the religious experience of men in preparing them for the gospel (ver. 20; 3 : 20; Gal. 3 : 24).

21. The triumphs of grace over sin are glorious. The gospel is more than sufficient to repair the ruins of the fall, and to raise the race to heaven. How eager should we be to enjoy its blessings! What folly, what sin to neglect its provisions! (Ver. 21; 1 Peter 1 : 10–12; Heb. 2 : 3.)

CHAPTER VI.

In this chapter, and the two succeeding ones, the apostle shows that the doctrine of salvation through free justification by faith, so far from encouraging sin, insures the believer's personal holiness and final salvation. The discussion, while growing out of the doctrine of justification, is connected largely with the doctrine of sanctification. In this chapter, and as far as 7 : 6, Paul shows that gratuitous justification does not lead to sinful indulgence; for the believer is united by faith with the ever-living Christ, with whom he has died to sin and risen to a new life, as illustrated in his baptism

(ver. 1–14); and, being no longer under law but under grace, he is no longer a servant of sin but a servant of righteousness, and is constrained to loving obedience (ver. 15–23). This new life and its happy fruits are illustrated by a well-known principle of Jewish law (7 : 1–6).

1–23. THE MORAL INFLUENCE OF THE *doctrine of salvation through gratuitous* JUSTIFICATION BY FAITH IN CHRIST. This doctrine does not lessen the obligation or the incentives to holy living: because the believer has become dead to sin and has risen to a new life (ver. 1–14); and because freed from the bondage of the law under which he was a slave to sin, he is now under grace with a spirit of obedience unto righteousness (ver. 15–23).

1. Thus far Paul had been dealing largely with the past; now he turns to the future. **What**—in view of what he had said in 5 : 20, 21—**shall we say then?** (Comp. 3 : 5; 4 : 1.) Shall we say, *Let us* **continue in sin,** or according to another reading, *Are we to* **continue in sin that grace may abound?** A common objection to justification by faith apart from the works of the law, which Paul must often have met, was that it tended to immorality. This objection would be suggested anew by the statement, "Where sin abounded, grace superabounded" (5 : 20). This had led some to charge them with saying, "Let us do evil, that good may come" (3 : 8). Some regard the question here as the language of an objector. This is not necessary. It is better to regard it as one which Paul had met in his own experience, and which he now uses in expostulating with believers against such an abuse of the doctrine. Paul proceeds to show that it does not encourage sin, nor weaken the incentives to holiness.

2. God forbid. Perish the thought! (See on 3 : 4.) He had already disclaimed

3 longer therein? Know ye not, that so many of us as were baptized into Jesus Christ were baptized into his death? Therefore we are buried with him by baptism into death: that like as Christ was raised up from the dead by the glory of the Father, even so we also should walk in newness of

3 therein? Or, are ye ignorant, that all we who were baptized into Christ Jesus were baptized into his death? 4 We were buried therefore with him through the baptism into his death? that as Christ was raised from the dead through the glory of the Father, so we also might walk in newness of

e 1 Cor. 12 : 13 ; Gal. 3 : 27.   *f* Ver. 4, 5, 8 ; 1 Cor. 15 : 29 ; Gal. 2 : 20.   *g* Col. 2 : 12, 13.
h 8 : 11 ; 2 Cor. 13 : 4.   *i* 7 : 6 ; 12 : 1, 2 ; Eph. 4 : 22-24.

it in 3 : 7, 8. **How shall we that are dead**, rather, *that died*, **to sin live any longer therein?** The absurdity of remaining in sin is most strikingly shown. We having *died to sin* and yet *live* therein? Impossible! To have *died* to sin is to have utterly renounced it and forsaken it, and to be no longer under it as a ruling power. (Comp. Gal. 2 : 19.) In justification the believer also is separated from the guilt of sin (ver. 7 ; 1 Peter 2 : 24). Accepting Christ as our Saviour and Lord, and consecrating ourselves to him, is renouncing allegiance to sin as our master; and by virtue of our union with Christ, we are delivered from the dominion of sin (ver. 8-11). Paul does not yet refer to baptism, but to that spiritual change that preceded baptism. Baptism is a burial and has reference to death, but death precedes burial. The thought suggested by this question is illustrated and enlarged upon in the next nine verses.

3. Know ye not introduces an expression of earnest remonstrance. More exactly: *Or*, is it possible, that *you are ignorant* of the significance of your own baptism? Surely you cannot be ignorant of its lessons. **That so many of us,** etc.—*that all we who were baptized into Christ Jesus*, into a professed allegiance and subjection to and fellowship with Christ (Gal. 3 : 27). This was represented symbolically in their baptism, and truly so if they were what they professed. **Were baptized into his death**—for sin; into a professed conformity to his death, that as he "put away sin by the sacrifice of himself" (Heb. 9 : 26), so we have died to sin, and put it away, as it were, from us. This we did symbolically and professedly, and truly so if we had really been regenerated. We should remember that in the apostolic age baptism generally implied genuine conversion;

yet there were exceptions, as in the case of Simon Magus. Instead of **into**, some eminent scholars prefer to render *unto*, and it is so rendered in the margin of the Improved Bible Union version. Thus baptized *unto* Christ means with distinct and exclusive reference to him as our Lord and Redeemer; and *unto* his death, means with especial reference to his death as suffered for sin and for the believing sinner. Symbolically "it is just as if, at that moment, Christ suffered, died, and were buried for such a man, and as if such a man suffered, died, and were buried with Christ" (BENGEL). (Gal. 2 : 19.) It is evident from this passage that baptism is an intelligent act on the part of the one baptized and that he cannot be an unconscious infant; and also that it does not confer regeneration, since that is symbolized by the act, and in the preceding verse it is implied as possessed before the act.

4. The question of ver. 3 implies that they admitted the significance of their baptism. **Therefore,** it follows in view of this, **we are**, rather, *were*, **buried with him,** after the manner of his literal burial **by** or *through the baptism into death*, symbolically representing that we were spiritually dead to sin. See on preceding verse. Burial is a consequent and proof of death, and it puts the dead out of sight. " Dead and buried," as we say. (Comp. John 11 : 17.) There is a plain reference here to immersion as the act in baptism. So commentators generally. **That like as Christ was raised up from the dead**—in order that Christ in his resurrection also might be our example, *so that we also might* **walk in newness of life,** in a newer, higher course or manner of life. Christ was raised **by,** or *through*, **the glory of the Father**—that power which exhibits God's glory (1 Cor. 6 : 14,   2 Cor. 13 : 4 ; Col.

5 life. *For if we have been planted together in the likeness of his death, we shall be also *in the likeness* of *his* resur-
6 rection: knowing this, that ⁱour old man is crucified with *him*, that ᵐ the body of sin might be destroyed, ⁿ that henceforth we should not serve sin.
7 For ᵒ he that is dead is freed from sin.

5 life. For if we have become united with the likeness of his death, we shall be with that of his resurrection
6 also; knowing this, that our old man was crucified with him, that the body of sin might be destroyed, in order that we might no more be in bondage
7 to sin. For he that died has been jus-

k Col. 3 : 1-4.   *l* Gal. 5 : 24; Eph. 4 : 22; Col. 3 : 5, 9, 10.   *m* 7 : 24; Col. 2 : 11.   *n* John 8 : 34-36.   *o* Ver. 2; 1 Peter 4 : 1.

1 : 11). God was glorified in Christ's resurrection (John 17 : 1). It is the divine purpose that we should die that we might live, and so in our baptism we profess what is symbolically represents—our death to sin and our resurrection to a new life.

5. For, in confirmation of what has just been said, **if we have been planted**—rather, *if we have become grown together*, or *united with* **the likeness of his death.** This likeness consists in being dead to sin, and in having had our corruption and wickedness slain and buried, as it were, in Christ's tomb. **We shall also be** united *with* **the likeness of his resurrection**, which will be shown in a new life consecrated to God. That the reference is to a new spiritual life on earth, and not to the future resurrection of the body, is evident from ver. 4. Two statements are made in this verse: First, that we have become like Christ in his death, further illustrated in ver. 6 and 7. Second, so we shall also be in his resurrection, further illustrated in ver. 8-11. Both of these are put forth as true, it being taken for granted that they were genuine Christians. Schleiermacher has an eloquent discourse on "Christ's Resurrection a Pattern of our New Life." See "Fish's Masterpieces," Vol. I., p. 525.

6. Knowing this—asserting a fact of experimental knowledge. **The old man**—the former self in our unrenewed state, in distinction from the new life, the renewed man (Col. 3 : 9. 10; Eph. 4 : 22-24; 2 Cor. 5 : 17). The remnants and tendencies of the former are represented elsewhere as still continuing in the believer, opposing the spirit and temper of the renewed heart, and struggling for the ascendency (7 : 17-20; 1 Cor. 9 : 27; Gal. 5 : 17). **Is**—rather, *was*, **crucified with him** (Gal. 2 : 20). The pain and shame of this mode of death well represented the pangs and self-

abasement of Paul at his conversion (1 Tim. 1 : 13), and the figure of such a death suggests how radical the change at conversion is. The old impulses and passions give way to new impulses and desires (2 Cor. 5 : 15-17). **The body of sin**—sinful and ruled by sin, our sinful nature (8 : 13; Col. 3 : 5), **might be destroyed**, *rendered inoperative and powerless*; that its power might be abolished, done away, and as it were destroyed, *in order that we might no longer be in bondage to* **sin.** Sin is personified as a master to whom we had once given willing service. (Comp. Eph. 2 : 1-7.)

7. This verse is regarded as very difficult, arising from its conciseness and axiomatic form. It may be more literally rendered, *For he that died has been justified from* **sin.** It is plainly added, as confirmatory of what the apostle had just said in ver. 6. Dr. A. N. Arnold refers this to Christ, who could be said to be justified from sin, when, having died on account of sin, he was raised to the right hand of God, "separated from sinners" (Heb. 7 : 26). This is true in a sense, but the reference seems to be, both in the preceding verse and at the beginning of the next verse, to the believer's death to sin, and it would naturally be the same in this. The statement of the next verse, *If we died with Christ*, suggests a connection here between the believer's death to sin and Christ's death for sin. Enjoying the fruit of his atoning death, he is *justified, absolved*, and separated *from* sin, as a ruling force, and *accounted righteous*. (See on 1 : 17 (3).) As sin is personified as a master throughout this passage (last verse), so here *justified from sin* suggests a deliverance from the body of sin as a ruling power (ver. 14). And inferentially we may say, that as death changes the relation of a slave to his master, making him a free man, so the believer's death to sin with Christ so changes his relation to sin

8 Now p if we be dead with Christ, q we believe that we shall also live with
9 him: knowing that r Christ being raised from the dead dieth no more; death hath no more dominion over
10 him. For in that he died, s he died unto sin once: but in that he liveth,
11 t he liveth unto God. Likewise reckon ye also yourselves to be dead indeed unto sin, but u alive unto God through Jesus Christ our Lord.

8 tified from sin. And if we died with Christ, we believe that we shall also
9 live with him; knowing that Christ, being raised from the dead, dies no more; death has dominion over him
10 no more. For the death that he died, he died to sin once for all; but the life
11 that he lives, he lives to God. Thus reckon ye also yourselves to be dead to sin, but alive to God in Christ Jesus.

p Ver. 3-5; 2 Tim. 2 : 11, 12.　q 2 Cor. 4 : 10-14.　r See refs. Ps. 16 : 9-11; Rev. 1 : 18.
s Heb. 9 : 25-28.　t See refs. Luke 20 : 38.　u 2 Cor. 5 : 15; Gal. 2 : 19, 20.

that he is no longer its slave, but assured of perpetual life (ver. 8, 9).

8. Now—rather, *And*, continuing the same fact, *if we died with Christ*, and adding an additional thought, growing out of it, **we believe that we also shall live with him.** Being partakers of Christ's death, we are sure that we shall live with him, participate in his new and endless life both here and hereafter (ver. 11-13; 8:1, 2, 10; Gal. 2:20; 2 Tim. 2:11, 12; 1 Thess. 4:17). We must not limit our idea of Christ's death to his physical sufferings (Heb. 5:7-9; Matt. 27:46).

9. Knowing—introducing the reason for the statement of the last verse. *Since we know* **that Christ being raised from the dead dieth no more; death hath no more dominion,** *rules over him no more*. Christ's obedience and death were voluntary. As connected with our race, and as making satisfaction to Divine holiness and justice, sin had dominion over him (John 10:18; Matt. 20:28; Phil. 2:7 ff.). His resurrection was a proof and a proclamation that the power of death was broken (1:4; 1 Cor. 15:55-57).

10. This verse explains and confirms the preceding. **For in that he died**—equivalent to *For the death that he died*. **He died unto sin**—on account of sin; he bore the penalty of sin, which is death. Having suffered that **once** *for all*, death has no more claim upon him (Heb. 7:27; 9:12; comp. Heb. 10:10; Jude 3). It needs never to be repeated. He can henceforth live unto God, enjoying his reward. **But in that he liveth**—*But the life that he liveth*, **he liveth unto God.** This does not mean that, in a sense, he did not live unto God while in this world, but his life was one of voluntary obedience to all the requirements of God, even unto death for the sins of men. Having fully satisfied the penal demands on account of sin, he has only to live; and this life he lives to God, to glorify him (John 17:1, 2), in bringing many sons to glory (Heb. 2:10), in putting all enemies under his feet, establishing and consummating his kingdom, which he will finally deliver up to God and the Father (1 Cor. 15:24).

11. Application of the preceding verse. **Likewise,** in like manner with Christ, **reckon ye also yourselves to be dead** *to* **sin.** Christians are dead to sin, not in the same sense that Christ was. He died on account of sin and for sin (ver. 10), being himself without sin (1 Peter 2:22); Christians die in renouncing and forsaking sin, and in this change of relation to it, through the death of Christ. Dying in their stead, they are partakers of the benefits of his death. So that they are to consider themselves not only dead to sin, **but alive to God,** partakers of Christ's life (Heb. 3:14; 2 Peter 1:4; 2 Tim. 1:10). And this is **through,** rather *in* **Jesus Christ,** in fellowship and union with him. Thus it is *in* Christ that believers become dead to sin and alive to God (8:1, 2; 2 Cor. 5:17). And being thus united with Christ, he lives in them (Gal. 2:20). Alford remarks that in this chapter it is not Christ's Mediatorship, but his Headship which is made prominent. **Our Lord**—omitted by best authorities. Thus far Paul has shown that the believer's relation to Christ, and the consequent change effected in him thereby, are diametrically opposed to the idea of continuing in sin that grace may abound (ver. 1).

BAPTISM AS A FIGURE. We may speak of baptism as a sign, an antitype, an emblem, or a symbol. An emblem is generally used as suggestive of some

12 ¹ Let not sin therefore reign in your mortal body, ² that ye should obey it in
13 the lusts thereof; neither yield ye your ³ members *as* instruments of unrighteousness unto sin; but ⁴ yield

12 Let not sin therefore reign in your mortal body, that ye should obey its
13 desires; nor present your members to sin as weapons of unrighteousness;

x Ps. 19 : 13 ; 119 : 133.   *y* Gal. 5 : 16, 24 ; 1 Peter 2 : 11 ; 4 : 2, 3.
z 7 : 5, 23 ; 1 Cor. 6 : 15 ; Col. 3 : 5 ; James 4 : 1.   *a* 12 : 1 ; 2 Chron. 30 : 8 ; 1 Peter 2 : 24.

natural fitness; a symbol is generally chosen or agreed upon to represent something moral or spiritual by the figures or properties of natural things. The two may unite in one. Thus the bread and wine in the Lord's Supper are appropriate emblems of our Lord's body and blood, and his own chosen symbols of his sufferings and death. So the waters of baptism may be a fitting emblem of purification from sin, an emblematic washing away of sin, and Paul's chosen symbol of the believer's death and life to God.

But to be more particular. (1) Baptism *symbolizes* the believer's union with Christ ("baptized into Christ"), the submerging of the whole man into the Christly spirit of a new life; and thus united to the spiritual body of Christ he has put on the garb of Christ to wear it in the church of Christ (Gal. 3 : 27 ; 1 Cor. 12 : 13). (2) It symbolizes a burial with Christ—the believer's consciousness of a spiritual death and of a dying to all ungodliness, and of a burial to a sinful life, and a rising with Christ, a consciousness of the birth of a new life, henceforth to be lived unto God. (3) And growing out of this reference to the death and the resurrection of Christ, it symbolizes the believer's resurrection and blissful immortality.

Baptism may be conceived of as a *sign*. As circumcision was a sign of a natural connection with Abraham and Israel, so baptism as an external rite is a sign or token of an outward profession of Christ and of connection with the Christian church. It cannot however be so truthfully spoken of as a *seal*. Circumcision was a seal of Abraham's faith which he exercised before he was circumcised, a pledge and an assurance of the righteousness of faith (Rom. 4 : 11). So believers are sealed with Holy Spirit of promise, impressing the image of Christ on the soul, and giving an assurance of an everlasting inheritance (Eph. 1 : 14 ; 4 : 30. Comp. 2 Tim. 2 : 19). Baptism is nowhere spoken of as a seal in the New Testament.

As an *antitype* baptism is mentioned in 1 Peter 3 : 21. An antitype is that which corresponds to its type. Peter speaks of baptism as the antitype "after a true likeness," as the Revised version paraphrases it, answering or corresponding to the waters of the deluge which prefigured it in the Old Testament. Baptism symbolizes the resurrection of Christ, the foundation of the believer's hope, and, if truly received, is more than the putting away of the filth of the flesh; it presupposes and symbolizes all that a good conscience toward God requires, namely, a soul renewed and consecrated to him.

12. In this and the two following verses the apostle enforces the practical results of what he had just gone over. **Let not sin therefore,** in view of the fact that you are to account yourselves as dead to sin (ver. 11), **reign** as a king, **in your mortal body,** a body subject to death and in which death is at work. The effects of sin and death were so marked and obvious in the body that Paul calls especial attention to it. **That ye should obey the lusts,** or *desires,* **thereof.** The best critical text omits **it in.** The idea is, Let not sin, your former master, continue to reign in your body, that ye should obey its inordinate and sinful appetites. "The bodily appetites are the fuel; sin is the fire" (BENGEL). Rather in your new life let sin be banished, and your body be a temple of the Holy Spirit (1 Cor. 6 : 19).

13. Neither yield your members—the organs of the body, such as the tongue, eye, hands, and feet, implying, however, the mental activities working with them. The figure of **sin,** as a king, is continued in this verse, who is waging war against righteousness, to whom is *presented* the members of the body as **instruments,** or *weapons,* literally, *heavy armor,* **of**

yourselves unto God, as those that are alive from the dead, and your members *as instruments of righteousness* 14 unto God. For sin shall not have dominion over you: *b for ye are not under the law, but under grace.*
15 What then? Shall we sin, because we are not under the law, *c but under grace."*
16 God forbid. Know ye not, that *d to*

but present yourselves to God, as alive from the dead, and your members to 14 God as weapons of righteousness. For sin shall not have dominion over you : for ye are not under law, but under grace.
15 What then? Are we to sin, because we are not under law, but under 16 grace? Far be it! Know ye not, that

b 7 : 4–11 ; 8 : 2.   *c* Eph. 2 : 8–10.   *d* John 8 : 34.

---

righteousness. But yield, or *present,* **yourselves to God, as those that are alive from the dead,** as having become dead with Christ to sin, and living with him to God (Eph. 2 : 5, 6), **and your members** *as weapons,* or *heavy armor of righteousness,* **to God.** (Comp. 12 : 1; 13 : 12.) There is no middle ground in this service. Either sin or righteousness rules the man. The believer's service is also a voluntary service—*present yourselves.* The different tenses of the same verb is thus distinguished by BARTLETT ("Christian Scriptures") : " Neither *be ever presenting* your members unto sin, . . . but *once for all present* yourselves unto God," etc. An excellent exhortation to inconstant Christians.

14. Paul presents the concluding and crowning argument of this discussion. Not only in view of what he had already said, but also for the reason about to be given, he asserts: **For sin shall not have dominion over you,** shall not have *lordship* over you ; sin is no longer to be your master. **For ye are not** *under law,* through which is a knowledge of sin (3 : 20), and which even intensifies sin and causes it to abound (5 : 20), **but ye are under grace** which reigns through righteousness, not only in the justification of the believer, but also in his sanctification (5 : 21). They were not under a system of law, but under a system of grace. It sounds like a Christian axiom. Law could only command, it could not effect reconciliation, nor give the spirit obedience ; but grace through Jesus Christ effects the one with God and gives the other to man. Law had no power to deliver the sinner from the mastery of sin, but grace through a spiritual union with Christ frees the believer from the lordship of sin, and through motives of love and hope ensures grateful and cheerful obedience to God. The thought

in regard to law is developed in chapter 7 ; that in regard to grace in chapter 8. This whole discussion was important in developing the gospel in its relation to the law and to meet needed instruction both among Jewish and Gentile converts. Paul wrote this Epistle at Corinth. He saw there how improper views had led into false liberties and wicked indulgences (1 Cor. 5 : 1-6 ; 20). It was doubtless so elsewhere (Gal. 5 : 13). It was necessary to check such tendencies, to define the Christian's relation to the law, to sin, to grace, and to holiness.

15. Paul proceeds to illustrate further the relation to sin under law, and to righteousness under grace, by the case of master and servant. He had shown that we cannot continue in sin, because we are dead to Christ ; he now proceeds to show that acts of sin are to be avoided, because we cannot serve two masters. **What then** are we to conclude? Paul sees that an inference, directly opposite from what he was enforcing, might be drawn from the statement he had just made. **Shall we,** rather, *Are we,* **to sin,** commit acts of transgression, **because we are not under law but under grace?** This is more definite than to *continue in sin,* in ver. 1. This he repels at once. **God forbid.** *Away the thought!* There has been a tendency in every age to make the liberty of the gospel a license to sin. " Such has been the objection to the doctrines of grace in all ages. And the fact that this objection was made to Paul's teachings, proves that his doctrine is the same with that against which the same objection is still urged " (HODGE).

16. Know ye not—you surely know. The question is in the form that assumes an affirmative answer. **That to whom ye yield,** or *present,* **your-**

whom ye yield yourselves servants to obey, his servants ye are to whom ye obey; whether of sin unto death, or of 17 obedience unto righteousness? But God be thanked, that ye were the servants of sin, but ye have obeyed from the heart *that form of doctrine which 18 was delivered you. Being then ƒmade free from sin, ye became the servants 19 of righteousness. I speak after the manner of men, because of the infirmity of your flesh: for *as ye have

to whom ye present yourselves servants unto obedience, his servants ye are whom ye obey; whether of sin unto death, or of obedience unto 17 righteousness? But thanks be to God, that ye were servants of sin, but obeyed from the heart that form of teaching unto which ye were delivered; and being made free from sin, 19 became servants of righteousness. I speak after the manner of men, because of the infirmity of your flesh

e 2 Tim. 1 : 13-16.   *f* See refs. John 8 : 32.   *g* Ver. 13, 17.

selves as *bond-servants* or *slaves*, to obey, etc. Paul appeals to a general and well-known fact. When any one enters into service, he binds himself to obedience to the one he serves. **Whether . . . or.** It must be to one, or to the other. He cannot serve two masters at the same time (Matt. 6 : 24). **Unto death.** The result of the service of sin, not merely physical death, but especially spiritual and eternal death. So the service of God results in righteousness, holy living, "the fruits of holiness" (ver. 22), embracing and ending in eternal life. Serving sin implies the practice of sin; so the service of righteousness implies the practice of righteousness.

17. Assuming the full assent of his readers to what he had said, the apostle exclaims in application to them, **But God be thanked that ye were the servants of sin,** once yet no longer. Their servitude is viewed at a single glance, as in the past. And at the same glance he sees in glorious contrast a changed life of obedience unto righteousness. That such a change had been effected, and that too, upon the slaves of sin by the grace of God, calls forth his hearty thanksgiving. Their terrible slavery made their deliverance and the gift of God the more conspicuous. **But ye have obeyed,** rather, *But ye obeyed* or *became obedient* when ye entered the state of grace (ver. 14), and became servants of righteousness (ver. 18). And this obedience was willing, inward, and spiritual, **from the heart.** What they obeyed was **that form of doctrine which was delivered you,** rather, *that form of teaching unto which ye were delivered* by God at your conversion, and symbolically and professedly at your baptism. *The form of teaching* was that Christian faith and practice which Paul had received and taught. That *form* may be regarded, with Wordsworth and some others, as *that mold of doctrine,* or *teaching,* into which (like molten metal) ye were delivered, soft and ductile, yielding to the burning efficacy of the truth taught you. It was the *model,* the *original pattern,* "the gospel of that pronounced evangelical type, as distinct from Judaism, which Paul always preached" (BOISE).

18. Closely connected with the preceding verse. **And**—continuing the thought, **being made free from sin**—delivered and set at liberty from sin as a master, **ye became servants** (*bond-servants* or *slaves*) **to righteousness.** Free yet slaves! Yet in this consisted their highest freedom (John 8 : 36. Comp. 1 Cor. 7 : 22). Such service being hearty, willing, and elevating, it could not be expected that they would return to the master and the bondage from which they had been emancipated. In their new service they were enabled and obliged to live a life of piety.

19. The apostle apologizes for using such an illustration, especially for the phrase *bond-servants* or *slaves to righteousness.* Slavery was terrible and well understood at Rome. **I speak after the manner of men**—as men usually do, in an imperfect way, in order that you may rightly contrast your present condition with your past, **because of the infirmity of your flesh.** Some regard this as an *intellectual* infirmity; others as a *moral.* Both seem to be included. By *weakness of the flesh* Paul means, that they were yet carnal and sensuous, and unaccustomed to those spiritual views of divine subjects which would render unnecessary such illustrations drawn from earthly objects and relations. (Comp. 5 : 12-14 ; 1 Cor.

yielded your members servants to uncleanness and to iniquity unto iniquity; even so now yield your members servants to righteousness unto holiness. 20 For when ye were ᵇ the servants of sin, ye were free from righteousness. 21 ⁱ What fruit had ye then in those things whereof ye are now ashamed? for ᵏ the end of those things is death. 22 But now ˡ being made free from sin, and become servants to God, ᵐ ye have your fruit unto holiness, and the 23 end everlasting life. For ⁿ the wages

For as ye presented your members servants to uncleanness, and to iniquity unto iniquity; so now present your members servants to righteousness 20 unto sanctification. For when ye were servants of sin, ye were free as to righteousness. 21 What fruit therefore had ye then in those things of which ye are now ashamed? For the end of those 22 things is death. But now, being made free from sin, and become servants to God, ye have your fruit unto sanctification, and the end eternal life. For

h John 8 : 34.   i 7 : 5.
m Eph. 5 : 9 ; Phil. 1 : 11 ; Col 1 : 10.

k Ver. 23 ; 1 : 32.   l Ver. 14, 18.
n 5 : 12 ; Gal. 6 : 7, 8 ; James 1 : 15.

3 : 1.) He had used the word *slave* not because the believer is really a slave, but to make his meaning plain; besides through their low spiritual condition, Christ's service might sometimes seem hard to them—more of a task than a privilege, performed more in the spirit of servitude than of liberty. All this thus far in ver. 19 is parenthetical. Paul now returns to develop his meaning as expressed in ver. 18. **For,** my meaning is, *that as ye presented* **your members** *slaves* **to uncleanness—** lustful, vicious sins, especially against one's self, **and to iniquity**—*leading into iniquity*—sins of *lawlessness*, especially against God, *so now present* **your members** *slaves* **to righteousness,** leading unto *sanctification*. Sanctification, here and in ver. 22, means the effect or result of consecration, *holiness* of heart and life. He would have them subject themselves as thoroughly to righteousness as they had formerly to wickedness.

20. In this verse to the end of the chapter the apostle enforces the exhortation of ver. 19, from the consequences attending each kind of service. **For** consider this fact that **when ye were the servants,** or *slaves,* **of sin,** ye **were free** so far *as respects* **righteousness—**of your own will and pleasure you acknowledged no allegiance to, no control of, righteousness; ye were free from any such relation to righteousness, as is represented by the relation of slaves to their master.

21. What fruit *therefore* **had ye then in those things whereof ye are now ashamed?** What good did your freedom do you? The answer implied is, *None.* You gained no advantage, you received no moral good. You now remember your service of sin with shame, and it yielded only death. Some end the question with *then*, thus, *What fruit therefore had ye at that time?* The answer is, *Those things of which ye are now ashamed.* This seems the more natural way of dividing the sentence. It is simpler and the thought is clearer. *Fruit* also is sometimes applied to that which is evil (7 : 5 ; Matt. 1 : 17-20 ; 12 : 33). **For the end of those things is death—**spiritual and eternal death, in contrast to *eternal life* (ver. 22).

22. But now—in contrast to your former state—**being made free from sin** as a master (see on ver. 18), **and become servants,** or *slaves,* (the same figure continued) **to God** (ver. 18), **you have your fruit unto holiness,** or *sanctification,* **and the end everlasting life**—spiritual and eternal life in contrast to death (ver. 21). Notice Paul deals with the present time looking onward to the future and full consummation, *Ye are having your fruit* issuing into *sanctification* which is thus a progressive work, and as an end of all your fruit and fruitfulness, *eternal life.* We enjoy the beginnings of eternal life here (John 3 : 36 ; Heb. 12 : 14), and its fullness hereafter (1 John 3 : 2). "As when the soul is living in sin it is not obedient to righteousness, so, when it is living in righteousness it cannot be obedient to sin. For the two are contrary one to the other" (ABBOTT).

23. Paul restates what he had said in the two preceding verses, and he does it in such a way as to show the difference in the two kinds of service which he had been contrasting. **For,** summing up and confirming what had been said, **the wages—**the word in the original signifies the pay of a soldier,

of sin *is* death; but ᵒthe gift of God *is* eternal life through Jesus Christ our Lord.

the wages of sin is death; but the gift of God is eternal life, in Christ Jesus our Lord.

ᵒ 5 : 17, 21; see refs. John 3 : 14–17; 1 John 5 : 11, 12.

and also of a servant—the *hire* that sin pays is **death,** spiritual and eternal. **But the gift of God**—that which God bestows is not viewed as wages, but as a gratuitous favor, and that gift is **eternal life,** life in its highest and noblest sense, **through,** rather *in,* **Christ Jesus our Lord.** Christ is our life (Col. 3 : 3, 4), and we have eternal life by virtue of our union with him. Notice death is wages; life a gift. The sinner earns the one; the believer receives the other. The service of sin is indeed slavery and ever downward; the service of righteousness is ennobling and ever upward, developing through God's grace into the highest liberty and the noblest form of creative existence. No wonder that Paul apologizes (ver. 19) for applying the idea of slavery to such a service. In his entire self-surrender to God, and in his devotedness to righteousness, the Christian was indeed as a slave, but in this very devotion and in this very relation he was to find his truest freedom, his highest exaltation, and the enjoyment of the crowning gift of God's favor. Notice also that the apostle ends this chapter the same as chap. 5. Whether he is tracing the results of justification or sanctification, he ends with Christ and the eternal life which comes through him.

PRACTICAL REMARKS.

1. We have in this chapter an antidote to antinomianism (ver. 2, 11, 12, 18, 22).

2. Any doctrine or system that encourages sin is not of God (ver. 1, 2; Gal. 5 : 13, 16, 21; 6 : 7).

3. It is a contradiction to profess to be a Christian and to live a life of sin (ver. 2, 3; 2 Cor. 6 : 15–17).

4. Baptism is an intelligent act, a profession of Christ, a putting on of Christ (ver. 3; Gal. 3 : 27).

5. Baptism is a burial in water and a symbolical burial of the old man with Christ (ver. 4; Col. 2 : 12).

6. Baptism is a resurrection from its watery grave, and a symbolical resurrection of the new man with Christ (ver. 5, 6; Acts 2 : 37, 38; 1 Cor. 10 : 1–4). Having reference to Christ's resurrection it, through him, implies the believer's resurrection (1 Cor. 15 : 23, 29).

7. Our union with Christ is the source and the assurance of a life of holiness (ver. 5–7; John 15 : 1–10).

8. In our fallen state life comes through death (ver. 6–8; John 12 : 24).

9. Soul crucifixion attending repentance marks, in the experience of Christians, the beginning of their life with Christ (ver. 6; Acts 2 : 37, 38; 2 Cor. 7 : 11).

10. "To be in Christ is the source of the Christian's life; to be like Christ is the sum of his excellence; to be with Christ is the fullness of his joy" (HODGE). (Ver. 5–11; Col. 3 : 3, 4; 1 John 3 : 2.)

11. Christ has broken the power of sin and through him the Christian, though still weak and imperfect, is no longer under its dominion (ver. 9, 10; 7 : 25; Rev. 1 : 18; 1 Cor. 15 : 57).

12. Faith in Christ is the means of both our justification and our sanctification (ver. 11, 22, 23; Heb. 11 : 5, 6).

13. The Christian should guard against the sins of the body as well as of the soul (ver. 12; 1 Cor. 6 : 13; 9 : 27).

14. We should devote every member of the body—hands, feet, tongue, and eyes—to Christ and his service (ver. 13; 12 : 1).

15. The Christian is not under a legal system which brings only condemnation, but under a system of grace which brings justification, holiness, and the gift of God, eternal life (ver. 14, 15, 23; 8 : 3, 4; Acts 13 : 39).

16. They who hold that under grace the moral law is of no obligation pervert both the law and the gospel (ver. 15; 8 : 4; 13 : 8–10; Gal. 5 : 14).

17. Every one is a servant either of sin or of righteousness. There can be no middle ground (ver. 16; Luke 16 : 13; Josh. 24 : 15).

18. Sin makes an infraction upon every law of our being. Its service is therefore slavery and its end death (ver. 17 : 19–21; Eph. 2 : 2, 3).

19. The service of righteousness accords

CH. VII.] ROMANS 91

Sanctification; the believer no longer under the Law which cannot save, illustrated by experience.

7 KNOW ye not, brethren, (for I speak ᵖto them that know the law,) how that the law hath dominion over a 2 man as long as he liveth? For ᵠthe woman which hath an husband is bound by the law to *her* husband so long as he liveth; but if the husband be dead, she is loosed from the law of

p 2 : 17, 18.

7 OR, are ye ignorant, brethren (for I am speaking to men who know law), that the law has dominion over the 2 man for so long time as he lives? For the married woman is bound by law to the living husband: but if the husband dies, she is loosed from the law

q Gen. 2 : 23, 24; 1 Cor. 7 : 39.

with our physical, mental, and spiritual constitution, and secures our highest good; and thus, though service, it is connected with our highest freedom. But it must be "from the heart" (ver. 17; 8 : 14–16; Gal. 5 : 13, 16).

20. All thanks and praise to God if, once the servants of sin, we are now the servants of God (ver. 17; 1 Tim. 1 : 12, 17; 1 Cor. 15 : 10).

21. In illustrating and enforcing doctrine and practice we must often take into account the mental and spiritual weakness of men (ver. 19; 1 Cor. 3 : 1–3; 1 Peter 2 : 2; John 16 : 12).

22. We should expect the Christian to remember with shame the sinful fruits of his life in impenitence (ver. 21; Eph. 5 : 12; 1 Tim. 1 : 13).

23. Under the law sinners work for wages and they get what they earn. Under the gospel the Christian's service is a consecration; salvation is through grace, and eternal life, the gracious gift of God (ver. 22, 23; 4 : 4; 8 : 13, 14; Eph. 2 : 8–10).

CHAPTER VII.

This chapter continues the discussion of the preceding chapter; and first illustrates (ver. 1–6) the believer's changed relation from law to grace by the law of marriage. He is thus devoted to Christ's spiritual service. Incidental questions then arise (ver. 7, 13), regarding the law, which he answers and illustrates from his own experience, both in his unregenerate and regenerate state, showing that sin was the great troubler of his heart, and that the evil is not in the law but in man's corrupt nature; that the law is alike powerless both for man's justification and sanctification, and that deliverance can come only through Jesus Christ (ver. 7–25).

1-6. THE BELIEVER'S CONDITION, not under law but under grace, ILLUSTRATED BY A FAMILIAR PRINCIPLE OF THE LAW OF MARRIAGE. The believer is made dead to law that he may be united to Christ.

1. Know ye not—or, *are ye ignorant*—an expression of earnest expostulation, as in 6 : 3, in support of the statement in 6 : 14. The latter part of chap. 6 is parenthetical. Having answered the objection, "Are we to sin because we are not under law, but under grace" (6 : 15), Paul now returns to the thought, "Sin shall not have dominion over you, for ye are not under law, but under grace" (6 : 14). It was a principle familiar to both Jew and Gentile, that death dissolves all legal ties. Or, if you are disposed to doubt that you are released from the law, am I to suppose *you are ignorant*, etc. **Brethren** and *my* **brethren** (ver. 4), addressed to the whole church, Jew and Gentile. **For I speak to them that know,** or *are acquainted with,* **law.** The principle he is about to state was a general legal principle, recognized both by Roman and Jewish law, but especially by the latter; and so **the law,** with undoubted reference to the Mosaic law, **hath dominion over** *the* **man,** *the human being,* male or female, *for so long a time as he liveth.*

2. Having stated the general principle, he now illustrated it by a simple case. **For,** in confirmation and illustration, **the woman that hath an husband,** rather, *is subject to a husband,* that is, a married woman, **is bound** *by law to the living husband,* while he lives (1 Cor. 7 : 39). **But if the husband** *die,* **she is loosed,** *put beyond the operation* **of the law** binding her to **her husband.** She is no longer under the influence of that law, or in

3 *her* husband. So then ¹if, while *her* husband liveth, she be married to another man, she shall be called an adulteress: but if her husband be dead, she is free from that law; so that she is no adulteress, though she be married to another man.
4 Wherefore, my brethren, ye also are become ˢdead to the law by the body of Christ: ᵗthat ye should be married to another, *even* to him who is raised from the dead, that we should ᵘbring
5 forth fruit unto God. For when we were ˣ in the flesh, the motions of sins, ʸ which were by the law, ᶻ did work in our members ᵃ to bring forth fruit unto

3 of the husband. So then if, while the husband is living, she is married to another man, she shall be called an adulteress; but if the husband dies, she is free from the law, so that she is no adulteress, though she is married to another man.
4 Wherefore, my brethren, ye also were made dead to the law through the body of Christ, that ye might be married to another, to him who was raised from the dead, in order that we
5 might bear fruit to God. For when we were in the flesh, the passions of sins, which were through the law, wrought in our members to bear fruit unto

r Matt. 5 : 32. *s* 8 : 2; Gal. 2 : 19, 20; Eph. 2 : 15; Col. 2 : 14; 1 Peter 2 : 24. *t* 2 Cor. 11 : 2; Eph. 5 : 22–32.
u See refs. 6 : 22.   *x* 8 : 5–8; Eph. 2 : 3.   *y* 3 : 20; 5 : 20.   *z* Ver. 8–13; 6 : 13.
a 6 : 21, 23; James 1 : 15.

any way affected by it. The principle is, that the relation is dissolved by the death of either party. But as believers are the bride of Christ, and are so represented elsewhere, their relation to the law and to Christ, is more aptly represented here by that of the wife to her husband (Eph. 5 : 23, 24; John 3 : 29; Rev. 2 : 2, 9).

3. So then, in view of what I have just said, **if while *the* husband liveth she be married to another man** *she shall receive the name of an* **adulteress. But if *the* husband *die*, she is free from *the* law,** relating to husband and wife, *that she may not be an adulteress,* etc. Paul now has stated the principle and given a particular illustration. In the application he uses the single fact, that death dissolves legal ties. As death dissolves the relation between husband and wife, so the believer's death in Christ dissolves his relation to the law, to which he was subject as the wife to her husband, till death dissolved the connection (ver. 4–6). In our application we must beware and not go beyond Paul. In so doing we may draw analogies that Paul never intended.

4. Therefore, my brethren, ye also, as in the case of the wife from her husband (ver. 2, 3), *were made* **dead to the law,** released from it by death, *through* **the body of Christ.** It was in his body that he suffered the penalty of sin (Col. 1 : 21, 22; 1 Peter 2 : 24; Eph. 2 : 15; Heb. 10 : 10). Even the mental sufferings of our Lord were connected with, and outwardly manifested through his bodily sufferings (Luke 22 : 44; Matt. 27 : 46). **That ye should**—expresses the design and end in view. *In order that ye might be married to another,* than the law, **to him who was raised from the dead.** They had become dead to the law through the death of Christ in order that they might be united to Christ under a new bond of love and obedience, expressed under the figure of marriage (Eph. 5 : 23, 32. Comp. 6 : 4, 9, 10). And all of this, dead to the law and married to Christ, was for this purpose, *that we might* **bring forth fruit unto God.** Notice the apostle includes himself. Fruit is the natural result, it is God's design (John 15 : 2–8). Our union with Christ is an assurance that we will not present ourselves to sin, but will bring forth fruit to God. See Gal. 5 : 22, 23 for the kind of fruit. It does not appear to have been Paul's design to represent "fruit" here under the figure of offspring.

5. In this, and the following verse, Paul confirms what he had just said, contrasting and stating more fully the difference between their present and former relation. He had hinted at it in the last clause of 6 : 14; and in the rest of this chapter he discusses it more fully. **For when we were in the flesh,** in our natural, unrenewed state (John 3 : 6), slaves to sin and rebellious against God's will, **the motions,** *the passions of sins,* that is, the sinful passions, **which were excited by the** holy restraints and requirements **of the law, did work in our members** (6 : 13) *that we should* **bring forth**

6 death. But now we are delivered from the law, *b* that being dead wherein we were held; that we should serve *c* in newness of spirit, and not *in* the oldness of the letter.

6 death. But now we have been loosed from the law, having died to that in which we were held; so that we serve in newness of the Spirit, and not in oldness of the letter.

b Ver. 4, 6:2.   *c* 6:4; 2 Cor. 3:6.

---

fruit unto death. This is enlarged upon in ver. 7-11. See Gal. 5:19, 20, for the fruits of the flesh. These lead on to, and terminate in, eternal death.

6. But now, in our new relation under grace, **we are delivered,** *loosed* or *freed* (ver. 2), **from the law,** as a ground of acceptance with God. We are not bound to it in any way as a means and ground of justification. Paul of course cannot mean that we are loosed from the requirements of the law, so far as they are not done away in Christ, for he had said that the gospel establishes the law (3:31, which see). **That being dead,** rather, *having died to that,* that is, to the law *in which* **we were held,** firmly bound as by a legal and marriage obligation. (Comp. Gal. 3:23.) It is not the law that is dead to us, but we have died to the law "through the body of Christ" (ver. 4, which see). **That,** etc., rather, *So that we serve* God, giving him a habitual service as faithful and as binding as that of a bond-servant, *in the* **newness of** *the* **spirit and not in the oldness of the letter.** Some take *spirit* for the Holy Spirit; but it is better to regard the phraseology as Hebraistic, meaning a new and spiritual service in distinction from a literal and legal service. They now served God from the free prompting of a new spiritual life, and not in the servile observance of the letter. That which was an outward requirement in the dead letter of the law has now become the living law of the spirit of the believer. (Comp. 2 Cor. 3:6.) Paul has thus shown that salvation through faith tends to holy living; that freed from the bondage of the law under which he was continually sinning, he is free to serve God in a new life.

7-25. IT IS NOT THE FAULT OF THE LAW THAT IT CANNOT SECURE THE CONVERSION AND SANCTIFICATION OF THE SINNER. The evil is in man, in the opposition of his carnal heart to the requirements of the divine law which is holy, just, and good.

Ever since the days of Augustine it has been discussed whether Paul here speaks of his own experience, and if so, whether he refers to his regenerate or unregenerate state. As he speaks in the first person the presumption is that he speaks of himself. He often in the Epistles refers to his own experience (9:1, 10:1; 1 Cor. 9:26, 27; 2 Cor. 12:1-10; Phil. 3:4-14, etc.). This is generally admitted; and also that he presents his case here as a representative one, as he does sometimes elsewhere (1 Cor. 13:11). Paul appears to have regarded himself "an example of them who should thereafter believe on him (Jesus Christ) unto eternal life" (1 Tim. 1:16). As far as ver. 14 he speaks in the past tense, and it is very generally admitted that he refers to his unregenerate state. But in regard to the rest of the chapter there is not so general an agreement. From ver. 14 however he speaks in the present tense, and the presumption is that he speaks of his present state as a Christian. This is confirmed by the fact that the experience presented (ver. 7-25) is progressive. At first he is "deceived" and "slain" by the law, yet "the law was holy" (ver. 11). Then he was brought to "consent to the law that it was good" (ver. 16); and finally he says, "I delight in the law of God after the inward man" (ver. 22). How natural to refer these expressions to his own experience, now in his unregenerate and now in his regenerate state. In the one the law is rebelled against; in the other it is approved and delighted in. So also the two natures implied, according to scriptural analogy, point to the Christian. Paul nowhere represents the unregenerate as possessing two natures as here described. But he does so represent the Christian in Gal. 5:17, "For the flesh lusteth against the Spirit, and the Spirit against the flesh; and these are contrary one to the other, so that ye may not do the things that ye would." Moreover, some of the expressions seem only applicable to

7 What shall we say then? Is the law sin? God forbid. Nay, a I had not known

7 What then shall we say? Is the law sin? Far be it! But I should not

a 3 : 20.

Christian experience. For example: "I *delight* in the law of God after the inward man" (ver. 22); "with the mind I myself serve the law of God" (ver. 25). But the Bible nowhere represents the sinner as serving that law which Paul says is spiritual. On the contrary, it represents him as dead in trespasses and sins, receiving not the things of the Spirit, neither knowing them, for they are spiritually discerned. He is blind and dead and cannot himself perceive, much less approve and delight in, the things of the Spirit.

The context and the course of argument appear to demand the above view. Paul had asserted that the Christian is not under law but under grace (6 : 14), which he illustrates and enforces in such a manner that the incidental question arises, "Is the law sin?" From ver. 7 to the end of the chapter Paul answers by showing that the evil was not in the law but in man's corrupt nature. And in doing this how natural for Paul to refer both to his unregenerate and his regenerate state, showing that not only formerly, but also at present, sin was the great troubler of his heart. Indeed, without this reference the argument would have been incomplete. For, as the gospel is not the cause of sin in the Christian's heart, so the law is not the cause of sin in the sinner's heart. Some have supposed that the context demands that this whole passage should refer to the unregenerate. Their principal arguments are founded on a *supposed antithesis* between the seventh and eighth chapters. And to show that there is such an antithesis they *presuppose* that an unrenewed man speaks throughout the seventh chapter, which is the point to be proved. Thus they reason in a circle. But as we have already shown, ver. 14-25 appear to describe a struggle often experienced in the Christian. It presents him in relation to the law in connection with an evil heart, but in the eighth chapter it views him from a different basis, under grace, with the same heart indeed, but justified, and going on in sanctification.

And finally this view of the passage accords with Christian experience. The Christian has a conflict which he did not experience in his unrenewed state. Then indeed he had a contest at times, but he yielded to the wrong with his whole heart. His conscience was perverted and his reason led him astray. He approved of sin and therefore did it. But now when he does the same things he approves not. A struggle such as he never knew in his former state takes place between the old and new man. So long as a single sin remains he struggles against it. The more he learns of himself the more does he see how deep the roots and how strong the remnants of sin are in his heart. And though he may have grown in grace many years he discovers such dregs of sin in himself and experiences such fresh conflicts that he cries out, "O wretched man that I am." Yet he sees victory at hand and exclaims, "I thank God, through Jesus Christ our Lord." For an opposite view, see Dr. A. C. Kendrick, on "The Moral Conflict of Humanity" (American Baptist Publication Society, 1894), and for a similar view see Dr. W. N. Clarke on Romans 7 : 7-25 in " Baptist Quarterly," October, 1875, p. 385 ff.

7. If the sentiment of ver. 5 and 6 be true, that to be under the law was not productive of a life of holiness (5 : 20), that it was necessary to change one's relation to God from under law to under grace, in order to bring forth fruit to God, the devout but uninstructed Jew might exclaim: **What shall we say then?** Shall we say, **Is the law sin?** Are law and sin in a certain sense convertible terms, so much so that the former cannot exist without the latter being in some way the cause of it? Is the law immoral in its tendency and sin-producing? To this the apostle gives an emphatic denial—**God forbid.** Let such a thing not be once thought of! He then proceeds to show, by the actual effect of the law upon himself, both **before** and after conversion, that it **is** only indirectly the occasion of sin; that its nature and

[CH. VII.] ROMANS 95

sin, but by the law: for I had not known lust, except the law had said,
8 *Thou shalt not covet. But ʳsin, taking occasion by the commandment, ᵍwrought in me all manner of concupiscence. For ʰ without the law sin
9 was dead. For I was alive without the law once: but when the commandment came, ⁱsin revived, and I died:
10 and the commandment, ᵏ which was *ordained* to life, I found *to be* unto

have known sin, unless through law; for I should not know coveting, if the law did not say, Thou shalt not covet.
8 But sin, finding occasion through the commandment, wrought in me all manner of coveting. For apart from
9 law, sin is dead. And I was alive apart from law once; but when the commandment came, sin revived,
10 and I died. And the commandment which was unto life, that I found to be

e See refs. Exod. 20 : 17.   f Ver. 13, 17 ; 5 : 20.   g James 1 : 14, 15.   h 4 : 15 ; 1 Cor. 15 . 56.
i Ver. 8, 21–23.   k See refs. Luke 18 : 5.

influence are holy and good, and that the evil is in us. In this verse he says it was the law that taught him what sin is. **Nay,** rather, *But,* **I had not known sin,** *except through* **the law; for I had not known lust,** *evil desire* or *coveting,* **except** the law had said, **Thou shalt not covet** (Exod. 20 : 17). He would not have known sin as sin, nor regarded it as such, except through the law. For example, it was the law that showed him the sin of coveting, both as a matter of judgment and of experience (next verse).

8. But sin. Notice that *sin* here is more than an isolated transgression. It is personified, and means the depraved principle or tendency in man's moral nature. It also includes to a greater or less extent a sense of guilt, and the painful consciousness of wrong. **But sin,** the evil principle within me, **taking,** or *finding,* **occasion** *through* **the commandment,** which forbade the natural but wrong desire, defining its character, showing that to be sinful which otherwise might have been regarded as natural and innocent, **wrought in me all manner of concupiscence,** *of evil desire* or *coveting.* What this evil principle had prompted me to do without regarding it as wrong, now, when enlightened by the commandment, it still prompts me to do, with the knowledge that it is sinful. And this extended to all evil desires of every kind. The commandment only forbade; it did not give power to refrain. **For** *apart from* **law, sin is dead.** Where there is no law to fix and define particular acts of transgression, and hence no intentional violation of law and right, *sin is dead,* dormant and has no life, so to speak; there is no sense of sin and of guilt. The evil in the heart is com-

paratively inactive, until excited by the law's restraints. It is natural for the evil heart to strive for what is forbidden, and to desire what is denied (Prov. 9 : 17. Comp. 1 Cor. 15 : 56). What is true of the written law, is true also of the inner law of man's moral nature. (See 2 : 14, 15.)

9. The last clause of the preceding verse Paul corroborates from his own experience. **For,** rather, *And,* **I was alive**—*was living,* having a sense of personal rectitude and a feeling of security, peaceful and self-satisfied, **without,** or *apart from,* **the law once,** before the law with its spiritual and heart-searching requirements came home to my conscience. He cannot mean that he was not under the law or ignorant of it, for he knew it from childhood, but that he was insensible to its spirituality and to the extent of its requirements. *Once* is general and indefinite, and refers to the period before conversion, and may include both the innocent period of childhood and also that of his Pharisaic self-righteousness and blindness to the law. **But when the commandment**—some particular requirement, like that mentioned in ver. 7—**came,** vividly and powerfully to my consciousness and conscience, **sin revived**—sprang into life, being no longer dead—**and I died,** I lost my personal sense of rectitude and feeling of security, and under a sense of sin I was conscious of guilt and exposure to Divine wrath. He found the law exceeding broad and far too strict for him. And this may have occurred repeatedly, as in the experience of most unconverted persons.

10. And the commandment which was ordained to life, rather, *which was unto life,* designed originally for it and leading to it. The

11 death. For ᶦsin, taking occasion by the commandment, ᵐdeceived me, and
12 by it slew me. Wherefore ⁿthe law is holy, and the commandment holy, and just, and good.
13 ºWas then that which is good made death unto me? God forbid. But sin, that it might appear sin, working death in me by that which is good; that sin by the commandment might become exceed-

11 unto death. For sin, finding occasion through the commandment deceived
12 me, and through it slew me. So that the law is holy, and the commandment holy and righteous and good.
13 Did then that which is good become death to me? Far be it! But sin, that it might be shown to be sin, by working death to me through that which is good; that sin through the commandment might become exceedingly sin-

l Ver. 8, 13.   *m* Eph. 4 : 22 ; Heb. 3 : 13.   *n* Ver. 14 ; Ps. 19 : 7-9 ; 1 Tim. 1 : 8.   *o* Ver. 7.

law was given that man might know God's will, and doing it enjoy his favor. A perfect life and perfect obedience would have insured life and well-being (Luke 10 : 28). **I found to be unto death**—leading into death, into a conscious loss of God's favor and of self-righteous peace and security, into a conviction of sin and of **exposure** to the Divine wrath.

11. The apostle explains how in his experience he found the commandment to be unto death. **For sin taking, or** *finding*, **occasion** *through* **the commandment**—as in ver. 8 (which see). **Deceived and seduced me.** Sin, personified under the figure of an enemy, used the commandment as a basis and means of temptation, as the serpent did to Eve (Gen. 3 : 1, 4, 5), and as Satan did to Christ (Matt. 4 : 6), and thus lured him on from the right way to destruction (2 Cor. 11 : 3). **And by it slew me**—destroyed his false security and his sense of rectitude, as in ver. 9. Thus the effect of the law upon his conscience was to disclose his actual condition, and cut off the hope of God's favor, without providing a remedy. He saw himself a lost sinner under the condemnation of God's holy law.

12. From these facts in Paul's experience, by which he showed that the law brought sin to view in its true character (ver. 8) and aroused his conscience to a sense of sin and guilt (ver. 9-11), it follows that the law is not to blame, that it is not sin, nor the colleague of sin, but the very opposite. **Where-fore**, or, *So that*, **the law**, as a whole, **is holy** in its own nature and as a revelation demanding holiness, **and the commandment**, any particular command in the law **is holy**, being of the same in nature as the law itself, **and just**, *righteous*, in its claims and sanctions, and in its relation both

to God **and men, and good**, salutary and beneficial in its aims and tendencies.

13. The statement that the commandment was good might appear inconsistent with the statement in ver. 10, that he had found the commandment to be unto death. Paul therefore resumes the thought and anticipates an objection. Was then that which **was** good made death to me, or, *Did* it then *become death to me?* Was it the direct and immediate cause of this death of which I speak? This he most emphatically **denies.** *Let it not be thought of!* **But sin** became death unto me, that **it might appear sin,** and be shown to be sin, *by working out death to me through* **that which is good ; that** sin *through* **the commandment,** which in its nature, aims, and tendency is good, **might become exceeding,** or *beyond measure,* sinful. The commandment furnished the ground **or occasion** for the inward depravity to manifest itself, and **to** show outwardly its malignant character, by making such base use of that which is good and bringing forth such disastrous results. The law gave the knowledge of sin (3 : 20), defined transgression (4 : 15), and brought wrath **and condemnation.** Thus the law **led on to death; but it was** sin that caused the death, and thus in the light of the good, in opposition to the good, **and in the perversion of the** good, **it showed its true nature and** real **character as sin**, *pre-eminently sinful.*

14. There is manifestly a change in this verse in point of view. The change to the present tense is surely not accidental, nor merely rhetorical; nor is it to be explained merely by the vividness of Paul's conception. The most natural reason is that he includes his present **state as a Christian.** His vividness

14 ing sinful. For we know that ᵖthe law is spiritual: but I am carnal, ᵍ sold
15 under sin. For that which I do I allow not: for ʳ what I would, that do
16 I not; but what I hate, that do I. If then I do that which I would not, I consent unto the law that *it is* good.

14 ful. For we know that the law is spiritual: but I am carnal, sold under sin.
15 For what I perform, I know not; for not what I wish, that do I practice;
16 but what I hate, that I do. But if what I wish not, that I do, I consent to

p Matt. 5 : 22, 28; Heb. 4 : 12. *q* Ver. 23; 1 Kings 21 : 20, 25; 2 Kings 17 : 17. *r* Gal. 5 : 17.

would naturally increase as he progressed from past to present experience. The train of thought in ver. 14–16 accords with such a transition to his renewed state. The sentiment in this verse can be applied, though not in the same degree, to both the renewed and unrenewed man, and appears to be so expressed as not to exclude either. This was perfectly natural in such a transition. While it is true that the natural man sins against his better judgment and conscience, it is true in a higher sense of the renewed man, and it is evident from what follows that the apostle's mind was fixed more directly on the latter (ver. 18, 22, 25). See discussion at the beginning of this section. **For** introduces the reasons why the results stated in the preceding verse necessarily take place, namely, That the law and its subjects are different in their natures; the requirements of the former do not accord with the nature of the latter, hence a conflict. **For we,** as Christians, **know that the law is spiritual** in its quality, nature, and character, being a transcript of God's holy will, requiring spiritual service and spiritual purity. **But I am carnal,** *fleshly,* living in the flesh, being more or less under its influence, having fleshly appetites and passions to contend against, and to lead me astray. Paul here points to his human nature apart from divine grace. That he could thus refer to himself as a Christian is evident, for he addresses the Corinthians "as carnal, as babes in Christ" (1 Cor. 3 : 1). There are two adjectives in Greek, derived from the noun meaning flesh, differing in form only by a single letter and by the position of the accent, the one referring more to flesh as the material, *fleshy* (2 Cor. 3 : 3), the other to the quality, *fleshly* (1 Cor. 9 : 11). The former, according to most manuscripts, is used here and in 1 Cor. 3 : 1, and 2 Cor. 3 : 3; the latter in 15 : 27; 1 Cor. 3 : 3; 9 : 11; 2 Cor. 1 : 12; 10 : 4;

Heb. 7 : 16, and 1 Peter 2 : 11. In later Greek the forms were often confounded and there appears to have been some confusion in their use, so that the difference in their meaning was not always marked. Thus in 1 Cor. 3 : 1 the first is applied to the Corinthian Christians, and immediately in ver. 3 the second is twice applied to them in about the same sense. "There is," says PROF. BOISE, "no important distinction between them. See Liddell and Scott." **Sold under sin,** *having been sold under sin* in his past state, the result of the bondage still continuing. Notice how applicable this is to the renewed man, for it may denote unwilling bondage; and every Christian is more or less an unwilling servant to sin, while the unrenewed man is its willing slave. Paul's terrible conflicts with the remains of sin in his own heart makes him use strong language.

15. Paul confirms and explains what he had just said, continuing the figure of one in bondage, "sold under sin." **For that which I do,** or *perform* in action. **I allow not**—rather, *I know not,* I do it unknowingly, like a slave who acts blindly at the bidding of another—the act is unintelligent, and my soul does not recognize it as really its own. **For what I would,** etc.— rather, *For not what I wish do I practise,* the practice of my life by no means comes up to my desire; **but what I hate, that do I**—I find that I am doing acts that I hate. All this is the evidence of the power of sin in me. Many Christians have found these words descriptive of their inward conflicts. The struggle is between the better self, the renewed nature and the lower nature, the remains of sin, as appears from what follows (ver. 17 ff.).

16. Paul clinches the argument and exculpates the law. **If then I do that which I would not,** or, *which I wish not,* **I consent to the law that it is good**—my unwillingness to do

G

17 Now then it is no more I that do it,
18 but sin that dwelleth in me. For I know that *in me (that is, in my flesh,) dwelleth no good thing: for to will is present with me; but *how* to perform
19 that which is good I find not. For the good that I would, I do not: but the evil which I would not, that I do.
20 Now if I do that I would not, it is no more I that do it, but sin that dwelleth

17 the law that it is good. Now then, it is no longer I that perform it, but the
18 sin that dwells in me. For I know that there dwells not in me, that is, in my flesh, any good: for to wish is present with me; but to perform that
19 which is good is not. For the good that I wish, I do not; but the evil that
20 I wish not, that I practice. But if what I wish not, that I do, it is no

Ver. 23.   † See refs. Gen. 6 : 5; Ps. 51 : 5; Isa. 64 . 6.   u Ver. 15, 25.

wrong bears witness to the excellence of the law. It is a recognition and a confession that the law is right. It also indicates that there is a better nature in me, distinct from and in conflict with the old nature of sin which dwells in me (ver. 17).

17. In this and the three following verses, the apostle shows that it is the influence of indwelling sin which prevents his perfect obedience to God's law. **Now then**, or, *But now*, as things now are, suggestive of the fact that there was a time when there was not this inward struggle, **it is no more I that do it**—better, *it is no longer I that perform it*, my true and better self is not the prime mover, **but sin that dwelleth in me**. The word translated **do,** or *perform*, means *to work out*, and expresses here the primary efficient cause. Indwelling sin, the old man, is the primary cause of disobedience, and this the apostle proceeds to illustrate in ver. 18, 19.

18. For I know, by experience, **that in me, that is, in my flesh,** in my lower carnal nature, **dwelleth,** referring to the language of the preceding verse, **no good thing.** This shows that Paul recognized in himself both a higher spiritual, and a lower carnal nature. He further explains: **For to will,** better, *to wish*, **is present with me, but how to perform,** etc., rather, *but to perform that which is good is not* present with me. **I find not**—should be omitted, according to the best authorities. The verb **to will** is found seven times in this section, and is translated, *would* except here. It may be rendered *will* or *wish*. Its contrast to *I hate* (ver. 15) indicates that its meaning partakes largely of the emotions, the desires, hence *to wish*. "This is not *the full determination of the will*, the standing with the bow drawn and the arrow aimed,

but rather the *inclination* of the will— the taking up the bow and pointing at the mark" (ALFORD).

19. Explains the preceding clause. **For the good that I** *wish*, **I do not,** *I am not doing*, **but the evil which** *I do not wish*, **that I practise.** This is popular language of every-day life, intended to be understood by the common mind. The apostle does not say that he ever did any particular act which his will opposed at the moment of doing it. This would be impossible in any one. He is rather looking at the habit and currents of his life, his desires for the good which he failed to attain on account of the inroads of evil. And what was this good? Was it not conformity to the Divine will, perfect obedience to the divine law? Every failure would lead him to say, "The good I wish, I do not." On the other hand, any departure from this perfect standard, any wandering of the affections from God, any conformity to the world, would lead him to say, "The evil I wish not, that I practise," "What I hate that do I." The Christian is more or less liable to such experiences. Bunyan thus expresses himself: "The evil that dwells in me is so universal, that as sure as there is any motion to what is good, so sure is evil present with us. Desires come warm with the Spirit and grace of God in us, but as warm waters running through cold pipes, or as clear water running through dirty conveyances, so our desires are chilled and defiled by the corruptions of the flesh" (Condensed from "Devotional Works," pp. 210–215).

20. A conclusion drawn from the two preceding verses, thereby restating and confirming what he had said in ver. 19. **For the good that I** *wish*, **I do not; but the evil I** *wish* **not, that I** *practise.* There has been an advance in thought since ver. 17. The

21 in me. I find then a law, that, when I would do good, evil is present with 22 me. For I *delight in the law of God 23 after *y* the inward man: but *a* I see another law in *b* my members, warring against the law of my mind, and *b* bringing me into captivity to the law 24 of sin which is in my members. *c* O more I that perform it, but the sin that 21 dwells in me. I find then the law, that, when I wish to do good, evil is 22 present with me. For I delight in the 23 law of God after the inward man. But I see a different law in my members, warring against the law of my mind, and bringing me into captivity to the law of sin which is in my members

x Ps. 1 : 2 ; 19 : 7–11 ; 119 : 97–104.   *y* 2 Cor. 4 : 16 ; Eph. 3 : 16.   *z* 8 : 2 ; Gal. 5 : 17.
a 6 : 13, 19.   *b* Ver. 14.   *c* 1 Kings 8 : 38.

apostle makes it clearer, that it is the higher and better self that wishes the good, and that it is the lower self in which sin rules. And so the way is prepared for the important conclusion in the next verse.

21. General conclusion of ver. 17–20. **I find then** *the* **law** under which I stand, this law of my being, **that when I** *wish to* **do good, evil is present with me.** Some suppose the law of Moses to be meant. But most expositors take law in the sense of principle, which is the most natural and simplest interpretation. Paul found himself subjected to this law of his being—that opposite principles or elements were co-existing in him, and contending for the mastery. This is true in a certain sense of the unconverted who sin against their reason and conscience, but it is true in a higher degree of the Christian. That this is its reference is evident from the next verse.

22. Confirming and explaining what he had just said. **For I delight,** or *take pleasure,* **in the law of God,** that law which is from God and of which he is the author, **after,** or *according to,* **the inward man.** Notice that *delight* is a stronger word than *consent* in ver. 16. It expresses the pleasure that the renewed soul takes in God's commandments. Thus the psalmist exclaimed, "Oh, how love I thy law! I will delight myself in thy statutes" (Ps. 119 : 16, 97). This emotion of pleasure is very different from that feeling of dread of the law in the unrenewed heart, which sometimes arouses a conflict. *Inward man* is a Pauline phrase, found besides here in 2 Cor. 4 : 16 and Eph. 3 : 16, in both of which the Christian is spoken of in reference to his intelligent moral nature, acted upon, renewed, and strengthened by the Holy Spirit. And in this verse the *inward* man must be in a renewed state in order to *delight* in the law of God. Moreover, *inward man* is in opposition to *members* in the next verse, which appears to have the same application as "flesh" in ver. 18, which means his lower, carnal nature, and therefore inward man naturally refers to his higher or moral nature as renewed. (Comp. 1 Peter 3 : 4.) See also next verse on *mind.*

23. But, alas! **I see another** and *different* **law in my members** (ver. 5 ; 6 : 13) **warring against the law of my mind.** *Members* are properly the limbs and organs of the body, but since moral actions cannot be ascribed to the material members of the body the word takes a figurative sense like "flesh," meaning the lower, unsanctified propensities of our natures. It is used in opposition to *inward man* of the last verse and of *mind* in this verse. The *law in my members* is **the law of sin which is in my members,** the principle of evil (ver. 21) which still has a seat and exercises power in the tendencies and remaining corruptions of my nature. *The law of my mind* is the opposite of "the law in my members," and refers not to the law of God but rather to that principle (ver. 21) that has its seat, and exercises control in the mind, in delighting in and serving the law of God (ver. 22, 25). In opposition to "my members" *my mind*—strictly my reason or understanding—has a wider reference to the inward man (ver. 22). According to Eph. 4 : 23 the mind is subject to the renewing of the Holy Spirit. In ver. 25 it is opposed to "the flesh," the lower sinful propensities. The manifest reference therefore is to the renewed or sanctified nature. The Christian goes against the dictates of his enlightened reason and conscience when he yields to the lower sinful propensities. Pagan and Pla-

wretched man that I am! Who shall deliver me from *the body of this death? ʳI thank God through Jesus Christ our Lord. ᶠSo then with the mind I myself serve the law of God; but with the flesh the law of sin.

24 Wretched man that I am! Who will deliver me from the body of this death? Thanks be to God, through Jesus Christ our Lord! So then I myself with the mind serve the law of God, but with the flesh the law of sin.

d 6:6. *e* Matt. 1:21; 1 Cor. 15:57; 2 Cor. 12:9, 10. *f* Gal. 5:17-24.

tonic ideas of the inner and outer man should be guarded against. Plato regarded the body as the corrupt part of man, and the intellect and reason as the purer and nobler part, the latter obstructed, corrupted, and debased by the former. But the Scriptures place the seat of evil in the moral nature, by which the understanding and reason are perverted and misled. The mind is defiled and needs renewing; and by a depraved will the members of the body are used as instruments of unrighteousness. **Bringing me,** in the act of bringing my real self, **into captivity,** though not ultimately, and only partially successful. The verb in the original is very strong, *taking captive by the spear,* forcibly and against one's will. And this captivity would have been complete and final except for the victory through Christ (ver. 25). Note the three laws, "law of God," "law of sin," and "law of my mind."

24. The apostle reaches the climax of this terrible experience. It is the agonizing cry of what he then felt, longing for complete deliverance from a bondage which he hated. **O wretched man that I am!** *O me, miserable man!* **Who shall deliver me from the body of this death?** "the body of sin" (6:6), with its passions of sin bringing forth fruit unto death (ver. 5)— this state of sin leading to death, which is the wages of sin (6:23). This is the earnest and ever-present longing of the spiritually minded soul for deliverance from the power of sin. The higher the attainment the more terrible is the presence of any influence of sin. This accords with Paul's experience and language regarding himself. Before his conversion, in the light of the letter of the law he was "blameless" (Phil. 3:6); in A. D. 58, with over twenty years' growth as a Christian, he views himself "the least of the apostles, not fit to be called an apostle" (1 Cor. 15:9); in A. D. 63, with his increased spiritual knowledge, he styles himself "less than the least of all saints" (Eph. 3:8); and in A. D. 65, nearer the goal of final victory, he is in his own estimation "the chief of sinners" (1 Tim. 1:15). Some have likened the body of this death to the dead carcass which was sometimes tied to criminals to drag around wherever they went. This is better as an illustration than an interpretation.

25. But his exclamation was not a wail of despair, but rather of agony, in view of sin, and its remaining power within him, and of longing for deliverance of which he was assured through faith. **I thank God,** rather, according to the best reading, *thanks to God,* I have deliverance **through Jesus Christ our Lord.** A joyous outburst of thanksgiving for the deliverance assured him and already partially experienced through Christ. Paul is not representing the Christian life as merely a conflict. He is showing that the evil is not in the law but in the heart. Though he has a struggle he is under grace (6:14). As he advances in the divine life the power of sin within him grows less, though he may have deeper views of himself. He may generally overcome, but when he yields to its power he has new evidence of the strength of sin in his heart, which requires so much grace to overcome it, and he cries out: "Wretched me! Who shall deliver me?" But he sees victory at hand and exclaims, "Through Jesus Christ our Lord!" **So then,** summing up the whole passage especially from ver. 14, **with the mind,** renewed by the spirit (ver. 23), **I myself,** that which really constitutes me, **serve the law of God,** showing that it is holy and good; **but with the flesh,** my lower, corrupt, unsanctified nature (ver. 18), **the law of sin,** showing that the evil in me is the cause of the trouble. Thus the questions are answered: "Is the law sin?" (ver. 7) and "Did then that which was good become death to me?" (ver. 13.) The answer to both is, No. It is the evil in me that is sin and germinates sin, and leads on to death. Notice that *mind* and *flesh* are placed in opposition to each other, representing the new and old man. Since the law is spiritual and its requirements are not met by one that is carnal (ver. 14), nor with the *flesh* (this verse), it follows that *the mind* which serves the law of God is spiritual and renewed. We see also the position of these two natures: The higher, spiritual nature on the one hand, and the lower, carnal nature, with its appetites and passions, on the other. And also that the renewed nature is the stronger. For Paul, before his conversion, was under the entire control of the flesh; but now as a Christian he serves God in spite of his flesh, overcoming its opposition and crucifying its affections and lusts. See next chapter.

PRACTICAL REMARKS.

1. The marriage contract is for life. That which is ratified by God, can be annulled only according to his word (ver. 1, 2; Matt. 19 : 6-9 ; 1 Cor. 7 : 15).

2. To be under grace does not imply liberty to sin, for that would entail slavery to sin; but rather deliverance from the law, as a covenant of works and a ground of justification (ver. 1-6; 6 : 12-14).

3. The Christian is bound and subject to Christ in a living and inseparable union, symbolized by the marriage relation (ver. 2-6; 8 : 35-39).

4. Sin is active and dominant in our unregenerate state, and its fruit is death (ver. 5; 6 : 20).

5. Through faith we are united to Christ, and its fruit is a life unto God (ver. 4 6; 6 : 22, 23).

6. The freedom of the Christian is in his filial spirit and his prevailing desire to obey God (ver. 6 ; 8 : 2-4).

7. The law serves an important purpose in the salvation of men, in enlightening and educating the conscience (ver. 7, 8; Ps. 19 : 7, 8).

8. The law of God should be faithfully preached, for while it cannot save, it prepares the way for salvation (ver. 8 ; 2 Cor. 5 : 11 ; Gal. 3 : 24).

9. A correct view of the spirituality and extent of the law is necessary to a right knowledge of the nature and power of sin (ver. 9-11, 14; Matt. 5 : 22, 28).

10. Conviction of sin is an essential part of an experience from death unto life (ver. 9-11 ; John 16 : 9 ; Acts 2 : 37; 1 Cor. 14 : 24, 25).

11. Paul's religion was rooted in an experience. Our religion should be experimental (ver. 11, 13; Acts 22 and 26; Gal. 1 : 15, 16; Eph. 2 : 4, 5).

12. The more we truly know ourselves, the more are we convinced of the purity of God's law; and the holier we are, the clearer are our views of its requirements (ver. 12, 16 ; 2 Peter 3 : 18).

13. The heinousness of sin is seen in its opposition to holiness, and to a holy law (ver. 8, 11, 13).

14. The law is spiritual, demanding spiritual service, which the carnal heart, from its own nature, is unable to give (ver. 14 ; 8 : 7, 8).

15. The regenerate heart sins not willingly nor knowingly (ver. 14, 15; John 5 : 18).

16. It is an evidence of the new nature that it hates sin, and approves and delights in the law of God (ver. 16, 22; 2 Cor. 5 : 17; Gal. 6 : 15).

17. There are two principles in the Christian—the higher and the lower—the new and the old man (ver. 17, 18, 21, 22, 23 ; Gal. 5 : 17).

18. The religious life is necessarily a conflict. Religion is aggressive, and it must struggle against sin, so long as it remains (ver. 19-21; Gal. 5 : 17 ; 2 Cor. 6 : 14).

19. The new nature in the Christian is the higher and the stronger. It is that which makes the man, and generally rules the Christian (ver. 20, 22, 25 ; 1 Cor. 9 : 27; Eph. 4 : 20-24).

20. Learn the cause of religious declension—not keeping up the conflict (ver. 16-21; 1 Cor. 10 : 12 ; Rev. 2 : 4).

21. Paul's experience affords no apology for sin. It is rather a self-condemnation on account of sin, and a longing to be freed from its power (ver. 14, 24).

22. Learn the deep depravity of the human heart. "In me, that is, in my flesh, dwelleth no good thing" (ver. 18, 21-24; Jer. 17 : 9).

23. Paul could not save himself, nei-

Sanctification; the salvation of the believer in Christ, present, complete and eternal.

8 THERE is therefore now ᵍno condemnation to them which are ʰ in Christ Jesus, who ⁱ walk not after 2 the flesh, but after the Spirit. For ᵏ the law of ˡ the Spirit of life in Christ

8 THERE is therefore now no condemnation to those who are in Christ 2 Jesus. For the law of the Spirit of life in Christ Jesus set me free from

g John 3 : 18, 36 ; 5 : 24.   *h* John 15 : 4 ; Phil. 3 : 9.   *i* Gal. 5 : 16, 19-25.   *k* 6 : 18, 22 ; John 8 : 36.
l Ver. 10, 11 ; John 7 : 38, 39 ; 1 Cor. 15 : 45 ; 2 Cor. 3 : 6.

ther could his good resolutions save him (ver. 14, 18, 21).
24. The Christian's salvation and victory over sin are only through Jesus Christ (ver. 25 ; 8 : 37 ; 1 Cor. 15 : 57).
25. The Christian finds his greatest enemy in his own heart (ver. 23-25).
26. If the Christian must meet such conflicts, how helpless the sinner (ver. 24, 25 ; 1 Peter 4 : 18).

CHAPTER VIII.

Paul had presented the Christian with the remains of sin in his heart, in relation to the law ; he now proceeds to view him in relation to grace, free from condemnation, a spiritual child of God, whose Spirit dwells within him, producing and maintaining both purity of life and right affections toward God (ver. 1-17). True, all God's children suffer here, yet these sufferings are not inconsistent with their sonship. Having suffered with Christ they shall be glorified with him. Thus their sufferings will be outweighed by the glory that will result from them ; and so work for their good, according to the will and the high purpose of God (ver. 17-30). The final issue is thus assured. God is for us, and nothing can break that bond, of his own will and love, between him and us (ver. 31-39). The apostle treats here of sanctification in the believer, but as inseparably connected with his justification. The chapter really presents the results of the apostle's discussion thus far.

1-17. NO CONDEMNATION NOW RESTS ON THE BELIEVER. Christ has delivered us from the law of sin and death, and brought us into the new relationship of spiritual children to God. What the law could not do, God has accomplished by Christ, under the guidance of the Spirit in us (ver. 3-8). Believers are not in the flesh, but in the Spirit ; and the Spirit of Christ is a Spirit of life, which ends in a glorious resurrection of the body (ver. 9-11). We are therefore not debtors to live according to the flesh, but led by the Spirit we are sons of God and sure of the glory to come. Having received the spirit of sonship, we have become heirs of God and joint-heirs with Christ (ver. 12-17).

1. There is therefore—in view of the whole discussion thus far, especially 5 : 1 to 7 : 6, and of the deliverance through Jesus Christ (7 : 25). The discussion in 7 : 7-25 is however somewhat incidental, and complete in itself, and ends with the assertion that the struggle of the soul still exists. The eighth chapter does not suppose the struggle ended, but rather its continuance with faith and hope, led on and invigorated by the Holy Spirit. It is a life conflict, but a successful one (1 Cor. 9 : 26, 27 ; Phil. 3 : 10-16 ; 2 Tim. 4 : 7, 8). **Now**—under the gospel. **No**—emphatic. From the very nature of the case there can be *no* condemnation, it is not to be thought of. **Condemnation**—condemnatory sentence or judgment resulting from sin ; suggested by 5 : 16, 18, where the word here used, is only found elsewhere in the New Testament. **In Christ Jesus**—in fellowship with him (6 : 11 ; 12 : 5 ; 2 Cor. 5 : 17. Comp. Eph. 5 : 30). The phrase expresses our relation to God, which relation the apostle develops in the next seven verses. Such "shall not come into condemnation, but are passed from death unto life" (John 5 : 24. Comp. ver. 34). **Who walk . . . Spirit.** This sentence belongs to ver. 4, and is omitted here by the best text.

2. For—introduces the reason of the foregoing statement. **For the law** of the Spirit, the rule and principle by which the Spirit works, producing holy love and obedience. **Of the Spirit**—the Holy Spirit, who is the giver of spiritual and eternal *life* (John 7 : 39 ; 1 Peter 1 : 2 ; Rom. 5 : 18). The Holy Spirit ap-

Jesus hath made me free from the law of sin and death. For ᵐ what the law could not do, in that ⁰ it was weak through the flesh, God sending his own Son ᵉ in the likeness of sinful flesh, and ᴾ for sin, ᑫ condemned sin in 4 the flesh; ʳ that the righteousness of the law might be fulfilled in us, who walk not after the flesh, but after the Spirit.

3 the law of sin and death. For—what the law could not do, in that it was weak through the flesh—God, sending his own Son in the likeness of sinful flesh and for sin, condemned sin in the 4 flesh; that the requirement of the law might be fulfilled in us, who walk not according to the flesh, but according

m 3 : 20 ; Gal. 3 : 21 ; Heb. 7 : 18, 19.   n 7 : 5–11.   o Phil. 2 : 7 ; Heb. 2 : 17.   p Heb. 10 : 1–14.
q 1 Peter 4 : 1, 2.   r Col. 1 : 22 ; Jude 24.

pears to be meant, as it is the reference and meaning of the word generally throughout the whole chapter. **In Christ Jesus**—the believer's union and relation to him. (See on ver. 1.) **Hath made me free**—*set me free*, referring to a definite past time, when he was justified and accepted in Christ. The same thought as expressed in 7 : 4–6. **From the law of sin and death**—the outer law of works, whether it is the Mosaic law or any code of morality and ceremony on which a person depends. Any such law leads to sin and death, and is incapable of producing holiness of heart and life (2 Cor. 3 : 6; Gal. 2 : 19, 20). Paul looks back to his justification when he was delivered from the condemning power of the law because Christ had satisfied all its claims, and at the same time he views the working of the Spirit who dwells in us. Both justification and sanctification are essential to salvation (ver. 4).

3. **For**—introduces another consideration, expressed in this verse and the next, in support of the statement in ver. 1. It is thus confirmatory of the preceding verse. **What the law could not do**—it could not render satisfaction for sin and free man from its guilt and power (Acts 13 : 39 ; Gal. 3 : 21 ; Heb. 7 : 18, 19). **In that it was weak through the flesh.** The fault was not in the law, which was holy, righteous, and good (7 : 12), but in man's sinful nature (7 : 7–13). **God sending his own Son**—recognizing the pre-existence of Christ. **In the likeness of sinful flesh**—not in our flesh of sin, but in its *likeness*, liable to all its needs and infirmities, and tempted in all points as we are, though in him was no sin (Heb. 4 : 15; 1 Peter 2 : 22 ; Phil. 2 : 7). **And for sin**, or, *on account of sin*—a general but emphatic idea. It was on account of sin that God sent his Son in order that he might expiate it and destroy it. He was manifested to take away sins, and destroy the works of the devil (1 John 3 : 5, 8). **Condemned sin in the flesh**—in the very nature which he had assumed: in our nature he suffered the penalty of sin (7 : 4; Heb. 2 : 10; 1 Peter 2 : 24) and kept the law perfectly (1 Peter 2 : 22 ; Heb. 7 : 26), exhibiting the righteousness of the law and its adaptability to men. Thus he condemned sin, *decided against* it, and did judgment upon it, exposing and condemning its malignity, breaking its power, and procuring its overthrow. Thus also he did what the law could not do—subduing sin in us by the indwelling Spirit and fulfilling the law in those that believe (next verse).

4. The object of all this. **That the righteousness**—*the things accounted right*—that is, *the requirements*, the righteous precepts of the law. (See on 1 : 17 (5) : 2 : 26.) **Might be fulfilled in us**—that these requirements of the law might be met and performed in us who walk, etc. Not only is Christ's righteousness accounted to us in justification, but it results in a life of faith and obedience through the Spirit in our sanctification (Heb. 8 : 10–12). **Who walk not**—*those walking not according to the flesh, but according to the Spirit*—according to his dictates, following him as a guide. The idea is not absolute perfection, for this is not attainable in our present state (1 John 1 : 8), but so far as they do walk. (Comp. 1 John 5 : 18.) "Whosoever is born of God sinneth not," that is, so far as he is born of God, since nothing unholy can proceed from God. So of the renewed man, so far as he is spiritually minded, his aims and services are in complete obedience to the divine law. This accords also with the conflict described in 7 : 7–25. It is because the Christian is

5 For *they that are after the flesh do mind the things of the flesh; but they that are after the spirit *the things of
6 the Spirit. For "to be carnally minded is death; but to be spiritually minded
7 is life and peace. Because *the carnal mind is enmity against God: for it is not subject to the law of God, *neither in-
8 deed can be. So then they that are in the flesh cannot please God.
9 But ye are not in the flesh, but in the Spirit, if so be that *the Spirit of

5 to the Spirit. For they that are according to the flesh mind the things of the flesh; but they that are according to the spirit, the things of the Spirit.
6 For the mind of the flesh is death; but the mind of the Spirit is life and
7 peace. Because the mind of the flesh is enmity against God; for .t does not subject itself to the law of God,
8 neither indeed can it; and they that are in the flesh can not please God.
9 But ye are not in the flesh, but in the Spirit, if indeed the Spirit of God

s John 3 : 6 ; 1 Cor. 2 : 14.   *t* Gal. 5 : 22, 25.   *u* Ver. 13 ; 6 : 21, 23 ; Eph. 5 : 3-5.
v 1 : 28-30 ; James 4 : 4 ; 1 John 2 : 15, 16.   *x* 1 Cor. 2 : 14.   *y* 1 Cor. 3 : 16.

walking according to the Spirit that the conflict occurs. If he did not thus walk there would be no conflict, but the law of sin in his members would have full control.

5. Development and confirmation of the preceding clause. **For they that are after the flesh**—presenting the state of those "who walk after the flesh." **Do mind the things of the flesh**—are carnally minded. Earthly things are the objects of their choice, and with them they are fully occupied and engrossed. **They that are after the Spirit**—in a state of regeneration, who have the presence of the Holy Spirit, and are under his influence. Paul knows of but two classes among men. **The things of the Spirit**—are spiritually minded, guided by the Spirit, and loving spiritual things (Col. 3 : 2 ; Phil. 3 : 19, 20 ; Rom. 12 : 16).

6. For—explanatory, introducing a radical difference between being carnally minded and spiritually minded, and thereby making it evident that only the latter is not subject to condemnation. **To be carnally minded**—or, *The mind of the flesh*, the thought and purposes of the soul devoted to earthly things, and under their control. The words are descriptive of the unrenewed state of man, estranged from God. Such a state is **death**, alienation from God, and leading on to eternal death. Death never means annihilation in Scripture. **To be spiritually minded**—or, *The mind of the Spirit*—the thoughts, purposes, and affections imbued with the Spirit, and under his control. Descriptive of the renewed state. Such a state is **life**, in the enjoyment of God's favor, in fellowship with him, and leading on in eternal life. Connected also with religious **peace**, which is an evidence of a justified state (5 : 1).

7. Because—introduces the reason of the preceding assertion. **The carnal mind**, or the mind of the flesh—the natural unrenewed state, the same as in the preceding verse. **Is enmity against God**—is opposed to the Divine will, and in its very nature is at war with the Divine nature, which is holiness and love. Sin and holiness, hatred and love, are diametrically opposed. **For it is not subject**—or better, *for it does not subject itself to the law of God;* it persists in disobedience and rebellion. **Neither indeed can be**—better, *Neither indeed can it* submit itself. It is incapable of so doing, for that would involve a change of its own nature, and it cannot change itself. In its own nature it is the very opposite of that required by the law.

8. The result stated as a matter of fact in the experience of individuals. **So then they**—rather, *And they* **that are in the flesh cannot please God.** Closely connected with the preceding verse. Walking after the flesh and pleasing God cannot exist at the same time in the same person. Thus we are brought to the inference that only those in Christ can please God, and therefore are under no condemnation, which is the general sentiment of the whole passage.

9. But ye, the disciples of Christ, **are not in the flesh**—in an unrenewed state, as just described (ver. 8), **but in the Spirit**, in that renewed state in which the Holy Spirit is the ruling influence. Such "walk after the Spirit" (ver. 4). **If so be**—provided that. Paul's language is assuring

God dwell in you. Now if any man have not *the Spirit of Christ, he is none
10 of his. And if Christ be ᵃin you, the body is dead because of sin; ᵇbut the spirit is life ᶜbecause of righteousness.
11 But if the Spirit of him that raised up Jesus from the dead dwell in you, ᵈhe that raised up Christ from the dead shall also quicken your mortal bodies by his Spirit that dwelleth in you.
12 ᵉTherefore, brethren, we are debtors, not to the flesh, to live after the flesh.
13 For ᶠif ye live after the flesh, ye shall die: but if ye through the Spirit do

dwells in you. And if any one have not the Spirit of Christ, he is none of
10 his. And if Christ is in you, the body is dead because of sin; but the spirit
11 is life because of righteousness. And if the Spirit of him who raised Jesus from the dead dwells in you, he who raised Christ from the dead will make alive your mortal bodies also, because of his Spirit that dwells in you.
12 So then, brethren, we are debtors, not to the flesh, to live according to the
13 flesh. For if ye are living according to the flesh, ye are going to die; but if

z Gal. 4 : 6; Phil. 1 : 19. *a* 2 Cor. 13 : 5; Eph. 3 : 17; Col. 1 : 27. *b* John 11 : 25, 26. *c* Phil. 3 : 9.
d 6 : 4, 5; John 14 : 19; 1 Cor. 6 : 14. *e* 6 : 2–15; 1 Cor. 6 : 19, 20; 1 Peter 4 : 2, 3. *f* Ver. 6; Gal. 6 : 8.

and consoling, yet suggestive of such doubt and inquiry as to lead to self-examination (1 Cor. 13 : 5; Heb. 6 : 9). **The Spirit of God**—the Holy Spirit, **dwell in you**—denoting his habitual presence and influence (1 Cor. 3 : 16). **Now if any man have not**—is destitute of **the Spirit of Christ,** the Holy Spirit, of his indwelling presence and influence, **he is none of his**—he has no connection with Christ and no part in these consoling views. "The Spirit of God" and "the Spirit of Christ" are the same (Gal. 4 : 6; 1 Peter 1 : 11). Christ possessed the Spirit without measure (John 3 : 34; Acts 10 : 38); and he imparts it to his people (John 15 : 26; 16 : 7; Luke 24 : 49; Eph. 3 : 16).

10. And if Christ *is in you*, as a matter of fact, through the Spirit, as just stated in the preceding verse. **The body is** *indeed* **dead,** mortal, subject to death, **because of sin.** The believer is still in a measure subject to sin (7 : 17–25), and therefore to its penalty so far as the body is concerned. **But the Spirit**—permeating the human spirit, or the human spirit permeated by the Holy Spirit. The principle thus divinely planted has no connection with sin, and hence has no taint of death, but has **life**, not only in promise but in reality, "living unto God." **Because of righteousness**—the implanted righteousness of sanctification which carries life along with it (6 : 22, 23). Justification through the righteousness of Christ however is implied.

11. A further result of the indwelling Spirit of Christ. The effect on the soul in the last verse; on the body in this. **But if,** as a matter of fact, the

Spirit of him, God the Father (6 : 4; Heb. 13 : 20), **that raised up Jesus,** personally, **from the dead** *dwell in you*, **he that raised up Christ,** the Head of his people and as a first-fruits of them that have fallen asleep (1 Cor. 15 : 20), **shall also quicken,** or *make alive*, **your mortal bodies,** subject to death, **through**—rather, *because of*, **the Spirit that dwelleth in you;** gives the reason, the indwelling Spirit. The body having become the temple of the Holy Spirit is precious in the sight of God (1 Cor. 6 : 19). The natural reference here is to the resurrection of the body (2 Cor. 4 : 14). The same verb, *quicken*, is used with the same reference in 1 Cor. 15 : 22. It is broader than *raised up*, and thus may include the change effected in those that remain at our Lord's coming (1 Cor. 15 : 51). Thus the death of the body is but for a season.

12. From the preceding views the apostle draws practical admonitions and encouragements. **Therefore, brethren, we are debtors,** we are under obligation, **not to the flesh,** to which we owe nothing, and from which we have suffered much. But rather to the Spirit to live after the Spirit. We are under no obligation to the law of the flesh; another law, that of the Spirit, is now the ruling principle, which demands absolute obedience.

13. Enforces the foregoing statement, non-compliance results in death. **For if** *ye are living according to the flesh ye are going to die.* The result is impending and sure (James 1 : 15). **But if ye through the Spirit,** who produces in you spiritual affections and exercises of the mind, **do mortify the**

e mortify the deeds of the body, ye shall live.
14 For b as many as are led by the Spirit of God, i they are the sons of God.
15 For ye have not received the spirit of bondage again k to fear; but ye have received the l Spirit of adoption,
16 whereby we cry, m Abba, Father. n The Spirit itself beareth witness with our spirit, that we are the children of God;
17 and if children, then o heirs; p heirs of by the Spirit ye put to death the deeds
14 of the body, ye will live. For as many as are led by the Spirit of God, these
15 are sons of God. For ye did not receive a spirit of bondage again unto fear; but ye received a spirit of adoption, whereby we cry, Abba, Father.
16 The Spirit himself testifies with our spirit, that we are children of God;
17 and if children, also heirs: heirs of

g 1 Cor. 9 : 27 ; Gal. 5 : 24 ; Col. 3 : 5-8.   h Ver. 5, 9 ; Gal. 5 : 18.   l 1 John 3 : 1, 2.
k 2 Tim. 1 : 7 ; 1 John 4 : 18.   l Gal. 4 : 5-7.   m Mark 14 : 36.   n 2 Cor. 1 : 22 ; 5 : 5.
o Acts 26 : 18 ; 1 Peter 1 : 4.   p Gal. 4 : 7.

deeds of the body, *do habitually put to death the practices of the body*, **ye shall live.** The end already begun is certain of completion. The struggle taught in chap. 7 is going on toward ultimate victory (12 : 2 ; Col. 3 : 5-10 ; Gal. 5 : 16).

14. Confirms the assertion just made, "Ye shall live," by the fact that they are sons of God. **For as many as are led by the Spirit of God,** as intimated in the preceding verse (Gal. 5 : 18, 22-24), **they are the sons of God ;** they partake of his nature and shall live. Neither God nor his sons can die. Concerning sons of God, see 2 Cor. 6 : 16-18 ; Gal. 3 : 26 ; Matt. 5 : 9, 45 ; Phil. 2 : 15 ; 1 John 3 : 1-3. This sonship is proved and explained in the two following verses.

15. **For,** to show that ye are the sons of Gods, **ye have not received**—rather, *ye did not receive*, when ye became Christians, **the spirit of bondage**—of servitude, slavery—*tending again unto fear.* Such was not the spirit and temper of your minds which ye received in connection with the Holy Spirit. **But ye have received a** *spirit* **of adoption,** or *sonship*—that spirit and temper of mind connected with sonship, **whereby we cry, Abba, Father.** The word *adoption* or *sonship* is the same as that in Gal. 4 : 5 ; Eph. 1 : 5. It is used only by Paul in the New Testament, who never applies it to sonship by birth, but always to adopted sonship. The figure is borrowed not from Jewish, but from Roman law, which recognized a fully adopted sonship. There is a clear distinction made in the New Testament between "the sons," or "the children of God," in a religious and spiritual sense, and "the offspring" of God (Acts 17 : 28) in the natural. One is not evolved from the other. One is by nature; the other by grace and through the Spirit. (See *Bib. Sac.*, July, 1895, pp. 439-457.) Becoming the sons of God through the Spirit of God, they have the spirit of children, so that with affection, reverence, and confidence they call him **Abba,** the Aramaic word for **Father,** which was one expressing a high degree of love and confidence, and used from early childhood. It was the word employed by our Lord in Gethsemane (Mark 14 : 36), and seems to have passed into general use among Christians. As applied to God it was equivalent to "Heavenly Father." "The knowledge of the Father as our Father, because the Father of the Son, is among the greatest of the treasures of grace" (H. C. G. MOULE). Thus the first proof given of sonship is from Christian consciousness (1 John 3 : 19-24).

16. A second proof of our sonship from the testimony of the Holy Spirit witnessing with ours. Both proofs are connected with Christian experience. **The Spirit** *himself* **beareth witness,** or *testifies,* **with our Spirit,** which also witnesseth in our own consciousness, **that we are the children,** a more tender word than sons, **of God.** Paul recognizes the Holy Spirit and our spirit as distinct. The testimony of our spirit is verified by that of the Holy Spirit. We are conscious that we love the Father, and that we have fellowship with the Son, and we are also conscious of the love of God shed abroad by the Spirit in our hearts (5 : 5 ; 1 John 1 : 3 ; 3 : 14 ; 4 : 13 ; 5 : 7).

17. Hence being God's children they are sure of the glory to come. **If children,** as you are in fact (John 1 : 12),

God, and joint heirs with Christ; q if so be that we suffer with *him*, that we may be also glorified together.

18 For I reckon that *r* the sufferings of this present time *are* not worthy *to be compared* with the glory which shall
19 be revealed in us. For the earnest expectation of the creature *s* waiteth for

God, and joint heirs with Christ; if indeed we suffer with him, that we may also be glorified with him.

18 For I reckon that the sufferings of this present time are of no account, in comparison with the glory which is going
19 to be revealed for us. For the earnest longing of the creation is waiting for

q Phil. 1 : 29 ; 2 Tim. 2 : 10–12 ; Rev. 3 : 21.   *r* Acts 20 : 24 ; 2 Cor. 4 : 17, 18 ; 1 Peter 1 : 6, 7 ; 4 : 13.
s 1 Cor. 1 : 7 ; Gal. 5 : 5.

---

then, as a matter of course, **heirs,** a figure borrowed from the human relation; **heirs of God** to a glorious inheritance by virtue of adoption and birth into the family of God (Gal. 4 : 4–7 ; Matt. 25 : 34; Acts 20 : 32; 1 Peter 1 : 4) ; **joint heirs,** *fellow-heirs*, **with Christ,** who by union with him becomes our divine and human Elder Brother (ver. 29) and we participants in his glory (John 17 : 22, 24). **If so be that,** *if indeed*, suggesting self-examination (ver. 9), **we suffer with him**—suffer as he suffered in inward and outward conflict with sin, Satan, and the world (Heb. 12 : 3), and suffering for his sake and the gospel. If we are one with him in divine relationship we must be sharers in his sufferings, *in order that* **we may be also glorified** *with him.* The one is a necessary antecedent, the needful preparation ; the other the necessary consequent, the obvious result (1 Peter 4 : 5–7). An inheritance of suffering here and of glory hereafter (Mark 10 : 29, 30 ; Rom. 4 : 13, 14 ; Rev. 3 : 21 ; 22 : 5). The *state of adoption* involves three things : (1) Freedom from the law as a ground of justification ; (2) enjoyment of the spirit of sonship ; (3) heirship, a right to a future inheritance. Of this they have foretastes here, in the spiritual freedom, in spiritual-mindedness, and in spiritual victories.

18–39. GROUNDS OF ENCOURAGEMENT IN THE MIDST OF SUFFERING. Future glory far outweighs all present suffering (ver. 18–25) ; the Holy Spirit helps us (ver. 26, 27) ; all things work for good to them that love God according to his purpose (ver. 28–30) ; the final issue is assured. God is for us and nothing can break the bond between us and him (ver. 31–39).

18. The *first* ground of encouragement. The reference to suffering and glory, in the last verse, suggests the train of thought that follows. **For—** to confirm what has been said and to encourage in the midst of sufferings. **I reckon that the sufferings of this present time,** and Paul well knew by experience what these sufferings meant (2 Cor. 7 : 5 ; 11 : 23–28), **are not worthy to be compared,** are insignificant and of no account in comparison **with the glory which shall be revealed in us,** literally, *into us.* It is not a glory that merely passes *before* us, or is exercised *toward* us, but which enters *in* and is wrought within us, of which we are the recipients and the subjects (2 Cor. 3 : 18 ; Col. 3 : 4 ; 1 John 3 : 2). It is evident also from the next verse that we are to be the subjects of this glory. *The present time* has the idea of brevity—this brief, passing, limited time. Dr. A. Carson has an eloquent sermon on this verse. See "Fish's Masterpieces," Vol. I., p. 594 ff.

19. The meaning of this and the four verses that follow has been discussed for ages. The chief difficulty is in the word translated *creature* and *creation* (ver. 22). Derived from a verb meaning *to create,* the word denotes primarily *the act of creating.* In the New Testament it is used in this sense only in Rom. 1 : 20. Its secondary and common meaning is *the thing created, the creation.* In ordinary use it has about the same latitude as the word creation, and thus may be mentally limited by the nature of the action ascribed to it or exerted on it. For example, in Mark 16 : 15, "Preach the gospel to every creature," or *the whole creation,* the word is evidently limited to rational or human beings on earth, no others being the objects of such action. So also it is limited to *any created thing* in ver. 39 and 1 : 25 ; also Heb. 4 : 13. In Gal. 6 : 15 ; 2 Cor. 5 : 17, *new creation* or *creature* is evidently limited by the connection and the adjective *new* to the regenerate man in Christ Jesus. In Mark 10 : 6 ; 13 :

the ᵗ manifestation of the sons of God.
20 For ᵘ the creature was made subject to vanity, not willingly, but by reason of him who hath subjected *the same* in
21 hope; because the creature itself also shall be delivered from the bondage of corruption into the glorious liberty of

the revelation of the sons of God.
20 For the creation was made subject to vanity, not by its own will, but because of him who made it subject, in
21 hope that the creation itself also will be set free from the bondage of corruption into the freedom of the glory of

t Mal. 3 : 17, 18; 1 John 3 : 2.   *u* Gen. 3 : 19.

19; 2 Peter 3 : 4; Rev. 3 : 14, the reference is plainly to the sum or aggregate of created things (comp. Heb. 9 : 11) "not of this building" or *creation*, not this kind of *created things*, not of this material creation. In the general sense of *creation* it appears to be used in this passage. But is the word at all restricted in meaning by its connection with the words and thoughts of the passage? And if so, to what extent? I answer, the word creation cannot here include Christians, the converted; for they, "the sons of God" are here distinguished from the creation (so also in ver. 22, 23), the creation is waiting for their manifestation. Neither does it appear to include mankind; for man was not subjected unwillingly to vanity (Gen. 3 : 1-7); and mankind outside of believers cannot be said to be looking with earnest longing for the resurrection and its consequent glories, which are included in "the manifestation of the sons of God"; neither can it be said of humanity as a whole that it shall participate in this glorious deliverance. The word creation therefore seems to be limited here to the inanimate and irrational creation and quite equivalent to our word *nature*. As irrational animals were involved in the curse we need not suppose them to be excluded here. (Comp. Isa. 11 : 1-9.) Only so far, however, as the general resurrection and the renovation of our earth may exclude them (2 Peter 3 : 10-16; 1 Cor. 15; 1 Thess. 4 : 13-18). By a bold and animated personification, as in Old Testament prophecies, Paul introduces universal nature as waiting and longing for the full deliverance and glory of the sons of God. See Dr A. C. Kendrick, "Moral Conflict of Humanity," American Baptist Publication Society, 1894; Dr. Arnold, "Baptist Quarterly," 1867, p. 143 ff. For introduces the proof of the greatness and certainty of the future glorification which he had just contrasted with the brief and insignificant sufferings here (ver. 18). *For creation* or *nature with earnest* and persistent *expectation waits for* **the manifestation,** or revelation, **of the sons of God—** patiently waiting and longing for those glorious events, that renovation which shall attend and attest the revealing of the sons of God (ver. 18, 19), when it shall be freed from the curse of the fall (Gen. 3 : 17, 18). **Earnest expectation**—a peculiar word with an emphatic meaning. Nature is represented as *stretching forth her neck* in strained attention, as it were, to some distant portion of the heavens from which deliverance was to come. In regard to this manifestation see 1 John 3 : 2; and of the renovation, see 2 Peter 3 : 12, 13; Rev. 21 : 1, ff.

20, 21. The reason of this longing. **For the creature,** *nature* or creation, **was made subject to vanity,** *imperfection* and *frailty*, **not willingly,** not of its own choice, *but of the will of him who made it subject*, that is, of God, who subjected it for the wisest ends and his own glory. Through man's sin the earth was cursed for his sake (Gen. 3 : 17), and unable to realize the ends for which it was created. In regard to *vanity* compare Ps. 39 : 5, 6. **In hope.** This should be separated from the preceding by a comma, and joined to ver. 21, *In hope that even nature itself*, emphatically indicating a descent from a higher and nobler to a lower order of beings. **Shall be delivered,** *will be set free*, **from the bondage,** the servitude, **of corruption,** connected with and resulting from the vanity to which it was subjected. So far as nature is concerned the *corruption* is a physical imperfection and detriment; some change for the worse came upon man's abode when he fell (Gen. 3 : 17-19), and nature suffered and still suffers from the consequences of the fall and of sin. **Into the glorious liberty**—pregnant with meaning; and brought *into the freedom of the glory* **of the children of God.**

22 the children of God. For we know that the whole creation groaneth and travaileth in pain together until now: 23 and not only *they*, but ourselves also, which have ᵡ the firstfruits of the Spirit, ʸ even we ourselves groan within ourselves, waiting for the adoption, *to wit*, the ᶻ redemption of our body. 24 For we are saved ᵃ by hope: but hope

22 the children of God. For we know that the whole creation groans and travails in pain together until now. 23 And not only so, but ourselves also, though we have the first-fruits of the Spirit, even we ourselves groan within ourselves, waiting for the adoption, the redemption of our body. 24 For by hope we were saved; but hope

---

ᵡ 2 Cor. 5 : 5.   ʸ 2 Cor. 5 : 2-4.   ᶻ Luke 21 : 28; Eph. 4 : 30.   ᵃ Heb. 6 : 18, 19.

Creation or nature shall share in the freedom connected with and involved in the glory of the saints, but in a way adapted to its character, that is being physically restored to its primeval beauty and excellence. (Comp. Isa. 65: 17-25; Ezek. 34:25-27; Matt. 19: 28; Acts 3: 21; 2 Peter 3: 13.) We may believe that in the beginning God adapted every other being and event of our world to man's character and condition, as foreknown, thus making man a central figure in our world and producing harmony in all his works. See Hitchcock's "Religion and Geology," pp. 104-111.

22. And this is a truthful representation, **For we know**, from universal experience, **that the whole creation**, or *all nature*, **groaneth** *together* in all its parts **and travaileth in pain together**, as it were, in childbirth, **until now**, from the beginning up to this time. A vivid and strong personification of the suffering and distress connected with the curse from man's sin. (Compare similar pictorial language in the Old Testament.) "For this shall the earth mourn" (Jer. 4:28); "Howl, ye ships of Tarshish" (Isa. 23:1); "The land mourneth and languisheth, Lebanon is ashamed and withereth away" (Isa. 33:9); "The voice of thy brother's blood crieth unto me from the ground" (Gen. 4:10); "How doth the city sit solitary that was full of people! . . . She weepeth sore in the night, and her tears are on her cheek" (Lamen. 1:1,2). The pangs here, however, are not of despair and death but of hope and life.

23. And not only they, rather, *And not only so*, does the whole creation groan together, etc., **but ourselves also**, who are believers, *though* **we have the firstfruits of the Spirit** which we have received, an earnest and pledge of heavenly bliss (2 Cor. 1:22), **even we ourselves** (repeated for emphasis) **groan within ourselves** (7: 14-24; 1 Cor. 9:27. Comp. Jesus groaning, John 11: 33, 38), **waiting** patiently and with expectation **for the adoption**, or *sonship*, the Spirit of which we have received (ver. 15), but the full consummation and recognition of which do not yet appear (1 John 3:2), **the redemption**, or *ransoming*, **of our body** from the curse and bondage of sin, and a transformation into a glorious body like that of the risen Christ (Phil. 3: 21; 2 Cor. 5:2). As Paul is speaking of bodily sufferings largely, so he directs attention to the redemption of the body. Without the glorified body redemption would not be complete, and in that body it becomes complete. And so a glorified body is necessary to the full realization of sonship. On *first-fruits* see Deut. 26: 1-11; 1 Cor. 15: 20. First-fruits were the first handful from the fields, which was a foretoken and a pledge of the whole. So the reception of the Spirit by believers is a token and a pledge of its fuller and more perfect enjoyment hereafter (Eph. 1: 13, 14). Thus ver. 22, 23 illustrate and expand the thought of ver. 20, 21, especially *the hope* that creation shall be delivered and this hope extended to the children of God. The glory for the future deliverance is advanced, not only by the prophetic birth-pangs of the whole creation, but also by the agonizing longings of those who have received the first-fruits and foretastes of the Spirit.

24. The apostle has presented hope connected with suffering nature and with sighing and agonizing believers. Hence he continues: **For**, introducing the reason of this expectancy, **we are**, rather, *were*, **saved**, at the time of exercising faith in conversion, **by**, or *in*, **hope**. *By means of hope* as an extended faith, or, *in the hope* which we exercised in view of the final and

that is seen is not hope: for what a man seeth, why doth he yet hope for? 25 But if we hope for that we see not, then do we with patience wait for it. 26 Likewise the Spirit also helpeth our infirmities: for [b] we know not what we should pray for as we ought: but the Spirit itself maketh intercession for us with groanings which cannot be 27 uttered. And [c] he that searcheth the hearts knoweth what is the mind of the Spirit, because he maketh intercession for the saints according to the will of God.

seen is not hope: for what one sees, 25 why does he also hope for? But if we hope for what we do not see, we wait 26 for it with patience. And in like manner the Spirit also helps our weakness; for we know not what to pray for as we ought; but the Spirit himself makes intercession for us with groan-27 ings which cannot be uttered. And he who searches the hearts knows what is the mind of the Spirit, because he makes intercession for the saints according to the will of God.

[b] Matt. 20 : 22 ; James 4 : 3.   [c] See refs. 1 Chron. 28 : 9 ; Acts 1 : 24 ; 1 Thess. 2 : 4.

glorious salvation (1 Peter 1 : 5; Titus 1 : 2; Rom. 12 : 12). Both of these ideas are suggested. Our salvation was not an immediate, but a prospective one. Paul distinguishes between hope and faith (1 Cor. 13 : 13), and everywhere emphasizes salvation by faith. "Inasmuch as the object of salvation is both relatively present and also relatively future, hope is produced from faith and indissolubly linked with it; for faith apprehends the object, in so far as it is present; hope, in so far as it is still future" (PHILIPPI). **But hope that is seen**—realized in having its object present and thus seen, **is not hope**, it ceases to be hope, it is sight; for it is evident that a **man cannot hope for** that which he sees and enjoys.

25. The thought of the preceding verse is applied to the subject in hand: patient waiting for our full salvation. **But if we** are *hoping for what we do not see*, **then do we with patience**, with constancy, and *through patience*, in steadfastness **wait for it** and *expecting* it, the adoption and the redemption of our body being included in our full salvation (ver. 23).

26. In this and the next verse Paul presents a *second* ground of encouragement in the midst of sufferings: the Holy Spirit helps us. **Likewise**—*in like manner*. As in our earnest longing for deliverance hope helped us with patience and in expectancy of future glory, so in like manner the Holy Spirit helps our infirmities, rather, *our infirmity* or *weakness* (2 Cor. 12 : 10); he *shares a part with us*, helping us to bear, in our infirmity, our load of suffering; and this he does in guiding and assisting us in prayer with groanings unutterable. The reference is manifestly to the Holy Spirit, as else-

where in this chapter. **For,** to show how the Spirit helps us, **we know not what we should pray for as we ought**—our inability to know *what* and *how* to pray, is one example of our weakness (2 Cor. 12 : 7-9), and the Spirit's aid in prayer is one of the principal ways in which he helps us bear the groanings within while we wait (ver. 23). **But** in this weakness **the Spirit** *himself* **maketh intercession**, by awakening desires and longing in our own spirits which are proper and according to the will of God. Christ calls the Holy Spirit another Comforter, or Advocate (John 14 : 16, 26 ; 16 : 13), who would teach them and guide them. So the Spirit, as an advocate to his client, may prompt and counsel as to our petitions. And these intercessions for us, are **with groanings which cannot be uttered**—exciting desires and longings of soul too vast to be uttered in human language, but only in the groanings, the unutterable language of the human heart (Eph. 3 : 20 ; 6 : 18).

27. But though these longings, which are originated and excited by the Spirit, cannot be expressed, yet they are known to him **that searcheth**, or *sears*, human **hearts** (1 Sam. 16 : 7 ; Jer. 17 : 9, 10 ; Heb. 4 : 13), *and he* **knoweth**, he understands and regards with approval, **what is the mind of the Spirit**, those aspirations and longings which are produced by the Spirit; he understands their intent and meaning. **Because he**, the Spirit, **maketh intercession for the saints**, rather omitting the article, *for saints*, thus designating the renewed character of the persons in whose hearts he carries on his intercessions. And he does this **according to the will of God**, literally, *according to God*, in agree-

28 And we know that ᵈ all things work together for good to them that love God, to them who are ᵉ the called ᶠ according to *his* purpose. For whom ᵍ he did foreknow, ʰ he also did predestinate ⁱ *to be* conformed to the image of his Son, ᵏ that he might be the first-30 born among many brethren. Moreover whom he did predestinate, them he also ˡ called: and whom he called, them he also ᵐ justified: and whom he justified, them he also ⁿ glorified.

28 And we know that all things work together for good to those who love God, to those who are called according to his purpose. Because whom he foreknew, he also predestined to be conformed to the image of his Son, that he might be the first born among many 30 brethren. And whom he predestined, them he also called; and whom he called, them he also justified; and whom he justified, them he also glorified.

d Gen. 50 : 20 ; Heb. 12 : 6–11 ; 1 Peter : 7. 11.   *e* See refs. 1 : 6, 7.   *f* 9 : 11, 23, 24 ; Eph. 1 : 11 ; 2 Tim. 1 : 9.
g Jer. 1 : 5 ; 1 Peter 1 : 2.   *h* Eph. 1 : 4–6, 11.   *i* 1 John 3 : 2.   *k* Col. 6 : 15–18 ; Heb. 1 : 5, 6 ; Rev. 1 : 5.
l Heb. 9 : 15 ; 1 Peter 2 : 9.   *m* 3 : 22–26 ; 1 Cor. 6 : 11.   *n* John 17 : 22, 24 ; Heb. 10 : 14 ; 1 Peter 5 : 10.

ment with his will; and this affords the reason of the preceding assertion. Such unuttered prayers will meet God's approval and be answered (1 John 5 : 14).
28. A *third* encouragement amid trials (ver. 28-30). All things working together for good to God's children. **And,** in addition to all I have said, **we know,** having the assurance of faith and of the Spirit in our hearts, in our Christian consciousness, **that all things,** in the widest sense, including afflictions, trials, and persecutions (ver. 38), **work together,** uniting and conspiring to one end, **for good,** present and future, until the time of their glorification (ver. 30), **to them that love God,** a designation of God's children (1 Cor. 2 : 9 ; Eph. 6 : 24), in whose hearts the love of God has been poured forth (5 : 5), **to them who are the called according to his purpose,** the divine side, as love was the human side. God's children are effectually *called* by the word (James 1 : 18) and the Holy Spirit (1 Thess. 1 : 5), begotten and made partakers of divine grace (Gal. 1 : 15 ; Heb. 6 : 4), called to be saints (1 : 6, 7 ; Rev. 17 : 14), *according to his purpose* as set forth in the following verses. As God is the greatest, wisest, and best, his purpose must be that which he "purposed in himself," "according to his good pleasure" (11 : 34 ; Eph. 1 : 9, 11, Comp. 2 Tim. 1 : 9 ; Rom. 9 : 11). Some would translate the last clause, *Since they are the called according to his purpose.* The other rendering is the usual and preferable one.
29. For—assigns the grounds of the statement just made. **For whom he did foreknow**—as such, as the objects of his purposed grace. The application of the word must be thus restricted, else there would be no distinction in their case, for, of course, he foreknew all men. **He also did predestinate,** *pre-determined, fore-ordained* (comp. Eph. 1 : 4), **to be conformed to the image of his Son**—their complete salvation, their glorious destiny, assured by his own unchangeable purpose (1 Peter 1 : 2 ; 2 Cor. 3 : 18). Conformity to Christ is the chief thing here in the apostle's thought. **That he might be the first-born,** prior in time and in dignity, in all things pre-eminent (Col. 1 : 15, 18 ; Heb. 1 : 6 ; Rev. 1 : 5), **among many brethren,** a numberless company (Rev. 1 : 4-9), joint heirs with him (ver. 17) and partakers of his glory and heavenly kingdom (John 17 : 22-24). The purpose and calling of God make it certain that the object of Christ's life, death, and resurrection will be attained.
30. Moreover, or *And,* **whom he did predestinate,** as above, **them he also called** by his word and accompanying Spirit (see on ver. 28) effecting regeneration; **and whom he called them he also justified,** acquitted them of all guilt and accepted them as righteous (3 : 26) ; **and whom he justified them he also glorified**—the consummated salvation of soul and body in heaven. In this chain of past tenses Paul views the whole process in its final completeness. His point of view is final glory. The five links of this golden chain are the divine acts connected with our salvation. The human acts, such as faith, turning, and other exercises in repentance, conversion, and the exercise of holiness, are accordingly omitted. The links are consecutive, and from the first all the rest follow with certainty.

31 What shall we then say to these things? ᵒIf God *be* for us, who *can be* 32 against us? ᵖHe that spared not his own Son, but delivered him up for us all, ᑫhow shall he not with him also 33 freely give us all things? Who shall lay anything to the charge of God's 34 elect? ʳ*It is* God that justifieth. Who *is* he that condemneth? ˢ*It is* Christ that died, yea rather, that is risen again, ᵗwho is even at the right hand of God, ᵘwho also maketh intercession for us.

31 What then shall we say to these things? If God is for us, who is 32 against us? He who spared not his own son, but delivered him up for us all, how will he not also with him freely give us all things? Who will lay anything to the charge of God's elect? 34 God is he that justifies; who is he that condemns? Christ is he that died, yea rather, was raised, who is also at the right hand of God, who also intercedes for us.

---

o Num. 14 : 9 ; Ps. 118 : 6.   p 5 : 6-10.   q 1 Cor. 3 : 21-23.   r 3 : 26 ; Isa. 50 : 8, 9.   s 4 : 25 ; 14 : 9.
t Mark 16 : 19 ; Col. 3 : 1 ; Heb. 12 : 2.   u See refs. Isa. 53 : 12.

---

31. What God does for us (ver. 29, 30), Paul eloquently shows in the remainder of this chapter. Nothing, according to this, can prevent the ultimate glorification and salvation of God's children. For first, against all opposition, God's gift of his Son is a pledge that he will bestow all that is essential to our well-being (ver. 31, 32); second, the consequent impossibility of any charge whatever being made available against God's chosen ones (ver. 33, 34); or third, of anything being able to separate us from God's love as manifested in Christ. This is one of those passages of Paul in which eloquence finds its climax in the force, beauty, and sublimity of its thought and language. **What shall we then say to these things**—in view of the things that God does for us, just enumerated in ver. 29, 30? And what shall we infer? **If God** *is for us, who is* **against us?**—implying that all opposition is comparatively as nothing. (Comp. 2 Kings 6 : 16, 17 ; Heb. 13 : 6.)

32. The reason for believing that God is for us and will do all things in our behalf. *Surely* **he that spared not his own Son**—his *own* in the highest and mysterious sense (John 1 : 18; 3 : 16; Col. 1 : 15; Heb. 1 : 2, 3); who did not spare him from all the humiliation and anguish of his incarnation and sufferings, **but delivered him up** unto sufferings and death *in behalf of* **us all** (Isa. 53 : 5, 10; Matt. 26 : 38, 39), so that every believer has his share in him, **how shall he not** (it cannot be otherwise) **with him** also **freely,** *graciously,* **give us all things,** that are needful for our safety and complete salvation? With Christ and because of Christ all else connected with our salvation will come. The argument is from the greater to the less. Since God has done the greater, he will not leave the less undone. (Comp. 5 : 9, 10.) Also "All things are yours," etc. (1 Cor. 3 : 21-23).

33. Exultantly we may ask, **Who shall lay anything to the** charge **of**—*who will bring any charge against*—**God's elect,** against those whom God has chosen? **It is God,** he is the one, **that justifieth,** that acquits from all guilt and accounts them righteous (3 : 26). All charges therefore must fall to the ground before his ultimate and righteous tribunal; and no accuser can stand before him.

34. Who is he that condemneth—who can and who dares *give judgment against?* **It is Christ that died** for us (5 : 8), thus atoning for our sins and removing all condemnation, **yea, rather that** *was raised*, proving the divine efficacy of his death (see on "raised for our justification," 4 : 25), **who is** *also* **at the right hand of God,** exalted as a Prince and a Saviour (Acts 5 : 31; Heb. 1 : 3; Rev. 5 : 6-9), "This is the only direct reference to the ascension in this Epistle; but what a pregnant reference!" (MOULE.) **Who also maketh intercession for us**—like an advocate undertaking the management of our case and pleading our cause, presenting as it were his mediatorial and atoning work, which secures our pardon and the continued supplies of divine grace (Heb. 4 : 14-16; 7 : 25; 9 : 24; 1 John 2 : 1). Compare how Jesus prayed for Peter, "that thy faith fail not" (Luke 22 : 31, 32. See on ver 26). Many with Augustine, Alford, and others, prefer the interrogative form throughout the whole passage (ver. 31-35),

CH. VIII.]   ROMANS   113

35 ᶻ Who shall separate us from the love of Christ? ʸ shall tribulation, or distress, or persecution, or famine, or 36 nakedness, or peril, or sword? As it is written, ᵃ For thy sake we are killed all the day long ; we are accounted 37 as sheep for the slaughter. ᵃ Nay, in all these things we are more than conquerors through him that loved us. 38 For I am persuaded, ᵇ that neither death, nor life, nor angels, nor ᶜ prin-

35 for us. Who will separate us from the love of Christ? Will tribulation, or distress, or persecution, or famine, or 36 nakedness, or peril, or sword? As it is written,
  For thy sake we are killed all the day long ;
  We were accounted as sheep for slaughter.
37 Nay, in all these things we are more than conquerors through him who 38 loved us. For I am persuaded, that neither death nor life, nor angels nor

z John 10 : 28.   y Luke 21 : 12-19.   z 1 Cor. 4 : 9; 15 : 30, 31 ; 2 Cor. 4 : 11.,
a 1 Cor. 15 : 54–57 ; 2 Cor. 2 : 14 ; 12 : 9, 10.   b 14 : 8.   c Eph. 6 : 11, 12 ; Col. 2 : 15 ; 1 Peter 3 : 22.

which the Greek allows with the same essential meaning, and in ver. 33 and 34 punctuate thus : " Who shall lay anything to the charge of God's elect? Shall God, he who justifieth? Who is he that condemneth? Is it Christ, he who died, yea rather, was raised, who is also at the right hand of God, who also intercedes for us?" The questions imply their own answers. The majority of critics, however, punctuate as in the English version.

35. Finally, in view of God's love in Christ, exhibited in what Christ has done and is doing for us, Paul reaches the climax, and triumphantly asks, **Who shall separate us from the love of Christ?**—that is, Christ's love for us, not ours for him (2 Cor. 5 : 14 : Eph. 3 : 19). Compare on "the love of God" (5 : 5). Our love, however, grows out of Christ's love, and is inseparably connected with God's love in Christ, shed abroad in our hearts (5 : 5). **Us** is somewhat emphatic—*us,* for whom Christ died and intercedes. **Shall tribulation, or distress, or persecution,** etc.—any, or all of these things, which he and other Christians were suffering from their adversaries, the world, the flesh, and the devil ? (2 Cor. 11 : 23-27 ; 2 Tim. 3 : 10-12.) These at times might arouse fear, or cause despondency, or, joining hands with weak faith, tempt them to think that God was forsaking them, but they could not separate them from the strong hold of Christ's love (John 10 : 28, 29).

36. As it is written (Ps. 44 : 22), quoted from the Septuagint version, and suggested by the last word *sword,* in the preceding verse. **For thy sake we are killed all the day long**—at all times of the day we are liable to be put to death, and at all hours it occurs to one or another ; **we are accounted as sheep for the slaughter,** rather, *for slaughter,* destined for it and regarded as suitable for it by their adversaries. Paul quotes this as true of saints of all ages, applicable to those of his day as well as to those of Old Testament times. (Comp. Heb. 11 : 35–36.) We suffer as they suffered, and their sufferings were a foreshadowing of ours.

37. *But* or **Nay**, so far from being overcome and separated from Christ's love, **in all these things,** sufferings, persecutions, and deaths, enumerated in ver. 35, 36, **we are more than conquerors,** we gain triumphant and surpassing victories, **through him that loved us,** through Christ (ver. 35, 39), who is thus styled in Rev. 1 : 5. (Comp. Gal. 2 : 20.) In these very things in which we may appear to be vanquished we come forth with a stronger faith and a more ardent love here, and a larger capacity for enjoying the eternal weight of glory hereafter (2 Cor. 4 : 16–18).

38. Paul confirms what he had said, of being more than victorious, by an enthusiastic expression of his assured convictions : **For I am persuaded,** having full assurance (comp. same word in 14 : 14 ; 15 : 14), **that neither death nor life**—two states or conditions which must confront every individual, the one, the last enemy, with its terrors, the other with its charms or sufferings, but both must yield to the power of Christ (14 : 8, 9 ; Phil. 1 : 21–23 ; 1 Cor. 15 : 26), **Nor angels, nor principalities**—superhuman beings and dominions in general, including both good and bad (Eph. 3 : 10 ; Col. 1 : 16). In Eph. 6 : 12 Paul refers to the conflict against principali-

H

cipalities, nor powers, nor things pres
39 ent, nor things to come, nor height,
nor depth, nor any other creature,
ᵈshall be able to separate us from the
love of God, which is in Christ Jesus
our Lord.

principalities, nor things present nor
39 things to come, nor height
nor depth, nor any other created thing,
will be able to separate us from the
love of God, which is in Christ Jesus our
Lord.

d John 10 : 28-30.

---

ties, etc., and in Eph. 1 : 21 to Christ as above all these, and in Col. 2 : 15 as despoiling and triumphing over them. **Nor powers.** If this word is placed here, it naturally refers to superhuman powers in the same sphere as angels. But the best critical authorities place it at the end of the verse after "things to come," where it must be used of powers in the widest sense, forces of every description. **Nor things present, nor things to come**—events of all time, present and future. None of these shall separate us. Christ is the first and the last, who is and is to come (Rev. 1 : 8, 17, 18) and will ever be present to deliver.

39. Nor height, nor depth—no extent of space will be great enough to separate us. No matter how high Christ may be above us, nor how low we may be beneath him, he still embraces us in his love. (Comp. Ps. 139 : 7-10; Eph. 4 : 8-10.) **Nor any other creature,** or *created thing,* including all else that has been created, **shall** in any future time **be able to separate us,** all or any of us who are truly his, **from the love of God,** of the Almighty and Unchangeable One, **which is in** and through **Christ Jesus our Lord** (Eph. 1 : 6; Heb. 13 : 8). Notice that this "love of God in Christ" is styled "the love of Christ," in ver. 35, the love of God to us in Christ, indicating the divinity of Christ and the union of the Father and the Son in their love for us (John 3 : 16; Gal. 2 : 20). "What a commentary is this whole passage on ver. 28" (MEYER). "What did Cicero ever say more eloquent?" (ERASMUS.)

PRACTICAL REMARKS.

1. The sinner finds only condemnation out of Christ; but in Christ, united with him by faith and in fellowship with him through the Spirit, he finds pardon, peace, and safety (ver. 1, 31; 5 : 1; John 3 : 17).

2. The Holy Spirit is life-giving and through Christ gives true freedom from

the controlling influences of sin and death (ver. 2; Gal. 3 : 3; 4 : 6, 7).

3. The atonement is the product of Divine love, and its necessity is seen in the evils of sin, and in the demands of God's justice and holiness (ver. 3; John 3 : 16; Heb. 9 : 22, 23).

4. The Christian life is opposed to a life of self-gratification, and is characterized by devotedness to God and by loving obedience to him (ver. 4; Gal. 5 : 22-26).

5. The bent of one's thoughts, affections, and pursuits is a true index and decisive test of character (ver. 5; Matt 7 : 16-20).

6. Sin and misery, holiness and happiness, are necessarily and inseparably connected (ver. 6; Matt. 6 : 22-24).

7. Submission of the soul to God is an evidence of regeneration (ver. 7; James 4 : 4-7).

8. A change of heart is necessary to pleasing God (ver. 8; John 3 : 3).

9. One may know that he is a Christian by the indwelling of the Spirit (ver. 9; 1 Cor. 6 : 18-20).

10. How carefully should we keep our bodies from defilement, since they are temples of the Holy Spirit (ver. 9, 10; 1 Cor. 3 : 16, 17).

11. Though the body is still mortal and suffering from the effects of sin, yet the redemptive work of Christ extends to the bodies as well as to the souls of believers (ver. 10, 11, 23; John 11 : 23-26; Phil. 3 : 21).

12. By his indwelling Spirit, God delivers believers from the controlling power of the old nature, and obligates them to live for him (ver. 12; 12 : 1, 2).

13. We must either put our sins to death, or they will put us to death eternally. We cannot be saved in our sins (ver. 13; Luke 16 : 13; Gal. 6 : 8).

14. A sure sign of divine sonship. "led by the Spirit of God" (ver. 14; 2 Cor. 6 : 16, 17; Matt. 5 : 9).

15. A spirit of fear and servitude is un-

Christian. A filial spirit is the true spirit of religion, and is begotten only by the Holy Spirit (ver. 15; Gal. 4 : 6 ; John 1 : 12).

16. The Christian has the evidence of his sonship, in his own experience, by the testimony of the Spirit (ver. 16; Gal. 4 : 6).

17. Christ, a son and heir by nature; believers, by adoption. To what an inheritance! Finite suffering! Infinite glory! (ver. 17; 1 Peter 1 : 4).

18. The sufferings and trials of Christians are as nothing in both duration and degree to the future glory of their sonship (ver. 18; Col. 1 : 27 ; 2 Cor. 4 : 17).

19. Man stands at the head of creation. His fall was creation's curse; his restoration to the glory of sonship, creation's blessing (ver. 19; Gen. 3 : 17 ; Rev. 22 : 3).

20. God had a benevolent design in subjecting creation to suffering, decay, and death (ver. 20, 21; Acts 2 : 26). See Hitchcock's "Religion of Geology," p. 85, ff.

21. Creation is to be freed from its present state of degradation, and made partaker, according to its nature, of the glories connected with God's children (ver. 21; Acts 3 : 21 ; Matt. 19 : 28).

22. How infinitely great the future glory of believers if the whole creation from the beginning groans and longs for its manifestation (ver. 22; Rev. 12 : 6, 16).

23. The children of God will not find the full satisfaction of their earnest longings till they have attained the full glories of their sonship in the resurrection state (ver. 23 ; 1 Cor. 15 : 54-57).

24. Inasmuch as the Christian life is a growth, and sanctification progressive, hope holds an important place as a support and solace (ver. 24; Heb. 6 : 18, 19).

25. Hope and patience go together and help the believer waiting for the full enjoyment of his sonship (ver. 25 ; 5 : 4, 5 ; Heb. 6 : 11, 12).

26. We should ever recognize the office of the Spirit as our Advocate, and seek and gratefully acknowledge his help (ver. 26 ; Luke 11 : 13; Eph. 4 : 30).

27. Whatever prayer the Spirit incites, is according to God's will, and will be answered. He therefore is the safest who yields himself up most entirely to the Spirit (ver. 27; 1 John 5 : 14).

28. The facts of the believers loving God and God's purpose regarding them, should be a solace in trials, since all events are under his control for their good (ver. 28 ; Heb. 12 : 11; Ps. 119 : 67, 71).

29. Foreknowledge and decrees may be regarded as co-existent in the Divine mind (1 Peter 1 : 2). A Christlike spirit and life are a sure evidence that we are the subjects of God's gracious purpose (ver. 29; Eph. 1 : 4; 1 Cor. 15 : 49).

30. Man's free agency and God's sovereign purpose unite in human salvation (ver. 29, 30; John 6 : 44 : 5 : 40; Rev. 22 : 17). None will be saved but those who love God and follow after holiness (ver. 28, 29; Heb. 12 : 10, 14).

31. The perseverance of the saints is assured, since there is an inseparable connection between predestination and final glorification (ver. 30; Phil. 1 : 6).

32. With God for us we are in the majority and stronger than all the universe besides (ver. 31 ; Ps. 118 : 6).

33. God's infinite friendship and love for us have been tested and assured by his highest possible gift (ver. 32 ; 1 John 4 : 9, 10).

34. God's people are his chosen and justified ones. It is absurd to suppose that he would ever desert them (ver. 33 ; Heb. 13 : 5, 6).

35. Christ came not to condemn, but to save. His death, resurrection, exaltation, and intercession, all assure the salvation of believers (ver. 34 ; Eph. 1 : 20-23 ; John 3 : 17).

36. Our love results from Christ's love (John 4 : 19), and as nothing can destroy his love toward us, so nothing will destroy our love toward him (ver. 35, 38, 39 ; Jer. 31 : 3).

37. Scripture, history, and experience, all testify that God's people must expect opposition and persecution from a wicked world (ver. 37; 2 Tim. 3 : 12).

38. How triumphant our victory through Christ! His enemies are already a conquered foe. Tribulations become a means of blessing and glory (ver. 37 ; 1 Peter 4 : 13 ; James 1 : 2).

39. The present and eternal safety of the Christian is as sure as the love of God, the merit, power, and love of Christ can make it (ver. 31-39; John 10 : 28, 29).

Vindication of God's dealings with Jews and Gentiles.

9 ^c I SAY the truth in Christ, I lie not,
^f my conscience also bearing me wit-
2 ness in the Holy Ghost, that I have
great heaviness and continual sorrow
3 in my heart. For ^g I could wish that

9 I SAY the truth in Christ, I lie not,
my conscience also testifying with me
2 in the Holy Spirit, that I have great
grief and unceasing anguish in my
3 heart. For I could wish to be myself

<small>c Gal. 1 : 20 ; 1 Tim. 2 : 7.   f John 14 : 19-21.   g Exod. 32 : 32 ; 2 Sam. 18 : 33.</small>

10. What an honor to be a Christian! How grateful should we be for the love of God in Christ Jesus! What obligations it puts upon us! Woe to us if we love not in return! (ver. 31-39 ; 1 Cor. 16 : 22).

CHAPTER IX.

Paul now proceeds to consider the problem arising from the fact that a greater part of the Jews rejected Christianity. He had shown that salvation was only through faith in Christ. He had answered the objection, common to all ages, that such a doctrine tended to immorality, and had shown that on the contrary it insured holiness and final salvation. But still it would be objected from a Jewish standpoint that this doctrine involved unfaithfulness in God to the Jewish people. This was a living question peculiar to that age. Paul was constantly meeting it, and he had gone through it in his own experience, and under Divine guidance had wrought out an answer. This he presents in the ninth, tenth, and eleventh chapters.

In this chapter he vindicates the justice of God in passing over the unbelieving Jews and extending the gospel to the Gentiles. First of all he expresses his deep sorrow for his own people and his earnest desire for their welfare (ver. 1-5). But the promise of God had not failed, for mere natural descent from Abraham did not constitute a right to the promise (ver. 6-13), but the right depended entirely on the free favor and choice of God, with whom there is no unrighteousness (ver. 14-18). In this he exercised his unquestionable right and prerogative as the Creator in such a manner as to display his justice and his mercy (ver. 19-24), which was also according to prophecy (ver. 25-29), without interfering with the free exercise of faith or unbelief on the part of either Jew or Gentile (ver. 30-33). In this discussion Paul accepts the absolute righteousness of God as unquestionable, and the Old Testament Scriptures as of supreme authority.

1-5. PAUL EXPRESSES HIS DEEP SORROW FOR HIS OWN PEOPLE AND HIS EARNEST DESIRE FOR THEIR WELFARE, especially in view of their great privileges. As a Jew he would naturally do this for he had specially desired to preach the gospel to them (Acts 9 : 28, 29 ; 22 : 19, 20) ; as an apostle to the Gentiles he would be equally desirous of assuring them, notwithstanding this, of his deep interest and love for them. As he was also about to speak of matters especially distasteful to the Jews, such as God's passing over Israel and the calling of Gentiles, he was moved to use the strongest language in speaking of his deep concern for them.

1. What a contrast to the exultant strains at the end of the last chapter! But to Paul, in that high state of triumphant joy, the condition of unbelieving Israel would, in contrast, seem the more deplorable. As it burst afresh on his mind he could not but speak in language most intense. **I say the truth in Christ**, with a solemn sense of my union with Christ, as a believer in him, and in a manner becoming that relation. Though a Christian he would assure them that he had lost none of his interest in his own people. **I lie not, my conscience also bearing me witness,** or *testifying with me in the Holy Spirit,* imbued and enlightened by the Holy Spirit. The consciousness of the Spirit's presence and power increased confidence in the testimony of conscience. Such strong language was needful in view of the doctrine of the chapter which follows, and because as an apostle to the Gentiles the Jews might think he had quite forgotten them.

2. That I have great heaviness, or *grief,* **and continued sorrow,** or *unceasing pain,* **in my heart,** a living and abiding sorrow in my inmost

myself were accursed from Christ for my brethren, my kinsmen according to 4 the flesh: who are Israelites: ᵇ to whom *pertaineth* the adoption, and ⁱ the glory, and ᵏ the covenants, and ˡ the giving of the law, and ᵐ the service *of* 5 *God*, and ⁿ the promises; whose *are* the fathers; and ᵒ of whom as concerning the flesh Christ *came*, ᵖ who is over all, God ᑫ blessed forever. Amen.

accursed from Christ for my brethren, my kinsmen according to the flesh; 4 who are Israelites; whose is the adoption, and the glory, and the covenants, and the giving of the law, and the ser- 5 vice, and the promises; whose are the fathers, and of whom as to the flesh is the Christ, who is over all, God blessed forever. Amen.

ʰ Exod. 4 : 22; Deut. 14 : 1.   ⁱ Exod. 29 : 43; 1 Sam. 4 : 21, 22.
ᵏ Gen. 15 : 18; Exod. 24 : 7, 8; Eph. 2 : 12. Heb. 8 : 8–10.   ˡ Exod. 20.   ᵐ Heb. 9 : 1, 10.
ⁿ Luke 1 : 54, 55, 69–75.   ᵒ Luke 3 : 23.   ᵖ 10 : 12; Jer. 23 : 6; John 1 : 1–3.   ᑫ 2 Cor. 11 : 31.

being, in view of what has happened and will happen to my people.

3. For I could wish, even now if such a thing were possible and hence proper, but in the very nature of the case inadmissible! **that myself were accursed from Christ,** *an anathema*, devoted to ruin by a solemn curse *from Christ*, **for,** *in behalf of*, **my brethren, my kinsmen according to the flesh,** if such a thing could accomplish their salvation. I could for their sakes be willing to be treated as Christ was—bearing, as an object accursed, the sins of my people. Compare the same sentiment expressed by Moses (Exod. 32 : 32). It would be necessary for any one to enter into the experience and the very Christlike heart of the apostle in order to appreciate the full meaning of his language. (Comp. 1 John 3 : 16.) Anathema means, properly, anything consecrated to God, a votive offering. But anything thus devoted could not be redeemed, and if an animal, must be slain (Lev. 27 : 28, 29); and therefore applied to a person or thing doomed to destruction (Josh. 6 : 17; 7 : 12), and hence in the New Testament a *curse, devoted to ruin, to the direst woes.* This is the meaning of the word wherever used by Paul (1 Cor. 12 : 3 ; 16 : 22 ; Gal. 1 : 3, 9, see also Acts. 23 : 14). Instead of *I could wish* (above) some translate, *I was wishing,* describing an actual state of his mind at some former time. But this is less to be preferred. Most adopt the common rendering of our English text. See the same construction in Gal. 4 : 20 and Acts 25 : 22 in the Greek, and their translation in the Revised version.

4. Who are Israelites—their most sacred, honorable, and distinguished name (11 : 1; John 1 : 47). See Gen. 32 : 28 when the name Israel was given to Jacob. Note the six prerogatives which are now mentioned as peculiar to them as a people and greatly to their advantage. **To whom,** etc.; better, *whose is the adoption* or *the sonship*, that is as a nation taken into a near and peculiar relationship (Exod. 4 : 22 ; Deut. 14 : 1; Hosea 11 : 1, 8), a grand privilege, but not so great as the personal sonship of believers in Christ (8 : 15). **And the glory**—doubtless referring to the symbol of God's presence as manifested in the cloud in the wilderness, over the tabernacle, and at times on the mercy seat of the ark (Exod. 13 : 21. 24 : 16; 40 : 34; Lev. 16 : 2). **And the covenants** made with the patriarchs (Gen. 15 : 18; 17 : 2, 4. 7–11; 26 : 24; 28 : 13–15. See also Exod. 24 : 7, 8; 31 : 16; 34 : 28; Ps. 89 : 28, 34). **And the giving of the law** on Mount Sinai (Exod. chap. 19–23). Compare how Moses and Nehemiah dwell upon the excellencies of the law (Deut. 4 : 8; Neh. 9 : 13, 14). **And the service of God** (omit *of God*, not being in the original), *the religious service*, the entire system of ritual and ceremonial service ordained through Moses and performed in the tabernacle and the temple (Heb. 9 : 1). **And the promises** —especially those relating to the Messiah (John 4 : 22; Matt. 1 : 1).

5. Whose are the fathers (11 : 28), Abraham, Isaac, and Jacob, *the fathers* of the nation (Exod. 3 : 15 : 4 : 5 ; Acts 3 : 13; 7 : 32). **And of whom as concerning the flesh,** as to his human nature and descent, **Christ came,** the most important distinction of the Jewish people. The language implies that Christ had also a higher nature. (Comp. 1 : 3, 4.) **Who is over all,** Jew and Gentile, **God blessed forever**—referring most naturally to Christ and affirming his supreme divinity. This accords with what is taught concerning

6 *r* Not as though the word of God hath taken none effect. For *they are* not all Israel, which are of Israel: 7 *t* neither, because they are the seed of Abraham, *are they* all children: but, In Isaac shall thy seed be called. 8 That is, *u* They which are the children of the flesh, these *are* not the children of God: but the children of the promise *z* are counted for the seed. For 9 this *is* the word of promise, At this time will I come, and Sarah shall have a son.

6 But not as though the word of God has failed. For not all they are Is- 7 rael, who are of Israel; neither, because they are Abraham's seed, are they all children; but, in Isaac shall 8 thy seed be called. That is, not they who are the children of the flesh are children of God; but the children of 9 the promise are reckoned as seed. For the word of promise is this, At this season I will come, and Sarah shall have a son.

r 3 : 3 ; 11 : 1, 2.   *s* 2 : 28, 29.   *t* Luke 3 : 8 ; Phil. 3 : 3.   *u* Gal. 4 : 22–31.   *z* Gal. 3 : 26–29.

Christ in John 1 : 1, 18 ; 20 : 28. (Comp. Acts 20 : 28; Titus 2 : 13, and John 12 : 41, with Isa. 6 : 5.) Some however put a period after *flesh*, and make this an independent sentence, a doxology, *May God who is over all be blessed*, or *praised forever*. A strong objection to this is that *who*, coming immediately after *Christ as to the flesh*, naturally refers to Christ, and that a change of subject from Christ to God is improbable. Besides, the position of the word *blessed* in the original should be placed at the beginning of the sentence, as a doxology, but it is placed in the middle where it would naturally be in describing Christ. Others place a period after *over all*, referring to the providential oversight of Christ, and make a sentence and doxology of the clause, *Blessed be God forever*. But in the original the word *God* comes first and without the article which is right in a descriptive sentence, but in a doxology *God* should have the article and *blessed* should come first. To regard either of the above as an independent doxology, is abrupt, and so far unnatural. It was however most natural after referring to the human nature of Christ, *as to the flesh*, to speak of his divinity. Most scholars, both ancient and modern, adopt this view. That such language having so much of the character of the doxology should refer to Christ, accords with 2 Peter 3 : 18; Rev. 1 : 6; 5 : 13. (Comp. 2 Tim. 4 : 18; 1 Peter 4 : 11.) **Amen.** (See on 1 : 25.)

6–13. NOTWITHSTANDING ISRAEL'S UNBELIEF, THE PROMISE OF GOD HAS NOT FAILED.

6. Paul's sad lament over Israel implied that the great mass of his people were failing of salvation. *But* while this was the case it was **not as though** it were a fact—that **the word of God had taken none effect,** *had failed.* He did not mean to say or imply that the promise made to Abraham, regarding his seed being blessed and a blessing, had come to nought. For, to explain, **they are not all true Israel, which are** descended *from* **Israel.** There is a spiritual in distinction from a literal, national Israel. Notice Paul's argument in Gal. 3 : 7–29. Compare our Saviour's words, John 8 : 39, "If ye were children of Abraham, ye would do the works of Abraham."

7. Neither, to illustrate, **because they are the seed,** the natural descendants, **of Abraham, are, they all children** in the sense contemplated in the promise, **but** God limited his promise, leaving out Ishmael and his descendants, saying, **In Isaac shall thy seed be called,** or reckoned as heirs (Gen. 21 : 12). Paul thus shows that a promise such as God gave to Abraham which apparently included all his descendants (Gen. 17 : 7), might be limited as in the cases of Ishmael and Isaac (Gen. 17 : 20–23).

8. That is, explaining and applying the quotation, *it is not* the **children of the flesh,** the mere natural descendants, *that are* **the children of God, but the children of promise are counted,** or *reckoned as seed*—those defined by special promise are regarded as the genuine posterity in question.

9. For, to confirm what he had said about "the children of promise," this **is the word of promise, as follows: At this time,** or *season* of the year, **will I come and Sarah shall have a son,** and hence this was the son of promise. This is quoted (Gen. 18 : 10) almost literally from the

10 And not only this; but when Rebecca also had conceived by one, even by our
11 father Isaac; for the children being not yet born, neither having done any good or evil, (*that the purpose of God according to election might stand, * not of works, but of him that calleth;)
12 it was said unto her, The elder shall
13 serve the younger. As it is written, Jacob have I loved, but Esau have I hated.

10 son. And not only so; but when Rebecca also had conceived by one, our
11 father Isaac (for they being not yet born, nor having done anything good or evil, that the purpose of God according to election might stand, not of
12 works, but of him who calls), it was said to her, the elder shall serve the
13 younger. Even as it is written, Jacob I loved, But Esau I hated.

y 4 : 17 ; 8 : 28–30.   z 11 : 6 ; Eph. 2 : 9.

Hebrew, varying slightly from the Septuagint. Its only bearing on the argument is to show that the son in whose line the seed should be reckoned, was called by a specific promise. The promise was limited to Sarah's son. Hagar's son was also Abraham's seed, but not a son of promise.

10. And not only this, rather, *And not only so*, as in the example just cited, illustrating how God called and limited his people even among the descendants of Abraham; but, in a more marked example, **when Rebecca had conceived by one,** by one and the same person, even **our father Isaac.** Isaac and Ishmael had only one parent in common; but Isaac and Esau had both in common. Both the latter though treated so differently were of the one and same father, even Isaac, in whose line the seed of Abraham was to be reckoned, showing that not all the seed of even Isaac was the true Israel. The original is very concise, both in this and the next verse.

11. The whole of this verse may be regarded as in a parenthesis. The choice of Isaac had been made known after the birth and childhood of Ishmael (Gen. 17 : 18, 19), but the choice of Jacob rather than Esau was declared before they were born. **For the children,** the twins, **being not yet born, neither having done any good or evil,** *in order* **that the purpose,** the predetermination, **of God, according to election,** a choice or selection in the Divine mind, **might stand,** *remain* permanently, **not of works but of him that calleth.** The reasons of this choice lay wholly in the Divine mind and not in the works or characters of those chosen. It was "according to the good pleasure of his will" (Eph. 1 : 5). The purpose here has not a special reference to the election to eternal salvation, but to the choice of Jacob with his descendants as his chosen people. The account in Genesis (25 : 23) and the quotation in the thirteenth verse of this chapter, show that the descendants from the two brothers were especially intended, and that thus the choice affected all their posterity. Paul is treating of God's choice or election in its widest and most absolute respects.

12. It was said unto her, The elder shall serve the younger—quoted from the Septuagint from Gen. 25 : 23. In this verse "two nations" and "two peoples" are spoken of, and it is added, "One people will be stronger than the other people; and the elder will serve the younger." In the personal history of these two brothers, Esau's privileges, interest, and birthright, were subjected to Jacob. In the history of their descendants it was frequently literally fulfilled. Thus David subdued the Edomites (2 Sam. 8 : 14), and subsequent conquests are mentioned (2 Kings 8 : 21 ; 14 : 7 ; 22, etc.). Finally they were conquered by John Hyrcanus and incorporated into the Jewish nation ("Jos. Antiq." XIII., 9, 1).

13. And with this accords the word of the prophet : **As it is written,** in Mal. 1 ; 23 ; **Jacob have,** etc.—rather, *Jacob I loved, but Esau I hated.* Paul is very concise, but his readers were doubtless familiar with the prophecy of Malachi and the history of Esau. More fully the passage reads; "Jacob I loved ; but Esau I hated and made his mountains a desolation, and gave his heritage to the jackals of the wilderness." Paul appears to quote this to show that the Divine purpose quoted in ver. 12 had actually been carried out. Some, however, refer the words to God's original purpose respecting the brothers, giving Jacob the preference, allotting to him a

14 What shall we say then? *Is there unrighteousness with God? God forbid.
15 For he saith to Moses, I will have mercy on whom I will have mercy, and I will have compassion on
16 whom I will have compassion. So then ᵇ*it is* not of him that willeth, nor of him that runneth, but of God that
17 showeth mercy. For the Scripture saith unto Pharaoh, Even for this same purpose have I raised thee up,

14 What then shall we say? Is there unrighteousness with God? Far be it!
15 For he says to Moses, I will have mercy on whomsoever I have mercy, and I will have compassion on whom-
16 soever I have compassion. So then it is not of him who wills, nor of him who runs, but of God who has
17 mercy. For the Scripture says to Pharaoh, For this very purpose did I raise thee up, that I might show forth

a See refs. Gen. 18 : 25.   *b* John 1 : 12, 13; 1 Cor. 1 : 26-31; Heb. 12 : 17.

---

goodly land, and barren mountains to Esau. Thus he treated one with tenderness and affection, and the other with severity. The word *hate* when used in contrast to love sometimes means not positive hatred, but *less love*, or the *absence of love*. (See Gen. 29 : 30, 33.) But there is really no need of this explanation here, since Malachi (1 : 4) says, "The people against whom the Lord hath indignation forever." God's indignation does not partake of the unholy, passionate anger of man, but of righteous opposition to sin. Thus far Paul has shown that the right to be the children of promise depends not on mere natural descent from Abraham, nor upon any works of our own, but absolutely upon the good pleasure and free favor of God.

14-18. Paul proceeds to show that so far from there being any injustice in God's dealings with men, according to his own purpose, THAT THESE DEALINGS WERE DESIGNED FOR WISE AND MERCIFUL ENDS. This is illustrated by the case of Pharaoh.

14. What shall we say then? What shall we infer? **Is there unrighteousness with God.** *Away the thought.* The question is general, referring not merely to the case of Jacob and Esau, but to the general principle of God's government which it illustrated. The Jew, the Christian, and every believer in the Old Testament, would alike hold that God is supremely righteous (Ps. 92 : 15).

15. For—to confirm and illustrate the negative answer which he had just given in the preceding verse. **He saith to Moses,** whose name would add emphasis, and whose writings were to be received as of unquestioned authority. To Paul God's word was final. The quotation is from Exod. 33 : 19, in the words of the Septuagint version. More exactly translated : **I Will have mercy on whom** *I have mercy* **and I will have compassion on whom** *I have compassion.* In this, God declares that he has the absolute right of choice in the exercise of his mercy and compassion. Both *mercy* and *compassion* have reference to the exercise of sympathy and favor toward the miserable and wretched, but the latter is the stronger term, a bewailing sympathy, suited to exclamation and tears. Read the whole account in Exod. 33 : 17-23 and 34 : 5-10. Notice that in this verse God is speaking of the exercise of his *mercy*. He is perfectly free from obligation to any one in choosing the objects of his mercy.

16. So then it is evident from the declaration of God himself that **it is not of him that willeth** (John 1 : 13), **nor of him that runneth,** it is not of any act of the human will however strong, nor of any personal effort however great (the figure is derived from the race), **but of God that showeth mercy.** God's mercy and grace are prominent in the apostle's mind. (Comp. Phil. 2 : 13.) Running in the footrace was a favorite figure with Paul (1 Cor. 9 : 24-26; Gal. 2 : 2; 5 : 7; Phil. 2 : 16).

17. In this verse the apostle instances the case of Pharaoh, upon whom, according to the principle of ver. 15, God did not exercise mercy, but left him to his own wicked ways, and gave him up to hardness of heart. **The Scripture**—that is, God through the Scripture, recognizing God as its author (Comp. Gal. 3 : 8, 22.) **Pharaoh,** in the very time of Moses, and a prominent representative case. The quotation is from Exod. 9 : 16, following the Septuagint, except in the first clause. **Even for this same purpose,** *for this very end in view,* **I raised thee up.** The exact meaning is much dis-

that I might show my power in thee, and that my name might be declared
18 throughout all the earth. Therefore hath he mercy on whom he will have mercy, and whom he will « he hardeneth.

my power in thee, and that my name might be announced in all the earth.
18 So then, on whom he will he has mercy, and whom he will he hardens.

c See refs. Exod. 4 : 21.

puted. The Hebrew is: "I made thee to stand," which the Septuagint translates, "Thou wast preserved," or "maintained." Since God said this after the sixth plague, he may mean that Pharaoh had been kept in his position as an illustrious man and king thus far. But this hardly comes up to the full meaning of the Hebrew. Some translate the Greek as given by Paul, *roused thee' up*—that is, to resistance, referring to the effect of God's dealings upon the heart of the wicked monarch. It is said that Paul draws from ver. 17 what he says in ver. 18, and therefore *rouse thee up* in its effect must be nearly synonymous with *hardeneth*. It is an objection to this interpretation that it is too far removed from the natural meaning of the Hebrew, *made thee to stand*. The more natural meaning of the Greek is, *I raised thee up*, either, brought thee into existence, or raised thee up to a public position as a king, or including both ideas. This latter, however, seems too strong for the Hebrew. The general idea, " I have raised thee up as a man, and a king to thy present position, seems better to accord with all the circumstances of the case. Almost to the same effect, DR. ARNOLD (" Am. Com."), extending this idea a little, says: "'I have given thee thy place in history', as the verb is used in Matt. 11 : 11; 24 : 11; John 7 : 52, etc. This general sense alone suits the context and the apostle's argument." **That I might show** *forth* **my power in thee**, in thy overthrow, **and that my name**, in consequence of my righteous judgments upon thee, **might be declared**, *published abroad in* **all the earth**, through all time and unto most distant places. This was in accordance with his own will, but for wise and beneficent ends. Thereby his name was glorified and his holy and righteous character was made known.

18. Therefore—a conclusion from the last verse and also from ver. 14–17, **hath he mercy on whom he will**, **and whom he will he hardeneth.** In the Mosaic account the two sides of this hardening are presented : (1) Pharaoh's agency in producing it (Exod. 8 : 15. 32 : 9 : 34); (2) God's agency in effecting it (Exod. 4 : 21; 7 : 3; 9 : 12; 10 : 20, 27; 11 : 10). Everywhere in the New Testament the word translated *harden* is used in a moral sense to *render obstinate* or *stubborn* in impenitence (Acts 19 : 9; Heb. 3 : 13, etc.). But in what sense is it said that God hardened Pharaoh's heart? (1) God is said sometimes to do that which he permits. Thus God is said to have moved David to number Israel (2 Sam. 24 : 1), when he permitted Satan to move David to do it (1 Chron. 21 : 1); (2) God gives over men to their own ways, to hardness and impenitence of heart (1 : 24, 28; 2 Thess. 2 : 11); (3) God is said to do that which indirectly and incidentally results from his agency. Thus in Isa. 6 : 10 the prophet is commanded to make the heart of this people fat and their ears heavy, etc., which would be the indirect and incidental result of his preaching. It is possible that the last two may have been united in Pharaoh's case. He was not obliged to sin; but in the judgments upon him for his cruelty and impiety, he appears like one given over to a delusion, and what would have influenced aright a well-constituted mind, led him to greater wickedness. God exercised toward him great forbearance (ver. 22), but this only helped him forward in his wicked course. (Comp. 2 : 2, 4; 2 Peter 3 : 4, 9, 15, 16.) If any one thinks that the language demands more than the above, then it is possible that in his case God took away supernaturally his fear of consequences, and thus he was left free to act out his own evil inclinations without restraint or dread of punishment. The moral character of his actions would not be changed, and the strong expression and Pharaoh's blindness to consequences, are both accounted for. " Whatever difficulty there lies in the assertion, that God *hardeneth*

19 Thou wilt say then unto me, Why doth he yet find fault? For ᵈ who hath resisted his will?
20 Nay but, O man, ᵉ who art thou that repliest against God? ᶠShall the thing formed say to him that formed it, Why hast thou made me thus? Hath not the ᵍpotter power over the clay, of the same lump to make ʰ one vessel unto honour,
22 and another unto dishonour? What if

19 Thou wilt say then to me, Why then does he still find fault? For who resists his will? Nay but, O man, who art thou that repliest against God? Shall the thing formed say to him who formed it, Why didst thou make me
21 thus? Has not the potter a right over the clay, out of the same lump to make one part a vessel unto honor,
22 and another unto dishonor. And

ᵈ Job 23 : 13 ; Dan. 4 : 35.   ᵉ Job 33 : 13 ; 36 : 23.   ᶠ See refs. Isa. 64 : 8.   ᵍ Prov. 16 : 4 ; Jer. 18 : 6.
ʰ Jer. 22 : 28 ; Acts 9 : 15 ; 2 Tim. 2 : 20.

whom he will, lies also *in the daily course of his providence*, in which we see this hardening process going on in the case of the prosperous ungodly man" (ALFORD).

19–29. MAN NOT COMPETENT TO CALL IN QUESTION GOD'S DEALINGS. GOD'S RIGHT AND PREROGATIVE AS CREATOR EXERCISED IN SUCH A MANNER AS TO DISPLAY HIS JUSTICE AND HIS MERCY. AND THIS ACCORDS WITH PROPHECY.

19. In view of the statement of ver. 18, Paul presents an objection which he must have met in his own experience and which has been common with the unrenewed in every age. **Thou wilt say then unto me,** from the low plane of human reason, **Why doth he** *still* **find fault,** and blame me as responsible, when he controls all things according to his own will? The question implies that there is no reason for finding fault. **For who hath resisted,** *who withstands his* **will** or *purpose?* The Jew was accustomed to regard all Jews elect, and all non-Jews substantially non-elect and reprobate. The idea that the Jews were largely passed over and that the true Israel was largely from among Gentiles aroused his rebellious nature against God, and even the Christian Jew found it difficult to adjust his thoughts and emotions to the idea of God's supreme and absolute right to select Gentiles rather than Jews as members of his kingdom. It often must have produced a severe struggle, and aroused the old nature.

20. Nay—*Who then art thou, forsooth*—an expression of some severity and rebuke, and perhaps of contempt. **O man,** *O human being,* weak, insignificant, and ignorant, **that thou repliest against God,** acting like a judge, questioning, disputing with him, the All Wise, the Almighty, and the Holy One. Unbecoming, incapable, and arrogant.   (Comp. Job 38 : 1, 2 ; 40 : 1–5 ; 42 : 1–6.) **Shall the thing formed,** or *molded,* **say to him that formed,** or *molded it, Why didst* **thou** *make me* **thus?** The language of Isa. 29 : 16 and 45 : 9 used in part. The form of the question demands a negative answer—*By no means*—Not to a human molder, much less to the Divine Molder. The very thought is absurd. The conception here is not so much the creating as the forming, shaping, arranging, and adjusting, that already created. It is however the Creator who is doing this. The creature is not in the position to judge his Maker, or question his wisdom or his right to do as he pleases.

21. Hath not the potter power, or *a right,* to decide **over the clay of the same lump,** or *mass,* mixed with water and kneaded, **to make one vessel unto honor,** to be put to that use, **and another unto dishonor,** for an ignoble use.   (Comp. 2 Tim. 2 : 20 ; 1 Cor. 12 : 23.) There seems a free reference to Jer. 18 : 4–6. Such familiar allusions and comparisons from the Old Testament would come with special force to believing Jewish readers. In the application of this question to our race, **the lump** would represent the mass of sinful men, who had no claim to be made vessels unto honor. The main thought, here, however, is, that God, the Maker, has the absolute right to act his own pleasure in the formation and government of his creatures. And accordingly, while he does not make them evil, he may exercise sovereign grace, as their Creator, in choosing some from among sinful men for a nobler use, while he may employ others differently; but in either case he is under no obligation to give account to any of his creatures.

God, willing to show *his* wrath, and to make his power known, ¹endured with much longsuffering the vessels of 23 wrath ᵏ fitted to destruction; and that he might make known ˡthe riches of his glory on the vessels of mercy, which he had ᵐafore prepared unto 24 glory, even us, ⁿ whom he hath called, º not of the Jews only, but also ᵖ of the Gentiles?

what if God, willing to show forth his wrath, and to make known his power, endured in much long-suffering ves-23 sels of wrath fitted for perdition; and that he might make known the riches of his glory on vessels of mercy, which he before prepared for glory; 24 whom he also called, even us, not from Jews only, but also from Gentiles?

i Num. 14:11, 18; 1 Peter 3:20. *k* 1 Peter 2:8; Jude 4. *l* 2:4; Col. 1:27. *m* 1 Thess. 5:9. *n* 8:28-30; 1 Cor. 1:9. *o* Eph. 2:11-18. *p* Ps. 22:27.

22. Having rebuked the spirit of the objector in ver. 19, and shown the right of the maker in forming the thing made, the apostle now proceeds to apply the principle to God in his prerogative as Creator, in forming and governing all things. *And* **what will** any created being have to say, **if God willing,** *choosing* **to show** *forth* **his wrath and to make known his power,** *that which was possible on his part,* that is, to exhibit his displeasure against sin and his power to punish it, **endured with much long-suffering vessels of wrath fitted for destruction,** ready to enter into utter ruin (Phil. 3:19). Notice, (1) That while the right of God as Creator and Judge is absolute, he exercises this right with **long-suffering.** (2) That the *will* and the *power* to maintain right are two grand essentials of a moral government. (3) That the long-suffering and the displeasure are both exercised toward *vessels of wrath,* those already connected with the Divine wrath and fallen under it. (4) It is not said of the vessels of wrath, as of those of mercy, that they were "afore prepared" (ver. 23), but merely *fitted,* that is, prepared by obstinate perseverance in unbelief *for destruction* or perdition. Some take the verb in the middle voice and translate *fitting themselves* for destruction. But the meaning is essentially the same in either rendering. It could hardly be said that God endures with much long-suffering what he himself has prepared. The reader might be reminded of the case of Pharaoh (ver. 17), but the immediate reference was to the unbelieving Jews.

23. And that he might. Something needs to be mentally supplied, such as, "What if he did this?" or "What if he endured?" *in order* **that he might make known the riches,** etc. The idea of the patience of God seems connected with both the vessels of wrath and of mercy. "The instant destruction of the *vessels of wrath* (in this case the unbelieving Jews) would have been perfectly just; but God endured them with long-suffering (thus tempering his justice with kindness) both the aim and the result of this being the more striking display (by the contrast) of the greatness of his grace toward the vessels of mercy" (WINER'S GRAM., p. 570). **The riches,** or *wealth,* **of his glory,** of his goodness, grace, mercy, wisdom, and power, displayed and bestowed *upon vessels of mercy* (Eph.1:6). **"Of mercy** (ver. 15, 16, 18, 23), which assumes the former misery of the vessels" (BENGEL). **Which he had afore,** or *which he before prepared for glory,* by the divine process given in 8:29, 30, and according to the arrangements of his providence and grace. In thus presenting God as acting according to his own will, it is nowhere implied that he acts arbitrarily and without reasons. Read Jer. 18:1-12 as a sidelight upon this passage.

24. A continuation and expansion of the last part of the preceding verse. **Even us,** etc.—better, *Whom*—"the vessels of mercy," *he also called, even us, not from Jews only but also from Gentiles.* The two classes are kept prominent here and throughout the Epistle—Jews and Gentiles; and also God's plans and dealings with them, especially in this and the two following chapters. The Jews are being passed over, and the Gentiles are being called; but the heirs of promise, the vessels of mercy, are not confined to national lines. The object of God's long-suffering now appears. He might have cast off the unbelieving Jews forever, but

25 As he saith also in Osee, *I will call them my people, which were not my people; and her beloved, which was 26 not beloved. And it shall come to pass, that in the place where it was said unto them, Ye are not my people; there shall they be called the children of the living God. 27 Esaias also crieth concerning Israel, Though the number of the children of Israel be as the sand of the sea, *a 28 remnant shall be saved: for he will finish the work, and cut it short in righteousness: because a short work will the Lord make upon the earth. 29 And as Esaias said before, Except the

25 As he says also, in Hosea,
I will call that my people, which was not my people;
And her beloved, who was not beloved.
26 And it shall be, that in the place where it was said to them, Ye are not my people, there will they be called,
27 Sons of the living God. And Isaiah cries concerning Israel,
If the number of the sons of Israel be as the sand of the sea,
It is the remnant that will be saved;
28 For the Lord will do a work on the earth,
Finishing it and cutting it short.
29 And as Isaiah has said before,

q 1 Peter 2 : 10.   *r* 11 : 5.

he spared them that the subjects of his grace might be brought to the acknowledgment of the truth through the appointed means. (Comp. 2 Peter 3 : 9.)

25. That God has exercised his own divine and absolute right of choice is shown by quotations from the Old Testament: (1) In regard to Gentiles (ver. 25, 26). (2) In regard to Israel (ver. 27-29). **As he saith also in Osee**—the Greek for the Hebrew *Hosea*. The apostle gives the general sense, not the form of the Hebrew (Hosea 2 : 23). **I will call,** *the one,* **my people which** *was* **not my people; and her beloved,** *who* **was not beloved.** The primary reference is to the bringing back of the ten apostate tribes to allegiance to God. But the words illustrate a principle, and thus have a wider application. God's receiving Gentile sinners is in accordance with what he had in the past declared to be his mode of procedure. Compare the same text quoted in 1 Peter 2 : 10, which is an important parallel passage.

26. Another quotation to the same effect from Hosea 1 : 10, given almost exactly from the Septuagint. **And it shall** *be,* **that in the place**—whether in the temple, in Palestine, or wherever it may be—**where it was said unto them,** etc. By analogy and implication Gentiles are included in this Old Testament prophecy. (Comp. Eph. 2 : 11, 19-22.)

27. Esaias also, etc. Rather, *And Isaiah crieth aloud* **concerning Israel.** Paul proceeds to confirm what he had said and implied in ver. 24, in regard to the Jews. While they would be largely passed over, some

would be saved. The quotation is from Isa. 10 : 22, 23, nearly as in the Septuagint, giving the general sense of the passage, which is peculiarly difficult in the Hebrew. **Though**—better, *If*—**the number of the children of Israel be as the sand of the sea,** *it is the* **remnant** only *that* **shall be saved.** The apostle does not say, nor does he mean, that these words, primarily referred to the particular case he had in hand, but he uses them to illustrate a principle, which if applicable in one case would be applicable in this analogous case. **Shall be saved**—in Hebrew *shall return.* The return is to God by repentance (Isa. 10 : 21), which results in *salvation* (Acts 2 : 37).

28. The quotation is continued, declaring that what was predicted would be certainly and speedily executed. **For he will finish the work,** etc. The readings of manuscripts vary much here. The most approved is: *The Lord will execute his word upon the earth, finishing it and cutting it short.* He would bring the work to which his word referred to an end, and hasten it to a conclusion. Paul brings out the point of the Hebrew sufficiently and fairly for his purpose. The Lord will execute summary judgments on Israel, leaving only a remnant saved through mercy. So a remnant will now be saved through the same mercy.

29. A further confirmation from prophecy regarding the remnant only that should be saved. **And,** the small number of Jewish believers fulfills another prediction, **as Isaiah said before,** earlier than the one just

Lord of Sabaoth had left us a seed, *we had been as Sodoma, and been made like unto Gomorrah.

The Jews rejected for unbelief; faith indispensable to salvation.

30 WHAT shall we say then? *That the Gentiles, which followed not after righteousness, have attained to righteousness, ʸeven the righteousness 31 which is of faith: but Israel, ˣ which followed after the law of righteousness, hath not attained to the law of 32 righteousness. Wherefore? ᶻ Because *they sought it* not by faith, but as it were by the works of the law. For ᵗ they

If the Lord of Sabaoth had not left us a seed, We should have become as Sodom, And been made like to Gomorrah. 30 What then shall we say? That Gentiles, who were not following after righteousness, obtained righteousness, but righteousness which is of faith; 31 but Israel, following after a law of righteousness, did not arrive at [such] 32 a law. Wherefore? Because [they sought it] not by faith, but as if it were by works of law. They stumbled

a Isa. 13 : 19 ; Jer. 50 : 40.   *t* 1 : 18-32 ; 10 : 20.   *u* 1 : 17 ; Phil. 3 : 9.   *x* 10 : 2 ; 11 : 7.
y 4 : 16 ; 10 : 3.   *z* Luke 2 : 34 ; 1 Cor. 1 : 23.

quoted. This is from Isa. 1 : 9, and quoted exactly from the Septuagint. **Except the Lord of Sabaoth** (*of Hosts*, or *Armies*, as often in the Old Testament) **had left us a seed** (the Hebrew equivalent is, "a small remnant"), **we had** *become as Sodom,* **and had been made like unto Gomorrah.** The prophet describes the temporal calamity then endured by the people, which would have resulted in their total destruction had it not been for God's sparing mercy. They were indeed representatives and types of the spiritual future. The fact that they were Jews did not then save them, neither would it now. Notice through all the argument of this chapter how the mercy, long-suffering, and patient endurance of God are kept prominent (ver. 6, 15, 16, 18, 22, 24, 25, etc.). Had it not been for Divine love, all, both Jews and Gentiles, would have been lost.

30-33. Conclusion of the discussion of the chapter. THE PASSING OVER OF ISRAEL, THOUGH COMPREHENDED IN THE DIVINE PURPOSE, WAS THROUGH THEIR OWN FAULT. How Gentiles attained unto righteousness. The reason of Israel's failure.

30. What shall we say then to this? What conclusion shall we draw from this argument? The result was not such as either Jew or Gentile would have expected. But Paul answers in the light of the whole preceding discussion, and of the righteousness through faith which he had developed. We say then, **That the Gentiles,** better, *That Gentiles,* that portion of them that had believed on Christ, *who* **followed not after righteousness,** having no revelation to hold up this object for their attainment, *obtained* **righteousness,** not of works as man might expect, *but righteousness* **which is of faith,** the true righteousness. The figure of the race-course and obtaining the prize is used. Gentiles, though they ran not after righteousness, yet obtained righteousness at the goal of the race-course, but not of works, or merits of their own, but through faith, as a result from faith.

31. But Israel, the greater part of the nation, *who* **followed after a** *law* **of righteousness,** this being their object in observing the Mosaic law, and its perfect observance would have secured righteousness (Luke 10 : 28), *did not arrive at that law,* or *at such a law.* They did not attain their object, the law did not prove to be a law of righteousness to them ; they did not attain to that principle of holy life which would insure their acceptance with God. The last *righteousness* is not found in the best manuscripts; but it is clearly understood.

32. Wherefore this failure on Israel's part? This was the special question that now needed solving. He had suggested the answer regarding Gentiles. God had called them (ver. 23, 24), and they had attained it through faith (ver. 31). But why did Israel fail, when Gentiles succeeded? **Because** they sought it **not by faith, but as it were,** better, *but as being from works of law,* as though righteousness were to be attained in that way. "**'As**' suggests that such a pursuit was only a vain imagination" (BOISE). According to many critics, **of the law** should be

33 stumbled at that stumblingstone; as it is written, Behold, I lay in Sion a stumblingstone and rock of offence: and *whosoever believeth on him shall not be ashamed.

33 against the stone of stumbling; as it is written, Behold, I lay in Zion a stone of stumbing, and a rock of offense; and he that believes on him shall not be put to shame.

a 10 : 11.

omitted. In either case the meaning is the same. The word *law*, if omitted, is implied, and there is much manuscript authority for it. **For,** is omitted by the best authorities. The thought however is implied. **They stumbled at that stumblingstone,** better, *against the stone of stumbling*, the well-known stone, foretold in the next verse.

33. This is a composite quotation, uniting two passages from Isaiah (28:16; 8:14) and follows closely the Hebrew. The Jews referred both quotations to the Messiah. The former declares, **Behold I lay in Zion** "a stone, a tried stone, a precious corner stone of a sure foundation." Instead of these words in quotation marks, Paul substitutes from the latter passage, *a stone of stumbling and a rock of offense*, which evidently referred to the Messiah. Compare the same passages, quoted in 1 Peter 2 : 6, 8. See also Simeon's allusion to Isa. 8 : 14, 15, in speaking of Jesus as "set for the falling and rising of many in Israel" (Luke 2:34). Such references in ancient prophecy were often made in times of calamity to the Messiah as an encouragement to his people. They showed that God had purposes which ensured their safety. They implied that many would stumble and be offended at the Messiah, and perish ; but that those who believed on him *should* not *be put to shame*, but would realize all their hopes. **Shall not be ashamed**—from the Septuagint. The Hebrew is "shall not make haste," that is, shall not flee in terror. This yields a secondary meaning, shall have no reason for fear or shame, shall not be confounded. Thus while Paul gives the reason of Israel's failing so largely of the benefits of the Messiah, he indicates that it was their own fault. "He came to his own and his own received him not" (John 1 : 11).

PRACTICAL REMARKS.

1. Christian experience has to do with the innermost depths of the heart, and is attested by conscience and the Spirit (ver. 1 ; Acts 23 : 1 ; 8 : 16, 26).

2. The extremes of joy and sorrow often meet in the Christian's soul (ver. 2 ; 8 : 38, 39 ; 2 Cor. 2 : 2–4, 12-14).

3. It is a distinguishing mark of soul-winners that they are deeply concerned and often heavily burdened for the salvation of sinners (ver. 1-3 ; Phil. 3 : 18 ; Gal. 4 : 19).

4. It is natural and right that we should be anxious for the salvation of our kindred (ver. 3, 4 ; 10 : 1 ; Esther 8 : 6).

5. Our external relations to the people of God may prove our ruin (ver. 4, 5 ; 10 : 2, 3).

6. Christ is the God-man who is over all, blessed forever (ver. 5 ; 1 : 3, 4 ; Matt. 28 : 18 ; John 1 : 1, 18).

7. God knows no failure in his promises or his purposes (ver. 6 ; 2 Peter 3 : 9 ; Isa. 55 : 11).

8. No external circumstances such as pious parents, church ordinances and privileges, can make us true children of God (ver. 6-8, 4, 15 ; 3 : 9-18 ; Luke 3 : 8).

9. They only who are born of the Spirit are the children of promise, and hence the true children of God (ver. 6-9 ; John 1 : 13).

10. "Though children prior to birth do neither good nor evil, yet they may be naturally depraved. They neither hunger nor thirst, yet are hunger and thirst natural appetites. They exercise neither love nor anger, yet these are natural passions. They know probably neither joy nor sorrow, yet these are natural emotions" (HODGE). (Ver. 9-11; Gen. 6 : 5 : 8 : 21 ; Jer. 17 : 9 ; Ps. 51 : 3-5 ; 58 : 3, 4).

11. God had a plan in making all things, a purpose in arranging all events, and an election or selection of his people (ver. 11-13 ; Heb. 3 : 4 ; 1 Thess. 1 : 4 ; Eph. 3 : 11).

12. Election is according to the foreknowledge of God. As we cannot conceive a time when the Allwise God had not decreed, nor when he did not fore-

know, we must conclude that his decrees and foreknowledge were coexistent and coeternal (ver. 11-13; 8 : 29; 1 Peter 1 : 2).

13. The thought that there can be any unrighteousness in God is repugnant to a rightly constituted mind and cannot for a moment be entertained. He is the immutable standard of right and truth (ver. 4; 3 : 6; Gen. 18 : 25).

14. Scriptural election is unconditional but beneficent, according to God's own good and absolute pleasure. Men are elected to salvation but not to perdition (ver. 14-16; Eph. 1 : 11, 12; 1 Tim. 2 : 4.)

15. God is in no sense the author of sin. The wicked are their own destroyers. If left to their own wicked course they have no right to complain (ver. 17-20; Rev. 15 : 4; Hosea 13 : 9).

16. God's glory, the manifestation of his perfections, is the greatest and highest end of all things (ver. 17, 22, 23 ; Rev. 4 : 11).

17. "It is not optional with God whether he shall be wise, or great, or just, or true, or holy; but it is optional with him whether he shall show mercy to sinners or leave them to perish in their sins. How appropriate then the publican's prayer, 'God be merciful to me, a sinner'" (PENDLETON). (Ver. 17-20; Matt. 20 : 15 ; 2 Tim. 2 : 13; Luke 18 : 13).

18. God's sovereignty and man's free agency must both be accepted as the teaching of Scripture. We must believe that they are in complete harmony. The free moral agency of men and human responsibility appear to be not only a matter of fact but also a divine decree (ver. 19-24; Ps. 110 : 3; Ezek. 18 : 4, 20-32).

19. It is because man is ignorant and depraved that he finds fault with his Maker (ver. 19 ; Job 42 : 3-6).

20. The doctrine of election appears as a fact and a principle of the divine government in the case of Israel (ver. 12-18, 27-29; 11 : 7).

21. In election God is but carrying out his own inherent right as Creator and Former of all things and Ruler of the universe (ver. 19-24; Dan. 4 : 35).

22. God may also exercise a personal election in the choice of individuals to eternal life (ver. 24, 27, 29; 8 : 28-30; Acts 13 : 48).

23. Men as fallen intelligent beings are considered as objects of election (ver. 21 ; Eph. 2 : 10).

24. Opposition to the doctrine of election shows a want of confidence in God as the moral governor of the universe (ver. 19-21 ; Ps. 91 : 10).

25. How wonderful the patience of God toward sinners, and how surprising their abuse of it (ver. 22; 2 : 2-4; 1 Peter 3 : 9, 15 ; 2 Peter 2 : 1-3).

26. God has his own wise and good reasons, which if known would explain why some are saved and some are lost, the ground of the condemnation of sinners being always in themselves (ver. 25-33 ; John 3 : 18, 19).

27. In the doctrine of election we catch a glimpse of God's plan of working, of the secret things that belong to him ; but in other things revealed we see plainly our duty (ver. 30; Deut. 29 : 29).

28. The doctrine of election should produce humility, submission, confidence, peace, and diligence (ver. 22-33; Ps. 115 : 1; 2 Peter 1 : 10; Phil. 2 : 12, 13).

29. The doctrine of election should be preached only in love and in great tenderness (ver. 1, 2, 22, 29; 10 : 1 ; 11 : 20, 21 ; Luke 19 : 41, 42). See "Homiletic Uses of the Doctrine of Election," *Bibliotheca Sacra*, Jan., 1893, pp. 79-92.

30. Salvation does not come to men arbitrarily but is obtained through faith, or lost through unbelief (ver. 30-32; Mark 16 : 16).

31. Error and self-righteousness often prove a greater hindrance to salvation than vice or crime (ver. 30-32; Matt. 21 : 31).

32. Christ becomes to every man under the gospel either a sure foundation or a stone of stumbling (ver. 33 ; 1 Cor. 1 : 23, 24 ; 2 Cor. 2 : 16).

33. The Christian will never be disappointed or brought to shame through Christ (ver. 33 ; 7 : 25; 8 : 37).

CHAPTER X.

In this chapter Paul views Israel as unsaved through misguided zeal and ignorance, though the gospel is adapted and designed for all, and should be preached to all. In chap. 9 the passing over Israel is viewed from the Divine

10 BRETHREN, *my heart's desire and prayer to God for Israel is, that they 2 might be saved. For I bear them record *that they have a zeal of God, *but not according to knowledge. 3 For they being ignorant of *God's righteousness, and going about to establish their own *righteousness, have not submitted themselves unto the 4 righteousness of God. For *Christ is

10 BRETHREN, my heart's desire and prayer to God on their behalf, is that 2 they may be saved. For I testify for them, that they have a zeal for God, 3 but not according to knowledge. For being ignorant of the righteousness of God, and seeking to establish their own, they did not subject themselves 4 to the righteousness of God. For

b 9 : 1-3 ; 1 Cor. 9 : 20-22.   *c* 9 : 31 ; John 16 : 2 ; Acts 22 : 3 ; Gal. 1 : 14.
d 1 Tim. 1 : 13.   *e* 1 : 17 ; 9 : 30.   *f* Luke 16 : 15 ; Phil. 3 : 9 ; Rev. 3 : 17, 18.
g 3 : 25-31 ; Matt. 5 : 17 ; Acts 13 : 38, 39 ; 1 Cor. 1 : 30 ; Gal. 3 : 24 ; Heb. 9 : 7-14.

side ; in chap. 10, from the human side. In the former, Paul more especially views his kindred as lost, with a remnant saved ; in this, as savable, from the salvation side, though as a people rebellious. In both chapters God is just, faithful, and righteous, and the guilt of Israel entirely their own. In both the extension of the gospel to Gentiles is shown to be according to prophecy.

1-4. JEWS SAVABLE, YET UNSAVED. THE REASONS GIVEN.

1. Brethren—both Jews and Gentiles of the church at Rome. Therefore he speaks of Israel in the third instead of the second person. **My heart's desire,** *longing preference indeed,* implying some thought to be supplied. It would indeed be the joy and preference of my heart, though I know it is otherwise ordered. The obstacles to their salvation are brought out in the two following verses. **And prayer to God for Israel**—rather, according to the best text, *for them is* (that is, for Israel, 9 : 31), **that they might be saved**—literally, *for their salvation.* Their salvation would fill his heart with delight, and for this he prayed. While he knew that they were rebellious and God had otherwise directed, he did not regard their case as hopeless. In order to understand Paul fully in this verse and 9 : 1-3, we must put ourselves back in his place. The Jews considered themselves superior to all other nations in matters of religion, and the idea that Gentiles were as good as they, and could be saved as well, was exceedingly repugnant to their feelings. The apostle knew this dislike, and he wished to impress his brethren with his intense desire and love for them. Compare Acts 22 : 21, 22, describing a scene a few months later.

2. In this and the next verses Paul gives reasons for his affectionate longings for their salvation, and why they did not attain it. **For I bear them record,** *I testify for them,* as one who knows by intimate acquaintance and also by experience, **that they have a zeal of God**—better, *for God*—**but not according to knowledge,** *to full* knowledge of God and his plan of salvation. Their knowledge was not in proportion to their zeal. Like himself once, they acted "ignorantly in unbelief" (1 Tim. 1 : 13 ; Acts 13 : 27). But ignorance under the full light of the gospel, and their own Scriptures, was a crime ; and thus their misdirected zeal was sinful.

3. For, thus acting not according to a full and proper knowledge, **they being ignorant of God's righteousness,** of which he is the author, and which he reveals and imparts (3:21), **and going about,** or, *seeking,* **to establish their own righteousness** —to found a righteousness by their own acts—**have not submitted**—better, *did not subject themselves,* **to the righteousness of God,** and thus did not accept in submission and faith the righteousness which he has offered, and which avails before him. The second *righteousness* in this verse is omitted by the best authorities. *Seeking to establish their own,* they withheld from God his due, and rejected his offered righteousness. That their misguided zeal and ignorance might be removed was doubtless the apostle's earnest prayer.

4. For introduces an important declaration, and an explanation of their failure in not subjecting themselves to the righteousness of God. Literally, *For the end of the law is Christ into righteousness,* leading into righteousness, as a means of attaining right-

the end of the law for righteousness to every one that believeth.
5 For Moses describeth the righteousness which is of the law, [b]That the man which doeth those things shall

Christ is the end of law for righteousness, to every one that believes.
5 For Moses writes that the man who has done the righteousness which is of
6 the law, shall live in it. But the right-

[b] Neh. 9 : 29; Ezek. 20 : 11.

eousness *to every one that believeth.* Instead of seeking to establish their own, they ought, therefore, to have accepted God's righteousness. But how is Christ *the* **end** of the law? According to some he is the *end* or *termination* of the law as a system or means of obtaining righteousness, so that every believer may be justified as such by faith apart from legal obedience (6 : 14; 7 : 4, 6; Gal. 3 : 11, 12). According to others, Christ is *the end* or *aim* of the law—its *aim* being the coming and work of Christ, who alone is able to secure righteousness for us. The aim of the law was to make men righteous, and this alone is accomplished in Christ. Or the aim of the law as a schoolmaster was to lead to Christ (Gal. 3 : 23, 24; comp. 1 Peter 1 : 9; 1 Tim. 1 : 5). Others, that he is *the end, the fulfiller* of the law, having perfectly obeyed its moral precepts in his life, and fulfilled its types and sacrifices in his death and resurrection. And thus he wrought out a righteousness which is accounted reckoned to the believer. The word *law* is here emphatic, and the scope of the passage is very broad, and much of all pertaining to the above views may be included. Christ is the *consummation* of the law, including necessarily the *aim* or scope of the law which *terminates* as a covenant of works in him. He accomplishes for the believer that which the law, if perfectly obeyed, would have secured, namely, acceptance with God and consequent holiness. This accords well not only with what precedes, but with the comparison which follows in ver. 5–10. The apostle thus prepares the way also for showing that Christ should be preached **To every one that believeth.** It was very offensive to the self-righteous Jew to think that the Gentile whom he despised should stand on the same level with himself. His heart revolted at the thought of salvation through faith on the same terms to all (ver. 12).

5-13. THE GOSPEL IS ADAPTED AND DESIGNED FOR ALL.

5. Confirmatory of the truth stated in ver. 4, Paul introduces a comparison between the righteousness of the law and the righteousness of faith. **For Moses describeth,** or *writeth*, etc. According to the best Greek text, *For Moses writeth that the man who has done the righteousness which is of the law shall live in it*, in that righteousness as a basis or sphere of life. (Comp. 6 : 2; Col. 3 : 7.) He that obeys the law's demands shall live, enjoy God's favor, on the ground of perfect obedience. "This do and thou shalt live" (Luke 10 : 28). But this very standard brought condemnation ; for no one can keep the law (chap. 1–3). Even one transgression broke the law, and condemnation ensued (Gal. 3 : 10-12). The quotation is from Lev. 18 : 5. **Shall live**—not in the lower sense of a prosperous life in the land of promise, but in the higher sense of eternal life, the favor of God and eternal happiness. "Jewish interpreters themselves included in it (*life*) more than mere earthly felicity in Canaan, and extended their view to a better life hereafter" (ALFORD). It should be noted that Paul attributes Leviticus to Moses as its author.

6, 7, 8. Paul contrasts the righteousness which is of faith with the righteousness which is of the law, using Deut. 30 : 11-14, quoted freely, with a running commentary upon it, and applying it to Christ who is the end of the law, and to the gospel to which the law was preparatory. Paul does not mean to say that Moses applied the words as he applies them here. But Moses was speaking of future departures of Israel from God and his law, and of future returns to him. And he affirms that this commandment which he gives them is not far off, but near them and easily to be ascertained. They were to turn to the Lord with all their heart and all their soul (Deut. 30 : 10). In this they would exercise repentance and faith. The righteous under the old dispensation lived by faith (Heb. 11), and faith was accounted for righteousness (4 : 9). The prominent thing in Lev. 18 : 5

6 live by them. *But the righteousness which is of faith speaketh on this wise, say not in thine heart, Who shall ascend into heaven? (that is, to bring
7 Christ down *from above*:) or, Who shall descend into the deep? (that is, to bring up Christ again from the dead.)
8 But what saith it? The word is nigh thee, *even* in thy mouth, and in thy heart: that is, *k* the word of faith,
9 which we preach; that *l* if thou shalt confess with thy mouth the Lord Jesus, and shalt believe in thine heart that God hath raised him from the
10 dead, thou shalt be saved. For with the

cousness which is of faith says thus, Say not in thy heart, Who shall ascend into heaven? (that is, to bring Christ
7 down,) or, who shall descend into the abyss? (that is, to bring up Christ from
8 the dead.) But what says it? The word is near thee, in thy mouth, and in thy heart; that is, the word of faith, which
9 we preach; because, if thou confess with thy mouth Jesus as Lord, and believe in thy heart that God raised him from the dead, thou shalt be saved.

i 3 : 22, 25.   *k* 1 Tim. 4 : 6 ; 1 Peter 1 : 23, 25.   *l* Matt. 10 . 32, 33 ; Luke 12 : 8 . Phil. 2 : 9-11.

---

is *doing* the statutes of the law; the prominent thing in this passage is *turning* with all the heart, *loving* the Lord, and *obeying* his voice (Deut. 30 : 10, 20), which imply faith in God. In the former, immediate action in keeping the law is demanded; in the latter, a future return to God is spoken of. The one especially demanded works; the latter faith and obedience. This passage is therefore not only appropriate as the language of faith, but is also fittingly so used by Paul. If it could be thus used of heart service under the law, much more under the gospel. If true of the shadow, much more of the substance. If true of the spiritual requirements of the law, much more of the spiritual service of him who is the end of the law.

But the righteousness which is of faith, which comes from and is obtained by faith, **speaketh on this wise**—*speaks thus*. Moses naturally represents the law (John 1 : 17); so the apostle does not present him as speaking, but the righteousness of faith, personified, speaks: **Say not in thy heart, Who shall ascend into heaven**—as if it were an impossible thing, and far off. **That is,** applying the words to the present case and argument, **to bring Christ down,** as if the Messiah had not yet come, and in order to be saved he must be brought down and be personally present. **Or, who shall descend into the deep** —*the abyss.* The Hebrew has, "Who shall go over the sea" (Deut. 30 : 13). Both Paul and Moses took the sea, or the great deep, as the antithesis of heaven, but Paul here gives the idea instead of the exact word. *The abyss*—

the *bottomless* depths — the common realm of the dead. **That is, to bring up Christ from the dead** (omitting again), as though his resurrection was impossible, or had not taken place. The caution is against unbelief in regard to the two main points of faith: (1) That Christ had come; (2) that he had died and risen. The strength of the unbelief, whether mingled with anxiety and perplexity or not, would depend on the spiritual condition of the interrogator. The one merely convinced of sin intellectually would ask these questions differently from one deeply convicted of sin.

But what saith it? the righteousness which is of faith? **The word,** the message with the terms of the covenant from God **is nigh thee,** close to thee, **in thy mouth,** ready to be professed and proclaimed, **and in thy heart,** ready to be accepted, remembered, and practised. **That is,** to apply it under the gospel dispensation, **the word of faith,** the message which points to faith in Christ, ever holding it up as necessary to salvation, **which we preach.**

9. That, introducing a fuller statement of the preceding sentence, the substance of what was preached. But most recent interpreters translate, *Because,* giving the reason for and confirming the preceding application of the Mosaic saying to the preaching of the gospel. *Because* **if thou shalt confess,** or more exactly, *if thou confess with thy mouth Jesus as Lord,* in submission owning him as your supreme Lord and Master (1 Cor. 12 : 3 ; Matt. 10 : 32), *and believe in thy heart,* not a mere intellectual assent and belief, but a deeply

heart man ᵐbelieveth unto righteousness, and with the mouth confession is made unto salvation.
11 For the Scripture saith, ⁿWhosoever believeth on him shall not be ashamed.
12 For ᵒthere is no difference between the Jew and the Greek: for the same Lord over all ᵖis rich unto all that call
13 upon him. For whosoever shall call upon the name of the Lord shall be saved.

10 For with the heart man believes unto righteousness; and with the mouth confession is made unto salvation.
11 For the Scripture says, whoever believes on him shall not be put to
12 shame. For there is no distinction between Jew and Greek; for the same one is Lord of all, rich toward all that
13 call on him; for every one who calls on the name of the Lord will be saved.

_{m Gal. 2 : 16 ; Phil. 3 . 9. n 9 . 33. Jer. 17 : 7. o 3 . 22. 29. 30; Acts 15 ; 9; Gal. 3 ; 25. p Eph. 1 ; 7 ; 2 : 4, 7.}

fixed, cordial, loving faith, *that God raised* **him from the dead, thou shalt be saved**, from death and have eternal life (4 : 24, 25 ; 5 : 1 ; 1 Thess. 1 : 10; Heb. 13 : 20). Notice that *mouth* and *heart* are in the same order as in the preceding verse; that whoever confessed Jesus as Lord would have no need to say, "Who shall ascend," etc. (ver. 6), nor would he who believed in the heart have need to ask, "Who shall descend?" etc. Also that *shall be saved* corresponds with *shall live* (ver. 5), though embracing a fuller meaning. Thus the order in this verse was fixed by the order which precedes. Notice that Paul has taken a step in advance of ver. 4, namely, that faith in the risen Christ and confession of his name are sufficient for salvation.

10. The statement of the preceding verse is explained by what occurs in actual experience. The apostle now naturally puts faith and confession in the order in which they take place. **For with the heart man believeth,** or *For with the heart faith is exercised,* **unto righteousness,** unto the attainment of righteousness in justification. But this is not enough. Faith must be followed by confession, without which it is but a dead faith. **And with the mouth confession is made unto salvation,** unto its complete attainment. As faith manifests itself in confession and a life of obedience, so true confession implies faith. The two mutually act on each other. The process goes on. Faith is exercised unto righteousness not only in justification, but also in sanctification (Gal. 2 : 20), and confession is exercised unto a complete salvation in the development of a full Christian life and a perfect Christian manhood. Thus "the end of your faith" is "the salvation of your souls" (1 Peter 1 : 9).

11. For, in confirmation of this glorious result of faith and its consequent confession, **the Scripture saith** (Isa. 28 : 16, quoted already in 9 : 33), **Whosoever believeth on him shall not be ashamed**—*shall not be put to shame*—but shall attain the salvation promised and which they expected (5 : 5. See on 9 : 33). Both the Hebrew and the Septuagint read, *He that believeth*, etc. This the apostle broadens into, *Every one*, or, *Whoever believeth*, this universal application being in accord with the present state of his argument. This he sustains in the next verse. Here and through the rest of the argument faith only is mentioned, but the confession of Christ as Lord was a necessary consequent of faith, and needed no further separate mention. Notice that the apostle passes here in his quotations from Moses to the prophets, who also taught the salvation of believers and the rejection of unbelievers, whether Jews or Gentiles (ver. 13, 19-21).

12. For—used to confirm the "Whosoever" of ver. 11. Every one, I say, **For there is no difference,** or distinction, made respecting those who have faith, *between Jew and Greek* (1 : 16); **for the same** *is Lord of all,* **rich unto all that call upon him.** *Lord* refers naturally to Christ (ver. 9. 13, 16). And all the passages quoted refer primarily to the time of the Messiah. *Rich*—his *wealth* abounds to accept and pardon (Isa. 55 : 1-7), *toward all,* however numerous the suppliants (Rev. 22 : 17). Further in regard to the Lordship of Christ, see 14 : 9; Acts 10 : 36; Phil. 2 : 11. (See also on 9 : 5.)

13. To confirm and emphasize the "all" in ver. 12. Paul quotes (from the Septuagint) Joel 2 : 32: **For whosoever**—literally, *For every one whoever,* **shall call upon the name of the Lord shall be saved.** The same

14 How then shall they call on him in whom they have not believed? And how shall they believe in him of whom they have not heard? And how shall
15 they hear *q* without a preacher? And how shall they preach, *r* except they be sent? As it is written, *s* How beautiful are the feet of them that preach the gospel of peace, and bring glad
16 tidings of good things. But *t* they

14 How then are they to call on him in whom they believed not? And how are they to believe in him of whom they heard not? And how are they to hear
15 without a preacher? And how are they to preach, unless they are sent forth? As it is written,
How beautiful are the feet of those who bring glad tidings of good things!
16 But they did not all obey the glad

q Titus 1 : 3.   *r* Matt. 28 : 18-20 ; 2 Cor. 5 :-18-20.   *s* Nahum 1 : 15.   *t* John 12 : 37 ; Heb. 4 : 2.

---

passage was quoted more fully at Pentecost (Acts 2 : 21), and refers to Messianic times. The *name of the Lord* applies to Christ, and includes all that his name imports—Redeemer, Saviour, Lord, and final Judge. The Hebrew in Joel is "the name of Jehovah." Its application to Christ in this verse, which is also demanded by the next verse, distinctly marks the divinity of our Lord. *Shall call* implies faith (next verse), and a recognition and acknowledgment of Christ as a Saviour exalted to give repentance and the forgiveness of sins (Acts 5 : 31).

14-21. THE GOSPEL SHOULD BE PREACHED TO ALL. The heathen must be evangelized. Missionary intimations in the Old Testament.

14. If the prophets foretold salvation to all, Jews and Gentiles, who should turn to the Messiah, then there was need of preachers and missionaries. Here we have an argument for evangelizing the heathen against Pharisaic jealousy and exclusiveness. If then this is the case, as just stated, with Jews and Gentiles (ver. 13), **How then shall they call on him in whom they have not believed?** Calling on the name of the Lord supposes faith in the message. Such calling as resulted in salvation supposed saving faith (ver. 4-10). But salvation was only to those believing; and hence the language is equally applicable to unbelieving Jews and Gentiles. If the Jews, for example, believe not on the Messiah when he comes, as was foretold (ver. 16), then how shall they call upon him and be saved? **And how shall they believe in him of whom they heard not.** Thus faith pre-supposes hearing, and hearing a preacher. The language is applicable to both Jews and Gentiles, especially to the latter. Without this universal proclamation of the gospel, God's design to extend universally the gospel could not be accomplished.

15. And how shall they preach except they be sent *forth* by the Lord and the churches (Acts 13 : 2, 3). If they failed to do this through indifference or through prejudice or jealousy, how then could the predicted evangelization take place? **As it is written**—showing God's design to have such messengers, and the glad welcome given to their message. The quotation is a free rendering of Isa. 52 : 7, and has primary reference to the return of the people from captivity, which return was typical of a more glorious one of the true Israel under the gospel. **How beautiful the feet**—the very footsteps bearing them on over mountain and vale in their divine mission—**of them that preach** *the glad tidings* **of peace** (5 : 1 ; 8 : 6 ; Eph. 2 : 14, 15, 17 ; 4 : 3 ; 6 : 15), **and bring glad tidings of good things,** the rich saving blessings of salvation. The words **preach the gospel of peace and,** are not found in some of the oldest and best manuscripts and are omitted by some of the best latest critics. Preachers called of God and directed by the Spirit must be sent forth so that Jews and Gentiles might hear and be saved, or be without excuse if they believed not (ver. 16-18). Comp. Isa. 52 : 10 : "The Lord hath laid bare his holy arm in the eyes of all nations; and all the ends of the earth shall see the salvation of our God." Paul uses the plural **them** for the Hebrew singular *him.* The one represents a class; the other, individuals of that class.

16. But while the glad tidings were joyfully welcomed by many, they were rejected also, especially by a large portion of Israel. It might be urged as an objection, that the messengers and mes-

have not all obeyed the gospel. For Esaias saith, "Lord, who hath be-
17 lieved our report? So then *faith *cometh* by hearing, and hearing by the word of God.
18 But I say, Have they not heard? Yes verily, *their sound went into all the earth,* and their words unto the
19 ends of the world. But I say, Did not Israel know? First Moses saith, *I

tidings. For Isaiah says, Lord, who
17 believed our report? So then faith comes of hearing, and hearing through
18 the word of Christ. But I say, did they not hear? Yes, verily;
Their sound went out into all the earth,
And their words to the ends of the world.
19 But I say, did Israel not know? First Moses says,

---

u John 12 : 38.   z Ver. 14; 1 Thess. 2 : 13.   y Matt. 24 : 14; 26 : 19; Col. 1 : 6, 23.
z See 1 Kings 18 : 10; Matt. 4 : 8.   a 11 : 11.

---

sage had only partially succeeded. But this is what was foretold. **But,** though thus proclaimed, **they have not**—rather, *they did not all obey the glad tidings*—this preaching of the gospel viewed as ideally past. And this accords with the words of the prophet, **For Esaias saith,** *Who believed* **our report?** A question suggesting a negative answer, implying a very general unbelief, as exhibited by the Jews. The question is from Isa. 53 : 1, according to the Septuagint. **Report**—literally, *the things heard*, which were to be believed, resulting in salvation, or disbelieved, resulting in inexcusable condemnation.

17. An immediate conclusion from the preceding verse, and also of the argument from ver. 14. *Accordingly* **then faith cometh by hearing,** as a result of hearing. *The things heard* (ver. 16) were regarded by the prophet as the appointed means for believing ("Who hath believed?"). Hence hearing precedes faith, and the right kind of hearing results in faith. **And hearing comes by,** or *through*, **the word of God,** or according to many authorities, *the word of Christ*, that which has been spoken of God, or of Christ. The meaning is essentially the same. It is implied that the revealed message must be proclaimed in order to hearing. The several links of the evangelizing chain of ver. 14 and 15 are necessary. The gospel should be preached even though many reject it, both to Jews and Gentiles.

18. But I say, Have they, or better, *did they not hear?* this universal message. Has the word of God been proclaimed, and the revelation of Christ made known, and yet not heard? By no means. **Yes, verily,** to use the language of the psalmist (Ps. 19 : 4) in reference to the heavens which declare the glory of God, **their sound,** the proclamation of these messengers, **went into all the earth, and their words unto the ends of the world,** *the inhabited world.* It was natural for Paul, as often now with preachers, to clothe his thoughts with the words of Scripture. And most appropriately too, for Paul saw in the universal revelation in the natural world an illustration and type of the world-wide message of the gospel. All revelation of God, whether natural or revealed, came through Christ (John 1 : 9). A certain uniformity and analogy prevails in God's words and works. The universal voice of the one was the prelude of the universal voice of the other. It had become a fact too in Paul's day. Not only was the gospel proclaimed to both Jews and Gentiles, but starting from Pentecost it had gone with the converts to their homes "in every nation under heaven" (Acts 2 : 5). The apostles, the disciples "scattered abroad" (Acts 8 : 5), missionaries and evangelists, had penetrated the uttermost parts of the earth (15 : 19; James 1 : 1; Col. 1 : 23; 1 Peter 1 : 1; 5 : 13). The quotation is from the Septuagint. The Hebrew *line* is used of a *string* of a musical instrument and thence a *sound*, "Their sound," etc.

19. But I say, perhaps anticipating a possible objection, **Did not Israel know?** Is it possible that Israel was ignorant of this, the preaching of the gospel to both Jews and Gentiles? Was he ignorant of the purposes of God in respect to the reception of the gospel by the Gentiles, and their own unbelief? No, it was not possible, for **first,** in order of time and of a line of like predictions and warnings, **Moses saith** (Deut. 32 : 21), in reference to the extension of the gospel to the Gentiles,

will provoke you to jealousy by them that are no people, and by a foolish na-
20 tion I will anger you. But Esaias is very bold, and saith, ᵇ I was found of them that sought me not; I was made manifest unto them that asked not
21 after me. But to Israel he saith, All day long I have stretched forth my hands unto a disobedient and gainsaying people.

I will provoke you to jealousy by those who are no people,
By a nation without understanding I will provoke you to anger.
20 But Isaiah is very bold, and says,
I was found by those who sought me not;
I became manifest to those who asked not after me.
21 But as to Israel he says,
All the day long, I spread out my hands
To a disobedient and gainsaying people.

ᵇ 9 : 30.

I will provoke you to jealousy by them that are no people in the eyes of Israel, despised by them, and **by a foolish nation**, one without understanding, unenlightened. **I will anger you**, or *provoke you to anger*. Their jealousy and anger would be aroused in seeing their privileges and blessing transferred to nations whom they had regarded as degraded and foolish. How striking the meaning and fulfillment of these words to Paul's mind as he saw the prejudice and opposition of the Jews to Gentile Christianity and to himself as an apostle to the Gentiles. The quotation is from the Septuagint of Deut. 32 : 21. But from this the Jews might have known that if they forsook God he would transfer their privileges to others.

20. But Esaias is very bold and more decisive than Moses, **and saith** in regard to the Gentiles, **I was found of them that sought me not, I was made manifest unto them that asked not after me.** This is from Isa. 65 : 1, quoted from the Septuagint, the two clauses being inverted by the apostle, perhaps to emphasize "I have found." This verse runs parallel with 9 : 30. The closing words of Isaiah 65 : 1, "Unto a nation that was not called by my name," plainly shows that the reference is to Gentiles. And so Paul understood it and used it.

21. But God, through Isaiah, **to Israel, saith,** immediately after in the same chapter (Isa. 65 : 2). **All day long** (comp. Jer. 7 : 13) **I have stretched forth my hands**, in the attitude of earnest entreaty, **unto a disobedient and gainsaying**, or *contradicting*, **people.** Quoted from the Sep- tuagint. The Hebrew has "a rebellious people." Free agency and human responsibility are here recognized. The apostle is very brief and his argument is somewhat obscure, quoting Scripture without comment and allowing it to speak for itself. His general design is plain. The Jews knew, or ought to have known, from Moses and the prophets, that the gospel was to be extended to the Gentiles, and therefore should be preached to them. They had also been fully warned of their own rebellion and unbelief.

PRACTICAL REMARKS.

1. So long as there is any hope for the salvation of a sinner, we should labor and pray for him (ver. 1; Gen. 18 : 23-32).

2. Zeal may be productive of great good or great evil. It should be tested in the light of God's truth (ver. 2; Acts 26 : 9-11, 20, 22, 23).

3. Ignorance under the gospel may be a palliation, but not an excuse for rejecting it (ver. 3; 1 Tim. 1 : 13; Luke 23 : 34; 2 Peter 3 : 5).

4. There is no greater hindrance to salvation than self-righteousness. Without renouncing it, the sinner cannot submit himself to the righteousness of God (ver. 3; Luke 18 : 11-13; Phil. 3 : 3-11).

5. The law system ˙as a covenant of works is ended in Christ (ver. 4; Gal 3 : 21, 22; Heb. 8 : 13; 12 : 24).

6. "The law says, 'Do this and live'; the gospel says, 'Live, and do this'" (PENDLETON). The spiritual life through faith in Christ is the source of all right doing (ver. 5-8; John 5 : 24; Gal. 5 : 22-25).

7. Salvation by works is as impracticable for a sinner as ascending into

The rejection of the Jews neither total nor final; their future recovery life to the world.

11 I SAY then, ^c Hath God cast away his people?

11 I SAY then, did God cast away his people? Far be it! For I also am an

<small>c 1 Sam. 12 : 22 ; Jer. 31 : 37 ; Amos 9 : 8.</small>

heaven, or descending into the abyss (ver. 6, 7; 3 : 20; 11 : 6).

8. The terms of salvation are so simple, plain, and easy, that no one need perish (ver. 8. 9; Isa. 35 : 8; Rev. 22 : 17).

9. Professing religion is as much a duty as believing (ver. 9; Mark 16 : 16; Acts 2 : 38; Luke 12 : 8, 9).

10. Saving faith is more than an intellectual assent. It is a moral exercise of the soul in which the will, the affections, and the conscience unite (ver. 9, 10; Heb. 11 : 1).

11. The resurrection of Christ is a fundamental fact and doctrine in the Christian system. Faith in a risen Saviour cannot end in disappointment, nor in anything short of complete salvation (ver. 9, 11 ; 1 Cor. 15 : 20, 57 ; 1 Peter 1 : 5).

12. Paul's argument for preaching the gospel to all; (1) Christ has put an end to the Old Testament economy, and to the peculiar privileges of the Jews, which are accessible to all who believe (ver. 4); (2) faith in Christ and confession of his name are alone sufficient for salvation (ver. 9); (3) that this declaration is universal—all are included (ver. 11).

13. Christianity is in its nature a universal religion, adapted to every nation and to every age ; to the savage as well as to the most highly civilized (ver. 12, 13 ; John 4 : 21-24 ; Acts 10 : 34, 35).

14. Paul's missionary argument. The invitation and assurances of the gospel extend to all (ver. 13), but calling implies believing, and believing hearing, and hearing preaching, and preaching missionaries or preachers sent to all (ver. 14, 15 ; Mark 16 : 15).

15. It is the duty of Christians to send missionaries to the heathen and to the spiritually destitute everywhere. "How can they preach, except they be sent" (ver. 15 ; Matt. 28 : 19, 20).

16. Missionaries of the gospel are heaven-sent, honored of God, bearing glad tidings productive of salvation, and they

should receive encouragement and a glad welcome (ver. 15 ; 15 : 29; 1 Thess. 1 : 5).

17. The fact that only a few may believe does not alter the duty of preaching. All should have an opportunity, since they cannot believe unless they hear (ver. 16, 17).

18. The missionary activities of the apostolic age should stimulate Christians to a like work in every age (ver. 18; 1 : 8; 1 Thess. 1 : 8; Phil. 4 : 15-18).

19. The seeds of New Testament doctrine are found in the Old (ver. 19-21 ; Heb. 10 : 1).

20. God often takes away blessings from the highly favored, who abuse his mercies, and bestows them upon those less favored (ver. 19, 20; Matt. 21 : 43).

21. The forbearance of God toward sinful men is truly marvelous, but the day of reckoning approaches (ver. 21 ; 2 : 4, 10 ; Prov. 1 : 24-26).

22. God will withhold his favors from those peoples and nations that continue disobedient and rebellious. God judges nations in this world, individuals in the next (ver. 21; Gen. 15 : 14).

CHAPTER XI.

In this chapter Paul discusses God's plan in passing over the larger part of Israel. This passing over is not total (ver. 1-10), nor is it designed to be final ; but in the meantime it gives occasion for the call of the Gentiles (ver. 11-16) who are warned not to be high-minded but to exercise humility, reverence, and gratitude (ver. 17-24). It is however a part of God's purpose and plan, resulting in the ultimate gathering in of the Jews with the Gentiles (ver. 25-32), in all which God's infinite wisdom is gloriously displayed (ver. 33-36).

1-10. GOD HAS NOT WHOLLY PASSED OVER HIS PEOPLE. It is not so now, nor has it ever been so in the past. A remnant has been and is being saved.

1. God has not absolutely cast away his people. A false conclusion might

God forbid. For ⁴I also am an Israelite, of the seed of Abraham, *of the* 2 tribe of Benjamin. God hath not cast away his people which • he foreknew. Wot ye not what the Scripture saith of Elias? how he maketh intercession to 3 God against Israel, saying, ᶠLord, they have killed thy prophets, and digged down thine altars; and I am left alone, 4 and they seek my life. But what saith the answer of God unto him? I have

Israelite, from the seed of Abraham, 2 of the tribe of Benjamin. God did not cast away his people that he foreknew. Or know ye not what the Scripture says in Elijah; how he intercedes with God 3 against Israel, saying, Lord, they have killed thy prophets. have digged down thine altars, and I am left alone, and 4 they seek my life. But what says the answer of God to him? I have left to

d 9 : 3; Acts 22 : 3; 2 Cor. 11 : 22; Phil. 3 : 5.   *e* 8 : 29; Acts 15 : 18.   *f* 1 Kings 19 : 10-18.

be drawn from the passages quoted in 10 : 19-21, which the apostle voices in his own language. **Hath God,** rather, *Did God cast off his own people?* implying the impossibility of such a thing. The form of the question in the original calls for a negative answer; he repels the thought; **God forbid,** *No, by no means!* My own case proves that God has not cast off his people as such. **For I also am** not only a believer in the Messiah, but **an Israelite of the tribe of Benjamin,** one of the two royal tribes of Israel (1 Sam. 10 : 20, 21), and both tribes long known as the chief representatives of Israel. Paul appears to have regarded himself as a representative believer, and so he seems to have classed himself here (1 Tim. 1 : 13-16; Phil. 3 : 4-6). He was a true representative of the remnant saved (ver. 5). Admitting the supposition, it would exclude the writer himself from God's kingdom. From this particular reference to himself it has been inferred that a larger part of the church of Rome was of Gentile origin. Some interpret **For I also,** etc., as containing the ground for **God forbid.** *For I also,* as a true Israelite, cannot admit that the nation is excluded. The other, the more common view is, however, the more natural.

2. God hath, rather, *God did not cast away his own people whom he foreknew* and decided upon as such. God could not change his original plan formed from eternity with infinite knowledge (comp. Ps. 94 : 14), which seems to be quoted here. Paul may mean either Israel as a *nation,* whom God had foreknown and chosen to be entrusted with the oracles of truth (3 : 1, 2), or the *true* Israel whom he had foreknown and chosen as the "Israel of God" (2 : 28, 29; 9 : 6). The former is held by most modern interpreters; the latter by the older expositors. Either construction is grammatically possible. The latter, however, seems to be more natural and more in accord with what immediately follows (ver. 3, 4, 5), and with Paul's general teaching throughout the Epistle, that the people of God are not the natural but the spiritual children of Abraham (4 : 11-18). God's true people have alway been believers (Heb. 11). Literal Israel is indeed beloved for the father's sake (ver. 28); but none are true children but such as are Abraham's seed by faith (9 : 7, 8; Gal. 3 : 7, 8, 9, 29; see also our Saviour's words, John 8 : 39). **Or wot,** or *know,* **ye not what the Scripture saith of Elias?** literally, *in Elijah,* that is, in the narrative of Elijah's life. The ancients used names of persons or things for designating passages to which they wished to refer. Compare Luke 20 : 37 and Mark 12 : 26, *at the bush. How he intercedes with God,* for himself and in behalf of the true worship of God, **against Israel.** Paul introduces an analogous case to show that God had not rejected Israel.

3, 4. Paul refers to 1 Kings 19 : 10-18, and quotes very briefly, assuming his readers to be familiar with this incident in the life of Elijah. Ver. 3 differs slightly from the Septuagint of 1 Kings 19 : 10; ver. 4 is from 1 Kings 19 : 18, and varies from the Septuagint, but accords with the sense of the Hebrew, though not in form. **The answer of God,** *the divine response.* **Seven thousand men**—their wives and children are to be added. In numbering the people men were chiefly reckoned. **Baal**—a Phœnician god, probably representing the sun, though some suppose it to represent the planet Jupiter. "*Baal,* here in the feminine, *image* understood, the *image* of Baal, used contemptuously and opposed to *men*" (BENGEL). But elsewhere Baal

reserved to myself seven thousand men, who have not bowed the knee to
5 *the image of* Baal. ᶡEven so then at this present time also there is a remnant according to ᵇ the election of
6 grace. And ˡ if by grace, then *is it* no more of works: otherwise grace is no more grace. But if *it be* of works, then is it no more grace: otherwise work is no more work.
7 What then? ᵏ Israel hath not obtained that which he seeketh for. But the election hath obtained it, and
8 the rest were ˡ blinded: according as it is written, ᵐ God hath given them the spirit of slumber, ⁿ eyes that they should not see, and ears that they
9 should not hear; ᵖ unto this day. And

myself seven thousand men, who have
5 not bowed the knee to Baal. Even so then, at this present time also, there is a remnant according to the election of
6 grace. And if by grace, it is no longer of works; otherwise the grace becomes no longer grace. But if of works, it is no longer grace; otherwise the work is no longer work.
7 What then? What Israel seeks, that he obtained not; but the election obtained it, and the rest were hardened.
8 As it is written, God gave them a spirit of stupor, eyes that they should not see, and ears that they should not
9 hear, unto this very day. And David says,

g 9 : 27 ; Isa. 6 : 13.   *h* 9 : 11 ; Eph. 1 : 5.   *i* 4 : 4, 5.   *k* 9 : 31, 32 ; 10 : 3.
l See Isa. 6 : 10 ; Mark 6 : 52 ; John 12 : 40 ; 2 Cor. 3 : 14.   *m* Isa. 29 : 10.
n Isa. 6 : 9 ; Jer. 5 : 21 ; Matt. 13 : 14.   *p* 2 Cor. 3 : 14, 15.

is used sometimes in the masculine and sometimes in the feminine. The suggestion has been made that Baal is viewed as having two sexes and combining the mental characteristics of both. **I have reserved,** *I have left.* From this verb is derived the noun translated *remnant* in the next verse.

5. Even so then, reasoning analogically from this fact in Old Testament history, **at this present time also,** of general unbelief of Israel, **there is a remnant** which at times was very numerous (Acts 6 : 7 ; 21 : 20), **according to the election of grace,** that divine choice, grounded not on merit but on grace as an act of favor to the undeserving (9 : 11). This remnant was the salt of the nation now as in the past (Isa. 1 : 9; Rom. 9 : 27). We are therefore no more to expect that the present passing over of Israel is to be total than was the one just cited.

6. Paul pauses in his argument to emphasize "the election of grace," defining it negatively. And thus he opposes the Jewish idea of justification by keeping the law. **And if** this remnant has been elected or chosen **by grace,** by a divine gracious choice, **then it is no more of works; otherwise grace is no more grace,** *since in that case the grace,* the divine favor thus exercised ceases to be grace. This verse ends here according to many ancient manuscripts. There is however much authority for retaining the remaining words in the text. **But if** the election be grounded upon **works,** **then is it no more grace,** of divine favor; *since in that case,* of grace, *the work* ceases to be work. Salvation through the divine favor and salvation by man's works are directly opposed to each other. There can be no compromise. The two principles are mutually destructive (4 : 4).

7. What then is our conclusion? The apostle answers: **Israel** as a nation or people (9 : 6) *obtained not that* righteousness as a ground of acceptance before God, **which he seeketh for** in a wrong way (10 : 3); **but the election,** those elected, the *elect obtained it.* Compare 4 : 9, where "the circumcision" means *the circumcised.* **And the rest were blinded**—rather, *were hardened* in their impenitence; dullness and insensibility took possession of their understanding and hearts (2 Cor. 3 : 14, 15). Israel as a people are viewed in two parts, the chosen remnant forming the true Israel, and the rest, self-righteous and hardened, forming the mass of literal Israel.

8. And this Paul says is **as it is written.** Moses and Isaiah had written concerning the unbelief of Israel, and their abandonment by God to the insensibility of their own hearts. Two passages are combined (Isa. 29 : 10; Deut. 29 : 4) and freely quoted according to the sense. (Comp. Isa. 6 : 9, 10; Matt. 13 : 14.) **God gave them,** in righteous judgment, *a spirit of stupor,* which renders their souls torpid and insensible, so that they are not affected by the offers of salvation made them through the Messiah.

David saith, Let their table be made a snare, and a trap, and a stumblingblock, and a recompense unto them:
10 let their eyes be darkened, that they may not see, and bow down their back alway.
11 I say then, Have they stumbled that they should fall? God forbid: but *rather* ᑫthrough their fall salvation *is come* unto the

Let their table be made a snare, and a trap,
And a stumbling-block, and a recompense to them;
10 Let their eyes be darkened, that they may not see,
And bow thou down their back always.
11 I say then, did they stumble in order that they might fall? Far be it! But by their trespass salvation is come to

---

ᑫ Acts 13 : 42, 46, 47 ; 18 : 6 ; 22 : 18, 21.

Unto this day is a part of the quotation, and denotes a continuance of this condition. There should be no parenthesis in this verse. Thus it is shown that this condition of Israel is nothing new, that God has ever dealt in this way with his rebellious people, and that this continues to this very day. This was especially the case of Israel then.

9, 10. And to the same effect **David says** (Ps. 69 : 22). The quotation varies but little from the Septuagint. The natural inference is that David is quoted as the author of the psalm; but some regard the word David used as the title of the whole collection of the Psalms. "The question of authorship does not affect the question of the propriety of the phrase, *David saith:* but when it is so likely that David did write the psalm, inventing theories to prove that he did not seems to be useless ingenuity" (M. R. RIDDLE, in *Lange*). The sixty-ninth Psalm seems to be full of the Messiah, and is quoted in Matt. 27 : 34 ; John 2 : 17 ; Acts 1 : 20. This passage appears to have typical reference to him. The quotation is applicable here, whether the psalm be regarded as Messianic or not. **Let their table,** where they sit feasting and suspecting no evil, **be made,** turned into, **a snare and a trap, and a stumblingblock, and** so let their prosperity be turned into **a recompense unto them.** Paul freely quotes and develops the idea of requital. *And do thou* **bow down their back alway** in the servile condition of slavery and of bearing burdens. We must bear in mind that this comes upon them as a retribution, a punishment of sin. The point of the quotation is the judicial turning of blessings into curses, and visiting the enemies of the Messiah with blindness, servility, and impotence of soul, thus setting forth the desert and doom of obstinate unbelievers. Some shrink from such imprecations, but they are not the expressions of human anger, malignant selfishness, or of personal grievance, but of a wholesome and righteous abhorrence of evil, and a deep sense of its desert. They were the utterances of a soul in full sympathy with God's righteous government, and speaking under the guidance of his Spirit and in his name, in reference to those who had grossly violated his holy laws.

11-24. NOR DOES GOD DESIGN THEIR FINAL REJECTION, BUT RATHER AS AN OCCASION FOR CALLING THE GENTILES. *Israel's restoration is desirable for its influence, and probable from the nature of the case.*

11. I say then—calling attention to a false conclusion which some might draw, and guarding against it. **Have they stumbled**—rather, *Did they stumble,* when as a nation they rejected the Messiah *in order that they might fall* absolutely and finally, as a judgment upon them, and never be won back to Christ? This may be asked of the nation (9 : 32), or of *the rest* who were hardened, the representatives of the nation (ver. 7). It is said *they stumbled* with reference to 9 : 32, though a different word is used, but both words refer to their rejection of Christ. (Comp. 1 Cor. 1 : 23 ; Gal. 5 : 11.) The fall resulting from the stumbling implies ruin, destruction. The *stumbling* denotes a temporary lapse; the *fall*, final, absolute ruin. Paul admits the former, but denies the latter. **God forbid,** *Far from it.* The word **that,** *in order that,* introduced a false purpose, but at the same time suggested that there might be some other purpose. **But rather through their fall,** *offense* or *trespass,* as the word is rendered in 5 : 15–17,

Gentiles, *for to provoke them to jealousy. Now if the fall of them *be* "the riches of the world, and the diminishing of them the riches of the Gentiles; 13 how much more 'their fulness! For I speak to you Gentiles, inasmuch as "I am the apostle of the Gentiles, I mag-

the Gentiles, to provoke them to rivalry. Now if their trespass is the riches of the world, and their diminution the riches of the Gentiles, how much more their fulness? But I am speaking to you the Gentiles. Inasmuch then as I am an apostle of the

r Ver. 14 ; 10 : 19.   *s* Ver. 15.   *t* Isa. 11 : 11-16 ; Micah 4 : 1, 2 ; 5 : 7.
u 15 : 16 ; Acts 9 : 15 ; 13 : 2 ; Gal. 2 : 2, 7-9 ; Eph. 3 : 8 ; 1 Tim. 2 : 7.

18, 20, literally their *falling aside*. The idea is a temporary not final falling aside into unbelief and rejecting Christ. By it an occasion occurred, so that **salvation** (which was "of the Jews," (John 4 : 22)) **is come unto the Gentiles** (Acts 28 : 28) **for to provoke them,** the Jews, **to jealousy,** or *rivalry*—excite them to emulation to recover the blessings they had lost (Phil. 1 : 15-18). Thus the unbelief of the Jews benefited the Gentiles, in immediate offers of the gospel to them (ver. 18 : 6), and also in depriving the Jews of the power of insisting that Gentiles should come under the Mosaic law. "The salvation of Gentiles was indeed always in the Divine purpose; but Jewish unbelief was the occasion which that purpose took for its actual development" (MOULE). (Matt. 21 : 43 ; 22 : 9 ; Acts 13 : 46 ; 15 : 16, 17.)

12. In this argument Paul has in mind the future restoration of Israel. If their stumbling and rejection were the occasion of so much good, how much more good must result from their restoration (ver. 12, 15)? **Now if** *their* **fall,** *trespass, falling aside* into unbelief, **be the riches of the world,** in salvation to the Gentiles, bringing to them "the unsearchable riches of Christ" (Eph. 3 : 8) ; **and the diminishing of them,** *their reduction* to an inferior spiritual state or condition through unbelief, **the riches of the Gentiles, how much more their fulness,** their restoration to all the blessings of Christ's kingdom and to the full enjoyment of them! How much more will this result in the spiritual riches of the world and of the Gentiles! The word translated **diminishing** means *a lessening, a being made less,* hence *a reduction,* to an inferior state or condition. It is found elsewhere only in 1 Cor. 6 : 7, and in Isa. 31 : 8 (Septuagint). It is here opposed to *fulness, the filling* of them which is spoken of the restoration of the Jews to the blessings of the kingdom of God. Notice that the words **them, them,** and **their** refer to the Jews as a people or nation. Some find the idea of numbers in the words *diminishing* and *fulness,* thus : If *their reduction* as God's people *to a small number* is *the riches of the Gentiles, how much more* their increase to the *full number.* I prefer, however, the former interpretation, as it accords better with the spiritual idea of Jewish condition implied in ver. 15 and in the whole context.

13. **For**—according to the most approved reading, *But,* **I speak,** or *say,* this **to you** *the* **Gentiles,** referring to the thought in the two preceding verses. He now and throughout the rest of the chapter addresses the Gentile converts as distinct from the Jewish believers in the church at Rome. He speaks of the Jews in the third person and treats the Gentiles as a body to be benefited. He thus showed both his devotion to his Gentile apostleship, and his earnest desire for the spiritual welfare of his own kindred. It has also been inferred from this that the main body of Roman Christians were Gentiles. There was in Paul's day a great gulf of prejudice between Jews and Gentiles. This would naturally show itself in churches composed of both classes. The apostle had endeavored to lessen this prejudice among his Jewish brethren. He now strives to overcome it among Gentile believers. The Jews had been a channel and occasion of blessing to them; and their debtors they were. (Comp. 15 : 27). Compare Acts 16 : 20-22, where we get a glimpse of the Roman contempt for the Jews.

Inasmuch as—giving his reason for personally addressing them, **I am** *an* **apostle of the Gentiles** (15 : 12-19 ; Acts 9 : 15 ; Gal. 2 : 7, 8 ; Eph. 3 : 8 ; 1 Thess. 1 : 14-16). A self-consciousness of his noble mission here finds expression. **I magnify mine office,** or *glorify my ministry,*

tify mine office: if by any means I may provoke to emulation *them which are* my flesh, and might save some of 15 them. For if *the casting away of them be the reconciling of the world, what *shall* the receiving *of them* be, but 16 life from the dead? For if *the first-fruit be* holy, the lump *is* also *holy:*

14 Gentiles, I glorify my ministry; if by any means I may provoke to rivalry 15 my flesh, and save some of them. For if the casting away of them is the reconciling of the world, what shall the receiving of them be, but life from the 16 dead? And if the first-fruit is holy, so is the mass; and if the root is holy, so

x Ver. 11, 12.   *y* Num. 15 : 18-21.

making the most of it, and exerting myself to the utmost for its success, thereby moving my kindred to emulation (ver. 14). He hoped through the Gentiles to reach the Jews, and that the prosperity of the work among the former would arouse the latter to attention and inquiry.

14. If by any means I may provoke to emulation, or *rivalry* (the same word as used in ver. 11) **my flesh,** my kindred, **and might save some of them,** implying that he did not expect to save a large number of them through his own ministry. They were mostly too prejudiced against him, too blinded to see the truth, and too self-righteous to feel their need of a Saviour (2 Cor. 3 : 15, 16). But the saving of *some* was worthy of the highest efforts of his ministry (1 Cor. 9 : 22). He would overcome prejudices on the part of both Jew and Gentile, and break down the middle wall of partition that separated them and make them one in Christ (Gal. 3 : 28; Eph. 2 : 14-18). In these *some* he saw a pledge and first-fruits of the coming glorious harvest.

15. Returning from the digression in the last two verses the apostle passes to the topic of ver. 11, 12. **For**—confirms what he had already said and introduces a reason for his deep interest in the salvation of Israel. **If the casting away of them,** a different word from that used in ver. 1, 2, with a different reference. It is opposed to "the receiving of them," and implies that the casting away was not final, and that it was to be followed by a restoration. **Be,** proves to be, the occasion **of reconciling the world,** the Gentiles composing the main part of the world. The circumstances attending the casting away of Israel, their unbelief, the crucifixion of Christ and their rejection of the gospel, resulted in providing the world's reconciliation and in the enjoyment of it by the vast company of Gentile believers (Eph. 2 : 11-17). If this is so, **what shall the receiving of them be but life from the dead,** that is, like it in its effects upon others. Their reception into the kingdom will be attended with a revival of true religion so vast and wonderful that it will be like a translation from death to life. It will usher in the latter day glory. Some early and late expositors suppose *life from the dead* to mean the resurrection at the end of the world. But this is not the ordinary use of life in the New Testament. The connection also appears to demand a reference to the spiritual blessings conferred upon the Gentiles through the Jews. These would be so worldwide and so glorious as to form a fitting climax to the reconciling of the world just spoken of.

16. The apostle has already implied the restoration of Israel, and that for its effects upon the world it would be desirable. He now treats it as probable in the nature of the case. **For,** rather, *And,* **if the first fruit be holy,** *set apart, consecrated* to God, **the lump,** or *mass,* **is also holy.** The first-fruit here means, not the first gathered fruit of the field in their natural state (Lev. 23 : 10), but a portion of this when prepared for use, for example a cake of the dough first prepared (Num. 15 : 20). The offering of this was an acknowledgment that the whole belonged rightfully to God, and was consecrated to him, and was to be used and enjoyed as such. And this Paul uses to illustrate the restoration of Israel implied in the preceding verse, and as a reason for expecting it. *If the first-fruit is holy,* if the first body of Jewish believers are holy, *consecrated* to God as they evidently are and constituting the true Israel (ver. 2), then we may look upon their consecration as in effect implying the consecration of all, and their conversion as an earnest of the great spiritual harvest and conversion of Israel.

and if the root be holy, so are the branches.

17 And if some of the branches be broken off, *and thou, being a wild olive tree, wert graffed in among them, and with them partakest of the root

18 and fatness of the olive tree, boast not against the branches. But if thou boast, thou bearest not the root, but are the branches. And if some of the branches were broken off, and thou, being a wild olive-branch, wast graffed in among them, and became a partaker with them of the root of the fatness of the olive-tree; exult not over the branches. But if thou gloriest, it is not thou that bearest the root, but

*Eph. 2 : 11–13 ; 3 : 6.

And so also in regard to the patriarchs who were consecrated and dear to God. **If the root be holy,** if the fathers of the nation were separated and consecrated to peculiar privileges and blessings, **so are the branches,** so their descendants may be likewise regarded in the Divine purpose, and in the end may be expected to be so. *Holy* is used in the Old Testament sense of **consecration,** being *set apart* to God and to his purposes. It was said of Israel, that they were holy to the Lord, implying that there ought to be an inward corresponding holiness, but not affirming or implying that this was actually the case. By this figure the apostle means that the branches sustain the same relation as the root, that the fathers of Israel and their descendants both sustain the same peculiar relation to God, namely, consecrated to him as his peculiar people. Many suppose both "firstfruits" and "root" to refer to the fathers. But to me it seems more probable that the second emblem means something different from the first. It seems natural after implying the restoration and conversion of Israel in ver. 15, to speak of the first converts, so aptly represented by "first-fruits," as an earnest of the conversion of all. And it was equally natural then to fortify that argument by the fact that Israel had from the fathers downward been set apart to God as a peculiar people.

17. Paul continues to use the figure of *root* and *branches* to illustrate the true relation of Jewish and Gentile converts to each other, and to give words of caution to the latter. **If some of the branches be broken off,** that is, some of the Jews through their rejection of Christ. The branches not broken off would then of course represent those Jewish converts who were of the true Israel, and were occupying their original position in relation to the blessings to be received from the Messiah's kingdom. **And thou,** a Gentile, **being a wild olive** *branch* **wert graffed** (*grafted*) **in among them** that remained, **and with them partakest of the root and fatness,** that is, of the fatness of the root, participating in the blessing of the divine kingdom, etc. The wild olive must not be considered as barren. Its fruit is not so rich and abundant as that of the cultivated tree, and has a sharp acid taste. The *grafting* has reference not to the common effects of grafting. It is "contrary to nature" (ver. 24) and the effects are inverted. It rather refers to a participation of blessing, and a community of privilege. The Gentile converts had by divine grace been transferred to a position they did not originally hold, and through Christ had been made partakers of the divine kingdom and members of the true Israel. (Comp. Eph. 2 : 11-13.)

18. Continuation of the sentence. And since thou art a wild branch on an originally nobler stock, **Boast not against the branches,** or *Glory not over the branches*—over those broken off, the unbelieving Jews. **But if** thou art tempted *to glory,* remember that **thou bearest not the root, but the root thee,** that thou art not first in dignity and place, that the Jews had the priority in the divine arrangement and in the blessings pertaining to the Messiah and his kingdom. Compare "To the Jew first and also to the Greek" (1 : 16) ; our Lord's words, "Go not into a way of the Gentiles, . . . but go rather to the lost sheep of the house of Israel" (Matt. 10 : 5, 6) ; and Paul's words, "It was necessary that the word of God should first be spoken to you," etc. (Acts 13 : 46). Notice that those *broken off* through unbelief though of the literal Israel were not of the true Israel (9 : 6). And also that believing Gentiles were admitted as a part of

19 the root thee. Thou wilt say then, The branches were broken off, *a* that I
20 might be graffed in. Well; *b* because of unbelief they were broken off, and thou standest by faith. *c* Be not high-
21 minded, but *d* fear: for if God *e* spared not the natural branches, *take heed* lest he also spare not thee.
22 Behold therefore the goodness and severity of God: on them which fell, severity; but toward thee, goodness, *f* if thou continue in *his* goodness: otherwise *g* thou also shalt be cut off.
23 And they also, *h* if they abide not in unbelief, shall be graffed in: for God
24 is able to graff them in again. For if

19 the root thee. Thou wilt say then, branches were broken off, that I might
20 be grafted in. Well; by their unbelief they were broken off, and thou standest by thy belief. Be not high-
21 minded, but fear: for if God spared not the natural branches, neither will he spare thee.
22 Behold then God's kindness and severity; toward those who fell, severity; but toward thee, God's kindness, if thou continue in his kindness; otherwise, thou also shalt be cut off. And
23 they also, if they continue not in their unbelief, shall be grafted in; for God is able to graft them in again.

a Ver. 11, 12, 17.　*b* Acts 13 : 46, 47.　*c* 1 Cor. 4 : 7.　*d* Prov. 28 : 14; Phil. 2 : 12.
e Ver. 17, 19 ; 1 Cor. 10 : 1-12.　*f* Heb. 3 : 14 ; 10 : 23, 38.　*g* John 15 : 2.　*h* 2 Cor. 3 : 16.

the true Israel (ver. 29). A distinction should be made between the theocracy which answers to Israel, as a people, under the government of God; true Israel, answering to the divine kingdom, or kingdom of God; and the church, the professed discipleship of Jesus. Of the latter Paul is not here speaking.

19. Thou wilt say then, or *therefore*, in order to meet my reasoning and suggest some ground at least for glorifying. **Branches were broken off** *in order that I* **might be graffed** (*grafted*) **in,** as though some preference were shown you over the Jew. The should be omitted. The pronoun **I** is emphatic, indicative of a boasting spirit.

20. Well, *very good,* I admit that there was a preference, but it was not on account of any personal merit in you, and is therefore no ground of boasting. **Because of unbelief,** or *their disbelief,* **they were broken off, and thou standest by faith**—rather, by *thy faith,* or *belief.* Thou standest in thy present relation as a branch grafted into the good olive. Paul is here viewing the human side merely. **Be not high-minded,** *haughty,* with a spirit of boasting, **but fear,** exercise a reverential and humble spirit, lest through sins and unbelief thou forfeit the blessings and privileges to which thou hast been raised.

21. For if God spared not the natural branches—those of literal Israel in distinction from those grafted in—**take heed lest** *in any way* he also spare not thee. According to the Greek text most generally approved,

omit *take heed lest,* and translate, *Neither will he spare thee,* if thou fall into unbelief. There is indeed less reason to expect the forbearance of God toward the Gentiles who had thus been made partakers of blessings and privileges, if they misused them, than toward his own people who were beloved for their fathers' sake.

22. In view of what I have just said (ver. 20, 21), **Behold therefore the goodness,** *the kindness* (2 : 4), **and severity of God,** with the idea of stern sharpness and strictness. **On them which fell,** being broken off through unbelief, **severity; but toward thee,** grafted in among the branches of the olive, *God's goodness* **if thou continue,** or *abide,* by faith **in** *that* **goodness**—in that state into which his goodness has brought thee. Grace produces perseverance by nourishing and maintaining faith (1 Peter 1 : 5); it uses all gospel means, and among these means are warnings against apostasy (Heb. 6 : 4-9 ; Jude 17-23). **Otherwise,** *since in that case,* if thou abide not in that goodness, **thou also shalt be cut off.**

23. The apostle again takes up the fitness and propriety of the restoration of Israel. **And they also,** the broken-off olive branches, the Jews, **if they abide,** or *continue,* **not still in unbelief shall be graffed** (*grafted*), as well as the branches from the wild olive tree. **For God is able to graff** (*graft*) **them in again.** Every Jewish convert was a witness of the truth of this statement. Paul is treating now with individual Jews and Gentiles, as branches grafted or re-

thou wert cut out of the olive tree which is wild by nature, and wert graffed contrary to nature into a good olive tree: how much more shall these, which be the natural *branches*, be graffed into their own olive tree!
25 For I would not, brethren, that ye should be ignorant of this mystery, lest ye should be wise in your own conceits, that *i* blindness in part is happened to Israel, *k* until the fulness of
26 the Gentiles be come in. And so *l* all Israel shall be saved: as it is written,

24 For if thou wast cut out of that which is by nature a wild olive-tree and wast grafted contrary to nature into a good olive-tree; how much more shall these, who are the natural branches, be grafted into their own olive-tree?
25 For I do not wish you, brethren, to be ignorant of this mystery, lest ye be wise in your own conceits, that hardness has come upon Israel in part, until the fullness of the Gentiles come
26 in. And so all Israel will be saved;

i 2 Cor. 3 : 14–16.   *k* Luke 21 : 24.   *l* Isa. 45 : 17 ; Jer. 30 : 17–22.

grafted through faith into the good olive tree.

24. For if thou . . . wild by nature. (See on ver. 17.) **Wert graffed** (*grafted*) **contrary to nature into a good olive tree.** The superior is generally grafted into the inferior stock. But here the case is reversed; the poorer is grafted into the better, with excellent results. "The wild olive tree, whose fruit is larger and more meaty, but whose oil is less valuable and used only for ointments, has the curious quality that, when grafted on a cultivated tree it bears excellent fruit, which is just the reverse of the general effect of grafting" (SCHAFF-HERZOG). **How much more shall these that be the natural branches,** the unbelieving Jews, **be graffed** (*grafted*) **into their own olive tree,** which is theirs by nature. Israel was God's peculiar people, distinguished for ages by tokens of his regard, and still beloved for the fathers' sake. But Gentiles who had no such titles and tokens of his favor have obtained it; much more may Jews regain it. The restoration of Israel is a more probable event, judging from God's dealings in the past, than was the introduction of Gentiles into the true Israel.

25-32. THE RESTORATION OF ISRAEL ACCORDING TO GOD'S WORD AND PURPOSES. The ultimate gathering in of Jews and Gentiles.

25. Leaving the figure of the olive tree, Paul now speaks in plain language, and enlarges upon a great future restoration. **For,** confirmatory of the brighter future suggested by ver. 24. **I would not,** *I do not wish you*, **brethren,** *to be* **ignorant,** a common way with Paul in calling attention to some- thing important (1 : 13 ; 1 Cor. 10 : 1 ; 12 : 1 ; 2 Cor. 1 : 8 ; 1 Thess. 4 : 13), **of this mystery,** according to New Testament usage, *a secret or hidden thing* of God, not generally understood, and generally known only by revelation (1 Cor. 15 : 51 ; comp. Rom. 16 : 25 ; 1 Cor. 4 : 1). Why he wished them to know this mystery: **Lest ye should be wise,** or *in order that ye may not be wise*, **in your own conceits**—in your own estimation, and think too highly of yourselves because of the preference given you. He would check pride in Gentile Christians. They must not be wise above, or contrary, to what was written, nor suppose they understood better than Jews the plans of God's grace. The mystery was, **That blindness**—rather, *hardness* (ver. 7), **in part is happened,** or *come upon*, **Israel,** a large part of the nation, some in every age having accepted Christ, **until the fulness,** the full number, the multitudes, **of the Gentiles be come in,** or (omitting **be**), *come in* to the Messiah's kingdom and the enjoyment of his salvation. (Comp. Rev. 7 : 9.) See ver. 15, where it is intimated that the conversion of Israel would result in great crowning spiritual blessings to the world, which necessarily includes the Gentiles. So it is not necessary to explain this verse to mean the entire gathering of the Gentiles into the kingdom before the restoration of Israel.

26. And so, or *thus*, in the arrangement of God's grace, the hardness of Israel having ended with the coming in of the fullness of the Gentiles, **all Israel** as **a people shall be saved** through faith in Christ (ver. 28). It is most natural to refer this to the future, and to literal, rather than spiritual, Israel, when the great body of Israel

There shall come out of Zion the Deliverer, and shall turn away ungodli-
27 ness from Jacob: ⁿ for this *is* my covenant unto them, ᵒ when I shall take
28 away their sins. As concerning the gospel, *they are* enemies for your sakes: but as touching the election, *they are*
29 ᵖ beloved for the fathers' sakes. For the gifts and calling of God *are* ᵠ without repentance. For as ye ˢ in times

as it is written, there will come out of Zion the Deliverer; he will turn away
27 ungodliness from Jacob; and this is the covenant from me unto them,
28 when I shall take away their sins. As concerning the gospel, they are enemies for your sake; but as concerning the election, they are beloved for the
29 fathers' sake. For the gifts and the calling of God are not repented of.

m Jer. 31 : 31-37.   *n* Ezek. 36 : 25-29.   *o* Deut. 9 : 5 ; 10 : 15.   *p* See refs. Num. 23 : 19.   *q* 1 Peter 2 : 10.

then living will be brought to the acknowledgment of the truth. The context and the course of argument both require these. **As it is written.** The quotation is freely given from memory, gathered from Isa. 59 : 20, 21 ; 27 : 9, and perhaps Ps. 14 : 7. It was not necessary for the apostle to quote carefully, for *the coming of a Deliverer* was all that was essential to his argument. **There shall come out of Zion** (comp. Ps. 14 : 7), conceived as the capital of the theocracy, from the seed of David, **the Deliverer** (spoken of the Messiah), which might be referred to either his first or second coming. It seems however more natural, and it accords better with the next verse, to regard the reference here to the second coming, in connection with which this great work will be consummated. **And, rather,** *he will,* **turn away ungodliness from Jacob,** as a people or nation. He would overcome their unbelief and rebellion, and they would forsake their ungodly deeds and accept him as their deliverer from coming wrath (2 Thess. 1 : 9). The quotation speaks of his coming in general terms, but Paul manifestly views the future results in the conversion of Israel to Christianity. There are present indications that the fulfillment of the apostle's predictions may be near at hand. The gospel is being preached to, and converts gathered from, all nations. A widespread religious and spiritual awakening is occurring among the Jews; and a general tendency among them to return to their own land. Local Christian missions also are established in their behalf. (See on Acts 3 : 21.)

27. Continues the quotation (Isa. 59 : 21): **For this is my covenant,** or, *the covenant* granted *from me to them.* The apostle gives only the first

words of a well-known promise, often repeated and familiar to his readers, containing the gracious results of pardon, peace, and renewal to Israel. For the fuller terms of God's gracious covenant see Jer. 31 : 31-34, and Heb. 8 : 8-12 ; 10 : 16, 17. **This** refers backward to the promised work of the Messiah in the preceding verse, and forward to its accomplishment, when **I shall take away their sins** (Isa. 27 : 9), pardon them and restore them to the Divine favor. (Comp. Isa. 4 : 4.) This forgiveness is included in the covenant.

28. Summing up and confirming the thought just brought to view. **As concerning the gospel,** as unbelievers and rejecters of it, **they are enemies,** treated with strictness and given over to hardness **for your sakes,** in favor of you, so that you may be brought into the Messiah's kingdom and enjoy its favor and privileges. **But as touching,** or, *as concerning,* **the election,** God's choice of them as a people, **they are beloved,** and still within his gracious purposes, **for the fathers' sake,** the patriarchs of the nation (Deut. 7 : 8 ; 9 : 5 ; 10 : 15). Some refer the *election* to "the remnant" (ver. 5), and *enemies* to "the rest" of ver. 8. It accords better, however, with the context to regard them both as referring to Israel, as a people or nation.

29. This verse confirms the last clause of the preceding verse. **For the** gracious **gifts and calling of God**—his purpose and act in calling—**are without repentance,** the same word as in 2 Cor. 7 : 10, and here very emphatic. Paul means to put it very strongly, that God's purposes are immutable. God has not repented of the covenant and promises made to Abraham, Isaac, and Jacob, and so Israel, though passed over for a time, is still

past have not believed God, yet have now obtained mercy *through their unbelief; even so have these also now not believed, that through your mercy they also may obtain mercy. For *God hath concluded them all in unbelief, that he might have mercy upon all.

30 For just as ye in times past disobeyed God, but have now obtained mercy by their disobedience; so have these also now disobeyed, that by the mercy shown to you they also may now obtain mercy. For God shut up all unto disobedience, that he might have mercy on all.

r Ver. 11-19.   *s* 3 : 9; Gal. 3 : 22.

within the purposes of Divine love (Num. 23 : 19; 1 Sam. 15 : 29; Phil. 1 : 6; Heb. 13 : 8; 2 Tim. 2 : 13).

30, 31. In these verses the apostle illustrates and confirms the statement of ver. 29. **For as ye**—Gentiles—**in times past have not believed,** omit *have* and translate, *disobeyed God.* (Comp. 1 : 18-32.) **Yet have now obtained mercy through their unbelief,** *their disobedience,* that is, of Israel—the Jews. Through this disobedience Christ was crucified and became a propitiation for our sins, and it became also the occasion of preaching the gospel to the Gentiles. **So have these**—Israel, the Jews—**also now not believed,** or *now disobeyed,* **that through your mercy,** better, *that through mercy shown to you* by God in the gospel **they also may obtain mercy,** being influenced thereby and excited to emulation. (See on ver. 14, 15.) The emphatic idea in these two verses is *mercy.* Jewish unbelief and consequent disobedience was the occasion of mercy to the Gentiles; and this mercy to the Gentiles will be the occasion of, and will result in, the Jews obtaining mercy. Thus the seeming rejection of Israel will be only for a time, and God's immutable purposes of mercy toward them will ultimately have a fulfillment.

32. The Divine plan in a nutshell; consummated in the world's redemption. **For God** *shut up all,* Jews and Gentiles, **in unbelief,** or *disobedience,* the Gentiles in the past, the Jews at present, **that he might have mercy on all,** in bringing the multitudes of both Gentiles and Jews ultimately into his kingdom. **Concluded,** or *shut up,* so as to be helpless—without means of escape. (Comp. Gal. 3 : 22; Rom. 3 : 19.) All are indeed put on the same footing—that of *mercy*—and for all mercy is provided, and offered to all, on condition of acceptance by faith. But this does not appear to have been all that was in the apostle's mind, which drew forth his acclamation of praise. He saw, in the future Israel's restoration and conversion, with the Gentile fullness, bringing the whole world to Christ. He beheld God's plan in treating both Jews and Gentiles alike, with like glorious results, when the whole race living at the time would be redeemed to God. Surely such a view was enough to call forth his highest admiration and his unspeakable praise.

ISRAEL'S RESTORATION. There appear to be unfulfilled prophecies concerning Judah and Israel, such as Joel 3 : 1-21; Amos 9 : 8-15. Paul saw the fulfillment of such prophecies in the conversion and restoration of Israel. Much has been written upon this subject, some spiritualizing these prophecies, and others taking them with extreme literalness. Perhaps their true and intended meaning lies between the two. There never has been a time since apostolic days when there was so much to indicate their near fulfillment as now. A wonderful awakening is going on among the Jewish people, a national and a spiritual. This extends to all parts of the world. There is the Zionist movement toward spiritual truth and the Promised Land. Already there are said to be twenty-nine Jewish colonies in Palestine, and it is estimated that there are not less than one hundred thousand Jews there. And the Anglo-Saxon race—whether we regard it as more largely representing spiritual Israel than any other, or, with some, as the actual continuance of the ten lost tribes of Israel—this race is the great propagator of Christianity, the great Christian missionary race of the world. The conversion of the Israelitish people will be the climax of triumphant Christianity, and will add a stimulus and force to missionary enterprises unprecedented in history. In regard to the Jew and Christianity, it may be added, that it

K

33 O the depth of the riches both of the wisdom and knowledge of God! 'How unsearchable *are* his judgments, and
34 his ways past finding out! "For who hath known the mind of the Lord? Or who hath been his counsellor?
35 Or ª who hath first given to him, and it shall be recompensed unto him again?
36 For ʸ of him, and through him, and to

33 Oh, the depth of the riches, both of the wisdom and the knowledge of God! How unsearchable are his judgments,
34 and his ways past tracing out! For, Who knew the mind of the Lord? Or who became his counsellor?
35 Or who first gave to him, and it shall be given back to him again? For
36 from him, and through him, and for

t Ps. 36 : 6 ; 92 : 5.   *u* Job 15 : 8 , 1 Cor. 2 : 16.   *x* Job 35 : 7 ; 11 : 11.   *y* 1 Chron. 29 : 11, 12 ; Col. 1 : 16.

should not be demanded that he render himself less a Jew, but that he accept Jesus as his Messiah, the promised One of Israel. This is plainly in harmony with the fifteenth chapter of the Acts.

33-35. EXCLAMATIONS OF WONDER AT THIS SUBLIME MYSTERY, AND ASCRIPTIONS OF PRAISE TO THE AUTHOR AND RULER OF ALL. This naturally concludes the discussion in the ninth, tenth, and eleventh chapters. It is also a fitting conclusion to the whole doctrinal discussion of the Epistle which ends here. Compare the exultant endings of chapters seven and eight.

33. With this lofty and wide range of view of God's mysterious plan involving the glorious results of redemption, the apostle gives vent to his emotions in expression of admiration and praise. **O the depth,** as of the great deep, hidden and beyond man's scrutiny (1 Cor. 2 : 10 ; Ps. 36 : 6), **of the riches,** inexhaustible abundance, a word frequently used by Paul of God's goodness, grace, and glory (2 : 4 ; 9 : 23 ; 10 : 12 ; Eph. 1 : 7, 8 ; 2 : 7 ; 3 : 8, 16 ; Col. 1 : 27 ; 2 : 2), **both of the wisdom,** in planning, arranging, and carrying out all his purposes, **and knowledge,** in knowing all things from the beginning. "Where knowledge and wisdom are used together, the former seems to be knowledge regarded by itself, the latter wisdom as exhibited in action (1 Cor. 12 : 8 ; Col. 2 : 3). . . Knowledge applies chiefly to the apprehension of truths, wisdom superadds the power of reasoning about them and tracing their relations." (THAYER, "N. T. Lex."). MEYER regards *wisdom*, the more general term, "ruling everything in the best way for the best end." *Knowledge*, the more special term, of all relations, means, and methods. A large number of scholars translate, O depth of riches *and of wisdom and of knowledge of God!* **How unsearchable,** even to the inspired vision of the apostle, **are his judgments,** the purposes and decisions of wisdom, especially in chastisement and punishment (Ps. 97 : 2) ; **and his ways,** his methods of procedure in carrying out his plans, bringing good out of evil, and causing all things to redound to his glory, **past finding out**—beyond human ability to trace from the beginning to the end (Eph. 3 : 8 ; Job 9 : 10). His ways so *known* to him, so *unknown* to us.

34. The apostle uses the words of Isaiah (40 : 13), quoted from the Septuagint, as suited to his thought and confirmatory of it. **For who** *knew* **the mind of the Lord** in the beginning of creation, who had knowledge of what he would do, **or who** *become* **his counsellor,** who had wisdom to enter into his methods and advise him about carrying out his plans? (Comp. 1 Cor. 2 : 16 ; Jer. 23 : 18.)

35. In this verse Paul uses language from Job 41 : 11 (comp. Job. 35 : 7), according to the Hebrew. **Or who first** *gave* **to him and it shall be recompensed to him again?** This question naturally refers to his *riches* (ver. 33). No one has ever, or can ever, lay him under obligation. He is the giver, not the receiver—rich unto all that call upon him (10 : 12).

36. "An emphatic negative answer (*no one*) is implied in the foregoing questions; and **For,** *because,* introduces a conclusive reason for this emphatic negation" (BOISE). **For of him,** as the Creator and source of all things, **and through him,** or *by means of him,* sustaining, overruling, and governing—the channel of all blessings—**and to him,** the final cause and end, **are all things.** He is the source, the instrumentality, and the end of all created things. (Comp. Col.

him, *are* all things: ᵃ to whom *be* glory for ever. Amen.

him, are all things; to him be the glory forever. Amen.

ᵃ Gal. 1 : 5 ; 1 Tim. 1 : 17 ; Heb. 13 : 21 ; 1 Peter 5 : 11 ; Rev. 1 : 6.

1 : 16.) Alford, following Origen, finds here an implied reference to the attributes of God manifested in three persons of the Godhead. **To whom be glory forever,** through all the periods and developments of the future. **Amen.** (See on 1 : 25.) "Paul in chapter nine had been sailing, as it were, on a strait : he is now on the ocean" (BENGEL). "Never was a survey taken more vast of the Divine plan in the history of the world" (GODET).

PREACHING — DOCTRINAL, EXPERIMENTAL, AND PRACTICAL. Paul grounded his preaching and teaching in doctrine. This is exemplified in all his Epistles to the churches, in which he first unfolds doctrine and then enforces practice. He also wrote and spoke from a deep experience. The present generation would do well to take lessons from him. Since the great revival movement of 1858 doctrinal preaching has declined and ethical and practical instruction has largely taken its place. Converts have greatly multiplied, but without the corresponding increase of knowledge in the Scriptures and of the truth. As might be expected there has been a great lack of doctrinal knowledge among church-members generally. Sunday-school teachers have often shrunk from the thought of giving doctrinal instruction. Many therefore have grown up with superficial views and weak convictions. There needs to be a return to doctrinal study and experience. Doctrines not only need to be learned from the Scriptures, but also verified in personal experience. The result will be men and women of deep religious convictions. Knowing Christ and knowing his doctrine they will speak from the heart, and hence to the heart. They will be eminently doctrinal and eminently practical. They will be in touch with Christ and in touch with their fellow-men. Their influence will be felt among all classes, and in all the walks of life, upon the intellectual, social, and political, as well as upon the religious world.

PRACTICAL REMARKS.

1. God is ever faithful to his promises and to his people (ver. 1; Heb. 11 : 13; 1 Peter 4 : 19 ; 2 Peter 3 : 4-10).

2. Paul was a remarkable example of salvation by grace, of God's faithfulness to Israel, and of his mercy toward Gentiles (ver. 1, 6 ; 1 Tim. 1 : 12-16).

3. The salvation of God's true people is safe and assured in his hands (ver. 2; John 10 : 28, 29).

4. The best of saints sometimes give way to despondency and unbelief. Christians should not be pessimists (ver. 3, 4 ; Ps. 42 : 5, 11.

5. God has so exercised his gracious election that no age of the world will be without a remnant of his people (ver. 5 ; Isa. 62 : 1, 3).

6. Salvation by grace excludes the idea of merit founded on works. The sinner is utterly unworthy and helpless (ver. 6 ; 4 : 4 ; Eph. 2 : 8, 9).

7. The right seeking of salvation is in harmony with God's electing grace, and implies submitting to God's righteousness (ver. 7; 10 : 3 ; 9 : 16).

8. When people are left by God to themselves, their spiritual powers become permanently darkened and their blessings turn into curses (ver. 8-10 ; Acts 28 : 26, 27 ; 2 Cor. 4 : 4).

9. Even the means of grace and gospel privileges become malevolent to those who persistently reject God (ver. 9, 10 ; Acts 7 : 51; 2 Cor. 2 : 16).

10. Individuals and peoples sink down into the most wretched moral and spiritual slavery by departing from God (ver. 10 ; 6 : 16).

11. In God's dealing with the Jews we have an illustration of how he brings good out of evil, and makes even sin result in the race's welfare, and in his own glory (Ps. 76 : 10). The barrier between Jew and Gentile was broken down. The destruction of Jerusalem, of the temple, and of the ceremonial rites, took away barriers to the propagation of the true spiritual worship of the gospel (ver. 11 : John 4 : 18-24).

12. The conversion of Israel would greatly facilitate the conversion of the

world. Scattered everywhere they would become a band of most efficient missionaries among all nations. Even their conversion would, like a miracle, impress the world. It may be the design of God that they should be the *last* as well as the *first* missionaries (ver. 12, 15).

13. The mutual relation into which the gospel brings Jews and Gentiles should lead them to banish all feelings of hatred or contempt, to pray and put forth efforts for each other's salvation, and to unite in bringing the world to Christ (ver. 13-16).

14. We should ponder well our debt to God's ancient people, both in civil and religious matters. Salvation is of the Jews (John 4 : 22). Through them the Saviour and Christianity have come to us. "The germs of popular government are all to be found in the elements of the Hebraic commonwealth under Moses: popular suffrage; government organized into three departments—the legislative, the executive, and the judicial; two great representative assemblies—a house of deputies and a senate; a system of laws independent of, not emanating from, the will of a single despot; provisions of mercy mitigating the severity of absolute justice, and forbidding the cruelty of personal revenge; . . . liberty, law, order, the revelation of a personal God, the incarnation of a spiritual righteousness, a divinely inspired ethics, and the world's Redeemer, the source and the inspiration of all redemptive influences are all included in our debt to Judaism" (LYMAN ABBOTT). (Ver. 16-18. See "Wines' Laws of the Ancient Hebrews.")

15. The Jewish theocracy and the church are not the same. The former included all Israel by natural birth, the latter is made up only of those who have exercised personal faith. The one was national, the other included many local organizations (ver. 14-16, 32).

16. Infant baptism finds no place in this chapter. The church is not here discussed as an organization. The theocracy and the kingdom of God are rather brought into view (ver. 16-18).

17. The Gentile has no reason of boasting over the Jew. There is no special covenant pledging restoration to defaulting Gentiles. God would not probably bear so long with them as he did with Israel (ver. 18-24).

18. There is a tendency among those enjoying high privileges to be high-minded and to despise others less favored (ver. 18, 19; Luke 18 : 9-11, 19).

19. The exercise of true faith is productive of humility, and watchfulness, and of the use of means resulting in perseverance and final salvation (ver. 20, 21 ; 1 John 5 : 4; 1 Cor. 15 : 57).

20. We get a one-sided view of God if we lose sight of either his goodness or his justice (ver. 22, 23).

21. Faith and unbelief have been the two great deciding exercises in the religious experiences of men in all ages (ver. 23, 24; Heb. 11).

22. In this world God deals with nations, churches, and communities (ver. 14, 21; Gen. 15 : 14; Jer. 51 : 20, 21; Rev. 2 : 16).

23. The existence of sin in the world and the use God makes of it in his plans of grace and redemption are divine mysteries (ver. 25).

24. The conversion of Israel is foretold, but its details are not made known. Whether it is to precede, or follow our Lord's second coming, or whether they are to return to their own land and be converted there, Paul does not definitely say. Such questions should be treated cautiously, and their settlement left to their fulfillment (ver. 26, 27).

25. The promises of God to Israel encourage missionary labors among them (ver. 26-29).

26. Every effort made for the conversion of the Gentile world is something done toward the conversion of Israel (ver. 26-31).

27. All of God's designs of mercy will most surely be carried out. God will not forsake his people. No opposition can thwart his purpose to save them (ver. 29 ; Ps. 89 : 35, 36; Titus 1 : 2; Heb. 6 : 18 ; James 1 : 17).

28. Peoples and communities bear certain spiritual relations to one another. These should not be ignored, but if possible discovered and used for the advancement of Christ's cause (ver. 29, 30).

29. All men are sinners, and on a level before God, and can be saved only through his mercy (ver. 32).

Practical and ethical lessons.

12 I BESEECH you therefore, brethren, by the mercies of God, that ye ᵃpresent your bodies ᵇa living sacrifice, ᶜholy, acceptable unto God, *which is* your 2 reasonable service. And ᵈbe not conformed to this world; but ᵉ be ye transformed ᶠby the renewing of your mind,

12 I BESEECH you therefore, brethren, through the mercies of God, to present your bodies a living sacrifice, holy, well pleasing to God, which is your 2 rational service. And be not conformed to this age, but be transfigured by the renewing of your mind, that ye

a 6 : 13 ; 1 Cor. 6 : 13, 19, 20.   b Heb. 13 : 15, 16.   c See refs. Lev. 1 : 3.
d 2 Cor. 6 : 14-17 ; James 1 : 27 ; 4 : 4 ; 2 Peter 2 : 20 ; 1 John 2 : 15-17.   e 2 Cor. 5 : 17.
f John 3 : 3-7 ; Eph. 4 : 22-24 ; Col. 3 : 10.

30. We may hope from God's word for the time when the whole world will be converted to Christ (ver. 32; Isa. 11 : 9; Hab. 2 : 14; Rev. 20 : 4).

31. Since God is infinitely wise, just, and good, it becomes us to be humble and submissive to his will (ver. 33-36).

32. God is the Creator and Owner of all things. The universe evinces his power, wisdom, goodness, and glory (ver. 33-36; Ps. 19 : 1, 6).

33. Still greater wisdom and glory are displayed in his moral government and in his word (ver. 33-36; Ps. 19 : 7-14).

34. The wisdom, knowledge, and ways of God, will furnish themes of contemplation and of praise through all eternity (ver. 33-36).

35. God alone is absolutely great (ver. 35; Ps. 50 : 1-3, 12; 86 : 10; Rev. 4 : 11).

36. All truth tends to exalt God, and to present him as all and in all. All true religion comes from him, and to him ascribes all the glory (ver. 36; Rev. 7 : 10-12).

CHAPTER XII.

With the preceding chapter closes the doctrinal portion of the Epistle. With this chapter begins the practical portion, consisting of various precepts, admonitions, concluding remarks, messages, salutations, and benedictions. In this chapter Paul first enforces self-consecration (ver. 1, 2), and a sober, impartial judgment of self in the use of the spiritual gifts bestowed (ver. 3-8). He then exhorts to social duties, growing out of unfeigned love to one another as Christians (ver. 9-13), and to the world (ver. 14-21).

1-8. SELF-CONSECRATION TO GOD AND THE RIGHT USE OF SPIRITUAL GIFTS CONNECTED WITH AN IMPARTIAL JUDGMENT OF SELF.

1. Paul says, **Therefore,** with especial reference to the closing thoughts of the preceding chapter, and also with a general reference to **the mercies of God,** exhibited through the whole preceding doctrinal discussion. The Greek word for **beseech** cannot be exactly translated into English. It includes here the idea of entreaty and exhortation, *I entreat and exhort*. **Mercies,** the emotions of tenderness and pity, the compassionate dealings of God, which are unfolded in chapters 3-8. The word is also used in 2 Cor. 1 : 3; Phil. 2 : 1; Col. 3 : 12; Heb. 10 : 28. No motive could be stronger. **That ye present your bodies**—too little thought of that they should be temples of the Holy Spirit (1 Cor. 6 : 19). **A living sacrifice**—as animals before the altar, so present your bodies before God. God wishes not the dead bodies of irrational animals, but the living bodies of his true worshipers (Ps. 51 : 15-17), as a thank offering. (Comp. Lev. 3 : 1 ff.) **Holy**—free from defect and impurity. **Acceptable, or well-pleasing, unto God, which is your reasonable,** or *rational*, **service.** *Service* is properly religious service, opposed to a mere external ceremonial service (Heb. 12 : 28. Comp. Phil. 4 : 18.). As an expression of gratitude Paul would have them consecrate their powers and energies to God, not merely the soul, but the soul acting through the body, the hands, feet, eyes, tongue, and brain. The *body*, once polluted by sin, and a slave to sin (1 : 24; 6 : 12).

2. This consecration must extend to the soul and to the life. **And be not conformed to this world,** or *fashioned according to this age*, to the principles and practices of evil connected with this period of sin and death (2 Cor. 4 : 4; Gal. 1 : 4; Eph. 2 : 2); **but be ye transformed**—*changed in form* as to

that ye may ᵍprove what *is* that good, and acceptable, and perfect will of God.
3 For I say, ʰthrough the grace given unto me, to every man that is among you, ⁱnot to think *of himself* more highly than he ought to think ; but to think soberly, according as God hath dealt ᵏ to every man the measure of
4 faith. For as we have many members in one body, and all members have not
5 the same office; so ˡwe, *being* many, are one body in Christ, and every one members one of another.

may discern what is the will of God, the good and well pleasing and perfect.
3 For I say, through the grace that was given me, to every one that is among you, not to think of himself more highly than he ought to think ; but so to think as to think soberly, according as God divided to each one a measure
4 of faith. For even as we have many members in one body, and all the mem-
5 bers have not the same office ; so we, the many, are one body in Christ, and severally members one of another;

g Eph. 5 : 10.   *h* See refs. 1 : 5.   *i* 1 Cor. 4 : 7 ; 1 Peter 5 : 5.   *k* 1 Cor. 12 : 7-11.
l 1 Cor. 10 : 17 ; 12 : 12-30 ; Eph. 4 : 16, 25.

your moral character, **by, or through, the renewing by the Holy Spirit, of your mind,** to the end **that ye may prove,** or *test* and so *discern,* **what is that good,** rather, *what is the will of God,* namely, *that which is good and well pleasing* to him, *and perfect.* The word *conform* has an idea of being external and transient. Compare the same word in 1 Peter 1 : 14. The word *transform* refers to that which is real and permanent, and expresses a deep, abiding change. It is used in 2 Cor. 3 : 18; Phil. 2 : 6, 8. The *mind* strictly means *the thinking powers,* the intelligence, but here also includes in a popular sense other powers of the soul, such as affections and purposes, all of which are renewed (2 Cor. 5 : 17; Gal. 6 : 15). Compare the fuller phrase in Eph. 4 : 23. The *renewing* began in regeneration and continued in their sanctification and growth in grace (2 Cor. 4 : 16; Eph. 3 : 19). What is the will of God needs to be spiritually *discerned* (1 Cor. 2 : 14); hence the need of the renewing of the mind (comp. John 7 : 17) in order to discern it.
3. This consecration must be carried out humbly in the diligent use of such gifts as God has bestowed on each one. **For,** in regard to this self-consecration, **I say** and *exhort* **through the grace given me,** qualifying me as an inspired apostle (Eph. 3 : 2, 7; Gal. 2 : 9; 1 Cor. 3 : 10; Rom. 1 : 5; 15 : 15), **to every one among you,** whether a Jewish or a Gentile believer, **not to think of himself more highly than he ought to think,** etc. There is a play on words here which is difficult to express in another language. Alford presents it thus: "Not to be high-minded, above that which he ought to be minded, but to be so minded as to be sober-minded." They were to recognize the gifts of others as well as their own, and that whatever gifts they had they owed to the grace of God (ver. 6). Excessive self-depreciation is also impliedly condemned. **According as God has dealt,** or *in proportion as God has imparted to each one a measure of faith*—of dependent *trust* in Christ and confiding expectation. By faith we receive the workings of the Spirit, and the measure of our faith determines our capacity for all spiritual gifts and attainments. (Comp. Eph. 2 : 7. 8.) To **think soberly** involves true humility, a right and healthful view of ourselves and of our relation to others. **Among you,** as a community of Christians. The exhortation is to members of the church.
4. **For** introduces an illustration of the human **body** with its **members,** or *limbs,* each having its office, *function,* or *business,* which the apostle uses to enforce the exhortation of the preceding verse. This is one of Paul's favorite illustrations. It is given most fully in 1 Cor. 12 : 12-30. In Eph. 4 : 4-16 ; 5 : 23-30, Christ is presented as the lifegiving head. (See also 1 Cor. 10 : 17 ; Eph. 1 : 23; Col. 1 : 18, 24; 2 : 19; 3 : 15.) Here the connection of believers with each other, in a living union with Christ, is brought to view, and their different positions and functions.
5. **So we, who are many, are one body in Christ,** who is our bond of union by virtue of our union with him (8 : 1), **and every one,** or rather, *and individually,* **members one of another.** Through this union

6 Having then gifts differing according to the grace that is given to us, whether prophecy, *let us prophesy* according
7 to the proportion of faith; or ᵐ ministry, *let us wait* on *our* ministering; or he that teacheth, on teaching; or he that exhorteth, on exhortation. ⁿ He that giveth, *let him do it* with simplicity; °he that ruleth, with diligence; he that showeth mercy, ᵖ with cheerful-

6 and having gifts differing according to the grace that is given to us, whether prophecy, let it be according to the pro-
7 portion of our faith; or service, in the service; or he that teaches, in the
8 teaching; or he that exhorts, in the exhortation; he that imparts, in simplicity; he that leads, in diligence; he that shows mercy, in cheerfulness.

ᵐ Acts 6 : 4.   ⁿ Matt. 6 : 1–4, 22.   ° Acts 20 : 28; Heb. 13 : 7.   ᵖ 2 Cor. 9 : 7.

they are new creatures (2 Cor. 5 : 17) and related to each other. As a living body in Christ they are to use their differing gifts for the good of all (ver. 6–8). They must not regard themselves as standing alone, but as related to each other, and as members one of another they are to discharge their individual functions (14 : 7, 8).

6. Having then gifts differing in kind and degree, common or miraculous, **according to the grace that is given to us** (Matt. 25 : 14–30). It seems evident from the gifts mentioned in this and the two following verses, that Paul is not here limiting his directions to miraculous gifts. Whether miraculous or common, they were *gracious gifts* from the same Spirit. For the apostle's full discussion on spiritual gifts, see 1 Cor. chap. 12, 13, 14. The language here is very concise and elliptical. **Whether prophecy, let us prophesy according to the proportion of faith,** of that *trust* in Christ which lays hold of and receives the blessings of the Spirit. The phrase is substantially the same in meaning as "measure of faith" in ver. 3. Prophecy is the utterance of divine truth under the influence or inspiration of the Spirit. It is not confined to foretelling. He who has the gift of prophecy must exercise it within his own sphere in harmony with a sound, sober judgment (ver. 3). The truth he utters must be in accordance with the teachings of the Spirit, and in proportion to his faith which receives the divine influence (2 Cor. 4 : 13). Notice that the reference in this passage is not to church officers, but to the spiritual gifts and qualifications of the members. (Comp. on Acts 13 : 1; also 1 Cor. 12 : 4–11.)

7. Or if we have the spiritual qualification or gift of **ministry,** literally, *of service,* let us wait on and continue *in the service. Ministry* means any service in the church. In 11 : 13 it means apostolic service. In 15 : 31 is the *service* in bringing the money collected for the needy saints at Jerusalem. It here appears to be something different from "prophecy" and "teaching," but it is put in the important place between them. It would seem to be an active practical service, such as the young men performed at the death of Ananias and Sapphira (Acts 5 : 6, 10), or as the alms distributers in Acts 6 : 1–4; or the deacons in 1 Tim. 3 : 10, 11. **Or he that teacheth,** who has the gift and qualification for that work, let him continue *in teaching,* and be devoted to it. In Acts 13 : 1, prophets and teachers are mentioned as two distinct classes of workers. *Teachers* are also spoken of as in 1 Cor. 12 : 28, 29, and Eph. 4 : 11. It does not appear that they were officers in the church, but workers, their name indicating their work. They may have been expositors of the Scriptures and of apostolic preaching. Their special work was that of *instruction.*

8. Or he that exhorteth, having also qualifications for *entreating* and *consoling* (ver. 1), such as earnestness, unction, and an impressive voice, let him continue *in the exhortation* in that department of work. Exhortation is addressed more to the feelings; teaching to the understanding. More general directions now follow. **He that giveth,** having the means and the heart to distribute to the needy, **let him do it with simplicity,** without self-seeking, *in openness of heart,* the true spirit of *liberality* (2 Cor. 8 : 2; 9 : 11, 13; James 1 : 5). Notice that Paul speaks of the grace of giving (2 Cor. 8 : 1, 7). **He that ruleth,** that *presides* over others, as a leader in the church, among the deacons, or in the family, let him do it **with diligence,** with earnest and careful attention to duty. **He**

9 ness: ⁹ *let* love be without dissimulation. Abhor that which is evil; cleave to that which is good.
10 ʳ *Be* kindly affectioned one to another with brotherly love; ˢ in honour preferring one another; ᵗ not slothful in
11 business; fervent in spirit; ᵘ serving
12 the Lord: ˣ rejoicing in hope; ʸ patient in tribulation; ᶻ continuing instant in
13 prayer; ᵃ distributing to the necessity of saints; ᵇ given to hospitality.

9 Let love be unfeigned. Abhor that which is evil; cleave to that which is
10 good. In brotherly love, be tenderly affectionate one to another; in honor
11 preferring one another; in diligence not slothful; in spirit fervent; serving
12 the Lord; in hope rejoicing; in affliction enduring; in prayer persevering;
13 communicating to the necessities of the
14 saints; given to hospitality. Bless

q 1 Peter 1:22; 1 John 3:18.　r John 13:34, 35.　s Phil. 2:3; 1 Peter 5:5.　t 2 Thess 3:10, 11.
u 1 Cor. 10:31.　x 5:2; Luke 10:20.　y 5:3, 4; Luke 21:19.　z See refs. Luke 18:1.
a 1 Cor. 16:1, 2.　b See refs. Gen. 18:2; 1 Tim. 3:2.

that showeth mercy in acts of kindness and charity, succoring the afflicted and bringing help to the wretched, let him do it in **cheerfulness.** (Comp. 2 Cor. 9:7.)

9-21. UNFEIGNED LOVE AND DUTIES GROWING OUT THEREFROM TO ONE ANOTHER AS CHRISTIANS, AND TO THE WORLD.

9. The apostle passes from a wholesome estimate of one's self, which leads to a proper use of one's gifts, to the exercise of Christian love, which will lead them into lines of right action toward all. Let love, toward both Christians and others, **be without dissimulation,** *unfeigned,* without hypocrisy. This love is emphasized elsewhere (2 Cor. 6:6; 1 Tim. 1:5; 1 Peter 1:22). This is followed in the Greek by participles, *abhorring, cleaving,* etc., to the end of ver. 13. True Christian love joins itself in abhorring **evil,** whatever is hurtful and injurious, and in cleaving to the **good,** whatever is beneficial. It thus prepares the way for all the Christian exercises and works which are named in the following verses. (Comp. Ps. 97:10.) **Abhor**—a strong word, *having a horror of.* **Cleave**—*joining one's self steadfastly to* and laboring for **that which is good.**

10. *As to brotherly love* (1 Peter 1: 22; 3:8; 2 Peter 1:7) **be kindly affectioned one to another,** as belonging to one family and to one spiritual brotherhood. This *tenderly loving* is a word used in expressing family affection, chiefly of parents and children. **In honour,** *as to honor,* be from each to each and to all, **preferring one another** (Phil. 2:3; 1 Peter 5:5). The word translated *preferring* is found only here in the New Testament. Many understand it to mean *going before* as a leader, setting an example of deference or of mutual esteem. We should be forward in the manifestation of respect for others.

11. Not slothful in business, rather, *in diligence,* in performing Christian duty, in accomplishing, promoting, and striving after whatever you may have to do, *be not remiss.* (Comp. Eccl. 9:10.) **Fervent,** zealous for what is good, **in spirit,** in the human spirit, renewed and animated by the Holy Spirit. (Comp. Acts 18:25.) **Serving the Lord**—having his glory in view and with a sense of obligation to him. We have thus in this verse a reference to all the outward manifestations of the Christian life, to its inward promptings, and to its high purpose. Some ancient authorities read, *serving the occasion* or *opportunity* with moral discretion. But this reading is not well sustained.

12. Rejoicing in hope, as the ground of rejoicing. (Comp. 5:2; 1 Peter 1:3-9.) **Patient** and *enduring* in the midst of **tribulation,** or *affliction* (5:3; 8:35); be steadfast when in a state or condition of trial. **Continuing** instant, rather, *be persevering,* **in prayer,** both in its individual exercise (Matt. 6:6) and in union with others (Acts 1:14; 12:12). "Pray without ceasing" (1 Thess. 5:17). Give constant attention to prayer (Acts 2:42; 6:4; Col. 4:2).

13. Distributing to, or *sharing in,* the **necessity,** or *wants,* **of** the **saints;** so make their wants your own as to relieve them. (Comp. 15:27; Heb. 13:16; Gal. 2:10; 6:6). **Given to,** or *pursuing,* **hospitality,** practise it earnestly (Heb. 13:2). These exhortations were especially pertinent in those days of persecution, when many suffered loss of their goods and were driven

14 *Bless them which persecute you: bless, and curse not.
15 ᵈRejoice with them that do rejoice,
16 and *weep with them that weep. ᶠ*Be* of the same mind one toward another. ᵍMind not high things, but ʰ condescend to men of low estate. Be not wise in your own conceits.
17 ⁱRecompense to no man evil for evil. ʲProvide things honest in the sight of
18 all men. If it be possible, as much as those who persecute you; bless, and curse not. Rejoice with those who rejoice; weep with those who weep. Be of the same mind one toward another. Set not your mind on high things, but be carried away with lowly. Become not wise in your own conceits.
17 Recompense to no one evil for evil. Provide things honorable in the sight
18 of all men. If it be possible, as far as

---

e See refs. Matt. 5 : 44.   *d* 1 Cor. 12 : 26.   *e* See refs. Job 2 : 11.   *f* See refs. Acts 4 : 32.
g Matt. 18 : 1–4.   ʰ Job 31 : 13–16.   *i* Matt. 5 : 39.   *j* See refs. 2 Cor. 8 : 21.

---

from home; and of missionary labor, when apostles, evangelists, and others, were traveling everywhere preaching the word.

14. Treatment of persecutors. **Bless them.** *Be* in the habit of *blessing them that* **persecute you.** Let this be your habitual spirit and practice. Compare our Lord's precept (Luke 6 : 28) and his example (Luke 23 : 34). The persecution under Nero occurred six years later, but Christians were exposed to persecutions privately in various ways, and more or less publicly (2 Tim. 3 : 12). **Bless, and curse not,** invoke God's blessing, but do not invoke his curse on any one. Some suppose that Paul did not practise his own precept in Acts 23 : 3. But we may regard Paul there speaking as an inspired man and uttering words prophetic of Ananias' doom. (See on Acts 23 : 3.)

15. Exercise a sympathizing spirit. **Rejoice** *with those rejoicing, and* **weep** *with those weeping.* The carrying out of the law of love toward all. "Verse 14 defines the proper conduct in relation to personal *antipathy;* verse 15, the proper conduct in relation to personal *sympathy*" (LANGE). Compare John the Baptist's joy (John 3 : 29), and our Saviour's sympathy with the sisters of Lazarus (John 11 : 35). Paul carried out his own precept (2 Cor. 2 : 2–4; Phil. 1 : 4; 2 : 17, 18).

16. The temper of mind Christians should exercise. **Be of the same mind,** be alike in thinking the same thing **one toward another,** *not setting your mind,* etc. This "characterizes the loving *harmony,* when each in respect to his neighbor has one and the same thought and endeavor. Compare generally 15 : 5; Phil. 2 : 2; 4 : 2; 2 Cor. 13 : 11" (MEYER). **Mind not high things.** This needs to be separated only by a comma from the preceding (so Westcott and Hort): *not setting your mind on,* or *aiming at* **high things.** Be not ambitious in self-seeking and for personal and social positions. **But condescend to men of low estate,** rather, *but be carried away with the lowly,* have an absorbing interest in men or things that are lowly. The neuter seems to be demanded by the contrast, *high things;* but the masculine is not here inapt, and it is argued that in no other case in the New Testament is this adjective, rendered *lowly,* used of things. But whether used in the masculine or neuter, the general meaning is the same. Christ yielded himself to lowly things and conditions of life for our salvation, and associated with publicans and sinners in order that he might save them. (Comp. 1 Tim. 6 : 1–7.) **Be not wise in your own conceits** (11 : 25), in your own estimation, in your own eyes. This accords well with what precedes. Observance of this precept will help the observing of those which precede and follow.

17. Recompense to no man, *render back to no one,* whether a Christian or not, **evil for evil.** The law of retaliation is forbidden by Christian principle (Matt. 5 : 39, 43–48; 1 Thess. 5 : 15; 1 Peter 3 : 9). **Provide things honest,** rather, *take thought for things honorable* and becoming **in the sight of all men,** fair and right both in reality and appearance. This seems to be quoted from the Septuagint of Prov. 3 : 4. *Honest* in the Bible always means *honorable,* and is opposed to unbecoming. Our lives should be becoming our professions, and such as to recommend us as Christians. (Comp. Matt. 5 : 14–16.)

18. Live peaceably on your part. **If it be possible,** and often it will be difficult and sometimes impossible

lieth in you, live peaceably with all
19 men. Dearly beloved, *k*avenge not
yourselves, but *rather* *l*give place unto
wrath: for it is written, Vengeance *is*
mine; I will repay, saith the Lord.
20 Therefore if thine enemy hunger, feed
him; if he thirst, give him drink: for
in so doing thou shalt heap coals of
21 fire on his head. *m* Be not overcome of
evil, but overcome evil with good.

depends on you, be at peace with all
19 men. Avenge not yourselves, beloved,
but give place to the wrath [of God].
For it is written, To me belongs vengeance:
I will recompense, saith the
20 Lord. But,
If thine enemy hungers, feed him;
If he thirsts, give him drink.
For, in doing this,
Thou wilt heap coals of fire on his head.
21 Be not overcome by evil, but overcome
evil with good.

k See refs. Lev. 19 : 18.   *l* Matt. 5 : 39.   *m* Luke 6 : 27-30.

with imperfect and wicked people, **as much as lieth in you,** or *as much as depends on you,* **live peaceably with all men.** Have a peaceable disposition, and do and endure for the sake of peace, so that if it be broken it will be by others rather than by yourselves. (Comp. Matt. 5 : 39-41.) Universal peace, however, cannot be attained where sin exists. Besides, duty will at times require us to oppose or expose wrongdoing, which will naturally arouse opposition.

19. But at all events the Christian must not avenge himself, but leave that to God, who is holy, and whose right and business it is. **Dearly beloved.** An expression of beautiful tenderness, and of persuasive appeal. "The voice of love entreats to walk in love." **Avenge not yourselves**—do not exact justice to yourselves, do not undertake to vindicate yourselves and exact punishment. (Comp. Matt. 5 : 39.) Paul illustrates this precept in 1 Cor. 5 : 7, and Peter in 1 Peter 2 : 20-23. **But rather give place unto wrath,** rather, *the wrath,* that is of God. Not the wrath of the enemy, which they are not to return, nor their own wrath, which they are to restrain, but the wrath of God, which accords with the Scripture immediately quoted. **Vengeance is mine; I will repay, snith the Lord.** Quoted freely from the Septuagint of Deut. 32 : 35. It is also quoted in Heb. 10 : 30. *Mine* and *I* are emphatic. It is not the gratification of revenge, but the execution of deserved punishment, that is meant.

20. Therefore, in view of the preceding principles, **if thine enemy hunger, feed him;** kindly and attentively (1 Cor. 13 : 3). This verse is quoted from Prov. 25 : 21, 22. **For in so doing thou shalt heap coals of fire on his head.** The figure appears to be that of melting metals by covering them with burning charcoal. The idea is not the anticipated pleasure of producing pain and shame, which would be revenge and contrary to what precedes and follows; but that deeds of kindness and love, would tend to melt and subdue the heart into repentance, while they would be the most effectual rebuke of the wrong (Luke 6 : 27-36).

21. Be *thou* **not overcome** *with* **evil,** by retaliating and avenging thyself and by harboring an angry spirit, **but overcome evil with good,** by the spirit and deeds of kindness and love, as suggested in the preceding verse. In 1878 a little Christian community in China was severely used by a petty official, who some time after was sentenced to severe punishment. But one of his former victims interposed and procured his pardon; and thus their enemy was turned into a grateful friend (A. E. MOULE, "Story of the Chehkiang Mission").

PAUL'S ETHICS. In this chapter Paul bases moral duty and obligation on the mercies of God as a motive, and the will of God as a standard. But in his address upon Mars' Hill (Acts 17 : 24-29), he goes back of these and begins with the nature of God, and our relation to him as his offspring—the Author and Sustainer of our being. Thus the ultimate ground of our moral obligation must be found in the nature of God, from which nature our common nature has been derived, and to which nature, as expressed in the Divine will, we should be conformed. And this is reasonable, and accords with our rational, spiritual being and with our relations to God and our fellow-men. Inasmuch as God is holy our service should be holy, and every exercise of love and right should be in accordance with God's holiness. This can only be done in a renewed nature, and toward this every Christian should aim. Practically we are not to avenge evil, but overcome it with good. Vengeance we are to leave with God, and civil punishment to civil government.

PRACTICAL REMARKS.

1. Doctrine and practice should go hand in hand. We should make the former the foundation for the latter (ver. 1; Eph. 4 : 1; Col. 3 : 1).

2. Christian doctrine should be verified in Christian experience. It will thus become productive of holiness in heart and life (ver. 1, 2; John 17 : 17; Col. 2 : 6, 7).

3. The mercies of God as manifested in Jesus Christ, are the strongest motives for consecration and Christian living (ver. 1, 2; Phil. 2 : 1, 2, 12; 2 Cor. 5 : 14).

4. The Christian spirit of consecration is directly opposed to conformity to the world (ver. 2; James 4 : 4; Gal. 5 : 16).

5. Christian brethren, having different gifts, abilities, and stations, should especially guard against self-conceit and ambition on the one hand, and discontent and envy on the other (ver. 3, 4; 15 : 1; 1 Peter 2 : 1, 5).

6. The beauty of Christian brotherhood can only be fully manifested by each being in his place and doing his appropriate work (ver. 4, 5; Eph. 4 : 1, 3, 25, 32; 1 Cor. 14 : 33).

7. We owe it to Christ, as members of his spiritual body, to cultivate our gifts and discharge the duties of our calling for the glory of God and the good of others (ver. 6-8; Phil. 3 : 13-16; 1 Cor. 6 : 20).

8. "Real honor consists in doing what God calls us to do, and not in the possession of high offices or great talents. No man's usefulness is increased by going out of his sphere" (HODGE). (Ver. 6-8; 1 Sam. 2 : 30; John 12 : 26.)

9. Love is the fulfilling of the law and lies at the foundation of Christian practice (ver. 9, 10; 13 : 10; 1 John 4 : 7, 8).

10. There are different kinds of love. Christians, as members of a spiritual family, exercise for one another a love which is marked by a spiritual, brotherly affection (ver. 10; 1 John 4 : 7, 11, 12).

11. Laziness and indifference are incompatible with the Lord's service (ver. 11; Matt. 25 : 26; Heb. 6 : 12).

12. We need to be instant in prayer, since God is the source of our joy, patience, and every grace (ver. 12; 1 Thess. 1 : 2, 3; 2 Thess. 1 : 11, 12).

13. Christian charity and hospitality should be exercised by us, as the stewards of God, especially toward the household of faith (ver. 13; 1 John 3 : 17; Gal 6 : 10).

14. The perfection of Christian love is exhibited in its exercise toward an enemy, and is of God (ver. 14; 5 : 8; Matt. 5 : 44, 45).

15. Christian sympathy, ennobling and perfecting human sympathy, shares the joys and sorrows of others without respect of persons (ver. 15; 1 Thess. 5 : 14, 15).

16. A proper estimate of ourselves and of others will cure pride and self-conceit, and stimulate effort among the humble and lowly (ver. 16; Phil. 2 : 5, 14-17; Rom. 14 : 10, 19).

17. A spirit of retaliation is ignoble and brutish, much less is it Christian (ver. 17; James 4 : 1, 4).

18. Abstaining from doing evil is but a part of external duty. The Christian religion demands that which is becoming and honorable and peaceful (ver. 17, 18; 2 Cor. 8 : 21; 1 Peter 2 : 12).

19. Judgment and vengeance are prerogatives of God and are not to be exercised by men, except as he has, for the good of society and for his glory, given them authority (ver. 19; 13 : 1, 3; Matt. 18 : 17).

20. Nothing is so powerful as goodness and love, and nothing is more effective in subduing enemies and overcoming opposition (ver. 20; 2 : 4).

21. The surest way of not being overcome by evil, is to overcome it by good. This is true of individuals, of churches, and of Christianity in the conversion of the world (ver. 21; John 12 : 32).

CHAPTER XIII.

In this chapter Paul continues to enlarge upon Christian practice. Pass-

13 LET every soul ⁿ be subject unto the higher powers. For ᵒ there is no power but of God: the powers that be are ordained of God. Whosoever therefore resisteth the power, resisteth the ordinance of God: and they that resist shall receive to themselves damnation. For ᵖ rulers are not a terror to good works, but to the evil. Wilt thou then not be afraid of the power? Do that which is good, and thou shalt have praise of the same: for ᵠ he is the minister of God to thee for good. But if thou do that which is evil, be afraid; for he

13 LET every soul submit himself to the authorities that are over him. For there is no authority but from God, and those that are have been appointed by God. So that he that sets himself against the authority, resists the ordinance of God; and they that resist will receive to themselves condemnation. For rulers are not a terror to the good work, but to the evil. And dost thou wish not to fear the authority? Do that which is good, and thou wilt have praise from him; for he is God's minister to thee for good. But if thou

---

n Deut. 17:12; Titus 3:1; 1 Peter 2:13–17.
p Deut. 25:1.
o See refs. Prov. 8:15, 16; Dan. 4:32; John 19:11.
q 2 Chron. 19:6.

---

ing naturally from God, the Supreme Ruler and Judge, to civil governments, as ordained of God, he enforced subjection to rightful authority (ver. 1–5); and a faithful attention to civil duties as carrying out the great law of love (ver. 6–10); and as a motive for this and an entire consecration he presents the brevity of human life and the approach of final salvation (ver. 11–14).

1. Let every soul—*every man* (2:9), **be subject,** be in the habit of *submitting himself to* **the higher powers,** *to the authorities that are over him.* Peter gives a similar injunction (1 Peter 2:13, 14). Wrong views on this may have existed among Roman Christians at that time. The turbulent Jewish spirit may have had an influence upon them. Paul insists that every one should *submit himself* freely of his own accord. And his advice had its designed effect. Under the influence of such precepts, the early church won the moral victory over the Roman empire and heathendom. Thus it overcame evil with good. **For there is no power,** better, *no authority*, **but of God:** a statement of a general principle, that God is the source of the office and functions of government. The powers that be, *And those authorities that exist have been* **ordained** or *appointed by* **God.** That human government is of Divine appointment is here applied to existing governments. It is implied that God is supreme and his authority is above all. But a higher law is not here under consideration (Acts 4:19, 20); nor the right to change the structure or the rulers of government. Civil authority is subordinate under God, and in connection with the preceding chapter, it is implied that the civil is distinct from the spiritual. There is no ground here for a State church, or for a government's interfering in spiritual matters.

2. Whosoever, therefore—as a conclusion from the preceding statement, **resisteth,** or setteth himself against the authority (the same verb used in James 5:6), **resisteth** (a different verb from the preceding) **the ordinance of God.** Lawful authority is meant, that which accords with the standard of right. **Shall receive to themselves damnation,** rather, *condemnation*. Not eternal damnation, but temporal punishment which magistrates execute under the appointment of God.

3. For in confirmation of what I have said, **rulers,** as a class, are not an occasion of **terror** *to the good work* (according to the best Greek text), **but to the evil work.** The good and the evil work are personified. Paul is making a general statement. Rulers were designed to be such and generally were such. **Wilt thou then,** rather, *And wouldst thou have no fear of the authority?* **Do** habitually that **which is good, and thou shalt have praise of the same,** the one exercising the authority. This again is a general principle generally true. Fully carried out it would give us a model government. Paul has in mind a standard, an ideal government. Tholuck finds here an evidence that this Epistle **was written before the** Neronian persecution.

4. For he is the minister, or *a servant,* **of God to thee for good**—this is the end in view, hence you may

beareth not the sword in vain: for he is the minister of God, a revenger to execute wrath upon him that doeth evil.
5 Wherefore ye must needs be subject, not only for wrath, but also for *conscience' sake.
6 For, for this cause 'pay ye tribute also: for they are God's ministers, "attending continually upon this very thing.
7 *Render therefore to all their dues; tribute to whom tribute *is due*; custom to whom custom; *y* fear to whom fear: *honour to whom honour.
8 *Owe no man anything, but to love one another: for *b* he that loveth
9 another hath fulfilled the law. For this, Thou shalt not commit adultery, Thou shalt not kill, Thou shalt not

do that which is evil, fear, for he bears not the sword in vain: for he is God's minister, an avenger for wrath to him
5 that does evil. Wherefore it is necessary to submit yourselves, not only because of the wrath, but also because of conscience.
6 For, on this account ye pay tribute also; for they are God's ministers, attending continually to this very thing.
7 Render to all their dues; tribute to whom tribute is due; custom to whom custom; fear to whom fear; honor to
8 whom honor. Owe no one anything, but to love one another; for he that loves
9 another has fulfilled the law. For this, Thou shalt not commit adultery, Thou shalt not kill, Thou shalt not

r 12 : 19. *s* 1 Peter 2 : 13. *t* See Matt. 17 : 24–27. *u* See 1 Sam. 7 : 16. *x* Luke 20 : 25.
y Lev. 19 : 3 ; Prov. 21 : 21. *z* Exod. 20 : 12 ; Lev. 19 : 32 ; 1 Tim. 6 : 1. *a* Deut. 21 : 14, 15 ; Prov. 3 : 27, 28.
b Matt. 22 : 39, 40 ; Col. 3 : 14 ; 1 Tim. 1 : 5.

expect praise for practising the good. But if you are an evil-doer, **be afraid; for he beareth not the sword in vain.** The figure may have been suggested by the fact that the Cæsars wore a sword or dagger as an emblem of imperial power. **For he is the minister,** or *a servant*, **of God,** an avenger for wrath, for punishment **upon him that doeth,** *practiseth,* **evil.** The bearing of the sword betokens the right to execute capital punishments, and in connection with the **wrath,** betokens all lesser punishments.

5. Wherefore, in view of the ruler's authority under God, and his official power to execute whatever sentence he may impose, **ye must needs be subject,** rather, *it is necessary to submit yourselves,* to civil authority, **not only** *because of the* **wrath,** which in case of crime will issue in punishment, **but also for conscience' sake,** as a Christian man with an enlightened conscience who, in the divine order of things, recognizes his obligations to civil authority. (Comp. 1 Peter 2 : 13–15.) Yet when a ruler transcends his office and enjoins a direct violation of God's command, he becomes himself a violator of God's law, and the Christian can say, "We ought to obey God rather than man" (Acts 5 : 29).

6. Paul now passes to the enforcement of civil duties growing out of the principles just stated. **For** *on this account* **pay ye tribute also**—toll or taxes. This is declarative and in illustration of what he had said. The com-

mand is in the next verse. **For they are God's ministers** (not the word used in ver. 4, but *servants* of a public and sacred character as representing God), **attending continually** *to* **this very thing.** This is their business and duty.

7. Render therefore to all their dues. This refers to all magistrates; for of these he is speaking, and to such the rest of the verse evidently refers. **Tribute,** or *tax*, on person or property, **to whom tribute is due; custom,** or *duty*, on merchandise; **fear,** as to an avenger of wrong; **honour,** as to rightful authority. Compare our Lord's reply to the Herodians, which presents the divine as well as the human side: " Render to Cæsar the things that are Cæsar's, and to God the things that are God's" (Matt. 22 : 21).

8. Love is inculcated, a motive, and an essential element in Christian practice. **Owe no man anything,** whether it be a financial debt or any other obligation. See that your dues (preceding verse) and other obligations are promptly met. Avoid being unnecessarily in a state of debt (Prov. 3 : 27, 28). **But,** or *except,* **to love one another,** which is an ever-continuing and increasing obligation, and which therefore requires perpetual payment; and in the very nature of things can never be paid off. Paul has Christian love especially in view: " Love one another" (1 Thess. 4 : 9). **For he that loveth another,** his neighbor, hath **fulfilled the law** of Moses. Paul is

steal. Thou shalt not bear false witness. Thou shalt not covet: and if there be any other commandment, it is briefly comprehended in this saying, namely, *Thou shalt love thy neighbour as thyself. ᵈLove worketh no ill to his neighbour: therefore love is the fulfilling of the law.

11 And that ᵉknowing the time, that now it is high time ᶠto wake out of sleep: ᵍfor now is our salvation nearer

12 than when we believed. The night is far spent, ʰ the day is at hand : ⁱ let us therefore cast off the works of darkness, and ᵏlet us put on the armor of

steal, Thou shalt not covet; and if there is any other commandment, it is summed up in this word, namely, Thou shalt love thy neighbor as thyself.

10 Love works no ill to one's neighbor; therefore love is the fulfillment of the

11 law. And this, knowing the season, that it is high time already for you to be awaked out of sleep; for now is our salvation nearer than when we be-

12 lieved. The night is far advanced, the day is at hand. Let us therefore put off the works of darkness, and let

c See refs. Mark 12 : 31.   d 1 Cor. 13 : 4–7.   e 1 Thess. 5 : 1–3.   f 1 Cor. 15 : 34.   g See refs. Luke 21 : 28.
h Heb. 10 : 25.   i Eph. 5 : 11 ; 6 : 11–18 ; 1 Thess. 5 : 5–7 ; 1 John 1 : 5–7.   k 1 Thess. 5 : 8.

stating a principle, according to which all should aim to live. (Comp. in Gal. 5 : 13, 14 ; see also Matt. 22 : 37–40.) He is speaking only of the second table of the law ; but one must keep the first in order to fully keep the second. He who truly and fully loves his neighbor must truly love God also (1 John 4 : 7, 8, 20, 21).

9. The apostle proceeds to show how love to one's neighbor fulfills the law. **If there be any other commandment,** equivalent to "Every other commandment." The ninth, "Thou shalt not bear false witness," is omitted in the best manuscripts. The positive *love* of **thy neighbor as thyself** would insure the observing of all these negative requirements. These and all we owe to our neighbor is **briefly comprehended,** *is summed up* **in this saying.** Selfishness will be excluded and all sinful partiality (James 2 : 8).

10. Love worketh no ill to his neighbour; it will thus avoid the acts which the law forbids. Love is personified here, also in 1 Cor. 13 : 4–8, where its influence, in endurance, thought, and deed, is **strikingly portrayed.** Love therefore, is **the fulfilling,** rather, *the fulfilment of the law,* it is obedience to the law as an accomplished fact. Compare *hath fulfilled the law* (ver. 8)—by its very nature love has satisfied its demands.

11. The apostle uses the shortness of time as a motive. **And that,** rather, *And this* do, referring to ver. 8 and what follows. **Knowing the time,** *the season,* fixed and limited, a consideration of which will show you *that already it is time for you to be awaked* **out of sleep**—to be aroused from stupor, inactivity, and forgetfulness. **For now is our salvation,** or, *For salvation is nearer to us,* **than when we believed**—eternity is nearer, with its full salvation. A comparison of such passages as 1 Thess. 4 : 17 ; 5 : 6 ; 1 Cor. 15 : 51 ; Heb. 9 : 28, naturally leads to the conclusion that Paul must have had some reference, at least, to the second coming of Christ. The time of our Lord's return, whether near or remote, was unknown (Mark 13 : 32), but the certainty was assured (Acts 1 : 11); it was a strong motive in apostolic days (Matt. 24 : 42 ; 25 : 13 ; Rev. 3 : 3 ; 16 : 15). But whether this earthly life should end with death or with Christ's return, in either case salvation (1 : 16) was nearer.

12. Changing the figure, it is no longer *the season,* but *the night.* The **night** of imperfection, trial, and spiritual darkness **is far spent**—*is far advanced;* the dawn is approaching. **The day** of complete deliverance and salvation **is at hand.** To Paul's faith that day, whether it should begin with his departing and being with Christ (Phil. 1 : 21–23), or with Christ's second coming (Heb. 9 : 28), was near. **Let us therefore cast off,** or *put off,* **the works of darkness,** as one puts off his night garments. The reference is to the deeds of moral darkness, the besetting and other sins against which the Christian has to contend (Heb. 12 : 1 ; 2 Cor. 6 : 14 ; Eph. 6 : 12). **And** being robed **as for the day, let us put on the armor,** or *weapons,* **of light,** such as the light demands and is becoming to it. The Christian life is a warfare ; he needs therefore to be clothed with **the armor** of spiritual

13 light. *Let us walk honestly, as in the day; *not in rioting and drunkenness, *not in chambering and wantonness,
14 *not in strife and envying. But *put ye on the Lord Jesus Christ, and *make not provision for the flesh, to *fulfil* the lusts *thereof*.

13 us put on the weapons of light. Let us walk becomingly, as in the day; not in reveling and drunkenness, not in lewdness and wantonness, not in
14 strife and jealousy; but put on the Lord Jesus Christ, and make not provision for the flesh, to fulfill its desires.

l 1 Peter 2 : 12.　　m Luke 21 : 34.　　n 1 Cor. 6 : 9.　　o James 3 : 14–16.　　p Gal. 3 : 27.　　q Gal. 5 : 16, 17.

light—faith, love, hope, truth, righteousness, peace, and the graces of the Spirit (1 Thess. 5 : 8 ; 2 Cor. 6 : 7 ; Eph. 6 : 11–16).
13. Let us walk honestly—*becomingly*—**as in the day,** with the light about us, as the children of light (1 John 1 : 7); doing the deeds of the day, and such as shall bear the scrutiny of the light. Things not becoming are to be avoided, such as **rioting**—*reveling*, and carousing (1 Peter 4 : 3). **Drunkenness** — *drunken spells* (Gal. 5 : 21). **Chambering**—licentious indulgences. **Wantonness**—shameful and indecent words and acts, and unchaste conduct toward others. **Strife and envying,** or *jealousy*. Sins of temper, classed with lusts of the flesh (Gal. 5 : 20). This list of sinful acts and indulgences suggests what may have been the moral degradation of these Roman believers before their conversion and also of the moral corruption to which they were exposed (Eph. 2 : 2, 3). This and the following verse formed the turning point in the conversion of Augustine.
14. But, on the contrary, **put ye on,** as a garment and as an armor (ver. 12), **the Lord Jesus Christ,** breathe as it were his spirit, live as it were his life, be Christlike. Be so possessed with the mind of Christ as to resemble him, and reproduce as it were the life of Christ. (Comp. Gal. 3 : 27 ; Eph. 4 : 24 ; Col. 3 : 10.) Love is the motive (ver. 10), and Christ the pattern. **And make no provision,** by way of *forethought* **for the flesh,** the seat of sinful passions and lusts, *with a view of gratifying its evil desires*. Or, which amounts to substantially the same : indulge not the desires of your own corrupt human nature (6 : 12, 19 ; 1 Cor. 9 : 25–27).

CHRISTIAN ETHICS OF THE STATE. There are three institutions which may be said to be of Divine origin : the family, the State, and the Church. They may exist together, but each has its own sphere and functions ; each is independent, but each should work in harmony with the other two. The great principles of Christ's kingdom include the fundamental principles underlying the well-regulated family and the well-governed State, such as love to one's neighbor and the commands of the Decalogue relating to our fellow-men. Paul therefore recognizes the true basis of the State to be the will and law of God. The Christian and the gospel may and should exert a moral influence upon the State for its good. Since we find ourselves within the State and under its government, it is our duty to help support it, obey its laws, and defend it even unto death if need be. If it enacts wrong-doing, we should strive to change it if possible ; but if we cannot we can submissively suffer the penalty, choosing to obey God rather than men. Government may so persist in wrong-doing as to pervert its very nature and object, making resistance and revolution justifiable.

PRACTICAL REMARKS.

1. Civil authority is of Divine origin, but forms of government are human. Loyalty to God involves loyalty to law (ver. 1 ; Matt. 23 : 2, 3).

2. Nihilism is destructive of authority, and hence opposed to the ordinance of God. A bad government is better than anarchy (ver. 2).

3. Civil authority is distinct from religious authority. Neither has a right to control the other (ver. 1–7 ; Matt. 22 : 21).

4. The design of civil government is not for the ruler, but for the good of the ruled (ver. 3 ; Acts 23 : 3).

5. The principles of the gospel tend to rectify human government and to make both tyranny and anarchy impossible (ver. 1–7 ; Matt. 7 : 12).

6. There is a right of revolution. Set-

Concerning conscientious differences of opinion and practice.

14 HIM that is weak in the faith receive ye, *but* not to doubtful disputations—

14 HIM that is weak in the faith receive; not for decisions of disputes.

v 15 : 1, 7.

ting one's self against law and government, and trying to improve and change them, are two essentially different things. The one is anarchy, the other revolution. The Christian may not engage in the former, but there may be circumstances in which he may support the latter (ver. 1-6).

7. There is a law higher than government. The Christian may for conscience' sake obey the former, and hence endure the penalty of the latter (ver. 1-6; Acts 4 : 19 ; 5 : 29; Dan. 3 : 16-18; 6 : 10).

8. The Christian may take advantage of existing authority and law (ver. 1, 5; Acts 22 : 25 ; 25 : 11).

9. Government and nations are accountable to God, and will be judged by God (ver. 1-7).

10. Obligations and debts to government are as sacred as those to individuals (ver. 6-8).

11. It is the duty of Christians to be watchful against debt; to be industrious and to practise frugality in order to avoid it (ver. 8; 1 Thess. 4 : 11, 12; 2 Cor. 11 : 9; Eph. 4 : 28).

12. Love is most comprehensive and has to do with every form of moral obligation (ver. 8-10).

13. A deep conviction of the reality and nearness of eternity will prompt an upright life and an entire consecration to Christ's service (ver. 11-14; Acts 17 : 30, 31 ; 1 Thess. 4 : 16, 17).

14. The nearness of final salvation should fill the Christian with joy and hope, and arouse him to activity, and nerve him for meeting the trials of life (ver. 11, 12).

15. While Christians "put on Christ" in their baptismal confession (Gal. 3 : 27), they should put him on daily by exhibiting his spirit, character, and life (ver. 14).

CHAPTER XIV.

In this chapter Paul passes to the treatment that weak and over-scrupulous brethren should receive from their stronger but equally conscientious brethren. It would seem that a special application in regard to such was needed in the church at Rome. There were tendencies toward asceticism about which there were honest differences of opinion. They should exercise mutual forbearance and not judge one another (ver. 1-12). The strong should not put a means of stumbling in the way of the weak (ver. 13-18), but rather exercise self-denial for their sake (ver. 19-23).

1-12. THE CONDUCT TO BE EXERCISED TOWARD WEAK AND OVER-SCRUPULOUS BRETHREN. Mutual forbearance and the exercise of the law of love in regard to conscientious differences of opinion and practice. It does not seem that these views had gone so far as to affect their doctrines, as in Galatia, where there were Judaizing teachers (Gal. 1 : 7). Their case seems similar to that of the Corinthians, who were conscientiously troubled about meats offered to idols (1 Cor. 8 : 1-13; 10 : 25-33) ; fearing to eat meat or drink wine bought in the open market, lest they had been polluted by having been offered to idols, or by coming into contact with the unclean, they confined themselves to a vegetable diet, of the purity of which they were assured.

1. *But* him that is weak—a contrast from the exhortation of 13 : 14. *But*—while "making no provision for the flesh to fulfill the lusts thereof" (13 : 14)—in regard to those who go to an extreme in over-sensitiveness and in avoiding everything that seems to them to minister to the corruptions of the flesh. Weak in the faith in Christ, so that things indifferent and really not binding on the conscience trouble him. Compare ver. 14, where Paul, strong in the faith, rises above such matters. Receive ye *to yourselves*, into fellowship—the present tense. Receive him not only as a new believer, but continue to take him to your hearts and treat him as a brother Christian. But with this caution—not to doubtful

ROMANS

2 tions. For one believeth that he *may eat all things; another, who is weak,
3 eateth herbs. Let not him that eateth despise him that eateth not; and *let not him which eateth not judge him that eateth: for God hath received
4 him. ᵘWho art thou that judgest another man's servant? To his own master he standeth or falleth. Yea, ˣhe shall be holden up: for God is able to make him stand.
5 ʸOne man esteemeth one day above another: another esteemeth every day

2 One believes that he may eat all things; but he that is weak eats herbs.
3 Let not him that eats despise him that eats not; and let not him that eats not judge him that eats: for God received
4 him. Who art thou that judgest another's servant? To his own lord he stands or falls. But he shall be made to stand; for the Lord is able to make him stand.
5 One man esteems one day above another; another esteems every day

---

ˢ Titus 1 : 15.   *t* 1 Cor. 10 : 29, 30 ; Col. 2 : 16.   ᵘ Matt. 7 : 1, 2 ; Luke 12 : 14.
ˣ See refs. 8 : 31–39 ; 1 Peter 1 : 5.   ʸ Gal. 4 : 9 10.

---

disputations, rather, *not for the purpose of deciding* or *passing judgment on opinions,* as to which is the most correct. The word *disputations,* or *opinions,* is the same as used in 1 : 21, and there translated *imaginations,* and means *thoughts,* inward *reasonings,* speculations. The injunction is here made general, but as applied to the weak brother personally, it naturally refers to the thoughts and opinions that trouble him, in other words, to his *scruples.* Hence they were to receive him, but not for the purpose of discussing and passing judgment upon his scruples and such matters. He was not to decide upon things in dispute.

2. The apostle specifies two extremes. **For one,** who is strong, **believeth,** or, *has faith,* according to which he may eat all things without any conscientious scruples. He has faith to rise above all ceremonial observances of the law, and to see that his justification or condemnation does not depend on Mosaic rites. **Another, who is weak** in the faith, cannot rest so fully on Christ for his justification and complete salvation as to divest himself of anxiety and scruples regarding meats that are unclean. And so to escape all contamination he **eateth herbs.** This is his simplest solution of the question regarding clean and unclean animals, and also of meat defiled by idol sacrifices, or polluted in any other way.

3. But let not the strong despise the weak; nor the weak judge and condemn the strong. **For God hath,** rather, *did receive,* **him** at his conversion. This is true of either of the above parties; but it here applies especially to the strong, according to the next verse. This is a reason for forbearance and charitableness of judgment.

4. **Who art thou,** weak one, **that judgest another man's servant?** *household servant,* or *domestic.* This word for servant is also found in Acts 10 : 7; Luke 16 : 13; 1 Peter 2 : 18. The word *judge* here carries along with it the idea of censure and severity, and does not forbid the proper expressions of opinion on the subject. Paul does this in ver. 14. **To his own Master,** *the Lord Jesus Christ,* **he standeth or falleth.** To him alone is he amenable. **Yea,** rather, *But,* instead of falling, **he shall be holden up**—*made to stand,* and established through faith. **For God,** according to the best text, *For the Lord,* Christ, **is able,** *is powerful,* **to make him stand.** He supports the believer, and he who is strong in the faith will be supported and delivered in every hour of temptation. As a result also he will stand at the judgment day.

5. Two opposites again are presented. **One** who is weak **esteemeth one day above another**—*distinguishing* between days, and regarding one holier than another. **Another** who is strong **esteemeth every day alike**—*he judges* every day as good, and as a consecrated man (12 : 1, 2) he regards his whole time and life devoted to the Lord. As the apostle, both before and after this reference to days, is speaking of food and drink, it is natural to regard the reference here to be principally to feasts and fasts under the law. These were the feasts of the Passover, the Pentecost, the Tabernacle, the Trumpet, the Dedication, and Purim; the fasts on the Day of Atonement (Lev.

L

alike. ᵃ Let every man be fully per-
6 suaded in his own mind. He that regardeth the day, regardeth *it* unto the
Lord; and he that regardeth not the
day, to the Lord he doth not regard *it*.
He that eateth, eateth to the Lord, for
ᵃ he giveth God thanks; and he that
eateth not, to the Lord he eateth not,
7 and giveth God thanks. For ᵇ none of
us liveth to himself, and no man dieth
8 to himself. For whether we live, we
live unto the Lord; and whether we
die, we die unto the Lord: ᶜ whether
we live therefore, or die, we are the
9 Lord's. For ᵈ to this end Christ both
died, and rose, and revived, that he
might be ᵉ Lord both of the dead and
living.

alike. Let each one be fully per-
6 suaded in his own mind. He that regards the day, regards it to the Lord;
and he that eats, eats to the Lord, for
he gives thanks to God; and he that
eats not, to the Lord he eats not, and
7 gives thanks to God. For no one of us
lives to himself, and no one dies to
8 himself. For if we live, we live to the
Lord; and if we die, we die to the
Lord; whether we live therefore, or
9 die, we are the Lord's. For to this end
Christ died, and lived, that he might
10 be Lord of both dead and living. But

ᵃ Ver. 23; 1 John 3 : 19–21.   *a* 1 Cor. 10 : 30, 31; 1 Tim. 4 : 3–5.
ᵇ 2 Cor. 5 : 14, 15; Phil. 1 : 20–24; 1 Peter 4 : 2.   *c* 1 Cor. 3 : 21–23.   *d* 2 Cor. 5 : 15.   *e* Acts 10 : 36.

---

16 : 29–31), in the fourth, fifth, seventh, and tenth months (Zach. 8 : 19), and on Monday and Thursday of each week (Luke 18 : 12). Besides the weekly Sabbath there were seven days of holy convocation: the first and last days of the Passover festival, the first day of the feast of Tabernacles, and the day following the feast, the day of Pentecost, the day of Atonement, and the feast of Trumpets. As to how far this verse may apply to the Sabbath, I would say: Only in so far as it was an institution under the law. It does not touch the original *rest-day* of creation, one rest-day in seven (Gen. 2 : 3), nor the Lord's Day under the Christian dispensation (Gal. 4 : 10; Col. 2 : 16). The whole passage seems to indicate that reference is had to Jewish believers with Essenic and ascetic tendencies, and to Gentile and other believers who had come out into a fuller liberty of the gospel (Gal. 5 : 1 ff.). **Let every man be fully persuaded,** or *assured,* **in his own mind.** Let him not act against his own conscience, and remember that he is accountable to the Lord.

6. The true Christian position stated. **He that regardeth the day** as sacred, to be religiously observed, **regardeth it as** due **unto the Lord** Christ (ver. 9), to whom he feels responsible. **And he that regardeth not the day, to the Lord he doth not regard it.** These words should be omitted, as they are not in the best manuscripts. *And* **he that eateth,** etc. Both the eater of all kinds of food and the eater of herbs recognize their obligations to Christ for all their blessings, and have his glory in view (1 Cor. 10 : 31), and give **God thanks.** Both practise a spirit of devotion and thanksgiving. This would seem to indicate that the practice of giving thanks at meals was universal among early Christians.

7. For in confirmation of the thought, *to the Lord* (twice in ver. 6), it may be said that **none of us liveth to himself, and no man dieth to himself.** As Christians, self is subordinate both in life and in death, and Christ is uppermost as Lord. Both the eater and the abstainer are servants of Christ.

8. This verse carries out the thought of the preceding. **For** whether we live or die, we live or die **unto the Lord.** We are his by virtue of our union with him, and by being "bought with a price" (1 Cor. 6 : 20; 7 : 23). Christ owns us both in life and death. **Whether we live therefore, or die, we are the Lord's.** Both in life and death, here and hereafter, we belong to the Lord, and are to be devoted to him. Compare Paul's confession in Acts 28 : 23 and his ideal of Christian living in Phil. 1 : 21; Gal. 2 : 20.

9. For to this end, namely, that he might be Lord both of the dead and the living—of both classes, not to be separated, but together equally his —**Christ both died, and rose, and revived,** rather, according to the best text, *Christ died and lived,* that is, rose from the dead. It was necessary for

10 But why dost thou judge thy brother? Or why dost thou set at nought thy brother? For *we shall all stand be-
11 fore the judgment seat of Christ. For it is written, *As I live*, saith the Lord, every knee shall bow to me, and every
12 tongue shall confess to God. So then ᵍevery one of us shall give account of himself to God.
13 Let us therefore judge one another any more: but judge this rather, that ʰ no man put a stumbling-block or an occasion to fall in *his*

thou, why dost thou judge thy brother? Or thou also, why dost thou despise thy brother? For we shall all stand before
11 the judgment-seat of God. For it is written, As I live, says the Lord, to me every knee shall bow, and every
12 tongue shall confess to God. So then, each one of us will give account concerning himself to God.
13 Let us therefore no longer judge one another; but judge this rather, not to put a stumbling-block, or an occasion

f Eccl. 12 : 14; Matt. 25 : 31, 32; Acts 10 : 42.   *g* Matt. 12 : 36.   *h* Lev. 19 : 14; see refs. Matt. 18 : 6, 7.

Christ both to die and to rise again in order to become Lord (Phil. 2 : 8-11). By his death and his resurrection life he effected the purchase, and demonstrated his ownership of his followers; and thus showed that he was Lord both of their earthly and heavenly life. These matters of meat and drink therefore should not separate them, and one should not either despise or condemn the other.

10. Thou, in the first two clauses is very emphatic, in contrast to *Lord* in the preceding verse. The first clause is addressed to the *weak* one; the second to the *strong* one. *But thou,* weak one, **why dost thou judge** thy **brother,** who is strong in faith and in the liberty of the gospel? *Or thou also,* strong one, *why dost thou* set **at nought,** or *despise,* **thy brother,** weak and perplexed as he is with his conscientious scruples? **For we shall all,** both weak and strong, **stand before the judgment seat of Christ,** or *of God,* according to the most approved text. In 2 Cor. 5 : 10 it is called "the judgment seat of Christ." (Comp. Matt. 25 : 31.) That God will judge men by Jesus Christ is evident from 2 : 16; Acts 10 : 42; 17 : 31; John 5 : 22. In view of the judgment, how unbecoming for Christian brethren to be judging and despising one another.

11. The apostle confirms the preceding statement by Isa. 45 : 23. It is freely quoted and somewhat abbreviated. Compare the same in Phil. 2 : 10, 11, where it is especially applied to Christ. **As I live, saith the Lord—** a most solemn divine declaration, equivalent to swearing by himself— **every knee shall bow to me, and every tongue shall confess to**

God, or according to some, *shall give praise to God,* but the latter meaning includes the idea of confession, and the confession contains an element of praise for Jesus as Lord, because he saves his people from their sins (Phil. 2 : 11. Comp. Rev. 5 : 9, 10).

12. This verse sums up in a brief sentence the thought of the two preceding verses. So then **every one of** us, be he weak or strong, **shall give account of himself,** not of another, **to** God. The emphasis here is on *each one of us*. The judgment will be personal and individual; it will be to God, not to man. Brethren should therefore not assume the office of judge one of another. The thought is carried out in what follows, with reference to the duty of the strong to the weak.

13-23. THE STRONG SHOULD AVOID GIVING OFFENSE TO, BUT RATHER EXERCISE SELF-SACRIFICE FOR, THE WEAK.

13. Since **therefore** our brother is not our servant, but Christ's, and we both act in devotion to him, and all questions will be finally settled at the bar of God, **let us** *no longer continue to* **judge one another.** (Comp. Matt. 7 : 1.) Paul now passes to admonish the strong through the rest of this chapter. From this we may infer that they were the larger party in the Roman church. **But judge this rather,** be this your determination, **that no man put a stumbling-block,** that against which one stumbles and falls into sin, **or an occasion,** as a trap by which **to fall into sin,** *in a* **brother's way.** The two words "stumbling-block" and "an occasion of offense" are similar in meaning, and together give emphasis to the thought (as also in 9 : 33).

11 brother's way. I know, and am persuaded by the Lord Jesus, *i* that *there is* nothing unclean of itself : but *k* to him that esteemeth anything to be unclean,
15 to him *it is* unclean. But if thy brother be grieved with *thy* meat, now walkest thou not *l* charitably. *m* Destroy not him with thy meat, for whom Christ
16 died. Let not then your good be evil
17 spoken of. *n* For the kingdom of God *o* is not meat and drink ; but righteousness, and peace, and joy in the Holy

14 to fall, in a brother's way. I know, and am persuaded in the Lord Jesus, that nothing is defiled of itself ; but to him that accounts anything to be de-
15 filed, to him it is defiled. But if because of food thy brother is aggrieved, thou no longer walkest in accordance with love. Do not by thy food destroy
16 him for whom Christ died. Let not
17 then your good be evil spoken of. For the kingdom of God is not food and drink ; but righteousness, and peace,

i Ver. 20 ; Acts 10 : 15, 28.   *k* 1 Cor. 8 : 7, 10.   *l* 13 : 10 ; Gal. 5 : 13,   *m* 1 Cor. 8 : 11.
n See refs. Matt. 3 : 2.   *o* 1 Cor. 8 : 8.

The former is the more general word, representing a larger obstacle ; the latter the more specific—as a trap or trapstick—representing a smaller and more hidden obstacle. The former partakes more of the outward act ; the latter more of the thought. (Comp. 1 Cor. 8 : 1 ff.)

14. An important statement in which Paul places himself in agreement with the strong, and thus prepares the way for enforcing his admonition. **I know, and am persuaded by,** rather, *in,* **the Lord Jesus,** in living union and fellowship with him, having therefore the mind of Christ, and an assurance of the truth of what I am about to utter. A strong expression of his complete knowledge and assurance of the fact. An authoritative utterance. **That nothing** *is* **unclean of itself,** morally and religiously profane through its own nature. Paul regarded the Old Testament laws regarding food as no longer binding, since the Mosaic economy had come to an end in Christ (10 : 4 ; Col. 2 : 16 ff.; Acts 10 : 15, 16 ; Matt. 5 : 17). **But to him that esteemeth,** or *accounteth,* **anything to be unclean, to him it is unclean,** in his mind and feelings, and to his conscience. Conscience is not to be violated, but respected and followed. If it is wrong then it should be instructed and enlightened ; but never should it be rudely dealt with. A person's convictions must be respected.

15. But or *For.* Internal evidence rather favors *but ;* external, *for.* Granting what I have said, **if thy brother be grieved**—*put to pain,* and his conscience hurt *because of* **meat,** or *food,* **thou** *no longer* **walkest charitably,** *according to love.* They would transgress the rule of Christian love which he had laid down in 12 : 9, 10 ; 13 8.

Meat in the Common version does not mean *flesh* alone. Here it means food in general, including flesh. **Destroy not him,** do not begin the destruction of one **with thy meat,** or *food,* **for whom Christ died,** the deepest and strongest of motives for Christian tenderness and love. *Thy food*—suggestive of a **selfish** spirit and act. *Destroy* is in the present tense, and points to the beginning, not the accomplishment of the act. The violation of conscience and regarding iniquity in the heart (Ps. 66 : 18), if continued in, would result in destruction. (Comp. 1 Cor. 8 : 11.)

16. *Therefore,* in conclusion, **let not your good,** as Christians, including your liberty "in the kingdom of God" (ver. 17), which is good in itself, and which you mean for good (1 Cor. 10 : 29, 30), **be evil spoken of**—*be blasphemed, slandered,* both among yourselves and without, by being the occasion of censures and wrangling, of injured consciences, of violated love, of the falling away of some weak ones, and the lowering of the Christian life among all. (Comp. 1 Peter 2 : 12-16.)

17. For, as a reason for this exhortation (ver. 16), **the kingdom of God** —his reign in the hearts and lives of the redeemed (Luke 17 : 21 ; see note on Matt. 3 : 2), **is not meat** (*food*) **and drink** —does not consist in *eating and drinking* of this or that, or in abstaining from them. This is not its vital element ; it is not the nature of true religion under the gospel. But it consists *in* **righteousness,** in our relations to God and men as required in justification and sanctification, **and peace,** with God and one another, **and joy in the Holy Ghost,** of which he is the Author. On the use

CH. XIV.]   ROMANS   165

18 Ghost. For he that in these things serveth Christ *is* acceptable to God, ⁹ and approved of men.
19 ʳ Let us therefore follow after the things which make for peace, and things wherewith ˢ one may edify
20 another. ᵗ For meat destroy not the work of God. ᵘ All things indeed *are* pure; ᵛ but *it is* evil for that man who
21 eateth with offence. *It is* good neither to eat ˣ flesh, nor to drink wine, nor *any thing* ʸ whereby thy brother stum-

18 and joy in the Holy Spirit. For he that in these things serves Christ, is well pleasing to God and approved by men.
19 So then, let us pursue the things which make for peace, and things by
20 which one may build up another. Do not, for the sake of food destroy the work of God. All things indeed are clean; but it is evil for that man who
21 by eating makes another stumble. It is good neither to eat flesh, nor to drink wine, nor anything whereby thy

p 12 : 1, 2 ; Acts 10 : 35.   *q* 2 Cor. 4 : 2 ; James 2 ; 18-26.   *r* 12 : 18.   *s* 15 : 2.   *t* Ver. 15.
u Matt. 15 : 11 ; Acts 10 : 15.   *v* 1 Cor. 8 : 9-12.   *x* 15 : 1, 2 ; 1 Cor. 8 : 13.   *y* Ver. 13.

here of *kingdom of God*, see 1 Cor. 4 : 20; Col. 1 : 20. "The essence of the kingdom of God is not to be found in questions about eating and drinking" (THAYER'S "N. T. Lex."). Inasmuch as Paul in this Epistle has treated of righteousness and peace in relation to justification and sanctification, it seems best to extend the reference to both here. *Holy Spirit* qualifies *joy*. It is possible to connect it also with righteousness and peace, as the latter certainly are connected with the Spirit in the work of God in the soul (5 : 1-5).
18. **For,** in confirmation of the statement just made, **he that in these things**—righteousness, peace, and joy —**serveth Christ,** a servant notwithstanding his Christian liberty. Instead of *these things* most of the best manuscripts have *in this* or *herein*, which may refer to *the Holy Spirit* (ver. 17), or more probably to the whole idea of the preceding passage, and thus is substantially equivalent to the other reading. **Acceptable to God,** well pleasing to him, **and approved of men,** like gold tried and standing the test. The Christian in spirit and daily living should commend himself to the consciences of his fellow-men, both of believers and of the world (1 Cor. 8 : 8 ; 2 Cor. 4 : 2). True religion may be unpopular among men, but in the long run it will be acknowledged as true and real.
19. Paul draws a conclusion from the last few verses. *So then,* instead of exciting strife and debate in this matter, **let us follow,** or *pursue,* **the things** *of* **peace**—adopt peaceable measures and a course of conduct that tends to peace; **and,** avoiding that which will make others stumble and fall, let us pursue *the* **things where-** **with one may edify,** or *build up*, **another**—the things of *mutual upbuilding* in the Christian life. Let us strive to strengthen one another in his faith in Christ and in his participation in righteousness, peace, and joy in the Holy Spirit (ver. 17). On *edify* compare 15 : 2 ; 1 Cor. 14 : 4, 12, 26.
20. Paul exhorts the opposite of upbuilding, keeping the figure in mind (ver. 19). **For meat,** or *food*, about the eating of which there may be a question, or a conscientious scruple, **destroy not**—*pull not down*—**the work of God,** which he has built up in the heart, character, and life. On *destroy* compare Acts 6 : 14; 2 Cor. 5 : 1 ; Gal. 2 : 18. The apostle now briefly reaffirms and applies his statement in ver. 14. **All things**—all food, in regard to eating and abstaining—**indeed are pure,** or *clean*, **but,** though it be pure, **it is evil,** or *sinful to him eating* **with offence.** Literally, *by means of a stumbling-block*. Through the example of the stronger he is induced to eat, and so he suffers the condemnation of conscience (ver. 23). Of course, the strong will also injure himself by such a course of action, but that is not the special point here.
21. The apostle lays down a most important practical precept, applicable to all such cases. He has shown that eating with offense is *evil* to the weak one ; now he affirms in contrast that it is *good* and noble for the strong one to abstain from eating **flesh** or drinking **wine** or from **anything whereby thy brother stumbleth, or is offended, or** *weakened* (ver. 13). It is right and noble for the strong brother to forego his liberty and exercise self-denial rather than do injury to a weak one. "Not the *principle* of liberty,

bleth, or is offended, or is made weak.
22 Hast thou faith? Have *it to thyself before God. 'Happy *is* he that condemneth not himself in that thing
23 which he alloweth. And *he that doubteth is damned if he eat, because he cateth not of faith: for *whatsoever is not of faith is sin.

brother stumbles, or is made to offend,
22 or is weak. Hast thou faith? Have it to thyself before God. Happy is he that judges not himself in that which
23 he approves. And he that doubts is condemned if he eat, because it is not of faith; and all that is not of faith is sin.

*1 John 3 : 21.   *a* 1 Cor. 8 : 7.   *b* Titus 1 : 15.

but its *application* might be positively mischievous, and the practical breach of the theory might be its truest 'honor'" (MOULE). In 1 Cor. 8 : 12, 13 the apostle puts the case still stronger, as a "sin against Christ." Compare our Lord's words in Matt. 5 : 29, 30; Luke 17 : 1, 2. The Revised version ends the verse with *stumbleth*. But the Improved Bible Union version, on good manuscript authority, retains the words that follow, *or is made to offend or is weak*.

22. The apostle applies the principle of the chapter to the strong. **Thou,** emphatic, and addressed to the strong one. **Hast thou faith?** such confidence and assurance in Christ, as to be above the petty annoyances and scruples about food and days and ceremonial restrictions? **Have it to thyself before God**—keep it to thyself personally and in thy private life before God, but do not make a display of it before men, to the injury of the weak. **Happy is he** who acts consistently, and **condemneth,** or *judgeth* not himself in that thing which he **alloweth,** rather, in that which he *approves*. Happy he who has such faith, resulting in such full knowledge and persuasion (ver. 14), as to have no scruples and **no** self-condemnation in regard to what he **approves.** (Comp. Paul in 1 Cor. 6 : 12.)

23. The principle applied to the weak. **And, or** *But*, he that **doubteth**—wavers as to whether he **should** eat or not—**is damned, rather** *is condemned,* both by conscience and God, **because he eateth not of faith,** in such confidence in Christ and such apprehension of him as to overcome all scruples. Literally, *out of faith,* as the result of faith. Paul clinches what he says by adding a general Christian axiom: **For,** rather, *And,* **whatsoever is not of faith**—not growing *out of* faith and connected with faith—**is sin.** Faith is necessary to pleasing

God (Heb. 11 : 6). Faith is fundamental in Christian character (2 Peter 1 : 5). It is essential to Christian living (Gal. 2 : 20). "In every moral act there are two important elements to be considered: the act itself, and the state of the actor's conscience. In order to be wholly right, it must be right in *both* of these respects; but in order to be wrong, it need be faulty in only *one* of them" (AM. COMMENTARY). Hence in regard to conscience it may be said: "To do what it approves may not always be right, but to do what it questions is always wrong." Many give faith here the meaning of *belief* or *conviction*. But it seems to me better to take the word in its ordinary meaning of *trust* in Christ (ver. 1). A clear and growing faith naturally tends to right conceptions of Christian liberty in regard to questions of conscience and practice.

In many manuscripts, mostly later ones, the final doxology (16 : 25-27), occurs at the end of this chapter. "The cause of its insertion here," says WESCOTT and HORT, "cannot be known with certainty." Some suppose that this chapter ended a church lesson for public reading, and the doxology was added as a suitable close. While appropriate here, except that the apostle continues the discussion of the subject of the section in the next chapter, the weighty grandeur of the doxology seems more fitting at the close of the Epistle. The genuineness of the two chapters that follow is generally admitted.

CASUISTRY AND THE KINGDOM OF GOD. There is difficulty in deciding the right and wrong of certain human actions, such as cases of conscience, and of duty in doubtful emergencies. Casuistical questions are answered by our Lord (Matt. 22 : 17; Luke 14 : 3), and by Paul in this chapter and in the seventh and eighth of First Corinthians. But neither they, nor any of the New Testament writers attempt to lay down any code of laws for the endless diversities of such cases of human conduct. Yet they furnish principles and knowledge by which every one may decide with approximate accuracy what ought, or what ought not, to be done in cases as they may arise. It is implied that the moral character of actions is in the individual—in his motive, or rather, in his purpose, for his purpose implies a choice between what appears to him to be right or wrong (14:14; 1 Cor. 8:4; 10:19-22). But not everything that appears to be lawful and right is expedient. Regard must be had to the rights and scruples of others; neither making light of them, nor by word or example leading them to transgress their conscientious convictions. We may and should clearly present the truth and exercise the law of love toward our weak brother.

The simple and general principles of casuistry, as presented in the New Testament, are in marked contrast to the subtlety and hair-splitting distinctions which have been developed in the auricular confessions of the Roman Catholic Church and the subterfuges of the Jesuits. Paul plainly intimates that the essence of the kingdom of God is not in mere ritualistic observances—as, *e. g.*, eating and drinking; but in righteousness—that conformity of the soul to the Divine will which is produced by the Holy Spirit, and in that peace and joy in the Holy Spirit, which are opposed to a censorious judging or ignoring a brother's weaknesses.

It is also implied in the three preceding chapters that the kingdom of God has to do with all the affairs of this life, and that it should exert a healthful influence on the family, society, the State, and the world.

PRACTICAL REMARKS.

1. Faith tends to bind us to God and to our brethren. A weak faith therefore should be respected and fostered, and not rudely dealt with and despised (ver. 1-3; 15:7; Heb. 11:1-3).

2. True piety can exist with low views of gospel truths, and even with absurd scruples arising from prejudices and wrong education (ver. 1-3; 1 Cor. 3:13-15).

3. Brethren weak in the faith are to be welcomed into fellowship, but not made teachers and leaders (ver. 1-3; 1 Tim. 2:6; 5:22; Titus 1:9).

4. A contemptuous spirit on the one hand, and a censorious spirit on the other, toward Christian brethren, are alike unbecoming the gospel (ver. 3, 4; Matt. 7:1).

5. The Christian should be a man of decided convictions, and should seek after clear views of duty (ver. 5, 6; James 1:6, 7).

6. The Christian should guard against austerity and an over-sensitive conscience on the one hand, and on the other against license and the loosening of moral obligations (ver. 2-6; 3:8; Matt. 23:4, 23-26).

7. A man cannot separate himself from the race, neither can he isolate his own influence. No one therefore should seek to live for himself alone (ver. 7, 8; Amos 6:1, 6; 1 Cor. 13:4, 8).

8. The fact that Christians living or dying are the Lord's should ever influence their conduct toward God and one another (ver. 7, 8; 2 Peter 3:11; 1 Peter 4:1, 11).

9. Since Christ exercises universal dominion over both the dead and living, our lives should be devoted to him, and death but a portal to a higher service (ver. 9; Matt. 28:18; Gal. 6:10; Rev. 14:4, 5).

10. The thought that we must all alike be tried at the judgment, should temper our spirit and regulate our conduct toward others, especially toward our brethren (ver. 10-12; Eccl. 12:14; 2 Cor. 5:9, 10).

11. Christ must be divine, since we are to live to him, and he is Lord both of the dead and the living, and the judgment seat of God is the judgment seat of Christ (ver. 8-12; John 5:22-27; 2 Tim. 4:1).

12. If any have the ability or the propensity of passing judgment on others, let him use that ability for their good (ver. 13; 1 Peter 2:11, 12).

13. We should stand fast in gospel liberty, keeping our conscience subject only to God and the truth, and should

13 WE ᶜ then that are strong ought to	13 NOW we, the strong, ought to bear
ᶜ Gal. 6 : 2.	

not yield it to bondage to human opinion (ver. 13; Gal. 5 : 1).

14. True gospel liberty does not give one the right to commit either an act wrong in itself, or one which may lead another into wrong-doing (ver. 14, 15; 1 Cor. 10 : 24-31; Phil. 2 : 4).

15. Between things universally admitted as right and wrong, and things divinely commanded and divinely forbidden, there are many things, the doing or not doing of which must be decided by the individual conscience (ver. 13-23; 1 Cor. 10 : 25, 27; Heb. 13 : 18).

16. In these debatable questions the motive of the act, its environment, and its influence on others must be considered (ver. 14-18; 1 Cor. 15 : 33; 2 Cor. 1 : 12).

17. For the decision of these questions, conscience needs to be educated and enlightened by the Spirit (ver. 14-18; Heb. 9 : 14; 10 : 12-17).

18. The exercise of Christian liberty in debatable matters, should be united with the service of love. While opposing the form or the appearance of evil, we should not violate the law of love (ver. 15, 16; 1 Thess. 5 : 22; 1 Tim. 1 : 19; 1 Cor. 8 : 11).

19. True religion consists not in mere external observances, nor in conscientious scruples, but in the graces of the Spirit, the services of love, and obedience to Christ (ver. 17, 18; 1 Cor. 8 : 8; Col. 2 : 16, 17).

20. Moral character pertains to the agent and to his motives, rather than to acts in themselves. Nothing in the lower creation is really religiously unclean or profane. Neither is one day in itself more sacred than another (ver. 5, 14, 20; Gen. 1 : 31; Gal. 4 : 10; 1 Cor. 7 : 31; 10 : 19).

21. Christian liberty should be exercised for the good, not for the destruction of others. Total abstinence finds a firm foundation here (ver. 19, 21; Gal. 5 : 13).

22. A thing may be lawful but not expedient. What is considered innocent, may be the means of great evil (ver. 15, 16, 20, 21; 1 Cor. 6 : 12; 10 : 23).

23. It is our duty to exercise self-denial for the good of others, and avoid doing that which may occasion evil to our fellow-men. Here comes in the principle of total abstinence in our modern temperance movement (ver. 18, 21; 1 Cor. 8 : 13).

24. Faith as a guide in the matters of conscience. We should avoid doing that about which we have doubts, nor should we lead others to violate their conscientious scruples. Rather we should try to educate and enlighten conscience in regard to right principles and right doing (ver. 22, 23; 1 Cor. 8 : 11, 12).

CHAPTER XV.

This chapter continues the discussion of the last, enforced by the example of Christ (ver. 1-13), after which the apostle concludes the whole discussion. He then expresses his confidence in his Roman brethren and refers to his calling and extensive labors among the Gentiles (ver. 14-21). He also mentions his expected visit to Jerusalem, and thence to Rome and Spain (ver. 22-29), and asks their prayers for a prosperous journey and closes with a benediction (ver. 30, 31).

This, and the next chapter, have been supposed, by some later critics, to have been written originally by Paul for others than Roman Christians, or perhaps added later to the Epistle. This, however, is not sustained by manuscript authority, and the great majority of scholars have held that they are genuine and stand in the place where they belong. The connection of thought between the last chapter and this, and through these chapters to the end of the Epistle, is so natural that the perusal of them will satisfy the general reader that they are in the right position, and that they are not mere accidental additions.

1-13. DISCUSSION OF THE PRECEDING CHAPTER CONTINUED AND ENFORCED BY THE EXAMPLE OF CHRIST. The first four verses are addressed to the strong, followed by an exhortation for mutual Christlike conduct between Jewish and Gentile believers.

1. There appears to be a natural connection between this and the preceding chapter. We then, or, *Now we*, that are strong, or *able*, firm in faith and

bear the d infirmities of the weak, and not to please ourselves. e Let every one of us please his neighbour for his good to edification. f For even Christ pleased not himself; but, as it is written, The reproaches of them that reproached thee fell on me. g For whatsoever things were written aforetime were written for our learning, that we through patience h and comfort of the Scriptures might have hope.
5 i Now the God of patience k and consolation grant you l to be likeminded one toward another m according to

the infirmities of the weak, and not to please ourselves. Let each one of us please his neighbor, for his good, to upbuilding. For Christ also pleased not himself; but, as it is written, The reproaches of those who reproached thee, fell on me. For whatever things were written in former times were written for our instruction, that we through patience and through consolation of the Scriptures may have hope.
5 And the God of patience and consolation grant you to be of the same mind one with another, according to Christ

d 14 : 1, 21; Isa. 35 : 3, 4; 1 Cor. 9 : 22; Gal. 6 : 2.   e 14 : 19; 1 Cor. 9 : 19, 22; 10 : 24, 33; Phil. 2 : 4, 5.
f Matt. 26 : 38, 39.   g 4 : 23, 24; 1 Cor. 9 : 9, 19.   h Ps. 94 : 19; 119 : 81; Heb. 6 : 10-19.
i Exod. 34 : 6.   k 2 Cor. 1 : 3, 4; 7 : 6.   l 12 : 16.   m Eph. 5 : 2.

convictions. Notice that Paul includes himself among the *strong*, as in 14 : 14. **Ought**—we *owe* it to Christ and our weak brethren. (Comp. 1 : 14.) In 14 : 1 Paul exhorts; here he speaks of the matter as duty and obligation. **To bear**, as a burden patiently (Rev. 2 : 2, 3), **the infirmities,** or *weaknesses*, of mind, connected with error and scruples of conscience, and an undeveloped faith; **of the weak,** or *the unable*, of those not well able to bear their own burden (Gal. 6 : 2). **And not to please ourselves,** not seeking our own gratification of innocent appetites and desires. In other words, we are to exercise a self-denying love (1 Cor. 10 : 33).

2. On the contrary, **let every one of us please his neighbour,** whatever brother he comes in contact with, **for his good,** having his real spiritual welfare in view, **to edification,** to upbuilding him in his Christian character and life (14 : 19). Paul here defines the right way of seeking to please others. Otherwise would be wrong, which he elsewhere condemns (Gal. 1 : 10). Compare a worldly and evil pleasing of others in Mark 6 : 22.

3. For, introducing the strongest of reasons, the example of Christ, **even,** or *also*, **Christ pleased not himself** (Luke 22 : 42; John 4 : 34), but in his suffering for sinners "delighted to do the will of him who sent him." Paul in this Epistle has dwelt on Christ as a sacrifice; now he presents him as an example, which he often does elsewhere (1 Cor. 11 : 1; 2 Cor. 8 : 9; Phil. 2 : 5, 6; Heb. 12 : 2, 3). **But,** so far from pleasing himself, **as it is written.** The quotation is from Ps. 69 : 9 (the Septuagint), which is evidently Messianic in its character, the psalmist writing as a type of Christ. **The reproaches of them that reproached thee,** which wicked men cast upon God, **fell on me,** thus proving his unselfishness in doing his Father's will and in seeking to save men (Matt. 20 : 28; John 4 : 34).

4. For introduces a reason for the above quotation and a statement of a general principle, that the Old Testament Scriptures were intended for the instruction of Christian believers. **For whatsoever things were written aforetime,** *all* before this time, namely the whole Old Testament, **were written for our learning**—for our *instruction* and upbuilding (2 Tim. 3 : 15-17), *in order* **that we through patience and** *through* **comfort of the Scriptures**—patience and comfort produced by the study of Scripture—**might,** or *may,* **have hope of** glory and eternal life. On *patience* or *endurance* see 5 : 3. From the example, as foretold and fulfilled in our Saviour (ver. 3), we may derive comfort and be helped to endure unto the end (1 Peter 2 : 19-21).

5. Now, rather, *And,* introducing a wish, growing out of what precedes: *And may the God* **of patience and consolation,** or *comfort,* just spoken of, of which he is the Author, **grant you to be like-minded,** *of the same mind among one another,* not so much in unity of opinions as in the harmony of feeling, **according to Christ Jesus**—according to his spirit, example, and teachings. Just in proportion as the believer receives from God patience, comfort, and hope in the

6 Christ Jesus; that ye may ⁿwith one mind *and* one mouth glorify God, even ᵒthe Father of our Lord Jesus Christ.
7 Wherefore ᵖreceive ye one another, ᑫas Christ also received us, to the glory of God.
8 Now I say that ʳJesus Christ was a minister of the circumcision for the truth of God, ˢto confirm the promises
9 *made* unto the fathers: and ᵗthat the Gentiles might glorify God for *his* mercy; as it is written, For this cause I will confess to thee among the Gen-

6 Jesus; that with one accord ye may with one mouth glorify the God and Father of our Lord Jesus Christ.
7 Wherefore receive one another, as Christ also received you, to the glory of God. For I say that Christ has been made a minister of the circumcision, in behalf of God's truth, that he might confirm the promises made to
9 the fathers; and that the Gentiles might glorify God for his mercy; as it is written,
For this cause I will confess to thee among Gentiles,
And will sing to thy name.

ⁿ Zeph. 3 : 9 ; Acts 4 : 24, 32. ᵒ John 20 : 17. ᵖ 14 : 1–3. ᑫ 5 : 2 ; Luke 15 : 2 ; John 6 : 37 ; 13 : 34. ʳ 9 : 4, 5 ; Matt. 15 : 21 ; John 1 : 11. ˢ Micah 7 : 20 ; Luke 1 : 54, 55 ; 2 Cor. 1 : 20. ᵗ 9 : 23, 24 ; John 10 : 16.

study of the Scriptures, will he be raised above petty controversies and unchristian, unfraternal conduct (Col. 1 : 3–8).

6. Continuation of the preceding thought, **That ye may,** etc. *That with one mind,* with unanimity of spirit, *ye may with one mouth,* a oneness of outward utterance, **glorify God even the Father,** better, *the God and Father* **of our Lord Jesus Christ.** A two-fold idea is brought to view, namely, he whom Jesus, the Christ, served, and to whom he held the relation of Son. (Comp. Eph. 1 : 3 ; 1 Peter 1 : 3.) Through Christ the believer enjoys this two-fold relation to God and Father (John 20 : 17 ; Heb. 1 : 8, 9). The great end of God's people is to glorify him ; and all of his gifts and blessings tend to fit them for this end (11 : 33–36).

7. In order that the wish expressed in the last two verses might be fulfilled in his brethren at Rome, Paul exhorts them, both strong and weak : **Wherefore receive ye one another** to *yourselves—take one another* to your hearts in friendship and intercourse (14 : 1). "Do not wait one for the other, but each be ready to take the initiative steps" (BOISE). **As Christ also received** to himself **us,** or *you* (a better reading of the text) into his friendship and love (14 : 3). Those who were sinners and estranged from him Christ received, took to himself as brethren, **to the glory of God,** in order that God might be glorified (Eph. 1 : 6). Paul is addressing both Jewish and Gentile believers, as is evident from the next two verses.

8. Now, rather, *For,* according to the best text, introducing a reason and explanation of the preceding exhortation. Ver. 8 is addressed with special reference to Jewish believers ; ver. 9 with special reference to Gentile. **For I say**—*for,* to explain, *I mean*—**that Christ** (**Jesus** is omitted by the best texts) **was,** rather, *has become,* a **minister,** or *servant,* **of the circumcision.** Christ came and lived as a Jew, submitted to the law and was obedient to the law, and confined his ministry to the Jewish people (Matt. 15 : 24 ; 10 : 5, 6). The expression "minister of the circumcision," is only found here, and Alford suggests that it is used "to humble the pride of the strong, the Gentile Christians, by exalting God's covenant people to their true dignity." **For,** or *in behalf of God's truth,* that it might be fulfilled, and thus confirm the promises made unto the fathers (2 Cor. 1 : 20 ; Gal. 3 : 14). It had been foretold that the Messiah should descend from Abraham, through Judah and David (Gen. 12 : 3 ; Micah 5 : 2 ; Ps. 89 : 35, 36),

9. Continuing the sentence, **And that the Gentiles might glorify God for his mercy** so wonderfully exercised toward them. The promises had been given to Israel and through Israel the blessings of the promises had come upon Gentiles. The one had covenants, and the truthfulness of God was pledged in their behalf; the others were "strangers from the covenants of promise" (Eph. 2 : 12), and in a sense were peculiarly the objects of *mercy.* Yet in the divine arrangement all were objects of mercy (11 : 32) **As it is written.** In

10 tiles, and sing unto thy name. And again he saith, Rejoice, ye Gentiles, with his people.
11 with his people. And again, Praise the Lord, all ye Gentiles; and laud
12 him, all ye people. And again, Esaias saith, There shall be a ᵘ root of Jesse, and he that shall rise to reign over the Gentiles; in him shall the Gentiles trust.
13 Now the God of hope fill you with all ˣ joy and peace in believing, ʸ that ye may abound in hope, through the power of the Holy Ghost.

Personal notices, relating to the apostle and his ministry.

14 And ᵃ I myself also am persuaded of you, my brethren, that ye also are ᵃ full of goodness, filled with all knowledge, able also to admonish one

10 And again he says,
Rejoice, ye Gentiles, with his people.
11 And again,
Praise the Lord, all ye Gentiles;
And let all the peoples extol him.
12 And again, Isaiah says,
There shall be the root of Jesse,
And he who rises up to rule over Gentiles;
On him will Gentiles hope.
13 Now the God of hope fill you with all joy and peace in believing, that ye may abound in hope, in the power of the Holy Spirit.
14 And I myself also am persuaded of you, my brethren, that ye yourselves also are full of goodness, filled with all knowledge, able to admonish one an-

ᵘ Rev. 5 : 5 ; 22 : 16.   ˣ 14 : 17 ; John 14 : 1 ; 2 Thess. 2 : 16, 17.   ʸ 5 : 4, 5 ; Heb. 6 : 11.
ᶻ 2 Peter 1 : 12 ; 1 John 2 : 21.   ᵃ Phil. 1 : 11 ; Col. 1 : 8-10.

this and the three following verses Paul quotes from the Law, the Psalms, and the Prophets (Luke 24 : 44). The one in this verse is from Ps. 18 : 49, cited from the Septuagint. David is viewed as a type of Christ, who praises God for the Gentiles who are saved through him.

10-12. The quotations are cited quite exactly from the Septuagint. The first is from Deut. 32 : 43. **Again he,** or *it*, the Scripture, **saith.** The Gentile nations are prophetically presented as participating in the joys of the covenant people of Israel. The quotation in ver. 11 is from Ps. 117 : 1, and is a prophetic intimation of Gentiles joining with Israel in praising God for his mercy manifested in the gospel. The quotations thus far are general. In ver. 12 a more particular reference is made to Christ as the spiritual King and hope of Gentiles, quoted from Isa. 11 : 10. A **root**—*sprout, the shoot,* the descendant **of Jesse,** the father of David. **In him**—resting *upon him will* **Gentiles trust,** rather, *hope*. Faith is implied, hope is expressed. Exercised by them who before had no hope (Eph. 2 : 12). All of these passages confirm the statement of ver. 9, that Gentiles shall unite with Israel in glorifying God for his mercy through the Messiah.

13. Having proved the statement of ver. 9 by Scripture, Paul closes the paragraph with a benediction. Seizing upon the last word, *hope,* of the preceding quotation, he says: **Now the God of hope,** a name especially fitting to God and appropriate in addressing Gentiles at Rome. "For Hope had been a false divinity, whose temple at Rome, Livy, Book XXI., says, was struck with lightning, and again in Book XXIV., was consumed" (BENGEL). God is the Author of hope—the hope of glory and of eternal life. **In believing**—the condition and state in which are **all joy and peace,** connected with and springing out of hope. **Through,** rather, *In* the indwelling and inworking **power of the Holy Ghost**—*Spirit.* (Comp. 5 : 1-5.) This verse is a fitting close of the hortatory and practical part of the Epistle. Notice how faith, hope, joy, and peace, are all united. What follows is devoted to personal and incidental matters.

14 - 33. CONCLUDING AND PERSONAL TOPICS. See opening paragraph of this chapter.

14. Paul's confidence in his Roman brethren similar to that expressed in the introduction of this Epistle (1 : 8-12). In an emphatic manner he expresses his assured conviction concerning them: **And I myself also,** as well as those who have reported your faith (1 : 8), **am persuaded of you.** This appears to be addressed to them as a body. **That ye** *yourselves* **also,** independently of my exhortations and instructions, **are full of goodness,** excellent qualities (Eph. 5 : 9 ; 2 Thess. 1 : 11), **filled with all knowledge,** which all together

15 another. Nevertheless, brethren, I have written the more boldly unto you in some sort, ᵇ as putting you in mind, ᶜ because of the grace that is given to
16 me of God, that ᵈ I should be the minister of Jesus Christ to the Gentiles, ministering the gospel of God; that the ᵉ offering up of the Gentiles might be acceptable, being sanctified by the
15 other also. But I write the more boldly to you, in part as putting you in mind, because of the grace that was given to
16 me by God, that I should be a minister of Christ Jesus to the Gentiles, ministering in the gospel of God, that the offering up of the Gentiles may become acceptable, being sanctified by the

ᵇ 2 Peter 1 : 2-15.   ᶜ 1 : 5.   ᵈ 11 : 13.   ᵉ Isa. 66 : 20; 1 Peter 2 : 5.

are very necessary qualifications for being **able also to admonish one another**. This is not mere complimentary language. The whole Epistle shows that he was writing to Christians of spiritual strength and maturity.

15. His freedom in writing them was a discharge of his duty as an apostle to the Gentiles (ver. 15-21), and a compensation for his inability to visit them (ver. 22-24). **Nevertheless,** *But* **I have written,** literally, *I wrote.* So the time of the writing would be in the past to them when they came to read the letter. **In some sort,** or *measure*, that is, somewhat boldly. Others understand, *in part*, in certain portions of the Epistle, as in 6 : 17-21; 9 : 19, 20; 11 : 19-21, etc. But Godet and some others very naturally join it with the verb that follows: *In part*, or *partly,* **as putting you in mind, because of the grace that is given to me of God,** the divine favor in making him an apostle (1 : 5; Eph. 3 : 2-8), being the motive and ground of authority in calling these things to remembrance.

16. Continuing the sentence, **That I should be the,** rather, *a* **minister,** a public *servant* or attendant, **of Jesus Christ to the Gentiles.** This was the purpose or aim of God's grace given him (ver. 15), that he should be an apostle to the Gentiles. The word translated *minister* was originally used of a public officer at Athens, who administered his office at his own expense. In the New Testament it is applied to magistrates (Rom. 13 : 6), to angels (Heb. 1 : 7), to Christ as High Priest and Servant of the heavenly sanctuary (Heb. 8 : 2). In Phil. 2 : 25 it is applied to Epaphroditus, an attendant and minister to the apostle's wants. Paul here appropriately applies it to himself as one of the apostles who were attendants of Jesus Christ himself (Mark 3 : 14), and publicly "busied for him in holy things." The verb from which it is derived occurs in ver. 27 and in Acts 13 : 2, on which see note. Both noun and verb are noble words, applied to official and public services. Christ is here viewed as the Head and Ruler of his people, who appointed Paul as an apostle to the Gentiles. **Ministering** in religious services *in sacred things,* or *after the manner of a priest,* **the gospel of God.** This ministering consisted of preaching and in agonizing efforts and prayers for the salvation of souls (9 : 1-3; 10 : 1). The verb means to be *busied about sacred things*, and when used of a priest, means *to perform sacred rites.* It is found only here in the New Testament. In 4 Mac. 7 : 8, it is used of those who defend the sanctity of the law by undergoing a violent death. So here we may conceive of Paul *ministering in sacrifice* the gospel, by undergoing great trials in preaching the gospel, "in stripes above measure, in deaths oft" (2 Cor. 11 : 23-27). It appears evident that the word here is used figuratively. For Paul no more speaks of himself as a priest literally than he does of the Gentiles as a literal offering. (See below.) **That the offering up of the Gentiles,** the Gentile converts to God, **might be acceptable,** because they were **being sanctified,** or *made holy,* **by the Holy Ghost—**Spirit. Compare 2 Cor. 11 : 2, where there is a similar idea under the figure of presenting them as a betrothed bride, a pure virgin to Christ. This is the only passage in the New Testament where a word which may imply a priestly character or action is used of a preacher of the gospel. It is used here of Paul as an apostle to the Gentiles, and wholly in a figurative sense. Had Paul laid claim to sacerdotal functions, it is very unlikely that he would have been silent regarding it in the rest of his writings. He was not silent respecting his apostleship (1 Cor. 9 : 1). His

17 Holy Ghost. ʳI have therefore whereof I may glory through Jesus Christ ᵉin those things which pertain to God.
18 ʰ For I will not dare to speak of any of those things ⁱ which Christ hath not wrought by me, ᵏ to make the Gentiles
19 obedient, by word and deed, ˡ through mighty signs and wonders, by the power of the Spirit of God; so that from Jerusalem, and round about unto Illyricum, ᵐ I have fully preached the
20 gospel of Christ. Yea, so have I strived to preach the gospel, not where Christ

17 Holy Spirit. I have therefore my glorying in Christ Jesus, as to things
18 pertaining to God. For I will venture to speak only of those things which Christ wrought through me, to bring the Gentiles to obedience, by word and
19 work, in the power of signs and wonders, in the power of the Holy Spirit; so that from Jerusalem, and around as far as Illyricum, I have fully preached
20 the gospel of Christ; yea, making it my aim so to preach the gospel, not

f 2 Cor. 3 : 4–6 ; 11 : 16–30.   *g* Heb. 5 : 1.   *h* 2 Cor. 10 : 13–18.   *i* Acts 21 : 19 ; Gal. 2 : 8.   *k* 1 : 5 ; 16 : 26.
l Acts 14 : 8–12 ; 15 : 12 ; 19 : 11, 12 ; 2 Cor. 12 : 12.   *m* Acts 20 : 20 ; 2 Tim. 4 : 17.

silence is an argument against regarding the Christian ministry as a priesthood. Christ is presented as our High Priest in Heb. 3 : 1, etc. All mediating priests are taken away in the gospel. All believers have a holy priesthood unto God (1 Peter 2 : 5 ; Rev. 1 : 6), and all have free access to the throne of grace through Jesus Christ. Paul and the humblest believer stand on a level here.

17. I have therefore, in view of the above statement, *my glorying,* that which really belongs to me, *in Christ Jesus,* in him and him alone (see ver. 18) ; **in those things which pertain to God,** in my services as an apostle and minister of Christ. He owed it to Christ rather than to himself, that he was permitted to glory in these matters, pertaining to his commission (ver. 15, 16), labors, and successes (ver. 18, 19).

18. For, introduces his justification, in this and the three following verses, of the statement concerning his glorying in Christ (ver. 17). **For I will not dare to speak, . . which Christ hath not wrought** *through me.* Some put the emphasis on *through me,* in distinction from what Christ had wrought through others. It is better, however, to place it on *which Christ hath not wrought.* I will not dare to mention anything I have done; my appeal is only to what Christ has wrought through me in the conversion of the Gentiles. There is a transition from negative to the positive, but I would appeal to what Christ has done through me, **by word,** the preaching of the gospel, **and deed,** by his life, but especially by his miracles. (See next verse.) Paul enjoyed miraculous gifts and wrought miracles (1 Cor. 14 : 18 ; 2 Cor. 12 : 12).

19. The sentence is continued. **Through mighty signs and wonders,** rather, *In the power of signs and wonders,* miracles and supernatural works of all kinds (John 4 : 48 ; Acts 15 : 12), referring especially to Christ working through Paul by *deed* (ver. 18). *In* **power of the Spirit of God,** or better, *of the Holy Spirit,* in the conversion of men, referring more especially to Christ working through Paul by *word,* with reference also to *deed* (ver. 18). Miracles had their place and were used by the Holy Spirit, but it was the preaching of the gospel which especially resulted in the conversion of the Gentiles (Acts 19 : 8–12, 17–20). **So that from Jerusalem,** the ecclesiastical center and capital of Judaism, **and round about,** in the regions around, *as far as* **Illyricum,** a province northwest of Macedonia, eleven hundred miles northwest from Jerusalem, **I have fully preached the gospel of Christ,** literally, *I have fulfilled the gospel* by fully preaching it. Compare " to fulfill the word of God," fully exhibiting it, in Col. 1 : 25. From Acts 20 : 2 it appears that Paul traversed the regions of Macedonia, which bordered on Illyricum, shortly before completing this Epistle. Several years later Titus had gone to Dalmatia (2 Tim. 4 : 10), a part of the Roman province of Illyricum, which makes it not unlikely that Paul had labored there either before this, or after his first imprisonment. See CLARK'S " Harmonic Arrangement of the Acts," pp. 228, 229, 231.

20 - 21. The sentence continues. **Yea, so have I strived,** literally, *so making it a point of honor,* being ambitious, **to preach the gospel, not where Christ was named,**

was named, ⁿ lest I should build upon
21 another man's foundation : but as it is
written, To whom he was not spoken
of, they shall see : and they that have
not heard shall understand.
22 For which cause also ᵒ I have been
much hindered from coming to you.
23 But now having no more place in these
parts, and ᵖ having a great desire these
24 many years to come unto you ; whensoever I take my journey into Spain, I
will come to you ; for I trust to see you
in my journey, ᑫ and to be brought on
my way thitherward by you, if first
I be somewhat filled with your com-

where Christ was named, that I might
not build upon another's foundation ;
21 but as it is written,
They to whom nothing was announced concerning him shall see,
And they that have not heard shall
understand.
22 For which cause also, these many
times, I was hindered from coming to
23 you. But now having no longer a
place in these regions, and having a
longing these many years to come to
24 you, whenever I go to Spain ;—for I
hope in passing through to see you,
and to be sent forward thither by you,
if first I have been satisfied in a measure with your company.—

ⁿ See 1 Cor. 3 : 9-15 ; 2 Cor. 10 : 13, 15, 16.   ᵒ 1 : 13 ; 1 Thess. 2 : 17, 18.   ᵖ Ver. 32 ; 1 : 11-13 ; Acts 19 : 21.
ᑫ Acts 15 : 3.

where he had been made known, **lest
I should build upon another
man's foundation.** (Comp. 1 Cor. 3 : 10.)
The field was so vast that there was
room for all ; he would avoid needless collisions and discords ; and besides he had adopted the spirit of
Isa. 52 : 15 as his rule, which predicted
that the gospel should be preached to
those who never heard it. **As it is
written.** Cited exactly from the Septuagint. **To whom he was not
spoken of,** etc. The prophet is speaking of the servant of Jehovah, the
Messiah, who is for the first time announced to kings and nations.
22. Paul now speaks of his future
plans. **For which cause also,** because of the incessant and extensive
labors described above, **I have been
much hindered,** better, *I was for
the most part,* or *these many times,*
hindered from coming to you.
There had doubtless been other hindrances which he does not name. He
gives the main hindrance. This verse
is similar to 1 : 13, on which see notes.
About six years before this writing
Paul had met Aquila at Corinth, who
had come from Rome (A. D. 52, Acts 18 : 2),
from whom he doubtless learned much
about the Roman Christians ; and about
a year before this (A. D. 57), at Ephesus,
it is definitely stated that it was his purpose to visit Rome (Acts 19 : 21).
23. But now, having no more,
rather, *no longer place,* or opportunity (Acts 25 : 16), *in these regions,* between Jerusalem and Illyricum. Having preached the gospel throughout
these regions and planted churches at
central points, from which evangelists
could go forth, he felt that his work as
a pioneer missionary was accomplished.
He wished to go where Christ had not
been made known. **Having a great
desire,** an affectionate *longing,* **these
many years,** since he met Aquila at
Corinth (see on ver. 22), and perhaps before
that time, **to come unto you.** See
further, note on 1 : 11.
24. The sentence continues. **Whensoever I take my journey into
Spain**—to the far West. The Spanish
peninsula was also called *Hispania,*
but more commonly by the Greeks,
Iberia. According to the highest critical authorities, the words, **I will
come to you,** should be omitted.
This verse is variously punctuated.
That of the Improved Bible Union version is preferable, which places a comma
after ver. 23, a semicolon and a dash
after Spain, and a period and a dash at
the end of ver. 24. The words beginning with **for,** in this verse, and ending with the verse, are explanatory,
and somewhat parenthetical. **To see
you in my journey**—*in passing
through*—his stay would be short, as
" Christ had already been named " at
Rome (ver. 20). **To be brought on
my way,** etc., *to be sent forward
thither by you.* It was common to
escort persons on their way (Acts 15 : 3 ;
1 Cor. 16 : 6). Some of the Roman brethren might also go with him into Spain
(Acts 15 : 22). **Somewhat filled,** *in a
measure satisfied,* " a delicate expression
implying that he could not be satisfied
in full with their company " (BOISE).
(Comp. 1 : 12, and note).

25 pany. But now ⁿI go unto Jerusalem,
26 to minister unto the saints. For ᵒit hath pleased them of Macedonia and Achaia to make a certain contribution for the poor saints which are at Jeru-
27 salem. It hath pleased them verily; and their debtors they are. For if the Gentiles have been made partakers of their spiritual things, ᵖtheir duty is

25 But now I am going to Jerusalem to
26 minister to the saints. For Macedonia and Achaia thought it good to make some contribution for the poor among
27 the saints who are in Jerusalem. For they thought it good; and their debtors are they. For if the Gentiles have shared in their spiritual things, they

---

ⁿ Acts 19 : 21; 20 : 22; 24 : 17.   ᵒ Acts 11 : 27–30; 1 Cor. 16 : 1, 2; 2 Cor. 8 : 1–6; 9 : 2, 12.
ᵖ 1 Cor. 9 : 11; Gal. 6 : 6.

There need be no difficulty between Paul's principle of not building on another's foundation and his desire to visit Rome. For (1) it does not appear that the church at Rome had been planted by any of the apostles, or any one preacher. (2) Paul could fittingly visit them as an apostle to the Gentiles. (3) There were a number of his converts and acquaintances there (16 : 3-15). (4) Rome could be visited on his way to Spain. (5) When he did visit them he applied his principle at once by calling Jews who had not been evangelized, and afterward preaching to such as came to him. In the large city of Rome there was abundance of room. (See the Introduction to Romans.)

It has been much discussed whether Paul ever carried out this plan. It is probable that he was liberated from his first imprisonment, after which he visited Spain and the far west. So Clement in his first letter to the Corinthians (chap. 5), and other early writers. See CLARK'S "Harmonic Arrangement of the Acts," pp. 260, 261. An inscription found in Spain, of Nero's time, commemorates the riddance of the province of "robbers and of those who sought to instil a new superstition into mankind" (MR. LEWIN, "Life," etc., Vol. II., p. 363, note). This probably refers to Christianity, and perhaps to the results of Paul's labors.

25. This should begin a new paragraph. Paul states his present plan and work, which must be accomplished before he could visit Rome on his way to Spain (ver. 25-29). **But** although I am expecting to visit you, **now I go**, rather, *now I am going to Jerusalem*. He was really on his way from Ephesus through Macedonia and Greece, now temporarily at Corinth (Acts 20 : 1-3). **To minister**, or *ministering*, **to the saints**—carrying collections from the churches for their relief (Acts 24 : 17). *Ministering* is a present participle (the same verb as in Acts 6 : 2), and may include the gathering, the carrying, and the presenting of the collections to the *saints* (1 : 7). Paul and Barnabas had, A. D. 44, performed a similar service (Acts 11 : 29, 30; 12 : 25). In reference to this present ministering, in addition to the above references, see 1 Cor. 16 : 3, 4; 2 Cor. 8 : 1–4; 9 : 1, 2. A comparison of these strikingly illustrates the truthfulness of the sacred documents. (See "Har. Arrange. Acts," pp. 118, 119, 240, 241.)

26. For, to explain, **it hath pleased,** *it seemed good to* **them of Macedonia,** at Philippi, Thessalonica, etc., **and Achaia**—*Greece* (Acts 20 : 2), **to make a certain contribution for,** or *sharing with,* **the poor** *of* **the saints at Jerusalem.** It is implied that all were not poor. They had suffered persecutions (Acts 8 : 1; 12 : 1), and doubtless thereby many had been impoverished. It is also implied that the community of goods had ceased at the church at Jerusalem. *Contribution*—with the ground idea of sharing or participating with those receiving; translated *communion,* it is applied to the Lord's Supper (1 Cor. 10 : 16), in reference to Christians partaking symbolically of the body and blood of Christ. It is a beautiful thought that in contributing to others we are sharing with them our blessings. It is thus a *participation.* (See next verse.)

27. It hath pleased—*It seemed good to them*—an exact repetition of the first words of ver. 26. **And their debtors they are,** they *owe* it to them, it is their *duty*. (Comp. 1 : 14.) Jerusalem was the mother church; and Antioch, which sent forth Paul and others to the heathen, received her first preachers from Jerusalem (Acts 11 : 19-22). It

also to minister unto them in carnal
28 things. When therefore I have performed this, and have sealed to them
 ᵘthis fruit, I will come by you into
29 Spain. ˣAnd I am sure that, when I
come unto you, I shall come in the
fulness of the blessing of the gospel of
Christ.
30 Now I beseech you, brethren, for the
Lord Jesus Christ's sake, and ʸfor the
love of the Spirit, ᶻthat ye strive together with me in *your* prayers to God
31 for me; ᵃthat I may be delivered from
them that do not believe in Judæa;

ought also to minister to them in car-
28 nal things. When therefore I have
performed this, and have sealed to
them this fruit, I will go on by you to
29 Spain. And I know that, when I come
to you, I shall come in the fullness of
the blessing of Christ.
30 And I beseech you, brethren, by our
Lord Jesus Christ, and by the love of
the Spirit, to strive together with me
31 in your prayer to God for me; that I
may be delivered from the unbelieving

ᵘ Phil. 4 : 11.   ˣ 1 : 11, 12; Eph. 1 : 3.   ʸ Phil. 2 : 1.   ᶻ 2 Cor. 1 : 11; Eph. 6 : 19, 20; 1 Thess. 5 : 25.
ᵃ Acts 21 : 27-31; 23 : 12; 1 Thess. 2 : 15, 16; 2 Thess. 3 : 2.

was through the Jewish believers that
Gentiles received the gospel (Acts 10:
35-48). **For if the Gentiles have
been made partakers of,** or *shared
in* (the kindred verb of the noun *contribution*, ver. 26), **their spiritual**
blessings, **their duty is also,** *they
owe it* **to minister**—to do service (the
kindred verb of the noun *minister*,
in ver. 16), **to them in carnal,**
or *fleshly,* **things.** Paul regards the
making of contribution as a religious,
sacred service. The two reasons for
performing this service are given : their
good pleasure, **including** gratitude
(ver. 26), their duty as debtors (ver. 27).
These contributions were a bond of
sympathy between the Jewish and
Gentile churches, and tended **to the**
unity of the churches, both **of those**
giving and those receiving. The same
is true with our independent Baptist
churches to-day. The great missionary
enterprises tend to unify them in faith
and doctrine. Co-operation in Christian work produces a bond of brotherly
sympathy, better than that of a hierarchy.
28. *Having* **performed therefore
this** journey to Jerusalem and this
service to the saints there, **and sealed**
—authoritatively attesting and securing
to them **this fruit**—the proceeds of
the collections made in the churches :
an expression of their love. The word
sealed has an unusual use, meaning
an authoritative assurance that the
money was theirs, sealing or confirming
their ownership. *Fruit* refers directly
to the gathered collections, and perhaps
indirectly to the love and faith that
prompted the gifts. **I will come** by
you, or *I will go on through your city,*

into Spain, making a passing visit
at Rome.
29. **And I am sure,** *And I know,*
from past experience in other churches
(2 Cor. 1 : 15), from my deep convictions
and confidence in God. The words, **of
the gospel,** should be omitted, not
being found in the best manuscripts.
I will **come in the fulness of the
blessing of Christ** (Eph. 3 : 19), furnished with and wholly full of the
blessings which he abundantly imparts.
(See 1 : 11.) This was fulfilled in the
apostle's case, though very differently
from what he expected (Acts 28 : 15, 16,
30, 31). His ministry at Rome was attended with abundant blessing to both
saints and sinners (Phil. 1 : 12-14 ; 4 : 22).
The Epistles to the Ephesians, the
Colossians, the Philippians, and Philemon, written at Rome, attest how fully
he was enjoying the blessing of Christ.
They who argue that this chapter was
composed in the second century can
find no foundation here.
30. Paul entreats their prayers for
himself, by two strong motives : **For,**
or *by,* **our Lord Jesus Christ,**
through what he has done for us,
and for, or *by,* **the love of the
Spirit,** of which he is the Author, and
which as the Comforter he exercises
toward us (John 14 : 16-18), and sheds
abroad **in our hearts** (5 : 5 ; Gal. 5 : 22).
That ye strive together—*agonize*,
struggle intensely **with me in your
prayers.** (Comp. Col. 4 : 12.) "Paul is
the only apostle who asks the prayers
of believers for himself" (BENGEL).
(See 2 Cor. 1 : 11 ; Phil. 1 : 19 ; Col. 4 : 3, 4 ; Eph.
6 : 19 ; 1 Thess. 5 : 25 ; 2 Thess. 3 : 1 ; Philem. 22 ;
Heb. 13 : 18.)
31. He had forebodings of dangers

and that my service which *I have* for Jerusalem may be accepted of the 32 saints; ᵇ that I may come unto you with joy ᶜ by the will of God, and may 33 with you be ᵈ refreshed. Now ᵉ the God of peace *be* with you all. Amen.

in Judæa, and that my ministry for Jerusalem may prove acceptable to the 32 saints; that I may come in joy to you through the will of God, and may with 33 you be refreshed. And the God of peace be with you all. Amen.

b 1:10.   *c* Acts 18:21.   *d* 2 Cor. 7:13; 2 Tim. 1:16; Philem. 7:20.
e 16:20; 1 Cor. 14:33; 2 Cor. 13:11; Phil. 4:9; 1 Thess. 5:23; 2 Thess. 3:16; Heb. 13:20.

from Jewish unbelievers. He therefore wishes their prayers for his deliverance **from them.** He knew that in every city bonds and afflictions awaited him (Acts 20:22). Prayers were answered, though differently from the way in which he expected (Acts 21:31, 32; 23:12-24; 25:2-5, 12; 27:1). He also desired their prayers, that his **service,** or *ministry* (ver. 25), the benefactions, **for Jerusalem may be accepted of the saints**—may prove acceptable to them. Paul was conscious of the prejudice borne by Jewish Christians against him (Acts 21:20, 21), and doubtless also to some extent against Gentile Christians, and he feared that the gifts he bore might not be well received at Jerusalem.

32. Further objects of prayer. **That I may come unto you.** By what a remarkable journey he came to them is told us in the twenty-seventh and twenty-eighth chapters of the Acts. **With,** or *in,* **joy.** He came to them in the joy of great deliverances from dangers, of special favors from God and men (Acts 27:25, 34-36, 44; 28:5, 6, 8-10, 14-16; Phil. 1:12, 18). **By the will of God,** as willed in answer to your prayers. **And may with you be refreshed**—may have *restful refreshment* by mutual holy intercourse, a beautiful figure of the restful influence arising from their interchange of views, experiences, and prayers. The same word is used in 1 Cor. 16:18; 2 Cor. 7:13. (Comp. 1:12.) How much opportunity Paul had for this during his two years' imprisonment at Rome (Acts 28:16, 17, 30, 31).

33. Having besought their prayers, Paul craves a benediction upon them. **Now,** or **And the God of peace,** the Author of peace, of reconciliation (5:1), and of inward concord and outward quiet, **be with you all.** In those troublous times, and in view of dangers which were threatening and anxieties naturally arising therefrom, this was a becoming prayer. It would heal all differences between Jewish and Gentile Christians. **Amen**—so may it be fulfilled (1:25; 9:5; 11:36; 16:27).

This appears like an end of the Epistle, and especially of the last four chapters. It is not necessary to suppose that Paul wrote this letter in a week or a month. He may have written different portions of it at different intervals, while he was expecting to return to Jerusalem and then go to Rome. The next chapter, however, appears to have been penned just before sending it by Phebe of Cenchræa (16:1, 2).

PRACTICAL REMARKS.

1. Pleasing ourselves should always be subordinate to helping our brethren (ver. 1; 1 Cor. 9:19, 22; Phil. 2:4).

2. Our object in pleasing others should be their highest good and the glory of God (ver. 2; 14:12; 1 Cor. 10:24).

3. Christ is our example in seeking not his own comfort, but the will of God and our eternal good (ver. 3; John 17:5; Phil. 2:6-8; Heb. 10:4-10).

4. The Scriptures are intended for the instruction, guidance, comfort, and hope of Christians in all ages (ver. 4; John 5:39; 2 Tim. 3:15).

5. If all Christians should imitate the example and spirit of Christ, and obey his word, there would be no divisions among them (ver. 5, 6; John 17:21-23).

6. "The character and conduct of Jesus Christ are at once the most perfect model of excellence and the most persuasive motive to obedience" (HODGE). (Ver. 5, 6; John 13:15; 1 Peter 2:21.)

7. Concord and harmony among Christians are for God's glory, but contention among them dishonors him (ver. 7; Eph. 1:4-6; Isa. 58:4, 5).

8. It was necessary that the Messiah should be connected with some one race of man, and fittingly with God's chosen people (ver. 8; Heb. 2:14-17).

M

9. It is the duty of all, and especially of Gentiles, to glorify God for his mercy as exhibited in our salvation (ver. 6, 9; 11 : 32, 33).

10. The Scriptures are standards of appeal in doctrine and practice (ver. 10-12; 2 Tim. 3 : 16).

11. The salvation of Gentiles was no afterthought of God, but was according to his purpose from the beginning (ver. 10-12; Eph. 3 : 6-9).

12. There is no distinction between Jews and Gentiles in the terms and privileges of salvation (ver. 10-13; 10 : 12, 13).

13. The Christian's hope is anchored in God and can never fail him (ver. 13 : 5 : 5; Heb. 6 : 19).

14. We should always exercise a kind and conciliatory spirit in admonition and instruction (ver. 14; 2 Tim. 2 : 24-26; Titus 3 : 2).

15. While we should not flatter others, we should commend them as far as we honestly can, in order to encourage them and prompt them to activity (ver. 14, 15; 16 : 19; 2 Peter 1 : 12; Rev. 2 : 2, 3).

16. The ministry is a sacred calling and its converts are the offerings of a spiritual harvest to God (ver. 16; 1 Thess. 2 : 19).

17. While the Christian minister may rejoice in his successes, he should remember that they are through Christ's power and for Christ's glory (ver. 17; 2 Cor. 10 : 17; 12 : 9, 10).

18. Christ works as really and as effectually through the words and lives of his ministers now, as he did once through the supernatural gifts of the apostles (ver. 18, 19; 1 Cor. 2 : 2-4).

19. The Christian minister should preach a full gospel (ver. 19; 1 Cor. 1 : 25-28; Acts 20 : 26, 27).

20. Every one has his gift. Some are fitted to plant churches; some to build them up and comfort them; some to erect houses of worship (ver. 20; Acts 4 : 30; 11 : 24; 2 Cor. 10 : 13-16).

21. We should exercise great care lest we build improperly on another man's foundation. One plants and another waters, but God gives the increase (ver. 20, 21; John 4 : 35-38; 1 Cor. 3 : 6-8).

22. It is the highest honor to preach and plant churches in new fields, but still any work in church building is honorable (ver. 20-22; 1 Cor. 12 : 29, 30).

23. We should always be seeking new opportunities for doing good (ver. 23, 24; Gal. 6 : 10).

24. There is no satiety in true Christian fellowship. "We cannot see enough of those we love" (Boise). (Ver. 24; 1 Cor. 16 : 17, 18.)

25. To minister to the necessity of the saints is a work worthy of an apostle (ver. 25; Gal. 2 : 10).

26. The rich and poor should prove a mutual blessing in the development of Christian graces (ver. 26; 2 Cor. 8 : 12-15, 19).

27. Christian benevolence is a participation with others, rather than a contribution to others, and thereby we discharge a debt to the Lord and to one another (ver. 27; 2 Cor. 9 : 12-14).

28. The public religious contribution is of the nature of worship offered through others to Christ (ver. 27, 28; 2 Cor. 8 : 1-8; 1 John 3 : 17).

29. Wherever we go we should take Christ with us, and the full blessing of the gospel for others (ver. 29).

30. Prayer is a spiritual wrestling with God, and this should be especially exercised for the Christian minister (ver. 30; Gen. 32 : 24).

31. The prejudice of men should not hinder us from doing them good (ver. 31).

32. In all our prayers, labors, and journeys, it should be our supreme desire that the will of God be done (ver. 32; James 4 : 14, 15).

33. What greater blessing is there than the enjoyment of peace with God and man? (Ver. 33; John 14 : 27.)

CHAPTER XVI.

This chapter contains the final conclusion of the Epistle. Phœbe is commended (ver. 1, 2), followed by greetings (ver. 3-16), warnings against false teachers and against divisions (ver. 17-20); greetings from the apostle's companions (ver. 21-23), and the concluding doxology (ver. 24-27). In this chapter we get a view of Paul as a personal friend.

1. I introduce and commend **unto you Phœbe** (meaning *bright*, *radiant*), our sister in Christ, yours as

Salutations; warning against those who cause divisions; praise to God.

16 I COMMEND unto you Phœbe *our sister, which is a servant of the church 2 which is at ᵍCenchrea: ʰ that ye receive her in the Lord, as becometh saints, and that ye assist her in whatsoever business she hath need of you: for she hath been a succourer of many, and of myself also.

3 Greet ⁱ Priscilla and Aquila my help-

16 I commend to you Phœbe our sister, who is a servant of the church which is 2 at Cenchrea; that ye receive her in the Lord in a way worthy of saints, and assist her in whatever matter she may have need of you; for she herself also has been a helper of many, and of myself.

3 Salute Prisca and Aquila, my fellow-

---

f Matt. 12 : 50.   *g* Acts 18 : 18.   *h* Phil. 2 : 29 ; 3 John : 5, 6.   *i* Acts 18 : 2, 3, 18, 26 ; 2 Tim. 4 : 19.

---

well as mine, *being also* a **servant, a** *deaconess*, **of the church which is at Cenchrea,** or Cenchreæ, the eastern harbor of Corinth on the Saronic gulf, about eight or nine miles east of the city. From this place Paul sailed to Ephesus (Acts 18 : 18). It still retains its name among the educated. It seems that Phœbe went to Rome in connection with this Epistle, and she is generally regarded as the bearer of it. Nothing is known of her outside of this passage. Phœbe was a *servant* of the church in more than in a menial sense; she was evidently a consecrated helper, or what may be termed a *deaconess*, as the word was officially used in the second century. Some suppose that 1 Tim. 3 : 11 refers to this class of persons. Priscilla (ver. 3), Mary (ver. 6), Tryphena, Tryphosa, and Persis (ver. 12), probably belonged to the same class. About fifty years later, Pliny in his letter to Trajan speaks of deaconesses in the Bythinian churches. They were especially needed in Greek and Oriental churches, where the sexes were rigidly separated. They were chosen from pious women, chiefly widows, and they devoted themselves, among their own sex, to self-denying labors and charity. They were found at Constantinople at the end of the twelfth century. Their total disappearance was, "to a large extent, due to the State's having assumed the care of the poor and the sick, as also to the gradual introduction of infant baptism, and the administration of the rite by sprinkling, which made the assistance of women unnecessary" (HERZOG).

2. I commend Phœbe (previous verse), in order **that ye receive her in the Lord,** as a fellow-Christian, both she and you being in Christ and bearing the same relation to him, **as becometh saints**—*in a way worthy of saints*, with that loving and delicate attention which Christians should exercise toward each other, and especially toward a Christian sister. **And that ye assist,** literally, *stand by her*, **in whatsoever business** *she may have* **need of you.** What her business was is unknown. It may have concerned property, or perhaps business pertaining to her work as a deaconess. She would doubtless need their help, as seems evident from what follows. **For she** *herself* **hath been a succourer,** *a protectress and helper*, **of many, and of myself.** Omit **also.** The word translated *succourer* is an honorable one, and seems to be used with reference to her official work in caring for the affairs of the poor, the sick, and strangers, especially of her own sex. She may have been a helper of Paul in sickness, and also a protectress in danger. Possibly at this very time, when he was about to sail for Syria, she may have protected him against a plot laid against him by the Jews (Acts 20 : 3).

3. Greet, or *salute*, **Priscilla,** or rather, according to the best text, *Prisca*, the former a diminutive of the latter, a Latin name, meaning *ancient*, a similar variation in form being not uncommon among Romans. **And Aquila,** a Latin name, meaning *eagle*. These two eminent Christians were Jews, born in Pontus, and about A. D. 52 exiled from Rome, when they came to Corinth and were there with Paul eighteen or more months (Acts 18 : 2, 3, 11. 18); after which they went to Ephesus with Paul, probably starting a tent-making business, thus providing a home and preparing the way for Paul when he returned on his third missionary journey to labor there (Acts 18 : 18, 26; 1 Cor. 16 : 19). At the date of sending this

4 ers in Christ Jesus: who have for my
life laid down their own necks: unto
whom not only I give thanks, but also
5 all the churches of the Gentiles. Likewise greet ᵏ the church that is in their
house.
Salute my well beloved Epenetus,
who is ˡ the firstfruits of Achaia unto
6 Christ. Greet Mary, who bestowed
7 much labour on us. Salute Andronicus
and Junia, my kinsmen, and my fellow
prisoners, who are of note among the
apostles, who also were ᵐ in Christ before me.

4 workers in Christ Jesus, who for my
life laid down their own necks; to
whom not only I give thanks, but also
5 all the churches of the Gentiles; and
salute the church that is in their
house.
Salute Epenetus, my beloved, who is
the first-fruits of Asia unto Christ.
6 Salute Mary, who bestowed much labor
7 on you. Salute Andronicus and Junias, my kinsmen, and my fellow-prisoners, who are of note among the
apostles, who were in Christ even before me.

ᵏ Matt. 18 : 20 ; 1 Cor. 16 : 19 ; Col. 4 : 15 ; Philem. 2.   ˡ 1 Cor. 16 : 15.
ᵐ Gal. 1 : 22 ; 2 Cor. 5 : 17 ; 1 John 5 : 20.

Epistle (A. D. 58), they were again at Rome, having probably left Ephesus about the time that Paul left (Acts 20 : 1). They probably went to Rome expecting Paul to follow them in due time. Later, at the close of Paul's life, they appear to have been at Ephesus again (2 Tim. 4 : 19). Prisca's name stands first, implying that she was the leading and stronger character of the two. (Comp. notes on Acts 18 : 2, 26.) Paul styles them **my helpers**, or *fellow-workers*, **in Christ Jesus.** They were indeed fellow-workers at tent-making (Acts 18 : 3), but here the reference is to their religious work and co-operation in the Lord. It is not unlikely that Prisca acted as a deaconess.

4. Who (omit **have**) **for my life laid down their own necks.** The figure is that of presenting the neck to the executioner's axe. It is unknown when it was that Aquila and his wife risked their lives for Paul. It might have been at Corinth under the opposition and persecution of the Jews (Acts 18 : 6, 12; 2 Cor. 1 : 8-10), or at the great tumult at Ephesus (Acts 19 : 23, 28-31). But whenever it was, Paul gives **thanks** to them, as did **all the churches of the Gentiles**, to whom Paul was an apostle, for being spared to them.

5. Likewise greet, or *And salute*, **the church**—*the congregation* or *the meeting* **at their house.** They had had a congregation at their house **at Ephesus** (1 Cor. 16 : 19). Their business may have been such as to necessitate a large building, in which was a large room suitable for religious gatherings. There were doubtless several such meeting-places and gatherings at Rome (ver. 14, 15). See Col. 4 : 15 and Philem. 2 for allusion to churches or congregations in private houses. See note on ver. 14, and also on Acts 20 : 17, and at end of that chapter. **Salute my well-beloved Epenetus**, or, *Epænetus, my beloved*, probably one of Paul's own converts, **who is the firstfruits**, one of the first converts, **of Achaia** (Greece), rather, according to the best text, *of Asia*, the Roman province of that name, of which Ephesus was the capital, **unto Christ,** having been brought into union and a saving relation with him. (Comp. 1 Cor. 16 : 15.) Epenetus is a Greek name, meaning *approved, praised*. Nothing more is known of him.

6. Greet, *salute*, **Mary,** the only Hebrew name in this chapter, **who bestowed much labour,** wearisome effort and toil amid trials and perhaps dangers, **on us,** rather, according to the best text, *on you.* She had been an important helper. Nothing more is known of her.

7. Salute Andronicus (a Greek name, meaning *a man of victory*), **and Junia** (the feminine of a celebrated Latin name) Junia was probably the wife or sister of Andronicus. Many read *Junias*, masculine, but it is impossible from the text to decide. Some infer from what follows that this person was a man. **My kinsmen,** most naturally, referring to blood-relations. (Comp. Acts 23 : 16.) **My fellow-prisoners**—when and where is not known. The same word is found in Col. 4 : 10; Philem. 23. Paul himself says that he had been "in prisons more abundantly" (2 Cor. 11 : 23), **who are of note,** or *distinguished among the apostles.* This phrase is somewhat ambig-

8 Greet Amplias, my beloved in the Lord.
9 Salute Urbane, our helper in Christ, and Stachys, my beloved.
10 Salute Apelles, approved in Christ. Salute them which are of Aristobulus' household.
11 Salute Herodion, my kinsman. Greet them that be of the *household* of Narcissus, which are in the Lord.
12 Salute Tryphena and Tryphosa, who labour in the Lord. Salute the beloved Persis, which laboured much in the Lord.

8 fore me. Salute Ampliatus, my beloved in the Lord. Salute Urbanus, our fellow-worker in Christ, and
10 Stachys my beloved. Salute Apelles, the approved in Christ. Salute those who are of the household of Aristobulus.
11 Salute Herodian my kinsman. Salute those of the household of Narcissus
12 who are in the Lord. Salute Tryphaena and Tryphosa who labor in the Lord. Salute Persis the beloved who labored
13 much in the Lord. Salute Rufus, the

nous. It is held by some to mean, noted as apostles, taking the word apostles in the wider sense of messenger, or missionary. It is more natural, however, and freer from difficulties to take it as meaning, held in high repute by the apostles. The word *apostles* thus retains its usual restricted New Testament sense. They were early disciples **in Christ**, having become Christians **before me**, and were well known and honored by the apostolic body.

8. Greet, or *salute*, **Amplias,** or according to the best reading, Ampliatus (a Latin name, meaning *enlargement*); the former is an abbreviation of the latter. Paul held him in high esteem as a Christian brother, for he speaks of him as **my beloved in the Lord,** in Christian fellowship.

9. Salute Urbane, better *Urbanus* (a Latin name, meaning *pertaining to the city*, polished, genteel), **our helper,** or *fellow-worker*, a preacher or perhaps a deacon. *Our* includes both the writer and those to whom the Epistle is addressed. He appears to have been a spiritual helper to Paul in the past and at that time of the Roman brethren. **And Stachys** (a Greek name, meaning a growing *ear of grain*), **my beloved,** one dear to him personally.

10. Salute Apelles (a Greek name, meaning one *removed* or *separated*, and often borne by freedmen), **approved in Christ**—one who had been tried, tested, and found true as a Christian. In trials and sufferings he had probably shown steadfastness in faith. **Salute them which are of Aristobulus** (a Greek name, meaning *best counseling*). These were the Christians of his family or establishment—slaves, freedmen, and others. As he is not included, it might be inferred that he was not a Christian, or not living. (Comp. Phil. 4:22.) But no such inference can be drawn, for Paul speaks twice in the same way of Stephanas (1 Cor. 1:16; 16:15), yet from 1 Cor. 16:17 we learn that Stephanas was with Paul at Ephesus. It is possible that Aristobulus was with Paul at Corinth when he wrote this. Some would identify him with Arwystli, a man of Italy and one of the earliest missionaries to Britain, mentioned in the Welsh Genealogies of the Saints of Britain (Bibliotheca Sacra, 1875, pp. 656, 657).

11. Salute Herodion (a Greek name, meaning *sprung from a hero*), **my kinsman,** or *relative*. **Greet,** or *salute*, **them that be of the household of Narcissus** (a Greek name, *a daffodil*), who **are in the Lord,** those who are Christians. See on ver. 10. There was a noted Narcissus, a freedman of the Emperor Claudius, but he had been put to death two or three years before this was written. His household may have been still continuing. Another of the same name has been mentioned as an associate and a bad favorite of Nero. But as the name was common at Rome, inferences are mere guesses.

12. Salute Tryphena and Tryphosa (Greek names, *luxurious*, both from the same root), **who labour in the Lord**—now doing religious work. They were very likely deaconesses. **Salute the beloved Persis** (a Greek name, *a Persian woman*, just as Lydia denotes a Lydian (Acts 16:14)), **who laboured much,** at some previous time, **in the Lord,** perhaps also as a deaconess. Paul's great delicacy has frequently been noted in saying "*the* beloved" instead of "*my* beloved," as in ver. 8. Perhaps Persis was an aged believer, whose days of active toil were past.

13. Salute Rufus (a Latin name, *red*), *the* **chosen,** *the elect*, the choice

13 Salute °Rufus, °chosen in the Lord,
14 and his mother and mine. Salute Asyncritus, Phlegon, Hermas, Patrobas, Hermes, and the brethren which
15 are with them. Salute Philologus, and Julia, Nereus, and his sister, and Olympas, and all the saints which are with them.
16 *P*Salute one another with an holy kiss. The churches of Christ salute you.

elect in the Lord, and his mother and
14 mine. Salute Asyncritus, Phlegon, Hermes, Patrobas, Hermas, and the
15 brethren who are with them. Salute Philologus, and Julia, Nereus and his sister, and Olympas, and all the saints
16 who are with them. Salute one another with a holy kiss. All the churches of Christ salute you.

n Mark 15 : 21.   *o* 2 John 1.   *p* 2 Cor. 13 : 12; 1 Thess. 5 : 26; 1 Peter 5 : 14.

one **in the Lord**—a pre-eminent Christian; **and his mother**, naturally, **and mine**, by her motherly care for me. (Comp. John 19 : 27.) Rufus has generally been regarded as the one mentioned in Mark 15 : 21, the son of Simon the Cyrenæan, whom the Jews compelled to bear the cross of Jesus (Luke 23 : 26). He seems to have been well known, and if Mark wrote his Gospel at Rome it was natural that he should describe him. Yet all this is uncertain, as Rufus was a common name, and Mark and Paul may have had in mind different individuals.

14. Another list of persons having Greek names. **Asyncritus** (*incomparable*), **Phlegon** (*burning*), **Patrobas** (*paternal*), **Hermas, Hermes** (different forms of the name of the Greek god of speech, called by the Romans Mercurius). These persons are unknown beyond their names. The legends of the Romish church make most of the persons named in this chapter bishops or martyrs, but no reliance can be placed on these traditions. It should be noted that early Christian converts had no scruple in retaining their names, even though they were that of a heathen deity. **And the brethren** *that* **are with them**, probably forming a Christian assembly, church, or out-station. See on ver. 5. Origen and Eusebius supposed that Hermas was the author of the work entitled, "The Shepherd of Hermas," but that work is now regarded as belonging to the last half of the second century.

15. Salute Philologus (Greek name, *lover of the word*), **and Julia** (Greek name, *downy*), perhaps the wife of Philologus. Some suppose the latter name should be Julias, masculine, as in the case of Junia (ver. 7). **Nereus** (two syllables, a Greek name of a minor sea god, whose rule was thought to be on

the Mediterranean; see on ver. 14), **and his sister,** a Christian woman of some note, though her name may have have been unknown to Paul. Nothing more is certainly known of Nereus. **And Olympas** (a Greek name, *dwelling on Olympus*), a Christian man, perhaps of the household of Philologus. **And all the saints which are with them,** forming another church, assembly, or out-station. Whether there were several separate churches at Rome at this time, or one church with several meeting-places, we are not told. It should be noted that this Epistle is not addressed to the church at Rome, but to the saints in Rome (1 : 7). Neither is the church at Rome mentioned in the New Testament. It seems natural to infer that as there was one church at Jerusalem, at Antioch, and at Ephesus, with their plurality of elders, and various meeting-places, so it was at Rome.

16. Having completed his salutations, the apostle exhorts them to follow his example with mutual, loving greetings. **With a holy kiss** (1 Cor. 16 : 20, etc.). The Oriental salutation by means of a kiss was common then and still continues in the East. It is here styled *holy* as a religious act, an expression of chaste, godly affection and of Christian fellowship. Compare the "kiss of love" (1 Peter 5 : 14). The **churches of Christ,** in and around Corinth, where he had made known his intention of visiting Rome, **salute you.**

The number of persons to whom Paul sends salutations in a city he had never visited is remarkable, but not surprising. Rome was then the center of the world, where peoples from all countries met, and from whence journeys were taken to all parts of the Roman Empire. He had been a preacher

17 Now I beseech you, brethren, mark them ᵩwhich cause divisions and offences contrary to the doctrine which ye have learned; and ʳavoid them.
18 For they that are such serve not our Lord Jesus Christ, but ˢtheir own belly; and ᵗby good words and fair speeches deceive the hearts of the simple. For ᵘyour obedience is come
19 abroad unto all *men*. I am glad therefore on your behalf: but yet I would have you ˣwise unto that which is
20 good, and simple concerning evil. And

17 Now I beseech you, brethren, to mark those who are causing divisions and occasions of stumbling, contrary to the teaching which ye learned;
18 and turn away from them. For they that are such serve not our Lord Christ, but their own belly; and through their kind and smooth speech deceive the hearts of the guileless.
19 For your obedience is come abroad unto all men. I rejoice therefore over you; but I wish you to be wise as to that which is good, and simple as to

q Acts 15 : 1, 5, 24; 2 Thess. 3 : 6, 14, 15; 1 Tim. 6 : 3-5; 2 John 10, 11.   *r* 2 Tim. 3 : 5; Titus 3 : 10.
s Isa. 56 : 10-12; Phil. 3 : 19; 2 Peter 2 : 10-15.   *t* 2 Tim. 3 : 6; Titus 1 : 10; 2 Peter 2 : 3.
u 1 : 8; 1 Thess. 1 : 8, 9.   *x* Matt. 10 : 16.

over twenty years and a recognized missionary to the heathen for thirteen years throughout Cyprus, Asia Minor, Macedonia, and Greece. Some of these persons were relatives, others converts, and others noted fellow-laborers. Paul had strong social and religious attachments and made strong friends (Acts 27 : 43; 28 : 10, 14, 15, 16). The number of women named should be noted, indicating their position and importance in the early churches.

17. This and the three following verses contain a warning against false teachers and divisions. Paul entreats his Roman brethren to **mark** carefully, *keep an eye upon*, **them which cause**, or *are making, the* **divisions and offences,** or *occasions of stumbling*, **contrary to the doctrine,** *the teaching, which ye* **learned.** This false teaching is referred to as well known, but as the warning is so brief, it may be inferred that it had not made much progress, or even no progress, at Rome. Dr. Lightfoot on Phil. 3 : 18 thinks that the false teachers here were not Judaizers, but their opposites, Antinomians, the rejecters of all law, and belonging to the same party addressed in 6 : 1-23. But as the Epistles to the Galatians, the Corinthians, and the Romans were written in the same period, it is natural to suppose that the reference in them all is to the same class of false teachers, namely, Judaizers. He was meeting this opposition everywhere. At the same time he may have found both at Corinth and Ephesus a type of Antinomianism, afterward developed among some Gnostics, who held that the acts of the body were indifferent to the soul. Instead of having any private discussion or public controversy with such false teachers, Paul exhorts **to avoid them,** *to be turning away from them*—the present tense, denoting that they should be in the habit of so doing. A wise, effective, and peaceable way (2 Tim. 3 : 5; 2 John 10).

18. For introduces a confirmation of the preceding exhortation by giving three characteristics of these false teachers: they do not serve **our Lord Christ** (omit **Jesus,** according to the best text); they serve **their own** lower appetites and their selfish indulgences; and **by their good words and fair speeches,** by *kind language*, affecting goodness and piety, *and plausible words*, to make their teaching appear reasonable, **they deceive the hearts of the simple,** the innocent and the guileless, who are distrusting no one, and themselves unconscious of any bad intentions.

19. Paul feels that he can exhort his Roman brethren with full confidence that they would act accordingly, **For your obedience is**—*has*—**come abroad unto all men.** This was obedience to Christ and to the teachings of the gospel (1 : 5, 8). **I am glad,** or *rejoice,* **therefore on your behalf,** or *upon you,* as the foundation of my rejoicing. **But although I know of your obedience and rejoice over you, I would have you wise unto that which is good,** in respect to it, **and simple,** or *guileless as to that which is evil,* being untainted and having nothing to do with it. He thus very delicately explains his words of caution and warning. This looks as if he was warning them against false teachings

*the God of peace *shall **bruise Satan** under your feet shortly. *The grace of **our Lord Jesus Christ** be with you. Amen.
21 *Timotheus **my workfellow, and** *Lucius, and *Jason, and *Sosipater, my kinsmen, salute you.
22 I Tertius, who wrote *this* epistle, salute you in the Lord.
23 *Gaius mine host, and of the whole church, saluteth you. *Erastus the chamberlain of the city saluteth you, and Quartus a brother.

20 that which is evil. And the God of peace will bruise Satan under your feet speedily. The grace of our Lord Jesus Christ be with you.
21 Timothy, my fellow-worker, salutes you, and Lucius, and Jason, and Sosipater, my kinsmen. I, Tertius, who write the letter, salute you in the Lord.
23 Gaius my host, and of the whole church, salutes you. Erastus the treasurer of the city salutes you. And Quartus the brother.

y 15 : 33. z Gen. 3 : 15. a 2 Cor. 13 : 14. Phil. 4 : 23 ; Rev. 22 : 21. b See refs. Acts 16 : 1. c Acts 13 : 1. d Acts 17 : 5. e Acts 20 : 4, *Sopater*. f 1 Cor. 1 : 14 ; 3 John 1–6. g See refs. Acts 19 : 22.

with which they had not come into actual conflict.
20. Paul's exhortation and expression of confidence is followed by an assurance of their safety and victory. **And the God of peace** (see on 15 : 33), the very opposite of divisions and occasions of stumblings (ver. 17), **shall bruise,** or *trample,* as a conqueror, **Satan under your feet,** with reference to the first promise of a Saviour (Gen. 3 : 15). Satan is the great *adversary* of Christ and his people, the author of error and strife. **Shortly** — *quickly* (Luke 18 : 8 ; Rev. 22 : 6). The God of peace will give you speedily a complete victory over these that trouble you. (Comp. 13 : 11, 12.) In the meantime **the grace of our Lord Jesus Christ be with you,** in and for the strife. **Amen**— not found in the best manuscripts, and should be omitted. Again Paul appears to end his letter, but he adds salutations from his companions in Corinth and a doxology. But this was often Paul's manner (Phil. 4 : 20, 24 ; 2 Thess. 3 : 16, 18 ; 1 Tim. 6 : 16, 21 ; 2 Tim. 4 : 18, 22).
21. Timotheus, or, *Timothy* (a Greek name, *honor of God*), **my fellow-worker,** as an evangelist and fellow-missionary (Acts 16 : 1–3 ; 18 : 5 ; 20 : 4 ; Phil. 2 : 19–22). His name appears in all of Paul's Epistles and to the Hebrews, except Ephesians and Titus. **Lucius** (a Latin name, *luminous*), not the same name as Luke, possibly the prophet and teacher in the church at Antioch (Acts 13 : 1, on which see note). **Jason** (a Greek name, *he that cures*), possibly the host of Paul at Thessalonica (Acts 17 : 5, 6). And **Sosipater** (a Greek name, *saver of a father*), possibly the same as Sopater of Berea (Acts 20 : 4). But these names were common, and the three are styled by Paul **my kinsmen,** or *relatives.* Doubtless all of these mentioned in this verse were known to many in Rome. Compare on ver. 16.
22. I Tertius (Latin name, *third*), **who wrote this epistle,** as Paul's amanuensis, **salute you in the Lord,** as one in union with Christ as a Christian. He doubtless knew personally some of them at Rome. Paul may have employed an amanuensis on account of the weakness of his eyes (Gal. 4 : 15). In his earlier Epistles, at least, it was his custom to write a few words at the close with his own hand (2 Thess. 3 : 17 ; Gal. 6 : 11. See also 1 Cor. 16 : 21 ; Col. 4 : 18).
23. Gaius (a Latin name, *lord,* the same as Caius), a very common name. There was Gaius of Macedonia (Acts 19 : 29), of Derbe (Acts 20 : 4), and 3 John 1. This one was Paul's **host** at Corinth **and of the whole church;** his hospitality was exercised toward them all, his house open to them and to all guests of the church, and without doubt the same Gaius as that of 1 Cor. 1 : 14. **Erastus** (a Greek name, *beloved*), **the chamberlain,** rather, *the treasurer,* **of the city** of Corinth. This indicates where this letter was written. Erastus must have been of some social standing and political influence. But few such converts are recorded in apostolic history (Acts 13 : 12 ; 17 : 4, 34). "Not many wise after the flesh, mighty, or noble," were called (1 Cor. 1 : 26). Erastus, of Acts 19 : 22, an assistant of Paul, was probably another, but perhaps the same as the one mentioned in 2 Tim. 4 : 20. **Quartus** (Latin name, *fourth*), **a,** or rather, *the,* **brother** in Christ and well known, doubtless, **to some** in Rome, either personally or by reputation. Nothing

24 The grace of our Lord Jesus Christ *be* with you all. Amen.
25 Now ʰ to him that is of power to stablish you according to my gospel, and the preaching of Jesus Christ, ⁱ according to the revelation of the mystery, which was kept secret since the
26 world began, but ᵏ now is made manifest, ˡ and by the Scriptures of the prophets, ᵐ according to the commandment of the everlasting God, made known to all nations ⁿ for the obedience
27 of faith—to ᵒ God only wise, *be* glory through Jesus Christ for ever. Amen.

25 Now to him who is able to establish you, according to my gospel and the preaching of Jesus Christ, according to the revelation of the mystery kept
26 in silence during eternal ages but now made manifest, and through prophetic Scriptures, according to the commandment of the eternal God, made known to all nations for obedience to the
27 faith, to God only wise, through Jesus Christ, to whom be the glory forever. Amen.

Written to the Romans from Corinthus, *and sent* by Phœbe servant of the church at Cenchrea.

ʰ 2 Thess. 3 : 3 ; Jude 24.
ᵏ Eph. 1 : 9 ; 2 Tim. 1 : 10 ; 1 Peter 1 : 20.
ᴸ 15 : 18.
ⁱ Eph. 3 : 3–5, 9 ; Col. 1 : 26, 27.
ˡ 1 : 2 ; 3 : 21.   ᵐ Matt. 28 : 19 ; Acts 13 : 47.
ᵒ 1 Tim. 1 : 17 ; Jude 25.

more is known of him. Perhaps both he and Tertius (ver. 22) were Romans.

24. The grace, etc. A repetition of ver. 20. It is omitted by the oldest manuscripts, but some ancient documents omit ver. 20 and retain this verse. It has been suggested by Alford and others that the amanuensis wrote as far as this, and that Paul penned the fervid doxology that follows with his own hand.

25. This doxology is rapturous and sublime; its position at the end of the Epistle is natural; its structure is irregular, indicating struggling thoughts and emotions; its thought and style are Pauline. (Comp. 1 Tim. 6 : 15, 16.). It is a brief and beautiful summary of the essential teachings of the Epistle, and a general ascription of praise for the redemption detailed therein. Jude's (ver. 24, 25) doxology may be an imitation of this. **Now to him that is of power**, or *who is able*, **to stablish you,** amid oppositions and erroneous doctrines (6 : 1 ; 9 : 14, 19 ; 14 : 1 ; 16 : 17), **according to my gospel,** which I preach (see on 2 : 16), **and the preaching of Jesus Christ,** the great theme of gospel preaching and the only ground and hope of salvation, which gospel and preaching are according **to the revelation of the mystery**—salvation by faith to Jew and Gentile alike, as brought out in this Epistle (comp. Eph. 3 : 3–9), **which was kept secret since the world began,** or *during eternal ages*. Paul had received his commission from Christ and had been taught by revelation (Gal. 1 : 1, 11, 12). The divine manifestation of salvation in the cross of Christ and its proclamation to all nations were new. The incarnation and its results formed new manifestations of Divine wisdom and love, even to angels (Eph. 3 : 10 ; 1 Peter 1 : 12).

26. The sentence continues. **But now is made manifest,** or *made plain,* this mystery now made plain to the saints (Col. 1 : 26), **and by *means of*,** or *through*, **the Scriptures of the prophets** — the prophetic writings which foretold Christ and contained the germs of the gospel. Wherever the apostle went he took as his text the Old Testament Scriptures (Acts 13 : 17 ff. ; 26 : 22, 23). **According to the commandment of the everlasting,** rather, *the eternal,* **God,** whose will is that the gospel should be preached to every creature (Matt. 28 : 19 ; Mark 16 : 15), and who commands all to repent (Acts 17 : 30). And this glorious mystery, this secret counsel of God, the dying and risen Christ, "the end of the law for righteousness to every one that believeth" (10 : 4), **is made known to all nations,** especially the Gentiles, **for** the purpose of producing and obtaining **obedience** *to the* **faith** and which accompanies faith. (See note on 1 : 5.)

27. To God only wise, who is absolutely the only wise Being, and whose supreme wisdom to man is revealed in the gospel **through Jesus Christ,** the Mediator and channel of our thanks and praise. This is connected with the beginning of ver. 25, thus: "Now to him who is able," etc. .. "to God only wise, through Jesus Christ," etc. **Be glory**, rather, *to whom*—that is, to God—*be the glory*, which belongs to him, which is manifested in the gospel, and in the salvation of men, and which will be his **for ever. Amen**—so it is and so let it be. (See on 1 : 25.)

THE SUBSCRIPTION. This does not belong to the Epistle, but is no doubt true to fact. The subscriptions to Paul's Epistles are of later date and are said to have been the work of Euthalius, a bishop of the fifth century. They are of no historical authority, and some of them are inconsistent with the contents of the Epistles.

PRACTICAL REMARKS.

1. The only female office in the church mentioned in the New Testament is that of deaconess. Woman is spoken of as a "helper" and a "fellow-worker," but her official work in the church is *diaconal* rather than ministerial (ver. 1, 3, 6, 12).

2. We should appreciate, welcome, and utilize the influence and ability of Christian women in church and Christian work (ver. 2).

3. Christian women may be largely useful in Sunday-school, family, and private instruction. Priscilla, in connection with her husband, instructed Apollos (ver. 3; Acts 18 : 26; 2 Tim. 1 : 4, 5).

4. We, as individuals, and all the churches of God, have reasons for thankfulness for the martyrs of the past, and the dangers and sufferings of those through whom the gospel is enjoyed by us (ver. 4; Rev. 7: 13, 14).

5. Our love to Christ and for our brethren should make us willing to imperil our lives for his sake and in their behalf (ver. 4; 1 John 3 : 16).

6. Neither numbers nor a house of worship are essential to constitute a church. It may be small and meet in a private dwelling, yet be efficient (ver. 5, 14, 15).

7. Both individual and family religion should be cultivated. The Christian's home should be consecrated to Christ as much as if there were a church at his house (ver. 5, 10, 11, 14, 15).

8. From this list of names we learn much of Paul's personal and private life. His social regard, his Christian affection, and his influence over others. Twenty-six salutations to persons in a church he had never visited (ver. 3-16).

9. Whatever criticisms have been made upon Paul's views of women elsewhere, we learn from this chapter his high estimate of Christian womanhood (ver. 3, 6, 12; 2 Tim. 1 : 4, 5).

10. True religion does not ignore nor lessen natural affection, but rather ennobles, purifies, and utilizes it for God (ver. 7, 11).

11. Fellow-suffering and fellow-work, especially for Christ, tend to endear us to one another and to tighten the bonds of love (ver. 3, 7 ; Col. 4 : 10).

12. True religion binds the hearts of those who embrace it together as one family in tender ties and mutual interests (ver. 13; Matt. 12 : 47-50; John 19 : 26, 27).

13. The undying memory of so many mentioned by Paul is a type of the eternal blessing of those whose names are written in the Lamb's book of life (ver. 3-16).

14. In the Apostle Paul we have a striking example of a personal and individual worker. He lived in touch with men, knew them by name, cared, watched over, and prayed for them (ver. 1-16; Acts 17 : 17 ; 18 : 5-11, etc.).

15. We catch glimpses of the early constitution of the Christian churches. Their government was simple and congregational. There was no sign of a hierarchy at Rome in Paul's day (ver. 1-16).

16. Peter could not have been at Rome when Paul sent this Epistle. His name does not appear among the salutations. Paul surely would have greeted him had he been there (ver. 1-16).

17. Christian customs may change while the reality remains. We may not give the "kiss of peace" or the "holy kiss," but the underlying affection should find expression in forms consistent with the usages of our times (ver. 16).

18. Those who attempt to make divisions in churches and cause offenses to brethren are commonly actuated by some evil or ambitious motive (ver. 17, 18; Acts 15 : 1-24; 1 Cor. 3 : 3; Gal. 5 : 19, 20).

19. False teachers in the church are generally selfish, plausible, and deceitful (ver. 18, 19).
20. The best course with false teachers and false doctrines is to have nothing to do with them (ver. 17, 18; 2 John 10).
21. Obedience to Christ is an evidence of love and of a true faith (ver. 19, 26).
22. God is the author of peace and the gospel—a dispensation of peace (ver. 19, 20; Matt. 10 : 16).
23. Satan is the author of error and confusion, but he is a conquered foe and cannot prevail against those who contend in God's strength (ver. 20; Matt. 16 : 18).
24. The gospel and the preaching of Jesus Christ is the stability of Christians and of churches (ver. 25; Heb. 1 : 1-3; Isa. 33 : 6; 1 Tim. 3 : 15, 16).
25. The gospel brings to us the mystery of godliness which God has revealed for our faith and obedience; it should be preached to all nations (ver. 26; 1 Tim. 3 : 16; Eph. 6 : 19).
26. Our approach to God, whether in prayer or praise, should be through Jesus Christ (ver. 27; 11 : 33-36).

PAUL'S GOSPEL AND JOHN'S.

There is a tendency among some to magnify the differences between Paul and John, and even to represent the teachings of these two apostles as antagonistic. Both, however, were taught by the Lord (Gal. 1 : 1, 12; 1 John 1 : 1, 3), and both were guided by the Spirit. On the divine side they were chosen to represent and enforce respectively certain special doctrines of the great system of gospel truth. On the human side their differences may be traced first to their different mental endowments and mental conceptions. John centers on fewer points, and conceives of truth more absolutely. Paul is more systematic, and conceives of truth more in its relation to other truths.

But secondly, their writings were largely called forth by heretical teachings which led to the discussion of certain doctrines, and affected the manner of their presentation. Thus the Judaizers and legalists led Paul to treat of the great doctrine of justification by faith. Disorders in the church at Corinth led to his discussion of church order, the gifts of the Spirit, and the doctrine of the resurrection. The teaching of a false philosophy and Oriental mysticism occasioned the Epistles of his imprisonment, and led to a fuller exhibition of the majesty and glory of Christ, and of the church as the body of Christ. So also of John. Some who ignored the humanity of Christ, and others his divinity, and still others who would allow sinful indulgence and immorality, led John to dwell upon Christ as the Word, God manifest in the flesh, and to insist on fellowship with God and consequent purity of heart and life. Paul's later Epistles are connecting links with those of John.

Paul emphasizes faith, and John love, but the former held love to be the greatest of graces, and the latter shows his high estimate of faith by its frequent mention. Paul, while presenting the incarnation and the humiliation of Christ, makes prominent the resurrection, and views Christ as the exalted and living Saviour. John views them as the eternal word, incarnated, and now glorified through death and the resurrection. Paul dwells upon the atoning death of Christ; John, upon Christ as the Lamb of God, who is a propitiation for our sins. Both Paul and John divide the human race into two classes, the righteous and the wicked. Both view the Fatherhood of God, as related to Christ and believers. Both teach the divine dignity of Christ, as the Son of God, the God-man; the importance and work of the Holy Spirit, the new birth, and eternal life. There appears no contradiction between the two. John is the complement of Paul. His writings are the culmination of the divine revelation regarding salvation to man. Without either Paul or John revelation would be incomplete.

ANCIENT CORINTH

PAUL'S FIRST EPISTLE TO THE CORINTHIANS

Salutation and thanksgiving.

1 PAUL, [a]called *to be* an apostle of Jesus Christ [b] through the will of God, 2 and [c]Sosthenes, *our* brother, unto [d] the church of God which is at Corinth, [e] to them that are sanctified in Christ Jesus, [f]called *to be* saints, with all that in every place [g]call upon the name of

1 PAUL, called to be an apostle of Jesus Christ through the will of God, 2 and Sosthenes our brother, to the church of God which is in Corinth, those who are sanctified in Christ Jesus, called to be saints, with all that call on the name of our Lord Jesus

a Rom. 1:1; Gal. 1:1.   b Eph. 1:1; Col. 1:1.   c Acts 18:17.   d Acts 18:8-11.
e Ver. 30; 6:9-11; John 17:19; Jude 1.   f Rom. 1:7; 2 Tim. 1:9.   g Acts 9:14, 21.

TITLE. In the earliest manuscripts it is simply *First to the Corinthians.* The fuller title, added later, is a truthful designation and an abbreviation of the first two verses of the Epistle.

CHAPTER I.

Paul begins with an introduction (ver. 1-9) and proceeds at once to notice the party spirit existing in the church at Corinth, which he endeavors to correct (ver. 10-31).

1-9. INTRODUCTION. As a commissioned apostle Paul salutes the church at Corinth, and expresses his thanksgiving for the mercies given them, and his hope for their steadfastness unto the end.

1. Paul called to be an apostle, rather, *a called apostle.* See note on Rom. 1:1. Paul emphasizes his high and divine call in view of the fact that there were those who disputed it (9:1-12). In the two Epistles to the Thessalonians, before opposition to his apostleship became prominent, this clause is not found, but the Epistles written after generally begin in a manner similar to this (Rom. 1:1; 2 Cor. 2:1, etc.). He was called not through the will of man, but **through the will of God.** Notice how this thought is variously expressed in Gal. 1:1; 1 Tim. 1:1; 2 Tim. 1:2; Titus 1:1. His opposers might say that he was not called, as the Twelve were, by Christ himself; but it is such a call he claims (Acts 26:16-18; Gal. 1:1, 12). He associates with himself **Sosthenes our brother,** one of the Christian brotherhood. Concerning him we know nothing further. He appears to have been well known in Corinth. He may have been the ruler of the synagogue mentioned in Acts 18:17, who had become a convert and perhaps a minister. He could second what Paul writes. Paul very likely employed him as his amanuensis.

2. Unto the church of God, belonging to God (Acts 20:28); not to any party or human leader. **At Corinth.** See introduction, p. xv. The local church embraced all the professed believers at Corinth, though, doubtless, being unable to meet in one place, they had several meeting-places. The church consisted of converted people, **them that are sanctified,** consecrated and expiated for, **in Christ Jesus**—in union with him and by means of the atonement he had made. **Called to be saints**—divinely called. See note on Rom. 1:7. As Paul was a *called apostle* (ver. 1), so they were *called saints.* The word church means *called out,* and a church appropriately consists of *saints* called out from the world and consecrated to a life of holiness. The term *saint* is usually applied in the New Testament to believers and popularly applied to all professed believers. **With all that call,** etc.; equivalent to, As are all *who call upon*

189

Jesus Christ our Lord, ᵇ both theirs and
3 ours: ᶦGrace be unto you, and peace,
from God our Father, and *from* the
Lord Jesus Christ.
4 ᵏ I thank my God always on your behalf, for the grace of God which is
5 given you by Jesus Christ; that in
every thing ye are enriched by him,
ᶦin all utterance, and *in* all knowledge;
6 even as ᵐ the testimony of Christ was
7 confirmed in you: so that ᵒ ye come behind in no gift; ᵖ waiting for the coming [revelation ᵖ] of our Lord Jesus

Christ in every place, theirs and ours:
3 Grace to you, and peace, from God
our Father, and the Lord Jesus Christ.
4 I thank my God always on your behalf, for the grace of God which was
5 given you in Christ Jesus; that in
everything ye were made rich in him,
6 in all speech and all knowledge; even
as the testimony of Christ was con-
7 firmed in you; so that ye fall short
in no gift, waiting for the revelation of

ᵇ Rom. 10 : 12 ; Eph. 4 : 5.   ᶦ Rom. 1 : 7; Eph. 1 : 2.   ᵏ Rom. 1 : 8.   ᶦ 12 : 8, 10 ; Rom. 15 : 4 ; 2 Cor. 8 : 7.
ᵐ 2 : 1, 2 ; Mark 16 : 20.   ⁿ 2 Cor. 12 : 13.   ᵒ Phil. 3 : 20; Titus 2 : 13; Heb. 10 : 36, 37.
ᵖ Luke 17 : 30 ; Col. 3 : 4.

the name, etc. Sanctification and saint-
ship are extended to all believers.
They were sanctified and called to be
saints with the discipleship **in every
place.** The calling upon **the name
of Jesus Christ** indicates the general practice of praying to Christ. (Comp.
Acts 7 : 59; 9 : 14; Rom. 10 : 13.) The words
in every place, in the best text follow *our Lord Jesus Christ*. **Both
theirs and ours.** *Ours* refers to Paul
and the Corinthians; *theirs* to all
others. Some would refer it to place—
their locality and ours. But it seems
better to refer it to Christ—their Lord
and ours. He is Lord of all believers,
not of any party.

3. Grace be unto you, etc. The
same as in Rom. 1 : 7, on which see
note. **Peace** of God in the soul
would naturally lead to peace among
themselves. Its mention seems significant in view of their party strifes.
This ends the salutation.

4. In this and the three verses that
follow Paul expresses his thanksgiving
in their behalf. **I thank my God;**
the same in Rom. 1 : 8, on which see
note. Paul commonly began his Epis-
tles with thanksgiving (Phil. 1 : 3; Col. 1 : 3;
1 Thess. 1 : 2; 2 Thess. 1 : 3). Sometimes he
says, "Blessed be God" (2 Cor. 1 : 3 ; Eph.
1 : 3). **Always on your behalf.**
There were many things in general
among the Corinthians which were the
source of constant thankfulness, notwithstanding their party strifes and
imperfections. **For the grace,** or
favor, **of God which is,** rather, *was*,
given you *in* **Christ Jesus,** by virtue of your union with him. The
effect of this grace is described in the
next verse. "*Grace* is properly *in*

God: the gifts of grace in us, given by
that grace" (ALFORD). It is deserving of special notice that notwithstanding his severe censures in both of
his Epistles to the Corinthians, Paul
bestows on them so much praise. But
this praise was largely confined to
gifts, such as knowledge and wisdom,
which could be enjoyed by many
notwithstanding the low morality of
some of the church. It was also the
manner of the apostle to begin his
Epistles with words of commendation.
That to the Galatians is the only exception.

5. That, as a result of divine grace,
in everything, pertaining to your
Christian life, **ye are,** rather, *were*, at
your conversion and baptism **enriched
by,** rather, *in*, **him,** in union with
Christ and by means of that union,
in all utterance, or *speech*, preaching, prophesying, and speaking with
tongues (14 : 26), **and in all knowledge,** the apprehension of truth, the
discerning of spirits, and the understanding and interpretation of tongues.

6. Even as the testimony of—
concerning — **C h r i s t,** through the
preaching of the gospel by Paul and
his associates, **was confirmed in
you,** taking deep root and firmly fixed
in your souls.

7. The result of being well grounded
in the history and doctrine of Christ.
So that ye come behind, or *fall
short*, **in no gift,** in no spiritual gift,
ordinary and miraculous (ver. 5; 2 Cor.
8 : 7). **Waiting,** with believing and
hopeful expectation, **for the coming,**
rather, *the revelation*, **of our Lord
Jesus Christ,** when he will be revealed at his second coming (2 Thess. 1 : 7 ;

8 Christ: ᵠ who shall also confirm you unto the end, ʳ *that ye may be* blameless in the day of our Lord Jesus Christ.
9 ˢ God *is* faithful, by whom ye were called unto ᵗ the fellowship of his Son Jesus Christ our Lord.

The dissensions at Corinth described and rebuked.

10 Now I beseech you, brethren, by the name of our Lord Jesus Christ, ᵘ that ye all speak the same thing, and *that* there be no divisions among you; but

8 our Lord Jesus Christ; who will also confirm you unto the end, unaccused in the day of our Lord Jesus Christ.
9 God is faithful, through whom ye were called into the fellowship of his Son, Jesus Christ our Lord
10 But I beseech you, brethren, through the name of our Lord Jesus Christ, that ye all speak the same thing, and that there be no divisions among you;

ᵠ Phil. 1 : 6; 1 Thess. 3 : 13; Jude 24, 25.   ʳ Col. 1 : 22; 1 Thess. 5 : 23; 2 Peter 3 : 14.
ˢ 10 : 13; 2 Thess. 3 : 3; Heb. 10 : 23.   ᵗ John 15 : 1-9; Gal. 2 : 20; Phil. 3 : 10; 1 Peter 4 : 13; 1 John 1 : 3.
ᵘ Rom. 12 : 16; 2 Cor. 13 : 11.

1 Peter 1 : 7; Titus 2 : 13; 2 Tim. 4 : 8). The early Christians were looking for the speedy return of their Lord (1 Thess. 4 : 13-18; Phil. 3 : 20, etc.).

8. In this and the verse following Paul expresses his confidence in their continued steadfastness and final salvation. **Who** *will* **also confirm you unto the end.** As Christ in his doctrines and life was deeply and firmly grounded in their convictions, so would he also deeply fix and establish them unto the end. Many make *who* refer to God (ver. 4), but that is too remote; it naturally refers to **Christ,** who fills the thoughts of Paul. In the first nine verses he repeats the name of Christ nine times. It is entirely unnecessary to refer it to God, "either on account of *the Lord Jesus Christ* at the end of this verse, or of *God is faithful* immediately following; for what is here asserted of God, the calling into *the fellowship of Jesus Christ,* is at the same time a calling to being confirmed through Christ, which can take place only in the fellowship of Christ" (WINER, "N. T. Grammar"). **Unto the end**—not merely to the end of life, but of this dispensation, unto the second coming of Christ. **Blameless,** *unaccused,* free from reproach and sanctified unto holiness, **in the day of our Lord Jesus Christ,** when he shall come to judgment (Col. 1 : 28; Matt. 25 : 31 ff.).

9. The ground of this confidence respecting the saints at Corinth—the faithfulness of God. **God is faithful** in performing all that the calling of his people includes (10 : 13; 1 Thess. 5 : 24; 2 Thess. 3 : 3). **By whom ye were called;** implying promises and blessing of grace and salvation. **Unto,** rather, *into,* **the fellowship,** or *participation.* This word is variously rendered *communion* (10 : 16), *fellowship* (Gal. 2 : 9), *distribution* (2 Cor. 9 : 13). Its usual meaning appears to be a *sharing together, a joint participation* of anything. See on Rom. 15 : 26. It here refers to fellowship or participation in the blessings and dignity of **Christ** as the **Son** of God, joint-heirs with Christ (Rom. 8 : 17), no longer servants, but sons of God (Gal. 4 : 7), to be glorified with him (Rom. 8 : 21, 30; 2 Thess. 2 : 14; 2 Tim. 2 : 12; 1 John 3 : 2).

1 : 10-4 : 21. PAUL NOTICES THE PARTY SPIRIT AND DIVISIONS IN THE CORINTHIAN CHURCH; defends his method of teaching and the gospel he preached, and makes a pointed and affectionate application.

10-12. ENTREATS THEM TO LAY ASIDE ALL DIVISIONS. EXHORTS THEM TO UNITY.

10. Now, rather, *But,* in contrast to the things he had just commended, **I beseech you, brethren**—earnestness and tenderness united—**by the name of our Lord Jesus Christ,** by all that great and holy name implies, their Lord and Master and his, in whom they were one, and from whom came love and peace. Notice how emphatic he had made this name by frequent repetition—the tenth time since he began this Epistle. **That ye all speak the same thing**—that you agree in your utterances, for you are speaking different things (ver. 12), **and that there be no divisions,** or *schisms,* literally *rents,* internal *dissensions,* arising from party spirit **among you. But that ye be perfectly joined together—**

that ye be perfectly joined together in the same mind and in the same 11 judgment. For it hath been declared unto me of you, my brethren, by them *which are of the house* of Chloe, that 12 there are contentions among you. Now this I say, *that every one of you saith, I am of Paul; and I of ʷ Apollos; and I of ˣ Cephas; and I of Christ. 13 Is Christ divided? Was Paul crucified for you? Or were ye baptized in

but that ye be made complete in the same mind, and in the same judg- 11 ment. For it has been made manifest to me concerning you, my brethren, by those of the house of Chloe, that 12 there are contentions among you. And I mean this, that each of you says, I am of Paul, and I of Apollos, and I of 13 Cephas, and I of Christ. Is Christ divided? Was Paul crucified for you? Or were ye baptized into the name of

v 3 : 4-6 ; 4 : 6.   *w* Acts 18 : 24 ; 19 : 1.   *x* John 1 : 42.

fitted together, like that which had been broken or rent, and thus *made complete* **in the same mind**, perfectly united *in feelings* (Rom. 15 : 5), **and in the same judgment**, in *opinions* (7 : 40). He would have them free from all party feelings and purposes and party strifes.

11. Reason of the preceding exhortation. **For it hath been declared**, or, *it was made known to me*, on a recent occasion. Again he uses the endearing appellation, **my brethren.** Paul rises above kindred, race, or nation. Whoever had a spiritual, personal interest in Christ, be he Jew or Gentile, he was his brother (Mark 3 : 33-35). **Of the house of Chloe**; whether servants, children, or other kindred, we are not told. Chloe must have been a woman well known in Corinth, but whether a resident of Corinth or of Ephesus is unknown. **That there are contentions**—*strifes, wranglings*—**among you,** bringing into view the evil character and marked manifestations of the divisions among them (ver. 10).

12. Now this I say, what I mean is this, **that every one,** or *each one of you is saying*. Party spirit, like a contagion, was infecting the whole church. **Saith,** boastingly, **I am of Paul,** he is my leader. The parties are named historically as they arose in the church. Paul was the *planter* of the church. Apollos came later and *watered* (1 Cor. 3 : 6). The followers of Paul would represent the *faith* party, holding to Paul's teachings and opposing Judaizing tendencies in the church, **I of Apollos,** doubtless representing doctrines closely allied to those of Paul, with a rhetorical molding and tinged with Alexandrine philosophy. The frequent allusions to human learning and wisdom in this and the next chapters agree well with the party of

the learned Apollos. Some regard Apollos as the author of the Epistle to the Hebrews. See Acts 18 : 24-28 and notes. Apollos was an Alexandrine Jew, learned, eloquent, mighty in the Scriptures, and instructed more fully by Aquila and Priscilla, and on terms of friendship with Paul (16 : 12 and note; Titus 3 : 13). **I of Cephas,** Aramean for *Peter* (John 1 : 42). This probably represented the Judaizing and Pharisaic party which opposed Paul and questioned Paul's authority as an apostle. Peter had not been at Corinth, but they preferred him as the apostle of the circumcision (9 : 5; Gal. 2 : 7). **I of Christ.** Representing those who disclaimed human leaders and professed to follow the sayings and teachings of Christ, but interpreting them to suit themselves (2 Cor. 10 : 7). They very likely claimed large liberty, perhaps included those of Sadducean tendencies, who questioned a future bodily resurrection and held to a rationalized Christianity. They appear to be referred to as bitter opponents of the apostle in 2 Cor. 10 : 7 ; 11 : 13, 23, and as claiming for themselves certain apostolic authority. Their leaders, at least, appear to have been Jews, who probably had seen the Lord in the flesh (9 : 1; 2 Cor. 11 : 22-25).

13-17. PAUL SHOWS THE ABSURDITY OF SUCH DIVISIONS AND DISCLAIMS THE LEADERSHIP OF THE CHRISTIAN SYSTEM.

13. Is Christ divided? Some translate, *Christ is divided*. The interrogative form is to be preferred. But either **way the** thought is monstrous and absurd. Is Christ divided, into whom the whole church has been baptized (Gal. 3 : 27), and whose body the church is (Eph. 1 : 23)? **Was Paul crucified for you?** Did he suffer for you and become your Redeemer,

14 the name of Paul? I thank God that I baptized none of you, but *y* Crispus
15 and *z* Gaius; lest any should say that
16 I had baptized in mine own name. And I baptized also the household of *a* Stephanas: besides I know not whether I baptized any other.

Paul's manner of preaching defended.

17 For Christ sent me not to baptize, but to preach the gospel: *b* not with wisdom of words, lest the cross of Christ should be made of none effect.

14 Paul? I give thanks that I baptized no one of you, but Crispus and Gaius;
15 lest any one should say that ye were
16 baptized into my name. And I baptized also the household of Stephanas; besides, I know not whether I baptized
17 any other. For Christ did not send me to baptize, but to preach the gospel; not in wisdom of speech, lest the cross of Christ should be made of no effect.

y Acts 18 : 8.   *z* Rom. 16 : 23 ; 3 John : 1.   *a* 16 : 15, 17.   *b* 2 : 1, 4, 13 ; 2 Cor. 10 : 10.

your Saviour? **Or were you baptized in the name**, rather, *into*, or *unto, the* **name of Paul?** Into the recognition and profession of the name of Paul as one of dignity and divine authority? Were ye thus baptized into union with and dependence on him? Surely not! Such questions would receive nothing but a negative answer. Paul wisely begins with himself and with those who would use his name in an improper way.

14. Under these circumstances, and as results have turned out, **I thank God,** or according to some of the oldest manuscripts, *I give thanks that* **I baptized none of you but Crispus,** the ruler of the synagogue (Acts 18 : 8), **and Gaius,** "mine host and of the whole church" (Rom. 16 : 23, on which see note). These Paul seems to have baptized from special reasons of friendship. The rite was performed at Corinth at first doubtless by Silas and Timothy, Paul's attendants (Acts 18 : 5).

15. **Lest any of my opposers should say that I had baptized,** rather, according to the best critical authorities, *that ye were baptized into my name.* Paul anticipates any slanders that might arise and removes them. He had in no sense gathered a party.

16. While writing, Paul recalls that he had also baptized **the household of Stephanas**, perhaps reminded of it by his presence. He is mentioned in 16 : 15, 17, and his house is spoken of as "the firstfruits of Achaia and that they have addicted themselves to the ministry of the saints," implying that they were adults, or at least that there were no infants among them. The *household* consisted of inmates of the family, children and servants, and in this case Stephanas himself is included. Paul guards his statement against any possible error by adding, **I know not whether I baptized any other.** The baptism of believing households is not unusual among Baptists and in missionary fields.

17. Paul explains why he did not baptize. This verse forms a transition to what follows. **For Christ sent me not to baptize,** when he commissioned me as an apostle (Acts 26 : 16-18). This was not his special work. He does not undervalue baptism, but as Jesus baptized not, but his disciples (John 4 : 2), so Peter and Paul, and probably the other apostles, left baptism to their assistants, unless there were special reasons why they should administer the ordinance (Acts 10 : 48), **But to preach the gospel;** which was his great work as an apostle and a missionary, to announce the glad tidings, to evangelize. To lead men to Christ was the first and most important thing, and prepare them for baptism. When churches were formed, the elders or pastors, the officers or even members of the local church, could attend to baptizing. **Not with,** rather, *in*, **wisdom of words**—*of speech* (ver. 5), or *discourse* such as teachers give. Not merely the eloquent expression, nor the rhetorical form, but the subject-matter of the discourse is especially meant, the philosophic speculations. Paul used great plainness and simplicity of speech (2 Cor. 3 : 12), and doubtless differed from Apollos in this respect (3 : 4). This his opposers used to his disadvantage (2 Cor. 10 : 10). **Lest the cross of Christ,** the doctrine of the crucified Christ, of an atoning Saviour, **should be made of none effect,** should be lost sight of and deprived of its effect through such an array of wis-

194　I. CORINTHIANS　[Ch. I.

18 For ᵉ the preaching of the cross is to them that perish ᵈ foolishness; but unto us ᵉ which are saved it is the ᶠ power of God.
19 For it is written, ᵍ I will destroy the wisdom of the wise, and will bring to nothing the understanding of the pru-
20 dent. Where is the wise? where is the scribe? where is the disputer of this world? ʰ Hath not God made fool-
21 ish the wisdom of this world? ⁱ For after that in the wisdom of God the world by wisdom knew not God, it

18 For the word of the cross is to those who are perishing, foolishness; but to us who are being saved, it is the
19 power of God. For it is written,
    I will destroy the wisdom of the wise,
    And will reject the discernment of the discerning.
20 Where is the wise? Where is the scribe? Where is the disputer of this age? Did not God make foolish the
21 wisdom of the world? For since, in the wisdom of God, the world through its wisdom knew not God, God was

c 2 : 2 ; Gal. 6 : 12-14.　d Ver. 21, 23 ; 2 : 14 ; Acts 17 : 18.　e 15 : 2.　f Ver. 24 ; Rom. 1 : 16.
g 3 : 19-21 ; Job 5 : 12, 13.　h 2 Sam. 17 : 14 ; Job 12 : 17, 20, 24 ; Rom. 1 : 22.
i Luke 10 : 21 ; Rom. 1 : 20-22, 28.

dom and speculation. Paul presents Christ as the Head over all, and himself but under him, commissioned to preach the doctrine of the cross. Christ, not he, Paul, was the center of the Christian system.

Paul's reference to the cross of Christ leads him to dwell upon the subject and the method of his preaching from this point to the end of the next chapter.

18-25. THE PREACHING OF THE CROSS ABASING TO HUMAN PRIDE, BUT THE POWER AND WISDOM OF GOD TO THE HUMBLE AND BELIEVING. THE SIMPLICITY OF THE GOSPEL. HUMAN AND DIVINE WISDOM.

18. For, to explain what has just been stated, **the preaching,** literally, *the word*, the discourse or doctrine of the cross (see on ver. 17), **is indeed to them that perish,** better, *that are perishing*, **foolishness;** it appears as folly to them who are guided by human wisdom, and through unbelief are on the way to perdition. **But unto us which**—*who*—**are saved**, better, *are being saved*, who, through faith in the crucified and risen Christ, are in the way of salvation, **it is the power of God,** the manifestation of God's power, perceived by the understanding and felt and experienced in the soul. Compare note on Rom. 1 : 16. Notice the idea of salvation is here presented as still going on. The representation is common to the apostle (Phil. 2 : 12 ; Rom. 13 : 11 ; 2 Tim. 3 : 15). So also the destruction of the sinner is represented as progressing and incomplete (2 Cor. 2 : 15 ; 4 : 3).

19. The thought just presented is confirmed by Scripture, quoted freely from the Septuagint version of Isa. 29 : 14. **For** that *the word*, the doctrine of the cross, is "the power of God" (ver. 18), and that it must not be preached in "the wisdom of words" (ver. 17), is evident also from what is **written, I will destroy the wisdom of the wise,** the worldly wise, regarded by themselves and by others as wise. **And will bring to nothing,** *will set aside*, or *reject*, **the understanding**—*the prudence*—**of the prudent**, those who have insight and are sagacious and discreet in worldly matters and among men. (Comp. Matt. 11 : 25 ; 15 : 8, 9.)

20. In confirmation Paul utters a triumphant appeal and challenge to facts as they exist. Repetition and the interrogative form gives vividness and rhetorical force. The preaching of the cross had, according to the Scripture quoted (ver. 19), brought to nought, as it were, all other wisdom. **Where is the wise?** in general, but especially applicable to Grecian philosophers. **The scribe?** regarded as wise among the Jews. **The disputer of this world?** the learned disputant of schools and sects of this present evil world (Gal. 1 : 4). **Hath not God,** rather, *Did not God make*, **foolish the wisdom of this,** rather, *the world?* when the doctrine of the cross and salvation thereby was proclaimed? Compare James, who contrasts earthly wisdom with that which comes from above (James 3 : 15-17).

21. The apostle proves and illustrates the statement that God made foolish the wisdom of this world. **For after that, etc.,** rather, *For since* **in the wisdom of God the world** *through*

pleased God by the foolishness of preaching to save them that believe. 22 For the Jews require a sign, and the 23 Greeks seek after wisdom: but we preach Christ crucified, unto the Jews a stumblingblock, and unto the Greeks 24 foolishness; but unto them which are called, both Jews and Greeks, Christ the power of God, and the wisdom 25 of God. Because the foolishness of God is wiser than men; and the weakness of God is stronger than men.

pleased through the foolishness of preaching to save those who believe; 22 since both Jews ask for signs, and 23 Greeks seek after wisdom, but we preach Christ crucified, to Jews a stumblingblock, and to Gentiles fool- 24 ishness, but to those who are the called, both Jews and Greeks, Christ the power 25 of God, and the wisdom of God. Because the foolishness of God is wiser than men; and the weakness of God is stronger than men.

j Matt. 12 : 38, 39 ; 16 : 1. *k* Acts 17 : 18–21. *l* See refs. Isa. 8 : 14, 15. and Matt. 11 : 6.
m Ver. 18.   *n* Prov. 8 : 1, 22–30 ; Col. 2 : 3.   *o* Ver. 27–29.

its **wisdom knew not God,** did not learn to know him. This may mean either, since in God's wisdom he permitted human wisdom to show its inability to attain a saving knowledge of him; or, since amid the display of God's wisdom, as exhibited in creation and the light of nature, human wisdom failed seemingly to recognize him. The former is the more natural, and the one naturally to suggest itself to the reader; the latter accords with Paul's teachings in Rom. 1 : 19, 20, and Acts 17 : 27. And this is still the practical result of mere human wisdom. But this teaching of Paul may be combined with the first view: God, in his wisdom and his wise arrangements, permitted men through their wisdom to exhibit their failure and inability thereby to gain a saving knowledge of him, from the works of creation and the light he had given them. Since this was the case **it pleased God,** in his mercy, **by,** rather, *through the* so-called **foolishness of** *the* **preaching,** the well-known preaching of the cross (ver. 18), **to save them that believe.** The doctrine of a crucified and risen Saviour seemed foolishness to human wisdom (Acts 17 : 32); it required no high intellectual gift, no learning, no special ability, but simple faith in Christ. It was humbling to human pride and contrary to the speculations and the philosophy of the worldly wise.

22. Paul still further shows how God made foolish the wisdom of the world (ver. 20). **For the Jews,** better, *And since Jews,* **require a sign,** rather, according to the best reading, the plural, *signs,* miracles, probably some portents from heaven (Matt. 12 : 38; 16 : 1), to substantiate the word preached, as of divine authority. **And Greeks,** representing the Gentiles (ver. 24), the nations not Jews (Rom. 1 : 16), **seek after wisdom,** not external, but internal evidence, subtle speculations and depths of philosophy. Both Jews and Greeks made false demands, but differing according to their standards of truth and wisdom.

23. But we, in contrast to Jews and Greeks, and to what they desire, **preach Christ crucified,** *to Jews a* **stumblingblock** (Isa. 8 : 14), an offense, a hindrance to belief. A Messiah who was crucified was so opposed to their idea of a temporal Messiah, that they stumbled over his doctrine and rejected him. **And unto the Greeks,** rather, according to best text, *to Gentiles,* **foolishness** — to those seeking the guidance of human wisdom and philosophy, salvation through faith in one crucified seemed an absurdity (Luke 23 : 36–40; Acts 26 : 24).

24. But, in opposition to both classes just named, **to them,** personally, *who* **are called** of God through his Spirit and word (ver. 2), **both Jews and Greeks,** the offers and blessings of the gospel know no distinction of race and nation, **Christ the power of God, and the wisdom of God,** as he is revealed to the soul, a Saviour from sin. They see salvation through a crucified Redeemer, such as only Divine wisdom could devise, and Divine power accomplish (Rom. 8 : 3, 4; Eph. 3 : 10–12).

25. A reason given to substantiate the statement just made. **Because the foolishness of God,** comparatively so, the least manifestation of his wisdom, **is wiser than men**—than their wisdom; **and the weakness of God,** the smallest manifestation of his power, **is stronger than men**—

26 For ye see your calling, brethren, how that ᵖ not many wise men after the flesh, ᑫ not many mighty, not many 27 noble, *are called*: but ʳ God hath chosen the foolish things of the world to confound the wise; and God hath chosen

26 For see your calling, brethren, that not many are wise after the flesh, not 27 many mighty, not many noble; but the foolish things of the world God chose that he might put to shame the

p Matt. 11 : 25; John 7 : 48.   *q* James 2 : 5.   *r* Ps. 8 : 2; Acts 4 : 13-21.

than their power. For God's wisdom, see Rom. 11 : 33; Ps. 139 : 6; Isa. 40 : 28; God's power, Exod. 8 : 19; Job 9 : 4-10; 26 : 14; Ps. 9 : 8, etc. Paul seems not to be here referring to the greatness or smallness of the wisdom and power exhibited in the doctrines of the cross, but rather stating a fact which all reasonable persons must admit. And if so, it confirms and explains how it is that what appears folly and weakness in the gospel's way of salvation is really God's power and wisdom, greater than any of man's devising. The common explanation, however, of the *foolishness* and *wisdom* of God, is to take them as so called and so regarded by men—as what seem to men to have these qualities. This agrees well with the context, but I prefer the former view, as agreeing better with what follows.

DANGERS FROM THE SCIENTIFIC SPIRIT. True science is "the handmaid of religion." Each has its sphere. The perversion of either may render them antagonistic. When rightly understood and rightly cultivated they must be helpful to each other. We live in a scientific age. Wonderful advancement has been made in the discovery and confirmation of truth, and thus religion owes a debt to science; but no less is science indebted to religion from the stimulus and guidance it has received therefrom.

Yet science has its dangers. With its laboratories filled and fostered with a spirit of discovery, and its lecture rooms resounding with discussions of new theories of life and novel methods of reform, there is danger of drifting from the safe mooring of revealed religious truth. Flushed with successful investigation and intoxicated, as it were, with the inquiring spirit of the age, there is danger of harboring contempt for the past and undervaluing truth because it is old. There is danger of being too credulous of speedy improvements, too hopeful of discovering new panaceas, too ready to endorse whatever is new. With too limited a view and too great intentness on one line of study, there is danger of one's contracting a narrow, censorious spirit, and of becoming a radical of the radicals, an unsafe leader, even in social, moral, or political reform. And bordering on scientific bigotry there is danger of descending into a mental and moral degeneracy, and of leading men from, rather than to God and the truth. The Bible and the gospel are necessary for the even balancing of truth. Science, sanctified by religion, is needful for investigating the vast domain of God.

26-31. THIS CHARACTERISTIC OF THE GOSPEL ILLUSTRATED IN THE CORINTHIAN CONVERTS. The whole section (ver. 17-25), as well as ver. 25, finds an illustration and confirmation in these verses.

26. For ye see, rather an imperative appeal, *For see,* **your calling** of God (ver. 2, 24), **brethren, how that not many** *are* **wise after the flesh,** noted for human wisdom in distinction from the Divine wisdom in the Christian, which proceeds from the Holy Spirit. **Not many mighty,** of the world, such as statesmen and warriors, those powerful in authority. **Not many noble,** in rank, of distinguished descent. Corinth was noted for its nobility, its high-born families. "The majority of the first Christians were slaves and illiterate men, and the whole history of the growth of the church is substantially a progressive triumph of the unlearned over the learned, the lowly over the great, until the emperor himself laid his crown at the foot of the cross" (OLSHAUSEN).

27. Turning from the negative to the positive side, the apostle pushes his illustration to its utmost limit. **But God hath chosen,** or more exactly, *God chose,* **the foolish things of the world,** which were so accounted, **to confound,** better, *that he might put to shame,* **the wise** after the flesh (ver. 26),

the weak things of the world to confound the things which are mighty;
28 and base things of the world, and things which are despised, hath God chosen, yea, and things which are not, *to bring to nought things that are:
29 ᵗthat no flesh should glory in his presence.
30 But of him are ye ᵘin Christ Jesus, who of God is made unto us ᵛwisdom, and ˣrighteousness, and
31 ʸsanctification, and ᶻredemption: that, according as it is written, ᵃHe that glorieth, let him glory in the Lord.

wise; and the weak things of the world God chose that he might put to
28 shame the things which are strong; and the base things of the world, and the things which are despised, God chose, and the things which are not, that he might bring to nought things that are;
29 that no flesh should glory before God.
30 But of him are ye in Christ Jesus, who from God was made wisdom to us, both righteousness and sanctification,
31 and redemption; that, as it is written, He that glories, let him glory in the Lord.

*Ps. 37 : 35, 36; Isa. 2 : 11.   *t* Jer. 9 : 23; Rom. 3 : 27.   *u* Rom. 8 : 1.
w Isa. 11 : 2; Eph. 1 : 17, 18; Col. 2 : 2, 3.   *x* Isa. 45 : 24, 25; Rom. 4 : 25; 2 Cor. 5 : 21; Phil. 3 : 9.
y John 17 : 19; Acts 26 : 18; Eph. 5 : 26.   *z* 15 : 54-57; Rev. 5 : 9.   *a* 2 Cor. 10 : 17.

by accomplishing that which they notably failed to accomplish. They were thus disgraced, as it were, and put to shame. And to the same effect, **And . . . the weak things of the world,** *that he might put to shame* **the mighty,** or *the strong* of the world (ver. 26). To human eyes God chose the feeblest instrumentalities. See 6 : 9-11 for the character of some of the Corinthians before conversion.

28. And base things, of base birth or origin, those who among men are held of no account (James 2 : 5), **and things which are despised,** despicable in the world's estimation, *did God choose,* **and things that are not,** which are as good, comparatively, as nothing, **to bring to nought things that are—**regarded of great account among men. *And*, before *things which are not,* is omitted by some authorities, making only two instead of three classes in this verse. It seems, however, better to retain it, as above.

29. The reason for God's thus calling men. **That no flesh,** no man (Acts 2 : 17), **should glory in his presence;** according to the best manuscripts, *before God.* All ground of boasting or of self-glorification is taken away. "We may glory not *before* him but *in* him" (BENGEL). The Corinthian brethren might well infer that they must not glory in party leaders.

30. The ground and source of true wisdom and all excellence. Not of the world, with its wisdom and power, **but of him,** the source of your spiritual life (Rom. 11 : 36), **are ye in Christ Jesus,** in union with him, **who** *from* **God—**Christ is the gift of God to men (John 3 : 16)—*was* **made,** or *became*, **un-**

to us wisdom. "*From* the Father, *through* the Son, believers have their existence, not merely as regards their creation, but especially as regards their new creation, of whose several stages Christ is the essential representative" (OLSHAUSEN). Both by what Christ produces in us by the Spirit, and by his doctrine, life, death, and resurrection, he became *wisdom,* not by human research, *righteousness,* not by works of the law, *sanctification* or *holiness,* not by human merit and a legal morality, and *redemption,* not by paying the ransom ourselves. Some regard these terms as co-ordinate, as in our Common version. Others regard *wisdom* as the leading term and the other terms subordinate and explanatory. The latter is favored by the more exact translation, *was made unto us wisdom, both righteousness and sanctification and redemption;* and by the stress Paul lays upon wisdom throughout the chapter. According to this view these are the things in which Christ becomes to us *wisdom,* displaying infinite superiority over all human wisdom. *Both* **righteousness and sanctification—**closely united, as if designating two sides of the same work. *Righteousness,* the result of our being regenerated and justified through faith (Rom. 1 : 17; 3 : 21-24). *Sanctification,* in union with whom we grow in holiness—the new life grows on to perfection (Rom. 6 : 6-8). *Redemption,* Christ having paid the price of our deliverance from the captivity of sin. The term here appears to embrace the final and entire deliverance of the body, as well as the soul from all the consequences of sin (Rom. 8 : 23).

31. And this is in accordance with,

and in fulfillment of Scripture. As it is written, quoting freely from Jer. 9 : 23, 24, He that glorieth, let him glory in the Lord, not in himself, nor in any human leader, however illustrious. The whole work of salvation is of God, and the Corinthians are thus shown that their party spirit is opposed to the gospel.

PRACTICAL REMARKS.

1. Christians are called both into Christ's kingdom and to Christ's work (ver. 1, 2; 9 : 16; Rom. 12 : 6-8; John 17 : 18).

2. A New Testament church is composed of converted people who have been baptized upon a profession of their faith in Christ (ver. 2, 13-16; Acts 2 : 41; 10 : 47, 48).

3. True Christians everywhere have a spiritual union with Christ, and through him with one another (ver. 2, 3; John 17 : 21-23).

4. Both the Father and the Son are sources of peace and grace; but only through the Son are they manifested to men (ver. 3, 4; Col. 1 : 19; 2 : 9, 10).

5. Commend all you can first, and rebuke afterward (ver. 5-10; Rev. 2 : 2, 3, 13, 14).

6. If we must reprove, we should do it in a spirit that is glad to concede all that can be rightly demanded, and to commend all that is deserved (ver. 4-7; 2 Tim. 4 : 2).

7. A submissive waiting for, an earnest desire for, and a confident expectation of, our Lord's return is an evidence of true piety (ver. 7; Titus 2 : 13; 2 Peter 3 : 12; Heb. 9 : 28).

8. It is God's design to keep his people in the path of holiness unto the end (ver. 8, 9; 1 Thess. 4 : 3; Rom. 8 : 29).

9. Christians participate with Christ in spirit and heirship, in suffering and in glory (ver. 9; Rom. 8 : 9; 1 Peter 4 : 13; Rev. 3 : 21).

10. Christian unity can be truly realized only by oneness in Christ, in his Spirit and in the truth (ver. 10; John 17 : 19-22; Eph. 4 : 4, 5).

11. Discord and divisions in churches mar their moral beauty and weaken their efficiency (ver. 11-13; 3 : 3, 4).

12. Many who cause divisions exalt human leaders above Christ, or exalt Christ for selfish ends (ver. 12; Rev. 2, 9, 14, 20).

13. Many are devoted to the preacher rather than to Christ, and join the pastor rather than the church (ver. 12, 13; Rom. 1 : 25).

14. The true gospel minister shrinks from taking away the least glory from Christ (ver. 13-15; Gal. 6 : 14).

15. Baptism is so important that it is implied that all the Corinthian believers had been baptized (ver. 13-16).

16. Yet the reception of Christ by faith is more important than baptism, and preaching the gospel than baptizing (ver. 14-17).

17. Baptism is to be usually performed by the pastor and officers of the local church (ver. 14-17).

18. The object of gospel preaching is not to teach philosophy or to display learning, but to present Christ in his character and work for the salvation of men (ver. 17-20; 2 : 1, 5).

19. The humbling doctrines of the gospel are distasteful to the wise men of the world, and their power is such as to confound and perplex them (ver. 18, 19; Mark 10 : 15; Acts 8 : 13).

20. The plan of salvation is not what human wisdom would have devised. It is evidently not of man (ver. 18-21; John 1 : 11, 17; 3 : 11, 12).

21. In every age it has been true that the world through its wisdom failed to know God. Conceited human wisdom leads away from, rather than to God (ver. 21; 3 : 19; Gen. 6 : 5; 11 : 4; Rom. 1 : 22, 23).

22. We are to preach not what men desire, but what they need (ver. 24; Acts 20 : 20, 21).

23. A morbid desire for miracles and a conceit of wisdom both unfit men for the reception of the gospel (ver. 22, 23; Matt. 16 : 1; Acts 17 : 18).

24. The preaching of the cross can secure what no other teaching or preaching can secure—the conversion and salvation of men (ver. 21; John 3 : 14, 15; 1 Peter 1 : 23).

25. How great the power and wisdom of God, if his feeblest efforts surpass the wisest and mightiest efforts of men (ver. 25; Isa. 55 : 8, 9).

2 AND I, brethren, when I came to you, ᵇcame not with excellency of speech or of wisdom, declaring unto
2 you ᶜthe testimony of God. For I determined not to know any thing among yon, ᵈsave Jesus Christ, and him crucified. And ᵉI was with you ᶠin weakness, and in fear, and in much trem-

2 AND I, when I came to you, brethren, came not according to excellency of word or of wisdom, proclaiming to
2 you the testimony of God. For I determined not to know anything among you, but Jesus Christ, and him crucified. And I was with you in weakness and in fear and in much trem-

ᵇ 1 : 17 ; 2 Cor. 10 : 10.   ᶜ 1 : 6 ; Acts 20 : 20-27.   ᵈ Gal. 6 : 14 ; Phil. 3 : 8-10.   ᵉ Acts 18 : 1, 6-17.
ᶠ 2 Cor. 4 : 7 ; 10 : 1, 10 ; Gal. 4 : 13.

26. The great mass of true believers may ever be found among the humble in life (ver. 26-28; Matt. 11 : 5 ; Luke 4 : 18).

27. Men of rank and wealth are surrounded with peculiar temptations, which too generally keep them from accepting the gospel (ver. 26-28; Mark 10 : 24; 1 Tim. 6 : 9).

28. God shames the pride of men by choosing the weak and the lowly (ver. 26-29 ; James 2 : 5).

29. All men are on a level before God; all must become willing to give the entire glory of salvation to him (ver. 29; Rom. 10 : 4, 12, 13 ; Luke 18 : 14 ; Phil. 2 : 10, 11).

30. Christ is to the believer the source of Divine wisdom, of perfect righteousness, of true holiness, and of complete deliverance from all the effects of sin (ver. 30; Col. 2 : 3 ; Rom. 3 : 25, 26 ; Eph. 4 : 20-23 ; Col. 2 : 10).

31. A disposition to humble ourselves and exalt God is an evidence of true piety (ver. 31 ; Ps. 115 : 1).

CHAPTER II.

Paul describes how he had preached Christ only in great simplicity (ver. 1-5) ; yet the gospel contained the truest wisdom (ver. 6-9) ; was revealed by the Spirit (ver. 10-13) ; and must be spiritually discerned and received (ver. 14-16).

1-5. PAUL PREACHED NOT HIMSELF BUT CHRIST CRUCIFIED. He did not use words of worldly wisdom.

1. In view of what he had already said in the preceding chapter, Paul proceeds to justify his manner of preaching. **And I,** emphatic, returning to what he had said in 1 : 17, 23, with a view of showing that he had acted accordingly. **Not with excellency of speech,** the distinguished eloquence of the orator; **or of wisdom,** of the philosopher. **Declaring,** or announ- cing at once upon his coming. Note the three words for preaching, *bearing glad tidings* (1 : 17), *heralding,* publicly proclaiming (1 : 23), and here *announcing* the message. **The testimony of God,** concerning God, regarding Christ as God's gift for the sins of the world, for the salvation of men. (Comp. 1 : 6; 15 : 15.) The testimony of God and of Christ agree, and are substantially the same (John 3 : 34; 8 : 18). Some of the oldest manuscripts have *mystery,* the secret counsel of God, instead of *testimony.* Internal evidence favors the latter. It seems quite probable that the former crept in as a marginal gloss from ver. 7.

2. And this conduct was the result of a settled purpose. **For I determined not to know anything,** the sum and substance of my knowledge, **among you,** banishing everything else from my thoughts and teaching, **save Jesus Christ,** in his person and life, the risen and ascended Christ, the living Christ, **and him crucified,** as the one who was crucified, having suffered this shameful death for our sins. Thus he began by preaching the simple doctrine of salvation through the dying yet living Christ. Notice that he does not say to know *about* Christ, but *to know Jesus Christ,* the Saviour Messiah. Christ filled his consciousness, in living union with his soul, and he held up Christ as a living, glorious reality.

3. In the preceding verse Paul describes his theme, in this verse his preacher, and in the next his preaching. **And I,** emphatic. His theme had been the humbling doctrine of the cross and he, the preacher, also conscious of his own weakness. **In weakness, in fear and in much trembling.** He had no self-confidence, but rather a sense of insufficiency and unworthiness for so great a work, and self-mistrust and anxiety

4 bling. And my speech and my preaching *was* not with enticing words of man's wisdom, ᵇ but in demonstration
5 of the Spirit and of power: that your faith should not stand in the wisdom of men, but ʲ in the power of God.
6 Howbeit we speak wisdom among them that are ᵏ perfect: yet not ˡ the wisdom of this world, nor of the princes of this world, ᵐ that come to
7 nought: but we speak the wisdom of

4 bling. And my word and my preaching was not in persuasive words of wisdom, but in demonstration of the
5 Spirit and of power; that your faith might not be in the wisdom of men, but in the power of God.
6 But we speak wisdom among the perfect; yet a wisdom not of this age, nor of the rulers of this age, who are
7 coming to naught. But we speak

g 1 : 17; 2 Peter 1 : 16.   *h* Zech. 4 : 6; Rom. 15 : 19; 1 Thess. 1 : 5.   *i* 2 Cor. 4 : 7; 6 : 7.
k See refs. Matt. 5 : 48; Eph. 4 : 13; Phil. 3 : 15; Heb. 5 : 14; 6 : 12.   *l* 1 : 18-20; 3 : 19; 2 Cor.1 : 12.
m 1 : 28.

(2 Cor. 2 : 16). And the Lord encouraged him in a night vision (Acts 18 : 9, 10). Doubtless his bodily infirmity, to which he often alludes, contributed to his sense of weakness (Gal. 4 : 13; 2 Cor. 12 : 7; 11 : 30). **I was with you** at my coming (ver. 1), and continued to be with you (ver. 4) in this conscious state of weakness.

4. And also **my speech,** my conversation in private **and my preaching** in public **was not in enticing words,** *persuasive* arguments of wisdom, such as philosophers and the learned of the world were accustomed to use. **Man's** should be omitted, according to the highest authorities. It was in **demonstration,** the evidencing manifestation of the Holy **Spirit** and divine **power.** The word translated *demonstration* occurs only here in the New Testament and means *a showing faith,* and then *a proof.* It seems to refer here to the evidence or proof which the Spirit produced, working in and through the apostle upon the hearts of his hearers, showing that it was God's own truth (1 Thess. 1 : 5), and convicting of sin (1 John 3 : 5-8; Titus 3 : 5), and becoming the power of God unto salvation (Rom. 1 : 16; John 15 : 3; James 1 : 18; 1 Peter 1 : 23).

5. The result and Divine purpose of this. **That your faith** in Christ and in his gospel *might not* **stand,** *be based,* **in the wisdom,** the philosophy and reasonings, **of men, but in the power of God** accompanying the word preached. (See on 1 : 24.)

6-16. THE GOSPEL CONTAINS THE TRUE WISDOM, REVEALED BY THE SPIRIT, AND ONLY SPIRITUALLY DISCERNED.

6. Howbeit—but though we speak thus depreciatingly of worldly wisdom, we, as preachers of the gospel, do **speak wisdom among them that are perfect,** *full-grown, matured,* in contrast to *babes* in 3 : 1. The word *perfect* does not here mean absolute perfection; it is applied to mature Christians, to those who are *adults* in the Christian life (14 : 20; Eph. 4 : 13; Heb. 5 : 14). The apostle also meets the objection that might arise that he ignored all wisdom. God certainly had given man the faculties for receiving wisdom; and the Old Testament, especially Proverbs, chapters 8 and 9, had spoken of wisdom. He explains himself; he speaks wisdom, *but not a* **wisdom of this world,** such as argumentation, earthly reasoning, and disputations; **nor of the princes of this world,** the mighty and noble (1 : 26), especially *rulers* of the world (Acts 4 : 27; see on ver. 8); but of a higher order, of a nobler kind. **That come to nought** —*who are coming to nothing* (1 : 28), as to their plans, wisdom, pomp, and splendor (Isa. 14).

7. What this wisdom is. Notice that the apostle uses the words *declaring* (ver. 1) and *preaching* (ver. 4), referring to his early public proclamation of the gospel at Corinth; but here and in ver. 6 and 13 he uses the work **speak**—*to speak one's mind, disclose*—referring probably to later and more private instruction. "The primary meaning of the work **to speak**—*to utter one's self* —enables us easily to understand its very frequent use in the sacred writers to denote the utterances by which God indicates or gives proof of his mind and will, whether immediately or through the instrumentality of his messengers and heralds" (THAYER'S N. T. Lex.). **But we speak,** or *disclose,* **the wisdom of God,** or *God's wis*

God in a mystery, *even* the hidden *wisdom*, ⁿ which God ordained before the
8 world unto our glory: ᵒ which none of
the princes of this world knew: for
ᵖ had they known *it*, they would not
9 have crucified the Lord of glory. But
as it is written, Eye hath not seen,
nor ear heard, neither have entered
into the heart of man, the things
which God hath prepared for them
10 that love him. But ᑫGod hath revealed *them* unto us ʳ by his Spirit: for

God's wisdom in a mystery, the hidden
wisdom which God predestined be-
8 fore the ages to our glory; which no
one of the rulers of this age knows;
for had they known it, they would not
9 have crucified the Lord of glory; but
(as it is written),
Things which eye saw not, and ear
heard not,
And that entered not into man's
heart,
Whatsoever things God prepared for
those who love him;
10 but to us God revealed them through

ⁿ See refs. Rom. 16 : 25, 26.   ᵒ Matt. 11 : 25; Acts 13 : 27.   ᵖ Acts 3 : 17.
ᑫ Matt. 11 : 25–27; 13 : 11; 16 : 17; Eph. 3 : 5.   ʳ See refs. John 14 : 26.

---

dom (*God* is emphatic), **in,** or *as*, **a
mystery, even the hidden wisdom which God ordained,** or *foreordained*, **before the world unto,**
or *for*, **our glory.** *Mystery* is something *hidden* or *secret*, and among the
Greeks was used to denote those rites
which were confided only to the initiated, and were kept secret from the
outside world. It here means God's
secret purpose in providing salvation
for man, which was once *hidden*, but
now *revealed* (4 : 1; Eph. 3 : 3–5; Rom. 16 : 25;
Col. 1 : 26). It was *hidden* from angels
as well as from men (1 Peter 1 : 12). This
plan of redemption was in God's mind
before the world, or *the ages*, from
eternity (Acts 2 : 23; Eph. 3 : 9; Rev. 13 : 8).
And all this *for* **our glory,** the spiritual splendor of his people, in contrast
to the rulers of this world, who will be
brought to nothingness (ver. 6).

8. Which, wisdom, **none,** better,
no one, **of the princes,** or *rulers*, **of
this world knew,** or *has known*.
The Jewish leaders, Herod and Pontius
Pilate, were the representatives of this
world's rulers (Acts 4 : 26, 27). And their
ignorance is evident, **for had they
known it they would not have
crucified the Lord of glory** (Acts
3 : 17; Luke 23 : 34), who is the beginning
and end of this divine wisdom. Notice
the striking contrast between the shameful death upon the cross and *the Lord*,
the possessor and giver (James 2 : 1).
There seems to be an allusion to *our
glory* (ver. 7), and the epithet may be
translated *the Lord of that glory* of
which he is the embodiment and source
(John 17 : 1–5, 22).

9. This is closely connected with
what precedes, and should be only separated from ver. 8 by a semicolon. It
may be translated: *but* (*as it is written*)
*things which eye saw not and ear heard
not, and which entered not into the
heart of man, namely, the things which
God prepared for them that love him.*
There has been much discussion whence
these words are taken. They appear to
be a free quotation from Isa. 64 : 4,
combining with it truth taught in other
portions of the Old Testament. Some
would refer to such passages as Isa.
52 : 15; 65 : 16, 17. Or we may regard
the apostle as expanding and explaining the first three clauses by the last
clause. This wisdom consisted not
only of things unseen and unheard,
but also inconceivable, the things, he
adds, which God prepared for them
that love him. This does not refer to
the future happiness of the redeemed,
but to the wisdom which was revealed
by the Spirit and taught by the apostles (ver. 10). In Heb. 6 : 1, 2, we have
named the elements of the doctrines of
Christ, such as faith toward God, etc.
(Comp. Heb. 5 : 12.) Beyond the simple
and fundamental truths which would
be first preached to men were the deep
things of God (ver. 10), the great doctrines which Paul discusses in his
Epistles to the Romans, Galatians,
Philippians, Ephesians, **and** Colossians (Rom. 3 : 21–26; 11 : 33–36; Phil. 2 : 5–12, etc.).

10. In this and the two following
verses Paul speaks of the revelation of
this wisdom. **But God hath revealed**—*removed the veil, disclosed*,
that which was before unknown.
Them, the things spoken of in ver.
9; **unto us,** Paul and his fellow-apostles and teachers (ver. 6, 12, 13). **By,**

the Spirit searcheth all things, yea,
11 the deep things of God. For what
man knoweth the things of a man,
save the spirit of man which is in
him? even so the things of God
knoweth no man, but the Spirit of
God.
12 Now we have received, not the spirit
of the world, but *the spirit which is
of God; ʸthat we might know the
things that are ᶻfreely given to us of
13 God. ᵃWhich things also we speak,
not in the words which man's wisdom
teacheth, but which the Holy Ghost
teacheth; comparing spiritual things

the Spirit, for the Spirit searches all
11 things, even the depths of God. For
who among men knows the things of
the man, but the spirit of the man,
which is in him? So also the things of
God no one knows, but the Spirit of
12 God. And we received, not the spirit
of the world, but the spirit which is
from God; that we might know the
things that were freely given to us by
13 God. Which things also we speak, not
in words taught by human wisdom,
but in those taught by the Spirit;
combining spiritual things with spiritual.

ₛ See refs. 1 Chron. 28 : 9. ₜ Prov. 14 : 10; 20 : 27. ᵤ Rom. 11 : 33, 34. ᵥ Rom. 8 : 15, 16.
ᵧ John 16 : 14, 15; 1 John 2 : 20, 27. ᵤ Rom. 3 : 24; 8 : 32. ₐ See refs. ver. 4.

through, **his**, rather, *the*, **Spirit, the**
preferable text. The reason and proof
of this given as far as ver. 12. For
the Spirit searcheth, *examining into,* implying accurate knowledge (Rom. 8 : 27; Rev. 2 : 23), **all things, yea the
deep things,** or, *even the depths* **of**
God, his being, attributes, his counsels, and infinite fullness (Rom. 11 : 33).
Notice that the Holy Spirit is spoken
of in this and the next verse as distinct
from God the **Father.**

11. The knowledge **of God** concerning himself is illustrated analogically
by man's knowledge concerning himself. Since man was made in the image of God, the analogy holds good,
though man being finite, the knowledge in God's case is infinitely more
complete. **For what man,** etc.,
rather, *For who among men knoweth
the things* **of a man,** his inner
self, his thoughts and plans, **save
the spirit of man which is in
him.** No stranger can search into the
depths of another's soul; only the man
himself can do this. **Even so the
things of God knoweth no** *one*
but the Spirit of God, who alone
stands in such a relation as to know
what is in the Divine mind (Job 11 : 7; Isa. 40 : 28). The only point which Paul
here brings out and illustrates is that
the Spirit of God alone can reveal
the things of God. Hence the analogy
should not be carried further. (Comp. Matt. 11 : 27; John 14 : 26; 16 : 13.)

12. Note the argument: And we
have the Spirit (this verse), and the
Spirit knoweth all things (ver. 10, 11),
therefore are these things revealed to
us (ver. 10). **Now we have received,**

rather, *and we received,* when we became disciples. **Not the spirit of
the world,** "the spirit that now
worketh in the children of disobedience" (Eph. 2 : 2), the god of this world
(2 Cor. 4 : 4; John 12 : 31; 8 : 44; see James 3 : 15).
**But the Spirit, the Holy Spirit,
which is of,** rather, *from* **God** (John 15 : 26). The design of this reception of
the Spirit was **that we might know
the things that are freely given
to us of,** rather, *by* **God.** These
gifts of his grace are the treasures of
wisdom and glory revealed in the gospel
(ver. 9. Comp. Rom. 8 : 24-26; Eph. 2 : 4-10).

13. Which things, freely given us
by **God** (ver. 12), *we also* **speak, not in
the words,** the arguments and rhetorical forms, *taught by human wisdom,
but in those taught by the Spirit.* **Holy**
is omitted by the best critical authorities. **Comparing spiritual things
with spiritual.** These words have
been variously explained. Some: *Comparing* spiritual things, just as in secular matters we compare secular with
secular. Others: *Interpreting* or *explaining* (the word is so used in the
Septuagint, Gen. 40 : 8, 16, 22; 41 : 12, 15; Dan. 5 : 12) spiritual things in
spiritual words, or to spiritual men,
that is, conveying spiritual truths in
suitable words. But others more exactly translate, *Combining spiritual
things with spiritual,* that is, with
spiritual words, as taught by the Spirit.
Thus adapting the discourse to the
subject, putting together things that
agree and belong together side by side,
spiritual with spiritual, in speaking of
the things freely given us by God.
Seeking to convey spiritual truths by

14 with spiritual. *b* But the natural man *c* receiveth not the things of the Spirit of God: *d* for they are foolishness unto him: *e* neither can he know *them*, because
15 they are spiritually discerned. *f* But he that is spiritual *g* judgeth all things, yet he himself is judged of no man.
16 *h* For who hath known the mind of the Lord, that he may instruct him? *i* But we have the mind of Christ.

14 But a natural man receives not the things of the Spirit of God, for they are foolishness to him; and he can not know them, because they are
15 spiritually judged. But he that is spiritual judges all things; but he himself is judged by no one. For who has
16 known the mind of the Lord, that he should instruct him? But we have the mind of Christ.

b Matt. 16 : 23 ; Jude 19.   *c* John 3 . 3–6.   *d* 1 : 18, 23.   *e* John 6 : 44, 45 ; Acts 17 : 18 ; Rom. 8 : 5–8.
f 3 : 1 ; 14 : 37.   *g* Prov. 28 : 5 ; John 7 : 17 ; 1 John 4 : 1.   *h* See refs. Job 15 : 8.
i John 15 : 15 ; Gal. 1 : 12.

words of human wisdom would be incongruous.

14. But every one has not the capacity for receiving these spiritual truths. **But the natural man**, in his *physical*, natural state, under the control of his corrupt, sensuous, and animal nature, opposed to his spiritual man, which has been regenerated by the Holy Spirit (Jude 19 ; James 3 : 15), Paul presupposes the three-fold division of man into body, soul, and spirit (1 Thess. 5 : 23 ; Heb. 4 : 12). **The things of the Spirit of God . . . are foolishness,** appearing as folly (1 : 18), **to him,** *and he cannot* **know them,** not being able to understand them **because they are spiritually discerned,** or *judged of* (ver. 15 ; 4 : 3, 4). It is only as we have the Spirit of God that we can estimate and determine the blessedness of divine things. We must have the spiritual capacity.

15. But he that is spiritual, the spiritual man, who is under the control and enlightenment of God's Spirit (14 : 37 ; Gal. 6 : 1), **judgeth all things,** examines and determines concerning the things of God (ver. 12, 13), and all things necessary to salvation (1 Thess. 5 : 21). *But he* **himself is judged** *by no one* who is not spiritual. This is evidently the meaning; the privilege and ability of judging is given to the spiritual in this verse, and in 14 : 29 ; 1 John 4 : 1. He occupies a higher position than the natural man, and in his spiritual exercises is beyond the scrutiny of the natural, unrenewed man. Paul often exercised his spiritual judgment in his estimate of persons and things (chap. 7, 8 ; 16 : 1, 2 ; Gal. 2 : 14–16 ; Acts 13 : 9, etc.).

16. Proof of the foregoing by Scripture, quoted from the Septuagint of Isa. 40 : 13. **For who hath known the mind of the Lord,** the thoughts, purposes, and disposition of the Lord, **that he may instruct him? But we,** the spiritual, **have the mind of Christ,** which is here made identical with the mind of the Lord. As no one can know and instruct God, so the natural man cannot know and exercise judgment upon us who are spiritual and possessed of the thoughts and disposition of Christ. "The possession of this mind of Christ renders him who has it a mystery to him who has it not. The workings of his soul, thus enlightened by a higher power, are inscrutable to those who are destitute of spiritual vision" (J. J. LIAS).

PRACTICAL REMARKS.

1. Ministers of the gospel should faithfully speak God's bidding in language plain, simple, and intelligible to all (ver. 1 ; Jonah 3 : 2 ; Jer. 1 : 17 ; 23 : 28 ; Acts 5 : 20).

2. The Christian minister should *know* Christ, and live by faith in a crucified and risen Saviour (ver. 2 ; Gal. 2 : 20 ; Rom. 15 : 29).

3. The great purpose of the gospel preacher should be to present Christ crucified. The incarnation and the resurrection and all doctrine and teaching should bear relation to the great doctrine of the atonement (ver. 2 ; Rom. 3 : 23–26 ; Phil. 2 : 5–13).

4. The preaching of the cross, as Paul preached it, is the only kind of preaching that will be truly successful (ver. 1–4 ; 1 : 23, 24 ; John 3 : 14 ; 12 : 32).

5. Feeling our own insufficiency, we trust Christ the more and accomplish most for him (ver. 3–5 ; 2 Cor. 12 : 9, 10).

6. The gospel gives evidence to its divine origin and power in the conversion

Correction of party spirit; Paul's ministry exhibited and defended.

3 AND I, brethren, could not speak unto you as unto ᵏ spiritual, but as unto ˡ carnal, *even* as unto babes in Christ.

3 AND I, brethren, was not able to speak to you as spiritual, but as carnal,

ᵏ 2 : 15; Gal. 6 : 1.   ˡ Ver. 3, 4; 2 : 14.

of sinners and in the building up of Christians in heart and life (ver. 4, 5; 1 Thess. 1 : 5).

7. The Christian has in his own experience the proof that the gospel is of God and not of man (ver. 5; John 4 : 41; 9 : 25, 38).

8. The gospel reveals true and divine wisdom, and the more mature the Christian, the greater his power to receive it. The more he grows in grace, the greater his knowledge of the truth (ver. 6; Phil. 3 : 13-16; 2 Peter 3 : 18).

9. God has designed the gospel to redound to the final glory of believers (ver. 7; 2 Tim. 1 : 10; Rom. 2 : 7).

10. Unconscious sins may bring upon ourselves and others interminable evils. Yet ignorance is no excuse, since sufficient light has been given (ver. 8; John 5 : 36; 10 : 35; Luke 16 : 31).

11. Christians have spiritual views different from others—of God, of Christ, of truth and salvation, of heaven and eternity (ver. 9, 10; John 14 : 26; 16 : 12-14).

12. The Holy Spirit is a Divine Person. So also we read of Christ "the Lord of glory" (ver. 8), and of the "Father of glory" (Eph. 1 : 17), and the "Spirit of glory" (1 Peter 4 : 14), pointing to their equal divinity (ver. 10-12).

13. Through the Spirit the Christian may know of God, thus enjoy the illumination of the Spirit and know his gracious purposes toward him, and be assured of his own salvation. Consequently his spirit is different from that of the world (ver. 12; John 15 : 16).

14. Paul was inspired, and under the influence of the Spirit spoke the inspired truth of God. Inspiration is the guidance of the Holy Spirit in communicating divine revelation (ver. 13; 7 : 10, 12; 11 : 23; Gal. 1 : 1).

15. Men by nature are blind to the spirituality of the gospel and to the beauties of religion, and need enlightenment and regeneration by the Holy Spirit (ver. 14; Rom. 8 : 6-8; Rev. 3 : 17).

16. The truly spiritual man should live above the world, yet in the world, and interested in the duties and work of every-day life (ver. 5; John 17 : 15-18).

17. Our spiritual exercises should be in accordance with the mind and teaching of Christ, and regulated by his written word (ver. 16; 14 : 33, 40).

18. We should pray for the Spirit, that he may enable us to see and receive the truth. We need the illumination of the Spirit to understand revelation aright (ver. 6-16; Ps. 119 : 18; John 16 : 13).

CHAPTER III.

Paul returns to the partyism in the Corinthian church and applies what he had said, showing that they were carnally minded (ver. 1-4); and that Christian teachers are but servants and workers with God, who alone gives the increase (ver. 5-9); that he himself had laid Christ as the foundation among them and others had builded thereon (ver. 10, 11); and that each man's work would be tested at the judgment (ver. 12-15). Reminding them that they are the temple of God, he warns them of their danger and responsibility (ver. 16, 17), and exhorts them to renounce their false wisdom, and to willingly lose everything, and not glory in men, so that in Christ they may be wise and gain all things (ver. 18-23).

1-4. PARTY SPIRIT AND DIVISIONS PROVE THAT THE CORINTHIANS ARE CARNAL-MINDED.

1. What I have said was exemplified in your case, **and accordingly 1, brethren,** *was not able* **to speak unto you,** when I was with you, **as unto spiritual**—regenerate, under the control and enlightenment of the Holy Spirit—such persons as were referred to in 2 : 15; **but as carnal**—*as men of flesh,* influenced by animal appetites and a corrupt human nature, rather than by the Spirit of God. On the

2 I have fed you with ᵐ milk, and not with meat: ⁿ for hitherto ye were not able *to bear it*, neither yet now are ye
3 able; for ye are yet carnal. For ᵒ whereas *there is* among you envying, and strife, and divisions, are ye not
4 carnal, and walk as men? For while one saith, ᵖ I am of Paul; and another, I am of Apollos; are ye not carnal?
5 Who then is Paul, and who *is* Apollos, but ᵠ ministers by whom ye believed, ʳeven as the Lord gave to
6 every man? ˢ I have planted, ᵗ Apollos watered; ᵘ but God gave the increase.
7 So then ˣ neither is he that planteth any thing, neither he that watereth;
8 but God that giveth the increase. Now

2 as babes in Christ. I fed you with milk, and not with solid food: for ye were not yet able to bear it; nay, not
3 even now are ye able; for ye are yet carnal. For whereas there is among you envying and strife, are ye not carnal, and do ye not walk as men?
4 For whenever one says, I am of Paul; and another, I am of Apollos; are ye
5 not men? What then is Apollos? and what is Paul? Servants through whom ye believed, and that as the Lord gave
6 to each one. I planted, Apollos
7 watered; but God made it grow. So then neither is he that plants anything, nor he that waters; but God
8 who makes it grow. And he that plants

ᵐ Heb. 5 : 12-14.   ⁿ John 16 : 12.   ᵒ 11 : 16 ; Gal. 5 : 20, 21 ; James 3 : 16.   ᵖ 1 : 12.   ᵠ 2 Cor. 3 : 3, 6.
ʳ 12 : 4-11, 28 ; Rom. 12 : 3-6 ; 1 Peter 4 : 10, 11.   ˢ 4 : 14, 15 ; 9 : 1 ; Acts 18 : 4, 8, 11.
ᵗ Acts 18 : 24, 27 ; 19 : 1.   ᵘ 15 : 10.   ˣ 2 Cor. 3 : 5 ; 12 : 11.

meaning and use of *carnal*, see note on Rom. 7 : 14. It is not meant that they were really unregenerate, for Paul adds, **as unto babes in Christ.** He could not preach the divine wisdom in its fullness to them (2 : 6, 10), for they were not prepared to receive it (ver. 2. Comp. Heb. 5 : 11-15).

2. I have fed, rather, *I fed you,* when at Corinth, **with milk,** the simple elementary truths of the gospel. **Not with meat,** or *solid food,* the more difficult doctrines and higher views of the spiritual life (2 : 6, 7). Compare the higher flights in the Epistle to the Ephesians in contrast to the lower subjects principally dealt with in this Epistle. Such lofty views of spiritual thought they were not **yet able** to receive.

3. For ye are yet carnal—*fleshly,* exhibiting the influence of animal appetites and a corrupt human nature. The idea is not that the natural animal appetites are in themselves sinful, but rather that human nature is sinful. The bodily appetites are, however, often a source of temptation and sin. Their **envying and strife** were evidences of an animal and corrupt nature in them (Gal. 5 : 19-21), and that they were walking **as men** after the manner of men (15 : 32) in their natural, unrenewed state (Rom. 8 : 3).

4. Paul and **Apollos,** representing different classes of teachers. **Are ye not carnal?** or according to the majority of critical authorities, *Are ye not men?* purely human and exhibiting the natural, unrenewed state of men.

5-9. CHRISTIAN PREACHERS AND TEACHERS ONLY SERVANTS AND WORKMEN ; GOD GIVES THE INCREASE.

5. Who then is Paul, etc. The best critical authorities read, *What then is Apollos, and what is Paul?* **Ministers,** or *servants through whom ye believed,* **even as the Lord gave to each** one—and that too, as Christ has allotted to each one his labor and success (Eph. 4 : 7-12).

6. I have, rather, *I planted,* in preaching the gospel first at Corinth (Acts 18 : 1-11). **Apollos watered,** while Paul passed through the upper districts of Asia (Acts 19 : 1). Paul had peculiar ability in starting work and churches, as seen wherever he went. But Apollos appears to have had the ability of fostering and advancing the spiritual work already begun. **But** in both cases **God gave the increase,** or *caused it to grow*—made their labors effectual. The exact agreement of Paul's incidental reference here with the history in the Acts (18 : 1-27) is an evidence of the genuineness and truthfulness of both this Epistle and the Acts.

7. So then, an inference from the preceding, **neither is he that planteth or watereth anything,** of any consequence, but comparatively as nothing. **But God that** *giveth* **the increase,** better, *Makest it to grow.* "Gifts can effect as little in spiritual as diligence and expertness in temporal matters, without God's blessing" (OLSHAUSEN).

8 he that planteth and he that watereth are one; and every man shall receive his own reward according to his own 9 labour. For ᵃ we are labourers together with God: ye are ᵇ God's husbandry, 10 ye are ᶜ God's building. According to the grace of God which is given unto me, as a wise master-builder, I have laid ᵈ the foundation, and another buildeth thereon. But ᵉ let every man take heed how he buildeth thereupon. 11 For other foundation can no man lay than ᶠ that is laid, which is Jesus

and he that waters are one; but each will receive his own wages according 9 to his own labor. For we are God's fellow-workers; ye are God's field, God's building. 10 According to the grace of God which was given to me, as a wise master-builder I laid a foundation, and another builds thereon. But let each one take 11 heed how he builds thereon. For other foundation can no one lay than that which is laid, which is Jesus

y John 4 : 36–38.   z See refs. Job 34 : 11; Gal. 6 : 4, 5; Rev. 2 : 23.   a Mark 16 : 20; 2 Cor. 6 : 1.
b Isa. 5 : 1–7; Matt. 21 : 33–40; John 15 : 1, 2.   c Eph. 2 : 10, 20–22.   d 4 : 15; Rom. 15 : 20.
e 1 Peter 4 : 11.   f Matt. 16 : 18; Acts 4 : 11, 12; Gal. 1 : 7–9; Eph. 2 : 20.

8. Now, better, *And,* **he that planteth and he that watereth are one** thing, one instrumentality, they belong together, being fellow-laborers. This equality is opposed to any supposed superiority, or to any rivalry of teachers, or to party spirit among them. Notice how the neuter gender is used in this and preceding verses, as if to emphasize the contrast between the workers, who are servants and instruments, and God, who works through them. **And every man,** better, *each,* he that plants and he that waters, **shall receive his own reward,** or *wages,* **according to his own labour,** which he has done and his faithfulness in doing it (2 Cor. 5 : 10; 2 Tim. 4 : 8). They are but servants and responsible to God.

9. For introduces a reason for what he had just said, **For we are** *God's fellow-workers.* Being *fellow-workers* they were one in the nature and equality of their works, and being fellow-workers *of God* they were accountable to him and would receive their wages of him. While subordinate to him they are nevertheless God's helpers and workers together with him (2 Cor. 5 : 20; 6 : 1). They had also worked in one place and among one people. **Ye are God's husbandry,** or *field,* **ye are God's building**—the field and building were not theirs but God's, and to him they were responsible. Notice a distinction is here made between the preacher and the people. The last figure of a building is added to introduce what follows.

10–17. THE BUILDERS AND THE BUILDING. They build on Christ, but often with different materials. Their dangers and responsibility. Character building.

10. According to the grace, *the favor,* **of God which** *was* **given me** in my labors among you, fitting me for, and enabling me to do the work, not merely as a builder, but **as a wise** or *skillful* **masterbuilder,** or *architect,* **I laid** (omit have) **a foundation and another,** whoever he may be, **buildeth thereon,** carrying on the work begun. The work at Corinth he had presented under the figure of a field (ver. 5–8); now as a building. **But,** turning to a new point of view—the kind of building and the reward of the builders—**let every man,** *each one,* **take heed how he buildeth thereupon.** There may be many methods and materials in building thereon, but he assumes that there can be but one foundation, which he also asserts in the next verse.

11. I have taken for granted, Paul might have said, that there is but one foundation, **For other foundation can no man lay than that is laid,** by God himself (Isa. 28 : 16; Rom. 9 : 33), **which is Jesus Christ.** (See also Eph. 2 : 20; 1 Peter 2 : 6.) Notice that it is *Christ himself* who is the foundation, and not mere teaching *about* Christ. Yet Christ is the great Revealer, the sum and substance of the gospel, "the way, the truth, and the life" (John 14 : 6, on which see note: Col. 2 : 3). Paul had laid this foundation among the Corinthians (ver. 10) by preaching Christ crucified (2 : 1–5), Christ being received by them in faith, and formed in them by the Holy Spirit, the hope of glory (Col. 1 : 27). "Jesus Christ, the foundation of the whole church upon

12 Christ. Now *if any man build upon this foundation gold, silver, precious
13 stones, wood, hay, stubble; *every man's work shall be made manifest: for the day *shall declare it, because it shall be revealed by fire; and *the fire shall try every man's work of what
14 sort it is. *If any man's work abide which he hath built thereupon, he
15 shall receive a reward: if any man's work shall be burned, he shall suffer loss; but he himself shall be saved; *yet so as by fire.

12 Christ. And if any one builds on the foundation gold, silver, costly stones,
13 wood, hay, stubble; the work of each one will be made manifest; for the day will show it, because it is revealed in fire, and the fire itself will prove of
14 what sort is each one's work. If any one's work which he builds thereon shall remain, he will receive wages.
15 If any one's work shall be burned up, he will suffer loss; but he himself will be saved; yet so as through fire.

g Matt. 15 : 1-9 ; Gal. 4 : 10 ; Col. 2 : 6-8 ; 1 Tim. 4 : 1-3 ; Heb. 13 : 9 ; 2 Peter 1 : 5-7.   *h* Ver. 14, 15 ; 4 : 5.
i 1 : 8 ; 2 Thess. 1 : 7-10 ; 1 Peter 1 : 7.   *k* Isa. 4 : 4 ; Mal. 4 : 1.
l Dan. 12 : 3 ; 1 Thess. 2 : 19 ; 1 Peter 5 : 2, 4.   *m* Amos 4 : 11 ; Jude 23.

earth, must shew himself in his life-inspiring power at the rise of every individual church, nay, in every heart, if it is to be sanctified. The character of the great universal temple of God is thus repeated in every church, in every heart. Everywhere must be the living Christ be the corner-stone, the new man, born in regeneration" (OLSHAUSEN).

12. The different materials which may be built on Christ, the foundation. **If any** *one* **builds upon this foundation gold, silver, precious,** or *costly,* **stones,** as granite and marble—such doctrines and practices as shall be enduring and shall stand the test of the judgment; **wood, hay, stubble**—doctrines, practices, ceremonies, such as are perishable and cannot endure the test of the last great day. The figures here used are those materials which are and are not combustible. That the materials do not represent *persons,* false and true church-members, but true and false *teachings,* which contribute to the building of the characters and lives of Christians, appears evident from what follows. While this building on the true foundation has primary reference to Christian preachers and teachers, it may also be applied to every Christian, since every individual believer is founded on Christ and is building thereon (Acts 4 : 11, 12).

13. Every man's work *will* **be made manifest,** whether it is durable and valuable, or perishable and worthless. **For the day** *will* **declare,** better, *show it*—the judgment day at Christ's coming (4 : 5; Rom. 2 : 16; 2 Cor. 5 : 10) will show the character of the building, **because it**—the day—**shall be revealed,** rather, *because it is to be revealed in fire,* the very element which permeates and envelopes, as it were, that day. The *fire* is not that of punishment, but of testing and searching out and separating the true and the false; **the fire** *will* **try,** or *prove,* **every man's work of what sort it is.** (See 1 Peter 1 : 7; Matt. 3 : 12; Mal. 3 : 1-3; Heb. 12 : 29.) Fire represents the element of trial, bringing to light and consuming all that is perishable (4 : 5; Heb. 4 : 13).

14. The result of the test of the judgment upon the buildings on the true foundation. **If any man's work a b i d e**—*remains* unharmed, if it proves incombustible, if it consists of the pure and eternal truths of God's word, of the doctrines and practices which will stand the searching tests of the judgment, then **he shall receive a reward**—be recompensed for his faithful and effective labors.

15. If any man's work shall be burned *up*—if it consists of false principles and practices, then it will not stand the test of the judgment, but his hovel of wood, hay, and stubble will be consumed, and **he shall suffer loss** of wages and everything except the foundation. **Yet he himself shall be saved,** having believed and built on the true foundation, Jesus Christ. **Yet so** saved, **as by,** or *through* **fire,** saved with difficulty, like one just escaping with his life out of a burning building (Zech. 3 : 2; Mal. 4 : 1; 2 John 8). This passage gives no support to the doctrine of purgatory; it is not said that the man is saved by fire as a means of purification. But fire is used as an illustration, *so as through fire;* like one,

16 ᵃ Know ye not that ye are the temple of God, ᵒ and *that* the Spirit of God
17 dwelleth in you? ᵖ If any man defile the temple of God, him shall God destroy; for the temple of God is holy; which *temple* ye are.
18 ᵠ Let no man deceive himself: if any man among you seemeth to be wise in this world, ʳ let him become a fool, that
19 he may be wise. For ˢ the wisdom of this world is foolishness with God: for it is written, He taketh the wise
20 in their own craftiness: and again,

16 Know ye not that ye are God's temple, and that the Spirit of God
17 dwells in you? If any one destroys the temple of God, him will God destroy: for the temple of God is holy, and that ye are.
18 Let no one deceive himself. If any one among you thinks that he is wise in this age, let him become a fool, that
19 he may become wise. For the wisdom of this world is foolishness with God. For it is written, He that takes the wise
20 in their craftiness. And again,

n 6 : 19; 2 Cor. 6 : 16; Eph. 2 : 21, 22; 1 Peter 2 : 5.   o John 14 : 17; Rom. 8 : 11; 1 John 4 : 15, 16.
p Ezek. 5 : 11; 2 Peter 2 : 1.   q Isa. 5 : 21.   r Matt. 18 : 4; Luke 18 : 17.   s 1 : 19-21, 25-29.

passing through the fire, is saved at great risk and difficulty. Stanley thinks that the whole image of this passage " may have been suggested, or at least illustrated, by the conflagration of Corinth under Mummius (146 B. C.); the stately temples—one of them remaining to this day—standing amidst the universal destruction of the meaner buildings."

16. The figure of the building is carried further, and warning is addressed to the members of the Corinthian church. **Know ye not,** implying that they did know, or that they ought to know, yet their conduct seemed inconsistent with such knowledge. An expression as if surprising. **That ye are the temple**—*the sanctuary*, the inner temple—**of God;** spoken here of the church or company of believers at Corinth. (Comp. 2 Cor 6 : 16; Eph. 2 : 21.) The figure is applied to the bodies of believers in 6 : 19. Accordingly, as ye are the temple of God, **the Spirit of God dwelleth in you** (Eph. 2 : 22). The Spirit dwells in believers and among them. He is in the local church only as he is in the hearts of its members (Heb. 3 : 6; 1 Peter 2 : 5).

17. **If any man defile,** or *destroy,* **the temple of God, him shall God destroy.** The verb is the same in both members of the sentence. " Every Levitical defilement was considered a *destroying* of the temple, as was every injury to the buildings, and even every act of carelessness in the watching and superintendence of it" (MEYER). The violator of the sanctuary of the temple was punished with death. (Comp. Acts 21 : 28, on which see note.) **For the temple of God is holy,** consecrated to him, **which temple,** rather, *which sort*, **are ye.** *Which* refers not to *temple*, but to *holy* as a quality: The temple of God is holy and so are ye. Whoever shall pollute or destroy the church in any degree by sinful practice, or by false doctrine, or by party divisions, shall receive a like punishment from God. He that works ruin to God's church shall receive like ruin to himself. On these matters Paul enlarges in chapters five and six. Compare the builder with false material losing his building (ver. 15); also many sickly and dying churches (11 : 30; comp. also Matt. 18 : 6).

18-23. RENUNCIATION OF WORLDLY WISDOM IN ORDER TO THE TRUE WISDOM; AND OF GLORYING IN MEN, SINCE ALL THINGS ARE GOD'S.

18. Warning against self-deception and self-conceit. **Let no man deceive himself** in regard to these matters. **If any man** among you **seemeth to be wise,** rather, *thinks that he is wise,* **in this** world, having that conceit of superior wisdom which was largely the cause of the party strifes among them, and this was like the hay, wood, and stubble in the building, which was tending to destroy the church. **Let him become a fool** in his own present estimation and in the world's estimation, by accepting the gospel in its simplicity, that he **may be,** rather, *may become,* truly **wise,** in God's sight (2 : 7-16).

19. Enforces the preceding exhortation. **For the wisdom of this world**—worldly wisdom opposed to heavenly wisdom, **is foolishness with God**—*folly* in the sight of God. **For it is written** (Job. 5 : 13), **He taketh,** rather, *He that taketh* **the wise in their craftiness.** If God is thus spoken of as *grasping*, as it were,

The Lord knoweth the thoughts of the wise, that they are vain.
21 Therefore ᵗ let no man glory in men:
22 for ᵘ all things are yours; whether Paul, or Apollos, or ᵛ Cephas, or the world, or life, or death, or things present, or things to come; all are yours;
23 and ˣ ye are Christ's; and ʸ Christ is God's.

The Lord knows the reasonings of the wise,
That they are vain.
21 So then, let no one glory in men.
22 For all things are yours; whether Paul, or Apollos, or Cephas, or the world, or life, or death, or things present, or things to come, all are yours;
23 yours; and ye are Christ's, and Christ is God's.

t Ver. 4–7; 1 : 12; Jer. 9 : 23, 24.   *u 2 Cor. 4 : 5, 15; Eph. 4 : 11, 12.*   *v John 1 : 42.*
x Rom. 14 : 8; Gal. 3 : 29.   *y 11 : 3; Matt. 17 : 5; Phil. 2 : 6–11; Heb. 1 : 3.*

the wise in their craftiness, turning it to their own confusion, then their wisdom must be folly in his sight.

20. And again (Ps. 94 : 11), **The Lord knoweth the thoughts, or** *reasonings*, **of the wise that they are vain,** foolish and fruitless. In regard to their reasonings, compare Rom. 1 : 21; Eph. 4 : 17. In both of these quotations Paul follows the Septuagint with slight variations, showing that he substitutes his own translations in certain instances.

21. Therefore, or *So then,* to sum up, and in view of the folly of the world's wisdom before God, **let no man glory in men,** especially in party leaders. Let not Christians pride themselves against one another in their teachers (4 : 6). **For,** so far from your belonging to any human teachers, **all things** *belong to you*—all things are for your good (Rom. 8 : 28), and your teachers, so far from being regarded as your lords and masters, are rather your servants for Christ's sake in order that you may be saved (2 Cor. 4 : 5).

22. All things belong to you as God's children (ver. 21), **whether Paul, or Apollos, or Cephas** (1 : 12), whose gifts, abilities, and labors are the common property of all believers. Churches do not exist for teachers, but rather teachers for the planting and building up of churches. Notice he does not refer to the leaders of the Christ party (1 : 12). But the apostle does not stop with teachers, but pushes the thought still farther till he gets back to God. God's purposes begin and end in himself. **Or the world,** in its general and comprehensive sense, *the universe,* since ye are "heirs of the world" (Rom. 4 : 13; 8 : 19–23); **or life or death,** these two extremes including all possible conditions which work together for their good and their final salvation and glory; **or things present or things to come,** a vast sweep of the present and future, its joys and sorrows, its vicissitudes and its eternal weight of glory; **all are yours,** repeating what he had said and summing up with emphasis.

23. Nor does the apostle stop here, but note the change of ownership; all would be as nothing without Christ. **And ye are Christ's**—ye are not your own (6 : 20; 7 : 23), but you and all that belongs to you belong to Christ, and are to be used for him and to his glory; **and Christ is God's,** the human and divine Christ, the Mediator, belongs to God, the Father, for the fulfillment of his purposes and the extension of his glory, and the consequent good of all his creatures (15 : 28). Paul would have his readers live not as if they were their own for selfish purposes, but as Christ's, who lived not to do his own will, but the will of the Father who sent him (John 5 : 30). Thus Christ's prayer will be answered, "I in them, and thou in me, that they may be made perfect in one" (John 17 : 23).

PRACTICAL REMARKS.

1. All Christians are at first babes in Christ, but should not remain such, but grow up into the full stature of men in Christ Jesus (ver. 1; 2 Peter 3 : 18; Eph. 4 : 13).

2. The gospel has spiritual food for all capacities, and he is a wise minister who suits his instructions to the various necessities of his hearers (ver. 2; John 16 : 12).

3. Envy is a fruitful cause of strife, and both indicate a low state of religion among those who are exercised thereby (ver. 3; James 3 : 14, 16).

4. Party spirit in churches and among

Christians, and the following of party names, are opposed to the spirit of Christ and the gospel (ver. 4; John 17 : 21-23).

5. Ministers are indeed "servants," but they are honored of God and should receive the respect and affectionate regard of their people (ver. 5; 1 Tim. 1 : 12; 1 Thess. 5 : 12, 13).

6. God has wisely chosen preachers of different gifts and talents suited to the various conditions of communities and churches (ver. 6; Rom. 12 : 4-8).

7. All ministers are on a level as co-workers with God, whatever their talents, position, or fields of labor (ver. 8; Matt. 23 : 8-12).

8. Christians are alike a holy people and a royal priesthood, yet ministers are to be distinguished from their congregations in their official relations and labors (ver. 9; Mark 16 : 20; 2 Cor. 6 : 16).

9. Christ is the only foundation of every true church and every true believer (ver. 10, 11; Acts 4 : 12; Eph. 2 : 20).

10. Through the preaching of the gospel, and by faith, Christ is laid as the foundation in the heart of the Christian (ver. 10, 11; 2 : 1, 2; Col. 1 : 27, 28; 2 Cor. 13 : 5).

11. True believers as well as true gospel preachers build on Christ as a foundation, but some erect structures upon it widely different from others (ver. 12; Gal. 3 : 1-3; 5 : 22; 2 Peter 1 : 5, 6).

12. Christians will be tested at the judgment, not only as to their foundation, but also as to what they have built thereon (ver. 13; 2 Cor. 5 : 10).

13. Some, passing the test, will have an abundant entrance into the kingdom of glory; others will lose all but the foundation, and will be only "saved as through fire" (ver. 14, 15; Dan. 12 : 3; 2 Tim. 4 : 6-8; Rev. 2 : 15-20).

14. Also learn: (1) How important to hold Christ's doctrines and obey his commands. (2) To exercise liberality toward Christians who differ from us. Though their building may be defective, they may be on Christ as a foundation. (3) The certainty of the salvation of all true believers. Their building may be destroyed, but Christ, their foundation, cannot be. (4) The danger of being deceived. If some are deceived regarding the building, others may be regarding the foundation. (5) The greater danger of the sinner (1 Peter 4 : 17, 18; ver. 10-15).

15. A church should consist of a regenerate membership and thus be a body holy, consecrated to God, and a temple of the Holy Spirit (ver. 17; Matt. 18 : 6).

16. He who would become Christ's must be willing to be esteemed a fool for his sake (ver. 18; Matt. 16 : 24, 25).

17. A childlike and teachable spirit is the first step toward true wisdom (ver. 18, 19; Mark 18 : 4).

18. We should beware of speculations in religion, and of philosophies, falsely so called (ver. 18-20; Col. 2 : 8; Acts 17 : 21).

19. Our highest aim cannot be man's glory and God's glory at the same time (ver. 21; 1 Cor. 6 : 20; 10 : 3).

20. All things in the Divine purposes regarding man have reference to the good of God's people. Even death has lost its sting to the believer and become the gateway to glory (ver. 22; Eph. 1 : 9-14; 1 Cor. 15 : 55-57).

21. Christians are the only truly wise and rich among men (ver. 23; Rev. 2 : 9; James 2 : 5; 1 Tim. 6 : 18).

22. Christians should ever regard themselves as the Lord's. It is only as they become Christ's that Christ becomes theirs (ver. 23; 1 Cor. 7 : 23; John 15 : 16; 1 John 4 : 19).

CHAPTER IV.

Paul wishes to be regarded as a servant and steward of Christ, to whom he is responsible and to whose future judgment all decisions regarding himself must be referred (ver. 1-5). With Apollos and himself as examples, he exhorts the Corinthians to humility (ver. 6, 7), and contrasts the arrogant temper of the latter with the self-denying labors of the former (ver. 8-13). As their spiritual father he speaks with apostolic authority, tenderly entreating them to imitate him and solemnly warning the haughty of his speedy coming to them (ver. 14-21)

1-5. APOSTLES AND CHRISTIAN TEACHERS, STEWARDS OF THE MYSTERIES OF GOD, ACCOUNTABLE TO CHRIST, AND TO BE JUDGED BY HIM.

4 LET a man so account of us, as of the ministers of Christ, [a] and stewards 2 of the [b] mysteries of God. Moreover it is required in stewards, [c] that a man 3 be found faithful. But with me [d] it is a very small thing that I should be judged of you, or of man's judgment: 4 yea, I judge not mine own self. For [e] I know nothing by myself; [f] yet am I

4 LET a man so account us, as servants of Christ and stewards of the mysteries 2 of God. Here moreover, it is required in stewards, that one be found faithful. 3 But with me it is a very little thing that I should be judged by you, or by man's day: nay, neither do I 4 judge myself. For I am conscious to myself of nothing ; yet am I not hereby

[a] 3 : 5 ; 2 Cor. 5 : 18-20 ; Col. 1 : 25. [b] Luke 12 : 42 ; Titus 1 : 7. [c] Matt. 13 : 11. [d] Ezek. 3 : 17-21 ; Acts 20 : 31 ; 2 Cor. 4 : 2. [e] 1 Sam. 16 : 7. [f] 1 John 3 : 20, 21. [g] See refs. Job 9 : 2, 20 ; Prov. 21 : 2 ; Rom. 4 : 2.

1. **Let a man so account of us,** better, *So let a man account us as ministers* or *servants of Christ*. Let no man glory in us (3 : 22), but inasmuch as we belong to Christ (3 : 23), let them regard *us*, Paul and Apollos (ver. 6), such apostles and teachers as we, as Christ's servants, holding a position of service to and dependence on him. **Ministers,** better, *servants*. There is an idea of subordination in the word, of one who attends and assists a magistrate or renders any kind of service (Matt. 26 : 58; Luke 4 : 20). It is applied to religious service only here, Luke 1 : 2, and Acts 26 : 16, and to Mark as an *assistant* (Acts 13 : 5). **And stewards**—*managers* and *superintendents*, who were generally servants to whom were entrusted important affairs of a household (Matt. 24 : 45) ; here of religious affairs (Titus 1 : 7; 1 Peter 4 : 10) in the house of God, the Christian church (1 Tim. 3 : 15 ; 1 Peter 4 : 17). Paul would have them regard him and his co-laborers not as lords and masters, but as managing servants, to whom God, their supreme Ruler (3 : 23), had entrusted his mysteries, which were to be made known to men. Their position was inconsistent with boasting and party spirit. **Mysteries of God,** his *hidden* counsels in providing salvation for men through Christ. (See note on 2 : 7.) Compare "mystery of godliness" (1 Tim. 3 : 16). There is no reason here, or elsewhere in the New Testament, for regarding mysteries as referring to the so-called sacraments. Paul had himself said (1 : 17) that Christ did not send him to baptize, but to preach the gospel.

2. **Moreover.** The reading, according to the best manuscripts, should be : *Here moreover*, meaning, *In this state of things it only remains to be said, that it* **is required in stewards that a man be found faithful.** Faithfulness is so important a trust as that of a steward is a necessary and universal requirement, and it follows that it is emphatically so in stewards of religious things under God. Thus faithfulness is the great question; the other points about which the Corinthians might dispute and emphasize were of small moment.

3. In this and the two verses that follow Paul emphasizes the fact that the Lord is his judge in regard to his stewardship, and utters a warning against hasty judgment of ministers. **But with me it is a very small thing,** *it is of the least account*, **that I should be judged of,** rather, *by*, **you or of man's judgment,** literally, *by a human day* of judgment, any judicial day of men, that is, by human judgment. Human tribunals cannot discern and judge spiritually (2 : 14, 15), neither were these Corinthians fitted to exercise judgment, since they were carnal and babes in Christ, and walked as men (3 : 1-3). **Yea, even more, I judge not mine own self.** In his humility and honesty he would not trust his own opinion of himself, but leave all judgment to his Lord.

4. Paul states why he does not even judge himself. **For I know nothing by,** rather, *against*, **myself,** or, *I am conscious to myself of nothing*, of no unfaithfulness in my stewardship. Compare his declaration before the Sanhedrin, "I have lived in all good conscience before God until this day" (Acts 23 : 1 ; also Acts 24 : 16). **Yet am I not hereby justified**—*deemed righteous* and *guiltless* in regard to my stewardship. Paul is not referring to justification by faith ; he had no doubt of his forgiveness and of being in a state of grace. But he was conscious of many infirmities (15 : 9 ; Eph. 3 : 8 ; 1 Tim.

not hereby justified: but he that judgeth me is the Lord.

5 *Therefore* judge nothing before the time, until the Lord come, *who both will bring to light the hidden things of darkness, and will make manifest the counsels of the hearts: and *then shall every man have praise of God.

6 And these things, brethren, I have in a figure transferred to myself and *to Apollos, for your sakes; *that ye might learn in us not to think *of men above* that which is written, that no one of you be puffed up for one against

7 another. For who maketh thee to

justified, but he that judges me is the

5 Lord. So then do not judge anything before the time, until the Lord come, who will both bring to light the hidden things of darkness, and make manifest the counsels of the hearts; and then will each one have his praise from God.

6 And these things, brethren, I have in a figure transferred to myself and Apollos for your sakes; that in us ye may learn not to go beyond the things which ye have written, that ye be not puffed up each for the one against the

7 other. For who makes thee to differ?

g Matt. 7:1; Rev. 20:12.   *h* 3:13; Rom. 2:16.   *i* Rom. 2:6-11, 29, 1 Peter 1:7; 5:4.
k 3:5; Rom. 12:3.

1:13-15), and did not consider himself as already perfect (Phil. 3:15), and in regard to himself as a master-builder, building on Christ the foundation (3:10-14), he knew that the Lord could see in him imperfections which he could not see. The final decision must be put off to the day of the Lord (1:8; Rom. 2:16; Acts 17:31). **He that judgeth me is the Lord**, who is the only infallible Judge.

5. **Therefore,** in view of all this, **judge nothing before the time** to judge, in respect to me, **until the Lord come** to judgment (2 Tim. 4:1; 2 Thess. 1:7), **who both will bring to light the hidden things of darkness**—acts unknown and hidden from human knowledge, **and will make manifest the counsels of the hearts**—the purposes, thoughts, and motives which no human eye can reach (Heb. 4:13). **And then shall every, better, *each*, man have *his* praise from God.** (Comp. 3:14; Matt. 25:21; 2 Tim. 4:8.) **God** the Father judges through the Son (John 5:22, 27, 30). The apostle speaks only of the individual praise that shall be awarded to faithful stewards, implying reproof and punishment to the unfaithful. On judging others in general, see Rom. 2:1; Matt. 7:1. We are not to usurp Christ's place in passing judgments on his ministers, especially upon their thoughts and motives, nor are we to try to anticipate the decisions of the final judgment. This does not preclude our judging men and false prophets by their fruits (Matt. 23:15-29), trying the spirits whether they be of God (1 John 4:1-3), and testing the teachings of

ministers by God's word, and holding fast to that which is good (1 Thess. 5:21).

6-13. LET THERE BE NO STRIFE ABOUT TEACHERS. CONTRAST BETWEEN THE CORINTHIAN ARROGANCE AND PAUL'S HUMILITY AND SELF-DENIAL.

6. And these things, concerning ministerial stewardship and faithfulness, and judgments thereon, **brethren**, of the church generally, **I have**, or more exactly, *I transferred in a figure* **to myself and to Apollos** (notice the use of the first person in ver. 1, "Let a man so account of *us*") **for your sakes,** for your good and profit. What I might say of all your religious teachers, to avoid giving offense, I have applied to Apollos and myself as representatives of the whole. And wisely he thus did, for he and Apollos were one in spirit and in friendship. **That ye** *may in us learn this:* **Go not beyond that which is written,** in the Old Testament Scriptures. Of the New Testament, only James, First and Second Thessalonians, and probably Galatians, and possibly the Gospel of Matthew, were written It was too early to refer to the New Testament writers. The only such reference certainly made is in 2 Peter 3 16. The words **to think** is not found in the oldest and best manuscripts. **That no one of you be puffed up,** bearing yourself proudly and loftily *for the one* teacher **against another.**

7. Instead of exercising pride you should be filled with gratitude. **For who maketh thee to differ?** implying that it is God. **And what**

differ *from another?* And ¹what hast thou that thou didst not receive? Now if thou didst receive *it,* why dost thou glory, as if thou hadst not received *it?*
8 Now ye are full, ᵐ now ye are rich, ye have reigned as kings without us: and I would to God ye did reign, that we
9 also might reign with you. For ⁿ I think that God hath set forth us the apostles last, as it were appointed to death: for ᵒ we are made a spectacle unto the world, and to angels, and to
10 men. We *are* ᵖ fools for Christ's sake, but ye *are* wise in Christ; we *are* weak, but ye *are* strong; ye *are* honourable,
11 but we *are* despised. ᵠ Even unto this present hour we both hunger, and

And what hast thou which thou didst not receive? But if thou didst receive it, why dost thou glory, as if thou
8 hadst not received it? Already ye are filled full, already ye become rich, apart from us ye reigned as kings; yea I wish that ye did reign, that we
9 also might reign with you. For I think, God set forth us the apostles last, as condemned to death; because we have become a spectacle to the world, both to angels and to men.
10 We are fools for Christ's sake, but ye are wise in Christ; we are weak, but ye are strong; ye are glorious, but we are
11 without honor. Even until this present hour we both hunger and thirst and

l See refs. John 3 : 27; 1 Peter 4 : 10.　　*m* Rev. 3 : 17.　　*n* 15 : 30–32; Rom. 8 : 36; 2 Cor. 4 : 8–12.
o Heb. 10 : 33.　　*p* See refs. 1 : 18, etc; Acts 26 : 24.　　*q* 2 Cor. 6 : 4, 5; Phil. 4 : 12.

---

ability or gift **hast thou that thou didst not receive** from God? (John 3 : 27; James 1 : 17.) *But if* this is the case, **why dost thou glory** in any pre-eminence, as if all self-attained?

8. Paul pushes the thought to its opposite and ludicrous side, giving a sudden turn to his feelings, which is remarkable in the apostle's style. Note the climax in the verbs used, **are full, are rich, have reigned as kings.** This verse is commonly read as a declaration, thus heightening its irony. But to me it seems better, with Westcott and Hort and some others, to take it as a series of questions, thus: *Already are ye filled full? Already are ye rich? Without us have ye come to reign like kings?* Have ye become independent of us, your fathers in the gospel, fully satisfied, enjoying abundance and exercising lordship in your parties and party leaders? *Yea,* **I would ye did reign,** the apostle responds earnestly and solemnly, **that we also might reign with you,** and thus be rid of trials, distresses, and humiliations. The addition **to God** is not in the original and is not needed.

9. The last clause of the preceding verse prepares the way for exhibiting the afflicted state of the apostles themselves. **For,** to give the ground of the foregoing wish, **I think God set forth,** *exhibited,* **us the apostles,** all of them, including himself, **last,** as if the vilest and most worthless (ver. 13; Mark 9 : 35), **as it were** *approved* **to death,** rather, *as condemned* or *doomed to death.* The figure appears to be that of a procession of gladiators, of which the apostles were last, who came forth into the arena, saluting the ruler of the spectacle, as those who were about to die (comp. 15 : 32). **For we are made a spectacle unto the world,** on its broad stage to all created beings, **and to angels,** rather, *both,* **to angels and men,** all the intelligences of the universe (Heb. 10 : 33; 12 : 1), who gaze upon our death struggle. And, impliedly, ye Corinthians, engrossed in your own selves, remain unmoved and unconcerned at the awful tragedy!

10. Paul presents the contrast, implied in the two preceding verses, between the condition of the apostles and the Corinthians, in a vein of impassioned irony. **We are fools**—regarded and treated as such by the world, **for Christ's sake,** since we are intent on preaching Christ crucified (1 : 18, 23; 2 : 2); **but ye are wise,** "puffed up" and counting yourselves as such, **in Christ,** as Christians. **We are weak . . . despised**—so regarded by men, as we discard worldly instrumentality and power (2 Cor. 10 : 3), and labor in weakness and humility among those who are poor, dishonored, and without worldly influence (1 : 26–28; 2 Cor. 12 : 10). **But ye are strong . . . honorable,** *glorious,* in your own and each other's estimation. There is a vein of irony in this and the eighth verse. See examples of irony in Judges 10 : 14; Job 12 : 1; Amos 4 : 4.

11. Even unto this present hour, writing from Ephesus in the

thirst, and are naked and *are buffeted, and have no certain dwelling-
12 place; *and labour, working with our
own hands. *Being reviled, we bless:
13 *being persecuted, we suffer it: being
defamed, we intreat: *we are made
as the filth of the earth, *and are* the
offscouring of all things unto this
day.
14 I write not these things to shame
you; but *as my beloved sons I warn
15 *you*. For though ye have ten thousand
instructors in Christ, yet *have ye* not
many fathers: for *in Christ Jesus I

are naked and are buffeted and have
12 no fixed abode; and labor, working
with our own hands, being reviled,
we bless; being persecuted, we endure
13 it; being defamed, we beseech, we
have become as the filth of the world,
the offscouring of all things until
now.
14 I am not writing these things to
shame you, but to admonish you as
15 my beloved children. For if ye have
ten thousand tutors in Christ, yet not
many fathers; for in Christ Jesus it

r Acts 14 : 19 ; 23 : 2 ; 2 Cor. 11 : 23-25.   *s* See refs. Acts 18 : 3.   *t* See refs. Rom. 12 : 14, 20.
u 1 Peter 4 : 12-14, 19.   *x* Lam. 3 : 45 ; Acts 22 : 22.   *y* 2 Cor. 6 : 11-13 ; 1 Thess. 2 : 11.
z 3 : 6 ; 9 : 1, 2 ; 2 Cor. 3 : 2, 3 ; Gal. 4 : 19 ; James 1 : 18.

spring of A. D. 57, over twenty years
since his conversion, during all which
time he had endured privations in food
and clothing, suffered ill treatment,
being **buffeted**, like slaves, *beaten
with the fists*, having **no certain
dwellingplace** — *wanderers, with no
settled home*.

**12. And labor, working with
our own hands,** as he did when
among them at Corinth (Acts 18 : 3), and
now at Ephesus (Acts 20 : 34). Notice
how these words spoken on different
occasions agree with each other. Such
undesigned coincidences furnish the
very best proof of the genuineness of
both the Epistle and the Acts. (Comp.
also 9:6 and 1 Thess. 2:9; 2 Thess. 3:8.) **Being
reviled, we bless,** in accordance
with our Saviour's command (Matt. 5 : 44 ;
Luke 6 : 28), which possibly he had read
in Matthew. **Being persecuted,**
we *endure* it patiently, instead of
resenting it, defending ourselves, and
seeking vengeance.

13. Being defamed, not evil
spoken *to* as in "reviling" (ver. 12), but
evil spoken *about*, **we entreat,** try
to conciliate and appease. And now
Paul reaches the climax of disgrace
and contempt: **We are made as the
filth,** or *refuse*, **of the world** — that
which is removed by cleansing, meaning here the most abject and despicable
of men. Omitting **and are,** the preceding clause is enlarged upon: **the
offscouring,** *the scrapings*, **of all
things,** the despicable and worthless
of all things, or, perhaps, *of all men*,
unto this day. (Comp. Lam. 3 : 45.) Notice
that both here and in ver. 11 this terrible state of things continued to that

very time. Christians, and especially
their leaders, were the most misunderstood and the most unjustly despised
men of the times. (Comp. Acts 16 : 20, 21 ;
24 : 5 ; 28 : 22.)

**14-21. CONCLUSION OF THIS PART
OF THE EPISTLE. FATHERLY EN-
TREATY; APOSTOLIC DIRECTION AND
WARNING.**

14. At this point Paul changes the
plural form of address into the singular
and thus comes into personal relation
to the Corinthian believers as their
spiritual father and an apostle. They
may mistake the spirit and design of
the foregoing passage, and therefore he
states the object of his writing: **Not
to shame you, but as my beloved
sons I warn,** rather, *I admonish
you*. It is the admonition of a father,
not the indignant language of one who
would put them to confusion.

15. Paul justifies his right to admonish them. **For though ye have
ten thousand,** an indefinitely large
number, **of instructors,** or *tutors*,
**in Christ, yet have ye not many
fathers.** Among the Greeks and Romans *a tutor* designated a trustworthy
slave who supervised the morals and
lives of boys belonging to the better
class, being constantly with them till
they arrived at the age of manhood.
Both here and in Gal. 3 : 24 there is an
idea of severity attached to the name ;
the father seems here to be distinguished from the tutor as one whose discipline is usually milder. **For in
Christ Jesus,** words expressive of
that vital union with Christ which
forms the basis of the relation between
the believer and his spiritual Father,

have begotten you through the gospel.
16 Wherefore I beseech you, ᵃ be ye followers of me.
17 For this cause have I sent unto you ᵇ Timotheus, who is my beloved son, and faithful in the Lord, who shall bring you ᶜ into remembrance of my ways which be in Christ, as I teach every where in every church.
18 ᵈ Now some are puffed up, as though
19 I would not come to you. ᵉ But I will come to you shortly, ᶠ if the Lord will, and will know, not the speech of them which are puffed up, but the power.

was through the gospel I that begot
16 you. I beseech you therefore, become
17 imitators of me. For this very cause I sent to you Timothy, who is my child, beloved and faithful in the Lord, who will bring to your remembrance my ways which are in Christ, even as I teach everywhere in every church.
18 Now some were puffed up, as though I
19 were not coming to you. But I will come to you quickly, if the Lord will, and will know, not the word of those
20 who are puffed up, but the power. For

a 11:1; Phil. 3:17; 2 Thess. 3:9; Heb. 13:7.   *b* See refs. Acts 16:1.   *c* 11:2; 2 Tim. 3:10.
d 5:2.   *e* 16:5; Acts 19:21; 2 Cor. 1:15, 23.   *f* See refs. Acts 18:21.

through the gospel, the instrument in their renewal (Rom. 1:16; James 1:18), **I have begotten,** better, *I begot you,* as Christians (Gal. 4:19; Isa. 66:8). The higher and the more real spiritual fatherhood of God is implied and taken for granted in the words "in Christ Jesus" and "through the gospel," and is consistent with fathers and children in the gospel, all of whom have fathership in God (3:5-10).

16. Wherefore, since I am your father, **I beseech you,** with paternal tenderness, that with filial piety and duty *ye become imitators* of me in humility and self-denial, in teaching and practice. Such a spiritual father as Paul, who so closely imitated Christ, could justly ask imitation of his spiritual children. (Comp. 11:1; 1 Thess. 1:6; Phil. 3:17.)

17. For this cause, as I am your spiritual father and I wish you to become imitators of me, **have I sent,** rather, *I sent,* before this letter was written, *Timothy,* **who is my beloved son, and faithful in the Lord,** rather, *my child, beloved and faithful in the Lord,* implying that he owed his conversion to Paul (1 Tim. 1:2, 18; 2 Tim. 2:1-5; Acts 16:1), bearing the same relation to him that they did, and faithful to his teachings and practice. He was therefore a fit person to bring **into remembrance his ways which be in Christ,** a gentle hint that they had forgotten his humility and self-denying conduct in Christ's service (2 Tim. 3:10). Even **as I teach everywhere in every church,** his unvarying practice, an additional reason for their following his example. It appears that Timothy had been sent with Erastus, before the writing of this letter, into Macedonia on his way to Corinth (Acts 19:22), where Paul fully expected he would arrive after the reception of this letter (16:10), and later returned to Macedonia, meeting Paul there, who joined Timothy's name with his own in his second Epistle (2 Cor. 1:1). Compare "Clark's Har. Arrangement of the Acts," § 38 and note.

18. The mention of sending Timothy suggested his own expected coming, which some hoped and thought he would not undertake. **Now some are,** rather, *were,* **puffed up** with conceit and pride, **as though I would not come,** better, *were not coming to you,* as if I dared not come on account of opposers and the depreciation of his influence and apostolic authority (2 Cor. 10:1, 2, 10, 11). Compare Acts 19:22 and 2 Cor. 1:15-17; 2:3, 4, and notice how they tally and confirm the genuineness of these writings.

19. But, I say with emphasis, **I will come to you shortly** (16:8, 9), **if the Lord will,** who holds in his hands the lives and conditions of men. Paul speaks of "the will of *God*" in Rom. 1:10; 15:32; here, "if the *Lord* will," which accords with James 4:13-15. Meyer thinks that *Lord* here is to be understood of God rather than of Christ. But the apostle usually applies this term to Christ as the Son (ver. 4, 5; 1:2, 3, 7-9, etc.), and it seems more natural to refer it here to him. **And will know, not the speech,** the arrogant talk and boasting, **of them that are puffed up, but the power,** to act in Christ's service. He would then test whether their spiritual power and excellence corresponded with

20 For ᵍthe kingdom of God *is* not in word, but in power. What will ye?
21 ʰShall I come unto you with a rod, or in love, and *in* the spirit of meekness?

the kingdom of God is not in word, but
21 in power. What do ye wish? Shall I come to you with a rod, or in love and the spirit of gentleness?

ᵍ 2 : 4 ; 1 Thess. 1 : 5.   ʰ 2 Cor. 10 : 1, 2 ; 13 : 10.

---

their words. For this meaning of the word power, see 2 Cor. 4 : 7 ; Eph. 3 : 16 ; Col. 1 : 11.

20. For, to justify what he had just said, **the kingdom of God,** the reign of God established in the heart by a living fellowship with Christ (Rom. 14 : 17), and to be consummated when he returns with his saints (Phil. 3 : 20, 21 ; Eph. 5 : 5). Compare note on Matt. 3 : 2. **Is not in word**—talk and professions, **but in power**—in spiritual energy, manifested in moral excellence of character, in unction and the presence of the Spirit in preaching, and in Paul's case, in working of miracles and in spiritual gifts, and in apostolic authority.

21. In conclusion, **What will ye?** It is for you to decide how I am to come to you. **Shall I come to you with a rod,** literally, *in a rod,* in the spirit of a rod, of chastisement and severity, like a father (ver. 15) ready to chasten you; **or in love,** without the rod, the severity, and the chastening, **and the spirit of meekness,** of gentleness (Gal. 6 : 1 ; comp. 1 Tim. 6 : 11). Some refer *spirit* here to the Holy Spirit, but this is not necessary. Christian meekness however is one of the fruits of the Spirit, and is characteristic of the renewed human spirit (Gal. 5 : 23 ; Eph. 4 : 2). It is evident that Paul exercised apostolic authority among the churches where he labored, but he did it in a fatherly spirit and as an inspired man (7 : 10. 17, etc.).

THE KINGDOM OF GOD A REALITY. The kingdom of God is prominent in Paul's Epistles, and was a grand theme of his preaching (Acts 14 : 22 ; 19 : 8 ; 20 : 25 ; 28 : 23, 31). It is the Messianic kingdom under the gospel dispensation, already begun in the hearts of believers and advancing toward its full consummation. Its processes of growth and development are taught in some of the parables in the thirteenth chapter of Matthew. The kingdom is not the church ; but churches are the outward manifestations of the kingdom. Paul in his Epistles more frequently speaks of the church, but he does not overlook the kingdom as really existing (Rom. 14 : 17 ; 1 Cor. 4 : 20 ; 1 Thess. 2 : 12). It is a vital force in churches and believers, opposing all false influences and systems under the kingdom of darkness, whose head is Satan, the prince of this world. These must be overcome before the absolute consummation of the kingdom of God, when God shall be all in all (1 Cor. 15 : 28). It is to be feared that Christians too much overlook this kingdom. In so doing their vision and aims are narrowed, their motives are weakened, and they suffer loss in spiritual power. They should proclaim the present blessings and privileges of the kingdom and its future glories, and oppose with spiritual weapons whatever is wrong in the church and the world. The kingdom deals first with the individual, and through individuals with churches, and through these the family, society, and the State.

PRACTICAL REMARKS.

1. Ministers of the gospel are the servants of Christ, and should know no Master but him (ver. 1–4 ; Matt. 23 : 8–10).

2. No earthly position is more honorable and no trust more important than that of the Christian minister (ver. 1 ; Ezek. 33 : 2–8 ; 3 : 17).

3. Faithfulness to God and the souls of men is required of the minister of Christ (ver. 1–4 ; Ezek. 34 : 2 ff. ; Titus 1 : 7).

4. A good reputation is of great value, but greater is an unblemished character, and greatest the approbation of Christ, which will unfailingly follow such character (ver. 3, 4 ; 2 Tim. 2 : 15 ; 1 Sam. 16 : 7).

5. Our own judgment, or the judgment of others, is not a sure test of our fidelity to Christ and his cause (ver. 3–5 ; Ps. 139 : 23, 24 ; 143 : 2).

6. The judgment will be a revelation of secret things—of thoughts and motives ; its decisions will be just and impartial (ver. 5 ; Rev. 16 : 7).

7. All Christians stand on a level before

Moral disorders; regarding an immoral member in the church.

5 IT is reported commonly *that there is* fornication among you, and such fornication as is not so much as named among the Gentiles, [i] that one should

5 It is generally reported that there is fornication among you, and such fornication as is not even among the Gentiles, that one of you has his

[i] See refs. Lev. 18 : 8.

Christ and in the church. Party spirit is unbecoming (ver. 6; Luke 22 : 25, 26; Eph. 6 : 9).

8. We have nothing in ourselves which can give us an occasion for pride and vain boasting (ver. 7, 8; Ps. 115 : 1).

9. For every excellence of character or condition we are indebted to God, which we should humbly acknowledge with thanksgiving (ver. 7, 8 ; 15 : 10; James 1 : 17).

10. If we use irony or sarcasm it should be but rarely, and with great carefulness (ver. 8, 10; Col. 4 : 6).

11. We cannot safely estimate character by external conditions, or from the opinions which persons may form of themselves (ver. 8-10; Rev. 3 : 17).

12. Worldly and vital Christianity has always differed in the lives of its subjects (ver. 8-10 ; 2 Tim. 2 : 11-13).

13. From the experiences of Paul and the apostles we may learn how much true religion has cost. "The blood of martyrs has been the seed of the church" (ver. 9-13; Rev. 7 : 14).

14. The self-denying example and single devotedness of Paul may well put us to shame, in view of what we endure and accomplish in this age and country of soul-liberty (ver. 9-14).

15. It is a distinguished honor, involving great responsibilities, to have spiritual children in the gospel (ver. 15; 2 Cor. 12 : 14).

16. We should so live that we can say to others, "Be ye imitators of me" (ver. 16 ; 1 Tim. 4 : 12).

17. Christian churches should have a common rule of faith and practice (ver. 17; Eph. 4 : 5).

18. Arrogance in church-members indicates a heart and life estranged from Christ (ver. 18; Phil. 2 : 1-5).

19. There are times when church evils are to be corrected with a vigorous hand (ver. 19; Rev. 2 : 14, 20).

20. The power of the kingdom of God is in the mediatorial reign of Christ, and the regenerating and sanctifying work of the Spirit (ver. 20; 15 : 24, 25; 1 Peter 1 : 2 ; 2 Peter 1 : 4).

21. Church discipline is for the good of God's people and should be wisely maintained in all churches (ver. 21; 5 : 4, 5; Matt. 18 : 15-18 ; 1 Tim. 1 : 20).

CHAPTER V.

The apostle now gives attention to certain MORAL DISORDERS IN THE CORINTHIAN CHURCH (chap. 5, 6). In this chapter he first refers to a flagrant case of incest in the church, and to their failure in discipline (ver. 1, 2), and he requires that they should expel the offender (ver. 3-5) because the evil leaven will desecrate the whole (ver. 6-8). He then refers to a previous letter and explains its meaning. The church can exercise its judgment only upon its own members, which it must do in this case (ver. 9-13).

1. Having concluded his discussion and censure of party divisions, the apostle turns at once to moral evils in the church. What he had just said concerning dealing with offenders (4 : 21) prepared the way for this. **It is reported commonly,** better, *it is generally reported*, it is a popular rumor, **that there is fornication among you,** a common and notorious vice, including all unlawful lusts, **and such fornication,** for instance, **as is not so much as named,** rather, according to the best text, *as is not even*, **among the Gentiles, that one should have his father's wife,** should have married his *stepmother*. The father appears to have been still alive (2 Cor. 7 : 12). Some supposed she had been divorced, but this is unknown. Such cases were not allowed by their laws, and, though not absolutely unknown, were looked upon with abhorrence. It was equally against Jewish law (Lev. 18 : 8). Such a condition of

2 have his father's wife. ᵏ And ye are puffed up, and have not rather ˡ mourned, that he that hath done this deed ᵐ might be taken away from 3 among you. ⁿ For I verily, as absent in body, but present in spirit, have judged already, as though I were present, concerning him that hath so done this 4 deed, in the name of our Lord Jesus Christ, when ye are gathered together, and my spirit, ᵒ with the power of our 5 Lord Jesus Christ, ᵖ to deliver such an one unto Satan for the destruction of the flesh, ᵠ that the spirit may be saved in the day of the Lord Jesus.

2 father's wife. And ye are puffed up, and did not rather mourn, that he who did this deed might be taken 3 away from among you. For I verily, being absent in body, but present in spirit, have already, as if present, judged him who has so wrought this; 4 in the name of our Lord Jesus, when ye are gathered together, and my spirit, with the power of our Lord 5 Jesus, to deliver such a one to Satan for the destruction of the flesh, that the spirit may be saved in the day of the

ᵏ 4 : 18.   ˡ See 2 Cor. 7 : 7, 10.   ᵐ Ver. 5, 7, 13.   ⁿ Col. 2 : 5.
ᵒ Matt. 18 : 16–18, 20 ; John 20 : 23 ; 2 Cor. 2 : 10.   ᵖ 1 Tim. 1 : 20.   ᵠ See 2 Cor. 2 : 6–11.

things showed the influence of the loose and corrupt morals of Corinth upon the church. The early Gentile churches were by no means models. They were like our own missionary churches among the heathen, very imperfect. This instance of crime forms the climax of this portion of the Epistle. "It is, as it were, the burst of storm, the mutterings of which, as Chrysostom observes, had already been heard in the earlier chapters (3 : 16 ; 4 : 5, 20, 21), and of which the echoes are still discernible, not only in this Epistle (7 : 2 ; 10 : 8, 22 ; 15 : 33), but also in the second Epistle, the first half of which (chap. 1–7) is nothing less than an endeavor to allay the excitement and confusion created by this severe remonstrance" (DEAN STANLEY).

2. And ye are puffed up, self-complacent, boastful, and elated, *and did not* **rather mourn** over this scandalous sin, *that he that did* **this deed might be taken away from among you,** excluded from your fellowship. It seems better, with some critics, to regard this as a question, thus: *And ye, are ye puffed up, and did not rather mourn?* etc. But the sense in either case is the same. In their pride and by their silence they were sanctioning this sin. A becoming humility and mourning on account of it would have led them to deal as a church with the offender.

3. And he must be excluded, **For I verily, as absent,** rather, *being absent,* **in body, but present in spirit, have judged,** *him,* **already, as though I were present,** or, *have decided* **concerning him, that hath so done this deed,** in such a manner and under such circumstances.

4. The sentence continues to the end of ver. 5. **In the name of our Lord Jesus** (**Christ** should be omitted according to the best authorities), in his name and by his authority as his representative, **when ye are gathered together,** as a church, **and my spirit** with you, as it were, **with the power of our Lord Jesus** (omit **Christ** as above), his power being present in their assembly as promised in Matt. 18 : 20 ; 28 : 20, and with me as an apostle (comp. Acts 3 : 6, 16 ; 13 : 9–11 ; 16 : 18 ; 2 Thess. 3 : 6). The church was to act thus in Christ's name, in his power, and with the sanction of the apostle.

5. What they were to do. **To deliver such a one unto Satan,** a strong way of expressing excommunication from the church. He was to be delivered over as a heathen (Matt. 18 : 17) to the world over which Satan held special sway (2 Cor. 4 : 4 ; Eph. 2 : 2 ; 6 : 12). This seems to be the underlying conception (comp. 1 Tim. 1 : 20). The suffering as a result of this offender's conduct is conceived of as connected with Satan's kingdom. All moral and physical evils are conceived of as coming from him (Luke 13 : 16 ; 2 Cor. 12 : 7 ; Job 2 : 6), **For the destruction of the flesh,** implying some physical evil, as disease, afflictions, bodily sufferings, in which Satan may be conceived of as the instrument of divine justice. (Compare 11 : 30 ; Acts 5 : 5–10.) The object of this discipline is remedial. **That the spirit,** the center of his personality, or as we would say, that his soul, **may be saved,** from destruction,

6 *Your glorying is not good. Know ye not that *a little leaven leaveneth 7 the whole lump? *Purge out therefore the old leaven, that ye may be a new lump, as ye are unleavened. For even "Christ our Passover is sacrificed for 8 us. Therefore let us keep the feast, *not with old leaven, neither *with the leaven of malice and wickedness; but with the unleavened *bread* of sincerity and truth.	6 Lord. Your glorying is not good. Know ye not that a little leaven leavens 7 the whole mass? Cleanse out the old leaven, that ye may be a new mass, even as ye are unleavened. For our passover also, Christ, was sacrificed; 8 therefore let us keep the feast, not with old leaven, nor with the leaven of malice and wickedness, but with the unleavened bread of sincerity and truth.

r 4 : 19 ; James 4 : 16.   *s* 15 : 33 ; Gal. 5 : 9 ; Heb. 12 : 15.   *t* Ver. 13 ; see Exod. 12 : 15 ; Col. 3 : 5.
u See refs. John 1 : 29.   *x* Deut. 16 : 3 ; Eph. 4 : 17-24.   *y* See refs. Mark 8 : 15 ; 1 Peter 2 : 1, 2.

in the day of the Lord Jesus, the day of judgment (3 : 13). To the same effect is 1 Tim. 1 : 20, "That they may learn not to blaspheme," and also 3 : 15, "saved through fire." Through present sufferings the offender may be led to repentance and saved at last. As far as such consequences were connected with apostolic power (2 Cor. 13 : 10) they were peculiar to the apostolic age. The phrase "to deliver to Satan" does not occur in the ordinary forms of excommunication in the first four centuries (STANLEY). In regard to the wife (ver. 1) BENGEL says : "She was no doubt a heathen, therefore he does not rebuke her (ver. 12, 13)."

6. In such a state of things, **your glorying,** in your wisdom and spiritual gifts, **is not good,** is not becoming ; you have no ground for boasting. **Know ye not that a little leaven leaveneth the whole lump?** that sin is rapidly diffusive, that "one sinner destroyeth much good" (Eccl. 9 : 18). This appears to be a proverbial saying and occurs in Gal. 5 : 9. A similar proverb is given in 15 : 33. Leaven is used in the New Testament of an evil principle (Matt. 16 : 6, 11, 12), except in the parable of the leaven in the meal (Matt. 13 : 33). The presence of such sin among them, though confined to a few, and of such a sinner, gave a character to the whole church, and as long as they allowed this they were in a measure partakers of the sin.

7. The mention of leaven suggests the use of the figure of the Passover, when every particle of leaven was removed from their houses (Exod. 13 : 3-7). **Purge out therefore the old leaven,** the sins of the old man, of your unregenerate state, still clinging to you, **that ye may be a new lump even as ye are,** in Christ, un-

leavened, free from malice and wickedness (ver. 8). **Purge out,** a strong expression, *cleanse out,* every particle and taint. The later Jews searched with lighted candles the darkest holes and corners so that not the least leaven remained (Zeph. 1 : 12). The word *lump* means, literally, a *mass of dough.* The apostle would have them really as a church what they professed to be, a truly regenerate people. **For,** to carry out the figure and enforce the exhortation, **Christ our passover,** better, *For also our passover,* Christ, our Paschal Lamb, **was sacrificed for us** once for all (Heb. 7 : 27) in order that we might be saved from sin and its consequences (John 1 : 29). Let us therefore put away sin and keep ourselves free from the defilements of the world. The word translated *Passover* is used both of the feast and as here of the Paschal Lamb. For Christ as God's Paschal Lamb, see John 1 : 36 ; Rev. 13 : 8. *For us* is omitted by the highest critical authorities. The act of *slaying, sacrificing,* the victim is prominent here. It is needless, however, to press the illustration into supposing that Christ died at the very hour that the Passover lambs were killed. The main object of the illustration was the *cleansing out* of sins, as individuals and a church.

8. And since the lamb is slain and the feast is going on, **therefore let us keep the feast,** a perpetual festival, as it were, **not with the old leaven** of our former corrupt lives (Eph. 2 : 1-3), **neither,** to be more explicit, **with the leaven of malice and wickedness, but with the unleavened bread of sincerity and truth,** abstaining from the corrupting influences of sin and practising purity and truthfulness of heart and

I. CORINTHIANS [CH. V.

9 I wrote unto you in an epistle *not
10 to company with fornicators: *yet not
altogether with the fornicators of this
world, or with the covetous, or extortioners, or with idolaters; for then
must ye needs go ᵇout of the world.
11 But now I have written unto you not
to keep company, if any man that is
called a brother be a fornicator, or
covetous, or an idolater, or a railer, or
a drunkard, or an extortioner; ᶜwith
12 such an one no not to eat. For what
have I to do to judge ᵈ them also that
are without? Do not ye judge ᵉ them
13 that are within? But them that are

9 I wrote to you, in my letter, not to
10 keep company with fornicators; yet
not, altogether, with the fornicators of
this world, or with the covetous and
extortioners, or idolaters; for then ye
11 must needs go out of the world. But
as it is, I wrote to you not to keep
company, if any one called a brother
be a fornicator, or covetous, or an
idolater, or a reviler, or a drunkard, or
an extortioner, with such a one not
even to eat.
12 For what have I to do with judging
those who are without? Do not ye
13 judge those who are within? But

*2 Cor. 6 : 14, 17; Eph. 5 : 5, 11; 2 Thess. 3 : 14.   a 10 : 27.   b John 17 : 15; Phil. 2 : 15.
c Ver. 13; Matt. 18 : 17; Rom. 16 : 17; 2 Thess. 3 : 6; 2 John 10 : 11.
d Mark 4 : 11; Col. 4 : 5; 1 Thess. 4 : 12.   e 6 : 1-4.

---

life. "*Sincerity* takes care not to admit evil with the good; *truth*, not to admit evil instead of good" (BENGEL). "*Malice* denotes rather the vicious disposition; *wickedness*, the active exercise of the same" (THAYER'S "N. T. *Lex.*"). Paul wrote this Epistle about the time of the Passover (16 : 10, 11; see introduction), and perhaps this may have suggested this particular illustration.

9. I wrote unto you in an epistle, literally, *in the letter*, doubtless referring to an Epistle sent them a short time previous, but now lost. This is the view of the majority of commentators. **Not to**, *keep*, **company**, or, *be intimate*, **with fornicators** (2 Thess. 3 : 14). What he had just said in ver. 7, 8 leads him to notice a misunderstanding and a perversion by his adversaries of a passage in a former letter. He digresses to explain.

10. The warning to avoid association with dissolute persons among professed believers they had applied to all men. **Yet not altogether**, or, *not entirely with*, not in every case and under all circumstances with, **the fornicators of this world,** the unbelieving or heathen world; **or with the covetous,** *the greedy of gain*, **or**, rather, *and*, **extortioners**, unjust and violent graspers after other people's property; **or with idolaters**, here associated with the covetous, because covetousness is a kind of idolatry (Col. 3 : 5). **For then**, or *else ye must*, **needs go out of the world** altogether. You cannot help meeting such men in business and general society.

11. But now I have written unto you, better, *but as it is I wrote to you,* or *but now,* as the case stands in fact (Rom. 3 : 21), *I wrote to you*, in my former epistle, **if any man called a brother be a fornicator,** etc., as designated in ver. 10; to which are added, **a railer,** one who reviles, **or a drunkard.** Notice these six characters—all fitted to destroy the peace, life, and character of a church. Paul explains his meaning: with such professed brethren, you are not to keep company, **no not to eat,** *not even to eat* at ordinary meals. They are not to associate with such persons, nor to join them in festive and social intercourse. Of course, as an inference, such persons were not to partake with them of the Lord's Supper.

12. I make this limit to those who profess faith in Christ, **For,** *what have I,* as an apostle, **to do to judge,** rather, *with judging those,* **that are without,** the outside world, unbelievers. The phrase, *those without,* was the usual Jewish designation for the heathen. **Also** should be omitted. **Do not ye judge them that are within,** the church? Paul evidently has reference to "when ye are gathered together" (ver. 4). The question demands an affirmative answer. It was a strong way of saying, It is your province as a church to judge your own members. It would seem that Paul in this verse distinguishes his own authority as an inspired apostle, and that of the church. **But them that are without God judgeth,** neither you nor I have authority to do this.

13. Paul now applies what he had

without God judgeth. *ᶠTherefore put away from among yourselves that wicked person.* those who are without God judges. Put away that wicked man from among yourselves.

ᶠ Ver. 5, 7 ; Deut. 13 : 5 ; 21 : 21.

said to the person mentioned in ver. 1. **Therefore**, is not in the best text. The abruptness and strength of the exhortation accord with Paul's manner. **Put away,** *the wicked man,* **from among yourselves.** These are in the words of Deut. 24 : 7, and they indicate the usual formula in pronouncing punishment on great crimes (Deut. 13 : 5 ; 17 : 7 ; 21 : 21). This act of exclusion is to be their act. The apostle would not ignore the prerogative of the local church in exercising discipline.

CHURCH GOVERNMENT. Since the Christian church was divinely organized, if there is within it a governing power it must be of divine authority, and it is reasonable to expect to find what it is in the New Testament, both as to its nature and form. Such has been the general sense of Christendom in all ages, and hence the advocates of respective church governments have uniformly appealed to Scripture. An authoritative form is implied in such passages as, "We have no such custom, neither the churches of God" (1 Cor. 11 : 16). "God is not the author of confusion, but of peace, as in all the churches of the saints" (1 Cor. 14 : 33. Comp. 4 : 16, 17 ; 7 : 17 ; 11 : 2 ; 16 : 1 ; 1 Thess. 2 : 14 ; Titus 1 : 5).

The Epistles of Paul, especially those to the Corinthians, point to a democratic and independent government of local churches. Nowhere are officers or government of either a national or a universal church spoken of. Christ is represented as equally the Head of the universal church, of the local church, and of each individual member (1 Cor. 11 : 3 ; Col. 1 : 18 ; 2 : 10, 19). The Epistles to the Corinthians were addressed "to the church of God which is at Corinth" (1 Cor. 1 : 2 ; 2 Cor. 1 : 1). Paul recognizes the local church, not its officers, as vested with the power of excommunicating offenders, of receiving and restoring members, and as of the highest authority in giving final judgments and in settling personal difficulties (1 Cor. 5 : 4-7, 9, 12, 13 ; 6 : 1-4 ; 2 Cor. 2 : 6-8, etc. ; comp. Matt. 18 : 15-20). Paul gives not the least hint to the Corinthians that any other church or ecclesiastical body was responsible for their irregularities of discipline, or their disorders in connection with the Lord's Supper. The membership of the local church formed the responsible party ; and it he praises, or blames.

Dr. Alexander Carson, in his "Reasons for Separating from the General Synod of Ulster," very forcibly maintains that the democratic and independent government of churches is the most practicable in all countries, ages, and circumstances; that it is the least capable of abuse; and sufficient for subsisting in vigor and for preserving others from error; that it does not require human expedients and human wisdom in maintaining uniformity and purity of doctrine; but that it does require more than all other forms the most knowledge of the Scriptures; and constantly needs prayer and Divine guidance; that it also is the most favorable to soul liberty; and offers the fewest incitements to unhallowed ambition; that it is the best adapted to promote the welfare and growth of the membership; and that it most nearly resembles the simplicity of other gospel institutions." See also "Clark's Commentary on the Acts" on Church Polity, pp. 14, 15.

PRACTICAL REMARKS.

1. Evil rumors have generally some basis in facts. Churches should not allow such against their own members to go without investigation (ver. 1).

2. If a professed Christian gives way to a course of sin, he often descends lower than if he had never made a profession (ver. 1 ; 2 Peter 2 : 22 ; Zech. 13 : 6).

3. Pride and a boastful spirit tend to blind men to the nature and consequences of sin (ver. 2 ; 1 Tim. 3 : 6).

4. Discipline and the corrections of evils in a church should be undertaken in a tender and humble spirit (ver. 2 ; 2 Cor. 7 : 7, 11).

5. Discipline is to be exercised by the church itself, in its collective capacity,

Regarding going to law before the heathen; the limits of Christian liberty.

6 DARE any of you, having a matter against another, go to law before the 2 unjust, and not before the saints? Do

6 DARE any one of you, having a matter against another, go to law before the unrighteous, and not before 2 the saints? Or, know ye not that the

and not by individual members (ver. 3, 4, 13 ; Matt. 18 : 17).

6. Paul's authority was that of an apostle and an inspired man, but he did not so exercise it as to ignore the rights of the local church (ver. 4, 5, 13 ; 2 Cor. 7 : 12).

7. A special object in church discipline should be the spiritual good of the offender (ver. 4-6 ; 2 Cor. 7 : 7-13).

8. The least sin is dangerous. It may pollute the whole character and life of the individual, and mar the reputation and life of a church (ver. 6; James 1 : 15; 2 John 10).

9. Christians should strive to keep themselves free from the contaminations of sin and of the world (ver. 7, 8; 1 John 3 : 3 ; 1 Tim. 4 : 12).

10. A spirit of asceticism is not the spirit of the gospel. Christians are not of the world, yet they are in the world for the world's good (ver. 9, 10 ; John 17 : 15 ; Matt. 5 : 14, 15).

11. We learn what class of persons are not to be regarded as Christians: fornicators, covetous, idolaters, etc. (ver. 11 ; 6 : 9, 10).

12. We should refrain from making persons of depraved morals and irreligious lives our associates (ver. 11, 12 ; 6 : 17).

13. It is the duty of the church to deal promptly with public offenses, and to exclude public offenders (ver. 13 ; 2 Thess. 3 : 6).

14. It is a solemn thing to be excluded from a church of Christ (ver. 4, 5, 13 ; Matt. 18 : 17, 18).

15. It is also a solemn fact that the world of the ungodly is condemned already, and is to be finally judged by a holy and righteous God (ver. 13 ; Rev. 20 : 11-13).

CHAPTER VI.

With the distinction in mind, between the church and the world, Paul rebukes those Corinthian Christians who were taking their lawsuits before heathen tribunals, and shows the inconsistency of such conduct (ver. 1-11). He then re-

sumes the subject of fornication among them, and limits the law of Christian liberty and expediency which some had abused (ver. 12-14) ; and he admonishes them against licentiousness, since their own bodies were God's living temples, and a redeemed body should be used for God's glory (ver. 15-20).

1-11. LAWSUITS BEFORE HEATHEN TRIBUNALS.

1. The digression in this paragraph was naturally suggested by what Paul had just said in 5 : 12, 13. As they had nothing to do in judging the world, so they ought not to carry their disputes before unbelievers, and thus be judged by them. **Dare any,** *one,* **of you,** is it possible that any one of you can be so bold and imprudent, as **having a matter,** or *suit,* **against another** brother to **go to law before the unjust,** *the unrighteous,* **and not before the saints?** It was a matter of surprise. How could any one of them bring himself to do such a thing? Paul does not intimate that heathen magistrates were intentionally unjust, but he designates them as belonging to a class, the unrighteous, in contrast to the saints. In Matt. 18 : 17 we have Christ's precepts for the settlement of personal difficulties in the local church. It appears that Christians were accustomed to settle their disputes among themselves by arbitration, and that this custom continued till the establishment of Christianity as the religion of the Roman Empire. In the so-called Apostolical Constitutions, written as early as the second or third century, the existence of such courts of arbitration is implied, which were held early in the week, so that any disputes that arose might be settled before Sunday. The civil law also gave its sanction to decisions pronounced in such cases by arbitrators privately chosen. There was therefore no need for Christians to resort to heathen tribunals.

2. Do ye not know—according to the best text, *Or do ye not know,* can you be ignorant of such a well-known fact, as your conduct would seem to

CH. VI.] I. CORINTHIANS

ye not know that *the saints shall judge the world? And if the world shall be judged by you, are ye unworthy to judge the smallest matters? 3 Know ye not that we shall ᵇjudge angels? How much more things that 4 pertain to this life! ᶦIf then ye have judgments of things pertaining to this life, set them to judge who are 5 least esteemed in the church. I speak to your shame. Is it so, that there is not a wise man among you; no, not one that shall be able to judge between 6 his brethren? But brother goeth to law with brother, and that before the

saints will judge the world? And if the world is judged by you, are ye unworthy to judge the least matters? 3 Know ye not that we shall judge angels? How much more the things 4 of this life? If then ye have judgments about things of this life, set those to judge who are of no esteem in 5 the church. I speak to your shame. Is it so, that there can not be among you even one wise man who will be able to judge between his brethren, 6 but brother goeth to law with brother, 7 and that before unbelievers? Already,

g Ps. 49 : 14 ; Dan. 7 : 22 ; see refs. Matt. 19 : 28 ; Rev. 20 : 4. *h* 2 Peter 2 : 4 ; Jude 6. *i* 5 : 12.

imply, an ignorance which is entirely inexcusable, **that the saints shall judge the world** of unbelievers by virtue of their close and exalted union with Christ (ver. 15; 12 : 27; 2 Tim. 2 : 12). Thus Christ speaks of the apostles "judging the twelve tribes of Israel" (Matt. 19 : 28); and Daniel (7 : 22), of "judgment being given to the saints of the Most High"; and Jude (14), of "the Lord coming with ten thousand of his saints." **And if the world** *is* **judged by you,** in your presence, *before you,* as judges, **are ye unworthy,** unfit, **to judge the smallest matters,** the most trifling cases? Or as some would translate, "Are ye unworthy of the smallest tribunals"? The other rendering, however, is to be preferred.

3. **Know ye not,** as in ver. 2, and frequently used in this Epistle (3 : 16; 5 : 6; 9 : 13, 24), calling attention to something well known. **That we shall judge angels.** The climax in the thought regarding the high destiny of believers. Some suppose *good* angels are meant, because angels are generally used in the New Testament of good angels. But bad angels are referred to in Matt. 25 : 41; 2 Cor. 11 : 14; 12 : 7; 2 Peter 2 : 4; Jude 6; Rev. 9 : 11; 12 : 7, 9. Notice also that it is not *the* angels, but simply *angels*. Besides, it is nowhere stated that the good angels are to be judged (2 Thess. 1 : 7), and it is difficult to see how saints could judge them. But bad angels are to be judged (Matt. 25 : 41; Rev. 20 : 10; 2 Peter 2 : 4; Jude 6), and it is fitting that these great opposers of the saints should be judged and condemned by them. It seems better, therefore, to regard the reference here to bad

angels. **How much more** should we judge **in things that pertain to this life.** Or the thought may be expressed thus: Shall we judge angels, and *not indeed in things relating to ordinary life?*

4. **Judgments,** the word translated "matters" in ver. 2. **If then ye have judgments,** *causes* or *suits,* **pertaining to this life, set them to judge who are least esteemed,** or *accounted as nothing,* **in the church.** Some would make this a question: *Do ye set them to judge?* etc. But the common translation as above is preferable, as best suiting the context. The thought is: Since you are to judge angels, the least-esteemed among you surely can attend to these ordinary matters. And perhaps impliedly: If they are not able to do it, surely they ought to be.

5. Abruptly Paul explains his words. **I speak,** I say this (ver. 4) **to your shame,** to arouse your shame, that neither you nor your conduct are such as your exalted position as saints demands. **Is it so that there is not a "wise" man among you?** etc. Among you Corinthians, who regard yourselves as wise, and pride yourselves in your wisdom. Surely you should find some among you who could arbitrate such matters. This could not well apply where one party was an unbeliever.

6. **But,** so far from this, **brother goeth to law with brother, and that before unbelievers,** which was unbecoming, degrading, and inconsistent. By exposing their differences before the eyes of the heathen, they brought scandal upon themselves, and discredit upon the worthy name by which they were called. "A litigious

7 unbelievers. Now therefore there is utterly a fault among you, because ye go to law one with another. *Why do ye not rather take wrong? Why do ye not rather *suffer yourselves to be de-* 8 frauded? Nay, ye do wrong, and de- 9 fraud, and that *your* brethren. Know ye not that ᶩthe unrighteous shall not inherit the kingdom of God?

Be not deceived: ᵐ neither fornicators, nor idolaters, nor adulterers, nor effeminate, nor abusers of themselves 10 with mankind, nor thieves, nor covetous, nor drunkards, nor revilers, nor extortioners, shall inherit the 11 kingdom of God. And such were ⁿ some of you; ᵒ but ye are washed, but

it is indeed a defect in you, that ye have law-suits one with another. Why not rather suffer wrong? Why not 8 rather be defrauded? But ye yourselves do wrong, and defraud, and 9 that your brethren. Or know ye not that the unrighteous shall not inherit the kingdom of God? Be not deceived; neither fornicators, nor idolaters, nor adulterers, nor effeminate, nor abusers of themselves with men, 10 nor thieves, nor covetous, nor drunkards, nor revilers, nor extortioners, 11 will inherit the kingdom of God. And such were some of you; but ye were

k Prov. 20 : 22; Matt. 5 : 39–41; Rom. 12 : 17–19; 1 Thess. 5 : 15. *l* See refs. Lev. 19 : 15, 35; Isa. 10 : 1, 2.
m Gal. 5 : 19–21; Eph. 5 : 3–5; Heb. 12 : 14; 13 : 4; Rev. 22 : 15.
n Rom. 6 : 17–19; Eph. 2 : 1–3; Col. 3 : 5–8; Titus 3 : 3. *o* Eph. 5 : 26; Titus 3 : 5; Rev. 1 : 5, 6.

spirit is known to have characterized the Greek nation from the time of Aristophanes downward, and it is not wonderful that this should have cropped out in the Christians of Corinth" (*T. W. Chambers*, in MEYER).

7. Now therefore there is utterly a fault, etc., better, *It is indeed already a defect in general in you.* Your having lawsuits one with another shows a *defect* in your Christian love and sense of right; it implies selfishness and injustice. Already there is a *falling short* in your Christian characters and lives, which may result disastrously, since such sins exclude men from the kingdom of God (ver. 9, 10). **Why do ye not rather take, or *suffer*, wrong . . . rather be defrauded**, according to the command of Christ (Matt. 5 : 38–42).

8. Nay, *Instead of this*, **ye do wrong and defraud and that your brethren**, with whom you are bound in spiritual relations closer and dearer than the ties of blood (Matt. 23 : 8).

9. Paul strengthens his remonstrance by appealing to the well-known character of the kingdom of God as opposed to all unrighteousness. **Know ye not** (ver. 2, 3), the well-known fact, **that the unrighteous shall not inherit the kingdom of God**, which is to be consummated at Christ's coming? (See on 4 : 20.) Yet they were conducting themselves as if ignorant of this. Hence he warns them. **Be not deceived** in regard to yourselves and this matter. (Comp. 3 : 8, 10.) He then proceeds to particu-

lars, in order that there may be no misunderstanding of his meaning. The classes named are the same substantially as those in 5 : 11 (on which see), with four additional ones. They include those who lived for their own sensual indulgence, or for gain. **Effeminate**, the indulgers in soft and luxurious living. **Abusers of themselves with mankind,** *sodomites* (1 Tim. 1 : 10; Rom. 1 : 27).

10. Nor thieves, with probable reference to some of the lawsuits. Notice that **drunkards** and **revilers** are put together both here and in 5 : 11, as if suggested by the fact that drunkenness and strife usually go together. Paul doubtless had noticed that such classes of persons were common at Corinth, and he affirms that none of them **shall inherit the kingdom of God,** at "the restitution of all things" (Acts 3 : 21). Notice how the apostle returns to these great moral and social evils (5 : 9–11). It was their low spirituality and loose morals that lay at the foundation of their party strifes and other troubles (3 : 1–3).

11. And such classes of persons **were some of you,** before your conversion, but having been changed in heart and life, you should not have wrongdoing among yourselves, and disputes, and even lawsuits, before heathen tribunals. The contrast in what follows is made intense by the emphatic **but** repeated thrice. The three verbs—*washed, sanctified,* and *justified*—are in the past tense and form a climax comprehending three great

ye are p sanctified, but ye are q justified in the name of the Lord Jesus, and by the Spirit of our God.
12 r All things are lawful unto me; s but all things are not expedient [or, profitable]. All things are lawful for me; t but I will not be brought under the
13 power of any. u Meats for the belly, and the belly for meats: but God shall

washed, but ye were sanctified, but ye were justified in the name of the Lord Jesus Christ, and in the Spirit of our God.
12 All things are lawful for me, but not all things are profitable; all things are lawful for me, but I will not be brought under the control of anything.
13 Foods for the belly, and the belly for foods; but God will bring to nought

p 1 : 2, 30; 2 Thess. 2 : 13.   q Rom. 3 : 24, 26–30.   r 10 : 23; Rom. 14 : 14.
s 8 : 4, 7–13; 10 : 24–33; Rom. 14 : 15.   t 9 : 27.   u Matt. 15 : 17; Rom. 14 : 17.

facts of their Christian experience in conversion. **But ye are washed,** literally, *ye washed off*, or *bathed away*, these pollutions, the act properly referring to the whole body, and figuratively to the whole being. It is generally thought that there is here an allusion to baptism. The verb implies an intelligent agent in submitting to God, and in renouncing and forsaking sin, just as the believer submits voluntarily and intelligently to baptism, which symbolically represents the forgiveness and cleansing away of sins. See Acts 22 : 16 and note, where the same verb is used. There is, however, no more reference to self-baptism than there is to sinners changing their own hearts or forgiving their own sins. Compare such passages as James 4 : 8; Phil. 2 : 12; 2 Cor. 7 : 1, 11. **But ye were sanctified,** consecrated to God and a holy life (Eph. 5 : 26; Heb. 10 : 10, 14; Rom. 12 : 1). **But ye were justified,** including not only their acceptance by God as righteous, but also that moral righteousness of heart and life which results at conversion, through union with Christ and the operation of the Holy Spirit. *Justified* seems to contrast with *unrighteous* in ver. 9. (See on Rom. 1 : 17.) **In the name of the Lord Jesus,** *Christ*, **and by the Spirit of our God.** Both of these clauses refer to the three preceding verbs. The person and work of Christ, and the work of the Spirit, are both connected with our regeneration and forgiveness, our sanctification and justification, and brought vividly to view in our baptism. So also baptism and all it symbolizes are realities to us by faith and nothing to us without faith. How inconsistent the moral disorders in these Corinthian Christians! How should these words of the apostle have inspired them to a holier life!

12-20. RETURNING TO THE SIN OF FORNICATION, PAUL LIMITS THE LAW OF CHRISTIAN LIBERTY, WHICH SOME HAD ABUSED.

12. Paul proceeds to discuss this sin in view of their new spiritual life. **All things are lawful unto me,** were the apostle's own words, and were true in the sense and with the limitations in which he used them, but not in the sense that his opponent quoted and applied them; and doubtless they loved to refer to them in self-justification. He had used them especially with reference to food (ver. 13; 10 : 29). "All things are lawful to me, which can be lawful" (BENGEL). **But all things are not expedient,** rather, *profitable*, advantageous. **All things, I repeat, are lawful for me, but I will not be brought under the power of any,** or *under the control of anything.* As if he had said: All things are allowed me or in my power, but they must be for my good. All things are within my power, but I must not be brought under their power, even of my lawful desires; I must not become their slave. "Liberty, good in itself, is destroyed by its abuse (Gal. 5 : 13; 1 Peter 2 : 16)" (BENGEL). Paul speaks with the force of a maxim, as a representative of Christians.

13. In this verse Paul refers to *food* as a representative of things indifferent, to which he had especially referred in his maxim regarding liberty, and then he notices fornication as inapplicable to the law of Christian liberty because absolutely sinful. **Meats,** or *foods*, **for the belly,** the digestive organs generally, **and the belly for** *foods*, one destined for the other, appointed sustenance and the appointed receptacle. **But God shall destroy both it and them;** both are temporary and perishable. Food

P

destroy both it and them. Now the body *is* not for fornication, but ª for the Lord; ⁊ and the Lord for the body. 14 And ᶜ God hath both raised up the Lord, and will also raise up us ᵃ by his 15 own power. Know ye not that ᵇ your bodies are the members of Christ? Shall I then take the members of Christ, and make *them* the members of 16 an harlot? God forbid. What, know ye not that he which is joined to an harlot is one body? (For ᵉ two, saith 17 he, shall be one flesh.) ᵈ But he that is joined unto the Lord is one spirit.

both it and them. Now the body is not for fornication, but for the Lord; 14 and the Lord for the body. And God both raised the Lord, and will raise up us through his power. 15 Know ye not that your bodies are members of Christ? Shall I then take away the members of Christ, and make them members of a harlot? Far be it! 16 Or know ye not that he who is joined to the harlot is one body? For the two, 17 says he, shall be one flesh. But he that is joined to the Lord is one spirit.

z Ver. 15, 19, 20; 3:16, 17; Rom. 12:1; 1 Thess. 4:3-7.   *y* Eph. 5:23.
z Rom. 6:4-8; 8, 11; 2 Cor. 4:14.   *a* Eph. 1:19, 20.   *b* 12:27; Eph. 4:12, 15, 16; 5:29, 30.
c Matt. 19:5; Eph. 5:31.   *d* John 15:1-5; 17:21-23; Eph. 4:4.

is necessary in this present life; but in the future life we shall hunger and thirst no more (Rev. 7:16). At our Lord's second coming "the dead shall be raised incorruptible and we shall be changed" (15:51, 52). Food and digestive organs will no longer be needed. Questions concerning these are comparatively unimportant. But not so with fornication, which degrades the body, which was destined for the Lord and to immortality. *But* **the body is not for fornication,** it is not made for it, **but for the Lord,** for his service and glory (ver. 19; Rom. 12:1); **and the Lord for the body,** for its salvation and its glorification. Christ is Saviour of the body as well as of the soul (15:54-57). The transition from questions regarding food, especially that offered to idols (10:19-24), to the question regarding sins of sensuality, was comparatively easy then, from the frequent connection of licentious rites with idolatrous worship in heathen cities, and particularly in Corinth. Note how "things offered to idols" and "fornication" are joined together in Acts 15:29; Rev. 2:14. It is not strange that Paul found it necessary to refute and condemn licentious liberty.

14. The thought is continued: Paul bases the resurrection of the body and our future life on Christ's resurrection. **And God hath,** better, *God both raised the Lord, and will raise up us,* etc. **His own power,** too emphatic, rather, *his power,* referring to *God's* power (Rom. 8:11; 1 Cor. 15:12-19). Such is the glorious destiny of the believer's body. Surely it should not be degraded by licentious lusts.

15. In this and the two verses that follow Paul adduces a second general argument, from the believer's relation to, and connection with, Christ. **Know ye not,** ye certainly know (ver. 2), **that your bodies are members of Christ,** being so closely connected with him, who is head over all, as to be "members of his body," as it were, "of his flesh and of his bones" (Eph. 5:30). See the thought in 12:27, "Ye are Christ's body, and each one members of it." **Shall I then,** so far degrade myself as to *take away,* **the members of Christ,** my own members, and by fornication **make them members of a harlot?** To ask a question so abhorrent was its own answer. **God forbid!** *Far be it!* Away the thought!

16. **What! know ye not.** Rather, *Or, know ye not,* as in ver. 2. Can you be ignorant of the closeness of the union, that he that **is joined to** *the* **harlot** (her character expressed vividly and definitely), **is one body,** that is, he with her is now one, partaking of her character and of her sin. The consequence of this union is illustrated and confirmed by quoting Gen. 2:24, in the words of the Septuagint version, **For** *the* **two, saith he** (God was the speaker), **shall be one flesh.** This was originally said of marriage, but it illustrates the closeness of the sinful and unlawful relation of a person who joins himself to a harlot. Of course it separates him from Christ.

17. Having presented the human and fleshly side, Paul gives the Christ and spiritual side. **But he that is**

17 *Flee fornication. Every sin that a man doeth is without the body; but he that committeth fornication sinneth 19 *against his own body. What, *know ye not that your body is the temple of the Holy Ghost *which is* in you, which ye have of God? *And ye are not 20 your own; for *ye are bought with a price. Therefore *glorify God in your body, and in your spirit, which are God's.

18 Flee fornication. Every sin that a man commits is outside the body; but he that commits fornication, sins 19 against his own body. Or know ye not that your body is the Holy Spirit's temple, who is in you, whom ye have from God, and ye are not your own? 20 For ye were bought with a price; glorify God therefore in your body.

e Gen. 39 : 7–12; Rom. 6 : 12, 13, 2 Tim. 2 : 22.   *f* Prov. 5 : 8–11.   *g* See refs, 3 : 16.
h Rom. 14 : 7–9; 2 Cor. 5 : 15; Titus 2 : 14.   *i* 7 : 23; Acts 20 : 28; 1 Peter 1 : 18, 19; 2 Peter 2 : 1.
k 10 : 31; Rom. 12 : 1; 1 Peter 2 : 9.

joined, closely united, **to the Lord is one spirit,** indicating an inward spiritual union, the Lord's spirit pervading the believer's spirit, and the two in unison (John 17 : 21, 23; 15 : 1–7; comp. Eph. 5 : 23–32). It is impossible for such a one to be joined to a harlot without alienating himself from Christ and breaking this spiritual union.

18. No wonder, after such a presentation of the believer's close and vital union with Christ, that Paul exclaims, **Flee fornication,** including sensual lusts. This exhortation forms also the connecting link with what follows. The apostle now presents his third general argument, that fornication is a sin against one's own body, which, in the believer's case, is the temple of the Holy Spirit. **Every sin,** that is, as the connection demands, *Every other sin* **a man doeth is without,** *outside,* **the body,** external to it. Take the other sins forbidden in the Decalogue, they are directed against objects outside the body, or if they affect the body they come from without. This is true even of drunkenness, gluttony, and suicide, they come from outside the body. **But he that committeth fornication,** within himself, using his own sensuous nature as an instrument, **sinneth against his own body,** against its very nature and against the fundamental law of his being, that a man shall cleave to his wife and to her alone, and they two shall become one flesh (Gen. 2 : 24). He runs counter to this primal law of our being.

19. Paul substantiates what he had just said. **What, know ye not,** rather, *Or do you not certainly know* (see ver. 2) this fact, **that your body,** each one individually, **is the temple of the Holy Ghost,** *Spirit who,* **is in you.** It is because of the indwelling Spirit that the believer's body is God's temple. (See on 3 : 16. Comp. 2 Cor. 6 : 16; 2 Tim. 2 : 20; 1 Peter 2 : 9.) *Whom,* the Spirit, **ye have of,** *from,* **God,** not from yourselves, and thus **ye are not your own,** but God's. You have therefore no right to pollute the body and alienate it from its rightful owner.

20. Ye are not your own, **for ye are,** rather, *were,* **bought with a price,** from the slavery of sin (Rom. 3 : 19; 6 : 17, 18, 22) with the price, the blood of Christ in his sufferings and death (Matt. 20 : 28; Acts 20 : 28; 1 Peter 1 : 18, 19; Rev. 5 : 9). **Therefore glorify God in your body,** as in God's temple, or use your body as his sanctuary to his glory (Rom. 12 : 1), instead of dishonoring God, through unchaste passions and sensuous deeds. The remaining words, **And in your spirit which are God's,** while implied by the preceding clause, are not found in the best and oldest manuscripts. Paul's argument had special reference to the body, and so with it he naturally stops.

PRACTICAL REMARKS.

1. It is the duty of Christians to settle their differences among themselves, without appealing to civil tribunals (ver. 1; Matt. 5 : 23–25; 18 : 15).

2. How exalted the Christian in the future world, not only above wicked men, but in some respects above angels (ver. 2, 3; Rom. 8 : 17; Rev. 3 : 21).

3. A spirit of strife among Christians shows great immaturity, and a lack of spiritual wisdom (ver. 4, 5; 3 : 3).

4. With the spirit and wisdom of Christ Christians could settle their differences by arbitration (ver. 7; Matt. 5 : 43–45).

Replies to questions respecting marriage, divorce, and celibacy.

7 NOW concerning the things whereof ye wrote unto me: [1] *It is* good for a

7 NOW concerning the things of which ye wrote: It is good for a man not to

[1] Ver. 8, 26, 27, 37, 38.

5. For Christians to engage in lawsuits before unbelievers is a shame to themselves and a disgrace to Christ and his cause (ver. 5, 6; Zech. 13 : 6; James 2 : 7).

6. A willingness to suffer wrong, rather than to do wrong, if generally practised among Christians, would result in the peaceful settlement of all their differences (ver. 7; Matt. 5 : 39; Rom. 12 : 17-19; 1 Thess. 5 : 15).

7. No one should excel the Christian in honesty; dishonesty among themselves reveals deep depravity (ver. 8; Rom. 12 : 17; 2 Cor. 8 : 20-23).

8. The unholy, while they remain so, cannot be saved (ver. 9, 10; Heb. 12 : 14).

9. In how many ways and forms does sin manifest itself! How much does the term "unrighteous" include! (ver. 9, 10; Matt. 7 : 13.)

10. The remembrance of what we are saved from should produce in us humility, gratitude, and an earnest desire to serve God and save others (ver. 11; Eph. 2 : 1-7, 11-13; 5 : 8; Col. 3 : 7 12-15).

11. In view of what God has done for us we should forsake sin in every form and live a holy life (ver. 11; 2 Cor. 4 : 2; Rom. 12 : 1, 2).

12. Whatever is not profitable but rather injurious, should be abandoned. We should be masters, not slaves of habit (ver. 12; 8 : 13; 9 : 27).

13. We should give proper attention to food and the laws of our physical being, but not raise them in importance above the functions of our spiritual natures (ver. 13; Matt. 6 : 25, 31).

14. The thought that our bodies are for the Lord's use, and that they are to be raised into his likeness, should restrain us from improper and unholy practices (ver. 14; Phil. 3 : 21).

15. Our oneness with Christ demands that we should keep ourselves pure even as he is pure (ver. 15; Heb. 10 : 22; 1 John 3 : 3).

16. The marriage relation is so sacred that it is marred and violated by sensuality (ver. 16; Matt. 5 : 27-32).

17. The closer union of the spirit of the Christian with Christ's Spirit should be kept sacred and inviolable from all improper and sensual indulgences (ver. 17; John 15 : 1; Eph. 4 : 1-3, 25-32).

18. Licentiousness is a crying sin of our times and country. Witness the number of divorces. No sin so weakens the body, impairs the mind, and shortens life (ver. 18).

19. We are the Lord's—our bodies his temples; our spirits controlled and sanctified by his Spirit; and we his purchased possession (ver. 19, 20; Rom. 14 : 7-9).

20. Are we tempted to sin? Do we need incitements to bodily purity and personal holiness? Let us think of the cross and the price paid for our redemption (ver. 20; Eph. 4 : 17-24).

CHAPTER VII.

At this point Paul passes to the second and remaining part of his Epistle, and answers certain questions which had been asked him in a letter received from Corinth. In this chapter he treats of *marriage, divorce, and celibacy.* He first speaks of marriage and gives advice to the married (ver. 1-7) and then to the unmarried (ver. 8, 9); treats of divorce (ver. 10, 11), and of married persons where one party is a heathen (ver. 12-16); and then lays down a general rule, that the gospel does not ordinarily interfere with the outward position of Christians, and that generally each may remain in the calling which he had before conversion (ver. 17-24). Paul then proceeds to consider marriage, especially of maiden daughters, under present difficulties (ver. 25-34), the duty of parents to unmarried daughters (ver. 35-38), and finally the duty of widows (ver. 39, 40).

1-7. ADVICE AS TO MARRIAGE AND CELIBACY.

1. **Now concerning the things whereof ye wrote unto me.** *Unto me* is omitted by the highest critical

2 man not to touch a woman. Nevertheless, *to avoid* fornication, let every man have his own wife, and let every 3 woman have her own husband. ᵐ Let the husband render unto the wife due benevolence: ⁿ and likewise also the 4 wife unto the husband. The wife hath not power of her own body, but the husband: and likewise also the husband hath not power of his own body, 5 but the wife. ᵒ Defraud ye not one the other, ᵖ except *it be* with consent for a time, that ye may give yourselves to fasting and prayer; and come to-

2 touch a woman; but because of fornications, let each man have his own wife, and let each woman have her 3 own husband. Let the husband render to the wife her due: and in like man- 4 ner the wife also to the husband. The wife has not authority over her own body, but the husband; and in like manner the husband also has not authority over his own body, but the wife. 5 Defraud not one the other, unless it be by agreement for a season, that ye may give yourselves to prayer, and may

m Exod. 21 : 10; 1 Peter 3 : 7. *n* Eph. 5 : 22, 23. *o* Ver. 3.
p Joel 2 : 16; Zech. 12 : 12–14; see Exod. 19 : 15; 1 Sam. 21 : 4, 5.

authorities. The first question was in regard to scruples which some of them entertained concerning marriage. The Jewish converts would naturally hold to marriage, since the Jews, except the Essenes, held it to be a duty, and regarded it a sin not to be married by the age of twenty. The tendency among Gentiles, however, was toward celibacy, and some philosophers shared in this feeling, and so strong was it that Augustus enacted laws to counteract it. Very likely, then, the question originated with the Gentile converts, many of whom were the followers of Paul. The inquiry, however, appears to have come from the church itself, *whereof ye wrote*. Paul was a Jew, yet especially an apostle to the Gentiles. He perhaps had been married, but was now unmarried (ver. 8; 9: 5). Different parties might appeal to him from different motives. All would naturally desire his views on the subject. Alford adds in regard to the original text: "In hardly any portion of the Epistles has the hand of correctors and interpolaters of the text been busier than here. . . . In consequence, the textual critic finds himself in this chapter sometimes much perplexed between different readings, and in danger of on the one hand adopting, on overwhelming manuscript authority, corrections of the early ascetics, and on the other excluding, from a too cautious retention of the received text, the genuine but less strongly attested simplicity of the original." **It is good**, expedient, profitable, and salutary, **for a man not to touch a woman**, in marriage. This doubtless was the view of one party at Corinth, and Paul endorses it with certain limitations, which he proceeds to give in the next verse. He does not here mean *morally* "good," for in ver. 28 and throughout the chapter he holds that a person does not sin in marrying. In ver. 26 and 29 we get light on this passage and the reason for his advice.

2. Nevertheless to avoid fornication, or more exactly, *But because of fornications*, let each man and woman be married. Notice the vice is here in the plural, indicating the commonness of this sin at Corinth. (Comp. note on 6 : 13.) Paul here expresses his view in reference to this particular question. For his fuller and later teachings regarding marriage see Eph. 5 : 23–30; 1 Tim. 5 : 14. (Comp. Heb. 13 : 4 ; 1 Peter 3 : 1–7.)

3. Being in the married state they are to continue in it, and husband and wife are to render to each other **due benevolence**, rather, according to the best text, that which is *due*, the conjugal duty that is *due*, each to the other.

4. The apostle states a principle growing out of the oneness in the married relation. Being one flesh **the wife hath not power**, or *authority*, *over* **her own body, but the husband;** and so of the man. Each is the other's. Each is dependent on the other. The rights of each are substantially equal. Selfishness must not be the rule of either party.

5. As an inference from the principle stated in the preceding verse, Paul says, **Defraud ye not**, *withhold not that which is due* the one from the other, **except it be with consent**, better, *by agreement*, **for a short time that ye may give yourselves to**

gether again, that Satan tempt you not for your incontinency.
6 But I speak this by permission, *and
7 not of commandment. For I would that all men were *even as I myself: but *every man hath his proper gift of God, one after this manner, and
8 another after that. I say therefore to the unmarried and widows, *It is good
9 for them if they abide even as I. But *if they cannot contain, let them marry: for it is better to marry than to
10 burn. And unto the married I com-

again be together, that Satan may not tempt you on account of your incon-
6 tinency. But this I say by way of per-
7 mission, not of command. And I wish all men to be even as myself. But each one has his own gift from God, one after this manner, and another after that.
8 Now I say to the unmarried and the widows, it is good for them if they
9 remain as I also am. But if they have not self-control, let them marry; for it
10 is better to marry than to burn. And

---

q Ver. 12, 25; 2 Cor. 8 : 8; 11 : 17.   *r* 9 : 5, 15.   *s* 12 : 11; Matt. 19 : 12.
t Ver. 1, 26, 27, 32-35.   *u* Ver. 2, 28, 36, 39; 1 Tim. 5 : 11, 14.

---

a season of earnest **prayer.** The original conveys the idea both of brevity of time and devotedness and urgency of prayer. The concessions were to be mutual and the occasion extraordinary. **Fasting** should be omitted, doubtless added by later ascetics. **And come,** rather, according to the best reading, *Be* **together again,** **that Satan tempt you not for,** rather, *on account of,* **your incontinency,** *your want of self-control.* Substantially the same reason as that given in ver. 2 for being married.

6. But I speak this, the injunction with its limitation in ver. 5, **by permission**—*by way of permission* or *allowance,* **not of command.** The husband and wife were allowed to pursue this course, but not by positive command. This explanation of the apostle is brief and somewhat indefinite. It is referred by different ones to what follows, or to all that precedes in this chapter, or to ver. 1. It is better and more natural, with Alford, Meyer, and others, to refer it to the whole of ver. 5. The *permission* and the *command* had reference to the Corinthians, but they imply authority either in Paul as an apostle and an inspired man, or from the Lord himself. Whatever authority he had was indeed from the Lord (ver. 25).

7. For, rather, *but,* according to the most reliable text. *But,* while I have thus written, **I would that all men were even as myself,** having perfect self-control though without a wife (9 : 5). In reference to incontinency (ver. 5) all were not like himself. **But,** this power of self control is a moral and natural gift and **every man hath his proper,** *his own,* **gift,** his natural and gracious endowments, from **God, one after this manner and another after that,** so that each one is fitted for the state he is in, be it married or unmarried. (Comp. Matt. 19 : 11.)

8-24. ADVICE TO THE UNMARRIED AND TO THE MARRIED. Divorce. Regarding mixed marriages, where one party is an unbeliever. Christianity and social conditions.

8. I say therefore, rather, *But,* while remembering that persons are differently constituted and differently endowed (ver. 7), **I say to the unmarried,** of both sexes, **and widows,** especially widows who might be overlooked in this connection. Paul sums up what he has to say, addressing different classes: the unmarried (this verse), the married (ver. 10), "to the rest" (ver. 12). The *unmarried* are not here limited to widows, as some suppose, but include both sexes, since it is contrasted with "the married" (ver. 10), which includes both male and female. Widows are really included in the class of the unmarried, but they needed special mention, and are treated separately in ver. 39, 40. This verse decides nothing in regard to the question, whether Paul was a widower, only that he was then unmarried: **if they abide even as I.**

9. But if they cannot remain as I am without sin, **if they cannot contain,** *if they have not self-control* (ver. 5), **let them marry:** for it is **better to marry,** even in times of distress and persecution, than to **burn,** than to be inflamed with lusts. "Because to marry is no sin (ver. 28, 36), while to burn is sinful" (Matt. 5 : 28).

10. And unto the married, both husband and wife, who form a second

mand, * *yet* not I, but the Lord, *y* Let not the wife depart from *her* husband:
11 but and if she depart, let her remain unmarried, or be reconciled to *her* husband: *z* and let not the husband put away *his* wife.
12 But to the rest speak I, *a* not the Lord. If any brother hath a wife that believeth not, and she be pleased to dwell with him, let him not put her
13 away; and the woman which hath an husband that believeth not, and if he be pleased to dwell with her, let her not
14 leave him. For the unbelieving husband is sanctified by the wife, and the to the married I give command, not I, but the Lord,—That the wife depart
11 not from the husband, but if she even depart, let her remain unmarried, or let her be reconciled to her husband; and that the husband leave not his
12 wife. And to the rest say I, not the Lord: If any brother has an unbelieving wife, and she agrees to dwell with
13 him, let him not leave her. And if any wife has an unbelieving husband, and he agrees to dwell with her, let
14 her not leave her husband. For the unbelieving husband is sanctified in the

x See ver. 12, 25, 40.   *y* Mal. 2 : 14–16; Matt. 5 : 32; 19 : 6, 9; Mark 10 : 11, 12 , Luke 16 : 18.
z Mark 10 : 2–9.   *a* Ver. 6.

class, distinct from the class mentioned in ver. 8. **I command, yet not I,** indeed, **but the Lord,** who gave special injunctions to this class (Mark 10 : 11, 12). Paul could well command what the Lord commanded. He makes no reference here to what he might enjoin as a private, uninspired individual. He speaks with apostolic authority, but recognizes his Lord's authority as taking precedence of his own. (Comp. ver. 25, 40.) **Let not the wife,** rather, *that the wife,* **depart not,** or, *be not separated,* by divorce or otherwise, **from her husband.** The exception to this rule, "for the cause of fornication" (Matt. 5 : 32), is omitted as not involved in the cases Paul is now considering. He mentioned *the wife* first as perhaps the party with whom voluntary separations and divorces more usually at that time began.

11. But and if she depart, *however, if she should depart,* a supposable case which might occur in such a state of society as that at Corinth, then **let her remain unmarried,** for if she should marry she would commit adultery (Mark 10 : 12). **Or be reconciled to her husband**—this being the only marriage relation open to her. **And let not,** rather, as in ver. 10, continuing the Lord's command, *and that the husband put not away his wife* by divorce, or, *not leave his wife,* separate himself from her without a divorce for proper cause. Both ideas seem to be included in the verb. From the similarity of construction as well as from the teachings of Christ, we infer that what was said to the departing wife applies also here to the husband. The law of divorce among the Jews was very lax (Matt. 5 : 31, 32); and under Greek and Roman law in Paul's day there were great facilities for obtaining divorces, but greater for the husband than for the wife.

12. Paul now addresses a third class. **But to the rest** of the married believers whose companions were either heathen or unconverted Jews, **speak I, not the Lord.** Christ had left no special precept in respect to mixed marriages, and so Paul speaks under the general guidance of the Spirit, given him as an apostle (ver. 40). But Christ had laid down a general rule, and the apostle applied it to the case in hand. If the unbelieving wife **be pleased,** or *consents,* **to dwell** with the believing husband, then **let him not put her away,** or *leave her.* Thus the whole responsibility of the separation is thrown on the unbelieving wife.

13. And so of the believing wife with an unbelieving husband. **And the woman,** rather, according to the most approved text, *And any wife,* etc. So also the last clause should read, *let her not leave her husband.* The sacredness of the marriage tie is to be guarded under all possible circumstances. **Leave him.** The verb is the same as that translated put away, in ver. 11, 12.

14. This verse has given much trouble to commentators, and has been variously interpreted. We should approach it unbiased, and lay aside all preconceived notions regarding it. We simply wish to know what Paul meant. **For,** introduces the passage as giving a reason for the injunction in ver. 12, 13, why the believer should not leave

232 I. CORINTHIANS [CH. VII.

unbelieving wife is sanctified by the husband: else were your children un-
15 clean; ᵇ but now are they holy. But if the unbelieving depart, let him depart. A brother or a sister is not under bondage in such *cases:* but God hath

wife, and the unbelieving wife is sanctified in the brother; else your children are unclean; but as it is they are holy.
15 But if the unbelieving departs, let him depart. The brother or the sister is not under bondage in such cases; but God

ᵇ Mal. 2 : 15; Acts 2 : 39.

---

the unbelieving husband or wife, but continue to dwell with him or her. The key of the passage is in the word *unclean*. **Else were your children,** the children of Christians generally at Corinth, **unclean.** This appears to be ceremonial uncleanness, for it is opposed to *holy,* **but now are they holy.** But this holiness cannot be moral and spiritual holiness; for the same thing is said of unbelieving husbands and wives, that they were *sanctified* in their believing companions. Hence the holiness predicated of these children, husbands and wives of believers, must have been ceremonial, that cleanness or purity pertaining to social and domestic life. This is further confirmed by the fact brought out in ver. 16, that the unbelieving companion might be converted and saved. The question was evidently about cleanness and uncleanness, similar to that which troubled Peter when he said, "I have never eaten anything that is common or unclean," and "But God hath showed me that I should not call any man common or unclean" (Acts 10 : 14, 28). Yet several years later Peter, Barnabas, and others, under Jewish influence, separated themselves from eating with Gentiles at Antioch, and was rebuked by the Apostle Paul (Gal. 2 : 11, 12). Thus Jews did not associate socially with Gentiles, and both Ezra and Nehemiah had commanded Jews of their day to put away their heathen wives (Ezra 10 : 2, 11; Neh. 13 : 23 ff.). It seems that Judaizing influences were at work in the church at Corinth; and that some at least thought that they would be ritually contaminated by their conjugal relations with unbelievers. It became, doubtless, a matter of conscience with them, whether they ought not to put away their unbelieving husbands or wives. This question Paul meets and answers, as in the two preceding verses, and in this gives the reason. **For the unbelieving husband is sanctified,** *purified,* *cleansed* (1 Tim. 4 : 5; Heb. 9 : 15) **by,** more exactly, *in* **the wife,** in his close union with his believing wife (one flesh), so that she may lawfully dwell with him; and **the unbelieving wife is sanctified,** being under a cleansing influence *in* **the husband** (or *the brother,* according to the most approved text), so that he may lawfully dwell with her. **Else were your children unclean,** being unregenerate and having not yet believed, and none of you could dwell with them, a thought repugnant to every natural and religious feeling, and which needed only to be stated to be rejected. **But now,** or *as it is,* **they are holy,** they are not ceremonially profane, but they are clean.

This passage has been used in defense of infant baptism. But it may be remarked (1) That it affords no more ground for baptizing infants than it does for baptizing the unbelieving husbands or wives. Whatever is stated of infants is affirmed of these unconverted consorts. (2) It affords an argument against the existence of infant baptism in the apostolic church. If it had existed, the apostle would naturally have mentioned it, and thus clinched his argument by it. But he implies that the children of Christian parents had no nearer relations to the church than the unbelieving husband of a believing wife. (3) Neither can the doctrine of infant baptism be rightly developed from this passage. The holiness was not that of regeneration, nor was there the exercise of a personal faith. But baptism is everywhere conditioned upon repentance and faith.

15. But if the unbelieving, *the unbeliever,* **depart, let him depart,** let there be a separation; the responsibility is on him. **A brother or a sister is not under bondage** like a slave, not under the constraint of law or necessity **in such cases,** in such circumstances. He is discharged from future obligation as a husband or a

16 called us *c* to peace. For what knowest thou, O wife, whether thou shalt *d* save *thy* husband? Or how knowest thou, O man, whether thou shalt save *thy* wife?
17 But *e* as God hath distributed to every man, as the Lord hath *f* called every one, so let him walk. And *g* so ordain I in all churches. Is any man called *h* being circumcised? let him not become uncircumcised. Is any

16 has called us in peace. For what knowest thou, O wife, whether thou shalt save thy husband? Or what knowest thou, O husband, whether thou shalt save thy wife? Only, as the Lord has divided to each one, as God has called each one, so let him walk. And so I ordain in all the churches.
18 Was any one called being circumcised? Let him not become uncircumcised.

c 14 : 33; Rom. 12 : 18; 14 : 19; Heb. 12 : 14.   *d* 1 Peter 3 : 1.   *e* Ver. 7.   *f* Ver. 18, 21.
g 4 : 17; 2 Cor. 11 : 28.   *h* Acts 15 : 1, 19, 24, 28; Col. 3 : 11.

wife. Compare the words "bound," "loose," and "free from," in Rom. 7 : 2, 3. Desertion is thus a ground for the permanent separation of married persons, and if it amounts to an actual violation and breaking of the marriage tie, it is a sufficient ground for divorce. In this case there is no conflict between Christ and Paul. Both enjoin that a man shall not put away his wife, nor a wife her husband, except for adultery (Matt. 5 : 32). But Paul adds that if the unbelieving party is determined to leave, thus negatively putting the other away, let him go. The responsibility and the guilt are his. **But God has called us to,** literally, *in*, **peace,** to live in peace one with another. To exercise a spirit of peace in your married life, in permitting the unbelieving party to depart, and after the separation to exercise the same spirit.

16. For, introduces a reason for acquiescing in the separation permitted in the preceding verse and exercising a spirit of peace in relation to the unbelieving party. The prospect of his conversion would be small indeed in the midst of strife, and in a union which he was determined to dissolve, it was better to let him depart. **For what knowest thou,** or, *how knowest thou*, **O wife, whether thou shalt save thy husband?** What reason have you to expect to convert him under such circumstances? You certainly have no such prospect of saving him as to make it desirable to retain him if he is determined to leave you. This interpretation, which is held by the best late expositors, seems to be demanded by the logical connection and grammatical form of the passage. Yet it fails to entirely satisfy me. By a somewhat looser construction the older commentators, and some later ones, regard the apostle as urging a continuance of the marriage relation if possible rather than a separation. According to this view the last clause of ver. 15 presents a contrast: *But*, while I advise separation in this particular case, *God hath called us to be in peace*, "a peaceful disposition must always prevail in order not to give cause on his or her side for separation" (OLSHAUSEN). *For how knowest thou, O wife, but that thou shalt save thy husband?* Is it not possible that this may be the result, and is not this a sufficient reason for remaining together? This is the first meaning a person generally gets from this passage. It accords with its general design (beginning with ver. 14) to avoid all unnecessary separation, and also with the teachings of Scripture (1 Peter 3 : 1, 2).

17. The permission to live apart from a heathen husband or wife was a special case. But Paul goes on to show that Christianity does not disturb existing relations that are not sinful. **But,** rather *only*, by way of caution against an abuse of what he had said. Let the heathen depart if he wishes, *Only as the Lord has distributed to each man* his share or lot, *as*, in the state in which *God has called each one*, **so let him walk,** so let him live. **And so ordain I,** thus I command, **in all** *the* **churches,** in the exercise of apostolic authority. We have in 2 Thess. 3 : 6 an illustration of the manner in which Paul gave orders to the churches.

18. Paul proceeds to illustrate by examples the precept just given. **Is,** rather *was*, **any man called,,** converted to Christ, **being circumcised,** as a Jew? **Let him not become uncircumcised.** Some Jews were ashamed of their Judaism and strove to efface the outward signs of it by a

called in uncircumcision? ᶦ let him not
19 be circumcised. ᵏ Circumcision is
nothing, and uncircumcision is nothing, but ˡ the keeping of the com-
20 mandments of God. ᵐ Let every man
abide in the same calling wherein he
21 was called. Art thou called ⁿ *being
a servant?* care not for it: but if thou
mayest be made free, use *it* rather.
22 For he that is called in the Lord, *being*
a servant, is ᵒ the Lord's freeman: like-

Has any one been called in uncircumcision? Let him not be circum-
19 cised. Circumcision is nothing, and
uncircumcision is nothing; but the
keeping of the commandments of God.
20 Let each one abide in that calling in
21 which he was called. Wast thou called
being a servant, care not for it; but if
thou even canst become free, use it
22 rather. For he that was called in the
Lord, being a servant, is the Lord's

i Gal. 5 : 2.   *k* Rom. 2 : 25–29; Gal. 5 : 6; 6 : 15.   *l* 1 Sam. 15 : 22; 1 John 2 : 3, 4; 3 : 22–24.
m Ver. 17; Luke 3 : 10–14.   *n* 1 Tim. 6 : 1–3.   *o* John 8 : 32–36; Rom. 6 : 18–22.

surgical operation (1 Mac. 1 : 15; Jos. Ant. XII., 5 : 1). Jewish converts to Christianity mingling among Gentiles might desire to do this. But Paul condemns the practice. **Is**, rather, *has any one been* **called in uncircumcision,** being a Gentile? **let him not be circumcised.** As a reaction against heathenism some Gentile converts might be desirous of the outward sign of Israel. But Paul would have no change in these external national relations.
19. Circumcision is nothing and uncircumcision is nothing from a Christian point of view. It is a matter of indifference whether a person had been circumcised or not. Paul exemplified his independence in this matter by circumcising Timothy and refusing to circumcise Titus (Acts 16 : 3; Gal. 2 : 3). **But the keeping of the commandments of God** is everything. Obedience is the great thing. The two parallel passages (Gal. 5 : 6; 6 : 15) differ by substituting for this clause " But faith working by love " in the first, and " But a new creature " in the second. But faith and love produce obedience, and the new creature is one who is obedient (John 14 : 23; James 2 : 18; Heb. 8 : 10; Eph. 4 : 23, 24).
20. Paul comes back to a general principle in such cases. *Let every man, each one,* **abide in the same calling,** in that *state* or *condition*, whether circumcision or uncircumcision, slavery or freedom, **wherein he was called,** at his conversion. The *calling* does not here mean the vocation, but rather the state or condition in which the divine call into Christ's kingdom finds a person.
21. The second example. **Art thou,** rather, *wast thou*, **called being a servant?** or *slave?* The first example (ver. 18) refers to the great ex-

ternal distinction at that time in religious life; this example brings to view the great distinction that existed in social life. **Care not for it—** have no concern or anxiety about it. **But if thou mayest be made free,** etc., may be translated either, *But if thou canst also become free, rather use the opportunity*; or, *But if thou even canst become free, use it rather,* that is, remain in slavery, though the offer is made. In regard to these two views Dean Stanley says: " It is one of the most evenly balanced questions in the interpretation of the New Testament." He rather inclines to the second view, and to regard the whole passage as expressive of comfort to the slave under his hard lot, and if his master was a Christian the passage would be still further illustrated by 1 Tim. 6 : 2. " The commentators before the Reformation have chiefly been in favor of the second [view]; since, in favor of the first." But Meyer, Alford, and others prefer the second interpretation. Olshausen, Principal Brown, and Beet take the first view. To me it seems that **But if,** introduces a limitation to the direction just given (a peculiarity of Paul in this chapter, (ver. 2, 7, 9, 11)), and thus he modifies his advice. *But if also,* in addition to being called, *thou canst become free, use it rather*—rather take advantage of it. Thus this is added rather parenthetically. Paul's practice favored freedom and shows how highly he valued it (Acts 16 : 37; 22 : 28), and so does ver. 23. Upon the whole I incline to this view.
22. For he that is, rather, *was*, **called in the Lord,** to be in Christ, and of course called by him, **being a servant is the Lord's freeman,** rather, *freedman*, one who has been

CH. VII.] I. CORINTHIANS 235

wise also he that is called, *being* free, is
23 *p* Christ's servant. *q* Ye are bought
with a price; be not ye the servants of
24 men. Brethren, let every man, wherein he is called, therein abide *r* with
God.
25 Now concerning virgins *s* I have no
commandment of the Lord; yet I give
my judgment, as one that hath obtained mercy of the Lord *t* to be faith-
26 ful. I suppose therefore *u* that this is
good for the present distress, *I say*, that
27 *it is* good for a man so to be. Art thou
bound unto a wife? *x* Seek not to be
loosed. Art thou loosed from a wife?

freedman; in like manner also the
freeman, when he is called is Christ's
23 servant. Ye were bought with a price;
24 become not servants of men. Brethren, let each one abide with God in the
condition in which he was called.
25 Now concerning virgins I have no
commandment of the Lord's; but I
give a judgment, as having received
mercy from the Lord to be faithful.
26 I think therefore that this is good on
account of the impending necessity,
that it is good for a man to be thus.
27 Art thou bound to a wife? Seek not to
be loosed. Art thou loosed from a

p Eph. 6 : 6 ; Col. 3 : 23, 24 ; 1 Peter 2 : 16.   *q* 6 : 20 ; see Lev. 25 : 42.   *r* 10 : 31 ; Col. 3 : 17, 22.
s Ver. 6, 10, 12, 40 ; 2 Cor. 8 : 8, 10.   *t* 4 : 2 ; 1 Tim. 1 : 12.
u Ver. 1, 8, 26, 35-38 ; Matt. 24 : 19 ; Luke 23 : 28, 29.   *x* Ver. 12-14.

made free, in this case from the slavery of sin. He is the Lord's freedman in the sense that he has been made free by him (John 8 : 36). **Likewise also he that** *was* **called, being free, is Christ's servant**—belongs to him and bound to do his will. Yet this is the highest freedom (Eph. 6 : 6-9). "The Lord's freeman is one whom the Lord has redeemed from Satan and made his own; and the Lord's slave is one whom Christ has purchased for himself. So that master and slave stand on the same level before Christ" (HODGE).

23. The thought of belonging to Christ leads naturally to the exhortation, **Ye are,** rather, *were,* **bought with a price** (see note on 6 : 20); **be,** rather, *become,* **not servants,** or *slaves,* **of men;** whatever your condition, whether that of slavery or freedom, let not your minds and spirits become enslaved to the opinions and prejudices of men. Be not slaves to what men may wish and demand, but conform your conduct to Christ's will and service.

24. Paul again returns to the conclusion which he had enforced in ver. 17, 20. **Brethren, let every** *one,* **wherein he is,** *was,* **called,** the condition in which he was converted, **therein abide with God,** in fellowship with him, in harmony with his will, and content with the condition which he has ordained.

25-38. CONCERNING THE MARRIAGE OF VIRGINS, AND THE DUTIES OF PARENTS TO THEM. The impending trials. The shortened time.

25. Now concerning virgins, young maidens, as ver. 36 shows. Concerning this particular case he had **no commandment of the Lord,** neither spoken by him when upon earth, nor received from him by revelation (11 : 23 ; Gal. 1 : 11). **Yet,** *But,* **I give my judgment,** *an opinion,* **as one that hath obtained mercy of the Lord to be faithful,** *trustworthy,* to be relied upon, as a good steward of the gospel (4 : 2 ; 1 Tim. 1 : 12-16). As an apostle he utters an opinion and gives advice, as to what was the best thing to do in a temporary emergency for such a case.

26. According to his usual rule Paul first treats of the general principle and then of a particular case. **I suppose,** or, *I think,* **therefore that this is good for the present distress,** literally, *the impending necessity,* the calamities which were then threatening. What these were we do not fully know; but they were so great as to make the cares and responsibilities of the marriage state undesirable. Distress and anxiety attended a profession of Christianity. It would seem that Paul regarded these calamities as the tribulations which were to precede the coming of our Lord (Matt. 24 : 8). Those preceding the destruction of Jerusalem, the type of his second coming, were indeed impending. It was now thirteen years preceding that event, and matters already were converging toward it. **It is good for a man,** *a person* of either sex, **so to be,** or, *to be thus,* as he goes on to say—to remain as he is, married or unmarried.

27. This verse explains *so to be* of the last verse. **Art thou loosed from a wife**—spoken to a single man,

28 Seek not a wife. But and if thou marry, ⁷ thou hast not sinned; and if a virgin marry, she hath not sinned. ᶻ Nevertheless such shall have trouble in the flesh: but I spare you. 29 But *this I say, brethren, the time is short: it remaineth, that both they that have wives be as though they had 30 none; and they that weep, as though they wept not; and they that rejoice, as though they rejoiced not; and they that buy, as though they possessed 31 not; and ᵇ they that use this world, as not abusing it: for ᶜ the fashion of this wife? Seek not a wife. But if thou even marry, thou hast not sinned; and if a virgin marry, she has not sinned. Yet such shall have affliction in the 29 flesh; and I am sparing you. But this I say, brethren, the time is shortened; that henceforth both they who have wives be as though they had 30 none; and they that weep, as though they wept not; and they that rejoice, as though they rejoiced not; and they that buy, as though they possessed not; 31 and they that use the world, as not abusing it; for the fashion of this

y Ver. 36; Heb. 13 : 4.   *z* Ver. 26.
a Job 14 : 1, 2; Ps. 39 : 4–7; 90 : 5–10; Eccl. 9 : 10; 1 Peter 4 : 7; 1 John 2 : 17.
b Eccl. 9 : 7–10; 1 Tim. 6 : 17, 18.   *c* Eccl. 1 : 4; James 1 : 10, 11; 4 : 14; 1 Peter 1 : 24; 1 John 2 : 17.

whether he had ever had a wife or had never been married. *Loosed* is the opposite of **bound**, in the preceding question, and equivalent to *free from*. **Seek not a wife.** This is in harmony with ver. 10, 11.

28. Still addressing the single, unmarried man. **But and if,** *But even if* **thou marry, thou hast not sinned,** thou hast not incurred guilt, having acted according to the divine arrangement (Gen. 2 : 24). And so **if a virgin,** an unmarried daughter, **marry, she hath not sinned. Nevertheless,** simply, *But,* **such shall have trouble,** or *afflictions,* **in the flesh.** She shall not incur guilt, but she shall have trials. **But,** in giving this advice, **I spare you,** rather, *I am sparing you* from worldly trouble. My desire is to spare you from these afflictions. Some regard the meaning to be, I say no more about the sorrows that will befall you to spare your feelings, if you do marry (2 Cor. 12 : 6). But the other view, I think, is to be preferred.

29, 30. But this I say, in regard to this question and the present state of things, **the time is short,** literally, *is shortened, contracted,* as it were, into a brief period. Compare John's words, "It is the last time" (1 John 2 : 18). In connection with ver. 26 and 31, it seems that Paul here refers to the time or age preceding the coming of Christ. Compare "Except that the Lord had shortened those days" (Mark 13 : 20). We have here an illustration of our Lord's words in Mark 13 : 32, that no one, not even an inspired apostle, but the Father knew the day of his coming. **It re-** **maineth,** according to the best text, *That in the future,* **both they that have wives be as though they had none,** not wholly or unduly devoted to earthly relationships. Paul is describing the state of mind that the character of the times demanded. The heart must not be wholly given up to any human affection, or earthly possession. MEYER presents the meaning of the whole passage thus: "That the husband should not by his married state lose the moral freedom of his position as a Christian in heart and life; that the sorrowful should not do so through his tribulation, nor the joyful through his good fortune, nor the merchantman through his gain, nor he that uses the world through his use of it. We see the reverse of this independent attitude in Luke 14 : 18–20. There the heart cleaves to temporal things as its treasure" (Matt. 6 : 21). While living in the world they are to live above the world; and living among men, they are to live with God.

31. And they that use this world as not abusing it, or more exactly, *as not using it to the full,* using it with moderation, and as not their own. **For the fashion,** the outward *form* or *condition,* **of the world passeth,** rather *is passing, away,* like the scenes in a theatre, preparatory to the restitution of all things (Acts 3 : 21) and the new heaven and the new earth (Rev. 21 : 1). Give not yourselves up to the perishable things of the world; but live independent of it, and as citizens of a heavenly and continuing city (Phil. 3 : 20; 1 Peter 1 : 4). This passage illus-

32 world passeth away. ᵈ But I would have you without carefulness. ᵉ He that is unmarried careth for the things ᶠ that belong to the Lord, how he may
33 please the Lord : but he that is married careth for the things that are of the world, how he may please *his* wife.
34 There is difference *also* between a wife and a virgin. The unmarried woman ᵍ careth for the things of the Lord, that she may be holy both in body and in spirit : but she that is married careth for the things of the world, how she
35 may please *her* husband. And this I speak for your own profit ; not that I may cast a snare upon you, but for that which is comely, and that ye may attend upon the Lord without distraction.

32 world is passing away. But I wish you to be free from anxieties. The unmarried man is anxious for the things of the Lord, how he may please the
33 Lord ; but he that is married is anxious for the things of the world, how he
34 may please his wife. There is a difference also between the wife and the virgin. The unmarried woman is anxious for the things of the Lord, that she may be holy both in body and spirit : but she that is married is anxious for the things of the world, how she may please her husband.
35 And this I say for your own profit : not that I may put a constraint on you, but for that which is seemly, and that ye may attend upon the Lord

d See refs. Ps. 55 : 22 ; Phil. 4 : 6.   *e* 1 Tim. 5 : 5.   *f* Ver. 34.   *g* Luke 10 : 40, etc.

trates the expectation of the early Christians of the speedy return of Christ (Acts 1 : 11).
32. This verse introduces a new line of thought growing out of what he had just said. **But,** since the time is so short, **I would have you,** *I wish you to be*, **without carefulness,** rather, *free from anxiety*, pertaining to earthly matters. The word translated *carefulness* and *careth* in this and the two following verses is that used in Matt. 6 : 25, 27, 28, 31, 34, and there translated "take no thought," *be not anxious*, be not troubled with care. The variations of reading and punctuation in this and the next two verses, in the original, are numerous. The most approved text will be followed. **He that is unmarried careth,** *is anxious*, **for the things of the Lord, how he may please the Lord**—he has indeed anxiety, but it is for the cause of Christ.
33. But he that is married careth about, *is anxious for*, **the things of the world,** etc. The married man has in addition anxiety for worldly matters that he may please his wife. Thus he has double anxiety, and his interests are divided.
34. There is a difference also, or *a division*, in anxiety and pursuits, **between a wife and a virgin,** similar to that noted in ver. 32, 33. The **unmarried woman** *is anxious for* **the things of the Lord, that she may be holy,** entirely *consecrated*, to him, **both in body and in spirit.** But the **married** woman, like the married man (ver. 33) has additional anxiety about worldly matters. Husbands and wives, like Aquila and Priscilla, should be mutual helpers in the Lord's service ; but often it is not so. "This is how it happens that many a Christian woman comes to be found absenting herself from the place of prayer, frequenting the ball-room and theatre, giving parties on the Sabbath, and in other ways compromising her conscience to her own spiritual injury and the discredit of her profession. And it is to the danger of such evils, incurred by marriage, that the apostle points" (D. W. Poor, in *Lange*).
35. Paul explains himself lest he should be misunderstood. **And this I speak,** *this* recommendation in ver. 32-34, **for your own profit,** your best interests, your spiritual advantage and happiness. **Not that I may cast a snare,** or *a noose*, **upon you** (a figurative expression derived from hunting or from war), *constrain you* by command from that which God has instituted and which our state of nature requires, **but for that which is comely,** or *seemly*, to promote that which is *becoming*, in life and character (Rom. 13 : 13) ; **and that ye may attend upon the Lord without distraction** from worldly cares and anxieties, that ye may be continually devoted to the Lord and his cause. Dean Stanley refers to Luke 10 : 39-41 as an illustration of this expression : Martha "cumbered (or *distracted*) with much serving," Mary sitting at the feet of Jesus.

36 But if any man think that he behaveth himself uncomely toward his virgin, if she pass the flower of *her* age, and ʰ need so require, let him do what he will, ⁱ he sinneth not: let them
37 marry. Nevertheless he that standeth stedfast in his heart, having no necessity, but hath power over his own will, and hath so decreed in his heart that he will keep his virgin, ᵏ doeth well.
38 ˡ So then he that giveth *her* in marriage doeth well; but he that giveth *her* not in marriage, ᵐ doeth better.
39 ⁿ The wife is bound by the law as long as her husband liveth: but if her husband be dead, she is at liberty to

36 without distraction. But if any one thinks that he behaves himself unseemly toward his virgin, if she be past the flower of her age, and need so require, let him do what he wishes, he
37 sins not; let them marry. But he that stands stedfast in his heart, having no necessity, but has authority concerning his own wish, and has determined this in his own heart that he will keep his
38 virgin, will do well. So that both he that gives his own virgin in marriage does well, and he that gives her not in marriage will do better.
39 A wife is bound as long as her husband lives; but if her husband be fallen asleep, she is at liberty to

ʰ Ver. 9, 37. ⁱ Ver. 28; Heb. 13 : 4. ᵏ Ver. 2. ˡ Heb. 13 : 4. ᵐ Ver. 1, 8, 26, 32–34, 37.
ⁿ Ver. 10; Rom. 7 : 2, 3.

36. The apostle now gives advice to parents in regard to their unmarried daughters. It was the custom among Jews and Greeks, as it is in most Oriental countries, for the parents to decide upon the marriage of their children. What he had just said about being *comely*, or *seemly*, appears to have suggested this turn in his course of thought. **But if any man think that he behaveth himself uncomely,** unseemly and unbecomingly, **toward his virgin,** his daughter, by incurring disgrace for her in keeping her unmarried. Among the Jews continued maidenhood was regarded a disgrace. A rabbinical saying was: "If your daughter is past the marriageable age, release your slave to give him to her for a husband." Some suppose Paul here refers to exposing her to the temptations to which she would be liable by remaining unmarried. But the other view to me seems preferable. **If she pass the flower of her age,** *the bloom of life,* having fully attained maturity, **and need so require,** and *it needs so to be,* or, *so it ought to be,* if she is persistent in wishing marriage, and circumstances are such that it appears to be duty to accede to her desire, **let him do what he will,** what according to his best judgment he wishes to do; **he sinneth not,** in not following my advice as given above. Let them marry, the daughter and her lover.

37. Nevertheless, or, *But,* **he that standeth stedfast in his heart**—having a firm character and no misgiving about acting in an unseemly way toward his daughter, **having no necessity,** as in the other case (ver. 36), the daughter not being desirous or willing to be married, or her hand not being sought in marriage; **but hath power over his own will,** to do what he wishes and judges best, without regard to external circumstances; **and hath so decreed in his heart,** *hath determined this* privately and within himself, **that he will keep** at home his **virgin,** his daughter unmarried, **doeth well,** rather, according to the best text, *will do well,* acts morally right. This is the positive side of "sinneth not" (ver. 36). The whole passage brings to view the authority of the parent over the daughter at home, in Greek and Roman society, and his entire responsibility for her.

38. So then, better, according to the most approved reading, *So that,* to sum up the discussion, *both* **he that giveth** *his virgin* daughter **in marriage, doeth well;** *and* **he that giveth her not in marriage,** *will do* **better**—in point of "profit" (ver. 35), advantage, considering the troublous times, the indications of the Lord's coming (ver. 26, 29), and the duties to be performed. Note that both do well, but one will do better.

39, 40. CONCERNING THE SECOND MARRIAGE OF WOMEN.

39. The wife is bound by the law as long as her husband liveth, etc. The same stated in Rom. 7 : 2, on which see note. **If her husband be dead,** rather, *be fallen asleep,* the word generally used of the Christian's death (11 : 30; 15 : 6, 18, etc.

be married to whom she will; ⁰ only in the Lord. But she is happier if she so abide, ᵖ after my judgment: and ᵠ I think also that I have the Spirit of God.

married to whom she wishes; only in the Lord. But she is happier if she abides as she is, according to my judgment; and I think that I also have the Spirit of God.

o Deut. 7 : 3, 4; 2 Cor. 6 : 14-16.   p Ver. 25.   q 14 : 37; 1 Thess. 4 : 8.

Compare note on Acts 7 : 60). It is sometimes used of death in the Old Testament (Deut. 31 : 16; 1 Kings 2 : 10; Dan. 12 : 2). **Only in the Lord**—a limitation to the preceding phrase, **to whom she will,** or, *wishes*. She has full liberty to marry, but only in connection or union with the Lord, that is, only to a Christian (2 Cor. 6 : 14). The same principle would apply to a man. Under all circumstances mixed marriages were to be avoided. In certain cases Paul advised the marriage of widows (1 Tim. 5 : 11-14).

40. But she is happier if she so abide, after my judgment, being freer from trials and in troublous times, provided of course that she is wholly consecrated to Christ's service (ver. 34; 1 Tim. 5 : 9-14). **And I think,** speaking modestly, **also that I have,** rather, *that I also have,* as well as others, **the Spirit of God** (1 Thess. 4 : 8), and hence judge correctly. Paul does not express doubt about having the Spirit, but rather implies his full persuasion that he was speaking under the direction of the Spirit.

In summing up the teachings of this chapter, it must be remembered that Paul was answering particular questions under particular circumstances, and that we must therefore be cautious about deriving general principles from them. His preference for a single life was founded upon the impending calamities, and the greater freedom from worldly cares, and limited to such as could live chastely unmarried (ver. 9, 26-34). At a later time, when speaking upon the general duties of a Christian life (Eph. 5 : 22, 23), so far from representing marriage as an inferior state, he makes it a symbol of the highest and holiest fellowship, that between Christ and his church. There is nothing in Paul's teaching of the asceticism that prevailed a few centuries later; neither can the arbitrary Romish doctrine of the celibacy of the clergy and of monastic orders find support in this chapter. (Comp. 1 Tim. 4 : 1-3.)

PRACTICAL REMARKS.

1. How important, responsible, and sacred is the marriage union in the light of Paul's teaching (ver. 3, 10, 11, 16, 27, 33, 39; 1 Tim. 3 : 2).

2. Polygamy is unlawful under the gospel (ver. 2; 6 : 16; Matt. 19 : 4-6).

3. The marriage relation tends to promote purity, and prevents scandal (ver. 2, 9; 1 Tim. 5 : 11-14).

4. Husband and wife belong to each other, having mutual and respectively equal rights (ver. 3, 4, 32, 34; Eph. 5 : 21-28).

5. Self-control, or any other excellence of body or mind, is a gift of God (ver. 6, 7; Matt. 19 : 10-12; James 1 : 17).

6. A married or single life is advantageous to a person, according to his power over himself and his ability to serve God (ver. 7-9).

7. A single life is of special value only when the heart is pure and the life chaste (ver. 1, 2, 8, 9).

8. Paul gives no support to asceticism. An arbitrary prohibition of marriage is a doctrine of demons (ver. 7, 9, 38; 1 Tim. 4 : 1-4).

9. The marriage relation is intended to be as enduring as life, and can be broken only by the grossest of crimes (ver. 10, 13; Matt. 19 : 3-10).

10. If for any reason husband and wife separate to live apart, it must be with the understanding that neither is to marry again during the natural life of the other (ver. 11-13, 15).

11. Unity of religious faith is most desirable in married life, yet truth should not be sacrificed to error (ver. 11-13).

12. Christianity hallows the marriage relation. Is it sacred and indissoluble under the law? It is even more so under the gospel (ver. 14; Rom. 3 : 31; Matt. 5 : 17).

13. In the family and marriage relation there is a duty and also an encouragement to labor for the unbelieving (ver. 16; 1 Peter 3 : 1, 2; James 5 : 20).

14. Christianity is a pre-eminent and a universal religion, adapting itself to all races, ages, and conditions of men (ver. 17-21; Acts 10 : 34; Gal. 3 : 28).

15. It becomes the Christian to be content in whatever lot Providence has placed him (ver. 18, 21, 24; 1 Tim. 6 : 6-8; Phil. 4 : 11).

16. Obedience to Christ is supreme in all our services, relations, and conditions of life (ver. 19; 1 Sam. 15 : 22; 2 Cor. 10 : 5).

17. It is the duty of Christians to preserve social order, and to be faithful to God and men in every station of life (ver. 21, 22; 1 Peter 1 : 13-16; Rom. 13 : 6-10).

18. We should not turn our liberty into license, but use it for holiness and righteousness as servants of Christ (ver. 22, 23; 1 Peter 2 : 15, 16; Titus 2 : 3, 4).

19. We should ever be mindful how much our salvation cost Christ, and that we are at all times his servants (ver. 23; Acts 4 : 19; 5 : 29; Phil. 1 : 27, 28).

20. We should not lightly or hastily change our calling. But God has not called any one to a sinful vocation (ver. 24; 1 Tim. 5 : 22; Rev. 18 : 4).

21. We should be so grounded in the fundamental principles of the gospel as to be able to advise in matters not expressly decided in the Scriptures (ver. 25; 1 Tim. 3 : 15).

22. Parents owe an important and solemn duty to their children in regard to marriage (ver. 25, 36-38).

23. Marriage is in itself a sacred ordinance, established by God, and designed for the good of mankind (ver. 25, 26, 38; Heb. 13 : 4; Gen. 2 : 18, 24).

24. Marriage should not be hastily entered into. Wrong motives, persecution, great calamities, poverty, sickness, and approaching death, may be just reasons for refraining from this relationship (ver. 26-28; Mark 13 : 17).

25. We should live in view of the judgment, and of our Lord's return (ver. 29-32; Matt. 21 : 44-46; 1 Thess. 5 : 1, 2; 2 Peter 3 : 8-10).

26. All earthly relationships are fleeting and destined to dissolution. How should we use them for one another's good and the glory of God? and how should we not set our hearts upon them? (Ver. 25-32; 2 Peter 3 : 11.)

27. No earthly relationship, no earthly sorrow or joy, should keep us from God and duty. They should rather help us on to God (ver. 25, 32; 1 Peter 4 : 7-11; 2 Peter 3 : 14).

28. We should give way neither to immoderate joy, nor to immoderate grief (ver. 30; Phil. 4 : 7).

29. The fact that the fashion of the world is passing away, should lead us to properly estimate and use it, and to seek an enduring and heavenly inheritance (ver. 31; Matt. 6 : 20; Luke 16 : 1-9).

30. It is lawful and best for some, to whom God has given the needed power and grace, to remain unmarried, and to devote themselves entirely to the work of the Lord (ver. 32-34).

31. It should be the Christian's supreme desire, whether married or unmarried, to please the Lord (ver. 32-34; Heb. 11 : 5; 1 John 3 : 22).

32. Many a Christian husband has been injured by a gay and thoughtless wife, and many a Christian wife by a worldly and domineering husband (ver. 33-35).

33. Christians should so conduct themselves in the married relation as not to interfere with their personal piety or usefulness, but so as to promote both (ver. 32-35).

34. If in lighter matters children should regard the judgment of parents, much more in the important matter of marriage (ver. 36-38; Eph. 6 : 1-3).

35. Even in troublous times marriage is well to those who would be better off if unmarried (ver. 38, 40).

36. Christians should marry in the Lord, so as to be not only one in affection, but one in Christ (ver. 39; 2 Cor. 6 : 15).

37. We can lay down no definite rule for marrying or not marrying. Each case must be settled on its own merits, according to circumstances (ver. 1-40).

CHAPTER VIII.

Another question which had been asked the apostle, was concerning eating food offered in sacrifice to idols. The answer to this extends to 11 : 1. First of all in this chapter Paul lays down the principle that such matters are to be settled by love rather than by knowledge (ver. 1-3). He remarks that

On eating food offered to idols; the scruples of the weaker to be respected.

8 NOW as touching things offered unto idols, we know that we all have knowledge:—knowledge puffeth up, 2 but charity edifieth: and if any man think that he knoweth anything, he knoweth nothing yet as he ought to

8 NOW concerning the things offered to idols we know,—because we all have knowledge; knowledge puffs up, but 2 love builds up; if any one thinks that he knows anything, he has not yet 3 known as he ought to know: but

r Ver. 10; 10 : 19–22, 28; Acts 15 : 20, 29.
u 13 : 4–13.
s Rom. 14 : 14, 22.   *t* Rom. 14 : 3, 10.
x Prov. 26 : 12; Gal. 6 : 3.

while this is a matter of indifference (ver. 4–6), yet all are not equally enlightened regarding it (ver. 7), and that some may be led to violate their own consciences; and that thus leading a brother to sin against his conscience they were sinning against Christ (ver. 8–12). Paul then lays down a principle of abstaining for the sake of others (ver. 13).

1–3. THE QUESTION REGARDING FOOD SACRIFICED TO IDOLS TO BE SETTLED BY LOVE RATHER THAN BY KNOWLEDGE. (Comp. Rom. 14.)

1. Now as touching, or *concerning*, **things offered to idols,** those parts not consumed by fire at heathen sacrifices. These were used by the priests and the worshipers, and were eaten at feasts, or sold by the poor and miserly in the market. "Most public entertainments," says Dean Stanley, "and many private meals were more or less remotely the accompaniments of sacrifice. . . This identification of sacrifice and feast was carried to the highest point among the Greeks. . . At Corinth the conqueror in the Isthmian games used to give a banquet to the people immediately after the sacrifices in the temple itself of Poseidon." Jews were forbidden to partake of heathen sacrifices (Num. 25 : 2; Ps. 106 : 28; comp. Rev. 2 : 14). Gentiles were accustomed to them; some, especially proselytes, would naturally regard them lightly; others lately converted from heathenism might be unable to rid themselves of an idea of their sacredness (7 : 7). The apostolic conference had enjoined upon Gentile believers that they should abstain from the pollutions of idols for the sake especially of their Jewish brethren (Acts 15 : 20 : 21 : 25). Among those, therefore, gathered from Jews, proselytes, and heathen, the question was a pressing one and difficult of adjustment. The first clause of this verse is repeated in ver. 4. A parenthetical explanation intervenes. But all are not agreed as to where the parenthesis begins. Some begin it after **we know,** and translate, *Now concerning things offered to idols we know* about it—*because we all have knowledge. . .* (ver. 4), *we know,* I say, *that an idol,* etc. A larger number begin the parenthesis after "knowledge," thus: *Now concerning things offered to idols,* "*we know,*" as you say in your epistle, "*that we all have knowledge.*" Paul appears to quote what they had said, and then parenthetically digresses on *knowledge* in relation to *love,* and resumes the thread of discourse with ver. 4. The latter view seems to me to be preferable. **Knowledge** concerning idols (ver. 4) such as Christians possess, by itself, alone, without love, **puffeth up,** inflates with pride, fills with self-conceit, **but charity edifieth,** rather, *love* toward God and toward our neighbor *buildeth up* from the foundation. The figure is taken from the gradual building up of a house: Love promotes wisdom, self-denial, and every grace in Christian character and living, and the well-being and development of the church. "*Knowledge* only says, *all things are lawful for me;* love adds, *but all things do not build up*" (BENGEL). Knowledge must be tempered with love.

2. But knowledge without humility is very imperfect. At our best we know but in part (13 : 12). Knowledge without love is unchristian. As there is a false, a pretended wisdom (3 : 18), so there is a false and pretended knowledge. If any man is puffed up and self-conceited, **if any man think that he knoweth anything,** if he is self-opinionated, **he knoweth nothing yet as he ought to know,** and as it should be known. He has not really learned what he pretends to know.

3 know: but if any man love God, *y* the
4 same is known of him:—as concerning
therefore the eating of those things
that are offered in sacrifice unto idols,
we know that *a* an idol *is* nothing in
the world, *a* and that *there is* none other
5 God but one. For though there be
that are *b* called gods, whether in
heaven or in earth, (as there be gods
6 many, and lords many,) but *c* to us
there is but one God, the Father, *d* of
whom *are* all things, and we in [or,
for] him; and *e* one Lord Jesus Christ,

if any one loves God, this one is known
by him:—
4 Concerning then the eating of the
things offered to idols, we know that
there is no idol in the world, and that
5 there is no God but one. For though
there are gods so-called, whether in
heaven or on earth (as there are gods
6 many, and lords many), yet to us there
is one God, the Father, from whom are
all things, and we unto him; and one
Lord, Jesus Christ, through whom
are all things, and we through him.

y Exod. 33 : 12, 17; see refs. Ps. 1 : 6.   *z* 10 : 19; Ps. 115 : 4-8 : Isa. 41 : 24.
a Deut. 4 : 39; Mark 12 : 29; 1 Tim. 2 : 5.   *b* Ps. 96 : 5; Dan. 5 : 4.   *c* Mal. 2 : 10; Eph. 4 : 6.
d Acts 17 : 28; Rom. 11 : 36.   *e* John 13 : 13; Acts 2 : 36; Eph. 4 : 5; Phil. 2 : 11.

(Comp. note on 3 : 16. See also Gal. 6 : 3; 1 Tim. 6 : 3, 4.)

3. But if any man love God, and in that case he will love his neighbor also (1 John 4 : 7, 8, 20), **the same is known of him.** If we are known of God we must have some knowledge of him, and of divine things. The two are inseparable (Gal. 4 : 9 and John 17 : 3). Knowledge is thus deficient without love, and alone is not a sufficient guide. If any one boasts of knowledge, he needs to cultivate love. Love with knowledge is our only safe guide in dealing with our fellow-men (13 : 4-7).

4-6. TO THE ENLIGHTENED CHRISTIAN, EATING FOOD OFFERED TO IDOLS IS A MATTER OF INDIFFERENCE.

4. As concerning therefore the eating, etc. The apostle resumes the thought begun in ver. 1. **We know,** as you said in your Epistle, **that "an idol is nothing in the world,"** he has no true being and is nothing but a mere image in the temple, or as many prefer to translate, *And that there is no idol in the world*, there is no such thing as a pagan divinity in the universe. By *idol* is meant the deity it represents. A name without a reality; an image with nothing to represent. In the next clause *other* should be omitted: **"And that there is** *no* **God but one,"** which all Christians would admit. We may thus far regard this as a quotation from the letter to Paul from Corinth, which he adopts. If idols were nothing, if heathen deities, such as Jupiter and Apollo had no existence, then they could pollute nothing offered to them. The argument is so far correct. The thought is pursued a step further, and a new factor introduced in 10 : 20, which needed not to be noticed here. (See on ver. 10.)

5. The thought is expanded and explained in this and the next verse. **For though there be that are called gods.** Paul makes a supposition, without admitting a reality. *For though there are gods so called*, even supposing this to be the case, **whether in heaven** or *upon* **earth,** where the heathen conceived their divinities to exist. **As there be,** rather, *are*, **gods many and lords many,** whom the heathen worship. It was a fact that in heathen phraseology there were many, who bore the name, some of gods, and some of lords. **Lords** is added to include the whole range of heathen divinities, and perhaps also to correspond with *Lord* of the next verse. Many however interpret *gods many and lords many* as referring to superhuman beings, the angels mentioned in Deut. 10 : 17; Joshua 22 : 22; Dan. 2 : 47. Compare John 10 : 35; Ps. 82 : 6, where the term *gods* is applied to judges, even though unjust, because they were appointed to act in place of God on earth. And angels have their mission under God in respect to men (Dan. 8 : 16; 10 : 13; Heb. 1 : 14). It is possible in a general way to include both views.

6. But, or *yet*, whatever others may hold regarding the so-called gods of the heathen, **to us,** as Christians, **there is but one God, the Father, of,** or *from*, **whom are all things,** the source of all and upon whom all depend, **and we in,** rather, *unto* **him,** to serve his purposes, he is our object and end; **and one Lord,** namely, **Jesus Christ by,** or *through*, **whom are all things,** the divine agent in the

CH. VIII.] I. CORINTHIANS 243

ᶠ by whom *are* all things, and we by him. Howbeit *there is* not in every man that knowledge: for some *with conscience of the idol unto this hour eat *it* as a thing offered unto an idol; and their conscience being weak is ᵇ defiled.
8 But ⁱ meat commendeth us not to God: for neither, if we eat, are we the better; neither, if we eat not, are we
9 the worse. But ᵏ take heed lest by any means this liberty of yours become ˡ a stumblingblock to them that
10 are ᵐ weak. For if any man see thee ⁿ which hast knowledge sit at meat in the idol's temple, shall not the con-

7 Yet the knowledge is not in all; but some, being accustomed to the idol until now, eat it as a thing offered to an idol; and their conscience being
8 weak is defiled. But food will not commend us to God; for neither, if we eat not, are we lacking; nor, if we eat,
9 do we abound. But take heed, lest in any way this liberty of yours become a
10 stumbling-block to the weak. For if any one sees thee, who hast knowledge, reclining at table in an idol's temple, will not his conscience if he is

f John 1 : 3 ; Col. 1 : 16, 17 ; Heb. 2 : 10.   *g* 10 : 28, 29.   *h* Rom. 14 : 14, 23.   *i* Rom. 14 : 17.
k Rom. 14 : 21 ; Gal. 5 : 13.   *l* Rom. 14 : 13-15, 20.   *m* Rom. 14 : 1, 2 ; 15 : 1.   *n* Ver. 1.

creation and preservation of all things, **and we,** *through* **him,** in our new creation and redemption (John 1 : 3 ; Col. 1 : 16 ; Heb. 1 : 2 ; Eph. 4 : 5, 6 ; 1 Cor. 15 : 28).

7-13. ALL NOT BEING EQUALLY ENLIGHTENED, WE MUST HAVE REGARD IN OUR CONDUCT TO THE INFIRMITIES OF THE WEAK.

7. Thus far the apostle has treated the eating of things offered to idols as a matter of indifference to the Christian who has clear knowledge of things relating to God, and of the nothingness of idols. **Howbeit there is not in every man that knowledge**—all are not equally enlightened; they have not those clear views which have become deep convictions, and which lead to decided action. **For some with conscience,** having a conscientious fear or scruple, **of the idol unto this hour,** or, *until now,* which feeling they have not been able to divest themselves of. This might be true of certain Jewish believers and others. But the most approved text reads, *For some being used until now to the idol,* being accustomed to the idol as more or less real, have not been able to rid themselves entirely of the idea; so that to them the idol-sacrifice and eating things offered to idols are not matters of indifference. According to this these weak brethren belonged to the Gentile portion of the church, especially those converted recently from heathenism. **And their conscience being weak,** not strong to distinguish clearly between things lawful and unlawful to the Christian, **is defiled** by a sense of sin (ver. 10 ; comp. Rom. 14 : 14, 20, 23).

8. Paul gives a reason why the strong should have regard to the consciences of the weak. Both knowledge and liberty are not to be abused. **But meat,** or *food,* **commendeth us not,** according to the best text, *will not commend us* **to God,** *will not bring us near,* into fellowship with God. It is not perishable food (6 : 13), but Christ who brings us near and presents us to God (2 Cor. 4 : 14; Col. 1 : 22). **For neither, if we eat are we the better,** pre-eminent before God; **neither, if we eat not are we the worse** in excellence before him. The eating or the abstaining in itself will not affect our standing before God. (Comp. 7 : 19 ; Rom. 14 : 17.)

9. Such being the case, the important question is, How will our conduct affect others? And there is danger of affecting some disastrously. **But take heed lest by any means this liberty of yours,** *this right* of doing under the gospel, **become a stumbling-block to them that are weak,** over which they shall stumble into acting against their own conscience, which to them may result most seriously (ver. 11. Comp. Rom. 14 : 13, 20).

10. The apostle shows how an enlightened believer may be thus a stumbling-block. He selects an extreme case, a striking example of an abuse of Christian liberty. This would show the evil tendency of smaller abuses. **For if any man see thee which hast knowledge,** of what things are lawful and unlawful, **sit at meat,** rather, *reclining at table in an* **idol's temple, shall not the conscience**

science of him which is weak be emboldened to eat those things which are
11 offered to idols; and ᵒthrough thy knowledge shall the weak brother
12 perish, for whom Christ died? But ᵖwhen ye sin so against the brethren, and wound their weak conscience, ye
13 sin against Christ. Wherefore, ᵠif meat make my brother to offend, ʳI will eat no flesh while the world standeth, lest I make my brother to offend.

weak be built up to eat the things
11 offered to idols? For in thy knowledge he that is weak perishes, the brother on account of whom Christ died!
12 And thus sinning against the brethren, and wounding their weak conscience,
13 ye sin against Christ. Wherefore, if food makes my brother to stumble, I will eat no flesh for ever more, that I may not make my brother to stumble.

o Rom. 14 : 15, 20, 21.   p Matt. 25 : 40, 45; Acts 9 : 4, 5.   q Mark 9 : 42; Rom. 14 : 21.   r 9 : 17, 19-23.

of him that is weak, regarding thee as an example and guide in such matters, be emboldened, literally, *be built up into the eating of idol sacrifices*, and thus, his conscience being defiled, he may relapse into idolatry. He is thereby built up in wrong-doing. In 10 : 14-21 such participation is condemned as unlawful; here it is only condemned for the sake of others, that being the point of argument.

11. According to the most approved text the question ends with the preceding verse, and this reads : *And through thy knowledge he that is weak perishes, the brother for whose sake Christ died!* "*Died*—through the love thou art so far from imitating" (BENGEL). (Comp. note on Rom. 14 : 15; also Rom. 15 : 1-3.) *Perishes* denotes the final loss of the soul; but the present tense here employed brings into view this loss in its progress. Such warnings as this and Heb. 6 : 6 are doubtless used by the Holy Spirit to prevent the destruction of any of God's true children.

12. Having mentioned Christ, Paul traces the result of such conduct in relation to Christ. **But when ye so sin against the brethren and wound their weak conscience,** and thus do them moral injury by leading them to act contrary to their convictions, **ye sin against Christ.** Even the least are representatives of Christ (Matt. 25 : 40); and they are members of Christ (12 : 27; Rom. 12 : 5); and Christ dwells in their hearts by faith (Eph. 3 : 17). Sins against the brethren are most surely sins against Christ.

13. In view of all that he had said, Paul deduces a principle of abstaining from things indifferent for the good of others, which he states in the strongest possible manner, and to which he was ready to obligate himself as long as life. **Wherefore,** *for this very reason*, **if meat,** or *food*, **make my brother to offend,** or *to stumble* into sin, **I will eat no flesh** of any kind **while the world standeth,** or, *forevermore*, **lest I make my brother to offend.** He would never taste of flesh again, rather than be a stumbling-block in his brother's way. (Comp. note on Rom. 14 : 21. See also Mark 9 : 42; Luke 17 : 1, 2.) At this point Paul suspends his discussion on idol worship and resumes it in 10 : 14. The intervening digression is apposite and important.

CONSCIENCE, ITS USE IN THE NEW TESTAMENT.—According to our modern modes of thought, it is well to distinguish conscience, the faculty that judges one's moral acts, from moral consciousness, the state of the soul that accompanies conscience and recognizes its workings. Conscience should also be distinguished from the moral faculty. The former is specific, the latter more general and judges moral actions by whomsoever performed. The Hebrew has no word for conscience, but uses the general terms "inward parts," "reins," and "heart." John uses the word "heart" with reference to conscience in his First Epistle (3 : 21, 22). The Greek and also the Latin had but one word, which originally had no religious bearing. It was primarily used of consciousness; but before the Christian era began it was also applied by philosophical writers to conscience. It is not found in the Old Testament, and in the New only in the writings of Paul, Peter, and the author of the Epistle to the Hebrews, expressing the moral exercises and state of the soul. The exact meaning of each instance where the word appears must be learned from the connection.

(1) The clearest instance in the New Testament, where the word is used for moral consciousness, is in Heb. 10 : 2, "no more conscience," or *consciousness*, of sins. Also in 1 Cor. 8 : 7, "some with *consciousness* of the idol"; and less clearly in Acts 23 : 1 ; 24 : 16; 1 Tim. 1 : 5, 19 ; 3 : 9; Heb. 9 : 9; 1 Peter 3 : 16. (2) It appears to be used of the moral faculty in 2 Cor. 4 : 2 and 5 : 11, where the actions of others are judged. (3) In its limited and distinctive sense of deciding upon one's own moral actions, it is found in Rom. 2 : 15 ; 9 : 1; 13 : 5; 1 Cor. 8 : 7 (second instance), 10 ; 10 : 25, 27, 28, 29; 2 Cor. 1 : 12; 1 Peter 3 : 21. In examining these and other instances where the word occurs, it will be found that the meaning varies with shades between the above distinctions.

The supreme authority of conscience is implied in such passages as Rom. 2 : 15; 2 Cor. 1 : 12; 5 : 11; 1 Peter 2 : 19; 3 : 21. That it may be affected by education and its surroundings is indicated in such passages as 1 Cor. 8 : 12 ; 1 Tim. 4 : 2. The conscience, however, can become an infallible guide only as the soul is brought into perfect harmony with God and his law (Heb. 9 : 14; 10 : 22).

Liberty of conscience means that God, not man, may decide how one may worship; and that one has a right to follow the dictates of his conscience in so doing. But liberty is not license. It is abused when pretence to worship is turned into revelry and debauch, into blasphemy, or a pretext for immorality and crime.

PRACTICAL REMARKS.

1. True Christian knowledge is modest. That which is high-minded, contentious, and selfish, is so far false (ver. 1, 2 ; 13 : 34; Rom. 2 : 19-21).

2. Christian knowledge and Christian love are inseparable (ver. 1–3 ; 13 : 2 ; 1 John 4 : 7, 8).

3. A true Christian may have very wrong views and feelings in regard to many things; but love with spiritual knowledge and God's word will guide in such matters (ver. 1–3 ; 13 : 4, 5 ; Rom. 13 : 10).

4. That there is but one God is a fundamental truth in all true religion (ver. 4 ; Mark 12 : 29-32; 1 Tim. 2 : 5).

5. We know that heathen idols are nothing, but we should beware of idols in our hearts (ver. 4, 5 ; Ezek. 14 : 3).

6. Christ is the one Lord of his people, our supreme Lawgiver and King (ver. 3 ; John 13 : 13).

7. The unity of God and the Lordship of Christ are harmonious truths. The Father and the Son represent eternal distinctions in the Divine nature (ver. 6 ; John 1 : 1, 2; Heb. 1 : 2, 3).

8. We should seek to enlighten the conscience with spiritual knowledge and the word of God (ver. 7; 2 Cor. 1 : 12 ; 4 : 2).

9. All food that is healthful and nutritious should be received with thanksgiving; yet in itself it has no effect on our Christianity (ver. 8; 1 Tim. 4 : 3, 4 ; Rom. 14 : 17).

10. We ought to be careful lest our conduct, even in things that are lawful, should be an occasion of leading others into sin (ver. 9, 10; Gal. 5 : 13).

11. He who cares not for the influence of his example upon others has the spirit of Cain: "Am I my brother's keeper?" (ver. 10, 11 ; Gen. 4 : 9).

12. All sins against our neighbor are sins against God (ver. 12; 10 : 16, 29; Rom. 13 : 9).

13. It is not enough that a thing is not forbidden, or that it is not wrong in itself; we must consider how it will affect others for evil or for good (ver. 11, 12 ; Rom. 14 : 14, 15).

14. How noble Paul's principle of denying one's self of any gratification which might lead others into sin. How would the church, society, and the world be bettered by its general practice. How would the cause of temperance and social purity be advanced (ver. 13 ; Rom. 14 : 21).

CHAPTER IX.

The general subject of eating things offered to idols, and in particular the denying of ourselves for the good of others, Paul illustrates by his own conduct. He had foregone his rights as an apostle in living unmarried, and also had not availed himself of God's universal law that the laborer, man or beast, should receive the fruit of his labor (ver. 1-12); while God had appointed that they who preach the gospel should live by the gospel, he had

On eating food offered to idols; Paul's use of his Christian liberty.

9 ᵛAM I not an apostle? ᵗAm I not free? ᵘHave I not seen Jesus Christ our Lord? ˣAre not ye my work in
2 the Lord? If I be not an apostle unto others, yet doubtless I am to you: for ʸ the seal of mine apostleship are ye in
3 the Lord. Mine answer ᶻ to them that do examine me ᵃ is this:

9 Am I not free? Am I not an apostle? Have I not seen Jesus our Lord? Are not ye my work in the Lord?
2 If to others I am not an apostle, yet to you at least I am; for the seal of my apostleship are ye in the
3 Lord. My defense to those who ex-

s 1 : 1 ; see refs. Acts 9 : 15 ; 2 Cor. 12 : 12.   *t* Ver. 19.   *u* 15 : 8 ; Acts 9 : 3–6, 17 ; 22 : 14, 18.
x 4 : 14, 15.   *y* 2 Cor. 3 : 2, 3 ; 12 : 12.   *z* 2 Cor. 13 : 3.   *a* Ver. 4–6.

made it his glory and reward to preach the gospel without charge (ver. 13–18), and being free he had exercised his freedom in becoming the servant of all (ver. 19–23). He then urges upon the Corinthians self-restraint, since that was needful for their safety (ver. 24–27); which is further enforced in the next chapter.

1–23. HOW PAUL AS AN APOSTLE FOREWENT HIS RIGHTS FOR THE SAKE OF SAVING OTHERS. See preceding analysis of the chapter.

1. Paul proceeds to show that the principle of self-denial, which he had laid down for himself (8 : 13), was but a single expression of his general conduct as a freeman and an apostle. His freedom and apostleship he brings into the foreground and makes emphatic, both because he would make his self-denial for others stand out the more prominent, and also because there were those who were disposed to impugn his motives, to question his apostleship, or at least give him an inferior place among the apostles. He at once, in his fervid manner, plunges into the heart of the discussion, asking four questions, each of which demands an affirmative answer. To his Corinthian converts, the mere asking of them were but to expect a positive and affirmative reply. According to the oldest and best manuscripts the first two questions of the common reading are reversed, which is the more natural order. **Am I not free?** from all men (ver. 19) to act as I please in regard to self-denial for the good of others? **Am I not an apostle?** having all the rights and privileges, the authority and gifts pertaining to the office? (Matt. 10 : 1; Gal. 1 : 1; 2 :7-9.) **Have I not seen Jesus, the Lord?** as you have often heard me testify? **Christ** is omitted by the best text. He had seen the Lord at his conversion near to Damascus (15 : 8; Acts 9 : 17); on his return to Jerusalem (Acts 22 : 17, 18); later in a vision at Corinth (Acts 18 : 9); besides he had other visions and revelations of the Lord (2 Cor. 12 : 1). It was necessary that an apostle should be a witness to Christ's resurrection (Acts 1 : 22); and Paul fulfilled this condition. The other apostles had been associated with Jesus in his earthly ministry. But this deficiency was made up by his seeing the glorified Jesus, and the abundance of the revelations given him (2 Cor. 12 : 7). **Are not ye my work**, as an apostle, **in the Lord?** in fellowship with him and engaged in his service? As such they were the fruit and the evidences of his apostleship. See next verse, which expands this thought.

2. If I be, better, *If I am*, **not an apostle to others,** to those outside of you and in their estimation. These *others* included those who did not belong to their company, who had not been converted under his ministry, and they had not been molded under his spiritual power. They included Jewish emissaries and opposers. **Yet doubtless**, rather, *at least*, **I am to you.** Paul claimed to be an apostle, and God owned his claim. No other church had greater proofs of his apostleship than that at Corinth; among none had the fruits and signs of an apostle been more manifest. **For the seal,** the attestation and proof (comp. Rom. 4 : 11), **of mine apostleship are ye in the Lord,** in your fellowship with Christ, and in the enjoyment of spiritual gifts. The signs of his apostleship were manifested in them and among them (1 : 7; 2 Cor. 12 : 12) It was only in Christ, not out of him, that they could be an attestation of Paul's apostolic authority and work.

3. Mine answer, or *defense* (a

4 ᵇHave we not power to eat and to
5 drink? ᶜHave we not power to lead about a sister, a wife, as well as other apostles, and ᵃˢ ᵈthe brethren of the
6 Lord, and ᵉCephas? Or I only and ᶠBarnabas, ᵍhave not we power to forbear working?

4 amine me is this: Have we no right to
5 eat and drink? Have we no right to lead about a wife who is a sister, as also the rest of the apostles, and the
6 brothers of the Lord, and Cephas? Or have only I and Barnabas no right to
7 forbear working? Who ever serves as

b Ver. 7-14; Matt. 10:10; Gal. 6:6; 2 Thess. 3:9. *c* 1 Tim. 4:3; Heb. 13:4.
d See refs. Matt. 12:46, 47. *e* Matt. 8:14; John 1:42. *f* Acts 4:36. *g* See refs. Acts 18:3.

legal term as if in a court of justice (Acts 22:1; 25:16), **to them that do examine me** (another legal term, as if under a preliminary investigation, held for the purpose of gathering evidence for the information of the magistrates (Acts 4:9) **is this.** It is best to put a period here. But to what does the word *this* refer? Most late expositors refer it back to the Corinthian converts, this attestation of his apostleship (Acts 15:4, 12; Gal. 2:2, 9). What follows is not a defense of his apostleship, but of his full freedom while sacrificing for others. But most of the older interpreters refer it to what follows. So it is most natural to take the language. Paul's chief design in this chapter is to show how his conduct of self-denial accorded with the principle laid down in 8:13, and to defend this conduct. His brief reference and defense of his apostleship was incidental but important, and doubtless called forth by his knowledge of opposers. In the fervor of his thoughts, he would naturally take in his freedom and rights as well as his apostleship. His language may thus be both retrospective and prospective. What precedes was strictly a defense of his apostleship; what follows, a defense of his conduct as an apostle. He naturally goes from one to the other, and with some indefiniteness of expression.

4. Have we not power, *a right,* **to eat and to drink?** at the expense of the church (Luke 10:7). This was the thought he was about to develop (ver. 6 ff.). His well-known custom of supporting himself, while preaching the gospel (1 Thess. 2:8-10; 2 Thess. 3:7-9; Acts 20:34) was not a result of necessity, as some of his opposers might affirm, but a free act of devotion (2 Cor. 11:7-9; 12:15-18),

5. Have we not power, *a right,* **to lead about a sister** believer *as a* **wife,** at the expense of the churches,

as well as the other apostles—implying that they took their wives with them in their missionary journeys, and were both regarded as entitled to maintenance from the brethren. This passage plainly implies that Paul was unmarried, and that the other apostles generally were married. Some, to avoid this conclusion, translate the word *wife, a woman,* who attended them as an assistant, like the woman in Luke 8:2, 3. But in that case the word woman is superfluous, for a *sister* is a *woman.* Besides, it is not at all probable that the apostles would have adopted such a practice in society so corrupt as heathen society then was, nor would they have exposed themselves to the scandals arising therefrom. Neither is there any historical evidence of such a practice among them. Besides Peter (Hebrew name, Cephas) was married (Matt. 8:14). **By brethren of our Lord,** are meant the younger brothers of our Lord by Joseph and Mary. (See note on Mark 6:3.) Peter and the brethren of our Lord are mentioned, as those who were held in most esteem by the Jewish party.

6. Or I only, better, *or have only I,* **and Barnabas, not power,** *not a right,* **to forbear working?** for our support (4:12; Acts 18:3). Paul and Barnabas were missionaries among the heathen (Acts 13:2), and were together in Paul's first missionary journey (Acts 13:2-14:28); but separated before Paul's second journey (Acts 15:39). Barnabas is mentioned in connection with Paul at the apostolic conference in Acts 15:12 and Gal. 2:1, 9, 13. He had been in high esteem among the apostles (Acts 4:36; 9:27; 11:22), and would doubtless be well known, at least by reputation, among Jewish Christians at Corinth.

7. Paul now proceeds to defend his right to be supported by the churches. First, from the analogy of human conduct in other callings. He selects three, the soldier, the vinedresser, and the

7 Who goeth a warfare any time at his own charges? Who ᵇ planteth a vineyard, and eateth not of the fruit thereof? Or who feedeth a flock, and eateth
8 not of the milk of the flock? Say I these things as a man? Or ⁱ saith not
9 the law the same also? For it is written in the law of Moses, ᵏ Thou shalt not muzzle the mouth of the ox that treadeth out the corn. ˡ Doth God take
10 care for oxen? Or saith he *it* altogether for our sakes? ᵐ For our sakes, no doubt, *this* is written: that ⁿ he that ploweth should plow in hope: and that he that thresheth in hope should be
11 partaker of his hope. ᵒ If we have

a soldier at his own charges? Who plants a vineyard, and eats not of its fruit? Or who shepherds a flock, and
8 eats not of the milk of the flock? Am I saying these things after the manner of men? Or does not the law also say
9 these things? For in the law of Moses it is written, Thou shalt not muzzle an ox while treading out the grain? Is it
10 for the oxen that God cares? Or does he say it altogether for our sake? Yes, for our sake it was written; because he that plows ought to plow in hope; and he that threshes, in hope of partaking.
11 If we sowed for you spiritual things, is

ᵇ Deut. 20 : 6 ; Prov. 27 : 18.　ⁱ Isa. 8 : 20.　ᵏ 1 Tim. 5 : 18.　ˡ See Matt. 6 : 26.　ᵐ Rom. 15 : 4.
ⁿ John 4 : 36 ; 2 Tim. 2 : 6.　ᵒ Rom. 15 : 27 ; Gal. 6 : 6.

shepherd, who all subsist on the fruit of their labors. **At his own charges** —from his own resources. "The example from the army, like most of the military expressions in the Epistles, is true only of the later ages of Greece and Rome, when the voluntary service and the mixed pursuits of the ancient soldiers were superseded by the regular profession of a standing army" (STANLEY). **Of the milk**—from its food and from its sale. In the East a portion of the milk forms to this day a part of the shepherd's pay.

8. Say I these things as a man —after the manner of men, according to human judgment and from a human point of view? **Or saith not the law the same also.** The law is conceived of as something higher and more authoritative than human analogies and reasoning. The question is equal to a strong affirmation that the law does thus speak. And so Paul passes to his *second* argument, which is drawn from the law of Moses.

9. The apostle quotes Deut. 25 : 4, from the Septuagint version, **Thou shalt not muzzle the mouth of the ox that treadeth out the corn,** better, *the grain;* threshing the grain by treading it either with or without dragging the threshing machine. This is also quoted and similarly applied in 1 Tim. 5 : 18. In such an application it became almost a proverbial saying, **Doth God care for** *the* **oxen?** Comparatively not. Yet Paul does not deny God's care for them (Matt. 10 : 29), but so much more incomparably does he care for us that his care for them is as nothing. Paul's mind is on the

spiritual import of the passage, and its purport to us, teaching us by this kindness to the brute creation a lesson of humanity to men, and a kind consideration of all who labor (2 Cor. 3 : 6). Note too how Deut. 25 : 4 stands alone after and between humane precepts to men.

10. Or saith he it altogether for our sakes? or *assuredly for our sakes?* God spoke especially for those who could understand and who were capable of moral discipline. So Philo explains the spirit of the law, "that it speaks not in behalf of irrational creatures, but in behalf of those who have sense and reason." **For our sakes no doubt this** *was* **written.** While God feeds the young ravens when they cry (Ps. 147 : 9), yet this was spoken to God's people, and it had a higher reference than merely the brute creation ; it was an object lesson to man to teach him that all labor should have its due compensation, and that they that toil for others should share in the fruit of their labors. And so the apostle goes on to show. **That he that ploweth should plow in hope** of partaking of the harvest, **and he that thresheth,** or *treadeth out* (ver. 9), **in hope should be partaker of his hope,** rather, *in hope of partaking* of the crop. Spiritual plowing and threshing are here meant (1 Cor. 3 : 6, 9). All who labor should profit by it, especially Christian laborers in God's field.

11. Paul applies the argument from husbandry, appealing to the principles of gratitude as an additional reason. **If we,** especially himself, and probably including Silas and Timothy, who assisted him at Corinth (Acts 18 : 5). He

sown unto you spiritual things, *is it* a great thing if we shall reap your car-
12 nal things? If others be partakers of *this* power over you, *p are* not we rather? *q* Nevertheless we have not used this power; *r* but suffer all things, lest we should hinder the gospel of Christ.
13 *s* Do ye not know that they which minister about holy things live *of the things* of the temple; and they which wait at the altar are partakers with
14 the altar? Even so *t* hath the Lord ordained that they which preach the gospel should live of the gospel.
15 But *u* I have used none of these

it a great matter if we shall reap your
12 carnal things? If others partake of this right over you, do not we still more? But we used not this right; but we bear all things, that we may not cause any hindrance to the gospel of Christ.
13 Know ye not that they who minister about the holy things eat of the things of the temple, and they who wait at
14 the altar partake with the altar? Even so did the Lord appoint for those who proclaim the gospel, to live by the
15 gospel. I however have used none of

p Ver. 2. *q* 2 Cor. 11 : 7–12. *r* 4 : 11, 12. *s* See refs. Num. 5 : 9, 10; Deut. 10 : 9; 18 : 1.
t Ver. 4; Luke 10 : 7. *u* Ver. 12; Acts 18 : 3; 2 Cor. 12 : 13–19.

could not have included Barnabas (ver. 6), for we have no evidence that Barnabas ever labored at Corinth. **Have sown unto you,** rather, *If we sowed for you,* spiritual *blessing* of the gospel when we labored among you, **is it a great thing if we shall reap** *of you* **carnal things?** food and drink and raiment for our maintenance. The argument is from the greater to the less. For such great spiritual blessings and gifts, gratitude ought to prompt at least the bestowment of the lesser blessings of earthly support. Compare the same argument in Rom. 15 : 27; and in form of an injunction in Gal. 6 : 6.

12. The apostle strengthens his position by another argument drawn from a comparison of himself with others, who had a less claim upon them. **If others be partakers of this power over you,** *the right* of receiving support from you, *should* **not we rather** be partakers of it. They had had teachers, some of them inferior and misleading (2 Cor. 11 : 20), who had come in after the church was established, but he was the founder of the church, and they were largely the converts of his ministry (4 : 15). Through Christ they owed to him their Christian life. **Nevertheless we have not used,** rather, *we did not use* **this power,** or *right,* when among you. And this conduct of self-denial accorded with the principle laid down in 8 : 13. **But we suffer,** rather, *bear,* **all things,** hardships and privations arising from receiving no compensation (2 Cor. 11 : 27), and the object of this is, *that we may not cause any hindrance to* **the gospel of**

Christ, by being charged with interested and selfish motives (ver. 18; 1 Thess. 2 : 3–10). He would not cause any to stumble by anything he might do.

13. Paul returns to his argument, and appeals to the temple service. This was especially suited to the Jewish believers, as ver. 24–27, appealing to Gentile customs, was suited to Gentile believers. **Do ye not know**—appealing to a practice familiar to them and still existing. **That they that minister,** or *are busied,* **about holy,** or *sacred,* **things,** which pertain to the worship of God in the temple, **live,** or *eat,* **of the things of the temple?** *the sacred place;* and **they that wait at the altar are partakers with the altar.** The whole verse has reference to Jewish sacrifices and to the priesthood, the priests not including the Levites. The Jewish priests were maintained from the sacrifices, which were apportioned, a part to be burnt upon the altar, a part for the priests, and a part to be consumed by the worshiper (Lev. 6 : 16; Num. 5 : 8–10; 18 : 8–20; Deut. 18 : 1). As the priesthood was supported, so should the ministry be, whether apostles or not. This application Paul makes in the next verse.

14. **Even so hath the Lord,** *did the Lord,* when upon earth, **ordained,** *prescribe* by express precept (Matt. 10 : 10; Luke 10 : 7) *to those who proclaim the gospel, to live by the gospel.* This saying of our Lord to the apostles in Judea would have weight with Jewish converts at Corinth.

15. Paul reverts to his custom of denying himself for the good of others, according to the principle enunciated

things: neither have I written these things that it should be so done unto me. For *it were* better for me to die than that any man should make my
16 glorying void. For though I preach the gospel, I have nothing to glory of: for a necessity is laid upon me; yea, woe is unto me, if I preach not the
17 gospel! For *y* if I do this thing willingly, I have a reward: but if against my will, *a* dispensation *of the gospel* is
18 committed unto me. What is my reward then? *Verily* that, *z* when I preach the gospel, I may make the gospel of Christ without charge, that I abuse not my power in the gospel.

these things; and I write not these things, that it may be so done in my case; for it were better for me to die, than that any one should make my
16 glorying void. For if I preach the gospel, I have nothing to glory of; for a necessity is laid on me; for, woe is to me, if I preach not the gospel! For if
17 I do this willingly, I have a reward; but if unwillingly, I have a steward-
18 ship intrusted to me. What then is my reward? That, in preaching the gospel, I may make the gospel without charge, so as not to use to the full my right in

x Jer. 1 : 17; 20 : 9; Amos 3 : 8; Acts 4 : 20.   *y* 1 Peter 5 : 2-4.   *z* Phil. 1 : 17; Col. 1 : 25.
a Ver. 12; 10 : 33; 2 Cor. 11 : 7.

in 8 : 13. **But I** (emphatic) whatever others may do, **have used none of these things**, as was my right. Neither did he desire, by what he had just said, that his support should be provided for in the future: **Neither have I written**, more exactly, *did I write*, **these things that it should be so done unto me.** The abandonment of his rights was entirely voluntary on his part, and he does not propose to press their claims. There is here some confusion in the original text. That text which is best sustained may be rendered: *It is well for me to die rather than . . . my glorying*, that is, the ground of my glorying, *no one shall make it void!* The abruptness, the strength of expression, and its broken form, accords with its vehemence. (Comp. Rom 9 : 1.) To labor gratuitously was his glory, which he would suffer no one to take from him. It was a proof of integrity and of entire unselfishness on his part. And thus he could better keep his body under (ver. 23-27).

16. Paul gives a reason why he emphasizes his glorying in preaching the gospel gratuitously. **For though**, rather, *For if* **I preach the gospel, I have nothing to glory of.** He was but doing his duty. It was indeed a bounden duty for the faithful discharge of which he was most solemnly accountable: **For necessity is laid upon me;** feeling a moral compulsion by the call and commission of Jesus (Acts 22 : 10, 21. *see* 16-18), and for his pardoning grace (1 Tim. 1 : 12-16). Indeed, if he did not do it, he would be under condemnation and exposed to the judgment of God. **Yea,** better, *For*, **woe is me,** the threatened judgments of God betide me at the last great day, **if I preach not the gospel.**

17. Explains and applies this necessity in his own case still further. **For if I do this thing willingly,** preaching the gospel of mine own accord as a voluntary undertaking, which is not my case, **I have a reward.** He was taken, put into the service, and put under obligation (Acts 9 : 15, 16; Gal. 1 : 15, 16; Phil. 3 : 12; 2 Tim. 1 : 11). **But if against my will,** or *unwillingly*, not entering upon it of my own accord, an involuntary service which I am under obligation to do, which was really his case (Acts 9 : 16; 22 : 14), then **a dispensation of the gospel,** rather, *a stewardship is entrusted to me,* by God who is my absolute Lord, which I must discharge. A steward was usually chosen from among slaves (4 : 1). As the Lord's steward, however willingly and heartily he might perform his office, he had no option but to obey. After doing all, at his very best, he had only done what was his duty to do (Luke 17 : 10).

18. **What is my reward then?** my divine recompense under these circumstances? Wherein does it consist? **Verily that,** rather, *This, that* **when I preach the gospel, I may do it without charge, that I abuse not,** rather, *so that I use not to the full my right in the gospel*, that right of support conferred upon me in preaching the gospel (ver. 14); and having the consciousness of faithfully thus doing; and thereby gaining the more converts (ver. 20-23). The privilege and satisfaction of preaching the gospel without money and without price to those ad-

19 For though I be ᵇfree from all *men*, yet have ᶜI made myself servant unto
20 all, that I might gain the more. And ᵈ unto the Jews I became as a Jew, that I might gain the Jews; to them that are under the law, as under the law, that I might gain them that are under the
21 law; ᵉto them that are ᶠwithout law, as without law, (ᵍbeing not without law to God, but under the law to Christ,) that I might gain them that

19 the gospel. For being free from all men, I made myself servant to all, that
20 I might gain the most. And to the Jews I became as a Jew, that I might gain the Jews; to those under law, as under law, not being myself under law, that I might gain those under law;
21 to those without law, as without law (not being without law to God, but under law to Christ), that I might gain

ᵇ Ver. 1.   ᶜ Gal. 5 : 13 ; 1 Thess. 2 : 7.   ᵈ Acts 16 : 3 ; 21 : 20-26.   ᵉ Gal. 2 : 3-5, 11-14.
ᶠ Rom. 2 : 12, 14.   ᵍ 7 : 22 ; Rom. 7 : 22 ; Gal. 5 : 13, 14.

dressed was a sufficient recompense to him (1 Tim. 1 : 12-16). "He looks for no higher reward or pay than to preach the gospel without pay; he hopes for no higher freedom (returning to the image of a slave implied in 'a stewardship entrusted to me' (ver. 17)) than to become a slave to all" (STANLEY). (Comp. Rom. 1 : 14, 15.)

Calvin and some others adopt another interpretation of ver. 16, which is worthy of mention, although it does not so closely accord with the grammatical structure of the passage. They take Paul to mean: "For if I preach the gospel willingly, which indeed I do, I have a reward from God, though I receive no pay from men. But if I do it unwillingly, simply because I am compelled to do it, then I reduce myself to the condition of a servant who simply does what he is bidden. Since then I am performing a willing service, what is my reward?" etc. There is a sense in which Paul did this service willingly, and there is also a sense in which, being captured as it were, he did it unwillingly. But whether willingly or unwillingly, he could not escape his responsibility.

19. Paul proceeds to show in this and the four following verses, how for the good of others he had not fully used his rights in the gospel (ver. 18). **For though I** *was* **free from all men** (ver. 1), not dependent upon and not obligated to receive pay from them, *I made myself servant unto all*, I voluntarily enslaved myself to them, **that I might gain the more,** than I could otherwise. In other words, he gained *the most* converts in this way. By preaching the gospel gratuitously, thus attracting all, he would save more than he would being paid, attracting some and repelling others. The word *gain* is suggestive of reward. Saving more souls would enter into his reward (ver. 18 ; 1 Thess. 2 : 19, 20).

20. He enumerates how he accommodated himself to different classes and denied himself for his converts. He is speaking specially of his ministry at Corinth, as the tenses used and the connection indicate (ver. 1, 2, 11 ; 11 : 1). **Unto the Jews I became as a Jew,** as in circumcising Timothy (Acts 16 : 3), and in Jewish observances (Acts 18 : 18 ; 21 : 26). **To them that are under the law,** more exactly, *To those under law, as under law*—a broad designation, including proselytes, Jewish converts, and all who were under more or less legal bondage, adapting himself to them. According to the oldest and best manuscript, Paul adds, *not being myself under law*, not being under legal bondage and dependent upon law for salvation (Rom. 6 : 14 ; Gal. 2 : 13-21). Perhaps his ministry in Berea may illustrate this (Acts 17 : 11, 12 ; see also Acts 19 : 1-6).

21. To them that are without law, as without law—to the heathen as one standing on a level with them, and neither by example nor precept imposing upon them the positive enactments of the Jewish law (Col. 2 : 20). But to guard himself from being misunderstood Paul adds in parenthesis, **being not without law to God, but under law to Christ.** Alford renders, *Not being an outlaw from God, but a subject to the law of Christ*. Paul was no Antinomian. His freedom from the Mosaic law was not independence of God, but rather the greater dependence on him, by his subjection to the law of Christ, which is a law of love and obedience. He and the Gentiles were indeed under the inward law written on the heart (Rom. 2 : 14, 15 ; Jer. 31 : 33), and a heart consecrated to Christ recognized

22 are without law. *b* To the weak became I as weak, that I might gain the weak: *i* I am made all things to all men, *k* that I might by all means save 23 some. And this I do for the gospel's sake, that I might be partaker thereof with you.

On eating food offered to idols; self-restraint needful for our own safety.

24 Know ye not that they which run in a race, run all, but one receiveth the prize? *l* So run, that ye may obtain. 25 And every man that *m* striveth for the mastery is temperate in all things. Now they *do it* to obtain a corruptible

22 those without law. To the weak I became weak, that I might gain the weak. I have become all things to all, that I may by all means save some. 23 And all things I do for the gospel's sake, that I may become a partaker thereof with others.

24 Know ye not that they who run in a race, all indeed run, but one receives the prize? Thus run, in order that ye 25 may obtain. And every one who strives in the games is temperate in all things; they indeed to obtain a corruptible crown, but we an incorrupt-

h 8 : 13; Rom. 15 : 1 ; 2 Cor. 11 : 29.   *i* Ver. 19; 10 : 33.   *k* Rom. 11 : 14; 2 Tim. 2 : 10.
l Luke 13 : 24; Phil. 2 : 16; 3 : 14; 2 Tim. 4 : 7; Heb. 12 : 1.   *m* Eph. 6 : 12; 1 Tim. 6 : 12; 2 Tim. 2 : 5; 4 : 7.

this. Paul illustrated this at Athens (Acts 17 : 23 ff.; also see Gal. 2 : 3; Acts 14 : 14-18).
22. To the weak became I as weak, or according to the best text, *became I weak.* To the weak, superstitious, and scrupulous, I condescended so as to lovingly enter into their feelings and meet them on their own grounds. For illustrations see 8 : 13; Rom 15 : 1, 2; 2 Cor. 11 : 29; Gal. 6 : 2. To sum up, and to meet all cases not included in the foregoing, **I am made all things to all men, that I might by all means,** and ways, **save some.** This he did, not by the sacrifice of principle, but of his rights in matters indifferent, and in exercising sympathy without compromising his own convictions, and thus approaching men on their most accessible side.
23. And this I do, or according to the best text, *And all things,* spoken of in the preceding verses, **I do for the gospel's sake,** for its glory, extension, and blessings, **that I might be partaker thereof with you,** *that I may become a joint partaker thereof.* Paul does not mean that he might be saved, for he did not expect to be saved by preaching (ver. 27), but through faith in Christ. But he wished to be a fellow-partaker with them of those gospel blessings that are the privilege of the believer, and to enjoy the great pleasure arising from preaching the gospel and gaining converts to Christ (1 Thess. 2 : 19, 20). He would have stars in his crown. Notice that in this verse he includes self-denial for his own good also, as well as for others' good. In being a fellow-partaker he exhibits humility

and his affectionate condescension to the level and the wants of those whom he would save.
24-27. HE URGES UPON THEM SELF-RESTRAINT, AS NEEDFUL FOR THEIR OWN SAFETY.
24. Know ye not—you Corinthians are familiar with the Isthmian games which are celebrated every three years near the seacoast about eight miles from your city; and ye know that in the race-course *they that run,* **run all, but one receiveth the prize** of the victor (next verse). Not that this is so in the Christian race, for each one can obtain a crown; but he would have each **so run,** with such eagerness, concentrated effort, and persistence, as if the prize could be obtained by one only (Phil. 3 : 14). On his way from Athens to Corinth Paul would pass the stadium or race-course, to which in this and other passages he makes allusions. We have in this passage, the race, the racer, the prize, the self-restraint, the crown, the herald, and the rejected contestant.
25. And every man that striveth for the mastery, *that contends in the gymnastic games,* **is temperate in all things,** exercising self-control and self-restraint in regard to food and wine and every kind of sensual indulgence. The preparatory discipline lasted for ten months and was very severe, at times under a professional trainer (2 Tim. 2 : 5). **They to obtain a corruptible crown,** a wreath or garland of the green pine, which was usually awarded as a prize at the Isthmian games. So also the laurel, olive,

26 crown; but we *an incorruptible. I therefore so run, not as uncertainly; so fight I, not as one that beateth the 27 air: °but I keep under my body, and bring it into subjection; lest that by any means, when I have preached to others, I myself should be ᵖa castaway.

26 ible. I therefore thus run, as not uncertainly; thus fight I as not beating 27 the air. But I buffet my body, and bring it into bondage; lest by any means, after having preached to others, I myself should be rejected.

ⁿ 2 Tim. 4 : 8; James 1 : 12; 1 Peter 1 : 4; 5 : 4; Rev. 2 : 10; 3 : 11.
o 6 : 12; Rom. 8 : 13; Col. 3 : 5.   p 2 Cor. 13 : 5, 6.

and parsley were used. All these would dry up and fade. **But we an incorruptible**—of righteousness (2 Tim. 4 : 8), of life (James 1 : 12; Rev. 2 : 10), an unfading crown of glory (1 Peter 5 : 4).

26. I therefore run, not as uncertainly, leaving nothing to chance, but in such a way as to ensure the prize. He did not even count his life dear to him, if he might so complete his race with victory (Acts 20 : 24). Changing the figure to that of a boxer, he continues: **So fight I**, or *so box I*, **not as one that beateth the air**, striking at random into the air, thus missing his antagonist. The Christian life is a conflict as well as a race (Rom. 7 : 14-25). The conflict is against the world, the flesh, and the devil. Paul now represents himself in the midst of the contest. "It must be remembered . . . that from the national character and religion of the Greeks, these games derived an importance which raised them above the degrading associations of modern times. . . They were not merely exhibitions of bodily strength, but solemn trials of the excellence of the competitors in the gymnastic art, which was to the Greeks one-half of human education" (STANLEY). The names of the victors were handed to posterity, sung in triumphal odes, and their "likeness placed in the long line of statues which formed the approach of the adjacent temple."

27. But I keep under my body, literally, *I beat it black and blue, I buffet my body*, handle it roughly, discipline it with hardships. (Comp. Acts 20 : 33-35; 2 Cor. 11 : 23-28.) **And bring it into subjection:** *I enslave it*, bring my body with its appetites and passions in bondage under the power of my moral will and higher renewed nature. **Lest by any means having preached,** *having been a herald to others*, **I myself should be a castaway,** *I myself should be unable to stand the test*, and thus would be rejected as unworthy of the prize. There is an allusion here to the herald at the games whose business it was by voice or trumpet to summon the competitors to the contest. In the Christian warfare, the apostle finds a formidable antagonist in himself, and he would triumph over his own peculiar sins and temptations, lest having been a herald to others, he should in the final issue prove unsuccessful and unworthy. And he must also strive lawfully. (See 2 Tim. 2 : 5.) Such a striking reference to himself was indeed an exhortation and a warning to the Corinthian converts. If this was so necessary for himself, how necessary to them, to exercise self-denial and self-restraint for their own spiritual safety. The thought is additionally enforced in the next chapter.

PRACTICAL REMARKS.

1. The conversion of souls in one's ministry is an evidence of having been called of God to the work (ver. 1, 2; Acts 15 : 3, 7, 12).

2. The minister should so live and labor as to be able to appeal to his people that he is a true minister of Jesus Christ (ver. 2; 1 Tim. 2 : 1-11).

3. A necessary qualification of an apostle was to have seen the Lord. The apostles therefore could have had no successors (ver. 1-3; Acts 1 : 21, 22).

4. Ministers of the gospel have an unquestionable right to married life. The Romish doctrine of celibacy of priests is a denial of this right (ver. 4, 5; 1 Tim. 3 : 2; 4 : 3).

5. The Christian minister may give his services to his people, but his people cannot claim them as a gift (ver. 5, 15).

6. Ministers should not be rated according to the salaries they receive, but ac-

cording to their faithfulness (ver. 5, 12; 4 : 2).

7. Christian ministers have their rights, one of which is to receive support from those they serve (ver. 7-14).

8. The minister may be viewed as a soldier, a vineyardist, and a shepherd (ver. 7; 2 Tim. 2 : 3, 4; Matt. 21 : 28; John 21 : 16).

9. God's dealings with animals and the inanimate creation contain lessons for men (ver. 9, 10; Ps. 19; Luke 13 : 6-9; 12 : 6, 7).

10. It is both temporal and spiritual economy to support the preacher and the teacher (ver. 11; Rom. 15 : 21; Mal. 3 : 8-12).

11. Ministers belong to a high and holy calling, appointed of God to live from their people, not above, nor below, but as their people (ver. 12-14; 1 Peter 5 : 2 ; 1 Thess. 2 : 7, 8).

12. We should beware lest we lower the ministry into a mere profession, or to a mercenary calling (ver. 12-14; 1 Tim. 6 : 17-19).

13. We may hinder the cause of Christ even in doing things that are lawful, but not expedient (ver. 12; 8 : 13).

14. There may be circumstances which will require the preacher to labor at his own expense, if he can do so, for the sake of Christ and his cause (ver. 12. 15, 18; Acts 18 : 3).

15. By preaching the gospel without charge we can show the excellence of religion and gain a more glorious reward (ver. 15-18, 23).

16. He who preaches the gospel gratuitously imitates Christ as well as Paul (ver. 15-18; 2 Cor. 8 : 9).

17. They who are called of God to the ministry cannot be happy in any other calling (ver. 16; Jonah 1 : 9-12; Jer. 20 : 9).

18. We have no cause for glorying in that we became Christians and then became Christian workers. It is all of grace (ver. 17, 18; 15 : 10; 1 John 4 : 19).

19. Living and working for Christ brings its own reward. But the "crown of glory" is the gift of God (ver. 18 ; 2 Tim. 4 : 8).

20. Sacrificing for others in Christ's work will be gloriously rewarded in the salvation of souls (ver. 19-22).

21. Without compromising principle we should adapt ourselves to all classes in society in order to save souls (ver. 19-22 ; Rom. 1 : 14, 15).

22. The humility of Paul may well be made a study and an example. See how he puts himself on a level with his converts, that he may partake of their blessings, how he would put forth every effort, so as not to be lost. How does this contrast with the self-confidence of many at the present day (ver. 23, 27; Titus 2 : 12; Eph. 6 : 12).

23. No one can begin the Christian life or attain its good without persistent self-denial, effort, and conflict (ver. 24-26; Matt. 16 : 24, 25; 24 : 13; Luke 13 : 34; Rev. 2 : 7, 11, 17, 26, etc.).

24. Renouncing every sin, laying aside every weight, having the goal ever in view, keeping the eye fully fixed on Christ, and an entire consecration of soul and body to God, are needful for successfully running the Christian race (ver. 24, 25; Heb. 12 : 1, 2).

25. We must not take risks in religion, nor put forth efforts at random, since with Christ's help we can plan and act with certainty (ver. 26; 15 : 58; Rom. 7 : 24, 25).

26. The fact that one is a preacher, and even a successful one, does not ensure salvation. He must guard against sin and exercise personal godliness as long as life lasts (ver. 27; Gal. 5 : 24; Col. 3 : 5 ; Heb. 4 : 1).

27. The doctrine of the perseverance of the saints is in harmony with a conviction of a possibility of failure, and of the necessity of putting forth every effort for final success. God gives no such guarantee of salvation as to warrant spiritual repose. The influence of hope and fear are alike needful to the motive for persevering triumphantly to the end (ver. 27; Phil. 2 : 12, 13; 2 Peter 1 : 10).

CHAPTER X.

Still continuing on the general discussion regarding eating food offered to idols, Paul shows by the example of ancient Israel the danger of returning to idolatry and kindred vices through a lack of self-restraint (ver. 1-10), and utters a warning to Christians (ver. 11-13). He advises them to flee idolatry, and not participate in idols' feast, for there

10 MOREOVER, brethren, I would not
that ye should be ignorant, how that
all our fathers were under [q] the cloud,
2 and all passed through [r] the sea; and
were all baptized unto Moses in the
3 cloud and in the sea; and did all eat
4 the same [s] spiritual meat; and did all

10 FOR I do not wish you to be ignorant, brethren, that our fathers were
all under the cloud, and all passed
2 through the sea; and were all baptized
into Moses in the cloud and in the
3 sea; and all ate the same spiritual
4 food, and all drank the same spiritual

q See refs. Exod. 13 : 21, 22 ; 40 : 34. r See refs. Exod. 14 : 21, 22, 29 ; Josh. 4 : 23.
s See refs. Exod. 16 : 4, 15, 35.

cannot exist both fellowship with Christ and demons (ver. 14-22); and having regard for the scruples of others to abstain from food which they know to have been offered to idols (ver. 23-30); aiming as he did after God's glory and our neighbor's good (ver. 31-11 : 1).

1-13. THE EXAMPLE OF LACK OF SELF-RESTRAINT IN ISRAEL, A LESSON AND A WARNING TO CHRISTIANS. The baptism in the cloud and in the sea. The sin and overthrow of ancient Israel. Temptations must be avoided.

1. Instead of **Moreover,** the reading of the best text is, *For*, thus joining this verse closely with the warning implied in the last verse of the preceding chapter. See note at the end. "As it might be possible for me, so also is it for you, to be rejected; *for* the history of ancient Israel teaches this. It is needful therefore that we distrust ourselves and abstain from fully using our liberty." **I would not that ye should be ignorant,** a common expression of Paul (12 : 1; Rom. 1 : 13; 11 : 25), generally introducing something new and important, and a forcible way of saying, "I wish you to know." Notice Paul says, **our fathers,** recognizing his own descent from Israel. Many of the Corinthian brethren were Jews, and doubtless many of the Gentile converts had been proselytes; and all believers belonged to spiritual Israel (Rom. 4 : 16). Notice also that emphasis is laid upon **all**—it is repeated five times. *All* enjoyed the same privileges, all were admitted by a baptism, in the cloud and in the sea, to the privileges given through Moses, and all were sustained by miraculous provision. Notice again that all **were under the cloud** (Exod. 14 : 19, 20; Ps. 105 : 39), and **all passed through the sea** (Exod. 14 : 22; Num. 33 : 8; Ps. 78 : 13, 14).

2. The two privileges selected are those which most nearly correspond with the two ordinances of the Christian church. **And were all baptized unto Moses.** More exactly, *They baptized themselves, or had themselves baptized unto Moses.* The idea of a voluntary agent is implied. They received baptism voluntarily. How Paul conceived of an immersion of the ancient Israelites, appears from what follows, that it was **in the cloud and in the sea,** not in either one as separate from the other, but in the two combined. Paul's conception of the act appears also from the preceding verse, that they were "under the cloud" and "passed through the sea." (Comp. Num. 14 : 14, "Thy cloud standeth *over* them"; and Ps. 105 : 39, "He spread a cloud for a *covering*.") The cloud and the sea are both of the same nature, and the two represent the element into which they were baptized. According to Paul's conception the water stood on both sides of them, and the cloud over them, so much so that they were in the cloud and in the sea, hidden from the sight of the Egyptians. Whether the cloud, in removing from before them to behind them, passed over them and remained over them we are not told. Paul merely states the facts in general terms, and conceives of a submersion and an emersion which was voluntary on their part. **Unto Moses**—into connection with him as their leader sent by God, and into the privileges of the Mosaic economy. In passing through the sea they passed out of bondage into freedom, from the yoke of Pharaoh into the fatherly care of God. This would suggest to the Corinthians their own baptism unto Christ and its privileges.

3. The food and drink to which Paul passes are suggestive of the Lord's Supper. **And did all eat the same spiritual meat,** or *food*, meaning the manna, which is termed spiritual, because it was given supernaturally by God (Exod. 16 : 14-16) and is styled "bread

drink the same spiritual drink; for they drank of that spiritual Rock that *followed them: and that Rock was 5 Christ. But with many of them God was not well pleased; for they *were overthrown in the wilderness.

6 Now *these things were our examples, to the intent we should not lust after evil things, as *they also lusted.

7 Neither be ye idolaters, as *were some of them; as it is written, *The people sat down to eat and drink, and rose up

drink; for they drank of a spiritual rock that followed them, and the rock 5 was the Christ. But in the most of them God had no pleasure; for they were overthrown in the wilderness.

6 Now these things came to pass as examples to us, in order that we might not desire evil things, as they also 7 desired them. Nor become ye idolaters, as were some of them; as it is written, The people sat down to eat 8 and drink, and rose up to play. Nor

---

t See refs. Exod. 17:6.   u Ps. 105:41.   x Num. 14:11, 12, 28–33, 35; 26:64, 65; Heb. 3:17; Jude 5.   y Ver. 11; Heb. 4:11.   z Num. 11:4, 33, 34.   a Exod. 32:6, 17–19.

---

of heaven" (Ps. 78:24). The manna had a spiritual meaning and purpose, not merely to sustain life but to foreshadow "the true bread from heaven," which Christ declares is his flesh which he gives for the life of the world (John 6:32, 51).

4. And did all drink the same spiritual drink, that which was given supernaturally by God on two occasions, the one at Horeb near the beginning of their wanderings in the wilderness (Exod. 17:6), and the other at Kadesh about thirty-eight years later (Num. 20:1, 11). The spiritual meaning and purpose, Paul goes on to show (John 6:53–55). **For they drank of a spiritual rock that followed them.** We need not take this to mean that the rock literally followed them, according to a Jewish tradition, which Meyer thinks was a later invention of the rabbis; but that it was the rock in the stream that flowed from it, represented as an allowable use of language. Compare Deut. 9:21, "the brook that descended out of the mount." (See also Ps. 78:16; 105:41). **And that rock,** rather *the rock,* **was *the* Christ,** represented or typified Christ, the source of their material and spiritual sustenance and life. This is a common use of the verb *to be,* for example, "The seven good kine are seven years," that is, they represent seven years (Gen. 41:26. See note on Matt. 26:26). Christ "the rock" was uppermost in the mind of the apostle. Christ the Angel of the Covenant went with them as their guide and support (Exod. 23:20–23; 32:34; Josh. 5:13). The term rock is frequently applied to God (Deut. 32:4, 15, 18, 30, 31, 37, etc.) and to Christ (Rom. 9:33. See note on Matt. 16:18). Bengel suggests that if there had been more than two ordinances of

the church, Paul would have pointed out some spiritual resemblances to them.

5. But notwithstanding their great privilege and God's care and guidance, **with many of them,** rather, *with the most of them,* **God was not well pleased.** Only two of them, Caleb and Joshua, were permitted to enter the promised land (Num. 26:64, 65). This is evident, **for they were overthrown,** their bodies *were strewn* in the wilderness—a vivid portrayal of the Divine judgment upon them; "left to moulder on the sands of the desert" (STANLEY).

6. The apostle here begins a special application by referring to special sins of Israel in the wilderness and God's judgments upon them. **Now these things were our examples,** *came to pass as examples,* or patterns of warning, *to us,* designed to represent similar relations and experiences among Christians. The five instances given are those which resemble the sins to which the Corinthians were most liable. **To the intent,** better, *in order that* **we should not lust,** or *desire,* **evil things as they also lusted,** or *desired.* As a noted example of their lusting may be mentioned their desire for the flesh-pots of Egypt, the food they had enjoyed there, and the giving of quails which resulted so disastrously to them (Num. 11:4, 18, 33, 34). We should restrain our desires especially from those things which may result in evil to us, or to others.

7. Neither be ye idolaters, in connection with idol feasts, as **were some of them** in the worship of the golden calf, as it is written (Exod. 32:6), that after offering burnt offerings and peace offerings, the people sat down to eat and drink and rose up to

8 to play. ᵇ Neither let us commit fornication, as some of them committed, and ᶜ fell in one day three and twenty
9 thousand. Neither let us tempt Christ, as ᵈ some of them also tempted, and
10 were destroyed of serpents. Neither murmur ye, as ᵉ some of them also murmured, and ᶠ were destroyed of ᵍ the
11 destroyer. Now all these things happened unto them for ensamples: and let us commit fornication, as some of them did, and fell in one day three
9 and twenty thousand. Nor let us tempt the Lord, as some of them tempted, and perished by the serpents.
10 Nor murmur ye, as some of them murmured, and perished by the destroyer.
11 Now these things happened to them by way of example, and they were

ᵇ 6 : 18; Rev. 2 : 14.   ᶜ Num. 25 : 1–9.   ᵈ See refs. Exod. 17 : 2, 7 ; 23 : 20, 21 ; Num. 21 : 5, 6.
ᵉ See refs. Num. 14 : 2, 27–30 ; 16 : 41–49.   ᶠ Num. 14 : 37 ; 16 : 49.   ᵍ Exod. 12 : 23 ; 2 Sam. 24 : 16.

play, to be merry with song and dances, such as anciently accompanied heathen feasts.

8. Neither let us commit fornication as some of them did, in the licentious worship of Baal-peor (Num. 25 : 1-6). From Num. 31 : 16 and Rev. 2 : 14 we learn that Balaam instigated Balak to the use of these temptations against Israel. This warning was specially needed by the Corinthians, since at Corinth licentious rites were blended with the worship of Venus, in whose temple were a thousand licentious priestesses. Paul says that in consequence of this sin of Israel there **fell in one day three and twenty thousand,** while Moses, in Num. 25 : 9, says twenty-four thousand. The greater, of course, includes the less. But both state even approximate numbers. The Spirit designed that they should speak after the manner of men, and so in a general way both were correct.

9. Neither let us tempt, or *test,* **Christ** by our abuse of Christian liberty, as some of **them tempted,** or put to the test his patience and avenging power. There were several instances recorded of Israel tempting God (Num. 14 : 22 ; Exod. 17 : 7). The particular case referred to here was their discouragement because of the roughness of the way and their discontent with having merely manna to eat (Num. 21 : 6 ; Ps. 78 : 18), and speaking against God and against Moses ; and they **were destroyed of,** *by the,* **serpents,** well known as the fiery serpents of the Mosaic narrative. The majority of the best manuscripts have *Lord* instead of *Christ.* But Christ is meant in either reading (ver. 4). Paul would especially impress his Corinthian converts with the fact that it was against Christ that they were sinning (8 : 12), in being discontented in needful self-denial and restriction of their liberty. "How many, forgetting the blessing of their spiritual deliverance, might look back with a discontented longing to the license of the past" (MEYER).

10. Neither murmur ye, complain discontentedly, **as some of them also murmured.** *Also* should be omitted, not being in the best text. The Israelites often murmured (Exod. 16 : 2; 17 : 2 ; Num. 14 : 2), but the one referred to here seems to be that recorded in Num. 16 : 41-49, when they murmured against Moses and Aaron, and through them against God, because of the destruction of Korah, Dathan, and Abiram with their company. **And were destroyed of,** or *perished by,* **the destroyer.** The word rendered *the destroyer* is only found here, and means the pestilence which destroyed fourteen thousand seven hundred persons (Num. 16 : 49). The pestilence in David's day was administered by a destroying angel (2 Sam. 24 : 16, 17), and so some understand a destroying angel here. The angel in Exod. 12 : 23 is called the destroyer. The application to the Corinthians would be their complaints against Paul and other teachers that God had given them; and perhaps also regarding sickness and deaths among them (11 : 30). It should be noted (1) that in all the sins specified in the foregoing, Paul says, **some of them,** showing that it was not true of all the Israelites of that day. (2) That he regards all these sins as connected with and growing out of lusting. (Comp. James 1 : 14, 15 ; 1 John 2 : 16, 17.)

11. Confirmation of ver. 6. **Now all of these things happened unto them as ensamples,** or according to the most approved text, *by way of example,* as a typical warning to pos-

ʰ they are written for our admonition, ᶦ upon whom the ends of the world 12 are come. Wherefore ʲ let him that thinketh he **standeth take heed lest he fall.**

13 There hath **no** temptation **taken you** but such as is common to **man**: but ᵏ God *is* faithful, ˡ who will **not suffer you to be tempted above that ye are able**; but will with the temptation also make a way to escape, that ye may be able to bear *it.*

14 Wherefore, my dearly beloved, ᵐ flee 15 from idolatry. I speak as to wise men; 16 ⁿ judge ye what I say. ᵒ The cup of

written for our admonition, on whom 12 the ends of the ages are come. Wherefore let him that thinks he stands, take 13 heed lest he fall. There has no temptation taken you but such as belongs to man; and God is faithful, who will not suffer you to be tempted above what ye are able, but will with the temptation make also the way of escape, that ye may be able to bear it.

14 Wherefore, my beloved, flee from 15 idolatry. I am speaking as to wise 16 men; judge ye what I say. The cup of

h 9 : 10; Rom. 15 : 4.   *i* Heb. 10 : 25, 37; 1 Peter 4 : 7; 1 John 2 : 18.
j Matt. 26 : 33, 34, 40, 41, 69-75; Rom. 11 : 20.   *k* See refs. Deut. 7 : 9.
l Luke 22 : 32; 2 Cor. 12: 8-10; 2 Peter 2 : 9.   *m* Ver. 7; 2 Cor. 6 : 17; 1 John 5 : 21.   *n* 1 Thess. 5 : 21.
o Matt. 26 : 26-28.

terity. "Paul regards the types as actual prophecies, real images of subsequent occurrences, just as in the first germ or leaf-formation of a tree the future blossom is represented and shadowed forth. . . History is to be a living mirror for the present. *They were written for our admonition*" (OLSHAUSEN). **On whom the ends of the world,** or *ages,* **are come.** The plural *ends* is used, pointing to the successive epochs in these latter days before the coming of our Lord. The present gospel dispensation is the last time in reference to the old dispensation (1 John 2 : 18; Heb. 9 : 26). The apostles did not know the time of our Lord's coming, but were longing for it (Acts 1 : 7 ; 1 Peter 4 : 7 ; 2 Peter 3 : 8, 9).

12. The apostle utters a word of caution. **Wherefore,** in view of these admonitions of history, **let him that thinketh that he standeth,** as one of God's people, **take heed lest he fall,** as did these ancient Israelites. The Corinthians needed to be warned against self-confidence (3 : 18, 21; 4 : 8, 18). They must exercise watchfulness and fidelity.

13. Paul would not cause any to despair, and so adds a three-fold encouragement to all who would exercise watchfulness. (1) Your temptations are not so great and peculiar as to be outside of human experience. They are such as are **common to man,** they are *human,* such as belong to men. (2) *And* **God is faithful,** his fidelity to you and his promises. (1 Thess. 5 : 24; John 10 : 28, 29), and he *will not permit you to be tempted beyond* **that ye may be,**

are, **able to bear.** His faithfulness implied in your calling secures your safety. (3) **But will with the temptation also make a way,** rather, *the way,* **to escape,** suited to each temptation by which he permits your faith to be tried. "Were it not that God gave *the escape* along with *the temptation,* the latter would be too heavy for you, you would not be able to bear up under it, but would be crushed altogether. But this is not his *will*" (MEYER).

14-22. KEEP AWAY FROM IDOLATRY, AND PARTICIPATE NOT AT IDOL FEASTS.

14. Wherefore, in view of your exposure to temptation, and your danger of falling into sin, and God's faithfulness in succoring those who are watchful and trustful in him, **my dearly beloved** (omit *dearly*), **flee from idolatry.** The expression is a strong one: get out of the way of idolatry, avoid all that may lead to it, *for this very reason,* your own safety. This the apostle enforces in the next eight verses. Thus he returns to the direct discussion of eating things offered to idols, and of idols' feasts, from which he digressed at the beginning of chap. 9.

15. Paul appeals to their own sense of consistency and right. **I speak as to wise men,** men of insight, intelligence, able to discern the force of what I say (1 : 5; 8 : 1). **Judge ye,** be ye judges, **of what** *I am about to say* (ver. 16-22). He confidently leaves it to their own enlightened judgment to decide.

16. He first argues from the Lord's Supper. **The cup of blessing was**

blessing which we bless, is it not the *communion of the blood of Christ? *the bread which we break, is it not the communion of the body of Christ? 17 For *we *being* many are one bread, *and* one body: for we are all partakers 18 of that one bread. Behold *Israel after the flesh: *are not they which eat of the sacrifices partakers of the

blessing which we bless, is it not a partaking of the blood of Christ? The loaf which we break, is it not a par- 17 taking of the body of Christ? Because we, the many, are one loaf, one body; 18 for we all share in the one loaf. Behold Israel according to the flesh. Are not they who eat of the sacrifices

p John 6 : 53–55 ; 1 John 1 : 3, 7.   *q* 11 : 23, 24 ; Acts 2 : 42, 46.   *r* 12 : 12, 13 ; Rom. 12 : 5.
s Rom. 4 : 1 ; 9 : 3, 5.   *t* See refs. 9 : 13.

the name given to the cup at the passover, over which thanks were given. In connection with the Lord's Supper it was that over which they blessed God for his goodness in redemption. In regard to the two words, *blessing* God and *giving thanks*, used at the celebration of the Supper, see note on Matt. 26 : 26, 27. **Which we bless,** we all uniting in thanksgiving and prayer in setting it apart for its solemn and religious use, as commanded by Christ (11 : 25). **Is it not the communion,** *the partaking* or *participation,* **of the blood of Christ?** On the word *communion,* see note on 1 : 9. Paul speaks elsewhere of the participation or fellowship in the ministering to the saints (2 Cor. 8 : 4) ; of the Spirit (2 Cor. 13 : 14) ; of the gospel (Phil. 1 : 5) ; of suffering (Phil. 3 : 10). The participation here referred to cannot be literally of the substance of Christ's body and blood, for, besides other reasons, his body was not yet broken nor his blood shed, when the Supper was instituted. It must therefore refer to a spiritual participation of Christ's body and blood and of the benefits of his death. The bread and cup symbolically represented Christ's body and blood, and in receiving and partaking of them they signified that they accepted of Christ and his atonement by faith. Thus through the ordinance they by faith received and became partakers of the results of his sacrificial death. Hence many prefer to style this ordinance the Communion, thus bringing to view the spiritual participation and fellowship of the believer with Christ. (See John 6 : 51–54 and notes.) **The bread which we break,** connected with the formal setting it apart by prayer in which all could join mentally, orally, or responded to by Amen (14 : 16), in accordance with the example set by Christ (Matt. 26 : 26). The bread therefore should not be broken before it is

put on the table, nor the loaf passed around for the communicants to break off each a share.
17. This verse is confirmatory of the preceding verse. This may be translated, **For we,** *the* **many are one bread,** or *loaf*, by assimilation of the bread partaken, **one body** spiritually of Christ, of which the bread is the symbol. The one loaf enters our bodies and becomes a part of each of us, so symbolically and spiritually we become parts and members of the one body of Christ. Or with much the same meaning we may translate, *Since the bread is one*, which enters and becomes a part of us, *we the many are one body* spiritually; **for we are,** unitedly and jointly, **all partakers of that one bread,** or *of the one loaf*—we by faith all share in what it represents, with Christ and in his atoning work. (Comp. 12 : 12 ; John 6 : 35–56.) In the Lord's Supper our communion and fellowship are with Christ ; it is, however, a united service in which the many join, and through Christ they indirectly fellowship one another. We have fellowship with one another so far as we have fellowship with him. (Comp. 12 : 12 ; Eph. 4 : 4.) The bearing of this on partaking at idol feasts is brought out in ver. 21.
18. Another argument the apostle derives from the Jewish sacrifices. In thus passing from the Lord's Supper to the Jewish altar, he descends from the higher to the lower, from the superior and more spiritual to the inferior and the carnal. (Comp. Gal. 4 : 3, 6, 9.) Thus he gets nearer to the base heathen sacrifices and feasts. He appeals to something familiar to his Jewish and proselyte readers. **Behold Israel after the flesh,** literal Israel in distinction from the spiritual "Israel of God" (Gal. 6 : 16 ; Rom. 9 : 6). **Are not they which,** *who*, **eat of the sacri-**

19 altar? What say I then? "That the idol is any thing, or that which is offered in sacrifice to idols is any 20 thing? But *I say* that the things which the Gentiles *sacrifice, they sacrifice to devils, and not to God: and I would not that ye should have fellowship 21 with devils. *Ye cannot drink the cup of the Lord, and *the cup of devils: ye cannot be partakers of the Lord's table, and of the table of devils.

19 partakers of the altar? What then do I say? That what is offered to idols is anything, or that an idol is anything? 20 Nay; but that what they sacrifice, they sacrifice to demons, and not to God; and I do not wish you to become 21 partakers with the demons. Ye can not drink the cup of the Lord, and the cup of demons; ye can not share in the table of the Lord, and the table of

u 8:4.   v See refs. Lev. 17:7.   x 1 Kings 18:21; Matt. 6:24; 2 Cor. 6:15-17.   y Deut. 32:38.

fices, those parts not consumed (Lev. 3: 3-5; 7:15-18; 8:31; Deut. 12:18), **partakers of the altar**, at Jerusalem, on which the sacrifices are offered, the altar having a part and they a part. Are they not sharers in the Jewish worship? The word rendered *partakers* is not the same word as that translated *communion* in ver. 16 and 17, but a kindred word meaning substantially the same. It means *an associate*, a partaker, or a sharer, and it is implied that the altar and the partakers (the priests and worshipers), share together the victim, in connection with a religious service. (See note on 9:13.) The conclusion would be that those who partake of heathen feasts share in heathen worship. But this may seem to be inconsistent with what he had said in 8:4, that heathen divinities had no real existence. So he touches the point again in the next verse.

19. What say I then? The two clauses that follow should be transposed thus: Do I say, **That—a thing—which is offered in sacrifice to idols is anything,** as the heathen suppose, a genuine offering to a god? **Or that an idol is anything,** has any such real existence as the heathen suppose? A decided negative answer must be given.

20. But I say, better, *Nay*, I say not this, I hold still as I affirmed in 8:4, that an idol has no real existence, but for all that, idol and idol worship represent the kingdom of evil and the evil spirits that maintain it. I say then, **that the things which the Gentiles sacrifice**, to use the language of Moses (Deut. 32:17), **they sacrifice to devils**, *demons*, evil spirits, **and not to God** (Septuagint: the Hebrew reads, *to demons, which are no gods*). Their gods are not realities, but they are regarded as such by their worshipers. The powers of darkness are their governing principle; and their worship, both in its conception of their gods and in their sacrifices, partakes of the nature of evil spirits (vs. 106:37). So that in these sacrifices they are really partakers of, and sharers with, the powers of darkness. Paul could then well add to his Corinthian brethren, **and I would not**, *I do not wish*, **that ye should have fellowship**, or **become** *partakers with demons*, who are represented in heathen worship. The word translated fellowship is the same as that in ver. 18, which see. On the real existence of demons, see note on Matt. 4:24. To sum up thus far: As partaking of the Lord's Supper is an act of Christian service implying a union of believers with Christ, and a partaking of the Jewish sacrifice is an act of Jewish service, implying a participation in the worship of Jehovah, so partaking of an idol feast is an act of heathen service, implying participation in the worship of the kingdom of darkness.

21. In this verse we have both the ground of the wish he had just expressed, and a forcible conclusion of his argument thus far. Such a combining of opposite elements in religious service is incompatible, morally impossible, and hence inadmissible. **Ye cannot drink the cup of the Lord,** spiritually participating, **and the cup of** *demons*, the libation which was poured forth in honor of a false god at the beginning of a feast, or of a sacrifice. It was indeed a cup and a table of demons, being connected with worship to something besides Jehovah, and the exercise of homage to the powers of darkness. It obviously would unfit them for participating in the service and fellowship of Christ.

22 Do we ᶻprovoke the Lord to jealousy? ᵃAre we stronger than he? 23 ᵇAll things are lawful for me, but all things are not expedient: all things are lawful for me, but all things edify 24 not. ᶜLet no man seek his own, but 25 every man another's *wealth.* ᵈWhatsoever is sold in the shambles, *that* eat, asking no question ᵉfor conscience' 26 sake: for ᶠthe earth *is* the Lord's, and 27 the fulness thereof. ᵍIf any of them 22 demons. Or do we provoke the Lord to jealousy? Are we stronger than he? 23 All things are lawful, but not all things are profitable; all things are lawful, but not all things build up. 24 Let no one seek his own, but his 25 neighbor's good. Whatever is sold in the market eat, asking no question because of conscience; for the earth is 26 the Lord's, and the fullness thereof.

z Exod. 20 : 5; Deut. 32 : 21.   *a* Job 9 : 4; Ezek. 22 : 14.   *b* See refs. 6 : 12.
c Ver. 33; 9 : 19-23; 13 : 5; Rom. 15 : 1, 2; Phil. 2 : 4.   *d* 1 Tim. 4 : 4.   *e* Ver. 27-29; 8 : 7.
f See refs. Ps. 24 : 1; 1 Tim. 6 : 17.   *g* 5 : 9-11; Luke 5 : 29, 30; 19 : 7.

(Comp. 2 Cor. 6 : 14-16.) To the same effect our Lord said, "Ye cannot serve God and mammon" (Matt. 6 : 24).

22. Do we provoke, etc., rather, *Or,* by uniting these two discordant elements, *are we provoking,* **the Lord to jealousy?** is this the meaning of our conduct, do we wish to arouse his anger? As was the case of Israel (Deut. 32 : 21, where the phrase "provoke to jealousy" is found (Ps. 95 : 8; Heb. 3 : 16)). Jehovah is a jealous God (Exod. 20 : 4; 34 : 14), "who will not give his glory to another, nor his praise to graven images" (Isa. 42 : 8). **Are we stronger than he?** so that we can challenge his anger and resist his wrath. The very thought of this is absurd. It appears from 8 : 10, and the last few verses, that it is eating of the sacrificial feasts in idol temples which Paul here condemns, and to which he could fittingly apply the expressions "cup of demons" and "table of demons." As to the meat taken away or sold, thus disassociated from idol worship, it was to him a matter of indifference (ver. 25; 8 : 7, 8).

23-11 : 1. CONSIDERATION FOR OTHERS OUR RULE OF ACTION. SEEKING GOD'S GLORY AND THE GOOD OF OTHERS OUR AIM.

23. Paul turns abruptly to such eating of food offered to idols as was indifferent. He recurs to language which he had used in 6 : 12 in a different connection. **All things are lawful.** Omit **for me,** according to the best text. He used this in regard to Christian liberty, and it seems to have been quoted against him. At least he explains and limits its application in what follows. In things not in themselves sinful, Paul could say, All things are lawful; but the first modification is, **but all things are not expedient,** or rather, *profitable,* the same as in 6 : 12 (note on which see). The second modification is, **but all things edify not,** do *not build up* (8 : 1), in Christian character. Then they may rather injure.

24. Paul lays down a principle involved in 8 : 13, in form of a precept. According to the highest critical authorities it should read, *Let no one seek his own, but his neighbor's good,* in these matters (Rom. 15 : 2, 3). In using the law of liberty be not selfish, but unselfishly exercise the law of love (Phil. 2 : 4). "It will thus happen in our case, as in that of the apostle, that what may be quite wrong under one set of circumstances may be quite right in another, as in Gal. 2 : 3 and Acts 16 : 1" (J. J. LIAS).

25. Having given the restrictive precept in the preceding verse, the apostle gives a first permission in the use of one's liberty. **Whatsoever is sold in the shambles**—the provision market—**that eat, asking no question for conscience' sake,** not anxiously inquiring either in buying or eating, whether it had been left over from heathen sacrifices, *because of conscience,* that no religious scruple might be excited and your conscience offended. It is implied that the apostle regarded conscientious scruples unnecessary in this case. The reference is to the conscience of the individual buying and eating.

26. As a reason for the above permission he quotes Ps. 24 : 1, **For the earth is the Lord's, and the fulness thereof.** The earth and all that fills it is the Lord's, and for our use, especially for God's people. "For every creature of God is good, and nothing to be refused, if it be received

that believe not bid you *to a feast*, and ye be disposed to go; ʰ whatsoever is set before you, eat, asking no question 28 for conscience' sake. But if any man say unto you, This is offered in sacrifice unto idols, eat not, ⁱ for his sake that showed it, and for conscience' sake: for ᵏ the earth *is* the Lord's, and 29 the fulness thereof: conscience, I say, not thine own, but of the other: for ˡ why is my liberty judged of another 30 *man's* conscience? For if I by grace be a partaker, why am I evil spoken of for that ᵐ for which I give thanks? 31 ⁿ Whether therefore ye eat, or drink, or whatsoever ye do, do all to the

27 If one of the unbelieving invites you to a feast, and ye choose to go, whatever is set before you eat, asking no 28 question because of conscience. But if any one say to you, This has been offered in sacrifice, eat it not, for his sake that showed it, and because of 29 conscience. Conscience, I say, not thine own, but that of the other; for why is my freedom condemned by 30 another conscience? If I partake with thanks, why am I evil spoken of, for 31 that for which I give thanks? Whether therefore ye eat or drink, or whatever 32 ye do, do all to the glory of God. Give

---

ʰ Luke 10 : 7. ⁱ 8 : 10-13. ᵏ Ver. 26; Deut. 10 : 14. ˡ Rom. 14 : 16. ᵐ Rom. 14 : 6; 1 Tim. 4 : 3, 4. ⁿ Rom. 12 : 1; Col. 3 : 17, 23; 1 Peter 4 : 11.

---

with thanksgiving" (1 Tim. 4 : 4). How such things were defiled in actual heathen sacrificial worship is shown in ver. 19, 20. But this defilement does not remain, when the meat is taken away from the sacrifices, and from the actual associations of heathen worship.

27. The apostle gives a second permission in the use of one's liberty. If an unbeliever **bid you to a feast,** in a private house. Not a sacrificial feast, for that is forbidden (ver. 20-22). **And ye be disposed,** better, *And ye choose*, **to go; whatsoever is set before you, eat, asking no question,** etc. As in the preceding verse. You need feel no conscientious scruples, nor trouble yourselves about a matter which is perfectly indifferent, so far as you and your conscience are concerned.

28. Just here Paul places a limit to one's liberty on account of another. **But if any man say unto you,** be he a believer or unbeliever, one of the guests or even the host himself. **This is,** rather, *has been sacrificed to an idol*, **eat not for his sake that shewed it**—for his good, since, if he is a believer he may have scruples of conscience, or if an unbeliever he might infer that you approved of idol-worship; **and for conscience' sake,** since the question of idolatrous worship is now introduced, and your act might be wrongly interpreted, and thus be hurtful to others. Whose *conscience* is told us in the next verse. The next sentence, the repetition of the quotation in ver 26, is not found in the oldest and best manuscripts, and should be omitted.

29. Conscience, I say, not thine own, since you have no scruples about it, and can eat with thanksgiving to God (ver. 26), **but of the other,** who may have scruples, and who might be led to violate his own conscience. You are to act according to the principle laid down in 8 : 7-13. **For why is my liberty judged of,** better, *by*, **another man's conscience?** Why is my moral liberty in regard to such things, indifferent in themselves, condemned by another man's conscience? My only reason in refraining from eating is to spare his conscience from injury, not because there is any danger to my own. The question implied its own answer, and is equivalent to a positive affirmation, That his liberty should not be condemned by another's conscience—in this case, weak and unenlightened.

30. For if I by grace be a partaker, rather, *If I partake with thanksgiving* (ver. 26), being in a state of right feeling, **why am I evil spoken of for that for which I give thanks?** as if I were acting inconsistently and contrary to my own conscience (Rom. 14 : 6; 1 Tim. 4 : 3). "Thanksgiving sanctifies all food; it denies the authority of idols and asserts God's" (BENGEL).

31. Paul comes to the general conclusion of this discussion, and gives some general rules for guidance. The first has reference to God. **Whether therefore ye eat, or drink,** in general, **or whatsoever ye do** (whether eating, drinking, or acting), **do all to the glory of God.** Let this be your highest aim Do nothing to dishonor God, but all to honor him.

32 glory of God. °Give none offence, neither to the Jews, nor to the Gentiles,
33 nor to ᵖ the church of God; even as I please all *men* in all *things*, ᵠ not seeking mine own profit, but the *profit* of many, that they may be saved.
11 Be ʳ ye followers of me, even as I also *am* of Christ.

no occasion of stumbling, either to Jews or Greeks, or to the church of
33 God; as I also please all in all things, not seeking my own profit, but that of the many, that they may be saved.
11 Become imitators of me, even as I also am of Christ.

o 8 : 13; Rom. 14 : 13; Phil. 1 : 10; 2 : 15.   p 11 : 22; Acts 20 : 28.   q Ver. 24; 2 Cor. 12 : 19.
r 4 : 16; Eph. 5 : 1.

This applies to many things at the present day, and especially to the use of intoxicating liquors. The practice of drinking is dishonoring God; the abstaining from it tends to his glory.
32. The second rule or principle has reference to our fellow-men. **Give none offence,** better, *Give no occasion of stumbling* (8 : 9, 13), *either to Jews or Greeks,* those outside the church, or, **to the church of God**—the brethren. This presents the three classes of men, the *all men* of the next clause, with whom they would come in contact. Let not your acts be a temptation to others, and lead others into sin.
33. This last rule he enforces by his own practice. **Even as I,** *also,* **please all men in all things,** striving to be at their service, and becoming all things to all in matters that are indifferent (9 : 22), **not seeking my own profit,** advantage in any way, **but,** in contrast with my own, the true and highest *profit of the many,* **that they may be saved.** Their salvation was his great aim. In matters indifferent it was the standard of his expediency (9 : 19; Rom. 15 : 2).
11 : 1. Paul concludes with the exhortation, **Be ye followers of me**—*Become imitators of me,* in denying yourselves and foregoing your rights for others' good—**even as I also am of Christ,** who is our highest example in this respect (Phil. 2 : 4-8; Eph. 5 : 2; Rom. 15 : 3; Matt. 20 : 28). Thus he returns to his own example as in 9 : 1-22, and to that of Christ as in 8 : 11.

PRACTICAL REMARKS.

1. The symbolic or figurative baptism of Israel in the cloud and in the sea, gives no sanction to sprinkling, pouring, or the application of water to the recipient. They were baptized *in* not *by* the sea and the cloud (ver. 1, 2; Mark 1 : 5; Acts 8 : 38).

2. Baptism on the part of the candidate is an intelligent act, implying the giving up of the old life, the entering on a new life, and the accepting of Christ as our Leader, Saviour, and Lord (ver. 1, 2; Rom. 6 : 4, 5).

3. In the Lord's Supper we partake of the spiritual food and drink, not of the literal body and blood of Christ (ver. 3, 4; 11 : 23-26).

4. In our journey through life we need, like the Israelites, constant supplies for our spiritual necessities (ver. 3, 4; John 15 : 5).

5. The manna and the rock with its flowing stream strikingly represents the fullness of Christ and the abundance of his grace for his people (ver. 3; 2 Cor. 12 : 9; Heb. 4 : 16).

6. A public profession and availing ourselves of external ordinances and privileges will not alone save us (ver. 5, 6; Isa. 29 : 13, 14).

7. The sins and falls of ancient Israel stand as perpetual warnings to God's people in all ages (ver. 6-10; Heb. 4 : 1, 6-11).

8. The history of ancient Israel warns us against conformity to the world, and trying Christ by presumptuous sins (ver. 6-10; Rom. 2 : 4; 12 : 2).

9. The backslidings of Israel show the deep depravity of the human heart (ver. 7-10; Jer. 8 : 5; Rom. 7 : 7-11, 24).

10. The gospel dispensation is God's last will and call to men (ver. 11; Rev. 22 : 10, 11; Acts 2 : 17).

11. Confidence in our own security may be over-confidence, and an evidence of danger (ver. 12; Rom. 11 : 20; Phil. 2 : 12).

12. Christians in the times of their highest spiritual enjoyments should exercise special watchfulness, since they are most likely to be off their guard and

exposed to temptation to self-confidence (ver. 12, 13; 2 Cor. 12:7).

13. They who put their trust in God need not fear temptation (ver. 13; 2 Peter 2:9).

14. Though God is faithful to us, we must strive to be faithful to him, in fleeing from sin and not exposing ourselves to temptation (ver. 14; 1 John 5:21; Matt. 6:13).

15. The claims, principles, and precepts of the gospel are most reasonable (ver. 15; Rom. 12:1; 1 Peter 3:15; Isa. 1:18).

16. The Lord's Supper is not a sacrifice, but a memorial of Christ's death. It involves a communion, a participation, and fellowship with Christ in the benefits symbolized by his broken body and shed blood (ver. 16; 11:25, 26; Matt. 26:27).

17. In the Lord's Supper there is an idea of believers jointly fellowshiping Christ. So they are a unity in him (ver. 16:17; Eph. 4:4-6).

18. The Lord's Supper is a church ordinance. Not for the single individual, but for the assembled brotherhood (ver. 17; 11:20, 33).

19. That which is pure in itself may be rendered impure by association and circumstances (ver. 19; Rom. 14:14, 23).

20. All false worship belongs to the kingdom of darkness (ver. 20; Rev. 18:2, 4).

21. Bacchanalian feasts and parties of revelry are diametrically opposed in spirit to the Lord's Supper, and should not be attended by Christians (ver. 21; Rom. 13:13; 2 Cor. 6:17).

22. "The Lord is a jealous bridegroom of his bridal church, and to put contempt on him, or to provoke him to jealousy (Deut. 32:21), is to imitate the sin of Israel, who tempted Christ" (BESSER). (ver. 9-22).

23. No one has a right to patronize that which is really wrong, but in things indifferent he has a right to his own convictions (ver. 28, 29; Rom. 14:22).

24. However lawful a thing may be in the family, in social life, or in personal habits, if it tends to pull down, rather than to build up the cause of Christ and to save souls, it is among the things that are inexpedient (ver. 23; Rom. 14:14-18).

25. It is consistent with a proper self-love to make the good of others and their salvation our aim—a good antidote for selfishness (ver. 24; Phil. 2:4, 20, 21; Gal. 6:10).

26. In our private and personal acts we can generally be safely guided by an enlightened conscience (ver. 25, 27, 29; 2 Cor. 1:12).

27. The products of the earth are good. It is their *use* that affects others for good or for evil (ver. 26; Gen. 1:31).

28. We must not turn our liberty into license, nor lightly treat the consciences of others (ver. 28, 29; 8:12).

29. The strong must not despise the conscience of the weak, nor the weak censure the conscience of the strong (ver. 29).

30. The giving of thanks at meals accords with the practice and spirit of Christ and his apostles (ver. 30; John 6:11; Acts 27:35).

31. The glory of God is the uppermost thing in the universe; and what is for his glory is the highest good of all (ver. 31; 2 Cor. 4:15).

32. We should live blamelessly not only among brethren, but also in the world, lest we retard or hinder the salvation of any (ver. 32; Titus 2:11-14).

33. We can boldly enforce any duty when we can appeal to our own example (ver. 33; Acts 24:16).

34. Christ presents a perfect example, and his word, life, and example form our final bar of appeal (11:1; John 14:6; Heb. 12:2).

CHAPTER XI.

In the last four chapters Paul has treated of questions pertaining to private and social life. In this he passes to things relating to public assemblies and public worship. He first discusses the question concerning the conduct and dress of women in public services. Praising the Corinthians for observing his instructions (ver. 2), he enjoins that men should have their heads uncovered, and women have theirs covered in public worship, on the ground of the divine order in the world (ver. 3-6), and because of woman's relations to men (ver. 7-12). This is confirmed by a sense of natural fitness, and the uniform practice of the churches (ver. 13-16). The apostle then

Concerning public worship; the conduct and dress of women.

2 Now I praise you, brethren, that ye remember me in all things, and keep the ordinances [*or*, traditions*a*] as I
3 delivered *them* to you. But I would have you know, that *b* the head of every man is Christ; and *u* the head of the woman *is* the man: and *v* the head of
4 Christ *is* God. Every man praying or

2 Now I praise you, that ye remember me in all things, and hold fast the instructions, as I delivered them to you.
3 And I wish you to know, that the head of every man is Christ; and the head of the woman is the man; and the
4 head of Christ is God. Every man

a 2 Thess. 2 : 15; 3 : 6.   *t* Eph. 5 : 23; Phil. 2 : 9.   *u* See refs. Gen. 3 : 16.
v 3 : 23; 15 : 27, 28; John 14 : 28.

condemns certain disorders of the Corinthians in celebrating the Lord's Supper (ver. 17-22); gives the history, nature, and purpose of the ordinance (ver. 23–26), and the manner of its observance with a warning against an irreverent participation in it (ver. 27-34).

1. This verse completes the discussion on eating food offered to idols. See note on it at the end of the preceding chapter.

2-16. CONCERNING THE CONDUCT AND DRESS OF WOMEN AT PUBLIC SERVICES.

2. The Corinthians in their letter to the apostle (7 : 1) appear to have stated that they were holding fast to his instructions, and ask further his judgment about the unveiling of women during public worship. Paul in turn, according to his custom, commends them so far as it was possible. (See on 1 : 4.) **Now I praise you, brethren**, from many things I have heard from you, and as ye wrote me, **that you remember me in all things, and keep the ordinances,** *the deliverances* or *injunctions,* **as I delivered them to you.** The word rendered *ordinances* is derived from the verb translated *delivered* in this verse. It occurs thirteen times in the New Testament, and in every passage except this is translated "traditions." In general it is instruction, narrative, or precept given orally or in writing. The oral law and the doctrine of the rabbis were Jewish tradition (Matt. 15 : 2; Mark 7 : 3; Gal. 1 : 14). Here and in 2 Thess. 2 : 15; 3 : 6, Paul applies the word to the instructions he had given. These instructions the Corinthians had kept; but in carrying them out certain difficulties and disorders had arisen. (See on ver. 17.)

3. Paul lays down a principle in the divine order and nature of things as a ground of the injunctions he is about to give. **But** while thus praising you, and in addition to former instructions, *I wish you to know* (see on 10 : 1), **that the head of every man is Christ.** Paul is speaking to his Christian brethren, and of matters pertaining to Christians. He is therefore not referring so much to the general headship of Christ in creation (Col. 1 : 16; 2 : 10) as to his particular headship of the church (Eph. 1 : 22; 4 : 15; Col. 1 : 18; 2 : 19). "As in the human organization the exercise of dominion over all the members proceeds from the head; so in the family, from man; in the church, from Christ; in the universe, from God" (OLSHAUSEN). Before God all men stand on a level, and in Christ Jesus there is neither male nor female, but a oneness which overrides all earthly distinctions (Gal. 3 : 28). But in the nature of things and in the organization of society it is necessary that there be officers and headship. A man without a head would be an anomaly; with more than one head, a monstrosity. And so in the family. There must be a ruling, guiding hand, and God has placed man there as its natural and lawful head and representative. And so **the head of the woman is the man.** And the same holds true in the church, so far as its social and earthly relations and distinctions are concerned. And this is carried still further, **The head of Christ is God.** Christ is subordinate to the Father, as the God-man and Mediator (15 : 24-28; Phil. 2 : 7; John 14 : 28). Subordination pervades the universe and the Christian system, and it is the highest glory for each one to fill his own place. On account of sin and human frailty all, it is true, do not fill their places. Some are incompetent. But

¹ prophesying, having *his* head covered,
5 dishonoureth his head: but ʸevery
woman that prayeth or prophesieth
with *her* head uncovered dishonoureth her head: for that is even all one
6 as if she were shaven. For if the

praying or prophesying, having his
head covered, puts shame on his head.
5 But every woman praying or prophesying with the head unveiled, puts shame
on her head; for it is one and the same as
6 if she were shaven. For if a woman is

z 12 : 28 ; 14 : 1, etc.   y Acts 21 : 9.

exceptions by contrast only prove the rule.

4. Every man praying or prophesying, not so much foretelling future events as uttering inspired truth and instructing the people under the impulse of the Holy Spirit (12 : 10), in the public assembly. **Having his head covered dishonoureth his head,** because there is nothing higher than man in the visible creation (Ps. 8) nor in the visible church of Christ, and a covering of the head would be a sign of subjection, or subordination. It was the custom of the Jews, Romans, and Germans to pray with their heads covered or veiled, thus "showing themselves reverent and ashamed before God and unworthy with open face to behold him." But the Greeks worshiped with uncovered heads. Paul sees in this custom the true one for the Christian man, since he stands as the highest representative of Christ on earth, "not as a servant but a son" (Gal. 4 : 7), who can approach God with unveiled face (2 Cor. 3 : 14-18). On *He dishonoreth his head*, Stanley remarks: "Both the literal and the metaphorical sense are included. 'He dishonors his head by an unseemly effeminate practice (ver. 14); and thereby Christ, who is spiritual Head. The head as the symbol of Christ, is treated with the same religious reverence as is the body, in 6 : 19, as being the temple of the Spirit.'"

5. But every woman that **prayeth or** prophesieth (Acts 2 : 18; 21 : 9), in the meeting, **with** *the* **head uncovered,** contrary to the usual custom. This prayer or prophecy was doubtless under the impulse of the Holy Spirit, as in ver. 4. Prophetesses are mentioned in the Old Testament: Miriam, the sister of Moses (Exod. 15 : 20); Deborah (Judges 4 : 4); Huldah (2 Kings 22 : 14); Noadiah (Neh. 6 : 14). In the New Testament Anna is mentioned (Luke 2 : 36); and the four daughters of Philip (Acts 21 : 9). So also Mary the mother of Jesus prophesied (Luke 1 : 46-55). All these appear to have been under the inspiration of the Spirit, and perhaps with the exception of Mary spoke publicly. The apostle in this verse implies that women had spoken and would speak at certain times and places, and in some kinds of meetings, which was well understood by his readers. He speaks in a general way; but in 14 : 34 he enjoins silence in the public congregation. In Oriental countries women wore a veil, or in some countries a shawl, which on public occasions could be thrown over the head. It would seem that at Corinth both the men and the women needed instruction. Some men, following the Jewish custom, would appear in the public assemblies with covered heads. Paul decides as above for the Grecian custom, as being right in the nature of things. It would seem from this passage and 14 : 34, 35, that some women, on the ground of Christian liberty and the oneness of male and female in Christ (Gal. 3 : 28), had gone beyond the rules of propriety in Grecian and Oriental countries, and had appeared without the veil in public worship, and had prayed and prophesied in the public assemblies of the church. Paul disapproves of both of these innovations, the former here, the latter in 14 : 34, 35. Yet in this passage the apostle appears to permit, and not condemn, the praying and prophesying of women in certain gatherings. Meyer harmonizes this with 14 : 34, by supposing the latter to refer to the large public meetings of the whole church, and this to the smaller gatherings for social worship. **Dishonoureth her head**: brings shame on her head by appearing unwomanly. By laying aside a customary mark of her sex she exhibits a lack of modesty. Thus she dishonors the man as well as herself. **For that is even all one,** rather, *For it is one and the same,* **as if she were shaven**—it exhibits the same shamelessness, though different in

woman be not covered, let her also be shorn: but if it be a shame for a woman to be shorn or shaven, let her 7 be covered. For a man indeed ought not to cover *his* head, forasmuch as ᵃ he is the image and glory of God; but the woman is the glory of the man. 8 For ᵃ the man is not of the woman; 9 but the woman of the man; ᵇ neither was the man created for the woman; 10 but the woman for the man. For this cause ought the woman ᶜ to have power

not veiled, let her also be shorn; but if it is a shame for a woman to be 7 shorn or shaven, let her be veiled. For a man indeed ought not to veil his head, being God's image and glory; 8 but the woman is man's glory. For man is not from woman; but woman 9 from man. For man was also not created on account of the woman, but 10 woman on account of the man. For this cause ought the woman to have·

ᵃ See refs. Gen. 1, 26, 27.
ᵇ Gen. 2 : 18.

ᵃ Gen. 2 : 21, 22 ; 1 Tim. 2 : 13.
ᶜ Gen. 20 : 16 ; 24 : 65.

---

degree. The shaven head in a woman was a sign of a harlot, or of mourning, both in Judea and Greece.

6. Enforces what he had just said: **For if a woman be not covered, let her also be shaven.** Let her be consistent, and lay aside the natural covering of the head, as well as the artificial. But inasmuch as it was considered **a shame,** or *disgraceful,* for her to be shaven, **let her be covered.** "Before the gaze of masculinity it often is at once the modesty and dignity of woman to veil herself. That unrestrained gaze is often profane; and it is a divine reserve that shrinks and conceals from it. In that reserve is contained the proudest and noblest self-respect; so that under the forms of humiliation resides woman's exaltation. Thereby she becomes to man's idea a something sacred and imperial. Let her forfeit that ideal and she dethrones herself and becomes an unlovely being. By most divine law each sex is confined to its own nature. It is equally shameful for manhood to become effeminate, and for womanhood to become masculine" (WHEDON).

7. Paul proceeds to fortify what he had enjoined by the relation of man and woman in creation. **For a man indeed ought not to cover his head, forasmuch as he is the image** (in his rational, moral nature) **and the glory** (in his dignity and dominion over all things in the world) **of God.** (See Gen. 1 : 26 ; 3 : 16 ; Ps. 8 : 5–8.) **But the woman,** while she also is in the image of God (Gen. 1 : 27 ; 5 : 1, 2), **is the glory of the man**—reflects not the glory of God as a ruler, but rather that of man as the head of the household. "She receives and reveals what there is of majesty in him. She always

assumes his station; becomes a queen, if he is a king, and manifests to others the wealth and honor which belong to her husband" (DR. CHAMBERS, in *Meyer*). Thus a covering, as a sign of dependence, is fitting to her, but not becoming to him, being comparatively independent, and the highest creature in the visible creation (ver. 3). Notice Paul repeats not *image,* but *glory,* being the important thing in the argument.

8, 9. For, in confirmation of the preceding statement, **the man is not of,** or *from,* **the woman** in creation, **but the woman of,** or *from,* **the man.** Thus we read in Gen. 2 : 21, 22, that woman was taken out of the side of man. **Neither,** or *For* **neither was the man created for the woman; but the woman for the man.** Thus it is said in Gen 2 : 18, "That it was not good for man to be alone, and that woman was made a helper, suited to him." Thus in creation, woman being after man, from man, and for him, is naturally dependent and subordinate in her physical being, and ranks next to him.

10. Paul draws his inference in regard to the head-dress of women in public services. This is one of the most difficult passages in the New Testament, and has received numerous interpretations. There may be an allusion to some custom, expression, local or transitory term, now lost to us, which if known would make the thought clear and forcible. **For this cause,** because of the relation of woman to man as indicated in their creation (ver. 7-9), **ought the woman to have** a sign **of power,** or *authority,* **on her head,** as indicated by a veil or covering. This most naturally refers to man's authority or headship over her. Perhaps it

on her head, ᵈ because of the angels.
11 Nevertheless ᵉ neither is the man without the woman, neither the woman
12 without the man, in the Lord: for as the woman *is* of the man, even so *is* the man also by the woman; ᶠ but all things of God.
13 ᵍ Judge in yourselves: is it comely that a woman pray unto God un-
14 covered? Doth not even nature itself

[the token of] authority on her head,
11 because of the angels. Nevertheless, neither is woman apart from man, nor man apart from woman, in the Lord.
12 For as the woman is from the man, so is also the man through the woman;
13 but all things from God. Judge in your own selves; is it becoming that a
14 woman pray to God unveiled? Does

ᵈ Eccl. 5 : 6 ; 1 Tim. 5 : 21; Heb. 12 : 1.   ᵉ 7 : 10-14.   ᶠ 8 : 6 ; Rom. 11 : 36.
   ᵍ 10 : 15; Luke 12 : 57; 1 Thess. 5 : 21.

might refer to her delegated and dependent authority (Luke 4 : 6 ; 23 : 7 ; Mark 13 : 34) within her own sphere (6 : 12 ; 7 : 37). But in either case the subordinate relation of woman to man is indicated or implied. **Because of the angels,** probably referring to the presence of angels in their assemblies (Heb. 1 : 14), who also, according to a well-known Jewish view, would be grieved in witnessing any immodest and unbecoming conduct. In harmony with this view is the thought suggested by Isa. 6 : 2, that in the heavenly world angels indicate their subordinate relation by veiling their faces. Additional reference might be made to a very ancient Jewish belief in connection with the fall of angels before the deluge (Gen. 6 : 2 ; 2 Peter 2 : 4 ; Jude 6, 14), that evil spirits gained power over women with their heads bare. Thus the woman with becoming modesty and self-control, indicated by her covered head, would be protected. Still the term *angel* is generally applied to good angels in the New Testament. Another view worthy of mention is, that as the word *angel* means *messenger* (Luke 7 : 24 ; 9 : 52), it may refer to spies from the heathen, or to friendly visitors from other churches, who might be unfavorably impressed with what appeared immodest, and report it. It is better, however, to suppose reference to angels as above. (Comp. 4 : 9 ; 1 Tim. 5 : 21; 1 Peter 1 : 12 ; Heb. 12 : 1.)

11. Paul qualifies what he had said in ver. 8 and 9, so as not to be misunderstood. **Nevertheless**—woman should not be depreciated either by herself or by man, nor should they act independently of each other; for **neither is the man without the woman, neither the woman without the man, in the Lord,** in their relation to Christ and to each other as Christians. They are mutually dependent, and supplement each other.

12. For as the woman is of, rather, *from,* **the man,** by creation (Gen. 2 : 22), **even so is the man also by,** or *through,* **the woman,** by birth; **but all things of,** or *from,* **God,** the order, the relation, and the distinction between the sexes, are according to a divine arrangement. (Comp. 3 : 23.) Nature and grace are harmonious.

MAN'S AND WOMAN'S EQUALITY. Man and woman have spiritual equality. There is neither male nor female in Christ Jesus (Gal. 3 : 28). Each equally enjoys sonship in and with him (Rom. 8 : 17). But each has his or her own sphere. Man is superior in his sphere, and woman in hers; so there need be no conflict. The Father and the Son are equal in their essential natures, yet the Son in his mediatorial office is subordinate. So woman in her physical and family relations is subordinate to man. Yet the spheres of each border on and interlap each other, so that the one often shows a superiority in the sphere of the other. Yet woman's sphere is largely in the family and in the home, and she can best show her superiority in discharging the duties of her position in a superior manner. That their spheres should differ in church work accords with their nature and the constitution of things.

13. Paul appeals to the natural fitness of things and to their sense of propriety. **Judge in yourselves,** by your own instinctive feelings; exercise your common sense. **Is it comely,** *is it becoming,* **that a woman pray to God,** in the social gathering (ver. 5), **uncovered?** Does not nature itself teach you the opposite? (Next verse.)

14. But what is meant by **nature**

teach you, that, if a man have long
15 hair, it is a shame unto him? But if a woman have long hair, it is a glory to her: for *her* hair is given her for a covering.
16 But ᵇ if any man seem to be contentious, we have no such custom, ⁱ neither the churches of God.

Disorders at the Lord's Supper, and its proper observance.

17 Now in this that I declare *unto you* I praise *you* not, that ye come together not for the better, but for the
18 worse. For first of all, when ye come

not even nature itself teach you, that,
if a man have long hair, it is a dis-
15 honor to him? But if a woman have long hair, it is a glory to her; for her
16 hair is given her for a covering. But if any man seems to be contentious, we have no such custom, nor the churches of God.

17 And while I enjoin this, I praise you not, that ye come together not for the
18 better, but for the worse. For first of

ᵇ 1 Tim. 6 : 3, 4.   ⁱ 7 : 17; 14 : 33.

here? Does it mean the original course of nature which has made the distinction between the sexes by giving the woman's head the more abundant hair? Or does it refer to the instinctive feelings, the native sense of propriety, which may be more or less affected by custom and habit. Alford and Stanley take the former view; Meyer and Thayer's "Lexicon" take the latter. But may not *nature* be used in a popular way, not to be closely limited? Paul seems to refer to the sense of propriety having its roots in the nature of things. Does not this teach you, **that if a man have long hair it is a shame unto him?** There had been different customs among men, but in the apostle's day long hair in a man was a mark of effeminacy or of savage manners. The verdict of nature appeared in the instinctive sense of propriety and the general custom of civilized society.

15. But if a woman have long hair, it is a glory to her, it is an ornament. Beauty is the prerogative of woman, which is a right to be cherished and exercised, modestly and submissively, according to the laws of her own being. **For her hair is given her for a covering,** a natural veil and protection, a symbol of concealment and modesty. So nature suggests the propriety of the covered head for woman and the uncovered head for man in public worship. "Whatever contradicts feelings which are universally received, in questions of morality, propriety, and decency, is questionable, to say the least" (ROBERTSON).

16. But, to close this discussion with a final word, **if any man seem,** is disposed, **to be contentious** in regard to this matter, **we,** Paul and his associates in missionary work and in founding churches, **have no such custom,** as the practice of women praying uncovered, **neither the churches of God.** Thus the voice of the apostles and of Christendom was against them. Some refer *custom* to contention, "it is not our custom to be contentious." But as Alford remarks, this is a very unlikely reference after so long a treatment of a particular subject. It naturally refers to that, and thus gives the best sense. It will be noticed in this discussion that Paul's argument is partly from the divine law and order and partly from symbolic reasons, the sense of propriety and beauty, and from the practice of society and the custom of the churches. That which is of divine direction is permanent; but the rest is more or less temporary, as modified by circumstances and customs of different nations and ages.

17-34. CONCERNING DISORDERS AT THE LORD'S SUPPER, AND ITS PROPER OBSERVANCE.

17. Now in this that I declare unto you, rather, *And while I enjoin this* in regard to the head covering (ver. 2-16), and have praised you generally for keeping my instructions (ver. 2), there is a more important matter for which **I praise you not,** namely, **that ye come together,** in your assemblies, **not for the better, but for the worse,** resulting in your spiritual injury rather than spiritual improvement.

18. For first of all (comp. Rom. 1 : 8), mentioning no second. Paul would at once notice disorders in their religious gatherings, especially as connected

together in the church, *k* I hear that there be divisions among you, and I
19 partly believe it; for ¹there must be also heresies among you, ᵐ that they which are approved may be made manifest among you.
20 When ye come together therefore into one place, *this* is not to eat the
21 Lord's supper: for in eating every one taketh before *other* his own supper; and one is hungry, and ⁿ another is

all, when ye come together in church; I hear that divisions exist among you;
19 and I partly believe it. For there must be also factions among you, that they who are approved may be made manifest among you.
20 When therefore ye assemble yourselves together, it is not to eat a supper
21 of the Lord; for in eating, each takes before others his own supper; and one is hungry and another is drunken.

k 1 : 10-12 ; 3 : 3. *l* Matt. 18 : 7 ; Luke 17 : 1 ; Acts 20 : 30 ; 1 Tim. 4 : 1, 2 ; 2 Peter 2 : 1, 2.
m See Deut. 13 : 3 ; 1 John 2 : 19.   *n* 2 Peter 2 : 13 ; Jude 12.

with the Lord's Supper (ver. 20-34), and incidentally as connected with spiritual gifts (chap. 12-14). **When ye come together** *in church, in an assembly*, in a church gathering. This would seem to suggest that they had some general meeting place, while they often met in different places for smaller assemblies. **I hear that there be,** *are*, **divisions among you,** cliques, separations according to social distinctions and petty preferences; **and I partly believe it.** The reports may be exaggerated, but I am led to believe it in part, not only from the character of my informants, but for the reason I am about to state (next verse).

19. For there must be also heresies, better, *factions*, **among you,** such is your carnal condition (3 : 1-3), and it is a part of God's providence that there should be divisions, **that they which are approved,** they who are tried and stand the test, **may be made manifest among you.** The opposite of the *approved* is the *reprobated*, the *rejected* (9 : 27 ; 2 Cor. 13 : 7). Factions, like storms, often serve the purpose of purification. *Heresies*, translated *sects*, Acts 5 : 17 ; 15 : 5 ; 24 : 5 ; 26 : 5 ; 28 : 22, and *heresies* elsewhere in the Common version ; but in the Revised version *sect*, in Acts 24 : 14, *factions*, 1 Cor. 11 : 19 ; Gal. 5 : 20, and *heresies* once, 2 Peter 2 : 1. The term *factions* here is a stronger form of the *divisions* (ver. 18), a deliberate and chosen form of factious conduct, not of false doctrine, as in 2 Peter 2 : 1. It was not originally used in a bad sense, but implied *choice*, then *opinion*, and then *party*, as in schools of philosophy. It came to have a bad sense in Christian usage.

20. When ye come together therefore, there being such divisions and factions (ver. 18, 19), **into one place,** at the same place and time (Acts 2 : 1), **this is not to eat the Lord's Supper,** more exactly, *there is no eating of a supper of the Lord*, that instituted by him. Whatever you may call it, and whatever you may have designed to do, it is not eating a supper of the Lord, it is not worthy of the name. It is not possible to properly observe it under such circumstances. The reason Paul states in the next verse. The rendering of the Revised version, *It is not possible to eat the Lord's Supper*, is more of the nature of an inference as above, and of an interpretation than a translation. On *Lord's Supper* Stanley remarks: "Though the epithet is here used in contradistinction to *his own* supper (ver. 21), yet the adjectival form, as in Lord's Day (Rev. 1 : 10), indicates that it was already the fixed name of the institution."

21. For in eating every one taketh before *other* **his own supper,** not waiting one for the other, each one helped himself, or ate what he had brought himself. There was no sharing together in the meal. **And so one,** the poor man, **is hungry, and another,** the rich man, **is drunken.** Such indecent behavior was unbecoming a Christian assembly, and a perversion of Christ's ordinance. The wine appears to have been intoxicating. Many infer from this passage, and from Acts 2 : 42, 46 ; 20 : 7, 11, that the Lord's Supper took place at the end of a social meal. This meal they regard as the love feast, which was common in the primitive churches, and is first mentioned in Jude 12 and in 2 Peter 2 : 13. As in the dining club of the Greeks, so frequently each brought his own portion, and often the richer members supplied the wants of the poorer. Dis-

22 drunken. What! ᵒhave ye not houses to eat and to drink in? Or despise ye ᵖthe church of God, and ᵈshame them that have not? What shall I say to you? Shall I praise you in this? I praise *you* not.
23 For ʳI have received of the Lord that which also I delivered unto you, ˢThat the Lord Jesus the *same* night in which he was betrayed took bread:
24 and when he had given thanks, he brake *it*, and said, Take, eat: this is

22 What! have ye not houses to eat and to drink in? Or despise ye the church of God, and put shame on those who have not? What shall I say to you? Shall I praise you in this? I praise you not.
23 For I received from the Lord, what I also delivered to you, that the Lord Jesus, in the night in which he was be-
24 trayed, took a loaf; and having given thanks, he broke it, and said, This is

o Ver. 34.   p 10 : 32.   q James 2 : 5, 6.   r 15 : 3 ; Gal. 1 : 1, 11, 12.
s Matt. 26 : 26–28 ; Mark. 14 : 22 ; Luke 22 : 19.

orders arose in the love feasts similar to those described here. On account of this, love feasts began to disappear after the close of the fourth century. It is probable that the Lord's Supper was generally preceded by a common meal in the early churches, as was the case at the institution of the ordinance. But the absence of all reference to the feast of love in that memorable chapter on love, the thirteenth of this Epistle, renders doubtful its use at that time in the church at Corinth. In the earliest account we have of the manner of celebrating the Lord's Supper, by Justin Martyr, about A. D. 150, there is no mention of the love feast. (Neander, "Hist.")

22. What! have ye not houses, you surely have houses, **to eat and to drink in?** You could satisfy your appetites at home if this is your object. These exclamations of astonishment are forcible arguments. **Or despise ye the church of God,** the assembly called out from the world (see on Acts 5 : 11), and which belongs to God, and in which he dwells (3 : 16). Their disorders were contempt of Christ's body, the church, and of the brethren whom they treated as unworthy of a common footing with themselves. **And shame,** better, *put to shame,* **them that have not?** or, *have nothing,* the poor, making prominent their poverty. **What shall I say to you?** These questions contain mild rebukes. **Shall I praise you in this?** alluding to ver. 2. **I praise you not,** as in ver. 17. They had made it not only a common, social meal, but also an occasion for jealousies and wrangling. They had perverted its form, spirit, and design.

23. I cannot praise your manner of observing the Lord's Supper, **For I have received of the Lord that which also I delivered unto you;** this being among the instructions I gave you (ver. 2). How did Paul receive this? Directly from the Lord, or indirectly through Ananias at his baptism, or some other medium? The most natural meaning of the language is that he received it by direct revelation from the Lord. (Comp. 1 John 1 : 5.) **I** is emphatic in contrast to **you**. I personally received it and delivered it to you. It is natural to take both the deliverance and the reception as direct. This is confirmed by Paul's claim elsewhere that he received his gospel by direct revelation; also by his many revelations (2 Cor. 12 : 1). The similarity between this and Luke's account has often been noted. The differences are only such as we might expect, if Paul communicated it to Luke, his companion in travel, and if Luke prepared his Gospel under the general direction of Paul. **That the Lord Jesus**—an impressive and solemn beginning, making prominent the Lordship of the Saviour. *In the night* **in which he was betrayed,** more exactly, *in which he was being delivered up;* a vivid and solemn description. While the act of betrayal was going on and near completion the Supper was instituted. **Took bread,** *a loaf,* doubtless one left over from the Passover meal. (Comp. fuller notes to Luke 22 : 19–21.) The whole description suggests the solemnity, the importance, and religious character of the institution.

24. When he had given thanks. So Luke; Matthew and Mark say, "he blessed." Giving thanks was blessing God, and both were a blessing of the bread, setting it apart to a sacred use. (See 10 : 16.) **He brake it.** This act is

my body, which is broken for you:
25 this do in remembrance of me. *After the same manner also *he took* the cup, when he had supped, saying, This cup is the new testament in my blood: this do ye, as oft as ye drink *it*, in re-
26 membrance of me. For as often as ye eat this bread and drink this cup, ye do shew the Lord's death ⁿ till he come.
27 ˣ Wherefore whosoever shall eat this bread, and drink *this* cup of the Lord, unworthily, ʸ shall be guilty of the body

my body, which is for you: this do in
25 remembrance of me. In like manner also the cup, after they had supped, saying, This cup is the new covenant in my blood; this do, as often as ye
26 drink it, in remembrance of me. For as often as ye eat this bread, and drink the cup, ye proclaim the Lord's
27 death till he come. So that whoever eats the bread or drinks the cup of the Lord unworthily, will be guilty of the
28 body and the blood of the Lord. But

t Mark 14 : 23.
u 4 : 5; 15 : 23; John 14 : 3; Acts 1 : 11; 1 Thess. 4 : 16; 2 Thess. 1 : 10; Heb. 9 : 28; Jude 14; Rev. 1 : 7.
x Ver. 20-22; see Lev. 10 : 1-3; Num. 9 : 10, 13; 2 Chron. 30 : 18-20.   *y* Heb. 10 : 29.

related in all four accounts of the Supper, and ought not to be omitted. **And said, Take eat; this is my body,** etc. There is a variety of readings here, owing to the endeavor of early transcribers to assimilate the four accounts of what Jesus said. The most approved text reads, *And said, This is my body, which is for you; this do in remembrance of me.* The best text of Luke is the same as this, except that it has *given* added, thus: *which is given for you.* **This is my body**—represents my body, an emblem or symbol of it. (See note on 10 : 16, 17.) **In remembrance of me;** showing that this ordinance was to be observed, and that it was to vividly remind them of his sufferings and death for them.

25. After the same manner also he took the cup—in the like solemn and impressive manner taking it and giving thanks. Luke also says, *the cup*, probably referring to the cup used at the Passover. But Matthew and Mark say, *a cup*, implying that there were other cups on the table, probably one to each guest. **When he had supped,** rather, *when they had supped*—after they had eaten, the cup closing the meal. **This cup is the new testament,** rather, *the new covenant*, **in my blood**—the new covenant of grace and eternal salvation, which Christ has ratified in blood, being established by his undergoing death (2 Cor. 3 : 6; Heb. 8 : 6-8; 12 : 21). The word **testament** means *covenant*, God's compact, arrangement, and promises to men, and only once in the New Testament (Heb. 9 : 16) has it the meaning of testament. It was Christ's death that gave validity to this covenant which he

had entered into with man (Exod. 24 : 8; Matt. 26 : 28). **This do ye, as oft as ye drink it**—this is to be commemorative, but the frequency of the commemoration is to be governed by circumstances. It may have been daily at first (Acts 2 : 46), and weekly later on (Acts 20 : 7). But whenever it is observed it is to be **in remembrance of me,** a reminder and a memorial.

26. In this verse we have a blending together of our Lord's words, and of Paul's words. **For,** introduces a further explanation of the ordinance and reason for its observance. **For as often as ye eat:** showing that it is to be continued. Notice that after the giving thanks the emblems are still called *this bread* and *the cup.* So also in the next verse. There is no transubstantiation, no sacrifice, no sacramentalism here, or in this whole account of the ordinance. **Ye do show,** *announce,* or *proclaim,* **the Lord's death,** his sacrificial death for you, **till he come.** The Lord's Supper as a memorial points backward to our Lord's sufferings and death, and forward to his second coming. As Bengel says, it "unites the extremes of two periods" (Matt. 26 : 29).

27. Paul concludes by an application to the case in hand, the disorderly conduct of the **Corinthians.** **Where-fore**—*so that,* **whosoever** shall eat, *the bread,* **and,** rather, *or,* according to a great majority of the best manuscripts, **drink** *the* **cup unworthily,** irreverently, as brought to view in ver. 20-22, and "not discerning the Lord's body" (ver. 29), **shall be guilty of the body and blood of the Lord,** that is, guilty of a sin against Christ

28 and blood of the Lord. But *let a man examine himself, and so let him eat of 29 *that* bread and drink of *that* cup. For he that eateth and drinketh unworthily, eateth and drinketh damnation [*or*, judgment ᵃ] to himself, not discern- 30 ing the Lord's body. ᵇ For this cause many ᶜ *are* weak and sickly among you, 31 and many sleep. For ᵈ if we would

let a man prove himself, and so let him eat of the bread, and drink of the 29 cup. For he that eats and drinks, eats and drinks judgment to himself, if he 30 discern not the body. For this cause many among you are weak and sick, 31 and not a few sleep. But if we dis-

z Ver. 31; Ps.139 : 23, 24; 2 Cor. 13 : 5; Gal. 6 : 4; 1 John 3 : 20, 21. *a* Rom. 13 : 2. *b* Ver. 21.
c Ver. 32. *d* Ps. 32 : 3–5; Luke 15 : 18-20; 1 John 1 : 9.

(8 : 12), against his body and blood, the symbols of which had been dishonored. This expression has troubled many conscientious Christians. The reference and application is not to the fearful, timid, or weak believer, but to the careless and profane professor. Such a one may possibly go so far as to spiritually "crucify the Son of God afresh and put him to an open shame" (Heb. 6 : 6). A person is said to be guilty when he is in a condition which is amenable to punishment (ver. 29, 30). Moreover the passage refers not so much to personal qualifications as to the manner of observing the ordinance. The word is not *unworthy*, but *unworthily*. None can claim fitness in themselves. We are all unworthy; but with a sense of our sinfulness and with a trust in Christ as our Saviour, we may come to his table, and worthily partake of its emblems (Phil. 3 : 9-11; Luke 15 : 13, 14). It will help us, and be a most blessed means of grace.

28. How to partake. **Let a man examine himself,** scrutinize and prove his own heart and spiritual condition before God (2 Cor. 13 : 5; Gal. 6 : 4), to see if he is about to partake in a proper manner. **And so,** in this humble, careful, discriminating, and reverent spirit, **let him eat,** etc. Such an examination in case of a true believer would naturally lead to repentance of every sin and a humble trust in Christ.

29. An important reason for self-examination, so as to partake in a proper manner. **Unworthily,** omitted in the best texts. It may have been inserted by some scribe by way of explanation. So also is **Lord** omitted. The most approved text has simply *the body*, which of course means the Lord's body. **For he that eateth and drinketh,** *not discerning the body,* not distinguishing or discriminating the body of the Lord as symbolized in

the elements, and not making that proper distinction which he ought to make between this and ordinary food. Notice that it is Christ, not ourselves, nor our brethren, who is to be the subject of our thoughts and the object of our faith, in the Lord's Supper. Our communion is with Christ, not with our brethren. **Eateth and drinketh damnation,** rather, *judgment,* **to himself,** which he would have escaped had he judged himself (ver. 31). The word *damnation,* is too strong, which in our language is generally confined to final condemnation, not the meaning here (ver. 32). What kind of *judgment* is meant is explained in the next verse. And this is inflicted in order that they may escape final retribution (ver. 32). There is nothing in this verse to keep the humblest and weakest follower of Jesus from the Lord's table, if he can but realize, though with feeble faith and love, that Jesus died for him. The Lord would have him come, and not stay away. (Comp. Rom. 14 : 23.)

30. Paul points to their own experience for proof of what he had just said. **For this cause**—judgment coming upon those who eat in such a manner as not to discern the Lord's body—**many are weak,** *feeble,* **and sickly,** *diseased, invalids,* **among you, and many,** *not a few,* **sleep.** This naturally refers to bodily rather than spiritual infirmities. If *sleep* has reference to death (see on 7 : 39), then the other two words naturally refer to physical weakness and disease.

31. According to the best authorities this verse begins with *But,* instead of **For.** *But if we were judging ourselves,* looking discriminately into ourselves, or *discerning* (same word as in ver. 29) and deciding beforehand what was the proper and right moral con-

S

judge ourselves, we should not be
32 judged: but when we are judged, *we are chastened of the Lord, that we should not be condemned with the
33 world. Wherefore, my brethren, when ye come together to eat, tarry one for
34 another; and ⸢if any man hunger, let him eat at home; that ye come not together unto condemnation [*or*, judgment]. And the rest will I set in order when ᵍ I come.

cerned ourselves, we should not be
32 judged. But being judged, we are chastened by the Lord, that we may not be condemned with the world.
33 Wherefore, my brethren, when ye come together to eat, wait one for
34 another. If any one is hungry, let him eat at home; that ye come not together unto judgment. And the rest I will set in order when I come.

e Ver. 30; Deut. 8:5; Job 5:17; Heb. 12:5-11.   *f* Ver. 21, 22.   *g* 4:19; 16:5.

---

dition to be in, **we should not** afterward **be judged,** *we would not be incurring judgment*, from the hand of God. Notice how the apostle says "we," kindly putting himself among them and softening the application.

32. But when we are judged, or more exactly, *But being judged*, as we are in the temporal sufferings and afflictions that have befallen us (ver. 30), **we are chastened,** subjected to discipline **of,** or *by*, **the Lord** (Heb. 12:6-11), *in order that we may* **not be condemned,** at the last judgment, **with the world,** the unbelieving portion of mankind (John 15:18).

33. Conclusion of the whole subject. **Wherefore, my brethren,** addressing them in brotherly love, **when ye come together** in your religious assembly **to eat** of the Lord's Supper, **tarry one for another.** Let there be no haste, but kindly wait till the whole assembly may be convened, so that everything may be orderly and devoutly done (ver. 21). Remember that it is not an ordinary meal, or that its purpose is not to satisfy the appetite.

34. If any man hunger, let him eat at home; that ye come not together unto condemnation, *unto judgment* (ver. 29) upon yourselves. It seems that the apostle would have them separate it entirely from any other meal. **And the rest,** regarding details, **will I set in order when I come.** Thus abuses were abolished at Corinth. This passage has been appealed to by Romanists in support of tradition. But they who assert traditions fail to prove them as authentic. The apostles themselves referred back their instructions to the Lord and his word (7:10; 9:14; 11:23; Acts 15:15; 2 Peter 1:19-21). No ordinance can stand which is not grounded in the word of God.

QUESTIONS have arisen as to the nature of *the Lord's Supper, in its relation to social and church life.* Is it a social meal, to be observed at any time, privately or publicly, individually or collectively? Or is it a strictly religious ordinance to be observed by the church at its gatherings? Can a common meal partaken of devoutly and thankfully at home be a supper of the Lord, or must it be observed in the church or a religious assembly?

To this it may be replied:

1. That the Supper as instituted by our Lord was not a meal in the ordinary sense. For (1) Jesus took "a loaf" (Matt., Mark, Luke, and 1 Cor., according to the best text) and each of the eleven received but a part of it. The whole loaf (commonly thin, flat, and round) was not more than enough for the meal of a single person. (Comp. Luke 11:6.) And (2) Jesus took "a cup" (best text, Matt. and Mark) and said, "Drink ye all of it" (Matt.), and "they all drank of it" (Mark). And so a cup of wine hardly sufficient for a single meal of one person is shared in by the eleven. Thus as originally instituted the Supper could be styled a meal only in a limited sense. Each took a small portion of the same bread and the same cup. (Comp. 1 Cor. 10:16, 22.) And that it was not a social meal is evident from the fact that it was to be observed in remembrance of Christ and in communion with him (1 Cor. 10:16; 11:24-26).

2. After its institution there appears to be made a distinction between it and ordinary meals. In Acts 2:42 the disciples "were constantly attending upon the teaching of the apostles and fellowship (or the distribution), the breaking of bread and prayers." The Lord's Supper as a religious ordinance appears to be meant here by "breaking of

bread." But afterward it is said (ver. 46), "And daily attending with one accord in the temple, and breaking bread at their homes (at home) they partook of their food with gladness," the most natural reference being to their ordinary meals. So also in Acts 20 : 7, 11, "the breaking of bread" appears to have been the Lord's Supper in connection with a religious service, after which having "eaten," partaken of a more substantial meal, Paul talked a long while, and departed. Likewise in 1 Cor. 11 : 17 ff., Paul makes the same distinction. (1) He gives the model as Christ first instituted the Supper in which one loaf and one cup were used (ver. 23, 25), both in the singular number. (2) He condemns their perversion of the Supper, some feasting and some hungry, thus treating it as an ordinary social meal, showing that they had a wrong conception of the ordinance as well as a wrong method of observing it. And (3) he enjoined that they should not come to their assembly hungry, but having eaten at home, should wait for one another and observe the Supper together in an orderly manner. It was not for the satisfying of hunger nor for the meeting of any want in their social nature, but "to show the Lord's death till he come." It was for the discerning of the Lord's body, and in remembrance of him.

3. The Lord's Supper appears to have been an ordinance of the church to be observed when assembled for worship. In the eleventh chapter of 1 Cor., Paul speaks of certain customs or usages in church assemblies, or public services (1 Cor. 11 : 16). He first speaks of the conduct of women, and then of the observance of the Lord's Supper. In both of these there were irregularities among the Corinthians. The Supper he connects with a church service, for he says, "When ye come together in church" (1 Cor. 11 : 17), and also, "when ye assemble yourselves together" (1 Cor. 11 : 20). And as to their perversion of the Lord's Supper, he says, "Despise ye the church of God" (1 Cor. 11 : 22), thus connecting it with the local church. And again he says, "When ye come together to eat," that is, the Lord's Supper (1 Cor. 11 : 33), evidently addressing the church at Corinth (1 Cor. 1 : 2). Such language, used by the apostle, points to the Supper as a church ordinance. And this accords with the solemn and weighty manner in which he introduces its right observance in 11 : 23. Indeed he appears to regard it as worship, and throughout the chapter, to be solemnly connected with the public worship of their church assemblies. And this accords with the fact that it was first instituted with, and entrusted to, the eleven apostles, who were to be the inspired organizers of his churches in the world.

PRACTICAL REMARKS.

1. Every Christian should earnestly seek conformity to Christ in heart and life (ver. 1; Rom. 8 : 29; see Practical Remark 34, on chap. 10).

2. We should foster the disposition to commend whatever is commendable in others (ver. 2; Prov. 15 : 1; 25 : 15).

3. There is a divine order among all existences. There is a propriety in recognizing this order everywhere (ver. 3 : 12; Eph. 1 : 20-22).

4. We should observe the proprieties of life in religious matters as well as in worldly affairs (ver. 4 : 5; Rom. 14 : 16).

5. The two sexes are complements of each other, each having its place, and neither should assume the rank, the duties, or the usual costume of the other (ver. 5, 6, 11, 12).

6. We cannot dishonor ourselves without dishonoring those connected with us (ver. 5 : 6; Rom. 2 : 23).

7. God has made man the head and natural protector of the family and woman, the queen of the home, the helpmate of man (ver. 7-9; Prov. 31 : 23, 30).

8. "It is a perversion of God's ordinance when a woman usurps authority over her husband, or when a man from fond affection becomes a slave to his wife" (ver. 7-9, HEDINGER).

9. The New Testament confirms the Mosaic narrative as history and the word of God (ver. 7-9; Luke 24 : 27).

10. Christians should observe in public worship proper decorum and a respect for the common usages of society (ver. 7-10).

11. Angels are closely connected with the experience, worship, and work of Christians (ver. 10; Ps. 91 : 11; Luke 15 : 10; 16 : 22).

12. Woman is as essentially important in her place as man is in his, both in the kingdom of nature and of grace (ver. 11, 12).

13. The conduct of either sex in the worship of God should accord with the teachings of grace, nature, and common sense (ver. 13-15).

14. Both man and woman have a sphere in which each can attain the highest development (ver. 11-15).

15. Both in public and private, in the church and in the world, woman should evince that modesty and reserve which are her highest ornaments (ver. 15; 1 Peter 3 : 3, 4).

16. We may well hold to whatever has the sanction of apostolic authority and precedent (ver. 16; Eph. 2 : 20).

17. Faithful reproof is better than unqualified praise (ver. 17; Prov. 27 : 5, 6).

18. The Lord's Supper is a church ordinance. The church is "to come together" for its observance (ver. 18, 20, 33).

19. Divisions and factions in churches result from a low state of religion, and are opposed to the spirit of the gospel (ver. 19; 1 : 10; 3 : 3; Rom. 16 : 17).

20. God often uses divisions among Christians to show who are his true disciples (ver. 19; Rev. 3 : 10).

21. There is a tendency in even the best of Christians to degenerate and depart from the simplicity of the gospel (ver. 20-22; Gal. 1 : 6; 1 Tim. 4 : 6, 7).

22. The Lord's Supper cannot be properly observed by any one while exercising a spirit of selfishness and greed (ver. 21, 22, 31).

23. The abuses of the Lord's Supper have arisen in departing from its original simplicity. Thus in the popish mass and in the additions of ritual churches (ver. 23; 1 Tim. 4 : 6, 7).

24. The best way to uproot error is to preach the truth in all its simplicity (ver. 23, 24; 2 : 1, 5; Acts 20 : 27).

25. The Lord's Supper is not of the nature of a feast or of a sacrifice, but is a symbolic commemoration of the death of Christ (ver. 23, 26).

26. As to its design it is a memorial, a loving remembrance of his sufferings and death for us (ver. 24, 25).

27. It is not an ordinance of heaven, but of churches on earth to be continued till Christ's second coming. Then we shall no longer need it, for we shall see him and be like him (ver. 26; 1 John 3 : 2).

28. It is not a private but a public ordinance of the assembled church, proclaiming the Lord's death for them, and their belief in his second coming (ver. 26; Gal. 3 : 1; Heb. 9 : 28).

29. It should be approached reverently, and partaken of penitently in humble faith in Christ, as an atoning and all-sufficient Saviour (ver. 27-29).

30. It should be preceded by self-examination and a renewed consecration to Christ, and should be treated, not as a common meal, but as a solemn symbolization of the body and blood of Christ (ver. 28, 29; John 6 : 53, 54).

31. An improper and irreverent observance of the Lord's Supper is especially displeasing to God, and may be followed by Divine chastisement (ver. 27, 29, 30, 32).

32. If we would not incur the displeasure of our Lord we must deal honestly with ourselves, renounce our sins, and approach his table penitently with a desire to honor him and advance his cause (ver. 31).

33. God's design in chastisement is that his people may be reclaimed, not destroyed (ver. 32; Heb. 12 : 5-8; 2 Cor. 6 : 9).

34. At the Lord's table the rich and poor meet together, and all stand on a common level before God (ver. 21, 33, 34).

35. Human tradition is nothing, but God's word and ordinances, as they come to us through inspired men, are supreme (ver. 34; Col. 2 : 8; 2 Peter 1 : 21).

CHAPTER XII.

Paul passes to spiritual gifts concerning which it would seem the Corinthians had asked certain questions in their letter. The discussion is continued to the end of the fourteenth chapter. He first speaks of the nature and test of spiritual gifts (1-3); then treats of their unity and diversity (4-11); illustrates by the human body in which there are many members (12-14), but none to be overrated or despised (12-26). Application of these principles to the

Reproofs and instructions concerning spiritual gifts.

12 NOW ᵇconcerning spiritual *gifts*, brethren, I would not have you igno-
2 rant. Ye know ⁱ that ye were Gentiles, carried away unto these ʲ dumb idols,
3 even as ye were led. Wherefore I give you to understand, ᵏ that no man speaking by the Spirit of God calleth Jesus accursed: and ˡ *that* no man can

12 NOW concerning the spiritual gifts, brethren, I do not wish you to be ignorant.
2 Ye know that when ye were Gentiles ye were carried away to the dumb idols, in whatever way ye were led.
3 Wherefore I make known to you, that no one speaking in the spirit of God

h 14 : 1, 37.   *i* Eph. 2 : 11, 12 ; 1 Thess. 1 : 9 ; 1 Peter 4 : 3.   *j* Ps. 115 : 5, 7.   *k* 1 John 4 : 2, 3.
l Matt. 16 : 16, 17 ; John 15 : 26.

Corinthians, as a church of Christ (27-31). In this whole discussion we have a vivid picture of a remarkable period of Christianity, when supernatural gifts were enjoyed.

1-17. ORIGIN, NATURE, TEST, UNITY, AND DIVERSITY OF SPIRITUAL GIFTS.

1. The apostle commences as in 7 : 1; 7 : 25; and 8 : 1. **Now concerning spiritual gifts,** better, *Now concerning the spiritual*—well known to the Corinthian church, and about which they had probably consulted him (7 : 1). Some word is understood expressive of those agencies emanating from the Holy Spirit. Some supply *persons;* others supply *matters.* But *gifts* seems to be the best word, mentioned in ver. 4, upon which is the whole discussion, and which formed one of the characteristics of the apostolic churches. These gifts were supernatural endowments which came in accordance with prophecy (Joel 2 : 28) and the promise and prediction of our Saviour (John 14 : 16, 26 ; Mark 16 : 17, 18 ; Acts 1 : 5), and were generally diffused among believers (Acts 2 : 4 ; 10 : 44-46), and exhibited great diversity (ver. 28-30 ; Rom. 12 : 6-8 ; Eph. 4 : 7-11). It is not strange that certain disorders and abuses should arise. Some deceived, or deceiving, would claim what they did not possess, or more than they possessed. Some would be dissatisfied with their own gift and envy others. Some would be forward and ostentatious, and thus rivalries and confusion would arise in their public assemblies. It would seem also that the gift of tongues had come to be regarded as pre-eminent, even to the detraction of other gifts, such as the gift of prophecy. To correct these evils Paul proceeds to show that all gifts proceed from the Spirit, and in the next chapter that love is the greatest and guide of all, and finally in chapter fourteen, that the gift of prophecy was superior to that of tongues, and that order should prevail in all they did in their assemblies. **I would not have you ignorant,** better, *I do not wish you to be ignorant.* (See on 10 : 1.)

2. Ye know that ye were Gentiles—according to the most approved text, *that when ye were Gentiles,* heathen in fact as well as in name. The church at Corinth was largely Gentile (Acts 18 : 6-11). *Ye were* **carried away,** blindly led without reason, *to the* **dumb idols** *in whatever way* **ye were led.** The dumb, the deaf, and voiceless idol was suggestive, by way of contrast, of the speakings by prophecy, tongues, and otherwise of the Spirit. (Comp. Ps. 115 : 5; Hab. 2 : 18, 19.) Their former condition is emphasized when they were blindly carried away by the delusive utterance of pagan priests and priestesses to worship inanimate idols. A contrast indeed with the divine Spirit dwelling within them, and acting in harmony with the faculties of their souls.

3. Wherefore, because you have been in such a state, blinded and ignorant, **I give you to understand.** You need instruction in regard to the extraordinary gifts of the Spirit; and therefore *I make known to you* certain fundamental characteristics of the gifts, namely : "Jesus is not execrated, but confessed as Lord" (MEYER). **That no man speaking by,** rather, *in,* **the Spirit of God**—pervaded by the Spirit, **calleth Jesus accursed.** (See on Rom. 9 : 3). The very idea is excluded by the fact that the speaker dwells as it were in the Spirit. **And that no man can say** (omit that)

say that Jesus is the Lord, but by the Holy Ghost. 4 Now ᵐ there are diversities of gifts, 5 but ⁿ the same Spirit: ᵒ and there are differences of administrations, but the 6 same Lord: and there are diversities of operations, but it is the same God 7 ᵖ which worketh all in all. ᵍ But the manifestation of the Spirit is given to 8 every man to profit withal. For to one

says, Jesus is accursed; and no one can say, Jesus is Lord, but in the Holy Spirit. 4 Now there are diversities of gifts, 5 but the same Spirit. And there are diversities of services, and the same 6 Lord. And there are diversities of workings, but the same God who works 7 all in all. But to each one is given the manifestation of the Spirit, for profit-

ᵐ Heb. 2 : 4 ; 1 Peter 4 : 10.   ⁿ Eph. 4 : 4.   ᵒ Ver. 28, 29 ; Rom. 12 : 6–8 ; Eph. 4 : 11, 12.
p Eph. 1 : 23.   *q* Eph. 4 : 7 ; 1 Peter 4 : 10, 11.

Jesus is Lord, but by, rather, *in* **the Holy Ghost,** *Spirit,* as above. (Comp. Phil. 2 : 11). The apostle does not mean the mere utterance of these words, but the hearty and true confession of them which can only be spoken by one who is enlightened by the Holy Spirit. Compare, "Ye received the Spirit of adoption, whereby we cry, Abba, Father" (Rom. 8 : 15), and Peter's confession and our Lord's reply (Matt. 16 : 16, 17). See also a similar test in 1 John 4 : 1–3. "Paul furnishes a test of truth against Gentiles; John against false prophets" (BENGEL). Paul lays a broad foundation. The Spirit is not confined to extraordinary gifts, but extends in his influence to all gifts, and to the very beginnings of spiritual life. The Spirit is the origin of all; and we would naturally expect a great variety of gifts proceeding from him (next verse).

4. The diversity and unity of the gifts of the Spirit are stated and explained in this and the two following verses. **Now there are diversities,** *divisions* or *distributions,* **of gifts.** The word translated *gifts* is used only by Paul in the New Testament, except 1 Peter 4 : 10, and means a *gift of divine grace* or *favor*. (See 1 : 7 ; 7 : 7 ; 2 Cor. 1 : 11 ; Rom. 1 : 11 ; 5 : 15 ; 6 : 23 ; 11 : 29.) It is used almost always in this Epistle of *special gracious endowments* of the Holy Spirit; in addition to the ordinary fruits **of the** Spirit (Gal. 5 : 22), which exist in the believer in such a way as to fit him thereby to actively serve the cause of Christ (ver. 28–31 ; 1 Peter 4 : 10). **But the same Spirit,** bestows the gifts on believers "as he will" (ver. 11). Notice how the different persons **of the Trinity** are connected with these gracious endowments (this and next two verses).

5. **And there are differences,** rather, *diversities* (the same word as in ver. 4), **of administrations,** or serv-

ices, **but the same Lord,** under whom and to whom these services are performed.

6. **And there are diversities of operations,** *the workings,* the deeds wrought, the effects produced; **but** (omit **it is** according to the best text) **the same God which worketh all,** these workings of the Spirit, **in all,** upon whom they are bestowed. Notice how Paul presents three sides of these extraordinary gifts : gracious bestowments, services to the cause, and effective results ; and three sides of the Divine agency : the Holy Spirit who bestows the gift on each individual believer ; Christ, the Lord and Master, the Head of the church to whom and under whom the services are performed ; and God, the Father, the cause of all power, who gives efficiency to all workings of the Spirit. The same ascending divine gradation is observed here as elsewhere (Eph. 4 : 6), according to the parts performed by the Father, Son, and Spirit, in the work of redemption. Thus in these gracious endowments there is unity in their origin, in their ministry, and in their effects.

7. Paul states the object of these gifts—the benefit of others. **But the manifestation of the Spirit is given** *to each one,* to each Christian thus receiving the gift, **to profit withal,** *for profiting,* others. The Spirit indeed makes known his power in them, and they working with the Spirit (³ : ⁹), make known his power to others. Thus these extraordinary endowments become at once evidences that they were of God, and at the same time the means of conveying truth and the knowledge of salvation to others.

8. The apostle proceeds to confirm what he had said in ver. 7, at the same time specifying the various gracious gifts, which in their very nature are for

is given by the Spirit *the word of wisdom; to another *the word of knowledge by the same Spirit; *to another faith by the same Spirit; to another *the gifts of healing by the same Spirit; *to another the working of miracles; to another *prophecy; *to another discerning of spirits; to another *divers kinds of tongues; to

8 ing. For to one is given through the Spirit a word of wisdom; and to another a word of knowledge according to the same Spirit; to another faith, in the same Spirit; and to another gifts of healings in the one 10 Spirit; and to another workings of miracles; to another prophecy; to another discerning of spirits; to another various kinds of tongues; and

v 2 : 6, 7; Eph. 1 : 17.   *s* 1 : 5; 2 Cor. 8 : 7.   *t* 13 : 2; Matt. 17 : 19, 20.
u Mark 16 : 18; Acts 3 : 6; James 5 : 14.   *x* Mark 16 : 17; Acts 6 : 8.   *y* 14 : 1, etc.; Acts 11 : 28; Rom. 12 : 6
z 14 : 29; Acts 8 : 21; 1 John 4 : 1-3; Rev. 2 : 1, 2.   *a* 14 : 18; Acts 2 : 4; 10 : 46.

the good of others. **For,** to appeal to facts and illustrate, **to one is given by,** rather, *through,* **the Spirit the word,** rather, *a word,* a discourse or utterance, **of wisdom,** concerning the divine plan, previously hidden, of salvation for men through the death of Christ (2 : 6). **To another,** *a word,* discourse or utterance, **of knowledge,** showing deep insight into the truths of religion (13 : 2). The word of wisdom may be regarded as the gift of revealing the hidden truths of the gospel which belonged to the apostles and some other inspired men; the word of knowledge as a gift for understanding and explaining these truths, which belonged also to other teachers. **By,** better, *according to,* **the same Spirit.** Notice the unity of these various gifts is kept in view to the end of ver. 11. They emanate from the Spirit and are disposed to each as the Spirit wills.

9. To another faith. This is not saving faith, for that is common to all believers; nor a faith of miracles, for that is too narrow, and is also named in the next verse. It rather refers to an unusual confidence and assurance, bestowed by the Spirit on believers for great occasions, peculiar emergencies, or important missions. Such seems to have been the faith of Stephen (Acts 6 : 5, 15; 7 : 56); it is like the "fullness of faith" in Heb. 10 : 22, and of the martyrs in the eleventh chapter of the Hebrews. **To another the gifts of healing,** rather, *of healings.* The plural is used in reference to the different endowments exercised in healing different diseases. These gifts seem to have been common in the apostolic age (Mark 16 : 18; Acts 3 : 7; 5 : 15, 16; 9 : 34; 19 : 11, 12; 28 : 8, 9; James 5 : 14, 15). **By,** more exactly, *in,* by and through, **the same Spirit . . . one Spirit.** The expression varies, but the unity of the source and medium of the power is kept in view. The Spirit contains all these powers in himself and confers them.

10. To another, *workings of miracles*—effects produced by the exercise of miraculous power; the power of working miracles in general (Acts 9 : 40; 13 : 11; 16 : 18). The ability to understand and heal diseases (ver. 9) of course is not included. **To another prophecy;** speaking by the inspiration of the Spirit and declaring the purposes of God. (See on 11 : 4.) This is to be distinguished from ordinary prophesying and preaching. **To another discerning of spirits,** having the power to distinguish and decide whether one is speaking by the Spirit of God, by his own unaided power, or by an evil spirit (1 Tim. 4 : 1; 1 John 4 : 1). They could decide not only between the false and the true, but also in regard to the spiritual value of the utterances. (See on 14 : 29.) **To another divers kinds of tongues;** enabling him to speak in languages not his own (Acts 2 : 4, 11) and in tongues different from all known tongues (14 : 10). Those endowed with tongues appear to have been in a high state of spiritual ecstasy, speaking, singing, and praying (14 : 6, 14, 15; Acts 2 : 11). It seems to have been an act of worship rather than of teaching. There is no evidence that the apostles used it in preaching the gospel to foreign nations. Besides the description of the gift of tongues in this and the fourteenth chapters of this Epistle, the only direct information is found in Acts 2 : 1 ff., 10 : 46; 19 : 6; and Mark 16 : 17. It is not mentioned in the later Epistles, and it probably continued no longer than the apostolic age. (See note on Acts 2 : 4; and Schaff, "His. of Chris. Ch.," Vol. I., pp. 234-242). **To**

another ᵇ the interpretation of tongues.
11 But all these worketh that one and the selfsame Spirit, ᶜ dividing to every man severally ᵈ as he will.
12 For ᵉ as the body is one, and hath many members, and all the members of that one body, being many, are one
13 body; ᶠ so also *is* Christ. For ᵍ by one Spirit are we all baptized into one body, ʰ whether *we be* Jews or Gentiles, whether *we be* bond or free; and ⁱ have been all made to drink into one Spirit.

to another interpretation of tongues.
11 But all these works the one and the same Spirit, dividing to each one severally even as he will.
12 For as the body is one and has many members, and all the members of the body, being many, are one body, so
13 also is the Christ. For in one spirit we were all baptized into one body, whether Jews or Greeks, whether bond or free; and were all made to drink of one Spirit.

ᵇ 14 : 27.   ᶜ 7 : 7; Rom. 12 : 6.   ᵈ Heb. 2 : 4.   ᵉ Rom. 12 : 4, 5; Eph. 4 : 4, 16.   ᶠ Ver. 27; Gal. 3 : 16.
ᵍ Matt. 3 : 11; Eph. 4 : 4, 5.   ʰ Gal. 3 : 28; Eph. 2 : 13, 14, 16.   ⁱ John 7 : 37-39.

---

another the interpretation of tongues; the ability to translate the tongue, and explain its meaning. This was not needed at Pentecost, for every one heard in the language in which he was born (Acts 2 : 8). For further on this gift see 14 : 5, 23, 26, 27. There are nine gifts named here, eight implied in ver. 28, and seven in ver. 29, 30.

11. Having thus enumerated these gifts the apostle again emphasizes their unity, bestowed and wrought by the one Spirit. **But all these** diversities of gifts **worketh that one and the selfsame Spirit.** Notice that what is said of God in ver. 6, is here said of the Spirit, **dividing to every man** (compare the cloven or distributing tongues of Acts 2 : 3) **severally,** respectively and individually, **as he will,** not arbitrarily, but deliberately and discriminately, according to the capacity, disposition, and mental fitness of each believer. The personality of the Spirit is implied, as one who works and wills.

12. THE UNITY OF THESE DIVERSE GIFTS ILLUSTRATED BY THE HUMAN BODY; AND THE PRINCIPLE APPLIED TO THE CHURCH.

12. For as the body is one and hath many members, etc. This figure is a common one, and a favorite one with Paul (Rom. 12 : 4, 5; Eph. 4 : 16; 5 : 30; Col. 2 : 19). In the human organism there is diversity in unity. **So also is Christ** in relation to and in connection with his church (ver. 28; comp. 3 : 16; John 15 : 1). "The whole Christ ncludes the head and the body" (Augustine). Believers are spiritually in Christ (Rom. 12 : 5; 2 Cor. 5 : 17); and a spiritual unity pervades Christ and his people.

13. Confirms this unity of believers in Christ, by an appeal to facts in their own Christian experience. **For by,** rather, *in* **one Spirit,** regenerated and renewed (Eph. 3 : 24; Col. 3 : 10) **are we all,** rather, *we were all* **baptized into one body,** into one spiritual organism. Their unity was in one Spirit, in one baptism, and in the one spiritual body of Christ. Baptism has its spiritual side, which it symbolized by the outward form (Rom. 6 : 4, 5). Compare "in" or "into the name" (Matt. 28 : 19, on which see note) and "For as many of you as have been (*as were*) baptized into Christ have (*did*) put on Christ" (Gal. 3 : 27). Baptism implies not differences among believers but oneness, their unity, however opposite their nationalities, **whether Jews or Gentiles** (rather, *Greeks*), or however different their social conditions, **whether bond or free. And have been,** *were*, **all made to drink**—according to the best text—*of* one Spirit, a seeming allusion to the Lord's Supper, of which they first partook immediately after their baptism, spiritual partaking of Christ (10 : 16). What the apostle says in this verse can be true only of true believers, and he takes for granted that the Corinthian brethren are such. The partaking of the Lord's Supper points also to their oneness in Christ. In regard to the reference to *drinking*, rather than of eating, comp. 10 : 2-4; 11 : 26; John 4 : 14; 7 : 37, 38. "It is clear from this passage that Paul considers the unity of the church not as something formed from without, but as fashioned from within" (NEANDER). Some, however, see no allusion to the Supper, and refer it to the first reception of the Spirit when the soul is born from above (John 3 : 3-5),

14 For the body is not one member, but
15 many. If the foot shall say, Because I am not the hand, I am not of the body; is it therefore not of the body?
16 And if the ear shall say, Because I am not the eye, I am not of the body; is it
17 therefore not of the body? If the whole body were an eye, where were the hearing? If the whole were hear-
18 ing, where were the smelling? But now hath *k* God set the members every one of them in the body, *l* as it hath
19 pleased him. And if they were all one
20 member, where were the body? But

14 one Spirit. For the body also is not
15 one member, but many. If the foot say, Because I am not a hand, I am not of the body; it is not therefore not
16 of the body. And if the ear say, Because I am not an eye, I am not of the body; it is not therefore not of the
17 body. If the whole body were an eye, where were the hearing? If the whole were hearing, where were the smell-
18 ing? But as it is, God has set the members each one of them in the body,
19 even as he wished. And if they were all one member, where were the body?

k Ver. 28.   *l* Ver. 11; 3:5.

henceforth the Spirit becoming an abiding possession. Some of these would translate, *And all were watered with* (3:6,7), that is, figuratively, *imbued with one Spirit*, such as the miraculous endowments connected with the baptism of the Spirit at Pentecost.

14. The same leading thought is kept in view, unity yet diversity, and all in harmony. **For,** so it is, *also* with **the human body; it is not one member,** it does not consist of *one limb* with its particular office and function, **but of many,** each having its own office, function, and work, for the good of the whole. Having laid down this premise the apostle goes on to apply it to those who disparage their own gift on the one hand, and to those who despise the gifts of others on the other.

15, 16. You must not therefore underrate your own gift (ver. 15-20). **If the foot shall say, Because I am not the hand,** rather, *a hand,* **I am not of the body; is it therefore,** etc. This clause and the corresponding one in ver. 16 are not questions, but strong denials of the preceding declarations: *It is not, therefore,* on that account, *not of the body,* equivalent to, it is still, for all that, of the body, it belongs to it. The saying so does not make it so. The foot has its office, and functions, and is connected with the body, and the body cannot get along without it. No other member can take its place, and do its work. So also of the **ear** in its revelation to the eye. The application to Christians as members of Christ's body is evident. Each has his place, his gift, and work, according to his capacity and ability, and no one can fill his particular place or do his individual work. No one is unimportant in Christ's estimation; there is no cause for discontent (1 Tim. 6:6). It is sufficient that it is the will of the Spirit (ver. 11), and that each believer holds that relation which his Lord and Master would have him.

17. By two pointed interrogations Paul shows that the suppositions in the two preceding verses were preposterous and absurd. **If the whole body were an eye, where were the hearing?** the important function of the ear. How could the body do without the hearing and the smelling? To deprive the body of its members, or to make it consist of one or more conspicuous members, would be to destroy its organism, to throw it out of harmony with itself, and unfit it for usefulness. But as well might this be as for Christians to be all apostles, or all prophets, or all pastors, or all deacons. (Comp. ver. 29, 30.)

18. But now, as it really is, **hath God set,** or more exactly, *God set* or *disposed* **the members** generally, in the original constitution of the body at creation, **every one,** better, *each one,* **of them in the body,** each having its place and function, and hence important, **as it hath pleased him,** or, *as he wished.* God's good pleasure should be the end of argument. His wisdom and goodness are infinite and his right is unquestionable.

19. And if they were all one member, where were the body? what would become of the organization of the body as a whole? The thought is absurd and preposterous, as in ver. 17. The body having its many members concentrated into one would be no longer a body, but a monstrosity. As

now *are they* many members, yet but
21 one body. And the eye cannot say unto the hand, I have no need of thee: nor again the head to the feet, I have
22 no need of you. Nay, much more those members of the body which seem to be
23 more feeble are necessary: and those *members* of the body, which we think to be less honourable, upon these we bestow more abundant honour; and our uncomely *parts* have more abundant
24 comeliness: for our comely *parts* have no need. But God hath tempered the body together, having given more abundant honour to that *part* which
25 lacked: that there should be no schism

20 But now there are many members,
21 but one body. And the eye can not say to the hand, I have no need of thee; nor again the head to the feet, I have
22 no need of you. Nay, much more the members of the body which seem to be
23 more feeble, are necessary; and those parts of the body which we think to be less honorable, on these we bestow more abundant honor; and our uncomely parts have more abundant
24 comeliness; but our comely parts have no need. But God tempered the body together, giving more abundant
25 honor to that which lacked; that there might be no division in the

a body, performing the many duties of a body, it would cease to be.

20. But now, as it really is, **are they,** rather, *there are* **many members, yet but one body,** these all have their place, and go to make up the one body. As in all organisms, there is plurality in unity, and all in harmony. The perfection of the body consists in its many harmonious parts. The loss of even one mars its unity.

21. And so one member must not disparage or despise another. **And** since all the members are parts of the body, **the eye cannot say to the hand, I have no need of thee;** they are mutually dependent, and one is helpful to the other. The same is true of **the head** and **the feet.** One possessing superior gifts is not independent of one having inferior gifts; nor must he show pride because of his own, nor contempt toward those of the other. The illustration here is the reverse of that in ver. 15, 16.

22, 23. In contrast with the negative the apostle presents the positive side. **Nay, much more,** or, *nay, rather* than claiming no need of inferior members, even **those members of the body, which seem to be**—in their own nature—**more feeble, are necessary.** He does not name any, but simply affirms a fact, the weaker members are necessary. So there is no unnecessary gift or member in Christ's body, the feeblest are necessary as well as the strongest. **And those which we think to be less honourable upon those we bestow,** or *clothe with*, **more abundant honour,** such as the trunk and the limbs, **and our uncomely,** or, *unseemly*, **parts, have more abundant comeliness,** by means of covering and ornament. "'The weaker,' 'the less honorable,' and 'the uncomely,' are best left undefined, as the apostle has left them; the words being accumulated and varied designedly so as to include all parts of the human frame, without specifying any" (STANLEY). Christianity may exist without a Christian philosopher, or the brilliant pulpit orator, but the humble, every-day Christian is necessary to the maintenance of the Christian church. Churches do exist, though apostles have fulfilled their mission and passed away, but they could not exist without the prayers and godly lives of the great mass of its members in humble life.

24. The first clause, which is a contrast of the preceding statement, rightfully belongs to the preceding verse. **For,** rather, *But*, **our comely parts have no need,** of such care bestowed upon them, for example, the face, with its organs, needs no covering. **But,** begins a new sentence, and contrasts the divine side with the human. **But,** turning from what we do to the members individually, **God,** treating them as a whole with wise design (omit **hath**) **tempered the body,** caused its various parts to *unite together* in its organic structure at creation, having given, better, *giving*, **more abundant honour to that** part which **lacked,** the weak, the less honorable, and the uncomely of ver. 22, 23. By way of compensation God honors these through the natural instincts and feelings of men, which leads them to bestow upon them special care and protection.

25. God's object in so disposing the members of the body. **That there should be no schism in the body,** *no division* of feeling and interest as

in the body, but *that* the members should have the same care one for 26 another: ᵒ and whether one member suffer, all the members suffer with it; or one member be honoured, all the members rejoice with it.
27 Now ⁿ ye are the body of Christ, and 28 members in particular. And ᵒ God hath set some in the church, first ᵖ apostles,

body, but that the members might have the same care one for another.
26 And whether one member suffers, all the members suffer with it; or one member is honored, all the members rejoice with it.
27 Now ye are Christ's body and sever- 28 ally members of it. And God set some in the church, first apostles, secondly

<small>m Rom. 12 : 15; Gal. 6 : 2 ; 1 Peter 3 : 8.   n Rom. 12 : 5; Eph. 4 : 12 ; 5 : 23, 30; Col. 1 . 24.
o Ver. 7–11; Rom. 12 : 6–8; Eph. 4 : 11.   p Eph. 2 : 20; 3 : 5.</small>

displayed in ver. 21; **but that the members should have the same care one for another,** that there should be no partiality, but each exercising the same interest toward all the others. Paul has in mind the divisions at Corinth, and that they highly honored some gifts to the disparagement of others, and his language is modified thereby. For example it would seem from chap. 14 that they overvalued the gift of tongues and undervalued prophecy. There were also class distinctions among them (11 : 22), and other divisions (3 : 3).
26. Not only is there a care among all the members of the body individually (ver. 25), but there is a collective sympathy toward any one member. **And whether one member suffer, all the members suffer with it.** A common experience; pain even in the extremities of the body affects the whole. **Or one member be honoured, all the members rejoice with it.** "The head is crowned, and all the man is glorified ; the lips speak, and the eyes also laugh and rejoice" (CHRYSOSTOM). (Comp. ver. 22, 23, and Rom. 12 : 15; Gal. 6 : 1, 2.) This was suggestive to the Corinthians, that they should exercise mutual sympathy, honor one another's gifts, and rejoice in one another's prosperity (13 : 4–7).
27. Paul now applies what he had said of the human body to the church at Corinth. **Now ye,** the Corinthian church, **are the body of Christ,** or more exactly, *are Christ's body,* **and members in particular**—*individually members of it.* As the church at Corinth could be said to be God's temple, the Spirit of God dwelling in them (3 : 16), so in a like sense a local church can be styled Christ's body, since his Spirit is present with it, and dwells in its members individually (6 : 15, 19). Possessing the Spirit of Christ it partakes of the nature and quality of Christ, represents Christ and his collective discipleship, imaging forth spiritually their characteristics. Each member has his particular place, function, and work.
28. A more general application with reference to spiritual gifts. How God disposed these gifts in the church. **And God** (omit **hath**) **set some in the church,** when he constituted it. This is parallel with ver. 18. As "body" is used, though there be many bodies, so *church,* though there be many local churches. Paul is speaking of spiritual gifts, and he mentions those offices which were especially endowed with them, which endowment took place in the church at Jerusalem on the day of Pentecost, and afterward as it pleased God and the occasion demanded. The word *church* then can have a general reference to the Jerusalem church, or it may be used abstractly of churches in general, or generally of the aggregate discipleship throughout the world. Why may it not combine all these ideas in a general way? Is not the church here, according to Paul's idea, that of which any true Christian church was an exponent, and which could in a sense be applied to any local church, as he certainly does apply it in a general way to the church at Corinth. (See note on Acts 9 : 31.) Commentators generally apply it to the whole body of Christians scattered throughout the world. (See note on Matt. 16 : 18.) It will be noticed that Paul does not mention in the list that follows the officers of the local church, but what might be styled *the official organs* of the Spirit in the churches. **First apostles,** first chosen, first in rank, richly endowed with various gifts (Matt. 10 : 1), and the inspired organizers of churches. To the Twelve Paul was added. (See 9 : 1.) They belong to the churches in general. They were the

secondarily prophets, thirdly teachers, after that miracles, then gifts of healings, helps, governments, diversities of tongues. Are all apostles? Are all prophets? Are all teachers? 30 Are all workers of miracles? Have all the gifts of healing? Do all speak with tongues? Do all interpret? 31 But *covet earnestly the best gifts: and yet show I unto you a more excellent way.

prophets, thirdly teachers, then miracles, then gifts of healings, helps, governments, various kinds of tongues. Are all apostles? Are all prophets? Are all teachers? Are all workers of miracles? 30 Have all gifts of healings? Do all speak with tongues? Do all interpret? 31 But desire earnestly the greater gifts; and a still more excellent way I show you.

q Luke 6:13; Acts 13:1. r Ver. 10. s Ver. 9. t Num. 11:17; Acts 6:3, 4.
u 1 Tim. 5:17; Heb. 13:17, 24. z 14:1, 39.

connecting link between the spiritual kingdom and the outward church. They had no successors. Even when James, the brother of John, was slain, no successor was appointed (Acts 12:1. See note on Acts 1:26). **Secondarily,** better, *secondly,* **prophets** (see on ver. 10); **thirdly teachers,** endowed with special gifts of the Spirit for expounding the word of God. Both prophets and teachers are mentioned in Acts 13:1, as connected with the church at Antioch. (Comp. Rom. 12:4-8.) **After that miracles.** (See on ver. 10.) **Then gifts of healing.** (See on ver. 9.) **Helps,** often applied to the services of deacons, as helps to the pastors; but it is of wider signification, applicable to those who were endowed by the Spirit to be assistants and helpers in the work generally. Thus Mark was an assistant to Paul and Barnabas (Acts 12:25; 13:5. See also Rom. 16:3, 9). Dean Stanley supposes the gift to refer to "interpretation of tongues," and he could have added, to "discerning of spirits," enumerated in ver. 8, 10, but not mentioned here. It might include these as important helpers of others. **Governments,** rather, *governings;* that endowment of the Spirit fitting persons to preside, give counsel, and direct affairs in the work and administration of the church. **Diversities of tongues;** endowment to speak various kinds of tongues. (See note on ver. 10.) Notice how Paul places this gift, so highly prized by the Corinthians, last in the list, being of the least practical value. (See on 14: 18, 19.)

29, 30. The apostle eloquently bursts forth in a series of animated questions, demanding decidedly negative answers, showing that the extraordinary gifts of the Spirit are not common to all, but distributed according to the good pleasure of God (ver. 18, 28). **Are all apostles?** equivalent to, *Surely all are not apostles, all are not teachers,* etc. He mentions seven classes, selecting those the most manifest and which attracted the most attention. The other gifts were enjoyed by different ones of these, in greater or less measure.

31. But Paul adds a modifying exhortation. **But,** while I would have you to be content with your gift, and not exercise pride over your own, nor contempt toward those of others, yet I would not repress proper desire and efforts for higher attainments and for the bestowment of greater gifts; therefore I say, **covet,** *desire,* **earnestly the best,** rather, according to the highest critical authorities, *the greater* **gifts,** such as prophesying, teaching, and such as would especially profit the church (ver. 7; 14:26). These could be sought after by prayer, faith, and the diligent improvement of the talents and gifts they already possessed (Mark 4:25). Chapter fourteen is a good commentary on this. This clause properly closes this part of the discussion, and should end the chapter.

The last clause of this verse begins Paul's wonderful exhibition of the excellencies of love, and should be connected with the next chapter. **And yet shew I you,** rather, *And moreover the most excellent,* the pre-eminently excellent, *way I proceed to show you,* namely, the way of love, which you have not mentioned, and you must have quite overlooked, as your rivalries and jealousies show. In this way you can best attain, best enjoy, and best exercise these gifts to the good of others.

PRACTICAL REMARKS.

1. It is of the first importance for the Christian to understand the nature, work,

gifts, and graces of the Holy Spirit (ver. 1; John 16 : 14, 15).

2. It is often well to contrast our former miserable condition under the bondage of sin with our present state as Christians (ver. 2; Rom. 6 : 17; Eph. 2 : 11, 12; Titus 3 : 3-7).

3. All true religion is produced by the Holy Spirit, who leads repenting sinners to accept Christ as Lord, and to glorify him (ver. 3; John 3 : 5, 6; Rom. 8 : 14; John 16 : 14).

4. God is triune in his nature, and thus bears a three-fold relation to the gifts and graces of his people (ver. 4-6; 2 Cor. 13 : 14).

5. God bestows upon Christians all the gifts and graces they need in their inner lives, in their various callings, and in their work for Christ (ver. 4-6; 7 : 7; Heb. 4 : 16).

6. It is the duty of Christians to utilize their gifts and graces for the peace and edification of the whole church, and for the salvation of souls (ver. 7; Matt. 25 : 15; 1 Peter 4 : 10, 11).

7. A Divine unity as well as diversity is manifested in Christ's gifts and graces (ver. 4-11; Col. 1 : 3, 8; Eph. 4 : 4-7).

8. God is the source and fountain of wisdom and knowledge, and we should seek supplies from him (ver. 8; Rom. 11 : 33; James 1 : 5).

9. To saving faith God may add special boldness and power with him, in obtaining great blessings in spiritual and bodily health (ver. 9; James 5 : 13, 20).

10. In deed, word, and spiritual discernment we should seek the special help of the Spirit, in order that we may reject the false and support the true (ver. 10; Eph. 6 : 18, 20).

11. With every new experience we can speak to others with a new tongue (ver. 10; Ps. 40 : 3).

12. Since spiritual gifts and graces are bestowed according to the Spirit's wise and good pleasure, we should exercise them with humility and thankfulness, and treat all our fellow-laborers with kindness and honor (ver. 11, 18, 24; Phil. 1 : 3).

13. There is an analogy between nature and grace, between the natural and spiritual world (ver. 12-26; Heb. 8 : 5; 9 : 23; Matt. 13 : 18, etc.).

14. Baptism and the Lord's Supper should remind Christians that they are one in Christ, however diverse their condition in life (ver. 13; 10 : 1-3; Eph. 2 : 13-15).

15. To regard as useless any gift or grace bestowed upon us is to impugn the wisdom of God (ver. 7, 15, 16).

16. That which is most obscure in the kingdom of God is often most important (ver. 14, 15; Mark 4 : 26-29).

17. A variety of talents, attainments, and gifts is essential to the existence and growth of the church. If all were teachers where were the learners? (ver. 16, 17, 19).

18. Our graces and gifts are not according to our pleasure, but God's pleasure (ver. 18; Eph. 2 : 8-10; Rev. 4 : 11).

19. The perfection and highest usefulness of each Christian consist in possessing and using his own talents, and discharging his own duties (ver. 19, 20; Gal. 6 : 4; Phil. 2 : 12, 13).

20. Those having insight into Divine things (eyes) need their practical brethren (hands); those who direct affairs (head) need the burden-bearers (feet) (ver. 21).

21. Many Christians who are retiring and apparently feeble, but humble, meek, and prayerful, are often more necessary to the welfare of the church than the talented and the learned (ver. 22, 23; 1 : 20, 26-29).

22. God has so disposed of the gifts and graces of believers as to produce the highest harmony and perfection in them as a whole (ver. 24; Eph. 4 : 11-16).

23. Since Christ is as much to the humblest believer as to the most exalted, and the one cannot well do without the other, there should be no rivalries nor divisions of feeling among them (ver. 25; Phil. 2 : 5).

24. There should be no class distinctions in the church. Whatever tends to injure one portion is sure in the long run to injure the rest (ver. 25).

25. Every local church has its collective relationship to Christ, and each member an individual relation. The church has its duty as a whole: the members in addition their duties as parts (ver. 27; Rev. 3 : 2-6).

Love superior to all gifts, and chief among Christian graces.

13 THOUGH I speak with the tongues of men and of angels, ʸ and have not charity, I am become as sounding
2 brass, or a tinkling cymbal. And though I have *the gift of* ² prophecy,

13 IF I speak with the tongues of men and of angels, but have not love, I am become sounding brass, or a clanging
2 cymbal. And if I have prophecy, and

y 1 John 3 : 14 ; 4 : 20, 21.   z 12 : 8–10, 28 ; 14 : 1, etc. ; see Matt. 7 : 22.

26. God bestows gifts and graces, not alike upon all, but suited to their mental constitutions, their work among men, and their positions in the church (ver. 28; Eph. 3 : 7 ; 1 Tim. 4 : 14).

27. Some of the gifts of the early church were transient; and so were some of the offices in which these gifts were specially manifested (ver. 29, 30).

28. We should labor and pray for the greater gifts and attainments in the divine life, and also help others to do the same (ver. 31 ; Col. 1 : 28, 29).

29. The transient graces had their important uses, but the permanent and ordinary ones are of the most value (ver. 31 ; 13 : 13 ; 14 : 22).

CHAPTER XIII.

This prose poem, on the superiority of love to all spiritual gifts and graces, is one of surpassing beauty. Nowhere does Paul come so near the spirit and conceptions of John as here. "The periods roll on in rhythmic melody to the end of the chapter, like a strain of richest music dying, or a golden sunset" (PRINCIPAL BROWN). "On each side of this chapter the tumult of argument and remonstrance still rages; but within all is calm; the sentences move in almost rhythmical melody; the imagery unfolds itself in almost dramatic propriety; the language arranges itself in almost rhetorical accuracy" (STANLEY). The apostle first contrasts love with extraordinary gifts and graces, and declares it to be pre-eminently essential to religion (ver. 1–3), then presents its negative and positive characteristics (ver. 4–7), exhibits its permanence, and finally its pre-eminence as the chief of all (ver. 8–13).

1–3. LOVE CONTRASTED AND DECLARED TO BE PRE-EMINENTLY ESSENTIAL TO RELIGION.

1. Paul speaks in the first person to give emphasis and vividness. Assuming that to be the case which has never occurred, he gives great strength and force to his words ; **Though I speak with the tongues of men and of angels.** He mentions tongues first, as that gift was overvalued by the Corinthians. The rabbis speak of the language of angels. And surely they must have some mode of conveying their thoughts and conceptions. Paul speaks of having heard "unspeakable words which it is not lawful for man to utter" (2 Cor. 12 : 4). **And have not charity**, rather, *love*. The rendering, *charity*, has much obscured the meaning of this eloquent eulogy on love. The word here translated love is not found in classic writers. It first made its appearance in the Septuagint version in the Song of Songs. It is not found in the Acts, Mark, and James; it occurs only once in Matthew and Luke, twice in Hebrews and Revelation, but frequently in the writings of John, Paul, Peter, and Jude. It is the higher and nobler form of love, an active, fervid principle, having both God and men as its objects (1 John 4 : 20, 21). Its strong and self-sacrificing side is brought out by our Saviour, "as I have loved you" (John 15 : 12), and by John, "we ought to lay down our lives for the brethren" (1 John 3 : 16). Its highest and most perfect manifestation is found in God, "God is love" (1 John 4 : 8 ; 5 : 1–3). In this chapter Paul presents this love as principally exercised toward our fellow-men. **I am become as sounding brass**, a mere sounding piece of metal, **or as a tinkling cymbal**, a loud ringing, *a clanging cymbal*, mere noise without moral power. There may also be an allusion to the annoyance and din, as Chrysostom suggests, occasioned by some of the loud-mouthed talkers, exhorters, and speakers of tongues, in the Corinthian and other churches of that day.

2. **And though I have the gift of prophecy.** (See on 11 : 4.) Balaam had

and understand all mysteries, and all knowledge; and though I have all faith, ᵃso that I could remove mountains, and have not charity, I am
3 nothing. And ᵇthough I bestow all my goods to feed *the poor*, and though I give my body to be burned, and have not charity, it profiteth me nothing.
4   ᶜCharity suffereth long, and ᵈ is kind; charity envieth not; charity vaunteth
5 not itself, ᵉis not puffed up, doth not behave itself unseemly, ᶠseeketh not her own, is not easily provoked,

know all mysteries, and all knowledge; and if I have all faith, so as to remove mountains, but have not love,
3 I am nothing. And if I bestow all my goods in food, and if I give up my body to be burned, but have not love, it profits me nothing.
4 Love suffers long, is kind, love envies not, love vaunts not itself, is not
5 puffed up, does not behave unseemly, seeks not its own, is not provoked, im-

---

a Matt. 17 : 20; Mark 11 : 23; Luke 17 : 6.   b Matt. 6 : 1-4.   c Eph. 4 : 2; Col. 3 : 12, 13; 1 Peter 4 : 8.
d Luke 6 : 35, 36; Eph. 4 : 32; 1 John 3 : 16-18.   e Phil. 2 : 1-5.   f See refs. 10 : 24, 33.

---

that gift (Num. 23 : 7 ff.), but he "loved the wages of unrighteousness" (2 Peter 2 : 15). **And understand,** *know,* **all mysteries,** the hidden things which are revealed, connected with the divine plan of salvation (see on 2 : 7), **and all knowledge** pertaining to the gospel. Mysteries and knowledge correspond with wisdom and knowledge in 12 : 8 (on which see). Paul combines them here with prophecy, giving it fullness and perfection. **And though I have all faith,** all that the gift of miracle-working faith required, *so as to* **remove mountains,** with apparent reference to our Lord's words (Matt. 17 : 20; 21 : 21). Judas very likely wrought miracles with the other apostles (Matt. 10 : 1; Mark 6 : 13). This cannot mean justifying or saving faith, which is vitally connected with love and works through love (Gal. 5 : 6; Eph. 3 : 17-19; James 2 : 18-26). **And have not love, I am nothing;** though I appear to be so eminently favored by God, yet I am worthless in his sight, a mere nullity in spiritual worth and moral excellence.

3. He proceeds to the very highest outward works of love. **And though I bestow all my goods to feed** the needy and helpless. **Food** is not in the original. But the original has the idea of dealing out food as a mother to her babe, and distributing as to the hungry (Rom. 12 : 20). Zaccheus proposed to give but one-half of his goods to the poor (Luke 19 : 8). **And though I give my body to be burned;** a possible allusion to Dan. 3 : 19-26. A person could become a martyr from motives of ambition, fame, or fanaticism, and have no true underlying love. **And have** *not love,* my self-sacrifice and beneficence for others will be but an ostentatious display, **it profiteth me nothing,** it would be of no spiritual advantage, and avail nothing toward salvation.

4-7. EIGHT NEGATIVE AND SEVEN POSITIVE CHARACTERISTICS OF LOVE. "Paul exhibits love like a jeweler handling his most precious gem, turning it on every side" (KLING, *in Lange*).

4. The apostle speaks no longer in the first person, but personifies love. *Love* **suffers long,** under offenses and injuries; slow to anger and slow to avenge: *longsuffering* (Prov. 19 : 11; Matt. 18 : 26; 1 Thess. 5 : 14). **And is kind,** exercising a gracious, mild, and tender disposition toward others: *kindness.* These two characteristics are complements of each other, exhibiting opposite sides of love. *Love* **envieth not,** is free from envy and jealousy (Acts 7 : 9; 17 : 5); *generosity* (Gen. 50 : 15-21). **Vaunteth not itself,** is not vainglorious or self-boasting: *modesty.* **Is not puffed up,** not inflated with vanity and pride: *humility* (Rom. 12 : 3). Modesty and humility are closely allied, though not the same.

5. Doth not behave itself unseemly, does not act indecorously and unbecomingly, and is not forgetful of what is due to others: *courtesy* (1 Peter 3 : 8). **Seeketh not her own,** free from selfish seeking after one's own advantage, and grasping after one's rights, as had been exhibited in some of the Corinthians (11 : 19, 22); *unselfishness* (10 : 24, 33). **Is not** (omit **easily**) **provoked,** not irritated and aroused to anger, having a self-control over one's temper: *good temper.* Compare note

288   I. CORINTHIANS   [Ch. XIII.

6 *thinketh no evil; *rejoiceth not in iniquity, but ʲrejoiceth in the truth;
7 *beareth all things, believeth all things, hopeth all things, ᴵendureth all things.
8 Charity never faileth. But whether *there be* prophecies, they shall fail; whether *there be* tongues, they shall cease; whether *there be* knowledge, it
9 shall vanish away. ᵐFor we know
10 in part, and we prophesy in part: but when that which is perfect is come, then that which is in part shall be done

6 putes no evil, rejoices not at unrighteousness, but rejoices with the truth,
7 bears all things, believes all things, hopes all things, endures all things.
8 Love never fails; but whether there are prophecies, they will be done away; whether tongues, they will cease; whether knowledge, it will be done
9 away. For we know in part, and we
10 prophesy in part: but when that which is perfect is come, that which is in part will be done away.

g 1 Peter 4 : 8.   *h* Phil. 3 : 18.   *i* Acts 11 : 23 ; 2 John 4.   *k* Prov. 10 : 12 ; Rom. 15 : 1 ; 2 Tim. 2 : 24.
l 9 : 12.   *m* Ps. 40 : 5 ; 139 : 6.

on Acts 15 : 39, where the noun from this verb occurs. **Thinketh no evil,** *imputeth* or *taketh not account of evil,* of the evil done to her, but forgives it : *a forgiving disposition.* Compare the use of the verb in Rom 4 : 8 ; 2 Cor. 5 : 19.

6. Rejoiceth not in iniquity, better, *at unrighteousness,* in seeing it advanced and when she sees it in others (Ps. 5 : 4, 5) ; **but rejoiceth in,** rather, *with the truth,* when she sees it triumph in the world, with the consequent advance of righteousness and decline of wickedness (3 John 4). Love and truth rejoice together. We have here a sin-hating and a truth-loving disposition, two sides of a *godly temper,* or principle.

7. Beareth all things ; explained by some as *covering,* and excusing the errors and faults of others, but it is better to take it as used elsewhere in the New Testament (9 : 12 ; 1 Thess. 3 : 1, 5) to *endure* hardships, troubles, privations, and indignities, occasioned by others, without ceasing to love : *patience.* **Believeth all things,** is not distrustful and suspicious, disposed to make allowance and treat others in good faith : *trustfulness.* **Hopeth all things,** always hoping for the best, not despairing of the possible reformation of the most hardened offenders : *hopefulness.* **Endureth all things,** the afflictions and persecutions of this life, bravely and calmly, steadfast and unmoved, with a hopeful eye upon the future : *endurance,* or *perseverance.*

8-13. The permanence and preeminence of love. It is imperishable, and chief of even the permanent graces.

8. Having given the characteristics of love, Paul points out its chief glory, its imperishable nature. **Love never faileth,** it endures forever. In contrast is the perishableness of the gifts upon which the Corinthians had prided themselves. **Whether there be prophecies they shall fail** (not the same verb as that translated *fail* above), *they shall pass away,* or *be done away.* Prophecy is temporary, and for the good of Christians; but when it has accomplished its ends it will be no more needed (ver. 10). **Whether there be tongues they shall cease,** the gift being no longer required as a sign (14 : 22), and having accomplished its work. **Whether there be knowledge,** even this gift (12 : 8) **shall vanish,** or *be done away,* as no longer necessary "when the perfect has come" (ver. 10). These three gifts are taken as the representatives of all of the endowments of the Spirit in this contrast with love.

9, 10. Proof of what Paul had affirmed of knowledge and prophesying. Of the gift of tongues Paul did not think it necessary to speak. It was evidently temporary and very imperfect (14 : 6, 23). **For we know in part and we prophesy in part;** our deep knowledge of Divine things, and our prophesying concerning these things, are but partial views and revelations of the whole. So far they are imperfect. **But when that which is perfect is come,** at the consummation of God's kingdom (Acts 3 : 21 ; Hab. 2 : 14) **then that which is in part,** partial and imperfect, **shall be done away,** will give way before perfection. These gifts of the Spirit are necessary now, but will continue no longer than necessary ; but when the state of per-

11 away. When I was a child, I spake as a child, I understood as a child, I thought as a child: but when I became a man, I put away childish
12 things. For ᵒ now we see through a glass, darkly; but then ᵒ face to face: now I know in part; but then shall I know even as also I am known.
13 ᵖ And now abideth faith, hope, charity, these three; but ᵠ the greatest of these *is* charity.

11 When I was a child, I talked as a child, I thought as a child, I reasoned as a child; since I have become a man, I have done away with the
12 things of the child. For we see now through a mirror, obscurely; but then face to face. Now I know in part; but then I shall know fully, even as I was
13 also fully known. And now abides faith, hope, love, these three; and the greatest of these is love.

n 2 Cor. 5:7. o Exod. 33:11; Num. 12:8; Matt. 5:8; 1 John 3:2. p See ver. 8. q Col. 3:14; 1 John 4:7,8

fectness comes such imperfect conveyances will not be needed (ver. 12; 1 John 3:2).

11. Paul resumes the first person, and as a representative of others, illustrates his subject from his own growth in knowledge. **When I was a child,** in infancy and childhood, **I spake,** better, *I talked,* **as a child,** in infantile and childlike language; **I understood,** or *thought,* within a narrow range, **as a child; I thought,** rather, *I reasoned,* and formed my judgment, in a limited and imperfect manner, **as a child; but when,** rather, *since,* **I became a man,** *an adult, I have put away, done away,* brought to an end, **childish things.** These three verbs, *talked, thought,* and *reasoned* may have here some allusion to the gift of tongues, prophecy, and knowledge. It should be noted that the natural impressions of objects in childhood are true, so far as they go. So our present views of divine things are just and true so far as they are revealed to us by the word and the Spirit, but they are only partial, and suited to our present imperfect condition. They will give way to the full and complete views of our perfect manhood hereafter.

12. For now, to confirm what I have said and to illustrate, **we look through a glass,** rather, *through a mirror* (the object appearing to the observer through it and behind it) **darkly,** *obscurely,* and thus we see **an obscure thing.** The mirrors of the ancients were of steel or other metal, and reflected objects imperfectly. The word translated **darkly,** means literally, an *obscure saying,* an enigma (Num. 12:8; Judg. 14:13). Here it denotes the object which is imperfectly and obscurely seen in the mirror. We see divine truth in similitudes, symbols, words, and other imperfect human forms of conveying knowledge. **But then face to face,** with immediate vision without any intervening medium. (Comp. Num. 12:8; 2 Cor. 5:7; Rev. 22:4). **But then shall I know** *fully,* having thorough, complete knowledge, **even as also I am known,** rather, *was fully known,* by God at my conversion. Our knowledge of divine things rests on God's knowledge of us (8:3; Gal. 4:9; Matt. 11:27). In the future state our knowledge, though by no means equal with God's, will be like his, immediate and perfectly exact. Thus it is not our faculty for knowledge which is to be done away, but knowledge as a special gift and that which is suited to our present temporary and imperfect state. Our heavenly knowledge will be of a higher, purer quality than our present earthly.

13. And now, these things being so, these spiritual gifts being only temporary, **abideth,** unchanged and permanent, **faith** (not the transient gift of ver. 2), but the vision of the unseen and trust in God (Heb. 11:1), **hope,** with ever higher aspirations for future good (1 Peter 1:3, 4), **love,** necessary to dwelling in God and God in us (1 John 4:16). **These three** graces go hand in hand; Paul frequently associates them together (Col. 1:4, 5; 1 Thess. 1:3; 5:8). **The greatest of these** graces is **love.** Faith and hope belong to the creature; love to God himself (1 John 4:7, 8, 11, 12). Faith and hope benefit the one who exercises them, but love is diffusive and benefits others. Love is the most useful grace; and Paul valued the gifts according to their usefulness (12:7; 14:3, 4). Faith and hope will contribute to heaven; but love will pervade heaven —the atmosphere, as it were, of heaven. And thus also does the apostle show that ordinary graces are superior to the supernatural spiritual gifts in which they gloried.

T

The gift of prophecy superior to that of tongues; directions for public worship.

14 ʳFOLLOW after charity, and ˢdesire spiritual *gifts*, ᵗbut rather that ye may
2 prophesy. For he that ᵘspeaketh in an *unknown* tongue speaketh not unto

14 PURSUE love; and desire earnestly the spiritual gifts, but rather that ye
2 may prophesy. For he that speaks in a tongue speaks not to men, but to

r See refs. 13 : 1 ; Prov. 21 : 21 ; 2 Peter 1 : 5-8.   s 12 : 1, 31.   t Num. 11 : 25, 29 ; Rom. 12 : 6.
u Ver. 9-11, 16 ; Acts 2 : 4 ; 10 : 46.

Practical Remarks.

1. Love is a vital principle of all true religion (ver. 1-3 ; Matt. 25 : 37-40).
2. Some are ever seeking after the deep things, or the wonderful things of religion, when they should be learning its first principles (ver. 2 ; Luke 13 : 23, 24).
3. Others set more value on shining gifts than on spiritual graces (ver. 1-3 ; Matt. 23 : 5, 23).
4. Magnificent gifts and even heroic martyrdom can bring nothing but earthly glory without permanent benefits, except as we are actuated by right motives (ver. 3 ; 1 Peter 4 : 13-16).
5. How set with gems is true love to our fellow-men ! (Ver. 4-7 ; Gal. 5 : 22.)
6. Opposite to every gem of love stands some base evil or passion to mar and ruin human character (ver. 4-7 ; Gal. 5 : 19-21).
7. The characteristics of love are so active in their nature and marked in their effects that it should be easy for all to decide whether they possess it (ver. 4-7 ; 1 John 3 : 14-17).
8. That which is adapted to all circumstances and may be exercised always on earth and in heaven, is of the highest value (ver. 8 ; 2 Cor. 4 : 18).
9. Many gifts, which accomplish their purpose in this life, are useful, and should be prized and cultivated (ver. 8 ; 9 ; 14 : 1).
10. The Christian life is a growth and a training (ver. 10-12 ; 2 Tim. 1 : 5-7 ; Gal. 3 : 24, 25).
11. The Christian should rejoice that his present state of comparative ignorance is to be followed by one of inconceivable knowledge (ver. 12 ; Luke 10 : 20 ; 1 Peter 1 : 6-8.)
12. Moral and spiritual perfection is not to be attained this side of heaven (ver. 12 ; Phil. 3 : 12-16).
13. Everything of essential value to our souls will abide with us forever (ver. 13 ; Rev. 22 : 11).
14. Love is the heart of the redeemed earth and the glory of heaven (ver. 13 ; Rev. 1 : 5).

CHAPTER XIV.

Paul returns to the direct discussion of spiritual gifts, from which he had digressed at the end of the twelfth chapter. He first shows that the gift of prophecy is superior to that of tongues ; for it is a means of edification (ver. 1-5), while unknown tongues are not understood (ver. 6-9) and tend to confusion without an interpreter (ver. 10-19). They are also for a sign to unbelievers, while prophecy is especially for believers (ver. 20-25). He then gives directions to insure decorum and order ; as to the use of tongues and prophecy (ver. 26-33) ; as to the public use of gifts by women (ver. 34-36) ; exhortation to obedience and order (ver. 37-40).

1-25. THE SUPERIORITY OF THE GIFT OF PROPHECY OVER THAT OF TONGUES.

1. Follow after charity, *pursue after love*, which has been shown to be the chief of graces ; make it your first and highest aim ; and in connection with it, and under its guidance, *desire earnestly* (as in 12 : 31) *the* **spiritual gifts,** of which I have been speaking, **but rather** than the others, **that ye may prophesy.** This is the conclusion of the preceding chapter and the transition to this. Prophecy throughout this chapter is not so much the foretelling of events as the unfolding and applying of Divine truth by direct revelation or inspiration of the Holy Spirit (ver. 30 ; see on 12 : 10).

2. The reason for preferring prophesying. It is the more useful gift, especially as contrasted with that of tongues, which was so highly prized by the Corinthians, and had been the cause of much confusion among them. **For** he that speaks in a **tongue** (see on 12 : 10) speaks not to men, for he is not under-

men, but unto God: for no man understandeth *him*; howbeit in the spirit he
3 speaketh mysteries: but he that prophesieth speaketh unto men *to* edification, and exhortation, and comfort.
4 *He that speaketh in an *unknown* tongue edifieth himself; but he that
5 prophesieth *edifieth the church. I would that ye all spake with tongues, but rather that ye prophesied: for greater *is* he that prophesieth than he that speaketh with tongues, *except he interpret, that the church may receive edifying.
6 Now, brethren, if I come unto you speaking with tongues what shall I profit you, except I shall speak to you either by *revelation, or by knowledge, or by prophesying, or by doctrine?

God; for no one understands, but with the spirit he speaks mysteries.
3 But he that prophesies, speaks to men upbuilding and exhortation and comfort.
4 He that speaks in a tongue builds up himself; but he that prophesies
5 builds up the church. I wish you all to speak with tongues, but rather that ye should prophesy; and greater is he that prophesies than he that speaks with tongues, unless he interpret, that the church may receive upbuilding.
6 And now, brethren, if I come to you speaking with tongues, what shall I profit you, unless I speak to you either in revelation, or in knowledge, or in

x Ver. 14.   *y* Ver. 31.   *z* Ver. 12 : 13.   *a* Ver. 26.

---

stood by them, **but unto God,** who understands the deepest movements of the Spirit in praise, thanksgiving, and prayer (Rom. 8 : 26, 27). **Howbeit in,** or *with*, **the spirit,** his higher spiritual powers, **he speaketh mysteries,** the *hidden things* of God which are unknown to others and often unknown to himself. (See on 4 : 1.)

3. But, on the other hand, **he that prophesieth speaketh unto men edification,** that which *builds them up*, in the Christian life, **and exhortation,** that which moves them to greater activity and encourages them to more zealous endeavors, **and comfort,** that which calms and cheers them generally. It will be noticed that in this chapter, and elsewhere, the gifts of tongues and of prophecy are closely connected (12 : 10, 28; 13 :1; Acts 19 :6). They both were manifested through oral utterance, and very commonly went together. When the gift of tongues first appeared, Peter did not distinguish it from prophecy, but defended and described it under the name of prophesying (Acts 2 : 17-21).

4. He that speaketh in a tongue (omit **unknown**) **edifieth himself,** whether he understands or not what he is saying, because the Holy Spirit arouses his soul to holy emotions and to devout thanksgiving and praise. And there it ends with *building up* himself. **But he that prophesieth edifieth the church,** builds up in faith, holy emotion, and activity, the assembled discipleship.

5. But while Paul spoke thus, he would not discourage them in the exercise of any gift, and so he adds, **I would,** or *wish*, **that ye all spake with tongues;** but his preference is that they **prophesied.** And he affirms that prophecy is greater than tongues, unless he that speaketh with tongues **interpret** that which he has spoken, in order that **the church may receive edifying,** *building up*. It appears from this that one might speak in another language, without understanding what he himself said. Also that tongues when interpreted were for edification. It would seem also that tongues were in some intelligible language, and not in some ecstatic jargon, such as took place among the Montanists in ancient, and the Irvingites, in modern times.

6. *But,* **now,** since this is so with tongues without an interpreter, **if I come unto you speaking with tongues, what shall I profit you,** which is the most important thing in the exercise of spiritual gifts (12 : 7), **except I shall speak to you either by revelation,** concerning divine things, or mysteries, received from the unseen world, **or by knowledge,** by deep spiritual insight into truth (12 : 8), **or by prophesying,** unfolding truth in exhortation and consolation as in ver. 3, **or by doctrine,** *teaching*, instructing in longer or continuous discourses. He would be useful to them only as he, as an interpreter, united with tongues one of these four kinds of utterances. Many commentators reduce these to two kinds, classing reve-

7 And even things without life giving sound, whether pipe or harp, except they give a distinction in the sounds, how shall it be known what is piped
8 or harped? For if the trumpet give an uncertain sound, who shall prepare
9 himself to the battle? So likewise ye, except ye utter by the tongue words easy to be understood, how shall it be known what is spoken; for ye shall
10 speak into the air? There are, it may be, so many kinds of voices in the world, and none of them *is* without
11 signification. Therefore if I know not the meaning of the voice, I shall be unto him that speaketh a barbarian, and he that speaketh *shall be* a barbarian unto me.
12 Even so ye, forasmuch as ye are zealous of spiritual *gifts*, seek that ye may excel ᵇ to the edifying of the
13 church. Wherefore let him that speak-

7 prophesying or teaching. Even the lifeless things giving sound, whether pipe or harp, if they give no distinction in the sounds, how shall that which is piped or that which is harped
8 be known? For even if a trumpet give an uncertain sound, who will prepare for war? So also ye, unless ye
9 utter through the tongue speech easy to be understood, how will that which is spoken be known? For ye will be speaking into the air.
10 There are, it may be, so many kinds of voices in the world, and no one is
11 without meaning. If then I know not the force of the voice, I shall be to him that speaks a barbarian, and he that
12 speaks a barbarian to me. So also ye, since ye are eager for spiritual gifts, seek that ye may abound in them to
13 the upbuilding of the church. Where-

ᵇ Ver. 3, 4, 26.

---

lation with prophecy, and knowledge with teaching. They regard revelation and knowledge as means of knowledge, and prophecy and teaching the means of utterance. True, so far as it goes. But notice, Paul supposes that he may *speak* in all these four ways. For convenience however, they may be spoken of generally as prophecy and teaching.

7. The apostle illustrates his argument, showing the uselessness of unintelligible utterances, from the sounds of wind or stringed instruments. Omit **even.** Unless there is **a distinction in the sounds,** the particular notes of the music cannot be recognized. And so the sounds in human speech must be recognized in order to convey any definite ideas.

8. For, to use a stronger illustration, **if the trumpet give an uncertain sound,** an indistinct and obscure sound, **who shall prepare himself to the,** *for*, **battle.** Different sounds indicated different duties in military affairs, such as mustering, attacking, retreating, rallying. But even the clear and loud-sounding trumpet would be useless, if its sounds were indistinct. No clear impression would be conveyed to the mind.

9. Paul applies his argument from analogy. **So likewise ye, except ye utter by the tongue,** as through the musical instruments mentioned, **words easy to be understood,** *intelligible speech*, which has a discernible meaning, **how shall it be known what is spoken.** It will be but sound in **the air,** without reaching the minds of the hearers. Thus far the apostle has shown that u n k n o w n tongues, without an interpreter, are of no profit to others and thus inferior to prophecy.

10. So also without an interpreter tongues tend to confusion (this and nine following verses). Paul further illustrates from the languages of men. **There are, it may be, so many kind of voices,** or *sound in human speech*, **in the world, and none** (omit **of them,** according to the best text) **is without signification,** *is dumb, without meaning*. Every sound in language has its meaning. It is implied here that speaking in tongues was in human language and not jargon.

11. Therefore if I know not the meaning, literally, *the force*, the sense **of the voice,** or *sound*, **I shall be unto him that speaketh a barbarian,** *a foreigner*, whose speech is not intelligible. (Comp. Acts 28:2.)

12. Application of the argument to the Corinthians. **Even so ye,** etc. *So also ye, since ye are earnestly desirous of spiritual gifts*, **seek that ye may** *abound to the building up* **of the church,** in their graces and Christian lives. To do this they would so seek spiritual gifts, and exercise them in such a way, as to intelligently affect the members of the church and profit them.

13. W h e r e f o r e let him that

eth in an *unknown* tongue *pray that
14 he may interpret*. For if I pray in an
unknown tongue, my spirit prayeth, but
15 my understanding is unfruitful. What
is it then? I will pray with the spirit,
and I will pray [d] with the understanding also: *I will sing with the spirit,
and I will sing [f] with the understand-

fore let him that speaks in a tongue
14 pray that he may interpret. For if I
pray in a tongue, my spirit prays, but
15 my understanding is unfruitful. What
is it then? I will pray with the spirit,
and I will pray with the understanding also; I will sing with the spirit,
and I will sing with the understanding

c Ver. 27, 28; 12:10.   d John 4:23, 24.   e Eph. 5:19; Col. 3:16.   f Ps. 47:7.

speaketh in *a tongue*, **pray that he
may interpret.** This last clause has
been interpreted to mean either to
pray for the gift of interpretation, or to
pray in a language that he can interpret. The former seems to me to be the
preferable and most natural meaning,
and in harmony with what follows.
We learn from this passage, that interpretation was a distinct gift (ver. 5;
12:30); that interpretation was not always united with s p e a k i n g w i t h
tongues; and that spiritual gifts were
to be sought after by prayer.

14. For, to confirm and to illustrate
what I have said, **if I pray in** *a tongue*,
which I do not understand, **my spirit
prayeth** under the moving power of
the Holy Spirit. (Comp. Rom. 8:26.) I am
conscious of that, **but my understanding,** my mind, my intellectual
part being destitute of clear ideas, **is
unfruitful,** without benefit to others.
Hence the necessity of praying for the
gift of interpretation (ver. 13).

15. What is it then? What is
the conclusion to be deduced? What
follows? Since speaking with tongues
and interpreting of tongues may go together, Paul would combine them. **I
will pray,** in an unknown tongue,
**with the spirit, and I will pray
with the understanding,** with clear
ideas, so that, as an interpreter, I can
clearly convey them to the minds of
others. So also of singing, in which
the gift of tongues also manifested itself. (Comp. Eph. 5:19.) Paul appears to
have had the gift of interpretation as
well as of prophecy.

WORSHIP IN PRAYER AND SONG.
Prayer does not consist in mere words,
nor in beautiful and sublime expressions. It must be spiritual and intelligent, or it is not prayer. It may be
but a burden, a sigh, a falling tear, but
it must be a conscious expression of a
soul feeling its need, and craving help
from God.

"Prayer is the soul's sincere desire,
 Unuttered or expressed,
The motion of a hidden fire
 That trembles in the breast."

So music is not mere sound, but also
expression. Christian song is more
than harmony, it is worship. Its exercise must be spiritual; it should also
be intelligent. It is not mere art; it is
devotion. Many fail just here, and
mistake æsthetic emotions for devotional
feelings. Thus in prayer and song they
become ritualists rather than true spiritual worshipers.

"Pure, unalloyed musical enjoyment," says Professor Dickinson, "is
not worship, although easily mistaken
for it, and a musical impression disconnected from any other cannot in
the very nature of things conduce to a
spirit of prayer. It is only when the
prayerful mood already exists as the
definite tendency of the mind, induced
by the sense of love and duty, . . or
by any other agencies which turn the
heart of the believer in longing toward
the Mercy Seat—it is only in alliance
with such a state of desire and expectancy that music fulfills its true office in
the sanctuary. . . Certain it is, however, that the spirit of worship must
first exist; music may enhance and
direct it, but cannot be expected to
cause it" ("Bibliotheca Sacra," April,
1897, p. 330).

Art and an æsthetic taste are good in
their place, but they need to be sanctified by the truth and the Holy Spirit.
In worship they should hold a secondary place. In religious song the devotional element should be the controlling power. There should be intelligent service for God, and worship
of God. Many are carried away with
a brilliant ritual; the eye, the ear, the
refined taste are touched, but the heart
is not aroused to true spiritual worship.
They may worship God with their lips
and in melodious sounds, and their
hearts may be far from him. And the

16 ing also. Else when thou shalt bless with the spirit, how shall he that occupieth the room of the unlearned say ᶠ Amen at thy giving of thanks, seeing he understandeth not what thou sayest? 17 For thou verily givest thanks well, but the other is not edified. 18 I thank my God, I speak with tongues 19 more than ye all: yet in the church I had rather speak five words with my understanding, that *by my voice* I might teach others also, than ten thousand words in an *unknown* tongue. 20 Brethren, ʰ be not children in understanding: howbeit in malice be ye

16 also. Else, if thou bless with the spirit, how will he that fills the place of the ungifted say the Amen at thy thanksgiving, since he knows not 17 what thou sayest? For thou indeed givest thanks well, but the other is not 18 built up. I thank God, I speak with 19 tongues more than ye all. But in church I had rather speak five words through my understanding, that I may instruct others also, than ten thousand words in a tongue. 20 Brethren, be not children in understanding; yet in evil be babes, but in your understanding be full grown.

g Neh. 8 : 6.   *h* 3 : 1, 2 ; Rom. 16 : 19 ; Eph. 4 : 14 ; Phil. 1 : 9 ; Heb. 5 : 12, 13.

more art is cultivated, and the more cultured the age and people, the more should the Christian be on his guard. Temptations come through our higher as well as through our lower natures. An old precept that has come down to us from the fourth century is worthy of remembrance: "See that what thou singest with thy lips, thou believest in thy heart; and what thou believest in thy heart, thou dost exemplify in thy life."

16. A further argument for speaking plainly, or combining interpretation with speaking with tongues. **Else** *if thou* **bless with the Spirit,** using an unknown tongue, **how shall he that occupieth** *the place of the unlearned, the ungifted* in understanding tongues, **say Amen at thy giving of thanks?** The response Amen, *so be it*, passed over from the synagogue to Christian assemblies (Neh. 5 : 13 ; Rev. 5 : 14). Some suppose that the thanksgiving at the Lord's Supper is meant; but we should not limit its application here. Justin Martyr, about A. D. 150, speaks of the same response in his day. The word rendered *unlearned*, means here a *private*, one *unlearned*, not understanding unknown tongues, hence *the ungifted*, one who is not a prophet or an interpreter. It has no reference to whether he is an officer or a private member. "This is, as Doddridge has remarked, decisive against the practice of praying and praising in an unknown tongue, as ridiculously practised in the church of Rome" (ALFORD).

17. Paul would not be unfair to any, but would concede a right character to the thanksgiving: **For thou verily givest thanks well,** thou dost excellently in the act, and in the manner and spirit of the action, **but the other,** who is unlearned and ungifted so that he cannot understand, **is not edified,** profited (12 : 7), spiritually instructed and helped.

18. The apostle records his own experience in the case. **I thank** (my, omitted in the best text) **God,** to whom I owe every gift and grace (15 : 10), **I speak with tongues more than you all.** He would not depreciate a gift which had been richly bestowed upon himself, but would gratefully acknowledge God as the giver. Moreover it was not because of deficiency in this that he preferred the gift of prophecy.

19. Yet whatever I may do in private, **in the church,** *in an assembly,* **I had rather speak five words with my understanding,** having a clear idea of what I was saying (ver. 14, 15) in order **that I might teach others also,** *thoroughly instructing* them, **than ten thousand words** *in a tongue* unknown to them. Note the plural *tongues* in ver. 18, and the singular in this, implying that he enjoyed the gift of a plurality of tongues, but spoke only in one at a time. The Spirit in his case was the author of order, not of confusion.

20. Paul appeals to their common sense, and urges them to exercise their mature judgment on the matter. **Brethren, be not children in understanding,** in your faculty of perceiving and judging. A different word from that translated *understanding* in the preceding verses. He would not have them act like children with toys in showing their fondness for the gift of tongues. He would not have them carried away with sound and outward display. **Howbeit** I would not be

children, but in understanding be men.
21 ʲIn the law it is written, With *men of other tongues and other lips will I speak unto this people; and yet for all that will they not hear me, saith the
22 Lord. Wherefore tongues are ᵏ for a sign, not to them that believe, but to them that believe not: but prophesying *serveth* not for them that believe not, ˡ but for them which believe.
23 If therefore the whole church be come together into one place, and all speak with tongues, and there come in

21 In the law it is written,
With men of other tongues, and by lips of strangers,
I will speak to this people:
And not even so will they listen to me, saith the Lord.
22 So that the tongues are for a sign, not to those who believe, but to the unbelieving; but prophecy is not for the unbelieving, but for those who believe.
23 If therefore the whole church is assembled together, and all are speaking with tongues, and there come in those

---

ʲ John 10 : 34. ᵏ Mark 16 : 17; Acts 2 : 6-12. ˡ Ver. 3.

---

misunderstood, nor forget the teachings of my Master (Matt. 18:3), and therefore I add, **in malice,** or *wickedness,* **be ye children,** better, *be ye babes* even, but **in understanding be men,** *be mature,* and of ripe age (Eph. 4 : 14; Heb. 5 : 12).

21. He would have them exercise this mature and sound judgment in what he is about to say. **In the law;** referring to the whole Old Testament, not unusual with Paul, who looked upon the whole Mosaic economy as preparatory to Christ (Rom. 3 : 19; Gal. 3 : 23, 24; 4 : 5). The quotation is from Isa. 28 : 11, 12, partially and freely given. The Jewish priests and judges had complained that Jehovah had given them plain and reiterated teachings, only fit for children; and to this Jehovah responds that he would give them instructors of **other tongues,** namely, the Assyrian armies, yet it would be no benefit to them. Some regard this as a type of the pentecostal tongues. It is however better to take it as an illustration, which the apostle applies to the gift of tongues, from God's providential speaking through foreigners to Judah in chastisement and judgment. **And yet for all that,** etc., *And not even thus will they hear me;* an important part of the quotation, showing that Judah could have heard and should have heard God's providential voice, as well as his plain and simple instructions. The coming of the Assyrian armies would be to them a token of their unbelief in rejecting the words of the Lord. It should remind them of this warning and lead them to repentance, but such would not be the case.

22. Wherefore, according to the lesson taught by this Old Testament incident, **tongues are for a sign,** a convincing sign of God's presence and of his truth. The word translated *sign* is often applied to miracles (see on 1 : 22), indicating their design in authenticating the truth of God and his messengers. So of the miraculous gift of tongues, it was a proof of the presence of God in the opening of the new dispensation and of the truths of the gospel. **Not to them that believe,** for they were already convinced; **but to them that believe not,** who therefore needed some token. Some suppose that Paul teaches that the gift of tongues is a sign of judgment upon incorrigible unbelievers. But this is contrary to history, and unsustained by Paul's words. At Pentecost the gift of tongues was a call to the world to examine this new thing, to acknowledge God in it, and to repent (Acts 2 : 14-21, 38-41). And in the next two verses Paul points out a similar design. Like other calls and tokens, however, it might prove a savor of life or of death (2 Cor. 2 : 16). **But prophesying** (omit **serveth**) *is* **not for them that believe not,** is not a sign to unbelievers, for its higher instructions are not fitted to them, but **for them that believe,** bringing teachings suited to them, and authenticated by the inspiration and revelations of the Spirit.

23. The apostle appeals to facts and illustrates the different effects of all speaking with tongues (this verse), and all prophesying (next verse). **The whole church . . . and all speak with tongues;** must be taken in their popular sense, meaning a full and general assembly, and all who speak using tongues, thus limiting their exercises to that one form of address. The effect on those coming in, who were un-

those that are unlearned, or unbelievers, ᵐ will they not say that ye are mad?
24 But if all prophesy, and there come in one that believeth not, or one unlearned, ⁿ he is convinced of all, he
25 is judged of all: and thus are ᵒthe secrets of his heart made manifest: and so falling down on *his* face he will worship God, and report ᵖ that God is in you of a truth.
26 How is it then, brethren? When ye come together, every one of you hath a psalm, ᵠ hath a doctrine, hath a tongue, hath a revelation, hath an interpretation. ʳ Let all things be done unto edify-
27 ing. If any man speak in an *unknown* tongue, *let it be* by two, or at the most by three, and *that* by course; and let

who are ungifted, or unbelievers, will
24 they not say that ye are mad? But if all are prophesying, and there come in one that is an unbeliever, or ungifted, he is convicted by all, he is judged by
25 all. The secrets of his heart become manifest: and so falling on his face he will worship God, reporting that God is indeed among you.
26 What is it then, brethren? When ye come together, each of you has a psalm, has a teaching, has a revelation, has a tongue, has an interpretation. Let all things be done to upbuilding.
27 If any one speaks in a tongue, let it be by two, or at the most by three, and in

---

m Acts 2:13.   *n* Acts 2:37.   *o* Heb. 4:12.   *p* Isa. 45:14; Zech. 8:23.   *q* Ver. 6; 12:8–10.
r Ver. 12; 12:7; Rom. 14:19; Eph. 4:12.

---

learned, that is, *ungifted* (ver. 16), **or unbelievers,** would be to impress them **that ye are mad,** your tongues would seem to them like the ravings of persons not in their right minds. The effect would thus be bad rather than good.

24. But, on the contrary, **if all prophesy,** the effect upon an unbeliever or an ungifted person would be: **he is convinced of all,** rather, *convicted by all,* who speak in turn, their words penetrating with the Spirit's power, convicting him of his unbelief; **he is judged of all,** *by all,* their words arousing his conscience, leading to self-examination, and producing a sense of condemnation. This accords with the work of the Spirit in convicting of sin, righteousness, and judgment (John 16:8, 9).

25. The words **And thus** are omitted by the best manuscripts and highest authorities, but they do not give a wrong meaning. As a result, **are the secrets of his heart made manifest,** the listener sees his own inner life and spirit uncovered, laid open, not to others but to himself. (Comp. Heb. 4:12, 13; John 4:29.) **And so falling down on his face,** in humble reverence and as an act of homage (comp. Luke 5:12; 17:16; Matt. 26:39; Rev. 11:16) **he will worship God.** He came an unbeliever, but through the Spirit's power and the truth he is converted. **And report,** etc., rather, *reporting that God is really in you* and among you, working in each of you by his Spirit, and manifesting his enlightening power among you.

26–40. DIRECTIONS FOR INSURING DECENCY AND ORDER. These may be reduced to two rules: Let all things be done to edification (ver. 26); and, Let all things be done decently and orderly (ver. 40).

26. How, rather, *What,* **is it then, brethren?** as in ver. 15. What practical result follows? It is implied from what has been said that spiritual gifts must be restricted and guided by wise rules. And the facts are, that **when ye come together,** each of you who take part in your public assemblies has some gift which you wish to exercise: one has **a psalm,** a song of praise (ver. 15); another, **a doctrine,** or a teaching; another, an **unknown tongue;** another, **a revelation** of some mystery or hidden truth, or of the unseen world (ver. 6); another, **an interpretation** of a tongue or of some special truth (ver. 13). Each was anxious to speak as soon as the impulse seized him, forgetful of the common good; and thus disorders arose. In view of this, Paul in the first place enjoins, **Let all things be done unto edifying,** *unto building up* in the faith and the Christian life.

27. According to the above rule he proceeds to give directions, first in regard to the gifts of tongues. **Let it be by two, or at the most by three,** that the congregation be not wearied, and that unbelievers be not injured (ver. 23), **and that by course,** *in turn,* so that there be no confusion; **and let one interpret,** so that there be but one interpretation to each

28 one interpret. But if there be no interpreter, let him keep silence in the church; and let him speak to himself,
29 and to God. Let the prophets speak two or three, and ᵗ let the other judge.
30 If *any thing* ᵗ be revealed to another that sitteth by, let the first hold his
31 peace. For ye may all prophesy one by one, that all may learn, and all
32 may be comforted. And ᵘ the spirits of the prophets are subject to the
33 prophets: for God is not *the author* of

28 turn; and let one interpret. But if there be no interpreter, let him keep silence in church; and let him speak to himself, and to God.
29 And let prophets speak by two or
30 three, and the others judge. But if a revelation be made to another sitting
31 by, let the first keep silence. For ye all can prophesy one by one, that all
32 may learn, and all be exhorted. And spirits of prophets are subject to
33 prophets. For God is not a God of con-

*12 : 10; 1 John 4 : 1-3.   ᵗ Ver. 6, 26.   ᵘ Ver. 29, 30.

speech, and the congregation understand and be benefited.
28. But if there be no interpreter, let him keep silence in the church, in the public assembly, and thus avoid the difficulty, of being no benefit to others, mentioned in ver. 13-17. **Let him speak to himself, and to God,** avoiding what might be but a mere outward display, and contenting himself with inward communion with God. *Silence* however is enjoined only in the public worshiping congregation. There is no prohibition against exercising the gift in private and at home.
29. Directions in regard to prophesying. **Let the prophets speak two or three,** rather, *by two or three,* in turn. The same rule held good of preaching, as of the use of tongues. Two or three addresses took the place of the modern sermon. **And let the others judge,** or *discern,* discriminate the utterances and their value. (Comp. 11 : 29.) The word, *others,* grammatically refers to the rest of the prophets present, probably including the discerner of spirits (12 : 10). The spirits needed to be examined and judged, and the words of the prophets weighed and decided upon, by those spiritually fitted to do it (1 John 4 : 1). In regard to ordinary discourses, outside of spiritual gifts, the whole congregation of believers were to discern their spiritual value for themselves (10 : 15; 11 : 13; 1 John 2 : 20, 27).
30. If anything be revealed, better, *If a revelation be made,* **to another that sitteth by,** the fact of its being thus made indicating its importance, **let the first hold his peace,** *be silent.* The prophet speaking should at once give way, or bring his discourse to a close as soon as he possibly could in an orderly way. The good of the hearers must be kept in view. From this we may infer that the prophetic gift was connected with sudden impulses of inspiration and revelation.
31. Explanatory of the preceding verse. The waiting for the utterance of a fresh revelation need cause no anxiety or trouble, **For ye may,** rather, *can*, **all prophesy one by one,** if not at this meeting, then in subsequent meetings. By *all* is meant all those who should have a gift of prophecy, for all were not prophets (12 : 29). The object of the prophesying would be attained in this orderly way, **that all may learn, and all may be** *exhorted and* **comforted.** This agrees with what is said in ver. 3. The word translated *comforted,* means also to *exhort,* in such passages as Acts 2 : 40; 11 : 23; Rom. 12 : 8. All the prophets would in due time have an opportunity to speak, and all in the assembly would be admonished, consoled, and confirmed.
32. And to show that there need be no difficulty in following these directions, the apostle adds, **And the spirits of the prophets,** their own spirits under the inspiration of the Holy Spirit, **are subject to the prophets,** under their control, so that one can wait for another (ver. 30). Right impulses were to be directed; wrong ones resisted. This distinguishes God's prophets from the uncontrolled impulses of heathen prophets and sibyls, and from the fanaticism of those who have falsely claimed special gifts from God. Not every good emotion is an impulse of the Spirit.
33. And this must be so, **For God is not** *a God* **of confusion,** as would be the case if the prophets under his Spirit could not control themselves,

confusion, but *of peace. ⁷As in all churches of the saints.
34 ¹Let your women keep silence in the churches: for it is not permitted unto them to speak; but ᵇ*they are commanded* to be under obedience, as also saith
35 the ᵇ law. And if they will learn anything, let them ask their husbands at home: for it is a shame for women to speak in the church.

fusion, but of peace, as in all the churches of the saints.
34 Let your women keep silence in the churches; for it is not permitted to them to speak, but let them be in sub-
35 jection, as the law also says. And if they wish to learn anything, let them ask their own husbands at home; for it is shameful for a woman to speak in in church.

z 7 : 15; Rom. 15 : 33.   *y* 11 : 16.   *z* 1 Tim. 2 : 11, 12.
a 11 : 3, 7-9; Eph. 5 : 22; Col. 3 : 18; Titus 2 : 5; 1 Peter 3 : 1.   *b* See refs. Gen. 3 : 16.

but of peace, of harmony and good order; **as it is exemplified in all the churches of the saints.** Some high authorities join the last clause, **as in all**, etc., to the next verse. But it is more in accordance with Paul to place an appeal to general custom at the end of an argument, rather than at the beginning. (See 11 : 16.) Alford, Westcott and Hort, and the Bible Union versions join it to this verse.

34. The apostle advises in regard to the exercise of spiritual gifts by women in the public assembly. This is the most natural view, and to me seems to be the only admissible view. For immediately before (ver. 26-33) and immediately after (ver. 37-40) the subject discussed is spiritual gifts. **Let your women,** who may be possessors of gifts, **keep silence in the churches**—" in the larger and public assemblies of the church, which alone are under consideration in this chapter" (ELLICOTT). They were to exercise that self-control mentioned in ver. 30-32. **For it is not permitted unto them to speak, but they are commanded,** rather, according to the most approved text, *but let them be in subjection,* **as also saith the law,** recorded in Gen. 3 : 16. In 11 : 5, where Paul is not speaking specially of spiritual gifts, but rather of religious exercises in general, he assumes that on certain occasions and under certain circumstances a woman might speak or pray in a meeting. But in 1 Tim. 2 : 12 he says, "I permit not a woman to teach, nor to have authority over a man, but to be in quietness," referring to teaching or preaching in the public assembly. He would not have her do anything that was unbecoming to her position and sphere as a woman, or that would publicly imply authority over man. While in this passage Paul is speaking of the exercise of spiritual gifts in public assemblies, and in 1 Tim. 2 : 12, of preaching, in chap. 11 he may have had reference to smaller and less public meetings; and perhaps to praying and speaking, not only with covered head, but also in an unauthoritative manner, not suggestive of the public teacher or preacher. (See further on next verse.)

35. Additional directions, especially applicable to that age, to the Corinthians and to Oriental countries. **And if they will,** or, *wish to,* **learn anything, let them ask their** *own* **husbands at home,** who were regarded as their natural guides. The speaking of women was forbidden in Jewish synagogues, and while the presence of women was allowed in rabbinical schools they were not to speak or ask questions. Calvin has well remarked "that Paul does not prohibit women in case of need from consulting the prophets, since all husbands were not qualified to give information on such subjects." Yet such was the state of Eastern society that even this, unless carefully done, might lead to scandal. Unmarried women are not mentioned. Abuses had not probably arisen among them, and their greater modesty would keep them from breaking over the usages of society. **For it is a shame,** considered *disgraceful,* against the rules of propriety, **for a woman to speak in the church,** the public assembly. Greek and Roman, as well as Jewish custom, forbade the public speaking of women. In the East women were kept very much in seclusion, and could generally converse only with male relatives; and the same custom largely prevails to the present day. Paul would not have the cause scandalized. He insists upon a respectful regard to the customs of society. As these cus-

36 e What! came the word of God out from you? Or came it unto you only?
37 d If any man think himself to be a prophet, or spiritual, let him acknowledge that the things that I write unto you are the commandments of the
38 Lord: but e If any man be ignorant, let him be ignorant.

36 church. Or, was it from you that the word of God went forth? Or did it come unto you alone?
37 If any one thinks himself to be a prophet, or spiritual, let him recognize the things which I write to you, that they are the Lord's commandment.
38 But if any one is ignorant, let him be

c 4 : 7 ; Isa. 2 : 3.   d 3 : 1 ; 1 John 4 . 6.   e Hosea 4 : 17 ; Matt. 15 : 14 ; 1 Tim. 6 : 3–5.

toms change, his arguments, so far as they rest upon them, are modified, and the conclusions correspondingly modified.

The condition of woman among the Hebrews was superior to that among the heathen. There seems to have been comparative freedom of intercourse between the sexes in the early periods, though in later periods it was restricted. An important place was accorded woman in worship. "The Lord giveth the word; the women that publish the tidings are a great host" (Ps. 68 : 11, Revised ver. Comp. Exod. 15 : 20 ; 1 Sam. 18 : 6). Christianity has ever been favorable to woman, giving her the position accorded her at creation, that of social equality with man (Gal. 3 : 28). It recognizes her importance in worship (Mark 14 : 9; Luke 23 : 49 ; John 20 : 1 ff. ; Acts 1 : 14). The woman of Samaria successfully bore the glad tidings of Jesus as the Messiah to the citizens of Sychar (John 4 : 39–41). Dorcas was noted for her work of charity among the sick and the poor (Acts 9 : 36–39); Priscilla expounded the way of God more perfectly to Apollos (Acts 18 : 26); and Paul refers to Phœbe, Persis, and other women, as efficient fellow-helpers (Rom. 16 : 1, 12 ; Phil. 4 : 3, 4). But preaching which is unofficial is not to be restricted to ministers of the word. It is the function of all Christians, and it should be adapted to all human states and conditions. All as they have opportunity should tell the glad tidings (Acts 8 : 4). Both men and women should, in suitable ways, testify of the grace of God, according to their ability and their experiences and knowledge of divine things. There are abundant ways and opportunities, among the many classes of people, for all to find employment of the talents God has given them. But see Practical Remark 30, at the end of the chapter.

36. From this point to the end of the chapter we have a general conclusion to the discussion on spiritual gifts. Throughout the Epistle there are indications that the Corinthians had taken a course independent of other churches, and of Paul himself. This was probably the case in the exercise of spiritual gifts. He therefore reminds them : **What, or** Or, **came the word of God out from you?** It did not originate with you, nor did it first come through you. **Or came it unto you only,** *to you alone?* These very questions would remind them that they had received the gospel through the ministry of Paul; and that other churches had equal rights with them; and that all were amenable to the commands of the Lord.

37. Paul gives a test which would at once set aside the claims of arrogant and presumptuous teachers. **If any one think himself to be a prophet** (12 : 29), **or spiritual,** endowed with spiritual gifts, **let him acknowledge,** or *let him recognize the things I am writing that they are the Lord's commandment,* that is, of Christ. Paul emphatically affirms his own inspiration, and that in prescribing these regulations, especially the two rules given in verses 26 and 40, he had the mind of Christ and acted under the authority of Christ (2 : 16 ; 7 : 40 ; 11 : 2). Willingness to submit to Christ and to obey his command, as revealed by his word or his inspired apostles, were a necessary qualification of the true prophet or teacher.

38. With severity Paul proceeds. **If any man be ignorant** of the things I write, that they are the Lord's commandment, such willful ignorance and insubordination are hopeless ; **let him be ignorant,** I give him no more concern; it is a matter of indifference to me. Another reading with much manuscript authority has the last verb in the indicative instead of the imperative: *he is not known,* that

39 Wherefore, brethren, *covet to prophesy, and forbid not to speak with
40 tongues. *Let all things be done decently and in order.

39 ignorant. Wherefore, my brethren, desire earnestly to prophesy, and for-
40 bid not to speak with tongues. But let all things be done becomingly and in order.

f Ver. 1; 12:31.   *g* Ver. 26-33.

is, of God, he is ignored or disregarded by him. The verse may then be rendered, *If any man disregard them*, the things I am writing, *he is disregarded* of God (8:3). God will disregard him who disregards the directions of his inspired apostles. But the first and common reading seems preferable. Paul speaks with apostolic authority, and will waste no time with willful, ignorant opposers (11:16).

39. Wherefore, brethren, to sum up what has been said on this whole subject of spiritual gifts, **covet,** *desire earnestly* (12:31), **to prophesy,** without discouraging the speaking with tongues. This was advice to them both as a church and as individuals. Prophesying was to be sought after, yet speaking with tongues was not to be treated as undesirable.

40. According to the best text: *But* in all this exercising of gifts, **let all things be done decently,** *becomingly*, according to the rules of propriety, **and in order,** not tumultuously, but at the right time and place. This is Paul's second rule (ver. 26).

WAS THE HOLY SPIRIT IN THE OLD DISPENSATION, AND IN THE NEW. It is evident that the Holy Spirit was enjoyed in some measure under the old dispensation from the fact that prophets spoke as they were moved by him (2 Peter 1:21), and from such passages of Scripture as that uttered by Stephen, "Ye do always resist the Holy Spirit: as your fathers did, so do ye" (Acts 7:51). But wherein was the difference in respect to the Spirit's bestowment then and now?

(1) There was a difference as to *the extent* of the bestowment. The special power of the Spirit was granted to but few, to prophets—to such as Enoch, who "walked with God," and Moses, with whom Jehovah spake, as it were, "face to face," and who was permitted to behold some of his glory (Exod. 33:11, 18-23). In accord with this is the exclamation of Moses, "Would God that all the Lord's people were prophets, and that the Lord would put his Spirit upon them" (Num. 11:29). But now the presence of his Spirit is general and universal. "It shall come to pass in the last days, saith God, I will pour of my Spirit *upon all flesh*," etc. (Acts 2:17-21). (2) Another difference has respect to the *permanency* of the Spirit's presence. The manifestations of his presence then were comparatively few and far between. Prophets had their seasons of his presence and his absence; and there were times when there was no prophet in Israel, as between the days of Malachi and John the Baptist. But now the Spirit is among believers, and is to continue with them. "I will pray the Father, and he will give you another Comforter, that he may *abide with you forever*" (John 14:16). But (3) the great difference is in *the relative power* of the Spirit's manifestations. Souls were regenerated by the Spirit then as well as now. David recognized the creation of a clean heart and the renewing of a right spirit (Ps. 51:10). Abraham's faith was accounted to him for righteousness (Gen. 15:6), and thus he was justified, as were all who exercised a like faith. But justification implied regeneration. The two are inseparable. But while they were regenerated, their conversion was only into the light of the Old Dispensation. They lived under the shadow of the law, with types, sacrifices, and symbols. They were pupils in their minority, under the tutelage of the law; and the promises they saw afar off. But now regenerated souls are converted into the fuller light and on the higher plane of the gospel. Passing out from the tutelage of the law they enter upon the privileges of sonship under the gospel. They behold types and promises fulfilled in a risen, living, glorified Jesus. The Spirit takes and shows the things of Christ unto them (John 16:14, 15). He reveals to them things that eye had not seen, nor ear heard, nor had entered into the heart of man, the things that God had prepared for them that love

him (1 Cor. 2 : 9). This may be illustrated by the disciples before and after Pentecost.

A few words upon the difference between the Pentecostal enjoyment of the Spirit and that enjoyed at the present day. The prophecy of Joel had a special fulfillment in the pentecostal coming of the Spirit, but it also had reference to the whole period of the dispensation of the Spirit, until that great and notable day of the Lord should come (Acts 2 : 17-21). The pentecostal blessing was the fulfillment, not of the prophecy of Joel alone, but also the predictions of John the Baptist (Matt. 3 : 11), and of Christ himself (Luke 24 : 49). It was the baptism in the Spirit, the public manifestation of the church to the world, the ushering in of the gospel dispensation of the Spirit. It was fitting that it should be attended with miraculous gifts, the evidences of the presence and power of the Spirit. These continued for a time, and having answered their design, gradually passed away with the apostolic age. But all that was essential to the Spirit's presence and work among men remained. Indeed, the ordinary gifts and manifestations of the Spirit are oftener spoken of in the Epistles, and are more highly prized than the extraordinary ones. Above all miraculous gifts stand faith, hope, and love, and the greatest of these is love (1 Cor. 13 : 13). Believers are a royal priesthood, and stand on a level with the highest favored of the old dispensation, and above them in their relation to Christ and in their understanding of the great truths and mysteries of the gospel. This is their high privilege, but alas, how many fail to realize it! How many still live under the shadow of the old dispensation!

PRACTICAL REMARKS.

1. We must dwell in love. All our spiritual exercises and labors should be in the spirit of love (ver. 1; 1 John 4 : 16).

2. In speaking with tongues the Holy Spirit enabled the human spirit to utter prayer and praise to God in foreign languages (ver. 2, 13-16; Acts 2 : 11).

3. Prophecy was the greatest of the supernatural gifts to the apostolic church, because of its wide-embracing duties and its usefulness (ver. 3, 5, 19, 25, 39).

4. Spiritual gifts and talents are valuable in proportion to their usefulness (ver. 4-6, 19).

5. "The most brilliant accomplishments are worthless unless they are consecrated to the promotion of the cause of God in the world" (PENDLETON, ver. 5, 6, 9).

6. The various services in public worship should be plain and simple, and in a language understood by the worshipers (ver. 9, 16, 23, 28).

7. In the gift of tongues we see the power of the Spirit to reach all men and use all languages (ver. 7, 10-13 ; Acts 2 : 2-11 ; Matt. 28 : 19, 20).

8. In the gift of tongues and other supernatural gifts we get a glimpse of the greater things which God's children are to enjoy in the future world (ver. 7-16; 1 John 3 : 2; 2 Cor. 5 : 4).

9. In the supernatural endowments of the early church we have the symbolism of the future renewed and perfected humanity, in which boundless diversity will be harmoniously united (ver. 1-19; Rev. 7 : 9-12).

10. The chief object of the ministry, in studying different languages, should be to understand and express the truths of God the more clearly (ver. 10-12; Col. 4 : 2-6).

11. We should strive to excel in those things which build one another up in Christian doctrine and practice, in faith and holy living (ver. 12-14; 1 Thess. 5 : 11; Eph. 4 : 29; 2 Cor. 13 : 10).

12. Prayer should be from the heart, and public prayer in such language as can be understood and can be devoutly and silently entered into by the congregation (ver. 15, 16; Eph. 6 : 18).

13. Singing praises to God is an important part of Christian worship, and should be performed from the heart, and so enunciated in words as to be understood by, and profitable to, others (ver. 15; Col. 3 : 16; Eph. 5 : 19).

14. The audible "amen" is a beautiful and fitting endorsement by the congregation at the close of public prayer (ver. 16; 1 Chron. 16 : 36; Rev. 5 : 14 ; 19 : 4).

15. Preachers of the gospel, to be effective, must be understood by the hearers, and therefore they should study simplicity in style and language (ver. 19; 2 Cor. 4 : 2).

16. It is childish to be carried away with

showy gifts or external display, or with anything which does not minister to building up the life or purifying the heart (ver. 20; Eph. 4 : 13-16).

17. The gift of tongues was a miracle of the Holy Spirit at the beginning of the gospel dispensation, attesting his presence and power and in proof of the Christian religion to unbelievers (ver. 21, 22; Acts 10 : 46, 47).

18. The preacher should ever keep in view the good of all classes of his hearers, the building up of saints, and the conversion of sinners (ver. 22-24; 1 Tim. 5 : 1, 2).

19. The preached word in the hands of the Spirit comes with convincing power to the hearts of sinners (ver. 25; Acts 2 : 37; Heb. 4 : 12).

20. All religious services and worship, to be effective in glorifying God and benefiting men, must be under the guidance of the Holy Spirit (ver. 27-33; John 16 : 7-15).

21. It is evident that the apostles and early missionaries did not depend on the gift of tongues in preaching the gospel to the heathen (ver. 5, 13, 14, 16, 23, 28; Acts 14 : 11-14).

22. True religion is imbued with the Spirit of God, and leads to peace and decorum, and not to discord and tumult (ver. 27-33; Rom. 14 : 17).

23. Religious services should be both orderly and seasonable, noted neither for great length nor for great brevity (ver. 27-31).

24. The duty of silence in religious services is as imperative as the duty of speaking (ver. 28, 30, 34; Acts 15 : 12; Eccl. 3 : 7).

25. No preacher can claim that all he speaks is the truth unless he can give good reasons for it (ver. 29; 1 Tim. 4 : 11-16; Titus 2 : 7, 8).

26. Every Christian has the right of examining and weighing the truth for himself, and this he should do candidly, prayerfully, and earnestly (ver. 29; 1 Thess. 5 : 21; Acts 17, 11; 1 John 4 : 1).

27. Full liberty should be given at proper times and places for the exercise of the various talents of believers, provided it can be done to edification (ver. 31, 39).

28. The gift of prophecy and inspiration was bestowed on persons in harmony with their natural endowments, and did not interfere with self-control and free agency, and it was to be exercised in a reasonable manner (ver. 32, 33; Rev. 22 : 8, 9).

29. True religion is not boisterous, but orderly, peaceful, and thoughtful. The religious character of gatherings that are confused, noisy, and tumultuous, may well be questioned (ver. 33, 34; Acts 19 : 32-34).

30. Woman has an important sphere in church work; but it is more private than public in character. The question of her entering the public ministry is not one of native talent, mental and executive ability, eloquence, or pleasing address, but of a Divine call to the work, and of the teaching of the word of God. There is also a reason in the divine fitness of things. She should ever act consistently with the headship of man and her position as his helpmate (ver. 34, 35; Acts 9 : 39; 1 Tim. 2 : 11, 12).

31. The husband is the natural head of the family; and it is the duty of the Christian husband to try and fit himself for leadership in his household (ver. 35; 11 : 8).

32. Christ is our Lawgiver, and it is the part of the church not to make laws but to execute them (ver. 36).

33. The Lord's commands are supreme, and the inspired apostles derived their authority from him and spoke in his name (ver. 37; Acts 4 : 19; Gal. 1 : 1, 12).

34. A true prophet is shown by his regard for God's word (ver. 37; Jer. 23 : 28).

35. When the preacher has proclaimed the truth, he can then leave the responsibility upon his hearers (ver. 38; Acts 20 : 26, 27).

36. As in nature so in religion there is a divine order, and he who adapts himself the best to it, accomplishes the most for God and men (ver. 40; 1 Tim. 3 : 15).

37. While we are not to be slaves to custom, nor yield to that which may be opposed to God's word, yet in things indifferent and in customs which may largely accord with the word of God and the nature of things, we should have regard to the usages of the age and country in which we live (ver. 34-40; 11 : 13-16).

The Christian doctrine of the resurrection of the dead.

15 MOREOVER, brethren, I declare unto you the gospel ᵇ which I preached unto you, ⁱ which also ye have received, 2 and ᵏ wherein ye stand ; ˡ by which also ye are saved, ᵐ if ye keep in memory what I preached unto you ; unless 3 ⁿ ye have believed in vain. For ᵒ I delivered unto you first of all that which I also received, ᑫ how that Christ died for our sins ʳ according to the Scrip-

15 NOW I make known to you, brethren, the gospel which I preached to you, which also ye received, in which also 2 ye stand ; through which also ye are saved, if ye hold fast with what word I preached to you, unless ye believed 3 in vain. For I delivered to you first of all what I also received, that Christ died for our sins according to the

b Acts 13 : 1-16. *i* 1 : 4–8. *k* Rom. 5 : 2. *l* 1 : 21; Rom. 1 : 16. *m* John 8 : 31, 32 ; Col. 1 : 23. *n* Luke 8 : 13; James 2 : 20. *o* 11 : 23; Gal. 1 : 12. *q* 1 Peter 2 : 24. *r* See refs. Luke 24 : 26, 44–46 ; Acts 3 : 18.

CHAPTER XV.

This is one of the most wonderful chapters, not only in this Epistle, but in all of Paul's writings. It is the fullest and most forcible discussion in the New Testament of the doctrine of the resurrection. Some among the Corinthians doubted the resurrection of the dead (ver. 12), which fact had been told the apostle by those visiting him from Corinth, or communicated to him by letter with a request for his views thereon (7 : 1). The apostle begins by presenting Christ's resurrection as the primal theme of his preaching (ver. 1-4), and establishes it as a historical fact (ver. 5-11). He then proves that Christ's resurrection implies a general resurrection (ver. 12-19), both of which are essential to the scheme of redemption (ver. 20-28). The doctrine he fortifies by an appeal to the lives of believers (ver. 29-34). He then discusses the manner of the resurrection, and the nature of the resurrection body (ver. 35-49), and finally enlarges on the results of the resurrection (ver. 50-58).

1-11. THE RESURRECTION OF CHRIST A HISTORICAL FACT, AND THE CHIEF THEME OF PAUL'S PREACHING.

1. Moreover, *And* or *Now*, turning to a new subject. There appears to be no connection between this and what precedes. Paul reserves this most important subject to the last. **I declare,** *make known to you*, as you need instruction. (See on 12 : 3.) **The gospel,** the glad tidings of salvation (ver. 2), of which Christ's resurrection is a fundamental doctrine (ver. 3, 4). **Which also you** (omit have) **received** at your conversion. **Wherein ye** *now* **stand,** firm, maintaining the faith, so far as Christ is concerned. They had not fallen from their faith in Christ (10 : 12), but had resisted the assaults of unbelief (2 Cor. 1 : 24 ; Eph. 6 : 13–16).

2. By, or *through*, **which** gospel (ver. 1) **also ye are saved,** are being saved now, looking toward final salvation from sin and its consequences, **if ye keep in memory,** rather, *if ye hold fast the word*, the discourse, *with which I preached to you*, **unless ye have believed,** rather, *unless ye believed* in vain to no purpose ; unless your faith was fruitless and worthless (Gal. 3 : 4 ; 4 : 11) which is hardly to be supposed. The apostle regards a saving faith to be more than a momentary or intellectual exercise, to include a spiritual taking hold of and holding fast (Luke 8 : 15 ; Heb. 3 : 6, 14 ; 10 : 23) the great theme of his preaching, which was a suffering, dying, and risen Christ (ver. 3, 4), unless faith be altogether vain (ver. 14). The above **what I preached,** more exactly, *with what word*, discourse, instruction, *I preached to you* pointing not only to the theme, but also to the kind of theme. Paul emphasizes the gospel as he presented it (Gal. 1 : 8 ; Rom. 2 : 16 ; 16 : 25)

3. For, to explain what he had made known and preached to them (ver. 1, 2). **I delivered unto you first of all,** *chiefly*, **that which I also received** from the Lord (11 : 23), **how that Christ died for our sins,** *on account of, for the sake of*, our sins, in order to atone for them (Rom. 5 : 8–10 ; 3 : 23–26) **according to the Scriptures.** (Comp. Luke 24 : 27 ; Ps. 22 : 1 ; Isa. 53 : 1 ff. ; Zech. 12 : 10.) Notice how Paul begins the account of his gospel, not with Christ's birth, but with his death.

4 tures; and that he was buried, and that he rose again the third day according to the Scriptures; *and that

4 Scriptures; and that he was buried, and that he has been raised on the third day, according to the Scriptures;

*Ps. 2:7; 16:10; Isa. 53:10; Hosea 6:2; Luke 24:26, 34–43, 46; Acts 26:22, 23. †Luke 24:34.

This agrees with his preaching "Jesus Christ and him crucified" (2:2; 5:7; 8:11); and with the general tenor of his Epistles in chiefly insisting upon the death and resurrection of our Lord (Eph. 1:7–23; Col. 1:14–23; Rom. 6:1–4; 1 Tim. 3:16). Paul's Christ was not so much the living Jesus on earth as the exalted and living one in heaven.

THE CHRIST OF PAUL THE SAME AS THE CHRIST OF THE GOSPELS. None of Paul's Epistles touch so much upon gospel history as do those to the Corinthians. What then is their testimony upon the question, Does Paul's representation of Christ agree with that of the Gospels?

In answer it may be said that no real incongruity has been shown to exist. It should be noted however, (1) that when Paul wrote these Epistles he was dependent mostly, or wholly, on revelations from the Lord and oral Gospels handed down from eye and ear-witnesses of the Lord. None of the Gospels were then written except perhaps the Hebrew or Aramaic Gospel of Matthew, and there is no evidence that he had ever seen a copy of that. (2) Paul goes beyond all the Gospels, written or oral, in dwelling especially upon the risen, living Christ (2 Cor. 5:16). A general agreement prevails, however, as the following will show.

In regard to the *person* of Christ, Paul represents him in his humanity as the "second Adam," and in his divinity as the "one Lord Jesus Christ by whom are all things and we by him" (8:6). He appeals to him as the Lord, the one who has Divine authority (7:10; Matt. 28:18). As to his *character*, he speaks of him as the truth, the embodiment of truthfulness, through whom the promises of God are "yea and amen" (2 Cor. 1:20; John 18:37). Also of "the meekness and gentleness of Christ" (2 Cor. 10:1), and of his sinless life (2 Cor. 5:21; John 8:46). As to *doctrines*, Paul taught repentance (2 Cor. 7:10) and faith (15:2), and regeneration (2 Cor. 5:17), and adoption, God "our Father" and we his children (1:3), and the salvation of believers through the preaching of the cross (1:18, 24; John 3:14, 15). Paul regarded Christ as the way to the Father, and the knowledge of God and of Jesus Christ as eternal life (2 Cor. 3:18; 4:1–4; John 15:9, 10; 17:3). So also as to what Christ did for us. For our sakes he became poor (2 Cor. 8:9; Luke 9:58). He was our Passover, sacrificed for us (5:7; John 1:29), dying for our sins (15:3; Matt. 20:28), and made sin for us (2 Cor. 5:21; John 10:10, 14, 15). And what he does for us now, by the Holy Spirit in the hearts of believers (2:14; 6:19; John 14:26, etc.).

Many of Paul's words and phrases appear to have been quoted or molded from the words of the Lord Jesus. For instance, such expressions as they who "preach the gospel should live of the gospel" (9:14; Luke 10:7); "being reviled we bless" (4:12; Luke 6:28); "the saints will judge the world" (6:2; Luke 22:30); "though I have all faith so as to remove mountains" (13:2; Matt. 17:20). The same holds true as to his teaching concerning marriage and divorce (7:10 ff.; Matt. 5:32, etc.); concerning love as a grace or virtue (13:1 ff.; John 15:9, 10); as to the distinction between the letter and the spirit (2 Cor. 3:6; John 6:63). And finally, not to refer to other passages, we may mention Paul's account of the Lord's Supper (11:23–26), and of his appearances to the disciples after his resurrection (15:3–8).

All this, and much more that might be adduced, shows that Paul did not preach another gospel.

4. And that he was buried and that he rose again, rather, *that he hath been raised*, implying that he is alive, **the third day.** The tense of the first verb relates to the single act of Christ's burial; that of the second verb to his continued resurrection life. **According to the Scriptures.** Of course the Old Testament Scriptures, which were to him an infallible standard of appeal. (See Ps. 16:10; Isa. 53:10; Hosea 6:2; Jonah 2:10.) It should be noticed that it is distinctly said that he *was buried*; and the four Gospels give a distinct account of his burial. Thus there could be no doubt of his death;

5 he was seen of Cephas, then of the
6 twelve: after that, he was seen of
above five hundred brethren at once;
of whom the greater part remain unto
this present, but some are fallen asleep.
7 After that, he was seen of James; then
8 of all the apostles. And last of all
he was seen of me also, as of one born
9 out of due time. For I am the least
of all the apostles, that am not meet to

5 and that he appeared to Cephas, then
6 to the twelve; then he appeared to
above five hundred brethren at once,
of whom the greater part remain until
7 now, but some are fallen asleep. After
that, he appeared to James; then to all
8 the apostles. And last of all, as if to
the one born out of due time, he ap-
9 peared to me also. For I am the least
of the apostles, who am not fit to be

u Matt. 28 : 17; Mark 16 : 14; Acts 10 : 41.
y 9 : 1; Acts 9 : 4, 17 ; 22 : 14, 17, 18.

x Luke 24 : 50; Acts 1 : 2–12.
z Eph. 3 : 8.

he really entered the grave, and his soul descended into the regions of the dead (Acts 2 : 29–31), from both of which he came forth in his resurrection. Compare Acts 28 : 23, where we have an account of Paul's preaching the gospel to the Jews at Rome.

5. In this whole passage Paul speaks as one who knew and believed what he said. His words are not those of a fanatic, nor of an impostor, but are the utterances of truth and soberness (Acts 26 : 25). He now proceeds to prove the resurrection of Christ as a historical fact. **And that he was seen of Cephas,** the Aramaic form of the Greek name, Peter (John 1 : 42; Gal. 1 : 18), **then of the twelve,** a frequent designation of the company of the apostles (Matt. 26 : 20; Acts 6 : 2, etc.). These two appearances were on the day that Jesus rose, there being five appearances recorded for that day: (1) To Mary Magdalene (Mark 16 : 9 ; John 20 : 11) ; (2) to the other women (Matt. 28 : 9, 10) ; (3) to Peter (Luke 24 : 34; 1 Cor. 15 : 5) ; (4) to the two on their way to Emmaus (Mark 16 : 12; Luke 24 : 13) ; (5) to the apostles, Thomas being absent (Mark 16 : 14; Luke 24 : 36; John 20 : 19; 1 Cor. 15). A week later he appeared to the apostles, Thomas being present (John 20 : 26).

6. After that he was seen, rather, *he appeared*, **to above five hundred brethren at once.** This was probably on a mountain in Galilee (Matt. 28 : 16) by a special appointment of our Lord (Matt. 28 : 7; Mark 16 : 7), when he gave the last Commission (Matt. 28 : 16; Mark 16 : 15). See author's "Harmony of the Gospels," § 199, and note. **The greater part remain unto this present.** It was probably early in A. D. 58 when Paul wrote this, twenty-eight years after our Lord's resurrection, less than a generation. Thus there were many then living who saw Christ with their own eyes after he had risen. (See also next two verses.) "This was not done in a corner" (Acts 26 : 26). Jerusalem was easy of access from Corinth, and the apostle's assertions could have been easily disproved if disproof were possibly.

7. After that he was seen of, *appeared to,* **James,** brother of our Lord, writer of the Epistle of James, and pastor of the church at Jerusalem (Acts 15 : 13; see note on Acts 12 : 17). James may have believed on Jesus before the resurrection, and certainly believed after it (John 7 : 5), and our Lord appeared to him to prepare him for his great work at Jerusalem as a witness of the resurrection. While not called among the Twelve, he seems to have stood on a level with them at Jerusalem (Gal. 2 : 9). **Then of all the apostles,** doubtless the one recorded in Acts 1 : 9–12, at the ascension.

8. And last of all he was seen, better, *he appeared to me also* (Acts 9 : 17; 22 : 14; 26 : 16) near the gate of Damascus. **As of one born out of due time,** better, *As it were to the one untimely born*, of immature birth. The apostle's meaning is explained in the next verse, he presents himself as inferior to the rest of the apostles, like a small and weakly child, immature and unshapely. Some commentators notice here the suddenness, and strangeness of Paul's conversion, unparalleled in Scripture and in the church of God; coming into the apostle's office without a period of growth (Acts 26 : 14–18), while the Twelve had a previous companionship with Jesus (Luke 6 : 13).

9. Paul explains his language of self-reproach, and the reason for using it. In his great humiliation at having **persecuted the church of God** (Acts 7 : 58; 8 : 3), he speaks of himself as **the least of the apostles,** in rank,

he called an apostle, because "I perse-
10 cuted the church of God. But ᵇ by the grace of God I am what I am: and his grace which *was bestowed* upon me was not in vain; but ᶜ I laboured more abundantly than they all: ᵈ yet not I, but the grace of God which was with
11 me. Therefore whether *it were* I or they, so we preach, and so ye believed.
12 Now if Christ be preached that he rose from the dead, ᵉ how say some among you that there is no resurrec-

called an apostle, because I persecuted
10 the church of God. But by God's grace I am what I am; and his grace which was bestowed upon me did not prove vain; but I labored more abundantly than they all; yet not I, but the
11 grace of God with me. Whether then it be I or they, so we preach, and so ye believed.
12 But if Christ is preached that he has been raised from the dead, how say some among you that there is no resur-

---

a Acts 8 : 3 ; 9 : 1 ; Gal. 1 : 13 ; 1 Tim. 1 : 13.   *b* Eph. 3 : 7, 8 ; 1 Tim. 1 : 12–16.
c Rom. 15 : 17–20 ; 2 Cor. 11 : 23–30 ; 12 : 11.
d Matt. 10 : 20 ; 2 Cor. 3 : 5 ; Gal. 2 : 8 ; Eph. 3 : 7 ; Phil. 2 : 13 ; Col. 1 : 28, 29.   *e* Acts 17 : 18 ; 26 : 8.

---

in his own estimation; **and not meet,** *not fit,* **to be called an apostle.** He felt himself unworthy of even the name of an apostle (Eph 3 : 8; Gal. 1 : 13; 1 Tim. 1 : 13). *The church of God* refers primarily to the church at Jerusalem (Acts 8 : 3 ; 9 : 1), where his persecution began and from which place it proceeded. The church there represented the early discipleship generally, and, at the time of the death of Stephen and the subsequent persecution, it was probably the only church in the world. (See Acts 9 : 31, and note.)

10. Paul admits his personal inferiority to the other apostles, but he magnifies the grace of God that wrought through him. **But by the grace of God I am what I am,** whatever I am God's grace has made me, I owe all to the undeserved favor of God. And this grace **was not in vain,** was not without fruit. This is the negative side. **But,** on the positive side, **I laboured more abundantly than they all,** than the other apostles, any one of them individually. The Twelve, who labored more especially among the Jews, had a more circumscribed field than Paul in his extended Gentile work. The mission among the Gentiles had also its greater difficulties. But while he thus refers to the greatness of his work, he takes no glory to himself. **Yet not I** alone have accomplished this, **but the grace of God which was with me,** rather, according to the most approved text, *but the grace of God with me,* working effectively with me, wrought this. Paul was conscious of his own agency, but also of his dependence on God's gracious help, as the most important factor. (Comp. 3 : 9 ; 2 Cor. 3 : 5 ; Eph. 3 : 7 ; Phil. 2 : 12, 13.)

11. Paul returns to the great theme of preaching from this digression regarding himself and the other apostles. He was conscious of opposition, but this would weaken in view of his humility. Neither would he care for it. **Therefore whether it were I or they,** the other apostles, who labored most, there is an agreement in our preaching and in your believing. **So we preach, and so ye believed,** at your conversion, that Christ died, was buried, and rose again (ver. 3, 4).

12-19. THE RESURRECTION OF CHRIST IMPLIES THE RESURRECTION OF ALL BELIEVERS. IT IS A FUNDAMENTAL FACT IN THE CHRISTIAN RELIGION. The reference is specially to the resurrection of believers. The resurrection of the wicked is elsewhere taught (John 5 : 29 ; Acts 24 : 15).

12. The apostle takes the resurrection of Christ as an established fact, accepted by the Corinthian Church. His whole argument proceeds upon the supposition that this was not a matter of controversy. **Now if Christ be preached,** *But,* as it is an actual fact that Christ is preached, **that he rose from the dead, how** is it possible *that some among you say* **there is no resurrection of the dead,** or more strictly, *of dead men?* The reference is to a future general resurrection. The verse is a question implying surprise at such views, which carried to their logical conclusion must also deny Christ's resurrection (ver. 13, 14).

It has been much discussed as to the persons here meant and their phase of belief. Outside of early Christians, the Pharisees and certain portions of the Jews, there was a general disbelief

13 tion of the dead? But if there be no resurrection of the dead, *f* then is Christ
14 not risen: and if Christ be not risen, then *is* our preaching vain, and your
15 faith *is* also vain. Yea, and we are found false witnesses of God; because *g* we have testified of God that he raised up Christ: whom he raised not up, if
16 so be that the dead rise not. For if the dead rise not, then is not Christ raised:
17 and if Christ be not raised, your faith
18 *is* vain; *h* ye are yet in your sins. Then they also which are *i* fallen asleep in

13 rection of dead men? But if there is no resurrection of dead men, then
14 neither has Christ been raised; and if Christ has not been raised, then is our preaching vain, vain also your faith.
15 And we are found also false witnesses of God; because we testified in respect to God, that he raised up the Christ; whom he raised not, if it be so that no
16 dead are raised up. For if no dead are raised up, neither has Christ been
17 raised; and if Christ has not been raised, your faith is vain; ye are yet in
18 your sins. Then they also who have fallen asleep in Christ have perished.

f 1 Thess. 4 : 14. *g* Acts 2 : 24, 32; 4 : 10, 33, 13 : 30–37. *h* Rom. 4 : 25. Heb. 9 : 22–28.
i 1 Thess. 4 : 13, 14; Rev. 14 : 13.

in a bodily resurrection. The Sadducees among the Jews and the Epicureans among the heathen, held to the non-existence of man after death. The Stoics taught the pantheistic doctrine, the reabsorption of the soul into divinity. The Platonists maintained the immortality of the soul, but regarded matter as the cause of all evil, and the resurrection of the body as unreasonable. Among Christians, a little later than this, were some, like Hymenæus and Philetus (2 Tim. 2 : 17, 18), who held that the resurrection was already past, and that it was a spiritual quickening through Christ, perverting the teaching of Paul (Col. 3 : 1). The Gnostics later still held a similar heresy. It is probable that these, to whom Paul refers at Corinth, were mostly Gentile Christians, and perhaps some Jews of Sadduceean tendency, to whom the doctrine of a bodily resurrection appeared inadmissible, strange, or unwelcome (Acts 4 : 2; 5 : 17; 23 : 6–9; 17 : 32). It is possible that some of them belonged to the Christ's party (1 : 12). They seem to have held to a future life, and Paul's general argument, based on Christ's resurrection, was well suited to bring conviction to his opponents, whatever might have been the origin and phase of their error.

13. Paul shows the absurdity of the assertion of his opponents. **But if there be no resurrection of** *dead men*, then the reasons which would prove that would prove that **Christ is not risen,** which you are not ready to admit, and which is not to be thought of in view of the many proofs of his resurrection.

14. **And,** to carry out the thought logically, **if Christ be not risen,** and is still dead, **then is our preaching** a risen Christ and Saviour **vain,** unmeaning and useless, **and your faith,** which you have been exercising in the Author of life (Acts 3 : 15; 5 : 31), **is also vain,** since you have been exercising it upon a dead man. If dead, he could not be the Son of God with power (Rom. 1 : 4). The whole gospel is subverted.

15. **And,** terrible for us, **we are found false witnesses,** not mistaken, but *false* witnesses **of God,** concerning him, professing to witness for him; **because we have willfully testified** *in respect to* **God, that he raised up Christ,** a monstrous supposition, if not true. **Whom he raised not up, if so be the dead rise not.** If no dead are raised, then Christ is not raised. The resurrection of Christ is true or false. If the latter, then Peter, James, John, the other apostles, and Paul himself, were impostors; and the five hundred also who had joined them in their testimony—a most absurd and incredible supposition.

16. Repetition of the argument of ver. 13, for precision and emphasis, and for the purpose of carrying out the inference further in the next verse.

17. **And if Christ be not raised** (as in ver. 14), **vain,** empty and useless is **your faith** in him as a Redeemer and Saviour. **Ye are yet in your sins,** condemned and unforgiven, and exposed to all their terrible consequences. A dead Christ cannot atone for sin, nor justify the ungodly (Rom. 4 : 25).

18. And worse still. The darkness of the picture deepens; for then all in Christ are lost. **Then they that**

19 Christ are perished. *If in this life only we have hope in Christ, we are of all men most miserable.
20 But now ⁱis Christ risen from the dead, *and become ᵐthe firstfruits of
21 them that slept. For ⁿsince by man came death, ᵒby man came also the
22 resurrection of the dead. ᵖFor as in

19 If in this life only we have hoped in Christ, we are of all men most pitiable.
20 But as it is Christ has been raised from the dead, a first-fruit of those who
21 have fallen asleep. For since through man came death, through man came
22 also the resurrection of the dead. For

k 4 : 9-13 ; 2 Tim. 3 : 12.   *l* Ver. 4-8 ; 1 Peter 1 : 3.   *m* Ver. 23 ; Acts 26 : 23 ; Col. 1 : 18 ; Rev. 1 : 5.
n Rom. 5 : 12-21.   *o* John 11 : 25 ; Rom. 6 : 23.   *p* Ver. 47, 48 ; Gen. 3 : 19.

have fallen asleep in Jesus (see on 7 : 39); implying their continued existence after death. That this is a conscious existence is evident from many passages. See Luke 23 : 43, and note, and Practical Remarks on Luke 16. **Are perished,** *are lost* in perdition, having incurred the loss of eternal life (John 17 : 12). The word does not mean annihilation or extinction of being. (See its use in 1 : 18 ; 8 : 11 ; Rom. 2 : 12 ; 2 Cor. 2 : 15, etc.) "One of the most harrowing thoughts, as we see from 1 Thess. 4 : 13 to the apostolic Christians, was the fear lest their departed brethren by a premature death be debarred from that communion with the Lord which they hoped to enjoy; and in itself nothing could be more disheartening to the Christian's hope than to find that Christians had lived and died in vain" (STANLEY).

19. Paul still dwells upon the sad conclusion of the preceding verse. **If in this life only we have hope,** or *hoped* **in Christ,** to be disappointed in the next life; if our hope is a mere exercise, while we are yet in our sins and under condemnation, and in reality without hope and without God in the world, and at the same time subject to the privations, hatred, and persecutions pertaining to a Christian life, then **we are of all men most miserable,** or *the most to be pitied.* Suffering all this for a false hope, a delusion, which is to end in bitter disappointment. Paul does not teach that Christians are more pitiable than other men, for he elsewhere teaches the contrary (Rom. 5 : 1-4 ; 1 Tim. 4 : 8); but they are thus to be pitied, if they are deluded, and if Christ is not all in all to them in this and in the coming world, as they think him to be.

20-28. BOTH THE RESURRECTION OF CHRIST AND OF HIS FOLLOWERS IS ESSENTIAL TO THE GREAT SCHEME OF REDEMPTION.

20. From such a gloomy picture (ver. 13-19) Paul turns to one full of hope and triumph. He sees in Christ's resurrection a pledge of the resurrection of his people. **But now,** as it really is, **Christ is risen from the dead,** for which there is abundant proof (ver. 3-8), **and become the firstfruits,** the earnest and pledge of the resurrection **of them that slept.** The words *and become* should be omitted according to the best text. The last clause will then read, *a firstfruit of those that have fallen asleep.* The firstfruit was the beginning of the harvest, a pledge and promise of the rest of the harvest. So Christ's resurrection was the beginning of the resurrection, the guarantee of the future resurrection of Christians (Rom. 8 : 23 ; 1 Thess. 4 : 14 ; Rev. 1 : 5). It is significant that our Lord rose on the morrow after the Paschal Sabbath, the day when the firstfruits of the harvest were presented (Lev. 23 : 10, 11).

21. For, to explain and confirm the statement that Christ's resurrection was a firstfruit of the resurrection of his followers, **since by,** or *through,* **man came death** (Rom. 5 : 12), *through* **man came also the resurrection of the dead.** The reference is to physical death and the resurrection of the bodies of the dead, as the preceding context shows. Of course as Paul is treating of the resurrection of believers, it is implied that they are raised into a glorified life. It is fitting and in the nature of things, that as death came through man, so the resurrection should come through man. Like acts best on like. It was necessary that Christ should have a human nature, in order to accomplish his work in human redemption, and that includes a human body since the believer's body is to be saved and glorified. (Comp. Rom. 5 : 12-17 ; 1 Tim. 2 : 5).

22. Further confirmation by a direct application to Adam and Christ. **For**

Adam all die, even so in Christ shall 23 all be made alive. But *every man in his own order: Christ the firstfruits; afterward they that are Christ's *at his 24 coming. *Then *cometh* the end, when he shall have delivered up *the kingdom to God, even the Father; when as in Adam all die, so also in Christ 23 will all be made alive. But each in his own rank; Christ a first-fruit; then they who are Christ's at his coming. 24 Then comes the end, when he delivers up the kingdom to God and the Father;

q 1 Thess. 4 : 15–17.   *r* Matt. 25 : 31; John 5 : 25–29; 1 John 2 : 28.   *s* Dan. 12 : 4, 9; Matt. 13 : 39, 40.
t Dan. 7 : 13–27.

as in Adam, the representative and head of the race, whose common nature we all partake; all die, all become mortal and liable to death (Rom. 5 : 12, 15, 17); so in Christ, our spiritual representative and head, whose nature we partake of through faith, shall all be made alive, made partakers of that resurrection which he has already attained (John 6 : 39–44; 11 : 25). As the apostle is discussing the resurrection it is both natural and obvious that temporal death and bodily resurrection are referred to in this passage. Some would extend the reference to the whole race—the mortality of all in Adam, and the resurrection of all in Christ, because of his general relation to the whole race. The language will admit of that interpretation; but still the apostle is speaking of believers in this whole chapter, and he does not appear to be thinking of the wicked at all (ver. 2, 14, 19, 23). Further on Christ and the resurrection of believers, see Rom. 8 : 11.

23. Paul notes that there is a divine order in the resurrection, and that Christ must precede his followers. Three steps are noticed: first, Christ's resurrection, then that of believers, then the subjection of opposers to Christ as mediator. In the last must be included the resurrection of the wicked, which Paul does not speak of definitely, as he is here simply discussing the resurrection of believers.

Referring to what he had just said, that in Christ all should be made alive (ver. 22), Paul continues, **But every man in his own order,** as divinely constituted. The word translated *order* primarily means, *That which has been arranged,* or *placed in order*. In military affairs it was applied to a *troop* of soldiers, and in other matters to a *class* or *rank* of anything. The primary meaning, *order*, fits the connection and the thought here. **Christ the firstfruits.** It was necessary that Christ should rise first, as the Head of the church, and should present himself to God as the firstfruits, and carry on his mediatorial work (Col. 1 : 18; see on Acts 26 : 23). **Afterward,** or better, **Then they that are Christ's at his coming,** at his arrival and presence, his second coming (Matt. 24 : 3, 37, 39; 1 Thess. 3 : 13; 4 : 15, 16; James 5 : 7, etc.). Then will be the glorious harvest of his raised people, of which he himself had been the firstfruits. His dominion began with his own resurrection, exalted to the right hand of God (Acts 5 : 31; Phil. 2 : 9), and at his second coming he returns to establish and consummate his kingdom on earth. It will be a fitting time for the resurrection of believers—the Head and the members must be together (John 6 : 39). As the Jewish dispensation ended with his resurrection, so the present order of things will end with his coming and a new order begin (Rev. 11 : 15; 20 : 5).

24. Then cometh the end of the world (Matt. 24 : 6; 2 Thess. 2 : 8; 1 Peter 4 : 7), and of Christ's mediatorial kingdom, when the wicked shall have been raised and judged, and the power of sin and death destroyed (Rev. 20 : 7–15). How long this order of things shall continue Paul does not say. **When he shall have delivered,** rather, according to the best authorities, *when he delivers up* **the kingdom to God, even the Father.** The kingdom given him by the Father will then be given back by him to the Father. Like a prince bringing back the spoils and trophies of conquest to his father. The mediatorial kingdom is here meant, with which Christ was invested at his resurrection (Matt. 28 : 18), and which is to continue till his work of redemption is accomplished (Acts 2 : 21). He will then no longer reign over the universe as Mediator; but as the Incarnate Son of God and as the Head of his people he will still continue; and in this respect "his kingdom shall have no end" (Luke 1 : 33; Dan. 7 : 14; Heb.

he shall have put down all rule and 25 all authority and power. For he must reign, *till he hath put all enemies 26 under his feet. ᶻThe last enemy that 27 shall be destroyed *is* death. For he ʸhath put all things under his feet. But when he saith, All things are put under *him, it is* manifest that he is excepted which did put all things under 28 him. ᵃAnd when all things shall be subdued unto him, then *shall the Son also himself be subject unto him that

when he has done away every rule, 25 and every authority and power. For he must reign, till he has put all the 26 enemies under his feet. As the last enemy, Death is done away with. For he subjected all things under his feet. 27 But even when he says, All things are subjected, it is manifest that he is excepted, who subjected all things to him. 28 And whenever all things have been subjected to him, then will the Son also himself be subjected to him who

u Ps. 2 : 6–10 ; 110 : 1 ; Eph. 1 : 22 ; Heb. 10 : 13.   x Ver. 54–57 ; see ref. Isa. 25 : 8 ; Heb. 2 : 14.
y See ref. Matt. 28 : 18.   z Dan. 2 : 34, 35, 40–45 ; Rev. 19 : 11–21.   a 11 : 3 ; John 14 : 28.

1 : 8 ; 2 : 8). And this delivering up of his kingdom will occur, **when he shall have put down,** *brought to naught,* **all,** rather, *every,* **rule,** *dominion,* and *every* **authority and power,** except his own (Eph. 6 : 12 ; Rev. 19 : 11–16). Thus all hostile powers will be brought to an end, and every one will yield him homage (Phil. 2 : 10, 11).

25. **For,** according to the Divine arrangement and from the nature of his mediatorial work, *it is necessary* that he should **reign till he,** that is, Christ, **hath put all enemies under his feet.** His reign began with his ascension (Eph. 1 : 20–23 ; Col. 2 : 14, 15), and it must continue till he has subjugated all the enemies of himself and his kingdom, Satan and the powers of darkness, the wicked, and whatever of lust or pride, of material or immaterial things, that oppose or stand in the way of his sway. The putting down of all opposition is necessary to the perfection of his rule (Phil. 3 : 21). The apostle has in mind the words of Ps. 110 : 1, and Ps. 8 : 6, quoted in ver. 27.

26. Among the enemies the last one to be destroyed is mentioned, death, which is personified as a rival foe. **The last enemy that shall be destroyed,** better, *As a last enemy death is brought to naught.* The verb is in the present tense. The future is before the apostle's eye as a realized fact. Physical death is meant, and it shall be completely done away by the resurrection. "There shall be no more death" (Rev. 21 : 4), no more dissolution of soul and body. The destruction of this last vestige of the results of sin (Rom. 6 : 23) upon his followers will be the crowning act of the triumphant Messiah. (Comp. Rev. 20 : 14.)

27. **For,** to give a reason and proof of what he had just said, he quotes Ps. 8 : 6, *all things,* which must include death, *he put* **under his feet.** *All* is emphatic. It is the Father who is here represented as subjecting all things to the Son. What the psalmist said of man, as originally endowed at creation, the apostle sees typically fulfilled in Christ, to whom had been committed "all power in heaven and on earth" (Matt. 28 : 18 ; Heb. 2 : 7 ; Eph. 1 : 22). Paul proceeds to explain and apply the quotation, guarding against a misapplication. **But when he saith, All things are put under him,** or *all things are put in subjection, it is evident* that **he,** the Father, **is excepted, which,** *who,* **did put all things under** him, the Son. This is evident both from the quotation and from the relation of the Father to the Son. For the Father is not subjected to the Son, but the Son to the Father (ver. 28). Meyer and some others make this refer to the future announcement of God at the last, and render as follows : *But when he,* that is, God, *shall have declared that all things have been subjected,* etc. But it seems not to be necessary to deviate from the more natural meaning of the passage. Comp. Heb. 2 : 7–9, which is a counterpart of this passage.

28. Paul now traces the consummation of Christ's mediatorial work up to God the Father, the great Author of all (John 3 : 16). **And when all things shall be subdued,** or *subjected to* **him,** the Son, then the mediatorial kingdom which began at his resurrection will have fulfilled its purpose, and **then** *will* **the Son also himself be subject,** voluntarily, for there must be no divided dominion (John 10 : 30 ; 17 : 22 ; Matt. 26 : 39 ; John 6 : 38) **unto him,** the Father, *that subjected all things to him,*

put all things under him, that God may be all in all.

29 Else what shall they do which are baptized for the dead, if the dead rise not at all? Why are they then baptized

subjected all things to him, that God may be all in all.

29 Else what shall they do who are baptized for the dead? If no dead are raised at all, why then are they bap-

that God may be all things **in all** his people. He will then be recognized as the only Lord and King. Christ having performed his work in his mediatorial kingdom will give up his commission, as it were, to the Father, and introduce his followers into a state of closest nearness to him. They will need no longer a Mediator between them and the Father. As God had been all things to Christ's humanity, so will he be equally all things to theirs (John 11: 41, 42; 17: 23, 24; 14: 8-10; Eph. 2: 18-22). And so the believer will have intimate and individual relations with the triune God, the Father, the Son, and the Spirit. On **all in all** comp. Eph. 1: 23; Col. 3: 11. Paul is not speaking of Christ's pre-existent nature and of the personal relations of the divine Logos (John 1:1). "This subjection no more involves inferiority of essence, than his subjection to Joseph and Mary (Luke 2:51) involved inferiority of essence to them" (ATHANASIUS). It accords with the constitution, harmony, and order of the divine nature (Phil. 2: 6, 7; Eph. 1: 3-14).

29-34. FORTIFIES THE DOCTRINE BY AN APPEAL TO THE LIVES OF BELIEVERS.

29. Resumes the thought of ver. 19. **Else,** if it be *otherwise* than as we have just described (ver. 20-28), if there be no resurrection, and we are of all men the most miserable (ver. 19) **what shall they do,** what will become of them, what will they gain, **who are baptized for the dead?** Do they not act foolishly, performing an entirely useless act? The first question, according to the best recent authorities, ends here. The second question should be translated, according to the best texts, **If the dead rise not at all, why are they then baptized** *for them?* They surely act in that case without reason and sense. The meaning of *for* ("*for* the dead," "*for* them") must be noticed. Its first meaning is *over*, locally, but is not found in this sense in the New Testament. The figurative sense of *over*, that is, *above*, may possibly be its use here. Its general mean-

ing, however, is, *on behalf of, for the sake of*, and then a little more generally, *in reference to, in relation to.* It is thought to mean in some rare cases, *instead of*, but it is doubtful whether it is ever so used in the New Testament. (See on Rom. 5: 6.)

With these preliminary remarks we are prepared to look into the meaning of this passage, one of extreme difficulty and variously explained. (1) Many late prominent scholars hold to the literal interpretation, that the apostle refers to believers permitting themselves to be baptized on behalf of persons who had died unbaptized. But it hardly seems possible that Paul could have given even a quasi sanction to a superstition so inconsistent with the doctrines he preached. Besides there is no evidence of such a practice in the apostolic age, nor in the age immediately following. "The sum of the historical testimony then is, that nearly three hundred years after the apostles, in an age when the most exaggerated notions regarding the efficacy of baptism prevailed, the usage in question existed among one or two small and heretical and ignorant sects; yet not even then in the church generally, and not even among these at an early period" (A. C. KENDRICK, "Christian Review," Vol. XXVII., p. 153). It was even ridiculed by Chrysostom in the fourth century. Instead of being referred to in this verse it was rather based by some heretics, as by the modern Mormons, on their interpretation of this passage. And the interpretation is an illustration of Paul's words, "The letter killeth" (2 Cor. 3: 6). (2) Another interpretation may be thus stated: As baptism symbolizes a death unto sin and a resurrection unto righteousness (Rom. 6: 4), so they who are baptized are baptized for the dead, for themselves as spiritually dead, in hope of a resurrection (Acts 23: 6, etc.). The objection to this view is, that this is true of all believers who are baptized, while this passage seems to limit it to a certain class, "They who are baptized for the dead." (3) Another view takes *for* in the primary figurative sense of

30 for the dead? And ᵇ why stand we in
31 jeopardy every hour? I protest by
ᶜ your rejoicing which I have in Christ
32 Jesus our Lord. ᵈ I die daily If after
the manner of men ᵉ I have fought
with beasts at Ephesus, what advan-
30 tized for them? Why are we also in
31 peril every hour? Daily do I die, I
protest by the glorying in you, brethren, which I have in Christ Jesus our
32 Lord. If after the manner of men I
fought with wild beasts at Ephesus.

ᵇ Rom. 8 : 35, 36 ; 2 Cor. 4 : 7-12 ; 11 : 26.   ᶜ 1 Thess. 2 : 19.   ᵈ 4 : 9-13 ; Rom. 8 : 36 ; 2 Cor. 4 : 10, 11.
ᵉ 2 Cor. 1 : 8-10.

---

over, above: **Else what shall they do,** what advantage shall they *who are baptized* have *above the dead? If the dead rise not at all, why then are they baptized* as an advantage *above them?* In other words, they might as well be dead; so "let us eat and drink; for to-morrow we die" (ver. 32 ; Comp. "Winer's Grammar," p. 382). The objection to this is the same as in the preceding. It applies to all; but this passage limits the baptism in question to a class. Dr. J. L. Dagg ("Baptist Quarterly," 1875, p. 117), regards this baptism as figurative of sufferings and a violent death, baptized as it were *over* dead martyrs. "If all who have heretofore undergone the immersion of martyrdom have sunk hopelessly down, never to rise, what must be the end of those who are permitting themselves to be immersed over them with the same immersion?" This limits the baptism to a distinct class, and is to be preferred to the preceding, yet seems a little strained. (4) A better interpretation may be thus stated: *What will they do, what will they gain, who are baptized* as it were *for the dead,* as for the grave, or *in relation to the dead?* they who in their baptism see foreshadowed sufferings and death, and in the act regard themselves as delivered over to death (2 Cor. 4 : 11). This interpretation is favored by the expressions that follow: "Why stand we in jeopardy every hour?" "I die daily," and "I have fought with wild beasts at Ephesus." Many as they submitted, *literally,* to baptism foresaw the loss of all things, even of life itself. In their baptism they faced death; it was like a death-warrant. And many, like Paul and his fellow-laborers, as they faced martyrdom wherever they went, saw in their condition, *figuratively,* a baptism as it were for the dead (4 : 9-13 ; 2 Cor. 1 : 7-12 ; 6 : 4-10). This is substantially the view of Dr. A. C. Kendrick, unfolded in a very able article on this whole subject, in the "Christian Review," Vol. XXVII., p. 143-169. Republished in Dr. Kendrick's "The Moral Conflict of Humanity," pp. 220-252. Am. Bap. Pub. Soc. 1894.

30. And not only baptism (ver. 29) indicates the belief among Christians of a resurrection, but also the perils, to which Paul and his fellow-missionaries were exposed, showed their firm conviction of the truth of the doctrine. **And why stand we in jeopardy,** in peril of our lives, **every hour,** if the dead rise not? Such conduct would be foolish and without reason. Paul bases upon the resurrection of believers a blessed immortality (ver. 53).

31. And this peril was peculiarly his. **I die daily** (for so this verse should begin). I am daily exposed to death, in the dangers, opposition, and persecutions I encounter (Rom. 8 : 35, 36 ; 2 Cor. 4 : 10-12 ; 11 : 23-27. Comp. his inward dying. Rom. 7 : 24 ; 8 : 13 ; Gal. 6 : 14 ; Col. 3 : 5). **I protest,** I most earnestly and solemnly assert it, **by your rejoicing,** better, *by the glorying in you, brethren,* **which I have in Christ Jesus our Lord** (2 Cor 1 : 14 ; 1 Thess. 2 : 19, 20). Paul rejoiced in them as converts given him in Christ, and all this joy he was ready to stake on the truth of his assertion. And surely he would not thus encounter death daily if he was not assured of a resurrection and of a future blessed existence.

32. From a general description the apostle turns to a particular illustration. **If after the manner of men.** If only as men are wont to fight for earthly gain and glory, **I fought with wild beasts,** in the amphitheatre or stadium, **at Ephesus,** where I am now writing, *what doth it profit me?* Incurring such peril as to make death inevitable, what would be the use of it? The self-evident answer is, No use, no profit. The question ends here, according to the most approved punctuation. It is not generally supposed that

tageth it me? If the dead rise not, let us eat and drink; for to-morrow we 33 die. Be not deceived; *evil communi- 34 cations corrupt good manners. ᵍ Awake to righteousness, and sin not; ᵇ for some have not the knowledge of God: ⁱ I speak *this* to your shame.

35 But some *man* will say, ᵏ How are the dead raised up? And with what body do they come?

what is the profit to me? If the dead rise not,

Let us eat and drink;
For to-morrow we die.

33 Be not led astray; evil companion-
34 ships corrupt good morals. Awake righteously, and sin not; for some have not knowledge of God. I say it to shame you.

35 But some one will say, How are the dead raised? And with what kind of

---

f 5 : 6 ; Prov. 13 : 20 ; 2 Tim. 2 : 17.   *g* See ref. Matt. 25 : 5-7 ; Acts 17 : 30, 31 ; Rom. 13 : 11-14 ; Eph. 5 : 41.
    h 1 Thess. 4 : 5.   *i* 6 : 5.   *k* Ezek. 37 : 3.

Paul actually fought with wild beasts at Ephesus, but that he refers to his conflicts with brutal, beastly men. His Roman citizenship would protect him against being thrown to the lions in the arena; and neither Luke in the Acts, nor Paul in his Epistles, mentions it. The mob of Demetrius (Acts 19 : 23 ff.) occurred after this writing, and neither then was he in any special danger. Merely as a man he gained nothing by his conflicts with fierce and brutal men. But with the Christian hope of a resurrection and a blessed future life, his gain would be great. But all was darkness without this hope. **If the dead rise not,** and hence no blessed immortality, then, in the language of the sensual Israelites of Isaiah's day, **let us eat and drink, for to-morrow we die** (Isa. 22 : 13). His exposures, sufferings, and trials would be utterly gratuitous, his future hopeless. The sensual pleasures of life would be his only portion of happiness. They had better be Epicureans at once. To such gross and startling consequences did the denial of the doctrine of the resurrection lead him. The conclusion is more terrible than even in ver. 19.

33. But here he interposes a warning, **Be not deceived** (6 : 9) by such Epicurean utterances; be not led astray by accepting false principles, or by your intercourse with the deniers of the truth. To confirm his exhortation he quotes Menander, an Athenian poet, born 342 B. C. **Evil communications,** intercourse, companionship, **corrupt good manners,** better, *good morals,* thus affecting the character. Think not that you can have intercourse with that which is evil without suffering in morals and practice. Paul here, as elsewhere, shows acquaintance with heathen authors (Acts 17 : 28; Titus 1 : 12). This quotation may have passed into a proverb.

34. Possibly some of them were already contaminated, and Paul cries out abruptly, **Awake to righteousness,** or *righteously.* The figure is that of instant return from drunkenness to a sober state. *Wake righteously* **to soberness of mind,** *from your drunken dreams,* **and sin not** by continuing in your moral lethargy and evil associations. **For,** giving a reason why they should at once awake, **some have not the knowledge of God,** literally, *some have ignorance of God;* in questioning and denying the resurrection they showed that they "knew not the power of God." (Comp. Matt. 22 : 29.) **I speak this to your shame** (6 : 5), even stronger in the original, *to shame you,* that such errors are among you. He speaks boldly and severely in order to save them. While claiming great knowledge they might well be ashamed of their ignorance of God.

35–49. THE MANNER OF THE RESURRECTION AND THE NATURE OF THE RESURRECTION BODY.

35. Having maintained the fact of the resurrection, Paul proceeds to discuss its manner. **But some man,** some objector, **will say, How are the dead raised up?** the *manner.* **And with what body,** kind of organization, **do they come?** the *nature.* These two questions indicate differences of opinion, and the points at which some stumbled. Some held that the same body in every respect would rise from the grave, which was a great source of difficulty to others. Some also saw nothing but evil and corruption in the body, and could not see how any good could come from it. It is not probable that Paul had any distinct objector in mind. He rather

314   I. CORINTHIANS   [CH. XV.

36 ¹ Thou fool, ᵐ that which thou sowest
37 is not quickened, except it die: and that which thou sowest, thou sowest not that body that shall be, but bare grain, it may chance of wheat, or of some
38 other *grain:* ⁿ but God giveth it a body as it hath pleased him, and to every
39 seed his own body. All flesh *is* not the same flesh: but *there is one kind of* flesh of men, another flesh of beasts, another
40 of fishes, *and* another of birds. *There are* also celestial bodies, and bodies terrestrial: but the glory of the celestial *is* one, and the *glory* of the terres-

36 body do they come? Thou fool, what thou thyself sowest is not made alive,
37 except it die; and what thou sowest, not the body that will be sowest thou, but a bare grain, it may be of wheat,
38 or of some other kind. But God gives it a body just as he willed, and to each
39 of the seeds a body of its own. All flesh is not the same flesh; but there is one flesh of men, another flesh of beasts, another flesh of birds, another
40 of fishes. There are also heavenly bodies and earthly bodies; but the glory of the heavenly is one, and that

l Luke 12 : 20; 24 : 25; Rom. 1 : 22.   m John 12 : 24.   n Gen. 1 : 11, 12.

puts a common objection in the mouth of an ideal person.
36. Paul first argues from the analogy of the grain which dies in order to spring up into a new life. **Thou fool,** without understanding, without reflection. This word is used in 2 Cor. 11 : 16, 19; Eph. 5 : 17; 1 Peter 2 : 15; Luke 11 : 40; 12 : 20. **That which thou sowest.** The word *thou* is emphatic. To what *thou* sowest God gives a body; much more will he give a body to what he himself sows. **Is not quickened,** *made alive,* **except it die.** In the natural world, in the very products you raise death must precede life (John 12 : 24). So in the perishing body you have not an argument against the resurrection, but rather for it.
37. Thou sowest not that body that shall be, but bare grain. It is connected with the sown grain, and comes from it, and yet it is different. It is therefore in accordance with nature that our bodies should be raised like a plant with its rich foliage in comparison to the bare grain that was sown.
38. But God giveth it a body as it hath pleased him, or *as he willed* in creation. So our resurrection body depends upon the will of God, and the great physical and spiritual laws of our being which he has established. **And to every seed his own body.** It is the same body, yet not the same. It is the same body, yet a new body. The old life in the one is developed in a higher life in the other. Personal identity depends on the principle of continuity, not on the material particles of the body, which are said to change every seven years. The soul is the man, and though the body may constantly be undergoing change, yet a certain vital principle continues, and a vital connection exists, so that the body is ever its own body. Jesus rose with the same body (John 20 : 20, 27), yet it had new functions and new qualities (Luke 24 : 16, 31, 37; John 20 : 19, 26).
39. The analogy is traced in the animate creation. That the plant should have a form of organization different from that of the seed from which it sprang, is suggestive of the different varieties and forms of bodily organizations in animal life. The flesh of different creatures differs widely in quality. And this shows that God is not limited to any given form or qualities of bodily organisms, either in this or in higher spheres. According to the best text, **fishes** should come last in the text, which accords also with zoological order. This course of reasoning was suggested by the question, "With what body do they come?"
40. Paul advances a step higher to heavenly bodies. **There are also celestial bodies, and bodies terrestrial.** Some suppose what we call heavenly bodies, the sun, moon, and stars, to be meant. But such is not the use of the word translated *celestial* in the New Testament, its application being to heaven and to heavenly beings, such as the various classes of angels (John 3 : 12; Phil. 2 : 10). That they should have some kind of celestial bodies is certainly conceivable, and accords with, if not implied by, Matt. 22 : 30; Luke 20 : 36. The terrestrial bodies are those of men, animals, and plants, such as are *upon the earth.* **But the glory of the celestial is one,** being encompassed with a heavenly radiance (Matt. 17 : 2; 28 : 3; Acts 12 : 7); **and the glory of the terrestrial is another,** in kind and quality, the

41 trial is another. °*There is* one glory of the sun, and another glory of the moon, and another glory of the stars: for one star differeth from *another* star in glory.
42 ᵖSo also *is* the resurrection of the dead. It is sown ᑫ in corruption; it is
43 raised in incorruption: ʳit is sown in dishonour; it is raised in glory: it is sown in weakness; it is raised in
44 power: it is sown a natural body; it is raised a spiritual body. There is a natural body, and there is a spiritual
45 body. And so it is written, The first man Adam ˢ was made a living soul; ᵗ the last Adam *was made* ᵘ a quicken-

41 of the earthly is another. There is one glory of the sun, and another glory of the moon, and another glory of the stars; for star differs from star
42 in glory. So also is the resurrection of the dead. It is sown in corruption, it
43 is raised in incorruption. It is sown in dishonor, it is raised in glory. It is sown in weakness, it is raised in power.
44 It is sown a natural body, it is raised a spiritual body. If there is a natural
45 body, there is also a spiritual. So also it is written, The first man Adam became a living soul; the last Adam a

o Gen. 1 : 14-16.   p Dan. 12 : 3; Matt. 13 : 43.   q Gen. 3 : 19; Ps. 49 : 9, 14.   r Phil. 3 : 21.   s Gen. 2 : 7.
t Rom. 5 : 14.   u John 5 : 21; 6 : 33-40, 54, 57; 17 : 2; Phil. 3 : 21; Col. 3 : 4.

strength, grace, and beauty of material organizations. The idea is included of superiority of the celestial to the terrestrial. And this leads us to expect a corresponding superiority of the resurrection body to our present earthly bodies.

41. The analogy is extended to the heavenly luminaries, the **sun, moon,** and **stars,** showing that there is a diversity in their **glory** or lustre, and that *star differs from star in brilliancy*. Some make this to teach that saints in heaven will have different degrees of honor and glory. The rewards of the heavenly world will indeed differ (3 : 15 ; 2 Cor. 5 : 10 ; see note on Matt. 20 : 16), but this is not the point of illustration here; rather, is it that our resurrection body will differ from, and be superior to, our earthly body.

42. Application of the preceding analogies (ver. 36-41) to the resurrection of believers. **So also is the resurrection of the dead,** in regard to the difference in the constitution and glory of the resurrection body from the present earthly body. Several differences are now specified. **It is sown,** a figurative expression for *buried*, **in corruption,** in a condition of decay (Rom. 8 : 21) ; **it is raised in incorruption,** in a condition imperishable and exempt from decay (Rom. 2 : 7).

43. It is sown in dishonour, in a condition unseemly and offensive (Phil. 3 : 21) ; **it is raised in glory,** in a condition of majesty and splendor (Matt. 13 : 43; Dan. 12 : 3; Rev. 1 : 13-16). **It is sown in weakness,** its native weakness culminated in a condition of utter powerlessness; **it is raised in power,** in vigor, with new faculties

and in the fullness of life. Some, with less strictness of interpretation, refer these characteristics not alone to the dead body, but to the present living body, tending to decay, subject to sickness and death, and destined to dissolution.

44. It is sown a natural, or *psychical*, **body,** which men have in common with the beast. The apostle appears to have in mind the three-fold distinction of body, soul, and spirit (2 : 14). The natural body is that which is limited by, and suited to, the lower and animal life of man. **It is raised a spiritual body,** animated by a principle of spiritual life, and suited to the higher, immortal spirit of man (2 Cor. 5 : 1, 2, 4; Rom. 8 : 23). **There is,** etc.; rather, according to the highest critical authorities, *If there is a natural body, there is also a spiritual body.* This must be so from the nature of things. If our present lower life has a body according to its needs, then it follows that the higher spiritual life will have one also fitted to its higher capacities. The apostle assumes here, as elsewhere, that man would be incomplete without a bodily organization.

45. And this distinction between the natural and the spiritual is suggested by Scripture, with which it accords. **And so it is written** (Gen. 2 : 7). **The first man Adam was made,** better, *became*, **a living soul,** a living nature, having the principle of natural life. And as the spiritual is the counterpart of the natural or psychical, so **the last Adam** *became* **a quickening,** rather, *a life-giving,* **spirit,** with special reference to the giving of the resurrection life (ver. 22; John 5 : 21, 28; Phil.

46 ing spirit. Howbeit that was not first which is spiritual, but that which is natural; and afterward that which is
47 spiritual. ˣ The first man is of the earth, ʸearthy; the second man is ᶻ the
48 Lord from heaven. As is the earthy, ᵃsuch are they also that are earthy; ᵇand as is the heavenly, such are they
49 also that are heavenly. And ᶜas we have borne the image of the earthy, ᵈ we shall also bear the image of the heavenly.

46 life-giving spirit. Yet the spiritual is not first, but the natural; then the
47 spiritual. The first man is of the earth, earthy; the second man is from
48 heaven. As is the earthy, such are they also that are earthy; and as is the heavenly, such are they also that
49 are heavenly. And as we bore the image of the earthy, we shall also bear the image of the heavenly.

ˣ John 3 : 31.   ʸ Gen. 2 : 7 ; 3 : 19.   ᶻ Isa. 9 : 6 ; John 3 : 13, 31 ; 1 Tim. 3 : 16.
ᵃ Job 14 : 4 ; John 3 : 6.   ᵇ Phil. 3 : 20, 21.   ᶜ Gen. 5 : 3.
ᵈ Rom. 8 : 29 ; 2 Cor. 3 : 18 ; Phil. 3 : 21 ; 1 John 3 : 2.

3 : 21 ; 1 Thess. 4 : 16). The first clause alone is quoted. But the second part is its complement; and, equally true (John 6 : 33, 39, 40, 54, 57 ; 11 : 25), Christ was the second Adam, the rabbinical name applied to the Messiah, the head and beginner of a new, justified, and redeemed humanity (Rom. 5 : 12-21). So Christ himself taught (John 5 : 21, 26). He was the *last* Adam, as no one like him is to follow. The word translated *soul* is rendered both life and soul in the New Testament (Matt. 10 : 28, 39 ; 16 : 25, 26). The Hebrew word *soul* includes all animal life common to men and beasts, and is also applied to the higher nature of man. The first meaning seems to be prominent here. Yet the fact that Adam was a *living* soul points at least toward a higher and immortal existence. The higher nature of Adam is brought out more distinctly, however, in Gen. 1 : 26, where it is said that God made man in his own image.

46. Paul states the divine order of the lower forms of life preceding the higher. *Yet not the spiritual first, but the natural, and then the spiritual.* This may be illustrated by analogies in creation. Progress is a universal law. There is an ever-ascending scale from lower to higher organizations of life. So also the natural birth precedes the spiritual or second birth.

47. The statement of the preceding verse is confirmed. **The first man is of** (*from*) **the earth, earthy,** *of the dust*, in allusion to Gen. 2 : 7, where it is said that "God formed man of the dust of the ground." This refers to his bodily organization. **The second man is the Lord** (*the Lord* should be omitted according to the best text) **from heaven.** This may refer only to Christ's risen and glorified body; but it seems better to refer it to his body begotten by the Holy Spirit, yet connected with our humanity, and now raised and glorified (Matt. 1 : 20 ; Luke 1 : 35 ; Rev. 1 : 13-15). He is heavenly in his origin and heavenly in his relations. (Comp. John 3 : 13, 31 ; Phil. 3 : 20, 21.) Thus the divine order of progress is illustrated in the body of Adam returning to dust (Gen. 3 : 19), and the body of Christ, begotten of the Spirit, not returning to corruption (Acts 2 : 31), but purified from whatever there was mortal in its composition and refined into a glorified condition.

48. Application to the present and future bodily organizations of Christians. **As is the earthy,** Adam, **such are they also that are earthy,** the descendants of Adam, men in their mortal condition. **And as is the heavenly,** Christ, **such are they also that are heavenly,** those who are connected spiritually with Christ, they shall be glorified like Christ. Mortality shall be swallowed up of life (2 Cor. 5 : 4 ; see also Phil. 3 : 20, 21). "Man, united to Christ by faith, partakes of *both* natures. He is liable, therefore, still to the weakness and infirmities of the former. And this he must bear to the end. He must be subject to the law of the natural order of things before he attains fully to the spiritual order" (LIAS).

49. The application is still more closely carried out. **And as we have borne the image of the earthy,** like Adam, having a decaying, animal body (2 Cor. 5 : 2), **we shall also bear the image of the heavenly,** in the resurrection and glorified state (Rom. 8 : 29 ; Col. 3 : 10 ; 1 John 3 : 2), having spiritual bodies like to Christ's glorious body.

50 Now this I say, brethren, that *flesh and blood cannot inherit the kingdom of God: neither doth corruption inherit incorruption.
51 Behold, I shew you a mystery; *We shall not all sleep, *but we shall all be
52 changed, *in a moment, in the twinkling of an eye, at the last trump: *for the trumpet shall sound, and the dead shall be raised *incorruptible, and we
53 shall be changed. For this corruptible must put on incorruption, and *this mortal *must* put on immortality.

50 And this I say, brethren, that flesh and blood can not inherit the kingdom of God; nor does corruption inherit
51 incorruption. Behold, I tell you a mystery. We shall not all sleep, but
52 we shall all be changed, in a moment, in the twinkling of an eye, at the last trump: for the trumpet will sound, and the dead will be raised incorrupti-
53 ble, and we shall be changed. For this corruptible must put on incorruption, and this mortal must put on im-

e John 3 : 3, 5. f 1 Thess. 4 : 15–17. g Phil. 3 : 21. h See 2 Peter 3 : 10.
i Matt. 24 : 31; John 5 : 25; 1 Thess. 4 : 16. k Ver. 42, 50. l 2 Cor. 5 : 4.

Another reading, *Let us bear the image of the heavenly*, is sustained by external evidence, but internal evidence is decidedly against it. Expositors very generally favor the common reading. Meyer, in his textual notes, shows how this reading may have originated, being demanded, as some thought, by ver. 50.

50–58. RESULTS OF THE RESURRECTION. The glorification of the living saints as well as of those who had died.

50. Now this I say, an expression introducing an important and emphatic statement. Whatever may be the opinions and speculations concerning the resurrection, I affirm this, **that flesh and blood,** our mortal nature, our bodily organism with its infirmities as it now is (ver. 44), **cannot inherit the kingdom of God,** as it will be consummated at our Lord's second coming (6 : 10). **Neither doth corruption,** that which is decaying, or destined to decay, **inherit incorruption,** become partaker of an incorruptible and imperishable life. In the very nature of things our bodies must be changed from what they now are, in order to dwell in a glorified and immortal state.

51, 52. Consistently with this Paul had shown that the dead in Christ should be raised with spiritual bodies (42–49). But it might be asked, How will it be with those saints who are living at Christ's coming? The answer is here given. **Behold,** give attention to something wonderful and extraordinary, **I shew you a mystery,** a thing formerly hidden but now revealed. He had written the Thessalonians regarding it (1 Thess. 4 : 15–17), but it was still unknown to the Corinthians. **We shall not all sleep,** all believers will not die, including Paul and his readers. Many suppose that Paul expected that he, or some of his readers, would be alive at our Lord's coming. So he appears to have expected when he wrote 1 Thess. 4 : 15; but he had at least partly corrected himself in 2 Thess. 2 : 1 ff. But of the time of our Lord's return even inspired apostles were ignorant (Mark 13 : 32; Acts 1 : 7). **But we shall all be changed,** as described in ver. 53; and it shall be instantaneous, **in a moment, in the twinkling of an eye, at the last trump,** which shall call the dead from their graves (1 Thess. 4 : 16). At the Hebrew festivals the trumpet was used to summon the people together (Num. 10 : 1–10). So the sounding of the trumpet is used to represent the assembling of the saints at Christ's second coming (Matt. 24 : 31). The apostle goes on to say that at the sound of the trumpet, **the dead shall be raised incorruptible, and we,** who are alive, **shall be changed** (Phil. 3 : 21). Paul associates himself with the living at the last day. Whether he would live to see it or not, he did not know; but by faith he vividly saw that day, as if present, and he writes as if he were among them. Elsewhere his language implies that he himself expected to die and be raised (6 : 14; 2 Cor. 4 : 14). In regard to the change of the living, compare the translation of Enoch and Elijah (Gen. 5 : 24; 2 Kings 2 : 11, 12).

53. To confirm what he had just said, **For this corruptible,** pertaining to our decaying bodies, **must,** in the nature of things (ver. 50) **put on,** as a garment (2 Cor. 5 : 4), **incorruption, and this mortal,** liable and subject to death, **must put on immor-

54 So when this corruptible shall have put on incorruption, and this mortal shall have put on immortality, then shall be brought to pass the saying that is written, ᵐ Death is swallowed 55 up in victory. O death, where *is* thy sting? O grave, where *is* thy victory? 56 ⁿ The sting of death *is* sin; and ᵒ the 57 strength of sin *is* the law. But thanks be to God, which giveth us ᵖ the victory 58 through our Lord Jesus Christ. ᵠ Therefore, my beloved brethren, be ye sted-

54 mortality. And when this corruptible shall have put on incorruption, and this mortal shall have put on immortality, then will come to pass the word that is written, Death has been swal- 55 lowed up in victory. Where, O death, is thy victory? Where, O death, is thy 56 sting? The sting of death is sin; and 57 the power of sin is the law. But thanks be to God, who gives us the victory through our Lord Jesus Christ. 58 Therefore, my beloved brethren, be

---

m Heb. 2 : 14, 15. *n* Rom. 6 : 23. *o* Rom. 4 : 15; 5 : 13; 7 : 5–13.
p Rom. 8 : 37; 1 John 4 : 4; 5 : 4, 5; Rev. 12 : 11.   *q* 2 Peter 3 : 14, 17, 18.

---

tality. The mortal body is not to be entirely destroyed, but it will be swallowed up of life. Some would apply this whole verse to those living at our Lord's return. But connecting it with the last verse, the first clause may refer to "the dead who shall be raised incorruptible," and the second clause to the living "who shall be changed," and their mortal bodies assume immortality, a state free from disease and death.

54. *And* when all this shall have come to pass, the dead in Christ raised into an incorruptible state, and the living saints changed into an immortal condition, **then shall be brought to pass the saying that is written** (Isa. 25 : 8), **Death is swallowed up in victory,** utterly and forever overcome by a triumphant and victorious life. The reference is to bodily death, which shall cease to exist, and shall be completely overcome by a glorified life. In Isaiah's prediction of Israel's restoration Paul sees a more perfect and glorious application to the consummation of God's kingdom, and to the lifegiving blessings of the gospel.

55. The apostle bursts forth into expressions of exultant joy, using words freely quoted from Hosea 13 : 14. **O death, where is thy sting? O grave, where is thy victory?** According to the highest critical authorities this should read, *Where, O death, is thy victory? Where, O death, is thy sting?* The personification of death in the last verse is continued in this. The victory in which death had been wont to pride himself is gone, a thing of the past! The sting which death had used with such sudden and destructive power is taken from him, and he seeks for it in vain. Without his deadly weapon he lies prostrate, a vanquished foe.

56. **Death,** like a scorpion, has a **sting** (Rev. 9 : 10), a deadly weapon, inflicting pain and destruction. (Comp. Rom. 5 : 12.) **It is sin** that makes death terrible and gives it power to pierce the soul with anguish. **The strength,** or *power,* **of sin is the law.** Sin is a want of conformity to God's holy law, whether it be a sin of omission or of commission. The law being recognized gives to sin its power to wound the conscience and to condemn (Rom. 7 : 11). With its precepts and penalties the law makes known the consequences of sin, without giving any power of deliverance (Gal. 3 : 19–21). In this verse we have the germ, which Paul afterward brings out more fully and with much wider application in Rom. 5 : 12–21; 7 : 7–24.

57. But Paul no longer views death, sin, and the law with terror, but beholds them overcome in Christ, who has died for our sins, fulfilled the claims of the law, and risen for our justification (Rom. 8 : 1; Heb. 2 : 14, 15; Phil. 3 : 21). Victory is as if already present, and a glorious resurrection. The law is satisfied; sin is powerless, and death is vanquished, all through the redemptive work of our risen Lord. The apostle breaks forth in thanksgiving to **God, who giveth us the victory through our Lord Jesus Christ.** The victory over death, in a glorious resurrection, is a part of Christ's redemptive work, which includes the complete salvation of soul and body from all the consequences of sin.

58. Paul closes with a practical admonition to steadfastness and to increasing Christian activity. With him the doctrinal and practical go together. **Therefore,** in view of your victory over death, **my beloved brethren,**

fast, unmoveable, always abounding in ʳthe work of the Lord, forasmuch as ye know ˢ that your labour is not in vain ᵗ in the Lord.

steadfast, immovable, always abounding in the work of the Lord, knowing that your labor is not in vain in the Lord.

r Titus 2 : 14 ; Heb. 13 : 21. *s* Gal. 6 : 9 ; Heb. 6 : 10. *t* Matt. 10 : 40–42.

our brotherly affection hallowed with our common glorious hope of a future resurrection, **be ye stedfast** in your faith and hope, **unmoveable** by any person or thing from the truth ye have received (ver. 1), **always abounding in the work of the Lord,** which he is carrying forward, and which he has given us to do. This work includes the various activities in upbuilding the cause of Christ. And now the final reason for this labor, **Forasmuch as you know,** having an assurance, **that your labour,** involving effort, burdens, and self-denials, **is not in vain,** useless and without reward, as it would be if there were no future resurrection (ver. 12-19). **In the Lord,** in union and fellowship with him, who is the resurrection and the life (ver. 22, 23; Rom. 8 : 11, 28-30) ; and thus your labor will be amply rewarded.

PRACTICAL REMARKS.

1. We should hold strictly to the gospel as presented in the New Testament (ver. 1 ; Jude 3).

2. The death, burial, and resurrection of Christ are the fundamental facts which should be made prominent in both our preaching and believing (ver. 2, 3 ; Luke 24 : 26, 46, 47).

3. There is no more fully established historical fact than the resurrection of Christ (ver. 4-8 ; Acts 1 : 3-11).

4. A sense of unworthiness should not keep us from duty. Humility should rather lead us to obey God (ver. 9, 10 ; Exod. 4 : 10-12).

5. Christian activity is consistent with entire dependence on God's mercy and grace. The latter should excite the former (ver. 10 ; 1 Tim. 1 : 12-16).

6. The risen and ascended Lord should be the Christ of our faith and our preaching. In studying the earthly life of Christ we may lose sight of this (ver. 1, 2, 11 ; Acts 2 : 32-36).

7. Take away the resurrection of Christ, and the whole system of Christianity falls into hopeless ruin (ver. 12-19 ; Acts 4 : 8-12).

8. The resurrection of Christ insures the resurrection of his followers (ver. 20-23 ; Col. 3 : 3, 4).

9. The resurrection of believers will be the great harvest of which Christ was the first-fruits (ver. 20-23 ; Num. 18 : 29, 30).

10. The mediatorial reign of Christ must necessarily continue till the work of redemption is complete, in the salvation of his followers and the subjection of his foes (ver. 24-28 ; Phil. 2 : 9-11).

11. Though death is robbed of its terrors, yet he is an enemy and should be so regarded (ver. 26, 55 ; Rev. 20 : 14).

12. The eternal Son of God, the Word, is ever one with the Father, in the essence of his Divine nature (ver. 25-28 ; John 1 : 1 ; Heb. 1 : 3).

13. Though a person sees in his baptism sufferings, persecutions, and even his own death-warrant, as it were, yet it will bring to him the answer of a good conscience and a hope of a glorious resurrection (ver. 29 ; 1 Peter 3 : 21 ; Rom. 6 : 5).

14. Voluntary exposures to sufferings, persecution, and death, are indeed irrational, if there is no resurrection and blissful hereafter (ver. 30, 32).

15. Not only vicious intercourse, but even the silent influences of evil tend to corrupt the lives and morals of men (ver. 33, 34).

16. The same difficulty which is found in the doctrine of the resurrection is found to exist in things of daily observation (ver. 36-38 ; John 12 : 24).

17. Life and the world are full of mysteries. To believe nothing but what we can explain is the greatest folly (ver. 35-38 ; John 3 : 12).

18. As in nature we see infinite variety of organized forms, so we can conceive of vast possibilities in the resurrection body and life (ver. 39-41).

19. Whatever change may take place at the resurrection, everything essential to personal identity will be found in the risen body (ver. 42, 37).

20. Whatever a spiritual body is, we may

Directions concerning the collection; concluding exhortations and salutations.

16 NOW concerning "the collection for the saints, as I have given order to "the churches of Galatia, even so do 2 ye. *Upon the first day of the week

16 NOW concerning the collection for the saints, as I directed the churches 2 of Galatia, so also do ye. On the first day of the week, let each one of you

u Acts 11 : 28-30 ; Rom. 15 : 26 ; 2 Cor. 9 : 1, 12 ; Heb. 6 : 10 ; 1 John 3 : 17.
x Acts 16 : 6 ; Gal. 2 : 10.   z Acts 20 : 7 ; Rev. 1 : 10.

regard it as free from the grossness of the flesh, and partaking of many of the qualities and functions of the spirit (ver. 42-44, 50; Luke 20 : 36).

21. How superior was the last Adam to the first! The one entailed death; the other gave life (ver. 45-47; Rom. 5 : 12-19; John 1 : 4, 12, 13).

22. Order and progress are manifested in both nature and grace. God is a God of order, not of confusion (ver. 46-49; 1 Cor. 14 : 33).

23. The resurrection body of saints will be like that of Christ (ver. 49 ; Phil. 3 : 21).

24. The change in the living at the resurrection will be as necessary as the raising of the dead : and God can as easily do the former as the latter (ver. 50-53.)

25. The resurrection of saints and their glorified life hereafter are matters not of reason, but of revelation (ver. 50-53 ; Rev. 20 : 6 ; 21 : 2-7).

26. The triumph of the Christian over death will be final and complete (ver. 55, 56; Rom. 7 : 25).

27. We shall owe all to Christ for our victory over death, sin, and every foe (ver. 57 ; 8 : 37-39).

28. Christianity is the only religion that takes away the sting of death and illumines the grave with life and immortality (ver. 54-57; 2 Tim. 1 : 10).

29. The prospect of a future resurrection and of immortal glory should lead Christians to stability in belief and doctrine, and to a life of active toil and self-denial (ver. 58; Heb. 6 : 10-12 ; 10 : 23-25.)

CHAPTER XVI.

Paul concludes the Epistle by first giving some directions concerning collections for the saints (ver. 1-4) ; then he speaks of a proposed visit to them, which he hoped soon to accomplish (ver. 5-9) ; advises regarding Timothy, Apollos, and other brethren (ver. 10-18) ;

extends salutations, utters a warning, and closes with a benediction (ver. 19-24). Compare the conclusions to the Epistles to the Romans, Ephesians, Colossians, and 2 Timothy.

1-4. DIRECTIONS CONCERNING THE COLLECTION FOR THE SAINTS. After the exhortation to abound in the work of the Lord it was fitting to give the practical directions contained in this chapter.

1. Now concerning the collection, *the gathering together* of money, with perhaps the idea of *savings* from small incomes. **For the saints.** (See on 1 : 2.) Both the collection and the saints are spoken of as well known to the Corinthians. From 2 Cor. 8 : 10 ; 9 : 2, it appears that Paul had directed them to make this collection a year before the writing of the second Epistle, or about six months before writing this Epistle. The saints were those at Jerusalem (ver. 3). They are styled more definitely in Rom. 15 : 26 (see note), as "the poor among the saints in Jerusalem." Persecution and the troublous times, of which Josephus speaks, had contributed to their poverty. **As I have given orders,** or *directed,* **the churches of Galatia,** in the central portion of Asia Minor (see note on Acts 16 : 6), probably when he visited them last, about two years before (Acts 19 : 1) ; or perhaps he had sent them word later from Ephesus. It is interesting to compare Gal. 2 : 10; Rom. 15 : 26 ; Acts 24 : 17, this verse, and 9 : 11, and note their undesigned agreement, and how they evidence the truthfulness of both the Acts and the Epistles. **So** *also* **do ye;** with the idea of urgency. "He who gives quickly, gives twice."

2. Upon the first day of the week, that is, on *every* first day. (See note on Acts 20 : 7.) But why select this day if there was not some religious distinction put on it? Since giving to the poor saints was a religious service to

let every one of you lay by him in store, ⁷ as *God* hath prospered him, that there be no gatherings when I
3 come. And when I come, whomsoever ye shall approve by *your* letters, them will I send to bring your liberality
4 unto Jerusalem; ᶻ and if it be meet that I go also, they shall go with me.
5 Now I will come unto you, ᵃ when I shall pass through Macedonia: (for I
6 do pass through Macedonia:) and it may be that I will abide, yea, and

lay by him in store, according as he is prospered, that there may be no collec-
3 tions made when I come. And when I arrive, whomsoever ye shall approve. them I will send with letters to carry
4 your benefaction to Jerusalem. And if it be worth while for me also to go, they shall go with me.
5 And I will come to you, when I have passed through Macedonia. For I pass
6 through Macedonia; and it may be that I will remain, or even pass the

y Deut. 8 : 18 ; 2 Cor. 8 : 1-3, 12-15.   *z* 2 Cor. 8 : 4, 19.   *a* Acts 19 : 21 ; 2 Cor. 1 : 15. 16.

Christ (Rom. 15 : 27, note ; Matt. 25 : 40) it comported with the hallowed associations of the resurrection day, and suggests its sacred character as the Lord's Day (Rev. 1 : 10), **Let every one of you lay by him in store,** by himself, at his home, *treasuring up whatever he may be prospered in.* It is to be an individual and personal work, done systematically, according to the prosperity enjoyed. It is also to be accumulative, and kept sacred. **That there be no gatherings,** *no collections* (the same word as in ver. 1) *made* **when I come.** More could thus be gathered with less burdens to one and all. It would save confusion, excitement, and mere impulsive effort. It would enter into their spiritual life as a habitual service to Christ and his cause, and as an exercise of a Christian grace (2 Cor. 8 : 1-9).

3. And when I come, or *arrive,* which he expected to do in a few months (ver. 5, 8), **whomsoever ye shall approve,** or *deem worthy.* Paul would have the givers select their own agents. He would not do that which rightfully belonged to the church to do. (Comp. Acts 6 : 2, 3.) **By your letters, them will I send,** rather, *them will I send with letters,* that is, of commendation (Acts 18 : 27 ; Rom. 16 : 1 ; 2 Cor. 3 : 2). Thus letters of recommendation were common among Christians. How many of these doubtless Paul wrote. Only that to Philemon has come down to us. As the originator of this special effort for the saints at Jerusalem, Paul directed it, and would commend those whom the church approved as fit. **To bring your liberality,** *your favor,* the expressions of your favor, your benefactions. Literally, it is *your grace,* the tokens of grace and love. (Comp. 2 Cor. 8 : 1, 4, 6, 7.) Notice he does not say *alms,* but by the word *grace* he indi-

cates a higher kind of religious service in giving. **Unto Jerusalem,** the point of destination. Doubtless the memory of how he had persecuted and impoverished the saints was to him a powerful motive.

4. And if it be meet that I go also, rather, *If it be worthy of my going also,* if it, the collection, be sufficiently large, if it be worth my journey, **they shall go with me.** He would under no consideration take charge of the money himself, lest his motives might be impugned, or it should be said that he had put any of it to his own use (9 : 16, 19 ; 2 Cor. 11 : 7-9 ; 12 : 16-18). As it turned out, he went and they accompanied him (Rom. 15 : 25-27 ; Acts 24 : 17). Paul's presence with them gave dignity and importance to the mission.

5-9. PAUL'S PROPOSED VISIT TO CORINTH.

5. The apostle announces definitely his plan of coming to them, **when I shall pass through Macedonia.** It appears from 2 Cor. 1 : 15-17, that in a lost Epistle (5 : 9), or in some other way, he had previously announced to them that he would come first to Corinth, then go into Macedonia and return; and that on account of this change in his plans, some had charged him with fickleness. **For I do pass, through Macedonia.** The reason for changing his plan is given in 2 Cor. 1 : 23, 24 ; 2 : 1 ; 12 : 20, 21 ; 13 : 2, 10. (See on ver. 8.) And he desired to stay longer at Ephesus (ver. 9).

6. And it may be, *it may happen that I shall remain* a time with you, *and even pass the winter with you,* till the navigation of the Ægean Sea is open in the spring. (Comp. Acts 27 : 12.) This conception of his proposed visit was quite definite in his mind, and he

v

winter with you, that ye may ᵇ bring me on my journey whithersoever I go.
7 For I will not see you now by the way; but I trust to tarry awhile with you,
8 ᶜ if the Lord permit. But I will tarry
9 at Ephesus until Pentecost: for ᵈ a great door and effectual is opened unto me, and ᵉ there are many adversaries.
10 Now ᶠ if Timotheus come, see that he may be with you without fear: for

winter with you, that ye may bring me on my journey whithersoever I go.
7 For I am unwilling to see you now, in passing; for I hope to remain some time with you, if the Lord permit.
8 But I shall remain at Ephesus until
9 the Pentecost. For a great and effectual door is open to me, and there are many adversaries.
10 Now if Timothy come, see that he may be with you without fear; for he

b Acts 15 : 3 ; 17 : 15 ; 21 : 5 ; Rom. 15 : 24 ; 2 Cor. 1 : 16.   *c* 4 : 19 ; Acts 18 : 21 ; James 4 : 15.
d Acts 19 : 8-20 ; 2 Cor. 2 : 12 ; Col. 4 : 3.   *e* Acts 19 : 9, 23, etc. ; 2 Cor. 4 : 8-10.   *f* 4 : 17.

was enabled to carry it out the next winter (Acts 20 : 3). **That,** *In order that,* **ye** (emphatic) **and no other church may have the pleasure to bring me,** or *send me forward,* **on my journey whithersoever I go,** the direction and route being yet undecided upon. It was customary for churches to escort their minister, or missionaries, a little way on their journey, as a token of regard (Acts 21 : 5 ; 20 : 38 ; 15 : 3 ; Rom. 15 : 24 ; 2 Cor. 1 : 15).

7. He gives a reason for the plan he had adopted and made known in the preceding verse. **For I will not see you,** better, *For I wish not to see you now* **by the way,** or *in passing,* as a passing traveler. **But,** rather, *For,* according to the best manuscripts, giving a particular reason, **I trust,** or *hope,* **to tarry a while with you** (ver. 6), which he could not do if he came now direct by sea. When he should visit them he wished to remain long enough to do them permanent good. Other reasons he states in his Second Epistle. (See references at the end of ver. 5.) He doubtless wished that there might be time for this Epistle to produce its proper effect upon the Corinthians. He did not wish to use severity either in word or deed against the unruly and his opposers. **If the Lord permit,** through indications of the Spirit or Providence. (Comp. Acts 16 : 6, 7 ; see 4 : 19 ; Heb. 6 : 3 ; James 4 : 15.)

8. But I will tarry, better, *shall remain,* **at Ephesus until Pentecost,** which was in the month of May. Some suppose that the great uproar at Ephesus regarding Diana took place at about the same time; but this is uncertain, and it may have occurred late in the summer or early in the autumn. (See on Acts 19 : 22, 41.) There are indications in the Acts and the Epistles that Paul remained longer than he expected, and left Ephesus in the month of August, A. D. 57. See Clark's "Harmonic Arrangement of the Acts," pp. 226-230, for a full discussion.

9. Two reasons why he should remain awhile at Ephesus. **For a great door,** a great opportunity, a favorite expression with Paul (Acts 14 : 27 ; 2 Cor. 2 : 12 ; Col. 4 : 3), and *effectual,* productive of results. His opportunity for reaching the people was great in extent, and wonderful in effect. With this agrees Acts 19 : 10, 19, 20. **And there are many adversaries,** a remarkable reason, which would have daunted many, but only aroused the courage and zeal of Paul. (Comp. Acts 19 : 30.) The many adversaries were indications of his success (Acts 19 : 26), and he felt strong in the Lord to meet them (Acts 19 : 17). Under such circumstances the young church at Ephesus needed his presence for counsel and encouragement. These adversaries had been increasing with the progress of the gospel, and the uproar about Diana was their most remarkable manifestation; but this Epistle was written before that event, which occurred about Pentecost, or probably later. (See on ver. 8.)

10 - 18. DIRECTIONS REGARDING TIMOTHY, APOLLOS, AND OTHERS.

10. Now if Timotheus come, whom he had sent to Macedonia and thence to Corinth before sending this letter. But he would arrive after the letter, which would go direct over the Ægean Sea to Corinth. The apostle conceives of Timothy's arrival as conditioned on circumstances. But he doubtless reached there, as the after events are in harmony with it, and we hear nothing to the contrary. (See on 4 : 17.) **See that he may be with you without fear.** Timothy was

ᵉ he worketh the work of the Lord, as I also do. ʰ Let no man therefore despise him; but conduct him forth in peace, that he may come unto me: for I look for him with the brethren.
12 As touching our brother ⁱ Apollos, I greatly desired him to come unto you with the brethren: but his will was not at all to come at this time: but he will come when he shall have convenient time.
13 ᵏ Watch ye, ˡ stand fast in the faith,
14 ᵐ quit you like men, ⁿ be strong. ᵒ Let all your things be done with charity.
15 I beseech you, brethren, (ye know ᵖ the house of Stephanas, that it is ᵍ the

works the work of the Lord, as I also do. Let no one therefore despise him; but send him forward in peace, that he may come to me; for I look for him
12 with the brethren. And concerning Apollos the brother, I besought him much to come to you with the brethren; and it was not at all his will to come at this time, but he will come when he shall have opportunity.
13 Watch, stand fast in the faith, acquit
14 you like men, be strong. Let all your
15 acts be done in love. Now I beseech you, brethren, (ye know the house of Stephanas, that it is a first-fruit of

---

g Rom. 16 : 21 ; Phil. 2 : 19-22 ; 1 Thess. 3 : 2. *h* 1 Tim. 4 : 12. *i* 3 : 5 ; Acts 18 : 24.
k See ref. Matt. 24 : 42 ; 1 Peter 5 : 8. *l* Gal. 5 : 1 ; Phil. 1 : 27 ; 4 : 1 ; 2 Thess. 2 : 15 ; Jude 3.
m 1 Sam. 4 : 9 ; 2 Tim. 2 : 3-5. *n* Josh. 1 : 6 ; Isa. 35 : 4 ; Eph. 6 : 10 ; Col. 1 : 11.
o 13 : 1-7 ; 14 : 1 ; John 13 : 34, 35. *p* 1 : 16. *q* Rom. 16 : 5.

---

young (1 Tim. 4 : 12), probably about twenty-five years of age (Acts 16 : 1, note), and naturally timid (2 Tim. 1 : 6-8 ; 2 : 1, 3, 15). In the condition in which the Corinthian church was, there was special need of this injunction. It was high praise of Timothy that Paul could say, **For he worketh the work of the Lord, as I also do,** preaching the gospel faithfully (1 Thess. 3 : 2 ; Phil. 2 : 22).

11. Let no man despise him on account of his youth and natural modesty. (See preceding verse.) **But conduct him forth,** or *send him forth,* on his journey, as in ver. 6 (the note on which see). **In peace,** courteously and lovingly. **For I look for him with the brethren,** Erastus (Acts 18 : 22) and perhaps the bearers of this Epistle. Titus was also sent after Timothy's departure (2 Cor. 12 : 18).

12. As touching, or *And concerning,* **our brother Apollos** (1 : 12), **I greatly desired him,** better, *I besought him much,* **to come unto you with the brethren,** doubtless the bearers of this Epistle (ver. 17). Paul thought Apollos especially fitted to go to Corinth at this time, since he was held in such high esteem there. He was the best one to enforce the teachings of this Epistle. **But his will was not at all,** he was positively unwilling **to come at this time;** he may have feared that his presence would increase the party spirit, and he would do nothing of the kind. **But he will come when he shall have convenient time,** *a good time* both for him and you. And he might think this to be when their party strifes had ceased, and he himself personally should be left out of the question. It is implied that Apollos was at, or near Ephesus at this time, and that he was not a faction-maker, and was on good terms with Paul, and had his confidence and esteem.

13. Paul adds an exhortation, a short summary of their duty at this time. **Watch ye,** like sentinels on guard in face of the enemy, **stand fast in the faith,** steadfastly trust in Christ, and accept and believe his teachings. It was needful that watchfulness and steadfastness should go together. (Comp. 15 : 58 ; 2 Cor. 1 : 24 ; Eph. 6 : 13, 14.) **Quit you like men,** be not feeble and effeminate, but manly and courageous; show moral courage. **Be strong,** or *be strengthened,* not in yourselves, but with the strength provided for you (Eph. 3 : 16). This four-fold exhortation shows what their attitude should be toward their spiritual foes.

14. But toward one another as fellow-Christians, **Let all your things,** rather, *acts,* **be done** *in love,* let divisions and strifes cease, and let love be the element of all your activity. (Comp. chap. 13 ; 8 : 1.)

15. Paul entreats them to exercise a proper regard for faithful laborers, especially the brethren who had come from Corinth and would return with this Epistle. **I beseech you, brethren,** inasmuch as **ye know the house,** or family, **of Stephanas.** (See note on 1 : 16.) The words, *ye know,* to the

firstfruits of Achaia, and *that* they have addicted themselves to ʳ the ministry
16 of the saints,) ˢ that ye submit yourselves unto such, and to every one that helpeth with *us*, and laboureth.
17 I am glad of the coming of Stephanas and Fortunatus and Achaicus: ᵗ for that which was lacking on your part
18 they have supplied. For they have refreshed my spirit and yours. Therefore ᵘ acknowledge ye them that are such.
19 The churches of Asia salute you. ˣ Aquila and Priscilla salute you much in the Lord, ʸ with the church that is
20 in their house. All the brethren greet

Achaia, and that they have set themselves
16 to minister to the saints,) that ye also submit yourselves to such, and to every one that works with us, and
17 labors. And I rejoice at the coming of Stephanas and Fortunatus and Achaicus; for what was lacking on your part
18 they supplied. For they refreshed my spirit and yours; therefore recognize those who are such.
19 The churches of Asia salute you. Aquila and Prisca, with the church that is in their house, salute you much
20 in the Lord. All the brethren salute

r 2 Cor. 9 : 1; Heb. 6 : 10.   s Ver. 18 ; 1 Tim. 5 : 17.
x Acts 18 : 2; Rom. 16 : 3.

t 2 Cor. 11 : 9.   u Phil. 2 : 29 ; 1 Thess. 5 : 12, 13.
y Rom. 16 : 5 ; Philem. 2.

end of the verse, are commonly regarded as a parenthesis. **That it is the firstfruits,** rather, *a first-fruit,* **of Achaia,** the whole of Greece, south of Macedonia. It is not meant that Stephanas and his family were actually the first converts, but among the first converts in the province of Achaia. **And that they have addicted,** better, *devoted,* **themselves to the ministry,** or *service,* **of the saints.** They had voluntarily devoted themselves for the service of Christians, both as to their temporal necessities and spiritual needs (next verse).

16. That ye submit yourselves *also* in turn **unto such,** exercising due regard, heeding their exhortations and co-operating with them (Eph. 5 : 21 ; 1 Peter 5 : 5). **And to every one** *who* **helpeth us,** *works with us,* in the general work of the church, **and laboureth,** implying earnest and laborious toil.

17. I am glad of the coming, or *I rejoice over the presence,* **of Stephanas,** probably the one named in ver. 15, **and Fortunatus and Achaicus,** unknown except as here mentioned. There is a Fortunatus mentioned at the end of Clement's First Epistle to the Corinthians, who may be the one here named. These three have been supposed to be the bearers of the letter referred to in 7 : 1, and on their return to Corinth may have taken this Epistle. **For that which was lacking on your part they have supplied,** the void occasioned by your absence they *fully supplied,* not by pecuniary gifts, for he had not received these from the Corinthian church (2 Cor. 11 : 9), but by their sympathy and love (next verse).

18. For they have refreshed my spirit by their arrival, intercourse, and sympathy, and as a natural consequence *yours* also, since they were your representatives, and their joy was also yours. (Comp. 2 Cor. 1 : 3-7 ; 7 : 13.) Their visit to the apostle resulted in relieving anxiety in a measure of all parties concerned, and reinvigorating their spirits. It awakened hope that the matters in the church might be satisfactorily adjusted. The interest of both the church and the apostle would center in these representatives. **Therefore,** in view of their relation to you and me and their service, **acknowledge,** *recognize rightly and fully,* their character and work, as your guides and representatives (1 Thess. 5 : 12).

19-24. FINAL SALUTATIONS, A SOLEMN WARNING, AND THE CLOSING BENEDICTION.

19. The churches of Asia salute you—the churches in the cities of the Roman province of Asia, southwestern portion of Asia Minor, of which the church at Ephesus was chief. Of these at a later period seven are enumerated in Rev. 1 : 11. From this passage and Col. 4 : 16 we learn that Paul was in a measure acquainted with these churches, and that there existed a fraternal fellowship between the churches. **Aquila and Priscilla** (or *Prisca*), who returned to Rome after Paul left Ephesus, **salute you.** (See note on Rom. 16 : 3.) **With the church that is in their house,** the assembly that was accustomed to meet there for worship. Having a tent-making business they doubtless had room for meetings at their house. (See note on Rom. 16 : 5.)

you. ᶻGreet ye one another with an holy kiss.
21 ᵃThe salutation of *me* Paul with
22 mine own hand. If any man love not the Lord Jesus Christ, ᵇlet him be Anathema ᶜMaran-atha.
23 ᵈThe grace of our Lord Jesus Christ
24 be with you. My love *be* with you all in Christ Jesus. Amen.

The first *Epistle* to the Corinthians was written from Philippi by Stephanas, and Fortunatus, and Achaicus, and Timotheus.

you. Salute one another with a holy
21 kiss. The salutation of me, Paul, with my own hand.
22 If any one loves not the Lord Jesus Christ, let him be accursed. Maran atha.
23 The grace of our Lord be with you.
24 My love be with you all in Christ Jesus. Amen.

z Rom. 16 : 16 ; 1 Thess. 5 : 26 ; 1 Peter 5 : 14.   *a* 2 Thess. 3 : 17.   *b* Gal. 1 : 8, 9.
c Jude 14, 15.   *d* Rom. 16 : 20.

20. All the brethren of the Ephesian church **greet**, or *salute you*. **Greet**, or *salute*, **one another with a holy kiss**, a token of Christian affection and in contrast with anything unchaste and impure, so common in that age. (See note on Rom. 16 : 16.) Such Christian salutations of affection would tend to swallow up all divisions and strifes. In the East men and women sit apart, and salute one another apart. (Compare 2 Cor. 13 : 12, and the "kiss of love," 1 Peter 5 : 14.)

21. The salutation of me Paul with mine own hand. Paul usually employed an amanuensis (Rom. 16 : 22), but added a salutation in his own handwriting, as a mark of its genuineness, and as a personal token of interest and affection (2 Thess. 3 : 17 ; Col. 4 : 18).

22. The three independent sentences that close this Epistle, were also written by Paul in his own handwriting—words of earnest warning and of strong Christian affection. **If any man love not the Lord Jesus Christ,** and divisions and party strifes would indicate a defect or a want of that love (John 14 : 23 ; 1 John 4 : 20). The word translated *love* means intimate personal affection, and is the one that Peter used when he answered, "Thou knowest I *love* thee" (John 21 : 15, note). Paul elsewhere uses another word of Christian love (ver. 24 ; 2 : 9 ; Eph. 6 : 24 ; 1 Thess. 4 : 9), reverential and founded on high qualities of character—the word generally used to express that love which we exercise toward God or God toward us. Doubtless the lack of intimate personal affection among the Corinthians, and consequently toward Christ, suggested to Paul the use of this word. Christians are to cultivate a feeling of personal loyalty and affection for Jesus Christ, such as a soldier feels for his general, or a disciple for his Master" (LIAS). **Let him be anathema,** *accursed* (12 : 3 ; Rom. 9 : 3 ; Gal. 1 : 8). The word is used of a person or thing devoted to destruction without hope of redemption (Josh. 6 : 17 ; 7 : 12 ; comp. Lev. 27 : 28, 29). **Maran atha.** Two Aramaic words, meaning, *Our Lord cometh ;* he is near at hand, be ready to meet him, for he will judge those who reject him (Phil. 4 : 5 ; Mal. 4 : 6). The use of the Aramaic gave force and solemnity to his words. "The Lord cometh" sounds like a familiar watchword of early Christians, who were looking for the early return of their Lord, for the deliverance of his followers, and for vengeance on his foes (2 Thess. 1 : 6-10). These words of the apostle are not vindictive, but are expressive of the repugnance of holiness to sin, and of the righteous feeling of all holy beings toward the crowning sin of men in opposition to the infinite love of God in Christ.

23. But while severe in reproof and faithful in warning, he adds, **The grace of our Lord be with you,** the common closing prayer of his Epistles (Rom. 16 : 20, note ; Gal. 6 : 18 ; Phil. 4 : 23). As the anathema is everlasting perdition so the grace or favor of Christ is eternal life. The words **Jesus Christ** are omitted in the best text.

24. My love, that kind which one Christian exercises for another (ver. 22), **be with you all.** He loves them, though he had been compelled to use severe rebukes, and he loves them all. **In Christ Jesus,** in union and fellowship with him. How Christ is exalted, the all and in all! The Epistle begins and ends with Jesus Christ.

Amen. So it is and so let it be. (See Rom. 1:25.) The subscription is of uncertain authorship and of no authority. From ver. 8 it appears that Paul was at Ephesus, and not at Philippi, when he wrote this Epistle.

PRACTICAL REMARKS.

1. Christian beneficence is a Christian duty. Its exercise should be voluntary and cheerful; systematic and constant; universal, deliberate, and proportionate, according as each has been prospered (ver. 1, 2; Rom. 15:26, 27; 2 Cor. 8:7, 12-15; 9:5-9).

2. The first day of the week, as the resurrection day and the Lord's Day, should arouse such grateful emotions as to make it a fitting and the best time for the exercise of benevolence for Christ's cause and the wants of others (ver. 2; Matt. 12:12).

3. Christian benevolence is not an act of condescension, as often exhibited in almsgiving, but a brotherly exercise of gracious affection (ver. 3; 2 Cor. 8; 19-24).

4. Christian benevolence is a work worthy of an apostle, and of the best of Christ's servants (ver. 4; 2 Cor. 8:18-23).

5. While churches should be ready to commend faithful ministers, ministers should be careful of their conduct, especially in financial matters (ver. 3, 4).

6. We should form our plans and act in dependence upon God and under the direction of his will (ver. 5-8; Jer. 10:23; James 4:15).

7. There is no evidence of a Christian observance of Pentecost in the apostolic age, though doubtless Christians everywhere regarded it with interest, as the day when the Spirit came to be with the church (ver. 8; Acts 2:2; 20:16).

8. When great good is being done, and opposition is excited thereby, the minister, so far from being discouraged, should seize every opportunity for good with faith and boldness (ver. 9; Neh. 6:11).

9. Young preachers of the gospel, who are faithful to Christ, should be encouraged and helped by the churches and the brethren (ver. 10, 11; 3 John 7, 8).

10. So also young preachers should seek so to live as to be worthy of the support and esteem of their brethren (ver. 10, 11; 1 Tim. 4:12).

11. Though Christians differ in regard to methods and plans of work, they should mutually respect each other's opinions, and not be alienated from each other on account of differences in judgment (ver. 12-14).

12. Watchfulness, manliness, steadfastness, and love are most important elements in a life of Christian usefulness (ver. 13, 14; Eph. 6:10).

13. We ought to recognize the various gifts of our brethren, and honor those who have been called to the work of the ministry (ver. 15, 16; 1 Peter 5:5).

14. The meeting of brethren of the churches in conferences, associations, and conventions, should result in mutual edification, and in their increased usefulness (ver. 17, 18).

15. Churches as well as individual believers should exercise toward one another the common courtesies of life, and the attentions of fellowship and love (ver. 19, 20; Acts 15:23, 31; Col. 4:15).

16. How terrible the relation which one sustains to God, to man, and to himself, who loves not Christ (ver. 22; 1 John 4:20).

17. How important and fundamental is the grace of Christ; and among the subjects of grace what a bond is Christian love (ver. 23, 24; 15:10; Eph. 3:17-19).

PAUL'S SECOND EPISTLE TO THE CORINTHIANS

Salutation; Divine consolation and deliverance.

1 PAUL, *ᵃ an apostle of Jesus Christ by the will of God, and ᵇ Timothy *our* brother, ᶜ unto the church of God which is at Corinth, ᵈ with all the saints which
2 are in all Achaia: ᵉ Grace *be* to you and peace from God our Father, and *from* the Lord Jesus Christ.
3 ᶠ Blessed *be* God, even the Father of our Lord Jesus Christ, the Father of

1 PAUL, an apostle of Jesus Christ through the will of God, and Timothy our brother, to the church of God which is in Corinth, with all the saints
2 who are in all Achaia: Grace to you and peace from God our Father and the Lord Jesus Christ.
3 Blessed be the God and Father of our Lord Jesus Christ, the Father of mer-

---

a 1 Cor. 1 : 1 ; 1 Tim. 1 : 1 ; 2 Tim. 1 : 1.   *b* Acts 16 : 1.   *c* 1 Cor. 1 : 2.   *d* Phil. 1 : 1 ; Col. 1 : 2.
e Rom. 1 : 7 ; Gal. 1 : 3 ; Phil. 1 : 2 ; 1 Thess. 1 : 1 ; Philem. 3.   *f* Eph. 1 : 3 ; 1 Peter 1 : 3.

TITLE. Its earliest form is simply, *Second to the Corinthians*, designed merely as a mark of designation. The fuller and later title is embraced in the first verse of the Epistle.

CHAPTER I.

THE FIRST PART of this Epistle, extending to the end of chapter seven, explains why Paul went to Troas instead of coming to Corinth, and the principles on which Paul exercised his ministry. He begins the Epistle with a salutation (ver. 1, 2); then expresses his gratitude for divine consolations in sufferings (ver. 3, 4), whereby he was enabled to console others (ver. 5-7). He refers to his afflictions in Asia, to the mode of his deliverance, and the sympathy of the Corinthian Church (ver. 5-14). He passes to the reasons of delaying his visit to them, and going to Troas instead. That it was not fickleness on his part (ver. 15-22); but in order that he might spare them and help them (ver. 23, 24).

1, 2. SALUTATION.

1. **Paul, an apostle,** etc. (See on 1 Cor. 1 : 1.) As joint-sender of the letter he writes with his own name that of **Timothy our brother,** or more exactly, *the* brother, well known to them, as one who had labored with Paul among them (Acts 18 : 5), and who appears to have recently returned from the journey to Corinth. (See note on 1 Cor. 4 : 17; 16 : 10; Acts 19 : 22.) Timothy, perhaps acted as his amanuensis. **With all the saints which are in Achaia,** in Greece, south of Macedonia. Paul addresses the church at Corinth in particular; but sends salutations of grace and peace to all the saints outside in the province.

2. **Grace be to you and peace.** (See on Rom. 1 : 7; 1 Cor. 1 : 3.) This benediction occurs in eleven of Paul's Epistles. In First and Second Timothy it is "grace, mercy, and peace." Christ is made prominent in this as well as in the first Epistle. (See on 1 Cor. 1 : 8.)

3-7. GRATITUDE FOR DIVINE CONSOLATION AND THE POWER TO COMFORT OTHERS.

3. **Blessed,** or *praised,* **be God, even the Father of our Lord,** etc., he who is God, and at the same time the Father of our Lord Jesus Christ (1 Cor. 15 : 24). It is not "God of," but rather the "Father of our Lord," etc. Yet this relation to God, especially as to Christ's connection with our humanity, is elsewhere expressed (John 20 : 17; Eph. 1 : 17). Not only is God the Father of the Lord Jesus, and hence our Father in a like sense, we being in Christ, who is our elder brother (Rom. 8 : 17), but he also is **the Father of mercies,** one who is characterized by

327

mercies, and the God of all comfort;
4 ᵃ who comforteth us in all our tribulation, ᵇ that we may be able to comfort them which are in any trouble, by the comfort wherewith we ourselves are
5 comforted of God. For as ⁱ the sufferings of Christ abound in us, so our consolation also aboundeth by Christ.
6 And whether we be afflicted, ᵏ it is for your consolation and salvation, which is effectual in the enduring of the same sufferings which we also suffer; or whether we be comforted, it is for your
7 consolation and salvation. And our hope of you is stedfast, knowing, that

cies, and the God of all consolation;
4 who consoles us in all our affliction, that we may be able to console those who are in any affliction, through the consolation wherewith we ourselves
5 are consoled by God. Because, as the sufferings of Christ abound toward us, so through Christ our consolation also
6 abounds. But whether we are afflicted, it is for your consolation and salvation; or whether we are consoled, it is for your consolation, which is effective in the endurance of the same sufferings
7 which we also suffer. And our hope of you is steadfast, knowing, that as ye

g 7 : 6 ; Ps. 66 : 17 ; Isa. 51 : 12 ; John 14 : 16, 18, 26.   *h* Ver. 5, 6 ; Ps. 34 : 2–6 ; 66 : 16.
i 4 : 10, 11 ; 1 Cor. 4 : 16 ; Phil. 3 : 10 ; Col. 1 : 24 ; 1 Peter 4 : 13.   *k* Ver. 4 ; 4 : 15 ; 2 Tim. 2 : 10.

mercies, a quality of his very nature, and growing out of this, **the God of all comfort,** or *of all consolation.* The word "Father" as applied to God suggests the relation of God to man in the exercise of mercy, pity, and compassion (Ps. 103 : 13 ; James 5 : 11). His fatherly compassion succors us, and all the comfort or consolation comes from him, as "the God of all comfort." The word translated *comfort,* or its verb, occurs ten times in this and the next four verses. It is closely allied to *Paraclete,* the Comforter or the Helper (John 14 : 16). It means *consolation,* with the idea of imparting cheer or encouragement to those in afflictions.

4. It is worthy of notice that Paul mostly uses the first person plural in this Epistle, often including Timothy and others, according to the context. He frequently uses the singular, however, in speaking of matters which he would limit to himself individually (ver. 15 ; 2 : 1, etc.). **Who comforteth,** *consoles* and cheers, **us in all our tribulations,** in every kind of *affliction* or *pressure* that befalls us. (Comp. 1 Cor. 7 : 28.) The consolation was continued and constant. **That we may be able to comfort,** or *console* and cheer, **them which,** *that,* **are in any trouble,** *affliction* (the same word as in the preceding clause), **by,** or *through,* **the comfort,** or *consolation,* **wherewith we ourselves are comforted,** *consoled* and cheered, **of,** *by,* **God.** Experience enabled him to comfort and encourage others. Affliction was designed for his good and the good of others. For this reason Paul was willing to endure it, and praise God in connection with it (1 Cor. 10 : 24).

5. Paul gives the reason and explanation of what he had said in the preceding verse. **For as the sufferings of Christ abound in,** rather, *toward,* **us,** or *overflows unto us,* **so our consolation also aboundeth by,** or *through,* **Christ.** On account of our connection with Christ we become partakers in his sufferings, arising from opposition to him (4 : 10 ; Matt. 10 : 25 ; John 15 : 20 ; Col. 1 : 24 ; Gal. 6 : 17 ; Phil. 3 : 10). The consolation comes through Christ, and overflows, as it were, passing over abundantly to you (Rom. 5 : 3–5 ; 8 : 17). Paul regarded himself as one with Christ, and through him, one with his brethren.

6. While there is no difference in the sense of this verse, there is considerable difference in the order of the words in various manuscripts. The most approved text reads *And whether we are afflicted, it is for your consolation and salvation ; or whether we are consoled, it is for your consolation, which is effectual in the endurance of the same sufferings which we also suffer.* Thus according to the principle presented in ver. 4, 5, both affliction and consolation are productive of consolation and salvation in others (4 : 15 ; 2 Tim. 2 : 8–12). **Which is effectual,** or *which works* and *is effective* in steadfast endurance. The consolation enables them to endure and be steadfast in the faith (Heb. 10 : 23, 26). The sufferings and the consolation were both of the same kind in Paul and in them, though in their personal experiences they would vary and differ in degree ; and all were connected with Christ.

7. And our hope of you is steadfast for your consolation and

l as ye are partakers of the sufferings, so *shall ye be* also of the consolation.
8 For we would not, brethren, have you ignorant of m our trouble which came to us in Asia, that we were pressed out of measure, above strength, insomuch that we despaired even of
9 life: but we had the sentence of death in ourselves, that we should o not trust in ourselves, o but in God which raiseth
10 the dead: p who delivered us from so great a death, and doth deliver; in whom we trust that he will yet deliver

are partakers of the sufferings, so are ye of the consolation also.
8 For we do not wish you to be ignorant, brethren, of our affliction which befell us in Asia, that we were exceedingly weighed down beyond our power,
9 so that we despaired even of life. Yea, we ourselves had in ourselves the sentence of death, that we should not trust in ourselves, but in God who
10 raises the dead; who delivered us from so great a death, and will deliver; in whom is our hope that he will still de-

l Rom. 8 : 17, 18; 2 Tim. 2 : 12; 1 Peter 5 : 10. *m* Acts 19 : 23, 32-35; 1 Cor. 15 : 32. *n* Jer. 17 : 5, 7.
o 4 : 13, 14. *p* 1 Sam. 7 : 12; 17 : 37; 2 Tim. 4 : 17, 18; 2 Peter 2 : 9.

salvation; **knowing that as ye are partakers of the sufferings** for Christ, **so shall ye be**, rather, *so are ye also*, sharers **of the consolation** through Christ. It is a present possession, and an encouragement and promise of a glorious future (4 : 17; Rom. 8 : 14. 23). By virtue of his union with Christ, Paul was both afflicted and consoled; and his Corinthian brethren were joint-partakers of his joys and his sorrows. Notice how he identifies himself with them.

8-14. PAUL'S AFFLICTION IN ASIA, HIS DELIVERANCE, AND THE DESERVED SYMPATHY OF THE CORINTHIAN CHURCH.

8. For, connects the following incident with the preceding verses, and gives a reason for what he had said about their mutual dependence and sympathy. **We would not have you ignorant,** a favorite expression of Paul's. (See on 1 Cor. 10 : 1.) **Of our trouble,** rather, *our affliction* (the same word as that used twice in ver. 4), **which came to us in Asia,** in the Roman province of Asia. (See on 1 Cor. 16 : 19.) The plural here appears to include Timothy, who shared the affliction with him to a certain extent. What this affliction was is uncertain. It was not probably the tumult at Ephesus (Acts 19 : 28-31), for Paul seems to have been kept out of danger. (Comp. note on Rom. 16 : 4.) Yet it is possible that, notwithstanding his Roman citizenship, the people in excited frenzy might have compelled him to fight with wild beasts for his life. (Comp. 1 Cor. 15 : 32.) The affliction seems to have been recent and known somewhat to the Corinthians, and probably occurred since writing his First Epistle. It seems better, however, to regard this affliction as some severe and deadly sickness, perhaps some epidemic that prostrated both Paul and Timothy. This agrees with their being **pressed out of measure, above strength,** or *being exceedingly weighed down beyond our strength, so that* **we despaired even of life.** This agrees also with their feelings that they were going to die (next verse). This too, may have caused Paul to delay still longer at Ephesus, even beyond Pentecost (1 Cor. 16 : 8), before going to Corinth. (See discussion in Clark's "Harmonic Arrangement of the Acts," p. 227.)

9. But, rather, *Yea,* **we had the sentence,** or *response,* **of death in ourselves,** in our own consciousness. The word translated *sentence,* means an *answer* which a judge, for example, might give. To the question, What would be the result of this affliction? the answer in our own convictions was *Death.* There was an inward persuasion or conviction to this effect. The design of God in this was, **that we should not trust in ourselves, but in God which** (*who*) **raiseth the dead;** who possessed this almighty power, which, if not then exercised in our behalf, would be in a future resurrection.

10. Who delivered us *out of so great a death,* from so great exposure and danger of death; well expressive of some apparently deadly disease. **And doth deliver.** The common reading, that God *did, does,* and *will deliver,* is favored by internal evidence. But the highest critical authorities adopt from external evidence the reading *and will deliver; in whom is*

11 *us;* ye also helping together by prayer for us, that for the gift *bestowed* upon us by the means of many persons thanks may be given by many on our behalf.

Reasons for Paul's delay of his intended visit.

12 For our rejoicing is this, the testimony of our conscience, that in simplicity and godly sincerity, not with fleshly wisdom, but by the grace of God, we have had our conversation in the world, and more abundantly to you-
13 ward. For we write none other things unto you, than what ye read or acknowledge; and I trust ye shall acknowledge
14 knowledge even to the end; as also ye have acknowledged us in part, that

11 liver; ye also helping together on our behalf by your supplication, that for the mercy bestowed on us through many persons, thanks may be given
12 through many on our behalf. For our glorying is this, the testimony of our conscience, that in holiness and godly sincerity, not in fleshly wisdom, but in the grace of God, did we conduct ourselves in the world, and more abun-
13 dantly toward you. For we write no other things to you, than what ye read or even acknowledge, and I trust ye
14 will acknowledge even to the end; as also ye did acknowledge us in part,

q See refs. Rom. 15:30; Phil. 1:19; Philem. 22.   r 4:15; 9:11,12.   s See refs. Acts 23:1; Rom. 9:1.
t 2:17; 4:2.   u 1 Cor. 2:4, 5, 13.   x 5:11.   y 5:12; Phil. 1:26.

our hope that he will still deliver. Paul first expresses his belief that God will deliver in the future as in the past. Then he emphatically repeats this belief, presenting God as the ground of his confidence, upon whom he has set and fixed his hope, that he would still continue to exercise mighty, life-saving power. He looked upon himself as one raised, as it were, from the dead. (Comp. Acts 14:19, 20.)

11. Paul recognizes also the help they had received from the prayers of his Corinthian brethren: **Ye also helping together by prayer** *on our behalf;* by individual and united prayer (Phil. 1:19; Rom. 15:30, 31). **That for the gift,** the divine *favor,* the *mercy,* **bestowed upon us by the means of many persons, thanks may be given by many persons,** literally, *countenances,* a vivid representation of the multitude of upturned *faces* to God in thanksgiving. First prayer, then thanks, by the Corinthians **on our behalf.** We have here a striking illustration of the mutual interest, feeling, and sympathy between Paul and his converts. Between them was a unity of soul and heart.

12. Paul expresses his joy and exultation that this sympathy and interest were fitting and deserved. **For our rejoicing,** better, our cause of *glorying* **is this, which is the testimony of our conscience, that in simplicity,** rather, according to the best text, *in holiness,* **and godly sincerity,** or *sincerity of God* (1 Cor. 5:8), proceeding from and implanted by the Holy Spirit; **not with,** better, *in,* **fleshly wisdom,** not in the wisdom of worldly prudence and of unrenewed men, **but by the grace of God.** Not relying on carnal wisdom, but upon the favor of God, **we have had our conversation,** rather, *our conduct,* **in the world.** The word conversation is used in its old sense of *ordinary conduct.* The meaning is, *we conducted ourselves* in the world, among the heathen, **and more abundantly** *toward you,* as Christians, giving special proofs to you of our holiness and godly sincerity, in laboring so long and faithfully, and maintaining ourselves with the work of our own hands (11:7-10). And so they should give him their prayers (ver. 11).

13. Paul confirms the preceding assertion, and declares the honesty and candor of his writings. **For we write none other thing to you than what you read** (*know* by reading) in our Epistles—we disguise nothing, we mean exactly what we have written; **or, what ye acknowledge** by your observation of our conduct, and by your acquaintance and experience with us; **and I trust ye** *will* **acknowledge even to the end.** The verb translated *acknowledge* means *to know thoroughly,* and hence to *recognize* a thing as it really is.

14. As also ye *did* acknowledge **us in part,** comparing the future with the past. Only a part of the church fully recognized his true char-

we are your rejoicing, even as ᵃ ye also *are* ours, in the day of the Lord Jesus.
15 And in this confidence ᵃ I was minded to come unto you before, that ye might
16 have ᵇ a second benefit; and to pass by you into Macedonia, and ᶜ to come again out of Macedonia unto you, and of you to be brought on my way toward Judæa.
17 When I therefore was thus minded, did I use lightness? Or the things that I purpose, do I purpose ᵈ according to the flesh, that with me ᵉ there should
18 be yea yea, and nay nay? But *as* God

that we are your glorying, even as ye also are ours in the day of our Lord Jesus.
15 And in this confidence I intended to come to you before, that ye might have
16 a second benefit; and through you to go into Macedonia, and from Macedonia to come again to you, and by you to be helped forward on my way
17 to Judæa. When therefore I intended this, did I show fickleness? Or the things that I purpose, do I purpose according to the flesh, that with me there should be the yea, yea, and the

---

ᵃ Phil. 2 : 16; 4 : 1; 1 Thess. 2 : 19, 20.   ᵃ 1 Cor. 4 : 19.   ᵇ Rom. 1 : 11; 15 : 29; Phil. 1 : 25, 26.
ᶜ 1 Cor. 16 : 5, 6.   ᵈ 10 : 2.   ᵉ Matt. 5 : 37.

---

acter. But he hoped that they all would generally recognize and acknowledge, **that we are your rejoicing,** the object of *your glorying* (9 : 3) **even as ye also are ours,** the future is present, as it were, in Paul's eye of faith, **in the day of Jesus Christ,** at his second coming, when teachers and churches shall stand before him in their true relations and character (1 Cor. 3 : 13. note). They were and should be each other's boasts. Their interests were mutual, and their sympathy with one another complete. At the very beginning of his Epistle he would have them recognize this, and he thus affectionately expresses himself before he proceeds to vindicate himself.

15-24. WHY HE HAD DELAYED VISITING THE CORINTHIANS. He vindicates himself against any fickleness on his part, which some of his opposers were disposed to charge against him.

15. And in this confidence—in the conviction that his Corinthian converts had this mutual oneness of feelings with him (ver. 12-14) Paul had determined to visit them **before** going to Macedonia, in order that they **might have a second benefit,** a *second favor* of his presence with its accompanying blessings, by visiting them again on his return from Macedonia. It was because all his converts did not recognize this mutual relation and feeling that he wrote his First Epistle, (3 : 4) waiting to see its effect, and so delayed to come at once to them (ver. 23).

16. How they might have enjoyed this second benefit of his presence is here told. He had planned to give them a first favor by coming to them directly from Ephesus over the Ægean Sea to Corinth, remaining a short time, and so **by,** or *through you,* **to pass** by land **into Macedonia, and to come again out of Macedonia unto you,** thus giving a second benefit or favor, when he might tarry longer. He may have announced this plan in his lost Epistle (1 Cor. 5 : 9); and perhaps upon changing his plan, or contemplating such a change, he sent to them Timothy (1 Cor. 4 : 17; Acts 19 : 22) before writing his first Epistle. But after writing it, and finding that the condition of things at Corinth demanded urgent attention, he sent to them Titus (8 : 16; 12 : 17, 18). It would seem that the Corinthians had learned of this change of plan at that time. **And,** *by,* **you to be brought,** or *helped forward,* with kind attentions and an escort (see 1 Cor. 16 : 6, note) **on my way toward Judea.** This was the very opposite of the route he actually took. He went through Macedonia to Corinth, and then returned through Macedonia on his way to Judea (Acts 20 : 1-3).

17. When I therefore was thus minded, *when I purposed this,* **did I use lightness?** did I show *the lightheadedness* and *fickleness* with which I am charged? **Or the things that I purpose, do I purpose,** is it my habit to purpose, **according to the flesh,** like a worldly and unrenewed man to be actuated by worldly motives and subject to caprice. Has such been my habit *in order that* **there should be** *the* **yea yea, and** *the* **nay nay,** now a solemn affirmation and then an emphatic denial, forming my plans in such a manner as to carry them out or not, according to the dictates of pleasure

is true, our word toward you was not 19 yea and nay. For ʲthe Son of God, Jesus Christ, who was preached among you by us, even by me and ᵍSilvanus and Timotheus, ʰ was not yea and nay; 20 but in him was yea. ⁱFor all the promises of God in him *are* yea, and in him Amen, unto the glory of God by 21 us. Now he ᵏ which stablisheth us with you in Christ, and ˡ hath anointed

18 nay, nay? As God is faithful, our word 19 to you is not yea and nay. For the Son of God, Jesus Christ, who was preached among you through us, through me and Silvanus and Timothy, was not 20 yea and nay, but is yea in him. For however many are the promises of God, in him is the yea; wherefore also through him is the Amen, to the glory 21 of God through us. Now he who confirms us with you in Christ, and

ʲ See refs. Luke 1 : 35.   ᵍ Acts 18 : 5, Silas.   ʰ Exod. 3 : 14; Heb. 13 : 8; Rev. 3 : 14.
ⁱ Rom. 11 : 29; 15 : 8, 9.   ᵏ Rom. 16 : 25.   ˡ 1 John 2 : 20, 27.

or profit? The repetition of *yea* and *nay* expresses emphasis. Instead of such duplicity and fickleness it is implied that he had adhered to his purpose throughout of coming to them, according to the will of God and the promptings of the Spirit (1 Cor. 4 : 19; 16 : 7).

18. A solemn assertion of his sincere and honest consistency. **But as God is true,** rather, *faithful*. A solemn appeal to God, as if he had said, God is my faithful witness and judge, **our word,** whether by preaching, conversation, or letter, **toward,** or *to*, **you, was not,** rather, according to the best text, *is not*, **yea and nay,** double-tongued and wavering. God knows that my teachings among you have never been characterized by any capricious changeableness, or carnal self-seeking. His conduct and teaching were so closely connected that the vindication of the latter was the vindication of the former.

19. His preaching, **the Son of God, Jesus Christ,** his great theme, was an argument against any fickleness on his part. Both his manner of preaching and the truth he uttered were opposed to vacillation. This verse is confirmatory of the preceding. The us here were Paul, **Silvanus,** of which Silas was an abbreviation, **and Timothy.** Silas first appears at the council at Jerusalem, whence he goes as a delegate with Paul and Barnabas on their return to Antioch. He is afterward chosen by Paul to take the place of Mark on his second missionary journey (Acts 15 : 22, 25, 27, 32, 40). He was with Paul at Philippi (Acts 16 : 19), at Thessalonica (Acts 17 : 4), at Berea (Acts 17 : 10), and at Corinth (Acts 18 : 5). Both in the last passage (Acts 18 : 5) and **here Silas is** mentioned incidentally and

similarly. This undesigned agreement in such minute matters by the two authors, writing at different times and places, confirms the truthfulness of both writers. Silas and Timothy were Pauline preachers. Their preaching **was not yea and nay,** dubious and contradictory; **but in him,** in Christ, it **was yea,** rather, *is yea*, is positive, unchangeable truth (James 1 : 17; Num. 23 : 19; Heb. 13 : 8). With such a message their conduct must have been consistent, honest, and true.

20. For, to substantiate what I have just said, **all the promises,** rather, *however many are the promises of God, in him is the yea,* the positive, affirmative utterance and certain fulfillment. **And in him** *the* **Amen,** ratified in Christ. God's promises find their expression in Christ, and are assured to us in and through Christ (Rev. 3 : 14). But according to the most approved text, the latter clause should read, *Wherefore also through him is the Amen,* referring to the responsive Amen in their assemblies (1 Cor. 14 : 16, note), expressing acceptance of and full assurance in the promises as true through Christ, **unto the glory of God by,** rather, *through*, **us.** It is through the preaching of the gospel that men are brought to an assured faith in God's promises (Rom. 10 : 14), and thus to glorify him.

21. This fixed assurance he traces back to God. **Now he which,** *who*, **stablisheth,** *confirms*, **us with you,** firm and steadfast, **in Christ** (Heb. 6 : 19) **and hath anointed us,** by his Spirit, **is God.** Notice how Paul improves every occasion for expressing his common interest and complete union with the Corinthians, *you with us*. And also how he regards them all as closely united to and identified in Christ. We

22 us, is God; who hath also sealed us, and given the earnest of the Spirit in our hearts.
23 Moreover I call God for a record upon my soul, that to spare you I
24 came not as yet unto Corinth. Not for that we have dominion over your faith, but are helpers of your joy: for by faith ye stand.

22 anointed us, is God; he who also sealed us, and gave the earnest of the Spirit in our hearts
23 But I invoke God for a witness upon my soul, that to spare you I came not
24 yet to Corinth. Not that we lord it over your faith, but are helpers of your joy; for in faith ye stand fast.

m Ezek. 9 : 4; Eph. 1 : 13; 4 : 30; 2 Tim. 2 : 19; Rev. 2 : 17.   *n* 5 : 5; Rom. 8 : 16, 23; Eph. 1 : 14.
o Job 16 : 19; Rom. 1 : 9; Phil. 1 : 8; 1 Thess. 2 : 5.   *p* 10 : 2, 6–11; 13 : 2, 10; 1 Cor. 4 : 21.
q 4 : 5; Matt. 23 : 8–10; 2 Tim. 2 : 24–26; 1 Peter 5 : 3.   *r* Rom. 1 : 12, Phil. 1 : 25, 26.
s Rom. 11 : 20; 1 Peter 5 : 8, 9.

are established in *the Anointed who hath anointed us*, giving us the unction of the Spirit, the privilege of all believers (1 John 2 : 20), that they should be "a chosen generation, a royal priesthood, a holy nation, a people for a possession" (1 Peter 2 : 9). Compare the anointing of Christ by the Holy Spirit at his baptism (Acts 4 : 27; 10 : 38; Luke 3 : 22; 4 : 1, 18). So also kings, priests, and prophets were anointed under the old dispensation (Lev. 8 : 12; 1 Sam. 16 : 15; 1 Kings 19 : 16).

22. Who hath also sealed us, more exactly, *Who also sealed us and gave us the earnest of the Spirit in our hearts.* The sealing is derived from the practice of signing and attesting legal documents (comp. note on 1 Cor. 9 : 2) to prove them genuine and maintain them inviolate. So they had been attested by the Holy Spirit as genuine believers, and as belonging to God (2 Tim. 2 : 19). The word translated **earnest** is found only here, in 5 : 5, and Eph. 1 : 14, in the New Testament, which word passed from the Phœnician into the Greek, and was applied to money deposited as part payment and a pledge of the future full payment. The term is a strong one, indicating the indwelling Spirit *in our hearts* as an installment and pledge of what is to come in the state of future blessedness (Eph. 1 : 14). Thus the believer is anointed or consecrated, sealed or marked as God's own, and given the earnest, the pledge and foretaste, by the Spirit. On the human side the *anointing* was the reception of the Holy Spirit, the Comforter, by faith; and the conscious possession of the Spirit became the *earnest*, the foretaste and pledge, giving assurance; and on the divine side was the *sealing*, the attesting of the believers by the Spirit, as God's own, "a peculiar people, zealous of good works" (Titus 2 : 14). This the apostle, his assistants, and Corinthian believers had enjoyed, after they had believed (Eph. 1 : 13). And as an application to the subject in hand, he would say that one who enjoyed, held, and taught such doctrines could not be fickle or carnal (ver. 17) in conduct and method.

23. Having vindicated h i m s e l f against the charge of fickleness, Paul now states the reason why he had delayed visiting Corinth. **Moreover,** etc., rather, *But* **I,** for my part, whatever my opponents may say, **call God to witness upon my soul,** appealing to God as a witness to his sincerity. Some take the expression to mean *against my soul,* which would require the addition, "if I speak not the truth." It rather means, that he calls God to witness upon what was the dearest to him, his very life, his soul, that he speaks the truth (Rom. 1 : 9; 9 : 1). This solemn oath of the apostle was justified, because his word and conduct had been called in question at Corinth, and were connected with the honor of Christ and the cause of God. **That to spare you I came not as yet to Corinth.** He would spare them from any sharpness or severity which he might feel compelled to use. He hoped that his First Epistle would produce a good effect, so that he might bring them loving service in the spirit of meekness (1 Cor. 4 : 21).

24. Not that we have dominion, or *we lord it,* **over your faith.** Fearing that a misconstruction might be put upon his words, Paul disclaims lordship over their faith in Christ and in the truth. So far from that, **we are helpers of your joy.** Whatever he does, he acts as a co-operating friend, not for producing grief, but rather for increasing their ultimate joy. **For by,** rather, *in*, **faith ye stand** firm (Rom. 11:20). They exercised faith in Christ, each one for himself independently, and in that believing condition they stood steadfast amid all dangers; and this indeed was a source of joy. It was not their faith, but their conduct, that caused the apostle's anxiety and brought forth his rebuke. But even in this he was a helper of their joy which their disorders had marred.

PRACTICAL REMARKS.

1. We should seek the happy consciousness of being in Christ's work, and of doing it according to God's will (ver. 1; 2 Tim. 1:12).

2. A church is a company of saints called out from the world, in fellowship with Christ and his people (ver. 2; Acts 20:28).

3. God is our only and real source of mercy and consolation (ver. 3; John 3:16; James 1:17).

4. Our afflictions and consolations enable us to comfort and instruct others (ver. 4; Col. 1:24).

5. Through self-sacrifice and suffering the Christian lives over, as it were, the life of Christ for the good of others (ver. 5, 6; 4:10-12).

6. Our connection with Christ's sufferings connects us with the sufferings of others in sympathy and for doing them good (ver. 5; 1 Peter 4:13).

7. It is our duty to use the experiences God has given us for the salvation and comfort of our fellow-men (ver. 6; Rom. 5:3-5).

8. Sanctified sufferings give hope of future blessings and final salvation (ver. 7; Rom. 8:17, 18).

9. It is well at times to look death in the face, in order to be faithful to ourselves and to others (ver. 8, 9; 1 Cor. 7:29-31).

10. A view of our mortality should compel our trust in God for all the blessings of life and salvation (ver. 9, 10).

11. We should regard God as the source of deliverance from every trial with expectation and thanksgiving (ver. 10, 11).

12. The pastor should have the prayers of his people, who can thus help him as in no other way (ver. 11; 1 Thess. 5:25).

13. Seeking the Divine favor, our conduct should be honest, straightforward, and according to the dictates of an enlightened conscience (ver. 12; Acts 23:1; 24:16).

14. Honest words will find a response in the hearts of others (ver. 13; John 1:47).

15. There should be mutual confidence, mutual love, and mutual joy between pastor and people (ver. 14; Phil. 4:1).

16. How many things may modify or change our best-laid plans (ver. 15; Acts 16:6-8).

17. "The purer a man's intentions are, the more unsuspicious will he be, and the more free will he be to adjust his course to new circumstances."—RIEGER. (Ver. 15-17.)

18. Of all men, a Christian should be a man of truth (ver. 18).

19. There are no contradictions or falsehoods in Christ and his word (ver. 19; John 14:6; 18:37; Rev. 3:7).

20. The promises of God are for God's glory in and through Christ, and are certain of fulfillment (ver. 20; 2 Peter 3:9).

21. Christian stability is from God, in Christ, and by the Spirit (ver. 21, 22; 1 Peter 1:5).

22. It is a terrible sin for a Christian to grieve the Spirit, since through the Spirit he has his anointing, his sealing, his pledge, and foretaste of future blessedness (ver. 21, 22).

23. The enjoyment of the graces of the Spirit is an evidence of eternal life (ver. 22).

24. If an inspired apostle would not lord it over his own converts in respect to their belief and trust in Christ, how unbecoming to uninspired men, such as popes and bishops, is it to exercise spiritual dominion over the faith and consciences of others (ver. 23, 24; 1 Peter 5:2-5).

CHAPTER II.

Paul still continues his reasons for delaying his visit to the Corinthians. He would not come to them in sorrow (ver. 1-4). His object was the spiritual good of all; and now he advises that the penitent offender be forgiven and restored (ver. 5-11). He explains why he left Troas and came into Macedonia (ver. 12, 13); but, notwithstanding, ex-

2   BUT I determined this with myself, ‘that I would not come again to you in
2 heaviness. For if I make you sorry, who is he then that maketh me glad, but the same which is made sorry by
3 me? And I wrote this same unto you, lest, when I came, ᵘ I should have sorrow from them of whom I ought to rejoice; ˣ having confidence in you all, that my joy is *the joy* of you all.
4 For out of much affliction and anguish of heart I wrote unto you with many tears; ʸ not that ye should be grieved,

2 AND I determined this with myself, that I would not come again to you in
2 sorrow. For if I make you sorry, who then is he that makes me glad, but he
3 that is made sorry by me? And I wrote this very thing, that I might not, when I came, have sorrow from those of whom I ought to have joy; having confidence in you all, that my
4 joy is the joy of you all. For out of much affliction and anguish of heart I wrote to you, through many tears; not

t 12 : 20, 21 ; 13 : 10.   *u* 12 : 20, 21.   *x* 8 : 22 ; Gal. 5 : 10.   *y* 7 : 8, 9, 12.

ults at the thought of what God had wrought through him (ver. 14-16), humbly acknowledging his own insufficiency, yet affirming his sincerity (ver. 17).

1–4. HE WOULD NOT COME TO THEM IN SORROW. His object had not been to grieve them, but to manifest his love, and advance them spiritually.

1. But, rather, *And*, continuing the explanation why he stayed away from Corinth. In addition to sparing them the sharp reproofs which his immediate presence would have necessitated (1 : 23), he would bring joy instead of sorrow. **I determined with myself,** in my own mind and independently of others. (Comp. Acts 26 : 9.) Many, however, prefer to translate, *for myself*, that is, for my own sake and advantage I determined, etc. But it was more like Paul to state his own private determination, which was: **That I would not come again to you in heaviness,** better, *in grief*, or *sorrow*—I grieving you (ver. 2), and you grieving me (ver. 3). *Again* does not belong to *heaviness* (*sorrow*), but to *come*—he would not make his third visit (see on 12 : 14) in sorrow.

2. For if I, on my part, **make you sorry in coming to you, who is he then that maketh me glad, but the same which,** *that*, **is made sorry by me.** They must be his source of gladness, but his visit would have rather caused grief to them and consequent grief to him. He would ensure this source of his joy. Hence he delayed his coming in order that he might remove what would be a cause of sorrow.

3. And I wrote this same, *this very thing*, I wrote as I did **unto you** (1 Cor. 4 : 21; 5 : 5), rebuking you in re-

gard to laxity of discipline. Some would refer this to his announcement of his change of purpose in coming to them (1 Cor. 16 : 7); but this is not probable. What follows evidently refers to the rebukes of his former Epistle. The object of his writing was **lest,** better, *that I might not, when I come have sorrow from those of whom I ought to have joy.* Had he gone to them before writing he would have had sorrow and caused sorrow, because of their inconsistent and unchristian conduct (12 : 20, 21). But he felt assured, that if he wrote them things would be righted, and that there would be no necessity of severely rebuking them, **having confidence in you all, that my joy is the joy of you all.** He felt assured that he and they were one in feelings and interest, in hopes and love; that they all desired to do right and be led by the Spirit, and were so attached to him as to be won over by his words. His joy at such a result would be their joy (1 : 6); even to **all,** though some had been opposed to him, yet his joy would be shared by them all.

4. Explanatory of the preceding verse and containing a reason for his confidence as just expressed. **For out of much affliction and anguish,** *burden and distress*, **of heart** (Luke 21 : 25) **I wrote unto you with many tears,** which, in case of a man of strong intellect like Paul, showed intense grief. We see the spirit in which Paul wrote, and how painful it was for him to blame and rebuke them. His object was not to grieve them, but to make them know his great love for them, out of which his reproofs sprang. This would soften his words and their hearts, and produce that feeling and

but that ye might know the love which I have more abundantly unto you.

5 But *if any have caused grief, he hath not grieved me, but in part: that
6 I may not overcharge you all. Sufficient to such a man *is* this punishment,
7 which *was inflicted* ᵃ of many. ᵇ So that contrariwise ye *ought* rather to forgive *him*, and comfort *him*, ᶜ lest perhaps such an one should be swallowed up

that ye might have sorrow, but that ye might know the love which I have very abundantly toward you.

5 But if any one has caused sorrow, he has caused sorrow not to me, but in
6 part (not to be too severe) to you all. Sufficient for such a one is this punishment, which was afflicted by the many.
7 So that, on the contrary, ye ought rather to forgive and console him, lest perhaps such a one should be

z 7 : 11 ; 1 Cor. 5 : 1, 5.   *a* 1 Cor. 5 : 4, 5 ; 1 Tim. 5 : 20.   *b* Gal. 6 : 1 ; Eph. 4 : 32.   *c* Prov. 17 : 22.

action which would result in joy. We have here the complement, the other side, of what he had said in the preceding verse. **The love which I have more abundantly,** or *very abundantly, toward* **you.** They were especially dear to him, like children to a parent. And with this deep affection naturally went out his intense anxiety for their perfection.

5-11. ADVISES THE FORGIVENESS AND RESTORATION OF THE PENITENT OFFENDER. But who was this offender? Expositors generally have answered, The incestuous person named in 1 Cor. 5 : 1. This seems to be the natural conclusion from comparing this passage with that. But some think it must have been some leading and insulting opponent of the apostle, since the latter speaks of some offense against himself personally (ver. 10; 7 : 12). But it was only against himself in part. (See on ver. 10.) Besides the incestuous person very likely had opposed Paul after the advice given in the letter mentioned in 1 Cor. 5 : 9. Moreover, the theory that it was not this incestuous person necessitates the supposition that Paul wrote four Epistles to the Corinthians, a third having been written between this and our First Epistle. Upon the whole the common view seems to me beset with the fewest difficulties, and is the one adopted in these notes.

5. Having spoken of the deep anxiety in which he wrote them, and their implied sorrow, he very delicately refers to the one who had caused much of the trouble. **But if any** *one has* **caused grief,** or *sorrow*. Notice how he carefully refers to the incestuous person, without mentioning his name or his crime (1 Cor. 5 : 1). **He hath not grieved,** or *caused sorrow* to **me** personally; it being a public of-

fense, affecting the whole church. *Me* is emphatic and put in contrast with *you all;* **but in part,** or *in some degree to you all, not to be severe*, not to give pain to you and to him by speaking too severely. Paul has in mind that the offender had repented, and he would exercise forbearance and forgiveness (ver. 6-11), and he also would exonerate the church from his charge of indifference (1 Cor. 5 : 2) ; it is also implied that the church had mourned over the sin and exercised the proper discipline. The apostle now writes in mildness, since he would not cause further sorrow to any.

6. It would seem that Paul's former Epistle regarding the offender had aroused strong feelings against him (7 : 8 ff.), and now he strives to moderate this feeling. **Sufficient** in magnitude and severity **to such a man,** exercising such a spirit of repentance and renunciation of his sin, **is this punishment**—doubtless exclusion from the church, for in ver. 9 it is implied that they had been obedient in all things. (See 1 Cor. 5 : 3-5, 13.) **Which was inflicted of,** or *by the*, **many,** *the greater part* of you. This discipline was exercised not by the officers, but by the church (Matt. 18 : 17, 18). All of the church were probably not present when this punishment was inflicted. Some also may not have assented to the offender's exclusion, or may have declined to take part, or may have remained passive in the matter; for there were still opposers in the church to Paul's apostolic authority.

7. So now he counsels lenity. **So that** contrariwise **ye ought,** or *should*, **rather forgive and comfort,** or *console*, him with cheer and encouragement. (See note on 1 : 3.) **Lest such a one**, so Paul designates the well-known offender (1 Cor. 5 : 5), be

8 with overmuch sorrow. Wherefore I beseech you that ye would confirm
9 *your* love toward him. For to this end also did I write, that I might know the proof of you, whether ye be ⁴obedient
10 in all things. To whom ye forgive any thing, I *forgive* also: for if I forgave any thing, to whom I forgave *it*, for your sakes *forgave I it*, in the person of
11 Christ; ᵉlest Satan should get an advantage of us; for we are not ignorant of his devices.

swallowed up with his overmuch sorrow. Wherefore I beseech you to con-
8 firm your love toward him. For to this end also I wrote, that I might know the proof of you, whether ye are
10 obedient in all things. And to whom ye forgive anything, I forgive also; for what I also have forgiven, if I have forgiven anything, for your sakes I
11 forgave it in the person of Christ, that no advantage might be gained over us

d 7 : 15.   *e* 11 : 3, 14; Eph. 6 : 11, 12.

swallowed up, overwhelmed, **with overmuch sorrow.** This expresses figuratively the effect of extreme grief, lest he be consumed with grief, driven into a melancholy and despairing state. It is implied that he had repented and deeply mourned over his sin.

8. Wherefore, in view of this, **I beseech you** *to* **confirm your love,** or rather, *confirm love*, this fundamental, vital, Christian principle, **toward him.** The verb translated *confirm* is also used officially, as to *ratify* some public act or covenant (Gal. 3 : 15, 17). The meaning here appears to be, That ye publicly decide or declare that love be shown to him by granting him pardon and restoration. Thus the object of the discipline of the church would be attained.

9. Reason for adopting gentler means toward the offender, since the object of his writing had been attained. **For to this end also did I write,** in my former Epistle regarding the incestuous person (1 Cor. 5 : 2, 4, 7), **that I might know the proof of you,** the trial and test of your character (a proof as a result of testing), **whether ye be,** or *are*, **obedient in all things;** he would test their obedience to his directions as an inspired apostle. Here then was one reason for his writing the First Epistle. Not only did he wish his coming to them to be not painful but joyous, not only to do them good by inducing them to exercise healthful discipline, but also to know their readiness to obey his injunctions. This having been accomplished to his satisfaction, he enjoins the restoration of the offender, which, judging from their ready and obedient spirit, would be done.

10. Their forgiveness of the offender would receive his sanction. **To whom ye forgive anything, I forgive also.** He feels assured of the unity of the church with him in exercising love (ver. 8) toward the offender, and he is ready to ratify their action in advance. Notice how he honors the church, which must take the lead in its discipline. The pardon was of a public offense against the church, which Paul sanctioned and forgave as far as it affected him. **For if I forgave anything,** rather, according to best text, *For what I also have forgiven, if I have forgiven anything,* **for your sakes forgive I it.** If he had forgiven anything which affected him personally, he had done it not for selfish ends, but for their sakes and in the confidence that they would forgive. His ministry and apostleship were not for his own advantage, but for theirs. And this forgiveness he had exercised **in the person of Christ,** as Christ's representative. So in the *name of the Lord Jesus* he had ordered the exclusion of the offender (1 Cor. 5 : 4). Some translate and interpret, *in the presence of Christ,* as if Christ himself were present and looking on with approval. The first rendering is to be preferred, though the idea of an observing and approving Lord may be included.

11. A final motive for exercising forgiveness. **Lest Satan should get an advantage over us,** *overreach us,* in doing injury when we have an opportunity of doing good. In his exclusion from the church the offender had been delivered over to Satan (1 Cor. 5 : 5, note). But in his repentance he was renouncing the power and dominion of Satan. If the church refused forgiveness and restoration, then he might be discouraged and driven to despair (ver. 7). And in his despair he might plunge deeper into crime. **For we**

12 Furthermore, *when I came to Troas* by Satan; for we are not ignorant of his devices.
12 Now when I came to Troas to preach

f Acts 16 : 8 ; 20 : 6.

are not ignorant of his devices, his evil designs and plottings against Christ's people (Eph. 6 : 11; 1 Peter 5 : 8). *Satan* means *adversary*, and he is presented as the great adversary of believers. The design of the discipline had been the good and reformation of the offender, but this might be thwarted by Satan if an unforgiving spirit was manifested by the church. The personality and agency of Satan are here plainly recognized.

CHURCH DISCIPLINE, FORMATIVE AND CORRECTIVE. Discipline primarily is *training* by instruction and exercise, and then *reforming* by correcting and punishing. Accordingly church discipline should be first *formative*, training the members to a true Christian character; and when this fails, it must be reformative or *corrective*, for the good of the individual and for the honor of Christ and his cause.

Both of these forms of discipline were recognized by Paul. He preached Christ, "warning every man and teaching every man in all wisdom that he might present every man perfect in Christ" (Col. 1 : 28); but if necessary he would "come with a rod" (1 Cor. 4 : 21). His Epistles were largely in the line of formative discipline. Such were his instructions to the Corinthians in regard to spiritual gifts, the proper observance of the Lord's Supper, their orderly conduct in their public assemblies, marriage and celibacy, and eating meat offered to idols. So also was his advice to the different parties at Corinth and his fervent appeals to his opposers. Corrective discipline was his last resort for persistent or notorious offenders (1 Cor. 5 : 1 ff.).

Corrective discipline is important and often necessary, but it is sometimes exalted into undue prominence. They make a great mistake who act as if it were the great object of the church to punish the unruly. If formative discipline were properly attended to by pastors, officers, and workers in the church, there would generally be but little left for corrective discipline.

(Read Col. 3 : 16-25 ; 4 : 1-5 ; 2 Tim. 2 : 22, 23 ; Titus 2 : 1-15 ; 1 Peter 2 ; 11-18 ; 4 : 1-9.)

Yet "it must needs be that offences come," and the good of the church and the honor of Christ demand their correction in wisdom and love. Offenses may be classified as follows:

1. *Minor*, such as the infirmities of the weak, which are to be borne, with kind admonition and help. (Read Rom. 15 : 1 ; Gal. 6 : 1 ; 1 Thess. 5 : 14, 15 ; 2 Thess. 3 : 10-12 ; Titus 3 : 9 ; James 1 : 26.)

2. *Private*, such as cannot be proved, and therefore must be treated very carefully and privately, leaving the matter with God (Matt. 18 : 15; Prov. 25 : 9).

3. *Personal*, evident injuries of one brother by another, in person, reputation, or property. Our Lord has prescribed the treatment of these in Matt. 18 : 15-18; comp. 1 Cor. 6 : 1-6.

4. *Public*, such as affect all the members of the church. These are to be dealt with publicly, with penalties varying from censure to exclusion (1 Tim. 1 : 19, 20 ; 2 Tim. 3 : 2-7 ; Titus 1 : 13 ; 1 Cor. 5 : 10, 11).

But public, and even personal offenses, may become so malignant as to be insufferable, in which case immediate expulsion will be required (1 Cor. 5 : 13 ; 6 : 9, 10). But corrective discipline must in all cases be exercised kindly but faithfully for the good of the offender and for the glory of Christ (2 Cor. 2 : 5-10 ; 7 : 5 ff. ; 2 Thess. 3 : 14, 15 ; 2 Tim. 2 : 24. James 5 : 19, 20.) See " Church Discipline," by Rev. Eleazer Savage (Sheldon & Company, New York, 1863), which has a full treatment of this whole subject.

12-17. WHY HE LEFT TROAS AND CAME INTO MACEDONIA. EXULTS IN THE TRIUMPHS OF HIS MINISTRY. The crisis through which he passed.

12. Paul returns to the thread of his narrative, which he left at ver. 4. He had spoken of the deep anxiety in which he had written his former Epistle, and now he tells how this same anxiety urged him on from Troas to Macedonia. **Furthermore, when I came,** etc. Better, *And having come to Troas . . . and a door having been opened*. Though such was the case, yet

to *preach* Christ's gospel, and ᵍa door
13 was opened unto me of the Lord, ʰI
had no rest in my spirit, because I
found not Titus my brother: but taking
my leave of them, I went from thence
into Macedonia.

Digression respecting the character and results of his ministry.

14 Now thanks *be* unto God, ⁱwhich always causeth us to triumph in Christ,

the gospel of Christ, and a door was
13 opened to me in the Lord, I had no relief for my spirit, because I found not
Titus my brother; but bidding them
farewell, I went forth into Macedonia.
14 But thanks be to God, who always leads
us in triumph in Christ, and makes

---

g 1 Cor. 16 : 9.   *h* 7 . 5, 6.   *i* Rom. 8 : 37 ; 1 Cor. 15 : 57.

---

he had no rest because Titus had not come from Corinth. (See ver. 13.) **To Troas,** or, *to the Troad*, the angle of territory, south of the Hellespont, of which Troy was the principle point of interest, being an important commercial city and a Roman colony. It had been built, as Dr. Schliemann's discoveries appear to prove, on the ruins of the ancient city. (Comp. notes on Acts 16 : 8, 12.) Besides this visit, Paul was at Troas three times (Acts 16 : 8–11 ; 20 : 5, 6 ; 2 Tim. 4 : 13), Luke passes over this portion of Paul's history very rapidly in the Acts, and does not notice this visit nor the visits to other churches. Yet there is an undesigned agreement in his statement, that Paul went from Ephesus into Macedonia and thence to Greece, implying that he came northward by way of Troas. Paul's object in visiting Troas at this time was not merely as a traveler, but *for the gospel of Christ*; that is, to further it by preaching. *A door*, a great opportunity (see on 1 Cor. 16:9) for missionary work, was opened to him **of,** rather, *in the Lord*, in the service and cause of the Lord. Paul was not in a state of mind to do much then, but he returned a few months later (Acts 20 : 6) and spent a week.

13. I had no rest, *no relief,* from the distress **in my spirit,** my higher spiritual nature (comp. 1 Cor. 2 : 14), **because I found not Titus my brother.** Titus was a Gentile Christian (Gal. 2 : 1, 3), one of Paul's converts (Titus 1 : 4), a companion and fellow-helper of Paul. He is not mentioned in the Acts, but was with Paul at Ephesus in his third missionary journey. Timothy had been sent to Corinth and had returned (1 : 1; Acts 19 : 22) without fully carrying out Paul's plans. Paul had also sent Titus, one probably older and peculiarly fitted for the mission of pacifying matters, and looking

after the collections (7 : 13–15 ; 8 : 16, 17), and he was now anxiously expecting his return. Further regarding Titus, see Titus 1 : 5 ; 2 Tim. 4 : 10. Paul's great anxiety appears to have unfitted him for labor at Troas; besides the affairs at Corinth seemed more urgent. And therefore he says, *so* **taking my leave of them,** bidding them farewell (Acts 18 : 21), **I went** *forth* **into Macedonia,** the province north of Achaia. (See note on Acts 20 : 1.) This incident in Paul's history shows how great his interest and love were for his Corinthian converts.

14. We have here one of those abrupt digressions peculiar to Paul. The mention of Macedonia as well as the recollection of the great opportunity at Troas, and of how he was borne like a captive through deep anxiety to Macedonia, fills his mind with the memory of the severe conflicts and the signal triumphs of his ministry ; and perhaps the favorable intelligence from Corinth adds to his exultant joy, and he breaks forth into thanksgiving ; and he continues in the line of impassioned digressions till 7 : 5, when he returns to his coming into Macedonia and to the coming of Titus. **Now,** rather, *But*, in contrast to my unrest and anxiety, **thanks be to God,** the source of my strength in weakness, **which,** *who*, **always,** even in times of deepest distress, **causeth us to triumph in Christ,** in soul-nourishing fellowship with him. This causative sense of the verb is allowable (THAYER's "Lexicon" and WENER's "Grammar"); but its general meaning is, to *lead captive in triumph* (Col. 2 : 15). According to this, Paul regarded himself as taken captive at his conversion, and being led as a captive ever since. *Who always leads us in the train of his triumphs,* as in a triumphal procession. His success

and maketh manifest *the savour of his knowledge by us in every place. 15 For we are unto God ¹a sweet savour of Christ, ᵐ in them that are saved, and 16 ᵒ in them that perish: ᵒ to the one *we are* the savour of death unto death; and to the other the savour of life unto manifest through us in every place the 15 savour of the knowledge of him. Because we are to God a sweet savor of Christ, in those who are being saved, 16 and in those who are perishing; to the one a savor of death to death, to the other a savor of life to life. And who

k Sol. Song 1:3. *l* Gen. 8:21; Phil. 4:18.   *m* 1 Cor. 1:18.   *n* 4:3, 4.
o John 9:39; 1 Peter 2:7, 8.

in preaching the gospel is God's success over him. "But the sense of conquest and degradation is lost in the more general sense of 'making us to share his triumph'" (STANLEY). The "Speaker's Commentary" adopts Calvin's view: "Who at all times makes a triumphal pageant of us, as his victorious officers and soldiers." The following seems to be a natural view: Paul conceives of himself (1) as having been taken captive; (2) as such led in God's triumphal procession, a figure borrowed from the victorious procession of a Roman general, the most glorious spectacle then known; but (3) at the same time united in living union with Christ. He had been taken captive for a glorious purpose (Phil. 3:12), like the captive Daniel, he had been raised to noble service (Dan. 6:2, 26), and brought into a spiritual union with Christ (Rom. 8:2, 17). In view of such infinite grace, he bursts forth into exultant thanksgiving. Paul changes the figure and adds, **and maketh manifest the savour,** *the fragrant incense,* **of his knowledge by,** or *through,* **us,** as incense bearers, **in every place,** wherever they went preaching the gospel. It was customary to burn incense in honor of the conqueror as he and the procession passed along.

15. Confirmatory and explanatory of the preceding clause. **For,** or *Because,* **we are** *to* **God a sweet savor,** or *odor.* In the preceding verse Paul and his associates were incense bearers, here by a common change in figure they are the *fragrant odor,* or the burning incense, for that is what they are to God. The apostle here employs a word, *sweet odor,* used in the Septuagint in reference to the fragrance of sacrifices and oblations (Gen. 8:20; Exod. 29:18; Lev. 1:9, 13, 17, etc.), and used figuratively in Eph. 5:2 and Phil. 4:18, and spoken of as acceptable and well-pleasing to God. But here Paul is thinking not so much of the odor of sacrifice as of the odor of the incense that accompanied the triumphal procession. He and other preachers of the gospel were redolent with Christ, filled and interpenetrated with Christ, proclaiming and diffusing the gospel, and thus were a fragrance to God. They are a sweet odor **in,** or *among,* **them that are saved,** or *being saved,* **and in,** or *among,* **them that perish,** or *are perishing.* The process of life and death is regarded as going on, as the triumphal procession moves forward; some are on their way to deliverance, others on their way to death. But whether among one or the other class, and however differently the gospel may affect them, the preachers and the preached Christ are as fragrance to God. They are well-pleasing to him, whether men receive the gospel and are saved, or reject it and are lost. "The light is inestimably precious, whether the eye rejoices in it, or through disease is destroyed by it" (HODGE).

16. The relation of preachers and their preaching to different classes. The double working and effect of the gospel. Paul has the figure of the triumphal procession in the mind. **To the one,** as to an unpardoned prisoner about to be executed, **we are the,** *a,* **savour,** or *odor,* **of death unto death,** or, according to the most approved reading, *from death unto death;* **to the other,** as to a pardoned prisoner, soon to be released, *an odor* of life, or *from life,* **unto life.** To one rejecting the gospel message, spiritual death is developed into eternal death, to the other, life, begotten by the word of truth (James 1:18), passes on into a never-ending blessed existence. The repeated phrases may be regarded either as expressing the origin and the effect, **or as a** Hebrew superlative, ex-

life. And ᵖwho *is* sufficient for these 17 things? For we are not as many, which ᵠcorrupt the word of God: but as ʳof sincerity, but as of God, in the sight of God, speak we in Christ.

17 is sufficient for these things? For we are not as the many, corrupting the word of God; but as from sincerity, but as from God, in the sight of God we speak in Christ.

p 3 : 5, 6 ; 1 Cor. 15 : 10.   q 4 : 2 ; 1 Thess. 2 : 3-5 ; 1 Tim. 4 : 1 ; 2 Peter 2 : 1-3.   r 1 : 12 ; Acts 20 : 27.

pressing emphasis by repeating the emphatic word. To one death and that alone, from beginning to end ; to the other life, and that alone, etc. These opposite effects of the gospel are brought to view in Matt. 21 : 44; Luke 2 : 34; John 9 : 39; Rom. 9 : 32, 33; 1 Peter 2 : 8. In view of this presentation of the relation of preachers and the gospel to different classes, Paul abruptly asks: **For these things,** preaching, responsibilities, and never-ending results, **who is sufficient,** who is qualified, adequate, and competent for such a work? Evidently not false teachers ; nor were all true Christians duly qualified ; but such as himself and others who taught the truth in its purity and from God (next verse), and whose sufficiency was from God (3 : 5).

17. Without making a definite answer to the preceding question, Paul in this verse implies who are, and who are not, competent and sufficient for these things. **For we are not as many,** rather, *the many*, pointing to the erroneous teachers, who were opposing Paul, **who corrupt,** or *adulterate,* **the word of God.** These surely had shown that they were not worthy and competent. The word translated *corrupt* is found only here in the New Testament, and was applied to vendors of wines, who were in the habit of adulterating their commodities for the sake of gain ; and so the word came to mean *adulterate.* The word of God was adulterated by mixing in errors of doctrine and precept, by dishonest methods, and by making personal ends, worldly influence, and the praise of men take the place of the glory of God, and the highest interests of his cause (10 : 12 : 11 : 18 ; 1 Cor. 4 : 6 ; 2 Cor. 4 : 2, 4, 5). **But as of sincerity,** *from* pure motives and honest feelings, in opposition to *corrupting* by admixture. And not this alone, **but as of,** or *from*, **God,** the source of Christian truth, their authority and from whom they had their commission ; **in the sight of God,** conscious of his presence and that his all-seeing eye was upon them ; **speak we in Christ,** as those who are united to him, living, moving, and acting, as it were, in him. What a climax is here presented. All selfishness is excluded. Moved by God, inspired by his Spirit, in union with and encompassed as it were, with Christ. Such ones, speaking under such conditions, were sufficient, for evidently their sufficiency was not in themselves, but in God (3 : 5).

PRACTICAL REMARKS.

1. We can sometimes do more by our absence than by our presence (ver. 1 ; 2 Sam. 13 : 38, 39 ; John 16 : 7).

2. A mutual sympathy, love, and confidence between pastor and people are necessary to his highest enjoyment and their greatest profit (ver. 2-4 ; 1 : 6, 7).

3. We must sometimes grieve others that we may do them good (ver. 3 ; Prov. 27 : 5, 6 ; Gal. 2 : 11, 14).

4. Tenderness is consistent with courage and manliness. If we must reprove, let it be done in love (ver. 4 ; Acts 20 : 31 ; Phil. 3 : 17, 18).

5. Public offenses and scandals in churches injure the cause of Christ, and should be repugnant and a grief to Christians (ver. 5, 6 ; 1 Cor. 5 : 11, 13).

6. Church discipline should be administered faithfully, yet tenderly and in love (ver. 5, 6 ; 1 Cor. 5 : 3-7).

7. Church discipline has for its end not so much the punishment as the reformation and restoration of the offender (ver. 6-8 ; Matt. 18 : 15).

8. As soon as offenders give evidence of repentance they should be forgiven, both by individual Christians and the church (ver. 6-8 ; Matt. 18 : 21-35).

9. Church discipline should be exercised in loyal obedience to the commands and spirit of Christ (ver. 9 ; Eph. 4 : 32).

10. The local church is the highest ecclesiastical tribunal. Paul would not

3 DO *we begin again to commend ourselves? Or need we, as some *others*, †epistles of commendation to you, or
2 *letters* of commendation from you? ᵘYe are our epistle written in our hearts,
3 ˣknown and read of all men: *forasmuch*

3 ARE we beginning again to commend ourselves? Or need we, as do some, letters of commendation to you, or
2 from you? Ye are our letter, written in our hearts, known and read by all

*s 5 : 12 ; 12 : 11.   t Acts 16 : 27.   u 1 Cor. 9 : 1, 2.   x Rom. 1 : 8.

trespass on its functions or authority (ver. 10; Matt. 18 : 17).

11. The apostles acted, and true churches act, upon the authority of Christ in cases of discipline (ver. 10; Matt. 18 : 18 ; Acts 15 : 22).

12. In the exercise of church discipline, and in our conduct toward weak and erring brethren we are especially liable to have Satan get the advantage of us (ver. 11).

13. Ministers should hail with joy and embrace opportunities for preaching the gospel; yet opportunities are not always a sure sign of duty (ver. 12, 13 ; Acts 18 : 20).

14. Christian ministers belong to Christ and should be under the control of the Spirit and of providence in their work (ver. 13, 14; Luke 4 : 11; Acts 16 : 6-10).

15. True ministers of the gospel have always cause for joyous thanksgiving, since God is leading them in triumph, and making them share in the triumphs of Christ (ver. 14).

16. Faithful ministers are acceptable to God, whatever the result of their labors (ver. 15 ; 1 Cor. 4 : 2).

17. How awfully solemn and responsible the work of the ministry in relation to men (ver. 16; Acts 20 : 26-28).

18. They that handle the word of God should be good, true, and consecrated persons (ver. 17 ; 1 Tim. 3 : 9).

CHAPTER III.

From this point to the end of the seventh chapter, Paul explains his ministry—its principles, character, and results. He begins by pointing to his converts as the credentials of his ministry (ver. 1-3), and ascribes his sufficiency to God who had made him a minister of the new covenant (ver. 4-6), which is far superior to the law (ver. 7-11); so that he and his fellow-laborers, openly and with great plainness, proclaimed the gospel, and all Christians without hindrance behold the glory of Christ and become partakers of it (ver. 12-18).

1-11. HIS MINISTRY ACCREDITED BY HIS CONVERTS; ITS SUFFICIENCY NOT IN HIMSELF, BUT FROM GOD.

1. What he had just said regarding his preaching (2 : 17) reminds him that he had been charged with boasting, and he asks, *Are we beginning* **again to commend ourselves?** referring, probably, to such passages in his former Epistle, as 1 Cor. 2 : 16; 3 : 10; 9 : 20-27; 14 : 18, from which his opponents had derived their charge of self-laudation. The next question, according to the best text, should read, *Or need we, as do some, epistles of commendation to you or from you?* By **some,** Paul probably refers to certain opposers who had brought letters from churches in Judea and elsewhere, and had received letters from the Corinthian church on their departure. They indeed needed such letters; but Paul and Timothy, as he goes on to show, did not need them. The practice of giving letters of *introduction* and *commendation* (the word includes both ideas) is illustrated in the case of Titus (8 : 17-19) and of Apollos (Acts 18 : 27 ; comp. Rom. 16 : 1 ; Col. 4 : 10).

2. We have no need of such letters; **Ye are our epistle,** certifying us to the world, not written upon tablets or parchment, and carried in the hand, but **written in our hearts,** in our consciousness, in the deep conviction of our own inward experience (comp. 1 Cor. 9 : 2), **known and read of all men,** including the Corinthians, and others who knew them or heard the wonderful work wrought through the ministry of the apostle among them. There is a play upon the words in the original (*known* and *re-known* by reading) which cannot be rendered into English. (Comp. 1 : 13.) The great work done in one of the principal cities of the world would naturally have a world-wide notoriety. The Spirit's work in the hearts of Christians and in the salvation of sinners is generally noised abroad (Acts 2 : 2-6).

as ye are manifestly declared to be the epistle of Christ ministered by us, written not with ink, but with the Spirit of the living God; not ʸ in tables of stone, but ᶻ in fleshly tables of the heart.
4 And such trust have we through Christ
5 to God-ward: ᵃ not that we are sufficient of ourselves to think any thing as of ourselves; but ᵇ our sufficiency
6 is of God; who also hath made us able ᶜ ministers of ᵈ the new testament, not

3 men; being made manifest that ye are Christ's letter ministered by us, written not with ink, but with the Spirit of the living God; not in tablets of stone, but in tablets that are hearts of flesh.
4 And such confidence have we through
5 Christ, toward God. Not that we are sufficient of ourselves to think anything as from ourselves; but our suffi-
6 ciency is from God; who also made us sufficient as ministers of a new cove-

y Exod. 24 : 12 ; 34 : 1.   z Jer. 31 : 33 ; Ezek. 11 : 19.   a 2 : 16 ; John 15 : 5.
b 1 Cor. 15 : 10 ; Phil. 2 : 13 ; 4 : 13.   c 5 : 18–20 ; Eph. 3 : 7 ; Col. 1 : 25–29 ; 1 Tim. 1 : 11, 12.
d Jer. 31 : 31 ; Matt. 26 : 28 ; Heb. 8 : 6–10.

3. The figure is continued and further applied. **Forasmuch as ye are manifestly declared to be,** rather, *being manifested,* by your lives, gifts, and graces (1 Cor. 1 : 4–7), *that ye are an epistle of Christ,* or *Christ's letter,* of which Christ is the author, commending Paul and his associates, **ministered by us,** we being instrumental in its writing, serving, as it were, as scribes; **written not with ink,** which is material and perishable, **but with the Spirit of the living God,** the Holy Spirit entering in as a life-giving power, communicating the life of him who is the fountain of life (John 1 : 4 ; 14 : 6 ; Rom. 8 : 2, 10 ; 2 Tim. 1 : 10). Changing the figure from writing to engraving, and from letters to tablets, **not in tablets,** or *tablets,* **of stone,** as in case of the law (Exod. 34 : 1 ; Deut. 9 : 9–11), **but in fleshly tables of the heart,** or, according to the most approved text, *but in tablets,* namely, *hearts of flesh,* wrought upon by the Holy Spirit. The contrast between the Spirit in human hearts and the law on stone, was doubtless suggested by such passages as Jer. 31 : 33 ; Ezek. 11 : 19 ; 36 : 26. (Comp. Prov. 3 : 3 ; 7 : 3.) The distinction between the old and new covenant seems to have been in Paul's mind, which he considers in ver. 6–11. Such was the work that Christ had effected upon the Corinthian converts, by the Holy Spirit through the ministry of Paul. It was wrought internally upon the hearts, and manifested in the life to all beholders.

4. And such trust, rather, *confidence,* as expressed (2 : 17-3 : 1-3) in the preceding verses, and attested by our converts as living epistles, **have we through Christ,** who wrought through us, and who is the author, as it were, of these epistles; and this confidence, exercised in dependence on Christ, is **to Godward,** better, *toward God,* as its object, in reference to all our labors in his cause. In this assured confidence he had written 1 : 23, 24.

5. But while this confidence and assurance which Paul possessed was strong, it was tempered with humility. He would guard against every appearance of arrogance. It was implied in the preceding verse that he was not exercising self-confidence. But that there might be no doubt he emphasizes the thought: **Not that we are sufficient of ourselves,** by any means we may use (returning to the idea touched upon in 2 : 16), **to think anything,** and devise anything, relative to the promotion of the gospel, **as** *from* **ourselves,** as an original source, **but our sufficiency,** ability or competency, **is** *from* **God,** he is the source of all. The preposition **of** occurs three times in this verse; the last two are stronger than the first, and mean literally **out of,** as from an original source. Paul disclaims the idea that he has any ability in himself to think out and accomplish the results of the gospel. It was in no respect any invention of his.

6. Paul develops the thought of the last clause in reference to his own ministry. Continuing the sentence he says, **who also hath made us able ministers of the new testament,** rather, *who also made us sufficient as ministers of a new covenant,* the gospel in distinction from the law (1 Cor. 11 : 25 ; Gal. 4 : 24 ; Eph. 3 : 7 ; Col. 1 : 23). The emphasis is on the *new.* God had qualified them with adequate power to perform the duties as ministers not of an old but of a new covenant. By *covenant* is

of the letter, but of the spirit: for *the letter killeth, ^f but the spirit giveth life. 7 But if *the ministration of death, ^h written and engraven in stones, was glorious, ⁱ so that the children of Israel could not stedfastly behold the face of Moses for the glory of his countenance; 8 which glory was to be done away: how shall not ^k the ministration of the spirit 9 be rather glorious? For if ^lthe ministration of condemnation be glory,

nant; not of the letter, but of the Spirit; for the letter kills, but the Spirit makes alive. But if the ministration of death, engraven with letters on stones, came in glory, so that the sons of Israel could not look intently on the face of Moses on account of the glory of his face, which glory was passing away; how shall not rather the ministration of the Spirit be in glory? 9 For if the ministration of condemna-

e Rom. 4 : 15; 7 : 9-11; Gal. 3 : 10.   f John 6 : 63; Rom. 8 : 2.   g Rom. 7 : 10.
h Ver. 3; Deut. 10 : 1, etc.   i Exod. 34 : 29-35.   k 1 Cor. 12 : 4-11.   l See refs. ver. 6.

meant an arrangement which binds men to certain conditions, upon the fulfillment of which God promises eternal salvation. The old covenant required perfect obedience and conformity to the law; the new covenant requires faith in Christ (Rom. 10 : 5-13). This *new covenant* Paul characterizes as **not of the letter**, as was the law, **but of the Spirit**, a contrast suggested by the last clause of ver. 3 (Jer. 31 : 31-34). The *law* wrote out and prescribed what men should do, and there stopped without giving them power to obey; the gospel comes to the heart with the Spirit, creating a new life and enabling obedience and conformity to the divine will. (Comp. Rom. 2 : 29; 7 : 6.) The words, *of the letter* and *of the Spirit*, seem to depend not on the word *covenant*, but on the word *ministers*. This accords with *ministration* in the following verse. In either case the sense is substantially the same. **For**, introducing a reason for the sufficiency of their ministry of a new covenant, **the letter killeth, but the Spirit giveth life,** or *makes alive*. The *letter*, representing the law, *kills*, in demanding obedience which no man can render, in producing a knowledge of sin and of exposure to God's wrath and of just condemnation (Rom. 3 : 19, 20); but the *Spirit*, representing the gospel, *makes alive*, by revealing God's love and God's righteousness through faith in Jesus Christ, and renewing the heart and transforming the life by the Holy Spirit (Rom. 3 : 22; 7 : 25; 8 : 2-4).

7. From this to the end of the eleventh verse, Paul shows the superiority of the ministry of the Spirit under the gospel to that of Moses under the law. He reasons from the law to the gospel, from the less to the greater. **But if the ministration,** *ministry* or *service*, **of death,** that which threatens and brings death to the soul that sins (Ezek. 18 : 4; Rom. 6 : 12; 7 : 9; 1 Cor. 15 : 56; Gal. 3 : 10, 21), **written and engraven,** rather, according to the best text, *engraven with letters on stones*, referring to the two tables of the law (Exod. 31 : 18), **was glorious,** better, *came into being in glory*, attended with glory. The reference is to the second giving of the law (Exod. 34 : 4-8, 29-35), when Moses beheld the glory of the Lord, and his face shone. (Comp. Exod. 33 : 17-23.) **So that the children,** or *sons*, **of Israel could not stedfastly behold,** *fix their eyes upon,* **the face of Moses, for the glory of his countenance,** or *face*, the people being afraid to come near him (Exod. 34 : 30). **Which glory** of his face **was to be done away,** rather, *was passing away*. It was thus glorious and dazzling to the people, though it was transitory and fading.

8. If this was the effect of the transitory glory of Moses' ministry under the law, **how shall not the ministration,** *the ministry,* **of the Spirit,** under the gospel, operating through preachers and teachers (ver. 6), giving life and governing the lives of men (ver. 3), now, in the future, and permanently, **be rather glorious,** how shall it not rather *be* and remain *in glory?* It is the Spirit of the living God that thus ministers (ver. 3). The words *in glory*, denote permanency; and the future tense, the glory here and the greater glory hereafter. See on ver. 18 for the transformation effected in the believer's soul.

9. The apostle carries on the comparison still further, and explains more particularly the two ministries. **For,** to take an additional view, **if the ministration,** or *ministry,* **of condemnation** which pronounced con-

much more doth the ministration ᵐ of 10 righteousness exceed in glory. For even that which was made glorious had no glory in this respect, by reason 11 of the glory that excelleth. For ⁿ if that which is done away was glorious, much more that which remaineth is glorious.
12 Seeing then that we have such hope, ᵒ we use great plainness of speech: 13 and not as Moses, ᵖ which put a vail over his face, that the children of Israel could not stedfastly look to ᵍ the 14 end of that which is abolished. But

tion has glory, much more does the ministration of righteousness exceed in 10 glory. For even that which has been made glorious has not been made glorious in this respect, on account of 11 the glory that excels. For if that which is passing away is glorious, much more that which abides is glorious.
12 Having therefore such hope, we use 13 great plainness of speech; and are not as Moses who put a vail over his face, that the children of Israel might not intently look on the end of that which

---

ᵐ Rom 1 : 17; 5 : 15–21.   ⁿ Heb. 8 : 13; 12 : 25–29.   ᵒ 7 : 4; Eph. 6 : 19.   ᵖ Exod. 34 : 33, 35.
ᵍ Rom. 10 : 4; Eph. 2 : 14, 15; Heb. 10 : 1, 9.

---

demnation upon transgressors (Deut. 27 : 26; Rom. 7 : 12-14; Gal. 3 : 10), **be,** or *has*, **glory,** as we have already seen; **much more doth the ministration,** or *ministry*, **of righteousness,** which reveals a righteousness and how it may be obtained (5 : 21; Rom. 1 : 17; 3 : 21), **exceed in glory.** The latter surely abounds in glory in contrast to the glory of the former.

10. For, to explain and confirm what I have just said, **even that which was,** better, *has been*, **made glorious,** as brought to view in ver. 7, *has* **no glory in this respect,** namely, **by reason of,** or *on account of*, **the glory that excelleth.** The law has no glory in comparison with the surpassing glory of the gospel. The glory of the ministry under the old covenant disappears before the glory of the ministry under the new, like the light of the moon before the effulgence of the sun.

11. For, to clinch or rivet the argument, **if that which is done away,** or better, *is passing away* (see on ver. 7), was **glorious,** was accompanied with and in the midst of glory, **much more that which remaineth is glorious,** is attended with glory as a permanent attribute. The contrast is between that which passes away and ceaseth, and that which abides and is permanent. The ministry of Moses under the law was transitory; the ministry of the new covenant is abiding. If the former was attended with glory, much more must the latter remain in glory, both here in the present dispensation, and in the future heavenly kingdom.

12-18. PAUL AND HIS FELLOW-LA-

BORERS SUPERIOR TO MOSES IN THE RESULTS OF THEIR MINISTRY. ALL CHRISTIANS PARTAKERS OF ITS GLORIOUS RESULTS.

12. Seeing then that we have such hope, of the permanent glory pertaining to the new covenant and its ministry, **we use great plainness, great freedom and unreservedness, bordering on boldness, of speech.** The fullness and unreservedness of the gospel (this verse) is contrasted with the reserved and partial revelations of the law (next verse). "We speak everything with freedom, keeping back nothing, suspecting nothing, but speaking plainly" (CHRYSOSTOM). Notice that in ver. 4, Paul says *such trust*, or *confidence;* but here with a wider and further range of vision of future and unending glory, his confidence becomes *such a hope* (Phil. 2 : 15, 16; 1 Thess. 2 : 19; 2 Tim. 4 : 8. Comp. on 2 : 17).

13. And, we are, **not as Moses,** we do not do as he did, who **put a vail over his face, that the children of Israel could not,** rather, *might not*, **steadfastly look,** or *intently*, **to the end of that which is abolished,** better, *on the end of that which was passing away*, the transitory nature of the old covenant being prominent here. The Revised version of Exod. 34 : 33, reads, "And when Moses had done speaking with them, he put a vail on his face." And this accords with the Septuagint version of the same passage; and also agrees with the original here, which implies that Moses put the vail over his face *after* speaking to the people, in order that they might not behold the glory fading from his face. Paul uses an allegorical illustra-

'their minds were blinded: for until this day remaineth the same vail untaken away in the reading of the Old Testament: *which* vail is done away 15 in Christ: but even unto this day, when Moses is read, the vail is upon 16 their heart. Nevertheless *when it shall turn to the Lord,* "the vail shall 17 be taken away. Now *the Lord is that

14 was passing away but their understandings were hardened: for until this day on the reading of the old covenant the same vail abides, not being taken away; which vail is done away 15 in Christ. But even to this day, whenever Moses is read, a vail lies on their 16 heart. But whenever it turns to the 17 Lord, **the** vail is taken away. Now the

r 4 : 4; see refs. Deut. 29 : 4; John 12 : 40. *s* 4 : 6. *t* Deut. 30 : 10; Hosea 3 : 5. Rom. 11 : 23, 25-27.
u Isa. 25 : 7. *x* 1 Cor. 15 : 45.

tion, to **show** the transitory glory of the law, passing away like the glory of Moses' face. In ver. 7, Paul speaks from a different point of view. There, as in Exod. 34 : 30, 34, 35, the reference is to Moses putting on the vail, because of the terror of the Israelites at the brightness of his face, emphasizing the glory of the law, which glory the gospel greatly surpassed. Here the reference is to concealing the fading glory of his face, emphasizing the veiling of truth under the law in contrast to the open plainness of the gospel's proclamation. The law came with its types and shadows of good things to come; the gospel with its clear and full revelation of eternal life and future glory.

14. But their minds, or *understandings,* **were blinded,** *hardened or dulled.* The figure is that of a hard substance which may blind or dull the sight. Here their understandings or perceptions had been dulled and callonsed; and the gospel proclamation, though **so** plain, **was** of **no** avail. (Comp. 4 : 3, 4.) **For,** to prove and illustrate **the** fact of their hardened understandings, **until this day remaineth the same** vail untaken away **in the** reading **of the old testament,** rather, *for until this day, on reading the old covenant,* the law, *the books of* **Moses,** *the same vail remains, not being taken away,* the same hardness and blindness continues. **Which** vail **is done away,** *or is being removed,* **in Christ.** The work is going on, and the spiritual blindness and ignorance is being removed as they are converted. Many however prefer to translate and connect with what precedes, thus: *the same vail remains at the reading of the law, it not being discovered that it is done away in Christ.* While this is allowable and makes good sense, it does not seem to me to be the most natural meaning of the original.

(Compare **Winer's** "Grammar," p. 534.)

15. But even unto this day, *whenever* **Moses is read,** the writing of Moses, answering to the old covenant of the preceding verse, **the vail is upon their hearts.** The figure is changed; the veil is not over their faces, but lying upon their hearts. It was not an intellectual, but a moral blindness, affecting their whole inner being, which caused their unbelief and prevented them from seeing the transitory character of the old dispensation. Compare Stephen's speech and its results (Acts 7 : 51-54 and notes).

16. Nevertheless, when, better, *But whenever,* **it,** referring to *heart,* in the preceding clause. The reference is general and indefinite. But inasmuch as it was the Jewish heart that **was** veiled, so the same heart is meant. Whenever Jews individually or collectively **turn unto the Lord,** that is, unto Jesus Christ (ver. 14), **the vail shall be taken away,** rather, *is taken off,* as Moses took off his veil when he went in to speak to the Lord (Exod. 34 : 34). "When their heart goes in to speak with God, ceases to contemplate the dead letter, and begins to commune with the Spirit of the old covenant (the Spirit of God), then the veil is removed, as it was from the face of Moses" (ALFORD).

17. Paul explains what he had just said in ver. 16. **Now the Lord,** that is, Jesus Christ, **is that Spirit,** rather, *is the Spirit,* of God (ver. 3), spoken of in a general way and in opposition **to** the letter (ver. 6). He was the revealer of the Old Testament Scriptures, their sum and their substance (1 Peter 1 : 10, 11; Rev 19 : 10). "The last Adam was made a life-giving Spirit" (1 Cor. 15 : 45). He gives life to the letter of Scripture, and to believers eternal life (John 10 : 28; 17 : 3). He works through the Holy Spirit, as

Spirit; *and where the* **Spirit of the Lord** *is* **liberty. But we all, with open face** beholding *as in a glass* *the glory of the Lord,* *are* **changed into the same image** *from* **glory to glory,** *even as by the spirit of* **the Lord** [or, *of the Lord the spirit*].

y Isa. 61 : 1 ; John 8 : 36 ; Rom. 8 : 2, 15, 16.
b Rom. 8 : 29 ; 1 Cor. 15 : 49 ; Eph. 4 : 22–24.
z 1 Cor. 13 : 12.
c Ps. 84 : 7.
a 1 : 4, 6.

his agent **and** representative in the world (John 14 : 16, 17, 23, 26). They are viewed as one. As the Father and the Son are said to be one, so are the Son and the Spirit one in their working (John 16 : 13–15). Compare Matt. 28 : 20, "Lo, I am with you alway," by a living union and the Holy Spirit. Some think that "the Lord" is the Holy Spirit throughout this passage. But Paul says just after this (4 : 5) that Christ is Lord, and Lord is a common designation of Christ in the Epistles. **And where the Spirit of the Lord is, there is liberty,** *freedom,* from the bondage of the law (Rom. 8 : 14, 8 : 15), from the veil of blindness and hardness **on** the heart; freedom to enjoy a well-grounded hope and to speak plainly and boldly (ver. 12), and to look with unveiled face upon the glory of Christ (ver. 18). This is then a *spiritual freedom,* the opposite of *having a veil on the heart* (ver. 15; Rom. 8 : 9–11). That veil hindered, fettered, and kept in bondage the spiritual activities; but the Spirit removes the barriers, quickens and governs the spiritual powers and activities of the soul (John 8 : 32, 36; Rom. 6 : 18, 22; James 1 : 25; 1 Peter 2 : 16).

18. But, or *And,* having the Spirit of the Lord and enjoying this freedom, **we all,** that is, all Christians, **with open face,** rather, *with unveiled face,* instead of reading the letter of the law with veiled hearts, like the Jews, etc. The figure of the veil is still carried on. As Moses went in to speak with the Lord and saw his glory unveiled (Exod. 33 : 18–22; 34 : 5–8, 34), so now Christians are permitted to see that glory, both as it was dimly reflected in the old covenant, and also as it is brought more clearly into view in the new. **Beholding as in a glass the glory of the Lord,** *beholding for ourselves the glory of the Lord,* of Christ, *as in a mirror,* from which it is reflected. The mirror was polished metal. The veil is taken away from all believers in Christ (ver. 16), and they behold the glory of God in the face of Jesus Christ (4 : 6; Heb. 1 : 3; John 1 : 14; Col. 1 : 15). They see this glory in the word of God, both in the Old and New Testament, and by faith as it is revealed to them by the Spirit. Some translate, *And we all, with unveiled face, reflecting as a mirror the glory of the Lord,* just as Moses' face shone, reflecting God's glory. But this is not the more ordinary meaning of the word, and is not so natural as an interpretation. It is a true and beautiful inference of what is here said. Christians do behold Christ's glory, they are transformed thereby, and as a result they reflect Christ's image and glory. **Are changed,** *are transfigured* (the same used in Matt. 17 : 2; Mark **9 : 2**; Rom. 12 : 2), **into the same image,** that is, of Christ (Gal. 4 : 19; 1 John 3 : 2), **from glory to glory,** from one degree of glory to another, according to the distinctness of the view in the mirror. "Christians who look seldom and indistinctly into the mirror will have Christ's image in the soul more faintly and indistinctly. They who abide, constantly looking at Christ in the mirror of the gospel, will receive the impression of his character with a more striking likeness to the original" (A. CARSON). **As by the Spirit of the Lord,** a free translation of the original, *the Lord's Spirit,* that is, the Holy Spirit (Rom. 8 : 9; Gal. 4 : 6). The Holy Spirit is the representative of Christ in the world, the author of regeneration and sanctification, who takes the things of Christ and shows them to us (John 16 : 14; Rom. 8 : 10, 11, 29). Others prefer to render, *Even as from the Lord the Spirit,* as designated in ver. 17; as Christ was the Spirit of the law, so under his direction and influence the Divine Spirit effects this transformation. It is well to bear in mind in interpreting these verses that God is

4 THEREFORE seeing we have this ministry, ⁴ as we have received mercy,

4 THEREFORE having this ministry, as we received mercy, we faint not.

d 1 Tim. 1 : 13.

Spirit, and that the Father, Son, and Holy Spirit are one in essence, and that there is a unity in all their purposes and operations.

PRACTICAL REMARKS.

1. Letters of commendation are proper and often serviceable, but should be given only when deserved (ver. 1; Acts 18 : 27).
2. The less deserving, the greater the number, too often, of recommendations (ver. 1).
3. The minister's best recommendation may be read in the souls saved, and the Christians built up, by his ministry (ver. 2, 3 ; 1 Thess. 2 : 19).
4. True religion is of the heart and born of the Spirit. All else is superficial and false (ver. 3; John 3 : 3, 5).
5. God is the minister's sure support, in whom he finds a full supply, if he labors in a trustful and obedient spirit (ver. 4-6; Acts 26 : 22).
6. Christian ministers find their great encouragement in the fact that their sufficiency is from God (ver. 5; 1 Cor. 3 : 7).
7. A true gospel ministry is a spiritual ministry. It is evangelistic and spiritual in its results (ver. 6; Acts 19 : 10, 17-20).
8. The Christian ministry is glorious, having a glorious message, attended by a glorious spirit, and with glorious results. Its work is correspondingly solemn and responsible (ver. 7-11; 4 : 5, 6).
9. How vain to attempt to be justified by the law, whose ministry is that of condemnation and death (ver. 7, 9; Rom. 3 : 20).
10. How great the danger of grieving the Spirit, since the gospel ministry of the Spirit is our only hope (ver. 8; Eph. 4 : 30).
11. The Mosaic economy was introductory and preparatory. The gospel dispensation is final and permanent in its results. How gratefully should its superiority be acknowledged and its blessings improved (ver. 10, 11; Gal. 4 : 21-26).
12. Ministers owe it both to the gospel and to their hearers that they preach boldly, plainly, and intelligibly, so as to be clearly understood (ver. 12; 1 Cor. 2 : 1-5).
13. The Old Testament should be read under the light of the New (ver. 13-15; Luke 24 : 27).
14. The reason why the Jews misunderstand their own Scriptures is their blindness and hardness of heart. So many now read only the letter of the word and see not the spirit (ver. 13-15; Rom. 9 : 30-33).
15. Israel will in due time return to the Lord and acknowledge Christ (ver. 16; Rom. 11 : 26 ff.).
16. The true glory of the Scriptures is seen by any one only as he has turned to the Lord (ver. 16; 1 Cor. 2 : 14-16).
17. Christ is the revealer of truth, both in the Old and the New Testament (ver. 17; John 14 : 6; 18 : 36-38).
18. The gospel has a transforming power, reflecting the image of Christ and assimilating all true believers to his likeness (ver. 18; 4 : 6; 1 John 3 : 2; see Carson's "Knowledge of Jesus," pp. 203-233).

CHAPTER IV.

Having such a glorious ministry, the apostle affirms his courage in preaching the gospel conscientiously, honestly, and purely (ver. 1, 2), and if any perish, it is through shutting their eyes to the glory of Christ (ver. 3-6). Ministers are indeed weak in themselves, like earthen vessels, but this by contrast only sets off the power of God in their ministry (ver. 7-11), which is for the good of their converts and the glory of God (ver. 12-15). In their weakness they are cheered by the prospects of a glorious future life (ver. 16-18), confidently expecting a glorified body (5 : 1-4), having the earnest of the Spirit and stimulated by the judgment (5 : 5-10).

1-6. THEIR MINISTRY GENUINE AND FAITHFULLY EXERCISED IN THE SIGHT OF GOD, AND THEY WHO PERISH SHUT THEIR EYES TO THE GLORY WHICH IT PROCLAIMS.

1. **Therefore, seeing we have this ministry,** so glorious (3 : 7-16), and conferring such blessing and privi-

2 * we faint not; but have renounced the hidden things of dishonesty, not walking in craftiness, ᶠ nor handling the word of God deceitfully; but ᵍ by manifestation of the truth ʰ commending ourselves to every man's conscience in the sight of God.
3 But if our gospel be hid, ⁱ it is hid to
4 them that are lost: in whom ᵏ the god of this world ˡ hath blinded the minds of them which believe not, lest the light of the glorious gospel of Christ, ᵐ who is the image of God, should

2 But we renounced the hidden things of shame, not walking in craftiness, nor handling with guile the word of God; but, by the manifestation of the truth, commending ourselves to every man's conscience in the sight of God.
3 But even if our gospel is vailed, it is
4 vailed in those who are perishing; in whom the god of this age blinded the understandings of the unbelieving, that the light of the gospel of the glory of Christ, who is God's image, should

e Acts 20 : 23, 24.   *f* 2 : 17; 1 Thess. 2 : 3–5.   *g* 6 : 4–7.   *h* 5 : 11.   *i* 1 Cor. 1 : 18; 2 Thess. 2 : 10.
k Matt. 4 : 8, 9; John 12 : 31; Eph. 2 : 2; Rev. 20 : 2, 3.   *l* 3 : 14; John 12 : 40.   *m* See refs. John 14 : 9.

leges upon Christians (3 : 17, 18), **as we have received mercy,** *even as we obtained mercy*, at our conversion and our appointment to this work (Acts 26 : 16; 1 Tim. 1 : 12–16), **we faint not,** *we lose not courage*, in speaking and acting. Paul returns to the thread of thought, before expressed, in "having such confidence," "such hope," and "using such plainness of speech" (3 : 4–6, 12). Notice Paul's humility and how he regards himself as unworthy, "as we have received mercy" (ver. 5; 1 Cor. 15 : 9; Eph. 3 : 8).

2. But, or *And*, **have renounced the hidden things of dishonesty;** rather, *we renounced*, at the very beginning of our ministry, *the hidden, secret, things of shame*, those secret practices which shame conceals and of which one ought to be ashamed. **Not walking in craftiness,** not conducting ourselves in the ministry with contrivances and intrigues to attain our end; compare the craftiness of the Herodians (Luke 20 : 20–23). **Nor handling the word of God deceitfully,** *not adulterating* or *falsifying* the word of God, mixing it with false teachings. There may be a reference, by way of contrast, to the false teachers and opposers of the apostle. There is, however, a reaffirming of what he had said in 2 : 17. **But, by** (*the*) **manifestation of the truth,** plainly and clearly presenting the unadulterated truth of God, the gospel, in contrast to the crafty and the corrupting teachings just mentioned (1 Thess. 2 : 3, 4). **Commending ourselves to every man's conscience,** this plain preaching of Christ, forming, as it were, another letter of recommendation (3 : 3), addressed to the consciences of men in **the sight of God,** in the presence of

the all-seeing God, who searches the heart both of the speaker and hearer (2 : 17). The gospel, when thus proclaimed, has a self-evidencing power, witnessing to the honesty of those who preached it.

3. But, *even, if,* notwithstanding the evident truthfulness of the gospel and its clear and forcible presentation, **our gospel be hid,** rather, *is veiled*, as was the case with Israel in reading the law (3 : 14), **it is hid to them that are lost,** rather, *it is veiled in, or among those that are perishing*—in a perishing condition (1 Cor. 1 : 18; Luke 15 : 24, 32). The next verse explains how this veiling took place.

4. In whom the God of this world, a name applied to Satan, who rules in the hearts of worldly men, or the men of this wicked *age*. He is styled "the prince of this world" in John 12 : 31; 14 : 30, "the prince of the power of the air" in Eph. 2 : 2. (Comp. Eph. 6 : 12; Rev. 12 : 12.) **Hath blinded the minds of them that believe not,** more exactly, *Blinded the understandings* (see on 3 : 14) *of the unbelieving*, those disbelieving and rejecting the only way of salvation (John 3 : 18; 5 : 40; Acts 4 : 12). The word *blinded* is a literal translation and is not the word used in 3 : 14. Figuratively, it is applied to the blunting or darkening of the mental and moral perceptions. While all are spiritually blind by nature, this blindness is aggravated by rejecting the gospel. **Lest the light of the glorious gospel,** better, *that the brightness of the gospel of the glory of Christ*, **who is the image of God** (3 : 18; John 1 : 14–18; Col. 1 : 15; Heb. 1 : 3), *should not shine*, or *dawn*, upon them. The words **unto them,** are

350　　　　II. CORINTHIANS　　　[CH. IV.

5 shine unto them. ⁿFor we preach not
ourselves, ᵒbut Christ Jesus the Lord;
and ᵖourselves your servants for Jesus'
6 sake. For God, ᑫwho commanded the
light to shine out of darkness, hath
shined in our hearts, to give ʳthe light
of the knowledge of the glory of God
in the face of Jesus Christ.

Motives, responsibilities, trials, and supports of the apostolic ministry.

7 But we have this treasure in ˢearthen
vessels, ᵗthat the excellency of the
power may be of God, and not of us.

5 not shine. For we preach not ourselves, but Christ Jesus as Lord; and ourselves as your servants for Jesus'
6 sake. Because it is God, that said, Out of darkness light shall shine, who shined in our hearts, to give the light of the knowledge of the glory of God in the face of Christ.

7 But we have this treasure in earthen vessels, that the exceeding greatness of the power may be God's and, not

---

n John 3 : 27-31 ; Acts 14 : 11-15.　　　o 1 Cor. 1 : 23 ; Col. 1 : 27, 28.
p Matt. 10 : 25-28 ; John 13 : 12-15 ; 1 Cor. 9 : 19-23.　　　q Gen. 1 : 3.
r Ver. 4 ; 1 Cor. 2 : 12-15 ; 1 Peter 2 : 9.　　　s 1 Cor. 1 : 28 ; Heb. 5 : 2.　　　t 1 Cor. 2 : 3-5.

---

not in the original, but are naturally implied. Compare "shined in our hearts" (ver. 6). The gospel displays the glory of Christ and the glory of his work (Phil. 2 : 9-11), as the only begotten of the Father, full of grace and truth. The image of God is the perfection, the highest manifestation of his glory, as one with the Father (John 14 : 8-11).

5. The apostle gives a reason for the preceding statement. **For we preach not ourselves**, as masters or lords (1 : 24), but in preaching the glad tidings of the glory of Christ, we preach **Christ Jesus**, *as* **Lord**, as the supreme Lord and Master, **and ourselves**, in contrast, **your servants, your slaves** or bond-servants, **for Jesus' sake**. On account of Christ he feels constrained and under obligation to do this (5 : 14). In his humility how far was he from commending himself (3 : 1).

6. We preach Christ as Lord and ourselves as your servants, **For, God who commanded light to shine out of darkness**, first at creation and then in the moral and spiritual world (John 1 : 4, 5), **hath shined in our hearts.** The most approved text, however, reads, *For*, or *Because it is God that said, Light shall shine out of darkness* (Gen. 1 : 3), *who shined in our hearts* (John 8 : 12), the creator of light and the illuminator of the soul being the same, *that we may give the light of the knowledge of the glory of God*, substantially the same idea as "the light of the gospel of the glory of Christ" (ver. 4) *in the face of Christ*, as it shines in his face. The face of Christ is his character and person, which distinguishes him from all others, as the Mediator of the new covenant (Heb. 12 : 24); and his glory, the glory of the invisible God, far transcends the brightness on the face of Moses (3 : 13). The word rendered *face*, is translated *person* in 2 : 10. The light has shined in our hearts in order that we may spread the light (2 : 15, 16 ; 3 : 3, 6). In view of such an illumination of the apostle's soul he could not only be forgetful of self, but proclaim such excellence, glory, and grace.

7-15. THE BODILY AND OUTWARD WEAKNESS OF THE MINISTER BUT SETS OFF THE SPIRITUAL POWER AND DIGNITY OF HIS MINISTRY. The apostle's difficulties and supports.

7. In this and the three following verses the apostle describes his personal weakness, thereby showing that all is to be ascribed to God and not to men (3 : 5). **But, though there is such glory in the gospel we preach, we have this treasure,** especially "the light of the knowledge of the glory of God" in Christ (ver. 6), which the gospel ministry proclaims (ver. 1 ; 2 : 14), **in earthen vessels**, in weak, frail bodies (ver. 10, 16), affecting the whole being. Treasures were often kept in earthen jars. The figure, however, naturally reminds one of the torches in Gideon's pitchers (Judg. 7 : 16). The weakness of these vessels, *made of clay* (Gen. 2 : 7 ; 1 Cor. 15 : 47), is the prominent thought. The design of God in this is, **that the excellency,** *the superiority*, **of the power,** as exhibited in their ministry, **may be,** shown to be, **of God,** God's power, *and not from ourselves*, as a source.

CH. IV.] II. CORINTHIANS 351

8 We are ᵘtroubled on every side, ˣyet not distressed; we are perplexed, but
9 not in despair: persecuted, but not forsaken; ᶻ cast down, but not destroyed;
10 ᵃ Always bearing about in the body the dying of the Lord Jesus, ᵇ that the life also of Jesus might be made manifest
11 in our body. For we which live ᵇ are alway delivered unto death for Jesus' sake, that the life also of Jesus might be made manifest in our mortal flesh.
12 So then death worketh in us, but

8 from ourselves; being pressed in every way, yet not straitened; perplexed,
9 yet not despairing; pursued, yet not forsaken; smitten down, yet not destroyed; always carrying about in the
10 body the dying of Jesus, that the life also of Jesus may be manifested in our
11 body. For we who live are always delivered to death for Jesus' sake, that the life also of Jesus may be mani-
12 fested in our mortal flesh. So that death is working in us, but life in you.

ᵘ 7 : 5-7 ; 11 : 23-30.   ˣ 12 : 10 ; Prov. 14 : 26 ; Rom. 8 : 35-37.   ʸ 7 : 6 ; Ps. 37 : 24.
ᶻ Gal. 6 : 17 ; Col. 1 : 24.   ᵃ Rom. 8 : 17 ; 2 Tim. 2 : 11, 12 ; 1 Peter 4 : 13.   ᵇ See refs. Rom. 8 : 36.

8. In ver. 8–10 Paul illustrates the meaning of "earthen vessels" as applied to himself and his associates, and the superior power of God. All the verbs are participles, dependent on the preceding statement. "We have this treasure in earthen vessels" . . . *being* **troubled on every side,** *pressed in every way,* and from all directions, **yet not distressed,** *not straitened,* not put in a position from which there is no escape, *being* **perplexed,** not knowing what to do, *yet not despairing,* not hopeless. The contrast is between doubt and despair. "A way of escape is never wanting. *Perplexed* about the future, as *troubled* refers to the present" (BENGEL).

9. Being persecuted, but not forsaken, or *pursued* by enemies, persecutors, *yet not forsaken* by God; **cast down, but not destroyed,** struck down to the ground, yet not deprived of life, not left unable to renew the conflict. In the last verse and this, Paul appears to compare himself to a combatant, and the illustration here reaches a climax. First he is hardly pressed, then in straits as to what to do, then pursued, and then actually smitten down.

10. And this was not an occasional experience, but like Christ in the flesh, he was undergoing a continual succession of indignities and sufferings; and also like Christ he was having a succession of deliverances and victories by the power of God. **Always bearing about in the body the dying,** *the putting to death,* **of Jesus,** who was suffering, as it were, a protracted death in the trials, hardships, and sufferings manifested in the apostle's body (Col. 1 : 24). **Lord** is omitted in best text. **That the life of Jesus,** his triumphant, resurrection life, *may* **be manifest in our body,** in the repeated deliverances from the perils of death. Paul conceives himself as closely connected with Christ in his suffering and triumphs.

11. Paul explains still further. **For we which,** *who,* **live,** who are in the midst of life, **are alway delivered unto death,** a kind of living death ((comp. 1 : 8) ; "in deaths oft" (11 : 23) ; "I die daily" (1 Cor. 15 : 31)) **for Jesus' sake,** in his behalf and for his cause (ver. 16). And the divine design is, **that the life also of Jesus** *may be manifested* **in our mortal flesh,** in our flesh subject to death. This is an emphatic repetition of the last clause of ver. 10, the decaying nature of the body being brought into view. But even in this, Christ's life and power, whereby he conquered death, is shown forth in our dying flesh. "God exhibits death in the living, that he may exhibit life in the dying" (ALFORD).

12. Paul sums up what he had said, and brings in a new thought, the relation of his sufferings to his Corinthian converts. **So then death,** the dangers and suffering by which the dying of Jesus is manifested in our mortal bodies, **worketh,** is active in us, this mortal peril is our own (1 Cor. 4 : 9) ; **but life** which is exhibited in us, is for your benefit, and is working actively **in you** (ver. 14, 15 ; Rom. 8 : 16, 17). Through death comes life (John 12 : 24). "The death of Christ was the life of the world ; the dying daily (1 Cor. 15 : 31) of his disciples, by virtue of the same Spirit that lives in him, is the means whereby that life spreads among mankind. Death may be said to be working in Christ's ministers, because of their visible sorrows, anxieties, persecutions (ver. 16) ;

13 life in you. We having the same spirit of faith, according as it is written, I believed, and therefore have I spoken: we also believe, and therefore speak:
14 knowing that ᵈ he which raised up the Lord Jesus shall raise up also by Jesus,
15 ᵉ and shall present us with you. For ᶠ all things are for your sakes, that ᵍ the abundant grace might through the thanksgiving of many redound to the glory of God.
16 For which cause we faint not; but

13 But having the same spirit of faith, according to what is written, I believed, therefore did I speak, we also believe,
14 therefore also we speak : knowing that he who raised up the Lord Jesus will raise up us also through Jesus, and
15 will present us with you. For all the things are for your sakes ; that the grace, abounding through the many, may make the thanksgiving more abundant, to the glory of God.
16 Wherefore we faint not ; but though

c Rom. 1 : 12; 2 Peter 1 : 1.   d Rom. 8 : 11 ; 1 Cor. 6 : 14.   e Jude 24.   f 1 : 4–6 ; 1 Cor. 3 : 21.
g See refs. 1 : 11.

life in their converts because of the change in their character and acts" (J. J. LIAS). As Christ is one with his people, so "for Jesus' sake" (ver. 11) embraces his people. Paul's converts were not only comparatively free from the anxieties and persecutions to which he was exposed, but through these exposures he brought Christ to them as their spiritual and resurrection life (ver. 14, 15).

13. We having, rather, *But having the same spirit of faith,* as that which animated the psalmist, in the quotation that follows. There is a contrast with the statement just made. Though death works in us and life in you, yet we have this faith that leads us to speak openly and boldly. Notice how he returns again and again to this idea. In 3 : 4 it is "such confidence"; in 3 : 12 it is "such hope"; here it is "the same faith" as that indicated in Ps. 116 : 10. **I believed and therefore have I,** or more exactly, *did I speak* (quoted from the Septuagint version); **we also believe and therefore speak.** Both the Hebrew and the Greek contain the idea that speaking was the result of faith, which was the point in Paul's mind. The psalmist's faith enabled him to triumph over all his deadly troubles (Ps. 116 3. 8–14), and to declare the salvation of God; and so a similar faith enabled Paul and his associates to rise above the infirmities of the body and the exposures and dangers of death, and proclaim the saving power of the gospel.

14. His faith is grounded on the resurrection of Christ. **Knowing that he which,** *who,* **raised up the Lord Jesus,** he knew that the resurrection of Christ had actually occurred (1 Cor. 15 : 8). This knowledge gave him as-

surance and boldness (1 Cor. 15 : 58). **Shall raise up us also by Jesus,** or, according to the best authorities, *with Jesus,* not at the same time, but sharing the same life and condition. Paul uses the same argument as in 1 Cor. 15 : 20–24. He does not appear here, as at some other times (1 Thess. 4 : 15 ; 1 Cor. 15 : 51), to expect the second coming of Christ before his own death. His severe affliction (1 : 8) may have modified his anticipations. **And shall present us with you** before the Father in glory (11 : 1 ; Eph. 5 : 27 ; Col. 1 : 22 ; Jude 24). **With you,** in fellowship of love and of a glorious reward.

15. *With you,* I say, **for all things are for your sakes.** (See 1 Cor. 3 : 21, 22 ; 2 Tim. 2 : 10.) What he did and suffered were among the *all things* which were for their present good and eternal salvation. The divine purpose is, that **the abundant grace,** rather, *that the grace, abounding through the greater number* saved, *may make the thanksgiving more abundant to the glory of God.* The **more** grace the **more** saved, and the more saved the **greater** the thanksgiving to God. (Comp. 1 : 11.) He sees his work, through the salvation and thanksgiving of his converts, redounding to God's glory.

16–18. THE MINISTER OF THE GOSPEL SUSTAINED BY THE HOPE OF GLORIOUS IMMORTALITY. This thought is developed to the end of 5 : 10. Cheered by the prospect of an eternal life.

16. The apostle had referred to reasons "why we faint not," in ver. 1 ; he now draws an additional reason from what he had just said, regarding the certainty of the resurrection, and that all their sufferings were working out such glorious results. And this was continuously illustrated in his experi-

^b though our outward man perish, yet
¹ the inward *man* is renewed day by
17 day. For ᵏ our light affliction, ˡ which
is but for a moment, ᵐ worketh for us a
far more exceeding *and* eternal weight
18 of glory; ⁿ while we look not at the
things which are seen, but at the
things which are not seen : ᵒ for the
things which are seen *are* temporal;
but the things which are not seen *are*
eternal.

our outward man is decaying, yet our
inward man is renewed day by day.
17 For our light affliction, which is but
for a moment, is working out for us
more and more exceedingly an eternal
18 weight of glory; while we look not at
the things that are not seen, but at the
things that are not seen ; for the things
that are seen are for a season, but the
things that are not seen are eternal.

h Job 19 : 26, 27; Ps. 73 : 26.   *i* Rom. 7 : 22; Col. 3 : 10.   *k* Matt. 5 : 12; Rom. 8 : 18.
l 1 Peter 1 : 6; 5 : 10.   *m* Heb. 12 : 10, 11.   *n* 5 : 7; Rom. 8 : 24, 25; Heb. 11 : 1.   *o* 1 John 2 : 17.

ence. **But though our outward man**, the body, our physical nature, **perish**, *is decaying*, the wasting process all the time going on, as the result of sorrows, sufferings, and persecutions, yet our inward man, the soul, our spiritual nature, **is renewed** with spiritual strength and vigor (Col. 3 : 10) **day by day**. The process goes on from day to day, effected by the Holy Spirit (ver. 6 ; 3 : 17) and their afflictions (ver. 17). Notice how the vivid contrasts are ranged, from clause to clause, in this and several verses that follow.

17. This renewal in connection with suffering further explained. **For our light affliction which is for a moment,** more exactly, *the momentary lightness of our affliction*, **worketh out for us** *more and more exceedingly*, beyond all measure and beyond what language can express, **an eternal weight of glory**—vast, transcendent, never-ending glory. "The apostle opposes things present to things future ; a moment to eternity ; lightness to weight; affliction to glory. Nor is he satisfied with this, but he adds another word, *more exceedingly*, and doubles it " (CHRYSOSTOM). It is in this *exceeding excessive* manner that these afflictions, momentary and light comparatively, work out for us never-ending blessedness. "Even that *affliction* which is excessive, when compared with less afflictions (1 : 8), is yet light compared with the exceeding glory" (BENGEL).

18. While, or *since*, **we look not at the things which are seen, but at the things which,** *that*, **are not seen ;** the object of our gaze is not the things of this earthly life, but those beyond the reach of bodily sight. By faith the invisible becomes assured and real (Heb. 11 : 1, 27 ; 1 Cor. 2 : 9, 10). It is only the Christian who has this faith and this aim of life. **For the things which are seen are temporal,** are for a time, temporary, **but the things which are not seen are eternal.** The one pertains to the brief season of this life; the other to the unending ages of eternity. "This verse contains the whole philosophy of the Christian view of affliction. It does not deny the reality of earthly sorrows, or underrate their power, as did the stoics; but after allowing them all their force, calmly says that they dwindle into insignificance when compared with the exceeding and eternal glory to which they lead " (CHAMBERS IN MEYER). The thought is continued in the next chapter.

PRACTICAL REMARKS.

1. The Christian ministry is such that the preacher of the gospel should never lose courage in proclaiming the truth (ver. 1 ; Acts 20 : 24).

2. The gospel comes with a self-evidencing power to the consciences of men (ver. 2, 4 ; John 3 : 19-21 ; 17 : 3).

3. The gospel is pure, simple truth. Preachers and religious teachers should avoid shams and all deception, and proclaim the message plainly and fully (ver. 2 ; John 14 : 6 ; Acts 20 : 27).

4. It is not the fault of the gospel that sinners are not saved. They will not believe, and they are blinded and deluded by Satan (ver. 4 ; John 5 : 40 ; 8 : 44).

5. The great purpose of the Christian ministry is to make known Jesus Christ, as Saviour and Lord, to their fellow-men (ver. 5 ; 1 Cor. 2 : 2-4).

6. The God of nature is the God of grace (ver. 6 ; Acts 17 : 23-31).

7. The knowledge of Jesus is the highest

5 FOR we know that if *our* earthly house of *this* tabernacle were dissolved, we have a building of God, an house not made with hands, eternal in the

5 FOR we know that, if our earthy house of the tabernacle be dissolved, we have a building from God, a house not made with hands, eternal in the

p Job 4 : 19 ; 2 Peter 1 : 13, 14.   *q* John 14 : 2 ; Heb. 11 : 10.   *r* Heb. 9 : 11, 23.

of all knowledge, and the most excellent of sciences (ver. 6 ; John 11 : 6-12).

8. The triumphs of the gospel, notwithstanding the weakness and frailty of its proclaimers, is a proof of its Divine origin (ver. 7-9 ; 1 Cor. 1 : 26-31).

9. Christian missionaries exhibit in their own experience the sustaining power of the gospel under trial (ver. 8, 9 ; Acts 26 : 22).

10. If we realize in our experience the dying of the Lord Jesus we shall also partake of his life (ver. 10, 11 ; Phil. 3 : 8-11 ; Col. 1 : 24).

11. We should welcome trials for the sake of Jesus and the salvation of men (ver. 11, 12 ; Phil. 3 : 13, 14).

12. The results of the ministry is of far more value than all it costs (ver. 12 ; Acts 20 : 22-24 ; Dan. 12 : 3).

13. Ministers of the gospel should be men of convictions, and should also have the courage of their convictions (ver. 13 ; Acts 20 : 19-21, 26, 27).

14. In the resurrection of Christ we have a pledge of our own resurrection and future glory (ver. 14 ; Rom. 8 : 11, 23).

15. The glory of God is the highest motive in laboring for the salvation of men (ver. 15 ; 1 Cor. 10 : 31).

16. Though the body wearies, grows old, decays, and dies in Christ's service, the soul enjoys an ever-increasing and enlarging life (ver. 16 ; 2 Tim. 4 : 6-8).

17. We should learn from Paul how to bear affliction and anticipate future glory (ver. 17 ; 11 : 23-27 ; Rom. 8 : 31-37).

18. Let us so live as to view all things that come to us from the standpoint of eternity (ver. 18 ; 1 Cor. 7 : 29-31 ; 1 John 4 : 5, 6).

CHAPTER V.

Paul continues to show how in their ministry they are cheered by the hope of a glorious immortality : Looking for the future glorified body (ver. 1-4), having an earnest of this, though as yet absent from the Lord (ver. 5-8), and stimulated by the thought of the judgment (ver. 9, 10). He dwells upon the motives : the fear of the Lord and the love of Christ (ver. 11-15) ; and their changed condition and relation through the reconciliation which God has effected in Christ, of which reconciliation they were ministers (ver. 16-19), and which they earnestly preached and entreated sinners to accept (ver. 20, 21).

1-10. THE CHEERING AND STIMULATING INFLUENCES OF THE FUTURE LIFE ON THEIR MINISTRY. A glorified body, the earnest of the Spirit, and the judgment seat of Christ.

1. Continuing the thought, the apostle gives a further reason for what he had affirmed regarding the future glorious results of our present afflictions (4 : 17, 18). **For,** looking at the unseen, **we,** associating Timothy with me (1 : 1), **know,** having seen the risen and glorified Lord (see on ver. 4 : 14), and enjoyed the revelations and guidance of the Spirit, **that if,** instead of living to see the second coming of the Lord, **our earthly house of this tabernacle,** or *tent,* **be dissolved,** *be disunited,* if our earthly body be taken down like a tent. **Earthly, upon the earth** (1 Cor. 15 : 40), refers to the body, not as made of the earth, but as existing on the earth (Phil. 2 : 10). The body is spoken of as a *tent-house,* a frail, temporary *tenement,* in contrast to a *building,* or a permanent dwelling. Notice that Paul had an assurance, a certainty, amounting to actual knowledge. Also that he thought that he might live to welcome the return of Christ, and so he speaks doubtfully of death, though elsewhere he speaks of it as that which might come to him at any moment (Acts 20 : 22-24 ; 21 : 13). His recent affliction had brought death very near to him (1 : 8-10 ; 4 : 10-12). **We have a building of God,** etc., rather, *We have in the heavens a building from God,* originated and prepared by him, **eternal,** not only permanent, but existing forever, **a house not made with hands,** as earthly houses are. Paul passes over the intermediate state between death and the resurrection ; for elsewhere he represents the new body as given at the resurrection and Christ's

2 heavens. For in this *we groan, earnestly desiring ʰto be clothed upon with our house which is from heaven: 3 ᵍif so be that ˢbeing clothed we shall 4 not be found naked. For we that are in *this* tabernacle do groan, being burdened; not for that we would be unclothed, but clothed upon, ʸthat mortality might be swallowed up of life.
5 Now ᶻhe that hath wrought us for the selfsame thing *is* God, who also

2 heavens. For in this we groan, longing to be clothed upon with our habitation which is from heaven; 3 if indeed being clothed, we shall not be found 4 naked. For we that are in the tabernacle groan, being burdened; not that we wish to be unclothed, but to be clothed upon, that what is mortal may be swallowed up by life.
5 Now he that wrought us out for this very thing is God, who gave to us the

---

*Rom. 7 : 24; 8 : 23.   ᵗ 1 Cor. 15 : 53, 54.   ᵘ Phil. 3 : 11;   ᶻ Rev. 3 : 18; 16 : 15.
ʸ See refs. Isa. 25 : 8.   ᶻ Isa. 29 : 23; Eph. 2 : 10.

---

second coming (1 Thess. 4 : 16, 17; 1 Cor. 15 : 52; Phil. 3 : 21). But this need cause no difficulty, for in this animated discourse Paul speaks as if the future were present. This is often done in Scripture. The intermediate state did not engross his attention; he regarded it as temporary; he appears not to have received special revelations concerning it; and he regarded the second coming of Christ as speedy. And so he passes to the glorified state at once, where in heaven he sees the glorified body, heavenly and spiritual in its nature, prepared and given by God.

2. This verse is confirmatory of the preceding verse. **For,** this knowledge and assurance of an immortal body, in case of the dissolution of our present mortal tenement, is attested by the fact that **in this** body **we groan** (see Rom. 8 : 23) and sigh, **earnestly desiring,** or *longing,* **to be clothed upon,** as with an outer garment, **with our house,** or *dwelling-place,* **which is from heaven.** Compare "from God" (ver. 1). This intense longing of the renewed soul, begotten of the Spirit, would surely be satisfied. Notice the words *clothed upon,* implying the apostle's hope that he might be living at the Lord's coming. The words, however, may be applied to the restored body at the resurrection (1 Cor. 15 : 53).

3. If so be that being clothed, according to a preferable reading, *Seeing we shall be found clothed, not naked,* not disembodied. The word *naked* does not necessarily express absolute nakedness, but often means *ill-clad* (Matt. 25 : 36), or without the outer garment (John 21 : 7). Hence here, without the resurrection body. Both the righteous dead and the righteous living shall meet their Lord at his coming with glorified bodies (1 Cor. 15 : 51, 52; 1 Thess. 4 : 16, 17). Being assured of this, the apostle asserts it strongly; and this belief is a ground for his longing to be clothed upon with his building from heaven (ver. 2).

4. Paul confirms and explains what he had said in ver. 2. **For we that are in this,** rather, *the,* **tabernacle,** of which we have spoken, **do groan** and sigh, **being burdened,** *oppressed,* with the thoughts that death, with its preceding infirmities and its dissolution, naturally awakens. He now states negatively and positively for what he sighs: **not for that we would,** *we desire,* **to be unclothed,** be disembodied and remain so; **but rather that we may be clothed upon,** not that we wish to put off the mortal body, but rather *that which is mortal* **might be swallowed up of,** or *by,* **life,** and become immortal. As he was hoping for the speedy coming of Christ, it was his special desire that he might live till he came, and not put off this body by death, but rather like Elijah, be glorified living. He would anticipate death by life. Paul regarded death as an enemy (1 Cor. 15 : 26), and the disembodied spirit not in itself to be desired. It was the spiritual and glorified body for which he longed. Concerning the intermediate state, and a conscious state of existence between death and the resurrection, see Clark's volume on Luke, in "A People's Commentary," Chap. 16, Practical Remarks 24, 25, pp. 380, 381.

5. The apostle traces his longing, and the basis of his confidence, to the Spirit. **Now he that hath wrought us for the selfsame thing,** *now he that wrought us out,* fashioned and fitted us at conversion, *for this*

a hath given unto us the earnest of the
6 Spirit. Therefore *we are* always confident, knowing that, whilst we are at home in the body, we are absent from
7 the Lord: (for *b* we walk by faith, not
8 by sight: we are confident, *I say*, and *c* willing rather to be absent from the body, and to be present with the Lord.
9 Wherefore *d* we labour, that, *e* whether

6 earnest of the Spirit. Being therefore always of good courage, and knowing that while at home in the body we are
7 absent from the Lord (for we walk by
8 faith, not by sight), we are of good courage, and are well pleased rather to be absent from the body, and to be at home with the Lord.
9 Wherefore we also make it our aim,

a See refs. 1 : 22 ; Rom. 8 : 16 ; 1 John 2 : 20, 27.   *b* 4 : 18 ; 1 Cor. 13 : 12.   *c* Phil. 1 : 20-24.
d 1 Cor. 9 : 26, 27 ; 1 John 3 : 3.   *e* Rom. 14 : 8.

very thing, for the swallowing up of mortality by life, for the glorified body, **is God** (Isa. 25 : 8). The reference is to the resurrection body, whether of the living or the raised dead at Christ's coming. This seems evident from what follows. **Who also hath given,** rather, according to the best text, *who gave us*, **the earnest,** the pledge, **of the Spirit.** (See note on 1 : 22.) The gift of the Spirit and his work in their hearts at conversion was a foretaste and pledge of their sanctification and their glorification (Rom. 8 : 29, 30). And this was true of all believers, whether they should live to see the Lord's return or not (Rom. 8 : 23).

6. Therefore, in view of God's purpose and the pledge of the life-giving Spirit (ver. 5), **we are always confident,** rather, *being confident*, **or** *of good courage at all times*, whether living or dying, **and knowing that while we are at home in the body,** as the earthly abode of the Spirit, **we are absent,** away from home, **from the Lord.** Their citizenship is in heaven (Phil. 3 : 20, 21), and their permanent and final home is there. God is present with all men by his sustaining power (Acts 17 : 27, 28); and with his people by his Spirit, who notwithstanding are absent from him, from his glorious presence and the close intercourse with him which that presence involves. The sentence is somewhat broken but is resumed in ver. 8.

7. In a parenthesis, Paul explains how he was absent from the Lord. **For we walk,** pass our life, **by,** or *through*, **faith, not by,** or *through*, sight, *by what is seen*. The word translated *sight* does not mean *power of vision*, but the *thing seen*, what *visibly appears*. The life we live here is that of faith, having an assurance of things hoped for and a conviction of the reality of things not seen (4 : 18. Heb. 11 :

1, 13, 14 ; John 20 : 29); it is not that of sight, encompassed by the visible appearances of heavenly things. We see not the Lord Jesus face to face, and the attendant glories, but realize them in our spirits as they are granted to our faith by the Holy Spirit (Eph. 3 : 16-18).

8. The thought is resumed from the end of ver. 6. **We are confident, I say, and willing,** better, *we are confident*, of good courage, and *are well pleased*, **rather to be absent from the body,** as our earthly home, *to depart out of the body*, to die, **and to be present,** go home or be at home, **with the Lord.** While the apostle would prefer to live till Christ's second coming and "be clothed upon" with a glorified body (ver. 4), and though death itself is not desirable (ver. 4), yet in view of a future resurrection, and the blessedness of the disembodied state, he was well pleased to die and enter that state. He would be indeed without a bodily home, but he would have a spiritual home with the Lord, looking forward to a glorified body, at the return of his Lord to earth. This throws light upon the state of the saved between death and the resurrection. They are in a blissful condition, and hence conscious, and enjoy such nearness to Christ that in comparison with it his spiritual presence with them on earth is absence (Phil. 1 : 23; Heb. 12 : 23). Doubtless their place and their enjoyments are exactly suited to their disembodied condition. Their eternal intercourse with Christ has begun, although the resurrection to a glorified body is necessary to complete their redemption, and to enjoy fully its glories. (See on 12 : 2, 4, and note on Luke 23 : 43.)

9. Wherefore, as we are well pleased and prefer absence from the body and presence with the Lord (ver. 8), **we labour,** rather, *we make it our aim*, or *our ambition*, **that whether**

present or absent, we may be accepted of him. *For we must all appear before the judgment seat of Christ; *that every one may receive the things done in *his* body, according to that he hath done, whether *it be* good or bad.

11 Knowing therefore *h* the terror of the Lord, *i* we persuade men; but *k* we are made manifest unto God; *l* and I trust whether at home or absent, to be well 10 pleasing to him. For we must all be manifested before the judgment-seat of Christ; that each one may receive the things done through the body, according to the things which he practiced, whether good or evil.

11 Knowing therefore the fear of the Lord, we persuade men; but to God we have been manifested, and I hope that

f See refs. Rom. 14 : 10.   *g* See refs. Rom. 2 : 6; Rev. 22 : 12.
h Nahum 1 : 6; Matt. 10 : 28; Heb. 10 : 31; Jude 23.   *i* Ver. 20; 6 : 1.   *k* 1 : 12-14; 2 : 17.
l 4 : 1, 2; 1 Thess. 2 : 3-12.

present, *at home* **with the Lord, or absent** from him, **we may be accepted of him,** or better, *well pleasing to him.* The word translated *labor* denotes a striving, the end aimed at being regarded as a matter of honor, hence, *to be ambitious.* (See Rom. 15 : 20 and note.) It was the apostle's ambition, his present earnest aim, whether living or dying (1 Thess. 5 : 10), so to live as to be well pleasing to Christ.

10. Paul had just dwelt upon the inward feeling, the earnest impulse of his soul, his ambition to please his Lord. He now turns to an outward motive, the judgment seat of Christ. **For we** Christians **must all,** as a matter of necessity and of divine appointment which none can evade, **appear,** rather, *be manifested,* **before the judgment seat of Christ.** (Comp. Matt. 25 : 31; Rev. 20 : 11.) There is not to be merely an appearance, but a manifestation of what we are, including the secrets of the heart (1 Cor. 4 : 5), before the judgment seat. Notice that Paul includes himself, and that the prospect of this manifestation was to him a motive. The judgment of the wicked is elsewhere taught (Rev. 20 : 12-14). **That every one,** each one individually, **may receive the things done in** *the* **body,** coming back as it were in wages, in reward or punishment, *according to the things which he did,* **whether good or bad.** The deeds in the body will decide the wages at the judgment; the acts and changes, after the soul has left the body, will not be taken into the account in fixing the final state.

"This passage stands alone in the insight which it gives us into the apostle's feelings, under the sense of approaching decay and dissolution. The burst of triumphant exultation over the power of death in Rom. 8 : 30-39 and 1 Cor. 15 : 51-58, is more an expression of the sense of God's love through Christ, than of any personal expectation for himself. . . The two passages which most bear comparison with this (2 Tim. 4 : 6-8; Phil. 1 : 20-24) . . . represent his calm expectation of an event brought on by external circumstances, as a soldier on the eve of battle, rather than his contemplation of death in itself (this passage) as the natural termination of the exhaustive powers of his nature" (STANLEY, "Epistles to Cor.," p. 421). On the apostle's condition of mind and body at this time compare 1 : 8-10; 2 : 13; 4 : 7-11, 16-18; 5 : 1.

11-17. THE MOTIVES OF THEIR MINISTRY: THE FEAR OF THE LORD AND THE LOVE OF CHRIST.

11. This passage seems connected as an inference to the two preceding verses. At the same time mention of the judgment may have brought to mind certain charges of his opponents that he had used dishonest means in seeking to win men. **Knowing therefore the terror,** rather, *the fear,* **of the Lord,** being conscious of a wholesome fear of Christ as judge, **we persuade men,** or *we do "seek to win men,"* as objectors say. But it is not to win them to ourselves (Gal. 1 : 10), but to Christ and to the gospel, by every proper means and motive, by warnings and exhortations (Col. 1 : 28). A dread of God is natural to men because they are conscious of being sinners (Isa. 6 : 5; Luke 5 : 8). The thought of a future judgment strikes the wicked with terror and the righteous with awe. **But we are made manifest unto God,** better, *but to God we have been made manifest,* the purity of our conduct and motives, our character and preaching as ministers of the gospel, have all along been known to him. **And I trust also,** rather, *and I hope*

also are made manifest in your con-
12 sciences. For ᵐ we commend not ourselves again unto you, but give you
occasion to glory on our behalf, that
ye may have somewhat to *answer* them
which glory in appearance, and not in
13 heart. For ⁿ whether we be beside
ourselves, ᵒ *it is* to God: or whether we
14 be sober, *it is* ᵖ for your cause. For the
love of Christ ᑫ constraineth us; because we thus judge, that, ʳ if one died
15 for all, ˢ then were all dead: and *that*

we have been manifested also in your
12 consciences. We are not again commending ourselves to you, but giving
you occasion of glorying on our behalf,
that ye may have wherewith to answer
those who glory in appearance and not
13 in heart. For whether we were beside
ourselves, it was for God; or whether
we are of sound mind, it is for you.
14 For the love of Christ constrains us;
because we thus judged, that one died
15 for all, therefore they all died; and he

ᵐ 3 : 1.   ⁿ 12 : 6, 11 ; Acts 26 : 24, 25.   ᵒ See 2 Sam. 6 : 21, 22.   ᵖ 2 Tim. 2 : 10.
ᑫ Acts 4 : 19, 20.   ʳ Isa. 53 : 6 ; Rom. 5 : 15.   ˢ Rom. 5 : 12.

we have been made manifest also in your consciences, in our true charac-
ters as preachers of the truth. (See note on 4 : 2.) Notice how the apostle makes conscience a judge in religious matters.

12. For, omitted by the best au-
thorities. In writing thus, **we are not commending ourselves again unto you.** His opposers appear to have charged him with vanity and self-praise. (See on 3 : 1, and his vindication in 3 : 2–5.) **But give you,** more exactly, *giving you,* **occasion to glory,** exult, **in our behalf**—we are giving you the opportunity and a ground for answering those **who glory in ap-
pearance,** in what appears visible to the eye, in outward show (10 : 7) **and not in heart,** what is real and true inwardly. A brief and striking description of the hypocrisy of his opponents (11 : 12, 13). They made a show of piety in the flesh (Gal. 6 : 12), but were actuated by self-interest, rather than pure motives (1 Sam. 16 : 7). "In heart—such was Paul's nature—truth shone from his heart to the consciences of the Corinthians " (BENGEL).

13. Ye can well boast of us as your teachers, **For whether we be,** rather, *whether we were,* **beside our-
selves,** when we were with you, as some doubtless said, *it was* **to,** *for,* **God,** for his cause and glory, in his service; it was a holy madness. Festus after this charged Paul with madness (Acts 26 : 24; comp. 17 : 18, 32). **Or whether we are sober,** *sound minded,* **it is for you,** in your service and for your advantage. In either case Paul's conduct was praiseworthy. The *sound mind* was a right mind, having a healthful self-
control, opposed to madness, *beside our-
selves* (Mark 3 : 21 ; 5 : 15). Paul exhibited an enthusiasm on the one hand (1 Cor.

2 : 2 ; 2 Cor. 6 : 4–10) and a practical wisdom on the other, becoming all things to all men (1 Cor. 9 : 22). He exercised a holy shrewdness in his devotion to their spiritual interests.

14. The reason of his sole devotion to God and to his brethren, Christ's constraining love. **For the love of Christ constraineth us,** *impels us.* It is Christ's love to us, as seems evident from what follows, Christ's dying for us. (Comp. Rom. 5 : 5 ; 8 : 35.) The verb translated *constraineth* has the idea of pressing hard, and holding a person to one object. It is used of some strong outward pressure, as of a crowd (Luke 8 : 45), as of anxiety and sickness (Luke 4 : 38 ; 8 : 37; Phil. 1 : 23). Here it is Christ's love, passing over into a strong inward im-
pelling force, arousing and holding the apostle to one line of action. And this constraining power took effect in us, **because we thus** *judged,* at some pre-
vious time, probably at conversion, we came to this conclusion as a true and settled conviction, **that if one died for all, then were all dead,** rather, *that* (as) *one died for all, therefore they all died,* that is, his death was in a sense their death. The preposition translated *for* means *in behalf of.* (See on 1 Cor. 15 : 29.) *If* is omitted by the best textual authorities. These two clauses have given rise to much discussion. The simple meaning appears to be, that "they all," or more exactly, *the all,* in whose behalf Christ died, in a sense died in him. The death of Christ, which was for the sins of men, was regarded as the death of all men collectively. Christ was so related and identified with the race that he acted in their behalf and in their place. His death was on account of all and had reference to all (1 John 2 : 2). An atonement and recon-

he died for all, ⁱ that they which live should not henceforth live unto themselves, but unto him which died for them, and rose again.
16 ᵘ Wherefore henceforth know we no man after the flesh: yea, though we have known Christ after the flesh, yet now henceforth know we *him* no more.
17 Therefore if any man ʸ *be* in Christ, *he is* ᶻ a new creature; ᵃ old things are passed away; behold, all things are

died for all, that they who live should live no longer to themselves, but to him who for them died and rose again.
16 So that we henceforth know no one according to the flesh; even if we have known Christ according to the flesh, yet now we no longer know him.
17 So that if any one is in Christ, he is a new creature; the old things passed away; behold, they have become new.

t Rom. 6 : 1–13 ; 14 : 7–9 ; 1 Cor. 6 : 19, 20, Gal. 2 : 20 ; Titus 2 : 14.
u Deut. 33 : 9 ; see refs. Matt. 12 : 50 ; Gal. 2 : 5, 6.   *x* Rom. 8 : 1 ; Eph. 1 : 3, 4 : 1 John 5 : 20.
y John 3 : 3 ; Gal. 6 : 15 ; Col. 3 : 9, 10.   *z* Rom. 6 : 4–6 ; Eph. 4 : 22–24

ciliation was made, so that all might receive eternal life by accepting the gospel through faith in Christ. (See on ver. 21 ; also Rom. 3 : 25, 26.)

15. Paul continues his statement, bringing into view the object of Christ's death. **And that he died,** etc., better, *and he died for all in order that they who live,* by accepting the provisions of the gospel, *should no longer live unto themselves,* as they had done in their past lives before their conversion, *but to him who for them,* in their behalf, **died and rose again.** Notice that both Christ's death and resurrection was for their advantage (4 : 10, 11 ; Rom. 6 : 3–10 ; 14 : 9 ; Gal. 2 : 20 ; 5 : 24, 25 ; 6 : 14). In his death we are freed from the bondage of sin; in his risen life we through the Holy Spirit have life. Being in Christ Jesus we are not under condemnation and walk not after the flesh but after the Spirit (Rom. 8 : 1, 4 ; 5 : 10, 11 ; Col. 3 : 1–4). Thus we are brought into new relations and into a new life. Hence we see how the apostle was constrained by the love of Christ to an unreserved devotion to God and his cause (ver. 13).

16. Inference from the preceding verse. **Wherefore,** or *so that,* being in Christ, and entirely devoted to him (ver. 15), *we from the present time know no one,* **after the flesh,** according to his natural distinctions of birth, connections, and relations (Gal. 3 : 28). He regards his spiritual character. "He who knows no one *according to the flesh* has entirely left out of the account, in the Jew, his Jewish origin ; in the rich man, his riches ; in the scholar, his learning ; in the slave, his bondage, etc." (MEYER, Comp. 1 Cor. 2 : 10–16). **We** is emphatic, and suggests by implication that his opposers used a worldly, fleshly standard (10 : 7 ; 1 Cor. 1 : 12). This principle of action the apostle applied to his knowledge and estimate of Christ. **Yea, though,** or *even if,* **we have known Christ** *according to* **the flesh,** judging him according to natural and human standards, as of the tribe of Judah and as the son of David simply (Rom. 1 : 3), and not as the incarnate Son of God, the Divine Word, yet **now** *we no longer know him* after this manner. Before his conversion Paul had regarded Jesus as the despised and crucified Nazarene. And after his conversion, like many of the early teachers, he doubtless had some carnal conceptions which disappeared as he progressed in the knowledge of the truth. Besides, it was not so much Christ, as he lived on the earth, that so filled his mind as the risen Christ who now lives in heaven. There is nothing here, however, that implies that Paul had seen Jesus when in the flesh upon earth.

17. An inference from the two preceding verses. It follows that such as enjoy in themselves the benefits of Christ's death and possess the knowledge spoken of, are in Christ and are new creatures. **Therefore,** better, *So that if any one is,* **in Christ,** united spiritually in him, having become a Christian (12 : 2 ; Rom. 16 : 7), **he is a new creature.** According to a rabbinical usage a person converted from idolatry to Judaism was spoken of as a new creature, and the expression is used in a nobler application to one regenerated in Christ (Gal. 6 : 15). A radical change has been effected in his spiritual nature by the Holy Spirit (John 1 : 13 ; 3 : 3, 5 ; Titus 3 : 5). **Old things** *have* **passed away,** better, *the old things* of his former life, his former manner of living, *passed away* at his conversion. **Be-**

is become new. And *all things *are* of God, *b* who hath reconciled us to himself by Jesus Christ, and *c* hath given 19 to us the ministry of reconciliation; to wit, that *d* God was in Christ, *e* reconciling the world unto himself, *f* not imputing their trespasses unto them; and hath committed unto us the word of reconciliation.

18 And all things are from God, who reconciled us to himself through Christ, and gave to us the ministry of the 19 reconciliation; how that God was in Christ reconciling the world to himself, not reckoning to them their trespasses, and having committed to us the word of reconciliation.

a John 3 : 27; James 1 : 17.   *b* Dan. 9 : 24; Rom. 5 : 10; 1 John 2 : 2; 4 : 10.   *c* Ver. 20; Acts 13 : 38, 39.
d John 14 : 10, 11; 1 Tim. 3 : 16.   *e* See refs. Rom. 3 : 24-26.   *f* Ps. 32 : 1, 2.

hold, vividly calling attention to the great change that has taken place. **All things,** rather, according to the best text, *they,* the old things, **have become new,** in character, the whole man has been renewed; the tendencies and currents of his soul. Thoughts, motives, feelings, habits, and desires, have been changed according to the image of Christ. Compare "the old man" and "the new man" (Col. 3 : 9, 10; Eph. 4 : 22-24). On **creature** see note on Rom. 8 : 19.

18-21. THEIR MINISTRY ONE OF RECONCILIATION.

18. What the apostle had said about the new creature leads him back to God, and to the reconciliation which God has effected through Christ. **And all things are of God,** all this change, pertaining to the new creature (ver. 17) is *from* God, the author and source, **who hath reconciled us,** etc., rather, *who reconciled us,* Christians, *through Christ to himself, and gave us,* the apostles, teachers, and preachers, *the ministry of reconciliation.* **Jesus** is omitted in the best text. Some would make the first *us* refer to all men, making it parallel with *the world* in the next verse. But it is only in Christians that this reconciliation is a fully accomplished fact among men, and such it appears to be viewed by the apostle in this verse. The second *us* is limited still further to the ambassadors of Christ (ver. 20). Different views have been taken of *the reconciliation* here presented. Some limit it to a change in man's disposition toward God; others refer it entirely to a change in God's treatment of men, in which he causes his anger toward them to cease and takes them into his favor, and they become friends instead of enemies. To us the word, *an adjustment of a difference,* and the connection, **seem** to embrace both ideas. It appears to be in a certain sense a mutual reconciliation, but it begins with God in the manifestation of his grace. He is indeed the reconciler, but this is accepted by men in repentance and through faith in Jesus Christ. It only becomes thus an accomplished fact in human experience. The enmity between God and man is removed through Christ. God's wrath, his holy indignation against sin, is appeased (Rom. 3 : 25; Gal. 3 : 13), and men are drawn to exercise a willing and hearty love to God (John 12 : 32; Eph. 2 : 14-16; 1 John 4 : 19). On the words "reconcile" and "reconciliation" see further on Rom. 5 : 10, 11.

19. Explanatory of this ministry of reconciliation and of its message. **To wit,** better, *As that,* or *How that,* God **was in Christ,** identified with and dwelling in him (John 14 : 10; 17 : 21, 23; Col. 1 : 19), **reconciling the world unto himself,** through suffering, and death upon the cross (Col. 1 : 20; 1 John 2 : 2). **Not imputing,** better, *Not reckoning to them,* **not** accounting to them, **their trespasses.** (See note on Rom. 4 : 8 and 3 : 25.) In Christ's mediatorial work, God shows himself a gracious God, "forgiving iniquity, transgression, and sin." God sent not his Son to condemn, but to save (John 3 : 17). To the sinner he offers reconciliation through Christ with all its blessed results; and the believer in Christ he treats as if he had never sinned (Rom. 3 : 26; 8 : 1; comp. Heb. 9 : 12-14; 10 : 10-14). **And hath committed,** rather, *And having committed to us,* having placed (deposited as it were) in our minds, **the word of reconciliation,** the message or doctrine concerning it, which we are to make known to others. (Comp. Gal. 1 : 15; 1 Tim. 1 : 12.) Thus God's reconciliation in Christ includes, first the not reckoning to men their trespasses, and then, by his servants, beseeching men to be reconciled to him (ver. 20).

20 Now then we are *ambassadors for Christ, as though God did beseech you by us: we pray you in Christ's stead, 21 ᵇ be ye reconciled to God. For ʰhe hath made him *to be* sin for us, who knew no sin; that we might be made ᵏ the righteousness of God in him.

20 On behalf of Christ then we are ambassadors, as though God were beseeching through us; we entreat on behalf 21 of Christ: Be reconciled to God! Him who knew not sin he made to be sin for us, that we might become God's righteousness in him.

g Mal. 2 : 7; Eph. 6 : 20.   *h* See refs. Job 22 : 21.   *i* Isa. 53 : 4–6; 9–12; Gal. 3 : 13; Eph. 5 : 2.
k See refs. Rom. 3 : 21, 22.

20. The preacher's office and his general message to men. In view of the fact that God has committed to us the word of reconciliation, *We are therefore* **ambassadors**, acting in this high and honorable character, *on behalf* **of Christ,** one far greater than any earthly sovereign (Eph. 6 : 20; Phil. 2 : 9), **as though God did beseech you by us,** rather, *as though God were beseeching by us.* This is a general statement of the earnestness with which God's message is delivered to men. **We pray you in Christ's stead,** rather, *On behalf of Christ we pray,* we entreat men, the world (ver. 19). What divine condescension! This is a statement to the Corinthian Christians, not an entreaty to them, since they were already reconciled. **Be ye reconciled,** more exactly, *Be reconciled to God.* A passive active: Permit yourselves to be reconciled to God by accepting Christ and his righteousness; do not oppose your return to God's favor through unbelief, but lay hold of that favor now offered you in the "word of reconciliation." God is reconciled through Jesus Christ, and a way is provided for the reconciling of sinners who are still at enmity with him. This enmity must be subdued, and an active love must take its place. This is effected in regeneration and its accompanying exercises, the whole of which is popularly styled conversion. In regeneration God acts on the soul (John 1 : 13), but in the accompanying exercises of repentance and faith the will of man is brought into active exercise. We are begotten with the word of truth (James 1 : 18), and hence the necessity of proclaiming "the word of reconciliation" to men. The "beseeching," the earnest entreaty, is an appeal to the emotions and the will, which must be brought into active and loving exercise in order that reconciliation may be fully accomplished in the soul.

21. The reason or ground of the exhortation to be reconciled to God. Omit **For,** according to the highest critical authorities. Translate: *Him who knew not sin,* in its widest and deepest meaning, as a ruling power or principle (see on Rom. 5 : 12), who knew it not as an experience, either in positive acts or as a condition, but was perfectly innocent and guiltless (1 Peter 2 : 22), *he made to be sin for us*, in behalf of us; he was put into such connection with sin and such relation with us as sinners that he bore the curse of sin in our behalf (Gal. 3 : 13; Heb. 9 : 28). He took our place and suffered in our stead (1 Peter 2 : 24; 1 Tim. 2 : 6; Matt. 20 : 28). Some take *sin* in the sense of a sin offering; but of this there is not sufficient evidence. Christ was appointed to represent sin and the sinner, and, though holy, was treated as sin and sinners are treated (Acts 2 : 23; Rom. 8 : 3). He bore our sins, but he was not contaminated with sin (Heb. 7 : 26). And this was done in order **that we might be made,** better, *that we might become,* **the righteousness of God in him,** that we might be brought by faith into such connection with it, and into such relation to Christ, as to become possessors of this righteousness and its blessedness. In other words, that we, though sinners, might, on account of the death of Christ in our behalf, be treated as righteous, and become so, by the forgiveness of our sins and the renewal by the Holy Spirit. (See notes on Rom. 1 : 17; 3 : 21, 22.)

THE RELATION OF CHRISTIAN EXPERIENCE FOR ADMISSION TO BAPTISM AND THE CHURCH. Conversion, in a broad and popular sense of the word, may be said to be a spiritual change of a soul from a sinful state or course of sin to a life of love and of service of God, implying regeneration, repentance, and faith in Christ. Such a change is supernatural. It is a "new creation" (Gal. 6:15), not an evolution from the old sinful nature, but a holy seed implanted by the Spirit of God, and nourished by his Spirit, word, and grace. They who have undergone this change have entered upon a new life, having been "born again," "born of the Spirit" (John 3:3, 5). They are "in Christ" and are "new creatures: old things have passed away; behold, they have become new" (2 Cor. 5:17), and their "life is hidden with Christ in God" (Col. 3:3). In other words, this change is miraculous. They in whom it has been effected are "born, not of blood, nor of the will of man, but of God" (John 1:13). "He that believeth on me," says Jesus, "the works that I do shall he do also; and greater works than these shall he do; because I go to the Father" (John 14:12), referring to the works through the Holy Spirit, especially in the conversion of sinners. Supernatural works in the realm of Spirit are superior to those in the realm of sense. The raising of a soul from death into eternal life is a greater work than the raising of a dead body to life. I emphasize this change as supernatural and miraculous, because there appears to be in our time a tendency to strip off the supernatural from Scripture miracles and prophecy and from the Christian life. Evangelical Christian experience is as a consequence undervalued; a change of heart is to many a mere change of purpose; and a relation of a Christian experience is quite unimportant as an evidence for admission to baptism and to the church.

But if conversion is the superhuman work that Christ and his apostles declare it to be, then, as it is effected in the soul, it must become an experience, and no one can fully understand it but such as have come to know it by actual experience. Many passages of Scripture imply this experience, such as, "Come unto me and I will give you rest"; "As many as received him to them gave he power to become the sons of God"; "If any man is willing to do his will he shall know of the doctrine". "But when it pleased God, who called me by his grace, to reveal his Son in me." Doubtless many may not be able to point to the exact time when this change took place. The Spirit is sovereign and works as he pleases (John 3:8).

But yet there comes to their consciousness the fact that they were sinners in the sight of God, lost and helpless to save themselves, and that Jesus Christ is now their Saviour, suited to them, and "able to save to the uttermost (*completely*) them that come unto God by him."

In view of all this, it certainly appears that it is not enough to declare "a willingness to know and do the truth" in order to an entrance into the church. The first duty toward God should have been performed. Repentance toward God and faith in our Lord Jesus Christ should have been exercised. A consciousness of Jesus as a Saviour from sin, a personal Saviour, should have been felt. Such an experience is symbolized and professed in baptism (Rom. 6:4). Nothing short of this, it would seem, should be required for one to be publicly enrolled with the people of God. There should be an experience akin to that of the blind man: "One thing I know, that, whereas I was blind, now I see" (John 9:25). It is scriptural and reasonable that one be able to give an account of the hope that is in him (1 Peter 3:15).

PRACTICAL REMARKS.

1. It is the privilege of the Christian to have an assurance, practically amounting to knowledge, of a future glorified existence (ver. 1; 1 Cor. 15:58; John 14:2).

2. The pains and burdens incident to our frail mortal bodies are in striking contrast to the immortal vigor of the future glorified body (ver. 2-4; Cor. 15 53-55; Rev. 21:4).

3. The second coming of Christ will be a joyful day to all who shall be prepared to meet him (ver. 2-4; James 5:7, 8; 2 Tim. 4:8).

4. The Christian is designed for a blessed immortality; and the Spirit gives him evidences of it here (ver. 5; 2 Tim. 1:9, 10; Eph. 1:3).

5. The Christian's home is where Christ is (ver. 6; Phil. 1:23; Rev. 3:21).

6. The Christian's prospects are such that he can, whatever his circumstances, be of good courage (ver. 6, 8; Phil. 4:4).

7. In spiritual things, faith is at present better than sight (ver. 7; 4:18; John 20: 29; Heb. 11:27).

6 WE then, as [1] workers together *with him*, beseech *you* also [m] that ye receive

[1] 1 Cor. 3 : 9.

6 AND working together with him, we also beseech you that ye receive

[m] Titus 2 : 11; Heb. 12 : 15, 25.

8. The state between death and the resurrection is one of conscious, happy existence, and is far more desirable than our present state (ver. 8 ; Luke 23 : 43 ; Phil. 1 : 23).

9. The Christian should be ambitious, but it should be a sanctified ambition in all things, and first of all to please God (ver. 9; Heb. 11 : 5; 1 Cor. 10 : 31).

10. Our probation will close with this life. We are to be judged of the things done in the body (ver. 10; Acts 17 : 31; Eph. 6 : 8; Rev. 22 : 11).

11. We should present the terrors of the law, and the fearfulness of a coming judgment, not to frighten, but to persuade sinners to flee from the wrath to come and lay hold on eternal life (ver. 10; Acts 10 : 42; Luke 19 : 41, 42).

12. Godly sincerity, a conscious uprightness, and a real love for souls, are far more valuable than any external advantages or endowments (ver. 12 ; Acts 24 : 16).

13. The earnest, fervent Christian is sure to be misjudged by the indolent, lukewarm, and unbelieving (ver. 13 ; Mark 3 : 21; 5 : 15-17 ; Matt. 10 : 24, 25).

14. Nothing on earth equals the constraining power of Christ's love (ver. 14 ; Eph. 3 : 19).

15. Since Christ died in behalf of all men it is the duty of Christians to preach the gospel to all (ver. 15 ; Heb. 2 : 9 ; John 3 : 16).

16. True Christian living is unselfish living, devoted to Christ and his cause (ver. 15 ; Rom. 12 : 1 ; 2 Tim. 1 : 12, 13).

17. We should form our estimate of men and things from a spiritual standpoint, with a reference to both time and eternity (ver. 16 ; Phil. 3 : 3-10 ; Isa. 53 : 2, 3).

18. The new birth is a new creation. It is a radical change in the will and affections ; in the feelings and perceptions of the soul (ver. 17; John 1 : 13 ; Eph. 4 : 24).

19. God is infinitely desirous for the reconciliation of men. He has removed every obstacle on his part through Jesus Christ; and to effect it in man he has appointed a ministry of reconciliation (ver. 18, 20; John 3 : 16; Job 9 : 33).

20. How sublime the work of God in divine and human reconciliation, and how responsible and glorious the work of making it known to men (ver. 19, 20; Rom. 11 : 33 ; 1 Tim. 1 : 12).

21. How amazing the condescension of God in making a reconciliation possible, and in entreating men to be reconciled (ver. 20; Phil. 2 : 7, 8).

22. The sinner has something to do. He is to give up his opposition to God, accept the terms of mercy, and trust in Jesus Christ alone for salvation (ver. 20; Acts 2 : 38 ; 16 : 31).

23. The Lord is our sin-bearer and our righteousness (ver. 21; 1 Peter 2 : 24; Isa. 53 : 12; Jer. 23 : 6; 33 : 16).

CHAPTER VI.

The apostle admonishes the Corinthians not to receive the grace of God in vain (ver. 1, 2), and describes the aims of his ministry in cultivating every grace amid hardships and persecutions, and in accomplishing great and blessed results (ver. 3-10). He then makes an earnest appeal for an affectionate response (ver. 11-13), and warns the Corinthians against unbelief, impurity, and evil associations.

1-10. FURTHER DESCRIPTION OF THE AIMS AND WORK OF HIS MINISTRY, AS AN AMBASSADOR OF CHRIST. With the wonderful list of apostolic sufferings, comp. 4 : 8-12 and 11 : 23-27.

1. We then, as workers together. This is rather a continuation of the thought from the last chapter, *And working together with him*, with Christ, in whose behalf they entreated men to be reconciled, and who is the principal subject of thought in the preceding verse. (Comp. 1 Cor. 3 : 9.) **Beseech you also,** rather, *we also beseech you*, with the added idea, we give you this exhortation, **that ye receive not,** etc. As ambassadors of Christ they were exhorting men to be reconciled (5 : 20), and were thus fellow-helpers of Christ; and in pursuing this work they also entreated and exhorted the Corinthians that **the grace of God,** the grace of reconciliation, which had been extend-

2 not the grace of God in vain. (For he saith, ⁿI have heard thee in a time accepted, and in the day of salvation have I succoured thee. ᵒBehold, now is the accepted time; behold, now is
3 the day of salvation.) ᵖGiving no offence in any thing, that the ministry
4 be not blamed: but in all *things* approving ourselves ᑫas the ministers of God, ʳin much patience, in afflictions, ˢin
5 necessities, in distresses, ᵗin stripes, in imprisonments, ᵘin tumults, in labours,

2 not the grace of God in vain; (for he says,
　In an acceptable time I heard thee,
　And in a day of salvation I helped thee;
behold, now is the acceptable time, behold, now is the day of salvation;)
3 giving no cause of stumbling in anything, that our ministry be not blamed;
4 but in everything commending ourselves as God's ministers, in much patience, in afflictions, in necessities, in
5 distresses, in stripes, in imprisonments, in tumults, in labors, in watchings, in

n Luke 19 : 42–44. o Heb. 3 : 7, 13. p Rom. 14 : 13 ; 1 Cor. 10 : 32. q 12 : 12 ; 1 Cor. 4 : 1. r 2 Tim. 3 : 10. s 1 Cor. 4 : 11. t 11 : 23–27. u 1 : 8–10 ; Acts 17 : 4, 5.

---

ed to them in their conversion, should not be received in vain, to no purpose. Compare the rocky ground hearers who received the word with joy, but fell away (Matt. 13 : 20, 21; also comp. John 15 : 2). Their final salvation might depend instrumentally on such exhortations as this.

2. In a parenthetic sentence, including a quotation from Isa. 49 : 8, in the words of the Septuagint version, Paul gives a reason and an enforcement of the exhortation. **For he saith, I have heard,** better, *I heard thee,* etc., the quotation closing with the indefinite past, *I succored* or *helped thee.* These were the words of Jehovah to the Messiah, who is the head of his people. The **time accepted,** the time of exercising grace or favor, was **the day of salvation,** the day for announcing and communicating salvation to his people. This had been promised and its fulfillment was certain. So the apostle rightly applies these prophetic words to this gospel time and gospel message. **Behold, now,** since we are ambassadors on behalf of Christ, who has been made sin for us, and given us this earnest message of reconciliation, *now* is the *well* accepted **time; behold, now is the day of salvation,** the time and day of God's grace, which we beseech you not to receive in vain. The Christian should in his life and conduct continually acknowledge God's gracious message and the word of reconciliation which he has received.

3. This is closely connected with ver. 1. Paul enforced his exhortation "not to receive the grace of God in vain," by his own example. **Giving no offence,** *no cause of stumbling,* in **anything,** in any respect, **that the ministry,** of reconciliation, the office and its ministration, **be not blamed.** It was of the first importance that their ministry should be without reproach; for this might prove a cause of stumbling, leading some into error or sin.

4. The preceding verse presents the negative, this the positive side. **But in all things,** in everything, **approving,** or *commending* (the same word as in 3 : 1), **ourselves as the ministers of God,** better, *as God's ministers,* in the long list of particulars that follows. They did not *prove,* but rather *commended* themselves as God's ministers by their conduct. In 3 : 1 *ourselves* is emphatic; here it is not. Paul speaks modestly. The means by which Paul and his associates commended themselves may be divided into four classes. The *first,* extending to the end of ver. 5, relates to bodily sufferings in ten particulars. **In much patience,** endurance, steadfastness, unswerving in the greatest trials and sufferings. **In distresses,** great straits from which escape seems about hopeless (4 : 8).

5. **In stripes, in imprisonments,** or *in prisons* (11 : 23–25; Acts 16 : 22–24). The book of the Acts records but one of these, that at Philippi (Acts 16 : 22 ff.); but gives but a small part of Paul's ministry and sufferings. **In tumults,** civil disturbances, seditions. For some of these in the apostle's experience see Acts 13 : 50; 14 : 5, 19; 16 : 22; 17 : 5; 18 : 12; 19 : 23. **In labours,** for his own support (Acts 18 : 3; 20 : 34; 2 Thess. 3 : 8); spiritually, for Christ's cause (Col. 1 : 29; 1 Tim. 4 : 10). **Watchings,** sleepless nights in trav-

6 in watchings, in fastings; *by pureness, y by knowledge, by long-suffering, by kindness; ᶻ by the Holy Ghost, ᵃ by
7 love unfeigned, ᵇ by the word of truth, by ᶜ the power of God; by ᵈ the armour of righteousness on the right hand and
8 on the left, by honour and dishonour, ᵉ by evil report and good report; as de-
9 ceivers, and yet true; as unknown, and ᶠyet well known; ᵍas dying, and, behold, we live; as chastened, and not
10 killed; as sorrowful, ʰyet alway re-

6 fastings; in pureness, in knowledge, in long-suffering, in kindness, in the Holy
7 Spirit, in love unfeigned, in the word of truth, in the power of God; through the weapons of righteousness on the
8 right hand and on the left, through glory and dishonour, through evil report and good report; as deceivers,
9 and yet true; as unknown, and yet well known; as dying, and behold, we
10 live; as chastened, and not killed; as sorrowful, yet always rejoicing; as

---

ᶻ 1 Thess. 2 : 10.   y 11 : 6; Eph. 3 : 4.   ᶻ 3 : 3; Rom. 15 : 19; 1 Thess. 1 : 5, 6.   ᵃ See refs. Rom. 12 : 9.
ᵇ 4 : 2; Eph. 1 : 13.   ᶜ 1 Cor. 2 : 4, 5.   ᵈ 10 : 4; Eph. 6 : 11, 13, 14; 1 Thess. 5 : 8.   ᵉ Rom. 3 : 8.
ᶠ 4 : 2; 11 : 6; 1 Cor. 4 : 9.   ᵍ See refs. 4 : 10, 11.   ʰ 1 Thess. 3 : 7-10.

---

eling, praying, with anxious cares and the like (Acts 27 : 20, 33). **In fastings,** common with Paul (11 : 27; Acts 13 : 2, 3; 14 : 23). In all these he had showed "much patience" (ver. 4).

6, 7. The *second* class of the list begins here, consisting of eight internal virtues and endowments, ending with "the power of God" (ver. 7). **By,** more exactly, *in,* as far as the phrase "the armor of righteousness," in ver. 7. *In* **pureness,** from evil deeds and motives and sin generally (1 Tim. 5 : 22). **Knowledge,** of divine truth (1 Cor. 12 : 8). **Longsuffering,** or forbearance, which does not hastily retaliate wrong. *In* **the Holy Spirit,** having his presence, and enjoying his manifestations (Rom. 8 : 4, 5; 1 Cor. 12 : 8). **Love unfeigned,** real, sincere, free from selfish purposes, a marked characteristic of Paul (ver. 11; Rom. 12 : 9). *In* **the word of truth,** with which he was entrusted and which he preached (4 : 2; 5 : 19; Gal. 2 : 5). *In* **the power of God,** manifested in their preaching and work (4 : 7; 1 Cor. 2 : 4).

The *third* class of the list begins at this point, extending through "good report," in ver. 8, and consists of six things by means of which Paul advanced his work, thereby commending him as a minister of Christ. **By**—in this class the preposition is changed from *in* to *through* or *by means of.* **The armour,** or *weapons,* **of righteousness on the right hand and on the left,** both for offense and defense, the shield of faith as well as the sword of the Spirit (Eph 6 : 16, 17) and the spear of truth.

8. By honour, *through,* or *by means of glory,* the highest kind of honor, **and dishonour,** that cast upon him by the enemies of God's cause. *Through,* or *by means of,* **evil report and good report,** defamation and praise. Not only did the apostle pass through these opposite experiences, but they resulted in the furtherance of the gospel (Phil. 1 : 12). His conduct was such, and the results were such, as to commend him as God's servant (Gal. 1 : 10; 2 : 11 ff.).

The *fourth* and last class of the list commences here, ending with ver. 10, and consists of seven striking contrasts of the apparent and real condition of Paul and his associates, each contrast beginning with *as.* **As deceivers and yet true.** *Yet,* in this and the following contrasts, is not needed to express the sense. That God's enemies should call them *deceivers* was really a commendation, as well as the fact that they were really true.

9. As unknown, regarded as obscure persons by some (comp. Gal. 1 : 22), **and yet well known,** where he labored in the churches (3 : 1, 2; 5 : 11). **As dying,** so regarded from the standpoint of his sufferings, infirmities, and persecutions (4 : 10, 11; 1 Cor. 4 : 9), **and, behold, we live** (1 : 10; Acts 14 : 20); **as chastened, and not killed** (an allusion, perhaps, to Ps. 118 : 18), in deep affliction and apparently chastened of God, but not put to death. (Comp. 7 : 4; 12 : 7-9; Isa. 53 : 4.) Afflictions are not always chastisements, but often opportunities for glorifying God (John 17 : 1; James 5 : 11).

10. As sorrowful, full of sorrow, so it seems to the world, who witness our tears and anxieties, **yet alway rejoicing** in the Lord (4 : 17; Rom. 5 : 3, 11; Phil. 4 : 4, 12). There is joy in the Christian's tears; though trials abound, joy superabounds. **As poor,** needy

joicing; as poor, yet making many rich; ¹ as having nothing, and yet possessing all things.

The apostle's warnings to, and affection, for the Corinthian Christians, and his joy on receiving the report of Titus.

11 O ye Corinthians, our mouth is open
12 unto you, ᵏ our heart is enlarged. Ye are not straitened in us, but ¹ ye are
13 straitened in your own bowels. Now for a recompence in the same, (ᵐ I speak as unto *my* children,) be ye also enlarged.

poor, yet making many rich; as having nothing, and yet possessing all things.

11 Our mouth is open to you, O Corin-
12 thians, our heart is enlarged. Ye are not straitened in us, but ye are straitened in your own affections.
13 Now as a recompense in the same kind (I speak as to my children), be ye also enlarged.

i 1 Cor. 3 : 21, 22 ; James 2 : 5.   k 7 : 3.   l 12 : 15.   m 1 Cor. 4 : 14, 15.

---

and penniless, and looked upon as having nothing, and at the same time **making many rich** with spiritual blessings (1 Cor. 7 : 29-31; Eph. 3 : 8, 16-19), and indeed **possessing all things** in Christ, a boundless, an eternal, and a heavenly inheritance (1 Cor. 3 : 21-23; Rom. 8 : 32). A fitting climax of this wonderful description.

11-13. AN APPEAL FOR AN AFFECTIONATE RESPONSE.

11. After the remarkable description of his own sufferings in exercising his ministry, the way is prepared for this powerful appeal. **O ye Corinthians,** the only place where they are thus personally and pointedly addressed in the two Epistles. **Our mouth is open unto you,** full, frank, without reserve, the outlet of a large overflowing heart. "Out of the abundance of the heart the mouth speaketh" (Matt. 12 : 34). **Our heart is enlarged,** *has been* and is enlarged, expanded in sympathy, love, and interest for you. What makes this the more remarkable in Paul's case is that this enlargement takes place notwithstanding the provocations, opposition, and criticisms he had received from them. (Comp. Gal. 4 : 19.) This large-heartedness and warm, tender sympathy were among the secrets of Paul's success.

12. Ye are not straitened, compressed into a narrow space, **in us,** in our hearts; there is ample room for you; **but ye are straitened in your own bowels,** *in your own hearts,* or *affections,* and so you do not respond as ye should to our love. The fault is not in us, but in you. Your hearts, your affections, are not broad enough to receive us. The Hebrews regarded the bowels as we do the heart, as the seat of the tenderer affections, and so the word is better rendered here and in many places by *heart* or *affections* (Phil. 1 : 8; 2 : 1; Col. 3 : 12, etc.).

13. Now for, or *as*, **a recompense in the same** *kind*—that is, in love **(I speak as unto my children,** with paternal affection to children who should return filial love), **be ye also enlarged** in your hearts. Return love for love.

PAUL'S HEART. Paul was eminently a man of heart, and this was one secret of his power over men. At Ephesus, for the space of three years, he ceased not to admonish every one night and day "with all lowliness of mind and with tears" (Acts 20 : 19, 31). At Corinth he was "in weakness, and in fear, and in much trembling" (1 Cor. 2 : 3). To the Corinthians, in his Second Epistle, he especially reveals his heart. Whether afflicted or comforted, it was for their consolation and salvation (2 Cor. 1 : 6). "Out of much affliction and anguish of heart," he wrote to them, "with many tears" (2 Cor. 2 : 4). His mouth was open and his heart enlarged unto them (2 Cor. 6 : 11). How frankly, courageously, yet tenderly, he addresses his opposers at Corinth, face to face and heart to heart (2 Cor. 10 : 1-11 : 33). How full of love is his Epistle to the Philippians, overflowing even to Christless souls: "For many walk, of whom I have told you often, and now tell you even weeping, that they are the enemies of the cross of Christ" (Phil. 3 : 18). And in his last Epistle, on the eve of martyrdom, how lovingly, as a father, does he write to his spiritual son Timothy with his final benediction: "The Lord Jesus Christ be with thy spirit. Grace be with you" (2 Tim. 4 : 22).

14 ⁿBe ye not unequally yoked together with unbelievers. For ᵒwhat fellowship hath righteousness with unrighteousness? And what communion hath
15 light with darkness? And what concord hath Christ with Belial? Or what part hath he that believeth with an in-
16 fidel? And ᵖwhat agreement hath the temple of God with idols? For ᵠye are the temple of the living God; as God hath said, ʳI will dwell in them, and walk in *them;* and I will be their God,
17 and they shall be my people. ˢWhere-

14 Be not yoked unequally with unbelievers; for what fellowship has righteousness with lawlessness? And what communion has light with darkness?
15 And what concord has Christ with Belial? Or what portion has a believer
16 with an unbeliever? And what agreement has God's temple with idols? For we are the living God's temple, as God said, I will dwell in them, and walk among them; and I will be their God, and they shall be my people.

ⁿ Deut. 7 : 2, 3 ; 1 Cor. 7 : 39 ; James 4 : 4. ᵒ 2 Chron. 19 : 2 ; 1 Cor. 10 : 21 ; Eph. 5 : 7, 11 ; 1 John 3 : 12, 13
ᵖ 1 Sam. 5 : 2, 3 ; 1 King 18 : 21 ; Matt. 6 : 24. ᵠ 1 Cor. 3 : 16, 17.
ʳ Exod. 29 : 45 ; Ezek. 37 : 26, etc ; Zech. 13 : 9. ˢ See refs. Isa. 52 : 11.

14–7 : 1. WARNING AGAINST EVIL ASSOCIATIONS AND EXHORTATION TO INWARD HOLINESS. On account of the abruptness of these verses and their seeming want of connection with the context, some have considered them a part of a letter now lost and written before our present first Epistle (1 Cor. 5 : 9). Such a theory, however, is not necessary. Paul had exhorted them not to receive the grace of God in vain (ver. 1); and after the digression in ver. 3–10, it was not unnatural for him to urge their separation from unbelievers, as a means of more effectively enjoying the blessed results of the grace of God. Besides, the apostle, having expressed his warm affection for them (ver. 11–13), could get a full and hearty response only as they separated themselves from sin and sinners.

14. Be ye not unequally yoked together with unbelievers, which will be a hindrance to receiving and enjoying the grace of God and to the exercise of Christian affection. This is to be limited not merely to marriages of Christians to the heathen and the unbelieving, although including them, but must be extended to close and intimate relations and companionships. The figure is taken from yoking together two animals of different species, as the ox and ass (Deut. 22 : 10). They were to avoid such association with unbelievers as would involve complicity in their sins. **For what fellowship,** *what sharing* (the word thus rendered occurs only here in the New Testament), **hath righteousness with unrighteousness?** *lawlessness,* which was characteristic of heathen life. **And what communion hath light with darkness?** What has one in common with the other? *Light* represents the condition of the Christian (John 3 : 19), and darkness that of the heathen and the unbeliever (4 : 4; Eph. 5 : 8). The mere asking of such questions suggested their answer.

15. What concord, *agreement,* **hath Christ with Belial?** rather, *Beliar,* an epithet for Satan. *Beliar* is found in Deut. 13 : 13 ; Judg. 19 : 22 ; 1 Sam. 25 : 25, and means *worthlessness,* and appears to have been applied by the later Jews to Satan, the prince of evil spirits. **Or what part,** or *portion,* **hath he that believeth with an infidel?** *hath a believer with an unbeliever?* As there can be no compatibility between the two opposing principles of truth and error, between the heads of the two opposing kingdoms, Christ and Satan, so there can be none between the members of these kingdoms, believers and unbelievers.

16. What agreement, *partnership,* **hath the temple of God with idols?** The question suggests that there were still some at Corinth who were abusing their liberty (1 Cor. 8 : 10) and who needed to "flee from idolatry" (1 Cor. 10 : 14). **For ye are,** rather, *we are,* **the temple of the living God,** and therefore we should not enter into any alliance with idols. (See notes on 1 Cor. 3 : 16 and 6 : 19.) This is confirmed and explained by the quotations from the Old Testament which follow. The citation in this verse is a union of Lev. 26 : 11, 12 and Ezek. 37 : 27, quoted freely and doubtless from memory. The apostle infuses into them the gospel idea, and applies to spiritual Israel those predictions which referred pri-

fore come out from among them, and be ye separate, saith the Lord, and touch not the unclean *thing;* and 18 I will receive you, *t*and will be a Father unto you, *u*and ye shall be my sons and daughters, saith the Lord Almighty.

17 Wherefore, come out from the midst of them, and be separated, saith the Lord, and touch not anything unclean; and 18 I will receive you, and will be to you a Father, and ye shall be to me sons and daughters, saith the Lord Almighty.

t Jer. 31 : 9 ; Rev. 21 : 7.   *u* See refs. Rom. 8 : 14–17.

marily to literal Israel. Compare our Lord's words in John 17 : 21, 23; also Rom. 9 : 25, 26; 1 Peter 2 : 9, 10.

17, 18. In these two verses Paul draws a conclusion and makes an application in the language of Scripture. He combines Isa. 52 : 11; 2 Sam. 7 : 14, with Ezek. 20 : 33, 34; Isa. 43 : 6; Hosea 1 : 10; Amos 4 : 13, quoting and combining freely. **Wherefore,** since God has promised to dwell in you and walk in you and be your God, **come out from among them, and be ye separate,** let it be done at once and let the act be complete. The prophet had reference to the heathen; the apostle extends the reference to the wicked and the unbelieving generally. **And touch not,** do not continue to touch, as in the past, *anything* **unclean.** (Comp. 1 Cor. 5 : 10 and note.) There must be a separation from both unholy people and unholy things. This done, **and I** (emphatic) **will receive you, and will be a Father unto you,** I will enter into the relation of a Father to you, **and ye shall be my sons and daughters,** ye shall enter into the relation of sons and daughters to me. (Comp. John 17 : 15; Rev. 18 : 4; Lev. 11 : 8, 31–40; Ezek. 11 : 20.) **The Lord Almighty,** so the Hebrew "Lord of Hosts" is translated in the Seventy, and so the name of God frequently appears in the Revelation (1 : 8; 4 : 8; 11 : 17, etc.). In these last three verses we have an illustration of the way in which the Old Testament is frequently quoted in the New. The writers often quote according to sense and from memory, and often blend together different passages, and sometimes only give the general sense of Scripture. All these are illustrated here. On these promises the apostle grounds his exhortation in the first verse of the following chapter.

PRACTICAL REMARKS.

1. It is of the first importance, both for salvation and for usefulness, that Christians be exhorted not to receive the grace of God in vain (ver. 1; 1 Cor. 9 : 27; Heb. 12 : 14–17).

2. How much we owe to the intercession of Christ (Ps. 2 : 8; Isa. 59 : 16; Heb. 7 : 25).

3. The day of salvation is of infinite importance. To each individual it is the "now" (ver. 2; Heb. 3 : 7–13).

4. The minister of the gospel should be without reproach. Purity of character is necessary to his highest success (ver. 3; Matt. 10 : 16; 1 Cor. 10 : 32, 33).

5. The lives of ministers, and indeed of all Christians, should commend them and their works to their fellow-men (ver. 4; Phil. 2 : 14–16; 1 Thess. 2 : 10–12).

6. How often and how greatly do the bodily sufferings of Christians redound to the good of the world and the glory of God (ver. 4, 5; Rom. 5 : 3–5; Phil. 1 : 12–14).

7. A minister's success depends largely upon a holy life, and a consecrated service (ver. 6, 7; Mal. 2 : 1–7; 2 Tim. 2 : 3–5; 4 : 5).

8. We should seek to increase our efficiency by every instrumentality given us, and by making the most untoward circumstances contribute to that end (ver. 7, 8; Phil. 3 : 7–11; 1 Peter 4 : 1; Ps. 76 : 10).

9. A wicked world presents a fine field for exhibiting a true Christian character and life (ver. 8–10; Phil. 2 : 15, 16).

10. The true estimate and worth of a Christian is to be obtained by a deeper view than that of outward circumstances (ver. 10; 1 Sam. 16 : 7).

11. None but a minister or a pastor can know a pastor's heart (ver. 11; 12 : 14; Gal. 4 : 19).

12. A people should return a pastor's love. His best recompense is that they enlarge their love toward him, obey Christ, and be separated from the world (ver. 13–17; 3 John 3, 4; Philem. 19–21).

13. The cause of Christ suffers unless a

7 HAVING therefore these promises, dearly beloved, let us cleanse ourselves from all filthiness of the flesh and spirit, perfecting holiness in the fear of God.
2 Receive us; we have wronged no man, we have corrupted no man, we
3 have defrauded no man. I speak not

7 HAVING therefore these promises, beloved, let us cleanse ourselves from every defilement of flesh and spirit, perfecting holiness in the fear of God.
2 Open your hearts to us; we wronged no one, we corrupted no one, we de-
3 frauded no one. I say it not to con-

z 6 : 17, 18. *y* Ezek. 36 : 25, 26 ; 1 Peter 2 : 11 ; 1 John 3 : 1-3. *z* Phil. 3 : 12-15 ; 1 Thess. 3 : 13 ; Heb. 12 : 14. *a* See refs. 1 Sam. 12 : 3, 4.

line of separation is distinctly made and seen between Christians and unbelievers (ver. 14-16; 2 John 11 : 1 Tim. 5 : 22 ; Matt. 6 : 24).

14. Christians should avoid evil companionships and evil associations (ver. 14-16; 1 Cor. 15 : 33, 34).

15. Christians are God's temple. How pure their hearts should be ; how clean their consciences ; how holy their lives (ver. 16; 2 Tim. 2 : 19-21).

16. There must be a separation from the world, if we would enjoy the favor of God (ver. 17; Matt. 16 : 24, 25).

17. The Christian alone among men enjoys the true Fatherhood of God (ver. 17, 18; Rom. 8 : 15, 16).

18. How unspeakable the privilege to be a Christian, to be children of a king, and heirs of a heavenly kingdom (ver. 18; Rev. 1 : 6 ; Matt. 25 : 34).

CHAPTER VII.

Continuing the thought of the preceding chapter, Paul exhorts to inward holiness (ver. 1) ; and through the rest of the chapter treats of the results of his former Epistle, as he had learned from Titus. He exhorts them to trust him, and appeals to his uprightness (ver. 2-4). His affection for them proved by his experience in Macedonia, regarding the coming of Titus, his anxiety for them, and the letter he had written them, and his joy to hear that it had resulted in their reformation (ver. 5-16).

1. **Having therefore these promises,** just quoted (6 : 16-18), **dearly beloved,** a tender and loving epithet in harmony with 6 : 11, and preparatory to the affectionate appeal that follows. **Let us cleanse ourselves,** a condition on which God based his promise to receive them (6 : 17) **from all filthiness of the flesh and spirit,** better, *from every defile-* ment *of flesh and spirit,* both outward and inward, of word and act, of thought and desire, from physical and spiritual stains of sin. **Perfecting holiness,** the positive side of the exhortation— going on *to complete* holiness; to follow after holiness is the work of a Christian life (Heb. 12 : 14). **In the fear of God,** the feeling, the atmosphere as it were, in which holiness is to be pursued. A reverence for God and a fear of offending him, are necessary to our progress in sanctification (5 : 11; Matt. 10 : 28; 1 Peter 1 : 17).

2-16. PAUL'S APPEAL FOR THEIR FULL CONFIDENCE AND SYMPATHY. HIS JOY AT THE GOOD NEWS BROUGHT BY TITUS REGARDING THE EFFECT OF HIS FORMER LETTER. The change in tone at this point of the Epistle, gives force to the supposition that Titus had just arrived from Corinth. See introduction.

2. Having finished his exhortation (6 : 14; 7 : 1), Paul repeats his request of 6 : 13, in corresponding language. **Receive us**—rather, *Open your hearts to us,* make room for us in your affections. And there is no reason why you should not heartily receive us. **We have wronged,** rather, *We wronged,* **no man,** while exercising our ministry among you, we did no one injustice in any way, **we corrupted,** or *ruined no man* financially, **we defrauded,** *we overreached,* or *took advantage of no one.* (Comp. 8 : 19, 20 : 12 : 14-16.) In these vivid expressions Paul probably had reference to charges that his opponents had brought against him. They may have misinterpreted his preaching, and his conduct in matters of discipline, of lodging among them and dealings with them, and in gathering collections for the poor. (Comp. 10 : 7-11 ; 11 : 7 ; 1 Cor. 9 : 1-6.) Some refer *corrupted* to corrupting them by the preaching of false doctrine. (Comp. 2 : 17 ; 11 : 3.) But as the two other verbs denote, not inward, but

this to condemn *you*: for I have said before, that ye are in our hearts ᵇ to die
4 and live with *you*. ᶜ Great *is* my boldness of speech toward you, ᵈ great *is* my glorying of you: ᵉ I am filled with comfort, I am exceeding joyful in all our tribulations.
5 For, ᶠ when we were come into Macedonia, our flesh had no rest, but ᵍ we were troubled on every side; without *were* fightings, within *were* ʰ fears.
6 Nevertheless ⁱ God, that comforteth those that are cast down, comforted us
7 by ᵏ the coming of Titus; and not by his coming only, but by the consolation wherewith he was comforted in

demn you; for I have already said; that ye are in our hearts, to die together and to live together. Great is
4 my boldness toward you, great is my glorying on account of you; I am filled with consolation, I am made to abound with joy, in all our affliction.
5 For even when we were come into Macedonia, our flesh had no relief, but we were afflicted in every way; without were fightings; within were fears.
6 But God, who consoles the lowly, con-
7 soled us by the coming of Titus; and not by his coming only, but also by the consolation with which he was con-

---

ᵇ 1 Thess. 2 : 8.   ᶜ 3 : 12.   ᵈ 1 : 14; 9 : 2-4; 1 Cor. 1 : 4.   ᵉ Rom. 5 : 3; Phil. 2 : 17; 1 Thess. 3 : 7-9.
ᶠ 2 : 13; Acts 20 : 1.   ᵍ 4 : 8.   ʰ 12 : 20. 21.   ⁱ See refs. 1 : 3, 4; Jer. 31 : 13.   ᵏ 2 : 13.

---

outward injury, it is more natural to understand this of external hurt or ruin (1 Cor. 3 : 17), such as to *bring to beggary* or *want*.

3. But Paul would not be misunderstood by what he had just said. His words are not of condemnation, but of love and perhaps a challenge against reproach. **I speak not this to condemn you,** either directly or indirectly, of any injustice. **For I have said before** (5 : 11-13; 6 : 11-13) **that ye are in our hearts,** in our affections (Phil. 1 : 7), **to die and live with you,** or, *to die together and to live together*—in life and in death you will be in our affection. No change in my circumstances or condition can alter my love for you. An expression of highest friendship.

4. For the first time in this Epistle the first person plural is exchanged for the singular when Paul is speaking of himself. **Great is my boldness of speech** (omit *speech*), my fearless *confidence*, my bold assurance, **toward you, great is my glorying,** to others, *on account* **of you** (1 : 14; 3 : 2). How then could he speak words of condemnation? (Ver. 3.) They surely would not misconstrue his language. His heart was full to overflowing toward them, and on their account to others; and more: **I am filled with comfort,** and encouragement, *with the consolation* which I have received by the intelligence from you, through Titus, who had come from Corinth. **I am exceeding joyful in all our tribulation,** *I overflow with joy in all our affliction*. A climax of feeling and expression. The phrase, *in all our*

affliction, is to be joined to both of the preceding clauses.

5. **For, when,** rather, *For, even when* **we were come into Macedonia.** Not only in Troas was I filled with anxiety (2 : 13), but in Macedonia also I had no rest till I heard from Titus. **Our flesh** (not merely the body but our sensitive human nature, our frail human self) **had no rest,** or *relief;* **but we were troubled,** hard pressed, afflicted on every side, in every way, in everything. His mental anguish took hold of his body, affected his health; everything was a burden. **Without were fightings,** disputings, and opposition from avowed unbelievers and Judaizing Christians. (Comp. Acts 13 : 45; 14 : 4, 5, 19; 16 : 19, 20; 17 : 5-8, 13, 18-20.) **Within were fears,** for the Corinthians, regarding the mission of Titus, his reception at Corinth and the result. The conflicts with those outside the church doubtless also aroused fears and anxieties.

6. **Nevertheless God, that,** *who,* **comforteth,** and encourages (both ideas are in the word), who *consoles,* **those that are cast down,** those who are brought low with grief, depressed with sorrow, **comforted,** or *consoled,* **us by the coming of Titus,** and his presence with us. (Comp. 1 Thess. 3 : 6, 7.)

7. **And not by his coming only,** and presence (comp. 2 : 14), **but by the consolation wherewith he was comforted,** or *consoled,* **in you,** in respect to you as a ground of consolation. Titus was encouraged, consoled by the conduct of the Corinthians; and the rehearsal of what he had seen and

you, when he told us your earnest desire, your mourning, your fervent mind toward me; so that I rejoiced the
8 more. For ¹though I made you sorry with a letter, I do not repent, though I did repent: for I perceive that the same epistle hath made you sorry,
9 though *it were* but for a season. Now I rejoice, not that ye were made sorry, but that ye sorrowed to ᵐ repentance: for ye were made sorry after a godly manner, that ye might receive damage
10 by us in nothing. For ⁿ godly sorrow

soled in you, when he told us your earnest desire, your mourning, your zeal for me; so that I rejoiced the
8 more. Because, though I made you sorry by my letter, I do not regret it, though I did regret it; for I see that that letter made you sorry, though but
9 for a time. Now I rejoice, not that ye were made sorry, but that ye were made sorry to repentance; for ye were made sorry after a godly manner, that in nothing ye might receive harm from

---

l 2 : 2-4. m Ezek. 18 : 27-30; Jonah 3 : 8-10.   n 2 Sam. 12 : 13; Matt. 26 : 75.

heard among them was consoling to Paul. **When he told us your earnest desire** for me, longing to see me again among you, **your mourning** for having grieved me so by the divisions in the church, and especially in regard to the incestuous person (1 Cor. 3 : 3 : 5 : 1), **your fervent mind toward me,** better, *your zeal for me,* in defending me against enemies. The First Epistle had borne good fruit in their repentance, in obeying his directions, and in increasing their affection for him. **So that I rejoiced the more,** on the receipt of the good tidings. He had at first been made glad by the arrival of Titus; but the good news made him the more glad.

8. Paul proceeds to explain his "rejoicing the more," with reference to his First Epistle. **For,** or, *Because,* **though I made you sorry with a,** rather, *the,* **letter,** by means of my letter, **I do not repent,** rather, *regret it,* **though I did** *regret it.* The word translated *repent* is a more superficial and less noble word than the one usually used for *repent,* which means to *change our mind* (next verse). It is found in the New Testament only here, Matt. 21 : 29, 32; 27 : 3, and Heb. 7 : 21. The word *regret* best expresses its meaning here. It properly expresses an *after care, concern,* or *anxiety* for something done, which may indeed attend true repentance, but which may also be felt where there is no radical change, as in the case of Judas (Matt. 27 : 3). That an inspired apostle in his human weakness should have had a time when he regretted that he had given the Corinthians pain, by his letter, with perhaps no good results, is not strange. Inspiration does not use a man as a mere machine, the human element has a

place. And after the special impulse of the Spirit passes away, he may have the struggles and misgivings common to his frail nature (ver. 5; comp. John the Baptist, Matt. 11 : 2; Jer. 1 : 6-9; Jonah 1 : 3; 4 : 1-11). The apostle now gives a reason for what he had said in the first half of this verse. **For I perceive that** *that* **epistle** *grieved you,* **though but for a season.** He feared lest he had given unnecessary pain, and his mind was not fully set at rest till Titus arrived and he saw that God's Spirit had ordered all things right and for their highest good. Here we see the tender and conscientious heart of Paul.

9. Though for a time I felt misgivings and regret, **Now I rejoice, not that ye were made sorry,** I would not have you think that for a moment, your sorrow in itself gave me joy, **but that ye sorrowed,** better, *but that ye were made sorry unto* **repentance,** unto *a change of mind,* which was attended with such experiences and reformation as described below. Repentance is *a change of mind,* of purpose, feelings, and views, implying an abhorrence of and sorrow for sin, a turning to God, and hearty amendment of conduct or reformation of life as the fruits (Matt. 3 : 8-10). **For ye were made sorry after a godly manner,** literally, *according to God,* as he commands and wills, that is with repentance (Rom. 8 : 27). **That ye might receive damage,** or, *suffer harm, from* **us in nothing** pertaining to salvation. If they had not exercised this sorrow they might have been spiritually injured with a sorrow that "worketh death" (ver. 10).

10. This verse confirms and explains what he had just said of godly sorrow

worketh repentance to salvation not to be repented of; ⁰ but the sorrow of the world worketh death.

11 For behold this selfsame thing, that ye sorrowed after a godly sort, what carefulness it wrought in you; yea, *what* clearing of yourselves; yea, *what* indignation; yea, *what* ᵖ fear; yea, *what* ᵠ vehement desire; yea, *what* ʳ zeal; yea, *what* ˢ revenge! In all *things* ye have approved yourselves to be clear

12 in this matter. Wherefore, though I wrote unto you, *I did it* not ᵗ for his cause that had done the wrong, nor for his cause that suffered wrong, ᵘ but

10 us. For godly sorrow works repentance to salvation, not to be repented of; but the sorrow of the world works

11 out death. For behold this very thing, that ye were made sorry after a godly manner, what diligence it wrought in you; yea, what defence of yourselves; yea, what indignation; yea, what fear; yea, what longing desire; yea, what zeal; yea, what avenging! In every thing ye shewed yourselves to be pure

12 in the matter. So then, though I wrote to you, it was not on account of him who did the wrong, nor of him who suffered wrong, but that your care for

o Gen. 4 : 14; 1 Sam. 31 : 3–6; 2 Sam. 17 : 23; Matt. 27 : 4, 5.   p Ver. 1; Ps. 2 : 11; Heb. 4 : 1.
q Ps. 38 : 9; 42 : 1; Isa. 26 : 8.   r 9 : 2.   s Matt. 5 : 29, 30.   t 1 Cor. 5 : 1.   u 2 : 4; 1 John 3 : 18, 19.

and its negative effect. **For godly sorrow,** that sorrow which is according to God's mind and will, **worketh,** produces, **repentance,** *a change of mind,* leading **to salvation** through Christ, a salvation from sin, including pardon, newness of life, peace, and reconciliation with God; **not to be repented of,** rather, *not to be regretted.* (See on ver. 8.) Many refer this last clause to *salvation,* which cannot be attended with regret, or by a figure of speech, by which a positive is affirmed by a negative meaning here: salvation, affording supreme joy. Others refer it to *repentance,* since we cannot conceive of a salvation which is attended with regret; but a superficial or false repentance must necessarily be regretted. It seems to me that Paul had the whole phrase in mind, *repentance to salvation,* which in its nature and results was attended with no regret but joy. **But the sorrow of the world,** such as the unregenerate have, the opposite of godly sorrow, **worketh,** produces, **death,** alienation from God and eternal death. A godly sorrow abhors sin and is exercised on account of sin as sin; the sorrow of the world is exercised in view of consequences, and from fear of punishment, and leads to remorse and despair. The two are illustrated in the case of David (Ps. 51) and Saul (1 Sam. 15 : 24), Peter (Luke 22 : 62) and Judas (Matt. 27 : 3-5).

11. The apostle exhibits the good effects of godly sorrow in the Corinthians as a proof of what he had been saying. **For behold this selfsame thing,** *this very thing,* etc., what carefulness, rather, *what earnestness,* **it wrought in you,** to make amends for previous negligence and inactivity in removing offenses; this earnestness is expanded in six particulars: **yea, what clearing of yourselves,** or, *defense* of yourselves, to Titus, and through him to me; **yea, what indignation** against sin and at themselves in view of the scandal in the church; **yea, what fear** of the apostle's condemnation and rebukes (ver. 15; 1 Cor. 4 : 21) and of God's displeasure; **yea, what vehement,** *longing,* **desire** for me, to see me (ver. 7); **yea, what zeal** to punish the offender, in behalf of God, for his glory; **yea, what revenge,** infliction of punishment! This is one of Paul's climaxes. Bengel notes that two of these six particulars are in regard to themselves, two in regard to the apostle, and two in regard to the offender. *In everything* **ye have approved yourselves to be clear,** *ye commended yourselves as pure in the matter,* regarding the incestuous person which had so scandalized the church (1 Cor. 5 : 1). The church had acted as a church, and through its majority had inflicted needed discipline (2 : 5, 6). The blessed effects of godly sorrow were thus manifest.

12. The apostle deduces the inference, that he wrote them his former Epistle, not for any private considerations, but to bring out this earnestness and activity just described. **Wherefore,** *accordingly then,* **though I wrote you, I did it not for his cause that had done the wrong merely, nor for his cause that suffered wrong,** the father of the in-

that our care for you in the sight of God might appear unto you.

13 Therefore we were comforted in your comfort; yea, and exceedingly the more joyed we for the joy of Titus, because his spirit *x* was refreshed by you all.

14 For if I have boasted any thing to him of you, I am not ashamed; but as we spake all things to you in truth, even so our boasting, which *I* made before Titus, is found a truth.

15 And his inward affection is more abundant toward you, whilst he remembereth *y* the obedience of you all, how *z* with fear and trembling ye received us might be manifested to you in the

13 sight of God. For this cause we have been consoled; but in our consolation, we rejoiced abundantly more at the joy of Titus, because his spirit has

14 been refreshed by you all. For if in any thing I have gloried to him of you, I was not made ashamed; but as we spoke all things to you in truth, so also our glorying before Titus was found to

15 be truth. And his tender affection is more abundantly toward you, while he remembers the obedience of you all, how with fear and trembling ye received him.

x Rom. 15 : 32.   *y* 2 : 9 ; Phil. 2 : 12.   *z* Ver. 10, 11.

cestuous person (1 Cor. 5 : 1), it was not the private interests of individuals that caused me to write you, it was rather your good. Paul speaks of his chief and primary motive in writing as if it was his only motive. All else was subsidiary. This passage would seem to indicate that the father of the offender was still alive. **But that our care for you,** rather, according to the best texts, *But that your earnest care,* or, *regard,* diligence, earnestness (the same word as in ver. 11) *for us (your* and *us* are emphatic) **might appear, might be manifested, unto you in the sight of God,** pure and upright in his sight. His aim was the manifestation unto themselves of their zealous regard for him and his apostolic authority. In so doing they would in the highest degree show their faithfulness to Christ and his cause, since he was an ambassador of Christ, and represented Christ. And this would result in the highest good of all concerned.

13. The consoling effect of all this upon Paul himself. **Therefore,** the object of our writing having been accomplished, **we were,** rather, *we have been,* **comforted** and encouraged, *consoled.* This should be followed by a semicolon; and, according to the best text, Paul continues, *but in,* or *upon our,* **comfort,** or *consolation* (added to it), *we rejoiced exceedingly more at* **the joy of Titus** (see ver. 4), **because his spirit** *has been* **refreshed by you all.** The joy of Titus added abundant joy to the apostle's consolation, and Titus' joy resulted from the refreshment his soul had received in his intercourse with the Corinthians. (Comp. on ver. 7.)

14. An additional reason for the apostle's joy. **For if I have boasted,** or *gloried,* **any thing to him of you, I am not ashamed,** rather, *I was not put to shame,* on his return and his report, as if I had boasted falsely or without cause. **But as we spake all things to you in truth,** in all our teaching and intercourse while with you, **even so our boasting,** or *glorying,* **which I made before Titus, is found,** rather, *was found,* **a truth.** Paul had described their true condition to Titus, that, notwithstanding their divisions and disorders, they were true at heart and had strong regard and affection for himself, and this he doubtless had said to encourage Titus to perform the journey and the mission, which might be an unpleasant one. The repentance, the prompt obedience, the strong affection, shown toward Paul, and the kind reception Titus received, proved the apostle's words true.

15. The joyful result on Titus himself. **And his inward affection** (literally, *bowels,* as in 6 : 12, descriptive of the tender thoughts and affection of Titus) **is now more abundantly** turned **toward you, whilst he remembereth the obedience of you all,** how, as shown by the fact that **with fear and trembling ye received him,** with self-distrust and dread of doing wrong and anxiety to please and obey the apostle. (See on 1 Cor. 2 : 3.) The fear and trembling is not descriptive of any awe that they had of Titus, but of their obedience to Paul's injunctions. This had deeply impressed Titus, and the recollection of it intensified his affection toward them.

16. Paul abruptly concludes this portion of the Epistle, which had been

16 him. I rejoice therefore that ᵃI have confidence in you in all *things.*

16 I rejoice, that in everything I am of good courage concerning you.

a 2 Thess. 3 : 4; Philem. 21.

of a personal character—his relation to the Corinthians. **Therefore** should be omitted, not being found in the most ancient documents. Translate: *I rejoice that in everything I am of good courage in you* (ver. 7). The ground of his good courage was in them, in their good conduct and their careful obedience of his word. Being thus made of good courage by them, he could rejoice concerning them, with good prospects for their future. Having thus thoroughly settled the matter with the Corinthians, he leaves it to attend to other things in the next chapter.

PRACTICAL REMARKS.

1. It is our duty to aim after holiness and for its attainment. The promises of God are both an encouragement and a pledge (ver. 1; 1 : 20–22; 1 Peter 1 : 13–16).

2. Let us so live as to be able to appeal to our conduct before our fellow-men in proof of a blameless life (ver. 2; 1 Thess. 2 : 10–12).

3. We may defend ourselves against wrong accusations, but it should be done in a spirit of love and a willingness to devote ourselves to the good of others (ver. 3; 1 John 3 : 16).

4. The Christian life, and especially the Christian ministry, has its great trials, but also its overflowing joy (ver. 4–6; James 5 : 10; Eph. 1 : 3; 1 Peter 1 : 8).

5. The faithful preacher at home, or the missionary abroad, must expect seasons of outward and inward trial; but in all God will bring a corresponding deliverance (ver. 5; 2 : 13, 14; 2 Tim. 3 : 10–12).

6. God is the supreme source of all consolation, and one important means is through friends (ver. 6, 7; Acts 27 : 3; 28 : 15; Phil. 4 : 10).

7. Every true pastor has a deep interest in the spiritual welfare of his people. How cheering to the preacher's heart are good reports from former fields of labor! (Ver. 7; 1 Thess. 3 : 1–3, 6–9; Prov. 25 : 25.)

8. The inspiration of the sacred writers was in harmony with the free exercise of all their human faculties and feelings (ver. 8; 12 : 1, 7; Gal. 2 : 11–13).

9. To give reproof is sometimes needful, though painful. If done tenderly, and if heeded, it will result in good and be productive of joy to both the giver and the receiver (ver. 8; Prov. 27 : 6, 9).

10. No damage ever comes from true repentance. It is followed by reformation of life and a present and eternal salvation (ver. 9–11; Luke 3 : 8; Acts 11 : 18; 26 : 20).

11. Mere sorrow is not repentance. But if exercised toward God, in view of sin as against a holy God, it leads to repentance (ver. 10; Ps. 51 : 4).

12. A worldly sorrow is distress only, without looking to God for pardon and salvation. It sometimes shortens life, or leads to suicide, and always tends to eternal death (ver. 11; Gen. 4 : 6–8, 13; 1 Kings 21 : 27–29).

13. True repentance is a real and positive change in one's feelings and views in regard to God and sin. There comes to be a hatred of sin, condemnation of self, and an acknowledgment of God as righteous (ver. 11; Ezra 9 : 6, 7; Job 42 : 6; Luke 23 : 40–43).

14. We should especially aim to strengthen the Christian life and develop the Christian character of our brethren (ver. 12; 3 John 2–4).

15. We may have a two-fold joy in Christ's service: the joy of having done good, and the joy that others, with us, are doing and receiving good (ver. 13; 3 John 5–8).

16. Happy that man whose words are above reproach! (Ver. 14; 1 Peter 2 : 22.)

17. The renewed heart naturally goes out in tender affection toward those who manifest the evidences of true repentance (ver. 15; Luke 15 : 21–24).

18. Faithful dealing and honest explanations, where there are misunderstandings, will generally be followed by the joy and encouragement of renewed friendship and increased affection (ver. 16; Matt. 18 : 15).

CHAPTER VIII.

THE SECOND PART of this Epistle, the collection for the poor of the saints

The grace of giving to the poor Christians in Judea.

8 MOREOVER, brethren, we do you to wit of the grace of God bestowed
2 on ᵇthe churches of Macedonia; how that ᵈin a great trial of affliction ᵈ the abundance of their joy and ᵉtheir deep poverty abounded unto the riches of
3 their liberality. For to *their* power, I bear record, yea, and beyond *their*

8 AND we make known to you, brethren, the grace of God which has been bestowed in the churches of Mace-
2 donia; that in much trial of affliction was the abundance of their joy, and their deep poverty abounded to the
3 riches of their liberality. For according to their ability, I bear testimony,

ᵇ Rom. 15 : 26.   ᶜ 1 Thess. 1 : 6 ; 2 : 14.   ᵈ Neb. 8 : 10–12.   ᵉ Mark 12 : 44.

at Jerusalem, begins here, and extends to the end of the next chapter. In these two chapters we have the most extended discussion of the principles of benevolence to be found in the Bible. Instead of a systematic treatment we have an object lesson, a case which actually occurred, in which the duty, principles, spirit, manner, and motives of Christian giving are presented. It should receive the special study of ministers, pastors, and members of our churches.

Paul commences by adducing the example of the Macedonian Christians in the grace of giving, which he would have the Corinthians imitate (ver. 1–6); urges it also by the example of Christ (ver. 7–11), that it be done willingly and in fair proportion (ver. 12–15). He commends to them the brethren who have this business in charge as trustworthy (ver. 16–24).

1–6. PAUL PRESENTS THE MACEDONIAN CHURCHES IN THE GRACE OF GIVING AS AN EXAMPLE TO THE CORINTHIANS. What precedes in this Epistle was admirably adapted to introduce the subject of benevolence. Paul had expressed his deep affection for them, and his confidence in their faithfulness and readiness to do whatever he enjoined. They had complied with his directions, and he had boasted of them. All this was fitted to excite them to liberality.

1. Moreover, brethren, we do you to wit, rather, in more modern English, *And, brethren, we make known to you* **the grace,** or *favor*, **of God,** *which has been* **bestowed on,** better, *in,* **the churches,** in the hearts and manifested in the conduct of the members **of the churches of Macedonia,** the country north of Achaia. These churches were those of Philippi, Thessalonica, and Berea. The grace of God had, through the Holy Spirit, begotten a like grace, a spirit of *favor*, of liberality in the hearts of the Macedonian Christians. Every good and perfect gift is from God (James 1 : 17). The apostle uses the word *churches*, since the liberality exercised was a church act through the members (ver. 19). The abrupt beginning of this chapter is explained by the fact that he had spoken about it in his former Epistle, and it was well known to the Corinthians (1 Cor. 16 : 1–4 ; comp. Acts 24 : 17 ; Rom. 15 : 25–27) ; and that now, after completing the first part of this Epistle, it was the uppermost thing in Paul's mind (Gal. 2 : 10).

2. How this grace was manifested in and among the Macedonians. I make known to you (ver. 1), **how that in a great trial,** *in much proof*, **of affliction** *was* **the abundance of their joy** (Acts 17 : 5 ; 1 Thess. 1 : 6 ; 2 : 14) ; **and their deep poverty abounded, unto the riches of liberality,** into the wealth of openhearted generosity. The **trial** means a *test* which was a *proof* of their worth. "In spite of their troubled condition they had displayed great joy, and in spite of their poverty they had displayed great liberality" (DE WETTE). Macedonia had suffered severely from civil wars between Cæsar and Pompey, between the triumvirs and Brutus and Cassius, and between Augustus and Marc Antony. There was much desolation and distress. To give, under such circumstances, indicated the grace of God in their hearts. It was not so much the amount as the proportion to their means; and this proportion was so great that it was the very wealth of generosity.

3. In this and the two following verses the apostle gives a proof of their super-abounding liberality. **For to their power,** or *according to their*

power, *they were* willing of themselves:
4 praying us with much intreaty that we would receive the gift, and *take upon us* ᶠ the fellowship of the minis-
5 tering to the saints. And *this they did*, not as we hoped, but first ᵍ gave their own selves to the Lord, ʰ and unto us
6 by the will of God; insomuch that ⁱ we desired Titus, that as he had begun, so he would also finish in you the same ᵏ grace also.
7 Therefore, as ˡ ye abound in every *thing, in* faith, and utterance, and knowledge, and *in* all diligence, and *in* ᵐ your love to us, *see* ⁿ that ye abound

and beyond their ability, they gave of
4 their own accord; with much entreaty beseeching of us the grace and the participation in the ministering to the
5 saints; and not as we expected, but themselves they gave first to the Lord,
6 and to us through the will of God. So that we exhorted Titus, that as he had before made a beginning, so he would also finish among you this grace also.
7 But, as in everything ye abound, in faith, and speech, and knowledge, and all diligence, and your love to us, see
8 that ye abound in this grace also. I

f Acts 11 : 28-30; 24 : 17; Rom. 15 : 25, 26; 1 Cor. 16 : 1, 3, 4.   *g* Isa. 44 : 3; Rom. 14 : 7-9; 1 Cor. 6 : 19, 20.
h 1 Chron. 12 : 18; 2 Chron. 30 : 12.   *i* Ver. 17; 9 : 5; 12 : 18.   *k* Ver. 4, 19.
l 1 Cor. 1 : 5; 12 : 13.   *m* 7 : 7.   *n* 9 : 8.

---

ability, **and beyond their power,** or *ability*, **they were willing of themselves,** to give, they gave *of their own free choice.* Under the influence of the Spirit and with the grace of giving in their hearts, they gave beyond their means and of their own choice.

4. That we would receive, omitted by the best manuscripts. Translate: *beseeching of us with much entreaty in regard to the grace* of giving, *and the participation of the ministering to the saints.* They besought that they might exercise the grace of liberality and have a share in this contribution for the poor of the saints at Jerusalem. A most remarkable example. People too often need to be urged to give according to their means, instead of their entreating that they may give even beyond their means. Notice that *participation* in Christian beneficence is a privilege and joy to both the giver and the receiver. (See on Rom. 15 : 26.)

5. And this they did, not as we hoped, not simply *as we expected*, **but first gave their own selves to the Lord,** to Christ, **and unto us,** the apostle and his associates, to be at their service (Acts 20 : 4; Col. 4 : 10; Phil. 2 : 25, 30), an expression of self-surrender and entire consecration to Christ and his cause. And this was done **by,** or *through*, **the will of God,** the Spirit working in them and producing these results (Acts 15 : 28). Such was God's will, **and** through his will **they did this** (1 Thess. 5 : 18).

6. Application to the Corinthians. **Insomuch that we desired Titus,** rather, *so that,* in view of what the Macedonians had done, *we exhorted Titus,* **that as he had** *before* **begun,** on his first mission to the Corinthians (7 : 14; 12 : 18), **so he would,** in his second mission, **also finish,** or *complete among you,* **the same grace,** better, *this grace,* of liberality **also,** as well as other labors for your good. Some think Titus was one of the bearers of the First Epistle (16 : 12), and perhaps also of the second (ver. 18). The act of giving was an act of *grace* toward others, and an exercise of a gracious spirit.

7-15. EXHORTS THEM TO ABOUND IN THIS GRACE, ESPECIALLY BY THE EXAMPLE OF CHRIST; GIVING WILLINGLY AND PROPORTIONATELY.

7. Therefore, rather, *But* (turning away from the instruction given to Titus to direct exhortation); *as in everything* **ye abound,** especially in the graces here named, **in faith,** exercised actively and attended with good to others (1 : 24); **and utterance, or,** *speech,* aptness for speaking and reasoning; **and knowledge,** of the truth; **and all diligence,** earnest zeal in Christ's work (7 : 11); **and your love to us,** received and abiding in us, literally, *the love from you in us.* All these were graces, since they were begotten by God's grace and Spirit and by them good was conferred upon others. **See that ye abound in this** grace of benevolence **also.** Giving was the exercise of a gracious disposition for the good of others. It was the product of the Holy Spirit. The excellent gifts of the Corinthians (1 Cor.

8 in this grace also. *I speak not by commandment, p but by occasion of the forwardness of others, and to prove
9 the sincerity of your love. For ye know the grace of our Lord Jesus Christ, that, q though he was rich, yet for your sakes r he became poor, s that ye through his poverty might be rich.
10 And herein t I give *my* advice: for u this is expedient for you, who have begun before, not only to do, but also
11 to be x forward a year ago. Now therefore perform the doing *of it;* that as there *was* a readiness to will, so *there may be* a performance also out of that

say it not by way of command, but through the diligence of others proving also the sincerity of your love.
9 For ye know the grace of our Lord Jesus Christ, that, though he was rich, for your sakes he became poor, that ye through his poverty might become
10 rich. And I give my judgment in this matter; for this is profitable for you, who made a beginning before others, not only to do, but also to will, a year
11 ago. And now finish the doing of it also; that as there was the readiness to will, so there may be the finishing

o Ver. 10; 1 Cor. 7 : 6, 12, 25.   p 9 : 2; Heb. 10 : 24.
r Matt. 8 : 20; 17 : 27; Luke 9 : 58; Phil. 2 : 6-8.
t 1 Cor. 7 : 25.   u Prov. 19 : 17; Matt. 10 : 42; 1 Tim. 6 : 18, 19; Heb. 13 : 16.

q John 1 : 1-4; 16 : 15; Col. 1 : 16, 17; Heb. 1 : 6-12.
s Rom. 8 : 17, 32; 1 Cor. 3 : 21, 22; James 2 : 5.
x 9 : 2.

12 : 8, 9) were reasons for their excelling in the noble grace or gift of Christian beneficence.

8. But the apostle would not be misunderstood; he does not command, but, by exhortation and through the example of others, he would have them abound in this grace as an exercise of love. **I speak not by commandment,** *by way of command.* Paul does not mean that he has no command of God in the case, but that he does not intend to command. He would not be arbitrary; he did not dictate (ver. 10; 1 Cor. 7 : 25; Philem. 8, 9). **But I speak and urge this by occasion of the forwardness of others**, rather, *through the earnestness of others*, which I use as a test, *proving also* **the sincerity,** or *genuineness,* **of your love.** Paul would not coerce them to give, for that would not be liberality on their part. True benevolence must be voluntary.

9. He appeals to the greatest of all examples, that of Christ, by whose standard of love the benevolence of the Corinthians and of all others could be tested. **For**, in the exercise of this grace for the good of others, **ye know the grace of our Lord Jesus Christ,** who is both our Saviour and Lord, whose example, love, and grace are above all others and present a perfect standard; **that, though he was rich** (John 1 : 1-3; Heb. 1 : 3)**, yet for your sakes he became poor,** or *he beggared himself* (Phil. 2 : 6-8)**, that ye through his poverty might be rich,** gain spiritual wealth and be heirs and joint heirs with him. Our Lord's becoming poor has reference not merely to his outward earthly poverty, but to his emptying himself of his divine majesty and glory (Phil. 2 : 7), and taking upon himself the form of a servant (Matt. 8 : 17, 20). Through him we become partakers of the divine nature (Eph. 3 : 19; Col. 2 : 2, 3; 2 Peter 1 : 4), and heirs to a heavenly inheritance (Eph. 1 : 11, 18; 1 Peter 1 : 4). Such an example of self-renouncing and self-sacrificing benevolence and love, the apostle presents before the Corinthians to test their love and stimulate them to a like renunciation.

10. This verse is closely connected with ver. 8. The important and striking thought of ver. 9 is parenthetic. **And herein,** *in this matter*, I give no command, but, **I give my advice,** or *judgment* (1 Cor. 7 : 25). **For this,** giving an opinion or judgment in the matter, **is expedient** and profitable (1 Cor. 6 : 12) **for you,** *who began before others, a year ago, not only to will but also to do.* To command would be an injustice to you, ignoring the fact that you began a year ago; but to give my judgment as to what is best to be done now, under present circumstances, is expedient and profitable for you. It appears that the Corinthians had preceded the Macedonians, not only in beginning the collection, but also in the purpose of making it (9 : 2; 1 Cor. 16 : 1), and Paul gives them full credit before offering advice in the matter.

11. Now therefore, rather, *But now,* **perform,** *complete,* **the doing of it** *also;* carry out your resolution at once, and finish the task according to your ability. **That as there was a readiness to will, so there may be a performance,** *the completion,*

12 which ye have. For 7 if there be first a willing mind, *it is accepted according* to that a man hath, *and* not according 13 to that he hath not. For *I mean* not that other men be eased, and ye 14 burdened but by an equality, *that now at this time your abundance may be a supply* for their want, that their abundance also may be *a supply* for your want: that there may be equal- 15 ity as it is written, He that had *gathered* much had nothing over; and he that *had gathered* little had no lack.
16 But thanks *be* to God, which put the

12 according to what ye have. For if there be first the willing mind, it is accepted according to what one has, not according to what he has not. 13 For it is not that others may have 14 relief and ye distress; but, by the rule of equality, at this present time your abundance being a supply for their want, that also their abundance may become a supply for your want, that 15 there may be equality; as it is written, He that gathered much had nothing over, and he that gathered little did not lack.
16 But thanks be to God, who puts the

y See refs. Exod. 25 : 2 ; Mark 12 : 43, 44 ; Luke 21 : 3 ; 1 Peter 4 : 10.

also out of that which ye have, according to your means. The standard of their giving was to be from their possessions, according to their ability; and he would have them as ready to perform as they were to will; and by so doing they would show the sincerity of their love (ver. 7).

12. Explanatory of the last clause. I say, "according to what ye have," for if, as in your case, **there be first** *the* **willing mind,** *the inclination, the readiness* (the same word as in ver. 11 and 19), **it is accepted, by God,** *well pleasing* to him, according to **what** *one* **hath and not according to that he hath not.** The readiness is personified which is accepted according to the means it has. (Comp. Mark 12 41-44.) God looks at the **heart**; he asks not for what is beyond our power.

13. Paul further explains that it is not the object of the collection to distress the Corinthians in order to relieve the saints at Jerusalem. **For I mean not that other men be eased,** rather, *that others may have relief*, in this case the saints at Jerusalem, **and ye burdened,** *distressed*, **in poverty.** Perhaps some might have supposed that Paul was partial and over-much anxious for his Jewish brethren. This Paul denies and declares for the principle of equality (next verse).

14. But by the principle of **equality,** that there may be fairness and equitable dealing. Dean Stanley notes the similarity between this passage and several in the fifth book of Aristotle's "Ethics," in which the word is used in the sense of *fairness, reciprocal advantage*. **That now at this time,** in the present crisis, **your abundance may be,** or *being*, **a supply for**

their want, for their deficiency, **that their abundance** *may become* at some future time **a supply for your want; that there may be equality,** that there may be equitable dealing on the principle of an equal proportion. The supposition is that the situation might at some time be reversed, the saints at Jerusalem prosperous and they in distress. Paul evidently has no reference to the spiritual blessings which they would receive from the Jews. These they had already received (Rom. 15 : 27). The whole discussion is upon temporalities.

13. And this accords with Scripture, **As it is written** (Exod. 16 : 18, freely quoted from the Septuagint), showing how God bestowed the manna according to each man's need. **He that gathered much had nothing over; and he that gathered little had no lack.** In this miracle Paul sees an acted parable, illustrating the principle of equality, in that the gift to every man was proportionate to his wants. There is no communism in this passage (ver. 11-15). A man's property is recognized as his own. He is to give voluntarily and according to his means, not into a common fund for everybody, but for the relief of those in want. It was for the necessities of the saints, but not in the encouragement of idleness (2 Thess. 3 : 10).

16-24. TITUS AND THE TWO BRETHREN WHO HAVE CHARGE OF THE BUSINESS ARE TRUSTWORTHY.

16. Paul returns to Titus, whom he had mentioned in ver. 6, in order to speak of his mission to the Corinthians. The thought of his earnest zeal for them fills him with thanksgiving. **Thanks be to God, which put,** better, *who*

same earnest care into the heart of
17 Titus for you. For indeed he accepted
ᵃthe exhortation; but being more forward, of his own accord he went unto
18 you. And we have sent with him ᵃthe
brother, whose praise *is* in the gospel
19 throughout all the churches; and not
that only, but who was also ᵇchosen of
the churches to travel with us with
this ᶜgrace, which is administered by
us ᵈ to the glory of the same Lord, and
20 *declaration of* your ready mind : ᵉavoiding this, that no man should blame us

same diligence for you into the heart
17 of Titus. For he accepted indeed our
exhortation; but being very zealous,
he went forth to you of his own accord.
18 And together with him we sent the
brother, whose praise in the gospel is
19 throughout all the churches; and not
that only, but who was also appointed
by the churches, as our fellow-traveler
with this gift which is administered by
us, to further the glory of the Lord,
20 and our zeal; being careful of this,
that no one should blame us as to this

z Ver. 6.   *a* 12 : 18.   *b* 1 Cor. 16 : 3, 4.   *c* Ver. 4, 6, 7; 9 : 8.   *d* 4 : 15; 9 : 13.   *e* 11 : 12; 1 Thess. 5 : 22.

is putting, the same earnestness **into
the heart of Titus for you,** that
is in me and which I have expressed
(ver. 8-15). Paul has Titus and the work
he is doing vividly before his mind.

17. A proof of Titus' earnest zeal in
their behalf. **For indeed he accepted the,** rather, *our,* **exhortation,** to complete the collection which
he had begun (ver. 6); **but being
more forward,** *very earnest,* **of his
own accord he went unto you.**
Titus having returned from Corinth,
Paul may have exhorted him to stir up
the Corinthians by letter to complete
the collection. But being the more
zealous, he determined to go again to
Corinth and do the work personally.
Or it may mean that Titus was so
earnest in the matter that he went of
his own free choice independently of
the exhortation. The past tense would
rather indicate that he had already
gone when the apostle was writing.
Still, it may be the epistolary past,
according to which the most recent
events are represented as they would
appear to the readers of the letter, in
which case Titus would have been one
of the bearers of this Epistle.

18. Commendation of the first companion of Titus. **And we have sent,**
or more exactly, *we sent,* **with him
the brother.** Who this was it is impossible to say. It was however no
obscure member of a church; nor could
it have been so prominent a fellow-worker as Barnabas or Silas, since
they would not have been put subordinate to Titus. According to the next
verse he was appointed by the churches
to travel with Paul and take the proceeds of the collection; but there is no
evidence that either Barnabas or Silas
was a fellow-traveler of the apostle at

so late a date as this. If *the brother*
was a delegate of the Macedonian
churches, it was probably Luke (Acts
20 : 5), for he was at Philippi and traveled with Paul. And the commendation
is befitting Luke, **whose praise is in
the gospel,** as a Christian worker,
throughout all the churches.
(Comp. Col. 4 : 14; 2 Tim. 4 : 11.) But if he was
an Ephesian delegate, then it was probably either Trophimus or Tychicus,
both of whom traveled with the apostle
(Acts 20 : 4).

19. Further information regarding
this brother who was sent with Titus to
Corinth. **And not that only, but
who was also chosen,** *appointed,*
by a formal vote (see note Acts 14 : 23), **of
the churches to travel with us
with this grace,** *this favor,* or *gift,*
which is administered by us,
looked after and managed by us. The
whole matter of this collection was entrusted to them. From Acts 14 : 23,
1 Cor. 16 : 3, 4, and this verse, it appears that both officers and delegates of
churches were appointed by vote of the
local church. It was the custom among
them, as among the Greeks, to vote by
show of hands. The object of this appointment and the ministration of this
matter of grace, was **to the glory of
the same Lord,** etc., rather, according to the best text, *to the glory of the
Lord and our* earnest *readiness,* that is,
our readiness and zeal. It was in order
to subserve and further the glory of the
Lord and their readiness to undertake
and accomplish the work. How this
was done is told in the next two verses.

20. He would avoid suspicions which
were detrimental to Christ's glory and
to their reputation. **Avoiding this,**
rather, *taking care of this,* **that no
man should blame us in this**

in this abundance which is adminis-
21 tered by us: (providing for honest
things, not only in the sight of the
Lord, but also in the sight of men.
22 And we have sent with them our
brother, whom we have oftentimes
proved diligent in many things, but
now much more diligent, upon the
great confidence which *I have* in you.
23 Whether *any do inquire* of Titus, *he is*
my partner and fellowhelper concerning you; or our brethren *be inquired
of, they are* ʲthe messengers of the
churches, *and* the glory of Christ.
24 Wherefore show ye to them, and before
the churches, ᵍthe proof of your love,
and of our ʰboasting on your behalf.

bounty which is administered by us:
21 for we provide for what is honourable,
not only in the sight of the Lord, but
22 also in the sight of men. And we sent
with them our brother, whom we have
often in many things proved to be
diligent, but now much more diligent,
through the great confidence which he
23 has toward you. As to Titus, he is my
partner, and in regard to you a fellow-
worker; as to our brethren, they are
messengers **of** the churches, the glory
24 of Christ. Therefore show toward
them before the churches, the proof of
your love, and of our glorying on your
behalf.

ʲ Rom. 12 : 17; 14 : 16; Phil. 4 : 8; Col. 4 : 5; 1 Peter 2 : 12.   ᵍ Phil. 2 : 25.   ʰ Ver. 8.   ⁱ 7 : 14; 9 : 2.

abundance, *as to this great liberality,*
which is administered, managed,
superintended, **by us.** Paul's carefulness and wisdom in this financial matter is shown in the appointment of this
well-known and highly trusted brother
to accompany Titus. He thus avoided
all possible charges or suspicions of
dishonesty in administering the trust.
How necessary this precaution was may
be inferred from 12 : 17, 18.
21. Paul adds a personal reason for
this carefulness. **P r o v i d i n g for
honest things,** rather, according to
the most approved reading, *For we are*
accustomed to *provide*, take thought,
care, *for things honorable*, praiseworthy, morally good, noble, **not only in
the sight of the Lord,** who sees
both the appearance and the heart,
but also in the sight of men, who
see only the conduct and the outer life,
which therefore should be above suspicion. To appear right as well as to
be right, is necessary both before God
and men. *Honest* had this wider meaning when our Common version was
made.
22. Commendation of the second
companion of Titus. **And we have
sent,** more exactly, *we sent,* **with
them,** Titus and his companion (ver.
18), **our brother, whom we have
oftentimes proved diligent,** tested
and proved to be *earnest,* **in many
things, but now much more dil-
igent,** or, *earnest, through* **the great
confidence which** *he has toward
you.* This brother had doubtless been
at Corinth, and would be especially acceptable to the Corinthians, in whom
he had so much confidence. Who he

was is wholly unknown. It may have
been Trophimus or Tychicus, (See on
ver. 18.)
23. A general commendation of the
three brethren. **Whether** any do inquire *concerning* **Titus, he is my
partner,** a sharer of my labors and
cares, **and fellow helper,** or *worker*,
with me, *in regard to you.* **Or con-
cerning our brethren,** the two above
mentioned, **they are the messengers of the churches** (both appear
to have been appointed; comp. ver. 19).
And, should be omitted. *They are,*
the glory of Christ, in their work
and life they bring glory to Christ
(Matt. 5 : 16), and in their person and
character they manifest his Spirit, holiness, and power (3 : 18; Gal. 1 : 24; Acts
21 : 19, 20). Notice that the word translated *messengers* is *apostles*, when used
officially. It is here applied to these
delegates, since they were *sent* by the
churches, the word *apostle* in the original meaning *one sent*.
24. *Therefore*, **shew ye to them**
(omit **and**) **before the churches,**
of which they are representatives, and
who would report their reception and
their success to those who commissioned
them, **the proof of your love,** your
Christian love to them, and, by your
co-operation in raising the collection,
your love to the poor, **and the proof of
our boasting,** or *glorying*, **on your
behalf,** give proof that our boasting
was well grounded and true. (See on
9 : 2-4.) The Corinthians would show
this by their spirit and conduct. While
we are not to give to be seen of men
(Matt. 6 : 1, 2), it is proper to set an example to others of Christian liberality.

INTER-CHURCH RELATIONS. Paul recognized all believers and churches as belonging to a common brotherhood. He wrote not only to the Corinthians but "to all that call upon the name of our Lord Jesus Christ in every place" (1 Cor. 1 : 2, 3). He associated all these together in one kingdom and one family, in the expressions, "*our* Lord," "*our* Father." He would have the churches on an equality with one another (2 Cor. 12 : 13) and uniform in their practices (1 Cor. 11 : 2 ; 14 : 34 ; 16 : 1), like members of a family, independent yet dependent, with certain relations, duties, and obligations. Thus he would have them exercise a courteous and brotherly spirit toward one another (1 Cor. 16 : 19), and exchange acts of kindness (Col. 4 : 16). Churches also gave and received letters of commendation (2 Cor. 3 : 1). Certain churches also united in appointing messengers to take the donations to the poor of the saints at Jerusalem (2 Cor. 8 : 19, 23). The church at Antioch sent Paul, Barnabas, and others to consult the apostles and the church at Jerusalem, and these latter returned a letter of advice with messengers to Antioch and to the churches of Syria and Cilicia (Acts 15 : 22, 23 ; comp. Rom. 16 : 1, 2).

PAUL'S RELATION TO THE CHURCHES. Paul nowhere speaks of himself as an officer of any particular church. His relationship to the churches, which he emphasized, was spiritual: That of a father in 1 Cor. 4 : 15, "Yet have ye not many fathers; for in Christ Jesus I have begotten you through the gospel"; that of an apostle in 1 Cor. 9 : 2, "If I be not an apostle unto others, yet doubtless I am to you"; that of an ambassador in 2 Cor. 5 : 20, "Now then we are ambassadors for Christ, as though God did beseech you by us." Paul's authority was that of the truth, that of an inspired man, and of a preacher of the gospel. (Comp. 1 Peter 5 : 1–3.) All this went to make him the missionary that he was.

PRACTICAL REMARKS.

1. A true spirit of Christian benevolence is indicative of the favor of God. Fallen man is naturally selfish. The grace of God is needed to make him truly liberal (ver. 1 ; Ps. 112 : 9 ; 1 John 3 : 17).

2. Afflictions open the heart. Joy and true liberality are generally united (ver. 2, 3 ; Rom. 5 : 3 ; 1 Kings 17 : 11-14).

3. An encouragement to weak churches. The afflicted and the poor are often the most liberal (ver. 2, 3 ; Mark 12 : 43, 44).

4. It is a great privilege to give and participate with the truly benevolent. Think of the Macedonians beseeching the privilege! How many in our day would rather beg to be excused! (Ver. 4 ; Heb. 6 : 10 ; Acts 20 : 35.)

5. Our first gift to the Lord and his cause should be ourselves. Herein is the secret of true benevolence (ver. 5 ; Rom. 12 : 1 ; Prov. 23 : 26).

6. Christian giving is a grace, received from God, exercised toward others (ver. 6 ; Heb. 13 : 15, 16 ; Acts 2 : 43-46).

7. The grace of giving can be cultivated like any other grace (ver. 7 ; 1 Tim. 6 : 17-19 ; Eph. 4 : 28).

8. The Christian character is incomplete without the grace of beneficence (ver. 7 ; 1 Thess. 3 : 12, 13 ; 1 John 3 : 17).

9. The sincerity of our love should be tested by our Christian beneficence (ver. 8, 24 ; James 2 : 14-16).

10. The benevolence of others and especially the example of Christ should stimulate within us the grace of giving (ver. 8, 9 ; 9 : 2).

11. The grace of beneficence should be exercised in an earnest and ready spirit, in deeds, not mere words (ver. 10, 11 ; 2 Sam. 24 : 24 ; Acts 16 : 15).

12. Christian giving should be voluntary (ver. 12 ; 9 : 7 ; Exod. 35 : 21, 22).

13. Christian giving should be in honest proportion to one's means (ver. 12-14 ; 1 Cor. 16 : 2 ; Deut. 16 : 10, 17).

14. The exercise of the true spirit of Christian benevolence is pleasing to God, and will be rewarded (ver. 12-14 ; Heb. 13 : 16 ; Matt. 10 : 42).

15. The grace of benevolence should be justly and mutually exercised (ver. 13, 14 ; Gal. 6 : 2, 5).

16. God's dealings with men should instruct us in regard to our exercise of beneficence toward others (ver. 15 ; Matt. 5 : 45, 46).

17. The grace of beneficence in the heart of Christians is a cause of thanksgiving to God (ver. 16, 17 ; 9 : 11, 12).

18. A good reputation as well as a good

9 FOR as touching *the ministering to the saints, it is superfluous for me to 2 write to you. For I know 'the forwardness of your mind, ᵐfor which I boast of you to them of Macedonia, that ⁿAchaia was ready a year ago; and your zeal hath provoked very many. 3 ᵒYet have I sent the brethren, lest our boasting of you should be in vain in

9 FOR concerning the ministering to the saints, it is superfluous for me to 2 write to you. For I know your readiness of mind, of which I glory on your behalf to the Macedonians, that Achaia has been prepared for a year past; and your zeal stirred up the greater part of 3 them. But I sent the brethren, in order that our glorying on your behalf might not be made void in this respect;

k See refs. 8 : 4 ; Gal. 2 : 10.   *l* 8 : 19.   *m* 8 : 24.   *n* 8 : 10.   *o* 8 : 6, 17, 18, 22.

character is invaluable to a Christian minister (ver. 18, 22; 1 Tim. 3 : 7).

19. The apostolic churches were congregational in government (ver. 19; 2 : 6; Acts 15 : 4, 22).

20. The apostolic churches were fraternal in their intercourse with one another. Co-operation in beneficence was a bond of union (ver. 19, 23; Col. 4 : 16; Acts 15 : 22, 23).

21. Ministers should exercise great care and caution in financial matters (ver. 20, 21; Acts 6 : 2-4; Titus 1 : 7).

22. The Christian should live from two standpoints—Godward and manward (ver. 21; Acts 24 : 16).

23. Christian ministers should co-operate with one another, and exercise brotherly affection (ver. 23; Rom. 16 : 9, 21; 1 Cor. 16 : 12, 15, 16).

24. We should all strive so to live as to be "the glory of Christ" (ver. 23; 3 : 18; 1 Cor. 6 : 20; Acts 4 : 13).

CHAPTER IX.

Continuing on the exercise of the Christian grace of benevolence, Paul urges the Corinthians to sustain his boasts of them (ver. 1-5); reminds them of the rich blessings which will be returned to them (ver. 6-11); and which will come to others and redound to the glory of God (ver. 12-15).

1-5. PAUL EXPRESSES CONFIDENCE IN THE CORINTHIANS, AND URGES THEM TO SUSTAIN HIS BOASTS OF THEM.

1. With great delicacy the apostle returns to the collection, and, to spare their honor, touches it indirectly. **For,** connects this closely with "the proof of their love" in their reception of the delegates (8 : 24). **For as touching,** or *concerning,* **the ministering to the saints,** the making of the collection and conveying it to the saints at Jerusalem, **it is superfluous for me to write to you** (the present has the sense of continued action), *to be writing you, to write further to you.* A collection was assured; there was no necessity to write about that. But he would write about their reception of the delegates, and about having the collection all ready when he himself should come. He had not lost faith in his Corinthian brethren; he did not doubt their willingness; but he was earnestly desirous to have his boasting made good. (See next two verses.)

2. It is superfluous, For I know the forwardness of your mind, *your readiness* (9 : 12), **for which I boast,** *I am glorying concerning you,* **to them of Macedonia.** Paul was at that time in Macedonia. His boast was, **that Achaia was ready,** to make and forward the collection, **a year ago.** Paul probably reckons time as a Jew, meaning about the same as *last year,* with us. The Jewish civil year began late in September, the ecclesiastical year late in March. It was now autumn at the time of his writing. He probably uses the ecclesiastical year, in which case the Corinthians were ready to make their effort before the preceding Passover. The effect of this boasting on the Macedonians was, **your zeal hath provoked,** *stirred up,* stimulated, **very many,** *the greater part of them,* to contribute liberally and promptly.

3. But as a wise precaution he had sent the brethren, so that there might be no disappointment or shame on the part of any. **Yet have I sent,** rather, *But I sent,* **the brethren,** Titus and the two messengers of the churches (8 : 18, 22), **lest our ground of boasting** *in your behalf should be made void in this respect,* in respect to the collection. Paul expected a collection, but he feared that it would not be so large or

this behalf; that, as I said, ʳ ye may be
4 ready: lest haply if ᵗ they of Macedonia come with me, and find you unprepared, we (that we say not, ye) should be ashamed in this same confident boasting.
5 Therefore I thought it necessary to exhort the brethren, that they would go before unto you, and make up beforehand your ʳ bounty whereof ye had notice before, that the same might be ready, as *a matter of* bounty, and not as *of* covetousness.
6 ˢ But this *I say*, He which soweth sparingly shall reap also sparingly; and he which soweth bountifully shall
7 reap also bountifully. Every man ac-

that, as I said, ye may be prepared;
4 lest perchance, if Macedonians come with me, and find you unprepared, we (that we say not, ye) should be put to shame in this confidence.
5 I thought it necessary therefore to exhort the brethren, that they should go before to you, and make up beforehand your previously promised bounty, that this may be ready as a matter of
6 bounty and not as covetousness. But as to this, he that sows sparingly will also reap sparingly; and he that sows bountifully will also reap bountifully;
7 but let each one give as he has pur-

p 1 Cor. 16 : 2.   *q* Acts 20 : 4.   *r* Gen. 33 : 11; 1 Sam. 25 : 27; 2 Kings 5 : 15.
s Prov. 11 : 24, 25; Eccl. 11 : 1, 6; Luke 6 : 38; 19 : 16-26; Gal. 6 : 7-9.

so promptly taken, as he had led the Macedonians to expect. **That, as I said,** in the preceding verse, **ye may be ready,** *prepared*, with a suitable collection.

4. Lest haply, *perchance, if any* **of Macedonia come with me,** as company, or as bearers of the Macedonian collection, **and find you unprepared,** the collection unfinished (9:6), **we,** emphatically, who boasted of you (the reason **that we say not, ye,** is because we would treat delicately your sense of honor, yet *you* who so long ago began so promisingly are the most concerned in the matter), and so we who boasted of you **should be ashamed in this same confident boasting,** rather, according to the better text, *in this confidence*, which we have had in you. Notice here as well as elsewhere in this Epistle how delicately, frankly, and gentlemanly, the apostle writes. From this verse some have inferred that the brethren sent previously (8:18, 22) were not Macedonians. True Luke was not strictly a Macedonian (Acts 16:10). But it is quite probable that Jason, a Thessalonian, and Sopater, a Berean, accompanied Paul to Corinth (Rom. 16:21; Acts 17:5; 20:4).

5. Therefore, in view of what I have just said, **I thought it necessary to exhort the brethren,** Titus and the two others, **that they** *should* **go before unto you, and make up beforehand,** before my coming, **your bounty,** rather, *your previously promised bounty*. The word *before* is thus thrice repeated emphatically, as though he had said, "My watchword is, *Beforehand, Beforehand, Beforehand*" (STANLEY). *Bounty*, literally, *a blessing*, in word and deed, a benediction, a benefit, a gift. "It blesses him that gives and him that takes." It had been promised the year before by the Corinthians, and previously announced by Paul to the Macedonians. **Whereof ye had notice before,** should be according to the best manuscripts, *your previously promised, or announced,* b o u n t y, as above. The object of the brethren going to Corinth was not only to get the collection ready, but, **that the same might be ready, as a matter of bounty,** as a blessing, an act of real benevolence, **and not as of covetousness,** not a gift which betrays the giver's covetousness. A liberal and a grudging spirit is contrasted in the next verse.

6-11. LIBERAL AND CHEERFUL GIVING WILL BE REWARDED.

6. Giving is like sowing and reaping, it brings a rich harvest to those who exercise it. **But this I say,** or *But as to this* matter of giving, **He which,** *that*, **soweth sparingly** *will* **reap also sparingly; and he which,** *that,* **soweth bountifully,** scattering blessings, *will* **reap also bountifully,** attended with blessing. The reaping will correspond with the sowing. (Comp. Gal. 6:7; Prov. 11:18.) Chrysostom notes that as in the harvest, so in giving we receive more than we give (Acts 20:35). Paul would have them give in a spirit of liberality.

7. Paul continues to enforce the spirit in which we should give—freely and willingly. **Every man according**

cording as he purposeth in his heart, *so let him give;* ¹not grudgingly, or of necessity: for ᶻGod loveth a cheerful 8 giver. ᵃAnd God *is* able to make all grace abound toward you; that ye, always having all sufficiency in all *things,* may abound to every good work: 9 as it is written, He hath dispersed abroad; he hath given to the poor; his righteousness remaineth for ever. 10 Now he that ministereth seed to the sower both minister bread for *your* food, and multiply your seed sown, and increase the fruits of your ʸ righteous-

posed in his heart, not grudgingly or of necessity, for God loves a cheerful 8 giver. And God is able to make every grace abound toward you; that ye, always having all sufficiency in everything, may abound toward every good 9 work; (as it is written

He scattered, he gave to the poor;
His righteousness abides forever;)

10 and he who supplies seed to the sower and bread for food, will supply and multiply your seed for sowing, and increase the fruits of your righteousness;

---

t Deut. 15 : 7–11.   *u* 8 : 12 ; Exod. 25 . 2 ; 35 : 5 ; Acts 20 : 35 ; Rom. 12 : 8.
z Ps. 84 : 11 ; Prov. 3 : 9, 10 ; 11 : 24, 25 ; Mal. 3 : 10 ; Phil. 4 : 18, 19.   *y* Hosea 10 : 12 ; Matt. 6 : 1.

as he purposeth in his heart, a deliberate and cordial exercise of the will, *as he has before determined,* **so let him give; not grudgingly,** not from a regretting and unwilling heart, **or of necessity,** from constraint, or simply because he feels that he **must give** (Matt. 19 : 20–22 ; Deut. 15 : 10). **For God loveth a cheerful giver,** one who is prompt and joyous in doing it. A warm and joyous heart, if it has anything to give cannot do otherwise. This is quoted from the Septuagint (Prov. 22 : 8), but it is wanting in the Hebrew (Exod. 25 : 2 ; comp. Rom. 12 : 8).

8. In this and **the two following** verses the apostle encourages beneficence with the **assurance of God's help. And God is able to make all,** better, *every,* **grace, every favor and gift of** his **kindness,** *to* **abound toward** and in **you, with special** reference to earthly blessings and the collection; **that ye, always having all sufficiency** *in everything,* a sufficiency of the necessities of life, **may abound to every good work**—in every act of benevolence God will grant you the means and the disposition for exercising beneficence. You need not fear being reduced to want by your liberality. Notice how strongly Paul puts it, *all sufficiency in everything.* The word *sufficiency* is translated *contentment* in 1 Tim. 6 : 6, and its meaning is explained by 1 Tim. 6 : 8, " Having food and covering, with these we shall be content," or sufficiently satisfied. (Comp. Phil. 4 : 11.) It is the simple necessities of life with which a consecrated and gracious state of mind is satisfied. All besides is regarded as superfluous, to be given when the needs of others require

it. Some have noted Paul's use of "purposeth" (ver. 7) and of "sufficiency" (this ver.) as in Aristotle, inferring his acquaintance with the writings of that famous philosopher.

9. And the Scripture will be verified in your case, **As it is written,** quoted from Ps. 112 : 9 (Septuagint version), **He,** the man who fears the Lord, **hath dispersed,** or *scattered,* **abroad,** like one sowing seed; **he hath given to the poor,** to the laboring poor is meant, the needy; **his righteousness remaineth,** or *abides,* **for ever.** The scattering of good things and the giving to the worthy poor were proofs of his righteousness, his gracious goodness. And such righteousness abides; what is given thus is not lost; it will live in its blessed effects and will be held in everlasting remembrance. The blessing of God thus attends him. This verse is parenthetical, but not the next, as in the Common version.

10. This is connected with **ver. 8,** modified by **the** quotation in ver. 9. It is not a prayer, as in the Common version, but a promise. **Now he that ministereth seed,** rather, *And he who supplies seed for the sower and bread for food* (words quoted from Isa. 55 : 10), still keeping up the figure of sowing, *will supply* **and multiply your seed sown,** the money, the **gifts of your** collection, **and increase the fruits of your righteousness. The above** translation accords with the best text. God will supply and multiply the seed for works of mercy; and as the seed grows into an abundant harvest, so he will increase the harvest of righteousness, the blessings of multiplied human joy, and of lessened hu-

11 ness; being enriched in every thing to all bountifulness, ᵃ which causeth
12 through us thanksgiving to God. For ᵇ the administration of this service not only ᵇ supplieth the want of the saints, but is abundant also by many thanks-
13 givings unto God; whiles by the experiment of this ministration they ᶜ glorify God for your professed subjection unto the gospel of Christ, and for your liberal ᵈ distribution unto them,
14 and unto all men; and by their prayer for you, which long after you for

11 ye being enriched in everything to all liberality, which works through us
12 thanksgiving to God. Because the ministry of this service not only fully supplies the wants of the saints, but also abounds through many thanksgivings to God, while through the
13 proving of you by this ministration they glorify God on account of your obedience to your confession in respect to the gospel of Christ, and for the liberality of the contribution to
14 them, and to all; they also, with sup-

ᵃ 1 : 11 ; 4 : 15.   a Ver. 1 ; 8 : 4.   b 8 : 14.   c Matt. 5 : 16.   d Heb. 13 : 16.

man sorrow. God will increase the means and the blessed results of doing good. Both temporal and spiritual blessings are included. Notice how Paul progresses in his words of encouragement. In ver. 8, God is *able*; in this verse, he also *will* do it—words of promise and encouragement.

11. The way in which this promise will be fulfilled in actual experience. **Being enriched in everything to all bountifulness, to all liberality** (the same word as at the end of 8 : 2); here is the seed, the financial means and disposition for doing good; **which causeth,** or *worketh*, **through us,** who convey the gifts, thus representing our sowing; **thanksgiving to God,** on the part of those who receive it, which is a fruit of righteousness. The promise in these verses is not to be limited to either temporal or spiritual blessings, but includes both in different degrees according to circumstances. The tendency of righteousness is to blessedness; of evil to misery. In this life righteousness produces a hundred-fold more enjoyment than does unrighteousness. Even in this world it generally pays to do right. A liberal spirit and liberal acts meet generally with the approval of men, and have a softening effect upon the deserving recipient. There are many instances in our day of temporal blessings attending benevolent acts.

12-15. LIBERALITY RESULTING IN THE GOOD OF OTHERS AND REDOUNDING TO GOD'S GLORY.

12. Starting from the preceding clause the apostle explains and expands the thought. **For the administration of this** public religious service, or offering by the contributors (see on Rom. 15 : 27), **not only sup-** **plieth,** filling up the measure of **the temporal want of the saints, but is abundant also,** or *also abounded*, *through* **many thanksgivings unto God,** overflowing in other good results through the many thanksgivings that it causes to be sent up to God. It thus results in the glory of God (4 : 15 and next verse).

13. The recipients of these benefactions glorify God on two accounts. **While by the experiment,** or *proof*, **of this ministration,** or *service* of beneficence, **they glorify God.** Their beneficence was a proof of the Christian character of the Corinthians (2 : 9 ; 2 : 8); and this led the recipients of it to glorify God, (1) **for your professed subjection unto the gospel of Christ,** *for the obedience ye render to that which ye profess concerning the gospel of Christ.* Their acts agreed with their profession. They showed they were Christians in fact as well as in name. And (2) **for your liberal distribution unto them and unto all men,** *for the* openhearted *liberality of your contribution unto them and to all men*, equally ready and applicable to others as to them. The word *contribution* (Rom. 15 : 26) has in it the idea of *sharing*, participating with. The saints at Jerusalem will give glory to God for that common sharing or fellowship with them and with all Christians, which their liberality displays. It was not so much the greatness of the contribution, as the spirit in which it was made. (See next verse.)

14. Thankfulness leads them to pray for and to long after their benefactors. **And by their prayer for you,** rather, *While they themselves also*, the saints at Jerusalem, *with supplication*

the exceeding *grace of God in you.
15 Thanks *be* unto God *f* for his unspeakable gift.

plication for you, longing after you on account of the exceeding grace of God
15 upon you. Thanks be to God for his unspeakable gift!

e 8 : 1.   *f* John 3 : 16; Rom. 6 : 23

on your behalf, long after you, longing with pious, grateful love for personal acquaintance and fellowship with you, *on account of the exceeding grace of God upon you,* bestowed by God and evidenced by your liberal contributions. Paul begins this discussion (8 : 1) and ends it with a reference to the *grace* of liberality, given by God and exercised by Christians. Grace makes cheerful and liberal givers. Christian giving is first of all the exercise of the heart. Paul emphasizes the spirit of giving; it is a religious exercise, the outgoings of love to Christ and to our fellow-men. Large contributions are desirable, but the right spirit in giving is of the utmost importance.

15. An outburst of thanksgiving. As the apostle contemplates the hearty thanksgivings of the Jerusalem saints, and the evident power of the gospel of Christ upon the Corinthians, and all originating in and carried out by the grace of God, his own heart overflows with thankfulness for the supreme gift of God, which includes and insures all the blessings of his grace. **Thanks be unto God for his unspeakable gift.** This can be none less than Christ, who is the source and channel of all gospel graces. No other gift is so unspeakable. As in 8 : 9, so here, the apostle almost involuntarily turns to Christ as a Saviour, God's gift to the world. (Comp. Rom. 8 : 32, 34, 39 ; 11 : 33; John 3 : 16.) "This exquisite and resistless outburst of thanksgiving for that gift which not only transcends all our givings but originates them all, is as sublime as it is suitable at the close of the whole subject of the collection for the poor saints of Jerusalem" (PRINCIPAL BROWN).

GRECIAN CHRISTIANITY AND MACEDONIAN LIBERALITY. The Gentile Christianity of apostolic days may be styled Grecian. The Greeks were the leaders of religions, as well as of intellectual, thought. The Septuagint version of the Old Testament in Greek bore a rich harvest in proselytes to Judaism, in right conceptions of God, and in the reception of the gospel. The Gentile churches were largely composed of Grecian converts. We see here the importance of the Bible as an instrumentality in evangelization, and of its general distribution among the people. In both the eighth and ninth chapters, Paul uses the Scriptures in enforcing Christian beneficence.

The Greeks of Macedonia furnish the most remarkable example of benevolence to be found in the Scriptures. Its characteristics are well worth our study. (1) They made their greatest offering first (themselves), and then continued their gifts of service and money. In our day Christians generally begin with the smaller offerings, and need to be educated up to giving themselves fully to the work. (2) They gave out of the abundance of their poverty, and not out of a superabundance of worldly goods. (3) They willingly exceeded their ability in giving, and not as is too often the case, did their ability exceed their willingness. (4) They were urgent to be allowed to give; they besought the privilege and the opportunity; while those who received their offerings were reluctant to accept them, knowing their deep poverty. (5) Their gifts were valued not according to the amount given, but according to the willingness and cheerfulness manifested. (6) And to crown all, they regarded giving not as something to be dreaded and evaded, but as a grace and a blessing to be desired and cultivated. They doubtless found that increase comes not by keeping, but by giving; that the way to get more is to give more.

PRACTICAL REMARKS.

1. Christian benevolence is not merely giving a contribution or making a collection. Its spirit, manner, object, proportion, and system must be taken into account (ver. 1–4, 6, 7 ; 8 : 12 ; 1 Cor. 16 : 1).

2. It is proper to refer to the benevolence of a church or an individual, in order to

Paul's vindication of his apostolic authority and character.

10 NOW *I Paul myself beseech you ᵇ by

10 NOW I, Paul, myself beseech you

g Rom. 12 : 1.   *h* Zech. 9 : 9 ; Matt. 11 : 29.

excite benevolence in others (ver. 2 ; 8 : 2-4 ; Acts 11 : 29, 30).

3. Agents for developing the benevolence of churches and gathering collections are scriptural, necessary, and useful (ver. 3, 5 ; 8 : 6, 16, 24 ; Rom. 15 : 25, 31).

4. Agents for benevolent contributions should themselves be benevolent, active as Christian workers, and held in honor among the churches (ver. 3 ; 8 : 17-19, 22, 24).

5. It is proper and right to stimulate the benevolence of Christians and churches by appealing to their sense of honor, and the esteem and confidence of others in them (ver. 3-5 ; 8 : 22, 24).

6. Churches should live up to their engagements in financial and benevolent matters, exercising a prompt, generous, and loving spirit (ver. 5 ; Phil. 4 : 10, 15-17 ; 1 Cor. 13 : 1).

7. The abundant reward of giving to the Lord is a scriptural motive for Christian beneficence (ver. 6, 7 ; Ps. 41 : 1 ; Prov. 19 : 17 ; 22 : 9 ; Luke 6 : 38).

8. Christian giving should be deliberate, of free choice, cheerfully, honestly, and conscientiously carried out (ver. 7 ; Eph. 4 : 28 ; Acts 5 : 2-4).

9. We should not wait to become rich before we exercise liberality. We should rather give a part to God's service and expect his help and blessing (ver. 8-10 ; Exod. 35 : 21-29 ; Prov. 11 : 24, 25 ; 28 : 27 ; Eccl. 11 : 1).

10. The gift of a good man is his memorial ; the evidence also of God's help and grace (ver. 9 ; Acts 10 : 4 ; James 1 : 17).

11. Riches are not bestowed for luxury and self-gratification, but for doing good to others, blessing the world, and for the glory of God (ver. 11, 12 ; Luke 16 : 9 ; 1 Tim. 6 : 17-19 ; 1 Chron. 29 : 3, 14, 17).

12. The spiritual blessings of beneficence far exceed its temporal blessings (ver. 12 ; Matt. 25 : 40 ; Luke 16 : 9 ; Heb. 13 : 16).

13. A beneficent spirit is necessary to a consistent Christian profession (ver. 13 ; James 2 : 14-16 ; 1 John 3 : 17).

14. The gratitude and prayers of those who receive our benefactions often more than compensate us for our gifts (ver. 14 ; Acts 9 : 36-41).

15. Jesus Christ is God's greatest gift, and our greatest motive for giving to others (ver. 15 ; 8 : 9 ; 5 : 14).

CHAPTER X.

With this chapter begins the THIRD AND LAST PART of this Epistle, in which Paul defends himself against certain opponents and false teachers in the church, and vindicates his apostolic authority and personal character. The change from the conciliatory and affectionate tone, in the former part, to sternness and severity in this part, is very remarkable. It may be explained : (1) That Paul up to this point had associated Timothy and perhaps others with him in matters of more general interest, but now he turns to a matter personal to himself. (2) That before this he had addressed the better disposed of the church, who were in the majority, while now he addresses those who were disposed to make light of his apostolic character and authority. (3) That in writing he is not careful to separate them into distinct classes, but addresses them generally, the application and persons meant being evident in either case. So the preacher in popular discourse often addresses the people as a whole, while the application is intended and understood to be for various classes.

In this chapter the apostle defends himself against the charge that he is a different man when absent from what he is when present ; and at the same time he maintains the reality of his apostolic authority. Though weak and gentle he declares that he has spiritual power which he will exercise when needed (ver. 1-6) ; that his apostolic authority is a reality (ver. 7-11) ; and that he does not imitate the false pretences of his opponents (ver. 12-18).

1-6. THE SPIRITUAL NATURE AND POWER OF HIS APOSTOLIC MINISTRY.

1. Now I, Paul, myself, person-

the meekness and gentleness of Christ, [who in presence [*or*, in outward appearance] *am* base among you, but being absent ᵏ am bold toward you: but I beseech *you*, ᵏthat I may not be bold when I am present with that confidence, wherewith I think to be bold against some, which think of us ᵐ as if we walked according to the flesh. For though ⁿ we walk in the flesh, ᵒ we do not war after the flesh: (ᵖfor the weapons of our warfare *are* not carnal, but ᵠ mighty through God ʳ to the pull-

through the meekness and gentleness of Christ, who in your presence indeed am lowly among you, but being absent am of good courage toward you; but I entreat, that I may not when I am present be of good courage with the confidence, wherewith I think to be bold against some, who think of us as walking according to the flesh. For though walking in the flesh, we do not war according to the flesh; (for the weapons of our warfare are not fleshly, but mighty before God to the casting

---

ᵏ See refs. ver. 10. ᵏ 13 : 2 ; Rom. 15 : 15. ˡ 12 : 20 ; 13 : 10 ; 1 Cor. 4 : 21. ᵐ 12 : 13–19.
ⁿ Acts 14 : 15. ᵒ Gal. 2 : 20 ; 2 Tim. 2 : 3, 4. ᵖ Eph. 6 : 13–18 ; 1 Thess. 5 : 8.
ᵠ 13 : 3, 4 ; Rom. 15 : 19. ʳ Jer. 1 : 9, 10.

---

ally, turning my attention to most important personal matters. Every word is emphatic. **Beseech you,** I myself, such as I am, personally *entreat* and *exhort you* (both ideas are included in the verb). His entreaty partook also of the nature of an exhortation. **By the meekness,** *mildness,* and kindness (Matt. 11 : 29), **and gentleness,** *clemency,* "sweet reasonableness" (Acts 24 : 4), **of Christ,** which traits of character he uses as a motive, and as if he would add, Do not force me to adopt a treatment unlike Christ. These traits so remarkable in Christ's character, and so far as possessed by myself, are not of me naturally but of Christ. **Who in** *your* **presence am base,** *lowly, humble,* **among you, but being absent am bold,** *of good courage,* or courageous, **toward you.** There is probably an allusion to the language of his opponents and their estimate of him (ver. 10). We are not to infer, however, from this verse that Paul had an inferior personal appearance.

2. But I beseech, better, *Yea, I pray,* or *entreat you* (a different verb from "beseech" of ver. 1), that by your influence and conduct you may make it possible that I may **not** have occasion to be bold, *courageous,* when I am present, at my next visit, with that confidence wherewith I think to be bold against some persons which think of us as if we walked according to the flesh, like worldly, unconverted men, moved by worldly motives and seeking selfish interests. Two different verbs are translated *bold*; the first implies good courage in himself, the second boldness toward others. Notice Paul's diffi-

culty was not with the church, but with the certain persons who might mislead, or improperly influence the church. What Paul had in mind to do when he arrived at Corinth he does not definitely say. But from what follows it appears that he intended to use spiritual weapons, which would consist largely in the authoritative preaching of the gospel. This would result in leading to complete obedience, and in freeing the church from unworthy members and false teachers, and in the necessary exercise of discipline.

3. Explanatory of what he had just said. **For though we** "walk not according to the flesh" (ver. 2), we do indeed **walk in the flesh,** we possess mortal bodies, fleshly natures with their infirmities, yet, **we do not war after,** *according to,* **the flesh,** according to the principles of worldly, unregenerate men. The figure of a warfare in the Christian life is common with Paul. More commonly it is applied to the conflict between the old and new man in the Christian soul. (See Rom. 7 : 14–25 ; Gal. 5 : 16–18 ; 1 Cor. 9 : 26 ; Col. 3 : 5–13.) The warfare here is against sin and evil around us in the world. (1 Tim. 1 : 18 ; 6 : 12 ; 2 Tim. 2 : 3, 4 ; 4 : 7.)

4. We do not war according to the flesh (ver. 3). **For the weapons of our warfare are not carnal,** *of the flesh, fleshly,* they are not such as the world and worldly men use, hence it is implied that they are spiritual. The word *weapons* is the heavy armor, not merely the weapons in actual warfare, but figuratively the means, the craft, the devices, and the hypocritical policy which the world uses in warfare. **But** the weapons, or **heavy armor of our warfare are mighty through,** rather,

5 ing down of strong holds;) *casting down imaginations, and every high thing that exalteth itself against the knowledge of God, and bringing into captivity every thought to the obedi-
6 ence of Christ; ʳand having in a readiness to revenge all disobedience, when ᵘyour obedience is fulfilled.
7 ˣ Do ye look on things after the outward appearance? ʸ If any man trust to himself that he is Christ's, let him of himself think this again, that, as he is Christ's, even so ᶻ are we Christ's.

5 down of strongholds; casting down imaginations, and every high thing that exalts itself against the knowledge of God, and bringing every thought into captivity to the obedience of
6 Christ; and being in readiness to avenge every disobedience, when your obedience is made complete.
7 Ye look on the things that are after the outward appearance. If any one trusts to himself that he is Christ's, let him consider this again with himself, that, as he is Christ's, so also are we.

ˢ 1 Cor. 1 : 19, 27–29.   ᵗ 13 : 2, 10; 1 Cor. 5 : 3–5.   ᵘ 2 : 9; 7 : 15.
ˣ 1 Sam. 16 : 7; John 7 : 24; Rom. 2 : 28, 29.   ʸ 1 Cor. 14 : 37.   ᶻ 11 : 23; 1 John 4 : 6.

before, **God**, that is, in his sight. They are not such as are counted powerful among men (1 Cor. 1 : 21–25), but are mighty in God's estimation and according to the principles of his warfare. In the Divine view they are powerful **to the pulling down**, more exactly, the casting down, **of strong holds,** to the demolition of the spiritual fortifications of false doctrines and erroneous opinions and practices. (For a description of this armor see Eph. 6 : 10–17; 1 Thess. 5 : 8.)

5. The preceding thought expanded and explained. The warfare is carried on (1) in casting down, (2) bringing into captivity, and (3) inflicting punishment on the disobedient. **Casting down imaginations,** the *reasonings* of philosophers which are inimical to Christ, and, so far from being true, are but the imaginations of men; **and every high thing**, or *lofty rampart*, **that exalteth itself,** or is erected, **against the knowledge of God,** as it is revealed in the gospel. In this conflict Paul brings the wisdom of God against the wisdom of this world. The worldly wise regard the knowledge of God as foolishness. But the true character of their reasonings, as vain imaginings and conceited opinions, are brought to light by the Spirit, and demolished by the truth of God (1 Cor. 2 : 4). **And bringing into captivity every thought,** every evil in the mind, evil devices and purposes, **to the obedience of Christ,** into subjection to him. The figure of a warfare is still continued. The thoughts are the captives and obedience the fortress where they are brought into submission to Christ.

6. And having in a readiness, rather, *and being in readiness*, **to revenge,** or *punish*, **all disobedience, when your obedience is fulfilled,** *is made complete*, when all of you have obeyed who will obey. Paul would give ample opportunity for the gospel to do its work. He entreated, exhorted, and rebuked, in order that he might not use sharpness when he came (13 : 10). But having done all he could he proposed not to spare those who persisted in their opposition (13 : 2). How he would do this is left to the Corinthians to infer, probably by the exercise of his apostolic authority in delivering the obstinate over to Satan, and enjoining upon the church their excommunication (ver. 11; 1 Cor. 5 : 4, 5).

7-18. HIS APOSTOLIC AUTHORITY A REALITY, UNLIKE THE FALSE PRETENSES OF HIS OPPONENTS.

7. Do ye look on things after the outward appearance? or, *on that which lies before the eyes?* But judging in this manner, I can appeal to external things to show that I have as close a connection with Christ as any others have. Some translate this as a direct statement, *Ye look on things*, etc. Others translate as an imperative, *Look at that which is plainly before your eyes*, and see the genuineness of my mission. This does not suit the connection as well as the other two renderings. The first, however, which makes it a question seems to me preferable. **If any man trust to himself,** having confidence in himself, **that he is Christ's,** that he belongs to him, having reference perhaps to some Judaizing teachers in the Corinthian church, who claimed a special nearness or connection with Christ (1 Cor. 1 : 12); if this be so, **let him** *with him-*

8 For though I should boast somewhat more *of our authority, which the Lord hath given us for edification, and not for your destruction, ᵇ I should not
9 be ashamed. That I may not seem as
10 if I would terrify you by letters: for *his* letters, say they, *are* weighty and powerful; but ᶜ*his* bodily presence *is* weak, and *his* ᵈ speech contemptible.
11 Let ᵉ such an one think this, that, such as we are in word by letters when we

8 For even if I glory somewhat more abundantly concerning our authority, which the Lord gave us for building you up, and not for casting you down,
9 I shall not be put to shame; that I may not seem as if I would terrify you
10 through my letters. For his letters, says one, are weighty and strong, but his bodily presence is weak, and his
11 speech despicable. Let such a one consider this, that such as we are in

a 13:10.   *b* 7:14; 12:6.   *c* 12:5, 7, 9; 1 Cor. 2:3; Gal. 4:13.   *d* 11:6; 1 Cor. 1:17; 2:1, 4.
e 13:2, 3, 10.

self think, *consider*, **this again, that, as he is Christ's, even so are we,** in no sense are we inferior to him. If any one has come to this decision in his own mind, let him reconsider it with himself. He could belong to Christ in no sense that Paul did not. He could not claim superior power or authority to the apostle. The best text has *with himself*, as above, and omits *Christ's* at the end of the verse.

8. Paul proceeds through the rest of the Epistle to maintain his apostolic authority. And first he intimates that his authority was greater than he had hitherto asserted among them. And this claim for myself is true, **For though,** or according to the preferable text, *For even if* **I should boast,** or *glory*, **somewhat more** *abundantly* than I have done, **of our authority, which the Lord** *gave* **for edification,** *for building you up,* **and not for your destruction,** *not for casting you down, I shall not be put to shame,* as a vain boaster. Facts will sustain and results will justify my glorying. The comparison has reference not to the boasts of his opponents, but to the boast made in ver. 3-6. Notice that his apostolic authority was given for the building up of Christians and churches, not for their destruction. (Comp. 2:2, 3; 7:8-11.) *Us* is omitted by the best manuscripts, but is found in many others.

9. Even in greater glorying I shall not be put to shame, **That I may not seem,** or *appear*, **as if I would terrify you** by *my* **letters.** The Lord who gave me authority will save me from being made ashamed, and from seeming to be a man of terrific words in letters without corresponding power when present. It would be shown that he was not a braggart, and that he wrote not to terrify and destroy,

but rather as he had just said, to build up. Alford and some others would supply something, thus: "I say this, because I wish not to seem as if I would terrify you with my letters." But the former construction seems more faithful to the original, and is favored by Meyer and others.

10. Paul had good reason for making the reference he did to his letters. **For his letters, say they,** rather, *says one*, the language of an opposer, **are weighty and powerful,** *strong*, able, impressive, forcible, and commanding respect, **but his bodily presence is weak,** wanting in power and energy, manliness, and dignity, **and his speech contem**ptible, *is of no account*, such as to be despised. It must be borne in mind that this is the exaggerated language of his opponents. The traditions that he was short in stature, and that his body was disfigured by some lameness or distortion are of no value. The comparison of Barnabas to Jupiter, and Paul to Mercury, by the people of Lystra (Acts 14:12) implies that he was at least of fair bodily presence, though the less commanding of the two. The efficiency of his work, his unceasing labors for many years, his long journeys and great exposures, are proofs that he was not a man of feeble constitution. Doubtless there was some ground for such objections to him by his enemies, such as weakness of voice, or infirmity induced by exposures and overwork. (Comp. 12:7. 1 Cor. 2:3; Gal. 4: 13, 14.) That he rose at times to heights of eloquence is evident from Acts 17: 22, ff.; 26:24.

11. Let such an one, who speaks in this way, **think this,** *consider*, calculate on this, **that, such as we are in word by letters when we are absent, such will we be also in**

are absent, such *will we be* also in deed when we are present.

12 ᶠFor we dare not make ourselves of the number, or compare ourselves with some that commend themselves; but they measuring themselves by themselves, and comparing themselves among themselves, ᵍare not wise.

13 ʰBut we will not boast of things without *our* measure, ⁱbut according to the measure of the rule which God hath distributed to us, a measure to reach

14 ᵏeven unto you. For we stretch not ourselves beyond *our measure*, as though we reached not unto you : ˡfor we are come as far as to you also in

15 *preaching* the gospel of Christ : not

word through letters when absent, such will we be also in deed when present.

12 For we have not the boldness to pair or compare ourselves with some of those who commend themselves; but they, measuring themselves among themselves, and comparing themselves with themselves, are without under-

13 standing. But we will not glory beyond our measure, but according to the measure of the limit which God divided to us as a measure, to reach even to

14 you. For we do not stretch ourselves beyond our measure, as if we reached not to you; for as far as to you also did

15 we come, in the gospel of Christ; not

---

f 5 : 12 ; Prov. 25 : 27.   *g* Prov. 26 : 12.   *h* Ver. 15 ; Prov. 25 : 14.   *i* Matt. 25 : 15 ; Rom. 12 : 6.
k 1 : 14.   *l* Acts 18 : 1, 4 ; 1 Cor. 3 : 5, 10 ; 4 : 15 ; 9 : 1.

---

deed when we are present. We do not, and we will not, play such a double part as this. We will not act the coward when present. This verse is proof that the language of his enemies was exaggerated, that he was not so weak and despicable as they represented.

12. The apostle confirms what he had just said and rebukes his adversaries for their standard of judgment. **For we dare not,** *we are not bold,* or *we do not venture, to* **make ourselves of the number, or compare ourselves with some,** etc. Paul implies that there is a certain boldness or venturesomeness in self-praise, which he has not the hardihood to undertake. There is a play upon words here, common with Paul (1 : 13, 3 : 2) : *we venture not to judge ourselves among, or to judge ourselves with, some of those,* **that commend themselves.** We do not belong to that class of persons; we do not compare ourselves with Apollos or Cephas, nor commend ourselves as do our adversaries (3 : 1 ; 1 Cor. 1 : 12). **But they, measuring themselves by,** rather, *among,* **themselves,** among persons of their own class and by their own standard, and **comparing,** or *judging,* **themselves among,** *with,* **themselves,** making their own estimate of excellence a standard, **are not wise,** are without understanding, guilty of folly. Self-measurement was a false, foolish, and delusive standard. Calvin applies this whole passage to the monks in his day, who while ignorant were held to be learned, and verified the old proverb, "Ignorance is

bold," because they measured themselves by themselves.

13. But we, in contrast to these self-commenders, **will not** *glory* **without our measure,** *beyond our limit,* immeasurably, **but according to the measure,** or *the limit,* **of the rule,** better, *of the sphere,* of activity and labor, **which God hath distributed,** *apportioned to us, as a* **measure,** or *limit,* **to reach even unto you.** There is no limit to the commendation of those who measure themselves by themselves. They may go on immeasurably as far as self-conceit and vainglory will take them. Paul's standard was the one God gave him, and that was within the limit of the sphere of his own labors. God had given him his work as an apostle to the Gentiles, and his fields of labor ; so that the boundary line of his sphere reaches unto the Corinthians, who were converted under his ministry and owed the existence of their church to his labors (3 : 2, 3 ; 1 Cor. 3 : 6, 10 ; 9 : 2).

14. Explanatory. **For we stretch not ourselves beyond our measure,** beyond the prescribed limit, overmuch, **as though,** better, *as if,* **we reached not unto you; for we are come,** rather, *we came,* **as far as to you also in preaching the gospel of Christ.** The line and measure of his labors, given him by God, extended to them, and there was no need of any effort on his part in claiming them within his sphere of gospel activity. It is also implied that he was the first to preach the gospel to them. He had traveled from place to

boasting of things without *our* measure, *that is,* ᵐ of other men's labours; but having hope, when your faith is increased, that we shall be enlarged by you according to our rule abundantly,
16 to preach the gospel in the *regions* beyond you, *and* not to boast in another man's line of things made ready to our
17 hand. ⁿ But he that glorieth, let him
18 glory in the Lord. For ᵒ not he that commendeth himself is approved, but ᵖ whom the Lord commendeth.

glorying beyond our measure in other men's labors; but having hope that as your faith increases, we shall be enlarged among you according to our
16 limit to further abundance, so as to preach the gospel in the regions beyond you, not to glory within the limits assigned to another of things made ready
17 to our hand. But he that glories, let
18 him glory in the Lord. For not he that commends himself is approved, but he whom the Lord commends.

ᵐ Rom. 15 : 20.   ⁿ Jer. 9 : 23, 24 ; 1 Cor. 1 : 31; Gal. 6 : 14.   ᵒ Prov. 21 : 2 ; 27 : 2; Luke 16 : 15.
ᵖ Rom. 2 : 29 ; 1 Cor. 4 : 5.

place, gathering converts, until he had reached Corinth, at that time the farthest point he had gone westward.

15. The apostle repeats a thought at the beginning of ver. 13, but here directed against false teachers. **Not boasting,** etc., *Not glorying without measure in* **other men's labours,** as do some disturbers among you. Such having come to Corinth gloried in the fruits of Paul's labors as if they were their own. But Paul made it his aim to preach the gospel where Christ was not named, so as not to build on another's foundation (Rom. 15 : 20). His preaching at Rome after this, and his writing to the Christians there, were but a partial exception; for he proposed only to take Rome on his way to Spain (Rom. 15 : 24). Besides, the church at Rome does not appear to have been founded by any particular one, but to have been gathered from persons who came thither from all parts of the empire, among whom were some of Paul's own converts. As a prisoner at Rome he was shut off as it were to preaching the gospel in that city. **But,** while persisting in observing the rule laid down in ver. 13, **having hope, when your faith** *increases* (with their increased faith there would be increased growth, less need of apostolic watchcare, and increased usefulness both to them and to him), **that we shall be enlarged by,** rather, *among,* **you,** made more and more efficient in apostolic labors, **according to our rule abundantly,** according to our prescribed *sphere* of activity (ver. 13), superabounding and extending our field of labors. He identifies himself with his work. He is enlarged as his work is enlarged, and that enlargement at Corinth depended on their faith.

16. The result of this enlargement would be, **To preach the gospel in the regions beyond you,** such as Italy and Spain (Rom. 15 : 19, 24, 28); and also, **not to boast in another man's line,** or *not to glory within another's sphere,* **of things made ready to our hand.** Notice how frequently the apostle alludes to, and emphasizes, the practice of some who glory in the results, upon fields and to labors, not their own.

17. In contrast to the self-glorying of his opponents Paul gives the true and Divine rule. **But he that glorieth, let him glory in the Lord,** who is the source of all success (1 Cor. 3 : 6. 7). This is a free quotation from Jer. 9 : 24, and it also occurs in 1 Cor. 1 : 31. As an example of Paul's glorying in the Lord, see 1 Cor. 15 : 10; 2 Cor. 12 : 9, 10. He found it necessary at times to assert his apostolic character and claims, and to refer to his works, but while he did this he ascribed all the glory to God.

18. Paul's comment on the preceding verse. A reason and an application. **For not he that commendeth himself is approved,** stands the test of trial, and stands approved as a faithful servant (2 Tim. 2 : 15), **but whom the Lord commendeth,** by the deeds done through him (3 : 2. 3). The Lord's commendation whether by word or deed is according to truth and righteousness. "This will surely be the final verdict in regard to us all, whatever men may say of us now " (BOISE).

PRACTICAL REMARKS.

1. No Christian character is properly balanced without a Christlike meekness and gentleness (ver. 1; Matt. 11 : 29; 1 Tim. 2 : 15).

Paul's defence against the charges of false teachers.

11 WOULD to God ye could bear with

11 Would that ye could bear with me in

2. Formative church discipline is more important than corrective. Proper training will in most cases render corrective discipline needless (ver. 2; 2 Tim. 1 : 5, 7; Titus 2 : 11, 12).

3. Yet we must not shrink from disciplining offenses when necessary (ver. 2, 6; 1 Cor. 5 : 3-7; 1 Tim. 1 : 20).

4. The fact that Christians are in the world necessitates a warfare (ver. 3-5; John 17 : 16).

5. The Christian is to use the spiritual weapons of truth. He must not call to his aid the sword, or worldly devices and intrigues, for the extension of the Redeemer's kingdom (ver. 4, 5; 1 Tim. 1 : 18, 19).

6. Christ is our Captain in the Christian warfare, and victory over error and all spiritual evils is certain (ver. 5; Heb. 2 : 10; 1 Cor. 15 : 24).

7. Our encouragement in this warfare is in God. Our weapons are mighty through him (ver. 5, 6; 1 Cor. 1 : 27-29; Judg. 7 : 18, 20).

8. Not the outward appearance, but the heart and inward graces and gifts of the Spirit, determine the character of Christians and of ministers (ver. 7; John 7 : 24; 1 Sam. 16 : 7).

9. The authority and work of the gospel ministry is not for disciplining offenses, but in preaching and teaching and building up the cause of Christ (ver. 8, 14, 16; John 21 : 15, 17).

10. It is unbecoming the Christian and especially the gospel preacher to try to pass for what he is not (ver. 9; Matt. 23 : 3, 25, 26).

11. The letters of Paul are remarkable in doctrine, argument, force, pathos, individuality, and instruction (ver. 9, 10; 2 Peter 3 : 15, 16; 2 Tim. 3 : 16).

12. Paul was remarkable for his humility and honesty (ver. 9-11; 1 Cor. 15 : 6-10).

13. They who assume that the standard of moral excellence is in themselves, instead of in God and his truth, are striking examples of pride and folly (ver. 12, 17; Prov. 30 : 12, 13; 26 : 12; Rev. 2 : 2).

14. God assigns to each one of his children his mission and sphere of labor (ver. 13-16; Matt. 25 : 14, 15).

15. It should be our aim to enlarge our usefulness as far as possible for Christ and his cause (ver. 14-16; Acts 26 : 20-22; Rom. 1 : 13, 15; 15 : 19, 20).

16. There is a dependence and an interdependence among Christians in their spiritual growth and usefulness (ver. 15; Rom. 14 : 7).

17. A missionary spirit and a willingness to preach Christ to those who never heard of him, and to spend a life in labor and sufferings in extending the gospel, are apostolic, and make ministers in our day, in a high and noble sense, successors of the apostles (ver. 14-16; Matt. 28 : 20).

18. God is the absolute good, the source and standard of moral excellence (ver. 17, 18; Mark 10 : 18; Rev. 15 : 4).

19. Self-estimates are deceptive. The Divine estimate and approval will stand the test of time and eternity (ver. 18; Rom. 2 : 29; Gal. 1 : 10).

CHAPTER XI.

Paul defends himself against his accusers, who appear to have been Judaizing, false teachers (ver. 22). He begins the chapter by apologizing for his boasting which he indulged in because of his interest in his converts (ver. 1-6), his disinterested love (ver. 7-11), and his desire to guard them against dishonest men (ver. 12-15). He proceeds to show that he is equal to his opponents as to race (ver. 16-22), and superior to them in labors, sufferings, and deliverances (ver. 23-33).

1-15. THE APOSTLE APOLOGIZES FOR HIS BOASTING.

1. Translate according to the best text: *Would that ye would bear from me a little folly*, in boasting. Paul's sensitive nature recoils from speaking in praise of himself, but his opposers compelled him in self-defense. (ver. 16-18; 12 : 11; 1 Cor. 3 : 1.) In the light of 10 : 17, 18, it seemed foolish; and he speaks as if in doubt as to whether they would bear with him. And so to his wish he adds a request, **and indeed**, or *nay, indeed*, I beseech you, **bear with me,**

me a little in *my folly*; and indeed bear with me. For I am *jealous over you with godly jealousy*; for *I have espoused you to one husband, that I may present you *as a chaste virgin to Christ. But I fear, lest by any means, as *the serpent beguiled Eve through his subtilty, so your minds *should be corrupted from the simplicity that is in Christ. For if he that cometh preacheth *another Jesus, whom we have not preached, or *if ye receive *another spirit, which ye have not received, or *another gospel, which we have not accepted, ye might well bear a little folly! Nay, indeed ye do bear with me. For I am jealous over you with a godly jealousy; for I betrothed you to one husband, that I may present a pure virgin to Christ. But I fear, lest by any means, as the serpent deceived Eve in his craftiness, so your minds should be corrupted from your singleness and purity toward Christ. For if indeed he that comes preaches another Jesus, whom we did not preach, or if ye receive a different spirit, which ye did not receive, or a different gospel, which ye did not receive, ye might

q Ver. 16, 17, 19, 21; 5:13; 12:11. *r* Phil. 1:8.   *s* Hosea 2:19, 20.   *t* Eph. 5:27; Col. 1:28.
u Lev. 21:13.   *x* Gen. 3:4, 13; John 8:44.   *y* Col. 2:4, 8, 18; 1 Tim. 4:1; 2 Peter 3:17.
z Acts 4:12.   *a* 1 Cor. 12:4-11.   *b* Gal. 1:7, 8.

for I am jealous, etc. (next ver.). Most later interpreters, however, take the verb in the indicative instead of the imperative, thus: *But, indeed, you do bear with me;* some perhaps at Corinth had said, "His foolishness is unbearable," and yet the church bore with him. The first construction, however, seems to me to suit the connection better.

2. For I am jealous over you with *a* **godly jealousy,** a pure, godlike jealousy, earnestly desirous that you should not be led astray, and solicitous for your final salvation. **For I espoused you,** *I betrothed you* (referring to the engagement rather than to the actual marriage), **to one husband,** to whom alone you are to remain faithful, **that I may present you a chaste,** *a pure*, **virgin to Christ** (comp. Eph. 5:25; Rev. 19:7-9). Paul had been the means of their conversion. Like John the Baptist he represents himself as the friend of the bridegroom (John 3:29), who often took an important part in negotiating and arranging the marriage. As such he had secured, as it were, the Corinthian church as the bride of Christ. Hence he felt a deep concern and a weighty responsibility in their behalf, that they should not be unfaithful. (Comp. Isa. 54:5; Jer. 3:14; Hosea 2:19, 20.) His own honor, their honor and highest interest, and Christ's glory, were all involved.

3. As Satan led Eve astray, so the apostle fears that the Corinthians will be led astray by Satan's emissaries, the false teachers. **But I fear, lest by any means, as the serpent,** representing Satan (Rev. 12:9), **beguiled** Eve, *deceived* her, **through his sub-** **tilty,** *craftiness*, **so your minds,** or *thoughts*, **should be corrupted,** and turned away, **from the simplicity,** *and*, according to the preferable text, *purity toward* **Christ.** *Simplicity* means that which is unmixed, unadulterated; *purity* is chaste faithfulness to him. The whole phrase therefore means single-minded loyalty to Christ. The Corinthian church is mentioned in ver. 2 as the bride, and to preserve the figure Eve is mentioned here, instead of Adam, as in Rom. 5:12; 1 Cor. 15:22. Paul sees the danger of the Corinthians being led away from Christ by the manifold and strange teachings of Judaizing or other erroneous teachers (Heb. 13:8, 9).

4. The apostle gives a reason for this fear, in that they were willing to endure the false preaching of his opponents. The passage is a difficult one, and may be translated and expressed thus: *For if indeed he that comes*, representing the false teachers in general, or perhaps the prime mover, *proclaims another Jesus*, another deliverer, Saviour, *whom we did not preach, or if ye receive a different spirit, which ye did not receive* at first, *or a different gospel which ye did not receive and accept* at the first, if he indeed preaches another gospel altogether, a new and a better one, if it were possible to do this, *you might well endure it.* But this is not so; for he professes to proclaim the same Jesus, the same Spirit, and the same gospel, only he opposes and depreciates the authority of him from whom you first received it. Therefore you should not willingly listen to him, for I do not fall behind "the most em-

5 with *him*. For I suppose *I was not a whit behind the very chiefest apostles.
6 But though *d I be* rude in speech, yet not *in knowledge; but f we have been thoroughly made manifest among you in all things.
7 Have I committed an offence *g in abasing myself that ye might be exalted, because I have preached to you

5 well bear with it. For I reckon that I am in no respect behind those preeminent apostles. And though I be rude in speech, yet I am not in knowledge; but in everything we have manifested it among all, in respect to you.
7 Or did I commit a sin in humbling myself that ye might be exalted, because I preach to you the gospel of

c 12 : 11, 12 ; 1 Cor. 15 : 10.   d See refs. 10 : 10.   e Eph. 3 : 4.   f 4 : 2 ; 5 : 11 ; 12 : 12.
g 10 : 1 ; 12 : 13 ; Acts 18 : 1-3 ; 1 Cor. 9 : 3-18.

inent apostles" (ver. 5), and much less the "false apostles" (ver. 13), except in rhetorical d i s p l a y (ver. 6 ; 1 Cor. 2 : 1-4); and surely not in gospel knowledge and frank, open conduct (ver. 6), nor in toil and suffering (ver. 22. ff.).

Paul is very generally regarded by expositors as speaking here ironically, thus: *nobly would ye bear with him!* with reference to the ready reception given the false teachers. But it is not necessary to suppose irony since it can be very naturally explained without it. In the strong, impassioned language of Paul the temptation is very great to introduce the element of irony, where it is possible, to explain difficulties. It seems to me that this has sometimes been carried too far.

5. The sum of Paul's boasting stated. **For,** confirmatory of the thought implied in the preceding verse. You should not readily listen to these false teachers, **for I suppose,** rather, *I consider, judge* (a deliberate opinion), **I was not a whit behind the very chiefest apostles,** better, *that I am in nothing inferior to the most eminent apostles* (Thayer's Lex.). Ancient interpreters refer this to Peter and John or to the rest of the Twelve. This is in harmony with Gal. 2 : 6-14. It may however be regarded not as a personal reference, but a general statement. No apostles anywhere could claim superiority to him. Later interpreters, however, more generally refer the words here to the false teachers, the opposers of Paul, and translate here and in 12 : 11, *those pre-eminent*, or, *overmuch apostles*, implying censure and a tinge of irony. But the first interpretation really includes all. If he was not inferior to the most eminent apostles, then he was superior to any less eminent and to all who might aspire to and claim apostolic authority and power.

6. He explains more particularly what he had just asserted, conceding one point, and this largely for sake of argument. **But though I be rude in speech,** as my opponents affirm, *unskilled in eloquence*, laying no claim to that rhetorical finish which is learned in schools. *Rude* does not mean that a person has not natural eloquence, for Paul was an impressive and powerful speaker (Acts 19 : 8 ; 24 : 10, etc.), but that he did not use the methods of professional orators. Though indeed unskilled, unprofessional in speech, **yet I am not in knowledge,** of the gospel and Divine things (Eph. 3 : 4); and I could dwell upon this, **but we have been thoroughly made manifest,** rather, according to the preferable text, *but in everything we have manifested it*, the fact that we are not deficient and unskilled in our knowledge of Christ and the gospel; we have manifested this *among all men in relation to you*. Our teaching among you is generally known, and the benefit you have received from us (1 Cor. 1 : 5, 6). "They are his 'Epistles known and read of all men'; and by their knowledge of the truth, he shows among all men his knowledge as a teacher" (GOULD; 3 : 2). He needs to say no more regarding his apostolic knowledge of Divine revelations and spiritual truths. It was evident to all.

7. Have I committed an offence, rather, *Or*, turning to another objection of his opponents, *did I commit a sin*, inconsistent with my apostolic claims, **in abasing myself,** in working for a living instead of enjoying my privilege as an apostle in receiving support from you (1 Cor. 9 : 4-15; Acts 18 : 3), **that ye might be exalted,** from the degradation of heathenism to the high moral position of Christian salvation, **because I preached to you the gospel of God freely,** *gratuitously*, without cost? A pointed

8 the gospel of God freely? I robbed other churches, taking wages *of them*,
9 to do you service: and when I was present with you, and wanted, [b] I was chargeable to no man (for that which was lacking to me [l] the brethren which came from Macedonia supplied); and in all *things* I have kept myself [k] from being burdensome unto you, and so
10 will I keep *myself*. [l] As the truth of Christ is in me, [m] no man shall stop me of this boasting in the regions of
11 Achaia. Wherefore? [n] because I love
12 you not? God knoweth. But [o] what I do, that I will do, [p] that I may cut off

8 God without cost? I robbed other churches, taking wages of them, that
9 I might minister to you. And when I was present with you, and lacked, I was a charge to no one; for what was lacking to me the brethren when they came from Macedonia supplied; and in every thing I kept myself from being burdensome to you, and so will I
10 keep myself. As the truth of Christ is in me, this glorying shall not be stopped against me in the regions of
11 Achaia. Why? Because I love you
12 not? God knows. But what I do, and will do, is that I may cut off the

---

[h] 1 Thess. 2 : 9 ; 2 Thess. 3 : 8, 9.   [i] Phil. 4 : 10, 14–16.   [k] 12 : 14, 16.   [l] Rom. 1 : 9 ; 9 : 1.
[m] 1 Cor. 9 : 15.   [n] 6 : 11, 12 ; 7 : 3 ; 12 : 15.   [o] Ver. 9.   [p] 1 Cor. 9 : 12.

---

question, the natural answer of which would be: By no means; you committed no sin, but rather showed your disinterested love (ver. 11). But it would seem that his enemies had reproached him for this exhibition of unselfishness, and used it as an argument against his apostolic authority. They themselves had exacted pay for their services (ver. 20), and so far from entering into and appreciating Paul's feelings, they charged it to a consciousness that he was not an apostle.

8. I robbed, *despoiled,* as it were, **other churches, taking wages,** which some might think unfairly taken (Phil. 4 : 15–18), **to do you service,** *that I might minister to you.* A strong statement of fact. He received from other churches what they were not really called upon to supply; and what the Corinthians were bound to furnish as much as any others. Why he did this is told in ver. 12. The word translated *wages* is not the usual word for *pay for services,* but one used of the *allowance* or *rations* given to soldiers (Luke 3 : 14 ; 1 Cor. 9 : 7), and here equivalent to *support,* the means of subsistence. All he got was a bare support, and what he needed above his earnings (1 Cor. 9 : 6) was received from others (next ver.).

9. And when I was present with you, and wanted, having fallen behind in my resources, **I was chargeable,** *I was a burden,* **to no man:** for, to explain how this was, **that which was lacking to me,** the deficiency which I failed to earn, **the brethren,** perhaps Timothy and Silas (Acts 17 : 5), **which came from Macedonia supplied.** *And in* *everything* I carefully *kept myself, and will keep myself, from being a burden to you.* Such had been his practice toward them, and he proposed for reasons to be given to persist in the practice.

10. That he will in the future continue in this course he most solemnly declares. **As the truth of Christ is in me,** existing in me and making me truthful as he is truthful, **no man shall stop me of this boasting,** or *glorying,* by any strong or violent measure that may be adopted, **in the regions of Achaia.** (See 1 Cor. 9 : 19, 19, and note.) The word translated *stop* signifies to *fence in, hedge in,* and is used of *stopping the mouth* in Rom. 3 : 19; Heb. 11 : 33. No insinuations, charges, and efforts of opposers shall stop me in this glorying, nor shall any argument from my conduct prove that my glorying is empty.

11. Wherefore? *Why* hold so tenaciously to this resolution, to receive nothing from them? He answers this first negatively. **Because I love you not? God knoweth.** A practical and most solemn denial. The question itself suggests his positive affection for them. God knew that there was no lack of love, and how great his love for them. He thus anticipates any suspicion that his conduct arose from any coldness or distrustfulness on his part. Love indeed willingly accepts gifts from loved ones. But he had other reasons aside from any lack of love, for not doing thus, which he proceeds to give.

12. He answers the question, *Wherefore* (ver. 11), positively. **But what I do, that I will do,** or, *But what I do*

occasion from them which desire occasion; that wherein they glory, they may be found even as we.
13 For such *are* false apostles, deceitful workers, transforming themselves
14 into the apostles of Christ. And no marvel; for Satan himself is trans-
15 formed into an angel of light: therefore *it is* no great thing if his ministers also be transformed as the ministers of righteousness; whose end shall be according to their works.

occasion of those who desire an occasion, that wherein they glory they may
13 be found even as we. For such men are false apostles, deceitful workers, transforming themselves into apostles
14 of Christ. And no wonder; for Satan himself transforms himself into an
15 angel of light. It is no great thing then, if also his ministers transform themselves as ministers of righteousness; whose end will be according to their works.

q Rom. 16 : 18; Gal. 1 : 7; 2 Peter 2 : 1; 1 John 4 : 1; Rev. 2 : 2.   *r* Titus 1 : 10, 11.
s Ver. 3; Matt. 4 : 1-10.   *t* Phil. 3 : 19; 2 Peter 2 : 3, 13-22.

---

and will do is, **that I may cut off** *the* **occasion from them which desire an occasion** against me, to depreciate me and magnify themselves. **That,** *in order that,* **wherein they glory, they may be found even as we,** "that we may both be judged fairly according to the actual facts" (BOISE). They shall have no occasion for saying that I preach for money. And in regard to the claim of support wherein they glory they shall be estimated even as we. Their selfish and aggrandizing spirit would not stand the test a moment in comparison with the unselfish and disinterested principle upon which the apostle acted. If they continued to receive pay for services they would suffer disadvantage in comparison with him; or they would be compelled to act upon the same disinterested principle as he, which they were not likely to do. This is a difficult passage, and a number of interpretations are given by expositors. The above seems to me the preferable one.

13. A reason for the statement in the preceding verse. **For such** persons as they who desire an occasion for a handle to use against me, **are false apostles,** professing to be commissioned by Christ when they are not (Rev. 2 : 2), **deceitful workers,** crafty, dishonest, pretending to be devoted to the gospel but seeking their own selfish ends (2 : 17; Rom. 16 : 17, 18; Gal. 6 : 12), **transforming themselves into** (omit the) **apostles of Christ.** It is their habit (present tense) to assume the appearance and air of apostles of Christ. But judged fairly and according to actual facts (ver. 12) their mask will be stripped off (Rev. 2 : 9, 13). *Apostles*—those who trace back their authority and commission to Christ, instead of to any church (Acts 1 : 21, 22; Gal. 1 : 1).

14. And no marvel, *it is not a strange thing,* **for Satan himself is transformed into,** assumes the appearance of, **an angel of light** (2 : 11; 10 : 7). It would be hard to speak of Satan more strongly as a person than is done here. Angels of *light* are thus designated, because of the brightness which surrounds them (Acts 12 : 7; Ps. 104 : 4); and because they are the messengers of God who is light and dwells in light (1 John 1 : 5; 1 Tim. 6 : 16); and because they convey s p i r i t u a l light, knowledge, and truth. As opposed to the angels of light Satan is of the kingdom of darkness, practising the deeds of darkness in deceiving and seducing men (4 : 6; Acts 26 : 18; Col. 1 : 13; 2 Thess. 2 : 9; Rev. 12 : 9). Notice Satan does not come to us as Satan; he comes with false colors (Gen. 3 : 1-6).

15. T h e r e f o r e it is no great thing if his ministers, *his servants,* **also,** as well as he, *transform themselves,* **as the ministers of righteousness,** assume to themselves the appearance of *servants* of righteousness (Rom. 6 : 18), devoted to righteousness as it is in Christ (5 : 21; Rom. 1 : 17). Righteousness is a condition of Christ's kingdom and represents a power which is o p p o s e d to Satan (6 : 7, 14). **Whose end shall be according to their works,** according to their deeds as they actually were, not according to the outward appearances they had assumed. Being Satan's servants they must receive his wages (Rom. 6 : 23; Phil. 3 : 19). The word *end* is significant, *the final fate* or destiny, pointing to an unchanging future, with no hope of being restored and eventually saved (Rom. 2 : 6-11; Phil. 3 : 19; Prov. 24 : 12).

16 ª I say again, let no man think me a fool; if otherwise, yet as a fool receive me, that I may boast myself a little.
17 That which I speak, ˣ I speak *it* not after the Lord, but as it were foolishly,
18 in this confidence of boasting, ʸ seeing that many glory after the flesh, ᶻ I
19 will glory also. For ye suffer fools gladly, ᵃ seeing ye *yourselves* are wise.
20 For ye suffer, ᵇ if a man bring you into bondage, if a man devour *you*, if a man

16 I say again, let no one think me foolish: but if ye do, yet receive me even if as foolish, that I too may glory
17 a little. What I speak, I speak not according to the Lord, but as if in folly,
18 in this confidence of glorying. Since many glory according to the flesh, I
19 also will glory. For ye gladly bear with the foolish, being yourselves
20 wise. For ye bear with it, if one brings you into bondage, if one devours

ᵘ Ver. 1 . 12 . 6, 11.   ˣ 1 Cor. 7 : 6, 12.   ʸ Ver. 21–23 ; Phil. 3 : 3, 4.   ᶻ 12 : 5, 6, 9, 11.
ᵃ 1 Cor. 4 : 10.   ᵇ Gal. 2 : 4 ; 4 : 9.

16–33. Equal to his opponents as to race; superior to them in sufferings.

16. I say again. Paul has made three attempts to begin his glorying. First (10 : 7), he stops to give attention to the empty glorying of his opponents ; second (11 : 1), he pauses to express his anxiety for his converts under the influence of false teachers; and third (11 : 6), he again stops to answer the charge arising from not accepting support. Now he returns to the point and expresses himself fully as far as 12 : 13. **Let no man think me a fool,** *think me foolish*, senseless, acting without reflection. He shrinks from self-praise as unbecoming. He feels humiliated that he is compelled so to do (12 : 11). **If otherwise,** or *if ye do* think me foolish, **yet as a fool receive me,** yet receive me even if ye do regard me as *foolish*, **that I may boast myself,** *that I too, as well as they, may glory a little*. There seems to be an implied contrast: others are allowed to boast much, surely I may boast a little.

17. He enlarges on this boasting a little. That which **I speak, I speak it not** after the manner of **the Lord** Jesus, or *according to the Lord*. (See similar expressions, 1 : 17; 10 : 3 ; 1 Cor. 15 : 32.) Self-praise was not according to the example and spirit of Christ (Matt. 11 : 29 ; Luke 17 : 10; Rom. 15 : 3, 5 ; Phil. 2 : 5 ; 3 : 3), and as implied by this manner of speaking, was not through any direct instruction from him. (Comp. 1 Cor. 7 : 12, 25, 40.) **But,** I speak, **as it were foolishly,** *as if in* a state of *foolishness*, **in this confidence of boasting,** in the assurance that I have in this *glorying*. In this Paul displays great humility, and he ascribes all glory to God (10 : 13, 17), so that there was nothing wrong in his self-glorying. "Like an oath, self-praise may under certain circumstances become necessary, especially for those who, like St. Paul, have the public duties of a sacred ministry to discharge" (Wordsworth). He does it in self-defense and for the good of his converts. He stoops as it were to their weakness and suits his argument to their carnal ideas.

18. He begins his glorying, and he gives a reason for so doing. Seeing **that many glory after the flesh,** after the manner of worldly men who look only at the outward, and boast of birth, race, and wisdom, **I will glory also,** which he does beginning with ver. 22. If they have done it from unworthy motives, and with so much effect upon you, I also will do it, impliedly with worthy motives. As if he had added: Not in what I have done, but in what I have suffered, and in God's grace to me. He uses arguments which were found to be suited to them. "What is allowed to many, is the more easily granted to one" (Bengel).

19. A reason, humorously put, why they should bear with him in glorying. **For ye suffer,** or *gladly bear with*, **fools,** those without understanding, deficient in intelligence, **seeing ye yourselves are wise,** intelligent. It is characteristic of intelligent men to bear with those who are deficient in understanding.

20. Further reasons why they should bear with him. Paul humorously refers to their forbearance with others, in view of which they would surely bear with him. **For ye suffer,** or *bear with it*, **if a man,** doubtless a reference to their false teachers, **bring you into bondage,** lording it over you and binding you to a blind obedience ; **if a man devour you,** selfishly *strips you*

take *of you*, if a man exalt himself, if a
21 man smite you on the face. I speak as
concerning reproach, ᶜas though we
had been weak. Howbeit ᵈ whereinso-
ever any is bold, (I speak foolishly,) I
22 am bold also. Are they Hebrews? ᵉso
am I. Are they Israelites? so *am* I.
Are they the seed of Abraham? so *am* I.
23 Are they ministers of Christ? (I speak
as a fool) I *am* more; ᶠin labours more
abundant, ᵍin stripes above measure,
in prisons more frequent, ʰin deaths

you, if one takes you captive, if one exalts himself, if one beats you on the
21 face. I say it as a dishonor, as though
we had been weak. But in whatever
any one is bold (I say it in folly), I
22 also am bold. Are they Hebrews? So
am I. Are they Israelites? So am I.
Are they Abraham's seed? So am I.
23 Are they ministers of Christ? (I speak
as beside myself,) I am more; in labors
more abundantly, in prisons more
abundantly, in stripes above meas-

c 10 : 10.   d Phil. 3 : 4.   e Acts 22 : 3; Rom. 11 : 1; Phil. 3 : 5.   f 1 Cor. 15 : 10.
g 6 : 4. 5; Acts 9 : 16; 20 : 23; 21 : 11.   h 6 : 9, 10; 1 Cor. 15 : 30-32.

of your goods; **if a man take of
you,** rather, *take you captive,* like a
hunter, if by craft he ensnare and catch
you, and thus satisfies his ambition or
avarice; **if a man exalt himself,**
assuming airs of superiority; **if a
man smite you on the face,** treating you rudely in the exercise of authority. This was the climax of forbearance. That such acts of presumption and violence might be committed,
by arrogant teachers in the early
churches, may be inferred from the
command in 1 Tim. 3 : 3 and Titus 1 :
7, that a bishop or pastor must not be
"a striker." (Comp. Matt. 5 : 39; Luke 22 : 64;
Acts 23 : 2; 1 Kings 22 : 24.)

**21. I speak as concerning re-
proach,** better, *I say it as a reproach,*
or *by way of self-disparagement,* as
though it were a fact that **we had
been weak** when among you, and in
our relation to you since then (10 : 10;
1 Cor. 4 : 10). He had represented himself
as weak and as nothing in contrast to
the arrogant assumptions of the false
teachers (ver. 16-20). I have so spoken
indeed, *but wherein* **any is bold, (I
speak foolishly,** *in foolishness,* as
my enemies would say), **I am bold
also,** in speech. Whatever these men
can glory in, I can glory in the same.
And as a proof he enters upon an
eloquent and wonderful description of
his ministerial labors (ver. 22-27).

22. Hebrews are they? bearing
that ancient and most venerable national name, and attached to their na-
tionality and their language (Acts 6 : 1;
21 : 40; 22 : 2; Phil. 3 : 5). **So am I a Hebrew. Israelites are they?** belonging to the theocracy and attached to
their covenant privileges as God's
people (Rom. 9 : 4; Acts 13 : 16; 21 : 28). **Seed
of Abraham are they?** descendants

of the father of the faithful and sharers
in the Messianic promises (Rom. 9 : 7; 11 :
1; comp. Acts 22 : 3; Phil. 3 : 5). Paul repeats
the vocabulary of their boasting.
It is evident that they were Jewish
teachers.

23. Ministers, or *servants,* **of
Christ are they?** specially connected
with Christ in their service for him?
peculiarly his servants, his ministers?
With stronger language Paul exclaims,
(I speak as a fool,) rather, *as one
beside himself,* out of his senses. In
great humiliation he is compelled to
speak of his ministerial labors and sufferings. In God's sight all boasting is
excluded (Luke 17 : 10; Rom. 3 : 27); but
facts were facts, and he is compelled to
appeal to them in self-defense, and
against the glorification and pretensions of his opposers (12 : 11). **I am
more,** in a much greater degree am I
a servant or minister of Christ. "I am
that pre-eminently" (BOISE). In a
graphic statement of facts Paul gives
a proof of this. He points to a life
without precedent in the world. "Self-
devotion for some special national cause
had been often seen before; the career
of Socrates was a lifelong service to humanity; but a continual self-devotion,
involving hardships like those here described, and extending over so long a
period, and in behalf of no local or
family interest, but for the interest of
mankind at large, was down to this
time a thing unknown" (STANLEY).
In labours, hard and troublesome,
more abundant (1 Cor. 15 : 10; Acts 20 : 20,
31, 34; Rom. 15 : 19), **in stripes above
measure** (ver. 24), **in prisons more
frequent,** or *more abundantly* (Acts
16 : 23), **in deaths oft,** in the midst
of death and in imminent danger of
death (Acts 14 : 19; 1 Cor. 15 : 31; 2 Cor. 1 : 9, 10;

24 oft. Of the Jews five times received I 25 ¹ forty *stripes* save one, thrice was I ʲbeaten with rods, ᵏonce was I stoned, thrice I ˡsuffered shipwreck, a night 26 and a day I have been in the deep; *in* journeyings often, *in* perils of waters, *in* perils of robbers, ᵐ*in* perils by *mine own* countrymen, ⁿ*in* perils by the heathen, *in* perils in the city, *in* perils in the wilderness, *in* perils in the sea, 27 *in* perils among false brethren; in

24 ure, in deaths often; from the Jews five times I received forty stripes 25 save one; thrice I was beaten with rods; once I was stoned; thrice I suffered shipwreck; a night and a day 26 I have spent in the deep; in journeyings often, in perils of rivers, in perils of robbers, in perils from my countrymen, in perils from the heathen, in perils in the city, in perils in the wilderness, in perils in the sea, in

ⁱ Deut. 25 : 3.   ʲ Acts 16 : 22, 23 ; 21 : 32.   ᵏ Acts 14 : 19.   ˡ Acts 27 : 41.
ᵐ Acts 9 : 23–25; 13 : 50; 14 : 5; 17 : 5; 20 : 3; 21 : 28–31; 23 : 10, 11 ; 25 : 3.
ⁿ 1 : 8–10; Acts 14 : 5; 16 : 19–24; 19 : 23–41.

4 : 11). From this and the verses that follow it appears how little of Paul's life we have in the Acts of the Apostles. But though this account goes far beyond that of the Acts, yet it is remarkable that there is nothing here that contradicts that narrative. The incidental agreements, and the differences w i t h o u t contradictions, confirm the truthfulness of Luke and Paul. Unlike most biographies of heroes and saints, the memoirs of the apostle underrate instead of overrate his labors and sufferings.

24. In this verse and the next Paul specifies instances of the "stripes above measure" and of "deaths oft," of the preceding verse. **Of the Jews five times received I forty stripes save one** (Matt. 10:17). None of these are mentioned in the Acts. Jewish law forbade the inflicting of more than forty stripes. One below that number was given lest by mistake the prescribed number should be exceeded. (JOSEPHUS, *Antiq.*, IV., 8, 21.) 25. **Thrice was I beaten with rods.** Only one of these is mentioned in the Acts, that at Philippi (Acts 16 : 22, 23). This was a Roman punishment; inflicting stripes a Jewish. It was not unusual for death to result from the stripes or the rods; and so these may also be included in the statement "in deaths oft." **Once was I stoned,** at Lystra (Acts 14 : 19). Clement of Rome, a friend of Paul (Phil. 4:3), in his first "Epistle to the Corinthians," written perhaps, A. D. 90, says that Paul "was imprisoned seven times, was whipped (or *put to flight*), was stoned." **Thrice I suffered shipwreck.** We have no account of these. That in Acts 27 occurred after this. **A night and a day,** a period of twenty-four hours, beginning with sunset, **I have been,** rather, *I have spent,* **in the deep,** clinging probably to some piece of the wreck and exposed to the dangers of the ocean. The expression implies a vivid remembrance of the event.

26. The last two verses were somewhat parenthetical. This verse resumes the line of thought in ver. 23. "I am more," in a much greater degree a minister of Christ—in, or *by*, **journeyings often;** the Acts gives some of these; he was now on his third general missionary tour. In perils of **waters,** *dangers of rivers,* overflowing at times and bridges were rare, dangerous to ford, quite impassable. He may have met such dangers in Pamphylia and Pisidia in his first missionary journey (Acts 13 : 13, 14, and note). Of **robbers,** who infested mountainous and sparsely settled regions. (Comp. Luke 10 : 30.) **By my own countrymen,** the Jews, who often sought his life, and were ever on his track to arouse persecution (Acts 9 : 25, 29 ; 17 : 5, 13 ; 18 : 12, etc.). **By the heathen,** as at Lystra, Philippi, and Ephesus (Acts 14 : 19; 16 : 19–22; 19 : 23–34). **In the city,** as at Damascus (ver. 32) and at Jerusalem (Acts 9 : 28, 29), **in the wilderness,** *a desert,* an uninhabited region, where he was exposed to hunger and thirst, heat and cold, as well as to roving bands of robbers. (Comp. Gal. 1 : 17.) **In the sea,** from pirates and from long voyages, aside from shipwrecks. **Among false brethren**—Judaizing teachers and those pretending to be disciples or apostles of Christ (ver. 13; Gal. 2 : 4). This last is a climax. Almost anything could be better endured than this (Ps. 55 : 12–14).

27. **In weariness,** *labor,* toil, and

weariness and painfulness, ° in watchings often, ᵖ in hunger and thirst, in fastings often, in cold and nakedness: 28 beside those things that are without, that which cometh upon me daily, 29 ᵠ the care of all the churches. ʳ Who is weak, and I am not weak? Who is offended, and I burn not?
30 If I must needs glory, ˢ I will glory of the things which concern mine in-

27 perils among false brethren; in toil and hardship, in sleeplessness often, in hunger and thirst, in fastings often, in cold and nakedness. Apart from the things which I omit, there is that which comes upon me daily, 29 anxiety for all the churches. Who is weak, and I am not weak? Who is caused to stumble, and I do not 30 burn? If I must needs glory, I will glory of things which belong to my in-

o 6 : 5; Acts 20 : 31. p 1 Cor. 4 : 11.
r 1 Cor. 8 : 13; 9 : 22.
q See Acts 15 : 36, 41; 18 : 23; 20 : 18, etc.
s 12 : 5-10.

---

painfulness, *travail,* **hardship** (2 Thess. 3 : 8, the same words in the original); **in watchings often,** sleepless nights through anxiety, business, or suffering (Acts 17 : 10; 20 : 11, 31); **in hunger and thirst,** when traveling, in desert places, in poverty, and unable to obtain the necessities of life (1 Cor. 4 : 11; Phil. 4 : 12); **in fastings often,** voluntary self-denials in connection with prayer (6 : 5; 1 Cor. 9 : 27). Thus we have brought to view compulsory and voluntary fasting. **In cold and nakedness,** exposed to the cold of winter with scanty clothing. Absolute nakedness is not here meant, but a want of sufficient clothing. What a contrast to Jewish rabbis, who sought the best of everything (Matt. 8 : 20; 23 : 6).

28. The list could be extended; but Paul desists with a comprehensive summary of what remains. Beginning a new sentence he says, **Besides those things that are without,** rather, *Besides the things omitted,* in the preceding list, **that which cometh upon me daily, the care,** better, the *anxiety,* or *solicitude, for all the churches* I have planted. He felt his responsibility as an apostle and missionary. As our modern missionaries have a deep anxiety for the churches they have gathered, counseling, directing, and exercising a care for them, so it was with Paul (Gal. 2 : 7). His visits to them and his Epistles evince this, especially do his Epistles to the Galatians and the Corinthians. Another very ancient reading is, *there is to me the daily pressure, anxiety for all the churches.* This represents the Latin Vulgate and the most ancient Greek manuscripts of the fourth century. The other represents the Peshito Syriac version of the second century and some ancient manuscripts. I incline to this,

29. Paul briefly explains his care and anxiety. **Who is weak** among all my converts in the churches, **and I** (emphatic) **am not weak with him? Who is offended,** *is caused to stumble,* **and I** (emphatic) **burn not,** in pain with and for him. The word *burn* expresses strong feelings, here sympathetic pain or grief. He took upon himself their individual anxieties (Rom. 15 . 1). "The verse is very instructive and suggestive on vicarious sufferings" (GOULD. Comp. Matt. 8 : 17). How true Paul's words were, in his own experience, may be seen in such passages as 2 : 5-11; 1 Cor. 5 : 1; 6 : 1; 7 : 1; 8 : 1; 9 : 22; 10 : 33; Phil. 4 : 2, 3.

30. Paul, in conclusion, touches upon the nature of his boasting, so different from that of his opponents. **If I must needs glory,** if it is necessary as it appears to be, **I will glory of the things which concern mine infirmities,** pertaining to my weakness (12 : 5, 9; 13 : 9). Such weakness as that manifested in suffering, patience, endurance, sympathy, and self-sacrifice, stood out in bold contrast to the pretended strength and self-assertion of the false apostles who opposed him (ver. 20). These exhibitions of things belonging to his weakness he had already mentioned, and would also further speak of. In him was a living exemplification of the beatitudes (Matt. 5 : 1-12).

31. Having spoken of his sufferings, self-sacrifices, burdens, and intense sympathies for others, and his glorying in the things which pertaineth to his infirmities, he solemnly asserts their truthfulness. It was so different from the common glorying among men, that he may have felt that many would not appreciate his deep feelings, and would

31 firmities. **¹The God and Father of our Lord Jesus Christ,ᵘ which is blessed for** 32 **evermore, knoweth that I lie not. ˣIn Damascus the governor under Aretas the king kept the city of the Damascenes with a garrison, desirous to ap-** 33 **prehend me: and through a window in a basket was I let down by the wall, and escaped his hands.**

31 firmity. The God and Father of our Lord Jesus who is blessed forevermore, 32 knows that I lie not. In Damascus, the governor under Aretas the king kept guard over the city of the Damas- 33 cenes to arrest me: and through a window I was let down in a basket through the wall, and escaped his hands.

t 1 : 23; Rom. 1 : 9; Gal. 1 : 20; 1 Thess. 2 : 5.   u Rom. 9 : 5.   x Acts 9 : 24, 25.

listen to his words with astonishment or with doubt. **The God and Father of our Lord Jesus** (omit Christ) **who is blessed forevermore, knoweth that I lie not** in regard to the things of which I am speaking. This solemn affirmation is in keeping with the fervid character of the whole passage. It is thrown in somewhat independently after the manner of Paul, having reference to both what precedes and what follows. Compare similar affirmations (Rom. 9 : 1-4; Gal. 1 : 20; 1 Tim. 2 : 7).

32. He gives an instance of personal suffering and deliverance in his early ministry which is a sample of many others. Some think he began here a historical account of his sufferings, which for some reason he did not continue. **In Damascus,** situated at the base of the Anti-Lebanon mountains, one hundred and thirty-three miles northeast of Jerusalem and fifty miles east of the Mediterranean. (See note on Acts 9 : 2.) **The governor,** *the ethnarh,* or *ruler of a nation,* a title of a provincial governor. **Under Aretas, the king,** of Arabia Petræa, whose daughter had been divorced by Herod Antipas in order that he might marry Herodias, his brother Philip's wife (Matt. 14 : 3-5). It seems probable that in the changes following the death of the Emperor Tiberius, A. D 37, Aretas got possession of Damascus and held it a year or more till A. D. 38 or 39. (See Clark's "Harmonic Arrangement of the Acts," §§ 16, 17, notes, pp. 170, 174.) **Kept,** *was guarding,* **the city of the Damascenes, desirous to apprehend me.** In Acts 9 : 23, 24, we learn that the Jews plotted to kill Paul, and were watching the gates of the city day and night. They doubtless acted in concert with the guard of the governor. This made the escape of Paul the more difficult and the more wonderful. **Many** manuscripts omit **desirous.**

33. And through a window in a basket, made of ropes, **I was let down by,** *through* an opening in, **the wall and escaped his hands.** The house and wall were so connected that he might be said to be lowered in a basket through the window and through the wall. Perhaps the window belonged equally to the house and the wall (Comp. Josh. 2 : 15; 1 Sam. 19 : 12, and note on Acts 9 : 25.) Later, infidels ridiculed Paul as "a basket escaper." But the mode of his escape shows how great his danger, his helpless condition, and his great extremity. In these exhibitions of his weakness he gloried, for his deliverance was manifestly of the Lord.

PRACTICAL REMARKS.

1. Boasting in general is folly—the fruit of pride. But self-praise, when it accords with truth, is sometimes necessary for Christ and his cause (ver. 1; Acts 5 : 36; 2 Cor. 10 : 15).

2. The church, the "Lamb's wife," should be pure, having a converted and consecrated membership (ver. 2; Rev. 19 : 7; 21 : 9).

3. There is great danger that churches be led away from the simplicity and purity of Christ, in doctrine, in worship, and in practice and life (ver. 3; Jude 3; 1 Tim. 2 : 1-3, 8-10).

4. The way of salvation through Christ is as perfect as it can be, and any change in the gospel will be for the worse (ver. 4; 1 Cor. 3 : 11).

5. Paul's apostleship was pre-eminent in labors, sufferings, successes, and revelations (ver. 5, 23-28; 12 : 2-4).

6. In the apostleship of Paul we learn that God does not always follow a uniform order in calling men into the ministry (ver. 5; Luke 6 : 12; Gal. 1 : 1, 12).

7. Paul was pre-eminent in knowledge and spiritual attainments. His thirteen Epistles bear witness to this (ver. 6).

8. The sacrifices and unselfishness of devoted ministers are often misjudged (ver. 7-9; Rom. 15 : 3).

9. Ministers of the gospel are entitled to support; but under certain circumstances they may feel it a duty and privilege to preach without compensation (ver. 9-11; Luke 10 : 7; 1 Cor. 9 : 13-19).

10. Ministers should be specially careful in their money matters. They should guard against a grasping spirit for high positions and large salaries (ver. 10-12; 1 Tim. 3 : 4).

11. Selfishness, deceit, and crafty methods are characteristic of false preachers and impostors (ver. 13; 2 Peter 2 : 1-3).

12. Satan is a real person, possessing great power and practising skillful arts (ver. 14; 2 : 11; Rev. 12 : 9; 1 Peter 5 : 8).

13. True piety is deeper than outer appearances (ver. 13-15; 10 : 3-6; John 7 : 24).

14. It is a sad fact that Satan has some ministers among the followers of Christ (ver. 15; Rev. 2 : 9).

15. In speaking of ourselves we should exercise humility, care, and moderation (ver. 16; 12 : 5).

16. We may be in the spirit of Christ, though we may be compelled to act unlike Christ (ver. 17, 18).

17. Self-conceited people are very liable to be inconsistent in their treatment of others (ver. 19, 20).

18. A true man has no reason to be a coward. A man in the right can well exercise boldness (ver. 21; Prov. 28 : 1; 1 Thess. 2 : 2).

19. A good and noble ancestry is to be greatly prized; but a good character is of greater value (ver. 21, 22).

20. The preacher of the gospel should aim to be a true minister of Christ, not merely in name but also in deed; not alone in words, but in results (ver. 23).

21. Christianity has cost great sufferings. The blood of the martyrs has been the seed of the church (ver. 23-27).

22. How slight our trials, sufferings, and labors for Christ, as compared with Paul's (ver. 23-27).

23. What Paul endured proved not only his sincerity, but also his truthfulness in recording the facts which lie at the foundation of the Christian religion (ver. 23-27; 1 Cor. 15 : 1-8; Gal. 1 : 1).

24. Missionaries among the heathen have great responsibilities in connection with their converts and churches, as to matters of daily life, habits, order, and discipline (ver. 28, 29).

25. The preacher of the gospel should be a man of large sympathies, who can make the cares of others his own (ver. 29; Titus 1 : 8, 9).

26. It is the glory of the Christian religion that it takes hold of the weaknesses of men, and teaches sympathy with the joys and sorrows of the lowly (ver. 30, 31; 12 : 10).

27. The Christian is a true man, and in rich experiences can appeal to God for their truthfulness (ver. 31; Rom. 1 : 9).

28. There are times when it is proper to appeal to God in attesting our truthfulness (ver. 31; Heb. 6 : 17, 18).

29. The Christian should be willing to suffer for Christ (ver. 23-33; 1 Cor. 10 : 33; 11 : 1; 1 Peter 4 : 16).

30. "No man of the apostolic period had more thorough acquaintance with trials and sufferings than Paul; yet he says that 'the sufferings of this present time are not worthy to be compared with the glory which shall be revealed'" (PENDLETON). (Ver. 31-33; Rom. 8 : 18).

31. God knows how to deliver his people; yet we should use all proper means in our power, and not depend on God to do for us what we can do for ourselves (ver. 32, 33; Acts 23 : 17, ff.; 27 : 43, 44).

CHAPTER XII.

Continuing his defense, Paul shows his superiority to his opponents in the abundance of revelations given him (ver. 1-6), followed indeed with continued sufferings, but with a Divine promise of needed grace (ver. 7-10); and lastly he notices that they had compelled his boasting, and that the signs of his apostleship were wrought among them and ought to have secured their commendation (ver. 11-13). Paul now begins the conclusion of his Epistle by asserting that he will still act disinterestedly and honestly (ver. 14-18), and that his object is their reformation (ver. 19-21).

12 IT is not expedient for me doubtless to glory. I will come to ᵛ visions and
2 revelations of the Lord. I knew a man ᶻ in Christ above fourteen years ago, (whether in the body, I cannot tell; or whether out of the body, I cannot tell: God knoweth;) such an one caught up
3 to the third heaven. And I knew such a man, (whether in the body, or out of the body, I cannot tell: God knoweth;)
4 how that he was caught up into ᵇ paradise, and heard unspeakable words,

12 I MUST needs glory though it is not profitable; but I will come to visions and revelations of the Lord.
2 I know a man in Christ, fourteen years ago (whether in the body I know not, or whether out of the body I know not, God knows), such a one caught up even to the third heaven. And I know
3 such a man (whether in the body or apart from the body I know not,
4 God knows), that he was caught up into paradise, and heard unspeakable

y 11 : 16–30. z Num. 12 : 6 ; Ezek. 1 : 1 ; Acts 9 : 10 ; 22 : 17. a 5 : 17 ; Rom. 16 : 7 ; Gal. 1 : 22.
b Luke 23 : 43.

1-10. PAUL'S ABUNDANT REVELATIONS FOLLOWED BY TRIALS AND DIVINE ASSURANCES.

1. It is not expedient for me doubtless to glory. The Greek text here is confused. According to that now preferred by the highest authorities, it should read, *I must needs glory.* I am compelled to continue glorying by the conduct of others, *though it is not profitable,* it is not to my advantage, it adds nothing to my personal glory, it is dangerous also and distasteful to me, and I only do it from necessity in self-defense. So ceasing to give instances of great trials and deliverances, which he might have multiplied into a long catalogue, he turns away to supernatural experiences, directly from the Lord. *But* **I will come to visions and revelations of,** that is, *from,* **the Lord,** Jesus Christ. *Visions* are appearances seen, whether awake or asleep; *revelations* are mental and spiritual disclosures of facts, truths, and things to the soul, which may or may not be connected with and result from visions (Acts 16 : 9 ; 26 : 19 ; Gal. 1 : 12, 16 ; Eph. 3 : 3).

2. I knew a man in Christ, a Christian. Paul modestly speaks of himself in the third person. That he refers to himself is evident from verses five to seven, in which he makes the case his own and assumes that these revelations were made to himself. Translate, *I know a man who fourteen years ago (whether in the body, I know not, or whether out of the body,* in a disembodied state, *I know not, God knows).* He was certain of what he saw and heard, but he was doubtful whether the catching up was simply of the spirit, or of the whole man, body and spirit, that was known only to God. Such **a one caught up to,** *even to,* as far as, **the third heaven.** Some of the Jewish rabbins held that there were several heavens, some two, others as many as seven (Deut. 10 : 14). It does not appear that Paul speaks here according to either view, but that by the third heaven he means the highest heaven, the immediate and glorious presence of God (Heb. 9 : 11, 12, 24 ; Eph. 1 : 20 ; Heb. 4 : 14 ; 7 : 26). It was in A. D. 57 when Paul wrote this; and according to the Jewish mode of reckoning time the fourteen years take us back to A. D. 44, when Paul and Barnabas visited Jerusalem from Antioch (Acts 11 : 30 ; 12 : 25); or perhaps to Antioch after their return, when they were separated for apostolic and missionary work (Acts 13 : 3).

3, 4. The third verse repeats the idea of the second verse. **Such a man,** one in Christ and caught up even to the third heaven. **How that he was caught up into paradise,** the abode of the righteous dead until the resurrection (Luke 23 : 43 and note ; Rev. 2 : 7). Some have thought paradise a more exalted place than the third heaven, but this is not possible if the third heaven is the immediate presence of God. Others regard paradise and the third heaven one and the same. But the conjunction *And,* beginning the third verse, indicates a statement of an additional fact, and together with the prepositions *to* and *into (as far as,* the third heaven and *into* paradise) indicate that the terms are not identical. The conception appears to be of paradise being **lower** than the third heaven, but joining upon it. There is but one vision meant here; but it is the more definitely located in this verse. (Comp. Ezek. 3 : 14 ; 11 : 1 ; 43 : 5.) **And heard un-**

CH. XII.] II. CORINTHIANS 405

which it is not lawful for a man to utter.
5 Of such an one will I glory : *yet of myself I will not glory, but in mine
6 infirmities. For ᵈthough I would desire to glory, I shall not be a fool ; for I will say the truth ; but *now* I forbear, lest any man should think of me above that which he seeth me *to be*, or *that* he heareth of me.
7 And *lest I should be exalted above measure through the abundance of the revelations, there was given to me a ᶠthorn in the flesh, ᵍthe messenger of Satan to buffet me, lest I should be ex-

words, which it is not lawful for a man to utter.
5 On behalf of such a one I will glory ; but on my own behalf I will not glory,
6 save in my infirmities. For if I should desire to glory, I should not be foolish, for I should be speaking the truth ; but I forbear, lest any one should reckon of me above what he sees me to be, or
7 hears from me. And that I might not be exalted overmuch by the abundance of the revelations, there was given to me a thorn in the flesh, a messenger of Satan to buffet me, that I should not be exalted overmuch.

c 11 : 30.   d 10 : 8 ; 11 : 16.   e 1 Tim. 3 : 6.   *f* See refs. Num. 33 : 35 ; Gal. 4 : 13, 14.
g Job 2 : 7 ; Luke 13 : 16.

speakable words, not to be spoken on account of their sacredness, **which it is not lawful,** or *permitted to*, **a man to utter.** "There are some things in this world too low to be spoken of, and some things too high. You cannot discuss the latter without vulgarizing them" (F. W. ROBERTSON). The vision was intended for Paul, not for others. A like reticence was observed by Rev. Wm. Tennent (died at Freehold, N. J., 1777), who when a young man had a trance which lasted three days, during which time he said he heard "unutterable things." Such examples are in striking contrast to Mahomet and many others, who have given full details of the things they profess to have seen in their ecstasies.

5. Of such a one, who had been lifted out of himself, as it were, into this exalted condition, **will I glory; yet,** or *but*, **of myself** as I now am in my ordinary weak condition, **I will not glory** *except* **in my infirmities,** or *weaknesses* (11 : 30). In that extraordinary condition he was not his active, but passive self, wrought upon and glorified by God. Between such a one, and himself of every-day life and experience, he saw a marked distinction. While he might glory in the one, he could not in the other, save in those things which indicated weakness and humility. This was indeed a rebuke to the self-assertion and boasting of his opposers.

6. For though I would, rather, *should*, **desire to glory** respecting myself, as it is implied (in ver. 5) that I might glory, still **I shall not be a fool,** rather, *I should not be foolish, for I should speak* **the truth ;** what I say

will accord with fact. **But I forbear;** he refrains from this glorying because he would have no one overestimate him. **Lest any man should think of me,** estimate me, above that which **he seeth me to be, and that which he heareth of,** rather, *from*, **me.** He would have people judge of him by coming into personal contact, from seeing and hearing him, by his conduct, and the message and words he uttered.

7. Paul relates a humbling experience in which the grace of God was displayed in connection with his weakness. **And** in these circumstances as implied in the preceding verses, **lest I should be exalted above measure,** or *overmuch*, and become proud and boastful, **through the abundance of the revelations,** which I have spoken of (thus identifying the experiences of ver. 2–4 as his own), **there was given me a thorn,** *a sharp splinter*, **in my flesh,** or a *sharp stake* piercing my flesh, **a messenger of Satan,** perhaps with reference to Job's trial when Satan smote his flesh (Job 2 : 5, 7), **to buffet me,** to pierce and maltreat me, **lest I should be exalted** *overmuch*. The discipline and its purpose was of God, though Satan was permitted to act as the instrument. What this thorn or pointed stick was has been much discussed, but never definitely settled. From the statement that it was *in the flesh*, and that he was *buffeted* thereby, it is natural to infer that it was some physical malady, painful, like a continual *piercing* of the flesh with a thorn. Perhaps Paul refers to it in his Epistle to the Galatians by the "infirmity of the

8 alted above measure. *b* For this thing I besought the Lord thrice, that it
9 might depart from me. And he said unto me, *i* My grace is sufficient for thee; *k* for my strength is made perfect in weakness. Most gladly therefore *l* will I rather glory in my infirmities, *m* that the power of Christ may
10 rest upon me. Therefore *n* I take pleasure in infirmities, in reproaches, in necessities, in persecutions, in distresses *o* for Christ's sake: *p* for when I am weak, then am I strong.

8 Concerning this I besought the Lord thrice, that it might depart from me.
9 And he has said to me, My grace is sufficient for thee; for my power is made perfect in weakness. Most gladly therefore will I rather glory in my infirmities, that the power of Christ may abide on me.
10 Wherefore I take pleasure in infirmities, in reproaches, in necessities, in persecutions, in distresses for Christ's sake: for when I am weak, then I am powerful.

h See Deut. 3 : 23–27 ; Matt. 26 : 39–44. *i* 3 : 5 ; Isa. 43 : 2 ; 1 Cor. 10 : 13.
k Isa. 40 : 29–31 ; Phil. 4 : 13 ; Heb. 11 : 34. *l* 11 : 30. *m* 3 Peter 4 : 13, 14. *n* 7 : 4 ; Rom. 5 : 3.
o Matt. 5 : 11 ; 1 Cor. 4 : 10. *p* 13 : 4 ; Ps. 37 : 39 ; Hab. 3 : 17–19.

flesh" and the "temptation in the flesh" (Gal. 4 : 14), in which case it may have been some inflammation of the eyes (Gal. 4 : 15), brought on by exposure and fatigue in his travels in Asia Minor. And Gal. 6 : 11 may also contain a reference to this weakness of his eyes when he speaks of the "large letters he wrote with his own hand." The Corinthians probably knew what Paul meant, and it is enough for us to know that it was some trying and painful affliction.

8. For this thing, or *concerning this*, **I besought the Lord thrice,** at three different times in earnest pleadings (comp. our Lord's praying thrice in Gethsemane, Matt. 26 : 36–39), **that it,** the thorn, or according to some, *that he*, the messenger or angel of Satan, **might depart from me.** *Lord* here means Christ. In the answer (ver. 9) "my strength," or *power*, is promised, which Paul says is "the power of Christ." Like Stephen, Paul calls on the Lord Jesus (Acts 7 : 59; comp. Luke 23 : 42, 46). Such prayers as those of our Lord and of Paul were the cries of weak humanity, and perfectly right if made in submission to the Divine will.

9. Twice he prayed without an answer; the third time the answer came. **And he said to me,** more exactly, *and he hath said to me*, implying that the beneficent results of the answer still continued to him. How Christ said this we are not told, whether in a vision or through an inner voice. **My grace is sufficient for thee.** Leave all to me. My gracious favor imparted to thee will be enough. Even that which seems a hindrance will be made to thee a source of strength. For (introducing the reason why Christ's grace was enough) **my strength,** better, *my power*, **is made perfect in weakness,** it is developed and fostered by it in my disciple as it was in me (Heb. 5 : 7–9; comp. Rom. 5 : 3–5). Thus the Lord's power, exhibited in spiritual strength, is the most conspicuous in physical weakness. Christ gave him not what he asked, but what was better than he asked. **Most gladly therefore,** in view of this answer and its comforting assurances, this grace and its sufficiency, **will I rather glory in my infirmities that the power of Christ may rest,** *may abide*, **upon me,** literally, *may fix a tent over me;* that is, that the power of Christ may come down and dwell in me and pervade my whole being, working and giving me help. (Comp. John 1 : 14.) If he gloried in his own strength he could not receive power from Christ; but if by emphasizing his infirmities he gave God all the glory, then could the power of Christ have its abode upon him and be an ever-abiding force within him.

10. In this verse Paul gives one of his triumphant conclusions. **Therefore I take pleasure in infirmities,** in bodily weaknesses, **in reproaches,** or insults, **in necessities,** necessitous circumstances, **in persecutions, in distresses,** great straits (see on 6 : 4), **for Christ's sake.** All these things he endured in behalf of Christ, and for the promotion of his cause and glory. And for this reason: **For when I am weak,** in myself, **then am I strong,** rather, *powerful*, through Christ's power upon me and in me. I am powerful in enduring and overcoming. Paul was not merely re-

11 I am become a fool in glorying; ye have compelled me: for I ought to have been commended of you: for in nothing am I behind the very chiefest 12 apostles, though I be nothing. Truly the signs of an apostle were wrought among you in all patience, in signs, 13 and wonders, and mighty deeds. For what is it wherein ye were inferior to other churches, except *it be* that I myself was not burdensome to you? forgive me this wrong.

11 I have become foolish; ye compelled me. For I ought to have been commended by you; for in nothing was I behind these pre-eminent apostles, 12 though I am nothing. Truly the signs of an apostle were wrought among you in all patience, by signs, and 13 wonders, and miracles. For what is there, wherein ye were made inferior to the rest of the churches, except that I myself was not a charge to you? Forgive me this wrong.

q 11 : 1, 16, 17.   r 11 : 5 ; Gal. 2 : 6–14.   s 1 Cor. 15 : 8, 9 ; Eph. 3 : 8.
t 6 : 4–10 ; Rom. 15 : 18, 19 ; 1 Cor. 9 : 2.   u 11 : 8, 9.   x 11 : 7.

signed to sufferings, e n j o y i n g the peaceful fruits of resignation; but he also took pleasure in trials, because Christ was glorified thereby, and thus partook of the higher joys of Christ's glory and victorious work (Rom. 7 : 24, 25).

11-13. THEY HAD COMPELLED HIS BOASTING, THOUGH THE SIGNS OF HIS APOSTLESHIP WERE AMONG THEM.

11. Paul is now drawing to the close of his long, animated self-defense, and as he looks over what he had written, he says, **I am become a fool,** better, *I have become foolish*, in thus glorying. The meaning is expressed by the words, **in glorying,** but they are wanting in the best manuscripts. But his apology is, **ye have compelled me,** by your misjudgments of me and your conduct toward me, and the consequent spiritual danger to yourselves. In other words, the blame is not mine, but yours. **For,** instead of being compelled to defend myself, **I ought to have been commended by you.** Both *I* and *you* are emphatic. They had had abundant evidences of his apostleship; **for in nothing am I,** rather, *was I*, **behind the very chiefest apostles,** *the most eminent apostles* (see on 11 : 5), when I was among you, **though I be nothing** in myself (1 Cor. 15 : 8–10).

12. But though Paul speaks most humbly of himself, yet the grace of God had wrought mightily through him. **Truly the signs of an apostle,** of one who is truly such, **were wrought among you in all patience,** endurance, steadfastness, **in,** or *by,* **signs, wonders, and mighty deeds.** The three words in the original are those which denote miracles; see "Notes on Matthew," introductory note to chapter 8. Paul brings to view two kinds of evidences of his apostleship, his endurance for Christ's sake which was inward, and the miracles which were the outward credential of his mission from C h r i s t. And these two were united in him; and both were essential—the signs and the spirit in which they were wrought. Notice he does not say "I endured," for that was of grace, nor "I wrought," for that was of God.

13. And to justify what he had just said, and to answer every objection, he asks, **For what is it wherein ye were made i n f e r i o r to other churches,** in comparison with *the rest of the churches,* **except that I myself was not burdensome to you?** He had not done less work, nor performed less miracles, among them than among others. The only possible disparagement of them was that he had not been chargeable to them, which was his right (1 Cor. 9 : 1-6). In this respect they had indeed been made inferior to the other churches. He had treated them as poor, unable, or unwilling. And this receiving pay, it would seem, had been made by his opponents one of the signs of an apostle. He had done wrong in their eyes, and it had really been productive of some wrong among them, while the apostle had done it with good intentions and for good reasons (11 : 7, ff.). It was a small matter, and he already had justified his conduct (11 : 11, 12). Yet he adds, doubtless in gentle irony, **f o r g i v e me this wrong,** *this injustice,* whatever there may have been, in doing you such a favor as preaching to you the gospel for nothing.

14-21. WILL STILL CONTINUE TO ACT DISINTERESTEDLY AND HONESTLY; HIS OBJECT THEIR REFORMATION.

Concluding exhortations, warnings, and salutations.

14 ʸBehold, the third time I am ready to come to you; and I will not be burdensome to you; for ᶻI seek not yours, but you: ᵃfor the children ought not to lay up for the parents, but the
15 parents for the children. And ᵇI will very gladly spend and be spent ᶜfor you [*Greek*, your souls]: though ᵈthe more abundantly I love you, the less I be loved.
16 But be it so, ᵉI did not burden you: nevertheless, being crafty, I caught

14 Behold, this is the third time I am ready to come to you; and I will not be a charge to you; for I seek not yours, but you: for the children ought not to lay up for the parents, but the
15 parents for the children. And I will most gladly spend and be spent for your souls; if I love you more abundantly, am I to be loved the less?
16 But be it so, I was not myself a charge to you; but yet, being crafty, I caught

y 1. 15-18, 23; 13 : 1; 1 Cor. 16. 5-7.   z Acts 20 : 33; 1 Cor. 10 : 33; 1 Thess. 2 : 19, 20; 1 Peter 5 : 2-4.
a Prov. 13 : 22; 1 Tim. 5 : 8.   b Phil. 2 . 17; 1 Thess. 2 : 8.   c 7 : 3; John 10 : 10, 11; 2 Tim. 2 : 10.
d 6 : 12, 13.   e 11 : 9.

14. Paul here begins the conclusion of the Epistle. **Behold,** *this is* **the third time I am ready to come to you.** Some take this to mean the third intention of his coming, having been but once before, and that his intention had not been carried out but once (1 : 15-17). But the most natural meaning is that he had visited Corinth twice before, and this is confirmed by 13 : 1. When his second visit occurred we do not know. It must have been before he wrote the lost Epistle mentioned in 1 Cor. 5 : 9, possibly during the first eighteen months of his residence at Ephesus. But it seems to me better to suppose that a period of two or three months elapsed between the eleventh and twelfth verses of the eighteenth chapter of the Acts (on which see notes), when Paul left Corinth to go into Macedonia by way of Athens; but not completing his intended journey he comes back to Corinth a second time. (Comp. 1 Thess. 2 : 17, 18; 3 : 1.) This would make Acts 18 : 12-18 descriptive of his second visit. Confirmatory of this is the probability that this visit occurred before the coming of Apollos to Corinth (Acts 19 : 1; 1 Cor. 3 : 6). Paul was probably at Corinth in A. D. 55; and from the First Epistle to the Corinthians we can hardly suppose that he and Apollos were there at the same time, or that he came there after Apollos. So this second visit would come before he came to Ephesus on his third journey (Acts 19 : 1). (See this more fully discussed in "Clark's Harmonic Arrangement of the Acts," pp 216-218.) **And I will not be burdensome,** *a charge,* **to you,** as he had not been on his two previous visits (11 : 9). He proposed to continue the exercise of this disinterested affection. And the reason he gives: **For I seek not yours,** your money and your praise, **but you,** your souls for Christ, your salvation through him. And he justifies this conduct from the relation of parents to children, and the duty of the former to the latter. Not the children should lay up for their parents, **but the parents for the children.** The Corinthians were his spiritual children (1 Cor. 4 : 15); and he was laying up for them the spiritual treasures of the unsearchable riches of Christ's kingdom (Eph. 2 : 7; 3 : 6; Rom. 11 : 33).

15. And it was a matter of joy to Paul to do this. **And I will very gladly,** that is, *most gladly,* **spend** whatever I have **and be spent** *wholly,* time, strength, and even life itself, be *utterly worn out,* **for you,** rather, *for your souls.* Most gladly would he consecrate his money, strength, and life for their salvation. The rest of this verse is a question, according to the most approved text: *If I love you more abundantly, am I to be loved the less?* Am I to be misjudged and censured as some of you have done? and thus be less esteemed and loved? The implied answer is, By no means; but you should be loved the more. This passage shows how intense was Paul's affection for his converts, and how he yearned for their love.

16. But be it so, you may say; let it be regarded as a settled fact. I have made out my case. **I did not** *myself* **burden you.** You admit that it was all right. Nevertheless, or

17 you with guile. *Did I make a gain of you by any of them whom I sent unto 18 you? *I desired Titus, and with *him* I sent a *brother. Did Titus make a gain of you? Walked we not in the same spirit? *Walked we* not in the same steps?
19 *Again, think ye that we excuse ourselves unto you? *We speak before God in Christ: *but *we do* all things, 20 dearly beloved, for your edifying. For I fear lest, when I come, I shall not find you such as I would, and *that* *I* shall be found unto you such as ye would not: lest *there be* debates, envy-

17 you with guile. Did I make gain of you, through any of those whom I 18 have sent to you? I exhorted Titus [to go], and sent with him the brother. Did Titus make gain of you? Did we not walk in the same spirit; did we not in the same steps?
19 Do ye all this time suppose that we are excusing ourselves to you? Before God in Christ we are speaking; and all, beloved, for building you up. 20 For I fear, lest perhaps, when I come, I should find you not such as I wish, and that I too should be found by you such as ye wish not; lest there should

f 7 : 2.   *g* 8 : 6, 16, 22.   *h* 8 : 18.
i 10 : 8 ; 1 Cor. 10 : 33.

i 5 : 12.   *k* 11 : 31 ; Rom. 9 : 1.
m 13 : 2, 10 ; 1 Cor. 4 : 21.

But, some one may think and perhaps say, **being crafty,** *cunning*, **I caught you with guile**, by artifice and deceit, making gain of you through others; implying perhaps, getting money under pretext of a collection for the poor saints at Jerusalem. Paul is not describing his own course of conduct; but referring to a possible insinuation of his adversaries, which he proceeds in the next verse to refute. This was a perfectly natural suggestion for a suspicious, worldly-minded Christian professor to make, one who had some dislike to Paul, and who could not appreciate his self-sacrificing spirit and disinterested love.

17. Paul appeals to the conduct of Titus and his companions at Corinth, as a refutation of a possible charge that he had sought in an underhanded way to obtain money of the Corinthians. **Did I make a gain of you,** *take advantage of you*, **by any of them whom I have sent unto you?** Did I through them get money or any personal advantage of you? The question requires a negative answer.

18. I desired, rather, *exhorted*, **Titus** to go, **and with him sent a,** literally, *the*, **brother** (8 : 18-22). **Did Titus make a gain of you?** did he overreach and take advantage? **Walked we not in the same spirit** of self-sacrifice and disinterested love? **Walked we not in the same steps,** showing the same unselfish conduct? Both of these questions imply an affirmative answer. Paul appeals to facts which were unanswerable. The conduct of Paul and his messengers was in perfect accord. The brother spoken of was doubtless one well known to the Corinthians. Titus had just returned from a visit to them, reporting their penitence (7 : 6).

19. Paul has concluded his defense of himself. He now guards them from supposing that he stood before them in judgment, or that they were his judges. **Again,** or according to the preferable text, *Have ye long been thinking that we are excusing*, justifying, *ourselves to you?* Have you all the time that I have been defending myself supposed that I was at all accountable to you, and that our own reputation was the chief thought in our minds? Most solemnly does he correct any such erroneous idea. **We speak before God in Christ.** It is in the presence of God, who is his judge, that he as a Christian in fellowship with Christ speaks these things. He had not been writing in a human, selfish spirit, but as one spiritually united with Christ. (Comp. 1 : 18, 23 ; 2 : 17.) **But we do,** or *speak*, **all things for your edifying,** for your good and *for building you up* in your Christian faith and life. His defense had not been for personal and selfish ends; it was not for his own reputation, but for their spiritual upbuilding.

20. This verse is confirmatory of the preceding. There is much need that I do this for your edification. **For I fear lest** *possibly* **when I come I shall not find you such as I would,** but such as are described in the latter part of this verse; **and that I shall be found unto you such as ye would not,** an apostle of Christ exercising apostolic authority, as described in the next verse. **Lest there be debates,** rather,

ings, wraths, strifes, backbitings, whis-
21 perings, swellings, tumults: *and lest, when I come again, my God ⁿ will humble me among you, and that I shall bewail many ᵒ which have sinned already, and have not repented of the uncleanness and ᵖ fornication and lasciviousness which they have committed.

be strifes, jealousy, wraths, party spirit, backbitings, whisperings, swellings,
21 tumults; lest, when I come again, my God should humble me before you, and I should mourn for many of those who have sinned before, and repented not of the uncleanness, and fornication, and wantonness, which they practiced.

n 2 : 1–4 ; Phil. 3 : 18, 19.   o 13 : 2.   p 1 Cor. 5 : 1.

strifes; **envyings**, jealousy; **wrath**, angry passions; **strifes**, party spirit; **backbitings**, defamation ; **whisperings**, secret slanders; **swellings**, puffings up of soul ; **tumults**, disturbances and disorders. What a terrible condition among these Corinthian converts do these words describe as to their conduct and their relation one to another (1 Cor. 1 : 11).

21. I fear (ver. 20) **lest when I come again**, my God (recognizing God's close personal relation to myself in this matter) *should* **humble me before you**, should make me blush and suffer mortification in respect to your impurities. The apostle felt that there was enough possibility of this to make him anxious, and that too among those who had professed conversion under his ministry. **And that I** *should* **bewail** *many of those who have sinned before*, **and have not repented of the uncleanness and fornication and lasciviousness,** licentiousness, **which they have committed,** or *practised.* The sins of impurity connected with their private lives are here distinguished from those sins mentioned in the preceding verse. These sins of sensuality show the influence of Corinthian morals upon the Corinthian church; and they appear to have been common (1 Cor. 5 : 1 ; 6 : 12–20), and some had not repented. The apostle was willing to forgive offenders when they had abandoned their sin. But if any should be made the subject of church discipline and excluded, it would be a ground of sorrow to the apostle ; and he would mourn for them if he should be compelled to exercise apostolic authority in the matter (1 Cor. 5 : 3–7 ; 2 Cor. 7 : 8). The apostle hoped that those who had sinned *before* his writing would, after his letters were received, repent of their sins before his coming among them.

PRACTICAL REMARKS.

1. It is always safe to glory in what Christ has done for us (ver. 1 ; Gal. 6 : 11).

2. Paul believed that the soul is the man, and that it can act apart from the body (ver. 2, 4 ; Phil. 1 : 20–23).

3. We can learn much of the future life and of heaven from the Scriptures. Yet let us beware against being wise beyond what is written (ver. 2–4 ; 5 : 1–4 ; Rev. 21 : 1, ff. ; Deut. 29 : 29).

4. There is a conscious state between death and the resurrection (ver. 4 ; 5 : 8 ; Luke 23 : 43).

5. We may well glory in infirmities when they bring us great blessings, and draw us nearer to Christ (ver. 5 ; Col. 1 : 24 ; Phil. 3 : 10).

6. If Christ gives us special favors of his presence and spirit, we should give him corresponding honor in our lives. And we should be willing to be judged by our fellow-men according to our conduct, rather than any real or supposed revelations that we have enjoyed (ver. 6 ; Acts 20 : 18, 35).

7. Christians are in special danger of spiritual pride, and must guard against it. One of the designs of afflictions is to produce humility (ver. 7 ; 1 Tim. 3 : 6 ; 1 Peter 5 : 5–7 ; Dan. 6 : 20–23).

8. We should bring all our trials and afflictions to the Lord earnestly yet submissively (ver. 8 ; 2 Sam. 12 : 16–20 ; Mark 14 : 32–41).

9. The Lord answers prayer, but often in his own way, which is better than ours (ver. 9 ; Deut. 3 : 23–27 ; Job 42 : 1–6).

10. Christians are not losers but rather gainers through trials ; they may well rejoice (ver. 10 ; Rom. 5 : 3–5).

11. Humility is an ornament to the greatest saint (ver. 11, 12 ; Col. 3 : 12 ; 1 Peter 5 : 5).

13 THIS is *q* the third *time* I am coming to you. *r* In the mouth of two or three witnesses shall every word be estab-
2 lished. *s* I told you before, and foretell

13 THIS is the third time I am coming to you. At the mouth of two witnesses, and of three, shall every word
2 be established. I have before said,

q 12 : 14. *r* See refs. Deut. 17 : 6. *s* 10 : 2 ; 1 Cor. 4 : 19-21.

12. How painful to many a pastor's heart are the misjudgments of his hearers, and their lack of appreciation of his self-denying love (ver. 11, 15).

13. Those for whom we do the greatest kindness sometimes appreciate it the least (ver. 13).

14. While ministers of Christ can claim a competent support, their great object should be the present and final salvation of their hearers (ver. 14; Acts 20 : 33 ; John 10 : 11 ; 1 Cor. 10 : 33).

15. The faithful minister deserves the deepest love of his people. Yet even though he receive ingratitude, he should gladly employ his time and strength for their souls in obedience to Christ (ver. 15).

16. The best of men are exposed to slanders and evil surmisings (ver. 16 ; Matt. 10 : 24, 25).

17. It becomes ministers to be very careful in their financial matters (ver. 17, 18 ; 1 Cor. 16 : 3, 4).

18. It should be the aim of the Christian always to live in the full consciousness of doing right (ver. 18 ; Acts 23 : 1).

19. The minister should be frank and honest, laboring unselfishly for Christ and his cause (ver. 19 ; 5 : 13, 14).

20. Open and private sins, such as Paul names, deserve the severest penalties of church discipline (ver. 20, 21 ; 1 Cor. 5 : 4-7 ; 6 : 16-18).

21. It is a joy to the pastor to have his converts walk in the truth ; but it is a cause of deep sorrow to see them turn back into sin (ver. 21 ; Phil. 3 : 18, 19 ; 3 John 4).

22. Exclusion from the church should be inflicted in obedience to Christ, for the good of the church, in a spirit of sorrow and of love, and in prayer for the repentance of the offender (ver. 20, 21 ; 13 : 1-3 ; Matt. 18 : 17 ; 1 Cor. 5 : 4 ; 2 Cor. 2 : 5-8).

CHAPTER XIII.

Paul continues to dwell upon his apostolic conduct which he proposes to exercise toward them. When he comes he will enforce discipline (ver. 1-4) ; he exhorts them to self-examination (ver. 5, 6) ; prays for their perfection (ver. 7-9), and writes now in order to avoid severity when he comes (ver. 10). He concludes with exhortations, salutation, and an invocation (ver. 11-14).

1-10. THE EXERCISE OF HIS APOSTOLIC AUTHORITY AT HIS THIRD COMING TO CORINTH. Discipline will be enforced. Hence they should examine themselves ; and he prays that they may stand the test.

1. Paul affirms the certainty of his coming. This is closely connected with the preceding chapter. **This is the third time I am coming to you.** The language is positive, and implies that he had visited Corinth twice before. The second visit is not definitely referred to in the Acts. (See note on 12 : 14.) **In the mouth,** upon the oral testimony, **of two or three witnesses,** *of two witnesses and of three,* **shall every word be established.** This is quoted from Deut. 19 : 15. His two previous visits, with his own testimonies and warnings, were like two witnesses ; and his third visit would be the confirming evidence of the preceding. This has been the usual interpretation. But Meyer and some others understand that Paul proposes at his next visit to resort to the strictest legal proceedings. The usual interpretation seems to be the preferable one. His several visits were indeed repeated testimonies to the truth and against offenses and were suggestive of this Scripture, and were illustrated by it. Yet the language implies that he would proceed to the discipline of offenders. Not that he would do it alone, for this power belonged ordinarily to the church (Matt. 18 : 16 ; 1 Cor. 5 : 12, 13), and even in the exercise of apostolic authority he did not act altogether independently of the church (1 Cor. 5 : 3-5).

2. His repeated visits were not only in the nature of testimonies to them for the truth, but also as arguments for their obedience. **I told you before,** during my second visit, **and** *now* **fore-**

you, as if I were present, the second time ; and being absent now I write to them which heretofore have sinned, and to all other, that, if I come again,
3 I will not spare: since ye seek a proof of Christ *speaking in me, which to you-ward is not weak, but is ᵘ mighty
4 in you. ˣ For though he was crucified through weakness, yet ʸ he liveth by the power of God ; for ᶻ we also are weak in him, ᵃ but we shall live with him by the power of God toward you.
5 ᵇ Examine yourselves, whether ye be

and now say beforehand, as when I was present the second time, so also now being absent, to those who heretofore have sinned, and to all the rest, that if I come again I will not spare ;
3 since ye seek a proof of Christ who is speaking in me, who toward you is not
4 weak, but is powerful in you. For he was crucified through weakness, yet he lives through the power of God. For we also are weak in him, but we shall live with him through the power
5 of God toward you. Try your own selves, whether ye are in the faith ;

t Matt. 10 : 20 ; 1 Cor. 5 : 4 ; 9 : 1, 2.   *u* 12 : 12.   *x* Phil. 2 : 7, 8 ; 1 Peter 3 : 18.   *y* Eph. 1 : 19, 20.
z See 4 : 7–12 ; 10 : 3, 4.   *a* Rom. 6 : 8–11 ; 2 Tim. 2 : 11, 12.   *b* See refs. 1 Cor. 11 : 28.

tell you, as if, rather, *as when I was,* **present the second time,** *even now* **being absent I write to them who heretofore have sinned** (the same words translated *sinned, already* or *before,* in 12 : 21), **and to all** *the others,* all the other members of the church who might need warning on account of danger from, or some connection with those who had sinned, or who needed exhortation to firmness and obedience (1 : 23, 24) ; **that if I come again I will not spare,** I will not be lenient as in my second visit, but will see that discipline is faithfully exercised. His indulgence had led some to charge him with vacillation and weakness (10 : 1, 10) ; but now he assures the whole church that at his next coming he will act with firmness. The words, **I write,** are wanting in the most approved text and should be omitted.

3. This verse is closely connected with the preceding. It justifies and gives a reason for what Paul had just declared : *I will not spare,* **since ye seek a,** *the,* **proof of Christ speaking in me**—since ye seek a proof of the power of the indwelling Christ who speaks in and through me, ye shall have a **full proof of it.** On *proof,* see on 2 : 9 ; comp. Acts 13 : 9–11. Paul conceives of himself as in a living union with Christ, who dwells in him and exerts his power through him. **Which,** *who,* **to you-ward is not weak,** in gifts and miracles, in correcting and punishing, **but is mighty in you,** powerful in inflicting punishment on those who remain impenitent. Some of them had by their conduct challenged, as it were, his apostolic authority and the power of Christ in him. It was dangerous, Paul intimates, thus to provoke Christ, who spoke through him, whose power was also in the church and among them for exercising discipline and punishing offenders (Matt. 18 : 20).

4. According to the best text, **though** should be omitted. Translate : *For* to confirm what I have said regarding Christ's power, *he was also* **crucified through weakness,** having emptied himself of his glory and voluntarily assumed our human nature with all of its infirmities (8 : 9 ; Phil. 2 : 7, 8 ; Heb. 2 : 9, 10, 17, 18) ; *yet he lives through the power of God,* having been raised from the dead and exalted to glory by Divine power where he ever liveth (Phil. 2 : 9, 10 ; Rom. 1 : 3, 4 ; Eph. 1 : 20–22). **For,** to give a reason and to illustrate, **we also are weak in him,** in the same manner as he was, weak and forbearing, having voluntarily laid aside our power in sparing you ; **but we shall live with him** in the same manner as he lived, **by,** or *through,* **the power of God toward you,** when we come among you (ver. 3). It will be evident to the Corinthians that the power of God is working in and through the apostle. Notice how he identifies himself with Christ, **in him,** *with him,* both in his weakness and in his strength. (Comp. 4 : 10–12 ; 10 : 4–6 ; Gal. 6 : 17 ; 1 Cor. 1 : 18.) He had indeed been weak among them, but upon his coming again he would assume such authority and power as comes from a union with and as conferred by the risen and glorified Christ.

5. Instead of testing and proving me to see whether Christ is in me, **examine,** *try,* test, **yourselves** (emphatic), **whether ye be,** rather, *are,*

CH. XIII.] II. CORINTHIANS 413

6 in the faith; prove your own selves. ᶜKnow ye not your own selves, ᵈ how that Jesus Christ is in you, except ye be *reprobates? But I trust that ye shall know that we are not reprobates.
7 Now I pray to God that ye do no evil; not that we should appear approved, but that ye should do that which is ᶠhonest, though ᵍwe be as reprobates.
8 For we can do nothing against the
9 truth, but for the truth. For we are

6 prove your own selves. Or know ye not your own selves, that Jesus Christ is in you, unless ye are reprobate indeed. But I hope that ye will know, that we are not reprobate.
7 Now we pray to God that ye do no evil; not that we should appear approved, but that ye may do what is
8 good, though we be as reprobate. For we have no power against the truth,
9 but for the truth. For we rejoice,

ᶜ 1 John 3 : 14, 19, 24.   ᵈ 6 : 16; John 6 : 56; Rom. 8 : 10; Gal. 2 : 20.   ᵉ 1 Cor. 9 : 27.
ᶠ Rom. 12 : 17.   ᵍ 1 Cor. 4 : 9-13.

in the faith, whether you are actually united to Christ by a living faith, whether you are true Christians or not. Not only try yourselves, but as a result of the trial, **prove yourselves,** make it plain in your own consciousness and by your fruits as to whether Christ is in you. **Know ye not,** rather, *Or,* if you hesitate about doing this, *know ye not as to your own selves,* **that Jesus Christ is in you,** by the indwelling of the Holy Spirit, **except ye be reprobates,** *unless ye are reprobate indeed,* unable to stand the test, and thus shown to be hypocrites, mere pretenders. But such a supposition is not to be thought of, either by him or by them. The word translated *reprobates,* means those not approved, descriptive of those who have been tried and found wanting, and hence *rejected* (1 Cor. 9 : 27). The thought of the apostle here is: If ye prove your true discipleship, then you will prove that I, who taught you, am a true apostle. If you are not spurious Christians we are not spurious apostles. (Comp. 3 : 2; 1 Cor. 9 : 2.)

6. But whatever may be the result of your trying and testing yourselves, **I trust,** I cherish the hope, **that ye shall know that we are not reprobates,** *unable to stand the proof* of our apostleship, when we were among you, but able to give the evidence of Christ speaking in and through us, and thus entitled to the apostolic authority that we claim. *We,* is emphatic. Paul contrasts the testimony of their Christian character and the testing of his apostolic authority. In any case he believes the latter will stand.

7. The apostle prays that the Corinthians may be directed aright, so that there will be no need of exercising authority in severity (ver. 4). In this he has no selfish ends, but their good.

Now I pray, according to the best text, *we pray,* first negatively, **that ye do no evil,** individually and as a church in these matters, obtaining a complete victory over whatever is wrong, **not that we should appear approved,** not for any personal ends of our own. *Approved,* having stood the test, the opposite of *reprobate.* **But,** we pray in the second place positively, **that ye should,** rather, *may do* or practise, **that which is honest,** *good, honorable,* **though we be as reprobates,** *though we be apparently unable to stand the proof.* The apostle wishes the Corinthians to do what is right in the sight of God, even though he himself should appear unapproved in the judgment of men. He would sacrifice his own reputation for their good. (Comp. Rom. 9 : 1-3.)

8. Reason and explanation of Paul's aim as just expressed. **For we can do nothing,** more exactly, *For we have no power,* of Christ speaking in and through us (ver. 3), no apostolic power, **against the truth** of the gospel, **but for,** *in behalf of,* **the truth,** in its spread and furtherance. Paul had been speaking of the *power* which he had received from Christ; and the *truth* is that which is brought to view and embodied in the gospel. He had not received this power to exercise in his own interests against the truth, but only in its behalf for the glory of God. Hence the discipline of the church is valid only as it is in accordance with the truth. Whatever it binds on earth is not bound in heaven, if contrary to the truth.

9. The assertion of the preceding verse confirmed by the subjects of the apostle's joy and prayer. **For,** in accordance with these principles and motions, **we are glad,** better, *we rejoice,*

glad, *b when we are* **weak**, and ye are strong: and this also we wish, [*even* 10 *your perfection.* *k* Therefore I write these things being absent, lest being present I should use sharpness, *l according to the power which the Lord hath given* me *to edification, and not to destruction.*

11 Finally, brethren, farewell. *m* Be perfect, *n* be of good comfort, *o* be of one mind, *p* live in peace; and the God of love *q* and peace shall be with you.

when we are weak, and ye are powerful; this also we pray for, even your
10 perfection. For this cause I write these things while absent, that when present I may not deal sharply according to the authority which the Lord gave me for building up, and not casting down.
11 Finally, brethren, farewell. Be perfect, be of good comfort, be of the same mind, be at peace; and the God of love and peace will be with you.

h 1 Cor. 4 : 10.   *i* Phil. 3 : 12-15; Heb. 6 : 1; 13 : 20, 21.   *k* 12 : 20. 21.   *l* 10 : 8.   *m* See refs. Matt. 5 : 48.
n 2 Thess. 2 : 16, 17.   *o* See refs. Rom. 12 : 16.   *p* Gen. 45 : 24; Rom. 12 : 18.   *q* Rom. 15 : 33.

when we are weak, seeming to be weak, having no occasion to exercise our power in the exercise of discipline, **and ye are strong** in Christian graces, *powerful* in piety, requiring no exercise of our authority. Paul does not say that the Corinthians are really strong, but that he rejoices when they are strong. **And this,** that ye may be strong, **we also wish,** better, *pray for,* **even your perfection,** your complete reformation, the *perfecting,* the *complete setting in order,* of Christian conduct and life. (Comp. 1 Cor. 1 : 10; Gal. 6 : 1; Eph. 4 : 12.) In that case there would be no need of giving proof of his apostolic authority in reference to offenders, and in discipline (ver. 3).

10. Therefore, or *On this account,* because I wish you to become strong in piety and perfected in conduct and life, **I write these things,** this Epistle, especially the last part of it, **being absent, lest being present, I should use sharpness** (ver. 2; 1 : 23), that when present I may not use severity, **according to the power,** or *authority which the Lord gave me* when he called and commissioned me as an apostle (Acts 26 : 16-18), *for* **edification,** *building up,* **and not for destruction,** *casting down* (10 : 8), such as might result from discipline and judgment. He uses this severity in writing, hoping to accomplish their reformation, so that he will have no necessity to use it when he comes. And he did not wish to do anything when he came which might appear like casting out converts or pulling down churches. Paul uses his favorite figure of a builder (5 : 1; 1 Cor. 3 : 10). His great work was to gather and build up converts and churches. Discipline and punishment were at times a necessity (which should be exercised for the good of the individual and the church); but as with the Lord, it was not the object of his work (John 3 : 17; 12 : 47).

11-14. CLOSING WORDS.

11. Closing exhortation. The kind and tender spirit which had begun to show itself in the preceding verses, is now more prominently manifested in friendly admonition, which, if fully obeyed, would make the exercise of severe measures unnecessary. **Finally,** as to what remains to be said, **brethren,** used only four times in this Epistle, indicating here the importance of what he was saying, and the affectionate spirit in which he spoke; **farewell,** *joy to you, fare you well* in the Lord (Phil. 3 : 1; 4 : 4). It was common to use this word at the beginning of letters in the sense of *greeting* (Acts 15 : 23; 23 : 26), and in salutations in the sense of *hail* (Luke 1 : 28; Mark 15 : 18). It is fitting here in the beginning of closing and encouraging words. **Be perfect,** go on in perfecting your conduct and life (ver. 9); **be of good comfort,** combining the ideas of encouragement and comfort; **be of one mind,** think as it were the same thing, be harmonious in thought and sentiment (Rom. 12 : 16; Phil. 2 : 2); **live in peace** with one another, let there be no discord (1 Cor. 1 : 10); **and the God of love and peace,** who is the author and giver of these graces (1 Cor. 14 : 33; Heb. 13 : 20; Jude 2), **shall be with you**—you shall enjoy communion with God through the Holy Spirit, and shall be kept continually united in love and peace. Joy, comfort, peace, and love are all fruits of the Spirit (Gal. 5 : 22). If they follow the promptings of the Spirit, which accord

12 *Greet one another with an holy kiss.
13 All the saints salute you.
14 *The *grace of the Lord Jesus Christ, and the love of God, and *the communion of the Holy Ghost, be with you all. Amen.

The second *Epistle* to the Corinthians was written from Philippi, *a city* of Macedonia, by Titus and Lucas.

12 Salute one another with a holy kiss.
13 All the saints salute you.
14 The grace of the Lord Jesus Christ, and the love of God, and the communion of the Holy Spirit, be with you all.

r See refs. Rom. 16 : 16.   *s* See Num. 6 : 23–27 ; Rom. 16 : 24.   *t* John 1 : 16, 17.   *u* Rom. 8 : 9, 14–16.

with the preceding exhortations, then they have the promise and assurance that the God of love and peace will be, and continue to be, with them. All of the preceding imperatives are in the present tense, denoting **continued** action. God's presence produces love and peace, and we must have love and peace to enjoy his presence. Hatred and discord will drive the Spirit from us. The exhortation in all its parts was especially suited to the Corinthians.

12. Closing salutations. **Greet**, or, *salute*, **one another with a holy kiss.** The same as in 1 Cor. 16 : 20, on which see note. If on reading the Epistle they would thus express their brotherly love for one another the effect would be good.

13. **All the saints**, in the vicinity and the church where he was in Macedonia, **salute you.** Doubtless Paul, in a measure at least, unburdened his heart to his brethren in Macedonia, and made known his anxieties to them. Their interest and love would be kindled by Paul's.

14. Closing benediction. This is the fullest of Paul's benedictions and comes fitly at the end of the Epistle in which he the most fully opens and unburdens his heart. It is rather an invocation, since its closing words are in the form of a prayer, and not of a blessing. In its three parts it recognizes the personality and deity of the Father, the Son, and the Holy Spirit in their gracious relations to the believer and the church. (Comp. note on Rom. 1 : 7.) **The grace**, or *favor*, **of our Lord Jesus Christ** (notice the fullness of the title), the Lord and head of the church, through whom all the blessing of salvation reaches us, **the love of God** the Father, the author and source of redemption (John 3 : 16) whose love is shed abroad in our hearts (Rom. 5 : 5), **and the communion,** *the participation* and fellowship, **of the Holy Ghost,** *Spirit*, in his indwelling and sanctifying presence and power (Rom. 8 : 9–11, 14–16), **be with you all**, the erring, the opposer, the gainsayer, as well as the faithful and obedient. How overflowing the apostle's loving heart, though he had used severity. "*Love* is ascribed to the Father as the source from whence the grace of Christ pours itself forth as a stream, producing brotherly *communion* among believers in the Holy Spirit. That the Son obtains first mention is explained by the fact that divinity reveals itself immediately to man in Christ; the Son first guides him to the Father, and his life is finally perfected in the communion of the Holy Spirit" (OLSHAUSEN).

Amen, is omitted by the highest critical authorities. The subscription, except simply *To the Corinthians,* is wanting in the oldest and best manuscripts, and is of no authority.

We may reasonably conclude that the effect of this letter was good, from Rom. 15 : 25–27 and Acts 20 : 2, since soon after this Paul went to Corinth and remained there three months, as it would appear, in peace, which he could hardly have done if this letter had not prepared the way. No trace of opposition is afterward found in the Corinthian church to the apostolic claims of Paul. According to the Epistle of Clement, written shortly after the apostle's death, there were divisions in the Corinthian church, but Paul was held in affectionate remembrance.

PRACTICAL REMARKS.

1. Churches should exercise discipline firmly, kindly, and faithfully, not upon suspicions and prejudice, but upon clear evidence, according to the offenses committed (ver. 1. 2 ; 1 Cor. 4 : 20, 21).

2. If the preacher would have Christ speak through him, let him be in fellowship with Christ through the indwelling

Spirit and an experimental knowledge of the word (ver. 3; John 16 : 13; 17 : 14, 17, 23; 1 John 1 : 3).

3. The preacher's authority is that of the truth, and thereby he gives evidence of Christ speaking in and through him (ver. 3, 8; 4 : 3).

4. Christ in his sufferings identified himself with us, and in his life and exaltation we are identified with him (ver 4; 1 Peter 3 : 18; 2 Tim. 2 : 11, 12).

5. In view of human imperfections and the importance of true personal religion, we should frequently examine ourselves (ver. 5; 1 Cor. 11 : 28; 3 : 13).

6. The Christian may know whether he is a true child of God (ver. 5, 6; 2 Tim. 1 : 12; 1 John 3 : 14, 19, 24; 4 : 16).

7. The minister should unselfishly seek the highest good of his people whatever may be the estimate in which he himself is held (ver. 7, 9; 12 : 14).

8. If the preacher turns aside from the gospel system of truth, he exceeds his commission and is without authority (ver. 8; Mark 16 : 16, 17; Isa. 8 : 20).

9. Christian perfection consists not so much in sinlessness, as in the symmetrical development of Christian character (ver. 9, 11; 2 Peter 1 : 5-8).

10. Whatever authority Christ may have given us, as churches or individuals, we should use it carefully and wisely under the guidance of the Spirit according to the word (ver. 10; 10 : 8; Matt. 10: 16, 20).

11. When Christians love one another and live in peace, then they may expect the God of love and peace to be with them (ver. 11; Rom. 15 : 5, 6).

12. The closing verse of this Epistle is a prayer, and it teaches us that it is proper to pray to the Son and the Spirit as well as to the Father (ver. 14; Acts 7 : 59; Jude 20, 21; Rom. 8 : 26).

13. The Father, Son, and Holy Spirit, stand on an equality with one another, each bearing a distinctive relation to the Christian and to his salvation (ver. 14; Matt. 28 : 19; Phil. 2 : 6).

14. Salvation comes to us from God the Father, through God the Son, and by God the Holy Spirit (ver. 14; John 3 : 5-17).

CORINTH UNEARTHED.

Much of the Corinth of Paul's day has for centuries lain out of sight beneath the rubbish and the soil. Several standing columns of a Doric temple have been almost the only trace of the Greek city. Of great interest and importance, therefore, have been the explorations made in Corinth, the past year, 1896, by Americans under the guidance of Dr. R. B. Richardson. Much has been done in determining the site of the *agora*, and preparing the way for future excavations. The well-worn steps of the stairs which gave access to the seats of the ancient theatre have been discovered. Within two hundred feet of the present village a tomb was found, containing relics from prehistoric times—vases of marvelous pattern and of most ancient chromatic treatment. What hopes from archæological research in old Corinth are aroused! May we not have confirmations of Luke and Paul in the Acts and the Epistles? Perhaps we may learn more of the proconsul Gallio, or of Erastus the public treasurer of Corinth, or of Gaius the host of Paul, or of the synagogue with the rulers Crispus and Sosthenes, or of Chloe and Stephanas, or of Paul's lost epistle, or of his unrecorded second visit to the Corinthians. Much of this and of many others may yet come to light.

GENERAL INDEX

Abba, Father, 106.
Abraham: justified by faith, 63; his great faith, 66, 67; while yet uncircumcised, 65; circumcision a consequence of his faith, 65; a seal of his righteousness, 65; a father of the faithful, 65–67; heir of the world, 66; his faith and the promise, 66; a father of many nations, 67; believing in hope against hope, 67; a pattern to believers, 68.
"Absent from the body," "present with the Lord," 356.
Accursed from Christ, 117.
Adam: meaning of, 75; relation of, to the race, 75, 76, 77; type of Christ by contrast, 77; similitude of his transgression, 77.
Adam to Moses, death reigned from, 77.
Adoption, spirit of, 106.
Amplias, 181.
Analogy between Adam and Christ, 75, 78.
"Anathema Maranatha," 325.
Andronicus, 180.
Angels, Christian judging, 223.
Apollos, referred to, 323.
Apostolic benediction, 415.
Apostolic ministry of Paul: defense of, 387–389; its weapons and its warfare, 388; its authority real, 389; unlike that of his opposers, 389–392; false standard of judgment upon, 391; built not on others' foundations, 392; sufferings of, 400; caring for the churches in, 401; deliverance at Damascus for, 402; visions and revelations connected with, 404; signs of among the Corinthians, 407; its authoritative exercise, 411, 412.
Apelles, 181.
Aquila: mentioned, 179, 180; church at his house, 180, 324.
Aretas, 402.
Aristobulus: mentioned, 181; early missionary to Britain, 181.
"Armor of light," 158.

Atonement, the: Practical Remarks on, 61, 62, 114; relation of to the race, 80.

Baal, 136.
Baptism: a burial, 83; a likeness of death, 84; a likeness of resurrection, 84; a likeness of death to sin and a new life, 83–85; an intelligent act, 263.
Baptism as a figure: described, 85, 86; a symbol, 86; a sign, 86; an antitype, 86; not as a seal, 86.
"Baptized for the dead": different interpretations of, 311; the preferable view of, 312.
"Baptized into his death," 83.
Baptized unto Moses: meaning of, 255; in the cloud and in the sea, 255; Practical Remarks on, 263.
"Barbarian," 31.
"Beholding as in a glass the glory of the Lord," 347.
Believers not under law but under grace, 91, 92.
Benevolence: defined, 178; remarks on, 320, 326.
"Be ye reconciled to God," 361.
Bible, The: Practical Remarks on, 61.
Body of believers: a temple of the Holy Spirit, 327; Practical Remarks on, 228.
Body, a living sacrifice, 149.
"Brethren," 30.
Building on Christ: the builders thereon, 206; Christ the foundation, 206; tried by fire, 207; saved through fire, 207, 210.
"Body of this death," 100.

"Called according to his purpose," 111.
Calling: from God, 28; internal and external, 28.
"Carnal," 204.
Carnally minded, 104.
Casuistry: the kingdom of God and, 166; no code of laws laid down for, 167; principles and knowledge of furnished for

GENERAL INDEX

deciding in reference to human conduct, 167; in marked contrast to papal subtleties and Jesuitical subterfuges, 167.
Character building, 207, 210.
Charity, grace of. See Love, 286.
"Chiefest apostles," 395.
Children, "unclean," "holy," 232.
Chloe, house of, 192.
Christ: the seed of David, 26; the Son of God, 27; the Spirit of holiness, 27; his resurrection, 27; his gospel, 32; in Rom., chap. 1, see Practical Remarks, 40; a propitiatory sacrifice, 58; delivered for our offenses, 69; raised for our justification, 69; our substitute, 72, 73; head of the race, Practical Remarks, 81; holding a two-fold relation of servant and Son, 170; "a minister of the circumcision," 170; his relation to the Gentiles, 170, 171; his kingdom and reign, 309; delivering up the kingdom to the Father, 309; all enemies put under him, 310; one with the Father, 311; Adam and, contrasted, 74; crucified, preaching of, 199; death of, relation to the race, 79; the death of, the death of all, 358; "the end of the law for righteousness," 128, 129; grace of, abounding, 78, 80; interceding for us, 112; his inseparable love, 113; "our Passover," 219; as presented by Paul the same as Christ of the four Gospels, 304; in regard to his person, 304; his character, 304; his doctrine, 304; words and phrases of, 304; our substitute, our sin-bearer, 261, 263; the unspeakable gift, 386.
Church: its general and particular meaning, 283; Practical Remarks on, 285; discipline, 341, 342, Practical Remarks: formative and corrective, 338; when valid, 413; its government, 221; divinely organized, 221; democratic and independent, 221; Dr. Alexander Carson on, 221.
Church at Corinth: embraced what, 189, 190; divisions of, 192; the party of Paul in, 192; of Apollos, 192; of Cephas, 192; of Christ, 192; character of its members, 196; moral disorders in, 217; slack in discipline, 218; should have enforced discipline, 219-221; Practical Remarks on, 221, 222.
Churches and Christians, temples of God, 208.

Christian, The: in relation to law and to grace, 102; his complete, ultimate victory, 113; through Christ, 114.
Christians: belong to God, 209; Practical Remarks on, 210; all things belong to them, 209; stewards of the mysteries of God, 210, 211; how designated in the Epistles and elsewhere, 31
Christian benevolence, Practical Remarks on, 386, 387.
Christian experience: as related to baptism and admission to the church, 361; conversion and evidences of repentance should be required, 362.
Christian liberty: abused, 225; some things lawful but not expedient, 225; Practical Remarks on, 228; Paul's use of, 246, ff.; its relation to Paul's marriage, 247; Paul's support by the churches, 247-249; his self-support, 250, 251; Paul's becoming all things to all men, 251, 252; Paul's bearing toward persons of weak conscience, 261.
Circumcision: cannot save, 48, 49; in the flesh and in the heart, 49; as a sign, 48; Practical Remarks on, 50, 51; a seal of Abraham's faith, 65; a token of God's covenant, 65; baptism did not take place of, 70; nothing in itself, 234.
Civil government: subjection to, 156; rulers in, 156; limit of its power, 157; accountable to God, 156, 160; paying tribute to, 157; demands of, and the law of love, 157, 158; motives of obedience to, 158.
"Coals of fire on his head," 154.
Collection: for the saints, 320, 321; at stated times and proportionate, 321, 326.
"Comforted together," 30.
"Communion of the blood of Christ," 259.
"Comparing spiritual things with spiritual," 202.
Condemnation, no, to the believer, 102.
Confession and faith, 130, 131.
Conflict within the Christian, 99-101.
Conscience: its use of, in the New Testament, 244, 245; its modern use, 244; its ancient use, 244; its supreme authority, 245; liberty of, 245, 261.
Contribution: a participation with others, 175; for the poor saints at Jerusalem, 175; duty of, from Gentiles to Jews, 176; a bond between Jewish and Gentile churches, 176.
Corinth: the city of Paul's day, xv; con-

dition of the church at, xv; subsequent history of, xv, 415; unearthed, 416.
Corinthians, Epistles to: xv; confirmed by the Acts, xiv; practical uses of, to churches, xxi; to the ministry, xxi; to our age and country, xxii.
Corinthians, First Epistle to: discussed, xv; its title, occasion, and design, xvi; time and place of writing, xvi; features of, xvii; contents and analysis, xvii.
Corinthians, Second Epistle to: considered, xx; its title, occasion, and object, xx; characteristics of, xxi; contents and analysis of, xxii; its title, 189.
Corinthians: why Paul delayed visiting them, 331-333; Paul would not come to, in sorrow, 335.
Corrupting: the word of God, 341; Practical Remarks, 342.
Covenants made with Abraham, Remark 11, pp. 69, 70.
"Creature" or "creation": meaning of, 107; subject to vanity, 108; delivered into the liberty of the children of God, 108, 109; groaning and travailing in pain, 109.
"Cup of the Lord" and "cup of demons," 260, 261.

Dangers from a scientific spirit, 196.
David, justified by faith, 64.
Deaconess: Phœbe, 179; Prisca, 180; Persis, 181; Practical Remark on, 186.
"Death unto death, a savour of," 340.
"Delight in the law of God," 99.
Depravity, human, Practical Remarks, 41.
Divine government explained, 44.
"Doubtful disputations," 161.

"Earnest expectation," 108.
"Earnest of the Spirit," 333.
Election and foreknowledge, 126, 127.
Election of grace, 137.
Elijah and the seven thousand, 136.
Enemy, treatment of an, 154.
Epenetus, 180.
Epistles: in general, v; of Peter, Paul, and John, v; relation of, to the Gospels, v; relation of, to the Old Testament, v; addressed to Christians, v; chronological order of, vi.
Epistles to the Corinthians: their genuineness, xiv; confirmed by undesigned coincidences in the Acts, xiv; the two Epistles compared, xvii; special uses, xxi; addressed to churches, 28; to saints, 28.
Epistle, First, to the Corinthians: to whom addressed, xiv; reasons for writing, xvi; design of, xvi; time and place of writing, xvi; features of, xvi; contents and analysis, xvii; its title, 189; superscription to, 326.
Epistle, Second, to the Corinthians: to whom addressed, xiv, xx; place of writing, xx; occasion and object of, xx; its characteristics, xxi; contents and analysis of, xxii; its title, 327; salutation, 327; words of gratitude, 327-329; its effect on the Corinthians, 415.
Epistle to the Romans: Paul its author, viii; its last five chapters, viii; to whom addressed, viii; when and where written, x; its occasion and design, x; contents of, xi; analysis of, xii; its theme, 32; its end, 177, 186; not all written at once, 177.
Erastus, 215.
Erastus, treasurer of Corinth, 184.
Eternal life, 43.
Ethics: Paul's, 154; ultimate ground of obligation in, 154.
Ethics, Paul's Christian: of the State, 159; of the family, of State and Church, 159; are fundamental principles, 159; their basis in the will and law of God, 159; government as to, may be perverted, 159.
Evil associations, warning against, 367.
"Evil communications corrupt good manners," 313.
Evil, overcoming with good, 154.
Experience, Christian: Practical Remarks, 161.

Faith: considered, 27, 33; of Roman Christians, 29; advance in, 32; live by, 33; in Christ is faith in God, 68, 69; confession and, 130, 131; saving, 135; a guide to conscience, 168.
False teachers: at Rome, 183; to be avoided, 183; Practical Remarks on, 186, 187.
"Farewell," 414.
"Fleshly tables of the heart," 343.
"Form" or "mold of doctrine," 88.
Food, sacrificed to idols: subject of, considered, 240, ff.; the question of eating it to be settled by love, 241; to the enlightened Christian a matter of indifference, 242; the question of, with regard to the infirmities of the weak, 243, 261;

Remarks, 215; Paul illustrates usage concerning, by his own conduct, 246–251.
Fornication: treated of, 226; flee, 227; Practical Remarks, 228.
Fortunatus and Achaicus, 324.
"From faith to faith," 32.

Gentiles: called, 139–141; the wild olive, 141; their relation to Israel, 142; their need of humility, 142; fullness of, 143.
Gentile ministry of Paul: spoken of, 173; from Jerusalem to Illyricum, 173; not builded on another's foundation, 174; consistent with visiting Rome, 175.
Gifts, Spiritual: use of, 151; of prophecy, 151; of teaching, 151; of exhortation, giving, ruling, 151.
Giving: grace of, 375, 376; the Macedonian churches an example of, 375; a mutual participation, 376; should abound in all, 376; Christ's example of, 377; should be willing, 378; should be proportionate, 378; among the Corinthians, 382, 383; was to be liberal and cheerful, 383, 384; God's help in, 384; resulting in the good of others, 385; and God's glory, 385; brings blessings on the giver, 386; all traced to Christ, 386; among Macedonians, 386; Remarks on, 381, 382.
Glorification of God's children certain, 112.
Glory, honor, immortality, 43.
"Glory of God," 57.
God: revelation of, 35; invisible things of, 35; his eternal power, 36; "blessed forever," 117; dealing with the Jews and bringing good out of evil, Remark 11, p. 147; gifts and calling of. without repentance, 144; no respecter of persons, 44; just and the justifier of sinners, 59; hardening the heart, 121; prerogative and rights of, as Creator, 122; long-suffering and wrath of, 123; "riches of glory in," 123; sovereignty of and man's free agency, 127; three-fold revelation of, 35; wondrous wisdom and knowledge of, 146.
"God of hope," 171.
Godly sorrow, good results of, 372.
God's wrath: how revealed, 35; against what, 35; in giving men over to their own passions, 37, 38; Remarks on, 41.
"Good that I would I do not," 98.
Goodness of God: despised, 42; to lead men to repentance, 42; Practical Remarks on, 50.

Gospel, The: adapted and designed for all, 129; should be preached to all, 132, 135; Practical Remark on, 12; contains the true wisdom, 200; spiritually discerned, 203; the law and, in harmony, 61.
Grace: defined, 29; under, 87; illustrated by the marriage relation, 91, 92.
Grace and works exclusive of each other, 137.
Grecian Christianity and Macedonian liberality, 386.
"Greek," 31.

Hardships of the Christian ministry referred to, 364, 365.
Heathen: without excuse, 36; degradation of, 36, 37, 38; picture of in Rom. 1, 21–32, 38; condemned by their own consciences, 39, 40.
Hermes, 182.
"Hold the truth in unrighteousness," 35.
"Holy," 40.
Holy kiss, 325.
Holy Spirit, The: 72, 105; and Spirit of Sonship, 106; distinguished from our spirit, 106; witnessing with our spirit, 106; helping our infirmities, 110; Practical Remarks on, 204; in the Old Dispensation, 300; in the New, 300; in the two contrasted, 300, 301; at Pentecost and now, 301.
Honest—honorable, 153, 155.
Hope: saved by, 109; distinguished from faith, 110.
Hospitality, 152, 155.

Idolatry: in Greece, Egypt, and Rome, 37; in the heart and life, 37; flee from, 258; inconsistent with communion and fellowship at the Lord's Supper, 259, 260; involved in idols' feasts, 260, 261.
Imprecations in Scripture, 138.
Impute, imputed, 64, 65, 76.
Incestuous man at Corinth, 217; penitent, 336; Paul advises his forgiveness, 336.
Infant salvation, Practical Remark, 81.
Infirmity of your flesh, 88.
Inter-church relations, independent, yet dependent, 380, 381.
Inward holiness, exhortations to, 368, 369.
"Inward man," 99.
Isaac and Ishmael, 119.
Israel rejected and Gentiles called, 139, 140.
Israel: savable, yet unsaved, 128; at fault,

GENERAL INDEX 421

125; and prophecy, 124, 125; not wholly passed over, 136; conversion and attendant blessings on, 140, 145; Remarks, 147, 148; restoration of, 143-146; restoration of, foretold, 145; restoration of, being fulfilled, 145; hardness of, 143; covenant with, 144; election of, 144; and Gentiles, 143; praise to God for, 146; what we owe to, in religion, in government, 148.

Israelites mentioned, 117; their privileges, 117.

Isthmian games: introduced, 252; illustrating the Christian race, 252, 253; illustrating how Paul strove for the mastery, 253; Practical Remarks, 254.

Jew, The: first in privilege, 32, 44, 51; knowing the law, but not keeping it, 46-48.

Jews and Gentiles alike sinners and condemned, 51-54.

Judging others, 212.

Judgment, The: Practical Remarks on, 50; God righteous at, 53, 54.

Judgment seat of Christ, 357.

Judgment of self, should be impartial, 150, 151.

Junia, 180.

Justification: what? 34, 60; how used by Paul, 34; as an act of God, 34; its gratuitous nature, 57; its ground, the redemption and sacrifice of Christ, 58, 59; its object, that God may save sinners, 59; its results exclude boasting, 61; results on individuals, 71-73; results on the race, 74, ff.

"Justification," a divine requirement, 34.

Justification by faith: illustrated by Abraham, 62; by David, 64; Practical Remarks on, 69; results in peace with God, 71; moral influence of, 82; does not lead to sin, 83; leads to holiness, 89, 90, 93; of life, 79.

"Justified" or "freed from sin," 84.

"Justified—glorified," 111.

"Justify," use of the word by Paul, 34; importance of understanding this and kindred words, 33, 34.

Justice of God: vindicated in passing over Israel, 118, ff.; designed for wise and merciful ends, 120; illustrated by Jacob and Esau, 119; dealing with Pharaoh, 120; enduring with vessels of wrath, 123; a remnant saved, 124.

Keeping the law, and circumcision, 48.

Kingdom of God: a reality, 216; its relation to individuals and churches, 216; its relation to the world, 216; opposed to all unrighteousness, 224; not in food and drink, 164; in righteousness, peace, joy, 164, 165, 167; has to do with all the affairs of men, 167, 168, Remark 19.

Kiss, holy, 182; Practical Remark, 186.

Law, The: of Moses, 44; design of, 80; without, 44; justified by, 44; in the heart, 45; cannot save, 46; none justified by the deeds of, 55; established by the gospel, 61; is it sin? 94; its effect on a sinner, 95, 96; holy, just, and good, 96; how it makes sin appear, 96; what it could not do, 103; two-fold in the Christian, 99.

Law and grace, 87; Practical Remarks, 90, 91, 101.

"Law of sin," 99.

"Law of sin and death," 103.

Lawsuits by Christians: before heathen tribunals, 222; inconsistent, 222, 223; should be settled in the church, 223; Practical Remarks, 228.

"Letter killeth," 344.

Liberty, gospel and Christian, 168.

"Life unto life," a savor of, 340.

Living peacefully with all, 154.

Lord's Supper: Practical Remarks on, 263, 264, 276; its proper observance, 269-271; its relation to social and church life, 274, 275.

Love: the greatest of gifts, 286-288; essential to religion, 286; characteristics of, 287; fulfilling the law, 158; Practical Remarks on, 290; unfeigned, 152; duties growing out of, 152; brotherly, 152, 155.

Love of God: in our hearts, 72; for us, 73.

Love-feasts, 270, 271.

"Made the righteousness of God in him," 361.

Man, the natural, 203.

Man and woman equal, 268.

Marriage: Paul on, 239; rather than asceticism, or celibacy of the clergy, 239; Remarks, 239, 240; divorce and celibacy related to, 228, ff.; when good, 229, 230; relations in, that are not sinful should not be disturbed, 233, 234; second, of women, 238, 239; only in the Lord, 239.

Married, The: advice to, 236, 237; as to

the divorce or separation of, 231, 232; one of, an unbelieving husband or wife, 232.
Minded: carnally, 104; spiritually, 104.
Minister, A, of Jesus Christ: referred to, 172; ministering in sacred things, 172; not sacerdotal, 172; offering up the Gentiles, 172.
Ministers, Christian: superior to Moses, 346, 347; Remarks on, 348; their bodily weakness, 350-352; spiritual power and dignity of, 350-352; sustained by a hope of a glorious immortality, 352-354; cheered in view of a glorified body, 354-356; having the earnest of the Spirit, 356; exercised in view of the judgment, 357; constrained by the love of Christ. 358, 359; their ministry one of reconciliation, 360, 361; ambassadors of Christ, 361; alms and work, 363, 364.
Ministers should well be careful in money matters, 380, 403.
Ministry: a stewardship, 211; Practical Remarks on, 216.
Ministry of the Spirit, glorious, 344.
Miraculous gifts, 30.
Missionaries: spoken of, 132; need of, 133; duty to send, 135; Remarks, 147, 148.
Moral actions and character, 167, 168.
Moral disorders in church at Corinth, 217.
Mosaic Law, design and effect of, 80.
"Mystery," 201.
"Mysteries of God," 211.

Narcissus, some of that name, 181.
Nations, Gentiles or heathen, 28.
Necessity, laid upon Paul to preach, 250.
Nereus and his sister, 182.
New birth and reconciliation of men, 360; Practical Remarks, 363.
No condemnation to the believer, 102.

Olympas: mentioned, 182; church at house of, 182.
Ordinary spiritual gifts, most highly prized, 30.
"Our earthly house of this tabernacle": treated of, 354; gives place to "a building of God, a house not made with hands," 354, 355.
"Owe no man anything," 157; see Practical Remark 11, p. 160.

Paradise, 404.
Paul: meaning of, 25; and Saul, 25;

birth, training, and mental character of, vi; as writer of Epistles, vi; writing out of his own experience, vii; by revelation, vii; with love for the truth, vii; with intense love for souls, vii; with vehemence, vii; of the nature of oral discourse, vii; Epistle of, to the Romans, viii; to the Corinthians, xv; and First Corinthians, xv; and Second Corinthians, xix; a servant of Jesus Christ, 25; an apostle, 26, 27, 189; his salutation to the Romans, 25, 28; his inscription to the Romans, 26, 28; set apart to preaching, 26; introduction of, to Romans, 29; appropriating God to himself, 29; his purposed visit to Rome, 30; object of his visit, 30, 31; a debtor to all men, 31; his obligation and readiness, 32; not ashamed of the gospel, 32; the gospel preached by, 32; his view of the human race, 34; his experience as a sinner, 95; his experience as a Christian, 100; his eloquence, 112, 114; his love for his people, 116, 128; a Benjaminite, 136; his preaching, 147; his ethics, 148; his ethics of the State, 159; his views of casuistry and the kingdom of God, 166; apostleship of, to the Gentiles, 172-174; his ministry not sacerdotal, 172; his proposed journey to Spain, 174; his visit to Rome on his way, 176; his many friends at Rome, 182, 183; his mission to preach rather than to baptize, 193; how he preached, 193; his humility, 212; his exercise of apostolic authority, 216; his apostleship to the Corinthians, 246; his freedom and self-denial, 251; buffeting his body, 253; receiving from the Lord, as to the Lord's Supper, 271; his dying daily, 312; fighting with wild beasts at Ephesus, 312; proposed visit to Corinth, 321; tarrying till Pentecost, 322; salutation with his own hand, 325; affliction of, in Asia, 329; deliverance of, at Damascus, 402; caught up to the third heaven, 404; his thorn in the flesh, 405; besought the Lord thrice, 406; affection of, for the Corinthians, 370.
Paul's boasting: apologizes for it, 393; for the sake of his converts, 394; through disinterested love, 395, 396; as to equality with his opponents respecting race, 398; of being superior to them in labors, suffering, and deliverances, 399-402; as

to his infirmities, 405, 406; compelled by the Corinthians, 407.
Paul's feelings in view of approaching dissolution, 357.
Paul's heart, 366.
Paul's letters and bodily presence, 390.
Paul's ministry: accredited by his converts, 342; its sufficiency of God, 343; "triumphing in Christ," 339.
Paul's relations: to the churches, 381; not as an officer, but as a father, as an ambassador, a missionary, 381.
Paul's visits: second, to the Corinthians, 408; his third visit, 408; had not been burdensome, 407; and would not be, 408; and his fears and wish regarding the Corinthians, 410; in the exercise of apostolic authority, 411; Christ speaking through him therein, 412.
Peace, 29.
Persis, perhaps a deaconess, 181.
Persecutor, treatment of, 153.
Phœbe of Cenchreæ, deaconess, 178, 179.
Prayer, the Spirit making intercessions, 110.
Preacher, The: office and message of, 361.
Preachers and missionaries, 132, 133.
Preachers and teachers: servants and workmen, 205; fellow-workers with God, 206.
Preachers should be supported by the churches, 248, 249.
Preaching of the cross: considered, 194–196; its effect, 195; foolishness of, 195; Practical Remarks upon, 198.
Preaching of Paul: doctrinal, experimental, and practical, 147; a lesson for this day, 147; the effect of such preaching on all classes, 147.
"Predestinate," 111.
Priscilla, 179, 324.
"Propitiation," not the mercy-seat, but a propitiatory sacrifice, 58.
Prophesying; direction concerning, 297; women and, 298.

Quartus, 184.
"Quicken your mortal bodies," 105.

Reconciliation: meaning of, 74; two sides of, 74; in God and in men, 360; the word of, 360.
Redemption: in Christ, 57; of our body, 109; Practical Remarks, 114.
"Repent" and "regret," 371.

Repentance: true and false, 371, 372; proof of the true, 372, 373.
Resurrection of Christ: a historical fact, 303–306; the theme of Paul's preaching, 303; implies the resurrection of all believers, 306–308; the resurrection denied by whom, 306, 307; essential to the scheme of redemption, 308–310; the divine order, 309; fortified by an appeal to the lives of believers, 311–313; manner of, 313; illustrated by inanimate and animate creation, 314; nature of, 316; results of, 317–319; necessary to our salvation, 25; Practical Remarks on, 70, 319, 320.
Retribution, 44.
Revolution, the right of, 159, Practical Remarks 6, 7, pp. 159, 160.
"Righteous" or "just," its use by Paul, 33.
"Righteousness": its meaning in Paul's writings, 33; of God, 32; of faith, 129; of the law, 129.
Righteousness of God: noticed, 56; declared for the remission of sins, 59.
Righteousness and salvation alone through faith, 56–60.
Rock, that, was Christ, 256.
Roman Empire, 29.
Romans, Epistle to: considered, viii; its title, 25; to whom addressed, viii; when and where written, x; occasion and design of, x; contents of, xi; design of, xii; its theme, 34; its main divisions, 34; its doxology, 185; superscription, 186.
Rome: in the days of Nero ix, xi, 31; composition of the Christian congregation at, ix; origin of Christianity at, ix; the language of the saints principally Greek at, x; Paul's visit to, 31, 32, 176.
Rufus, of, 181, 182.

"Saints": defined, 28, 31; perseverance of, 115.
Salvation by works and by grace opposite of each other, 63.
Sanctification: progressive, 89; in connection with justification, 102.
Satan an angel of light, 397.
Second Corinthians: considered, 327; salutation of, 322; its good results, 415.
Scriptures, Holy: reference to, 26; given for our instruction, 169.
Science and religion, the mutual helpfulness of, 196.

"Sealed us—the earnest of the Spirit," 333.
Self-confidence, danger of, 258.
Self-consecration: to God, 149; must extend to both soul and body, 150; in the diligent use of gifts and graces, 150.
Self-restraint: needful for spiritual safety, 252; Israel's lack of, a warning, 255-258.
"Serve the law of sin," 100.
Seventh chapter of Romans: its application, 91; who speaks in, a regenerate or an unregenerate man? 93, 94, 96, 97; Paul speaking from experience therein, 93; applies to one in his unregenerate state, 94-97; applied to regenerate state, 96-101; discussing under law and under grace, 91, 94.
Sin: meaning and use, 75; its nature, 75, 76; and death, 75; as transgression, as filthy, and a crime, 64; of Adam and the race, 75-77; universality of, 76; imputed between Adam and Moses, 76; against what law, 77.
Sinfulness of men, universal, 54, 55.
Sinners: includes all men, 54; all guilty before God, 55; in condemning others, condemn themselves, 41; cannot escape through God's justice nor through despising his goodness, 42; no escape for, through the law, 46-48; none saved, by circumcision, 48; wages of, death, 89, 90.
"Sister," 31.
"Sold under sin," 98.
Song: devotion in song all important, 293, 301; an old precept, 294.
Sons of God, 106.
Sonship of the Christian: shown in spirit and word, 106; testified by the Holy Spirit, 106; implies heirship, 107; implies joint-heirship with Christ, 107.
Sonship, spiritual, 115.
Sosthenes, perhaps an amanuensis of Paul, 189.
Sowing and reaping, 283, 284.
Speaking after the manner of men, 88.
Spirit of holiness, 27.
"Spirit giveth life," 314.
Spirit of Christ in the Old Testament, 346.
Spiritual gifts: considered, 30, 277; their diversity, 278; their unity, 280; illustrated by the human body, 281; superiority of some of to others, 290-291; their relation to unbelievers, 295-296; decency and order in, 296.
Spiritually minded, 104.

Stephanas: spoken of, 193, 324; household of, 193.
"Stewards," 211.
Strong, Dr. A. H.: on Epistle to Romans, 33; on faith linking us to Christ, 57.
Strong brethren: duties of to the weak, 164, 168, 169; should avoid giving offense, 160-164; should exercise self-sacrifice for, 165; should walk charitably, 164; should not destroy him for whom Christ died, 165; the rule in such cases, 165; from the example of Christ, 169.
Style, peculiarities of Paul's, 25, 41.
Substitution, 73.
Sufferings, present: referred to, 107; encouragement in, 107-111; outweighed by future glory, 107, 108; all working for our good, 111.
Sympathy, exercise of, 153.
"Swallowed up of life," 355.

Temptation, deliverance in, to the believing and watchful, 258.
Tertius, an amanuensis of Paul, 184.
Timothy: considered, 184, 322, 327; sent to Macedonia and Corinth, 215.
"The time is short," 236.
Third heavens, 401.
Thorn in the flesh, 405.
Titus: mentioned, 339; in Corinth, 376, 378, 379, 382; and the brother whose praise is in all the churches, 379; representing the churches, 379; Paul's partner, 380.
Tribulation, its effect on character and life, 72.
Troas, 339; Paul's anxiety at, 339.
Tutor, 214.

Unbelieving husband: sanctified by the believing wife, etc., 232; may be converted by, 233.
Unclean food, nothing in itself, 164; according to one's estimate, 164, 166.
"Ungodliness" and "unrighteousness" of men, 35, 37.
Unmarried, The: advice to, 230; to remain as they are, under threatening calamities, 235; to be without care and worldly enticements, 237.
Unmarried daughters, duty of parents to, 238.
Urbane, 181.

Vengeance belongs to God, not to men, 154, 155.

GENERAL INDEX

"Vessels of wrath," 123.
Visit to Rome: Paul's considered, 176; the spirit in which the apostle would make, 176; his ministry therein, 176, 177.
Victory of the Christian: is sure, 100; through Christ, 100, 114.

Walking by faith, not by sight, 356.
"Washed," "justified," "sanctified," 224, 225.
Weak brethren: duties to, 160; exercise of mutual forbearance toward, 160, 161; to be considered in regard to food, 161; and days, 161, 162; must give account to God, 163; duties of the strong to self-sacrifice for the weak, 163, 164; mutual duties, 170.
"Whatsoever is not of faith is sin," 166.
"Where the Spirit of the Lord is, there is liberty," 317.
Wisdom of God: considered, 194; true wisdom revealed in the gospel, 201.

"Wisdom, righteousness, sanctification, and redemption," 197.
Women: condition of among the Hebrews, 299; under Christianity, 299.
Woman: in church work, 302; her conduct and dress at public services, 265–268; her relation to man, 265, 268; her equality with man, 268; head of, covered while praying or prophesying, 266; covered because of the angels, 268.
Women and Paul, Practical Remarks, 186.
World by wisdom: not knowing God, 195; renounced for true wisdom, 208.
Worship: in prayer and song, 293; should guard against ritualism; must not mistake æsthetic emotion for devotional feeling, 293.
"Works of darkness," 158.
Works and faith, salvation by, contrasted, 63.
Wrath: considered, 43; of God, 34, 52.

www.ingramcontent.com/pod-product-compliance
Lightning Source LLC
Chambersburg PA
CBHW020543300426
44111CB00008B/777